KODANSHA
ENCYCLOPEDIA OF
JAPAN

Distributors
JAPAN: KODANSHA LTD., Tokyo.
OVERSEAS: KODANSHA INTERNATIONAL LTD., Tokyo.
  U.S.A., Mexico, Central America, and South America: KODANSHA INTERNATIONAL/USA LTD.
    through HARPER & ROW, PUBLISHERS, INC., New York.
  Canada: FITZHENRY & WHITESIDE LTD., Ontario.
  U.K., Europe, the Middle East, and Africa: INTERNATIONAL BOOK DISTRIBUTORS LTD.,
    Hemel Hempstead, Herts., England.
  Australia and New Zealand: HARPER & ROW (AUSTRALASIA) PTY. LTD., Artarmon, N.S.W.
  Asia: TOPPAN COMPANY (S) PTE. LTD., Singapore.

Published by Kodansha Ltd., 12-21, Otowa 2-chome, Bunkyo-ku, Tokyo 112 and Kodansha
International/USA Ltd., 10 East 53rd Street, New York, New York 10022.
Copyright © 1983 by Kodansha Ltd.
All rights reserved.
Printed in Japan.
First edition, 1983.

LCC 83-80778
ISBN 0-87011-629-0 (Volume 9)
ISBN 0-87011-620-7 (Set)
ISBN 4-06-144539-1 (0) (in Japan)

Library of Congress Cataloging in Publication Data
Main entry under title:

Kodansha encyclopedia of Japan.

  Includes index.
  1. Japan—Dictionaries and encyclopedias. I. Title:
Encyclopedia of Japan.
DS805.K633 1983   952'.003'21   83-80778
ISBN 0-87011-620-7 (U.S.)

KODANSHA
ENCYCLOPEDIA OF
JAPAN

9

KODANSHA

ACADEMIC ADVISERS

ARUGA Yūshō — marine biology — Associate Professor
Department of Fisheries
Tōkyō University of Fisheries
Tōkyō

ASAI Kiyoshi — Japanese literature — Professor
Department of Letters and Education
Ochanomizu Women's University
Tōkyō

FUKUSHIMA Yasuto — military affairs — Professor
National Defense College
National Defense Agency
Tōkyō

HARADA Katsumasa — Japanese history — Lecturer
Wakō University
Machida, Tōkyō Prefecture

HOSHIKAWA Kiyochika — agriculture — Professor
Faculty of Agriculture
Tōhoku University
Sendai, Miyagi Prefecture

HOSHINO Yoshirō — natural science — Science commentator
Kyōto

HOSOYA Chihiro — international relations — Professor
Department of Law
Hitotsubashi University
Kunitachi, Tōkyō Prefecture

IMAIZUMI Yoshiharu — zoology — Professor
Department of Literature
Tsuru University
Tsuru, Yamanashi Prefecture

ISHII Shirō — law — Professor
Faculty of Law
Tōkyō University
Tōkyō

ISHIYAMA Akira — clothing — Professor
Department of Home Economics
Bunka Women's College
Tōkyō

ITŌ Mikiharu — ethnology — Professor
National Museum of Ethnology
Suita, Ōsaka Prefecture

IWAI Hiroaki — social problems — Professor
Department of Sociology
Tōyō University
Tōkyō

KAGESATO Tetsurō — Japanese art — Director
Mie Prefectural Art Museum
Tsu, Mie Prefecture

KANAI Madoka — Japanese history — Professor
Historiographical Institute
Tōkyō University
Tōkyō

KAWASAKI Shinjō — Buddhist philosophy — Assistant Professor
Institute of Philosophy
Tsukuba University
Tsukuba Academic New Town, Ibaraki Prefecture

KURITA Ken — labor relations — Professor
Department of Commerce
Meiji University
Tōkyō

MASHIMO Keimei — medicine — Director
Tōkyō Welfare Pension Hospital
Tōkyō

MATSUDA Osamu — plant folklore — President
Japan Association of the Friends of Plants
Tōkyō

MIYAZAWA Ken'ichi	economics	Professor, Department of Economics President, Hitotsubashi University Kunitachi, Tōkyō Prefecture
NAGAZUMI Akira	international relations	Professor Faculty of Letters Tōkyō University Tōkyō
NARA Hakujun	Buddhist philosophy	Assistant Professor Institute of Philosophy Tsukuba University Tsukuba Academic New Town, Ibaraki Prefecture
NISHIKAWA Osamu	geography	Professor College of Arts and Sciences Tōkyō University Tōkyō
NISHIMURA Masae	anthropology	Professor Department of Education Waseda University Tōkyō
NODA Kazuo	management	Professor Department of Sociology Rikkyō University Tōkyō
NOMACHI Akira	Western philosophy	Professor Institute of Philosophy Tsukuba University Tsukuba Academic New Town, Ibaraki Prefecture
OKAMURA Tadao	political science	Professor Faculty of General Education Hōsei University Tōkyō
ŌMORI Wataru	government administration	Assistant Professor College of Arts and Sciences Tōkyō University Tōkyō
ŌSHIMA Yasumasa	Western philosophy	Professor World Problems Research Institute Kyōto Sangyō University Kyōto
SAITŌ Shōji	animal and plant folklore	Professor Department of Science and Engineering Tōkyō Denki University Tōkyō
SEIKE Kiyosi	architecture	Professor and Dean School of Fine Arts Tōkyō University of Fine Arts and Music Tōkyō
SHIKI Masahide	geography	Professor Department of Letters and Education Ochanomizu Women's University Tōkyō
SUZUKI Zenji	biology	Professor Faculty of Liberal Arts Yamaguchi University Yamaguchi, Yamaguchi Prefecture
TADA Michitarō	cultural anthropology	Professor Research Institute for Humanistic Studies Kyōto University Kyōto
TAKAGI Keijirō	medicine	President Japan Society of Pharmacists Tōkyō
TAKAKUWA Yasuo	education	Professor Faculty of Education Nagoya University Nagoya, Aichi Prefecture

TAKUMI Hideo	Japanese art	Director Kanagawa Prefectural Museum of Modern Art Kamakura, Kanagawa Prefecture
TANAKA Akira	Japanese history	Professor Faculty of Letters Hokkaidō University Sapporo, Hokkaidō
TANAKA Hideo	law	Professor and Chairman Faculty of Law Tōkyō University Tōkyō
TSUJI Shizuo	Japanese cooking	President Tsuji Professional Culinary Institute Ōsaka
TSUKUBA Hisaharu	agriculture	Assistant Professor Department of Economics Waseda University Tōkyō
UMETANI Noboru	international relations	Professor Faculty of Letters Ōsaka University Ōsaka
UWANO Zendō	linguistics	Assistant Professor Faculty of Letters Tōkyō University Tōkyō
WAKASUGI Akira	accounting	Professor and Dean Department of Economics Yokohama National University Yokohama, Kanagawa Prefecture
WATANABE Tōru	sports	Professor College of Arts and Sciences Tōkyō University Tōkyō
YAMADA Terutane	traditional medicine	Standing Director Japan Institute of Traditional Medicine Tōkyō
YUI Tsunehiko	management	Professor Department of Business Management Meiji University Tōkyō

EDITORIAL CONSULTANTS

CAMBRIDGE

Tadatoshi AKIBA
Takashi EGUCHI
Robert FELDMAN
Glen S. FUKUSHIMA
Andrew GORDON
Hiroshi WATANABE

TŌKYŌ

AMAKI Shihomi
ARATA Yōji
ARITA Seiko
Theodore F. COOK
Louise CORT
ENOMOTO Tōru
FUJINAGA Tamotsu
HAMADA Kōsaku
HATANO Sumio
HIROI Yūichi
Dangshi HUANG
INUTA Mitsuru
IWATA Rei
Japan Academy
Japan Foundation
KANNO Hiroomi
KATŌ Yasutake
KAWAI Masakazu
KOBAYASHI Michihiko
KUBOTA Takeshi
Joseph LOVE
MACHIDA Kōichi
MAYUZUMI Hiromichi
MOMOSE Kesao
MUKAE Ryūji
MURATA Harumi
NAITŌ Masao
NAKAGAWA Fumio
NAKAI Jun
NAKAZATO Toshikatsu
NASU Kunio
NISHIMURA Hiroko
OKADA Shigehiro
OKUMURA Hideo
ŌTSUJI Kiyoshi
Lawrence REPETA
SAITŌ Masao
SATŌ Tadao
SEKI Nobuko
SUEMATSU Yasukazu
SUZUKI Tomonari
TAKEHANA Rintarō
TANAKA Masaaki
TOMOI Masatoshi
TONOOKA Shin'ichiro
TSUCHIANA Fumito
TSUJI Keigo
URANO Ayako
WASHI Haruo
YAUCHI Kenji

CONTRIBUTORS

ABE Gihei — Assistant Professor, National Museum of Japanese History, Chiba Prefecture, Japan

ABE Hiromu — Chief, Preservation Section, Shōsōin Office, Nara, Japan

ABE Mikio — Executive Vice-President, Nomura Research Institute, Kanagawa Prefecture, Japan

ABE Takeshi — President, Tōkyō Gakugei University, Tōkyō, Japan

ABE Tokiharu — Secretary, Itō Foundation for the Advancement of Ichthyology, Tōkyō, Japan

ABE Yasushi — Music commentator

James C. ABEGGLEN — Vice-President, Boston Consulting Group, Inc, Boston, Massachusetts, US

ACHIWA Gorō — Physician

Barbara C. ADACHI — Author of *The Living Treasures of Japan* (1973) and *The Voices and Hands of Bunraku* (1978)

ADACHI Tetsuo — Deputy Manager, London branch, Long-Term Credit Bank of Japan, Ltd, London, England

Stephen ADDISS — Associate Professor, Department of Art History, University of Kansas, Lawrence, Kansas, US

AIDA Kō — Professor, Department of Home Economics, Ochanomizu Women's University, Tōkyō, Japan

AKASHI Yōji — Professor, Department of Foreign Languages, Nanzan University, Aichi Prefecture, Japan

Tadatoshi AKIBA — Associate Professor, Tufts University, Medford, Massachusetts, US

AKIYAMA Terukazu — Professor, Department of Literature, Gakushūin University, Tōkyō, Japan

AMAGI Isao — Advisor to the Minister, Ministry of Education, Tōkyō, Japan

AMANO Ikuo — Associate Professor, Faculty of Education, Tōkyō University, Tōkyō, Japan

AMANO Takashi — Commentator on fishing topics

Walter AMES — Author of *Police and Community in Japan* (1981)

J. L. ANDERSON — Manager for operations at WGBH in Boston; President of Mass Comm/Masu Komi media consultants; coauthor of *The Japanese Film* (rev ed, 1982)

Nancy ANDREW — Translator of *Almost Transparent Blue* by Ryū Murakami (1976)

Allan A. ANDREWS — Associate Professor, Department of Religion, University of Vermont, Burlington, Vermont, US

ANZAI Shin — Professor, Department of Literature, Sophia University, Tōkyō, Japan

Haruo AOKI — Professor and Chairman, Department of Oriental Languages, University of California, Berkeley, Berkeley, California, US

Michiko Y. AOKI — Roger Williams College, Bristol, Rhode Island, US

AOKI Tamotsu — Associate Professor, Department of Anthropology and Sociology, Ōsaka University, Ōsaka, Japan

AOMI Jun'ichi — Professor, Faculty of Law, Tōkyō University, Tōkyō, Japan

ARA Hide — Dean, Institute of Social Sciences, Tsukuba University, Ibaraki Prefecture, Japan

ARAI Eiji (d 1981) — Professor, College of Humanities and Sciences, Nihon University, Tōkyō, Japan

ARAI Naoyuki — Professor, Department of Literature, Sōka University, Tōkyō Prefecture, Japan

James T. ARAKI — Professor, Department of East Asian Literature, University of Hawaii at Manoa, Honolulu, Hawaii, US

ARAMAKI Shigeo — Professor, Earthquake Research Institute, Tōkyō University, Tōkyō, Japan

ARASE Yutaka — Professor, Institute of Journalism and Communication, Tōkyō University, Tōkyō, Japan

Diane Wright ARIMOTO

ARIMOTO Takafumi — Lecturer, Department of Fisheries, Tōkyō University of Fisheries, Tōkyō, Japan

ARIYAMA Teruo — Associate Professor, Department of Sociology, Momoyama Gakuin University, Ōsaka Prefecture, Japan

Barbara L. ARNN — Department of Modern Languages and Literatures, University of Oklahoma, Norman, Oklahoma, US

Paul H. ARON — Executive Vice-President, Daiwa Securities America Inc, New York, New York, US

ARUGA Yūshō — Associate Professor, Department of Fisheries, Tōkyō University of Fisheries, Tōkyō, Japan

ASAI Kiyoshi — Professor, Department of Letters and Education, Ochanomizu Women's University, Tōkyō, Japan

ASAJIMA Shōichi — Professor, Department of Business Management, Senshū University, Tōkyō, Japan

Janet ASHBY — Staff Writer, *Encyclopedia of Japan*

AWAJI Takehisa — Professor, Department of Law, Rikkyō University, Tōkyō, Japan

AWAYA Kentarō — Associate Professor, Department of Literature, Rikkyō University, Tōkyō, Japan

AZUMA Hiroshi — Professor, Faculty of Education, Tōkyō University, Tōkyō, Japan

Jane BACHNIK — Assistant Professor, Department of Anthropology, University of North Carolina, Chapel Hill, North Carolina, US

Robert L. BACKUS — Associate Professor, Department of Eastern Languages, University of California, Santa Barbara, Santa Barbara, California, US

Frederick BAEKELAND — Associate Professor, Department of Psychiatry, State University of New York Downstate Medical Center, Brooklyn, New York, US

Hans H. BAERWALD — Professor, Department of Political Science, University of California, Los Angeles, Los Angeles, California, US

BAI Kōichi — Professor, Faculty of Law, Tōkyō Metropolitan University, Tōkyō, Japan

Robert J. BALLON — Chairman, Socio-Economic Institute, Sophia University, Tōkyō, Japan

BAMBA Nobuya — Professor, Faculty of Law, Ōsaka University, Ōsaka, Japan

BANNO Junji — Associate Professor, Institute of Social Science, Tōkyō University, Tōkyō, Japan

Susan BARBERI

Gina Lee BARNES — Assistant Lecturer, Department of Archaeology, University of Cambridge, Cambridge, United Kingdom

Mary W. BASKETT

James C. BAXTER — Acting Assistant Professor, Department of History, University of Virginia, Charlottesville, Virginia, US

Edward R. BEAUCHAMP — Associate Professor, College of Education, University of Hawaii at Manoa, Honolulu, Hawaii, US

Johanna BECKER — Professor, Department of Art, College of St. Benedict, St. Joseph, Minnesota, US

George BEDELL — Associate Professor, Department of Linguistics, University of California, Los Angeles, Los Angeles, California, US

Lawrence W. BEER — Kirby Professor of Civil Rights, Department of Government and Law, Lafayette College, Easton, Pennsylvania, US

Burton F. BEERS — Professor, Department of History, North Carolina State University at Raleigh, Raleigh, North Carolina, US

Harumi BEFU — Professor, Department of Anthropology, Stanford University, Stanford, California, US

BEKKI Atsuhiko — Professor Emeritus, Rikkyō University, Tōkyō, Japan

John W. BENNETT — Professor, Department of Anthropology, Washington University, St. Louis, Missouri, US

Gordon M. BERGER — Director, East Asian Studies Center and Associate Professor, Department of History, University of Southern California, Los Angeles, California, US

Gail Lee BERNSTEIN — Associate Professor, Department of Oriental Studies, University of Arizona, Tucson, Arizona, US

Paul BERRY

Jonathan W. BEST — Assistant Professor, Art Department, Wesleyan University, Middletown, Connecticut, US

John BESTER — Lecturer, College of Arts and Sciences, Tōkyō University, Tōkyō, Japan

Theodore C. BESTOR — Social Science Research Council, New York, New York, US

Monica BETHE — Coauthor of *Nō as Performance: An Analysis of the Kuse Scene of Yamaba* (1978).

BITŌ Masahide — Professor, Faculty of Letters, Tōkyō University, Tōkyō, Japan

Carmen BLACKER — Lecturer, Faculty of Oriental Studies, University of Cambridge, Cambridge, United Kingdom

Dorothy BLAIR — Retired Consultant, The Corning Museum of Glass, Corning, New York, US

Peter BLEED — Associate Professor and Chairman, Department of Anthropology, University of Nebraska at Lincoln, Lincoln, Nebraska, US

Alfred BLOOM — Professor, Department of Religion, University of Hawaii at Manoa, Honolulu, Hawaii, US

Tuvia BLUMENTHAL — Associate Professor, Department of Economics, Ben Gurion University, Israel

Audie BOCK — Pacific Film Archives, University Art Museum, Berkeley, California, US

Felicia G. BOCK — Translator of *Engi-shiki: Procedures of the Engi Era,* Books I-V (1970), Books VI-X (1972)

Harold BOLITHO — Associate Professor, Department of Japanese, Monash University, Clayton, Victoria, Australia

Andrea BOLTHO — Magdalen College, University of Oxford, Oxford, United Kingdom

Robert BORGEN — Assistant Professor, Department of East Asian Languages, University of Hawaii at Manoa, Honolulu, Hawaii, US

Adriana BOSCARO — Director, Seminario di Lingua e Letteratura Giapponese, Università degli Studi di Venezia, Venice, Italy

Roger W. BOWEN — Assistant Professor, Department of Government, Colby College, Waterville, Maine, US

Gordon T. BOWLES — Professor Emeritus, Department of Anthropology, Syracuse University, Syracuse, New York, US

C. R. BOXER — Professor Emeritus, University of London, London, United Kingdom

John H. BOYLE — Professor, Department of History, California State University, Chico, Chico, California, US

Karen BRAZELL — Professor, Department of Asian Studies, Cornell University, Ithaca, New York, US

Martin BRONFENBREN-NER — Professor, Department of Economics, Duke University, Durham, North Carolina, US

Robert H. BROWER — Professor, Department of Far Eastern Languages and Literatures, University of Michigan, Ann Arbor, Michigan, US

Delmer M. BROWN — Director, Inter-University Center for Japanese Language Studies in Tōkyō; Professor Emeritus, Department of History, University of California, Berkeley, Berkeley, California, US

Philip BROWN — Assistant Professor, University of North Carolina, North Carolina, US

Sidney DeVere BROWN — Professor, Department of History, University of Oklahoma, Norman, Oklahoma, US

Michael Lee BROWNE — Professor, Department of Art and History, Wayne State University, Detroit, Michigan, US

James CAHILL — Professor, Department of History of Art, University of California, Berkeley, Berkeley, California, US

Carlo CALDAROLA — Professor, Department of Sociology, University of Alberta, Edmonton, Alberta, Canada

Kent E. CALDER — Lecturer, Japan Institute and Member, Program on US–Japan Relations, Center for International Affairs, Harvard University, Cambridge, Massachusetts, US

Alan CAMPBELL — Executive Editor, *Encyclopedia of Japan*

John Creighton CAMPBELL	Associate Professor, Department of Political Science and Director, Center for Japanese Studies, University of Michigan, Ann Arbor, Michigan, US
Jeanne CARREAU	Potter
William R. CARTER	Historian; translator of *Guide to the Asuka Historical Museum* issued by the Nara National Research Institute of Cultural Properties (1978)
Ann B. CARY	Staff Writer, *Encyclopedia of Japan*
Ellen F. CARY	
Otis CARY	Professor, Department of Literature, Dōshisha University, Kyōto, Japan
Richard T. CHANG	Professor, Department of History, University of Florida, Gainesville, Florida, US
Edward I-te CHEN	Associate Professor, Department of History, Bowling Green State University, Bowling Green, Ohio, US
John J. CHEW	Professor, Department of Anthropology, University of Toronto, Toronto, Ontario, Canada
Madeleine CHI	Professor, Fu-jen University, Taipei, Taiwan
Soon Sung CHO	Professor, Department of Political Science, University of Missouri, Columbia, Missouri, US
Kee Il CHOI	Former Professor, College of Wooster, Wooster, Ohio, US
Thomas W. CLEAVER	Assistant Professor, Department of Economics, Villanova University, Villanova, Pennsylvania, US
Diane Shaver CLEMENS	Associate Professor, Department of History, University of California, Berkeley, Berkeley, California, US
Richard S. CLEVELAND	Curator of Oriental Art, St. Louis Art Museum, St. Louis, Missouri, US
Maida S. COALDRAKE	Senior Lecturer, Department of History, University of Tasmania, Hobart, Tasmania, Australia
William H. COALDRAKE	Department of Fine Arts, Harvard University, Cambridge, Massachusetts, US
Bruce A. COATS	
Joel COHN	Staff Writer, *Encyclopedia of Japan*
Robert E. COLE	Professor, Department of Sociology, University of Michigan, Ann Arbor, Michigan, US
Rex COLEMAN	Senior Partner, Coleman & Gresser, Attorneys at Law, Los Angeles, California, US
Samuel J. COLEMAN	Carolina Population Center, University of North Carolina, Chapel Hill, North Carolina, US
Martin C. COLLCUTT	Associate Professor, Department of East Asian Studies, Princeton University, Princeton, New Jersey, US
Walter Ames COMPTON	Author of *Nippon-tō: Art Swords of Japan* (1976)
Ellen P. CONANT	Lecturer and writer
Hilary CONROY	Professor, Department of History, University of Pennsylvania, Philadelphia, Pennsylvania, US

Michael COOPER	Editor, *Monumenta Nipponica*, Sophia University, Tōkyō, Japan
Louise Allison CORT	Freer Gallery of Art, Smithsonian Institution, Washington, DC, US
Teruko CRAIG	Staff Writer, *Encyclopedia of Japan*
Lloyd CRAIGHILL	Professor of East Asian Studies, Kansai University of Foreign Studies, Ōsaka Prefecture, Japan
Edwin A. CRANSTON	Professor and Chairman, Department of East Asian Languages and Civilizations, Harvard University, Cambridge, Massachusetts, US
Sydney CRAWCOUR	Professorial Fellow and Head, Department of Far Eastern History, Research School of Pacific Studies, Australian National University, Canberra, Australia
Liza CRIHFIELD	Author of *Ko Uta: Little Songs of the Geisha World* (1979).
Doris CROISSANT	Privatdozent, Kunsthistorisches Institut, Universität Heidelberg, Heidelberg, West Germany
William K. CUMMINGS	Department of Sociology, National University of Singapore, Singapore
Louisa CUNNINGHAM	Curatorial Assistant, Oriental Art Department, Yale University Art Gallery, New Haven, Connecticut, US
Michael CUNNINGHAM	Oriental Department, Cleveland Museum of Art, Cleveland, Ohio, US
Michael A. CUSUMANO	Staff Writer, *Encyclopedia of Japan*
Frederick F. CZUPRYNA	Staff Writer, *Encyclopedia of Japan*
Kenneth J. DALE	Professor, Japan Lutheran College and Theological Seminary, Tōkyō, Japan
Donald J. DALY	Professor, Faculty of Administrative Studies, York University, Downsview, Ontario, Canada
Eugene A. DANAHER	Milgrim Thomajan Jacobs & Lee, New York, New York, US
Roger DANIELS	Professor, Department of History, University of Cincinnati, Cincinnati, Ohio, US
Brett de BARY	Assistant Professor, Asian Studies Department, Cornell University, Ithaca, New York, US
Jane DEVITT	Research Fellow, Japanese Economic and Management Studies Center, University of New South Wales, Kensington, New South Wales, Australia
George DeVOS	Professor, Department of Anthropology, University of California, Berkeley, Berkeley, California, US
Roger DINGMAN	Associate Professor, Department of History, University of Southern California, Los Angeles, California, US
Donna L. DOANE	
Miyoko DOCHERTY	Lecturer, Department of the Far East, School of Oriental and African Studies, University of London, London, United Kingdom
Paula DOE	Author of *A Warbler's Song in the Dusk: The Life and Work of Ōtomo Yakamochi* (1982)

DOI Teruo — Professor, Department of Law, Waseda University, Tōkyō, Japan

Michael W. DONNELLY — Associate Professor, Department of Political Science, University of Toronto, Toronto, Ontario, Canada

Ronald P. DORE — Assistant Director, Technical Change Center, London, United Kingdom

Grisha DOTZENKO — Kodansha Famous Schools, Inc, Tōkyō, Japan

John W. DOWER — Professor, Department of History, University of Wisconsin–Madison, Madison, Wisconsin, US

Peter DRYSDALE — Professorial Fellow, Research School of Pacific Studies, Australia–Japan Research Center, Australian National University, Canberra, Australia

Heinrich DUMOULIN — Professor Emeritus, Sophia University, Tōkyō, Japan

Charles DUNN — Professor, Department of the Far East, School of Oriental and African Studies, University of London, London, United Kingdom

Jerry DUSENBURY

Mary DUSENBURY

David DUTCHER — Lecturer, Ōsaka University, Ōsaka, Japan

Masayo Umezawa DUUS — Author of *Tokyo Rose* (1979)

Peter DUUS — Professor, Department of History, Stanford University, Stanford, California, US

Richard E. DYCK — Specialty Materials Department, General Electric Company, Worthington, Ohio, US

Yoshiko Kurata DYKSTRA — Professor, Kansai University of Foreign Studies, Ōsaka Prefecture, Japan

H. Byron EARHART — Professor, Department of Religion, Western Michigan University, Kalamazoo, Michigan, US

David M. EARL — Department of History and Philosophy, Eastern Michigan University, Ypsilanti, Michigan, US

Lane R. EARNS

David G. EGLER — Assistant Professor, Department of History, Western Illinois University, Macomb, Illinois, US

EJIMA Yasunori — Assistant Professor, Faculty of Letters, Tōkyō University, Tōkyō, Japan

EJIRI Kōichi — Suwada Farm, Chiba Prefecture, Japan

George ELISON — Professor, Department of East Asian Languages and Cultures, Indiana University, Bloomington, Indiana, US

ENDŌ Hiroshi — Professor, Department of Law, Gakushūin University, Tōkyō, Japan

ENDŌ Takeshi — Head Professor and Curator, Dressmaking Museum, Bunka Women's University, Tōkyō, Japan

Gerhild ENDRESS — Dozent, Abteilung Für Ostasienwissenschaften, Universität Bochum, Bochum, West Germany

ENOKI Kazuo — Deputy Director, Oriental Library, Tōkyō, Japan

Robert ENTENMANN

Frances ERGEN

Mark D. ERICSON — American Consulate, Ottawa, Ontario, Canada

Steven J. ERICSON — Staff Writer, *Encyclopedia of Japan*

Earle ERNST — Senior Professor of Drama and Theatre (Emeritus), University of Hawaii at Manoa, Honolulu, Hawaii, US

ETŌ Fumio — Professor, Department of Literature, Seikei University, Tōkyō, Japan

ETŌ Kyōji — Professor, School of Education, Nagoya University, Aichi Prefecture, Japan

Robert EVANS, JR — Professor, Department of Economics, Brandeis University, Waltham, Massachusetts, US

Lee W. FARNSWORTH — Professor, Department of Political Science, Brigham Young University, Provo, Utah, US

Wayne FARRIS

Dallas FINN

Richard B. FINN — Administrative Director, Program on US–Japan Relations, Center for International Affairs, Harvard University, Cambridge, Massachusetts, US

Jerry K. FISHER — Associate Professor, Department of History, Macalester College, St. Paul, Minnesota, US

Pat FISTER

Scott C. FLANAGAN — Professor, Department of Government, Florida State University, Tallahassee, Florida, US

Wm. Miles FLETCHER III — Assistant Professor, Department of History, University of North Carolina at Chapel Hill, Chapel Hill, North Carolina, US

James H. FOARD — Assistant Professor, Department of Religious Studies, Arizona State University, Tempe, Arizona, US

Grace FOX — Author of *Britain and Japan 1858–1883* (1969)

Andrew FRASER — Senior Fellow, Department of Far Eastern History, Research School of Pacific Studies, Australian National University, Canberra, Australia

Cal FRENCH — Professor, Department of the History of Art, University of Michigan, Ann Arbor, Michigan, US

Peter FROST — Professor, Department of History, Williams College, Williamstown, Massachusetts, US

FUJII Toshiko — Chief, Women Workers Section, Women and Minors Bureau, Ministry of Labor, Tōkyō, Japan

FUJIKAWA Kinji — Curator, Japanese Sword Museum, Tōkyō; President, Society for the Preservation of Japanese Swords, Tōkyō, Japan

FUJIKURA Kōichirō — Professor, Faculty of Law, Tōkyō University, Tōkyō, Japan

FUJIMURA Michio — Professor, Department of Literature, Sophia University, Tōkyō, Japan

FUJINO Ichirō — Chief, Ōsaka branch of Nishikawa Industries, Ōsaka, Japan

FUJITA Tomio — Professor, Department of General Education, Rikkyō University, Tōkyō, Japan

FUKAGAWA Tsuneyoshi — Professor, Shōbi College of Music, Saitama Prefecture, Japan

FUKUDA Hideichi — Professor, National Institute of Japanese Literature, Tōkyō, Japan

FUKUDA Kizō (d 1982) — Professor, Department of Literature, Seikei University, Tōkyō, Japan

Haruhiro FUKUI — Professor, Department of Political Science, University of California, Santa Barbara, Santa Barbara, California, US

Glen S. FUKUSHIMA — Consultant, *Encyclopedia of Japan*

FUKUSHIMA Shingo — Professor, Department of Law and Head, Graduate School of Law Studies, Senshū University, Tōkyō, Japan

FUNAKOSHI Tōru — Professor, Department of Engineering, Tōkyō Denki University, Tōkyō, Japan

Jean FUNATSU

FURUTA Hikaru — Professor, Faculty of Education, Yokohama National University, Kanagawa Prefecture, Japan

FURUYA Kōzō — Former Chief, Tea Research Station, Ministry of Agriculture, Forestry, and Fisheries, Tōkyō, Japan

Toyomasa FUSÉ — Professor, Department of Sociology, Faculty of Arts, York University, Downsview, Ontario, Canada

GANBE Eiichi — Former Director, Electric Communication Research Institute, Nippon Telegraph and Telephone Public Corporation, Tōkyō, Japan

C. Harvey GARDINER — Research Professor of History (Emeritus), Southern Illinois University, Carbondale, Illinois, US

Kenneth GARDNER — Deputy Keeper, Department of Oriental Manuscripts and Printed Books, The British Library, London, United Kingdom

Robert GARFIAS — Professor, Department of Music, University of Washington, Seattle, Washington, US

B. J. GEORGE, JR — Professor, New York Law School, New York, New York, US

Van C. GESSEL — Assistant Professor, Department of Modern and Classical Languages, University of Notre Dame, Notre Dame, Indiana, US

Kalyan Kumar GHOSH — Reader, Center for Southeast Asia, Jadavpur University, Calcutta, India

GŌDA Yoshimasa — Assistant, Department of Literature, Aoyama Gakuin University, Tōkyō, Japan

David I. GOLDBERG — Professor, Leningrad State University, Leningrad, USSR

Grant K. GOODMAN — Professor, Department of History, University of Kansas, Lawrence, Kansas, US

Theodore W. GOOSSEN

Andrew GORDON — Instructor, Department of History, Harvard University, Cambridge, Massachusetts, US

GOTŌ Kazuhiko — NHK Theoretical Research Center, Tōkyō, Japan

Patricia J. GRAHAM

Allan G. GRAPARD — Assistant Professor, Department of Asian Studies, Cornell University, Ithaca, New York, US

Maribeth GRAYBILL — Acting Assistant Professor, Department of the History of Art, University of California, Berkeley, Berkeley, California, US

Edward G. GRIFFIN

Jane T. GRIFFIN

Peter M. GRILLI — Director, Education and Communications and Japan Film Center, Japan Society, Inc, New York, New York, US

Willem A. GROOTAERS — Formerly Lecturer, Graduate School of Linguistics, Sophia University, Tōkyō, Japan

HABE Tadashige — Professor, Faculty of Marine Science and Technology, Tōkai University, Shizuoka Prefecture, Japan

Roger F. HACKETT — Professor, Department of History, University of Michigan, Ann Arbor, Michigan, US

Eleanor M. HADLEY — Adjunct Professor, Department of Economics, George Washington University, Washington, DC, US

HAGA Namio — Adviser, Mining and Metallurgical Institute of Japan, Tōkyō, Japan

HAGA Noboru — Head Professor, Institute of History and Anthropology, Tsukuba University, Ibaraki Prefecture, Japan

HAGA Tōru — Professor, College of Arts and Sciences, Tōkyō University, Tōkyō, Japan

Kanji HAITANI — Professor, Department of Economics and Business Administration, State University of New York College at Fredonia, Fredonia, New York, US

Yoshito S. HAKEDA — Professor, Department of Religion, Columbia University, New York, New York, US

David HALE

John O. HALEY — Associate Professor, School of Law, University of Washington, Seattle, Washington, US

Ivan P. HALL — Associate Executive Director, Japan–US Friendship Commission, Tōkyō, Japan

John W. HALL — Professor, Department of History, Yale University, New Haven, Connecticut, US

Robert B. HALL — Professor, Department of History and Director, Center for Asian Studies, University of Rochester, Rochester, New York, US

Robert King HALL (d 1981) — Editor of *Kokutai no hongi: Cardinal Principles of the National Entity of Japan* (1949) and author of *Education for a New Japan* (1949, reprint 1971)

HAMAKAWA Yoshihiro — Professor, Department of Electrical Engineering, Faculty of Engineering Science, Ōsaka University, Ōsaka, Japan

HAMANO Takuya — Writer of children's books; Lecturer, Tōkyō Gakugei University and Nihon University, Tōkyō, Japan

HANAMI Tadashi — Dean, Department of Law, Sophia University, Tōkyō, Japan

HANAMURA Masaru — Lecturer and trustee, Kunitachi College of Music, Tōkyō Prefecture, Japan

Mikiso HANE — Professor, Department of History, Knox College, Galesburg, Illinois, US

Susan B. HANLEY — Associate Professor, School of International Studies, University of Washington, Seattle, Washington, US

HARADA Katsumasa — Lecturer, Wakō University, Tōkyō Prefecture, Japan

HARADA Yukihiro — Senior Economist, Economics Division, Long-Term Credit Bank of Japan, Ltd, Tōkyō, Japan

Helen HARDACRE — Assistant Professor, Department of Religion, Princeton University, Princeton, New Jersey, US

Eileen HARGADINE

Phillip T. HARRIES — Lecturer, School of Oriental and African Studies, University of London, London, United Kingdom

HARUHARA Akihiko — Professor and Chairman, School of Journalism, Department of Literature, Sophia University, Tōkyō, Japan

HASHIKAWA Bunzō — Professor, Department of Politics and Economics, Meiji University, Tōkyō, Japan

HASHIMOTO Nobuyuki — Associate Professor, Department of Law, Kansai Gakuin University, Ōsaka Prefecture, Japan

HASHIMOTO Sumiko — Senior Researcher, Tōkyō National Museum, Tōkyō, Japan

HASUMI Otohiko — Professor, Department of Education, Tōkyō Gakugei University, Tōkyō, Japan

HATA Ikuhiko — Professor, Department of Politics and Economics, Takushoku University, Tōkyō, Japan

HATORI Tetsuya — Professor, Department of Literature, Seikei University, Tōkyō, Japan

Milan HAUNER — Department of History, University of Wisconsin–Madison, Madison, Wisconsin, US

William B. HAUSER — Associate Professor and Chairman, Department of History, University of Rochester, Rochester, New York, US

T. R. H. HAVENS — Professor, Department of History, Connecticut College, New London, Connecticut, US

HAYAKAWA Kunihiko — Director, Hayakawa and Associates, Architects, Tōkyō, Japan

HAYAKAWA Zenjirō — Professor, Department of Sociology, Rikkyō University, Tōkyō, Japan

HAYASHI Kunio — Fashion commentator

HAYASHI Kyōhei — Tsubouchi Memorial Theater Museum, Waseda University, Tōkyō, Japan

HAYASHI Shigeju — Professor, Department of Literature, Seikei University, Tōkyō, Japan

HAYASHI Takeji — Former President, Miyagi University of Education, Miyagi Prefecture, Japan

HAYASHI Yasaka — Former Professor, Department of Agriculture, Tōkyō University of Agriculture, Tōkyō, Japan

HAYASHI Yutaka — *Go* commentator

HAYASHI Yūzō — Standing Director, Japan Physical Education Facilities Management Company, Tōkyō, Japan

Benjamin H. HAZARD — Professor, Department of History, San Jose State University, San Jose, California, US

Graham HEALEY — Acting Director, Center for Japanese Studies, University of Sheffield, Sheffield, United Kingdom

Waldo HEINRICHS — Professor, Department of History, Temple University, Philadelphia, Pennsylvania, US

HEMMI Takemitsu — Professor, School of Mental Health, Faculty of Medicine, Tōkyō University, Tōkyō, Japan

Dan Fenno HENDERSON — Professor, School of Law, University of Washington, Seattle, Washington, US

Paul HENRIQUES — Instructor, Asian Division, University of Maryland, Tōkyō Prefecture, Japan

Howard S. HIBBETT — Professor, Department of East Asian Languages and Civilizations, Harvard University, Cambridge, Massachusetts, US

HIBI Yutaka — Professor, Faculty of Education, Nagoya University, Aichi Prefecture, Japan

Brian HICKMAN — Assistant Librarian for Japanese and Korean Collections, School of Oriental and African Studies, University of London, London, United Kingdom

Money HICKMAN — Department of Asiatic Art, Museum of Fine Arts, Boston, Massachusetts, US

HIDANO Tadashi — Professor and Director, Research Division, National Center for University Entrance Examinations, Tōkyō, Japan

HIGASHI Jutarō — Professor, Department of Art and Science, Tsuda College, Tōkyō, Japan

HIJIKATA Kazuo — Professor, Faculty of General Education, Nagoya University, Aichi Prefecture, Japan

HINOTANI Akihiko — Professor, Department of Literature, Keiō University, Tōkyō, Japan

Noboru HIRAGA — Lecturer, Department of Asian Languages and Literatures, University of Washington, Seattle, Washington, US

Atsuko HIRAI — Department of History, Michigan State University, East Lansing, Michigan, US

HIRANO Kunio — Professor, Department of Arts and Science, Tōkyō Women's Christian University, Tōkyō, Japan

HIRANO Ryūichi — President and Professor, Faculty of Law, Tōkyō University, Tōkyō, Japan

HIRASAWA Yutaka — Professor, Department of Fisheries, Tōkyō University of Fisheries, Tōkyō, Japan

HIRATA Masami — Chief Editorial Writer, Kyōdō News Service, Tōkyō, Japan

HIRATSUKA Masunori (d 1981) — Director, National Institute for Educational Research, Tōkyō, and Professor Emeritus, Faculty of Education, Kyūshū University, Fukuoka Prefecture, Japan

HIROI Nobuko — Lecturer, Department of Fine Arts, Kyōto City University of Arts, Kyōto, Japan

HIRONAKA Wakako — Writer and translator

HIROSAKI Yoshitsugu — Director, Enoshima Aquarium, Kanagawa Prefecture, Japan

HIROSE Hideo (d 1981) — Professor, Senshū University, Tōkyō, Japan

Johannes HIRSCHMEIER (d 1983) — President, Nanzan University, Aichi Prefecture, Japan

HITOTSUMATSU Shin — Professor, Research Institute for Mathematical Sciences, Kyōto University, Kyōto, Japan

Frank HOFF — Associate Professor, Department of East Asian Studies, University of Toronto, Toronto, Ontario, Canada

HŌJŌ Yoshio — Chief of Research, Department of Physiology and Heredity, Agricultural Technology Research Institute, Ibaraki Prefecture, Japan

HOKAMA Hiroshi — Professor, Department of Law, Chūō University, Tōkyō, Japan

Wendy HOLDEN — Department of the History of Art, University of Michigan, Ann Arbor, Michigan, US

Leon HOLLERMAN — Professor Emeritus, Department of Economics, Claremont McKenna College, Claremont, California, US

Inger-Johanne HOLMBOE — Lund Law School, Malmo, Sweden

HOMMA Yasuhei — Professor, Department of Sociology, Rikkyō University, Tōkyō, Japan

William D. HOOVER — Associate Professor and Chairman, Department of History, University of Toledo, Toledo, Ohio, US

Kyotsu HORI — Tōkyō Risshō Junior College for Women, Tōkyō, Japan

HORIUCHI Mamoru — Professor, Department of Education, Nagoya University, Aichi Prefecture, Japan

H. Mack HORTON — Translator of *Architecture in the Shoin Style* by Fumio Hashimoto (1981)

HOSHIKAWA Kiyochika — Professor, Faculty of Agriculture, Tōhoku University, Miyagi Prefecture, Japan

HOSHINO Akira — Professor and Chairman, Division of Education, College of Liberal Arts, International Christian University, Tōkyō Prefecture, Japan

HOSHINO Eiki — Lecturer, Department of Literature, Taishō University, Tōkyō, Japan

HOSODA Kazuo — Professor, Department of Home Economics, Shōwa Women's University, Tōkyō, Japan

HOSOYA Chihiro — Professor, Department of Law, Hitotsubashi University, Tōkyō Prefecture, Japan

HOSOYA Toshio — Professor Emeritus, Tōkyō University, Tōkyō, Japan

John F. HOWES — Associate Professor, Department of Asian Studies, University of British Columbia, Vancouver, British Columbia, Canada

HOYANAGI Mutsumi — Vice-President, Tōkyō Geographical Society, Tōkyō, Japan

Francis L. K. HSU — Professor and Director, Center for the Study of Culture in Education, School of Education, University of San Francisco, San Francisco, California, US

Thomas M. HUBER — Assistant Professor, Department of History, Duke University, Durham, North Carolina, US

David W. HUGHES —

G. Cameron HURST III — Professor and Chairman, Department of East Asian Languages and Cultures, University of Kansas, Lawrence, Kansas, US

Julia HUTT — Research Assistant, Far Eastern Section, Victoria and Albert Museum, London, United Kingdom

ICHIKAWA Kenjirō — Professor, Department of Fisheries, Tōkyō University of Fisheries, Tōkyō, Japan

ICHIKI Toshio — National Defense College, Tōkyō, Japan

Fumiko IKAWA-SMITH — Associate Professor and Chairman, Department of Anthropology, McGill University, Montreal, Quebec, Canada

Hiroko IKEDA — Professor Emeritus, Department of East Asian Literature, University of Hawaii at Manoa, Honolulu, Hawaii, US

IMAI Jun — Professor, Department of Humanities, Musashi University, Tōkyō, Japan

IMAI Shigeru — Associate Professor, Kyūshū Institute of Design, Fukuoka Prefecture, Japan

IMAIZUMI Yoshiharu — Professor, Department of Literature, Tsuru University, Yamanashi Prefecture, Japan

IMAIZUMI Yoshinori — Visiting Professor, Tōkyō University of Agriculture, Tōkyō, Japan

IMAMICHI Tomonobu — Former Professor and Dean, Faculty of Letters, Tōkyō University, Tōkyō, Japan

IMAMURA Yoshio —

IMAZEKI Rokuya — Former President, Mycological Society of Japan, Tōkyō, Japan

INABA Eiko — Formerly on staff of the Long-Term Credit Bank of Japan, Ltd, Tōkyō, Japan

INAGAKI Shisei — Social historian

INŌ Tentarō — Professor, Department of Literature, Chūō University, Tōkyō, Japan

INOKUCHI Shōji — Director, Folklore Society of Japan, Tōkyō, Japan

INOUE Hiroshi — Deputy Chief, Department of Botany, National Science Museum, Tōkyō, Japan

INOUE Kaoru — Professor Emeritus, Ōsaka University, Ōsaka, Japan

INOUE Keizō — Inoue Ski School, Niigata Prefecture, Japan

INOUE Munemichi — Manager, Economic Research Section, Marubeni Corporation, Tōkyō, Japan

INOUE Shōbi — Professor, Department of Education, Tōkyō Gakugei University, Tōkyō, Japan

INOUE Shun — Professor, Faculty of General Education, Ōsaka University, Ōsaka, Japan

INOUE Teruko — Associate Professor, Department of the Humanities, Wakō University, Tōkyō Prefecture, Japan

Daniel K. INOUYE — United States Senator from Hawaii

Akira IRIYE	Professor and Chairman, Department of History, University of Chicago, Chicago, Illinois, US
Mitsuko IRIYE	
Chiyoko ISHIBASHI	
Hoyu ISHIDA	Staff Writer, *Encyclopedia of Japan*
ISHIDA Ichirō	Professor, Department of Literature, Tōkai University, Kanagawa Prefecture, Japan
ISHIGE Naomichi	Associate Professor, National Museum of Ethnology, Ōsaka Prefecture, Japan
ISHII Ryōsuke	Professor, Department of Law, Sōka University, Tōkyō Prefecture, Japan
ISHII Susumu	Professor, Faculty of Letters, Tōkyō University, Tōkyō, Japan
ISHIKAWA Minoru	Professor, Department of Law, Sophia University, Tōkyō, Japan
ISHIMINE Keitetsu	Professor, Department of Law and Letters, Ryūkū University, Naha, Okinawa Prefecture, Japan
ISHIMURA Zensuke	Professor, Department of Law, Tōkyō Metropolitan University, Tōkyō, Japan
ISHIYAMA Akira	Professor, Department of Home Economics, Bunka Women's College, Tōkyō, Japan
ISHIZAKA Etsuo	Professor, Department of Sociology, Hōsei University, Tōkyō, Japan
ISHIZAKI Jūrō	Advisor to Daikyō Oil Co, Ltd, and to Abu-Dhabi Oil Co, Ltd
ISOBE Kiichi	Professor Emeritus, Tōkyō Institute of Technology, Tōkyō, Japan
ITASAKA Tsuyoshi	Film commentator
ITŌ Hajime (d 1980)	Commentator on economic affairs
ITŌ Masami	Judge, Supreme Court, Tōkyō, Japan
ITŌ Mikiharu	Professor, National Museum of Ethnology, Ōsaka Prefecture, Japan
ITŌ Nobuo	Director, National Cultural Properties Research Institute, Tōkyō, Japan
ITŌ Shigeo	Instructor, Legal Training and Research Institute, Supreme Court, Tōkyō, Japan
ITŌ Zen'ichi	Professor, Department of Arts and Science, Tōkyō Women's Christian University, Tōkyō, Japan
Hiroshi ITOH	Professor, Department of Political Science, State University of New York College at Plattsburgh, Plattsburgh, New York, US
IWADARE Hiroshi	Editorial staff, *Asahi shimbun*, Tōkyō, Japan
IWAI Hiroaki	Professor, Department of Sociology, Tōyō University, Tōkyō, Japan
IWAMOTO Tokuichi	Professor, Department of Literature, Kokugakuin University, Tōkyō, Japan
Yoshio IWAMOTO	Professor, Department of East Asian Languages and Cultures, Indiana University, Bloomington, Indiana, US
IWANAGA Shinkichi	Managing Director, Shimbun Tsūshin Chōsakai; author of *The Story of Japanese News Agencies* (1980)
IWASHIMA Hisao	Professor and Director, First Research Office of War History, National Defense College, Tōkyō, Japan
Masakazu IWATA	Professor, Department of History, Biola College, La Mirada, California, US
Tōru IWATAKE	Postdoctoral Research Fellow, Department of Music, University of Queensland, Brisbane, Australia
IYANAGA Teizō	Professor, Department of Literature, Sophia University, Tōkyō, Japan
Marius B. JANSEN	Professor, Department of East Asian Studies, Princeton University, Princeton, New Jersey, US
Donald JENKINS	Director, Portland Art Association, Portland, Oregon, US
JIMBO Genji	Professor, Department of Chemical Engineering, Nagoya University, Aichi Prefecture, Japan
Chalmers JOHNSON	Professor and Chairman, Department of Political Science, University of California, Berkeley, Berkeley, California, US
Gine JOHNSON	
Eleanor H. JORDEN	Professor, Department of Modern Languages and Linguistics, Cornell University, Ithaca, New York, US
John JUNKERMAN	Staff Writer, *Encyclopedia of Japan*
KAGESATO Tetsurō	Director, Mie Prefectural Art Museum, Mie Prefecture, Japan
KAI Michitarō	Professor, Department of Law, Ōsaka City University, Ōsaka, Japan
KAKEGAWA Tomiko	Professor, Department of Sociology, Kansai University, Ōsaka Prefecture, Japan
Yoshiko KAKUDŌ	Curator of Japanese Art, Asian Art Museum of San Francisco, San Francisco, California, US
KAMACHI Noriko	Professor, Department of History, University of Michigan–Dearborn, Dearborn, Michigan, US
KANAI Madoka	Professor, Historiographical Institute, Tōkyō University, Tōkyō, Japan
KANASEKI Hiroshi	Professor and Dean, Department of Arts and Sciences, Tenri University, Nara Prefecture, Japan
KANAZAWA Yoshio	Attorney, Kanazawa Law Office, Tōkyō, Japan
Christine Guth KANDA	Assistant Professor, Department of Art and Archaeology, Princeton University, Princeton, New Jersey, US
James KANDA	
KANEKO Hiroshi	Professor, Faculty of Law, Tōkyō University, Tōkyō, Japan
KANEKO Yoshimasa	President, Seika Jikken Sha, Tōkyō, Japan
KANNO Kōki	Professor, Department of General Education, Iwate University of Medicine, Iwate Prefecture, Japan
KANŌ Hisashi	Nara National Cultural Properties Research Institute, Nara Prefecture, Japan
Eugene J. KAPLAN	Japan Economic Institute of America, Washington, DC, US
Catherine KAPUTA	Cotranslator of *Kanō Eitoku* by Tsuneo Takeda (1977)
KARASAWA Tomitarō	Professor, Department of Education, Sōka University, Tōkyō Prefecture, Japan

KARATSU Hajime — Managing Director, Matsushita Communication Industrial Co, Ltd, Kanagawa Prefecture, Japan

KARITA Yoshio — Chief, First Section, North American Bureau, Ministry of Foreign Affairs, Tōkyō, Japan

KATA Kōji — Commentator; formerly Editor, *Shisō no Kagaku*

KATAGIRI Kazuo — Professor, Department of Literature, Aoyama Gakuin University, Tōkyō, Japan

KATŌ Hiroaki

KATŌ Hiromi — Economic Research Institute, Economic Planning Agency, Tōkyō, Japan

KATŌ Hiroshi — Professor, Department of Economics, Keiō University, Tōkyō, Japan

KATŌ Ichirō — Professor Emeritus, Faculty of Law, Tōkyō University and Chancellor, Seijō Gakuen, Tōkyō, Japan

KATŌ Jōji — Vice-Director, Productivity Research Institute, Japan Productivity Center, Tōkyō, Japan

KATŌ Kōji — Senior Researcher, National Institute for Educational Research, Tōkyō, Japan

KATŌ Kōzaburō — Professor, Department of Economics, Senshū University, Tōkyō, Japan

KATŌ Masashi — Senior Planning Officer, Planning Bureau, Economic Planning Agency, Tōkyō, Japan

KATŌ Shunjirō — Lecturer, Tottori University, Tottori Prefecture, Japan

KATŌ Shunpei — Professor, Department of Engineering, Tōkyō Institute of Science and Technology, Tōkyō, Japan

KATORI Tadahiko — Tōkyō National Museum, Tōkyō, Japan

KATSURA Yoshio — Professor, Department of Education, Kōbe University, Hyōgo Prefecture, Japan

KAWAHARA Sumiyuki — Senior Specialist for Cultural Properties, Monuments and Sites Division, Agency for Cultural Affairs, Tōkyō, Japan

KAWAI Takeshi — Professor, Department of Law, Hitotsubashi University, Tōkyō Prefecture, Japan

KAWAKAMI Hiroshi — Professor, Department of Literature and Arts, Seijō University, Tōkyō, Japan

KAWAMOTO Akira — Professor and Dean, Department of Sociology, Meiji Gakuin University, Tōkyō, Japan

KAWAMOTO Ichirō — Professor, Faculty of Economics, Kōbe University, Hyōgo Prefecture, Japan

KAWAMOTO Takashi — Senior Vice-President, The Bank of Tōkyō Trust Company, New York, New York, US

Fujiya KAWASHIMA — Associate Professor, Department of History, Bowling Green State University, Bowling Green, Ohio, US

KAWAUCHI Hachirō — Professor, Department of Humanities, Ibaraki University, Ibaraki Prefecture, Japan

KAWAZOE Noboru — Director, Communication Design Institute, Kyōto, Japan

KAZAKI Hideo — Professor, Department of Science, Tōhō University, Tōkyō and Professor Emeritus, Tōkyō Metropolitan University, Tōkyō, Japan

Donald KEENE — Professor, Department of East Asian Languages and Cultures, Columbia University, New York, New York, US

James T. KENNEY — Staff Writer, *Encyclopedia of Japan*

Roger KEYES — Coauthor of *The Theatrical World of Osaka Prints* (1973)

KIDA Hiroshi — Director, National Institute for Educational Research, Tōkyō, Japan

KIDA Jun'ichirō — Commentator on publishing

J. Edward KIDDER, JR — Vice-President, and Professor, Division of Humanities, International Christian University, Tōkyō Prefecture, Japan

KIKKAWA Shūhei — Lecturer, Department of Literature, Kagoshima Women's University, Kagoshima Prefecture, Japan

Cornelius J. KILEY — Associate Professor, Department of History, Villanova University, Villanova, Pennsylvania, US

Hee-Jin KIM — Associate Professor, Department of Religious Studies, University of Oregon, Eugene, Oregon, US

Yongdeok KIM — Department of Asian History, College of Humanities, Seoul National University, Seoul, Korea

KIMURA Eiichi — Professor, Department of Commerce, Hitotsubashi University, Tōkyō Prefecture, Japan

KIMURA Hidemasa — Chairman, Japan Committee for Civil Aviation Studies, Tōkyō, Japan

KIMURA Hiroshi — Senior Researcher, National Institute for Education Research, Tōkyō, Japan

KIMURA Kiyotaka — Lecturer, Shitennōji International Buddhist University, Ōsaka Prefecture, Japan

KIMURA Masanori — Professor, Department of Literature, Gakushūin University, Tōkyō, Japan

KIMURA Shigemitsu — Associate Professor, Department of Education, Tōkyō Gakugei University, Tōkyō, Japan

KIMURA Tsuyoshi — Minister's Secretariat, Ministry of Posts and Telecommunications, Tōkyō, Japan

Masako KINOSHITA

KINOUCHI Kiyoko — Professor, Department of Home Economics, Ōtsuma Women's University, Tōkyō, Japan

Maurine A. KIRKPATRICK

KISAKA Jun'ichirō — Professor, Department of Law, Ryūkoku University, Kyōto, Japan

KISHINO Hisashi — Lecturer, Department of Education, Rikkyō University, Tōkyō, Japan

Sandy KITA — Elvejhem Museum of Art, University of Wisconsin–Madison, Madison, Wisconsin, US

Joseph M. KITAGAWA — Professor, Department of Far Eastern Languages and Civilizations, University of Chicago, Chicago, Illinois, US

KITAHARA Yasusada — Executive Vice-President, Nippon Telegraph and Telephone Public Corporation, Tōkyō, Japan

John KITAHARA-FRISCH — Professor, Life Science Institute, Sophia University, Tōkyō, Japan

KITAMURA Bunji — Professor, Department of Literature, Kokushikan University, Tōkyō, Japan

KITAZAWA Masahiro — Professor, Faculty of Law, Nagoya University, Aichi Prefecture, Japan

Gisaburō N. KIYOSE — Assistant Professor, Department of East Asian Languages, University of Hawaii at Manoa, Honolulu, Hawaii, US

Jill KLEINBERG — Staff Writer, *Encyclopedia of Japan*

Lothar G. KNAUTH — Professor, Universidad Nacional Autonoma de Mexico, Villa Obregon, Mexico

KOBAYAKAWA Yōichi

KOBAYASHI Kazuhiro — Publications specialist

KOBAYASHI Manabu — Professor, Department of Education, Tsukuba University, Ibaraki Prefecture, Japan

KOBAYASHI Saburō — Professor, Archaeological Institute, Meiji University, Tōkyō, Japan

T. James KODERA — Associate Professor, Department of Religion, Wellesley College, Wellesley, Massachusetts, US

KOGIKU Kiichirō — Professor, Department of Economics, University of California, US

Byung Chul KOH — Professor, Department of Political Science, University of Illinois at Chicago, Chicago, Illinois, US

KOIKE Chie — Professor, Department of Home Economics, Bunka Women's University, Tōkyō, Japan

KOIZUMI Iwao — Professor, Department of Technology, Kanazawa University, Ishikawa Prefecture, Japan

KOJIMA Kazuto — Associate Professor, Department of Liberal Arts, Saitama University, Saitama Prefecture, Japan

KOJIMA Takeshi — Professor, Department of Law, Chūō University, Tōkyō, Japan

KOJIMA Tomiko — Lecturer, Department of Music, Tōkyō University of Fine Arts and Music, Tōkyō, Japan

KOKUBO Takeshi — Executive Editor, *Encyclopedia of Japan*

Akira KOMAI — Professor, Department of Far Eastern Languages and Civilizations, University of Chicago, Chicago, Illinois, US

KOMATA Yūsuke — Lecturer, Tankang University, Taipei, Taiwan

KOMATSU Sakyō — Science fiction writer

KOMINE Takao — Domestic Research Section, Economic Planning Agency, Tōkyō, Japan

KONDŌ Shinji — National Defense College, Tōkyō, Japan

KONISHI Jin'ichi — Professor Emeritus, Tsukuba University, Ibaraki Prefecture, Japan

KŌNO Motomichi — Lecturer, Komazawa University, Tōkyō and at Hokkaidō Education University, Hokkaidō, Japan

KŌNO Tomomi — Professor, Ōsaka Kun'ei Women's College, Ōsaka and Director, Kōno Food Research Institute, Ōsaka, Japan

KOSHIBA Harumi — Associate Professor, Department of Humanities and Arts, Tōkai University, Tōkyō, Japan

KOTANI Kōzō — Deputy Director-General, Government Pension Bureau, Prime Minister's Office, Tōkyō, Japan

KŌUCHI Saburō — Professor, Institute of Journalism, Tōkyō University, Tōkyō, Japan

KOYANAGI Shun'ichirō — Lecturer, Faculty of Education, Yamanashi University, Yamanashi Prefecture, Japan

KOYASU Nobukuni — Professor, Faculty of Literature, Ōsaka University, Ōsaka, Japan

KOZAWA Tadahiro — Staff Writer, *Encyclopedia of Japan*

Klaus KRACHT — Lecturer, Abteilung für Ostasienwissenschaften, Ruhr-Universität Bochum, Bochum, West Germany

Ellis S. KRAUSS — Associate Professor, Department of Political Science, Western Washington University, Bellingham, Washington, US

Hyman KUBLIN — Professor, Department of History, Brooklyn College, Brooklyn, New York, US

KUBO Fuminae — Director-General, Japan Pharmaceutical Information Center, Tōkyō, Japan

KUBOTA Kinuko — Professor, Department of Law, Tōhoku Gakuin University, Miyagi Prefecture, Japan

KUBOTA Takeshi — Teacher, Tōkyō Metropolitan Nishi Senior High School, Tōkyō, Japan

KUDŌ Masanobu — Director, Japan Ikebana Art Society, Tōkyō, Japan

KUMA Rakuya — Executive Director and General Manager, Research Laboratory, Kobayashi Kōsē Co, Ltd, Tōkyō, Japan

Fumie KUMAGAI — Professor, Department of Sociology, University of New Hampshire, Durham, New Hampshire, US

KUMAGAI Hiroshi — President, Japanese Association of Medical Sciences, Tōkyō, Japan

KUMAKURA Isao — Associate Professor, Institute of History and Ethnology, Tsukuba University, Ibaraki Prefecture, Japan

KUMATORI Toshiyuki — Director-General, National Institute of Radiological Sciences, Chiba Prefecture, Japan

KURANISHI Shigeru — Professor, Department of Engineering, Tōhoku University, Miyagi Prefecture, Japan

KURATA Bunsaku (d 1983) — Director, Nara National Museum, Nara, Japan

KURAUCHI Shirō — Professor, Department of Literature, Tōyō University, Tōkyō, Japan

KURITA Ken — Professor, Department of Commerce, Meiji University, Tōkyō, Japan

KURIYAMA Shigehisa — Staff Writer, *Encyclopedia of Japan*

KURODA Nobuyuki — Professor, School of Law, Kansei Gakuin University, Hyōgo Prefecture, Japan

Michio KUSHI — Kushi Institute, Boston, Massachusetts, US

KUWATA Tadachika — Professor Emeritus, Department of Literature, Kokugakuin University, Tōkyō, Japan

George KUWAYAMA — Senior Curator, Far Eastern Art, Los Angeles County Museum of Art, Los Angeles, California, US

Patricia Hagan KUWAYAMA — Manager, Foreign Exchange Department, Federal Reserve Bank of New York, New York, New York, US

William R. LAFLEUR — Associate Professor, Department of Oriental Languages, University of California, Los Angeles, Los Angeles, California, US

Whalen LAI — Associate Professor, Department of Religious Studies, University of California, Davis, Davis, California, US

Harry J. LAMLEY — Professor, Department of History, University of Hawaii at Manoa, Honolulu, Hawaii, US

H. G. LAMONT — Department of Oriental Languages, University of California, Los Angeles, Los Angeles, California, US

Richard LANE — Author of *Masters of the Japanese Print* (1962), *Shunga Books of the Ukiyo-e School, Series I-VI* (1973–82), and *Images from the Floating World* (1978).

Betty B. LANHAM — Professor, Department of Sociology and Anthropology, Indiana University of Pennsylvania, Indiana, Pennsylvania, US

T. C. LARKIN — New Zealand Ambassador to Japan 1972–76; Consultant, International Trade Development, Asia Pacific Research Unit Limited, Wellington, New Zealand

Joyce C. LEBRA — Professor, Department of History, University of Colorado, Boulder, Colorado, US

Takie Sugiyama LEBRA — Professor, Department of Anthropology, University of Hawaii at Manoa, Honolulu, Hawaii, US

Gari LEDYARD — Professor and Chairman, Department of East Asian Languages and Cultures, Columbia University, New York, New York, US

Changsoo LEE — Assistant Professor, School of Public Administration, University of Southern California, Los Angeles, California, US

George Alexander LENSEN (d 1980) — Professor, Department of History, Florida State University, Tallahassee, Florida, US

Robert W. LEUTNER — Assistant Professor, Department of Asian Languages and Literature, University of Iowa, Iowa City, Iowa, US

Solomon B. LEVINE — Professor, School of Business, University of Wisconsin–Madison, Madison, Wisconsin, US

Young Ick LEW — Associate Professor, Department of History, University of Houston, Houston, Texas, US

Bruno H. LEWIN — Professor, Abteilung für Ostasienwissenschaften, Ruhr-Universität Bochum, Bochum, West Germany

Olof LIDIN — Professor, East Asian Institute, University of Copenhagen, Copenhagen, Denmark

Thomas B. LIFSON — Assistant Professor, Graduate School of Business Administration, Harvard University, Cambridge, Massachusetts, US

Anthony V. LIMAN — Associate Professor, Department of East Asian Studies, University of Toronto, Ontario, Canada

Edward J. LINCOLN — Vice-President, Japan Economic Institute of America, Washington, DC, US

Howard A. LINK — Curator of Asian Art, Honolulu Academy of Arts, Honolulu, Hawaii, US

Noriko Mizuta LIPPIT — Associate Professor, Department of East Asian Languages and Cultures, University of Southern California, Los Angeles, California, US

Victor D. LIPPIT — Associate Professor, Department of Economics, University of California, Riverside, Riverside, California, US

David J. LU — Professor, Department of History and Director, Center for Japanese Studies, Bucknell University, Lewisburg, Pennsylvania, US

Jack A. LUCKEN — Associate Professor, Graduate School of Management, Rutgers–The State University of New Jersey, Newark, New Jersey, US

Leonard LYNN — Associate Professor, Department of Social Sciences, Carnegie–Mellon University, Pittsburgh, Pennsylvania, US

Kathleen MCCARTHY

Paul MCCARTHY — Associate Professor, Faculty of General Education, Rikkyō University, Tōkyō, Japan

James D. MCCAWLEY — Professor, Department of Linguistics, University of Chicago, Chicago, Illinois, US

Harold A. MCCLEERY — Vice-President, Tōkyō office, Chemical Bank, Tōkyō, Japan

Edwin MCCLELLAN — Professor, Department of East Asian Languages and Literatures, Yale University, New Haven, Connecticut, US

Aya Louisa MCDONALD — Acting Assistant Professor, Department of Art, Wellesley College, Wellesley, Massachusetts, US

Terry Edward MACDOUGALL — Associate Professor, Department of Government, Harvard University, Cambridge, Massachusetts, US

Miles K. MCELRATH — Associate Professor, Department of East Asian Languages and Literatures, Ohio State University, Columbus, Ohio, US

MACHIDA Yōji — Manager, Industrial Research Division, Long-Term Credit Bank of Japan, Ltd, Tōkyō, Japan

James MCMULLEN — Lecturer, Oriental Institute, University of Oxford, Oxford, United Kingdom

Theodore MCNELLY — Professor, Department of Government and Politics, University of Maryland, College Park, Maryland, US

Wayne C. MCWILLIAMS — Associate Professor, Department of History, Towson State University, Towson, Maryland, US

MAEDA Kazutoshi — Professor, Department of Management, Komazawa University, Tōkyō, Japan

MAEDA Wakaki — Sports Section, Tōkyō Office, *Chūnichi shimbun*, Tōkyō, Japan

MAKABE Tetsuo — Deputy Manager, International Project Finance Division, Long-Term Credit Bank of Japan, Ltd, Tōkyō, Japan

John M. MAKI — Professor Emeritus, Department of Political Science, University of Massachusetts, Amherst, Massachusetts, US

MAKI Masami — Head, Section IV, Institute for National Educational Research, Tōkyō, Japan

MAKINO Noboru	Vice-President, Mitsubishi Research Institute, Inc, Tōkyō, Japan
William P. MALM	Professor, School of Music, University of Michigan, Ann Arbor, Michigan, US
Alfred H. MARKS	Professor, Department of English, State University of New York at New Paltz, New Paltz, New York, US
Susan H. MARSH	Associate Professor, Department of Political Science, Providence College, Providence, Rhode Island, US
Byron K. MARSHALL	Professor, Department of History, University of Minnesota at Minneapolis St. Paul, Minneapolis, Minnesota, US
Samuel E. MARTIN	Professor, Department of Linguistics, Yale University, New Haven, Connecticut, US
MARUOKA Hideko	Writer on Japanese women's problems
Penelope E. MASON	Associate Professor, Department of Art, Florida State University, Tallahassee, Florida, US
Jeffrey MASS	Professor, Department of History, Stanford University, Stanford, California, US
MASUDA Yoshio	Professor, College of Arts and Sciences, Tōkyō University, Tōkyō, Japan
MASUDA Yūji	Senior Researcher, Economic Research Institute, Japan Society for the Promotion of Machine Industry, Tōkyō, Japan
MASUI Ken'ichi	Professor, Department of Commerce, Keiō University, Tōkyō, Japan
MASUNAGA Shizuto	Executive, Iōkai Shiatsu Center, Tōkyō, Japan
Francis MATHY	Professor, Department of Literature, Sophia University, Tōkyō, Japan
Susan MATISOFF	Associate Professor, Department of Asian Languages, Stanford University, Stanford, California, US
MATSUBARA Mitsunori	Prior, Yakushiin, Okayama Prefecture, Japan
Naoko MATSUBARA	Artist, printmaker
MATSUDA Osamu	President, Japan Association of the Friends of Plants, Tōkyō, Japan
MATSUI Hideji	Director, Research Center of Health, Physical Fitness and Sports, University of Nagoya, Aichi Prefecture, Japan
Amy T. MATSUMOTO	Associate Professor, Department of East Asian Languages, University of Minnesota at Minneapolis St. Paul, Minneapolis, Minnesota, US
MATSUMOTO Saburō	Professor, Department of Law, Keiō University, Tōkyō, Japan
Tomone MATSUMOTO	Lecturer, School of Modern Asian Studies, Griffith University, Nathan, Queensland, Australia
MATSUNAGA Seiji	Deputy Manager, Operations Administration Division, Long-Term Credit Bank of Japan, Ltd, Tōkyō, Japan
MATSUNAMI Yoshihiro	Associate Professor, Department of Buddhism, Taishō University, Tōkyō, Japan
MATSUO Takayoshi	Professor, Faculty of Letters, Kyōto University, Kyōto, Japan
MATSUSHITA Mitsuo	Professor, Department of Law, Sophia University, Tōkyō, Japan
MATSUURA Kaoru	Professor, Faculty of Law, Nagoya University, Aichi Prefecture, Japan
Marlene J. MAYO	Associate Professor, Department of History, University of Maryland, College Park, Maryland, US
MAYUZUMI Hiromichi	Professor, Department of Literature, Gakushūin University, Tōkyō, Japan
Meron MEDZINI	Visiting Senior Lecturer, School for Overseas Students, Hebrew University, Jerusalem, Israel
Julia MEECH-PEKARIK	Associate Curator, Far Eastern Art, The Metropolitan Museum of Art, New York, New York, US
Joan MELLEN	Professor, Department of English, Temple University, Philadelphia, Pennsylvania, US
Richard L. MELLOTT	
MERA Kōichi	Professor, Institute of Socioeconomic Planning, Tsukuba University, Ibaraki Prefecture, Japan
Charles M. MERGENTIME	
Daniel A. METRAUX	Department of History, Philosophy, and Government, Anderson College, Anderson, Indiana, US
MIHARA Takeshi	Staff, General Research and Planning Department, Fukutoku Mutual Bank, Ōsaka, Japan
MIKAMI Terumi	Professor, Department of Literature, Chūō University, Tōkyō, Japan
MIKI Seiichirō	Assistant Professor, Faculty of Literature, Nagoya University, Aichi Prefecture, Japan
Frank O. MILLER	Chairman, Department of Political Science, College of Wooster, Wooster, Ohio, US
Roy Andrew MILLER	Professor, Department of Asian Languages and Literature, University of Washington, Seattle, Washington, US
Douglas E. MILLS	Lecturer, Faculty of Oriental Studies, University of Cambridge, Cambridge, United Kingdom
MINAMIZUKA Shingo	Assistant Professor, Faculty of Literature, Chiba University, Chiba Prefecture, Japan
Richard H. MINEAR	Professor, Department of History, University of Massachusetts, Amherst, Massachusetts, US
MINEGISHI Kentarō	Assistant Professor, Department of Humanities, Tōkyō Metropolitan University, Tōkyō, Japan
MINEGISHI Sumio	Assistant Professor, Department of Humanities, Tōkyō Metropolitan University, Tōkyō, Japan
Earl MINER	Professor, Department of East Asian Studies, Princeton University, Princeton, New Jersey, US
Sharon A. MINICHIELLO	Associate Professor, Department of History, Loyola Marymount University, Los Angeles, California, US
MISUMI Haruo	Tōkyō National Cultural Properties Research Institute, Tōkyō, Japan

Arthur M. MITCHELL	Attorney, Tanaka & Takahashi, Tōkyō, Japan
C. H. MITCHELL	Author of *The Illustrated Books of the Nanga, Maruyama, Shijō and Other Related Schools of Japan: A Biobibliography* (1972)
Richard H. MITCHELL	Professor, Department of History, University of Missouri at St. Louis, St. Louis, Missouri, US
MIYACHI Seiya	Professor, Department of Economics, Kokugakuin University, Tōkyō, Japan
Hiroshi MIYAJI	Professor, Department of Oriental Studies, University of Pennsylvania, Philadelphia, Pennsylvania, US
MIYAKE Hitoshi	Professor, Department of Literature, Keiō University, Tōkyō, Japan
MIYAKE Masahiko	Professor, Department of Education, Aichi University of Education, Aichi Prefecture, Japan
MIYAMOTO Mataji	Professor Emeritus, Ōsaka University, Ōsaka, Japan
MIYAMOTO Mizuo	Lecturer, Department of Literature, Waseda University, Tōkyō, Japan
MIYANO Nobuyuki	Director, Indirect Tax Division, Takamatsu National Tax Bureau, Kagawa Prefecture, Japan
MIYAO Shigeo (d 1982)	Cartoonist and folklore researcher
MIYATA Setsuko	Lecturer, Department of Literature, Waseda University, Tōkyō, Japan
Dixon Y. MIYAUCHI	Professor, Department of History, State University of New York at Plattsburgh, Plattsburgh, New York, US
MIYAWAKI Osamu	Professor, Faculty of Education, Yokohama National University, Yokohama, Japan
MIYAZAWA Ken'ichi	President, Hitotsubashi University, Tōkyō Prefecture, Japan
Masao MIYOSHI	Professor, Department of English, University of California, Berkeley, Berkeley, California, US
MIZOGUCHI Toshiyuki	Professor, Institute of Economic Research, Hitotsubashi University, Tōkyō Prefecture, Japan
MIZUBAYASHI Takeshi	Associate Professor, Faculty of Law, Tōkyō Metropolitan University, Tōkyō, Japan
MOCHIDA Minoru	Deputy Manager, Business Department, Meiji Mutual Life Insurance Company, Tōkyō, Japan
Brian MOERAN	Department of Anthropology and Sociology, School of Oriental and African Studies, University of London, London, United Kingdom
Robert MOES	Curator, Department of Oriental Art, The Brooklyn Museum, Brooklyn, New York, US
Kathleen MOLONY	
MOMOSE Hiroto	Deputy Manager, Business Development Division, Long-Term Credit Bank of Japan, Ltd, Tōkyō, Japan
MOMOSE Kesao	Professor, Office for the Compilation of Historical Materials, Tōkyō University, Tōkyō, Japan
Tazuko MONANE	Professor, Department of Foreign Languages, University of Hawaii at Hilo, Hilo, Hawaii, US
Betty Iverson MONROE	Associate Professor, Department of Art History, Northwestern University, Evanston, Illinois, US
Wilbur F. MONROE	Author of *Japanese Financial Markets and the World Economy* (1973) and *Japanese Exports to the United States* (1978)
MORI Masumi	Researcher, Japanese Business History Institute, Tōkyō, Japan
MORIMOTO Minoru	Section Chief, Ministry of Agriculture, Forestry, and Fisheries, Tōkyō, Japan
MORINAGA Hiroshi	Professor and Director, Misasa Branch, Okayama University Hospital, Okayama Prefecture, Japan
James R. MORITA	Associate Professor, Department of East Asian Languages and Literatures, Ohio State University, Columbus, Ohio, US
MORIYAMA Tsuneo	Professor, Faculty of Education, Kumamoto University, Kumamoto Prefecture, Japan
Carol MORLAND	
Robert E. MORRELL	Associate Professor, Department of Japanese and Chinese, Washington University, St. Louis, Missouri, US
Mark MORRIS	Lecturer, Centre for Asian Studies, University of Adelaide, Adelaide, South Australia, Australia
Helmut MORSBACH	Senior Lecturer, Department of Psychology, University of Glasgow, Glasgow, Scotland
Anne Nishimura MORSE	
Ronald A. MORSE	Director, East Asia Center for Scholars, Washington, DC, US
William F. MORTON	Associate Professor and Chairman, Department of History, York College of the City University of New York, Jamaica, New York, US
William G. MORTON	
Karl MOSKOWITZ	Assistant Professor, Department of East Asian Languages and Civilizations, Harvard University, Cambridge, Massachusetts, US
MOTEGI Kiyoko	Lecturer, Takasaki College of Music, Gumma Prefecture, Japan
Frank T. MOTOFUJI	Professor, Department of Oriental Languages, University of California, Berkeley, Berkeley, California, US
Ross MOUER	Lecturer, School of Modern Asian Studies, Griffith University, Nathan, Queensland, Australia
MOZAI Torao	Professor, Department of Oceanography, Tōkai University, Kanagawa Prefecture, Japan
Chieko MULHERN	Associate Professor, Center for East Asian Studies, University of Illinois, Urbana, Illinois, US

Hugo MÜNSTERBERG — Professor Emeritus, Department of Art History, State University of New York College at New Paltz, New Paltz, New York, US

MURAKAMI Shigeyoshi — Lecturer, Department of Social Sciences, Hitotsubashi University, Tōkyō Prefecture, Japan

MURAKAMI Yumi — Security Analyst, Paine, Webber, Mitchell Co, New York, New York, US

MURAKOSHI Sueo — Professor, Department of General Education, Ōsaka City University, Ōsaka, Japan

MURAMATSU Teijirō — Professor, Institute of Industrial Science, Tōkyō University, Tōkyō, Japan

MURATA Hiroshi — President, Japan Institute of Life Insurance, Tōkyō, Japan

MURATA Yoshio — Professor, Tōkyō University of Agriculture, Tōkyō, Japan

Patricia MURRAY — Executive Editor, The Japan Interpreter, Tōkyō, Japan

MUTŌ Shunkō — Judge, Tōkyō Higher Court, Tōkyō, Japan

MUTSU Gorō — Director, International Relations Office, National Defense College, National Defense Agency, Tōkyō, Japan

William E. NAFF — Professor, Department of Asian Languages and Literatures, University of Massachusetts, Amherst, Massachusetts, US

NAGAHAMA Yōichi — Professor, Department of Law, Waseda University, Tōkyō, Japan

NAGAHARA Keiji — Professor, Department of Economics, Hitotsubashi University, Tōkyō Prefecture, Japan

NAGAI Hiroo — Professor, Department of Science and Literature, Nihon University, Tōkyō, Japan

NAGANO Gorō — Lecturer, Seian Women's College, Kyōto, Japan

NAGAO Masakazu — Tokio Marine and Fire Insurance Co, Ltd, Vancouver, British Columbia, Canada

NAGAO Ryūichi — Professor, College of Arts and Sciences, Tōkyō University, Tōkyō, Japan

Susumu NAGARA — Professor, Department of Far Eastern Languages and Literatures, University of Michigan, Ann Arbor, Michigan, US

NAGASAWA Katsuo — Professor Emeritus, Chiba University, Chiba Prefecture, Japan

NAGASE Akira — Japan Equipment Inspection Institute, Tōkyō, Japan

NAGASHIMA Atsushi — Professor, Department of Law, Tōyō University, Tōkyō, Japan

NAGATOYA Yōji — Lecturer, School of Medicine, Ōsaka University, Ōsaka, Japan

NAGAZUMI Akira — Professor, Faculty of Letters, Tōkyō University, Tōkyō, Japan

NAITŌ Kinju — Research and Study Department, Japan Travel Bureau, Tōkyō, Japan

NAITŌ Motoo — Professor Emeritus, Tōkyō University, Tōkyō, Japan; Professor, Nippon College of Veterinary and Zootechnical Science, Tōkyō, Japan

Tetsuo NAJITA — Professor, Center for Far Eastern Studies, University of Chicago, Chicago, Illinois, US

NAKAGAWA Kōji — Deputy Executive Secretary, Economic and Social Commission for Asia and the Pacific, Bangkok, Thailand

NAKAGAWA Masayuki — Deputy Manager, Operations Administration Division, Long-Term Credit Bank of Japan, Ltd, Tōkyō, Japan

Kate NAKAI — Assistant Professor, Department of History, University of Oregon, Eugene, Oregon, US

Yoshiyuki NAKAI — Assistant Professor, Department of Chinese and Japanese, University of Oregon, Eugene, Oregon, US

NAKAJIMA Kawatarō — Professor, Department of Literature and Home Economics, Wayō Women's University, Chiba Prefecture, Japan

NAKAJIMA Kenzō — Professor, Department of Education, Tōkyō Gakugei University, Tōkyō, Japan

NAKAJIMA Naotada — Professor, Research Division, National Center for University Entrance Examination, Tōkyō, Japan

NAKAMURA Hajime — Director, The Eastern Institute, Inc, Tōkyō, Japan

Kyōko Motomochi NAKAMURA — Assistant Professor, Liberal Arts Division, Kawamura Junior College, Tōkyō, Japan

NAKAMURA Masanori — Professor, Department of Economics, Hitotsubashi University, Tōkyō Prefecture, Japan

NAKANE Chie — Professor, Institute of Oriental Culture, Tōkyō University, Tōkyō, Japan

NAKANE Takehiko — Professor, Department of Science, Kagoshima University, Kagoshima Prefecture, Japan

Don T. NAKANISHI — Assistant Professor, Asian American Studies Center, University of California, Los Angeles, Los Angeles, California, US

NAKASA Hideo — Chief, Programming Division, National Association of Commercial Broadcasters in Japan, Tōkyō, Japan

NAKASATO Toshikatsu — Head, First Section, Department of Restoration Techniques, Tōkyō National Research Institute of Cultural Properties, Tōkyō, Japan

NAKAUCHI Tsuneo — Professor, Department of Arts and Sciences, International Christian University, Tōkyō Prefecture, Japan

Shigeru NAKAYAMA — Lecturer, College of Arts and Sciences, Tōkyō University, Tōkyō, Japan

Dick K. NANTO — Assistant Professor, Department of Economics, Brigham Young University, Provo, Utah, US

NAOI Atsushi — Assistant Professor, Faculty of Letters, Tōkyō University, Tōkyō, Japan

NARAMOTO Tatsuya — Historian

NARITA Katsuya — Professor, Tōkyō University, Tōkyō, Japan

NARITA Yoriaki — Professor, Faculty of Economics, Yokohama National University, Kanagawa Prefecture, Japan

NASU Hiroshi (d 1979) — Professor, Department of Economics, Gifu University of Economics, Gifu Prefecture, Japan

Karin C. NELSON

Margret NEUSS — Professor, Abteilung Japanologie, Philipps-Universität, Marburg, West Germany

J. V. NEUSTUPNÝ — Chairman, Department of Japanese, Monash University, Clayton, Victoria, Australia

NIKI Isao — Japan Raw Silk and Sugar Price Stabilization Agency, Tōkyō, Japan

NINOMIYA Masato — Attorney

Ian NISH — Reader, London School of Economics, University of London, London, United Kingdom

NISHIDA Makoto — Professor, Faculty of Science, Chiba University, Chiba Prefecture, Japan

NISHIDA Shunji — Assistant Manager, Personnel Division, Long-Term Credit Bank of Japan, Ltd, Tōkyō, Japan

NISHIJIMA Sadao — Professor Emeritus, Tōkyō University; Professor, Department of Humanities, Niigata University, Niigata Prefecture, Japan

NISHIKAWA Osamu — Professor, College of Arts and Sciences, Tōkyō University, Tōkyō, Japan

NISHIMIZU Mieko — Assistant Professor, Department of Economics, Princeton University, Princeton, New Jersey, US

NISHIMOTO Yōichi — Professor, Department of Politics and Economics, Tōkai University, Tōkyō, Japan

NISHIMURA Makoto — Professor, Department of Literature, Tōyō University, Tōkyō, Japan

Harry K. NISHIO — Professor, Department of Sociology, University of Toronto, Toronto, Ontario, Canada

Tamako NIWA — Associate Professor, Department of Asian Languages and Literature, University of Washington, Seattle, Washington, US

NIWATA Noriaki — Professor, Department of Commerce, Keiō University, Tōkyō, Japan

Agnes M. NIYEKAWA — Professor, Department of East Asian Languages, University of Hawaii at Manoa, Honolulu, Hawaii, US

NODA Kazuo — Professor, Department of Sociology, Rikkyō University, Tōkyō, Japan

NOGUCHI Takehiko — Assistant Professor, Department of Literature, Kōbe University, Hyōgo Prefecture, Japan

NOGUCHI Takenori — Professor, Department of Literature and Arts, Seijō University, Tōkyō Prefecture, Japan

NOGUCHI Yukio — Professor, Department of Economics, Hitotsubashi University, Tōkyō Prefecture, Japan

NOHARA Hiroshi — Nohara Office for Technicians, Kanagawa Prefecture, Japan

Sharon NOLTE — Assistant Professor, Department of History, Southern Methodist University, Dallas, Texas, US

NOMURA Tadao — Managing Director, Hōsō Bunka Foundation, Tōkyō, Japan

NOMURA Yoshihiro — Professor, Faculty of Law, Tōkyō Metropolitan University, Tōkyō, Japan

Edward NORBECK — Professor, Department of Anthropology, Rice University, Houston, Texas, US

NOSE Takayuki — Professor, Department of Public Health, School of Medicine, Tottori University, Tottori Prefecture, Japan

F. G. NOTEHELFER — Associate Professor, Department of History, University of California, Los Angeles, Los Angeles, California, US

NOZAKI Shigeru — Director, Broadcasting Research Institute, National Association of Commercial Broadcasters in Japan, Tōkyō, Japan

NUMATA Satoshi — Assistant Professor, Department of Literature, Aoyama Gakuin University, Tōkyō, Japan

James A. O'BRIEN — Professor, Department of East Asian Languages and Literature, University of Wisconsin, Madison, Wisconsin, US

OCHIAI Shigenobu — Kōbe Municipal Central Library, Hyōgo Prefecture, Japan

ODA Takeo — Professor Emeritus, Kyōto University, Kyōto, Japan

ODA Yukio — Assistant Manager, General Planning and Administration Division, Long-Term Credit Bank of Japan, Ltd, Tōkyō, Japan

ODAKA Kōnosuke — Professor, Institute of Economic Research, Hitotsubashi University, Tōkyō Prefecture, Japan

OGASAWARA Nobuo — Senior Researcher, Industrial Arts Section, Art and Science Division, Tōkyō National Museum, Tōkyō, Japan

OGATA Shijūrō — Executive Director, Bank of Japan, Tōkyō, Japan

OGAWA Yoshio — Professor Emeritus, Tōkyō University of Foreign Studies, Tōkyō, Japan

ŌGUCHI Yūjirō — Professor, Department of Letters and Education, Ochanomizu Women's University, Tōkyō, Japan

OGURA Michio — Professor, Department of Fisheries, Tōkyō University of Fisheries, Tōkyō, Japan

OGURI Junko — Lecturer, Gakujutsu Kenkyūjo, Tōkyō, Japan

OHARA Satoru — Professor, Department of Literature, Sophia University, Tōkyō, Japan

ŌHARA Satoshi — Professor, Department of Economics, Tōkyō Keizai University, Tōkyō, Japan

OKA Takashi — Associate Professor, Department of Law, Hōsei University, Tōkyō, Japan

OKADA Yasushi — Manager, Industrial Research Divsion, Long-Term Credit Bank of Japan, Ltd, Tōkyō, Japan

Shumpei OKAMOTO — Professor, Department of History, Temple University, Philadelphia, Pennsylvania, US

Frank Masao OKAMURA — Brooklyn Botanic Garden, Brooklyn, New York, US

ŌKI Yasue — Director, Kanagawa Prefectural Hot Spring Institute, Kanagawa Prefecture, Japan

Daniel I. OKIMOTO — Assistant Professor, Department of Political Science, Stanford University, Stanford, California, US

OKONOGI Masao — Associate Professor, Department of Law, Keiō University, Tōkyō, Japan

OKUDA Shinjō — Professor, Faculty of Education, Yokohama National University, Kanagawa Prefecture, Japan

OKUDAIRA Yasuhiro	Professor, Institute of Social Science, Tōkyō University, Tōkyō, Japan
ŌMORI Kazuko	Professor, Department of Home Economics, Tōkyō Kasei University, Tōkyō, Japan
ŌNAMI Yūji	Priest, Russian Orthodox Church, Tōkyō, Japan
P. G. O'NEILL	Professor, School of Oriental and African Studies, University of London, London, United Kingdom
ŌNISHI Harutaka	Professor, Department of Literature, Nara University, Nara Prefecture, Japan
ONO Kōji	Dean, Department of Law, Daitō Bunka University, Tōkyō, Japan
ŌNO Tōru	Professor, Department of Foreign Languages, Ōsaka University of Foreign Studies, Ōsaka, Japan
ŌNO Tsutomu	Writer on Social Thought and Contemporary Social Problems
ONODA Yōichi	Director, Shin Nampeidai Clinic, Tōkyō, Japan
Herman OOMS	Associate Professor, Department of History, University of Illinois at Chicago Circle, Chicago, Illinois, US
Alfred C. OPPLER (d 1982)	Jurist; Author of *Contemporary Japan* (1952) and *Legal Reform in Occupied Japan: A Participant Looks Back* (1976)
ORITA Kōji	Chief, Production Room, Theatrical Division, National Theater of Japan, Tōkyō, Japan
Masako M. ŌSAKO	Assistant Professor, Department of Sociology, University of Illinois, Chicago, Illinois, US
OSHIMA Mitsuo	Professor Emeritus, Tōkyō Gakugei University, Tōkyō, Japan
ŌSUMI Seiji	Far Seas Fishery Research Laboratory, Fisheries Agency, Shizuoka Prefecture, Japan
ŌTA Rin'ichirō	Librarian, Keiō University Library, Tōkyō, Japan
ŌTA Yoshimaro	Professor, Department of Literature, Sophia University, Tōkyō, Japan
Yūzō ŌTA	Associate Professor, Department of History, McGill University, Montreal, Quebec, Canada
ŌTŌ Tokihiko	Professor Emeritus, Seijō University, Tōkyō, Japan
ŌTSUKA Shigeru	Councillor, Foreign Affairs Division, Japanese National Railways, Tōkyō, Japan
ŌTSUKA Shigeru	Professor, Department of Literature, Mukogawa Women's University, Hyōgo Prefecture, Japan
ŌTSUKA Sueko	President, Ōtsuka Gakuin, Tōkyō, Japan
ŌTSUKA Yasuo	Vice-President, Oriental Medicine Research Center, Kitasato Institute, Tōkyō, Japan
ŌUCHI Eishin	Abbot, Shōenji, Nagasaki Prefecture, Japan
ŌUCHI Minoru	Center for International Studies, Cornell University, Ithaca, New York, US
OWADA Hisashi	Minister, Japanese Embassy, Moscow, USSR
David OWENS	Japan Society, Inc, New York, New York, US
Robert S. OZAKI	Professor, Department of Economics, School of Business and Economics, California State College at Hayward, Hayward, California, US
OZAWA Terutomo	Professor, Department of Economics, Colorado State University, Fort Collins, Colorado, US
George R. PACKARD	Dean, School of Advanced International Studies, John Hopkins University, Washington, DC, US
Allan PALMER	Tea ceremony teacher, Urasenke Foundation, Kyōto, Japan
Hugh PATRICK	Professor, Department of Economics, Yale University, New Haven, Connecticut, US
Erich PAUER	Lecturer, Japanologisches Seminar, Universität Bonn, Bonn, West Germany
Diana PAUL	Assistant Professor, Department of Religious Studies, Stanford University, Stanford, California, US
Mark R. PEATTIE	Visiting Professor, Department of History, University of California, Los Angeles, Los Angeles, California, US
Joseph A. PECHMAN	Director, Economic Studies Program, The Brookings Institution, Washington, DC, US
T. J. PEMPEL	Director, China–Japan Program, Cornell University, Ithaca, New York, US
Susan J. PHARR	Professor, Department of Political Science, University of Wisconsin–Madison, Madison, Wisconsin, US
Rulan Chao PIAN	Professor, Department of East Asian Languages and Civilizations, Harvard University, Cambridge, Massachusetts, US
Stuart D. B. PICKEN	Professor, Division of Humanities, International Christian University, Tōkyō Prefecture, Japan
John D. PIERSON	Manager, Planning and Development, Signode Nippon, Ltd, Kōbe, Japan
Ernest D. PIRYNS	Lecturer, International Department, Sophia University, Tōkyō, Japan
Joseph PITTAU	Former President, Sophia University, Tōkyō, Japan
David W. PLATH	Professor, Department of Anthropology, University of Illinois, Urbana, Illinois, US
Herbert E. PLUTSCHOW	Associate Professor, Department of Oriental Languages, University of California, Los Angeles, Los Angeles, California, US
Christian POLAK	Research Scholar, Maison Franco-Japonaise, Tōkyō, Japan
David POLLACK	Assistant Professor, Department of Foreign Languages, Literatures, and Linguistics, University of Rochester, Rochester, New York, US
Junco Sato POLLACK	
Edythe POLSTER	
Barbara PORTER	
Brian POWELL	Lecturer, Oriental Institute, University of Oxford, Oxford, United Kingdom
Irena POWELL	Oriental Institute, University of Oxford, Oxford, United Kingdom

Cyril H. POWLES	Professor, Faculty of Divinity, Trinity College, Toronto, Ontario, Canada
C. Kenneth QUINONES	Assistant Professor, Department of History, Trinity College, Hartford, Connecticut, US
Judith N. RABINOVITCH	Assistant Professor, Department of East Asian Languages and Literatures, Yale University, New Haven, Connecticut, US
Robert B. RADIN	Former Director of Japanese Studies, Department of History, University of Miami, Coral Gables, Florida, US
Esperanza RAMIREZ-CHRISTENSEN	Staff Writer, Encyclopedia of Japan
Daniel B. RAMSDELL	Professor, Department of History, Central Washington State College, Ellensberg, Washington, US
William V. RAPP	Vice-President, Morgan Guaranty Trust Company, New York, New York, US
C. Tait RATCLIFFE	President, International Business Information, Inc, Tōkyō, Japan
Kirsten REFSING	Former Lecturer, Asahikawa College, Asahikawa, Hokkaidō, Japan
Michael R. REICH	Coauthor of Six Lives, Six Deaths: Portraits from Modern Japan (1979)
Haru REISCHAUER	Writer
David K. REYNOLDS	Director, ToDo Institute, Los Angeles, California, US
Robert RHODES	Lecturer, Department of Literature, Ōtani University, Kyōto, Japan
Richard RICE	Assistant Professor, Department of History, University of Tennessee, Knoxville, Tennessee, US
Kenneth L. RICHARD	Assistant Professor, Department of East Asian Studies, University of Toronto, Toronto, Ontario, Canada
Bradley RICHARDSON	Professor, Department of Political Science, Ohio State University, Columbus, Ohio, US
Donald RICHIE	Author of The Films of Akira Kurosawa (1965), Ozu (1971), and The Japanese Movie (rev ed, 1982) and coauthor of The Japanese Film (rev ed, 1982).
J. T. RIMER	Professor and Chairman, Department of Chinese and Japanese, Washington University, St. Louis, Missouri, US
Alan RIX	Australia–Japan Economics Research Project, Department of Economics, Australian National University, Canberra, Australia
Laurance ROBERTS	Author of A Dictionary of Japanese Artists (1976) and Roberts' Guide to Museums (1978)
Gary E. ROBERTSON	
B. W. ROBINSON	Keeper Emeritus, Far Eastern Section, Victoria and Albert Museum, London; Adviser, Sotheby's, London, United Kingdom
Lawrence W. ROGERS	Associate Professor, Department of East Asian Languages, University of Hawaii at Hilo, Hilo, Hawaii, US
Thomas P. ROHLEN	Research Associate, Stanford University, Stanford, California, US
Thomas ROHLICH	Assistant Professor, Department of Asian Languages and Literature, University of Iowa, Iowa City, Iowa, US
Robert ROLF	Foreign Instructor, Department of Education, Fukuoka University of Education, Fukuoka Prefecture, Japan
John M. ROSENFIELD	Professor, Department of Oriental Arts, Harvard University, Cambridge, Massachusetts, US
Eugene ROTWEIN	Professor, Department of Economics, Queens College of the City University of New York, Flushing, New York, US
Gilbert ROZMAN	Professor, Department of Sociology, Princeton University, Princeton, New Jersey, US
Barbara RUCH	Associate Professor, Department of Oriental Studies, and Director, Institute for Medieval Japanese Studies, University of Pennsylvania, Philadelphia, Pennsylvania, US
Marleigh Grayer RYAN	Dean, Department of Liberal Arts and Sciences, State University of New York College at New Paltz, New Paltz, New York, US
Carole A. RYAVEC	
SAEKI Arikiyo	Professor, Department of Literature, Seijō University, Tōkyō, Japan
SAEKI Shōichi	Professor, College of Arts and Sciences, Tōkyō University, Tōkyō, Japan
SAGARA Iichi	President, University of the Sacred Heart, Tōkyō, Japan
SAGARA Tōru	Professor, Department of Literature and Arts, Kyōritsu Women's University, Tōkyō, Japan
SAIKI Kazuma	Professor, Department of Literature, Taishō University, Tōkyō, Japan
SAITŌ Hiroshi	Professor, Centro de Estudos Japonêses, Universidade de São Paulo, São Paulo, Brazil
SAITŌ Kenjirō	Professor, Department of Education, Utsunomiya University, Tochigi Prefecture, Japan
SAITŌ Masako	Professor, Department of Literature, University of the Sacred Heart, Tōkyō, Japan
SAITŌ Ryōsuke	Editor, Asahi shimbun, Tōkyō, Japan
SAITŌ Shizuo	Professor, Faculty of International Politics and Economics, Aoyama Gakuin University, Tōkyō, Japan; Council Member, United Nations University, Tōkyō, Japan
SAITŌ Shōji	Professor, Department of Science and Engineering, Tōkyō Denki University, Tōkyō, Japan
SAITŌ Tadashi	Professor Emeritus, Taishō University, Tōkyō, Japan
SAKAGUCHI Nobuhiko	Nihon Shōgi Remmei, Tōkyō, Japan
Akira SAKAI	Tōkyō Regional Immigration Bureau, Tōkyō, Japan

Robert K. SAKAI — Professor, Department of History, University of Hawaii at Manoa, Honolulu, Hawaii, US

SAKAI Tadayasu — Curator, The Museum of Modern Art, Kanagawa Prefecture, Japan

Hiroshi SAKAMOTO — Senior Lecturer, Department of Asian Languages, Stanford University, Stanford, California, US

SAKANOUE Masanobu — Professor, Department of Sciences, Kanazawa University, Ishikawa Prefecture, Japan

Mitsugu SAKIHARA — Associate Professor, Department of History, University of Hawaii at Manoa, Honolulu, Hawaii, US

SAKURABAYASHI Makoto — Professor, Department of Economics, Teikyō University, Tōkyō, Japan

SAKURADA Katsunori (d 1977) — Professor, Shiraume Gakuen Junior. College, Tōkyō Prefecture, Japan

Ralph SAMUELSON

SANEYOSHI Tatsuo — Freelance nonfiction writer

James H. SANFORD — Associate Professor, Department of Religion, University of North Carolina at Chapel Hill, Chapel Hill, North Carolina, US

SAOTOME Masahiro — Researcher, Tōkyō National Museum, Tōkyō, Japan

SASABUCHI Tomoichi — Adviser, Modern Culture Research Institute, Shōwa Women's University, Tōkyō, Japan

SASAKI Kinzō — Professor, Department of Law, Senshū University, Tōkyō, Japan

SASAKI Tadayoshi — Former President, Tōkyō University of Fisheries, Tōkyō, Japan

SASAYAMA Haruo — Assistant Professor, Faculty of Letters, Tōkyō University, Tōkyō, Japan

Elizabeth S. SATŌ — Professor, Department of History, University of Cincinnati, Cincinnati, Ohio, US

SATŌ Hideo — Chief, Research Room for Educational Materials, National Institute for Educational Research, Tōkyō, Japan

Hiroaki SATŌ — Translator of Japanese poetry

Kazuo SATŌ — Professor, Department of Economics, State University of New York at Buffalo, Buffalo, New York, US

SATŌ Kōji — Professor, Faculty of Law, Kyōto University, Kyōto, Japan

Ryūzō SATŌ — Professor, Department of Economics, Brown University, Providence, Rhode Island, US

SATŌ Seizaburō — Professor, College of Arts and Sciences, Tōkyō University, Tōkyō, Japan

SATŌ Tadashi — Professor, Institute of Geoscience, Tsukuba University, Ibaraki Prefecture, Japan

SATŌ Tamotsu — Professor, Department of Letters and Education, Ochanomizu Women's University, Tōkyō, Japan

Toshihiko SATŌ — Professor, Department of English, Virginia State College, Petersburgh, Virginia, US

E. Dale SAUNDERS — Professor, Department of Oriental Studies, University of Pennsylvania, Philadelphia, Pennsylvania, US

SAWADA Keisuke — Professor, Department of Education, Sōka University, Tōkyō Prefecture, Japan

SAWAKI Takao — Chairman, Department of Law, Rikkyō University, Tōkyō, Japan

SAWANOBORI Toshio — Professor, Department of Law, Kokugakuin University, Tōkyō, Japan

SAWAYAMA Hiroshi — Assistant Manager, Economics Division, Long-Term Credit Bank of Japan, Ltd, Tōkyō, Japan

Gary R. SAXONHOUSE — Professor, Center for Research on Economic Development, University of Michigan, Ann Arbor, Michigan, US

C. Franklin SAYRE — Assistant Professor, Department of Art and Art History, Oakland University, Rochester, Michigan, US

Paul SCHALOW

Wolfgang SCHAMONI — Privatdozent, Institut für Ostasienkunde (Japanologie), Universität Munchen, Munich, West Germany

Irwin SCHEINER — Professor, Department of History, University of California, Berkeley, Berkeley, California, US

Kim SCHUEFFTAN — Editor, Kodansha International, Ltd, Tōkyō, Japan

A. C. SCOTT — Professor Emeritus, Department of Theater and Drama, University of Wisconsin, Madison, Wisconsin, US

Christopher SEELEY — Lecturer, Department of Asian Languages, University of Canterbury, Christchurch, New Zealand

Edward G. SEIDENSTICKER — Professor, Department of East Asian Languages and Cultures, Columbia University, New York, New York, US

SEIKE Kiyosi — Professor and Dean, School of Fine Arts, Tōkyō University of Fine Arts and Music, Tōkyō, Japan

Kyōko Iriye SELDEN

SENGEN Ryūichirō — Professor, Department of Law, Dōshisha University, Kyōto, Japan

SENSHŪ Shin'ichi — Director, Civil Engineering Technology Research Laboratory, Electric Power Central Research Institute, Tōkyō, Japan

Carl SESAR — Translator of *Takuboku: Poems to Eat* (1966)

Joseph SEUBERT

Jack SEWARD — Author of *Hara-kiri* (1968), *Japanese in Action* (1969), and *The Japanese* (1972)

Nancy SHATZMAN-STEINHARDT — Department of the History of Art, Bryn Mawr College, Bryn Mawr, Pennsylvania, US

Charles D. SHELDON — Lecturer, Faculty of Oriental Studies, University of Cambridge, Cambridge, United Kingdom

Paul SHEPHERD

James E. SHERIDAN — Professor, Department of History, Northwestern University, Evanston, Illinois, US

SHIBANUMA Susumu — Director, The National Chuō Youth Center, Tōkyō, Japan

SHIGEMATSU Itsuzō	Chairman, Radiation Effects Research Foundation, Hiroshima Prefecture, Japan
SHIKI Masahide	Professor, Department of Letters and Education, Ochanomizu Women's University, Tōkyō, Japan
Ben-Ami SHILLONY	Chairman, Department of East Asian Studies, Hebrew University, Jerusalem, Israel
SHIMADA Jirō	Professor, Department of Economics, Chūō University, Tōkyō, Japan
SHIMADA Masahiko	Professor, Department of Literature, Kanazawa University, Ishikawa Prefecture, Japan
SHIMBORI Michiya	Professor, School of Education, Hiroshima University, Hiroshima Prefecture, Japan
SHIMIZU Hideo	Professor, Department of Law, Aoyama Gakuin University, Tōkyō, Japan
SHIMIZU Tetsuo	Poet
Yoshiaki SHIMIZU	Curator of Japanese Art, Freer Gallery of Art, Smithsonian Institution, Washington, DC, US
SHIMMI Hiroshi (d 1979)	General Secretary, Japan Bible Society, Tōkyō, Japan
SHIMOKAWA Kōichi	Professor, Department of Business Management, Hōsei University, Tōkyō, Japan
SHINADA Yutaka	Inspector of Cultural Properties, Agency for Cultural Affairs, Ministry of Education, Tōkyō, Japan
SHINAGAWA Fujirō	Professor, Department of Music, Senzoku Gakuen University, Kanagawa Prefecture, Japan
SHINJI Isoya	Associate Professor, Department of Landscape Architecture, Tōkyō University of Agriculture, Tōkyō, Japan
Minoru SHINODA	Professor, Department of History, University of Hawaii at Manoa, Honolulu, Hawaii, US
SHINOMIYA Toshiyuki	Assistant Professor, Faculty of Humanities, Hirosaki University, Aomori Prefecture, Japan
SHINRA Ichirō	Professor Emeritus, Meiji University, Tōkyō, Japan
Hiroki SHIOJI	Staff Writer, *Encyclopedia of Japan*
SHIONO Hiroshi	Professor, Faculty of Law, Tōkyō University, Tōkyō, Japan
SHIRAI Kunihiko	Chief, Birds and Animals Research Section, Forestry Experimental Station, Ministry of Agriculture, Forestry, and Fisheries, Tōkyō, Japan
SHIRAI Yoshio	Director, Japanese Film Critics' Pen Club, Tōkyō, Japan
SHIRAISHI Masaya	Assistant Professor, Thai-Vietnamese Department, Ōsaka University of Foreign Studies, Ōsaka, Japan
SHIRAISHI Teizō	Professor, Department of Humanities, Fukuoka University, Fukuoka Prefecture, Japan
Zenryū SHIRAKAWA	Assistant Professor, Department of Modern Foreign Languages, Boston University, Boston, Massachusetts, US
Ichirō SHIRATO	Senior Lecturer, Department of East Asian Languages and Cultures, Columbia University, New York, New York, US
SHIROTA Fumihiko	Chief, Internal Medicine Department, Nissan Kōseikai Tamagawa Hospital, Tōkyō, Japan
SHISHIDO Toshio	Vice-President, International University of Japan, Niigata Prefecture, Japan
Donald H. SHIVELY	Professor, Department of Japanese History and Literature, Harvard University, Cambridge, Massachusetts, US
William F. SIBLEY	Associate Professor, Department of Far Eastern Languages and Civilizations, University of Chicago, Chicago, Illinois, US
Jeanne SIGÉE	Translator and Editor of *Les Spectres de Yotsuya* by Tsuruya Namboku (1979)
George A. R. SILVER	Professor, Department of History, Earlham College, Richmond, Indiana, US
Bradford L. SIMCOCK	Assistant Professor, Department of Sociology and Anthropology, Miami University, Oxford, Ohio, US
Robert T. SINGER	Art historian and writer
Patricia SIPPEL	
Joseph W. SLADE	Professor, Department of English, Long Island University, Brooklyn Center, Brooklyn, New York, US
Richard SMETHURST	Associate Professor, Department of History, University of Pittsburgh, Pittsburgh, Pennsylvania, US
Barbara F. SMITH	
Henry D. SMITH II	Associate Professor, Department of History, University of California, Santa Barbara, Santa Barbara, California, US
Lawrence SMITH	Keeper of Oriental Arts, The British Museum, London, United Kingdom
Malcolm D. SMITH	Visiting Professor, Department of Law, University of British Columbia, Vancouver, British Columbia, Canada
Robert J. SMITH	Professor, Department of Anthropology, Cornell University, Ithaca, New York, US
SŌDA Hajime	Managing Director, Japan Society of Medical History, Tōkyō, Japan
SOEDA Yoshiya	Professor, Institute of Sociology, Tsukuba University, Ibaraki Prefecture, Japan
Michael SOLOMON	Assistant Professor, Department of History, Oakland University, Rochester, Michigan, US
SOMEYA Shirō	Councillor and Professor Emeritus, Institute of Public Health, Tōkyō, Japan
SONE Ken'ya	Professor, Junior College of Mechanical Engineering, Nihon University, Tōkyō, Japan
SONODA Minoru	Professor, Department of Literature and Executive Secretary, Institute for Japanese Culture and Classics, Kokugakuin University, Tōkyō, Japan
Isao SORANAKA	Assistant Professor, Department of History, University of Western Ontario, London, Ontario, Canada
Eugene SOVIAK	Associate Professor, Department of History, Washington University, St. Louis, Missouri, US
Dennis M. SPACKMAN	Staff Writer, *Encyclopedia of Japan*
Douglas E. SPARKS	Gnostic Concepts, Inc, Menlo Park, California, US

Norman SPARNON	Author of *Japanese Flower Arrangement, Classical and Modern* (1960)
Robert M. SPAULDING	Associate Professor, Department of History, Oklahoma State University, Stillwater, Oklahoma, US
Thomas A. STANLEY	Department of Oriental Studies, University of Arizona, Tucson, Arizona, US
Richard STANLEY-BAKER	Department of History in Art, University of Victoria, Victoria, British Columbia, Canada
Oliver STATLER	Author of *Japanese Inn* (1961), *The Pilgrimage* (1983), and others
M. William STEELE	Associate Professor, Division of Humanities, International Christian University, Tōkyō Prefecture, Japan
Kurt STEINER	Professor Emeritus, Department of Political Science, Stanford University, Stanford, California, US
Patricia G. STEINHOFF	Professor, Department of Sociology, University of Hawaii at Manoa, Honolulu, Hawaii, US
John J. STEPHAN	Professor, Department of History, University of Hawaii at Manoa, Honolulu, Hawaii, US
William E. STESLICKE	Visiting Scholar, Department of Medical Care Organization, School of Public Health, University of Michigan, Ann Arbor, Michigan, US
Margo STIPE	
J. A. A. STOCKWIN	Director, Nissan Institute of Japanese Studies, Oxford, United Kingdom
Richard STORRY (d 1982)	Director, Far Eastern Centre, St. Antony's College, University of Oxford, Oxford, United Kingdom
Giuliana STRAMIGIOLI	Professor, Instituto di Studi dell'India e dell'Asia Orientale, Università degli Studi di Roma, Rome, Italy
Tal STREETER	Sculptor; author of *The Art of the Japanese Kite* (1974)
Kenneth STRONG	Former Lecturer, Department of the Far East, School of Oriental and African Studies, University of London, London, United Kingdom
Nathan O. STRONG	Assistant Professor, Curriculum and Instruction Program, University of San Francisco, San Francisco, California, US
SUCHI Tokuhei	Writer
SUDA Ken	Former Professor, Tōkyō University of Navigation, Tōkyō, Japan
SUDŌ Haruo	Assistant Professor, Department of Sociology, Hōsei University, Tōkyō, Japan
SUENAKA Tetsuo	Professor, Department of School Education, Hyōgo University of Education, Hyōgo Prefecture, Japan
SUGENO Kazuo	Professor, Faculty of Law, Tōkyō University, Tōkyō, Japan
SUGIHARA Shirō	President, Kōnan University, Hyōgo Prefecture, Japan
SUGIYAMA Akio	Professor, Department of Education, Kōbe University, Hyōgo Prefecture, Japan
SUGIYAMA Tadayoshi	Professor, Department of Agriculture, Tōkyō University of Agriculture, Tōkyō, Japan

SUGIYAMA Yasushi	Professor, School of International Affairs, Aoyama Gakuin University, Tōkyō, Japan
SUYAMA Kazuyuki	Deputy Manager, Yokohama Branch, Long-Term Credit Bank of Japan, Ltd, Kanagawa Prefecture, Japan
SUZUKI Eichi	Assistant Professor, Department of Education, Ibaraki University, Tochigi Prefecture, Japan
SUZUKI Hiroaki	Joint General Manager, Division II, Credit Analysis, Long-Term Credit Bank of Japan, Ltd, Tōkyō, Japan
SUZUKI Kōichi	Director, Bank of Japan Centennial History Project, Bank of Japan, Tōkyō, Japan
SUZUKI Masao	Chief Researcher, Chiyoda Ward Library, Tōkyō, Japan
SUZUKI Mitsuru	Professor, Faculty of Engineering, Hiroshima University, Hiroshima Prefecture, Japan
SUZUKI Norihisa	Professor, Department of Education, Rikkyō University, Tōkyō, Japan
SUZUKI Ryōichi	Historian
SUZUKI Yoshio	Director General, Correction Bureau, Ministry of Justice, Tōkyō, Japan
SUZUKI Yukihisa	Professor, Department of Foreign Languages, Kyōto University of Foreign Studies, Kyōto, Japan
SUZUKI Zenji	Professor, Faculty of Liberal Arts, Yamaguchi University, Yamaguchi Prefecture, Japan
David L. SWAIN	Editor, *Japan Christian Quarterly*, Tōkyō, Japan
Barbara Bowles SWANN	
Thomas E. SWANN	Visiting Assistant Professor, University of Minnesota, Minneapolis, Minnesota, US
Thomas D. SWIFT	Professor, Department of History, California State University, Sacramento, California, US
Elizabeth de Sabato SWINTON	Research Curator in Oriental Art, Worcester Art Museum, Worcester, Massachusetts, US
Kenneth M. TAGAWA	
Mildred TAHARA	Associate Professor, Department of East Asian Literature, University of Hawaii at Manoa, Honolulu, Hawaii, US
Kōji TAIRA	Professor, Department of Economics, University of Illinois, Urbana–Champaign, Urbana, Illinois, US
TAKABATAKE Michitoshi	Professor, Department of Law and Politics, Rikkyō University, Tōkyō, Japan
TAKAGI Noritsune	Professor, Institute of Journalism and Communication Studies, Tōkyō University, Tōkyō, Japan
TAKAGI Shōsaku	Professor, Historiographical Institute, Tōkyō University, Tōkyō, Japan
TAKAHASHI Ken'ichi	Professor, Department of Literature, Sophia University, Tōkyō, Japan
TAKAHASHI Masao	
TAKAHASHI Naoki	Senior Lecturer, Department of Law, Senshū University, Tōkyō, Japan

TAKAKURA Shō — Professor, Institute of Education, Tsukuba University, Ibaraki Prefecture, Japan

TAKAKUWA Yasuo — Professor, Faculty of Education, Nagoya University, Aichi Prefecture, Japan

TAKAMURA Hisao — Social Education Supervisor, Social Education Bureau, Ministry of Education, Tōkyō, Japan

TAKANO Keiichi — Professor, Faculty of Education, Kyūshū University, Fukuoka Prefecture, Japan

TAKANO Shinji — Director, Wild Bird Society of Japan, Tōkyō, Japan

Ted T. TAKAYA — Assistant Professor, Department of Modern Languages and Literature, University of the Pacific, Stockton, California, US

TAKEBE Yoshiaki — Professor, Institute of Language Teaching, Waseda University, Tōkyō, Japan

TAKEDA Fumio — Sports Writer, *Asahi shimbun*, Tōkyō, Japan

TAKEDA Katsuhiko — Professor, Department of Politics and Economics, Waseda University, Tōkyō, Japan

TAKEDA Yukimatsu — Adviser, Nippon Electric Company, Tōkyō, Japan

TAKEHISA Yoshihiko — Professor, Department of Literature, Nara Women's University, Nara Prefecture, Japan

TAKENAKA Kazurō — Professor, Department of Sociology, Tsukuba University, Ibaraki Prefecture, Japan

TAKEUCHI Akio — Professor, Faculty of Law, Tōkyō University, Tōkyō, Japan

TAKEUCHI Hitoshi — Professor Emeritus, Tōkyō University, Tōkyō, Japan

Melinda TAKEUCHI — Assistant Professor, School of Art, Stanford University, Stanford, California, US

TAKEUCHI Rizō — Former Professor, Faculty of History, Tōkyō University, Tōkyō, Japan

TAKUMA Shinpei — Director, Department of Educational Technology, National Institute of Special Education, Kanagawa Prefecture, Japan

TAKUMI Hideo — Director, Kanagawa Museum of Modern Art, Kanagawa Prefecture, Japan

TAMAI Kensuke — Director, Centro de Estudos Japonêses, Universidade de São Paulo, São Paulo, Brazil

TAMIYA Hiroshi — Professor, Department of Law, Rikkyō University, Tōkyō, Japan

George J. TANABE, JR — Professor, Department of Religion, University of Hawaii at Manoa, Honolulu, Hawaii, US

Atsuko TANABE DE BABA — Universidad Nacional Autónoma de México, Mexico City, Mexico

TANAKA Akira — Professor, Faculty of Letters, Hokkaidō University, Hokkaidō, Japan

TANAKA Jirō — National Research Institute of Aquaculture, Fisheries Agency, Mie Prefecture, Japan

TANAKA Masaaki — Professor, Department of Arts, The Women's College of Fine Arts, Tōkyō, Japan

TANAKA Minoru — Professor, Department of Law, Keiō University, Tōkyō, Japan

TANAKA Shigeaki — Professor, Faculty of Law, Kyōto University, Kyōto, Japan

TANAKA Takeo — Professor, Historiographical Institute, Tōkyō University, Tōkyō, Japan

TANAKA Yōnosuke — Chairman, Council for the Study of Industrial Information, Tōkyō, Japan

TANAKA Yutaka — Assistant Judge, Civil Affairs Bureau, The Supreme Court of Japan, Tōkyō, Japan

TANIGUCHI Yasuhei — Professor, Faculty of Law, Kyōto University, Kyōto, Japan

TANIKAWA Atsushi — Lecturer, Department of Literature, Kokugakuin University, Tōkyō, Japan

TANIKAWA Hisashi — Professor, Department of Law, Seikei University, Tōkyō, Japan

TANJI Kenzō — Chief, Yono City History Compilation Office, Yono City Municipal Office, Saitama Prefecture, Japan

TANSŌ Akinobu — Professor, Department of Law, Ritsumeikan University, Kyōto, Japan

TASHIMO Masaaki — Manager, Industrial Research Division, Long-Term Credit Bank of Japan, Ltd, Tōkyō, Japan

TASHIRO Hikaru

TATSUKI Mariko — Senior Lecturer, Department of Economics, Teikyō University, Tōkyō, Japan

TATSUTA Misao — Professor, Faculty of Law, Kyōto University, Kyōto, Japan

TAURA Takeo — Professor, Faculty of Education, Nagoya University, Aichi Prefecture, Japan

TERAI Minako — Kimono specialist

TERASAKI Masao — Professor, Faculty of Education, Tōkyō University, Tōkyō, Japan

John E. THAYER III — Director, The Peabody Museum of Salem, Salem, Massachusetts, US

Sarah THOMPSON — Department of Prints, Philadelphia Museum of Art, Philadelphia, Pennsylvania, US

Arthur H. THORNHILL III

Donald R. THURSTON — Associate Professor, Department of Political Science, Union College, Schenectady, New York, US

David A. TITUS — Professor, Department of Government, Wesleyan University, Middletown, Connecticut, US

Ronald P. TOBY — Assistant Professor, Department of History, University of Illinois, Urbana–Champaign, Urbana, Illinois, US

TODA Yoshio — Former Lecturer, Department of Literature, Kokugakuin University, Tōkyō, Japan

TOGAI Yoshio — Professor, Department of Business Management, Matsuyama University of Commerce, Ehime Prefecture, Japan

TOGANOO Shōzui — Asiatic Department, Boston Museum of Fine Arts, Boston, Massachusetts, US

TOKUZEN Yoshikazu — Professor, Japan Lutheran Theological College-Seminary, Tōkyō, Japan

TOMATSU Hidenori — Assistant Professor, Department of Law, Seijō University, Tōkyō, Japan

TOMIKI Kenji (d 1979) — Former President, Japan Aikidō Society, Tōkyō, Japan; Professor, Kokushikan University, Tōkyō, Japan

TOMISAWA Konomi	Industrial Research Division, Long-Term Credit Bank of Japan, Ltd, Tōkyō, Japan
TOMITA Torao	Professor, Department of Literature, Rikkyō University, Tōkyō, Japan
TONOKI Keiichi	Professor, School of Information and Communication, Bunkyō University, Saitama Prefecture, Japan
Conrad TOTMAN	Professor, Department of History, Northwestern University, Evanston, Illinois, US
George Oakley TOTTEN III	Professor, Department of Political Science, University of Southern California, Los Angeles, Los Angeles, California, US
TOYODA Takeshi	Former Professor, Department of Literature, Chūō University, Tōkyō, Japan
TSUCHIDA Mitsufumi	Professor, Bunkyō University's Women's College, Tōkyō, Japan
TSUCHIDA Naoshige	Curator, National Museum of Japanese History, Chiba Prefecture, Japan
TSUCHIDA Tomoaki	Staff Writer, *Encyclopedia of Japan*
TSUCHIYA Rokurō	Professor, Department of Economics, Chūō University, Tōkyō, Japan
TSUCHIYA Shin'ichi	Councillor, Secretariat, Ministry of Justice, Tōkyō, Japan
TSUDA Hideo	Professor, Department of Literature, Kansai University, Ōsaka Prefecture, Japan
TSUJI Shizuo	President, Tsuji Professional Culinary Institute, Ōsaka, Japan
Matsuo TSUKADA	Professor, Department of Botany, University of Washington, Seattle, Washington, US
Toshio G. TSUKAHIRA	Foreign Service Institute, US Department of State, Washington, DC, US
Reiko TSUKIMURA	Professor, Department of East Asian Studies, University of Toronto, Toronto, Ontario, Canada
TSUKUBA Hisaharu	Assistant Professor, Department of Economics, Waseda University, Tōkyō, Japan
TSUMORI Makoto	Professor, Department of Home Economics, Ochanomizu Women's University, Tōkyō, Japan
TSUMURA Akinobu	Executive Director, Japan National Oil Corporation, Tōkyō, Japan
E. Patricia TSURUMI	Associate Professor, Department of History, University of Victoria, Victoria, British Columbia, Canada
Yoshihiro TSURUMI	Professor, Department of Marketing, Baruch College, City University of New York, New York, New York, US
Kinya TSURUTA	Professor, Department of Asian Studies, University of British Columbia, Vancouver, British Columbia, Canada
TSUTSUI Michio	Professor, Faculty of Agriculture, Tōkyō University, Tōkyō, Japan
Royall TYLER	Assistant Professor, Department of East Asian Languages and Literatures, University of Wisconsin, Madison, Wisconsin, US
William J. TYLER	Assistant Professor, Department of Oriental Studies, University of Pennsylvania, Philadelphia, Pennsylvania, US
UCHIDA Michio	Professor, Department of Education, Tōkyō Gakugei University, Tōkyō, Japan
UCHIKAWA Yoshimi	Professor, Institute of Journalism and Communication Studies, Tōkyō University, Tōkyō, Japan
UDAGAWA Akihito	Professor, Faculty of Economics, Yokohama National University, Kanagawa Prefecture, Japan
UDAGAWA Masaru	Assistant Professor, Department of Business Management, Hōsei University, Tōkyō, Japan
UEDA Kenji	Professor, Department of Literature, Kokugakuin University, Tōkyō, Japan
UEDA Kiichi (d 1980)	Former Professor, Shōwa University, Tōkyō, Japan
Makoto UEDA	Professor, Department of Asian Languages, Stanford University, Stanford, California, US
UEDA Masaaki	Professor, Faculty of Liberal Arts, Kyōto University, Kyōto, Japan
UEDA Nobuhiro	Assistant, Faculty of Law, Tōkyō University, Tōkyō, Japan
Toyoaki UEHARA	Associate Professor, Department of East Asian Languages and Cultures, Indiana University, Bloomington, Indiana, US
UENO Yoshiya	Assistant Professor, Faculty of Letters, Tōkyō University, Tōkyō, Japan
UKAI Nobushige	Professor, Faculty of Law, Tōkyō University, Tōkyō, Japan
UMETANI Noboru	Professor, Faculty of Letters, Ōsaka University, Ōsaka, Japan
J. Marshall UNGER	Assistant Professor, Department of East Asian Languages, University of Hawaii at Manoa, Honolulu, Hawaii, US
UNNO Fukuju	Professor, Department of Literature, Meiji University, Tōkyō, Japan
Taitetsu UNNO	Professor, Department of Religion, Smith College, Northampton, Massachusetts, US
UNNO Yoshirō	Professor, Department of Law, Niigata University, Niigata Prefecture, Japan
Frank K. UPHAM	Visiting Professor of Law, Harvard Law School, Cambridge, Massachusetts, US
URANO Tatsuo	Assistant Professor, Department of Law, Nihon University, Tōkyō, Japan
Marian URY	Associate Professor, Comparative Literature Program, University of California, Davis, Davis, California, US
Sharlie Conroy USHIODA	Instructor, Saddleback Community College, Mission Viejo, California, US
USHIOGI Morikazu	Professor, Department of Education, Nagoya University, Aichi Prefecture, Japan
USHIRO Masatake	Management Consultant, McKinsey & Co, Ltd, Tōkyō, Japan
USUI Katsumi	Professor, Institute of Sociology, Tsukuba University, Ibaraki Prefecture, Japan
UWANO Zendō	Assistant Professor, Faculty of Letters, Tōkyō University, Tōkyō, Japan
Allie Marie UYEHARA	Author of *Ten Keys to Modern Japanese Flower Arrangement* (1975)
Cecil H. UYEHARA	Author of *Leftwing Social Movements in Japan: An Annotated Bibliography* (1959)

H. Paul VARLEY — Professor, Department of East Asian Languages and Cultures, Columbia University, New York, New York, US

Susan Downing VIDEEN

Valdo H. VIGLIELMO — Professor, Department of East Asian Literature, University of Hawaii at Manoa, Honolulu, Hawaii, US

Savitri VISHWANATHAN — Reader, Department of Chinese and Japanese Studies, University of Delhi, Delhi, India

Ezra F. VOGEL — Professor and Director, US–Japan Program, Harvard University, Cambridge, Massachusetts, US

Suzanne H. VOGEL — Supervisor, Clinical Social Work, University Health Services, Harvard University, Cambridge, Massachusetts, US

Frits VOS — Professor and Director, Center for Japanese and Korean Studies, Leiden State University, Leiden, Holland

Meredith WADDELL — Formerly at Dentsū Inc, New York, New York, US

Hiroshi WAGATSUMA — Professor, Department of Anthropology, University of California, Los Angeles, Los Angeles, California, US

WAGATSUMA Takashi — Chief, Department of Obstetrics and Gynecology, National Medical Center Hospital, Tōkyō, Japan

WAKASUGI Akira — Professor and Dean, Department of Economics, Yokohama National University, Kanagawa Prefecture, Japan

WAKITA Osamu — Assistant Professor, Faculty of Letters, Ōsaka University, Ōsaka, Japan

WATANABE Akira — Assistant Professor, Department of Education, Tōkyō Gakugei University, Tōkyō, Japan

WATANABE Hiroshi — Architectural critic; Principal Associate, Wathos Planning, Tōkyō, Japan

WATANABE Hiroshi — Assistant Professor, Faculty of Law, Tōkyō University, Tōkyō, Japan

WATANABE Ichirō — Professor, Institute of Physical Education, Tsukuba University, Ibaraki Prefecture, Japan

WATANABE Tadashi — Former Deputy Secretary General, Science Council of Japan, Tōkyō, Japan

WATANABE Takeshi — Director and Chief, Construction Headquarters, Teito Rapid Transit Authority, Tōkyō, Japan

WATANABE Tōru — Professor, College of Arts and Sciences, Tōkyō University, Tōkyō, Japan

Tsugumichi WATANABE — Milbank Tweed Hadley & McCloy, New York, New York, US

WATANABE Yoshirō — Professor, Institute of Socioeconomic Planning, Tsukuba University, Ibaraki Prefecture, Japan

David B. WATERHOUSE — Professor, Department of East Asian Studies, University of Toronto, Toronto, Ontario, Canada

Glenn T. WEBB — Associate Professor, Department of Art History, University of Washington, Seattle, Washington, US

Herschel WEBB — Professor, Department of East Asian Languages and Cultures, Columbia University, New York, New York, US

Peter WEBER-SCHÄFER — Professor, Politische Wissenschaft Sektion, Abteilung fur Ostasienwissenschaften, Ruhr-Universität Bochum, Bochum, West Germany

C. G. WEERAMANTRY — Professor, Faculty of Law, Monash University, Clayton, Victoria, Australia

Gail Capitol WEIGL — Assistant Professor, Department of Art, University of Maryland, College Park, Maryland, US

Lucie R. WEINSTEIN — Associate Professor, Department of Art, Southern Connecticut State College, New Haven, Connecticut, US

Stanley WEINSTEIN — Professor, Department of East Asian Languages and Literatures, Yale University, New Haven, Connecticut, US

Theodore F. WELCH — Assistant University Librarian and Lecturer, Oriental and African Languages Program, Northwestern University, Evanston, Illinois, US

D. Eleanor WESTNEY — Department of Sociology, Yale University, New Haven, Connecticut, US

William WETHERALL

Carolyn WHEELWRIGHT — Assistant Professor, Department of the History of Art, Yale University, New Haven, Connecticut, US

John A. WHITE — Professor, Department of History, University of Hawaii at Manoa, Honolulu, Hawaii, US

Merry I. WHITE — Associate in Research, Fairbank Center for East Asian Studies and Director, Project on Human Potential, Harvard Graduate School of Education, Cambridge, Massachusetts, US

George M. WILSON — Professor, Department of History, Indiana University, Bloomington, Indiana, US

William R. WILSON — Translator of *Hōgen monogatari: Tale of the Disorder in Hōgen* (1971)

Manfred WIMMER — Japan Go Association, Tōkyō, Japan

Clark WORSWICK — Editor of *Japan: Photographs 1854–1905* (1979) and *Imperial China: Photographs, 1850–1912* (1978)

Yasuko YABE

YAGI Atsuru — Professor, Department of Humanities, Yamaguchi University, Yamaguchi Prefecture, Japan

YAMADA Katsumi — Professor, Department of Foreign Languages, Tōkyō University of Foreign Studies, Tōkyō, Japan

YAMADA Makiko — Associate Professor, Graduate School, International University of Japan, Niigata Prefecture, Japan

YAMADA Terutane — Physician and Standing Director, Japan Institute of Traditional Medicine, Tōkyō, Japan

YAMADA Tokubei — Specialist in Japanese dolls; Yoshitoku Co, Tōkyō, Japan

YAMADA Toshio — Professor, Department of Art and Literature, Seijō University, Tōkyō, Japan

YAMAGUCHI Kazuo — Professor, Department of Business Management, Sōka University, Tōkyō Prefecture, Japan

YAMAGUCHI Makoto — Professor, Department of Elementary Education, Kantō Junior College, Gumma Prefecture, Japan

YAMAGUCHI Osamu — Professor, Department of Literature, University of the Sacred Heart, Tōkyō, Japan

George K. YAMAMOTO — Professor, Department of Sociology, University of Hawaii at Manoa, Honolulu, Hawaii, US

YAMAMOTO Tadashi (d 1981) — Former Chief, Tōkyō Clinical Medicine Comprehensive Research Institute, Tōkyō, Japan

YAMAMOTO Takeo — Professor, Historiographical Institute, Tōkyō University, Tōkyō, Japan

Kozo YAMAMURA — Professor, Department of East Asian Studies, University of Washington, Seattle, Washington, US

YAMANAKA Seigō — Professor, Department of Arts and Literature, Seijō University, Tōkyō, Japan

YAMANO Aiko — Principal, Yamano Beauty School, Tōkyō, Japan

YAMANOBE Tomoyuki — Director, Tōyama Memorial Hall Art Museum, Saitama Prefecture, Japan

YAMARYŌ Kenji — Teacher, Azabugakuen High School, Tōkyō, Japan

YAMASHITA Kikuko — Staff Writer, *Encyclopedia of Japan*

YAMASHITA Ryūji — Professor, Faculty of Letters, Nagoya University, Aichi Prefecture, Japan

YAMAZAKI Isao — Essayist; former member of the Editorial Board, *Yomiuri shimbun*, Tōkyō, Japan

YAMAZAKI Yukio — Assistant Professor, Department of Humanities, Niigata University, Niigata Prefecture, Japan

Philip YAMPOLSKY — Adjunct Professor, Department of East Asian Languages and Cultures, Columbia University, New York, New York, US

Minoru YANAGIHASHI — Assistant Professor, Department of Oriental Studies, University of Arizona, Tucson, Arizona, US

YANAI Kenji — Professor, Department of Literature, Komazawa University, Tōkyō, Japan

Minja YANG — Information Officer, Office of the United Nations High Commissioner for Refugees, Tōkyō, Japan

YANO Tōru — Professor and Chairman, Social Sciences Section, Center for Southeast Asian Studies, Kyōto University, Kyōto, Japan

Richard YASKO — Associate Professor, Department of History, University of Wisconsin–Whitewater, Whitewater, Wisconsin, US

Kenneth YASUDA — Professor, Department of East Asian Languages and Cultures, Indiana University, Bloomington, Indiana, US

YASUDA Motohisa — Professor, Department of Literature, Gakushūin University, Tōkyō, Japan

YAZAWA Taiji — Professor Emeritus, Tōkyō Metropolitan University, Tōkyō, Japan

M. YOCHUM

Karl G. YONEDA

YONEKURA Mamoru — Art writer, *Asahi shimbun*, Tōkyō, Japan

YONEMOTO Kanji — Executive Director, Japan Industrial Robot Association, Tōkyō, Japan

Ann YONEMURA — Assistant Curator of Japanese Art, Freer Gallery of Art, Smithsonian Institution, Washington, DC, US

YOSHIDA Hiroo — Professor, Department of Literature, Chiba University, Chiba Prefecture, Japan

YOSHIDA Hiroshi — Assistant Manager, Economic Welfare Policy Section, Economic Welfare Bureau, Economic Planning Agency, Tōkyō, Japan

YOSHIDA Yoshio — Professor, National Institute for Research on Polar Regions, Ibaraki Prefecture, Japan

Takehiko YOSHIHASHI (d 1978) — Formerly of the School of International Service, American University, Washington, DC, US

YOSHIKAWA Yōko — Assistant Professor, Department of Foreign Languages, Kyōto Sangyō University, Kyōto, Japan

YOSHIKOSHI Tatsuo — Photographer

I. Roger YOSHINO — Professor, Department of Sociology, University of Arizona, Tucson, Arizona, US

Masatoshi M. YOSHINO — Professor, Institute of Geoscience and Director, Environmental Research Center, Tsukuba University, Ibaraki Prefecture, Japan

Michael Y. YOSHINO — Professor, Department of Business Administration, Harvard Business School, Cambridge, Massachusetts, US

YOSHITAKE Yoshinori — Professor Emeritus, Musashino Women's College, Tōkyō Prefecture, Japan

YOSHITOSHI Yawara — President, School of Medicine, Hamamatsu University, Shizuoka Prefecture, Japan

YOSHIZAWA Akira — President, International Origami Society, Tōkyō, Japan

Ernest P. YOUNG — Professor, Department of History, University of Michigan, Ann Arbor, Michigan, US

John YOUNG — Professor and Director, Institute of Far Eastern Studies, Seton Hall University, South Orange, New Jersey, US

YUASA Michio — Professor, Department of Law, Aichi Gakuin University, Aichi Prefecture, Japan

Nobuyuki YUASA — Translator and editor of *The Zen Poems of Ryōkan* (1981)

YUI Tsunehiko — Professor, Department of Business Management, Meiji University, Tōkyō, Japan

YUKAWA Osamu — Professor Emeritus, Nihon University, Tōkyō, Japan

Leon M. ZOLBROD — Professor, Department of Asian Studies, University of British Columbia, Vancouver, British Columbia, Canada

TRANSLATORS

The *Encyclopedia* is particularly grateful to Professor Michael K. YOUNG of Columbia University for his translations and advice concerning Japanese law.

ARAI Yasuko
Janet ASHBY
Carol BABA
BABA Shin'ya
Jerome E. BARNETT
Monica BETHE
James R. BRECKENRIDGE
James H. BRODERICK Jr
Theodore COOK
Kenneth DALE
Barry DUELL
Richard J. EMMERT
ENDŌ Akira
Mark ERICSON
FURUTA Minako
Paul GRONER
William D. JOHNSON
KANEKO Yoshihisa
KUSAKA Sae
Edward J. LAMPERT
John C. MARALDO
Lewis MARKS
MARUMO Teruyoshi
Julia M. MATISOO
Roland MONSON
ŌE Hidefusa
Roderick H. SEEMAN
Paul SHEPHERD
TAMURA Keiichi
TSURUOKA Atsuo
UETSUHARA Tokio
Marian URY
Michiko Nakanishi VIGDEN
Erika D. WHITE

TRANSLATION SERVICES

ISS International, Inc
National Translation Institute of Science and Technology
Translation Center for Industry and Technology, Inc

ART AND DESIGN

Art director:	SUGIURA Kōhei
Assistant art director:	KAIHO Tōru
Illustration design:	Six, Co
	ITŌ Katsuko
	MIYASHITA Katsuyuki
	SHIBA Masami
	TAKEZAWA Shigeru
Cartography:	Tanshi Co
	KOZAKI Kenzō
	SUGAI Minoru
	Nihon Kōbō Co
	Morishita Co
	Chizuseihan Cartographic Co
	SHIRAMASA Akiyoshi

PRODUCTION

Dai Nippon Printing Co, Ltd
DNP America Inc
Kimura Zugei Co
Komiyama Printing Co
Lehigh/ROCAPPI
Ellen VANOOK

INDEX

Richardson Associates:
   Dr. William J. RICHARDSON (director)
   J. Edmund DE STEFANO (chief indexer)

ACKNOWLEDGMENTS

Photographs

ABE Michiaki
ADACHI Michio
Agricultural Land Development Public Corporation
ASANO Kiichi
Benridō
Bon Color Photo Agency Co, Ltd
Bridgestone Museum of Art, Ishibashi Foundation, Kurume
Bridgestone Museum of Art, Ishibashi Foundation, Tōkyō
Bunraku Society
Byōdōin
Camera Tōkyō Service Co, Ltd
CHINO Takayasu
Chion'in
Chishakuin
Chōgosonshiji
Chōkōji
Chūō Kōron Sha, Inc
Chūō Ward Office
Chūsonji
Daiichi Publication Center
Daikakuji
Daisen'in
Dandy Photo Co, Ltd
EBARA Takao
Education Commission, Higashi Ōsaka
Egawa Museum of Art
Eisei Bunko
ENDŌ Norikatsu
Engakuji
Enman'in, Onjōji
Enryakuji
Fine Photo Agency Co, Ltd
FUDEMOTO Hiromasa
FUJI Hiroko
FUJII Manabu
FUJIMORI Takeshi
FUJISHIMA Ayako
Fukuoka Art Museum
Fukuoka City Branch Office, Tōkyō
FUSE Masanao
Gakken Co, Ltd
Gakushūin Daigaku Shiryōkan
Gotō Art Museum
Government Buildings Department
    Minister's Secretariat, Ministry of Construction
HAGA Hideo
HAGIWARA Hidesaburō
HANAYAGI Shigeka
HATTORI Masatsugu
HAYASHI Shigeo
Henjōkōin
HIDAKA Katsuhiko

HIGUCHI Hatsuko
HIRATA Gōyō
Hōkyōji
Hōryūji
Hosokawaryū Bonseki Iemoto
HOSOMI Minoru
Idemitsu Art Gallery
Ii Art Museum
Ikenobō
Imperial Household Agency (Tōkyō)
    Katsura Detached Palace Office
    Kyōto Office of the Imperial Household
    Office of the Shōsōin Treasure House
Institute of Oriental Culture, Tōkyō University
IRIE Taikichi
ISHII Takanori
ISHIMOTO Yasuhiro
Ishiyamadera
Itsukushima Shrine
Itsuō Art Museum
Iwanami Shoten Publishers
Iwasaki Art Publications
IWASA Tamayo
IWATA Kikue
IZUMI Kōji
Izumo Shrine
Japanese National Railways
Japan Federation of Artists
Japan Film Library Council (Kawakita Memorial Film Institute)
Japan Magazine Publishers Association
Japan Press Photo Co, Ltd
Japan Travel Bureau Photo Library
Jingoji
Jingū Bunko
Jōbon Rendaiji
J. O. Co
Jōgon'in
Jōjuin, Kiyomizudera
Kagawa Prefectural Tourist Office, Tōkyō
Kakubei Jishi Hozonkai
KANAYA Fumio
KANEKO Keizō
Kangikōji
Kansai Electric Power Co, Inc
Kanshinji
Kantō Sha Co
KANZE Motomasa
Kararī Co, Ltd
Kawabata Yasunari Memorial Society
KAWAI Hajime
KAWAMURA Noriyuki
Keiō University
Kendō Nihon
Kenninji

Kinki Nippon Railway Co, Ltd
Kitano Temmangū Shrine
Kiyomizudera, Kyōto Prefecture
Kiyomizudera, Nagasaki Prefecture
Kiyoshikōjin Seichōji
K. Mikimoto & Co, Ltd
Kōbe City Branch Office, Tōkyō
Kōdaiji
Kōdansha International Ltd
Kōdansha Photography Department
Kōfukuji
Kojimadera
Kongōbuji
Kōryūji
Kōtokuin
Kōzanji
KUBO Katsutaka
Kyōdō News Service
Kyōto Furitsu Sōgō Shiryōkan
Kyōto National Museum
Kyūgetsu
Kyūkaen
Maeda Ikutokukai Foundation
MAEDA Setsu
MAEJIMA Hisao
Mainichi Shimbun
MATSUMOTO Norio
Matsuo Taisha Shrine
Meiji University Archaeological Collection
M. G. S. Photo Library
Mitsubishi Heavy Industries, Ltd
Mitsui Bunko
MITSUI Shinako
Miyagi Michio Memorial Museum
Miyagi Prefectural Office, Tōkyō
MIYAZAKI Kazuo
MIYAZAKI Manabu
MOA Museum of Art
MORI Atsuki
MŌRI Hōkōkai
MORITA Jūshirō
MORIYA Nobutaka
Motoori Norinaga Memorial Museum
Mōtsuji
Mt. Kōya Cultural Properties Preservation Society
MUNAKATA Chiya
Musashino Local Museum
Museum of Modern Japanese Literature
Myōchiin, Tenryūji
Myōhōin
Myōhokkeji
Myōshinji
Nagasaki Municipal Museum
Nagasaki Prefectural Museum of History and Folklore

Nagasaki Prefectural Tourist Office, Tōkyō
NAGATA Seiji
NAKAMATA Masayoshi
NAMBU Hideo
Nara National Research Institute of Cultural Properties
Nara Prefectural Trade Office, Tōkyō
NARIYAMA Tetsurō
National Theater
New Tōkyō International Airport Authority
Nezu Art Museum
NHK Service Center
Nijō Castle
Nikkō Tōshōgū
Nippon Express Co, Ltd
Nippon Gakki Co, Ltd
Nippon Steel Corporation
Nishi Honganji
Nishizawa Toy Collection
Ōbaiin, Daitokuji
Ōbunsha Publishing Co, Ltd
ODA Hideo
OGAWA Isshin
OGAWA Tomoji
Oguro Kikaku Co, Ltd
OKUMURA Akira
ONCHI Kunio
Ōsaka Castle Museum
ŌTA Eiichi
Ōtsuka Kōgei Sha Co, Ltd
ŌTSUKA Seigo
Pentax Gallery, Asahi Kōgaku Co, Ltd
Photo Pac Co
Riccar Art Museum
Rinnōji
Rokuharamitsuji
Rokuonji
Ryōanji
Ryūsen'an
Saidaiji
Saigō Family
Sainenji
SAKAI Tadamasa
Sakamoto Manshichi Photography Research Co, Ltd
SASAKI Fumitsuna
SATŌ Haruki
Sekai Bunka Photo
Sendai City Museum
Shibundō Publishing Co
Shitamachi Museum
Shitennōji
Shizuoka Prefectural Trade and Tourist Office, Tōkyō
Shōgakukan Publishing Co, Ltd
Shōjūji
Shōren'in

Silk Museum
Sōgetsu Shuppan, Inc
Sōgō Art Co
SUGANUMA Baku
Suntory Museum of Art
SUZUKI Jūzō
Taishūkan Publishing Co, Ltd
Taizōin
TAKAMURA Kimie
TAMURA Tadatsugu
Tekisui Art Museum
Tessai Art Museum
Tochigi Prefectural Tourist Office, Tōkyō
Tochigi Prefectural Trade Office, Tōkyō
Tōdaiji
Tōfukuji
Tōji
Tokugawa Reimeikai Foundation
Tōkyō Aerial Photo Research Institute
Tōkyō Gakuso
Tōkyō Metropolitan Central Library
Tōkyō Metropolitan Government Office
Tōkyō National Museum
Tōkyō National Museum of Modern Art
Tōkyō National Research Institute of Cultural Properties
Tōkyō University of Fine Arts and Music
Toppan Idea Center, Toppan Printing Co, Ltd
Tōshōdaiji
Tōyama Studio Co, Ltd
Tōyō Bunko
Toyokuni Shrine
Toyota Motor Corporation
Tsubouchi Memorial Theater Museum
Uesugi Shrine
UMEHARA Ryūzaburō
UMEWAKA Manzaburō
Umezawa Memorial Gallery
Uni Photos Co, Ltd
Urasenke Konnichian
USHIO Yoshimichi
Waseda University Library
WATANABE Manabu
Yaesu Art Gallery
Yagi Photo Library
Yakuōin
Yakushiji
YAMAHATA Yōsuke
YAMAZAKI Kane
Yamato Bunkakan
Yoita Kyōdo Shiryōkan
Yokkaichi City Branch Office, Tōkyō
Yokohama City Port Department
YOKOYAMA Takashi
YOSHIDA Chiaki

Yoshikawa Kōbunkan Publishing Co, Ltd
YOSHIKOSHI Tatsuo
Yoshitoku Collection
Yūzenshikai
Yuzu Henshū Kōbō Co
Zauhō Publications
Zenkōji
Zenrinji

Special Acknowledgment

KŌMA Yoshiko
OSAKU Taiko

AIZAWA Takeshi
Fuji Photo
IMAJIMA Minoru
Ina Kōgei
KANAI Hiroo
KATAKURA Nobuhiro
KAWAMATA Takashi
KENZO TANGE & URTEC
KIKUCHI Sadao
KOBAYASHI Tadashi
MIURA Tōseki
PEC Co, Ltd
TSUNODA Eriko
YANO Takehiko

THE ROMANIZATION RULES OF THE *ENCYCLOPEDIA OF JAPAN*

Spelling

Japanese words are spelled according to the Hepburn system of romanization with macrons being used to indicate long vowels. The *Encyclopedia* uses *m* instead of *n* before *p*, *b*, or *m*, and an apostrophe is used to distinguish syllable-final *n* from *n* at the beginning of a syllable. Foreign words in Japanese phrases are spelled as pronounced in Japanese.

Italicization

All Japanese words have been italicized except for proper nouns, which have been capitalized and set in roman letters. Certain Japanese words that were judged to be familiar to Western readers—such as *kabuki, haiku, kimono,* and *samurai*—were italicized on their first use in an article only and thereafter set in regular type.

Word division

The basic principle followed in word division was to divide Japanese words and phrases into units consisting of from one to three Chinese characters in the case of words of Chinese origin *(kango)* or from one to six syllables in

the case of words of native origin (Yamato *kotoba*). Words or phrases of more than three Chinese characters or six syllables were divided into smaller units according to meaning or grammatical relationship. However, prefixes or suffixes that would be spelled solid according to this rule were spelled open if they were joined in sense to compounds of two or more words as a whole rather than to the first or last word (e.g., *nihonshi* "Japanese history" vs *gendai nihon shi* "history of modern Japan"). In another exception, compounds of four Chinese characters—spelled open by this rule—were hyphenated if a change in sound had accompanied compounding (e.g., *temmoku-jawan*, from *temmoku* and *chawan*).

An effort was also made to avoid repeating information in Japanese and English when English paraphrases or equivalents were needed to clarify the meaning of Japanese terms. Thus, as *ji* means "temple" in Japanese, Tōdaiji, for example, would be referred to as "Tōdaiji" or "the temple Tōdaiji" and *not* as "Tōdaiji Temple." Common geographical suffixes in this category include *kawa/gawa* "river" ("Sumidagawa" or "the river Sumidagawa," not "the Sumida River" or "the Sumidagawa River"), *shima/jima* "island," and *san/zan* "mountain."

HOW TO USE THE INDEX

Typography

Boldface type (e.g., **Anglo-Japanese Alliance**) indicates entries for which there are articles in the *Encyclopedia of Japan* while lightface type is used for topics discussed within articles (e.g., Marxism). Indented headings indicate aspects of the entry:

> Scandinavia
> Japanese studies ················· **4:43b**

The heading "Japanese studies" under the index entry "Scandinavia" indicates the location of information on Japanese studies in Scandinavia. The page references present the volume number in boldface followed by the page number and a letter indicating the left half (a) or the right half (b) of the page. Thus the reference for Japanese studies in Scandinavia, 4:43b, indicates that this information will be found in volume 4 on page 43 in the righthand column. Numbers in italics direct the reader to photographs.

Headings in italics are the titles of books, newspapers, magazines, films, plays, or art works. Quotation marks indicate poems, short stories, sections of books, and slogans. Words in foreign languages, with the exception of the Latin names of plants, are not set in italics unless

they fall into the categories listed above.

Alphabetization

The entries in the index are alphabetized letter by letter, not word by word, so that not all of the entries beginning with the same word will fall together:

> **New Liberal Club**
> **New religions**
> **News agencies**
> **Newspapers**
> **New Tōkyō International Airport**

Mc is alphabetized as if it were spelled out as Mac and St. as Saint.

Chinese characters

Chinese characters are provided for all Japanese personal names, place names, and titles of books as well as for select words.

Cross references

Cross references direct the reader to the form used in the index (e.g., **Japan External Trade Organization.** *See* **JETRO**).

A

Aa gyokuhai ni hana ukete
····· ああ玉杯に花うけて ···· 7:166b
Aa mujō ········· 噫無情 ····· 4:316b
Abacus ··························· 1:1a
  wasan ·························· 8:231a
Abalones [(awabi) family Haliotidae]
···· 1:1a–1b; 2:284a; 7:81b
Abashiri (city) ········ 網走 ···· 1:1b, *1b*
Abashiri, Lake ··· 網走湖 ···· 1:1b–2a
Abashiri Quasi-National
  Park ······· 網走国定公園 ···· 1:1b
Abdomen ··················· 3:100a–100b
Abe Akira ······· 阿部昭 ········ 1:2a
Abe Collection
  Ōsaka Municipal Museum of Fine Arts
·························· 6:121b
Abe family 安倍氏, 阿部氏 ······ 1:2a
  samurai against ················· 7:7b
Abegawa. *See* Abekawa
Abe ichizoku ···· 阿部一族 ···· 4:85a
Abe Isoo ····· 安部磯雄 ······· 1:2a–2b;
                                    7:281a
  education ······················· 1:2a
  labor involvements ········· 1:2a–2b
  pacifism ······················ 6:144a
  political career ············· 1:2a–2b
  Shakai Minshutō ········ 7:74a–74b
  Shakai Taishūtō ·········· 7:74b
Abe Jirō ·········· 阿部次郎 ······· 1:2b
Abekawa ········· 安倍川 ······ 1:2b
Abe Kōbō ····· 安部公房 1:2b–3b; 7:38b
  life ·························· 1:2b–3a
  shingeki ···················· 7:113b
  works ······················· 1:3a–3b
    literary devices ··········· 1:3a
    prose themes ··············· 1:3a
    scientific ················· 1:3a
Abe Masahiro ···· 阿部正弘 ···· 1:3b
  kabunakama revival ········· 4:100a
  Perry, Matthew Calbraith ···· 3:189b
Abe Nobuyuki ···· 阿部信行 ··· 1:3b–4a
Abe no Hirafu · 阿倍比羅夫 · 1:4a; 7:263a
Abe no Munetō · 安倍宗任 ···· 1:4a
Abe no Nakamaro
············ 阿倍仲麻呂 ···· 1:4a
  Sui and Tang (T'ang) China, embassies to
························· 7:259a
Abe no Sadatō ··· 安倍貞任 ···· 1:4a
Abe Nōsei. *See* Abe Yoshishige
Abe no Yoritoki · 安倍頼時 ·· 1:4a–4b
Abe Shigetaka ··· 阿部重孝 ···· 1:4b
Abe Shinnosuke
············ 阿部真之助 ···· 1:4b
Abe Shōō ······· 阿部将翁 ···· 1:4b
Abe Shōzō. *See* **Minakami Takitarō**
Abe Tadaaki ····· 阿部忠秋 ···· 1:4b
Abe Tomoji ····· 阿部知二 ···· 1:4b
  Shinkō Geijutsu Ha ········· 7:119b
Abe Yoshishige · 安倍能成 ···· 1:5a
Abe Yutaka ······ 阿部豊 ····· 2:268b
Abhidharmakośa ············ 4:320a
Abhinayadarpanam ··········· 8:21b
Abiko ··········· 安孫子 ······ 1:5a
Aboku shingo ···· 亜墨新語 ···· 4:369b
A-bomb Medical Law ········· 1:110b
Abō Pass ······· 安房峠 ······ 1:5a
  northern Japan ·············· 2:238b

Abortion (datai) ·· 1:5a; 2:234b, 246b–247b;
              6:224a, 225a; 8:263a
  criminality ··················· 2:48a
Abu Dhabi Oil Co, Ltd ········· 2:61a
Abugawa ·········· 阿武川 ······ 1:5a
Abugawa Dam · 阿武川ダム ···· 1:5a
Abukumagawa ··· 阿武隈川 · 1:5a; 2:366b
Abukuma Mountains
············ 阿武隈山地 · 1:5b; 2:366b
Abuna-e (risqué pictures) ······· 7:187b
Aburakasu ········· 油糟 ····· 7:140a
Abura kōmori (*Pipistrellus abramus*)
·························· 1:146b
Aburatsubo ········ 油壺 ······ 1:5b
Abuse of right ················· 1:5b
  ownership rights ············· 6:137a
Abutsu Ni ······· 阿仏尼 · 1:5b–6a;
                                    2:356a
  life ·························· 1:5b
  works ······················· 1:6a
Academic Degree Order (1887) ···· 1:6a
Academic degrees ············· 1:6a
Academic freedom 1:6a–6b; 6:220b; 8:171a
  constitutional guarantee ····· 2:396b
  Kyōto University Incident ···· 4:339a–339b
  Morito Incident ············· 5:254a
Academy Prize ················· 4:9b
Accent in the Japanese language 1:6a–8a
  dialects ············· 1:7a–7b; 2:91a
  history ···················· 1:7b–8a
  modern standard
    intonation system ··········· 1:7a
    long syllables ··············· 1:6b
    mora ······················· 1:6b
    parts of speech ············· 1:7a
    short syllables ············· 1:6b
Accounting and auditing ··· 1:8a–10a
  auditing practices ············· 1:9a
  balance sheets ············· 1:9b–10a
  certified public accountant (kōnin
    kaikeishi) ··················· 1:266a
  consolidated financial statement
·················· 1:360a–360b
  early history ················· 1:8a
  income statements ··········· 1:10a
  principles ···················· 1:8b
  profession ················· 1:8b–9a
  professionalization ········· 1:8a–8b
  tax accounting ······ 1:10a; 7:351b–352a
  tax accountants ············· 7:351b
Acheson statement ·········· 1:10a–10b
Achievement tests ··········· 1:10b
Achilles Corporation ··········· 1:10b
Acquisition by prescription ······ 7:68a
Actors' Analects, The ·········· 8:21b
Acupressure ··················· 7:83b
Acupuncture ········ 1:10b; 5:146a
  psychotherapy ·············· 6:261a
Adachi Buntarō
············ 足立文太郎 ···· 1:11a
Adachi Kagemori 安達景盛 ···· 1:11a
Adachi Kenzō ··· 安達謙蔵 ···· 1:11a
  Kokumin Dōmei ············· 4:260a
Adachi Mineichirō
··········· 安達峰一郎 ···· 4:373b
Adachi Tadashi ··· 足立正 ···· 1:11a
Adachi Ward ····· 足立区 ···· 1:11a
Adams, William ···· 1:11a–11b; 5:3b
  Dutch trade ················ 2:135b
  Saris, John ·················· 7:22a
Adatarasan ···· 安達太良山 ···· 1:11b
Administered prices ·········· 1:11b
Administrative acts ······· 1:13a, 14a
  types ······················ 1:14a
Administrative Board (Mandokoro) 5:101a
Administrative Case Litigation Law · 1:13a
Administrative Court ··· 1:11b–12a, 13a;
                                    7:277b

  abolishment ················· 4:378a
  Okano Keijirō ··············· 6:80b
  public law ·················· 6:265b
  tax laws ··············· 7:355a–358a
''Administrative disposition'' ····· 1:13a
Administrative guidance ··· 1:12a–13a;
              2:118a, 316a; 4:379b
  description ················· 1:12a
  effectiveness ··············· 1:12b
  enforcement methods ········· 1:12b
  exports ···················· 1:12a
  foreign trade ··············· 2:326a
  industrial policy ············ 3:297a
  Industrial Structure Council ·· 3:302b
  legal challenges ············· 1:12b
  Ministry of International Trade and
    Industry ·················· 4:190b
  Securities Exchange Law ······ 1:8b
  technological development ···· 7:370a
Administrative law ···· 1:13a–13b, 14a
Administrative litigation ··· 1:13b–14a
  seizures ···················· 7:55b
  types ······················ 1:13b
Administrative Management Agency
  (AMA) ········· 1:14a, 219a; 2:118a
Administrative Management and
  Inspection Commission ········· 1:14a
Administrative procedure ····· 1:14a
Administrative Reform, Provisional
  Council on ··················· 1:14a
Administrative scrivener ··· 1:14a–14b
Adogawa ········· 安曇川 ···· 1:14b
Adoption · 1:14b–15b; 2:242a–242b; 6:163a
  characteristics ············ 1:14b–15a
  foundlings ·················· 1:15b
  historical perspective ········· 1:15a
  in literature ················· 1:15a
  marriage ··················· 5:116a
  modern Japan ·············· 1:15a–15b
  principle of succession ···· 3:259b–260a
  provisional or temporary ······ 1:15a
  purposes ··················· 1:14b
  urban ······················ 1:15b
Adoptive marriage ········· 2:242a–242b
ADR ······················ 1:51b–52a
Adult, legal definition of ····· 1:16a
Adultery ················ 1:15b–16a
Adulthood ············· 1:16a; 5:4b–5a
Adulthood Day ················ 3:17a
''Advance to the North'' (hokushinron)
  group ······················· 1:87b
''Advance to the South'' (nanshinron)
  group ······················· 1:87b
Advertising ·············· 1:16a–17b
  cost ······················· 1:16a
  financing ··················· 1:17b
  future prospects ············· 1:17b
  history ·················· 1:16b–17a
  industry structure ·········· 1:17a–17b
  Japan Advertisers Association ··· 4:9b
  Japan Advertising Review Organization
·························· 4:9b–10a
  postwar history ············· 1:17a
  self-regulation ··············· 4:9b
  signboards ············· 7:193b–194a
Advertising agencies ······· 1:17b–18a
  Daikō Advertising Inc ····· 2:60a–60b
  Dentsū ····················· 2:87a
  first ···················· 1:16b, 17b
  Hakuhōdō ··················· 3:88a
  number ············· 1:16a, 17b–18a
Advertising revenues ··········· 1:16a
  postwar growth ·············· 1:17a
Advisory Council on the Welfare of the
  Physically Handicapped ······· 6:186a
Adzuki beans. *See* Azuki
Aeba Kōson ···· 饗庭篁村 ···· 1:18a
Shinshōsetsu ················· 7:125a

Aeba Yosaburō. *See* **Aeba Kōson**
Ae no Koto ···················· 2:259a
　ta no kami ··················· 7:344a
Aerophones ···················· 5:282a
Aesop's Fables ········· 3:183b, 347b
Aesthetics ············· 1:18a-19a
　concepts
　　aware ················· 5:246b-247a
　　fūryū ················· 2:374a-374b
　　iki ·················· 3:267b-268a
　　ma ······················· 5:77a
　　mono no aware ········· 5:246b-247a
　　okashi ···················· 6:81a
　　sabi ················· 6:361a-361b
　　shibui ················· 7:85b-86a
　　wabi ····················· 8:197a
　　yojō ····················· 8:328b
　　yūgen ············· 8:355a-355b
　historical trends ········· 1:18a-18b
　　Edo period ················ 1:18b
　　Heian period ·············· 1:18a
　　medieval ················· 1:18b
　　modern ··················· 1:19a
　premodern characteristics ····· 1:18b
　　beauty ··················· 1:18b
　　elegance ················· 1:18b
　　impermanence ············· 1:18b
　　simplicity ················ 1:19a
　　symbolic representation ····· 1:18b
　shibui ················· 7:85b-86a
Africa and Japan ········· 1:19a-19b
　aid ······················· 1:19b
　diplomatic relations ··· 1:19a; 3:322a-323b
　trade ··········· 1:19a; 3:322a-323b
Africa Committee ·············· 4:188a
African Development Fund (AfDF) ··· 1:19b
Afro-Asian Conferences ····· 1:19a-20a
Afro-Asian Peoples' Solidarity
Conferences ·················· 1:19b
Afterlife ···················· 1:20a
　avatar ············· 1:122b-123a
　Buddhist view ·············· 1:20a
　Emma ····················· 2:201b
　realms ···················· 1:20a
　representations ············· 1:20a
　Shintō view ················ 1:20a
　this-worldliness ············ 8:24b
　traditional belief ··········· 1:20a
After the Banquet case ··· 1:20a-20b, 85a,
　　　　　　　　　　255a; 6:249b
Afurisan ·········· 雨降山 ······· 6:137b
Afuri Shrine　　雨降神社
　Ōyama ···················· 6:137b
Aganogawa ········ 阿賀野川 ····· 1:20b
Agano ware ······· 上野焼 · 1:20b; 2:295b
　Kobori Enshū ·············· 4:238b
Agatai ············ 県居 ····· 4:129a
Agatameshi no Jimoku
　·········· 県召の除目 ······· 4:57b
Agata no Inukai no
Tachibana no Michiyo
　········· 県犬養橘三千代 ···· 1:20b-21a
Agatanushi ········· 県主 ····· 1:21a
Agatsumagawa ······ 吾妻川 ····· 1:21a
Agawa Hiroyuki · 阿川弘之 ········ 1:21a
Age, legal definition of ···· 1:21a-21b
Agechirei ········ 上地令 · 1:21a; 3:189b
Agedatami-bon ····· 上畳本 ···· 4:161b
Agency for Cultural Affairs (Bunkachō)
　·················· 1:75a; 5:186b
Agency for Spiritual Guidance · 7:245b
Agency of Industrial Science and
Technology ········ 1:21b; 6:304a
Agency system ··········· 2:66b-67a
Ageo ············· 上尾 ····· 1:21b
Age of Glass ················· 6:112a
Age of the Six Poetic Geniuses ··· 8:208b
Age reckoning ············· 5:3b-4a

Aging ······················ 5:149a
Ago Bay ·········· 英虞湾 ····· 1:21b
Agrarianism ··········· 6:32a-32b
Agrarian nationalism (nōhon shugi)
　·························· 6:205a
　Gondō Seikyō ·············· 3:45a
　Ishiguro Tadaatsu ··········· 3:341a
　Tachibana Kōzaburō ········· 7:292a
　ultranationalism ············ 8:144b
Agrarian Reform Recording Committee
　·························· 8:289a
Agricultural Administration Council 1:32a
Agricultural Chemicals Control Law 1:30b
Agricultural cooperative associations
(nōkyō) · 1:21b-22b, 139b; 6:238a; 7:214a
　land reform programs ········· 1:24b
　Nōrin Chūkin Bank ·········· 6:37b
　postwar ················ 1:22a-22b
　　membership ·············· 1:22a
　　problems ················ 1:22a
　　structure ················ 1:22a
　prewar ···················· 1:21b
　　government support ········· 1:21b
　　national networks ·········· 1:22a
　　prefectural federations ······ 1:21b
Agricultural rites ···· 1:22b-23a, 23a, 160b,
　　　　　　　　　194b; 2:258a
　corn raising ················ 1:22b
　folk religion ··········· 2:298a-300b
　harvest ···················· 1:22b
　New Year ·················· 1:23a
　rice growing ················ 1:22b
Agriculture ······· 1:23b-32a; 2:284a
　in Asia, development of ······ 7:178a-178b
　brewing ··············· 1:169b-170a
　climate ··············· 1:327b-328a
　commercial ········· 2:148a, 150a-150b
　early modern economy ····· 2:153a-153b
　farming techniques ········· 1:28b-31a
　　animal husbandry ········· 1:29b-30a
　　chemicals ················ 1:30b
　　dry field farming ········· 1:29a-29b
　　fertilizers ················ 1:30b
　　horticulture ·············· 1:30a
　　implements ··········· 1:30a-30b
　　insect pests ·············· 1:30b
　　irrigation ················ 1:29b
　　land improvement ·········· 1:29b
　　new varieties (plant breeding) ···· 1:30a
　　plant diseases ············· 1:30b
　　rice planting ··········· 1:28b-29a
　farmland ·················· 1:26a
　　climate ·················· 1:26a
　　cultivation areas ··········· 1:26a
　　farm households ··········· 1:26a
　　volcanoes ················ 1:26a
　financial depression of 1930s ····· 7:173b
　forestry ··············· 2:326b-327a
　gōnō (rich farmers) ········· 3:45b-46a
　governmental policy ······· 1:31a-32a
　　Basic Agriculture Law of 1961 ···· 1:31b
　　income doubling plan ········ 1:31b
　　present problems ··········· 1:32a
　　self-sufficiency ·········· 1:31a-32a
　　tenant-farming ············ 1:31a
　government policy
　　bakuhan system ········ 1:131a-133a
　history ···················· 1:23b
　　Edo period ················ 1:24a
　　modern era ················ 1:24a
　　political power ·········· 1:23b-24a
　horticulture ················ 3:231b
　industrial structure ········ 3:299b-302a
　labor movement ············· 4:353b
　landlordism ················ 4:362b
　land reclamation ········· 7:109b-110a
　livestock production ········ 1:27b-28b
　　beef cattle ················ 1:28b

　　chicken ·················· 1:28b
　　climate for ············ 1:27b-28a
　　dairy cattle ··············· 1:28b
　　history ················ 1:27b-28a
　　native breeds ·············· 1:28b
　　pork ····················· 1:28b
　mechanization ··········· 1:25a, 26a
　modernization ··········· 1:24a-26a
　　land reform and migration ······ 1:24b
　　postwar changes ········· 1:24b-26a
　part-time basis ············· 2:308a
　plant crops ············ 1:26b-27b
　　apples ··················· 1:71a
　　azuki bean ··········· 1:27a, 127a
　　chestnuts ················ 1:270a
　　cucurbits ············ 2:52a-52b
　　eggplants ················ 2:184b
　　fruit trees ················ 1:27a
　　grapes ············· 1:27a; 3:60b
　　green tea ················· 1:27b
　　industrial ················ 1:27b
　　mikan ············· 1:27b; 5:170a-170b
　　mushrooms ········· 1:27b; 5:282a-282b
　　peaches ··········· 1:27b; 6:169b
　　pears ···················· 6:170a
　　persimmons ··············· 6:178a
　　potatoes and yams ·········· 6:231b
　　radishes ·········· 1:27a; 6:276a-276b
　　rice ············· 1:26b; 6:308a-310a
　　soybeans ··········· 1:27a; 7:239a
　　vegetables, green ··········· 8:189a
　　vegetables, Western ······ 8:189a-189b
　　Welsh onions ·············· 8:241a
　　wheat and barley ······· 1:26b; 8:251a
　premodern economy ······· 2:147a-148a
　primary industries ··········· 6:240a
　religious aspects ········· 2:252b-254a
　sericulture ·············· 7:68b-69a
　tea ·················· 7:359b-360a
　terrace farming ············· 1:25a
Agriculture, White Paper on ······· 1:32a
"Agriculture-first" (nōhon shugi) ··· 1:26a
Agriculturists
　Andō Hirotarō ·············· 1:55a
　Fesca, Max ················· 2:252a
　Fukuba Hayato ·············· 2:361b
　Kellner, Oscar ·········· 4:190b-191a
　Miyazaki Yasusada ··········· 5:222b
　Ōkura Nagatsune ············ 6:98a
　Satō Nobuhiro ·············· 7:28b
　Yokoi Tokiyoshi ············· 8:331b
Agronome français: Dictionaire
économique ················· 4:294b
Aguinaldo, Emilio ········· 1:32a-32b
Agura ····················· 7:248b
Agura nabe ······· 安愚楽鍋 ···· 4:135a
Ai ······················· 3:290a
Aichi Canal ······· 愛知用水 · 1:32b, *32b*
Aichi Irrigation Project ········· 8:237a
Aichi Machine Industry Co, Ltd 1:32b-33a
Aichi Prefecture ····· 愛知県 ···· 1:33a
Aichi Steel Works, Ltd ····· 1:33a-33b
　Toyoda Automatic Loom Works, Ltd
　·························· 8:90a
Aida Gozan ······· 会田吾山 ···· 4:31b
Aida Masae ······ 会田昌江 ···· 3:102a
Aikawa ·········· 相川 ····· 1:33a
Aikawa Yoshisuke
　············· 鮎川義介 ········ 1:33b
Aikidō ·········· 合気道 · 1:34a, *34b*
　jūjutsu ··················· 1:34a
　jūjutsu techniques ··········· 1:34a
　modern systematization ········ 1:34a
　practice forms ·············· 1:34a
Aikoku Fujinkai (Patriot's
Women's Association)
　········ 愛国婦人会 · 1:34a; 7:105a
　Okumura Ioko ········ 6:96b; 8:261a

Aikokuhan (patriotic groups) ········· 愛国班 ········· 4:284a
Aikoku Kinrōtō
　Shimpeitai Incident ········· 7:108a
Aikoku Kōtō (Public Party of Patriots) ········· 愛国公党 · 1:34b; 6:207a
　Freedom and People's Rights Movement ········· 2:334a
　Gotō Shōjirō ········· 3:54a
　Hayashi Yūzō ········· 3:118a
　Itagaki Taisuke ········· 3:349a
Aikokusha (Society of Patriots) ········· 愛国社 1:34b; 2:373b; 6:207a
　Freedom and People's Rights Movement ········· 2:334b
　Itagaki Taisuke ········· 3:349a
　League for Establishing a National Assembly ········· 4:372b-373a
Aikyōgen ········· 間狂言 4:324b, 326a
Aikyōjuku ········· 愛郷塾 1:34b
　Tachibana Kōzaburō ········· 7:292a
Ainotake ········· 間ノ岳
　Shirane Sanzan ········· 7:147a
Ai no kawaki (Thirst for Love) ········· 愛の渇き ········· 6:231a
Ai no korīda (Realm of the Senses) ········· 愛のコリーダ ········· 2:275a
Ainu ········· 1:34b-36a
　Batchelor, John ········· 1:145b
　dance ········· 1:36a
　dialects ········· 2:92a
　economy ········· 1:35b
　Ezo ········· 2:238b
　folk crafts ········· 2:294a
　folktales ········· 1:36a
　general description ········· 1:34b-35a
　Jōmon skulls ········· 4:34b
　Koganei Yoshikiyo's study of ········· 4:248a
　land rights ········· 4:113a
　language ········· 1:36a-37b
　　affinities ········· 1:37a-37b
　　general description ········· 1:36a-36b
　　Japanese language ········· 4:23b
　　Kindaichi Kyōsuke ········· 4:212a
　　literature ········· 1:37a
　　phonology ········· 1:36b
　　studies ········· 1:36b
　　syntax and grammar ········· 1:36b-37a
　　vocabulary ········· 1:37a
　lifestyle ········· 1:35b
　minorities ········· 5:195a
　music ········· 1:36a, 37b
　　affinities ········· 1:37a
　　general description ········· 1:37b
　　musical instruments ········· 1:37b
　　origins ········· 1:35b
　physical characteristics ········· 1:35b; 4:35a-38a
　population ········· 1:35a
　religion ········· 1:36a
　Russia ········· 6:340b
　Sakhalin ········· 7:1b
　social organization ········· 1:36a
Ainu-English-Japanese Dictionary 1:145b
Ainu jojishi yūkara no kenkyū I-II · 4:212a
Aioi ········· 相生 ········· 1:37b
Aircraft industry. See Aviation
Air pollution ········· 2:227b-228a
　coal ········· 2:216a
　control ········· 2:227a-229a
　diseases ········· 2:226b-227a
Airport Law of 1952 ········· 1:38a
Airports ········· 1:37b-38a
　classes ········· 1:37a
　maintenance ········· 1:38a
　New Tōkyō International (Narita) · 1:37b; 5:370b-371b
　Ōsaka International ········· 1:37b

Tōkyō International (Haneda) ········· 1:37b
Air Self Defense Force ········· 7:60a-60b
Air transportation ········· 8:102b-103a
Aisai monogatari
　Shindō Kaneto ········· 7:111a
Aisin Seiki Co, Ltd ········· 1:38a
　Toyota Motor Co, Ltd ········· 8:93b
Ai to ninshiki to no shuppatsu
　········· 愛と認識との出発 · 4:312a
Aizawa Seishisai
　········· 会沢正志斎 ········· 1:38a
　Fujita Tōko ········· 2:347a
　Fujita Yūkoku ········· 2:347a
　Mito school ········· 5:205a
　Shinron ········· 7:124a
Aizawa Tadahiro 相沢忠洋 ········· 1:38a
　Iwajuku site ········· 3:358a
Aizen katsura · 愛染かつら ········· 4:177b
Aizu, Battle of. See Boshin Civil War
Aizu Basin ········· 会津盆地 ········· 1:38a
Aizu Book of Agriculture ········· 1:38b
Aizu Hongō ware
　········· 会津本郷焼 ········· 1:38b
Aizukoma ········· 会津駒 ········· 4:265a
Aizu Komagatake
　········· 会津駒ケ岳 ········· 4:265a
Aizu nōsho ········· 会津農書 ········· 1:38b
Aizu Wakamatsu 会津若松 ········· 1:38b
Aizu Yaichi ········· 会津八一 ········· 1:38b
Ajia Afurika Kaigi ········· 1:19b-20a
Ajikawa ········· 安治川 ········· 1:38b
Ajinomoto Co, Inc ········· 1:38b-39a
Ajirogi ········· 網代木 ········· 4:180a
Ajisai. See Hydrangea, Japanese
Akabane Kōsaku Bunkyoku · 赤羽工作分局 ········· 1:39a
Akabane Manufacturing Branch ········· 1:39a
Akabira ········· 赤平 ········· 1:39a
Akabori Shirō ········· 赤堀四郎 ········· 1:39a
Akaezo fūsetsu kō
　········· 赤蝦夷風説考 · 1:39a; 4:302a
Akagami ········· 7:168a
Akagisan ········· 赤城山 ········· 1:39a
Akahata ········· 赤旗 · 1:39b; 2:339a; 4:180b; 7:91b
　circulation ········· 4:12a
　Japan Communist Party ········· 4:11a
Akahata Incident. See Red Flag Incident of 1908
Akahata Jiken. 赤旗事件 See Red Flag Incident of 1908
Akahito ········· 赤人 ········· 8:287b
Akahon. 赤本 See Kusazōshi
Akai daiya ····· 赤いダイヤ ········· 4:115a
Akai Electric Co, Ltd ········· 1:39b
Akaishidake ········· 赤石岳 ········· 1:39b
Akaishi Mountains
　········· 赤石山脈 ········· 1:39b
Akai tori ········· 赤い鳥 · 1:39b-40a
Akakurage ········· 4:50b
Akakura Hot Spring
　········· 赤倉温泉 ········· 1:40a
Akama Shrine ········· 赤間神宮 ········· 1:40a
　Shimonoseki ········· 7:105b
Akamatsu family ··· 赤松氏 · 1:40a; 7:8b
Akamatsu Katsumaro
　········· 赤松克麿 ········· 1:40a-40b
　Kokumin Kyōkai founder ··· 4:260b-261a
Akamatsu Mitsusuke
　········· 赤松満祐 ········· 1:40a
Akamatsu Sōtan 赤松宗旦
　Tonegawa zushi ········· 8:74a
Akame, 48 Falls of
　········· 赤目四十八滝 ········· 1:40a
Akan, Lake ········· 阿寒湖 ········· 1:40a
Akan National Park
　········· 阿寒国立公園 ········· 1:40a

Akasaka Detached Palace ········· 1:40b
Akashi (city) ········· 明石 ········· 1:40b-41a
Akashi Strait ········· 明石海峡 ········· 1:41a
Akashi Women's Normal School
　Shin Kyōiku Undō ········· 7:121b
Akashiya no Dairen
　········· アカシヤの大連 ········· 4:232b
Aka to kuro (Red and Black) ········· 赤と黒 · 3:76a; 4:183a
"Akatombo" (Red Dragonflies) ········· 赤とんぼ ········· 2:133b
Akatsuchi no ie · 赤土の家 ········· 4:139a
Akatsuki to yūbe no shi
　········· 暁と夕の詩 ········· 7:293a
Akazome Emon · 赤染衛門 · 1:41a; 5:37a
　Eiga monogatari ········· 3:153a
Akazukin-chan ki o tsukete
　赤頭巾ちゃん気をつけて ········· 7:163a
Akebi (Akebia quinata) · 1:41a; 2:305a
　baskets ········· 4:104b
Akebonokai ····· あけぼの会 ········· 5:19b
Akechi Mitsuhide 明智光秀 · 1:41a-41b; 2:280b, 361b; 7:104a
　Honnōji Incident ········· 3:224a
　Kameoka ········· 4:125b
Akegarasu nochi no masayume ··· 明烏後正夢 ········· 7:333b
Aki ········· 安芸 ········· 1:41b
Akiba Shrine ········· 秋葉神社 ········· 1:41b
Akibiyori ········· 秋日和 ········· 3:102b
Akigawa ········· 秋川 ········· 1:41b
Akihito, Crown Prince
　········· 明仁親王 · 1:41b-42a
　Imperial household ········· 3:277b
Akimoto Matsuyo 秋元松代 ········· 1:42a
Aki no hi ········· 秋の日 ········· 4:169a
Aki no hitomi ······ 秋の瞳 ········· 8:284a
Aki no koe (Voice of Autumn) ········· 秋の声 ········· 6:139b
Aki no yo no naga monogatari (Long Tale for an Autumn Night)
　otogi-zōshi ········· 6:130a
Akirame ········· あきらめ ········· 1:42a
Akishima ········· 昭島 ········· 1:42a
Akishinodera ········· 秋篠寺 ········· 1:42a
Akita ········· 秋田 ········· 1:42b
Akita Castle ········· 秋田城 ········· 1:42b
Akita Incident · 秋田事件 ········· 1:42b
Akitajō ········· 秋田城 ········· 1:42b
Akita Komagatake
　········· 秋田駒ケ岳 · 4:264b-265b
Akita Oil Fields · 秋田油田 ········· 1:42b
Akita Plain ········· 秋田平野 ········· 1:42b
Akita Prefecture · 秋田県 · 1:42b-43a
Akita school ········· 秋田派 · 1:43a-43b
　main principles ········· 1:43b
　major painters ········· 1:43a
　Odano Naotake ········· 6:65a
　Satake Shozan ········· 7:25b
Akitsu ········· 安芸津 ········· 1:43b
Akiyama Saneyuki
　········· 秋山真之 · 1:43b-44a
Akiyama Teisuke 秋山定輔 ········· 1:44a
Akiyoshidai ········· 秋吉台 · 1:44a, 44b
Akiyoshidai Quasi-National Park ····· 秋吉台国定公園 ········· 1:44b
Akiyoshidō ········· 秋芳洞 · 1:44a-44b; 5:352b
Akiyoshi Toshiko 秋吉敏子 ········· 1:44b
Akizuki Rebellion of 1876
　········· 秋月の乱 ········· 1:44b
　chitsuroku shobun ········· 1:297a
Akkadō ········· 安家洞 ········· 1:44b
Akō ········· 赤穂 ········· 1:44b-45a
Akogiaura. See Akogiura
Akogiura ········· 阿漕浦 ········· 1:45a

Akō Incident of 887
　　　阿衡事件 ········· **1**:45a
　Miyoshi Kiyoyuki ········· **5**:224a
　Uda, Emperor ········· **8**:125b
Akō Incident of 1703. *See* **Forty-Seven Rōnin Incident**
Akubasho ········· **4**:95b
Akuma ·········悪魔 **4**:160b; **7**:342b
Akuma ga kitarite fue o fuku
　　　悪魔が来りて笛を吹く ········· **8**:333b
Akumyō ·········悪名 **4**:174b
Akune ·········阿久根 **1**:45a
Aku okeno ·····灰汁桶の ········· **6**:299b
Akutagawa Prize
　Akutagawa Ryūnosuke (1935) ········· **1**:46a
　Endō Shūsaku ········· **2**:214a
　Gomi Yasusuke (1953) ········· **3**:44b
　Hotta Yoshie (1951) ········· **3**:239b–240a
　Inoue Yasushi ········· **3**:311b
　Ishihara Shintarō ········· **3**:341
　Ishikawa Tatsuzō ········· **3**:345a
　Kaikō Ken ········· **4**:111a
　Kikuchi Kan ········· **4**:206b
　Kita Morio (1960) ········· **4**:227a
　Kiyooka Takayuki (1969) ········· **4**:232b
　Lee Hwe-song (1972) ········· **4**:374b
　Matsumoto Seichō ········· **5**:138a
　Nakayama Gishū (1938) ········· **5**:318b
　Ōe Kenzaburō (1958) ········· **6**:66a
　Ozaki Kazuo (1937) ········· **6**:139b
　Shōji Kaoru (1969) ········· **7**:163a
　Shōno Junzō (1954) ········· **7**:167a
　Tanabe Seiko (1964) ········· **7**:335b
　Yasuoka Shōtarō (1953) ········· **8**:319b
Akutagawa Ryūnosuke
　　　芥川龍之介 **1**:45a–46a, 313b; **5**:13a, 55a–55b; **7**:26b, 72b, 81a, 103b; **8**:173a
　birth and education ········· **1**:45a
　death ········· **1**:46b
　earlier period ········· **1**:45a
　final period ········· **1**:45b
　Kokon chomonjū used ········· **4**:256b
　Konjaku monogatari's influence on ········· **4**:271a
　middle period ········· **1**:45b
　Shinchō ········· **7**:109a
　Shinshichō ········· **7**:125a
　Shinshōsetsu ········· **7**:125b
　works ········· **1**:45a–45b
Akutagawa Ryūnosuke Literary Prize. *See* **Akutagawa Prize**
Akutō ·········悪党 **1**:46a, 97b
Ālayavijñāna ········· **1**:177a
Album leaf (sōshi) ········· **6**:150a
Alcock, Rutherford ········· **1**:46a; **7**:29a
　Shimonoseki Bombardment ········· **7**:106a
Alcoholic beverages in Japanese society ········· **1**:46a–47a
　earliest record ········· **1**:46a
　premodern drinking habits ····· **1**:46a–46b
　present day use
　　among women ········· **1**:47a
　　consumption ········· **1**:47a
　　social ········· **1**:47a
　　urban life ········· **8**:179a
　　varieties ········· **1**:47a
　　wedding ceremony ········· **1**:47a
　sake ········· **7**:1a–1b
Aleutian Islands ········· **4**:223b
Alexander, Wallace McKinney ········· **1**:47a
Algae ········· **7**:46b
Alien Land Acts ········· **1**:47a–47b
　ineffectiveness ········· **1**:47b
　1913 ········· **1**:47a; **8**:155b
　1920 ········· **1**:47b
Alien registration ········· **1**:47b; **2**:314a

Alien Registration Law of 1952 ····· **1**:47b; **2**:313a
Aliens. *See* **Foreigners, legal status of**
Allegory. *See* **Waka**
Allerlie aus Japan ········· **6**:312a
Allied Council for Japan ········· **1**:47b–48a, 117a–117b
　Ball, William MacMahon ······· **1**:135a–135b
　Far Eastern Commission ········· **2**:248a
　land reforms of 1946 ········· **4**:364a
　Occupation ········· **6**:51b
　Sebald, William Joseph ········· **7**:47a
Allied Occupation. *See* **Occupation**
All-Japan Bookbinding Association (Zen Nihon Seihon Kōgyō Kumiai Rengōkai) ········· **6**:246b
All Japan Federation of Electrical Machine Workers' Unions ········· **2**:87a
All Japan Federation of Proletarian Arts (Zen Nihon Musansha Geijutsu Remmei) ········· **6**:255b
All Japan Kendō Federation (Zen Nihon Kendō Remmei) ········· **4**:196a
All-Japan Printing Association ········· **6**:246b
All Men Are Brothers ········· **8**:336a
All Nippon Airways Co, Ltd (ANA) · **1**:48a; **8**:102b
All Nippon News Network (ANN) ··· **1**:92a, 93a
Allowances
　nonstatutory ········· **8**:200a
　statutory ········· **8**:200a
All Quiet on the Western Front ········· **6**:255b
Almanac of Publishing ········· **6**:267b–268a
Almeida, Luis de ········· **2**:172b
Alphabet. *See* Language: Japanese language
Alps Electric Co, Ltd ········· **1**:48a
Altaic languages, Japanese and ········· **4**:18b–20a
Alternate attendance ········· **7**:14a–14b
Altiona peto ········· **6**:100a
Aluminum
　manufacturers ········· **6**:10b–11a; **7**:173a, 268b–269a
　smelters ········· **7**:173a
Ama ········· **1**:48a–48b
　female ········· **1**:48a–48b
　male ········· **1**:48a–48b
"Amabune" ·········海人舟 **4**:269b
Amache Relocation Center ········· **1**:48b
Amae ········· **1**:48b–49a; **4**:39b; **6**:261a; **7**:262b, 275b
　Doi Takeo ········· **1**:49a
　vs enryo ········· **2**:221a
　general description ········· **1**:48b
　usages ········· **1**:48b–49a
　　adult relationships ········· **1**:48b
　　child-parent ········· **1**:48b, 277b
Amae no kōzō·甘えの構造 **1**:49a
Amagasaki ·········尼ケ崎 **1**:49a
Amagatari ·········天語り **2**:138a
Amagi ·········甘木 **1**:49a
Amagi Pass ·········天城峠 **1**:49b; **4**:146a
Amagisan ·········天城山 **1**:49b; **2**:342b
Amagi Yugashima
　　　天城湯ケ島 ········· **8**:355a
Amagoi. *See* **Rain, rituals for**
Amako family ·········尼子氏 **1**:49b
Amakudari ········· **1**:49b
Amakusa (town) ·········天草 **1**:49b–50a
Amakusa Islands 天草諸島 **1**:50a, *50b*
Amakusa Sea ·········天草海 **1**:50a
Amakusa Shirō. 天草四郎 *See* **Shimabara Uprising**
Amami Islands 奄美諸島 ···**1**:50a; **7**:30a
　agricultural rites ········· **1**:23a
　Yoronjima ········· **8**:339a

Amami Ōshima ·奄美大島 ····**1**:50a, *50b*; **4**:105b, 205a
Amanohashidate ·········天橋立 **1**:50a, *51a*; **6**:152b
Amanojakko ········· **1**:50a
Amanojaku ········· **1**:50a–50b
Amanokaguyama 天香久山 **8**:310b
Amanosagume ········· **1**:50a
Amano Tameyuki 天野為之 **1**:50b–51a
Amano Teiyū ·········天野貞祐 **1**:51a
Amano Tōkage ·········天野遠景 **1**:51a
Amaterasu Ōmikami
　　　天照大神 ·**1**:51a–51b, 125a; **2**:2b; **4**:125b; **7**:15b, 276a, 278b, 280a; **8**:236b, 256b, 307b
　account ········· **1**:51b
　birth ········· **5**:293a
　Daijōsai ········· **2**:59a–59b
　disappearance ········· **5**:293b
　feuding with Susanoo ········· **5**:293a–293b
　Hirota Shrine ········· **3**:150b
　imperial descent ········· **4**:191b
　imperial regalia ········· **3**:278b–279a
　Ise Shrine ········· **3**:338a
　Izumo Shrine ········· **3**:367a
　Jinnō shōtō ki ········· **4**:59b–60a
　Kannamesai ········· **4**:144a
　kokutai concept ········· **4**:263a
　messengers ········· **5**:294a–294b
　Ryōbu Shintō ········· **6**:351a
　Shingon sect ········· **7**:115a
　Shinsen shōjiroku ········· **7**:124b
　Takachihonomine ········· **7**:310b
　Takamagahara ········· **7**:314a
　tama ········· **7**:332a
　worship ········· **1**:51b
Amateru Kami ·········天照神 **7**:276b
Amatsukami ·········天津神 **4**:125b
Amatsu Kominato
　　　天津小湊 ········· **1**:51b
Amatsu tsumi ·········天津罪 **3**:101a
Ame no Futodama no Mikoto ·········天太玉命 **1**:125a
Amenomori Hōshū
　　　雨森芳洲 ········· **1**:51b
American Communist Party ····· **7**:229a
American Depositary Receipts (ADR) ········· **1**:51b–52a
American Pacific Mail Steamship Company ········· **3**:362b
Amerika Hikozō. *See* **Hamada Hikozō**
Amerika jigoku meguri (Touring the American Hell) ···アメリカ地獄巡り ········· **8**:13a
Amerika kanjō ryokō
　　　アメリカ感情旅行 ········· **8**:319b
Amerika kyōiku shisetsudan ········· **8**:164a
Amerika Mura アメリカ村 ··· **1**:52a
"Amerikan Sukūru"
　　　アメリカンスクール ········· **4**:252a
Amida ····**1**:52a, 176a, 179a *201a*; **2**:360a; **4**:62a; **7**:63a, 67b
　Byōdōin temple ········· **1**:227a
　East Asian Buddhism ········· **1**:52a
　Jōdo Shin sect ········· **4**:68b
　Jōruriji ········· **4**:77b
　Kinkakuji ········· **4**:213a
　Kiyozawa Manshi ········· **4**:233a
　Kyōgyōshinshō and ········· **4**:330a
　monasticism ········· **5**:238a
　Namu Amida Butsu ········· **5**:327a–327b
　Ōjōyōshū ········· **6**:77a
　popularization of Buddhism ········· **3**:171a–172a
　Primal Vow ········· **1**:52a
　Tannishō ········· **7**:344a
　Pure Land Buddhism ········· **4**:144b
　raigōzu ········· **6**:276b
　Sanzen'in ········· **7**:19b

Shinran · · · · · · · · · · · · · **7:**123a
statues · · · · · · · · · · · · · · **4:**111a
thought and culture · · · **8:**27a–28a
visual arts · · · · · · · · · · · **1:**52a
worship · · · · · · · · · · · · · · **1:**52a
Amida no munewari
　　　阿弥陀の胸割 · · · **4:**76b
Amida sculpture · · · · · · · **4:**66b
Amida's Riven Breast · · · · · · **4:**76b
Amida triad · · · · · · · · · · · · **6:**124b
Amino Kiku · · · · 網野菊 · **1:**52a–52b
Ami school · · · · 阿弥派 · · · **1:**52b–53a
connoisseurship · · · · · · · **1:**53a
Geiami · · · · · · · · · · **1:**52b; **3:**14a
influence · · · · · · · · · · · · · **1:**53a
ink painting · · · · · · · · · · · **3:**306b
Nōami · · · · · · · **1:**52b; **6:**29b–30a
origin · · · · · · · · · · · · · · · · **1:**52b
painting · · · · · · · · · · · · · · **6:**151b
Sōami · · · · · · · · **1:**52b; **7:**207b
Amitābha Buddha · · · **3:**328b–329a
Amity, Commerce and
Navigation, Treaty of (between
Philippines and Japan) · · · **4:**370a; **6:**184b
Amma · · · · · · · · · · · · · · · · **1:**53a
Amnesty (taisha)
criminal law · · · · · · · · · · · **2:**49a
ritsuryō system · · · · · · · · **6:**328a
Amō Eiji · · · · · · 天羽英二 · **1:**53a
Amoenitatum Exoticum · · · **4:**102a
Amoghavajra
Shingon sect · · · · · · · · · · **7:**114a
Amō statement · · · 天羽声明 · **1:**53a; **7:**92a
Amphibians · · · · **1:**60a–60b, 62a
frogs · · · · · · · · · · · **2:**339b–340a
imori · · · · · · · · · · · · · · · · **3:**275a
salamanders · · · · · · · · · **7:**5a–5b
Ampo Riots of 1960
pacifism · · · · · · · · · · · · · · **6:**145a
Ampo tōsō. *See* **Peace movement**
Amur River Society · · · · · · · **1:**53b
annexation of Korea · · · · **4:**282a
Gen'yōsha · · · · · · · · · **3:**24b–25a
nationalism · · · · · · · · **5:**342b–343a
Russo-Japanese War · · · · **6:**346a
tairiku rōnin · · · · · · · · · · **7:**302b
Uchida Ryōhei · · · · · · · · · **8:**124a
ultranationalism · · · · · · · · **8:**145b
World War II · · · · · · · · · · · **8:**271b
Analects · · · · · · · · · **2:**57a; **4:**277a
Itō Jinsai's study · · · · · · · **4:**247b
Anami Korechika 阿南惟幾 · · **1:**53b
Anan (city) · · · · · · 阿南 · · · **1:**53b
Anan Coast · · · · 阿南海岸 · · **1:**53b
Anarchism · · · · **1:**53b–54a; **4:**345a
Anarchist League of Japan · **3:**344a
Anarcho-syndicalism · · · **5:**231a–231b
Anatomische Tabellen · · · · · · · **7:**258b
Anatomy of Dependence · · · · **1:**49a
Ancestor worship · · · **1:**54a–55a; **6:**295b
background · · · · · · · · · **1:**54a–54b
butsudan · · · · · · · · · · · · · **1:**225b
ceremonies and festivals · · · · · **1:**54b
features · · · · · · · · · · · **1:**54a–54b
in Hirata Atsutane's thought · · · **4:**259a
memorial tablets · · · · · · · **1:**54a
social control of household · · · **1:**54b
state influence · · · · · · · · **1:**54a
An Chung-gŭn · · · · · · · · · **1:**55a
Ancient Learning
(Kogaku) · · · · · · 古学 · **4:**246b–248a;
　　　　　　　　　　　　　8:290b
Ancient private records · · · · **4:**255a–255b
Ando · · · · · · · · · 安堵 · · · **1:**55a
Andō Hiroshige · 安藤広重 · **3:**148a–149b
Andō Hirotarō · 安藤広太郎 · **1:**55a
Andon. *See* **Lanterns**
Andō Nobumasa 安藤信正 · · · · **1:**55a–55b

Andō Sanesue · · · 安東実季 · · · **3:**179b
Andō Shōeki · · · · 安藤昌益 · **1:**55b–56a
egalitarian thought · · · · · **1:**55b–56a
metaphysics · · · · · · · · · **1:**55b–56a
theory of medicine · · · · · · · **1:**56a
Anegawa, Battle of
　　　　姉川の戦 · **1:**56a, 94a,
　　　　　　　　　　95a; **5:**300a
Asai Nagamasa · · · · · · · · · **1:**94a
firearms usage · · · · · · · · · · **2:**279a
Oda Nobunaga · · · · · · · · · · **6:**63a
Anemone, Japanese [(shūmeigiku)
Anemone japonica] · · · · · · **1:**56a
Anesaki Chōfū. 姉崎嘲風 *See* Anesaki
Masaharu
Anesaki Masaharu
　　　　姉崎正治 · · · · **1:**56b
Anglerfishes [(ankō) family Lopliidae]
　　　　　　　　　　　　1:56b
Anglican-Episcopal Church · · **7:**51b
Angling · · · · · · · · · · · · · · · **2:**287a
Anglo-Japanese Alliance · **1:**56b–57b, 87b,
238b; **2:**332b; **7:**29b, 198b; **8:**152a, 270b,
　　　　　　　　　　　　291b, 343b
abrogation · · · · · · · · · · · · **1:**237b
background · · · · · · · · · · · · **1:**56b
in Britain · · · · · · · · · · · · · · **1:**57a
Denison, Henry Willard · · · · **2:**86b
dissatisfaction
in Japan · · · · · · · · · · · · · · **1:**57a
from outside · · · · · · · · · · · **1:**57a
Hayashi Tadasu · · · · · · · · **3:**118a
international relations · · · · · **3:**321a
Japanese control in Korea · · · **4:**282a
Japanese factions · · · · · · · · **1:**57a
Komura Jutarō · · · · · · · · · · **4:**268a
Korea's annexation · · · · · · **4:**287a
neutrality · · · · · · · · · · · · · **3:**196b
original agreement and revisions
　　　　　　　　　　　1:56b–57a
Russo-Japanese agreements of 1907–
1916 · · · · · · · · · · · · · · · **6:**344b
Russo-Japanese War · · · · · · **6:**346a
termination · · · · · **1:**57a–57b; **2:**330a
Tripartite Pact · · · · · · · · · · **8:**107a
Twenty-One Demands · · · · · **8:**120b
United States · · · · · · · · · · · **8:**157a
Washington Conference · · · · **8:**234a
Anglo-Japanese Commercial Trade
Treaty of 1894
Denison, Henry Willard · · · · **2:**86b
**Anglo-Japanese Commercial Treaty of
1894** · · · · · · · · · · **1:**57b; **8:**152a
international relations · · · · · **3:**320b
Mutsu Munemitsu · · · · · · · **5:**289a
Treaty of Shimonoseki · · · · **7:**106a
Unequal Treaties revision · · · **8:**148a
Anglo-Japanese relations. *See* **United
Kingdom and Japan**
Angoin. 　　　　安居院
See **Asukadera**
Animals · · · · · · · · · · · · · **1:**57b–62a
agriculture · · · · · · · · **1:**27b–28b, 61b
amphibians · · · · · · · **1:**60a–60b, 62a
arthropods · · · · · · · · · · · · **1:**62a
birds · · · · · · · · · · **1:**59b–60a, 61b
characteristics · · · · · · · · **1:**57b–59a
endemic species · · · · · · · **1:**59a
living fossils · · · · · · · · · · **1:**59a
zoogeographic divisions · · · **1:**59a
in contemporary Japan · · · · **1:**61b
fishes · · · · · · · · · **1:**60b–61a, 61b–62a
husbandry · · · · · · · · · · **1:**29b–30a
insects · · · · · · · · · · · · · · · **1:**61a
in Japanese culture · · · · · **1:**61a–61b
mammals · · · · · · · **1:**59a–59b, 61b
prevention of cruelty · · · · · · **7:**167a
protected · · · · · · · · · · · · · **5:**352a

reptiles · · · · · · · **1:**60a–60b, 62a
Animism · · · · · · · · · · · · · · **1:**62a
Anjō · · · · · · · · · · 安城 · · · **1:**62a
An Jūkon · · · · · · · 安重根 · · · **1:**55a
Ankō · · · · · · · · · · · · · · · · **1:**56b
Ankokuji · · · · · · · 安国寺 · · · **3:**269b
Ankokuji Ekei · 安国寺恵瓊 · **1:**62a; **7:**56b
Anna Incident · · · 安和の変 · **1:**62a–62b
Annaka · · · · · · · · 安中 · · · **1:**62b
*Annals of the Institute of Statistical
Mathematics* · · · · · · · · · · **7:**246a
Annual events. *See* **Festivals**
"Annual tribute" · · · · · · · **5:**360a–361b
Anotsu · · · · · · · · 安濃津 · · · **1:**62b
Anrakuan Sakuden
　　　　安楽庵策伝 · · **1:**62b–63a
comic monologue · · · · · · · · **6:**282a
early life and education · · · · **1:**62b
literary pursuits · · · · · · · · · **1:**63a
prelate of Jōdo sect · · · · · · **1:**62b–63a
Anraku no mon · 安楽の門 · · **6:**81b
Ansei commercial treaties
　　　　安政五か国条約 · **1:**63a; **4:**333a;
　　　　　　　　　　　　7:29a
gaikoku bugyō · · · · · · · · · · **3:**3a
Harris Treaty · · · · · · · · · · · **3:**105a
import tariffs · · · · · · · · · · **4:**112b–113a
Iwakura mission · · · · · · · · **3:**359a
Kōbe · · · · · · · · · · · · · · · · **4:**238a
Kōmei, Emperor · · · · · · · · **4:**266a
Mutsu Munemitsu · · · · · · · **5:**288b
Nagai Uta · · · · · · · · · · · · **5:**301b
Nagasaki trade · · · · · · · · · · **5:**306a
naichi zakkyo · · · · · · · · · **5:**309b–310a
Netherlands · · · · · · · · · · · **5:**362a
Opening of Japan · · · · · · · · **6:**114b
Sakuradamongai Incident · · · · **7:**4b
Sawa Nobuyoshi · · · · · · · · · **7:**31a
Shimonoseki Bombardment · · **7:**106a
shogunate missions to the West · **7:**161a
Takenouchi Yasunori · · · · · · **7:**325a
territory of Japan · · · · · · · · **8:**13b
Tokugawa Iemochi · · · · · · · **8:**48a
Unequal Treaties revision · · · **8:**148a
Yokoi Shōnan · · · · · · · · · · **8:**331a
Ansei gokakoku jōyaku
　　　　安政五か国条約 · · · **1:**63a
Ansei Purge · · · 安政の大獄 · **1:**63a–64a
general description · · · · · · · **1:**63a–63b
Harris Treaty · · · · · · · · · · · **1:**63b
Hashimoto Sanai · · · · · · · · **3:**110a
Ii Naosuke · · · · · · · · · · · · **3:**263a
levels · · · · · · · · · · · · · · · · **1:**63b
Sakuradamongai Incident · · · **1:**63b; **7:**4b
shogunal succession · · · · · · **1:**63b
sonnō jōi · · · · · · · · · **5:**156a–156b
Umeda Umpin · · · · · · · · · · **8:**146b
Yoshida Shōin · · · · · · · · · · **8:**346a
Antarctic research · · · · · · · **1:**64a–64b
history · · · · · · · · · · · · · · · **1:**64a
Japanese Antarctic Research Expedition
(JARE) · · · · · · · · · · · · · · **1:**64a
present status · · · · · · · · · · **1:**64a
special features · · · · · · · · · **1:**64a
Antenna · · · · · · · · · · · · · · · **2:**192a
Anthologies
imperial. *See* **Imperial anthologies**
Man'yōshū. *See* **Man'yōshū**
"unofficial" or private (shisenshū) · **8:**204a
*Anthologies of the Thirty-six Poetic
Geniuses* · · · · · · · · · · · · **1:**234b, 234b
Anthropological Association
(Anthropological Society of Nippon),
　　　　　　　　　　　　8:110a
Anthropological Association of Tōkyō
　　　　　　　　　　　　1:77a
Anthropologists
Adachi Buntarō · · · · · · · · · **1:**11a

Benedict, Ruth Fulton ············· 1:149b
Embree, John Fee ················· 2:200a
Hasebe Kotondo ··················· 3:106b
Imanishi Kinji ···················· 3:274a
Ishida Eiichirō ··················· 3:340a
Izumi Seiichi ····················· 3:366a
Kida Minoru ······················ 4:202a
Kiyono Kenji ······················ 4:232b
Koganei Yoshikiyo ················ 4:248a
Nakane Chie ······················ 7:218a
Torii Ryūzō ······················· 8:79a
Tsuboi Shōgorō ··················· 8:110a
Anti-Christian edicts ····· 1:64b-65a; 3:185b
  Azuchi-Momoyama
    Oda Nobunaga ··············· 1:64b
    Toyotomi Hideyoshi ·········· 1:64b
  Edo period
    Madre de Deus Incident ······ 1:65a
    Tokugawa Ieyasu ············· 1:65a
  Nagasaki trade ················· 5:306a
  National Seclusion ············· 5:346b
  Ōmura Sumitada ················ 6:104b
  Ōtomo Sōrin ···················· 6:132b
  Takayama Ukon ················· 7:321a
Anti-Comintern Pact ····· 1:65a-65b, 88a;
        2:332b; 3:202a; 8:272a, 344a
  international relations ·········· 3:321b
  Ōshima Hiroshi ················· 6:125b
  Russia and Japan ··············· 6:343a
  Russo-Japanese fisheries ······· 6:345a
  Tripartite Pact ················· 8:107a
Anticommunism ··············· 7:201b-202a
Antimonopoly Law (1947) ·· 1:65b-67b;
        4:378b; 8:363a
  administrative guidance ········· 1:12b
  cartels ···················· 1:66b, 245a
  computer industry ·············· 1:345a
  enforcement procedures ········· 1:67b
  holding companies ···· 3:216a; 4:189b
  industrial organizations ········ 3:293b
  merger, corporate ·············· 5:164a
  private monopolization ····· 1:65b-66b
    control ····················· 1:66a
    definition ··················· 1:65b
    exclusion ··················· 1:65b
    mergers ················· 1:66a-66b
    particular field of trade ······ 1:66a
    public interest ··············· 1:66a
    stock acquisitions ········· 1:66a-66b
  unfair business practices ··· 1:67a-67b
    abuse of economic power ··· 1:67a-67b
    coercion ···················· 1:67a
    definition ··················· 1:67a
    discriminatory acts ··········· 1:67a
    inducement ·················· 1:67a
    price setting ················· 1:67a
    restrictive agreements ········ 1:67a
  unreasonable restraint
    cartel agreements ············ 1:66b
    definition ··················· 1:66b
    exemptions ·················· 1:66b
    trade associations ············ 1:66b
  unreasonable restraint of trade · 1:66b-67a
Anti-Russia Fellow Activists' Society
        ···························· 7:303a
"Antislavery" law ················ 6:257a
Antiwar movement. *See* Peace
  movement
Antoku, Emperor 安徳天皇 ·· 1:40a, 67b;
        4:1a
Ants [(ari) family Formicidae] ·· 1:67b-68a
An'ya kōro ······ 暗夜行路 ···· 4:114a
Anzai Fuyue ····· 安西冬衛 ··· 1:68a
Anzai Masaru. *See* Anzai Fuyue
ANZUS Pact ··············· 1:117a-117b
Aobeka monogatari
        ···· あおべか物語 ···· 8:299b
Aōdō Denzen · 亜欧堂田善 ···· 1:68a

Aohon ················· 青本 · 4:201b, 319b
Aoi Bunko. *See* Aoi Library
Aoi Festival ········ 葵祭 1:68a; 2:253a,
        4:130a, 164a, 174a, 336b
Aoi getsuyōbi 青い月曜日 ···· 4:111b
Aoi Library ········ 葵文庫 ·· 1:68a-68b
Aoi Matsuri. *See* Aoi Festival
Aoi sammyaku (Blue
  Mountains) ····· 青い山脈 ··· 6:221b
Aoki [(Japanese laurel) *Aucuba
  japonica*] ···················· 1:68b
Aoki-Kimberley Treaty ·········· 7:198a
Aoki Kon'yō ···· 青木昆陽 ··· 1:68b
Aoki Mokubei ··· 青木木米 · 1:68b, 211a
Aoki Shigeru ······ 青木繁 ·· 1:69a
  education ············· 1:69a; 6:155b
  romanticism ·················· 1:69a
  seascapes ···················· 1:69a
  Umi no Sachi (Gifts of the Sea) 1:69a-69b
  Wadatsumi no iroko no miya ·· 1:69a
Aoki Shūzō 青木周蔵 1:57b, 69a-69b
  shigi kempō ················· 7:92b
Aomori ················ 青森 ·· 1:69b
*Aomori ken no semushi
  otoko* (The Hunchback
  of Aomori)
        ····· 青森県のせむし男 ··· 8:13a
Aomori Prefectural Museum ·· 1:69b
Aomori Prefecture 青森県 ·· 1:69b-70a
  economy ····················· 1:70a
  festivals ····················· 1:70a
  geographical description ······· 1:69b
  tourist attractions ············· 1:70a
Aoneko ················· 青猫 · 3:76a
Aonodōmon ······· 青ノ洞門 ·· 1:70a
Aono Suekichi · 青野季吉 · 1:70a-70b;
        5:13a
  political involvements ·········· 1:70b
  principal works ··············· 1:70b
Aoshima ··············· 青島 · 1:70b
Aoto Fujitsuna · 青砥藤綱 · 1:70b-71a
Aoto-zōshi hana no nishiki-e ·· 4:95a
Aoyagi Tanenobu 青柳種信 ···· 1:76b
Aoyama Gakuin University ··· 1:71a
Aoyama Tanemichi
        ·············· 青山胤通 ··· 1:71a
Apartment living ················ 5:6a
Aporon no shima
        ······· アポロンの島 ···· 6:69b
"Apostate's oath" ·············· 7:186a
Apparel. *See* Clothing
Appeals (Jōso) ·················· 2:51a
Appellate courts ················ 4:81a
Apples [(ringo) *Malus pumila*] ··· 1:71a
Appliance industries 1:298a; 3:207a; 4:52b;
        5:141b; 7:14a
Apprentice system ·········· 1:71a-71b
April 16th Incident ·········· 1:71b
  Tanaka Giichi ············· 7:336a-336b
Aquapolis ····················· 4:207b
Aquariums ·················· 1:71b
  history ······················ 1:71b
  number and location ··········· 1:71b
Arabian Oil Co, Ltd ·· 1:71b-72a; 6:182a
Aragoto ·············· 荒事 · 3:257a;
        4:91a-91b, 97b
Arahata Kanson · 荒畑寒村 · 1:72a-72b,
        155a
  Japan Communist Party · 1:72a; 4:11a
  Japan Socialist Party ··········· 1:72a
  Kanno Suga ·················· 4:145a
  labor movement ··············· 1:72a
  Red Flag Incident ············· 6:285a
  socialism ···················· 1:72a
  works ···················· 1:72a-72b
Arahitogami ······· 現人神 ·· 6:204b
Arai (city) ··········· 新井 ·· 1:72b
Arai, Clarence ·················· 4:15a

Arai Hakuseki ·· 新井白石 · 1:72b-73a
  concept of periodization ········ 3:155a
  historiography ················ 3:155a
  political program ·············· 1:72b
  Shōtoku no Chi ··············· 7:171a
  training and samurai service ···· 1:72b
  works ···················· 1:72b-73a
    Confucianism ··············· 1:73a
    historical ··················· 1:73a
Arainegi ······················· 2:25a
Arai Ōsui ········ 新井奥邃 · 1:73a
  education ···················· 1:73a
  evangelical activities ·········· 1:73a
  Harris, Thomas Lake · 1:73a; 3:104a
  visit to United States ·········· 1:73a
  writings ····················· 1:73a
Arajotai (The New Household)
  Tokuda Shūsei ················ 8:45a
Arakawa ············· 荒川 · 1:73a-73b,
        272a
Arakawa Toyozō ·荒川豊蔵 · 1:73b
Arakawa Ward ····· 荒川区 · 1:73b
Arakida Moritake
        ·············· 荒木田守武 ·· 1:73b
Arakida Rei ······· 荒木田麗 · 1:73b-74a
Arakida Reijo 荒木田麗女 · 1:73b-74a
  novels ···················· 1:73b-74a
  poetry ···················· 1:73b-74a
  style ····················· 1:73b-74a
Araki Mataemon
        ············ 荒木又右衛門 ·· 3:108a
Araki Moriaki ···· 荒木守晨 · 4:194b
Araki Sadao ····· 荒木貞夫 · 1:74a
  February 26th Incident ········· 2:250a
  gumbatsu ················· 3:66a-66b
  Kōdōha leader ················ 4:243a
Araki Sōtarō · 荒木宗太郎 · 1:74a
Arakurekai ···················· 5:19a
Ara Masahito ····· 荒正人 · 1:74a;
        5:316b-317a
Arao ················· 荒尾 · 1:74b
Araragi ········· アララギ · 1:74b; 7:28b,
        99b
  Koizumi Chikashi ············· 4:250b
  Orikuchi Shinobu ············· 6:118b
  Saitō Mokichi ················ 6:374a
  Shimaki Akahito ··············· 7:99b
Araragi school アララギ派 ···· 5:19b
Arashi Kanjūrō · 嵐寛寿郎 · 1:74b
Arashi no nagori
        ········ あらしのなごり ···· 6:332a
Arashiyama ·········· 嵐山 · 1:74b; 6:24b
Aratama Michiyo 新珠三千代 · 2:273a
Arbitration · 1:74b-75a; 2:118b; 4:349b
  Tripartite commissions ········· 4:351b
Arc ·························· 7:324b
Archaeological museums ··· 5:277b-278a
Archaeological sites and remains
  Fukui Cave ·················· 2:363b
  Heijō Palace site ·············· 3:124a
  Hoshino ····················· 3:235a
  Iba ························· 3:253b
  Iha shell mound ··············· 3:262a
  Ishibutai tomb ················ 3:339b
  Iwajuku ····················· 3:358a
  Kamegaoka ·················· 4:125a
  Karako ······················ 4:157b
  Kasori shell mounds ··········· 4:163b
  Moyoro shell mound ··········· 5:261b
  Mukōgaoka shell mound ········ 5:262b
  Nintoku Mausoleum ·········· 6:8a-8b
  Nogawa ······················ 6:31a
  Ojin Mausoleum ··············· 6:76b
  Okinoshima site ··············· 6:92b
  Ōmori shell mounds ··········· 6:103b
  Ōyu Stone Circles ········· 6:138b-139a
  Suku ························ 7:266a
  Takamatsuzuka tomb ····· 7:314b-315a

Togariishi ···················· 8:35b–36a
Toro ·························· 8:80b
Archaeological Society (Archaeological
Society of Nippon) ···· 1:77a, 179b
Archaeologists
Aizawa Tadahiro ···············1:38a
Gotō Shuichi ··············3:54a–54b
Hamada Kōsaku ················3:89b
Harada Yoshito ···············3:100b
Kobayashi Yukio ·············8:306b
Miyake Yonekichi ·············5:219a
Morimoto Rokuji ·············5:250b
Takahashi Kenji ····· 7:312a; 8:306b
Torii Ryūzō ··················8:79a
Tsuboi Shōgorō ··············8:110a
Umehara Sueji ······· 8:147a, 306b
Yamanouchi Sugao ············8:302b
Archaeology ·············· 1:75a–80b
haniwa ················· 3:97b–98a
inscriptions ·········· 3:313b–314a
Jōmon culture ·········· 4:72a–74a
kofun ················ 4:244a–246a
mokkan (wooden tablets) ······ 5:234a
Okhotsk culture ·········· 6:83b–84a
Paleolithic culture ······· 6:159b–160a
Satsumon culture ·············7:30b
shell mounds ·········· 7:82b–83a
studies. See Archaeology, studies of
Yayoi culture ·········· 8:321a–322a
Archaeology, studies of
general characteristics ········· 1:75a
excavations ···············1:75a
popular and governmental support 1:75a
scholarly discipline ·········· 1:75a
historical ·············· 1:79a–80b
early period ···············1:79a
formal establishment (1926–1945) · 1:79b
late 19th and early 20th century
····················· 1:79a–79b
new trends in ·············· 1:80a
postwar period ············· 1:79b
ideographs ············· 4:142b–143a
inscriptions ·········· 3:313b–314a
prehistoric ············· 1:75a–76a
early period ·········· 1:75a–75b
modern period ············· 1:75b
protohistoric ··········· 1:76a–79a
early period ·········· 1:76a–76b
early 20th century: typological and
chronological studies ··· 1:77a–78a
immediate postwar period: academic
excavations and research · 1:77a–78a
late 19th century: postrestoration
innovations ········· 1:76b–77a
recent developments: salvage
excavations and tomb preservations
····················· 1:78b–79a
shell mounds ·········· 7:82b–83a
Archery (kyūdō) ·············· 4:340a
contests (tōshiya) ········· 7:13a–13b
civil ················· 4:340a–340b
military ·············· 4:340a–340b
mounted (yabusame) ········ 8:283a–283b
Archipelago
administrative divisions ·········· 4:2b
remodeling plan ·············5:381b
territory ····················4:2b
Architects
Bertin, Louis-Emile ··········1:150a
Conder, Josiah ··············1:349b
Horiguchi Sutemi ·············3:227b
Isozaki Arata ················3:348a
Kikutake Kiyonori ············4:207b
Kobori Enshū ················4:238b
Kurokawa Kishō ··············4:316b
Maekawa Kunio ···············5:82a
Maki Fumihiko ···············5:85b
Murano Tōgo ················5:267a

Raymond, Antonin ············6:284b
Satō Takeo ··················7:28b
Shirai Seiichi ···············7:145b
Tange Kenzō ················7:340b
Taniguchi Yoshirō ············7:341b
Tatsuno Kingo ···············7:349b
Taut, Bruno ············ 7:351a–351b
Waters, Thomas James ·········8:237a
Wright, Frank Lloyd ···········8:279a
Yoshida Isoya ···············8:341a
Yoshimura Junzō ·············8:348a
Architectural Institute of Japan ··· 1:81b;
7:349b
Architectural Standards Law ···· 1:80b
ownership rights ···········6:137a
Architecture ············· 1:80b–82b
bridges ·············· 1:170a–170b
Buddhist ············· 1:182a–184b
Genshin ·················1:189b
Pure Land ···············1:189b
castles (shiro) ·········· 1:245b–249a
domestic ············· 7:110a–111a
gates ················ 3:12a–13a
esoteric Buddhist ············1:188a
gasshō-zukuri
Shirakawa ··············7:146b
gates ················ 3:12a, 13a
Karayō ···················1:191b
Mahāyāna Buddhist ···········1:185b
modern ········· 1:80b–81b, 81a
post-World War II ····· 1:81a–81b
naval
Hiraga Yuzuru ············3:142b
Yamagata Masao ···········8:293b
new style ··················7:33a
Nippon ···················7:351b
residential ············ 7:162a–163a
Rokumeikan ················6:335a
rural, Hida Folklore Village ······· 3:129b
schools ··············· 7:33a–33b
Shinden-zukuri mode ··········1:189b
Shintō art ·················7:135b
Shoin-zukuri style ············1:227a
storehouses ················7:248a
Sukiya-zukuri techniques ········ 1:81a
temple gates ···············3:12a
traditional domestic ······ 1:81b–82b
climate ··················1:81b
construction ·········· 1:81b–82a
elements ·················3:244a
materials ············ 1:81b–82a
shoin-zukuri ·········· 7:162a–163b
spatial concepts ········ 1:82a–82b
unit of measure ············1:82b
Western influence ········· 1:80b–81a
Bank of Japan Building ········1:140b
criticism ·················1:80b
Meiji Restoration ············1:80b
Zen ················· 1:191b–192a
Archives ·············· 5:336a–336b
Archives and Mausolea
Department, Imperial
Household Agency ······· 1:82b; 8:381b
Archives of Great Japan ···········2:65a
Arechi 荒地 ········· 1:82b–83a
founding ·············· 1:125b–126a
Argot ················ 3:303b–304a
Ari ···················· 1:67b–68a
Ariake Bay 有明湾 1:83a, 83a
Aribaba ·········· アリババ ···· 4:157b
Arida 有田 ···········1:83a
Aridagawa 有田川 ···········1:83a
Arige Kemi ····· 有毛検見 ····4:191a
Arikata no kotoba
有形の言葉 ····7:281a
Arima, Prince
有間皇子 ···· 1:83b–84a

Arima Harunobu ·有馬晴信 ··· 1:83a–83b;
7:98b
alliances ··················1:83b
Christian daimyō ···········1:305a
conversion to Christianity ··· 1:83a–83b
exile and death ·············1:83b
foreign involvements ·········1:83b
Arima Hot Spring 有馬温泉 ··· 1:83b
Arima Ineko 有馬稲子 ··· 1:83b
Arima Shinshichi 有馬新七 ··· 1:84a
Arima Yoriyasu 有馬頼寧 ··· 1:84a
Arisaka Hideyo 有坂秀世 ··· 1:84a
Arisawa Hiromi · 有沢広巳 ··· 1:84a–84b
Arishima Ikumitsu
有島行光 ···· 5:250a
Arishima Takeo · 有島武郎 ·· 1:84b–85a;
7:27b, 103b, 109a
death ················ 1:84b–85a
humanism ·················1:84b
Shirakaba school ······ 7:145b–146a
works ····················1:84b
Aristocracy ················6:170a
Aristocratic age ·········· 3:152a–153a
periodization ···············6:176b
Arisugawa no Miya
Taruhito 有栖川宮熾仁親王· 1:85a, 165a;
7:16b
Arita 有田 ····1:85a
Arita Hachirō ··· 有田八郎 ··· 1:20b, 85a;
7:92a
Arita ware ·········· 有田焼 1:85a–85b, 85a,
260b; 4:337a
museums ···················5:279b
Wagener, Gottfried ··········8:199a
Ariwara family ··· 在原氏 ··· 1:85b
Ariwara no Narihira
········· 在原業平 ··· 1:85b–86a;
7:13a; 8:208a
Ise monogatari ··············3:337a
Kokinshū ··················4:254b
Kokinshū criticism ···········1:85b
Rokkasen ··················6:334b
Ariyoshi Sawako
有吉佐和子 · 1:86a; 7:103b
Armed forces, imperial Japanese
··················· 1:86b–88b
China War (Sino-Japanese War of
1937–1945) ······ 1:88a–88b; 7:198a–202a
civilian control ·············1:88a
disarmament era ············1:88a
foreign models ·············1:85a
founding ·············· 1:86a–86b
conscription ·········· 1:86a–86b
Japanese independence ···· 1:86a–86b
sonnō jōi ················1:86a
imperial expansion ···········1:87a
Korea ·········· 1:87a; 4:287a–287b
Russian threat ·············1:87a
size of military ·············1:87a
militarism ············ 5:173a–175a
militarism era ····· 1:88a; 5:173a–175a
national defense policy, split ······· 1:87b
"Advance to the North" group ······ 1:87b
"Advance to the South" group ··· 1:87b;
7:236a–237a
Pacific War and dissolution of military
defeat ···················1:88b
Potsdam Declaration ·········1:88b
size of military ·············1:88b
Russo-Japanese War ··········1:87b
Sino-Japanese War ···········1:87b
supreme command ····· 1:86b–87a; 8:85a
Army General Staff Office ····· 1:87b
Imperial Headquarters ··· 1:87a; 2:58b
independence of ············1:86a
Naval General Staff Office 1:87a; 5:358b
World War I ·········· 1:87b–88a
World War II ···············8:271b

Armor ·················· 1:89b
  dōmaru or haramaki type ······ 1:89b
  dyes and dye colors ········· 2:136a-136b
  Kofun period ·············· 1:89b
  ōyoroi ··················· 1:89b
  tōsei gusoku ·············· 1:90a
Arms and armor ······ 1:88b-89b, 90a-90b
  armor. See Armor
  bows ···················· 1:89b
  early weapons ············· 1:89a
  firearms ········· 1:89b; 2:279a-279b
  jitte ···················· 1:90a
  kusarigama ··············· 1:90a
  museums ················· 5:280a
  naginata ················· 1:89a-89b
  possession ··············· 1:88b-89a
  saddlery ················· 1:90a
  sasumata ················· 1:90a
  shields ·················· 1:89b
  sodegarami ··············· 1:90a
  spears ··················· 1:89b
  swords ············· 1:89a; 7:285a-288a
  tetsubō ·················· 1:90a
Arms Export, Three Principles of
  ························ 1:90a-90b
Army, Imperial. See Armed forces,
  imperial Japanese
Army Academy ············· 1:90b
  National Defense Academy ······ 5:338a
Army Academy Incident ········ 6:41b-42a
Army camps ··············· 1:292a
Army Day ················· 6:347a
Army General Staff Office ····· 1:90b-91a
  independence ············· 1:87a
  power ··················· 8:85a
  Sugiyama Hajime ··········· 7:258b
Army Ministry ············· 1:91a
  Navy Ministry ············· 5:358a
"Arranged marriage" (miai) ···· 5:320b
Arrest (taiho) ·············· 2:49b
Arsenals ················· 3:210a
Arsenic poisoning ··········· 6:219a
Art ····················· 1:91a-91b
  aesthetics ··············· 1:18a-19a
  architecture, traditional domestic
  ························ 1:81b-82b
  bonsai ·············· 1:161b-163a
  Buddhist architecture ········ 1:182a-184b
  Buddhist art ············· 1:184b-194b
  Buddhist sculpture ········· 1:197a-204a
  bunjinga ··············· 1:210a-211a
  calligraphy ············· 1:232a-236b
  ceramics ··············· 1:256a-265b
  crests ·················· 2:42a-43b
  design ················· 2:88a-90a
  emakimono ············· 2:198a-200a
  flower arrangement ········· 2:288a-292a
  folk crafts ············· 2:293b-296a
  folk pictures
    ōtsu-e ·············· 6:133b-134a
  gardens ················· 3:8a-11b
  influence of China ·········· 1:91a
  ink painting ············· 3:305b-307b
  inrō ··················· 3:313a-313b
  lacquer ware ············· 4:360b-362a
  masks ······· 1:93a, 197a; 5:125b-127b
  merging with religion ········ 1:18b
  modern prints ············ 5:232a-233b
  namban art ·············· 5:322a-323a
  netsuke ················· 5:363a-365a
  painting ··············· 6:147b-159a
  photography ············· 6:185a-186a
  religious symbolism ········· 6:295b-296a
  screen and wall painting ······ 7:41a-43b
  Shintō architecture ········· 7:132a-134a
  Shinto art ·············· 7:134b-137b
  Shōsōin art repository ···· 1:184b, 200b;
                            7:168a-170a

shunga ················· 7:187a-188a
swords ················· 7:285a-288a
textiles ················· 8:16b-20a
tie-dyeing ··············· 8:29b
tsuba ················· 8:108a-109a
ukiyo-e ················· 8:138a-144a
zenga ················· 8:374b-375a
Arte Breve da Lingoa Iapoa ····· 6:334a
Arte da Lingoa de Iapam ······ 6:334a
Articles of incorporation
  limited liability company ······ 5:10a
  limited partnership company ···· 5:10b
Artisans ················· 7:165a
Artistic names ············ 5:325a-326a
Artists. See Painters
Artists' Alliance of Farmers and
  Workers ················ 7:175a
Art Theatre Guild of Japan Co, Ltd 1:91b;
                            2:275b
Aruga Kizaemon
  ·········· 有賀喜左衛門 ···· 1:91b
Aru hareta hi ni
  ·········· ある晴れた日に ···· 4:169a
Aru onna ······· 或る女 ···· 1:84a
Aru otoko ······ 或る男 ···· 4:114a
Asa ···················· 1:91b
Asabuki Eiji ····· 朝吹英二 ···· 1:91b-92a
Asada Gōryū ····· 麻田剛立 ···· 1:92a
Asada Sōhaku ···· 浅田宗伯 ···· 1:92a
Asagao ················· 5:255a
Asagaoichi ··············· 5:255a
Asa-gasuri ··············· 4:164b
Asagiri gunka (War Song
  of the Morning Mist)
  ·········· 朝霧軍歌 ···· 8:319a
Asahi ··········· 旭 ···· 1:92a
Asahi Breweries, Ltd ······ 1:92a; 4:221a
Asahi Chemical Industry Co, Ltd
  ···················· 1:92a-92b;
                            7:57b
Asahi chōja ····· 朝日長者 ···· 7:269a
Asahi Denka Kōgyō ········· 1:92b
Asahigawa ······· 旭川 ···· 1:92b
Asahi Glass Co, Ltd ········· 1:92b
Asahikawa ······· 旭川 ···· 1:92b
Asahi Mountains 朝日山地 ···· 1:92b-93a,
                            136b
Asahi National Broadcasting Co, Ltd
  ········· 1:92a, 93a, 172b, 173b
Asahina Yasuhiko
  ·········· 朝比奈泰彦 ···· 1:93a, 268a
Asahi Optical Co, Ltd ········· 1:93a
Asahi Pentax ·············· 1:93a
Asahi shimbun ··· 朝日新聞 1:18a, 93a-93b;
  2:371b; 4:139b; 5:128b, 369b-370a; 7:258a
  founding ················ 1:93a
  Ikebe Sanzan ············· 3:264b
  other publications ·········· 1:93b
  Rice Riots of 1918 ·········· 1:93b
  self-censorship ············ 1:253a
Asahi ware ······· 朝日焼 ···· 1:93b
  Kobori Enshū ············ 4:238a
  Wagener, Gottfried ·········· 8:199a
Asai Chū ······· 浅井忠 ···· 1:93b
  Fontanesi, Antonio ·········· 2:304a
Asai family ······ 浅井氏 ···· 1:93b-94a
Asai Nagamasa ·· 浅井長政 · 1:94a; 7:84b
Asai Ryōi ······ 浅井了意 · 1:94a; 5:46a
  Ukiyo monogatari ·········· 4:136b
Asaka (city) ····· 朝霞 ···· 1:94a
Asaka Canal ····· 安積疏水 · 1:94a; 4:293b
  Inawashiro, Lake ··········· 3:283b
Asakasha ········ あさ香社 ···· 5:19b
Asaka Tampaku ··· 安積澹泊 ···· 1:94a
Asakawa Kan'ichi
  ·········· 朝河貫一 ···· 1:94a
Asakura family ···· 朝倉氏 · 1:94a; 7:84a
  fortress ················· 2:363b

mansion excavation ········ 1:80a-80b
Asakura Fumio ···· 朝倉文夫 ···· 1:94b
Asakura Takakage Jōjō
  ·········· 朝倉孝景条々 ···· 1:94b
Asakura Toshikage,
  17-Article Code of
  ·········· 朝倉敏景十七箇条 ···· 1:94b-95a
  kabegaki ················ 4:90a
Asakura Yoshikage
  ·········· 朝倉義景 ···· 1:95a; 7:84b
Asakusa Bunko ···· 浅草文庫 ···· 1:95a-95b;
                            5:1a
Asakusa Kannon (Sensōji) ······ 8:63a
Asakusa Kurenaidan
  ·········· 浅草紅団 ···· 4:176a; 7:175b
Asama Hot Spring
  ·········· 浅間温泉 ···· 1:95b
Asamayama ······· 浅間山 ···· 1:95a, 95b
  Onioshidashi ············· 6:107b
Asami Keisai ···· 浅見絅斎 · 1:95b; 7:27b
  Seiken igen ··············· 7:51b
Asamushi Hot Spring
  ·········· 浅虫温泉 ···· 1:95b
Asan Mountains 阿讃山脈 ···· 7:18b
Asano Cement. See Nihon Cement Co,
  Ltd
Asano Nagamasa 浅野長政 ···· 1:95b
Asano Naganori 浅野長矩 ···· 2:327a
Asano Sōichirō 浅野総一郎 ···· 1:95b-96a;
                            7:52a
Asano Yoshinaga 浅野幸長 ···· 1:96a
Asano zaibatsu ··· 浅野財閥 ···· 1:95b
Asanuma Gumi Co, Ltd ······ 1:96a
Asanuma Inejirō
  ·········· 浅沼稲次郎 ···· 1:96a
"Asanuma statement" ········· 1:96a
Asaoka Ruriko 浅丘ルリ子 ···· 2:275a
Asayama Bontō ··· 朝山梵燈 ···· 1:96a-96b
Asayama Nichijō 朝山日乗 ···· 1:96b
Asceticism ··············· 1:96b
  organizing ··············· 7:182a
  kugyō ·················· 1:96b
  mountain ················ 8:287b
  present day Japan ·········· 1:96b
  shamanism ··············· 7:76b
  shugyō ················· 1:96b
ASEAN and Japan ····· 1:96b-97a; 2:309a;
                            3:324b
Asebi [(Japanese andromeda) Pieris
  japonica] ················ 1:97a
Ash-glazed wares ·········· 1:261b-262a
Ashibetsu ········ 芦別 ···· 1:97a
Ashibetsudake ···· 芦別岳 · 1:97a; 8:354a
Ashibi ········· 馬酔木 · 1:74b; 4:169b;
                            5:307b
Ashida Enosuke
  ·········· 芦田恵之助 ···· 1:97a-97b
  Seikatsu Tsuzurikata Undō development
  ························ 7:51a
Ashida Hitoshi ···· 芦田均 ···· 1:97b
  Japan Socialist Party ········· 4:48a
Ashide ·········· 葦手 ···· 1:97b
Ashigaru ········ 足軽 ···· 1:97b-98a
  yoriki ·················· 8:338b
Ashihara Yoshishige
  ·········· 芦原義重 ···· 1:98a
Ashikaga (city) ··· 足利 ···· 1:98b
  silk weaving ·············· 2:296a
Ashikaga family ··· 足利氏 · 1:98b-99b;
                            7:25b
  Ashikaga Yoshimitsu ········· 1:99a
  decline of shogunate ········· 1:99b
  Muromachi history ····· 1:99a; 3:172b
  origins ················· 1:99a
  Patrons of the Arts ········· 1:99b
  rivalry for leadership ········· 3:173b
  Shiba family branch ········· 7:83b

Ashikaga Gakkō · 足利学校 ··· **1**:99b-100a, 151b; **4**:136a
  education ················· **2**:172b
Ashikaga Gakkō Bunko
        足利学校文庫 ··········· **5**:1a
Ashikaga Gakkō Iseki Toshokan
        足利学校遺跡図書館 ······ **1**:100a
Ashikaga Masatomo. 足利政知
  See **Horikoshi Kubō**
Ashikaga military government
  decrees (tokusei) ·········· **8**:58b
Ashikaga Mochiuji
        足利持氏 ············· **1**:99b
  Uesugi Norizane ·········· **8**:130a
Ashikaga shogunate. *See* **Muromachi shogunate**
Ashikaga Tadayoshi
        足利直義 ············· **1**:100a
  Kannō Disturbance ········ **4**:144b
Ashikaga Takauji 足利尊氏 ··· **1**:40a, 100a-101a; **2**:204b; **2**:265a; **8**:341b, 356a
  betrayal ················· **4**:192a
  Genkō Incident ··········· **3**:21a
  Kanenaga, Prince ········ **4**:139b-140a
  Kannō Disturbance ········ **4**:144b
  Kemmu Restoration ········ **4**:191a
  Muromachi shogunate ······ **5**:271a
  portrait ················ **1**:*100b*
  Sasaki Takauji ··········· **7**:23b
  Shiba family ············· **7**:84a
  warrior government ········ **8**:229b
Ashikaga Yoshiaki
        足利義昭 ············· **1**:101b; **3**:172b, 178b
  Shinchō kō ki ·········· **7**:109b
Ashikaga Yoshimasa
        足利義政 **1**:101a; **3**:173a; **7**:67a; **8**:301b
  Higashiyama culture ······· **3**:132b
  Hino Tomiko ············· **3**:141a
  posthumous portraits ······ **4**:147b
  shinden-zukuri ··········· **7**:110b
Ashikaga Yoshimitsu
        足利義満 ········· **1**:99a, 101a-101b; **2**:204b, 265a
  China ·················· **1**:283b
  Kaei sandai ki ·········· **4**:101b
  Kan'ami ················ **4**:135b
  Kitayama culture ·········· **4**:229a
  tally trade ·············· **7**:331b
Ashikaga Yoshimochi
        足利義持 · **1**:99a; **3**:173a
Ashikaga Yoshinori
        足利義教 ··· **1**:99a, 101b; **3**:174a
  assassination ··········· **4**:196b-197a
Ashikari ············· 蘆刈 **7**:342b
Ashinoko ··········· 芦ノ湖 **1**:101b; **2**:342b; **3**:*86a*
Ashio ················· 足尾 **1**:101b
Ashio Copper Mine
        足尾銅山 ··· **2**:372a-372b
Ashio Copper Mine Incident ·····
        足尾銅山鉱毒事件 · **1**:73a, 102b; **4**:349b; **7**:99a
  Fukuda Hideko ··········· **2**:362a-362b
  Tanaka Shōzō ············ **7**:338b-339b
  Yokohama mainichi shimbun **8**:330a
Ashio Copper Mine labor dispute · **1**:102a
Ashio Kōdoku Jiken. *See* **Ashio Copper Mine Incident**
Ashiya (Honshū) ····· 芦屋 **1**:102a
Ashiya (Kyūshū) ····· 芦屋 **1**:102a
Ashizurimisaki ····足摺岬 **1**:102a; **7**:334a
Ashizuri-Uwakai National Park 足摺宇和海国立公園 ···· **1**:102b
Ashura ·················· **4**:244b

Asia
  culture ················ **7**:177b-179a
  Japanese immigration ······ **2**:362a-362b
  Japanese studies ·········· **4**:44b
Asia Development Board ····· **1**:102b
Asia faction
  Shigemitsu Mamoru ······· **7**:91b-92b
Asian American concept ····· **4**:14b
Asian Americans ·········· **4**:14b
Asian Games ··········· **1**:102b
Asian Relations Conference ·· **1**:19b
Asia Trade Development Association ···················· **3**:319b
Aso ················· 阿蘇 **1**:102b
Asobase-kotoba ··········· **2**:251a
Asō Hisashi ······· 麻生久 **1**:102b-103a
  Shakai Taishūtō ·········· **7**:74b
  Shinjinkai ··············· **7**:115b
Ason ················· 朝臣 **1**:103a
Aso National Park
        阿蘇国立公園 ·········· **1**:103a
Asosan ··········· 阿蘇山 **1**:103a, *103a*
Aso Shrine ······ 阿蘇神社 **1**:103b
Aso Volcanic Zone ········· **7**:346a
Assembly and Political Association Law (Shūkai Oyobi Seisha Hō) ···· **6**:266a
Assembly of Prefectural Governors ······ **1**:103b; **4**:203a; **7**:16b
Association for Mystery Writers of Japan ················· **2**:170b
Association for the Study of Materialism (Yuibutsuron Kenkyūkai) ····· **8**:81b
Association of American Libraries · **6**:269a
Association of Booksellers ··· **6**:268a
Association of Eastern European Studies ················· **2**:142b
Association of Japanese Geographers ····················· **1**:103b
  Kiuchi Shinzō ··········· **4**:231b
  tachimono ·············· **7**:293b
Association of Patriotic Japanese Literature ··············· **7**:176b
Association of Southeast Asian Nations. *See* **ASEAN and Japan**
Assumption of risk ······· **1**:103b-104a
Aston, William George ····· **1**:104a
Astrology
  On'yōryō ··············· **6**:113b
Astronomical observatories · **1**:104a
  Kwasan (Kasan) Astronomical Observatory ············· **1**:104a
  Latitude Observatory of Mizusawa · **1**:104a
  Tōkyō Astronomical Observatory · **1**:104a
Astronomy ············· **1**:104a-104b
  history of studies ········· **1**:104a-104b
  On'yōryō ··············· **6**:113b
  Publications of The Astronomical Society of Japan ·············· **1**:104b
  recent developments ······· **1**:104b
    celestial physics ········ **1**:104b
    radio astronomy ········ **1**:104b
    universities training researchers · **1**:104b
Asuka (region) ······· 飛鳥 **1**:105a-105b
Asuka (village) ····· 明日香 **1**:104b-105a
Asukabehime ······ 安宿媛 **4**:268b
Asuka culture ····· 飛鳥文化 **1**:105b
Asuka Daibutsu 飛鳥大仏 **2**:55b
Asukadera ········ 飛鳥寺 **1**:105b-106b, 182a; **7**:85a
  history ················ **1**:106a
  temple ················ **1**:106a
  excavation ············· **1**:106a
Asukagawa ·········· 飛鳥川 **1**:106b
Asuka Historical Museum ··· **5**:333a
Asuka history. *See* **History of Japan**
Asukai Masaari 飛鳥井雅有 **1**:106b

Asukai Masatsune
        飛鳥井雅経 · **1**:106b-107a; **5**:41a
  Shin kokinshū ·········· **7**:119b
Asuka Kiyomihara Code
        飛鳥浄御原律令 · **1**:107a, 151a
  Dajōkan ··············· **2**:69b
  ritsuryō system ·········· **6**:331a
  Taika Reform ············ **7**:295b
Asuka Kiyomihara no Miya 飛鳥浄御原宮 **1**:107a; **2**:350a
Asuka period ····· 飛鳥時代 **1**:107a
Asukata Ichio · 飛鳥田一雄 **1**:107b
  Japan Socialist Party ······ **4**:48a-49a
Atae ················ 直 **4**:89a, 310a
Atagawa Hot Spring
        熱川温泉 **1**:107b; **2**:342b
Atago Daigongen
        愛宕大権現 ············ **1**:107b
Atago Jinja ······ 愛宕神社 **1**:107b
Atago Shrine ···· 愛宕神社 **1**:107b
Atagoyama ······· 愛宕山 **1**:107b
  Tamba Mountains ········· **7**:333a
Ataka ················ 安宅 **4**:98a
Atami ·············· 熱海 **1**:107b
Atarashiki Mura · 新しき村 **5**:281a-281b
Atarashiki tsuchi 新しき土 **3**:102b
Athenée Français ·········· **2**:332b
Ātman ················ **1**:176b
Atomic bomb ······ **1**:107b-111b; **8**:276a
  aftereffects ············· **1**:109a-110b
    deaths ··············· **1**:109a-109b
    family and livelihood ···· **1**:110a
    material loss ·········· **1**:109b
    medical effects ········· **1**:109b
    non-Japanese hibakusha · **1**:110a-110b
    psychological ········· **1**:110a
  American justification ····· **1**:108a
  destructive power ········ **1**:108a-109a
    blast effects ·········· **1**:108b
    fire storms ··········· **1**:109a
    radiation effects ······· **1**:109a
    thermal radiation effects · **1**:108a
  hibakusha
    message ············· **1**:111a-111b
    organizations ········· **1**:111a
  Hiroshima ········· **1**:*108b*; **3**:*149a*, 149b
  historical background ······ **1**:108a
  Nagasaki ······· **1**:*109a*; **5**:304a, *304b*
  Occupation ············· **6**:51a
  postwar developments ····· **1**:110b-111a
    foreign assistance ······ **1**:111a
    hibakusha organizations · **1**:111a
    Japanese government ···· **1**:110b
    local governments ······ **1**:110b-111a
    medical community ····· **1**:111a
    peace movement ······· **1**:111a
    religious leaders ······· **1**:111a
    United States government · **1**:110b
  Truman, Harry S ········· **8**:107b
Atomic Bomb Casualty Commission (ABCC) ······ **1**:110b, 111b; **4**:37b
Atomic bomb related disease **1**:111b-114a
  Bikini radiation injuries
    clinical course ········· **1**:113b-114a
    exposure mode ········ **1**:113b
    fallout exposure ······· **1**:113b
    periodic examinations ··· **1**:113b
  burns ················· **1**:112a
  clinical course of sustained injuries **1**:112a
  Hiroshima and Nagasaki ···· **1**:111b-112a
  mechanical injuries ······· **1**:112a
  radiation injuries
    acute effects ·········· **1**:112b
    exposure doses ········ **1**:112a-112b
    late ················· **1**:112b

Atomic Disasters Anniversary World Conference against Atomic and Hydrogen Bombs ·········· 6:166a
Atomic energy, laws concerning ·················· 1:114a-114b
Atomic Energy Commission ·········· 7:167a
Atomic Energy Research Institute, Japan ·········· 1:114b; 7:38a
Atomic weapons, movement to ban ········ 1:114b-115a; 6:144b
Atomi Gakuen Women's University 1:115a
Atomi Girls' School ·············· 1:115a
Atomi Kakei ······· 跡見花蹊 ·········· 1:115a
Ato ni tsuzuku o shinzu (They Will Follow) ········· 後に続くを信ず ······ 8:319a
Ato no Chitoko no nikki kokiroku ·················· 4:255a
Atsuakira, Prince 敦明親王 ······ 4:249b-250a
Atsugi ·············· 厚木 ·· 1:115a-115b
Atsugi Bonjin ···· 厚木凡人 ······ 2:76a
Atsugi Motor Parts Co, Ltd ····· 1:115b
Atsuita ·············· 厚板 ······ 1:115b
Nō theater ·················· 1:115b
origin and description ·········· 1:115b
Atsumichi, Prince 敦道親王 ······ 3:366a
Atsumi Kiyoshi ······· 渥美清 1:115b; 2:275a, 275b
Atsumi Peninsula 渥美半島 ····· 1:115b
Atsumonozaki ······· 厚物咲 ····· 5:318b
Atsumorisō ·················· 4:305a
Atsuta Shrine ···· 熱田神宮 · 1:115b-116a; 2:51a
imperial regalia ·············· 3:278b
Owari Province ·············· 6:136b
site ······················· 5:309a
Attaining Enlightenment in This Very Existence ·················· 7:114b
Attendant ·················· 4:296a
Attorneys. *See* **Lawyers**
Attorneys Law (Bengoshi Hō) ····· 4:371b
Attu ······················· 1:116a
Audio equipment industry ········· 7:17b
Audio industries
Nippon Columbia Co, Ltd ····· 6:8b
Pioneer Electronic Corporation · 6:189a
Sansui Electric Co. Ltd. (Sansui Denki) ·················· 7:17b
Trio-Kenwood Corporation ······· 8:92ba
Audiovisual education ·········· 1:116a
Auditing. *See* **Accounting and auditing**
Auditing standards ········ 1:116a-116b
field work ·············· 1:116a-116b
general ················ 1:116a-116b
reporting ·············· 1:116a-116b
Audit officers ·················· 4:104b
Audit options ·················· 1:9a
August First declaration ···· 1:116b, 289a; 7:47b-48a
Aung San ·················· 1:116b
Australia and Japan ······· 1:116b-118b
historical background ···· 1:116b-117a
immigration issue ······ 1:116b-117a
trade issue ·········· 1:116b-117a
Japanese studies ········· 4:44a-44b
language studies ··········· 4:21a
postwar development
ANZUS Pact ·············· 1:117a
Ball, William MacMahon · 1:117a-117b, 135a-135b
British Commonwealth Occupation Force ········· 1:117a-117b, 170a
Evatt, H.V. ········· 1:117a-117b
relation in 1970s
cultural ·············· 1:117b-118b
oil crisis of 1973-74 ····· 1:117b-118b
trade ·············· 1:117b-118b
trade ·················· 1:117b

Agreement on Commerce ········ 1:117b
Australia-Japan Business Cooperative Committee ·········· 1:117b, 118b-119a
beef ······················· 1:117b
General Agreement on Tariffs and Trade (GATT) ·············· 1:117b
mineral resources ·············· 1:117b
1970s ······················ 1:117b
pre-World War II ·············· 1:117a
sugar ····················· 1:117b
1970s ······················ 1:117b
World War II ·············· 1:117a-117b
Australia, Japan, and Western Pacific Economic Relations Research Project (1972) ·················· 1:117b-118b
Australia-Japan Business Cooperative Committee (AJBCC) ········ 1:118b-119a
Pacific Basin Economic Council · 6:143b
Australia-Japan Foundation · 1:117b-118b
Australian immigration policy and Japan ·················· 1:119a-119b
Austria and Japan ········· 1:119b-120b
between wars ·················· 1:120a
early Austro-Hungarian relations · 1:119b
Pfizmaier, August ·········· 1:119b
von Benyowsky, Moritz August · 1:119b
Japanese studies ············· 4:43a
Meiji Restoration to World War I
constitutional law ······· 1:119b-120a
diplomatic relations ······ 1:119b-120a
Iwakura mission ········· 1:119b-120a
scientific exchange with ···· 1:119b-120a
sericulture ············ 1:119b-120a
Siebold, Heinrich von ···· 1:119b-120a
trade ················ 1:119b-120a
Unequal Treaties ········ 1:119b-120a
World Exhibition of 1873 ·· 1:119b-120a
post-World War II ············ 1:120a
Austronesian ·············· 4:20a-20b
Authors (modern). *See* **Novelists**
Authors (premodern)
Anrakuan Sakuden ······· 1:62b-63a
Arakida Reijo ············ 1:73b-74a
Asai Ryōi ·················· 1:94a
Bakin ················ 1:130b-131a
Chikamatsu Monzaemon ····· 1:275a-276a
Ejima Kiseki ·············· 2:188a
Hanasanjin ··············· 3:94b
Hirata Atsutane ········· 3:145a-145b
Hirose Tansō ·············· 3:148a
Hōseidō Kisanji ············· 3:234b
Jippensha Ikku ·········· 4:61a-61b
Kada no Arimaro ············ 4:100b
Kamochi Masazumi ·········· 4:128a
Kamo no Chōmei ········· 4:128b-129a
Kamo no Mabuchi ········· 4:129a-129b
Kan Sazan ················ 4:152a
Katō Chikage ·············· 4:167b
Katori Nahiko ·············· 4:169a
Keichū ················ 4:187b-188a
Koikawa Harumachi ·········· 4:250a
Miyako no Nishiki ··········· 5:219b
Miyako no Yoshika ·········· 5:219b
Motoori Norinaga ········· 5:257a-258b
Motoori Ōhira ············· 5:259a
Murasaki Shikibu ··········· 5:267b
Murata Harumi ············· 5:269b
Nishizawa Ippū ············· 6:20a
Ōmi no Mifune ············· 6:102a
Ryūtei Rijō ················ 6:359a
Ryūtei Tanehiko ········· 6:359a-359b
Saikaku ·············· 6:369b-371a
Sakurada Jisuke ··········· 7:4a-4b
Santō Kyōden ··········· 7:18a-18b
Segawa Jokō ··············· 7:48b
Sei Shōnagon ············ 7:52a-54a
Shikitei Samba ·········· 7:96b-97a
Shimizu Hamaomi ············ 7:104a

Sugawara no Takasue no Musume 7:257b
Tamenaga Shunsui ·········· 7:333b-334a
Tayasu Munetake ·········· 7:359a
Tsuga Teishō ·············· 8:113a
Ueda Akinari ··········· 8:126a-126b
Yashiro Hirokata ············ 8:317a
Yoshida Kenkō ·········· 8:341a-342a
Yoshishige no Yasutane ········ 8:349b
Autobiography of Yukichi Fukuzawa, The ······················ 1:155a
Autoharp ·················· 6:354b
Automatic Train Control ·········· 7:118a
Automation ·················· 7:202b
quality control ·············· 6:274a
Automobile Company (Ōtomōbiru Shōkai) ·················· 1:120b
Automobile Damage Compensation Security Law, liability under ···· 4:384a
Automobile Liability Security Law 1:120b
compensation guarantee ········ 1:120b
compulsory liability ·········· 1:120b
heavy liability ·············· 1:120b
Automobile Liability Security Law of 1955 ···················· 1:120b
Automobile pollution ·········· 6:218a
Automotive industry · 1:120b-122b; 8:102a
companies
Aichi Machine Industry Co, Ltd · 1:32b-33a
Aisin Seiki, Co, Ltd ·········· 1:38a
Atsugi Motor Parts Co, Ltd · 1:115b
Automobile Company ········ 1:120b
Bridgestone Tire Co, Ltd ······· 1:170b
Daihatsu Motor Co, Ltd ······· 2:58b
Fuji Heavy Industries, Ltd ···· 2:343a
Hino Motors, Ltd ········· 3:140b-141a
Honda Motor Co, Ltd ····· 3:219a-219b
Isuzu Motors, Ltd ··········· 3:348b
Kantō Auto Works, Ltd ······· 4:153a
Mitsubishi Motors Corporation · 5:208b
Nihon Radiator Co, Ltd ······· 5:381a
Nippondensō Co, Ltd ·········· 6:9a
Nissan Diesel Motor Co, Ltd ···· 6:20b
Nissan Motor Co, Ltd ········ 6:20b
Nissan Shatai Co, Ltd ········ 6:20b
Suzuki Motor Co, Ltd ······· 7:283a
Tōyō Kōgyō Co, Ltd ·········· 8:92a
Toyota Auto Body Co, Ltd ····· 8:93a
Toyota Motor Corporation ····· 8:93b
Yamaha Motor Co, Ltd ······· 8:296a
Yokohama Rubber Co. Ltd ····· 8:330b
early history ·············· 1:120b-122b
foreign imports ·············· 1:121a
Military Vehicle Subsidy Law of 1918 ·················· 1:121a
problems ·················· 1:121a
trial productions ············ 1:121a
in 1970s ················ 1:122a
postwar developments ····· 1:121b-122b
government protection ····· 1:121b-122a
passenger car production ······· 1:122a
between Wars ············ 1:121a-121b
Automotive Manufacturing Industries Law of 1935 ·············· 1:121b
foreign vehicles restriction ····· 1:121b
zaibatsu ·················· 1:121b
World War II ·············· 1:121b
Automotive Manufacturing Industries Law of 1935 ·············· 1:121b
Autumn and Winter Landscapes ···· 7:*17a*
"Autumn in the Forest" ·········· 7:105b
Autumn Landscape ············ 1:68b
Avalokitésvara ············ 4:144b-145a
Avatar ·················· 1:122b-123a
Avertimentos y avisos acerca dos costumes e catangues de Jappão ·················· 8:189a
Aviation ············ 1:*123a*, 123b-124a

destruction and revival · · · · · · · · · · 1:124a
early history · · · · · · · · · · · · · · · · · 1:123a
foreign technology · · · · · · · · · · · · · 1:123a
gross sales · · · · · · · · · · · · · · · · · · 1:124a
warplanes · · · · · · · · · · · · · · · · · · · 1:123b
world records · · · · · · · · · · · · · · · · · 1:123b
Aviation Cadets of the Imperial
  Japanese Navy · · · · · · · · · · · · · · · 8:329a
Awabi · 1:1a-1b
Awa Dance · · · · · · · 阿波踊り · 1:124a, *124b*,
  161b
Awajishima · · · · · · · 淡路島 · · · · · 1:124a
Awakening of Japan, The · · 6:79b; 7:294b
Awa maru · · · · · · · · · 阿波丸 · · · · 1:124b
Awano Seiho · · · · · 阿波野青畝 · · · · 1:124b
Awara · · · · · · · · · · · · 芦原 · 1:124b-125a
Awards. *See* Decorations
Aware. *See* Mono no aware
Awase-jōyu · · · · · · · · · · · · · · · · · · 2:25b
Awasezu · 2:25b
Awashima · · · · · · · · · 粟島 · · · · · · 1:125a
Awa Shrine · · · · · · · 安房神社 · · · · 1:125a
Awataguchi Yoshimitsu
  · · · · · · · · · · · 粟田口吉光 · · · · 1:125a
Aya, Prince · · · · · · · · 礼宮 · · · · · 3:277*a*
Ayabe · · · · · · · · · · · · 綾部 · · · · · · 1:125a
Aya family · · · · · · · · · 漢氏 · · · · · · 1:125b
Ayame. *See* Irises
Ayase · · · · · · · · · · · · 綾瀬 · · · · · · 1:125b
Ayatakedai · · · · · · · · · · · · · · · · · · 4:308a
Ayatsuri jōruri · · · 操浄瑠璃 · 1:212a-215b
Ayrton, William Edward · · · · · · · · · 1:125b
Ayu [(sweetfish) *Plecoglossus altivelis*]
  · · 1:14b, 115b, 125b; 2:26a, 283b, 287b
Ayukawa Gisuke. *See* Aikawa
  Yoshisuke
Ayukawa Nobuo · 鮎川信夫 · · · · · · 1:82b,
  125b-126a
Ayumu hito · · · · · · · · 歩む人 · · · · 4:179b
Azai family. *See* Asai family
Azai Nagamasa. *See* Asai Nagamasa
Azaleas [(tsutsuji) family Ericaceae]
  · · · · · · · · · · · · · · · · · · · 1:126a-126b
Azami · 8:24b
Azamukazaru no ki
  欺かざるの記 · · · · · 4:309a
Azuchi · · · · · · · · · · · 安土 1:126b; 4:340b
Azuchi Castle · · · · 安土城 · 1:126b; 7:91a
  description · · · · · · · · · · · · · · · · · 1:248a
  Kanō Mitsunobu · · · · · · · · · · · · · 4:147b
  Oda Nobunaga · · · · · · · · · · · · · · · 6:63b
  paintings · · · · · · · · · · · · · 3:181b; 4:146a
Azuchi-Momoyama history. *See* History
  of Japan
Azuchi-Momoyama period
  安土桃山時代 · · · · · · 1:126b
Azuchi Shūron · · · 安土宗論 · · · 1:126b-127a
Azuki (*Phaseolus angularis*) · · · · · · 1:127a
Azuma kagami · · · · · 吾妻鏡 · 1:127a-127b,
  294b; 2:342b; 5:44b; 7:152b
  arrangement · · · · · · · · · · · · · · · · 1:127a
  extant editions · · · · · · · · · · · · · · 1:127b
    Kanazawa edition · · · · · · · · · · · · 1:127b
    Kikkawa edition · · · · · · · · · · · · · 1:127b
    Shimazu edition · · · · · · · · · · · · · 1:127b
  general description · · · · · · · · · · 1:127a-127b
  hentai kambun · · · · · · · · · · · · 3:126b-127a
  historiography · · · · · · · · · · · · · · · 3:154a
Azuma Ryōtarō · · · 東龍太郎 · · · · · 1:127b
Azumasan · · · · · · · · · 吾妻山 · · · · · 1:127b
Azumazasa (*Sasaella ramosa*) · · · · · 1:136a
Azusagawa · · · · · · · · · 梓川 · · · · · · 1:127b

B

Baba Katsuya · · · · 馬場勝弥 · · · · · · 1:129a
Baba Keiji · · · · · · · 馬場敬治 · · · · · · 1:129a
Baba Kochō · · · · · · 馬場孤蝶 · 1:129a; 7:54b
Baba Tatsui · · · · · · 馬場辰猪 · · · · · · 1:129a
  Kōjunsha formed · · · · · · · · · · · · · 4:252b
  naichi zakkyo · · · · · · · · · · · · · · · 5:309b
Baba Tsunego · · · · 馬場恒吾 · · · 1:129a-129b
Baby carriers · · · · · · · · · · · · · · · · 6:101a
Bachiru · 7:169b
Bacon, Alice Mabel · · · · · · · · · · · · 1:129b
  Iwakura mission · · · · · · · · · · · · · 1:129b
  Tsuda Umeko · · · · · · · · · · · · · · · 1:129b
  writings · · · · · · · · · · · · · · · · · · 1:129b
Bacteriologists
  Hata Sahachirō · · · · · · · · · · · · · · 3:112b
  Kitazato Shibasaburō · · · · · · · · · · 4:229a
  Noguchi Hideyo · · · · · · · · · · · · · · 6:31b
  Shiga Kiyoshi · · · · · · · · · · · · · · · 7:89b
Badger. *See* Tanuki
Badminton · · · · · · · · · · · · · · · · · · 1:129b
Baibunsha · · · · · · · · · 売文社 · · · 1:72a,
  129b-130a
Baien · · · · · · · · · · · · 煤煙 · · · · · · 5:253b
Baika namako (sea cucumber) · · · · · 7:45a
Baiken (deed) · · · · · · · · · · · · · · · · 4:253b
Baikenjō (deed) · · · · · · · · · · · · · · · 4:253b
Bail · · · · · · · · · · · · · · · 1:130a; 2:49b-50a
Baishin · · · · · · · · · · · 陪臣 · · · · · · 1:130a
Baishōron · · · · · · · · 梅松論 · · 1:130a-130b
  general description · · · · · · · · · · · · 1:130a
  historiography · · · · · · · · · · · · · · · 3:154a
  literary comparisons · · · · · · · · · · · 1:130b
  versions · · · · · · · · · · · · · · · 1:130a-130b
Baiu · 4:8a
Bakan Sensō · · · · 馬関戦争 · · 7:105b-106a
Bakemono · · · · · · · · · · · · · · · · · · 1:130b
  hitotsume kozō · · · · · · · · · · · · · · 3:208b
  kappa · 4:156b
  mononoke · · · · · · · · · · · · · · · · · 5:247a
  oni · 6:106a
  tengu · 8:5b
  yamamba · · · · · · · · · · · · · · · · · · 8:297a
Bakin · · · · · · · · · · · · 馬琴 · 1:130b-131a,
  211b, 295, 378a; 5:11b, 16b, 48b
  gesaku · 3:28b
  kusazōshi · · · · · · · · · · · · · · · · · · 1:130b
  life · 1:130b
  Nansō Satomi Hakkenden · · · · · · · 5:329a
  nonfiction writings · · · · · · · · · 1:130b-131a
  works of · · · · · · · · · · · · · · · 1:130b-131a
  yomihon · · · · · · · · · · · · · · · · · · · 1:130b
Bakufu. 幕府   *See* Shogunate
Bakufu kengai shisetsu
  幕府遣外使節 · 7:161a-161b
Bakuhan system · · · · · · · 1:131a-133a,
  211b; 2:1a, 108b; 3:186a; 4:377b
  chōnin · 1:301a
  farmers and taxes · · · · · · · · · · 1:131b-132a
  general description · · · · · · · · · · · · 1:131a
  governmental developments · · · · · · 1:133a
  hyakushō · · · · · · · · · · · · · · · · · · 3:249b
  landlordism · · · · · · · · · · · · · · · · 4:362b
  provinces · · · · · · · · · · · · · · · · · · 6:260a
  rural development · · · · · · · · · · 1:132a-132b
    oyakata · · · · · · · · · · · · · · · · · · 1:132b
    productivity · · · · · · · · · · · · · · · 1:132b

    profit · · · · · · · · · · · · · · · · · · · 1:132b
    taxation · · · · · · · · · · · · · · · 1:132a-132b
  Samurai and government · · · · 1:131a-131b
    mobilization · · · · · · · · · · · · 1:131a-131b
    prebureaucratic lines · · · · · · · · · 1:131b
    salaries · · · · · · · · · · · · · · · · · · 1:131a
  shogunate missions to the West · · · 7:161a
  social structure and class policy
    · · · · · · · · · · · · · · · · · · · 3:187b-188a
    tenryō · · · · · · · · · · · · · · · · · · · 8:10a
  Tokugawa shogunate · · · · · · · · · · 8:55b
  townsmen and commerce · · · · · · · 1:132a
    craftsmen · · · · · · · · · · · · · · · · · 1:132a
    merchants · · · · · · · · · · · · · · · · · 1:132a
  urban development · · · · · · · · · 1:132b-133a
    toiya and kabunakama · · · · · · · · · 1:132b
    uchikowashi · · · · · · · · · · · · · · · 1:132b
Bakushū · · · · · · · · · · 麦秋 · · · · · · 3:102b
Balance of payments · · · · · · · 1:133b-135a
  definitions and data summary 1:133b-134a
    current account balance · · · · · · · · 1:133b
    merchandise trade balance · · · · · · 1:133b
    net long-term capital · · · · · · · · · · 1:133b
    overall balance · · · · · · · · · · · · · 1:134a
  flow of funds · · · · · · · · · · · · · · · · 2:293a
  foreign exchange control · · · · · · · · 2:314b
  foreign trade · · · · · · · · · · · · · 2:324a-324b
  IMF · 3:274a
  Japan's performance · · · · · · · · 1:134a-135a
    1950s and 1960s · · · · · · · · · · 1:134a-135a
    1966-71 · · · · · · · · · · · · · · · · · · 1:135a
    1971- · · · · · · · · · · · · · · · · · · · 1:135a
  modern economy · · · · · · · · · · 2:163b-164a
  monetary policy · · · · · · · · · · · · · · 5:241a
  research and development · · · · · · · 6:305a
  tariffs · · · · · · · · · · · · · · · · · · 7:346b-347a
Balance of trade · · · · · · · · · · · · · · 2:314b
Balkan states · · · · · · · · · · · · · · · · 2:142a
Ball, William MacMahon · · 1:117a-117b,
  135a-135b
Ballad-drama (kōwaka) · · · · · · · · · · 5:45a
Ballet. *See* Dance, Western-style
Balloonflower · · · · · · · · · · · · · · · · 4:207b
Balneotherapy · · · · · · · · · · · · · 3:239a-239b
  history · 3:239a
  present conditions · · · · · · · · · 3:239a-239b
Balneotherapy Institute · · · · · · · · · 3:239a
Bälz, Erwin von · · · · · · · · · 1:135b, 4:35a
Ba Maw · 1:135b
  Greater East Asia conference · · · · · 3:61b
Bambetsu   蕃別
  Shinsen shōjiroku · · · · · · · · · · · · 7:124b
Bamboo [(take; sasa) family Gramineae]
  · · · · · · · · · · · · · · · · · · · 1:135b-136a
  baskets · · · · · · · · · · · · · · · · · 4:104b-105a
  traditional furniture material · · · · · 2:371b
Bamboo and White Crane · · · · · · · · 4:147b
Bamboo craftwork · · · · · · · · · · · · · 2:295b
"Bamboo horse" · · · · · · · · · · · · · · · 7:246a
Bamboo ware · · · · · · · · · · · · · 1:136a-136b
B-aminoisobutyric acid (BAIB) · · · · · 4:37a
Ban'ampō · · · · · · · 万安方 · · 4:114b-115a
Banchōkai
  Teijin Incident · · · · · · · · · · · · · · 7:375b
Bancroft, Edgar Addison · · · · · · · · · 1:136b
Bandai-Asahi National
  Park · · · 磐梯朝日国立公園 · · 1:11b, 127b,
  136b-137a; 2:366a-366b
Ban Dainagon ekotoba
  (Picture Story of the
  Courtier Ban Dainagon)
  · · · · · · · · · · · 伴大納言絵詞 1:137a; 6:*152a*;
    8:81b
  Ōtemmon Conspiracy · · · · · · · · · · 6:129b
Bandaisan · · · · · · · · · 磐梯山 · · · · · 1:37a
Bandō Tamasaburō
  · · · · · · · · · · · 坂東玉三郎 · · · · · 4:91a

Bandō Tsumasaburō
阪東妻三郎 ·· **1**:137a-137b;
2:268b
Bangkok Conference ············ **7**:197a
Banishment ················· **1**:137b
edo jūri shihō-barai ········· **1**:137b
tokoro-barai ··············· **1**:137b
Banka (Dirge) ········ 挽歌 ·· **8**:319b
Banka poems
defined ················· **5**:105a-105b
Bankata ·········· 番方 ··· **1**:137b
Bank Bookkeeping Guide (1872) ···· **1**:6a
Bankei Yōtaku ··· 盤珪永琢 ·· **1**:137b
Banking Bureau ············ **5**:188a
Banking system ······· **1**:137b-140a, 242a
corporate finance ······ **2**:28b-29b, 35a
corporate funds ··········· **4**:189a
economic growth ··········· **2**:161a
foreign exchange ··········· **1**:140b
functions ················ **1**:140a
bonds ·················· **1**:140a
debenture floatation ······· **1**:140a
financing ··············· **1**:140a
securities ·············· **1**:140a
small business ··········· **7**:164a
trust transactions ········· **1**:140a
history ··············· **1**:137b-139a
agriculture and industrial banks · **1**:139a
Bank of Japan ··········· **1**:138b
Bank of Japan Law of 1942 ·· **1**:139a
central bank ············· **1**:138b
consolidation ············ **1**:139a
early modern ······· **2**:151b-152a, 153a
Financial Crisis of 1927 ······· **1**:139a
foreign exchange ······· **1**:138b-139a
Kawase kaisha ············ **1**:138a
long-term credit banks ······· **1**:139a
Mitsui ················· **1**:138a
National Bank Ordinance of 1872 **1**:138a
national banks ········· **1**:138a-138b
Ono houses ············· **1**:138a
post-World War II · **1**:139a; **2**:155b-156a
Ryōgaeshō ·············· **1**:137b
Savings Bank Ordinance of 1890 · **1**:138b
savings banks ············ **1**:138b
monetary policy ··········· **5**:240a
mutual financing ··········· **5**:262b
overloan ············· **2**:158a-158b
present ··············· **1**:139a-140a
Bank of Japan ············ **1**:139a
commercial banks ······· **1**:139a-139b
cooperative associations ····· **1**:139b-140a
credit association ·········· **1**:139b
exports ·············· **1**:139a-140a
foreign banks ············ **1**:139b
long-term credit banks ······· **1**:139b
mutual savings and loan banks
(sōgo ginkō) ········· **1**:139a-140a
postal savings system ······ **1**:139b-140a
public corporation ·········· **1**:139b
trust banks ···· **1**:139a-140a; **3**:327b-328a
Shibusawa Eiichi ········· **7**:86a-86b
Taika Shakkandan ······· **7**:297a-297b
Bank of Japan (Nippon Ginkō or Nihon
Ginkō) ·············· **1**:140a-140b
business cycles ··········· **1**:224b
domestic exchange ········· **2**:130b
establishment ············· **1**:140a
Financial Crisis of 1927 ····· **2**:277a-277b
Financial System Research Committee
···················· **2**:278b
flow of funds compilation ······ **2**:292a
foreign trade controls ········ **2**:320a
founding ················· **2**:30b
general description ········· **1**:140b
Inoue Junnosuke ·········· **3**:309b
interest rate structure ······· **3**:317b-318a
Matsukata fiscal policy ····· **5**:133b-134a

monetary policy ·········· **5**:239b-241b
national banks ············ **5**:336b
reorganization ············ **1**:140b
role ··················· **1**:140b
technological development ···· **7**:369a-369b
Bank of Japan Building ········ **1**:140b
Tatsuno Kingo ············ **7**:349b
Bank of Japan Case ·········· **6**:201b
Bank of Japan Law of 1942 ····· **1**:139a
Bank of Korea ············· **1**:303b
Bank of Taiwan ········· **7**:307b, 309b
Bank of Tōkyō, Ltd (Tōkyō Ginkō)
···················· **1**:140b-141a
Yokohama Specie Bank ······· **8**:330b
Bank of Yokohama, Ltd ······· **1**:141a
Banko ware ······· 万古焼 · **1**:141a, 264a
Bankruptcy ·············· **1**:141a
alternatives ·············· **1**:141a
Bankruptcy Law of 1922 ······ **1**:141a
Okano Keijirō ············· **6**:81a
Banks
Bank of Japan ········· **1**:140a-140b
Bank of Korea ············ **1**:303b
Bank of Tōkyō, Ltd (Tōkyō Ginkō) **1**:140b
Bank of Yokohama, Ltd ······ **1**:141a
Dai-Ichi Kangyō Bank, Ltd ···· **2**:58b
Daiwa Bank, Ltd ·········· **2**:68b
Export-Import Bank of Japan ··· **2**:237b
Fuji Bank, Ltd ············ **2**:342a
Hokkaidō Takushoku Bank, Ltd ·· **3**:214a
Industrial Bank of Japan, Ltd ··· **3**:291a
Japan Development Bank ······· **4**:12b
Kyōwa Bank Ltd ········ **4**:339b-340a
Long-Term Credit Bank of Japan, Ltd
···················· **5**:73a
Mitsubishi Bank, Ltd ····· **5**:206b-207a
Mitsubishi Trust & Banking
Corporation ············ **5**:209a
Mitsui Bank, Ltd ·········· **5**:211a
Mitsui Trust & Banking Co, Ltd
··················· **5**:212b-213a
Nippon Credit Bank, Ltd ······ **6**:9a
Nōrin Chūkin Bank ········· **6**:37b
Saitama Bank, Ltd ········· **6**:372b
Sanwa Bank, Ltd ········ **7**:18b-19a
Shōkō Chūkin Bank ········· **7**:164a
Sumitomo Bank, Ltd ········ **7**:267b
Sumitomo Trust & Banking Co, Ltd
···················· **7**:269b
Taiyō Kobe Bank, Ltd. ······· **7**:310a
Tōkai Bank, Ltd ··········· **8**:40b
Tōyō Trust & Banking Co, Ltd · **8**:93b-94a
Yasuda Trust & Banking Co, Ltd · **8**:318a
Yokohama Specie Bank ······· **8**:330b
Bannermen (hatamoto) ······ **3**:111b-112a
Ban Nobutomo ···· 伴信友 ·· **1**:141b
Ban on Heterodox (Kansei Igaku no Kin)
············ **2**:174a; **4**:152b; **5**:132a
"Banreki aka-e" · 万暦赤絵 ·· **7**:176a
Bansha ·········· 蛮社 ·· **1**:141b
Bansha no Goku · 蛮社の獄 · **1**:141b, 211b
Shinkiron ·············· **7**:119a
Takano Chōei ············ **7**:316a
Torii Yōzō ··············· **8**:80a
Banshi ··········· 番士 ·· **1**:137b
Banshokō ········· 蕃薯考 ·· **1**:68b
Bansho Shirabesho
··············· 蕃書調所 · **1**:141b-142a
French-Japanese relations ····· **2**:331a
Western learning ··········· **8**:243a
Banshū ··········· 番衆 ·· **1**:137b
Banshun ········· 晩春 ·· **3**:102b
Banshū-ori ····· 播州織 ·· **4**:160b
Banshū Plain ···· 播州平野 ·· **3**:139a
Bansugoroku ··············· **7**:259a
Ban-the-bomb movement ········ **1**:114b
Ban Tsuma ········· 阪妻 ·· **1**:137b
Banzai ················· **1**:142a

Banzuke ················ **7**:272a
Baptist Church ············ **1**:142a
Bar Association. *See* **Japan Federation
of Bar Associations**
"Bara tōnin" ····· 薔薇盗人 ···· **7**:176a
Barley. *See* **Wheat and barley**
Barrier of Nakoso ············ **5**:321b
Barriers, ancient fortified ······· **5**:321b
Barrier stations ············· **7**:57a
Basal metabolism ············ **4**:37a
Baseball ············· **1**:142a-143a
amateur ················ **1**:142b
nonstudent ············ **1**:142b
student ··············· **1**:142b
Japan-United States games ··· **1**:142b-143a
professional ············· **1**:142b
Dai Nihon Baseball Club ····· **1**:142b
two-league system ········ **1**:142b
rubber ball ·············· **1**:142b
Bashaku ········· 馬借 ·· **1**:143a-143b
Bashaku ikki ····· 馬借一揆 ·· **1**:143b-144a
Bashō ··········· 芭蕉 ·· **1**:144a-145b,
181b-182a, 276a; **5**:12a, 16a, 39a;
6:297a-297b, 298b, 299b; **7**:5b, 24a, 259a
disciples
Hattori Ransetsu ········· **3**:114a
Kagami Shikō ··········· **4**:102b
Kawai Sora ············· **4**:179a
Morikawa Kyoroku ········ **5**:250a
Mukai Kyorai ··········· **5**:262a
Naitō Jōsō ·············· **5**:311a
Ochi Etsujin ············ **6**:59b
Sugiyama Sampū ········· **7**:259a
Takarai Kikaku ·········· **7**:318a
Fūryū concept ············ **2**:374b
haibun ················· **3**:77b
haiku ················ **3**:78b-79a
Issa ·················· **3**:348a
life ················· **1**:144a-145a
Masaoka Shiki's criticisms ····· **5**:123b
northern journey ········ **1**:144b-145a
Shinkei ················ **7**:119a
Shin kokinshū ··········· **7**:120b
studies
Hattori Tohō ············ **3**:114a
westward journies ······· **1**:144a-144b
1684 ················· **1**:144a
1687 ················· **1**:144b
works
Fuyu no hi ············ **1**:144a
"Genjūan no ki" ········· **1**:145a
Haikai shichibushū ······· **3**:78a
Kashima mōde ·········· **8**:105b
Minashiguri ············ **1**:144a
Nozarashi kikō ·········· **1**:144a
"Oi no kobumi" ·········· **1**:144b
Oku no hosomichi ········ **1**:145a
"Saga nikki" ············ **1**:145a
Sarashina kikō ·········· **1**:144b
"Sarumino" ············· **1**:145a
Sumidawara ············ **1**:145a
Tōsei montei dokugin nijikkasen · **1**:144a
Bashō kukai ····· 芭蕉句解 ·· **6**:126a
Bashō school ············· **5**:18a
Basic Agriculture Law of 1961 ··· **1**:32a
Basic Law concerning Atomic Energy
of 1955 ················ **1**:114a
Basic Law concerning the Execution of
Duties by Police Officials ······ **8**:171a
Basic Law for Environmental Pollution
Control ····· **2**:224b-225b, 228a-228b
Basic Relations between Japan and the
Republic of Korea, Treaty on ···· **4**:287b
Basins
Chichibu ··············· **1**:271b
Hita ·················· **3**:206a
Hitoyoshi ··············· **3**:208b
Ina ··················· **3**:281b

Kamikawa · · · · · · · · · · · · · · · 4:126b
Kitakami · · · · · · · · · · · · · · · 4:226a
Kōfu · · · · · · · · · · · · · · · 4:243b; 8:301a
Kōriyama · · · · · · · · · · · · · · · 4:293b
Kyōto · · · · · · · · · · · · · · · 4:336b–337a
Matsumoto · · · · · · · · · · · · · · · 5:137b
Miyakonojō · · · · · · · · · · · · · · · 5:219b
Miyoshi · · · · · · · · · · · · · · · 5:223b
Nara · · · · · · · · · · · · · · · 5:332a–332b
Ōdate · · · · · · · · · · · · · · · 6:65a
Ōmi · · · · · · · · · · · · · · · 6:101a
Saku · · · · · · · · · · · · · · · 7:3a
Takayama · · · · · · · · · · · · · · · 7:320a
Tsuyama · · · · · · · · · · · · · · · 8:119b
Ueno · · · · · · · · · · · · · · · 8:128b
Yamaguchi · · · · · · · · · · · · · · · 8:294a
Bassui Tokushō 抜隊得勝 · · · 1:145b
Bataan · · · · · · · · · · · · · · · 1:145b
Batchelor, John · · · · · · · · · · · · · · · 1:145b
Bateren · · · · · · · · · · · · · · · 1:145b–146a
Bath · · · · · · · · · · · · · · · 1:146a
  customs · · · · · · · · · · · · · · · 1:146b
  mixed · · · · · · · · · · · · · · · 1:146b
  modern family · · · · · · · · · · · · 1:146a–146b
  public · · · · · · · · · · · · · · · 1:146a
    sentō · · · · · · · · · · · · · · · 1:146a
    temple · · · · · · · · · · · · · · · 1:146a
Batik · · · · · · · · · · · · · · · 7:21a
Bats [(kōmori) order Chiroptera] · · 1:146b
Batsu · · · · · · · 1:146b–147b; 6:205b; 7:62b
  general description · · · · · · · · · · 1:147a
  types · · · · · · · · · · · · · · · 1:146b–147a
    gakubatsu · · · · · · · · · · 1:147a; 3:3b
    gumbatsu · · · · · · · · · · 1:147a; 3:65b–67a
    habatsu · · · · · · · · · · 1:147a; 3:73a
    hambatsu · · · · · · · · · · 1:147b; 3:91b–92a
    keibatsu · · · · · · · · · · · · · · · 1:147a
    mombatsu · · · · · · · · · · · · · · · 1:147a
    zaibatsu · · · · · · · 1:147a; 8:361a–363b
Batsuzoku · · · · · · · · · · · · · · · 3:92a
Battledore · · · · · · · · · · · · · · · 3:77a
Battle of the Carriages · · · · · 4:148b, 149b
Bays
  Ago · · · · · · · · · · · · · · · 1:21b
  Ariake · · · · · · · · · · · · · · · 1:83a
  Dōkai · · · · · · · · · · · · · · · 2:127b
  Hiroshima · · · · · · · · · · · · · · · 3:149b
  Ise · · · · · · · · · · · · · · · 3:336b–337a
  Kagoshima · · · · · · · · · · · · · · · 4:105a
  Kojima · · · · · · · · · · · · · · · 4:251b
  Matsushima · · · · · · · · · · · · · · · 5:140a
  Mikawa · · · · · · · · · · · · · · · 5:170b
  Mutsu · · · · · · · · · · · · · · · 5:288b
  Nago · · · · · · · · · · · · · · · 5:308b
  Ōsaka · · · · · · · · · · · · · · · 6:120a
  Sagami · · · · · · · · · · · · · · · 6:363b
  Sendai · · · · · · · · · · · · · · · 7:63b
  Sukumo · · · · · · · · · · · · · · · 7:266a
  Suruga · · · · · · · · · · · · · · · 7:278b
  Tōkyō · · · · · · · · · · · · · · · 8:66a
  Tosa · · · · · · · · · · · · · · · 8:81a
  Toyama · · · · · · · · · · · · · · · 8:88a
  Tsuruga · · · · · · · · · · · · · · · 8:116b
  Uchiura · · · · · · · · · · · · · · · 8:125a
Be · · · · · · · · · 部 · 1:125b, 147b;
       2:103b; 4:166b; 7:256a
  classification · · · · · · · · · · · · · · · 1:147b
  ownership · · · · · · · · · · · · · · · 1:147b
  prototype · · · · · · · · · · · · · · · 1:147b
  Shintō · · · · · · · · · · · · · · · 7:126a
  uji-kabane system · · · · · · · · · · · · · · · 8:131b
Beads, ancient · · · · · · · · · · · · · · · 1:147b–148a
  bead-making sites · · · · · · · · · · · · · · · 1:148a
  glass · · · · · · · · · · · · · · · 3:35b
  kofun deposits · · · · · · · · · · · · · · · 4:244b
  Shintō art · · · · · · · · · · · · · · · 7:134b
  types · · · · · · · · · · · · · · · 1:148a
Beanbag · · · · · · · · · · · · · · · 1:148a

Bean curd · · · · · · · · · · · · · · · 8:35a
Bean paste. *See* **Miso**
Bean-scattering ceremony · · · · · · · 7:71b
Beard, Charles Austin · · · · · 1:148a–148b
Bears [(kuma) family Ursidae] · · 1:148b
"Beatles" · · · · · · · · · · · · · · · 6:112a
"Beatnik" movement · · · · · · · · · · 7:207a
Beauties beneath Trees (juka bijin)
   · · · · · · · · · · · · · · · 6:*149a*
Bedding · · · · · · · · 1:148b–149a; 2:371a
  kakebuton · · · · · · · · · · · · · · · 1:149a
  mosquito nets · · · · · · · · · · · · · · · 1:149a
  pillows · · · · · · · · · · · · · · · 1:148b
  shikibuton · · · · · · · · · · · · · · · 1:149a
Beef production · · · · · · · · · · · · · · · 1:28b
Bees and wasps [(hachi) order
  Hymenoptera] · · · · · · · · · · · · · · · 1:149a
Beetle, Japanese · · · · · · · · · · · · · · · 4:22b
Before the Dawn · · · · · · · · · · · · · · · 4:103b
Beheiren. *See* **Peace for Vietnam
  Committee**
Beigoma · · · · · · · · · · · · · · · 1:149b
Beijing (Peking) Customs Conference
   · · · · · · · · · · · · · · · 7:88b
Beijing (Peking) theater · · · · · · 8:22b–23a
Beijing Treaty of 1905 · · · · · · · · · · 6:228a
Beiō kairan jikki
  米欧回覧実記 3:359b; 4:307b
Bekkōbachi (spider wasps) · · · · · · · 1:149a
Bekkō-zaiku · · · · · · · · · · · · · · · 8:80b–81a
Belgium, Japanese studies · · · · 4:43a–43b
Bells, wind · · · · · · · · · · · · · · · 8:254a
Benedict, Ruth Fulton · 1:149b; 4:38a, 39a
Ben'en · · · · · · · · · · · · · · · 1:*192b*
Benevolence (jin) · · · · · · · · · · · · · · · 4:141b
Bengaru no tora
  ベンガルの虎 4:157b
Benikujaku · · · · · · 紅孔雀 8:339a
Benizuri-e ("safflower
  printed pictures") 紅摺絵 8:141a
Benkei · · · · · · · 弁慶 · 1:149b
  kabuki depiction · · · · · · · · · · · · · · · 4:97b
  Gikeiki · · · · · · · · · · · · · · · 3:32b
Benshi · · · · · · · · · · · · · · · 2:267b–268a
Benten · · · · · · · · · · · · 弁天 5:296a
Bentenjima · · · · · 弁天島 · 1:150a; 4:2b
Benzaiten. *See* **Tembu**
Benzoin umbellatum · · · · · · · · · · · · · · · 4:316b
Beppu · · · · · · · · · · · · 別府 1:150a
Beppu Bay · · · · · · · · 別府湾 1:150a
Bereaved Families Association · · · 8:319a
Beriberi Investigation Committee · · 7:311a
Berrien, F.K. · · · · · · · · · · · · 4:39b–40a
Berry, John Cutting · 1:150a; 2:51b
Bertin, Louis-Emile · · · · · · · · · · 1:150a
Berurin hyōhaku
  ベルリン漂泊 4:162b
Besshi Copper Mine
   · · · · · · · 別子銅山 4:182b
Besshi Copper Mine labor disputes
   · · · · · · · · · · · · · · · 1:150a–150b
Besshi Dōzan sōgi
   · · · · · · · 別子銅山争議 1:150a
Bessho · · · · · · · · · · · · · · · 3:137a
Betonamu ni Heiwa o Shimin Rengō
   · · · · · · · · · · · · · · · 6:145b, 166a
Betsugen Enshi 別源円旨 · · · 1:150b
Betsuri · · · · · · · · · 別離 8:219a
Bettelheim, B.J. · · · · · · · · · · · · 4:32a
Bibai · · · · · · · · · · · · 美唄 1:150b
Bible, translations of · · · · 1:150b–151a
  colloquial · · · · · · · · · · · · · · · 1:151a
  Japanese Common Bible Translation
  project · · · · · · · · · · · · · · · 1:151a
  Meiji version · · · · · · · · · · · · · · · 1:150b
  oldest extant · · · · · · · · · · · · · · · 1:150b
  Protestant · · · · · · · · · · · · · · · 1:150b
  Roman Catholic · · · · · · · · · · 1:150b–151a

16th century · · · · · · · · · · · · · · · 1:150b
Bible studies. *See* *Seisho no kenkyū*
Bibliography · · · · · · · · · · 1:151a–154a
  characteristics of extant manuscripts and
  printed books · · · · · · · · · · 1:153a–154a
    external · · · · · · · · · · · · · · · 1:153a–153b
    internal · · · · · · · · · · · · · · · 1:153b–154a
  descriptive · · · · · · · · · · · · · · · 1:154a
  form and characteristic of Japanese
  books · · · · · · · · · · · · · · · 1:151b–153a
    manuscripts · · · · · · · · · · · · · · · 1:152a
    printed books · · · · · · · · · · · · 1:152a–153a
  origin and transmission of books
   · · · · · · · · · · · · · · · 1:151a–151b
Bicycle theft · · · · · · · · · · · · · · · 4:86b
Biddle, Francis · · · · · · · · · · · · · · · 4:17b
Bigelow, William Sturgis · · · · 1:154b
Big Four combines · · · · · · 8:361b, 364a
Bigot, Georges · · · · · · · · · · 1:154b–155a
Bijin · · · · · · · · · · · · · 4:109b, 201a
Bijinga · · · · · · · · · · · · · · · 6:158b
  Itō Shinsui · · · · · · · · · · · · · · · 3:356a
  Kaburagi Kiyokata · · · · · · · · · · 4:100a
Bikini Island · · · · · · · · · 1:114b; 5:75b
Bikini radiation injuries · · · · · 1:113a–114a
Bills and Notes Law · · · · · · · 1:339a–339b
Bimbōgami · · · · · · · · · · · · · · · 1:155a
Bimbō monogatari (Story
  of the Poor) 貧乏物語 4:180b; 8:264b
Bindweed · · · · · · · · · · · · · · · 3:151a
Bingata. *See* **Okinawan textiles**
Biochemistry · · · · · · · · · · · · · · · 1:156a
Biochemists
  Akabori Shirō · · · · · · · · · · · · · · · 1:39a
  Hayaishi Osamu · · · · · · · · · · · · · · · 3:114b
  Shibata Keita · · · · · · · · · · · · · · · 7:84b
**Biography and
biographical fiction** · · · 1:155a–155b
  autobiographical · · · · · · · · · 1:155a–155b
  biographical · · · · · · · · · · · · 1:155a–155b
Biologists
  Fujii Kenjirō · · · · · · · · · · · · · · · 2:343a
  Imanishi Kinji · · · · · · · · · · · · · · · 3:274a
  Kihara Hitoshi · · · · · · · · · · · · · · · 4:204b
  Makino Tomitarō · · · · · · · · · · · · · · · 5:87a
  Minakata Kumakusu · · · · · · · · · · 5:176a
  Morse, Edward Sylvester · · · · · · · · · · 5:256a
  Oka Asajirō · · · · · · · · · · · · · · · 6:77b
  Ono Ranzan · · · · · · · · · · · · · · · 6:111b
  Thunberg, Carl Peter · · · · · · · · · · 8:29b
  Toyama Kametarō · · · · · · · · · · 8:88a
  Whitman, Charles Otis · · · · · · · · · · 8:252b
  Yamamoto Senji · · · · · · · · · · 8:299a
  Yatabe Ryōkichi · · · · · · · · · · 8:319b–320a
Biology · · · · · · · · · · · · · · · 1:155b–156a
  biochemistry · · · · · · · · · · · · · · · 1:156a
  genetics · · · · · · · · · · · · · · · 1:156a
  Meiji period · · · · · · · · · · · · 1:155b–156a
  physiology · · · · · · · · · · · · · · · 1:156a
  premodern · · · · · · · · · · · · · · · 1:155b
Bird-and-flower painting (kachōga)
   · · · · · · · · · 1:156a–156b; 6:158b–159a
Bird, Isabella Lucy · · · · · · · · · · 1:156b
"Bird rattles" · · · · · · · · · · · · · · · 5:334b
Birds · · · · · · · · · · · 1:59b–60a, 61b
  bush warbler · · · · · · · · · · 1:223b–224a
  chicken, Japanese · · · · · · · · · 1:272b–273b
  cranes · · · · · · · · · · · · · · · 2:41b
  crows · · · · · · · · · · · · · · · 2:51b–52a
  cuckoos · · · · · · · · · · · · · · · 2:52a
  geese · · · · · · · · · · · · · · · 3:13b
  gulls · · · · · · · · · · · · · · · 3:65b
  hawks and eagles · · · · · · · · · · 3:114b
  herons · · · · · · · · · · · · · · · 3:127b–128a
  kite, black · · · · · · · · · · · · · · · 4:229b
  komadori · · · · · · · · · · · · · · · 4:264b
  larks · · · · · · · · · · · · · · · 4:368b
  mandarin duck · · · · · · · · · · 5:100b–101b

pheasants ·················· 6:182b
plovers ···················· 6:192b
ptarmigan ·················· 6:262b
rails ······················ 6:277b
reed warblers ·············· 6:285b
sparrows ·················· 7:241a
thrushes ·················· 8:29b
wagtails ·············· 8:200b-201a
wild ducks ············ 8:253a-253b
woodpeckers ··············· 8:269b
Birds and Flowers ········ 4:110b
Birds and Flowers of the Four Seasons
····················· 4:150b
Birds of Prey ············· 4:148b
Birōjima ······· 枇榔島 ··· 1:156b
Birth control ······· 6:224b; 7:11a
family planning ······ 2:246b-247b
Birthday celebrations ······· 4:151a
Birthplace history ·········· 5:71b
Birth rate ·· 2:246b-247a; 6:222a, 223b-224a, 225a
economic implications ······ 6:232a
Bisai ············ 尾西 ··· 1:156b
Bishamonten ····· 毘沙門天 ·· 5:296a
''Bishō'' (The Smile) 微笑 ···· 8:333b
Bishū ············· 尾州 ··· 6:136b
Bitasen ········· 鐚銭 ·· 1:156b-157a
copper ·················· 1:156a
iron and brass ·········· 1:156b-157a
Bitchūguwa ················ 4:322a
Bitō Nishū ···· 尾藤二洲 ··· 1:157a
Biwa, Lake ······ 琵琶湖 ··· 1:*157a*, 157b-158a; 7:90b
Biwa (lute) ········· 琵琶 · 1:*157a*-157b; 2:301a; 7:*168b*, 195a
Chikuzen ·············· 1:157a-157b
court music ············· 1:157a
gagaku ·················· 3:2a
general description ········ 1:157a
gunka ·················· 3:69a
national anthem ·········· 5:336a
Satsuma mōsō ············ 1:157a
Biwa hōshi ··· 琵琶法師 · 1:157b; 5:44a; 7:61b
Biwako Canal · 琵琶湖疏水 1:157b; 4:336a
Bizen ············ 備前 ··· 1:158a
Bizenkurage ··············· 4:50b
Bizen ware · 備前焼 · 1:158a, 263a; 7:256a
early ···················· 1:158a
Edo-period ··············· 1:158a
general description ········ 1:158a
jar ···················· 1:*259a*
Kaneshige Tōyō ············ 4:140a
Momoyama period ········· 1:158a
museums ················ 5:279b
present ·················· 1:158a
Black Cat ··············· 6:*157a*
Black Dragon Society. *See* **Amur River Society**
Black, John Reddie ······· 1:158b; 4:46a
Black Ocean Society (Gen'yōsha)
····················· 3:24b-25a
Black Rain ··············· 3:255a
Blacks, attitudes toward ····· 2:312a-313a
Black-seal certificate ········ 7:184a
Black Stream (kuroshio) ······ 4:318b
Bloch, Bernard ··········· 1:158b
Blood chemistry ·········· 4:35b-36b
''Blood Debt'' Incident 1:158b-159a; 5:88a; 7:196b
''Blood seal'' ·············· 4:200a
''Blood tax'' riots (Ketsuzei ikki)
····················· 4:200a-200b
Blue Cat ················· 3:76a
''Bluestocking Society'' ····· 7:54a-54b
Board of Audit ········· 1:159a; 2:276b; 3:56a; 6:264b

Board of Censors ··········· 4:185b
ritsuryō system ··········· 6:323a
Board of directors ······· 1:159a-159b
Board of Inquiry (Monchūjo) · 5:239a
Board of Retainers (Samurai-dokoro)
····················· 7:8b
Boats, traditional. *See* **Ships**
Bōchō kaiten shi
········ 防長回天史 1:159b; 7:255b
Bodhicitta ················ 4:67b
Bodhidharma ·············· 4:158a
Bodhisattva · 1:159b; 4:66a, 144b; 7:169a
Jizō ···················· 4:66a
Bodhisena ················ 3:288a
Bōeichō ········ 防衛庁 ··· 2:82a
Bōei Daigakkō ··········· 5:338b
Bōei hakusho ············· 2:82b
Bōei Kenshūsho ·········· 5:338b
Bōfū ···················· 3:127b
Bohai (Po-hai) ········ 1:159b-160a; 2:347b; 7:257a, 261a
China invaded ············ 4:277b
Boissonade de Fontarabie, Gustave Emile ····· 1:160a, 166a; 4:378a
Civil Code ············· 1:316b-317a
French-Japanese relations ··· 2:332a
legal reform activities ······ 2:316b, 319a
Sandai Jiken Kempaku Movement (Movement to Memorialize Three Important Items) ········· 7:9b
Bojutsu yume monogatari
·········· 戊辰夢物語 1:141b; 7:316a
Bo Juyi ·················· 8:210a
Bokkai ········· 渤海 · 1:159b-160a
Bōkokurei Jiken. *See* **Grain embargo controversy**
Boku Eikō ······· 朴泳孝 ·· 6:159b
Boku Retsu ······ 朴烈 ·· 6:159a-159b
Boku Seiki ······· 朴正熙 ·· 6:159a
Bokuseki ················ 1:192b
Sōhō Myōchō ············ 1:*235a*
Bokuseki no utsushi
············ 墨跡の写し · 1:236a
Bokuseki soshi den
············ 墨跡祖師伝 · 1:236a
Boller, Anton ·············· 4:18b
Bolshevik Revolution (1917) · 6:342b-343a; 7:192a; 8:271a
Bolshevism ················ 5:231b
''Bolshevist Group'' ········· 6:255a
Bolshoi Ballet ············· 2:76a
Bombori lanterns ·········· 4:368a
Bommōkyō ······· 梵網経 · 1:234a
Bon dance. *See* **Bon odori**
Bond market ·············· 1:242b
Bonds, public ··········· 1:160a
foreign exchange control ···· 2:315a
public investment ········· 6:265a
Bone articles ············ 1:160a-160b
Jōmon culture ·········· 4:72a-74a
Kamegaoka site ·········· 4:125a
Okhotsk culture ··········· 6:84a
paleolithic culture ········ 6:159b-160a
Bon Festival ········· 盆 · 1:20a, 124a, 160b; 2:258a; 5:4b; 7:246a, 249b
chūgen ·················· 1:312a
cooking ·················· 2:22a
Daimonji Okuribi ·········· 2:61a
dance ···················· 2:75a
funerals ·················· 2:370a
dances ··················· 2:374a
importance ··············· 2:299a
nembutsu odori ··········· 5:360a
religion ·················· 6:291a
Tanabata Festival ········ 7:334b-335a
Bongaku Shinryō 梵学津梁 ·· 4:64a
Bonin Islands · ボニン諸島 ·· 4:7a

Bonito [(katsuo) family Scombridae]
····················· 1:160b-161a
Bonkei and bonseki ······· 1:161a
Bon odori ··············· 1:160b
Awa ···················· 1:124a
Bō no Tsu ······ 坊津 ··· 1:161b
Bonsai ······· 1:*162a*, 161b-163a
abroad ·················· 1:163a
aesthetics and philosophy ··· 1:162a-163a
ferns ···················· 2:252a
general description ········ 1:161b-162a
growing ················· 1:162a
fertilizer ················ 1:162a
instruments ············· 1:162a
seasons ················· 1:162a
soil ··················· 1:162a
temperature and moisture ··· 1:162a
varieties ················ 1:162a
major styles ············· 1:161b-162a
cascading ··············· 1:161b
clumped ················ 1:162a
forest ·················· 1:162a
rock planting ············ 1:162a
slanting ················ 1:161b
twin-trunk ·············· 1:162a
twisting-trunk ··········· 1:161b
upright ················· 1:161b-162a
weeping-cascade ·········· 1:161b
Shin-zen-bi ·············· 1:163a
styles
classic ················· 1:162a-162b
dramatic ················ 1:162a-162b
Bontō An ······· 梵燈庵 ·· 1:96a-96b
Bonus · 1:163a-163b; 2:18b, 243b; 4:348a
seasonal ················ 8:200a
Book catalogs ············· 3:219a
Book and magazine distributors ··· 1:163b
Bookbinding
modern ················· 6:245b
types ················ 1:153a-153b
traditional types ········ 1:153a-153b
Book illustration ········· 1:163b-164a
emakimono ············ 2:198a-200b
kusazōshi ·············· 4:319b-320a
Bookkeeping methods
accounting ············· 1:8a-10a
auditing ··············· 1:8a-10a
Book of Changes
omikuji ················ 6:101b
ommyōdō ··············· 6:103a
Book of Filial Piety · 孝経 ·· 2:57a
Book of History
in Ogyū Sorai's thought ···· 4:247b
Book of Odes
in Ogyū Sorai's thought ···· 4:247b
Book of Tea, The ···· 5:12a; 6:79b; 7:294b
Books
censorship ·············· 1:252a
external characteristics ····· 1:153a-153b
bindings ················ 1:153a-153b
paper ·················· 1:153b
scripts and writing styles ··· 1:153b
form ·················· 1:151b-153a
manuscripts ············· 1:152a
printed books ·········· 1:152a-153a
internal characteristics ···· 1:153b-154a
''one-yen'' (empon) ········ 2:212b
origin and transmission ···· 1:151a-151b
early ·················· 1:151a
Kana ·················· 1:151b
preservation ············ 1:151b
8th century ·············· 1:151b
9th century ·············· 1:151b
publishing ·············· 6:267b
Books of the floating world · 8:144a-144b
Booth, Eugene ··········· 1:164a
''Boroya no shunjū''
········ ボロ屋の春秋 ······· 8:147b

Bosatsu · · · · · · · · · · · · · · · · 1:159b; 7:169a
Bose, Rash Behari · · · · · · 1:164a-164b
Bose, Subhas Chandra · · · · 1:164b-165a
  Indian National Army · · · · · · · · 3:289b
Bōshibari · · · · · · · · 棒縛 · · 4:326b, 327a
Boshi jojō · · · · · · · 母子叙情 · · · · · · 6:80a
Boshin Civil War 戊辰戦争 · 1:165a-165b
  debate · · · · · · · · · · · · · · · · 1:165a-165b
  events · 1:165a
  French-Japanese relations · · · · · · 2:331b
  Goryōkaku, Battle of · · · · · · · · · · 3:47a
  Itagaki Taisuke · · · · · · · · · · · · · 3:349a
  Kabayama Sukenori · · · · · · · · · · · 4:89b
  Kan'eiji destruction · · · · · · · · · · 4:138a
  Kawai Tsugunosuke · · · · · · · · · · 4:179b
  Kawakami Sōroku · · · · · · · · · · · 4:181b
  Kido Takayoshi · · · · · · · · · · · · 4:202b
  Kiheitai · · · · · · · · · · · · · · · · · · 4:204b
  Kogosho Kaigi · · · · · · · · · · · · · 4:249b
  Meiji Restoration · · · · · · · · · · · · 5:159b
  Ōuetsu Reppan Dōmei · · · · · · · · 6:135b
  Shinsengumi · · · · · · · · · · · · · · 7:124b
  Takenouchi Tsuna · · · · · · · · · · · 7:325a
  Tōgō Heihachirō · · · · · · · · · · · · 8:36a
  Tokugawa Yoshinobu · · · · · · · · · 8:57b
  United Kingdom · · · · · · · · · · · · 8:151a
  White Tiger Brigade · · · · · · · · · 1:226b
  Willis, William · · · · · · · · · · · · 8:253b
Boshin Shōsho · 戊申詔書 · · · · · · · 1:165b
Bōshū · · · · · · · · · · 防州 · · 7:276b-277a
Bōsō Peninsula · 房総半島 · · · · 1:165b
Boston Symphony Orchestra
  Ozawa Seiji · · · · · · · · · · · · · · · 6:140b
Botan. *See* **Peonies**
Botanical Garden (Leyden) · · · · · · 7:193a
Botanical gardens · · · · · · · 1:165b-166a
  nonuniversity · · · · · · · · · · · · · · 1:165b
  specialty · · · · · · · · · · · · · · 1:165b-166a
  university · · · · · · · · · · · · · · · · 1:165b
Botanists
  Hirase Sakugorō · · · · · · · · · · · · 3:144b
  Iinuma Yokusai · · · · · · · · · · · · 3:263b
  Ikeno Seiichirō · · · · · · · · · · · · · 3:266b
  Itō Keisuke · · · · · · · · · · · · · · · 3:354b
  Makino Tomitarō · · · · · · · · · · · · 5:87a
  Maksimovich, Kark Ivanovich · · · · · 5:87b
  Matsumura Jinzō · · · · · · · · · · · · 5:138a
  Miyabe Kingo · · · · · · · · · · · · · 5:216b
  Miyoshi Manabu · · · · · · · · · · · · 5:224a
  Nakao Sasuke · · · · · · · · · · · · · 7:177b
  Noro Genjō · · · · · · · · · · · · · · · 6:39a
  Siebold, Philipp Franz von · · · 7:192b-193a
  Thunberg, Carl Peter · · · · · · · · · 8:29b
  Yatabe Ryōkichi · · · · · · · · · · 8:319b-320a
Botchan · · · · · · 坊ちゃん · · · · · 5:350a
Botekishū · · · · · · · 暮笛集 · · · · 7:279b
Bousquet, Georges Hilaire · · · · · · 1:166a
Bowing · · · · · · · · · · · · · · · · · · · 6:76a
Bows and arrows. *See* **Arms and armor**
Boxer Protocol of 1901 · · · · · · · · 7:199a
Boxer Rebellion 1:166a-166b, 287a; 3:196b;
                      5:9b; 7:29a, 198b
  aftereffects · · · · · · · · · · · · · 1:166a-166b
  cause · · · · · · · · · · · · · · · · · · · 1:166a
  climax · · · · · · · · · · · · · · · · · · 1:166a
  Fukushima Yasumasa · · · · · · · · · 2:367a
  Komura Jutarō · · · · · · · · · · · · · 4:268a
  Russia and Japan · · · · · · · · · · · 6:342a
  Russo-Japanese War · · · · · · · · · 6:346a
  Tairo Dōshikai · · · · · · · · · · · · 7:303a
  Tōgō Heihachirō · · · · · · · · · · · · 8:36a
  "Boxers" · · · · · · · · · · · · · · · · · 1:166a
Boxes · · · · · · · · · · · · · · · 1:166b-167a
  design · · · · · · · · · · · · · · · · 1:166b-167a
  haribako · · · · · · · · · · · · · · · · · 3:103b
  Kōrin · · · · · · · · · · · · · · · · · · · 1:166b
  materials · · · · · · · · · · · · · · · · 1:166b
  types · · · · · · · · · · · · · · · · · · · 1:166b

  writing box (suzuribako) · · · · 1:166b, *166b*
Box Man, The · · · · · · · · · · · · · · · 1:3a
Boycotts · · · · · · · · · · · · · · · · · · 2:14b
Boy Scouts · · · · · · · · · · · · · · · 1:167a
Boy's Day. *See* **Children's Day**
Braccialini, Scipione · · · · · · · · · · 3:350b
Bracelets, ancient · · · · · · · 1:148a, 167a
  chokkomon · · · · · · · · · · · · · · · 1:299b
  Jōmon · · · · · · · · · · · · · · · · · · 1:167a
  Kofun · · · · · · · · · · · · · · · · · · 1:167a
  Yayoi · · · · · · · · · · · · · · · · · · 1:167a
Brandt, Max August Scipio von · · · 1:167a;
                             3:26b
Brass bands · · · · · · · · · · · · · · · 5:286a
Braun, Hans Wolfgang · · · · · · · · · 3:26a
Brazil and Japan · · · · · · · · 1:167a-169a
  early relations · · · · · · · · · · · · · 1:167b
    immigration contracts · · · · · · · · 1:167b
    treaty of amity (1895) · · · · · · · · 1:167b
  Japanese immigrants · · · · · · 1:169a-169b;
                      2:200b-201b
    community leaders · · · · · · · 3:142b; 5:317b;
              7:105a; 8:130b, 221b, 298b
  large-scale economic cooperation
                    · · · 1:168b-169a
  postwar relations
    investments · · · · · · · · · · · · 1:168a-168b
    trade · · · · · · · · · · · · · · · · · · 1:168b
  prewar commerce · · · · · · · · 1:167b-168a
Brazilian-Japanese Cultural Association
  (Aliança Cultural Brasil-Japão) · · · · 8:298b
Bretton Woods Agreement · · · · · · · 8:161a
  IMF · · · · · · · · · · · · · · · · · · · 3:274b
Brewing · · · · · · · · · · · · · · 1:169b-170a
  method · · · · · · · · · · · · · · · 1:169b-170a
  miso · · · · · · · · · · · · · · · · · · · 1:170a
  sake · · · · · · · · · · · · · · · · · · · 1:170a
  soy sauce · · · · · · · · · · · · · · · · 1:170a
Bribery, political · · · · · · · · · · · · 6:202a
Bridges · · · · · · · · · · · · · · 1:170a-170b
  European techniques · · · · · · · · · 1:170a
  modern technology · · · · · · · · · · 1:170b
  premodern · · · · · · · · · · · · · · · 1:170a
Bridgestone Museum of Art · · · · · · 3:339b
Bridgestone Tire Co, Ltd · · · · · · · 1:170b
  Ishibashi Shōjirō · · · · · · · · · · · · 3:339a
Brinkley, Frank · · · · · · 1:170b-171a; 2:311a
British Commonwealth Occupation
Force (BCOF) · 1:117a-117b, 171a; 7:32b;
                        8:152b
British Commonwealth Peace
  Conference · · · · · · · · · · · · · · · 1:117a
British Origami Society · · · · · · · · 6:118b
Broadcast College · · · · · · · · 1:171a-171b
Broadcasting · · · · · · · · · · · 1:171b-173b
  commercial · · · · · · · · · · · · 1:173a-173b
  educational · · · · · · · · · · · · · · · 2:179a
  history · · · · · · · · · · · · · · · 1:171b-172b
    first · · · · · · · · · · · · · · · · · · 1:171b
    FM · · · · · · · · · · · · · · · · · · · 1:172b
    government control · · · · · · · · · 1:171b
    Nippon Hōsō Kyōkai (NHK)
      · · · · · · · · · · · 1:171b-173b; 5:374a
    postwar · · · · · · · · · · · · · · 1:172a-172b
    television · · · · · · · · · · · · · 1:172a-172b
    "Three Radio Laws" · · · · · · · · · 1:172a
  late-night · · · · · · · · · · · · · · · 1:173b
  present-day · · · · · · · · · · · · 1:172b-173a
    financing · · · · · · · · · · · · · · · 1:173a
    general characteristics · · · · · · · 1:172b
    networks · · · · · · · · · · · · · 1:172b-173a
    programming · · · · · · · · · · · · · 1:172b
    television viewing · · · · · · · · · · 1:173a
  public · · · · · · · · · · · · · · · · · · · 1:93a
  radio · · · · · · · · · · · · · · · · · · · 4:382a
  wire-relayed · · · · · · · · · · · · · · 8:254b

Broadcasting companies
  Asahi Broadcasting Corporation (ABC)
                         1:92a
  Asahi National Broadcasting Co, Ltd.
                         1:93a
  Chūbu Nippon Broadcasting Co, Ltd
                       1:311a
  Far East Network (FEN) · · · · · 2:248b-249a
  Fuji Telecasting Co, Ltd · · · · · · · 2:347b
  Kyokutō Hōsō · · · · · · · · · · · · · 4:332b
  Mainichi Broadcasting System Inc (MBS)
                        5:84b
  Nippon Broadcasting System, Inc · · · · 6:8b
  Nippon Cultural Broadcasting, Inc · · · 6:9a
  Nippon Television Network
    Corporation · · · · · · · · · · · 6:13a-13b
  Television Tōkyō Channel 12, Ltd · 7:380a
  Tōkyō Broadcasting System, Inc (TBS)
                        8:66a
  Yomiuri Telecasting Corporation · · 8:337a
Broadcasting Law of 1950 · · 1:171b-172b,
                         173b
  freedom of speech regulation · · · · 2:339a
  freedom of the press · · · · · · · · · 2:339a
Brocade (nishiki) · · · · · · · · · · · · 6:17b
Broken Thread · · · · · · · · · · · · · 6:188a
Bronze age · · · · · · · · · · · · 1:173b-174a
Bronze bell · · · · · · · · · · · · · · · · 1:78b
Bronze mirrors · · · · 1:77a, 78a, 167a, 174a,
           174b; 7:266a, 280a-280b
  chokkomon · · · · · · · · · · · · · · · 1:299b
  history · · · · · · · · · · · · · · · · · · 1:174a
  Imperial Regalia · · · · · · · · 1:174a; 3:278b
  inscriptions · · · · · · · · · · 1:174a; 3:314a
  Kagami to ken to tama · · · · · · · · 7:312a
  kofun · · · · · · · · · · · · · · · · · · 4:244a
  Ōzuka tomb · · · · · · · · · · · · · · 6:141a
  treasures and ritual implements · · · 1:174a
Bronze weapons 1:167a, 174a-175a; 7:266a
  Dōhoko dōken no kenkyū · · · · · · 7:312a
  fern frond design · · · · · · · · · · · 2:252a
  halberd heads · · · · · · · · · · · · · 1:175a
  history · · · · · · · · · · · · · · 1:174a-175a
  spearheads · · · · · · · · · · · · · · · 1:175a
  swords · · · · · · · · · · · · · · · · · 1:175a
Brooke, John Mercer · · · · · · 1:175a-175b
  Hamada Hikozō · · · · · · · · · · · · · 3:89a
  Kanrin maru · · · · · · · · · · · · · · 4:151b
Brotherhood of the New Life · · · · · 3:104a
Brother Industries, Ltd · · · · · · · · 1:175b
Brown algae · · · · · · · · · · · · · · · 7:46b
Brown, Nathan · · · · · · · · · · · · · 1:142a
Brown, Samuel Robbins · · · · · · · 1:175b
Brown, Winthrop Gilman · · · · · · · 4:285b
Bruno Taut · · · · · · · · · · · · · · · · 3:10a
Brunton, Richard Henry · · · 1:175b; 2:311a
Brussels Conference · · · · · · 1:175b-176a
Brussels Tariff Nomenclature
  United States (1945-1973) · · · · · · 8:161b
Bryan note · · · · · · · · · · · · · · · 1:176a
B-29 bomber · · · · · · · · · · · · · · 1:176a
  World War II · · · · · · · · · · · · · 8:276a
Bu · 4:193b
Buckwheat, cultivation of · · · · 7:178b-179a
Buddha · · · · · · · · · · · · · · · · · 1:52a
  Amida
  Dainichi ("Great Sun") · · · · 1:176a; 2:64b
  epithet · · · · · · · · · · · · · · · 6:281a-281b
  images · · · · · · · · · · · · 1:201b-203a; 7:67b
  power of · · · · · · · · · · · · · · · · 7:347a
  Shaka · · · · · · · · · · · · · · · · · 1:176a
  Yakushi · · · · · · · · · · · · · · · · 8:285b
"Buddha's-Footprint-Stone-Songs,
  The" · · · · · · · · · · · · · · · · · · 2:137b
Buddha tiles · · · · · · · · · · · 1:176a-176b
Buddhism · 1:176b-180a; 7:122b-123b, 217a
  Asian diffusion · · · · · · · · · · 1:177b-178a
  China · · · · · · · · · · · · · · · · · 1:178a

Southeast · · · · · · · · · · · · · 1:177b–178a
Azuchi Disputation · · · · · · · · 1:126b–127a
bodhisattva · · · · · · · · · · · · · · · · · 1:159b
canon of texts · · · · · · · · · · · · · · · 1:187b
ceremonies
  Gosaie · 8:286a
  incense · 3:284b
  Kōfukuji (place) · · · · · · · · · · · · 8:286a
  Saishōe · 8:286a
  Yakushiji · · · · · · · · · · · · · · · · · · 8:286a
  Yuimae · 8:286a
China and Japan · · · · · · · · · · 1:281b–282a
coexistence with Shintō · · · · · · · · 7:126b
dharma · 2:91b
doctrines
  emptiness · · · · · · · · · · · · 2:212b–213a
  hongaku (primordial enlightenment)
   · 3:221a
  inga · 3:303b
  interdependent origination (engi)
   · 2:217a–217b
  mujō · 5:262a
  satori (awakening; enlightenment) · 7:28b
  this-worldliness · · · · · · · · · · · · · 8:24b
early · 1:176b–177a
  Brahmanism · · · · · · · · · · · · · · · · 1:176b
  doctrine · · · · · · · · · · · · · · · 1:176b–177a
  economic principles · · · · · · · · · · 1:177a
  literature · · · · · · · · · · · · · · · · · · · 1:177a
  rules for religious life · · · · · · · · 1:177a
  sangha · 1:177a
  state theory · · · · · · · · · · · · · · · · 1:177a
education · 2:173a
esoteric (mikkyō) · · · · · · · · · · · 2:231a–231b
financial support · · · · · · · · · · · · · · 6:293a
flower arrangement · · · · · · · · · 2:288a–290a
folk religion · · · · · · · · · · · · · · · · · · 2:298a
fund-raising · · · · · · · · · · · · · · 3:136b–137a
gankake · 3:7b
Good Law
  Tale of Genji · · · · · · · · · · · · · 7:330b–331a
hijiri · 3:136b–137a
holy men · · · · · · · · · · · · · · · · 3:136b–137a
iconography · · · · · · · · · · · · · · · · · · · 7:381a
India and Japan · · · · · · · · · · · · · · · · 3:288a
influence on housing · · · · · · · · 3:243a–243b
inzō · 3:328a
Japanese sects · · · · · · · · · · · · · 1:178a–180a
  characteristics · · · · · · · · · · · · 1:179b–180a
  history · · · · · · · · · · · · · · · · · 1:178a–179a
  introduction · · · · · · · · · · · · · 1:178a–179b
  Jōdo · 4:67a–68a
  Jōdo Shin · · · · · · · · · · · · · · · · · 4:68a–69a
  Nara Buddhism · · · · · · · · · · · · · · 5:332b
  Nichiren sect · · · · · · 1:179a; 5:376b–377a
  present · 1:180a
  Pure Land Buddhism · · · · · · · · · 1:179a;
   6:270a–270b
  Ritsu · 6:332a
  Shingon sect · · 1:178b–179a; 7:113b–115a
  Tendai sect · · · · · · · · · 1:178b; 8:4a–5b
  Yūzū Nembutsu · · · · · · · · · · · · · 8:359b
  Zen Buddhism · · · · · · · · · 1:179a–179b;
   6:318a–320a; 7:233a–234b; 8:370a–374b
Japanese literature · · · · · · · · · 1:180a–182a;
   1:292a–296a; 6:194a
kikajin introduction · · · · · · · · · · · · · 4:205b
lay believers (danka) · · · · · 4:362b; 4:372a;
   8:123a
lay devotional associations · · · · · · · · 4:372a
literature · · · · · 1:292a–295b; 5:26a; 6:194a
monasticism · · · · · · · · · · · · · · · 5:236a–239a
money offerings · · · · · · · · · · · · · · · 5:242a
music · · · · · · · · · · · · · · · · · · · 5:283a–283b
nature · 5:357b
new religions · · · · · · · · · · · 5:366b; 7:224b
Okinawa · 6:85a
oshi · 6:124b

portrait painting · · · · · · · · · · · · · · 6:226b
prayer · 6:233a
priesthood · · · · · · · · · · · · · · · 6:238b–239a
priests. See individual sect
religion · · · · · · · · · · · · · · · · · 6:290b–293b
rites. See Buddhist rites
ritual implements. See Buddhist ritual
elements
rosaries · 1:197a
sculpture. See Buddhist sculpture
setsuwa bungaku · · · · · · · · · · · · · · · 7:72a
Shingaku · 7:112a
Shintoism · · · · · · · · · · · · · · · · 1:179b–180a
shrines. See Shrines
spread · · · · · · · · · · · · · · · · · · 1:177a–177b
  Brahmanism · · · · · · · · · · · · · · · · · 1:177b
  Mahāyāna · · · · · · · · · · · · · · · · · · 1:177b
syncretism · · · · · · · · · · · · · · · 7:289a–290a
temples. See Temples
thought and culture · · · · · · · · · · · · 8:24b
  community-ism vs. universalism · 8:27b
  functionalism and classicism · · 8:28a–29a
  life-centeredness vs. transcendence
   · 8:26b–27a
Tokugawa shogunate · · · · · · · · · · · · 8:53a
tolerance in Japanese religion · · · · · · 8:70b
warrior-monks · · · · · · · · · · · · 8:230b–231a
weddings · 8:239a
women in · · · · · · · · · · · · · · · · 8:256b, 258b
Buddhist architecture · · · · · · 1:182a–184b
bell tower · 1:183a
buildings for monks · · · · · · · · · · · 1:183a
gates and corridor · · · · · · · · · 1:182b–183a
pagoda and principal temple halls
   · 1:182a–182b
storehouse · · · · · · · · · · · · · · · · · · · 1:183a
styles · 1:183a–183b
  Asuka · 1:183a
  daibutsuyō · · · · · · · · · · · · · · · · · · 1:183b
  eclectic · 1:183b
  Karayō · 1:191b
  Tang · 1:183a
  wayō · 1:183a
Sutra repository · · · · · · · · · · · · · · 1:183a
Buddhist art · · · · · · · · · · · · · 1:184b–194b
Daruma · 1:193a
emakimono · · · · · · · · · · · · · · · · · · 1:191a
esoteric · · · · · · · · · · · · · · · · · 1:187b–189a
  architecture · · · · · · · · · · · · · · · · · 1:188a
  Goma ceremony · · · · · · · · · · · · · 1:188a
  Kannon, Eleven-Headed · · · 1:187b, 189a
  mandala · 1:188a
  painting · · · · · · · · · · · · · · · · 1:188b–189a
  Ryōbu Shintō · · · · · · · · · · · · 1:187b–188a
  sculpture · · · · · · · · · · · · · · · 1:188b–189a
  statues, wood · · · · · · · · · · · · · · · 1:189a
  types of buildings · · · · · · · · · · · · 1:188a
Hakuin · 1:193a
Heian-period · · · · · · · · · · · · · · · · · 1:189a
Hōryūji · 1:185a
Kichijōten · · · · · · · · · · · · · · · · · · · 1:185a
latter-day · · · · · · · · · · · · · · · · 1:193a–194b
  painting · · · · · · · · · · · · · · · · 1:193b–194a
  sculpture · · · · · · · · · · · · · · · · · · · 1:194a
Lotus Sutra · · · · · · · · · · · · · · · · 1:186a, 187b
Mahāyāna · · · · · · · · · · · · · · · · 1:184b–187b
  architecture · · · · · · · · · · · · · · · · · 1:185b
  calligraphy · · · · · · · · · · · · · · 1:187a–187b
  emakimono · · · · · · · · · · · · · · 1:186b–187a
  painting · · · · · · · · · · · · · · · · 1:185b–187a
  printing · · · · · · · · · · · · · · · · 1:187a–187b
  sculpture · · · · · · · · · · · · · · · · 1:185b–187a
masks · 1:189b
Minchō · 1:192b
Pure Land · · · · · · · · · · · · · · · · 1:189a–194a
  architecture · · · · · · · · · · · · · · · · · 1:189b
  painting · · · · · · · · · · · · · · · · 1:189b–191a
  sculpture · · · · · · · · · · · · · · · 1:189b–191a

Raigōzu · · · · · · · · · · · 1:190a, 190a–190b
Relic hall (shariden) · · · · · · · · · · · 1:191a
Sanjūsangendō · · · · · · · · · · · · · · · 1:189a
Scroll of Hungry Ghosts · · · · · · · · 1:191a
sculpture. See Buddhist sculpture
Takuma School · · · · · · · · · · · · · · · 1:190a
tapestry · 1:189b
Tosa school · · · · · · · · · · · · · · · · · · 1:193b
Zen · 1:191a–193a
  architecture · · · · · · · · · · · · · 1:191b–192a
  painting · · · · · · · · · · 1:192a–193a, 193a
  portraits · · · · · · · · · · · · · · · · · · · 1:192a
  sculpture · · · · · · · · · · · · · · · 1:192a–193a
  zenga · 1:193a
Buddhist castings · · · · · · · · · · · · · · 6:125a
Buddhist family altar · · · · · · · · · · · 2:307a
Buddhist images · · · · · · · · · · · · · · · · 7:94a
Buddhist rites · · · · · · · · · · · 1:194b–195a
agricultural rites · · · · · · · · · · · · · · 1:194b
esoteric
  Goma ceremony · · · · · · · · · · · · · 1:195a
musical instruments · · · · · · · · 1:195b–196a
nembutsu · · · · · · · · · · · · · · · · · · · 1:194b
pilgrimages · · · · · · · · · · · · · · · · · · 1:194b
Buddhist ritual implements · 1:195a–196b
esoteric Buddhism · · · · · · · · · · · · 1:196a
keman · 1:196b
Pure Land Buddhism · · · · · · · 1:196a–196b
reliquary (sharitō) · · · · · · · · · · · · 1:195a
vajra · 1:196b
Zen · 1:196b
Buddhist rosaries · · · · · · · · · · · · 1:197a
Buddhist sculpture · · · 1:197a–204a; 2:327a
Amida · 1:201a
Ashura · 4:244b
daibutsu · 2:55a
Five Wisdom Kings · · · · · · · · · · · · 1:200b
Fukūkenjaku Kannon · · · · · · · · · · 1:187a
Gakkō, statue of · · · · · · · · · · · · · · 1:198a
Ganjin, statue of · · · · · · · · · · · · · · · · 3:7a
Hakuhō culture · · · · · · · · · · · · · 3:87b–88a
Heian period · · · · · · · · · · · · · 1:198a–199a
historical survey · · · · · · · · · · · 1:197a–199b
iconography and sizes · · · · · · · 1:202b–203a
image types · · · · · · · · · · · · · · · · · · 1:201b
inscriptions inside · · · · · · · · · · · · 1:203b
Jizō · 1:201a, 201a
Jōchō · 1:201a
Kaikei · 1:201a
Kamakura period · · · · · · · · · · · 1:199a–199b
Kuratsukuri no Tori · · · · · · · · · · · 1:197a
materials and construction
  trees · 1:201b
materials and techniques · · · · · 1:200a–202a
  clay figures · · · · · · · · · · · · · · · · · 1:200a
  dry-lacquer statues · · · · · · · · · · · 1:200a
  gilt-bronze Buddhist images · · · · · 1:200a
  Respoussé bronze placques · · · · · 1:201a
  stone sculpture · · · · · · · · · · · 1:200a–201a
  tiles · 1:200b
  wood-core dry-lacquer images
   · 1:200a–200b
  wood sculpture · · · · · · · · · · · 1:201a–201b
Miroku, statue of · · · · · · · · · · · · · 1:197b
Muchaku · 1:186b
Niō · 1:186b
Nyoirin Kannon · · · · · · · · · · · · · · 1:188b
objects inside Buddhist images · · · 1:203b
pre-Buddhist clay figures · · · · · 1:197a–197b
preservation programs · · · · · · · 1:203b–204a
Renge Kokūzō · · · · · · · · · · · · · · · · 1:187a
Rushana · 1:199a
sculptors · · · · · · · · · · · · · · · · 1:199b–200a
  See also Sculptors
Shaka Triad · · · · · · · · · · · · · · · · · · 1:197a
Shikkongōshin, statue of · · · · · · · · 1:198b
Tempyō culture · · · · · · · · · · · · · · · · 8:3b
tools · 1:201b

Unkei · 1:*186b*
Yakushi · · · · · · · · · · · · · · · · · · · 1:*188b*
Yakushi Triad · · · · · · · · · · · · · · 1:*199a*
Budget, national · · · · · · · · · 1:204b-206a
  Diet · 2:95a
  education · · · · · · · · · · · · · · · · · · 1:205b
  Foodstuff Control Special Account · 1:205b
  local allocation tax · · · · · · · 1:205b-206a
  public works · · · · · · · · · · · · · 1:205a-205b
  roads · 6:332b
  social security· · · · · · · · · · · · 1:204b-205a
Budget Bureau · · · · · · · · · · · · · · 5:187b
Budō · · · · · · · · · · · · 3:60b; 5:118b-120a
Budō shoshin shū
  (Introduction to the Way
  of the Warrior)
  · · · · · · · · · · · 武道初心集 · · · · · · · 2:56b
Bugaku · · · · · · · · 舞楽 · · 2:*73a*; 3:1a;
                                  7:22a
  costumes · · · · · · · · · · · · · · · 8:23a-23b
  dance · 3:47b
  masks · · · · · · · · · · · · · · · · 5:126a-126b
  gosechi no mai · · · · · · · · · · · · · · 3:47b
Bugaku zusetsu (music)
  · · · · · · · · · · · · · · 舞楽図説 · · · · · 6:134b
Bugei jūhappan
  · · · · · · · · · · 武芸十八般 · · · · · 1:206a
Bugyō · · · · · · · · · · 奉行 · · · · · 1:206a
  jisha · 4:62b
Buildings Protection Law · · · · · · 4:374a
Bukan · · · · · · · · · · · · 武鑑 · · 1:206a
Buke (age of military houses) · · 6:176b
Buke densō · · 武家伝奏 · 1:206a-206b
Buke giri monogatari
  · · · · · · · · · 武家義理物語 · · · · · 8:144a
Bukehō · · · · · · · · 武家法 · · · · · 1:206b
  Goseibai Shikimoku · · · · · · · · 3:47b-48a
Buke-mono (aspects of
  samurai life) · · · · · 武家物 · · · 8:144a
Buke myōmoku shō
  · · · · · · · · · · · · 武家名目抄 · · · · · 8:358b
Buke nikki · · · 武家日記 · · · · · 4:101b
Buke seiji · · · · · · · · · · · · · · · 8:228a-230b
Buke Shohatto 武家諸法度 · 1:206b-207a;
                         3:187a; 4:85a
  laws · 1:206b
  samurai declassment · · · · · · · · · 4:108b
  Tokugawa Ieyasu · · · · · · · · · · · 8:50b
  Tokugawa shogunate · · · · · · · · · 8:53a
Buki Yushutsu Sangensoku · · · · 1:90a-90b
Bukka Tōsei Rei
  · · · · · · · · · · 物価統制令 · · · · · 6:238b
Bukkenron · · 物権論 · · · · · 7:255b
Bukkyō Daigaku · · · · · · · · · · · · 7:342a
Bukkyōgo daijiten
  · · · · · · · · · · 仏教語大辞典 · · 5:314a-315a
Bukōsan · · · · · · · · 武甲山 · · · · · 1:207a
"Bullet Train" · · · · · · · · · · · 7:116b-119a
Bullfighting · · · · · · · · · · · 1:207a, 251b
Bumbuku chagama
  · · · · · · · · · · · 分福茶釜 · · 1:207a-207b
  tanuki · 7:345a
Bummei Ittōki · 文明一統記 · 1:207b
Bummei Kaika · · 文明開化 3:359a; 5:154a
Bummeiron no gairyaku
  · · · · · · · · · · 文明論之概略 1:207b; 2:368a
  historiography · · · · · · · · · · · · · 3:156a
  kokutai · · · · · · · · · · · · · · · · · · · 4:263a
Bun · · · · · · · · · · · · · · · · 1:207b; 4:123b
Bunchi seigen rei
  · · · · · · · · · · 分地制限令 · · · · · 1:208a
Bunchō. *See* **Tani Bunchō**
Bunchō gadan · · 文晁画談 · · · · · 7:341a
Bundan · · · · · · · · · · · · · · · 1:208a-208b
Bundy, William Putnam · · · · · · · 4:285b
Bungaku jidai · · 文学時代 · · · · · 7:175b
Bungakukai · · · · · · · 文学界·1:208b-209a;
              4:69a, 180a; 6:66a

Kitamura Tōkoku · · · · · · · · · · · 4:227b
Bungakukai group · · · · · · · · · · · · 5:52a
Bungaku no sanjūnen
  (Thirty Years of
  Literature) · 文学の三十年 · · · 8:173b
Bungakuza
  shingeki · · · · · · · · · · · · · · · · · · 7:113a
  Tokugawa Musei · · · · · · · · · · · · 8:52a
Bungei · · · · · · · · · · · 文芸 · · · · 1:209a
Bungei jidai · · · · · 文芸時代 · 1:209a-209b
  founding · 5:19a
  Shinkankaku school · · · · · · · 7:116a-116b
Bungei Kakushin Kai · · · · · · · · · · · 5:19a
Bungei kurabu 文芸倶楽部 1:209b; 7:309b
Bungei Kyōkai · · · 文芸協会 · · · 5:18b
  shingeki · · · · · · · · · · · · · · · · · · 7:112b
Bungei seiki · · 文芸世紀 · · · · · 7:176a
Bungei sensen · · · 文芸戦線 · 1:209b
  leading theoretician · · · · · · · · · · 7:175a
  proletarian literature movement · · · 6:254b
  Senki · 7:66b
  Tanemakuhito · · · · · · · · · 7:340a-340b
Bungei shunjū · · 文芸春秋·1:209b-210a
Bungei Shunjū, Ltd · 1:210a; 2:373a
  Ikejima Shimpei · · · · · · · · · · · · 3:266b
Bungo Channel · · 豊後水道 · 1:210a
Bungo Takada · · · 豊後高田 · 1:210a
Bun'ikō · · · · · · · · · 文意考 · · · 4:129b
Bunjin artists · · · · · · · · · · · 1:210a; 3:28b
  Ike no Taiga · · · · · · · · · · · · · · · · 1:*210b*
  Jūben jūgi (The Ten Conveniences and Ten
  Pleasures) · · · · · · · · · · · · · · · · 1:*210b*
  Okada Beisanjin · · · · · · · · · · · · · 6:77b
  Okada Hankō · · · · · · · · · · · · · · · 6:78a
  Okamoto Toyohiko · · · · · · · · · · · 6:80b
  Tazaki Sōun · · · · · · · · · · · · · · · 7:359a
  Yosa Buson · · · · · · · · · · · · · · · 1:*210b*
Bunjinga · · · · · · · · · 文人画·1:210a-211a;
                              6:154a
  screen and wall painting · · · · · · · · 7:43a
Bunji seiji · · · · · · 文治政治 · 3:189a
Bunka and Bunsei eras
  · · · · · · · · · · 文化文政時代 · 1:211a-211b
  culture and learning · · · · · · · · · 1:211b
  foreign ships · · · · · · · · · · · · · · 1:211b
  shogunate and economy · · · · · · · 1:211b
Bunka Gakuin · · · · · · · · · · · · · · · 4:184a
Bunka Hōsō. *See* **Nippon Cultural**
Broadcasting, Inc
Bunkai hitsuroku (Reading
  Notes) · · · · · · · · · 文会筆録 · · · 8:312a
Bunka shūreishū
  · · · · · · · · · · 文華秀麗集·1:211b-212a;
              2:350b; 4:189a; 5:29b
Bunkazai Hogo Hō · · · · · · · 2:52b-53a
Bunke · 1:218a
Bunkengaku · · · · · 文献学 · · · 1:154a
Bunko · · · · · · · · · · 文庫 · · · · 4:199a
Bunkobon · · · · · · · · · · · · · · · · · · 6:162a
Bunkoku · · · · · · · · · · · 分国 · · · 1:274a
Bunkokuhō · · · · · · · · 分国法 · 1:212a
  bukehō · · · · · · · · · · · · · · · · · · · 1:206b
  Imagawa Kana Mokuroku · · · · · · 3:271b
  kabegaki · · · · · · · · · · · · · · · · · · · 4:90a
  kakun · 4:119a
  Ōuchike Kabegaki · · · · · · · · · · · 6:135b
  Shingen Kahō · · · · · · · · · · · · · · 7:113b
  Yūkike Hatto · · · · · · · · · · · · · · 8:357a
Bunkyō Ward · · · · 文京区 · · 1:212a
Bunkyū Sannen
  Hachigatsu Jūhachinichi no Seihen
  文久三年八月十八日の政変 · · · 2:39a-39b
Bunraku · · · · · · · · 文楽·1:212a-215b;
                2:274a; 8:21b-22a
  costumes · · · · · · · · · · · · · · · 8:23b-24a
  early history · · · · · · · · · · · · 1:213b-214a
  final stage · · · · · · · · · · · · · 1:215a-215b
  Kanadehon chūshingura · · · · · · · 1:*212b*

Kiritake Monjūrō II · · · · · · · · · · 4:222a
  puppeteer · · · · · · · · · · · · · · · · · 1:*213a*
  puppet heads · · · · · · · · · · · · · · 1:*214b*
  Sonezaki shinjū · · · · · · · · · · · · · 1:*212b*
  stage, chanter, and audience · · · · 1:*213a*
  stages of development · · · · · 1:214a-215a
  Takemoto Gidayū I · · · · · · · · · · 7:324b
  theater conventions · · · · · · · 1:212b-213b
  Toyotake Yamashiro no Shōjō · · · · 8:93b
  See also **Jōruri**
Bunroku Keichō no Eki
  (Bunroku Campaign)
  · · · · · · · · 文禄・慶長の役·3:326b-327a
Bunshō sekai · · · 文章世界 4:148b; 7:309b
Bunshoshō · · · · · · · 聞書抄 · · · 7:342b
Bunten · · · · · · · · · · · 文展·1:215b; 8:328a
  Japan Art Academy · · · · · · · · · · · 4:10b
  modern painting · · · · · · · · · · · · 6:158a
Bun'ya no Yasuhide
  · · · · · · · · · · · · · 文屋康秀 · · · 4:254b
Buraiha writers · · · · · · · · · · · · · 6:230b
"Buraikan" · · · · · · · · · 無頼漢 · · 7:122b
Burakumin · · · · · · 1:216a-217a, 324a; 7:217a
  minorities · · · · · · · · · · · · · · · · · 5:195a
Bureaucracy · · 1:217a-221a; 6:214a; 7:214a
  administrative guidance · · · · · · · 1:220b
  Administrative Management Agency 1:14a
  Cabinet Orders · · · · · · · · · · · · · 1:220b
  competition · · · · · · · · · · · · · · · · 1:220a
  Constitution of 1947 · · · · · · · · · 2:11b-12a
  coordination · · · · · · · · · · · · · · · 1:220a
  court rank (ikai) · · · · · · · · · · · · · 2:39b
  executive branch (government) · 3:55b-56a
  gakubatsu · · · · · · · · · · · · · · · · · · 3:3b-4a
  history and development · · · · · 1:217a-220a
  Imperial Ordinances · · · · · · · · · · 1:218a
  Meiji Constitution · · · · · · · · · · · 1:217b
  ministries · · · · · · · · · · · · · · 1:218b-219a
  national civil service system · 1:219b-220a
  politics · · · · · · · · · · · · · · · 1:220a-220b
  post-World War I return · · · · 3:199b-200a
  premodern · · · · · · · · · · · · · 1:217a-217b
  present day · · · · · · · · · · · · · 1:218b-219a
  Privy Council · · · · · · · · · · · · · · 1:217b
  public policy formation · · · · · 1:220a-220b
  public unionization · · · · · · · · · · 1:220b
  reform · · · · · · · · · · · · · · · · 1:220b-221a
  strikes · · · · · · · · · · · · · · · · · · · 1:220b
Bureaucrats, ritsuryō system · 7:150b-151a
  court ranks · · · · · · · · · · · · · · 2:39b-41a
"Bureaucrats' parties" · · · · · · · · · 6:321b
Bureau of Archivists · · · · · · · · · · 4:315b
Bureau of Books · · · · · · · · · · 8:381a-381b
Bureau of Poetry · · · · · · · · · · · · · · 4:1b
Bureau of Yin and Yang · · · · · 6:113a-113b
Buri · 8:323b
Burials, prehistoric · · · · · · · · 4:244a-246b;
                      6:235a-235b
  dolmen (shisekibo) · · · · · · · · 6:235a-235b
  flexed (kussō) · · · · · · · · · · · · · · 6:235a
  hōkei shūkōbo ("square, ditched graves")
  · 6:235b
  jar (kamekan) · · · · · · · · · · · · · · 6:235a
  shell mounds · · · · · · · · · · · · · · · 7:83a
Burma and Japan · · · · · · · 1:221a-221b
  Aung San · · · · · · · · · · · · · · · · · 1:116b
  Ba Maw · · · · · · · · · · · · · · · · · · 1:135b
Burners, hibachi · · · · · · · · · 3:128b-129a
Bushi ("military gentry")
  · · · · · · · · · · · · · · · 武士 · · · · · 7:7a
Bushidan · · · · · · · · · 武士団 · 1:221b
  ienoko and rōtō · · · · · · · · · · · · · 3:261a
  Kammu Heishi · · · · · · · · · · · · · 7:299a
  kokufu · · · · · · · · · · · · · · · · · · · 4:257a
  myōshu · · · · · · · · · · · · · · · · · · · 5:291b
  samurai · 7:7a
  Seiwa Genji · · · · · · · · · · · · · · · 5:177b
  shōen · 7:155a

sōryō system · · · · · · · · · · · · · · · 7:232a
yorioya and yoriko · · · · · · · · · · 8:338b
Bushidō · · · 1:20a, 221b-223b; 4:85a; 8:290a
early warrior society · · · · · · · · · 1:222a
Hagakure · · · · · · · · · · · · · · · · **3**:75a
legacy · · · · · · · · · · · · · · · 1:223a-223b
samurai · · · · · · · · · · · · · · · · · · **7**:8a
tea ceremony · · · · · · · · · · · · · 4:159a
transition to Tokugawa · · · 1:222a-223a
Bushū · · · · · · · · · · · 武州 · · · 5:275a-275b
Bush warbler [(uguisu) *Cettia diphone*]
· 1:223b-224a

Business
and government · · · · · · · · · · · · 5:92b
code of ethics · · · · · · · · · 1:302b-303a
Commercial Code · · · · · · · 1:337b-339a
concentration · · · · · · · · · · · · · 1:224a
consumer movement · · · · · · 2:14a-15b
contemporary economy · · · · · 2:158b-159a
cooperative associations (kyōdō kumiai)
· 2:25b
corporate culture · · · · · · · · · 2:26a-28b
corporate history · · · · · · · · · 2:29b-33b
corporations · · · · · · · · · · · · · 2:34b-37a
cycles · · · · · · · · · · · · · · · 1:224a-224b
funding · · · · · · · · · · · · · · · · 2:161a
practices. *See* Business practices
post–World War II, one-set principle
· 6:106a
stability laws · · · · · · · · · · · · · 7:205b
wholesale and retail · · · · · · · · 1:224b
Business Accounting Council (BAC) **1**:8b
Business and Professional Women's
Clubs, Federation of · · · · · · · · 8:263b
Business guidance laws · · · · · · · · 7:205b
Business leaders
Adachi Tadashi · · · · · · · · · · · · 1:11a
Aikawa Yoshisuke · · · · · · · · · · 1:33b
Asabuki Eiji · · · · · · · · · · · 1:91b-92a
Asano Sōichirō · · · · · · · · · 1:95b-96a
Ashihara Yoshishige · · · · · · · · · 1:98a
Dan Takuma · · · · · · · · · · · · · 2:77b
Dokō Toshio · · · · · · · · · · · · · 2:127b
Fujii Heigo · · · · · · · · · · · · · · 2:343b
Fujita Denzaburō · · · · · · · · · · 2:346a
Fujiwara Ginjirō · · · · · · · · · · · 2:348b
Fujiyama Aiichirō · · · · · · · · · · 2:359a
Fujiyama Raita · · · · · · · · · · · · 2:359a
Furukawa Ichibei · · · · · · · 2:372b-373a
Gō Seinosuke · · · · · · · · · · · · · 3:48a
Gotō Keita · · · · · · · · · · · · · · · 3:53a
Hara Yasusaburō · · · · · · · · · · · 3:103b
Hattori Kintarō · · · · · · · · · · · · 3:113b
Hibi Ōsuke · · · · · · · · · · · · · · 3:129a
Hiratsuka Tsunejirō · · · · · · · · · 3:146a
Hirose Saihei · · · · · · · · · · · · · 3:147b
Honda Sōichirō · · · · · · · · · · · · 3:219b
Horie Shigeo · · · · · · · · · · · · · 3:227b
Hori Kyūsaku · · · · · · · · · · · · · 3:228a
Hotta Shōzō · · · · · · · · · · · · · · 3:239b
Ibuka Masaru · · · · · · · · · · · · · 3:254a
Ichimura Kiyoshi · · · · · · · · · · · 3:258a
Idemitsu Sazō · · · · · · · · · · · · · 3:259a
Ikeda Shigeaki · · · · · · · · · · · · 3:266a
Inayama Yoshihiro · · · · · · · · · · 3:284a
Ishibashi Shōjirō · · · · · · · · · · · 3:339a
Ishida Taizō · · · · · · · · · · · · · · 3:340b
Ishikawa Ichirō · · · · · · · · · · · · 3:342a
Ishizaka Taizō · · · · · · · · · 3:347a; 8:304b
Iwasaki Koyata · · · · · 3:361b-362a; 8:289a
Kagami Kenkichi · · · · · · · · · · · 4:102b
Kaneko Naokichi · · · · · · · · · · · 4:139a
Katō Takeo · · · · · · · · · · · · · · 4:170b
Kawakami Gen'ichi · · · · · · · · · · 4:180b
Kikawada Kazutaka · · · · · · · · · · 4:205b
Kobayashi Ataru · · · · · · · · · · · 8:304b
Kobayashi Ichizō · · · · · · · · · · · 4:236b
Kuhara Fusanosuke · · · · · · 4:302b-303a

Kurata Chikara · · · · · · · · · 4:311b-312a
Magoshi Kyōhei · · · · · · · · · · · · 5:83b
Masuda Takashi · · · · · · · · · 5:129b-130a
Matsunaga Yasuzaemon · · · · · · · 5:139a
Matsushita Kōnosuke · · · · · · · · · 5:141a
Minomura Rizaemon · · · · · · · · · 5:195a
Miyajima Seijirō · · · · · · · · · · · 5:218a
Mizuno Shigeo · · · · · · · · · · · · 5:226b
Mogi Keizaburō · · · · · · · · · · · · 5:233b
Mori Nobuteru · · · · · · · · · · · · 5:251b
Morita Akio · · · · · · · · · · · · · · 5:253a
Motoyama Hikoichi · · · · · · · · · · 5:259a
Mukai Tadaharu · · · · · · · · · · · · 5:262a
Murata Shōzō · · · · · · · · · · · · · 5:270a
Mutō Sanji · · · · · · · · · · · · · · · 5:288a
Nagano Shigeo · · · · · · · · · · · · 5:303a
Nakajima Chikuhei · · · · · · · · · · 5:313b
Nakamigawa Hikojirō · · · · · · 5:314a-314b
Nakano Tomonori · · · · · · · · · · · 5:317a
Nakayama Sohei · · · · · · · · · 5:319a-319b
Nezu Kaichirō · · · · · · · · · · 5:373b-374a
Noguchi Shitagau · · · · · · · · · · · 6:32a
Odaira Namihei · · · · · · · · · · · · 6:61a
Ogura Masatsune · · · · · · · · · · · 6:71a
Ōhara Magosaburō · · · · · · · · · · 6:73b
Ōhara Sōichirō · · · · · · · · · · · · 6:73b
Okauchi Hideo · · · · · · · · · · · 6:81a-81b
Ōkawa Heizaburō · · · · · · · · · · · 6:81b
Ōkura Kihachirō · · · · · · · · · · · · 6:98a
Saji Keizō · · · · · · · · · · · · · · · 6:375a
Sakurada Takeshi · · · · · · · · · · · · 7:4b
Seki Hironao · · · · · · · · · · · · · · 7:56b
Shibusawa Eiichi · · · · · · · · · 7:86a-86b
Shibusawa Keizō · · · · · · · · · · · · 7:86b
Shōda Heigorō · · · · · · · · · · · · · 7:154a
Shōda Hidesaburō · · · · · · · · · · · 7:154a
Shōriki Matsutarō · · · · · · · · · · · 7:167a
Sugi Michisuke · · · · · · · · · · · · 7:257b
Suzuki Masaya · · · · · · · · · · · · 7:282b
Takahata Seiichi · · · · · · · · · · · · 7:313b
Tashiro Shigeki · · · · · · · · · · · · 7:347b
Torii Shinjirō · · · · · · · · · · · · · · 8:79b
Tsutsumi Yasujirō · · · · · · · · · · · 8:119a
Uemura Kōgorō · · · · · · · · · · · · 8:127b
Watanabe Tetsuzō · · · · · · · · · · · 8:236b
Yamamoto Jōtarō · · · · · · · · 8:298a-298b
Yamamoto Tamesaburō · · · · · · · · 8:299b
Yamashita Tarō · · · · · · · · · · · · 8:304b
Yano Tsuneta · · · · · · · · · · · · · 8:316a
Yasukawa Daigorō · · · · · · · · · · 8:319a
Yoshida Tadao · · · · · · · · · · · · 8:346a
Business machines · · · · · · · · · · · · 5:359a
Businessmen's Association · · · · · · · · 4:64a
Business practices
amakudari · · · · · · · · · · · · · · · · 1:49b
bankruptcy · · · · · · · · · · · · · · · 1:141a
pricing · · · · · · · · · · · · · · · · · · 1:11b
unfair · · · · · · · · · · · · · · · · · 1:67a-67b
abuse of economic power · · · · 1:67a-67b
coercion and inducement · · · · · 1:67a
definition · · · · · · · · · · · · · · · 1:67a
discriminatory acts · · · · · · · · · 1:67a
price settings · · · · · · · · · · · · 1:67a
restrictive agreements · · · · · · · 1:67a
Business stability laws · · · · · · · · · 7:205b
Buson · · · · · · · · · · 蕪村 · 1:*144b*, 211a,
224b-225a, 181b; 5:12a, 16a; 6:297b, 298b,
299b; 7:5b, 17b
haibun · · · · · · · · · · · · · · · · · · 3:78a
Bussangaku · · · · · · · 物産学 · · 1:225a
Bussan kaisho · · · 物産会所 · · 4:262a
Bussho · · · · · · · 仏所 · 1:225a-225b
founder · · · · · · · · · · · · · · · · · 1:303b
Bussokuseki · · · · · 仏足石 · · 1:225b
Bussokuseki no uta or "Buddha's
Foot-Stone Poem" · · · · · · · · · · 8:202b
Butsuda · · · · · · · · · · · · · · · · · · 1:176a
Butsudan · · · · · · · · · · · · 1:160b, 225b

Butsugu · · · · · · · · · · · · · · 1:195a-196b
*Butsumo dai kujaku myōō
kyō* · · · 佛母題孔雀明王経 · · 6:248a
Butsurui shōko · · 物類称呼 · · · 1:225b
Japanese dialects · · · · · · · · · · · 4:31b
Butterbur · · · · · · · · · · · · · · · · 2:360a
Butterflies [(chō) order Lepidoptera]
· 1:225b-226a
Buyaku · · · · · · · · · 夫役 · 1:226a-226b
Buyō (dance) · · · · · · · · · · · · · · · 8:63b
Buyō Inshi · · · · · · · 武陽陰士 · · 7:55b
Buzen · · · · · · · · · · 豊前 · · · 1:226b
Byakkotai · · · · · · · · 白虎隊 · · · 1:38b, 226b
Iimoriyama · · · · · · · · · · · · · · · 3:262b
"Byakuya" · · · · · · · · · 白夜 · · · 7:176a
Byōbu · · · · · · · · · · · · 2:371a; 7:41a-43b
Byōbu-e (paintings on screens) · · · 7:41b
Byōbugaura · · · · · 屏風ケ浦 · · 1:226b-227a
Byōdōin · · · · · · · · 平等院 · · 1:227a-227b;
2:358a; 7:41b
door panels · · · · · · · · · · · · · · 7:328a
gardens · · · · · · · · · · · · · · · · · · 3:9a
Phoenix Hall (Hōōdō) · · · 1:*226b*; 7:328a
raigōzu · · · · · · · · · · · · · · · · · 6:277a
By the Lake · · · · · · · · · · · · · · · 6:*156b*

C

Cabinet. *See* **Prime minister and
cabinet**
Cabinet Information Bureau · · · · · · 2:339a;
7:176a
Cabinet Law · · · · · · · · · · · 1:13a; 2:6b
Cabinet Library · · · · · · · · · · · · 1:229a
National Archives · · · · · · · · 5:336a-336b
Cabinet order · · · · · · · · · · · · · 1:229a
Cabinet Order concerning the Definition
of Nuclear Raw Materials of 1957
· 1:114b
Cable television · · · · · · · · · · · · 1:229a
Cabral, Francisco · · · · · · · · · 1:229a-229b
Cachon, Mermet de · · · · · · · · · · 1:229b
Cadastral register (Ōtabumi). *See*
Census
Cai E (Ts'ai O) · · · · · · · · · · · · 1:229b
Cairo Conference · · · · · · · · 1:229b, 290a
Taiwan · · · · · · · · · · · · · · · · · 7:309a
Calendar, dates, and time · · 1:229b-232b;
2:258a, 259a-259b, 299a
annual calendar · · · · · · · · · · · · 2:205a
festivals · · · · · · · · · · · · · · 2:258a-262a
Japanese, "National Era" · · · · · · 1:232a
jikkan jūnishi · · · · · · · · · · · · · · 4:57a
Jingūreki (Ise Shrine Calendar) · · 1:*231a*
months · · · · · · · · · · · · · · 1:232a-232b
nengō · · · · · · · · · · · 1:231b-232a; 6:174b
old civil · · · · · · · · · · · · · · 1:231a-231b
old solar · · · · · · · · · · · · · · · · 1:230b
periodization · · · · · · · · · · · · · · 6:175a
reign years · · · · · · · · · · · · · · · 1:232a
sexagenary cycle · · · · · · · · · · · 1:232a
solar and lunar · · · · · · · · · 1:230a-230b
times of day · · · · · · · · · · · · · · 1:232b
Calico · 7:21a
Calligraphers
Fujiwara no Sukemasa · · · · · · · · 2:355a
Fujiwara no Yukinari · · · · · · · · · 2:358b
Gion Nankai · · · · · · · · · · · · · · 3:34a
Gyokuen Bompō · · · · · · · · · 3:71a-71b

Hakuin · 3:88a
Hon'ami Kōetsu · · · · · · · · · · · · · · · · 3:218b
Hosoi Kōtaku · · · · · · · · · · · · · · · · · · 3:236a
Ichikawa Beian · · · · · · · · · · · · · · · · · 3:256b
Ike no Taiga · · · · · · · · · · · · · · · · · · · 3:267a
Ikkyū · · · · · · · · · · · · · · · · · · · 3:269b–270a
Jakugon · 4:1a–1b
Kang Hŭi-an · · · · · · · · · · · · · · · · · · · 8:325a
Kitao Shigemasa · · · · · · · · · · · · · · · · 4:228b
Konoe Iehiro · · · · · · · · · · · · · · · · · · · 4:273b
Konoe Nobutada · · · · · · · · · · · · · · · · 4:273b
Kūkai · 1:187b
Maki Ryōko · · · · · · · · · · · · · · · · · 5:87a–87b
Matsumura Goshun · · · · · · · · · · · · · · 5:138a
Miyamoto Musashi · · · · · · · · · · · · · · 5:220a
Nakamura Fusetsu · · · · · · · · · · · · · · 5:314a
Onoe Saishū · · · · · · · · · · · · · · · · · · · 6:110a
Ono no Tōfū · · · · · · · · · · · · · · · · · · · 6:111b
Ōtagaki Rengetsu · · · · · · · · · · · · · · · 6:128b
Ryōkan · 6:352a
Saichō · 1:187b
Sengai Gibon · · · · · · · · · · · · · · · · · · · 7:63b
Shōkadō Shōjō · · · · · · · · · · · · · · · · · 7:163a
Takuan Sōhō · · · · · · · · · · · · · · · · · · · 7:237b
Tesshū Tokusai · · · · · · · · · · · · · · · · · 8:16a
Calligraphy · · · · · · · · · 1:232b–236b; 2:358b
Azuchi-Momoyama period · · · · · · · · · 1:236a
bokuseki · · · · · · · · · · · · · 1:192b, 235b–236a
Chinese · · · · · · · · · · 1:283a; 4:142b; 7:170a
diplomatics · 2:97b
early history · · · · · · · · · · · · · · 1:233b–234a
Edo period · 1:236a
education · 2:172b
general description · · · · · · · · · 1:232b–233b
aim · 1:232b
Chinese-character scripts · · · · · · · 1:233b
connoisseurship and collection
activities · · · · · · · · · · · · · · · · · · · 1:233b
history · · · · · · · · · · · · · · · · · 1:232b–233b
implements · · · · · · · · · · · · · · · · · · 1:233b
Heian period · · · · · · · · · · · · · · 1:234a–235b
Hosshōji school · · · · · · · · · · · · · · · 1:236a
Kokinshū poems · · · · · · · · · · · · · · 1:234b
Kōzei style · · · · · · · · · · · · · · 1:235b–236a
Kūkai · 1:234a
Saga, Emperor · · · · · · · · · · · · · · · 1:234a
Sampitsu · · · · · · · · · · · · · · · · · · · 1:234a
Sanseki · · · · · · · · · · · · · · · · 1:234a–234b
Tachibana no Hayanari · · · · · · · · · 1:234a
wayō trend · · · · · · · · · · · · · · 1:234b–235b
implements · *1:233a*
ink painting · · · · · · · · · · · · · · · · · · · 3:305b
"ink traces" · · · · · · · · · · · · · · · · · · · 1:192b
kaisho · 7:170a
Kamakura and Muromachi periods 1:235b
Chinese Song calligraphy · · · · · · · 1:235b
Fujiwara no Sadaie · · · · · · · · · · · · 1:235b
Fujiwara no Toshinari · · · · · · · · · · 1:235b
Sesonji school · · · · · · · · · · · · · · · 1:235b
Sugawara no Michizane · · · · · · · · 1:235b
Kantei style · · · · · · · · · · · · · · · · · · · 4:153a
kinki shoga · · · · · · · · · · · · · · · · · · · 4:213b
Mahāyāna Buddhist · · · · · · · · 1:187a–187b
daizōkyō · · · · · · · · · · · · · · · · · · · 1:187b
issaikyō · 1:187b
minchōtai · 7:170a
museums · 5:280a
new Chinese influences · · · · · · · · · · 1:236a
script style, Chinese · · · · · · · · · · · · 7:170a
seichōtai · 7:170a
sōchōtai · 7:170a
style
Ashide · 1:97b
Western-style painting · · · · · · · · · · 8:328a
Calligraphy Museum · · · · · · · · · · · · · 5:314b
Calpico · 1:236b
Calpis · 7:220b
Calpis Food Industry Co, Ltd · · · · · 1:236b

Cambodia and Japan · · · · · · · · · · · 1:236b
refugees · 6:286a
Camellias [(tsubaki) *Camellia* spp.]
· · · · · · · · · · · · · · · · · 1:236b–237a; 2:326b
Cameras · 6:233b
Camphor tree [(kusunoki) *Cinnamomum
camphora*] · · · · · · · · · · · 1:237a; 2:326b
Canada and Japan · · · · · · · · · 1:237b–238a
Japanese immigrants · · · · · · · 1:238b–239b
post-1949 · · · · · · · · · · · · · · · · · · 1:239b
1877-1941 · · · · · · · · · · · · · · · · · · 1:238b
1941-1949 · · · · · · · · · · · · · · 1:238b–239a
Japanese studies · · · · · · · · · · · · · · · 4:42a
postwar relations · · · · · · · · · · 1:237b–238a
prewar relations · · · · · · · · · · · · · · · 1:237b
relations today · · · · · · · · · · · · · · · · 1:238a
Canals
Aichi · 1:32b
Asaka · · · · · · · · · · · · · · · · · · · 1:94a–94b
Biwako · 1:157b
Hakone · 3:86a
Meiji · 5:153a
Minumadai · · · · · · · · · · · · · · · · · · · 5:198a
Takasegawa · · · · · · · · · · · · · · · · · · 7:318b
Teizambori · · · · · · · · · · · · · · · · · · · 7:377a
Toyogawa · 8:90b
Cancer, medical research · · · · 5:151b–152a
Candles · 5:9a
Cannibalism · · · · · · · · · · · · · · · · · · · 7:323b
Canon, Inc. · · · · · · · · · · · · · · · · · · · 1:239b
Cant. *See* Ingo
Cao Rulin (Ts'ao Ju-lin) · · · · · · · · · 1:239b
Capacity to act · · · · · · · · · · · 1:239b–240a
Capacity to enjoy rights · · · · · · · · · 1:240a
Capes
Ashizurimisaki · · · · · · · · · · · · · · · · 1:102a
Daiōzaki · 2:66b
Echizemmisaki · · · · · · · · · · · · · · · · 2:144a
Erimomisaki · · · · · · · · · · · · · · · · · · 2:230b
Hinomisaki · · · · · · · · · · · · · · · · · · · 3:140b
Inubōzaki · 3:325b
Iragomisaki · · · · · · · · · · · · · · · · · · 3:329b
Irōzaki · 3:336a
Murotozaki · · · · · · · · · · · · · · · · · · · 5:274b
Nagasakibana · · · · · · · · · · · · · · · · · 5:304a
Nosappumisaki · · · · · · · · · · · · · · · · 6:40b
Noshappumisaki · · · · · · · · · · · · · · · 6:41a
Notsukezaki · · · · · · · · · · · · · · · · · · 6:41b
Omaezaki · 6:100b
Ōmazaki · 6:100b
Satamisaki · 7:25b
Shionomisaki · · · · · · · · · · · · · · · · · 7:141a
Sōyamisaki · · · · · · · · · · · · · · · · · · · 7:239a
Tappizaki · 7:346a
Toimisaki · 8:38a
Capital
foreign · 2:315b
industrial funds · · · · · · · · · · · 3:291b–292a
Capital formation · · · · · · · · · 1:240a–242a
developments in 1970s · · · · · · · · · · 1:242a
general description · · · · · · · · · 1:240a–241a
historical and international
comparisons · · · · · · · · · · · · · 1:241a–241b
production and welfare · · · · · · · · · · 1:241b
saving · 1:241a
Capitalism
debate · · · · · · · · · · · · · · · · · · · 5:382–383b
"Lectures on the History of the
Development of
Japanese Capitalism" · · · · · · · · · · 5:382b
Capitalism, Japanese. *See* **Nihon shihon
shugi ronsō**
Capital-liability ratio · · · · · · · · · · · · 1:243b
Capital markets · · · · · · 1:242a–243a; 2:35a,
276a–276b
banks and bond market · · · · · · · · · 1:242b
equity market · · · · · · · · · · · · · · · · · 1:242b
internationalization · · · · · · · · · · · · 1:243a

Japanese · 1:242a
Capital of the Tycoon · · · · · · · · · · · · 1:46a
Capital Outflow Prevention Law · · · 2:314b
Capital Provinces · · · · · · · · · · · 4:211b–212a
Capital punishment · · · 1:243a–243b; 6:172b
Capital Region Development
Commission · · · · · · · · · · · · · · · · · · 8:180b
Capital Region Development Plan · 8:180b
Capital stock · · · · · · · · · · · · · · 2:160a–160b
Capital structure · · · · · · · · · · · · · · · 1:243b
Capron, Horace · · · · · · · · · · · 1:243b; 2:311a
Caraway, Paul Wyatt · · · · · · · · 1:243b–244a
Card games · 4:381b
*Cardinal Principles of the National Entity
of Japan* · 4:264a
Career-long employment · · · · 2:210b–211a;
8:6a
Caretaker · 6:347a
Carp [(koi) *Cyprinus carpio*] 1:244a; 2:26a,
281b
Carpenters' tools · · · · · · · · · · 1:244a–245a
Carriage · 6:301a
Carrying poles. *See* **Tembimbō**
Cartels · · · · · · · 1:66b, 245a; 2:32a–32b, 324b
industrial organization · · · · · · 3:295b–296a
international · · · · · · · · · · · · · · · · 1:66b–67a
legal · · · · · · · · · · · · · · · · · · · 3:295b–296a
administrative guidance · · · · · 3:295b–296a
depression · · · · · · · · · · · · · · · · · · · 3:296a
private government control over · · · 4:370b
Cary, Otis · · · · · · · · · · · · · · · · 1:245a–245b
Casio Computer Co, Ltd · · · · 1:245b; 7:80a
Caste system · · · · · · · · · · · · · · · · · · · 6:324b
Castellan · 4:66b
"Castle culture" · · · · · · · · · · · · · · · · · 3:178a
Castles · · · · · · · · · · · · · · · · · · 1:245b–249b
ancient fortifications · · · · · · · · 1:245b–246b
grid-pattern city · · · · · · · · · · · 1:245b–246a
mountain fortress · · · · · · · · · · · · · · 1:246a
palisade · 1:246b
Azuchi-Momoyama and Edo periods
· · · · · · · · · · · · · · · · · · 1:247b–248a; 2:170a
decline of castle · · · · · · · · · · · · · · · 1:248a
rise of castle · · · · · · · · · · · · · · · · · 1:248a
building techniques and design
· · · · · · · · · · · · · · · · · 1:248a–249a; 2:279a
Fushimi · 2:375a
gates · 3:13a
Himeji · · · · · · · · · · · · · · · · · · 1:247*a*; 3:139a
Itojō · 3:354b
Matsumoto · · · · · · · · · · · · · · · · · · · 5:137b
medieval · · · · · · · · · · · · · · · · · 1:246b–247b
mountain fort · · · · · · · · · · · · · 1:246b–247b
plain castle · · · · · · · · · · · · · · · · · · 1:247b
museums · 5:278b
Nagoya · · · · · · · · · · · · · · · · · · 5:309a–309b
Ōsaka · · · · · · · · · · · · · · · · · · · 6:120a–120b
remains · 1:248b
Tagajō · 7:294a
warfare · 2:266a
Castle towns (jōka machi) · · · · · · 1:131a,
249a–249b; 2:266b
chōnin · 1:301a
development · · · · · · · · · · · · · · · · · · 1:248a
economy · 2:149b
map · *2:62a–62b*
premodern economy · · · · · · · · · · · · 2:148b
samurai · 4:194a
urbanization · · · · · · · · · · · · · · · · · · 8:176a
urban life · 8:177b
urban planning · · · · · · · · · · · · · · · · 8:179b
warrior government · · · · · · · · · · · · · 8:230a
"Catching a Catfish with a Gourd"
· 4:77b
Catfishes [(namazu) family Siluridae]
· 1:249b
Cathode-ray tube · · · · · · · · · · · · · · · 2:192a

Catholic Church. *See* **Christianity**
Catholicism. *See* **Christianity**
Catholic missionaries, modern
·········· 1:249b–251a; **4:**52a
  charitable and social welfare institutions
·········· 1:250b
  contemplatives ·········· 1:250b–251a
  current ·········· 1:250b
  educational institutions ·········· 1:250a
  Kōlbe, Maxmilian ·········· 1:250b
  origins ·········· 1:249b–250a
  scholars ·········· 1:250a–250b
Cats [(neko) *Felis catus*] ·········· 1:251a
  mythology ·········· **5:**296b
  Utagawa Kuniyoshi ·········· 1:*251a*
Cattle (ushi) ·········· 1:251a–251b
Cattle production ·········· 1:28b
CATV (Community Antenna Television)
·········· 1:229a
Caudill, William ·········· **4:**39b
Caves, paleolithic ·········· **6:**159b–160a
Cedar, Japanese. *See* **Sugi**
Celebrations. *See* **Ceremonies; Festivals**
Celestial beings, mythology ·· **5:**295a–295b
Celestial physics ·········· 1:104b
Cement industry ·········· 1:251b
Censorship ·········· 1:251b–255a
  early Shōwa period
    books ·········· 1:253a–253b
    newspapers ·········· 1:253a
    political and social movements ·· 1:253a
  Edo period ·········· 1:251b–252a
    Christian writings ·········· 1:251b
    sexual materials ·········· 1:252a
    shogunal government and official
      ideology ·········· 1:252a
    Tokugawa Ieyasu and Tokugawa
      family ·········· 1:251b–252a
  films ·········· **2:**339a
  freedom of speech ·········· **2:**338a
  freedom of speech, regulation of
·········· **2:**338a–338b
  Ienaga textbook review case ······· **3:**261a
  laws ·········· **2:**338b
  literary societies ·········· 1:208b
  Meiji period ·········· 1:252a–252b
    freedom of speech ·········· 1:252a–252b
    Libel Law of 1875 ·········· 1:252a–252b
    newspapers ·········· 1:252a
    prepublication ·········· 1:252b
    Press Law of 1909 ·········· **6:**236a
    Press Ordinance of 1875 (Shimbunshi
      Jōrei) ·········· 1:252b
    Publication Law of 1893 (Shuppan Hō)
·········· **6:**262b
    Publication Ordinance of 1869 ··· 1:252a
    Publication Ordinance Penalties
      (Shuppan Jōrei Bassoku) ·········· 1:252b
    socialism ·········· 1:252b
  Motion Picture Code Committee ·· **5:**256b
  newspapers and other publications
·········· **2:**338b–339a
  Occupation period ·········· 1:254a–254b
    China and Soviet Union ·········· 1:254b
    elimination of censorships procedures
·········· 1:254a
    Occupation Press Code ·········· 1:254a
    writings censored ·········· 1:254b
  Ōsaka Asahi Hikka Incident ······· **6:**120a
  post-Occupation period ·········· 1:254b–255a
    citizen organizations ·········· 1:255a
    Constitution of 1947 ·········· 1:254b
    invasion of privacy ·········· 1:255a
    obscenity and Supreme Court
·········· 1:254b–255a
    political pressure ·········· 1:255a
    self-censorship codes ····· 1:254b–255a

Subversive Activities Prevention Law
·········· **7:**254a–254b
  textbook authorization ·········· 1:255a
  radio broadcasting ·········· **2:**339a
    Broadcasting Law of 1950 ·········· 1:173b
  Taishō period ·········· 1:252b–253a
    magazines ·········· 1:252b
    newspapers ·········· 1:252b
    Peace Preservation Law of 1925 ·· 1:253a
  War period ·········· 1:253b–254a
    National Mobilization Law of 1941
·········· 1:253b
    Nihon Shuppankai (Japan Publishers
      Association) ·········· 1:253b
    penalties ·········· 1:253b
    Publications Control Committee · 1:253b
    social thought and history ·· 1:253b–254a
Census ······ 1:255a–255b; **2:**107a; **6:**223b
  ritsuryō system ·········· **6:**330a
Census registration ·········· **4:**60b–61a
  ritsuryō system ·········· **6:**324a
Center for Archaeological Operations
·········· **5:**333b
Center for Japanese-Brazilian Studies
·········· **5:**317b
Central America
  diplomatic relations ·········· **3:**323a–323b
  Japanese studies ·········· **4:**45a
  trade ·········· **3:**323a–323b
Central Council for Education ·· 1:51a,
255b; **5:**254b
Central Council on Youth Problems
·········· 1:255a
Central East Atlantic Fisheries
  Commission ·········· **2:**283a
Central Eugenic Protection Council
·········· **2:**234b
Central Finance Corporation for
  Commercial and Industrial
  Cooperatives ·········· **7:**204b
Central Glass Co, Ltd ·········· 1:255b–256a
Central Labor Relations Commission
  (Chūō Rōdō Iinkai) 1:218b, 256a; **4:**358b;
7:189b, 255b
  Ōta Kaoru ·········· **6:**129a
  strike injunctions ·········· **4:**352a
Central West Atlantic Fisheries
  Commission ·········· **2:**283a
Centro Diffusione Origami ·········· **6:**118b
Ceramic bowl ·········· **7:***168b*
Ceramic industries
  NGK Insulators, Ltd ·········· **5:**374a
  Noritake Co, Ltd ·········· **6:**37b–38a
  Tōtō, Ltd ·········· **8:**85b
Ceramics ·········· 1:256a–265b
  Agano ware ·········· 1:20b
  Aizu Hongō ware ·········· 1:38b
  Arita ware ·········· 1:85b, *260b*
  ash-glazed (shirashi) · 1:261b–262a; **7:**71a
    Chinese influence ·········· 1:262a
    kilns ·········· 1:262a
    Sue ware ·········· 1:261b
  Banko ware ·········· 1:141a
  Bizan ware ·········· 1:158a–259a
  Bizen ware jar ·········· 1:*259a*
  design techniques ·········· **7:**266b
  Echizen ware ·········· **2:**144a
  Edo period ·········· 1:263b–264a
    decline and resurgence ·········· 1:264a
    decorated wares ·········· 1:263b
    general ·········· 1:263b
    Korean noborigama (climbing kiln)
·········· 1:263b
    Rimpa ·········· 1:264a
    utilitarian wares ·········· 1:263b
  folk craft ·········· **2:**295b–296a
  furniture material, traditional ····· **2:**371b
  Hagi ware ·········· **3:**76b–77a

  Haji ware ·········· **3:**84a
  Hirashimizu ware ·········· **3:**145a
  history ·········· 1:256a–261b
  Iga ware ·········· **3:**261b
  Imari ware ·········· 1:*260b*
  iron-glazed ·········· **7:**71b
  Kakiemon ware ·········· 1:*261a*; **4:**116b
  Karatsu ware ·········· 1:*260b*; **4:**159a
  Kutani ware ·········· 1:*261a*; **4:**321b
  Kyōto ·········· 1:*262b*; **4:**337a–337b
  lead-glazed ·········· 1:262a–263a
    Kyōto ·········· 1:262b
    origin ·········· 1:262a–262b
    Sanage ·········· 1:263a
    technique ·········· 1:262a–262b
    types ·········· 1:262b
  Mashiko ware ·········· **2:**294b; **5:**125a
  medieval ·········· 1:263a
    Kamakura period ·········· 1:263a
    Muromachi period ·········· 1:263a
    "Six Old Kilns" ·········· 1:263a
    types ·········· 1:263a
  Mino ware ·········· **5:**196a–196b
  Nabeshima ware ·········· **5:**299a–299b
  Ogidō shell mound ·········· **6:**70a
  Onta ware ·········· **6:**113a
  Oribe ware ·········· 1:*258b*; **5:**196a–196b
  production techniques ······ 1:264a–265b
    glazes ·········· 1:265a–265b
    kilns ·········· 1:264b–265a
    tools ·········· 1:264b
  Raku ware ·········· 1:*258b*; **6:**283a
  Sanage ·········· **7:**9a–9b
  Satsuma ware (satsuma-yaki) ······· **7:**30a
  Seto ware ·········· 1:*257b*; **7:**71a–71b
  Shigaraki ware ·········· **7:**91a–91b
  Shino ware ·········· 1:*259a*; **5:**196a–196b
  Sōma ware ·········· **7:**226b–227a
  Sue ware ·········· 1:*257a*; **7:**256a
  Takatori ware ·········· **7:**319b–320a
  Tamba ware ·········· **7:**333a
  Tokoname ware ·········· **8:**43b–44a
  Tsuboya ware ·········· **8:**111a
  Tsutsumi ware ·········· **8:**119a
  Yayoi pottery ·········· **8:**322a–322b
Ceramics museums ·········· **5:**279b
Ceramists
  modern
    Arakawa Toyozō ·········· 1:73b
    Hamada Shōji ·········· **3:**89b
    Ishiguro Munemaro ·········· **3:**340a–341b
    Itaya Hazan ·········· **3:**351b
    Kaneshige Tōyō ·········· **4:**140a
    Katō Hajime ·········· **4:**168a
    Katō Tōkurō ·········· **4:**170b
    Kawai Kanjirō ·········· **4:**178a–179b
    Kitaōji Rosanjin ·········· **4:**228a
    Miwa Kyūwa ·········· **5:**216a
    Tomimoto Kenkichi ·········· **8:**71a–71b
  premodern
    Aoki Mokubei ·········· 1:68b
    Chōjirō ·········· 1:298b
    Eiraku Hozen ·········· **2:**186b
    Hon'ami Kōetsu ·········· **3:**218b–219a
    Kenzan ·········· **4:**199b–200a
    Miura Ken'ya ·········· **5:**215b
    Nin'ami Dōhachi ·········· **6:**4b
    Nonomura Ninsei ·········· **6:**35a
    Okuda Eisen ·········· **6:**95a
    Ri Sampei ·········· **6:**320b
    Sakaida Kakiemon ·········· **4:**116b
Cerebral apoplexy ·········· **5:**147b
Ceremonies
  coming-of-age ·········· **3:**17a
  gempuku ·········· **3:**17a
  yūsoku kojitsu ·········· **8:**358a–358b
Cerqueira, Luis de ·········· 1:265b–266a
Certain Woman, A ·········· 1:84b; **4:**309a

Certificate of Alien Registration ···· 1:47b
Certified public accountant (CPA) ·· **1:8b**, 266a
Certified Public Accountants Law (1948) ················ 1:8b
Cha. See Tea
Chabana (tea-ceremony flower arrangement) ················ 2:289a
Chadō. See Tea ceremony
Chaguchagu Umakko ······· チャグチャグ馬子 ········ 1:266a
Chairs ················ 2:371a
Chaji ················ 7:361b
Chakaiseki ryōri ······· 茶懐石料理 ··· 2:21a, 305a, 306a
Chakaiseki ryōri cuisine ···· 2:21b-22a
Chakushi ················ 6:326a
Chambara ········· 1:266a; 2:271a, 274b
Chamberlain, Basil Hall ····· 1:266a-266b; 2:311a
Hearn, Lafcadio ········· 3:120b
Chamberlains' Office ········· 4:315b
Chamber music ensembles ····· 4:65a
Chamber of Elders ·········· 3:22a
Chambers of commerce establishment ·········· 2:32a
regional ················ 4:11a
Changed circumstances, principle of ················ 6:245a-245b
Changgufeng (Ch'ang-ku-feng) Incident ················ 1:266b
Chang Hsüeh-liang. See **Zhang Xueliang (Chang Hsüeh-liang)**
Chang Myŏn ·········· 4:285a
Chang Po-go ············ 1:266b
Silla's trade controlled by ······· 4:277b
Chang Tso-lin. See **Zhang Zuolin (Chang Tso-lin)**
Chang Tzu-p'ing. See **Zhang Ziping (Chang Tzu-p'ing)**
Chanoine, Charles Sulpice Jules ················ 1:266b-267a; 2:331b
Cha no yu. 茶の湯 See **Tea ceremony**
Chanson ················ 6:354b
Chanter, puppet theater ········· 1:213b
Chants, religious ········ 5:283a-283b
Chao Fu ················ 4:146b
Chapbooks ············· 4:221b
Characters. See **Kanji**
Character sketches ···· 2:188a; 5:48b
"Charcoal-Maker Millionaire, The" ················ 7:269b-270a
Charcoal making ············ 1:267a
Chartered merchants ·········· 3:57a
Charter Oath · 1:267a-267b; 2:310b; 6:204a; 7:54a, 55a
composition ·········· 1:267a-267b
Fukuoka Takachika ········ 2:365b
Iwakura mission ········ 3:193b
Kido Takayoshi ········· 4:203a
kōgi seitai ron ········· 4:248b
Meiji Restoration ········ 5:159b
purpose ················ 1:267a
text ················ 1:267a
Yuri Kimimasa ·········· 8:358a
"Chart of the 50 sounds" ······ 3:40b-41a
Chasen ················ 1:136a
Chashaku ················ 1:136a
Chashitsu ·········· 7:361b-362a
Chausudake. 茶臼岳 See **Nasudake**
Chawan ·········· 7:363b-364a
Chaya Shirojirō ······· 茶屋四郎次郎 ········ 1:267b
Cheerleading ················ 6:66b
Chemical industry ········ 1:267b-268a

companies
Asahi Chemical Industry Co, Ltd. ················ 1:92a-92b
Asahi Denka Kōgyō ·········· 1:92b
Chisso Corporation ·········· 1:297b
Daicel Chemical Industries, Ltd ··· 2:56a
Hitachi Chemical Co, Ltd ··· 3:206b
Kanegafuchi Chemical Industry Co, Ltd ················ 4:137b
Kaō Corporation ·········· 4:156a
Kumiai Chemical Industry Co, Ltd ················ 4:308a
Kyōwa Hakkō Kōgyō Co, Ltd ··· 4:340a
Lion Corporation ·········· 5:10b
Mitsubishi Chemical Industries, Ltd ················ 5:207a
Mitsubishi Gas Chemical Co, Inc ················ 5:207b-208a
Mitsubishi Petrochemical Industries, Ltd ················ 5:212a
Mitsui Petrochemical Industries, Ltd ················ 5:212a
Mitsui Tōatsu Chemicals, Inc ··· 5:212b
Nippon Kayaku Co, Ltd ······· 6:10a
Nippon Shokubai Kagaku Kōgyō ················ 6:12a-12b
Nippon Soda Co, Ltd ········ 6:12b
Nippon Zeon Co, Ltd ········ 6:13b
Nissan Chemical Industries, Ltd ··· 6:20a
Nittō Chemical Industry Co, Ltd ··· 6:22b
Sekisui Chemical Co, Ltd ····· 7:57b
Shin-Etsu Chemical Co, Ltd ······ 7:11b
Shōwa Denkō ·········· 7:173a
Sumitomo Chemical Co, Ltd 7:267b-268a
Teijin, Ltd ·········· 7:375b
Tōagōsei Chemical Industry Co, Ltd ················ 8:30b
Tokuyama Soda Co, Ltd ······· 8:60b
Tōray Industries, Inc ········ 8:76b-77a
Tōyō Soda Mfg Co, Ltd ········· 8:93a
Ube Industries, Ltd ········· 8:123a
Chemical Society of Japan Award · 1:268a
Chemistry ············ 1:268a-268b
Japanese achievements ·········· 1:268b
Chemists
Akabori Shirō ·········· 1:39a
Asahina Yasuhiko ·········· 1:93a
Divers, Edward ·········· 2:120a
Fukui Ken'ichi ·········· 2:363b
Ikeda Kikunae ·········· 3:265b
Kondō Heisaburō ·········· 4:269a
Majima Toshiyuki ·········· 5:85a
Mizushima San'ichirō ····· 5:227b-228a
Nagai Nagayoshi ·········· 5:301a
Nitta Isamu ·········· 6:22a
Nozoe Tetsuo ·········· 6:42a
Ochiai Eiji ·········· 6:59a
Sakurada Ichirō ·········· 7:4a
Takamine Jōkichi ·········· 7:315b
Yabuta Teijirō ·········· 8:283b
Chemulp'o, Treaty of 1:268b; 4:280a-280b; 7:68b
Cheng Ch'eng-kung. See **Zheng Chenggong (Cheng Ch'eng-kung)**
Cheng Hsiao-hsü. See **Zheng Xiaoxu (Cheng Hsiao-hsü)**
Chen Mingshu (Ch'en Ming-shu) ·· 2:342a
Chen Shou (Ch'en Shou) ······ 8:305a
Chen Tianhua (Ch'en T'ien-hua) · 1:269a
Ch'en T'ien-hua. See **Chen Tianhua (Ch'en T'ien-hua)**
Cherries and Maples (panels) ·· 7:41a-41b
Cherry, flowering [(sakura) *Prunus* spp.] ················ 1:269a-270a
culture ················ 1:269a-269b
foreign ················ 1:269b-270a
varieties ················ 1:269b
Cherry Blossom Society ·········· 7:5a

Cherry blossom viewing ········ 3:94a-94b
Chestnut [(kuri) *Castanea crenata*] 1:270a
Chests ················ 2:371a
Chi ················ 4:141b
Chiang Kai-shek ······· 1:270a-270b, 288b; 6:260a, 285b, 302a; 7:228a; 8:377b
He-Umezu (Ho-Umezu) Agreement ················ 3:128b
Nanjing (Nanking) Incident ·· 5:328b-329a
Second United Front ······ 7:47b-48a
Shanghai Incident ·········· 7:77b
World War II ·········· 8:275a
Xi'an (Sian) Incident ·········· 8:281a
Chian Iji Hō ···· 治安維持法 ·· 6:168a-169b
Chian Keisatsu Hō. 治安警察法 See **Public Order and Police Law of 1900**
Chiaochou concession. See **Jiaozhou (Kiaochow)**
Chiba ············ 千葉 ········· 1:271a
Chiba Nikkō Company ·········· 2:304b
Chiba Prefecture ··· 千葉県 ········ 1:271a
Chiba Shūsaku ·· 千葉周作 ·· 8:303a
Chiba University ·········· 1:271a
Chibetto ryokōki ······· チベット旅行記 ········ 4:177b
Chichi ariki (There was a Father) ········· 父ありき ·· 6:141b
Chichibu, Prince ··· 秩父宮 ······ 1:272a
February 26th Incident ·········· 2:250a
Chichibu (city) ······· 秩父 ·· 1:271a-271b
Chichibu Basin · 秩父盆地 ···· 1:271b
Chichibu Cement Co, Ltd ········· 1:271b
Chichibu geosyncline ······· 秩父地向斜 ·········· 4:9a
Chichibu Incident ······· 秩父事件 ··· 1:271b-272a
Farmers' Movement ·········· 2:249a
Iida Incident ·········· 3:262b
Jiyūtō ················ 4:65b
Chichibu-Tama National Park ··· 秩父多摩国立公園 1:272a; 5:318b
Chichijima ···· 父島 ··· 1:272a-272b
Chichi no shanikusai (Father's Carnival) ······· 父の謝肉祭 ·········· 8:289b
Chicken, Japanese [(nipponkei) *Gallus gallus domesticus*] ·· 1:272b-273b
breeds and varieties ·········· 1:272b-273a
history and folklore ·········· 1:273a-273b
introduction ·········· 1:273a
Chicken production ·········· 1:30a
Chidori ················ 6:192b
Chifuren ················ 1:273b
Chigasaki ············ 茅ケ崎 ·········· 1:274a
Chigo ············ 稚児 ········ 1:274a
Chigo monogatari 稚児物語 ······· 6:130a
Chigyō ············ 知行 1:274a; 2:265a
Chigyōkoku system ······· 知行国制 ·········· 1:274a
Chihōban ················ 1:152b
Chihōkan Kaigi 地方官会議 ·········· 1:103b
Chihōshi ············ 地方史 ·· 5:71a-71b
Chihōzei. See **Taxes, national and local**
Chiji ············ 知事 ·· 4:197b
Chijimi ················ 1:274b
Chijin no ai ······ 痴人の愛 ·· 7:342b
Chijiwa Miguel ······· 千々石ミゲル ·········· 1:274b
Chikamatsu Hanji ······· 近松半二 ·· 1:274b, 276a; 5:49b
Naniwa miyage ·········· 5:328b
Chikamatsu Monzaemon ······· 近松門左衛門 ·········· 1:275a, 275b-276a; 2:274a; 3:22b; 4:77a; 5:16a, 47a; 6:269b; 7:262a
bunraku ················ 1:214a
Forty-Seven Rōnin Incident ······· 2:328a

giri and ninjō ·········· 3:34b
kabuki works ····· 1:276a; 4:91b
Naniwa miyage ·········· 5:328a
puppet plays ····· 1:275a–276a
Sakata Tōjūrō collaboration ··· 4:91a–19b; 6:379b
Semimaru ·········· 7:62a
works ·········· 5:47a
Chikamatsu Shūkō
近松秋江 ··· 1:276a
Chiken (title deed) ········· 4:253b
Chikubashō 竹馬抄 · 1:276b; 7:84a
Chikubujima Festival Mandala ····· 7:136b
Chikubushima 竹生島 · 1:276b
Chikugo ······ 筑後 ··· 1:276b
Chikugogawa ······ 筑後川 · 1:83a, 276b
Chikugo shōshi gundan
筑後将士軍談 ···1:76b
Chikuhakukai 竹柏会 ··· 5:19b
Chikuhō Coalfield
筑豊炭田 · 1:276b; 5:314a
Tagawa ·········· 7:294a
Chikujō Daiten · 竺常大典 · 3:353b
Chikumagawa ··· 千曲川 · 1:276b
Shinanogawa ·········· 7:109a
Chikuma Shobō Publishing Co, Ltd
·········· 1:276b
Chikura ········· 千倉 ··· 1:277a
Chikusai 竹斎 · 4:136b
Chikushino 筑紫野 · 1:277a
Childbirth ·········· 2:234b
Child Care Leave Bill of 1975 · 8:262a
Childhood and child rearing 1:277a–278b; 4:38a–38b
age and sex differences · 1:278a–278b
children in folk culture ·········· 1:277a
contemporary culture ·········· 1:277b
father and mother as disciplinarians
·········· 1:278a
games ·········· 3:6a
legal definition ·········· 1:277a
moral masochism and feelings of guilt
·········· 1:278a
physical and emotional closeness ··· 1:48b, 277b
recent developments ·········· 1:278b
shitsuke ·········· 1:277b–278a
Children
abandonment ·········· 7:279b
entertainment for ·········· 6:275b
and television ·········· 1:278b–279a
"Children for Hire" ·········· 8:173b
Children's Day ··· 1:146b, 277b, *279a,* 279a–279b; 2:*261a,* 262a; 5:4a
carp streamers ·········· 1:244a
dolls ·········· 2:129b
flags and banners ·········· 2:288a
kites ·········· 4:229b
Children's groups ·········· 5:4a
Children's literature ··· 1:279b–280a
Akaitori ·········· 1:39b
Iwaya Sazanami ·········· 3:364a
Ogawa Mimei ·········· 6:70a
Suzuki Miekichi ·········· 7:282b
Children's songs ··· 1:280a; 2:301a
Child Welfare Law · 1:280a–280b; 6:235b; 7:55b, 209b, 212a; 8:265b
juvenile crime ·········· 4:86b
Chile ·········· 4:369a
Chimakizasa *(Sasa paniculata)* · 1:136a
Chimmoku 沈黙 ··· 2:214a
Chin ·········· 4:40b–41a
China and Japan ········· 1:280b–291b
Buddhism ······ 1:178a; 2:186a–186b
calligraphic styles of ·········· 7:170a
Chinese-Japanese character dictionary
·········· 2:93a–93b
cultural sphere ·········· 2:141b–142a

diplomatic envoys, ancient ··· 7:259b–261a
ethics ·········· 2:232a
influence in medicine ······· 5:145b–146b
kampō (Chinese medicine) · 5:150b–151b
Neo-Confucianism ······· 7:190a–191b
(to 1911) ·········· 1:280b–287b
ancient period ············ 1:281a–283a
Edo period ·········· 1:284b–286a
medieval period ·········· 1:283a–284b
Meiji period ·········· 1:286a–287b
prehistory ·········· 1:281a
(after 1912) ·········· 1:287b–291b
anti-warlord and anti-imperialist
movements ·········· 1:288a–288b
Chinese Revolution of 1911 and
Twenty-One Demands ·········· 1:287b; 8:120b–121a
diplomatic relations ····· 1:291a–291b
Manchurian Incident ··· 1:288b–289a; 5:97b–98a
May Fourth Movement and Washington
Conference ··· 1:287b–288a; 5:143a–143b
North China problem · 1:289a–289b
outbreak of Pacific War and Japan's
defeat ·········· 1:289a–290a
postwar relations ···· 1:290a–290b; 3:205b
Sino-Japanese War of 1894–1895
·········· 7:197b–198b
Sino-Japanese War of 1937–1945 1:289b; 7:199a–202a
trade with China and Nationalist
government opposition ····· 1:290b–291a
unification of China by Nationalist
government ·········· 1:288b
wakō ·········· 8:220b
postwar relations ·········· 3:205b
religion ·········· 6:290a–293b
songs from ·········· 5:197a–197b
Taiwan ·········· 7:306a–309a
Chinaberry [(sendan) *Melia azedarach*
var. *japonica*] ·········· 1:291b
China Critic ·········· 7:337b
China Enterprise Company ·········· 5:249b
China Incident of 1937. *See*
Sino-Japanese War of 1937–1945
**China-Japan Peace and Friendship
Treaty** ·········· 1:291a–292a; 7:202a
antihegemony principle ·········· 1:292a
China War (1937–1945) ······ 3:201a–202a; 7:199a–202a
Ch'in-ch'i shu-hua ·········· 4:213b–214a
Chindai 鎮台 ··· 1:292a
Chinese
minorities ·········· 5:195a–195b
resident foreigners ·········· 2:313a–313b
Chinese bellflower ·········· 4:207b
Chinese characters. *See* **Kanji**
Chinese Communist Party
August First declaration ·········· 1:116b
Second United Front ··· 7:47b–48a
Chinese Eastern Railway (CER)
·········· 1:292a–292b; 7:237a
Hirota Kōki ·········· 3:150a
Ioffe (Joffe), Adolf Abramovich · 3:328a
Russia and Japan ······ 6:341b, 343a
World War I ·········· 8:270b
Chinese Exclusion Act (US) ······· 4:14a
Chinese Guomindang (Kuomintang)
Party. *See* Guomingdang
Chinese Lions (Karajishi zu) ··· 4:146b, *146a–146b*
**Chinese literature and
Japanese literature** ·········· 1:292a–296a; 5:195a–196a
characteristics ·········· 5:25a–25b
Edo period ·········· 1:294b–295b
Heian period ·········· 1:293a–294a

Kamakura and Muromachi periods
·········· 1:294a–294b
modern period ·········· 1:295b–296a
Nara period ·········· 1:293a
poetry ·········· 5:29a–32a
prose ·········· 5:29b–30a
recording and transmission ··· 5:26a–27a
Yamato period · 1:292b–293a; 5:193b–194a
Chinese-style painting ·········· 4:157a
Ching ·········· 8:119a–119b
Chinjufu 鎮守府 · 1:296a
Chinju no kami 鎮守の神 · 1:296a–296b
Chinkasai (Soothing of the
Flowers) 鎮花祭 ··· 6:191b
Chinkon ritual ·········· 4:107a
Chin Nampin 沈南蘋 ··· 7:83b
Chino ······ 茅野 ··· 1:296a
Chinowa ·········· 5:308a
Chinsetsu yumiharizuki
椿説弓張月 ··· 1:130b
Chinsō ·········· 1:192a; 6:227b
Chin Tenka 陳天華 ··· 1:269a
Chion'in 知恩院 1:296b; 4:336b
Chiossone, Edoardo ··· 1:296b; 2:311b
cultural exchange ·········· 3:350b–351a
Chiran ········· 知覧 ··· 1:297a
Chirigaku hyōron
地理学評論 ··· 1:103b
Chiri Mashiho · 知里真志保 ··· 1:36b
Chirimen ·········· 1:297a
Chiritsubaki ·········· 1:237a
"Chirizuka" 塵塚 ··· 4:179b
Chiryū 知立 ··· 1:297a
Chishakuin 智積院 · 1:297a
Shingon sect ·········· 7:115a
Shinshōji ·········· 7:125a
Chishima Islands. *See* **Kuril Islands**
Chishimakan Incident
千島艦事件 ··· 1:297a
Chishima Rettō · 千島列島 · 4:313a
Chishima Volcanic Zone
千島火山帯 ··· 1:297a
Chishimazasa *(Sasa kurilensis)* · 1:136a
Chishitsu Chōsajo ·········· 3:26a
Chiso Kaisei ····· 地租改正 · 4:365b–366b
Chisso Chemical Company · 2:304a
Chisso Corporation ·········· 1:297b
pollution ·········· 2:226a
Chisuji no kurokami
千すじの黒髪 · 7:335b
Chita ········· 知多 ··· 1:297b
Chita Peninsula · 知多半島 · 1:297b
Chiteiki ········· 池亭記 · 4:129a
Chitose ········· 千歳 ··· 1:297b
Chitose ware ···· 千歳焼 · 3:145a
Chitsuroku shobun
秩禄処分···1:297b–298a
dissolution of samurai class ··· 7:8b
Chi-tung Fang-kung Tzu-chih Cheng-fu
·········· 2:142b
Chiyari Fuji ······ 血槍富士 · 4:166a
**Chiyoda Chemical Engineering &
Construction Co, Ltd** ··· 1:298a
Chiyoda Saiichi
千代田才一 · 4:189b
Chiyoda Ward ··· 千代田区 · 1:298a
Chiyogami ·········· 1:298b
Chiyo Ni kushū 千代尼句集 · 4:102b
Chlorella *(Chlorella* spp.) · 1:298b; 7:334a
Chō ·········· 1:225b–226a
Chōchin lanterns ·········· 4:368a
Chōchō satsujin jiken
蝶々殺人事件 ·········· 8:333b
Chōdensu. *See* **Minchō**
Ch'oe Mu-sŏn ·········· 4:278a
Ch'oe Yŏng ·········· 4:278a
Chōfu (city) ······ 調布 ··· 1:298b
Chōfu (district) ······ 長府 ··· 1:298b

Chō Gakuryō ········ 張学良 ······· 8:377b
Chōhei hantai ikki
········· 徴兵反対一揆 ······ 4:200a
Chōheirei ········· 徴兵令 ····· 1:359a
Cho Hōkō ········· 張宝高 ····· 1:266b
Chōjirō ········· 長次郎 1:298b; 2:346a;
4:337a
Chōjū giga ····· 鳥獣戯画 · 1:298b-299a;
2:199a-199b; 8:32a
Chōka ········· 1:299a-299b
decline ········· 4:115b
Heian period ········· 5:30a
Kakinomoto no Hitomaro ······· 4:117a
waka ········· 8:202b
Chōkaisan ········· 鳥海山 ······· 1:299b
Chokāi shōsetsu tengu
········· 嘲戒小説天狗 ······ 8:288b
Chōkai Volcanic Zone
········· 鳥海火山帯 ······· 1:299b
Chōkata ········· 帳方 ····· 4:119b
Chōkei, Emperor 長慶天皇 ··· 1:299b
Chokkomon ········· 直弧文 · 1:160b, 167a,
299b
Chōkōdō ryō ····· 長講堂領 · 1:299b-300a
Chōkohō Jiken 張鼓峰事件 ···· 1:266b
Chō kokka shugi
········· 超国家主義 ·· 8:144b-146a
Chōkokuji. 長谷寺 See Hasedera
Chokurei ········· 3:278b
Chokusenshū ········· 勅撰集 ···· 3:275b
Chokushimon ········· 1:183a
Chokusho ········· 勅書 ···· 7:62a
Chōkyōsai Eiri 鳥橋斎栄里 ····· 1:300a
Chommage ········· 4:127b
Chōmonkyō ········· 長門峡 ···· 1:5a, 300a
Chōna hajime ···· 手斧始め ···· 4:195a
Chōnaikai ········· 1:300a; 5:359b
Chongguo Renmin Renmin Jiukuo Hui ··· 5:346a
Chongqing (Chungking) government
········· 1:300b
Chōnin ········· 町人 ···· 1:132a,
300a-302b; 3:191a
culture ········· 1:302b
daily life ········· 1:302a-302b
early history ········· 1:301a
Edo ········· 2:168b-169b
emergence ········· 1:301a-301b
further development ····· 1:301b-302a
Hiroshige ········· 1:300b
Junkeichō yomise no zu (Night Stalls in
Junkeichō) ········· 1:300b
shi-nō-kō-shō ········· 7:122b
strata ········· 1:302a
urban life ········· 8:177b
Chōnindō ········· 町人道 · 1:302a-303a
Chōnin kōken roku
········· 町人考見録 ····· 1:303a
Chōnin-mono (economic
life) ········· 町人物 ···· 8:144a
Ch'ŏphaesinŏ ········· 7:163a
Chopping board (manaita) ···· 2:24b
Chopsticks ········· 2:305b
Chordophones ········· 5:282b
Chōri Co, Ltd ········· 1:303a
Chō Sakurin ········· 張作霖 ···· 8:378a
Chōsan ········· 逃散 · 1:303a-303b
Chōsei ········· 長勢 1:199b, 303a,
303b
Chōsen ········· 庁宣 ···· 1:303b
Chōsen Ginkō ········· 1:303b
Chōsen Kaikyō. See Korea Strait
Chōsen Sensō ··· 朝鮮戦争 · 4:292a-292b
Chōsen tsūshinshi
········· 朝鮮通信使 · 1:303b-304a
Chōsenjin shisetsu raihei daigyōretsu ryakuzu
(Sketches of the Procession of the Korean
Tributary Mission) ····· 1:304a-304b
Korean-Japanese relations ······· 4:279a

Choshi
bibliography ········· 1:153b
Chōshi ········· 銚子 1:153b, 304a
Chō Shihei ········· 張資平 · 8:377b-378a
Chōshū domain 長州藩
Western naval expedition against ·· 7:105b
Chōshū Expeditions
········· 長州征伐 ····· 1:86a,
304a-304b
Meiji Restoration ····· 5:158a-158b
Satsuma-Chōshū Alliance ····· 7:29b
Tokugawa Iemochi ········· 8:48a
Tokugawa Yoshinobu ········· 8:57b
yonaoshi rebellions ········· 8:337b
Chōsokabe family
········· 長宗我部氏 ···· 1:304b
Chōsokabe Motochika
········· 長宗我部元親 1:304b; 8:302a
Chōsokabe Motochika,
100-Article Code of
········· 長宗我部元親百箇条 · 1:304b
Chōsokabe Okitegaki
········· 長宗我部掟書 ···· 1:304b
Chosŏn. See Taehan Empire
Chōson gappei ·· ········· 8:87b
Chōtei. See Conciliation
Chou En-lai. See Zhou Enlai (Chou
En-lai)
Chou Hung-ch'ing Incident. See Zhou
Hongqing (Chou Hung-ch'ing) Incident
Chou Tso-jen. See Zhou Zuoren (Chou
Tso-jen)
Chōya gunsai ··· 朝野群載 ···· 1:305a
Chōya shimbun ··· 朝野新聞 ···· 1:129a
Chōzen naikaku ··· 超然内閣 ···· 8:97b
Christian art, 16th and 17th centuries.
See Namban art
Christian Churches, Japan Association
of ········· 1:305a
Christian daimyō ···· 1:64b, 305a-306a
Arima Harunobu ········· 1:83a
Konishi Yukinaga ········· 4:270b
Ōmura Sumitada ········· 6:104b
Takayama Ukon ········· 7:321a
Christianity ········· 1:306a-310a; 6:290a
Anti-Christian edicts ···· 1:64b-65a
Azuchi-Momoyama ········· 3:183a
bateren ········· 1:145b-146a
Catholic ········· 1:308a
Deusu ········· 2:91a
Edo period ········· 4:32a
education ········· 2:172b; 6:293a
expansion ········· 1:306b-307a
government censorship ········· 1:251b
introduction to Japan ········· 1:306b
Japanese literature ········· 4:32a
Kakure Kirishitan · 1:308a; 4:119a
martyrdoms ········· 1:307a
missionaries ···· 1:249b-250b; 6:257a-258b
mission to Europe of 1582 ···· 5:203a
music ········· 5:283b
Nagasaki ········· 5:304a
nationalism ········· 1:309a-309b
"national isolation directives" ····· 7:186a
natural sciences ········· 5:355b
nonchurch (mukyōkai) ···· 5:262b-263a
Okinawa ········· 6:87a
Orthodox ········· 1:308a-308b
persecution and suppression · 1:307a-308a;
7:185b
Protestant ········· 1:308b
publications ········· 6:248a
reintroduction ········· 1:308a
sects ········· 7:242b
social activity ········· 1:309a
social work ········· 6:293a
statistics ········· 1:309b
Tokugawa shogunate ········· 8:53a

tolerance in Japanese religion ··· 8:70b
Toyotomi Hideyoshi ········· 8:95a
Urakami persecutions ········· 6:178a
warrior government ········· 8:230b
weddings ········· 8:239a
women in ········· 8:256b
Christian Mansion ···· 4:221b-222a
Christian schools ········· 6:295b
mission schools ········· 5:202b-203a
Christmas ········· 1:310a
Chronicle of Gods and
Sovereigns, A ········· 4:59b-60a
Chronicle of Great Peace. See Taiheiki
Chronicle of Japan · 1:141b; 5:383b-384a
Chronicle of the Kemmu Era ···· 4:191b
Chronicles, historiography ··· 3:152a-158a
Chronicles of Masakado ···· 7:165b
"Chronicles of the Three Kingdoms"
········· 8:240b
Chronological Records of the
Money-Changing Houses ···· 6:351b
Chrysanthemum and the Sword ··· 1:149b
Chrysanthemum Festival · 1:310a; 2:260b
Chrysanthemums [(kiku)
Chrysanthemum morifolium]
········· 1:310a-311a
Chūbu Electric Power Co, Inc ···· 1:311a
Chūbu-Nippon Broadcasting Co, Ltd
(CBC) ········· 1:311a
Chūbu region ··· 中部地方 · 1:311a-311b
Chūbu Sangaku National
Park ··· 中部山岳国立公園 · 1:5a, 127b,
311b
Chūchō jijitsu ··· 中朝事実 1:311b; 8:290b
Chūgan Engetsu 中巌円月 · 1:311b; 3:58b
Chūgen (retainer)
········· 中間 · 1:311b-
312a
Chūgen (gifts) ········· 中元 · 1:312a; 7:49a
kaeshi ········· 3:30b; 4:102a
kokorozuke ········· 4:256b
Chūgoku Electric Power Co, Inc · 1:312a
Chūgoku Mountains
········· 中国山脈 ········· 1:312a
Chūgoku region · 中国地方 · 1:312a-312b;
4:151b
Chūgū ········· 中宮 ···· 1:312b
Chūgūji ········· 中宮寺 ···· 1:312b
Chu Hsi school. See Shushigaku
Chu Hsi studies ········· 7:190a-191b
Chūji tabi nikki (Chūji's Travel Diary)
········· 忠治旅日記 ···· 2:268b
Chūkai ········· 中海 ···· 5:318b
Chūka Minkoku Ishin
Seifu · 中華民国維新政府 · 6:285b-286a
Chūka Minkoku Rinji
Seifu · 中華民国臨時政府 · 6:260a-260b
Chūkan shōsetsu ········· 1:312b-313a
postwar literature ········· 6:231a
Chūken kigyō ········· 7:205a
Chūki ········· 中気 ···· 1:231a
Chūkyō, Emperor 仲恭天皇 ··· 4:72a
Chūkyō Industrial Zone
········· 中京工業地帯 ···· 1:313a
Nagoya ········· 5:308b-309a
Chūkyōshin ········· 1:255b
Chūma ········· 中馬 ···· 1:313a
Chūmon (inner gate) 1:182b; 3:12b; 7:111a
Chung-hua Min-kuo Linshih Cheng-fu
········· 6:260a-260b
Chung-hua Min-kuo Wei-hsin
Cheng-fu ········· 6:285b-286a
Chungking government. See Chongqing
(Chungking) government
Chung Kuei ········· 7:163b
Chung-kuo Jen-min Chiu-kuo Hui 5:346a
Chūnichi shimbun
········· 中日新聞 ···· 1:313a

Chūō kōron ···· 中央公論 ·· 1:313a-313b;
4:114a; 6:267b; 7:100a, 309b, 338a; 8:348b
  banning ··············· 1:252b
  Kajii Motojirō ··········· 4:114a
  Takita Choin ··········· 7:327a
  Yokohama Incident ······ 8:330a
Chūō Kōron New Writer's Prize ··· 7:163a
Chūō Kōron Sha, Inc ····· 1:313b; 2:343a
  Shimanaka Yūsaku, president 7:100a-100b
Chūō Kyōiku Shingikai ········· 1:255b
Chūō Rōdō Iinkai ············ 1:256a
Chūō University ············· 1:313b
Chūō Ward ······· 中央区 ···· 1:313b
Churchill, Winston
  Yalta Conference ········ 8:286b
Church of Perfect Liberty, The ··· 6:192b
Chūritsu Rōren (Federation of Independent Labor
  Unions) ·········· 中立労連 · 1:313b-314a;
4:347b, 360a; 6:238a; 7:189b
Chūseikai ················· 1:314a
  Kenseikai ············· 4:198a
Chūshin ··················· 4:247b
Chūshingura ········ 忠臣蔵 · 4:171b, 275a;
5:49b; 8:184a
Chūshingura okame hyōban · 忠臣蔵岡目評判 ··· 4:61a
Chu Shun-shui ············· 7:191b
Chūsonji ········· 中尊寺 ···· 1:195b,
314a-314b
Chūuki. 中右記 **See Chūyūki**
Chūyūki ········· 中右記 ···· 1:314b
Chūzan'ō ········ 中山王 ···· 1:314b
Chūzenji, Lake ·· 中禅寺湖 ·· 1:315a; 6:*3a*
Cicadas [(semi) family Cicadidae] ··· 1:315a
Cien Dashi ················· 8:286a
Circle, Triangle, and Square ····· 8:*374b*
Cities
  Amami
    Naze ··············· 5:359a
  Awajishima
    Sumoto ············· 7:274b
  China
    Harbin ·············· 3:103b
  Hokkaidō
    Abashiri ·············· 1:1b
    Akabira ·············· 1:39a
    Asahikawa ··········· 1:92b
    Ashibetsu ············ 1:97a
    Bibai ··············· 1:150b
    Chitose ············· 1:297b
    Date ················ 2:78a
    Ebetsu ·············· 2:143a
    Eniwa ··············· 2:218a
    Fukagawa ··········· 2:359b
    Furano ·············· 2:370b
    Hakodate ············· 3:85b
    Iwamizawa ··········· 3:360b
    Kitami ·············· 4:226b
    Kushiro ············· 4:320b
    Mikasa ·············· 5:170b
    Mombetsu ··········· 5:236a
    Muroran ············· 5:274b
    Nayoro ············· 5:358b
    Nemuro ············· 5:360a
    Noboribetsu ··········· 6:30a
    Obihiro ·············· 6:49a
    Otaru ··········· 6:129a-129b
    Rumoi ·············· 6:340b
    Sapporo ············· 7:20a
    Shibetsu ············· 7:85b
    Sunagawa ··········· 7:274b
    Takikawa ············ 7:326b
    Tomakomai ··········· 8:70b
    Utashinai ············ 8:187a
    Wakkanai ············ 8:220a
    Yūbari ·············· 8:354b

  Honshū
    Abiko ················ 1:5a
    Ageo ··············· 1:21b
    Aioi ················ 1:37b
    Aizu Wakamatsu ······· 1:38b
    Akashi ············ 1:40b-41a
    Akigawa ············· 1:41b
    Akishima ············· 1:42a
    Akita ··············· 1:42b
    Akō ················· 1:45a
    Amagasaki ············ 1:49a
    Anjō ················ 1:62a
    Annaka ·············· 1:62b
    Aomori ·············· 1:69b
    Arai ················ 1:72b
    Arida ··············· 1:83a
    Asahi ··············· 1:92a
    Asaka ··············· 1:94a
    Ashikaga ············· 1:98b
    Ashiya ·············· 1:102a
    Atami ·············· 1:107b
    Atsugi ·············· 1:115a
    Ayabe ·············· 1:125a
    Ayase ·············· 1:125b
    Bisai ··············· 1:156b
    Bizen ··············· 1:158a
    Chiba ·············· 1:271a
    Chichibu ········· 1:271a-271b
    Chigasaki ············ 1:274a
    Chino ·············· 1:296b
    Chiryū ············· 1:297a
    Chita ·············· 1:297b
    Chōfu ·············· 1:298b
    Chōshi ············· 1:304a
    Daitō ··············· 2:67b
    Ebina ·············· 2:143a
    Ena ················ 2:213a
    Enzan ·············· 2:229b
    Esashi ·············· 2:231a
    Fuchū (Tōkyō Prefecture) ··· 2:340a
    Fuchū (Hiroshima Prefecture) ··· 2:340a
    Fuji ··············· 2:341a
    Fujieda ············· 2:342a
    Fujiidera ············ 2:343a
    Fujimi ·············· 2:343b
    Fujinomiya ··········· 2:344a
    Fujioka ············· 2:344a
    Fujisawa ············ 2:345a
    Fuji Yoshida ········· 2:359a
    Fukaya ············· 2:359b
    Fukuchiyama ········· 2:361b
    Fukui ·············· 2:363a
    Fukuroi ············· 2:365a
    Fukushima ··········· 2:366a
    Fukuyama ··········· 2:367b
    Funabashi ··········· 2:368a
    Furukawa ··········· 2:372a
    Fussa ·············· 2:375a
    Futtsu ············· 2:376b
    Gamagōri ············ 3:5a
    Gifu ··············· 3:31a
    Gobō ··············· 3:38b
    Gojō ··············· 3:40b
    Gose ··············· 3:47b
    Gosen ·············· 3:48b
    Goshogawara ········· 3:50a
    Gotemba ············· 3:51a
    Gōtsu ··············· 3:54b
    Gyōda ··············· 3:71a
    Habikino ············· 3:73a
    Hachinohe ············ 3:74a
    Hachiōji ············· 3:74b
    Hadano ·············· 3:75a
    Hagi ················ 3:75b
    Hakui ··············· 3:88a
    Hamada ·············· 3:89a
    Hamakita ············ 3:90a
    Hamamatsu ··········· 3:90b

    Hanamaki ············ 3:94a
    Handa ·············· 3:95a
    Hannō ·············· 3:99b
    Hanyū ············· 3:100a
    Haramachi ··········· 3:102a
    Hashima ············· 3:109b
    Hashimoto ··········· 3:109b
    Hasuda ············· 3:111a
    Hatogaya ············ 3:112b
    Hekinan ············· 3:126a
    Higashi Hiroshima ······ 3:131b
    Higashi Kurume ········ 3:132a
    Higashi Matsuyama ····· 3:132a
    Higashi Murayama ······ 3:132a
    Higashine ············ 3:132a
    Higashi Ōsaka ····· 3:132a-132b
    Higashi Yamato ········ 3:132b
    Hikari ·············· 3:137b
    Hikone ············· 3:138b
    Himeji ·············· 3:139a
    Himi ··············· 3:139b
    Hino ··············· 3:140b
    Hirakata ············· 3:143a
    Hirata ·············· 3:145a
    Hiratsuka ············ 3:146a
    Hirosaki ············· 3:147b
    Hiroshima ············ 3:149b
    Hisai ·············· 3:151a
    Hitachi ············· 3:206b
    Hitachi Ōta ·········· 3:207a
    Hōfu ··············· 3:209a
    Honjō (Akita Prefecture) ··· 3:223a
    Honjō (Saitama Prefecture) ··· 3:223a
    Hōya ··············· 3:246b
    Ibara ·············· 3:253a
    Ibaraki ············· 3:253a
    Ichihara ············· 3:255b
    Ichikawa ············ 3:256b
    Ichinomiya ··········· 3:258a
    Ichinoseki ··········· 3:258b
    Iida ··············· 3:262a
    Iiyama ············· 3:263b
    Ikeda ··········· 3:264b-265a
    Ikoma ·············· 3:270b
    Imaichi ·········· 3:272b-273a
    Ina ················ 3:281b
    Inagi ·············· 3:282b
    Inazawa ············· 3:284a
    Innoshima ··········· 3:308b
    Inuyama ············· 3:326b
    Iruma ·············· 3:336a
    Ise ················ 3:336b
    Isehara ············· 3:337a
    Isesaki ············· 3:338a
    Ishinomaki ··········· 3:345a
    Ishioka ············· 3:345a
    Itami ·············· 3:351b
    Itō ················ 3:351b
    Itoigawa ············· 3:353b
    Iwai ··············· 3:357b
    Iwaki ·············· 3:358a
    Iwakuni ············· 3:358a
    Iwakura ············· 3:358b
    Iwanuma ············· 3:361b
    Iwata ·············· 3:363b
    Iwatsuki ············· 3:364a
    Izumi (Miyagi Prefecture) ··· 3:365a
    Izumi (Ōsaka Prefecture) ··· 3:365a
    Izumi Ōtsu ·········· 3:366a
    Izumi Sano ··········· 3:366a
    Izumo ·············· 3:367b
    Jōetsu ··············· 4:69a
    Jōyō ··············· 4:78b
    Kadoma ············· 4:101a
    Kaga ··············· 4:102a
    Kainan ············· 4:111b
    Kaizuka ············· 4:114a
    Kakamigahara ········· 4:115a

Kakegawa	**4:115a**	
Kakogawa	**4:117b**	
Kakuda	**4:118a**	
Kamagaya	**4:120b**	
Kamaishi	**4:120b**	
Kamakura	**4:120b**	
Kameoka	**4:125b**	
Kameyama	**4:125b**	
Kami Fukuoka	**4:126a**	
Kaminoyama	**4:127a**	
Kamo	**4:128a**	
Kamogawa	**4:128a**	
Kanazawa	**4:136a**	
Kanuma	**4:154a**	
Kariya	**4:160a**	
Kasai	**4:160b**	
Kasama	**4:161a**	
Kasaoka	**4:161a**	
Kashihara	**4:162a**	
Kashiwa	**4:162b**	
Kashiwara	**4:162b-163a**	
Kashiwazaki	**4:163a**	
Kasugai	**4:163b**	
Kasukabe	**4:164a**	
Katano	**4:166a**	
Katsuta	**4:174b**	
Katsuura	**4:174b**	
Katsuyama	**4:175a**	
Kawachi Nagano	**4:177a**	
Kawagoe	**4:177b**	
Kawaguchi	**4:177b**	
Kawanishi	**4:182a**	
Kawasaki	**4:183a**	
Kazo	**4:185b**	
Kazuno	**4:185b**	
Kesennuma	**4:200a**	
Kimitsu	**4:208a**	
Kiryū	**4:222a**	
Kisarazu	**4:222b**	
Kishiwada	**4:223b**	
Kita Ibaraki	**4:225b**	
Kitakami	**4:226a**	
Kitakata	**4:226b**	
Kitamoto	**4:227a**	
Kiyose	**4:232b**	
Kōbe	**4:238a**	
Kodaira	**4:241a**	
Kōfu	**4:243b**	
Koga	**4:246a**	
Koganei	**4:248a**	
Kokubunji	**4:257a**	
Komae	**4:264b**	
Komagane	**4:264b**	
Komaki	**4:265a**	
Komatsu	**4:265b**	
Komoro	**4:267b**	
Kōnan	**4:268b**	
Kōnosu	**4:275a**	
Kōriyama	**4:293b**	
Kosai	**4:294b**	
Koshigaya	**4:295b**	
Kōshoku	**4:296a**	
Kudamatsu	**4:302a**	
Kuji	**4:303a**	
Kuki	**4:304a**	
Kumagaya	**4:305b**	
Kumano	**4:306b**	
Kunitachi	**4:310a**	
Kurashiki	**4:311b**	
Kurayoshi	**4:312a**	
Kure	**4:312b**	
Kurobe	**4:313b**	
Kuroishi	**4:316a**	
Kuroiso	**4:316a**	
Kusatsu	**4:319a-319b**	
Kuwana	**4:322a**	
Kyōto	**4:334a**	
Machida	**5:78b**	
Maebashi	**5:79b**	
Maizuru	**5:85a**	
Masuda	**5:129b**	
Matsubara	**5:131a**	
Matsudo	**5:132a**	
Matsue	**5:132b**	
Matsumoto	**5:137b**	
Matsusaka	**5:140a**	
Mattō	**5:142a**	
Mihara	**5:168b-169a**	
Miki	**5:171a**	
Minami Ashigara	**5:176b**	
Mine	**5:184a**	
Mino	**5:194a**	
Mino Kamo	**5:194b**	
Minoo	**5:195a**	
Misato	**5:198a**	
Misawa	**5:198a**	
Mishima	**5:199a**	
Mitaka	**5:203b-204a**	
Mito	**5:204b**	
Mitsukaidō	**5:213a**	
Mitsuke	**5:213a**	
Miura	**5:214a-214b**	
Miyako	**5:219a**	
Miyazu	**5:223b**	
Miyoshi	**5:223b**	
Mizunami	**5:226a**	
Mizusawa	**5:227b**	
Mobara	**5:228a**	
Mōka	**5:234a**	
Moriguchi	**5:249b**	
Morioka	**5:252b**	
Moriyama	**5:254b**	
Mukō	**5:262b**	
Murakami	**5:266a**	
Murayama	**5:270a**	
Musashi Murayama	**5:275a**	
Musashino	**5:275a**	
Mutsu	**5:288a**	
Nabari	**5:299a**	
Nagahama	**5:300a**	
Nagai	**5:300a**	
Nagano	**5:302a**	
Nagaoka	**5:303b**	
Nagaokakyō	**5:303b**	
Nagareyama	**5:303b**	
Nagato	**5:307a**	
Nagoya	**5:308b-309a**	
Nakaminato	**5:314b**	
Nakano	**5:315b-316a**	
Namerikawa	**5:324a**	
Nanao	**5:327b**	
Nan'yō	**5:330a**	
Nara	**5:331b-332a**	
Narashino	**5:334a**	
Narita	**5:334b**	
Natori	**5:349b**	
Neyagawa	**5:373a**	
Nihommatsu	**5:378b**	
Niigata	**5:385b**	
Niimi	**5:386b**	
Niitsu	**5:386b**	
Niiza	**5:386b**	
Nikkō	**6:2b-3a**	
Ninohe	**6:7a**	
Nirasaki	**6:13b-14a**	
Nishinomiya	**6:19a**	
Nishio	**6:19a**	
Nishiwaki	**6:19b**	
Noda	**6:30a-30b**	
Noshiro	**6:41a**	
Numata	**6:44b**	
Numazu	**6:44b**	
Obama	**6:47b**	
Obanazawa	**6:48a**	
Ōbu	**6:50b**	
Ōda	**6:60b**	
Ōdate	**6:65a**	
Odawara	**6:65b**	
Ōfunato	**6:67b**	
Oga	**6:68a**	
Ōgaki	**6:68a**	
Ojiya	**6:77a**	
Okaya	**6:82b**	
Okayama	**6:82b**	
Okazaki	**6:83a**	
Okegawa	**6:83b**	
Ōmachi	**6:100a-100b**	
Ōmagari	**6:100b**	
Ōme	**6:101a**	
Ōmi Hachiman	**6:101b**	
Ōmiya	**6:102b**	
Ono (Hyōgo Prefecture)	**6:108b**	
Ono (Fukui Prefecture)	**6:108b**	
Onoda	**6:109a**	
Onomichi	**6:110b**	
Ōsaka	**6:120a**	
Ōta	**6:128a**	
Ōtake	**6:129a**	
Ōtawara	**6:129b**	
Ōtsu	**6:133b**	
Ōtsuki	**6:134a**	
Owari Asahi	**6:136b**	
Owase	**6:136b**	
Oyabe	**6:137a**	
Oyama	**6:137b**	
Rikuzen Takata	**6:317b**	
Ryōtsu	**6:353a**	
Ryūgasaki	**6:353b**	
Sabae	**6:361a**	
Sagae	**6:363a**	
Sagamihara	**6:363b**	
Sakado	**6:375a**	
Sakai	**6:375b**	
Sakaiminato	**6:376b**	
Sakata	**6:379b**	
Saku	**7:3a**	
Sakura	**7:4a**	
Sakurai	**7:4b**	
Sanda	**7:9b**	
Sanjō	**7:12a**	
Sano	**7:15b**	
Sawara	**7:31b**	
Sayama	**7:31b**	
Seki	**7:56a**	
Sendai	**7:63b**	
Sennan	**7:66b**	
Seto	**7:71a**	
Settsu	**7:73a**	
Shibata	**7:84b**	
Shibukawa	**7:86a**	
Shijōnawate	**7:94a**	
Shiki	**7:95b**	
Shimada	**7:99a**	
Shimizu	**7:104a**	
Shimminato	**7:104b**	
Shimoda	**7:104b**	
Shimodate	**7:104b**	
Shimonoseki	**7:105b**	
Shimotsuma	**7:107a**	
Shingū	**7:115a**	
Shinjō	**7:116a**	
Shin Nan'yō	**7:121b**	
Shinshiro	**7:125a**	
Shiogama	**7:140a**	
Shiojiri	**7:140b**	
Shirakawa	**7:146b**	
Shiroishi	**7:148a**	
Shirone	**7:148a**	
Shizuoka	**7:153a**	
Shōbara	**7:154a**	
Sōja	**7:224a**	
Sōka	**7:224b**	
Sōma	**7:226b**	
Suita	**7:264b**	

Sukagawa · · · · · · · · · · · **7:265a**	Yachiyo · · · · · · · · · · · **8:283b**	Nōgata · · · · · · · · · · · **6:31a**
Sumoto · · · · · · · · · · · **7:274b**	Yaita · · · · · · · · · · · **8:284b**	Ogōri · · · · · · · · · · · **6:71a**
Susono · · · · · · · · · · · **7:279a**	Yaizu · · · · · · · · · · · **8:284b**	Ōita · · · · · · · · · · · **6:75b**
Suwa · · · · · · · · · · · **7:280a**	Yamagata · · · · · · · · · · · **8:290b**	Ōkawa · · · · · · · · · · · **6:81b**
Suzu · · · · · · · · · · · **7:280b**	Yamaguchi · · · · · · · · · · · **8:294a**	Ōkuchi · · · · · · · · · · · **6:95a**
Suzuka · · · · · · · · · · · **7:280b**	Yamanashi · · · · · · · · · · · **8:301a**	Ōmura · · · · · · · · · · · **6:104a**
Tachikawa · · · · · · · · · · · **7:293a**	Yamato · · · · · · · · · · · **8:308a**	Ōmuta · · · · · · · · · **6:104b–105a**
Tagajō · · · · · · · · · · · **7:294a**	Yamato Kōriyama · · · · · · · · · · · **8:310a**	Ōnojō · · · · · · · · · · · **6:110a**
Tajimi · · · · · · · · · · · **7:310a**	Yamato Takada · · · · · · · · · · · **8:310b**	Saga · · · · · · · · · · · **6:363a**
Takahagi · · · · · · · · · · · **7:311a**	Yanai · · · · · · · · · · · **8:315b**	Saiki · · · · · · · · · · · **6:371a**
Takahama · · · · · · · · · · · **7:311a**	Yao · · · · · · · · · · · **8:316a**	Saito · · · · · · · · · · · **6:373a**
Takahashi · · · · · · · · · · · **7:311b**	Yashio · · · · · · · · · · · **8:317a**	Sasebo · · · · · · · · · · · **7:24a**
Takaishi · · · · · · · · · · · **7:314a**	Yasugi · · · · · · · · · · · **8:318b**	Sendai · · · · · · · · · · · **7:63b**
Takaoka · · · · · · · · · · · **7:317b**	Yawata · · · · · · · · · **8:320a–320b**	Shimabara · · · · · · · · · · · **7:98b**
Takarazuka · · · · · · · · · · · **7:318a**	Yōkaichi · · · · · · · · · · · **8:329a**	Tagawa · · · · · · · · · · · **7:294a**
Takasago · · · · · · · · · · · **7:318b**	Yōkaichiba · · · · · · · · · · · **8:329a**	Takeo · · · · · · · · · · · **7:325a**
Takasaki · · · · · · · · · · · **7:318b**	Yokkaichi · · · · · · · · · · · **8:329b**	Taketa · · · · · · · · · · · **7:325b**
Takatsuki · · · · · · · · · · · **7:320a**	Yokohama · · · · · · · · · · · **8:329b**	Taku · · · · · · · · · · · **7:327b**
Takayama · · · · · · · · · · · **7:320a**	Yokosuka · · · · · · · · · · · **8:334a**	Tamana · · · · · · · · · · · **7:332b**
Takefu · · · · · · · · · · · **7:323b**	Yokote · · · · · · · · · · · **8:334a**	Tarumizu · · · · · · · · · · · **7:347b**
Takehara · · · · · · · · · · · **7:324a**	Yonago · · · · · · · · · · · **8:337a**	Tosu · · · · · · · · · · · **8:85a**
Tama · · · · · · · · · · · **7:332a**	Yonezawa · · · · · · · · · · · **8:338a**	Tsukumi · · · · · · · · · · · **8:115a**
Tamano · · · · · · · · · · · **7:332b**	Yono · · · · · · · · · · · **8:338a**	Usa · · · · · · · · · · · **8:181a**
Tanabe · · · · · · · · · · · **7:335a**	Yūki · · · · · · · · · · · **8:356b**	Ushibuka · · · · · · · · · · · **8:181b**
Tanashi · · · · · · · · · · · **7:339b**	Yuzawa · · · · · · · · · · · **8:358b**	Usuki · · · · · · · · · · · **8:182a**
Tatebayashi · · · · · · · · · · · **7:348b**	Zama · · · · · · · · · · · **8:367b**	Uto · · · · · · · · · · · **8:187b**
Tateyama · · · · · · · · · · · **7:349b**	Zushi · · · · · · · · · · · **8:381a**	Yamada · · · · · · · · · · · **8:288b**
Tatsuno · · · · · · · · · · · **7:349b**	**Kyūshū**	Yamaga · · · · · · · · · · · **8:290a**
Tendō · · · · · · · · · · · **8:5b**	Akune · · · · · · · · · · · **1:45a**	Yame · · · · · · · · · · · **8:313a**
Tenri · · · · · · · · · · · **8:8b**	Amagi · · · · · · · · · · · **1:49a**	Yanagawa · · · · · · · · · · · **8:313b**
Tenryū · · · · · · · · · · · **8:10a**	Arao · · · · · · · · · · · **1:74b**	Yatsushiro · · · · · · · · · · · **8:320a**
Toba · · · · · · · · · · · **8:31a**	Beppu · · · · · · · · · · · **1:150a**	Yukuhashi · · · · · · · · · · · **8:357b**
Tochigi · · · · · · · · · · · **8:33a**	Bungo Takada · · · · · · · · · · · **1:210a**	**Okinawa**
Tochio · · · · · · · · · **8:33a–33b**	Buzen · · · · · · · · · · · **1:226b**	Ginowan · · · · · · · · · · · **3:33b**
Toda · · · · · · · · · · · **8:33b**	Chikugo · · · · · · · · · · · **1:276b**	Gushikawa · · · · · · · · · · · **3:70b**
Tōgane · · · · · · · · · · · **8:35b**	Chikushino · · · · · · · · · · · **1:277a**	Hirara · · · · · · · · · · · **3:144b**
Tōkai · · · · · · · · · · · **8:40b**	Dazaifu · · · · · · · · · · · **2:79a**	Ishigaki · · · · · · · · · · · **3:340b**
Tōkamachi · · · · · · · **8:42a–42b**	Ebino · · · · · · · · · · · **2:143b**	Ishikawa · · · · · · · · · · · **3:342a**
Toki · · · · · · · · · · · **8:42b**	Fukue · · · · · · · · · · · **2:362b**	Itoman · · · · · · · · · · · **3:354b**
Tokoname · · · · · · · · · · · **8:43b**	Fukuoka · · · · · · · · · · · **2:364b**	Nago · · · · · · · · · · · **5:308b**
Tokorozawa · · · · · · · · · · · **8:44a**	Hirado · · · · · · · · · · · **3:141b**	Naha · · · · · · · · · · · **5:309b**
Tokuyama · · · · · · · · · · · **8:60b**	Hita · · · · · · · · · · · **3:206a**	Okinawa · · · · · · · · · · · **6:84b**
Tōkyō · · · · · · · · · **8:60b–66a**	Hitoyoshi · · · · · · · · · · · **3:208b**	Urasoe · · · · · · · · · · · **8:175b**
Tomioka · · · · · · · · · **8:71b–72a**	Hondo · · · · · · · · · · · **3:220a**	**Shikoku**
Tonami · · · · · · · · · · · **8:73a**	Hyūga · · · · · · · · · · · **3:252b**	Aki · · · · · · · · · · · **1:41b**
Tondabayashi · · · · · · · · · · · **8:74a**	Ibusuki · · · · · · · · · · · **3:255b**	Anan · · · · · · · · · · · **1:53b**
Tōno · · · · · · · · · · · **8:75a**	Iizuka · · · · · · · · · · · **3:264a**	Hōjō · · · · · · · · · · · **3:210b**
Toride · · · · · · · · · · · **8:77a**	Imari · · · · · · · · · · · **3:274a**	Imabari · · · · · · · · · · · **3:271b**
Tottori · · · · · · · · · **8:85b–86a**	Isahaya · · · · · · · · · · · **3:336b**	Iyo · · · · · · · · · · · **3:364a**
Towada · · · · · · · · · · · **8:86b**	Izumi · · · · · · · · · **3:365a–365b**	Iyo Mishima · · · · · · · · · · · **3:364b**
Toyama · · · · · · · · · · · **8:87b**	Kagoshima · · · · · · · · · · · **4:105a**	Kan'onji · · · · · · · · · · · **4:148b**
Toyoake · · · · · · · · · · · **8:89a**	Kanoya · · · · · · · · · · · **4:151a**	Kawanoe · · · · · · · · · · · **4:182a**
Toyohashi · · · · · · · · · · · **8:90b**	Karatsu · · · · · · · · · · · **4:159a**	Kōchi · · · · · · · · · · · **4:239b**
Toyokawa · · · · · · · · · · · **8:91b**	Kaseda · · · · · · · · · · · **4:161a**	Komatsushima · · · · · · · · · · · **4:266a**
Toyonaka · · · · · · · **8:92a–92b**	Kashima · · · · · · · · · · · **4:162a**	Marugame · · · · · · · · · · · **5:120b**
Toyooka · · · · · · · · · · · **8:92b**	Kasuga · · · · · · · · · · · **4:163b**	Matsuyama · · · · · · · · · · · **5:141b**
Toyosaka · · · · · · · · · · · **8:92b**	Kikuchi · · · · · · · · · · · **4:206a**	Muroto · · · · · · · · · · · **5:274b**
Toyota · · · · · · · · · · · **8:93a**	Kita Kyūshū · · · · · · · · · · · **4:226a**	Nakamura · · · · · · · · · · · **5:314b**
Tsu · · · · · · · · · · · **8:108a**	Kitsuki · · · · · · · · · · · **4:231b**	Nankoku · · · · · · · · · · · **5:329a**
Tsubame · · · · · · · · · · · **8:109b**	Kobayashi · · · · · · · · · · · **4:236a**	Naruto · · · · · · · · · · · **5:335b**
Tsuchiura · · · · · · · · · · · **8:112a**	Kokubu · · · · · · · · · · · **4:256b**	Niihama · · · · · · · · · · · **5:386a**
Tsuru · · · · · · · · · · · **8:116b**	Kumagaya · · · · · · · · · · · **4:305a**	Ōzu · · · · · · · · · · · **6:141a**
Tsuruga · · · · · · · · · · · **8:116b**	Kumamoto · · · · · · · · · · · **4:305b**	Saijō · · · · · · · · · · · **6:369b**
Tsuruoka · · · · · · · · · · · **8:117a**	Kurume · · · · · · · · · · · **4:318b**	Sakaide · · · · · · · · · · · **6:376a**
Tsushima · · · · · · · · · · · **8:117b**	Kushikino · · · · · · · · · · · **4:320a**	Sukumo · · · · · · · · · · · **7:266a**
Tsuyama · · · · · · · · · · · **8:119b**	Kushima · · · · · · · · · · · **4:320a**	Susaki · · · · · · · · · · · **7:278b**
Ube · · · · · · · · · · · **8:123a**	Makurazaki · · · · · · · · · · · **5:88a**	Takamatsu · · · · · · · **7:314a–314b**
Ueda · · · · · · · · · · · **8:125b**	Matsuura · · · · · · · · · · · **5:141b**	Tokushima · · · · · · · · · · · **8:58a**
Ueno · · · · · · · · · · · **8:128b**	Minamata · · · · · · · · · · · **5:176a**	Tosa · · · · · · · · · · · **8:81a**
Uji · · · · · · · · · · · **8:131a**	Miyakonojō · · · · · · · · · · · **5:219b**	Tosa Shimizu · · · · · · · **8:82a–82b**
Uozu · · · · · · · · · · · **8:174b**	Miyazaki · · · · · · · **5:221a–221b**	Tōyo · · · · · · · · · · · **8:89a**
Urawa · · · · · · · · · · · **8:175b**	Nagasaki · · · · · · · · · · · **5:303b**	Uwajima · · · · · · · · · · · **8:188b**
Urayasu · · · · · · · · · · · **8:176a**	Nakama · · · · · · · · · · · **5:314a**	Yawatahama · · · · · · · · · · · **8:320b**
Utsunomiya · · · · · · · · · · · **8:188a**	Nakatsu · · · · · · · · · · · **5:318a**	Zentsūji · · · · · · · · · · · **8:377a**
Wajima · · · · · · · · · · · **8:201a**	Naze · · · · · · · · · · · **5:359a**	Cities, new industrial · · · · · · · **5:365a**
Wakayama · · · · · · · · · · · **8:219a**	Nichinan · · · · · · · · · · · **5:375a**	Citizenship, naturalization · · · · · · · **5:351b**
Wakō · · · · · · · · · · · **8:220a**	Nishinoomote · · · · · · · · · · · **6:19a**	**Citizens' movements** 1:315a–316a; 6:206b,
Warabi · · · · · · · · · · · **8:223a**	Nobeoka · · · · · · · · · · · **6:30a**	215b, 237b

consumer movement · · · · · · · · · · · 2:14b
early postwar · · · · · · · · · · · · · · · · 1:315a
environmental · · · · · · · · · · · · · · · · 1:315a
major pollution suits · · · · · · · · · · · 1:315b
organization · · · · · · · · · · · · · · · · · 1:315b
victims' movements · · · · · · · · · 1:315a-315b
lawsuits · · · · · · · · · · · · · · · · · · · 1:315
women in · · · · · · · · · · · · · · · · · · · 8:263b
Citizen Watch Co, Ltd · · · · · · · · · · · 1:316a
C. Itoh & Co, Ltd · · · · · · · 1:316a; 2:344a
City commissioner · · · · · · · · · · · · · · 5:78b
City elders · · · · · · · · · · · · · · · 2:184b-185a
City Planning Law · · · · · · · · · · · · · · 8:180b
Civic education · · · · · · · · · · · · · · · · 1:316a
Civil Code · · · · · · 1:160a, 166a, 316b; 2:6b;
3:240a-241a; 5:118a-118b; 6:162b-163a
abuse of rights · · · · · · · · · · · · · · · · 1:5b
administrative law · · · · · · · · · · · 1:13a-13b
adulthood · · · · · · · · · · · · · · · · · · · 1:16a
bankruptcy · · · · · · · · · · · · · · · · · · 1:141a
capacity to act · · · · · · · · · · · · · 1:239b-240a
capacity to enjoy rights · · · · · · · · · · 1:240a
contracts · · · · · · · · · · · · · · · · · · · 2:20a
assumption of risk · · · · · · · · 1:103b-104a
customary · · · · · · · · · · · · · · · · · · · 2:53b
dairi · 2:66b-67a
damages, compensation for · · · · · · · · · 2:72a
divorce · 2:121b
of 1898
marriage law · · · · · · · · · · · · · · · 5:118a
women's suffrage · · · · · · · · · · · · 8:268b
environmental law · · · · · · · · · · · · · · 2:225a
environmental rights · · · · · · · · · 2:229a-229b
foreign juristic persons · · · · · · · · · · · 3:3a
foreign law influence · · · · · · · · · · · · 2:319a
government compensation · · · · · · · · · 3:55a
guardians (kōkennin) · · · · · · · · 4:253b-254a
inheritance law · · · · · · · · · · · · · · · · 3:304a
inkyo · 3:307a
juristic acts · · · · · · · · · · · · · · · · · · 4:86a
kōjo ryōzoku · · · · · · · · · · · · · · · · · 4:252b
kōkennin · · · · · · · · · · · · · · · · · · · 4:253b
liability for negligence · · · · · · · · · · · 4:383b
liability without fault · · · · · · · · · · · · 4:383b
old age and retirement · · · · · · · · · · · 6:99a
Oppler, Alfred C. · · · · · · · · · · · · · · 6:115a
ownership rights · · · · · · · · · · · · · · 6:136b
parental power · · · · · · · · · · · · · · · · 6:162b
partnership · · · · · · · · · · · · · · · · · · 6:164a
person without capacity · · · · · · · · · · 6:178a
prescriptive period · · · · · · · · · · · · · 6:235b
privacy, right to · · · · · · · · · · · · · · · 6:249b
problems · · · · · · · · · · · · · · · · · · · 4:378b
product liability · · · · · · · · · · · · · · · 6:253b
public law · · · · · · · · · · · · · · · · · · · 6:265b
revision · 2:332a
sex discrimination · · · · · · · · · · · · · · 2:362a
support provisions · · · · · · · · · · · · · · 7:277a
Tomii Masaaki · · · · · · · · · · · · · · · · 8:71a
torts · 8:81a
trust · 8:107b
Wagatsuma Sakae · · · · · · · · · · · · · · 8:198b
wills · 8:254a
women in · · · · · · · · · · · · · · · · · · · 8:261b
Civil Code controversy · · · · · · 1:316b-317b
Civil Engineering Society · · · · · · · · · · 2:372a
Civil Execution Law (Minji Shikkō Hō)
· 6:260a
Civilian control of the military · · · · · 1:317b
Civil Information and Education Section
of SCAP · · · · · · · · · · · · · · · · · 1:254b, 317b
Civil liberties, protection of · · 1:317b-318a
1947 constitution · · · · · · · · · · · · · · 4:378a
Civil Liberties Bureau · · · · · · · · · · · · 2:118a
Oppler, Alfred C. · · · · · · · · · · · · · · 6:115a
Civil Procedure, Code of · · · 1:318a-321a

appellate system · · · · · · · · · · · · · · · 1:321a
comparisons between Japanese and
American systems · · · · · · · · · · 1:320a-321a
compulsory execution · · · · · · · · · · · · 1:321a
court system · · · · · · · · · · · · · · · · · · 1:319a
definitions · · · · · · · · · · · · · · · · · · · 1:318a
discovery procedures · · · · · · · · · · · · · 1:320b
format · · · · · · · · · · · · · · · · · · 1:319a-320a
function · · · · · · · · · · · · · · · · · 1:318a-318b
historical background · · · · · · · · · 1:318b-319a
law of evidence · · · · · · · · · · · · · · · · 4:371a
private international law · · · · · · · · · · 6:251b
provisional disposition · · · · · · · · · · · 6:260a
relation to other laws · · · · · · · · 1:319a-319b
remedies, legal · · · · · · · · · · · · · · · · 1:321a
seizure · 7:55b
witnesses · · · · · · · · · · · · · · · · · · · 8:255a
Civil rights, 1889 Constitution and · 4:378a
Civil service · · · · · · · · 1:219b-220a; 6:264b
examination · · · · · · · · · · · · · · · · · 8:326a
National Personnel Authority · · · · · · · 5:344b
Civil Service Appointment Ordinance
(Bunkan
Nin'yō Rei) · · · · · · · · · · · · · · · · · 1:217b
Civil War of 672 · · · · · · · · · · · · 4:60a-60b
Clan · 8:131a
Clan names · · · · · · · · · · · · · · · 5:324b-325a
Clark, Edward Warren · · · 1:321b; 2:311a
Clark, William Smith 1:321b; 2:311b; 7:20a
Class consciousness · · · · · · · · · · · · · 7:216b
rise · 7:218a
Classical Japanese · · · 1:321b-322b; 7:34b
grammar · · · · · · · · · · · · · · · · · · · 1:322b
kakari-musubi · · · · · · · · · · · · · · · · 4:115a
orthography · · · · · · · · · · · · · · 1:322a-322b
Classical Standard · · · · · · · · · · · · · · · 3:16b
Classicism · · · · · · · · · · · · · · · · · · · 8:27b
Classified Collection of Japanese
Classics · 3:69b
Classified National History · · · · · · · · · 6:340a
Classroom plans · · · · · · · · · · · · · · · · 7:33b
Class structure · 1:322b-325a; 2:107a-107b
continuities from past · · · · · · · 1:324a-325a
elitism · 1:324b
Meiji era · · · · · · · · · · · · · · · · · · · 1:323b
modern classes · · · · · · · · · · · · · · · · 1:323b
modern debate over · · · · · · · · · 1:323b-324a
villages · 6:119b
Claudel, Paul Louis Charles · · · · 1:325a;
2:332b
Clause final expressions · · · · · · · · · · 7:231b
Clean Government Party · · · · · 4:266b-267a
Clerks · 4:308b
Climate · · · · · · · · · · · · · · · · · 1:325a-328a
cyclones · · · · · · · · · · · · · · · · · 1:328a-328b
early summer · · · · · · · · · · · · · · · · · 1:325b
heating · 1:327b
land utilization · · · · · · · · · · · · · 1:327b-328a
crop damage due to weather · · · · · · 1:328a
drought · · · · · · · · · · · · · · · · · · · 1:328a
floods · 1:328a
foehn phenomenon · · · · · · · · · · · 1:328a
highland areas · · · · · · · · · · · · · · · 1:328a
rice cultivation · · · · · · · · · · · · 1:327b-328a
warm districts · · · · · · · · · · · · · · · 1:328a
monsoons · · · · · · · · · · · · · · · · 1:327a-327b
rice cultivation · · · · · · · · · · · · · · · · 1:328a
seasons · · · · · · · · · · · · · 1:325b-326b; 4:7b-8a
baiu · · · · · · · · · · · · · · · · · · · 1:325b-326a
fall · 1:326b
midsummer · · · · · · · · · · · · · · 1:326a-326b
monsoon · · · · · · · · · · · · · · · · · · 1:325b
shūrin · 1:326b
spring · 1:325b
summer · · · · · · · · · · · · · · · · 1:325b-326b
winter · 1:325b
snow country · · · · · · · · · · · · · · · · · 1:327a
typhoons · · · · · · · · · · · · · · · · · · · 1:326b

weather and Japanese life · · · · 1:326b-327b
heating and changes in lifestyle · · 1:327b
monsoons · · · · · · · · · · · · · · · · · 1:327a
snow country · · · · · · · · · · · · · · · 1:327a
summer lifestyle and air conditioning
· 1:327b
Clinics, health care · · · · · · · · · · · · · 3:120b
Cliques. See **Batsu**
Cloisonné · · · · · · · · · · · · · · · 1:328b-329a
Cloister government · · · · · · · · · 3:314b-315a
Cloister Office · · · · · · · · · · · · · · · · · 3:315a
Clothing · · · · · · · · · · · · · · · · 1:329a-333a
Azuchi-Momoyama period · · · · · · · 1:332b
Edo period · · · · · · · · · · · · · · · 1:332b-333a
footwear · 3:30a
headgear · · · · · · · · · · · · · · · · 3:118b-119b
Heian period · · · · · · · · · · · · · · 1:329b-332a
men's · · · · · · · · · · · · · · · · · 1:330a-330b
women's · · · · · · · · · · · · · · · 1:331a-332a
Kamakura and Muromachi periods 1:332a
men's · 1:332a
women's · · · · · · · · · · · · · · · · · · 1:332a
kimono · · · · · · · · · · · · · · · · · 4:209a-210b
komon used for · · · · · · · · · · · · · · · 4:267a
modern developments · · · · · · · · · · · 1:333a
obi · 6:48b-49a
prehistoric · · · · · · · · · · 1:329b; 8:321b-322a
raingear · 6:280a
sashiko · · · · · · · · · · · · · · · · · · 7:24a-24b
tabi · 7:291a
tasuki · 7:348a
tekkō · 7:377a
uchikake · · · · · · · · · · · · · · · · 1:332a-332b
uchiki · 1:332a
uniforms · · · · · · · · · · · · · · · · 8:149b-150a
Western influence · · · · · · · · · · · · · · 1:333a
Yamato and Nara periods · · · · · · · · 1:329b
Clouds and Dragons · · · · · · · · · 4:110a-110b
Coal · · · · · · · · · · · · · · · 1:333a-333b; 5:352b
alternate energy source · · · · · · · · · · 2:215a
power · · · · · · · · · · · · · · · · · · 2:191a-191b
Coastal areas
Dannoura · · · · · · · · · · · · · · · · · · · 2:76b
Fukiagehama · · · · · · · · · · · · · · · · · 2:360a
Futamigaura · · · · · · · · · · · · · · · · · 2:376a
Jōdogahama · · · · · · · · · · · · · · · · · · 4:67a
Katsurahama · · · · · · · · · · · · · · · · · 4:173a
Kujūkurihama · · · · · · · · · · · · · · · · 4:303b
Maiko · 5:84b
Sanriku Coast · · · · · · · · · · · · · · · · · 7:16a
Shichirigahama · · · · · · · · · · · · · · · · 7:88a
Sosogi Coast · · · · · · · · · · · · · · · · · 7:232b
Sotomo · 7:233a
Tōjimbō · 8:39a
Tottori Sand Dunes · · · · · · · · · · · · · 8:86b
Coastal Fishing Ground Improvement
Law · 2:285a
Cochran, George · · · · · · · · · · · · · · · 1:237b
Cockfighting · · · · · · · · · · · · · 1:333b-334a
Cocks, Richard · · · · · · · · · · 1:334a; 7:22a
Coeducation · · · · · · · · · · · · · · · · · · 1:334a
Coffee houses · · · · · · · · · · · · 1:334a-334b
Cofradia · 7:241a
Coins
eirakusen · · · · · · · · · · · · · · · · · · · 2:186b
ginza (silver) · · · · · · · · · · · · · · 4:219b-220a
kinza (gold) · · · · · · · · · · · · · · 4:219b-220a
koban · 4:234b
kōchō jūnisen · · · · · · · · · · · · · · · · 4:239b
minting · · · · · · · · · · · · · · · · · 5:242b-243a
ōban · 6:47b-48a
premodern · · · · · · · · · · · · · · · · · · 5:242a
selecting (erizeni) · · · · · · · · 2:230b; 3:176a
yen · 8:323b
Wadō kaihō · · · · · · · · · · · · · · · · · 8:198a
zeniza (lesser) · · · · · · · · · · · · 4:219b-222a
Cold War · 3:324a
Cold-war diplomacy · · · · · · · · · · · · · · 7:10a

Collection for Ten Thousand
  Generations or Collection of Ten
  Thousand Leaves ········ **5**:26a; **8**:287b
Collection of a Thousand Years **7**:68a–68b
Collection of Chinese and Japanese
  Poems for Singing ············· **8**:218a
Collection of Gleanings ··· **7**:184b–185a
Collection of Golden Leaves · **4**:219a–219b
Collection of Jeweled Leaves ·· **3**:71b–72b
Collection of Sand and Pebbles **7**:80b–81a
Collection of Verbal Flowers ··· **7**:95a–95b
Collective bargaining right 1:334b; **2**:369a;
  4:347a–348a, 360a; **7**:188b–189a
Collective labor agreements ····· **1**:334b
  grievance procedure ··············· **3**:62b
Colloquial Standard ··············· **3**:16b
Colonialism ············ **1**:335b–336b; **4**:7a
  goals and outcome ·············· **1**:336b
  Guandong Peninsula ·· **1**:335b; **3**:64b–65a
  institution ················ **1**:335b–336a
  Sakhalin (Karafuto) ···· **1**:335b; **7**:2a
  Taiwan ·················· **7**:307b
Colonization Office. *See* **Kaitakushi**
Colorado River Indian Reservation **6**:229b
Color blindness ················· **4**:36b
Color of Stream and Hue of Mountains
  ···································· **7**:181a
Color television industry, Japanese, in
  U.S ······························· **4**:23a
Combined Fleet, Imperial Japanese
  Navy ·························· **1**:336b
Combs ························· **1**:337a
  hairstyles ······················· **3**:83a
Comedy ·························· **6**:281b
Comic magazines ·············· **1**:337a
Comic pictures ·········· **5**:101b–102a
Coming Nation, The ············· **4**:138b
Coming-of-age ceremonies. *See*
  Gempuku
Coming-of-Age Day ········ **2**:254a; **5**:4b
Comintern ······················· **7**:229a
Comintern 1927 Thesis ········· **1**:337b
  Japan Communist Party ········· **4**:11b
Comintern 1932 Thesis ········· **1**:337b
Commentary on the Constitution
  ······························ **4**:192b–193a
Commentary on the Lotus Sutra · **1**:234a
Commerce, Navigation, and Delimitation,
  Treaty of, (1855; between Russia and
  Japan) ······················· **8**:13b
Commercial banks ········· **1**:139a–139b
  city (toshi ginkō) ············· **1**:139b
  establishment ·················· **1**:139a
  function ················· **1**:139a–139b
  regional (chihō ginkō) ········· **1**:139a
Commercial Code ····· **1**:159a, 337b–339a;
  5:10b, 164a; **7**:48a, 247a–247b
  attitudes toward ················ **1**:339a
  Checks Law ···················· **1**:339a
  commercial entities ············· **1**:338b
  Commercial Law in Japan's industrial
  economy ················ **1**:337b–338a
  commercial transactions ······ **1**:338b–339a
  contracts ····················· **1**:338b
  development ············· **1**:338a–338b
  financial reporting requirements
  ······························ **2**:277b–278a
  foreign law influence ············ **2**:319a
  joint-stock company ········ **4**:70a–71a
  limited liability company ········· **1**:337b
  Okano Keijirō ·················· **6**:81a
  other commercial laws ··········· **1**:338b
  partnership ···················· **6**:164a
  private international law ·········· **6**:251b
  public law ····················· **6**:265b
  Roesler, Karl Friedrich Hermann ·· **6**:334a
  tax laws ······················· **7**:357b
  Ume Kenjirō ··················· **8**:147a

unlimited partnership company ···· **8**:173a
Commercial districts ········ **7**:149b–150b
Commercialization
  before 1600 ················· **2**:148a
  Edo-period ·············· **2**:149b–150a
Commercial law
  codification ···················· **1**:8a
  tax accounting ················· **7**:352a
Commercial paper ········· **1**:339a–339b
Commissariat rice ·········· **3**:252a–252b
Commissioner of foreign affairs ···· **3**:3a
Commissioner of Hakodate ········· **3**:86a
Commissioner of Sado ············· **6**:363a
Commissioners, premodern Japan **1**:206a
Commissioners of finance ···· **4**:143b–144a
Commissioners of temples and shrines
  ······························ **4**:62b
Commission on the Constitution
  ···················· **1**:339b–340a; **2**:13b–14a
Commission to Investigate the National
  Language ···················· **4**:31b
Committee for the Compilation of
  Documents ·················· **7**:335b
Committee of Seven to Appeal for World
  Peace ······················· **1**:340a
Committee to Promote Anti-Prostitution
  Laws ························ **6**:257b
Commonage rights ·············· **8**:71a
Commoners ···················· **3**:125b
Commoner's News ··············· **3**:125b
Common-law marriage ····· **1**:340a–340b
  Factory Law of 1911 ··········· **1**:340a
  Workers' Compensation ········· **1**:340a
Communication, symbolic ········ **2**:233b
Communication gestures ····· **3**:29a–30a
Communications
  international ·············· **3**:318b–319a
  telecommunications systems · **7**:377a–379b
  telephones ·············· **7**:379b–380a
Communion. *See* **Naorai**
Communism ············· **5**:229b–232a
  April 16th Incident ············· **1**:71b
  censorship ·············· **1**:252a, 254b
  labor federations ··············· **4**:346b
  March 15th Incident ············ **5**:113a
  Matsukawa Incident ······· **5**:136a–136b
  Mitaka Incident ················ **5**:204a
  Proletarian literature movement ··· **6**:255b
  publications ··················· **2**:339a
  Sino-Japanese War of 1937–1945
  ······························ **7**:201b–202a
  Yokohama Incident ············· **8**:330a
Communist associations ·········· **2**:337b
Communist League ·············· **6**:284b
Communist Manifesto ············ **4**:297b
Communist movement
  Comintern 1927 Thesis ········· **1**:337b
  Comintern 1932 Thesis ········· **1**:337b
Communist Party. *See* **Japan**
  Communist Party
Communists, public trial of · **1**:340b–341a
Community centers ········ **1**:314b, 341a
Community Chest ·········· **1**:341a–341b
Community education ······ **1**:341b–342a
  future issues ·················· **1**:342a
  history ························· **1**:341b
  system and present conditions
  ······························ **1**:341b–342a
Community education officers ···· **1**:342a
Commutation (genkei) ············ **2**:49a
Commuting ··············· **1**:342a–342b
"Companions of Barbarian Studies"
  ······························ **7**:167b
Companion stories
  otogishū ····················· **6**:129b
  otogi-zōshi ··············· **6**:129b–130a
Company welfare system ··· **1**:342b–343b;
  4:344b

Factory Law of 1911 ··············· **1**:342b
  future ························· **1**:343b
  growth ························ **1**:342b
  level ···················· **1**:343a–343b
  paternalism ··················· **6**:165a
  post-World War II development
  ······························ **1**:342b–343a
Compendiums of Edo period (1600–1868)
  ······························ **4**:233b
Compensation
  company welfare system ········· **1**:343a
  for damages ··················· **7**:226a
  government ··············· **3**:54b–55b
Compilation of Japanese History · **4**:262b
Complete Catalog of Japanese Books
  ······························ **1**:154b
Comprehensive National Development
  Law (1950) ··················· **8**:180a
Comprehensive National Land
  Development Plan ··· **1**:343b–344a; **8**:180a
Compromise ·············· **2**:118b–119a
Comptrollers ··················· **4**:144a
Compulsory education ····· **1**:344a; **2**:176b,
  223b
  school system ·················· **2**:177a
  elementary and secondary education
  ······························ **2**:195a–195b
Computer industry ········· **1**:344a–346b;
  2:167a–167b
  companies
  Fujitsū, Ltd ·················· **2**:347b
  Hitachi, Ltd ·············· **3**:206b–307a
  IBM Japan, Ltd ··············· **3**:253b
  Japan Electronic Computer Company
  (JECC) ···················· **1**:345a
  Nippon Electric Co, Ltd (NEC) ·· **6**:9a–9b
  Nippon Univac Kaisha, Ltd ······ **6**:13b
  Tōshiba Corporation ··········· **8**:82b
  governmental role ·········· **1**:345a–345b
  hardware and software incentives **1**:345b
  Information Technology Promotion
  Agency (IPA) ················· **1**:345b
  Japan Electronic Computer Company
  (JECC) ·················· **1**:345a–345b
  research and development projects
  ······························ **1**:345b
  history ··················· **1**:345b–346b
  incentives for development ······· **1**:345b
  Information Technology Promotion
  Agency (IPA) ················· **1**:345b
  Ministry of International Trade and
  Industry (MITI) ··············· **1**:345b
  research and development projects **1**:345b
  state ····················· **1**:344a–344b
  structure ················· **1**:344b–345a
Computer technology ········ **1**:346b–349a
  communications ··········· **1**:347b–349a
  development ··················· **2**:194a
  mainframe makers ·············· **1**:347b
  national projects ··········· **1**:347a–347b
  relations with IBM ············· **1**:347a
  research and development ········ **1**:347a
  trends ························· **1**:347b
Comte de Monte Cristo, Le ······· **4**:316b
COMTRAC
  Shinkansen ·············· **7**:118a–118b
Conciliation ··· **1**:349a; **2**:117a, 118b; **4**:81b
  contemporary law ·········· **4**:379a–380b
  labor ························· **4**:349b
  Tripartite commissions ········· **4**:351b
  litigation vs ·············· **4**:370a–370b
Concordia Society 1:349a–349b; **5**:96b–97a
Conder, Josiah ······· **1**:80b, 349b; **2**:292a;
  6:335a–335b
Condolence gifts ·········· **1**:349b–350a
  kaeshi ························· **4**:102a
Conduct codes ············· **1**:206b–207a
Confections ·············· **1**:350a–350b

azuki ················· 1:127a
Western influence ········· 1:350a
Conference of Administrative Vice-
Ministers ·············· 6:244a
Conference of Asian and Pacific
Accountants (1951) ········ 1:8b
Conference on Modern Japan
··················· 5:228b-229a
Confession ······· 1:350b; 2:49b
law of evidence ········· 4:371a
Confessions of Lady Nijō, The ····· 8:87a
Confiscation (bosshū) ········ 2:49a
Conflict resolution ····· 1:350b-352b
conflict ············ 1:350b-351b
factional ············ 1:351a
group ·············· 1:351a
individual versus group ····· 1:351a
vertical ············ 1:350b-351a
consensus decision making ····· 1:351b
institutionalized ········ 1:351b-352a
mediation ············ 1:351b
processes ··········· 1:351a-351b
ritualization ········· 1:352a-352b
Confucianism 1:352b-358b; 6:290a; 7:213b
Ancient Learning (Kogaku) ··· 4:246b-248a
Chinese
ancient ··········· 1:352b-353a
medieval ·········· 1:354b-355a
corporate culture ········ 2:26a-27a
Edo period ·········· 1:355b-357b
patronage and education ··· 1:355b-356b
thought ·········· 1:356b-357b
education ··········· 2:173a-173b
Five Classics ·········· 2:329b
Four Books ············ 2:329b
Japanese
ancient ··········· 1:353a-354b
medieval ·········· 1:355a-355b
Kobunjigaku ·········· 4:239a
limitations to influence ····· 1:356b
meritocracy ········· 1:354a, 358a
modern ············ 1:357b-358b
Ogyū Sorai ·········· 6:72b-73a
Okinawa ············· 6:85a
rei ················ 6:288b
religion and society ······ 6:294a
religious dimension ······· 1:354a
scholars ············ 7:191b
Setchūgaku ··········· 7:71a
Shingaku ············ 7:112a
Shushigaku ········· 7:190a-191b
tolerance in Japanese religion ····· 8:70b
virtues ·············· 5:87b
women in ············ 8:258a
Congress of Industrial Labor Unions of
Japan (Zen Nihon Sangyōbetsu Rōdō
Kumai Kaigi) ······· 6:212b; 7:6a
Connoisseurs ··········· 4:83a
"Conquer Korea" debate. *See*
Seikanron
Conroy, Hilary ··········· 4:22a
Consanguineous marriages ····· 4:38a
Consanguinity ········· 1:358b-359a
Conscription
ancient Japan ········· 7:2a-2b
modern ·········· 1:86a, 359a
ritsuryō system ········ 6:330a
Conscription Ordinance of 1873 ··· 1:86a,
359a; 2:361a; 8:190a, 291a
Chitsuroku shobun ········ 1:297b
ketsuzei ikki ··········· 4:200a
militarism ·········· 5:173a-173b
Nishi Amane ·········· 6:14a
shizoku ············· 7:151a
Yamagata Aritomo ········ 4:204b

Conservation ········· 1:359a-360a
Association for the Preservation of
Historic Sites, Places of Scenic Beauty,
and Natural Monuments ····· 1:359b
Comprehensive National Development
Plan ··············· 1:359b
Comprehensive National Land
Development Law ········· 1:359b
energy ·········· 2:215b-216a
Environment Agency ······· 1:359b
Japan Union of Nature Conservation
··················· 1:359b
Law for the Preservation of Historic Sites,
Places of Scenic Beauty, and Natural
Monuments ············ 1:359b
Law for the Protection of Cultural
Properties ············ 1:359b
National Parks Association of Japan
··················· 1:359b
National Parks Law ········ 1:359b
Natural Environment Preservation Law
··················· 1:359b
Natural Parks Law ········ 1:359b
Nature Conservation Society of Japan
··················· 1:359b
Conservative Faction ········ 7:259b
Consolidated financial statements
··················· 1:360a-360b
Consort ·············· 1:312b
Constitution. *See* Constitution of 1947;
Constitution of the Empire of Japan
(Meiji Constitution)
Constitution, dispute over revision of
··················· 2:13b-14a
Constitutional Association ······· 4:198a
Constitutional Association of Friends
··················· 6:314b
Constitutional Democratic Party · 6:315a
Constitutional Imperial Rule Party · 6:315b
Constitutional litigation ······· 2:13a-13b
Constitutional Nationalist Party
··················· 6:314b-315a
Constitutional Party ········ 4:198a-198b
Constitutional Problems Study Group
··················· 2:13b; 5:223b
Constitutional Reform Party ····· 6:314b
Constitution of 1868. *See* **Seitaisho**
Constitution of 1947 ········ 2:3b-7a
Bill of Rights ········· 2:5a-5b
cabinet ············· 2:5b-6a
civil liberties ········· 1:317b
Commission ········· 1:339b-340a
courts ·············· 2:6a
democracy ············ 2:84b
enactment ··········· 2:3b-4b
executive branch of government 3:55b-56a
finance ············· 2:6a
fundamental freedoms
assembly ············ 2:337a
association ·········· 2:337a-337b
religious faith ········ 2:337b-338a
speech ············· 2:338a
press ··············· 2:339a
Habeas Corpus Law ······· 3:73a
interpretation ········· 2:6a-6b
labor rights ············ 2:369a
liberties ·········· 2:369a; 5:62a-62b
local autonomy ·········· 2:6a
minority rights ········· 5:195b-196a
national defense ········· 5:336b-338b
national legislature ········ 2:5b
no-war, no-arms provision ····· 2:5a
pacifism ·············· 6:144b
political system ········ 6:214b-215a
popular sovereignty ······· 2:4b-5a
practice ············· 2:6b-7a
text ·············· 2:9b-13a
Amendments ········· 2:12b-13a

Cabinet ············· 2:11b-12a
Diet ·············· 2:11a-11b
Emperor ············· 2:9b-10a
finances ············· 2:12b
Judiciary ··········· 2:12a-12b
local self-government ······ 2:12b
preamble ············· 2:9b
renunciation of war ········ 2:10a
rights and duties of people ···· 2:10a-11a
supplementary provisions ····· 2:13a
supreme law ··········· 2:13a
women in ············· 8:261b
Constitution of the Empire of Japan
(Meiji Constitution) 2:1a-3b; 3:195b-196b
constitutional government ······ 2:3a
debates ············· 2:1a-2a
foreign models ········· 2:2a
Fukuzawa Yukichi ········ 2:2a
Genrōin draft ·········· 2:1b
Inoue Kaoru ·········· 2:1b
Inoue Kowashi ········· 2:1b-2a
Itagaki Taisuke ········· 2:1b
Itō Hirobumi ·········· 2:1b
Iwakura Tomomi ········· 2:1b
Kido Takayoshi ········· 2:1a
kokutai ············· 2:2a
Motoda Nagazane ········ 2:2a
newspaper ············ 2:2a
Ōki Takatō ············ 2:2a
Ōkubo Toshimichi ········ 2:1a-1b
Ōkuma Shigenobu ········ 2:1b
shigi kempō ··········· 7:92b
Ueki Emori ············ 2:2a
Yamagata Aritomo ········ 2:1b
democracy ············ 2:84b
drafting ·············· 2:2b
drafters ············· 2:2b
Emperors' authority ······· 2:2b-3a
European influence ········ 2:2b
Peerage Ordinance of July 1884 ·· 2:2b
promulgation ·········· 2:2b
general description ········ 2:1a
Genrōin ············· 3:22a
Great Court of Cassation ······ 3:60b
Inoue Kowashi ········· 3:311a
Itō Hirobumi ·········· 3:353a
Itō Miyoji ············ 3:355a
Iwakura Tomomi ········· 3:360a
Kaneko Kentarō ········· 4:138b
political system ········ 6:213b-214b
rights of people ·········· 2:3a
Roesler, Hermann ········ 6:334a
text ·············· 2:7b-9b
Emperor ··········· 2:7b-8a
Finance ············ 2:9a-9b
Imperial Diet ········· 2:8a-8b
imperial oath ·········· 2:7a
Judicature ············ 2:9a
Ministers of State and Privy Council
··················· 2:8b
preamble [or edict] (Jōyu) ····· 2:7b
promulgation rescript ······· 2:7b
rights and duties of subjects ···· 2:8a
supplementary rules ········ 2:9b
Construction industry ········· 2:14a
Construction industry companies
Asanuma Gumi Co, Ltd ······ 1:96a
Chichibu Cement Co, Ltd ····· 1:271b
Chiyoda Chemical Engineering &
Construction Co, Ltd ······· 1:298a
Fujita Corporation ········ 2:346a
Hazama-Gumi Ltd ········ 3:118b
Hitachi Plant Engineering & Construction
Co, Ltd ············· 3:207a
Kajima Corporation ········ 4:114b
Kumagai Gumi Co, Ltd ······ 4:304b
Maeda Construction Co, Ltd ···· 5:79b
Misawa Homes Co, Ltd ······ 5:198b

Mitsubishi Mining & Cement Co, Ltd ·············· **5:208a-208b**
Mitsui Construction Co, Ltd ·· **5:211a-211b**
Nihon Cement Co, Ltd ··········· **5:379a**
Nishimatsu Construction Co, Ltd ··· **6:17b**
Ohbayashi-Gumi, Ltd ············· **6:74a**
Okumura Corporation ············· **6:96b**
Onoda Cement Co, Ltd ·········· **6:109a**
Ōsaka Cement Co, Ltd ······ **6:120b-121a**
Penta-Ocean Construction Co, Ltd · **6:173b**
Satō Kōgyō Co, Ltd ············· **7:27a-27b**
Sekisui House, Ltd ··············· **7:57b**
Shimizu Construction Co, Ltd ··· **7:104a**
Sumitomo Cement Co, Ltd ······ **7:267a**
Sumitomo Construction Co, Ltd ··· **7:268a**
Taisei Corporation ··············· **7:303a**
Takenaka Kōmuten Co, Ltd ··· **7:324b**
Tobishima Corporation ············ **8:32b**
Toda Construction Co, Ltd ······· **8:33b**
Tōkyū Construction Co, Ltd ····· **8:70a**
Zenitaka Corporation ············· **8:375b**
Construction machinery industry ··· **2:14a**
Construction Standards Law ······ **6:313a**
Consumer credit ················· **2:17b**
Consumer expenditures ······· **2:17a-17b**
Consumer goods, durable ··········· **5:7a**
Consumer movement ········· **2:14a-15b,**
304a-304b
international influence ··········· **2:14b**
issues of ·························· **1:315b**
Consumer organizations ········· **7:181b**
Consumer price index ··········· **3:303a**
Consumer protection laws ····· **2:15b-16b**
characteristics of basic ········· **2:15b-16a**
local level ······················ **2:16b**
private laws ····················· **2:16b**
specific statutes ················· **2:16a**
Consumers ··············· **2:16b-17b, 243b**
expenditure patterns ········ **2:17a-17b**
apparel ······················ **2:17a**
credit ························· **2:17b**
discretionary ··············· **2:17a-17b**
food ·························· **2:17a**
housing ······················ **2:17a**
market segments ············ **2:17b**
savings ······················· **2:17b**
income ····················· **2:16b-17a**
population ····················· **2:16b**
role in economy ··········· **2:168a-168b**
shopping patterns ············· **2:119b**
Consumers' cooperatives · **2:14b, 17b-18a**
Consumption and saving behavior
················· **2:18a-20a; 5:7b**
asset portfolio ············· **2:18b-19a**
economic growth ············· **2:161a**
expenditure patterns ······· **2:19a-20a**
saving out of income ······· **2:18a-18b**
Containers
hisago ······················· **3:151b**
lacquer ware ·················· **3:313a**
wooden utensils ··············· **6:83b**
Contemporary Japan ··········· **4:44a**
Contraception ·················· **6:224a**
Contracts ··········· **2:20a-20b; 4:86a**
assumption of risk ········ **1:103b-104a**
employment ·············· **2:209a-209b**
formal legal principles ··········· **2:20a**
freedom of ····················· **2:337b**
jidan ··························· **4:53b**
managerial ideology ············· **5:92a**
principle of changed circumstances
······················ **6:245a-245b**
role and use ···················· **2:20b**
standard-form ·················· **7:243b**
technological assistance ······ **2:315b-316a**
Contract workers ················ **2:212a**

Control faction, Imperial Army. *See* Tōseiha
Cooking, Japanese ····· **1:**314b**; 2:20b-25b;**
3:127b
general description ··········· **2:20b-21b**
history ···················· **2:304b-306b**
implements ················· **2:24b-25b**
hōchō (knives) ··············· **2:24b**
kama and kamado (rice pot and
hearth) ·················· **2:25a**
makisu (bamboo for rolling and
shaping) ·················· **2:25a**
manaita (chopping board) ······· **2:24b**
nabe (saucepans or pots) ········ **2:24b**
nagashikan (mold with dual bottoms)
···························· **2:25a**
oroshigane (grater) ·············· **2:25a**
shamoji (spatula) ··············· **2:25a**
suribachi and surikogi (mortar and
pestle) ················· **2:24b-25a**
zaru (basket) ··················· **2:25a**
methods, general ············· **2:22b-24b**
agemono (deep-fried) ········ **2:23a-23b**
aemono ···················· **2:23b-24a**
dashijiru (stock) and condiments · **2:22b**
gohan-mono (white rice with water)
···························· **2:24a**
menrui (noodles) ············ **2:24a-24b**
mushimono (steamed) ·········· **2:23b**
nabemono (at table) ············· **2:24b**
nerimono (mashed) ·············· **2:24a**
nimono (stewed) ················ **2:23a**
shirumono (soups) ·············· **2:22b**
sunomono (vinegared) ······· **2:23a-24b**
yakimono (grilled or broiled) · **2:22b-23a**
yosemono (molded) ·············· **2:24a**
methods, specific
meshi ························· **5:164a**
miso ·························· **5:202a**
nattō ·························· **5:351a**
nori ························ **6:37a-37b**
pickles ························ **6:187b**
rāmen ························· **6:283a**
sashimi ························· **7:24b**
soy sauce ················· **7:239a-239b**
sukiyaki ······················ **7:265b**
sushi ····················· **7:278b-279a**
tempura ···················· **8:3a-3b**
teriyaki ························ **8:13a**
tōfu ··························· **8:35a**
umeboshi ······················ **8:146b**
regional ···················· **2:22a-22b**
tableware ················ **2:25a, 307a**
chawan (ceramic bowl) ·········· **2:25a**
hachi (deep bowl) ··············· **2:25a**
hashi (chopsticks) ··············· **2:25a**
kyūsu and dobin (teapots) ········ **2:25a**
sara (ceramic plate or dish) ······ **2:25a**
tokkuri and sakazuki (bottle and cup)
···························· **2:25a**
wan (soup bowl) ················· **2:25a**
zen (little table for one person) ···· **2:25a**
terms ······················· **2:25a-25b**
arainegi (long green onion) ········ **2:25a**
awase-jōyu (soy sauce) ·········· **2:25b**
awasezu (dressing) ··············· **2:25b**
itamae (cook) ··················· **2:25b**
kaishiki (leaves or paper) ········· **2:25b**
kakushiaji (hidden flavor) ········· **2:25b**
keshōjio (salt) ·················· **2:25b**
momijioroshi (red pepper) ········· **2:25b**
nerimiso (paste) ················· **2:25b**
sakana (appetizer with sake) ······ **2:25b**
sammaioroshi (cut fish) ··········· **2:25b**
shimofuri (fat or taint treatment) · **2:25b**
sujime (treatment to eliminate fishy
smell) ···················· **2:25b**
traditional ··················· **2:21b-22a**

chakaiseki ryōri ············· **2:21b-22a**
gyōji ryōri ···················· **2:22a**
honzen ryōri ··················· **2:21b**
kaiseki ryōri ··················· **2:22a**
shōjin ryōri ···················· **2:22a**
Cooperative associations ······· **2:25b**
Cooperative communities ········ **7:121b**
Cooperative Democratic Party (Kyōdō
Minshutō) ···················· **4:260b**
Cooperatives
agricultural ···················· **1:21b**
business ························ **2:25b**
consumers' ·················· **2:17b-18a**
Cooperativism, theory of ········· **7:174b**
Copernican theory ··········· **5:355b-356a**
Copper
mining ························ **5:185a**
mining companies ········· **7:266b-267a**
Copper coins
eirakusen ······················ **2:186b**
kōchō jūnisen ·················· **4:239b**
Wadō kaihō ···················· **8:198a**
zeniza ························· **4:220a**
Copyright Law ········· **2:25b-26a; 6:262b**
Design Law ······················ **2:91a**
translation rights ················· **8:98a**
Coral Island ···················· **7:324b**
Cormorant fishing ······· **2:26a,** *26a,* **287b**
in Nagaragawa ················· **5:303b**
Corporate culture ·············· **2:26a-28b**
Confucian and Utilitarian influences **2:27a**
emergence ·················· **2:26b-27a**
general description ············· **2:26a-26b**
ideology and practice ··· **2:27a-27b; 4:344b**
informal reinforcement ············ **2:28a**
multinational enterprises ·········· **5:263b**
socialization of new employees · **2:27b-28a**
Corporate diversification ········· **3:318a**
Corporate finance ············· **2:28b-29b**
capital structure ················· **1:243b**
creditworthiness ············· **2:28b-29a**
funds ························· **4:189a**
future trends ·················· **2:29a-29b**
origins ························· **2:29a**
Corporate history ·············· **2:29b-33b**
business development, Japanese-style
···························· **2:33a**
business organizations ········· **2:32a-32b**
Edo-period merchants ············ **2:29b**
entrepreneurs and business leaders
······················· **2:30a-30b**
forms of business ············· **2:31b-32a**
joint-stock company ············ **2:31b**
limited liability ················· **2:31b**
limited partnership ············· **2:31b**
unlimited partnership ··········· **2:31b**
zaibatsu ··················· **2:31b-32a**
management of labor ········· **2:32b-33a**
Meiji government as modernizer
······················· **2:29b-30a**
modern business ············· **2:30b-31b**
banks ························· **2:30b**
cotton spinning ················ **2:31a**
foreign trade ··············· **2:30b-31a**
internal commerce ·············· **2:30b**
mining ···················· **2:31a-31b**
periods ························ **2:30b**
railways ······················· **2:31a**
shipbuilding ··················· **2:31a**
shipping ······················ **2:31a**
Corporate recruitment ·········· **2:33b**
Corporate Reorganization Law · **1:141a;**
2:33b-34a; 4:378b
Corporate stock ················ **2:34a**
Corporate Tax Law ·············· **7:352a**
Corporate training programs ·· **2:34a-34b**
Corporations ·················· **2:34b-38b**
board of directors ··············· **1:159a**

bureaucracies ············ 1:219a-219b
changing ················· 2:37a
corporate identity ········· 2:37a
corporate image ··········· 2:317b
employment practices ······ 2:36a-36b
enterprise groups and subsidiaries
··························· 2:35b-36a
establishment ··········· 2:37b-38a
expense accounts ········ 2:237a-237b
financial characteristics ···· 2:34b-35a
governmental relations ····· 2:35b
labor union relations ······ 2:36b-37a
overseer ················· 6:136a
publicly traded
exchanges for ········· 7:246b-247a
stockholders' general meeting ···· 7:247a
purchase of equity ········ 2:315b
Corrections Bureau ·········· 6:249a
Correspondence forms ········ 7:376a
Corvée labor ··············· 8:327a
Cosigner ·················· 6:301a
Cosmetics ··············· 2:38a-38b
beni (rouge) ············· 2:38a
mayuzumi (eyebrow-paint) ····· 2:38a-38b
ohaguro (tooth blackening) ··· 2:38a
oshiroi (white powder) ······ 2:38a
Shiseidō Co, Ltd ·········· 7:148b
Cosmogony ·············· 2:38b; 6:290b
Cosmos ··················· 8:138a
Cost accounting standards ······· 2:38b
Cotia Cooperative Society ···· 5:317b
Shimomoto Kenkichi ········ 7:105a
Cotton ················· 8:16b, 19b
India and Japan ·········· 3:288b
sarasa (calico; batik) ······· 7:21a
Councillor (sangi) ········· 7:11a-11b
Councillors, junior (wakadoshiyori) 8:217a
-217b
Council of Business Accounting of the
Ministry of Finance ········ 2:38b
Council of Public Corporation and
National Enterprise Workers' Unions
··························· 4:294a
Council of State ············ 3:252a
Council on the National Language
(Kokugo Shingikai) ····· 2:38b-39a; 4:78b
Ueda Kazutoshi ·········· 8:127a
Counseling, educational ····· 2:179a-179b
"Counterculture" ·········· 6:206b
Counters ················· 2:39a
Coups d'État, periodization ······· 6:175a
Coup d'Etat of 30 September 1863
······ 2:39a-39b; 5:317b; 7:12b, 31b, 102a
Chōshū Expeditions ········ 1:304a
Hamaguri Gomon Incident ········ 3:90a
Hirano Kuniomi ··········· 3:143b
Kido Takayoshi ··········· 4:202b
Shichikyō Ochi ············ 7:88a
Tenchūgumi Rebellion ······· 8:4a
Couriers ················· 3:138b-139a
Court-appointed attorneys ······· 2:39b
Courtesans
portrayal of, in sharebon ······ 7:79b-80a
women in ················ 8:259b
Courtet, Guillaume ·········· 2:330b
Court for the Impeachment of Judges
··························· 3:275a
Court liaison officers ········ 1:206a-206b
Court Music Bureau ········· 2:74a
Court nobles. See **Kugyō**
Court Organization Law ·· 2:6a; 4:80b-81a
Oppler, Alfred C. ·········· 6:115a
Court ranks ·············· 2:39b-41a
Courts. See Judiciary
Courtyards ················ 7:147a
shirasu ·················· 7:147a
Cowra Prisoner-of-War Outbreak ··· 2:41a

Coxinga. See **Zheng Chenggong
(Cheng Ch'eng-kung)**
Crabs [(kani) tribe Brachyura] · 2:41a-41b,
285b
horseshoe ················ 3:231a
Crafts. See **Folk crafts**
Craftsmen of Various Trades ····· 4:150a
Cram schools ·········· 2:41b; 4:83b-84a
entrance examinations ········· 2:223a
universities and colleges ········· 8:170a
Cranes [(tsuru) family Gruidae] ···· 2:41b
Crane Wife, The ············· 8:117a
Crawford, Sir John Grenfell · 1:118a-118b;
2:41b
Creation Society ······· 3:70a; 8:355a, 378a
Creation story. See **Cosmogony**
Credit Guaranty Associations Law 7:205b
Credit unions, agricultural ·········· 1:22a
Crepe fabrics ··············· 1:274b
Crests ·············· 2:42a-43b, 280b
categories ··············· 2:43b
clothing ················· 2:43a-43b
general description ········· 2:42a
8th century ············· 2:42a
12th-13th centuries ········· 2:42b-43a
14th-16th centuries ········· 2:43a
texts ·················· 2:43a
Crickets [(kōrogi) subfamily Gryllinae]
··················· 2:43b-44b;
4:220b
Crime ················ 2:44a-46a
areas of concern ········· 2:44b-45a
drug abuse ············· 2:45a
female ················ 2:45a
juvenile delinquency ········ 2:44b-45a
organized ·············· 2:45a
political terrorism ········· 2:45a
white collar ············ 2:45a
collective responsibility of family (enza)
··························· 2:229a
Criminal Justice Administration 2:45b-46a
clearance rate ··········· 2:45b
imprisonment ··········· 2:46a
juvenile cases ··········· 2:45b-46a
penalties ··············· 2:45b
pretrial screening ·········· 2:45b
Daibon Sankajō ··········· 2:55b
international ············· 3:319a
shioki ·················· 7:140b
Shipbuilding Scandal of 1954 ···· 7:143a
Shōchū Conspiracy ········· 7:154b
social factors ············ 2:46a
statistics ··············· 2:46a-46b
historical trends ·········· 2:46a
international comparison ····· 2:46a-46b
Teigin Incident ·········· 7:375b
Crime victims, compensation for ··· 2:46b
Criminal code ··············· 1:160a
abortion ················ 1:5a
capital punishment (shikei) ·· 1:243a-243b
parenticide ·············· 6:163a
privacy, right to ··········· 6:249a
Criminal Compensation Law of 1950
··························· 2:47a
Criminal investigation ······· 2:47a-47b
Criminal justice administration · 2:45b-46a
clearance rate ············ 2:45b
imprisonment ············ 2:45b
juvenile cases ············ 2:45b-46a
penalties ················ 2:45b
pretrial screening ·········· 2:45b
penalties ················ 2:45b
Criminal law ············ 2:47b-49b
general doctrine
immaturity ············· 2:48a
general doctrines ········· 2:48a-48b
impaired mental condition ···· 2:48a
intoxication ············· 2:48a

mistake ················· 2:48a
necessity ··············· 2:48a-48b
principle of legality ········· 2:48a
self-denunciation ·········· 2:48b
history ·················· 2:47b
pardon ················· 2:49a
penal code organization ······· 2:47b-48b
provisional release ·········· 2:49a
punishment of attempts ······· 2:48b-49a
abettor ················ 2:48b
accessories ············· 2:48b
conspirational coprincipals ··· 2:48b
coprincipals ············ 2:48b
death ················· 2:48b
incarceration ············ 2:48b-49a
misui ················· 2:48b
pecuniary sanctions ······· 2:49a
Criminal penalty ········· 2:45b; 6:339b
Criminal procedure (Keiji Soshō Kisoku)
··························· 2:49b-51b
appeal (jōso) ············ 2:51a
basic characteristics ········· 2:50a
decision ················ 2:50b-51a
acquittal ··············· 2:51a
criminality and punishment ····· 2:51a
guilty ················· 2:50b
defendant's constitutional rights 2:50a-50b
compulsory process ········ 2:50a
impartial tribunal ········· 2:50a
presence of defendant ········ 2:50a
privilege against self-incrimination 2:50a
protection against repeated
prosecutions ·········· 2:50b
public trial ············· 2:50a
punishment according to procedures
established by law ········· 2:50b
right to counsel ·········· 2:50a
speedy trial ············· 2:50a
detention (kōryū) ········· 2:49b-50a
extraordinary remedial proceedings
··························· 2:51a-51b
extraordinary appeal ········ 2:51b
reopening ·············· 2:51a
history ················· 2:49b
institution of charges
accusations (kokuhatsu) ······ 2:50a
complaints (kokuso) ········· 2:50a
prosecution ············· 2:50a
investigation ············· 2:49b
arrest ················ 2:49b
interrogation ············ 2:49b
search and seizure ········ 2:49b; 7:55b
law of evidence ··········· 4:371a
Minor Offenses Law ········· 5:196a
noncoercive ············· 2:49b
revision ················ 4:378a
trial procedure ············ 2:50b
Criminology ·············· 2:51b
Hanzai ron josetsu ········· 7:327a
"Cross recognition", policy of ···· 4:287a
Crows [(karasu) *Corvus* spp.] · 2:51b-52a
Crows Rising in Spring Mist ····· 6:78a
Crucian carp [(funa) *Carassius* spp.]
··················· 2:26a, 52a
Crustaceans ··············· 7:179b
Crypto-Christians ········· 7:185b, 186b
Cuckoos [(hototogisu) family Cuculidae]
··························· 2:52a
Cucurbits (family Cucurbitaceae)
··················· 2:52a-52b
cucumber ·············· 2:52a
general ················ 2:52a
melons ················ 2:52b
squashes ··············· 2:52b
Cuisine, Japanese. See **Cooking,
Japanese**
Culpability ················ 2:48a
Cultivators' rights ··········· 7:5a

Culturalism · · · · · · · · · · · **5:**230b–231a
Cultural Properties Law · **1:**75a; **2:**52b–53a, 295b
   administrative acts · · · · · · · · **2:**52b–53a
   cultural properties · · · · · · · · · · · **2:**52b
   promulgation · · · · · · · · · · · · · · · **2:**52b
   purpose · · · · · · · · · · · · · · · · · · · **2:**52b
Culture and personality · · · · · · · **4:**39a
Cumulative guidance record · **2:**53a
   report cards · · · · · · · · · · · · · · · **6:**302b
Cuong De · · · · · · · · · · · · · · · · · **2:**53a
Currency
   bitasen · · · · · · · · · · · · · · **1:**156b–157a
   coins. *See* Coins
   Dajōkan satsu · · · · · · · · · · · · · · **2:**70b
   hansatsu · · · · · · · · · · · · · · · · · · **3:**99b
   Matsukata fiscal policy · · · · · · **5:**133b
   premodern · · · · · · · · · · · · · · · · **5:**243a
   ryō · **6:**347b
   yen · · · · · · · · · · · · · · · · **8:**323b–324a
Currency management · · · · · · · **7:**174a
Current Contents of Academic Journals
 · **4:**46a
Currents, ocean · · · · · · · · · · · · · **5:**114b
Curriculum · · · · · · · · · · · · · · **7:**34a–36a
   Japanese children abroad · · · · **7:**37a–37b
Customary law · **2:**53b; **4:**379b–380a
Cuttlefish. *See* **Squid and cuttlefish**
Cycling · **2:**53c
Cymbidium · · · · · · · · · · · · · · · · · **7:**188b
Cypresses [(hinoki) *Chamaecyparis obtusa*] · · · · · · · · · · · · · · · **2:**53b–54b
Cypress Trees · · · · · · · · · · · · · · **4:**146b
Cypripedium japonicum · · · · · · · **4:**305a
"Cyrano de Bergerac" · · · · · · · · **7:**121a
Czechoslovakia · · · · · · **2:**142b; **7:**192a
   Japanese studies · · · · · · · · · · · · **4:**43b

D

Dahl, Otto Christian · · · · · · · · · · · **4:**20a
Daianji · · · · · · · 大安寺 · · · · · **1:**182a; **2:**55a–55b; **7:**16b
Daibikan · · · · · · · · · · · · · · · · · · · **7:**107b
Daibon Sankajō
   · · · · · · · · · 大犯三箇条 · · · · · **2:**55b
Daibosatsu Mountains
   · · · · · · · · · · 大菩薩連嶺 · · · · · **2:**55b
Daibosatsu Pass 大菩薩峠 · · · · · **2:**55b
Daibosatsu Tōge · · · 大菩薩峠
   · · · · · · **5:**320a; **6:**221a; **8:**339a
Daibutsu · · · · · 大仏 · · · **2:**55b–56a; **4:**120b; **7:**168a
Daibutsuden (great Buddha hall) · · **8:**33a
Daibutsuyō · · · · · 大仏様 · · · · · **1:**183b
Daicel Chemical Industries, Ltd · · **2:**56a
   Fuji Photo Film Co., Ltd · · · · · · · **2:**56a
Daichō · · · · · · · · · 大帳 · · · · · **4:**187b
Daidairi · · · · · · · · · 大内裏 · · · · · **3:**122a
Daidairi zu kōshō
   · · · · · · · 大内裏図考証 · · · · · **1:**79a
Daidairon · · · · 大々論 · **3:**59a; **5:**101b
Dai Dembōin · · · 大伝法院 · · · · · **4:**118a
Daidō Danketsu Movement 大同団結運動 · · **2:**56a, 336a
Daidōji Yūzan · 大道寺友山 · **2:**56a–56b
Daidō Steel Co, Ltd · · · · · · · · · **2:**56b
Daiei Co, Ltd · · · · **2:**56b, 271b–272a
Daiei, Inc · · · · · · · · · · · · · · · · · **2:**56b

Daigakuin · · · · · · · · · · · · · · · · · · **3:**59b
Daigaku Rei (University Order) · · · **6:**252b
Daigakuryō · · · 大学寮 · · · **2:**56b–57a; **7:**256b
   court ranks · · · · · · · · · · · · · · · · **2:**40b
   decline · · · · · · · · · · · · · · · · · · · **2:**172b
   establishment · · · · · · · · · · · · · · **2:**172b
   Kangakuin · · · · · · · · · · · · · · · · **4:**140a
Daigaku wakumon 大学或問 · · · · · **4:**307a
Daigenkai · · · 大言海 · **2:**57a; **6:**134a
Daigennin (advocates) · · · · · · · · **4:**371b
Daigo · · · · · · · · · · 大子 · · · · · **2:**57a
Daigo, Emperor
   · · · · · · · · · · 醍醐天皇 · · · · · **2:**57a
   Engi Tenryaku no chi · · · · · · · · **2:**217b
   Fujiwara family · · · · · · · **2:**348a–348b
   Shin kokinshū · · · · · · · · · · · · · **7:**120a
   Shinkokushi · · · · · · · · · · · · · · · **7:**121b
   Sugawara no Michizane · · · · · · **7:**257a
Daigo Fukuryū maru
   · · · · · · 第五福竜丸 · · · **1:**113b; **5:**75b–76a
Daigo Fukuryū maru
   Jiken · · · 第五福竜丸事件 · **4:**75b–76a
Daigoji · · · · · · · 醍醐寺 · · · **1:**183a; **2:**57a–58a
   Shingon sect · · · · · · · · · · · · · · · **7:**115a
Daigoji Treasure House · · · · · · · **2:**58a
Daigokuden · · · 大極殿 · **1:**79b; **2:**58a
   Heiankyō · · · · · · · · · · · · **3:**122a–122b
Daihannyaharamitta kyō
   · · · · · · 大般若波羅蜜多経 · · · · · **4:**322b
Daihatsu Motor Co, Ltd · · · · · · · **2:**58b
   passenger car production · · · · · · **1:**122a
   Toyota Motor Co., Ltd. · · · · · · · **8:**93b
Daihon'ei · · · · · 大本営 · **1:**87a; **2:**58b
Dai-Ichi Bank, Ltd · · · · · · · · · · **2:**58b
Daiichi Chūō Kisen Kaisha · · · · · **2:**58b
Daiichi Electric Railway Co · · · · · · **4:**188b
Dai-Ichi Kangyō Bank, Ltd · **1:**140a; **2:**58b
Dai-Ichi Mutual Life Insurance Co
   · · · · · · · · · · · · · · · · · **2:**58b–59a
Daiinkun. 大院君 · · · · · *See* **Taewon'gun**
"**Dai isshō**" · · · · · · 第一章 · · · · · **7:**176a
Dai Jitao (Tai Chi-t'ao) · · · · · · · **2:**59a
Daijiten · · · · · · · · 大辞典 · **2:**93b; **4:**31b
Daijōe bemmō ·大嘗会便蒙 · · · · · · **4:**100b
Daijōin jisha zōji ki
   · · · · · · 大乗院寺社雑事記 · · · · · **2:**59a
Daijōkan. 太政官 · · · · · · · *See* **Dajōkan**
Daijō kishin ron (The Awakening of Mahāyāna Faith) 大乗起信論 · · · **6:**247b
Daijōsai · · · · · · 大嘗祭 · · · **2:**59a–59b, 298b
   kagura uta · · · · · · · · · · · · · · · · · **4:**108a
   Shintō rites · · · · · · · · · · · · · · · · **7:**139a
Daijō tennō (retired sovereign) · · · 太上天皇 · · · · · **4:**64a
Dai kagura · · · · 太神楽 **4:**107b; **7:**250a
Daikakuji · · · · · · 大覚寺 · **2:**59b, 289a
Daikan · · · · · · · · · 代官 · · · **2:**60a; **8:**9b–10a
   kanjō bugyō · · · · · · · · · · · **4:**143b–144a
Daikan Daiji · · · 大官大寺 · · · · · **2:**55a
Daikan Teikoku · 大韓帝国 · · · · · **7:**293b
Dai kanwa jiten 大漢和辞典 · · **2:**60a, 93b; **5:**255a–255b
Daikeichō · · · · · · 大計帳 · · · · · **4:**187b
Daiken Home Co · · · · · · · · · · · **2:**60a
Daiken Trade & Industry Co, Ltd · · **2:**60a
   Daiken Home Co · · · · · · · · · · · **2:**60a
Daikin Kōgyō Co, Ltd · · · · · · · · **2:**60a
Daikō Advertising, Inc · **1:**17a; **2:**60a–60b
Daikōgi · · · · · · · · 大公儀 · · · · · **4:**248b
Daikoku · · · · · · · · 大黒 · **2:**60b; **5:**296a
Daikoku dancers · · · · · · · · · · · · **4:**101b
Daikoku-mai · · · 大黒舞 · · · · · **7:**250a
Daikokuten · · · 大黒天 · **2:**60b; **7:**73a

   Shintō family altars · · · · · · · · · · **7:**137b
Daikokuya Kōdayū
   · · · · · · 大黒屋光太夫 · **2:**60b; **4:**173a
Daikon · · · · · · · · · · · · · · · **6:**276a–276b
Daikuhara Gintarō
   · · · · · · 大工原銀太郎 · · · · · **2:**60b
Daikyoku · · · · · · 太極 · · · · · **3:**126a
Daikyō Oil Co, Ltd · · **2:**60b–61a; **6:**182a
Daily Japan Herald · · · · · · · · · · **4:**46a
Daimaru, Inc · · · · · · · · · · · · · · **2:**61a
Daimoku · · · · · · 題目 **1:**179a; **5:**327a
Daimonji Okuribi
   · · · · · · 大文字送り火 · **1:**160b; **2:**61a
Daimonjiyama · 大文字山 · **2:**61a; **4:**336b
Daimyō · · · · · · · · 大名 · · · **1:**131b; **2:**61a–64b; **4:**7a, 55a; **7:**256b
   Abe Masahiro · · · · · · · · · · · · · · · **1:**3b
   Abe Tadaaki · · · · · · · · · · · · · · · · **1:**4b
   accounting agents · · · · · · · · · · · **4:**116a
   Amako family · · · · · · · · · · · · · · **1:**49b
   Andō Nobumasa · · · · · · · · · · · · **1:**55a
   Arima Harunobu · · · · · · · · **1:**83a–83b
   Asai Nagamasa · · · · · · · · · · · · · **1:**94a
   Asakura Yoshikage · · · · · · · · · · · **1:**95a
   bakuhan system · · · · · · · · · **2:**63a–64a
   codes of conduct · · · · · · · **1:**206b–207a
   declassment · · · · · · · · · · · · · · · **4:**108b
   domains · · · · · · · · · · · · · · · · · · **1:**221b
   Edo period · · · · · · · · · · · **2:**63b, 171b
   education · · · · · · · · · · · · · · · · · **2:**174a
   feudalism · · · · · · · · · · · · **2:**265a–267a
   Fukushima Masanori · · · · · · · · · **2:**366b
   Gamō Ujisato · · · · · · · · · · · · · · · **3:**6b
   genealogies · · · · · · · · · · · · · · · · **4:**138a
   general description · · · · · · · · · · · **2:**61a
   Gosanke · · · · · · · · · · · · · · · · · · **3:**47b
   hatamoto · · · · · · · · · · · · · · · · · **3:**111b
   highway travel · · · · · · · · · · · · · **4:**108b
   Hoshina Masayuki · · · · · · · · · · · **3:**235a
   Hosokawa Tadaoki · · · · · · · · · · **3:**236b
   Hosokawa Yūsai · · · · · · · · · · · · **3:**237a
   Hotta Masayoshi · · · · · · · · · · · · **3:**239b
   Ii Naosuke · · · · · · · · · · · · · · · · · **3:**263a
   Ikeda Mitsumasa · · · · · · · · · · · · **3:**265b
   Ikeda Terumasa · · · · · · · · · · · · · **3:**266a
   Imagawa Yoshimoto · · · · · · · · · **3:**272b
   inns · **3:**223a
   Itakura Katsukiyo · · · · · · · · · · · **3:**350a
   Kaisakuhō · · · · · · · · · · · · · · · · · **4:**112a
   Kamakura shogunate · · · · · **2:**61a–61b
   Kan'eiji · · · · · · · · · · · · · · **4:**137b–138a
   Katō Kiyomasa · · · · · · · · · · · · · **4:**168b
   Kuroda Nagamasa · · · · · · · · · · · **4:**314b
   Kuroda Yoshitaka · · · · · · · · · · · **4:**315a
   Kutsuki Masatsuna · · · · · · · · · · **4:**321b
   Kuze Hirochika · · · · · · · · **4:**322b–323a
   land laws · · · · · · · · · · · · · · · · · **1:**208a
   Maeda Toshiie · · · · · · · · · · **5:**80b–81a
   Maeda Tsunanori · · · · · · · · · **5:**81a–81b
   Matsudaira Katamori · · · · · **5:**131a–131b
   Matsudaira Sadanobu · · · · · **5:**131b–132a
   Matsudaira Tadanao · · · · · · · · · **5:**132a
   Matsudaira Tadayoshi · · · · · · · · **5:**132b
   Matsudaira Yoshinaga · · · · · · · · **5:**132b
   Matsukura Shigemasa · · · · · **5:**136b–137a
   Meiji Restoration · · · · **2:**64a; **5:**156a–157a
   military unification · · · · · · · **2:**61b, 63a
   Mizuno Tadakuni · · · · · · · **5:**226b–227b
   Mōri Motonari · · · · · · · · · · · · · **5:**250b
   Muromachi shogunate · · · · · · · · **2:**61b
   Nabeshima Kansō · · · · · · · · · · · **5:**299a
   Oda Nobunaga reforms · · · · · **2:**61b, 63a
   Ōuchi Yoshitaka · · · · · · · · · · · · **6:**135b
   registers · · · · · · · · · · · · · · · · · · **1:**206a
   rice tax transport · · · · · · · · · · · **4:**112b
   ryōshu · · · · · · · · · · · · · · · · · · · **6:**353a
   sankin kōtai (alternate attendance) rule
   · **7:**14a

Satake Shozan · · · · · · · · · · · · · · · 7:25b
sengoku · · · · · · · · · · · · · · 2:61b; 7:64a
Shimazu Nariakira · · · · · · · 7:102a–102b
Shimazu Yoshihiro · · · · · · · · · · · 7:102b
shōgun · · · · · · · · · · · · · · · · · · · 7:160b
shugo · 2:61b
Takeda Katsuyori · · · · · · · · · · · · 7:322b
Takeda Shingen · · · · · · · · · 7:323a–323b
Tōdō Takatora · · · · · · · · · · · · 8:34b–35a
Tokugawa Akitake · · · · · · · · · · · · 8:45b
Tokugawa Mitsukuni · · · · · · · 8:51b–52a
Tokugawa Nariaki · · · · · · · · · · · · 8:52a
Tokugawa shogunate · · · · · · · · · · 8:55a
Toyotomi Hideyoshi reforms · · · · 2:63a
Tsutsui Junkei · · · · · · · · · · · · · 8:118b
Uesugi Harunori · · · · · · · · · · · · 8:129a
Uesugi Kagekatsu · · · · · · · · · · · 8:129b
Uesugi Kenshin · · · · · · · · · 8:129b–130a
Ukita Hideie · · · · · · · · · · · 8:137b–138a
Yamanouchi Toyoshige · · · · · · · · 8:302b
Daimyō disturbances · · · · · · · · 6:74a–74b
Daimyō loans · · · · 大名貸 · · · · 2:64b
Kajimaya · · · · · · · · · · · · · · · · 4:114b
kakeya · · · · · · · · · · · · · · · · · · 4:116a
Kōnoike family · · · · · · · · · · · · 4:274a
Daimyō plays · · · · · · · · · · · · · · · 4:327a
Daimyō processions 大名行列 · · · · · 2:64b
sankin kōtai · · · · · · · · · · · · · · · 7:14a
Dainichi · · · · · · 1:176a, 184b, 187b; 2:64b
dual aspects · · · · · 4:269b–270a; 7:310a
Pure Land worship · · · · · · · · · · 4:118a
Shingon sect · · · · · · · · · · · 7:113b–115a
Dainichikyō · · · · · · 大日経 · · · · · 7:310a
Dainichi-Nippon Cables, Ltd · · · · 2:65a
Dainichi Nyoraï · · 大日如来 · · · 4:269b
Dai Nihon Butokukai (All Japan Martial
Virtues Society) · · · · · · · · · · · 4:196a
Dai Nihon chimei jisho
· · · · · · · · · · 大日本地名辞書 · 2:65a; 6:288a;
8:127a
Dai Nihon chishi
· · · · · · · · · · · · · · 大日本地誌 · · · · 6:288a
Dai Nihon Eiga Kyōkai · · · · · · · · 4:202a
Dai Nihon enkai jissoku
zenzu 大日本沿海実測全図 · 2:65a; 5:112b
Dai Nihon hennenshi
· · · · · · · · · · 大日本編年史 · · · 4:307b
Dai Nihon kahei shi
· · · · · · · · · · 大日本貨幣史 · · · 8:240a
Dai Nihon Kajin Kai
· · · · · · · · · · · 大日本歌人会 · · 5:19b
Dai Nihon Kajin Kyōkai
· · · · · · · · · · 大日本歌人協会 · · 5:19b
Dai Nihon Kannon Kai · · · · · · · · · 6:78b
Dai Nihon kokugo jiten
· · · · · · · · 大日本国語辞典 · · 2:57a, 65a,
377a
*Dainihonkoku zokusannō Shōtoku taishi
hōsan* · · · · · · · · · · · · · · · · · · 8:231a
Dai Nihon komonjo
· · · · · · · · · · 大日本古文書 · · 2:65a, 105a
Dai Nihon Sangyō Kumiai Chūōkai · 1:21b
Dai Nihon shi (History of
Great Japan) · · · 大日本史 · 1:94b, 285b,
357b; 2:65a–65b
historiography · · · · · · · · · · · · · 3:154b
Kuriyama Sempō, compiler · · · · · 4:313b
Mito school · · · · · · · · · · · · · · · 5:205a
Miyake Kanran · · · · · · · · · · · · · 5:218b
Nagakubo Sekisui · · · · · · · · · · · 5:302a
Shōkōkan · · · · · · · · · · · · · · · · 2:347a
Tokugawa Mitsukuni · · · · · 2:347a;8:51b
Dai Nihon shiryō
· · · · · · · · · · 大日本史料 · · · · 2:65b
Dai Nihon Teikoku Kempō
· · · · · · · · 大日本帝国憲法 · · 2:1a–3b

Dai Nippon Fujinkai
(Great Japan Women's
Society) · · · 大日本婦人会 · 1:34a; 2:65b;
8:261a
Dai Nippon hennenshi
· · · · · · · · · · 大日本編年史 · · 3:156a
Dainippon Ink & Chemicals, Inc · · · · 2:66a
Takenaka Kōmuten Co, Ltd · · · · · 7:324b
Dai Nippon Kokubō
Fujinkai (National
Defense Women's
Association)
· · · · · · 大日本国防婦人会 · · 2:66a; 8:261a
Dai Nippon Kokusuikai
(Great Japan National
Essence Society)
· · · · · · · · · · 大日本国粋会 · · · 2:66a
Tokonami Takejirō · · · · · · · · · · · 8:44a
Dai Nippon Pharmaceuticals · · · · · · 8:21a
Dai Nippon Printing Co, Ltd · · · 2:66a–66b
Toppan Printing Co, Ltd · · · · · · · 8:76a
Dai Nippon Rengō Seinendan · · · · · 2:66b
Tanaka Giichi · · · · · · · · · 7:336a–336b
Dai Nippon Seisantō · · · · · · 3:25a; 7:108a
*Dai Nippon shōgyō shi: Fu Hirado bōeki
shi* · 7:256b
**Dai-Nippon Sugar Manufacturing Co,
Ltd** · · · · · · · · · · · · · · · 2:66b, 359a
Dai Nippon Teikoku
· · · · · · · · · · 大日本帝国 · · · 2:66b
Dai Nippon Teikoku
Kaigun · · 大日本帝国海軍 · · 3:278a
Dai Nippon Teikoku
Rikugun · 大日本帝国陸軍 · · 3:278a
Daini Seikōsha Co · · · · · · · · · · · 4:200b
Daiōzaki · · · · · · · · · 大王崎 · · 2:66b
Dairi · · · · · · · · · · · · · 内裏 · · 2:66b–67a
Dairi (inner palace grounds)
Heiankyō · · · · · · · · · · · · · · · · 3:122a
Heijōkyō · · · · · · · · · · · · · · · · · 3:124a
Dairy cattle production · · · · · · · · · 1:28b
Daisen · · · · · · · · · 大山 · · 2:67a; 7:66a
Daisen-Oki National Park
· · · · · · · · 大山隠岐国立公園 · · 2:67a–67b;
6:83a; 7:101b
Daisetsuzan · · · · · · · 大雪山 · · 2:67b
Daisetsuzan National Park
· · · · · · · · 大雪山国立公園 · 1:92b; 2:67b,
370b
Daishin'in · · · · · · · · · 大審院 · · 3:60b
Daishōwa Paper Mfg Co, Ltd · · · · 2:67b
Daisūteki seisūron
· · · · · · · · · · 代数的整数論 · · 7:311a
Daitō · · · · · · · · · · · · 大東 · · 2:67b
Dai Tōa Kyōeiken
· · · · · · · · 大東亜共栄圏 · · 3:60b–62a
Daitō Islands · · · · · · 大東諸島 · · 4:224b
Daitōjuku · · · · · · · 大東塾 · · 2:67b–68a
Daitokuji · · · · · · · 大徳寺 · · 2:68a–68b;
4:336b; 7:67a
Ikkyū · · · · · · · · · · · · · · · 3:269b–270a
paintings · · · · · · · · · · · · · · · · · 4:148a
Daiwa Bank, Ltd · · · · · · · · · · · · 2:68b
Daiwa House Industry Co, Ltd · · · · 2:68b
Daiwa Securities Co, Ltd · · · · · · · 2:68b
Daiwa Spinning Co, Ltd · · · · · 2:68b–69a
Daizōkyō · · · · · · · · · 大蔵経 · · 1:187b
Daizu · 7:239a
Dajōkampu · · · · · · · 太政官符 · · 4:130a
Dajōkan (Grand Council
of State) · · · · · · · 太政官 · 2:2b, 69a–70b,
104a; 6:246a; 7:16b
early Meiji · · · 2:70a–70b; 3:193a–194a
authority under Seitaisho · · · · · · · 7:54a
censorship · · · · · · · · · · · · · · · · 1:252a
Navy Ministry · · · · · · · · · · · · · 5:358b

Sanshoku · · · · · · · · · · · · · 7:16b–17a
Taikyō Sempu · · · · · · · · · · · · · 7:297b
ritsuryō system · · · · 2:69a–70a; 3:163b;
6:329b–330a
ryōge no kan · · · · · · · · · · · · · · 6:351b
regency government · · · · · · 6:286b–288a
Dajōkan satsu · · · · 太政官札 · · · 2:70b
Dake Hot Spring · · · 岳温泉 · · 2:70b–72a
Damages, compensation for · · · · · 2:72a
Damask · · · · · · · · · · · · · · · · · · 2:131a
Dampatsurei · · · · · · 断髪令 · 2:72a; 4:127b
Dampatsushiki · · · · · · · · · · · · · 7:272b
Dams · · · · · · · · · · · · · · · · 2:72a–73b
classification · · · · · · · · · · · · · · · 2:72b
construction history · · · · · · · 2:72b–73a
Futagawa · · · · · · · · · · · · · · · · · 1:83a
Kurobe · · · · · · · · · · · · · · · · · · 4:313b
Mihoro · · · · · · · · · · · · · · · · · · 5:169a
Ogōchi · · · · · · · · · · · · · · · · · · · 6:71a
Oku Tadami · · · · · · · · · · · · · · · 6:98b
postwar · · · · · · · · · · · · · · · · · · 2:73a
Sakuma · · · · · · · · · · · · · · · · 7:3a–3b
Tagokura · · · · · · · · · · · · · · · · · 7:294b
Dance
Ainu · 1:36a
Awa · 1:124a
Bon odori · · · · · · · · · · · · · · · · 1:161a
dengaku · · · · · · · · · · · · · · 2:86a–86b
dojōsukui · · · · · · · · · · · · · · · · · 2:127b
masks · · · · · · · · · · · · · · · 5:126a–126b
sculpture · · · · · · · · · · · · · · · · · 1:197a
shishi-mai · · · · · · · · · · · · 7:148b–149a
shishi odori · · · · · · · · · · · · · · · 7:149a
traditional · · · · · · · · · · · · 2:73b–75b
bugaku · · · · · · · · · · · · 2:73a; 3:1b
Hanayagiryū · · · · · · · · · · · · · 2:74b
kabuki · · · · · · · · · · · · · · · · · 2:74b
since Meiji Restoration · · · · · · · 2:75b
Nō · · · · · · · · · · · · · 2:73a, 74b–75a
Western-style · · · · · · · · · · 2:75b–76b
Danchi · · · · · · · · · · · · · · · 3:244b, 254a
Dancing religion. *See* Tenshō Kōtai
Jingūkyō
Dangai. *See* Impeachment
Danger years (yakudoshi) · · · · 8:285a–285b
Dangibon · · · · · · · · · · · · · · · · · 4:256a
Dangyokei · · · · · · · · 断魚渓 · · 2:76b
Dan Ikuma · · · · · · · 團伊玖磨 · · 2:76b
Danjōdai · · · · · · · · · 弾正台 · · 4:185b
Danjō Garan · · · · · · · 壇場伽藍 · · 4:269b
Danka · · · · · · · · · · · · · · · · · · 2:76b
Kakure Kirishitan · · · · · · · · 4:119a–120a
Dan Kazuo · · · · · · · 檀一雄 · · 2:76b
Dan Kizui · · · · · · · · · 段祺瑞 · · 2:134b
Dannoura · · · · · · · · · 壇ノ浦 · · 2:76b
Dannoura, Battle of
· · · · · · · · 壇ノ浦の戦 · 1:67b; 2:77a;
7:263a
imperial regalia · · · · · · · · · · · · · 3:279a
Minamoto no Yoshitsune · · · · · · · 5:183a
Shimonoseki · · · · · · · · · · · · · · · 7:105b
Taira-Minamoto War · · · · · · · · · · 7:300b
Taira no Munemori · · · · · · · · · · · 7:301b
Taira no Tomomori · · · · · · · · · · · 7:302b
Danrin, Empress 檀林皇后 · · 2:77a
Danrin school · · · · · · 談林派 · · 2:77a–77b;
4:270a; 5:18a, 46b; 6:297a
yakazuhaikai · · · · · · · · · · · · · · · 3:79a
Danrin toppyakuin
· · · · · · · · · · 談林十百韻 · 2:77b; 6:20a
Danshi (" 'creped" paper)
· · · · · · · · · · · · · · 檀紙 · · 8:233a
Dan Takuma · · · · · · · 団琢磨 · · 2:77b
assassination · · · · · · · · · · 2:32a; 4:373a
Dantani Plywood Co, Ltd · · · · · · · 2:77b
Danzan Shrine tower · · · · · · · · · · 6:147b
Daochuo · · · · · · · · · · · · · · · · · · 4:67a
Daoxuan · · · · · · · · · · · · · · · · · · 2:131b

"Darakuron" ······ 堕落論 · **6**:230b, 375b
Dare da? Hanazono o arasu mono wa!
·················· **7**:119b
Darkness in Summer ·········· **4**:111b
Dart fishing ················ **2**:287a
Daruma ······················ **1**:*193a*
Daruma dolls ·················· **2**:77b
Daruma fairs ····· 達磨市 **2**:77a, 77b-78a
  Takasaki ··················· **7**:318b
Dashi ···················· 山車 · **2**:78a
Das Japanische Inselreich ······ **6**:288a
Das Kapital ················ **7**:310a
Date (city) ·············· 伊達 · **2**:78a
Date Chihiro ····· 伊達千広 · **3**:155b
Date family ········· 伊達氏 · **2**:78a
Date Masamune 伊達政宗 · **2**:78a-78b;
                          3:179b; **7**:63b
  Date family ················ **2**:78a
  French and Japanese relations ··· **2**:330a
  Hasekura Tsunenaga ········· **3**:109a
  Sekigahara, Battle of ········· **7**:56b
  Vatican expedition ·········· **4**:369a
Date Sōdō ·········· 伊達騒動 · **2**:78b
Davydov, Gavrill Ivanovich ········ **6**:341a
Day-care centers ·············· **6**:235b
Day laborers ·················· **7**:202b
Day lilies [(kisuge) *Hemerocallis
  thunbergii*] ················ **2**:78b-79a
Dazaifu ················ 太宰府 · **2**:79a
Dazaifu (Government
  Headquarters) ······· 大宰府 · **1**:4a;
    2:79a-79b, 104b, 364b-365a; **8**:303a
  Kōrokan ················· **4**:293a-294b
  Mongol invasions of Japan ··· **5**:243b-244b
  sakimori ···················· **7**:2a
  Sugawara no Michizane ······· **7**:257a
  urbanization ················ **8**:176a
Dazaifu Shrine
      ······· 太宰府天満宮 · **2**:79b; **7**:257a
  temmangū ················· **7**:381a
Dazai Osamu ····· 太宰治 · **2**:79b-80a,
                  274a; **6**:230b; **7**:176a
Dazai Shundai ··· 太宰春台 · **2**:80b
Death ················· **2**:80b-81a
  euthanasia ·············· **2**:235b-236a
  Death day anniversary ··········· **5**:5a
  Death penalty ········· **2**:48b; **6**:172b
  Death rate ············· **6**:223b-224a
  Debayashi ···················· **4**:99a
Debenture ················· **2**:81a
  joint-stock company ········ **4**:70a-71b
  Debtors, seizure ············· **7**:55b
December Ninth Movement ···· **2**:81a-81b
  Doihara-Qin (Doihara-Ch'in) Agreement
    ····················· **2**:126b
  National Salvation Association ····· **5**:346a
  Decision making
    leader's role ················ **5**:90b
    participants ·············· **5**:90b-91a
    process ··············· **5**:90a-91a
Declining industries ········ **2**:81b
Decorations (awards) ··· **2**:41a, 81b
  Decorative techniques
    cloisonné ················· **1**:328b
    kirikane (gold- or silver-leaf) · **4**:220b-221a
    lacquer ·············· **4**:361a-361b
    maki-e ················· **5**:85a-85b
    mother-of-pearl inlay (raden) · **5**:256b
    Rimpa ················ **6**:317b-318a
    string (mizuhiki) ······· **5**:225b-226a
    tortoiseshell work ········ **8**:80b-81a
  Decorum (rei) ············· **4**:141b
  Decoux, Jean ················ **2**:333a
  Decree of the Cancellation of Debts
    ······················ **4**:152b
Deer, Japanese [(shika) *Cervus nippon*]
    ······················· **2**:82a
  Deer Cry Pavilion ·········· **6**:335a-335b

Deer dance ·················· **7**:149a
Defendant
  acquittal ·················· **2**:51a
  constitutional rights ········ **2**:50a-50b
    compulsory process (shōnin o motomeru
      kenri) ··················· **2**:50a
    impartial tribunal (kōhei na saibansho)
      ······················· **2**:50a
    presence (shuttō) ············ **2**:55a
    public trial (kōkai saiban no kenri) **2**:50a
    punishment, legally mandated ···· **2**:50b
    repeated prosecutions, protection against
      (ichiji fusairi) ············ **2**:50b
    right to counsel (bengonin o irai suru
      kenri) ··················· **2**:50a
    self-incrimination, privilege against
      (mokuhiken) ·············· **2**:50a
    speedy trial (jinsoku na saiban o ukeru
      kenri) ··················· **2**:50a
  conviction ················· **2**:51a
Defense, national ········· **5**:336b-338b
Defense Agency (Bōeichō) · **1**:218b; **2**:5a,
        82a; **6**:242b, 264b; **7**:59a
Defense Facilities Administration
  Agency ············· **2**:82a; **7**:59b
Defense industry ········· **2**:82a-82b
  Defense Secrets Protection Law · **2**:339a
Defense White Paper ········ **2**:82b
  Defilement ············· **4**:186a-186b
Deguchi Nao ····· 出口なを · **2**:82b-83a;
                            7:76b
Deguchi Nobuyoshi
      ·············· 出口延佳 · **4**:59a
Deguchi Onisaburō
      ········· 出口王仁三郎 · **2**:83a
Deification. *See* **Ikigami**
Deities
  bimbōgami-type ············ **1**:155a
  Buddhist prototype ······· **3**:222b-223a
  creation of ················ **3**:364b
  Daikokuten (god of wealth) ······· **2**:60b
  feast days (ennichi) ·········· **2**:219a
  festivals ·················· **2**:254a
  Izanagi and Izanami ······ **3**:364b-365a
  Jizō ······················ **5**:4a
  ubusunagami ··············· **8**:123a
  water (suijin) ·············· **7**:263b
  yakubyōgami ················ **1**:155a
  zashiki warashi ············· **8**:368b
  See also **Kami**
Dejima ·········· 出島 **2**:*83a*, 83a-83b;
                            5:306a
  Dutch trading enclave ········ **2**:330b
  Kaempfer, Engelbert ······· **4**:101b-102a
  National Seclusion ·········· **5**:347b
  Takashima Shūhan ·········· **7**:319a
Dekasegi ··· **2**:83b-84a; **4**:343b, 356b
  industrial structure ········· **3**:301a
Delegation of power to legislate · **2**:84a
De Long, Charles E. ········ **2**:84a
Dembō kanjō ··· 伝法灌頂 · **4**:117b
Demetaka ··········· 出目高 · **2**:84a
Democracy ········· **2**:84a-85a; **7**:215b
  history ···················· **2**:84b
  modernization ·············· **5**:229a
  postwar development ········ **2**:84b-85a
Democratic education ··········· **2**:223b
Democratic Liberal Party
  Occupation ················· **6**:54a
Democratic Party ·············· **5**:197b
  Occupation ················· **6**:54a
Democratic People's Republic of Korea,
  Japanese relations with. *See* **Korea
  and Japan**
Democratic Socialist Party [(DSP)
  Minshatō] ··· **2**:85a-85b; **6**:212b; **7**:215b
  ban-the-bomb movement ···· **1**:114b-115a
  Diet ······················ **2**:96b

Dōmei ····················· **2**:130a
  Kasuga Ikkō ················ **4**:163b
  labor unions ················ **4**:347a
  national defense ········· **5**:336b-338b
  Nishio Suehiro ·············· **6**:19a
  peace movement ············· **6**:166b
  pressure groups ············· **6**:238a
  Sasaki Ryōsaku ·············· **7**:23a
Demokurashī ····· デモクラシー · **7**:115b
Demons
  mononoke ·················· **5**:247a
  oni ······················ **6**:106a
  pacification ················ **8**:285a
  yamamba ·················· **8**:297a
Dempata Eitai Baibai Kinshi Rei. *See*
  Tahata Eitai Baibai Kinshi Rei
Dempwolff, Otto ··············· **4**:20a
Denden taiko ··········· **2**:85b-86a
Den'en ni shisu (To Die in
  the Country) ·田園に死す · **8**:13a
Dengaku ··········· 田楽 · **2**:86a-86b,
                  297b, *298b*, 301a
  dance, traditional ·········· **2**:73b-74a
  furyū development ··········· **2**:374a
  Nō ······················· **6**:23b
  sarugaku ··················· **7**:22a
Dengaku nō ······ 田楽能 · **4**:324b
Den Hideo ········· 田英夫 · **2**:86b
Denison, Henry Willard ··· **2**:86b, 311a
Denki bungaku ········· **1**:155a-155b
Denki Kagaku Kōgyō ······ **2**:86b-87a
Denki Rōren ················ **2**:87a
Denkōroku ········· 伝光録 · **4**:190b
Denmark
  Japanese studies ············ **4**:43b
Denryoku Chūō Kenkyūjo ········ **2**:192a
"Densely inhabited district" (DID) · **8**:176b
Denshi Gijutsu Sōgō Kenkyūjo ···· **2**:195a
Dentists ··················· **3**:120a
Dentsū, Inc ······· **1**:17a; **2**:87a; **7**:56b
Department stores ···· **2**:30b, 87a-87b
Deposit money ············· **2**:87b
Depression ·········· **2**:153b; **3**:200a
Depression of the 1930s ········· **2**:320a
De Rijke, Johannes ·········· **2**:87b
Dermatoglyphs ··············· **4**:35b
De Sade case ······· **2**:87b-88a; **4**:362a
  obscenity ·················· **6**:50b
Descendants of Cain, The ······· **1**:84b
Design ················· **2**:88a-90a
  modern ·················· **2**:89a-90a
    commercial ············· **2**:89b-90a
    industrial ·············· **2**:89b-89b
  premodern ··············· **2**:88a-88b
Design in textiles ········ **2**:90a-91a
Design Law of 1959 ···· **2**:91a; **6**:164b
Desks ···················· **2**:371a
Detective Story Writers Club ···· **2**:170b
Deusu (*Deus*) ·············· **2**:91a
Deutzias. *See* **Unohana**
Deva ····················· **7**:381a
Deva Seizing a Demon ········· **4**:147a
Devils ···················· **5**:296a
DeVos, George ················ **4**:39b
Dewa Mountains 出羽山脈 · **1**:136b; **2**:91a
Dewa Sanzan Shrines
      ······· 出羽三山神社 ···· **2**:91a-91b
Dewey, John ················· **2**:180b
De Witt, John L. ·········· **4**:17b-18a
Dharma ············ **1**:192a; **2**:91b
  footprints of Buddha ········· **1**:225b
Dharma Bums, The ············ **7**:207a
Dharmakāya ················· **4**:68b
Dhyāna ····················· **1**:179b
Dialectical materialism theory ····· **3**:141a
Dialects ········ **2**:91b-93a; **4**:23b-24a
  boundaries ················· **2**:91b
  centers ···················· **2**:91b

divisions ···················· 2:91b
  Honshū ····················· 2:91b-92a
  Kyūshū ······················ 2:91b
East-West boundary ············ 2:92a-92b
social ······················· 2:92a-93a
"Dialogue on Poverty" ("Hinkyū
mondō") ···················· 8:303a
Diamond realm ·········· 4:269b-270a
Diamond realm mandala ······· 6:150b
Diana ·· 5:100a; 6:270b, 349a-351a; 7:141b
Diaries ··············· 5:33b; 6:2a-2b
  Chichi no shūen nikki ········· 3:348a
  Chūyūki ····················· 1:314b
  description ·················· 6:2a
  Gaun nikkenroku ············· 3:13b
  Hanazono Tennō shinki ········ 3:95a
  Izayoi nikki ················· 1:6a
  Izumi Shikibu nikki ··········· 3:366b
  Kagerō nikki ··········· 4:104a-104b
  Murasaki Shikibu nikki ······· 5:267b
  Nakatsukasa Naishi no nikki ··· 5:318a-318b
  Sanuki no Suke no nikki ······ 7:18b
  Sarashina nikki ············ 7:21a-21b
  Tosa nikki ··················· 4:216b
  Towazugatari ············· 8:87a-87b
  travel ···················· 8:104b-106a
  Umezu Masakage nikki ········ 8:147b
  Uwai Kakuken nikki ·········· 8:188b
Diary of a Japanese Convert ····· 1:155a
Diary of Lady Sanuki, The ········ 7:18b
Diary of Nakatsukasa Naishi · 5:318a-318b
Dictionaries ················ 2:93a-94a
  Butsurui shōko ··············· 1:225b
  Daigenkai ··················· 2:56a
  Dai kanwa jiten ·············· 3:60a
  Dai Nihon kokugo jiten ········ 2:65a
  Gagen shūran ················ 3:3a
  Gensen ·················· 3:23a-23b
  Iroha jirui shō ··············· 3:332a
  Nihon daijisho ··············· 5:379a
  Nippo jisho ·················· 6:8b
  Rigen shūran ················· 6:312a
  Ruiju myōgi shō ·············· 6:340a
  Setsuyōshū ··············· 7:72b-73a
  shinsen jikyō ················· 7:124b
  Wakun no shiori ·············· 8:221b
  Wamyō ruiju shō ············· 8:222a
Dictionnaire historique du Japon ·· 4:42b
Didactic writing ·············· 5:50a
Diesel Kiki Co, Ltd ············ 2:94a
Diet ······ 2:94a, 94b-96b; 4:37a
  cabinet orders ··············· 1:229a
  Constitution of 1947 ·········· 2:11a-11b
  delegation to power ··········· 2:84a
  democracy ··················· 2:84b
  elections ················· 2:189a-190a
  executive branch of government 3:55b-56a
  history ···················· 2:94a-94b
  Occupation ·················· 6:52a
  organization ·············· 2:94b-95a
  revision of tax system ········· 7:172b
  workings ·················· 2:95a-96b
  See also Imperial Diet
Diet Law ··················· 2:6b
Diet member legislation ········ 2:96b
Ding Ruchang (Ting Ju-ch'ang)
····················· 2:96b-97a; 8:287a
Diplomatics ······· 2:97a-100b, 112b-115a
  documents. See Documents
  external characteristics of documents
  ························· 2:97a-98b
    calligraphy styles ·········· 2:97b
    language styles ··········· 2:97b
    orthography ··············· 2:97b
    semantic problems ········ 2:97b-98b
    writing materials ········· 2:97a-97b
  hammotsu ················ 2:100a-100b
  historical documents ········ 2:99a-100b

Azuchi-Momoyama and Edo
  periods ·················· 2:100a-100b
  Kamakura and Muromachi
  periods ··················· 2:99b-100a
  Nara and Heian periods ···· 2:99a-99b
  internal characteristics
    date ····················· 2:99a
    issuing agent ············· 2:98b
    main text ·············· 2:98b-99a
    recipient ················· 2:98b
Diplomatic seals ············· 7:184a
Diplomats
  Aoki Shūzō ················· 1:69a-69b
  Arita Hachirō ··············· 1:85a
  Ashida Hitoshi ·············· 1:97b
  Enomoto Takeaki ·········· 2:219b-220a
  Gotō Shimpei ·············· 3:53b-54a
  Hayashi Tadasu ············· 3:118a
  Inoue Kaoru ············· 3:310a-310b
  Ishii Kikujirō ··············· 3:341a
  Iwakura Tomomi ············· 3:360a
  Katō Takaaki ············ 4:169b-170b
  Katsura Tarō ·············· 4:173b-174a
  Komura Jutarō ··········· 4:268a-268b
  Makino Nobuaki ············· 5:86b
  Matsuoka Yōsuke ·········· 5:139a-139b
  Mutsu Munemitsu ·········· 5:288b-289a
  Nomura Kichisaburō ·········· 6:34a
  Ōkuma Shigenobu ·········· 6:95b-96b
  Saitō Hiroshi ············· 6:373b-374a
  Satō Naotake ··············· 7:28a
  Shidehara Kijūrō ··········· 7:88a-89a
  Shigemitsu Mamoru ········· 7:91b-92b
  Soejima Taneomi ············ 7:219a
  Tanaka Giichi ············ 7:336a-336b
  Tōgō Shigenori ·············· 8:36b
  Uchida Kōsai ··············· 8:123b
  Ugaki Kazushige ·········· 8:130b-131a
  Yoshida Shigeru ··········· 8:343a-345a
  Yoshizawa Kenkichi ·········· 8:352a
Direct demand ············ 2:100b-101a
Disabled persons ············· 4:353a
Disarmament
  post-World War I ············ 1:88a
  post-World War II ········· 6:301a-301b;
  ························· 8:276a-277a
Discipline of Japanese history: a guide
  to research ·············· 2:101a-116b
  See also Historical scholarship
Discrimination ······· 1:216a-216b; 2:314a;
  ························ 5:195a-195b
Diseases ················· 5:147b-149a
  allergic disorders ············ 5:148b
  atomic bomb related ········ 1:111b-114a
  blood ····················· 5:148b
  circulatory ··············· 5:148a-148b
  collagen ··················· 5:148b
  digestive ··················· 5:148b
  endocrine and metabolic ······· 5:148b
  infectious ··············· 5:147b-148a
    prevention ··············· 5:149b
  intractable ················· 2:116b
  neoplasm ··················· 5:148a
  nervous disorders ············ 5:148b
  occupational ················ 6:55b
  parasitic ··················· 5:148a
  poisoning ················ 5:148b-149a
  pollution-related diseases ···· 6:217b-220a
  quarantine ················· 6:274a
  respiratory ················· 5:148a
  venereal ··················· 8:189b
Dismissal of an employee ······· 2:117a
Dispute resolution systems other than
  litigation ················ 2:117a-119a
  in court ················· 2:118b-119a
    arbitration ········· 1:74a-75a; 2:118b
    compromise ············ 2:118b-119a
    conciliation (chōtei) ········· 2:118b

  historical background ······ 2:117a-117b
  social methods ··········· 2:117b-118a
Dispute settlement ············ 4:53b
Distilling industries
  Nikka Whisky Distilling Co, Ltd ···· 6:1b
  Suntory, Ltd ················ 7:276a
  Takara Shuzō Co, Ltd ········· 7:318a
Distribution system ········ 2:119b-120b
  business ···················· 1:224b
  1868-1937 ················· 2:30b
  fragmented
    implications ·············· 2:120a
    sources ··············· 2:119b-120a
  trends of change ············· 2:120b
District courts ············ 4:80b-81b
Divers, Edward ·············· 2:121a
Divers ················· 2:286b; 4:37a
Dividends (kabushiki haitō) ······ 2:121a
Divination ················ 2:121a-121b
  futomani ··················· 2:121a
  incubation ·················· 2:121b
  kiboku ····················· 2:121a
  kites ······················ 2:230a
  shamanistic medium ·········· 2:121b
  Yi jing ····················· 2:121b
"Divine Soldiers" Incident ··· 7:108a-108b
Divine Wind League ··········· 4:58a
Divorce (rikon) · 2:121b-122b, 244b; 7:214b
  adultery ·················· 1:15b-16a
  settlements ················· 2:122a
    custody of children ········· 2:122a
    disposition of property ······· 2:122a
    general terms ············· 2:122a
    trends ················· 2:122a-122b
  types ··················· 2:121b-122a
    agreement ················ 2:121b
    arbitration ··············· 2:121b
    family court ··············· 2:121b
    judicial decision ········· 2:121b-122a
Divorce temple. See Kakekomidera
Doboku Kenkyūjo ············· 6:267a
Dōbōshū   同朋衆 ······ 4:62a
Dobu ················· どぶ ····· 7:111a
Dochirina kirishitan
  どちりな・きりしたん ····· 4:119b
Dōchū hizakurige
  ········· 道中膝栗毛 ····· 4:61a
Doctrina Christan ········· 4:52b, 119b
Documents
  bugyōnin hōsho ·············· 2:99b
  diplomatics. See Diplomatics
  gejijō ····················· 3:15b
  imperial edict ··············· 3:277a
  inzen ····················· 2:99b
  kampu ····················· 4:130a
  kaō ··················· 4:155a-156a
  kudashibumi ················· 4:302a
  migyōsho ················ 2:98a-99a
  mokkan ·············· 2:99a; 5:234a
  seals ····················· 7:45a
  semmyō ···················· 7:62a
  shotai ····················· 7:170a
  shuinjō ···················· 7:184a
  tasshi ····················· 2:100a
Dodge, Joseph M. ···· 2:122b-123a, 157b
Dodge line ··········· 2:122b-123a; 4:347a
  business cycles ··············· 1:224a
  economy ················· 2:157b-158a
  Ministry of International Trade and
  Industry ··················· 5:190b
  Price Control Order of 1946 ······ 6:238b
  Shimoyama Incident ··········· 7:107a
Doeff, Hendrik ··············· 2:123a
  French-Japanese relations ······· 2:330a
Dog, Japanese [(nihonken) Canis
  familiaris var. japonicus] ··· 2:124b-126a
  folklore ················· 2:125b-126a
  history ················· 2:125a-125b

types ············ 2:124b-125a
  large (ōgata)········ 2:124b-125a
  medium (chūgata)······ 2:125a
  small (kogata)········· 2:125a
Dōgashima········ 堂ヶ島 ··· 2:123a
Dōgen········ 道元 1:179b; 2:123a,
            123b-124a; 7:154a
  calligraphic works ········ 1:235b
  education ·············· 2:172b
  Eiheiji temple ········ 2:186a-186b
  Rinzai sect ············ 6:319a
  Sōtō sect ·········· 7:233b-234a
  Watsuji Tetsurō ········· 8:237b
Dogfighting (tōken) ····· 2:124a-124b
  Tosa dog ··············· 8:81b
Dōgo Hot Spring 道後温泉 2:126a; 5:141a
Dōgoyama ········ 道後山 ··· 2:126a
Dog shooting (inuoumono) ··· 2:125b
Dogtooth violet ··········· 4:165b
Dogū ·············· 土偶 4:74a-74b
Dogū mokugū ····· 土偶木偶 ·· 4:242b
Dohi Keizō ······ 土肥慶蔵 ·· 2:126a
Dōhō ············ 同胞 ···· 7:115b
Dōhoko ················ 1:175a
Dohyō ················· 7:271b
Dohyō's shōmen ··········· 7:272b
Doi Bansui ····· 土井晩翠 · 2:126a-126b;
                   5:12a
Doigahama ······ 土井ヶ浜 ·· 6:235a
  excavation of ············ 1:78a
Doihara-Chi'n Agreement. *See*
  Doihara-Qin (Doihara-Ch'in)
  Agreement
Doihara Kenji 土肥原賢二 · 2:126b
Doihara-Qin (Doihara-Ch'in) Agreement
                   2:126b
  Doihara Kenji ··········· 2:126b
Doi Kiyoyoshi ··· 土居清良 ·· 7:52a
Do ikki. 土一揆 **See Tsuchi ikki**
Doi Takeo ······ 土居健郎 ··· 1:49a
Doi Tatsuo ····· 土井辰雄 ·· 2:126b
Doi Toshikatsu 土井利勝 · 2:126b-127a
Dōji ············ 道慈 ···· 2:55a
Dōjima Rice Market
          堂島米市場 ···· 2:127a
  chōnin ················ 1:301b
  Kajimaya ·············· 4:114a
Dōjinsha school ··· 同人社 ·· 5:315a
Dojōgaku kenkyū
         土壌学研究 ···· 7:140b
Dōjōji ········ 道成寺 · 4:154b, 326a
Dojōsukui ············· 2:127b
Dōka ················· 1:175a
Dōkai Bay ······ 洞海湾 ·· 2:127b
Dōken ················· 1:175a
Dokkoishi ·············· 7:248a
Dokō Toshio ···· 土光敏夫 ·· 2:127b
Dokuganryū Masamune
        独眼竜政宗 · 2:78a; 4:166a
Dokugen aika ··· 独絃哀歌 ·· 4:123a
Dokugin hyakuin 独吟百韻 ···· 1:73b
Dokuritsu Bijutsu Kyōkai (Independent
  Art Association) ·········· 6:157a
Dokuritsu hyōron
  (Independent Review)
        独立評論 ····· 8:296a
Dokuro hai ····· どくろ杯 ·· 4:139a
Dokusen Kinshi Hō ······· 1:65b-67b
Dōkyō ·········· 道鏡 ··· 2:127b
  Fujiwara no Nakamaro ····· 2:353a
Doll Festival ····· 1:277b, 279b; 2:127a,
             127b-128a; 5:4a
  festivals ·············· 2:260b
  katashiro ·············· 4:166b
  origami ··············· 6:116b
  religious symbolism ······· 6:296a
  sekku ················ 7:58a
  shiohigari ·············· 7:140b

Dolls ·············· 2:128a-130a
  dogū ················ 2:128a
  Doll Festival. *See* **Doll Festival**
  Edo period ·········· 2:129a-130a
  gosho ningyō ········ 2:128b, 129b
  haniwa ··············· 2:128a
  Heian through Azuchi-Momoyama
    periods ··········· 2:128a-128b
  Hirata Gōyō ········· 2:129b, 130b
  inu hariko ············· 3:325b
  ishō ningyō ········· 2:129a, 129b
  kokeshi ··············· 4:254a
  Meiji period to present ····· 2:130a
  Saga ningyō ········· 2:129a, 129b
  Sakuma Kōho ········ 2:129a, 129b
  tsuchiningyō (earthen or clay) ·· 2:129b
Doll's House, A ··········· 7:112b
Dolmen burials. *See* **Prehistoric burials**
Dolphins. *See* **Whales**
Domain ················ 3:92b
  monopolies ············· 3:96a
Domainal code. *See* **Bunkokuhō**
Domainal paper money ······ 3:99b
Domain clique ········· 3:91b-92a
Domain currency ·········· 3:99b
Domain economies ········· 2:149a
Domain schools ······· 2:174a-174b
Dōmei (Japanese Confederation of
  Labor) ·········· 同盟 2:85b, 130a;
        4:347a-347b, 360a; 6:238a; 7:189a
  labor unions ········ 1:313b-314a
  Shinsambetsu ··········· 7:124a
  Takita Minoru ·········· 7:327a
Dōmei Tsūshinsha (Domei News
  Agency) ········ 2:130a; 4:54b; 5:369a
  censorship ············· 1:254a
  presidents ············· 2:373a
Domestic Affairs Adjustment Law · 2:118b,
                   246a
Domestic colonization doctrine ·· 7:236b
Domestic Competitive Painting
  Exhibitions (Naikoku Kaiga Kyōshinkai)
                   8:327b
Domestic exchange ····· 2:130a-130b
Domestic Painting Competitive
  Exhibitions ············ 7:359a
Dominicans ············ 2:130b
Dōmino ················ 7:249a
Dōmoto Inshō ··· 堂本印象 ·· 2:57b, 130b
Donchō ·············· 2:130b
Don Francisco de Velasco. *See* **Tanaka**
  Shōsuke
Dong Du Movement ········ 6:182a
Dongya Heqin Hui ········· 8:31a
Dōni ō dōwa ···· 道二翁道話 ·· 5:320a
Donjon ················ 1:248a
Donker Curtius, Jan Hendrik 2:130b-131a
Donsu (damask) ········· 2:131a
Door-to-Door Sales Law ····· 2:131a
Doppo gin ········ 独歩吟 ·· 4:309a
Dore, Ronald ············· 4:42a
Dōri no kankaku
        道理の感覚 ····· 1:51a
Dormouse, Japanese ····· 2:131a-131b
Doro-e ········· 泥絵 ··· 2:131b
Dorokyō ········ 瀞峡 ··· 2:131b
  Shingū ··············· 7:115a
Dōsen ·········· 道璿 ··· 2:131b
Dōshikai. *See* **Rikken Dōshikai**
Dōshin ········ 同心 ··· 8:338a
Dōshisha University · 2:131b-132a; 5:386a;
                  6:258a
Dōshō ·········· 道昭 1:106a; 2:132a
Dōshū ·········· 堂衆 ··· 2:132a
Dosō ············ 土倉 · 2:132a-132b;
              4:161b; 7:266b
  Shinran ··············· 7:122b
Dōsojin ········ 道祖神 ·· 2:132b

konsei, variation ········· 4:275b
Dōsōkai (alumni group) ····· 6:205b
Dōtaku ········ 銅鐸 1:257b; 2:132b
  Karako site ············· 4:157b
  Shintō ··············· 7:126a
Dōtoku ··········· 2:232b; 5:248a
Dōtombori ······ 道頓堀 ·· 6:119a
Double Fantasy ·········· 6:112a
"Doughnut phenomenon" ···· 8:176b
Douglas, Archibald ········· 7:242b
Douglas Reef ············· 6:93a
Dōwa Mining Co, Ltd ····· 2:132b-133a
Dōyaku (or *Zūfu*) *Haruma*
  (Halma Translated by
  Doeff) ····· 道訳法児馬 2:123a; 8:242b
Doyō fujin ······ 土曜夫人 ·· 6:65a
Dozō ················· 7:248b
Dōzoku ·········· 4:218a; 7:214b
Draft Law to Control Radical Social
  Movements ········· 2:133a-133b
Draft notification slips ····· 7:167b-168a
Dragon and Tiger ·········· 3:109b
Dragonflies ············ 2:133b
Dragon Palace ············ 5:295b
Drama
  modern ············· 5:57b-60a
    post-World War II ····· 5:59b-60a
    pre-World War II ····· 5:58a-59a
  radio ················ 6:275a
  Shingeki ·········· 7:112a-113b
  Shingeki ············· 7:112a
  Western
    criticism ········· 7:124b-125a
Draper, William ··········· 4:69b
Dress. *See* **Clothing**
Drivers' licenses ······· 2:133b-134a
  Road Traffic Law ········· 6:333a
Drug abuse ······· 2:45a, 134a-134b
  deaths ················ 4:86b
  Narcotics Control Law ····· 5:334b
Drugs ············ 5:150a-150b
  kampō ················ 5:151a
  medicine ·········· 5:150a-150b
  psychotherapy ··········· 6:261a
Drums ················ 5:282b
  taiko ················ 7:297b
  tsuzumi ·········· 8:119b-120a
Drunken drivers ··········· 6:333a
Dry field farming ········ 1:29a-29b
Drying Fishnets ··········· 4:111a
DSP ··············· 2:85a-85b
Dual Shintō (Ryōbu Shintō) ··· 4:188a;
               6:351a-351b
Dual sovereignty ··········· 6:86a
Dual structure ············ 2:324a
Duan Qirui (Tuan-Ch'i-jui) ··· 2:134b
Duan Qirui cabinet ········· 4:384b
Du Bousquet, Albert Charles · 1:166a;
               2:134b-135a
Du Fu ················ 6:297b
Dulles, John Foster · 2:135a-135b; 6:302b;
               7:10b-11a
Dutch East India Company
  Dutch Factory ··········· 2:135b
  Dutch trade ············ 2:135b
Dutch Factory ·········· 2:135b
  Doeff, Hendrik ·········· 2:123a
Dutch interpreters. *See* **Oranda tsūji**
Dutch-Japanese Treaty of Amity
              2:130b-131a
Dutch-language interpreters ···· 6:116a
Dutch Learning. *See* **Western Learning**
Dutch New Year ··········· 6:116a
Dutch reports ············ 6:115b
Dutch trade ·········· 2:135b-136a
Dyeing ········· 7:13b; 8:16b-21a, 29b-30a,
            237b-238a, 359a
Dyen, Isidore ············ 4:20a

Dyes and dye colors ··· 2:136a-136b; 8:18a
  design ················· 2:90a
  indigo ················· 3:290a
  murasaki root ··············· 5:267b

E

Eagles ··················· 3:114b
Earlier Nine Years' War ·· 1:4a-4b; 2:137a
  samurai in ················ 7:7b
Early Japanese History ·········· 6:288b
Early Japanese song. See Music, song, early
Early literature. See Literature
Ear ornaments, ancient ··········· 2:138b
  Kofun period ·········· 2:138b; 4:245a
Earthenware ············· 1:256b-258a
  Haji ware ·············· 3:84a-84b
  Jōmon pottery ············ 4:75a-75b
Earthquake Disaster Prevention,
  Committee for ············· 2:140b
Earthquake Research Institute ··· 2:141a;
    6:305b
Earthquakes ········· 2:138b-140a; 4:7b
  causes and distribution ···· 2:139a-139b
    crustal distortion and faulting ···· 2:139a
    mantle convection and horizontal
    displacement ············ 2:139b
  crustal movement ··········· 4:8b-9a
  prediction ················ 2:139b
    damage prevention ······· 2:139b-140a
    research ················ 2:139b
  Tōkyō Earthquake of 1923. See Tōkyō
  Earthquake of 1923
Earthquake scale ············· 2:140a
Earth sciences ·········· 2:140a-141a
  geology ················· 2:141a
  Meiji period ··········· 2:140a-141a
  seismology ············ 2:140b-141a
Earthworms [(mimizu) class Oligochaeta]
  ····················· 2:141a-141b
East Asia Common Culture Society 8:30a
East Asia cultural sphere ···· 2:141a-142a
East Asia Friendship Society ······· 8:31a
East Asian League ············ 8:30b
East Asia Research Institute ······· 8:289a
East Asia: The Great Tradition ····· 6:289a
East Asia: The Modern Transformation
  ····················· 6:289a
East China Sea ·············· 2:142a
Eastern European nations and
  Japan ·············· 2:142a-142b
  diplomatic relations ········· 3:323a-323b
  Japanese studies ··········· 4:43b-44a
  trade ················· 3:323a-323b
Eastern Japan ·············· 2:142b
Eastern Sea Road ··········· 8:40b-41b
East Germany ······· 3:27b; 4:43b-44a
East Hebei (Hopeh) Anticommunist
  Autonomous Government ···· 2:142b
  December Ninth Movement ········ 2:81a
  Yin Rugeng ··············· 8:325b
East India Company (Dutch). See Dutch
  East India Company
East India Company (English) ···· 1:334a
E-awase ········· 絵合せ ···· 7:167a
Ebara Corporation ········ 2:142b-143a
Ebashi Setsurō ··江橋節郎 ···· 2:143a
Ebetsu ············· 江別 ··· 2:143a

Ebi ···················· 7:179b
Ebina ·········· 海老名 ··· 2:143a
Ebina Danjō ······ 海老名弾正 ··· 2:143a
Ebine (Calanthe discolor) ···· 2:143a-143b
Ebino ············· えびの ··· 2:143b
Ebino Kōgen ····· えびの高原 2:143b; 4:221b
Ebisu ··········· 恵比須 2:143b; 5:296a
  Shintō family altars ··········· 7:137b
Ebisukaki ····· 恵比須舁き ···· 6:269b
Ebune ··················· 1:324a
Eburimanshi no yūga na seikatsu
  ··· 江分利満氏の優雅な生活 ··· 8:294b
Ebusshi ········· 絵仏師 ···· 2:143b
  Jigoku-zōshi ··············· 4:54b
  Kose school ··············· 4:295a
  Takuma school ············· 7:328a
Echigo-jishi ········ 越後獅子 ··· 4:118a
Echigo Mountains
  ············· 越後山脈 2:143b, 336b
Echizemmisaki ······ 越前岬 ··· 2:144a
Echizen ware ······· 越前焼 ··· 2:144a
  museums ················· 5:279b
Echizen'ya Chōjirō.
   越前屋長次郎
  See Tamenaga Shunsui
Eckert, Franz ·············· 5:286a
Econometric models ········ 2:144a-145a
  economic planning ··········· 2:144a
  Japanese planning ··········· 2:144a
  macroeconomic ·········· 2:144a-144b
  microeconomic ············· 2:144b
  recent developments and future
   prospects ············ 2:144b-145a
  regional industry ············ 2:144b
  static ··················· 2:144b
  turnpike ················· 2:144b
Economic Aspects of Japan, The ·7:324a
Economic cooperation ········· 1:205b
Economic Council ········· 2:167a-167b
Economic efficiency ······· 2:145a-146b
Economic growth, contemporary
  ···················· 2:163a-165a
  first phase ················ 2:163b
  government's role ········ 2:163a-163b
  major continuities ··········· 2:163a
  turning points ·········· 2:163b-165a
Economic history. See Economy,
  contemporary; Economy, early modern;
  Economy, Occupation-period;
  Economy, premodern
Economic independence ········ 2:165b
Economic planning ········· 2:165b-167b
  foreign investment control ······· 2:317a
  Income-Doubling Plan ·········· 3:287a
  industry choice ·········· 2:167a-167b
  managerial ideology ··········· 5:92b
  models ·················· 2:144a
  modern ·················· 2:163a
Economic Planning Agency (EPA)
  ············· 2:167b-168a; 4:190b
  function ·············· 2:165b-167a
  Income-Doubling Plan ·········· 3:287a
  national wealth ··········· 5:349a-349b
  White Paper on the Economy ····· 8:251b
  White Paper on the National Standard of
   Living ················· 8:251b
Economic Reconstruction Round
  Table ··················· 4:385b
Economic stabilization ········ 6:4b-5b
Economic Stabilization Board (ESB)
  ················· 1:8b; 2:168a
  Economic Planning Agency ··2:167b-168a
  economic reform ····· 2:155b-156a, 157a
  Nagano Shigeo ············· 5:303b
Economic Welfare Council ·· 2:168a-168b
Economists
  Amano Tameyuki ·········· 1:50b-51a
  Arisawa Hiromi ············ 1:84a-84b

  Crawford, Sir John Grenfell ······· 2:41b
  Fukuda Tokuzō ············· 2:362b
  Hirano Yoshitarō ············ 3:143b
  Inomata Tsunao ············· 3:309a
  Ishibashi Tanzan ············ 3:339b
  Kaiho Seiryō ·············· 4:110a
  Kanai Noburu ············· 4:135b
  Kawakami Hajime ············ 4:180b
  Koizumi Shinzō ············· 4:250b
  Kushida Tamizō ············· 4:320a
  Masuchi Yōjirō ············· 5:129b
  Mayet, Paul ··············· 5:142b
  Minobe Ryōkichi ············ 5:194a
  Morishima Michio ············ 5:253a
  Morito Tatsuo ············· 5:254b
  Nakayama Ichirō ············ 5:318b
  Noro Eitarō ··············· 6:38b
  Ōshima Sadamasu ············ 6:126a
  Ōtsuka Hisao ·············· 6:134a
  Ōuchi Hyōe ············ 6:135a-135b
  Sakisaka Itsurō ············· 7:2b-3a
  Shiozawa Masasada ··········· 7:141b
  Sōda Kiichirō ·············· 7:219a
  Sugimoto Eiichi ············· 7:258a
  Sugimura Kōzō ············· 7:258a
  Taguchi Ukichi ············· 7:294b
  Takata Yasuma ············· 7:319b
  Uno Kōzō ·············· 8:173b-174a
  Yamada Moritarō ············ 8:289a
  Yanaihara Tadao ············ 8:315b
  Yasui Takuma ··········· 8:318b-319a
Economy
  balance of payments ······· 1:133b-135a
  business concentration ········· 1:224a
  business cycles ·········· 1:224a-224b
  hunting and gathering ·········· 4:72a
  income distribution ········ 3:285b-287a
  industrial organization ····· 3:292a-296b
  industrial revolution in Japan ····· 3:298a
  industrial structure ········ 3:299b-302a
  Industrial Structure Council ······ 3:302a
  inflation and price stability ······ 3:303a
  input-output analysis ······· 3:312b-313a
  Matsukata era ············· 3:194b
  Matsukata fiscal policy ········· 5:134b
  maturing process ········· 5:241a-241b
  Meiji period ············ 2:29b-30a
  occupational structure ········ 6:55b-57b
  postwar growth ·········· 3:203a-203b
  occupation ················ 3:240a
  pre-World War II recovery ······· 3:201a
  price guidelines
   incomes policy ············ 3:287b
  recovery of during Shōwa depression
  ····················· 7:174a
  White Paper on the Economy ····· 8:251b
  White Paper on the National Standard of
   Living ················· 8:251b
  wholesale and retail ·········· 1:224b
  World War I ············ 3:199b-200a
Economy, premodern (to 1867)
  ···················· 2:146b-151a
  before 1600 ············ 2:147a-149a
   autonomous domains ·········· 2:148b
   commercialization and monetary
    expansion ··········· 2:148a-148b
   domain economics ··········· 2:149a
   foreign trade ·············· 2:148a
   protohistorical period ········· 2:147a
   ritsuryō system ·········· 2:147a-147b
   shōen ················ 2:147b-148a
   unification ··············· 2:149a
   urbanization ··········· 2:148b-149a
  Edo period ············· 2:149a-151a
   commercial expansion ······ 2:149a-150a
   diffusion of trade and handicraft
    industry ················ 2:150a
   employment options ·········· 2:150b

fiscal deficits and impoverished
samurai ················· **2:150b**
foreign trade ············· **2:150a**
regional variation ········ 2:150a-150b
shipping ················ **2:149b**
urbanization ·········· 2:149a-149b

Economy, early modern (1868-1945)
···················· **2:151a-154a**
foreign capital and commerce 2:151a-151b
growth industries ········ **2:152b-153a**
growth problems ········· **2:153a-154a**
industrialization and modernization
···················· **2:151a-152a**
private sector ············ **2:152a**
production ·············· 2:152a-152b

Economy, Occupation-period (1945-52)
···················· **2:154a-158b**
conclusions ·············· **2:158b**
Dodge line ·············· **2:157b-158a**
end of war ·············· 2:154a-155a
policy makers ·········· **2:154b**
SCAP ················· **2:154b-155a**
Korean War ············· 2:158a-158b
reform ················· 2:155a-156b
economic aid ·········· **2:155a**
economic purgation ······ **2:155a**
inflation and inflation control
··················· **2:155a-156b**
reparation payments ····· **2:155a**
reverse course ········· **2:156b-157a**

Economy, contemporary (from 1952)
···················· **2:158b-165b**
economic heritage ········ **2:158b-159a**
economic performance overview
···················· **2:159a-161a**
growth ················ **2:159b-160b**
investment and saving ····· 2:160b-161a
labor force ············ 2:161a-161b
technology ············· **2:161b**
growth benefits and costs ······· **2:165a**
growth environment ······ **2:163a-165b**
first phase ············· **2:163b**
government's role ······· 2:163a-163b
major continuities ······ **2:163a**
turning points ········· 2:163b-165a
structural changes ······· 2:161b-162a
industrial organization ·· **2:162b-163a**
production and workers distribution
···················· **2:162a-162b**

Edachi ············· 役立ち ··· **8:327a**
E-dai ···················· **4:164b**
Eda Saburō ········ 江田三郎 ··· **2:168b**
Japan Socialist Party ······· **4:49a**
Eda Satsuki ········ 江田五月 ··· **2:168b**
Edict of Expulsion ········· **8:95a**
"Edicts on Compassion for Living
Things" (Shōrui awaremi no rei)
···················· **8:56a-56b**
Edo ············· 江戸 ·· **2:168b-169b**
castle town ·············· **1:249a**
chōnin class ············· **1:301b**
development ············· **2:168b-169a**
influence ··············· **2:169b**
journeys to ·············· **2:171b**
land reclamation ········· **4:364a**
land use ·············· 2:169a-169b
population ·············· **8:178a**
rice riot ··············· **8:124a**
urbanization ·········· **8:176a, 177b**
Edo Castle ········· 江戸城 ··· 2:169b-170a
chōnin ················ **1:301b**
Kaempfer, Engelbert ········ **4:101b**
Nakaoku ················ **2:170a**
Ōhiroma ················ **6:74a**
Ōoku ·················· **6:113b**
Ōta Dōkan ·············· **6:128b**
Tokugawa Ieyasu ·········· **8:50a**
paintings ··············· **4:151a**

Edo city commissioners ········ **2:171a**
Edogawa ·········· 江戸川 ··· **2:170b**
Edogawa Rampo
·········· 江戸川乱歩 ·· 2:170b-171a;
5:291b
Edogawa Rampo Prize ········ **2:171a**
Edogawa Ward ··· 江戸川区 ········ **2:171a**
*Edo hakkei (Eight Views
of Edo)* ····· 江戸八景 ··· **8:184b**
Edo hanjō ki ··· 江戸繁昌記 ··· **8:11b**
Edo history. *See* **History of Japan**
Edokko ··············· 江戸子 ··· **4:61b**
Edokoro ············ 絵所 ··· **2:171a**
Edo kouta ········ 江戸小唄 ··· **4:298a**
Edokyahan ··············· **4:323b**
Edo literature. *See* **Literature**
Edo machi bugyō
·········· 江戸町奉行 · **2:171a; 5:78b;
7:6a**
Itakura Katsushige ············ **3:350a**
Ōoka Tadasuke ············· **6:113b**
Tōyama Kinshirō ············ **8:88a**
Edo Murasaki ······ 江戸紫 ··· **4:199a**
Edo period ········ 江戸時代 · **2:171a-171b**
Edo-period education. *See* **Education**
Edo-period wares. *See* **Ceramics**
Edo sampu ······ 江戸参府 ··· **2:171b**
Dejima ················· **2:83a**
Dutch Factory ············ **2:135b**
Kaempfer, Engelbert ········ **4:101b**
EDR ··················· **2:235b**
Education ·············· **2:171b-179a**
academic degrees ·········· **1:6a**
academic freedom ········· 1:6a-6b
academic pressures ········ **5:6b**
administration ········· **2:177a-178b, 181a**
local ················· 2:177b-178a
national ·············· **2:177b**
adult ················· **1:341b-342a**
audiovisual ············· 1:116a; **2:181b**
authorization system ········ **7:37b**
before 1600 ············ 2:172a-172b
ancient Japan ········· 2:172a-172b
medieval education ······ **2:172b**
boards ················· **2:178a**
Central Council for Education ·· **1:255b**
children of returnees ······ **2:182a**
Chinese characters required ······ **4:331b**
civic ················· **1:316a**
civil service ·········· 1:218a, 219b-220a
coeducation ············· **1:334a**
commoners school ··· **4:113b, 340a; 7:182a**
community ········· 1:341a, 342a; **2:182a**
compulsory ········· 1:344a; **2:183a-183b,
195a-195b, 223b; 7:35b**
corporate management ········ **2:32b**
corporate training and ········· **2:28a**
correspondence ········· **2:181b-182a**
cram schools ············· **2:41b**
cumulative guidance record (shidō
yōroku) ·············· **2:53a**
curriculum ············· **7:34a-36a**
elementary and secondary ··· 7:34a-35a
extracurricular activities ······ **7:35b**
foreign language training ··· **2:318b; 7:35b**
health and physical education ···· **7:35b**
history ················ **7:35b-36a**
home economics ········· **7:35b**
language ·············· **7:34b**
mathematics ············ **7:35a**
music and art ··········· **7:35b**
physics ··············· **4:10a; 6:186b**
school course guidelines ······ **7:34a**
science ··············· **7:35a**
social studies ·········· 7:34b-35a
structure ·············· **7:34b-35a**
democratization ········· 2:180a-180b
Edo period ············· **2:172b-175a**

Confucian scholarship and school
formation ·············· **2:173a-173b**
domain schools ········· **2:174a-174b**
heterodoxy and new orthodoxy ·· **2:173b**
other schools ·········· **2:174b-175a**
elementary ············· **2:195a-196a**
entrance examinations ·· **2:181a, 222a-223a**
environmental ············ **2:224a**
expenses ·············· **2:179b-180a**
finance ················ **2:178a-178b**
local ················· **2:178a**
national ·············· **2:178a**
financial aid ············· **2:277a**
foreign students in Japan ····· **2:319a**
schools ················ **3:3a**
gakubatsu ············ **1:147a; 3:3b-4a**
government policy ········· **2:178b**
decentralization ········· **2:178b**
equal opportunity ······ **2:178b, 230b**
finance ·············· **2:178b-179a**
private schools ········· **2:179a**
single-track school system ··· **2:178b**
teacher status, quality, and
renumeration ········· **2:178b**
graduate schools ·········· **3:59b**
higher. *See* **Higher education**
home ················· **2:181b**
humanization ············ **2:180b**
Iwakura mission and ········· **3:359b**
Japanese children abroad ···· **7:36a-37b,
48b-49a**
judges
Legal Training and Research Institute
···················· **1:320b**
levels
elementary (shotō kyōiku) · **2:194a-195b**
high schools (kōtō gakkō) ······· **2:195b**
junior colleges ········· **4:84a-84b**
preschool ············· **6:235b**
secondary (chūtō kyōiku) · **2:194a; 7:52a**
university. *See* **Universities and colleges**
lifelong learning ··········· **5:5b**
lifestyles ·············· **5:6b, 8b**
literacy ··········· **2:172b-173a; 5:10b-11a**
management ············· **5:89b**
mass communications ······· **5:129a-129b**
medical ·············· **3:120a-120b**
Meiji period ············· **2:152b**
militaristic ····· **2:176a-176b, 183b; 5:175a;
7:52a**
miscellaneous schools ······· **2:198b**
mission schools ········· **5:202b-203a**
modern ·············· **2:175a-176b**
characteristics ········· **2:175a-175b**
consolidation ··········· **2:176a**
establishment ········· **2:175b-176a**
expansion ·············· **2:176a**
post-World War II reforms ··· **2:176b**
wartime ·············· **2:176a-176b**
moral ··········· **5:248a-248b; 7:191b**
music ················· **5:285a**
national budget ··········· **1:204b**
nationalism ··········· **2:176a, 183b**
private schools ·········· **7:94a-94b**
professional schools ········· **7:62a**
progressive ·············· **7:31b**
provision, by parent or guardian ···· **1:21b**
PTAs ················· **6:262b**
reform ········· **2:176a-176b; 2:183a-184a**
early 20th century ········· **2:183b**
interwar period ········· **2:183b**
Meiji period ·········· 2:183a-183b
of 1947 ·············· **2:180a-180b**
post-World War II ······· **2:183b-184a**
religious ······ **6:290b, 295a-295b; 7:191a**
report cards ············· **6:302b**
research ·············· **2:180b-181a**
Shin Kyōiku Undō ·········· **7:121b**

scholastic ability measurement
········ 2:180b-181a
school administration ··········· 7:33a
school orders (gakkōrei) ········· 7:36b
school system ·········· 2:176b-177a
secondary ················ 2:195b
sex ···················· 7:73b
single-track system ········· 2:178b
special ·················· 7:241b
teachers ·············· 7:365a-367a
teacher-training systems ···· 6:38a; 7:365b
teaching methods ·········· 7:367a-367b
testing ·················· 1:10b
textbooks ················ 7:37b
tutoring schools (juku) ········ 2:223a
United States education missions to
Japan ················ 8:164b
universities and colleges ····· 3:133a-135a;
8:170a-171a
village schools (gōgaku) ·········· 3:40a
vocational ············ 8:192b-193a
Vocational Training Law · 8:193a-193b
Western Learning ···· 4:306a; 8:241a-243a
Western influence ········· 2:175b-176a
women ········· 8:260a; 267a-268a
contemporary ········· 8:262b-263a
youth schools ·············· 7:52a
Education, Fundamental Law of
···················· 2:182a-182b
aims ·················· 2:180a
content ················ 2:178b
Education Act of 1872 ········· 7:191b
Educational broadcasting ······ 2:179a
Educational counseling ····· 2:179a-179b
cases ················· 2:179b
Educational expenses ····· 2:179b-180a
Educational Personnel Certification Law
···················· 7:366a
Educational Public Employees Special
Law ················· 8:171a
Educational Reforms of 1947 2:180a-180b
coeducation ·············· 1:334a
Educational research ······· 2:180b-181a
administration ············ 2:181a
entrance examination system ····· 2:181a
humanization and curriculum revision
···················· 2:180b
moral education ··········· 2:181a
National Institute for ········ 2:181a
scholastic ability measurement
···················· 2:180b-181a
school role and function ········ 2:181a
Educational Research, National Institute
for ·················· 2:181a
Educational technology ········· 2:181b
Education law ·············· 2:182b
"Education mother" ··········· 2:181b
Education Order of 1872 ····· 2:175b,
182b-183a, 230b, 361a; 3:193b; 5:11a;
7:241b
coeducation ·············· 1:334a
compulsory education ········· 1:344a
Murray, David ············· 5:275a
normal schools ············· 6:38a
Ōseidasaresho ············· 6:124a
private schools ············ 6:252a
Tanaka Fujimaro ··········· 7:336a
teachers ·············· 7:365a-365b
Verbeck, Guido Herman Fridolin · 8:190a
women's education ··········· 8:267b
Education Order of 1879 ······ 2:183a
Education Reform Council ··· 1:51a, 255b;
2:183a
Fundamental Law of Education ···· 2:182a
Occupation ·············· 6:53a
United States education missions to
Japan ················ 8:164b

Educators
American
Bacon, Alice Mabel ··········· 1:129b
Berry, John Cutting ··········· 1:150a
Brown, Samuel Robbins ········ 1:175b
Clark, Edward Warren ········· 1:321b
Clark, William Smith ········· 1:321b
Fenollosa, Ernest Francisco · 2:251b-252a
Griffis, William Elliot ········· 3:62b
Janes, Leroy Lansing ··········· 4:2a
Kauffman, James Lee ·········· 4:175a
Mason, Luther Whiting ···· 5:127b-128a
Murray, David ············· 5:275a
Scott, Marion McCarrell ········ 7:41a
Shaw, Glenn William ··········· 7:81a
Vining, Elizabeth Gray ········· 8:192a
Vories, William Merrel ········· 8:195b
Warner, Langdon ··········· 8:228a
British
Conder, Josiah ············· 1:349b
Murdoch, James ············ 5:270b
German
Fröbel, Friedrich Wilhelm August 2:339b
Hausknecht, Emile ········· 3:114a-114b
Hearn, Lafcadio ·········· 3:120b-121a
Japanese
Abe Isoo ················· 1:2a
Abe Jirō ················· 1:2b
Abe Shigetaka ·············· 1:4b
Abe Yoshishige ·············· 1:5a
Amano Tameyuki ········· 1:50b-51a
Amano Teiyū ·············· 1:51a
Ashida Enosuke ········· 1:97a-97b
Atomi Kakei ·············· 1:115a
Azuma Ryōtarō ············ 1:127b
Daikuhara Gintarō ··········· 2:60b
Fukuzawa Yukichi ······· 2:367b-368a
Hamao Arata ·············· 3:91a
Hasegawa Tai ·············· 3:108a
Hatano Kanji ·············· 3:112a
Hatoyama Haruko ············ 3:112b
Hirose Tansō ·············· 3:148a
Inoue Enryō ·············· 3:309b
Inoue Tetsujirō ············· 3:311a
Itō Jinsai ················ 3:354a
Iwamoto Yoshiharu ··········· 3:360b
Izawa Shūji ··············· 3:365a
Kaigo Tokiomi ············· 4:109b
Kanō Jigorō ·············· 4:147a
Kawai Michi ·············· 4:179a
Kawasaki Natsu ············· 4:184a
Kikuchi Dairoku ············ 4:206a
Kozaki Hiromichi ··········· 4:300a
Maeda Tamon ·············· 5:80b
Makiguchi Tsunesaburō ········· 5:85b
Miura Baien ··········· 5:214b-215a
Miwata Masako ········· 5:216a-216b
Miyake Yonekichi ············ 5:219a
Mori Arinori ·········· 5:248b-249a
Morito Tatsuo ············· 5:254b
Motoda Nagazane ············ 5:257a
Nakai Chikuzan ············· 8:292a
Nakai Riken ··············· 8:292a
Nambara Shigeru ············ 5:323b
Naruse Jinzō ·············· 5:335a
Nishi Amane ············ 6:14a-14b
Nishimura Shigeki ········· 6:17b-18b
Nitobe Inazō ············ 6:21b-22a
Obara Kuniyoshi ············ 6:48a
Ogura Kinnosuke ············ 6:71a
Ōhara Yūgaku ·············· 6:73b
Oikawa Heiji ·········· 6:74b-75a
Okamoto Kansuke ············ 6:80a
Ōse Jintarō ············ 6:124a-124b
Ototake Iwazō ············· 6:133b
Sawayanagi Masatarō ·········· 7:31a
Shimoda Utako ············· 7:105a
Sugiura Shigetake ··········· 7:258a

Tachibana Kōzaburō ······ 7:292a-292b
Takada Sanae ············· 7:310b
Takagi Kenkan ············· 7:311a
Takamine Hideo ········· 7:315a-315b
Tanaka Fujimaro ··········· 7:336a
Tanimoto Tomeri ············ 7:342a
Tejima Seiichi ············· 7:377a
Tosaka Jun ··············· 8:81b
Toyama Masakazu ············ 8:88a
Tsuda Umeko ·········· 8:112b-113a
Tsunoda Ryūsaku ············ 8:116a
Yajima Kajiko ············· 8:284b
Yanaihara Tadao ············ 8:315b
Yasui Tetsu ··············· 8:319a
Yoshida Shōin ········· 8:345b-346a
Yuasa Hachirō ············· 8:354b
Eejanaika ·ええじゃないか· 2:184a
Eel, Japanese [(unagi) Anguilla
japonica] ··········· 2:184a, 287b
Efu ··············衛府···· 2:184a
Efumi ·············絵踏···· 4:119a
Egami Namio 江上波夫 ······ 1:78b
horse-rider theory ··········· 3:230a
E-gasuri ················· 4:164b
Egawa Hidetatsu ·江川英龍······ 2:184b
Egawa Tan'an. 江川坦庵
See **Egawa Tarōzaemon**
Egawa Tarōzaemon
············江川太郎左衛門···· 2:184b
Eggplant [(nasu) Solanum melongena]
···················· 2:184b
Ego ··················· 2:184b
Egonoki [(Japanese snowbell) Styrax
japonica] ··············· 2:184b
Egōshū ··········会合衆·· 2:184b-185a
Eguchi ·············江口···· 4:135b
Ehime Prefecture ·愛媛県·· 2:185a-185b
Ehon butai ōgi 絵本舞台扇 ······ 8:141a
Ehon mushi erami 画本虫撰· 8:142a, 185b
Eibutsuka poems ············· 5:106a
Eichelberger, Robert Lawrence ······ 2:185b;
7:33a
Eidaka ···············永高··2:185b-186a;
4:137a
Eifuku Mon'in ···永福門院···· 2:186a
Eiga monogatari ·栄華物語· 2:186a; 5:37a,
246a
Akazome Emon ············· 1:41a
Fujiwara no Michinaga ········· 2:186a
historiography ············· 3:153a
*Eigen Jakushitsu wajō
goroku* 永源寂室和上語録 ······ 4:2a
Eighteen Kabuki numbers ······ 4:97b-99a
Eight Eight Fleet ············· 3:73b
Eight Outrages ·············· 3:73b
Eight Provinces of Kantō ········ 4:141b
Eight Views of Ōmi ············ 6:101b
Eight Views of the Xiao (Hsiao) and
Xiang (Hsiang) Rivers ··· 7:167b; 8:13a
Eiheiji ···············永平寺·· 2:186a-186b,
364a
training ················· 2:172b
Eihei shingi ··········永平清規···· 2:172b
*Eikoku sangyō kakumei
shi ron* 英国産業革命史論 ······ 8:127a
Eikosaku ············永小作···· 2:186b
Eikyō Disturbance ··········· 7:322a
E inga kyō ······ 絵因果経 2:199a; 6:148a,
149a
Eiraku Hozen ········永楽保全···· 2:186b
Eirakusen ··········永楽銭···· 1:156b;
2:186b; 5:242b
erizeni ················· 2:230b
kandaka ················· 4:137a
Eirin ·················· 5:256b
Eisai ·················栄西· 1:179b, 294a;
2:187a-187b; 3:171b
calligraphic works ··········· 1:235b

Rinzai sect ··············· **6:319a**
Eisai Co, Ltd ·············· **2:187b**
Eisei Bunko Foundation ········· **5:276b**
Eison ··········· 叡尊 ··· **2:187b-188a**
Eiten ····················· **2:187b**
Eitoku. 永徳 ····· *See* **Kanō Eitoku**
Eiyokei ··········· 栄誉刑 ····· **7:140b**
Eiyū taibōron (Awaiting
   Heroes) ······· 英雄待望論 ····· **8:117a**
Eizon ·············· 叡尊 ··· **2:187b-188a**
   monasticism ··············· **5:238b**
Eji ······················· 衛士 ····· **2:184a**
Ejima Incident ····· 絵島事件 ····· **2:188a**
   Kaigetsudō Ando ············ **4:109b**
Ejima Kiseki ···· 江島其磧 **2:188a; 5:48b**
   fūzoku shōsetsu ··········· **2:278a**
Ejō ····················· 懐奘 ····· **2:186b**
Ekayāna (One Vehicle) doctrine · **4:67b**
Ekiben ················ **2:188a-188b**
Ekisei ··············· 駅制 ····· **2:188b**
Elderly ····················· **5:5a**
   institutions ··········· **7:211b-212a**
   lifestyles ················· **5:7a**
   otona ···················· **6:132b**
   respect for ··············· **5:5a**
   social security ············ **4:353a**
   suicides among ··········· **7:209a**
   welfare ············· **7:211b-212a**
Elder statesmen ··········· **3:21b-22a**
Election Law of 1945 ········ **8:263a**
Elections ··········· **2:188b-190a**
   democracy ·········· **2:84b-85a**
   Diet ····················· **2:94a**
   Imperial Diet ············ **3:276a**
   registration ·············· **2:190a**
   voter participation ········ **2:190a**
Electoral system ··········· **2:190a**
Electrical products
   manufacturers ··········· **7:174a**
Electric power ········· **2:190a-191b**
   companies
      Chūbu Electric Power Co, Inc ···· **1:311a**
      Chūgoku Electric Power Co, Inc ·· **1:312a**
      Hokkaidō Electric Power Co, Inc · **3:214a**
      Hokuriku Electric Power Co, Inc · **3:215a**
      Kansai Electric Power Co, Inc
                        ····· **4:151b-152a**
      Kyūshū Electric Power Co, Inc ··· **4:340b**
      Shikoku Electric Power Co, Ltd ··· **7:97b**
      Tōhoku Electric Power Co, Inc ··· **8:37a**
      Tōkyō Electric Power Co, Inc ··· **8:37a**
   dams ················ **2:72a-73b**
   development ············ **2:191b**
   distribution ········· **2:191a-191b**
   industrialization ·········· **2:191a**
   periods
      first ··················· **2:190b**
      second ················· **2:190b**
      third ·············· **2:190b-191a**
   suppliers ················· **4:10b**
   system ··················· **2:191a**
   transmission ········ **2:191a-191b**
**Electric Power Development Co,
   Ltd** ················ **2:191b-192a**
**Electric Power Industry, Central
   Research Institute of** ······ **2:192a**
Electric Power Management Law · **2:191b**
Electric power system ········ **2:191a**
Electronics ············ **2:192a-195a**
   companies
      Akai Electric Co, Ltd ······· **1:39b**
      Alps Electric Co, Ltd ······· **1:48a**
      Casio Computer Co, Ltd (Kashio
         Keisanki) ··············· **1:245b**
      Fujitsū, Ltd ··············· **2:347b**
      Hitachi, Ltd ········· **3:206b-207a**
      Matsushita Electric Industrial Co, Ltd
                              ····· **5:140b**

Matsushita-Kotobuki Electronics
   Industries, Ltd ········ **5:141a-141b**
Mitsubishi Electric Corporation
                        ····· **5:207a-207b**
Nippon Electric Co, Ltd ····· **6:9a-9b**
Oki Electric Industry Co, Ltd ··· **6:84a**
Omron Tateisi Electronics Co, Ltd
                        ····· **6:104a**
Pioneer Electronic Corporation ··· **6:189a**
San'yō Electric Co, Ltd ····· **7:19a**
Sharp Corporation ····· **7:80a-80b**
Sony Corporation ····· **7:228b-229a**
Tōshiba Corporation ········· **8:82b**
Trio–Kenwood Corporation ··· **8:106a**
Victor Co. of Japan, Ltd ····· **8:191b**
   consumer grade ······· **2:194a-194b**
   computer industry ········· **1:344a**
   development ·············· **2:192a**
      after 1955 ········· **2:193b-194a**
      postwar (1945-54) ········· **2:193b**
   industry structure ····· **2:194a-195a**
   manufacturers ············ **2:194a**
   Shinagawa Ward ··········· **7:108b**
   to 1945 ·················· **2:192a**
Electrotechnical Laboratory · **2:195a;
                              6:305b**
Elementary and secondary education
                        ····· **2:195b-196a**
*Elementary Japanese for College
   Students* ··············· **2:196b**
El Filibusterismo ··········· **6:332b**
Eliot, Charles Norton Edgcumbe · **1:149b;
                              2:196a**
Elisséeff, Serge ····· **2:196a-196b; 4:42b**
Elite, political and social ······· **8:325a**
Elizabeth Saunders Home · **2:196b; 7:30b**
   konketsuji in ············· **4:271b**
Ema ············ 絵馬 · **2:196b, 197a,
                        197b-198a; 7:144b, 256b**
   Kanō school ·············· **4:149b**
Emaki. *See* **Emakimono**
Emakimono ····· 絵巻物 · **2:198a-200a;
                              6:150a**
   Ban Dainagon ekotoba ······ **1:137a; 6:152a**
   Buddhist art ········· **1:186b-187a**
   Chōjū giga (Scrolls of Frolicking Animals
      and Humans) ········· **1:298b; 2:199a-199b**
   format ············· **2:198a-199b**
   Gaki-zōshi ············· **1:190b, 191a**
   Genji monogatari emaki · **1:163b; 2:198a-198b**
   Heiji monogatari emaki ····· **3:123b; 6:152a**
   history ············· **2:199a-200a**
   Jigoku-zōshi ············· **1:190b**
   Kanō school ·············· **4:149b**
   Scrolls of Hungry Ghosts ····· **1:190b**
   Shigisan engi emaki ····· **7:92b-93a, 93a**
   Sumiyoshi school ·········· **7:270a**
   Toba Sōjō ········ **2:199a-199b; 8:31b-32a**
   Tosa school ··············· **8:82a**
Embree, John Fee ··· **2:200a; 4:38b; 7:73b,
                              255a**
Embroidery ··············· **2:200a**
Embushū ··········· 閻浮集 ····· **8:16a**
Emigrant Protection Art ······· **2:200b**
Emigration ··········· **2:200a-201b**
   early ····················· **2:200b**
   effects ··················· **2:201b**
   exclusionism ············· **2:200b**
   growth of empire ·········· **2:200b**
   to Latin America ·········· **4:369a**
   Okinawa ················· **6:87b**
   postwar ············ **2:201a-201b**
   prewar ············ **2:200b-201a**
   See also **Immigration**
Emigration and immigration control
                        ····· **2:201b**
Emigration Bureau ··········· **2:200b**

Emi no Oshikatsu
                  恵美押勝 ······· **2:353b**
Emishi. 蝦夷 *See* **Ezo**
Emi Suiin ······· 江見水蔭 ····· **4:199a**
Emma ····················· **2:201b**
   hell ····················· **3:126a**
Emmeiji ··········· 延命寺 ····· **4:177a**
Emperor ············· **2:202a-209a**
   early ············· **2:203a-204b**
   Edo period ········· **2:204b-205b**
   "Emperor System" (Tennōsei) ····· **2:207b**
   Heian period ············ **2:204a**
   hōō (priestly retired sovereign) ·· **3:227a**
   Kamakura period ······ **2:204a-204b**
   legal status ·········· **2:208b-209a**
   list of ··············· **2:202a-203a**
   meaning ············ **2:208a-208b**
   Meiji Constitution ····· **2:2b-3a; 3:195b**
   Meiji period ······ **2:206b; 5:153a-154a**
   Meiji Restoration ····· **2:205b-206b**
   Muromachi and Azuchi-Momoyama
      periods ·············· **2:204b**
   1947 Constitution ····· **2:207b-208a**
   organ-of-state theory ······· **8:8a**
   present ············ **2:207a-207b**
   religion ·················· **6:291a**
   renunciation of divinity ······· **2:209a**
   "Symbol Emperor System" (Shōchō
      Tennō Sei) ············ **2:208a**
   Taishō period ········ **2:206b-207a**
   theocracy ················ **8:24a**
   veneration of ············ **6:290b**
"Emperor art" ··········· **7:351a-351b**
Emperor-as-organ theory. *See* **Tennō
   kikan setsu**
Emperors ············· **2:202a-203a**
   Antoku ············ **1:40a, 67b**
   Chōkei ··················· **1:299b**
   Daigo ···················· **2:57a**
   En'yū ···················· **1:62b**
   Fushimi ·················· **2:375a**
   Go-Daigo ····· **1:99a, 100a-100b; 3:39a**
   Go-Fukakusa ············· **3:39b**
   Go-Hanazono ············· **3:40a**
   Go-Ichijō ··········· **3:40a-40b**
   Go-Kameyama ········· **3:41b-42a**
   Go-Komatsu ·············· **3:43b**
   Go-Mizunoo ········· **1:193b; 3:44b**
   Go-Saga ·················· **3:47a**
   Go-Sanjō ················· **3:47a**
   Go-Shirakawa ········· **1:189b; 3:49b**
   Go-Toba ·················· **1:40a**
   Go-Uda ··················· **3:54b**
   Hirohito ········· **1:41b; 3:147a**
   Ichijō ··········· **3:255b-256a**
   Jimmu ············· **4:57a-57b**
   Juntoku ·················· **4:85a**
   Kameyama ··············· **4:125a**
   Kammu ··················· **4:128a**
   Kazan ···················· **4:185a**
   Keikō ···················· **4:189a**
   Keitai ··········· **4:190a-190b**
   Kimmei ·················· **4:208a**
   Kōbun ··················· **4:238b**
   Kōgon ··················· **4:249a**
   Kōkō ····················· **1:45a**
   Kōmei ············· **4:266a-266b**
   Kōtoku ··················· **4:297b**
   Meiji ············· **5:153a-154a**
   Mommu ·················· **5:236a**
   Nintoku ·················· **6:8a**
   Ōjin ·············· **6:76a-76b**
   Reizei ···················· **1:62a**
   Saga ····················· **6:363b**
   Sanjō ···················· **7:12a**
   Shirakawa ················ **7:146b**
   Shōmu ············· **1:184b, 198a**
   Sujin ···················· **7:264b**

Sutoku · · · · · · · · · · · · · · · · · **7:279b–280a**
Taishō · · · · · · · · · · · · · · · · **7:305a–305b**
Temmu · · · · · · · · · · · · · · · · **7:381b–382b**
Tenji · **8:5b–6a**
Toba · **8:31b**
Tsuchimikado · · · · · · · · · · · · · · **8:112a**
Uda · · · · · · · · · · · · · · · · **1:45a; 8:125b**
Empire of Great Japan · · · · · · · · · **2:66b**
growth · **2:200b**
Employee benefits
company welfare system · · · · · **1:342b–343b**
Employees' Pension Insurance · · **6:173a;**
7:211b
Employees' Pension Law · · · **6:173a**
Employers' liability · · · · · · · · **2:209a**
Employment
compensation · · · · · · · · · · · · **5:90a**
recruitment (saiyō) · · · · · · · · **2:33a**
training programs (shanai kenshū)
· **2:34a–34b**
corporate culture · · · · · · · · **2:26b–27a**
dismissal · · · · · · · · **2:117b; 4:349a**
Edo period · · · · · · · · · **2:211b–212a, 2:150b**
fudai · · · · · · · · · · · · · · · **2:211b–212a**
hiyō · · · · · · · · · · · · · · · **2:211b–212a**
hōkōnin · · · · · · · · · · · · · **2:211b–212a**
nenki hōkōnin · · · · · · · · · **2:211b–212a**
forms · · · · · · · · · · · · · · · · · · **2:209b**
group hiring · · · · · · · · · · · **3:62b–63a**
high level · · · · **2:159a–159b, 160b**
ie concept · · · · · · · · · · · · · · **3:260b**
industrial robots · · · · · · · · **3:298b–299b**
investigations · · · · · · · · · · · · **1:217a**
medical and health insurance **5:144b–145a**
modern · · · · · · · · · · · · · **2:210a–211a**
career-long · · · · · · · · **2:210b–211a**
"closed" · · · · · · · · · · · · · · **4:344b**
enterprise unionism · · · · · · **2:211a**
seniority system · · · · · · · · **2:211a**
trends · · · · · · · · · · · **2:210a–210b**
variations · · · · · · · · · · · · · **2:211a**
motivation
internal organization of Japanese
companies · · · · · · · · · · · · **3:318a**
permanent · · · · · · · · · · · · · · **2:33a**
personnel reassignment · · · · · · · **7:185a**
practices · · · · · · · · · · · · · **2:36a–36b**
premodern · · · · · · · · · · **2:211b–212b**
contract workers · · · · · · · · **2:212a–212b**
Edo period · · · · · · · · · **2:211b–212a**
rights of employees · · · · · · **2:212b**
before 17th century · · · · · · **2:211b**
promotion · · · · · · · · · · · · · · **2:211a**
resignations · · · · · · · · · · · · · **2:211a**
reward system · · · · · · · · · · · **5:90a**
self · **7:60b**
seniority system · · · · · · **5:90a; 7:65a**
socialization · · · · · · · · · · · · · **2:27b**
trends · · · · · · · · · · · **2:210a, 210b**
wage differentials · · · · · · · · **8:198b**
wage system · · · · · · · · · **8:199b–200b**
women · · · · · · · · · · · · · · · · · · **5:7a**
work-related accidents
industrial injuries · · · · · · · · **3:292a**
Employment contracts · · · **2:209a–209b**
work regulations · · · · · · · · **8:270b**
Employment Measures Law · · · **2:210a**
Employment Promotion Corporation
Vocational Training Law · · · · · · **8:193b**
Employment Referral Law of 1921
(Shokugyō Shōkai Hō) · · · · · **6:265a**
Employment security · · · · · · · **4:347a**
labor disputes · · · · · · · · · · · **4:350a**
Employment Security Law of 1947
(Shokugyō Antei Hō) · · · · **2:210a; 4:352b,**
358a; 6:265a
Employment system · · · · · · **2:210a–212b**
teinensei · · · · · · · · · · · · · · · **7:376b**

Empon · · · · · · · · · · · 円本 · · · · **2:212b**
Empress, nonreigning. See **Chūgū;**
Kōgō
Empresses · · · · · · · · · · · · · · **1:312b**
Gemmei · · · · · · · · · · · · · · · **3:124a**
Jitō · · · · · · · · · · · · · · · · **4:63b–64a**
Kōgyoku · · · · · · · · · · · · · · **7:371a**
Kōken · · · · · · · · · · · · · · · · **4:253b**
Saimei · · · · · · · · · · · · · · · **7:371a**
Shōtoku · · · · · · · · · · · · · · **4:253a**
Suiko · · · · · · · · · · · **1:197b; 7:264a**
Emptiness · · · · · · · · **2:212b–213a; 7:16a**
En · · · · · · · · · · · 縁 · · · · · · **7:359a;**
8:323b–324a
Ena · · · · · · · · · · · · 恵那 · · · · · **2:213a**
Enakyō · · · · · · · · · 恵那峡 · · · · **2:213a**
Enameling · · · · · · · · · · · **1:328b–329a**
Enami Kiemon
· · · · · · · · · 榎並喜右衛門 · · · · **4:214a**
Enasan · · · · · · · · · 恵那山 · · · · · **2:213a**
Enchi Fumiko · 円地文子 · · · · **2:213b**
Enchin · · · · · · · · · · 円珍 · · · · · **2:213b**
Encouragement of Learning, An · **3:4a–4b**
Enden · · · · · · · · · · · · · · · · · · **2:213b**
Endogamy · · · · · · · · · · · **5:116b–117a**
Endō Shūsaku · 遠藤周作 · **2:214a; 7:103b**
Christianity · · · · · · · · · · · · · · **4:32a**
education · · · · · · · · · · · · · · · **2:214a**
fiction · · · · · · · · · · · · · · · · · **2:214a**
Endowment insurance · · · · · · · · · **5:5b**
Endō Yukio · 遠藤幸雄 · · · · **2:214a**
Enduring Art of Japan, The · · · · **8:228a**
En el Pais del Sol · · · · · · · · · · **7:291a**
Energy
balance · · · · · · · · · · · · · · · · **2:217a**
conservation · · · · · · · · · **2:215b–216a**
nuclear power · · · · · · · · · · · **2:214b**
Energy industries · · · · · · **2:214a–214b**
Energy revolution · · · · · · · · **2:214b**
Energy sources · · · · · · · · **2:214b–217a**
alternatives · · · · · · · · · **2:215b–217a**
coal · · · · · · **1:333a–333b; 2:216a**
dams · · · · · · · · · · · · · · · · · · **2:72b**
electric power · · · · · · · · **2:190a–191a**
natural gas · · · · · · · · · · · · · **2:216a**
nuclear · · · · · · · · · · · **2:216b–217a**
oil crisis · · · · · · · · · · · **2:215a–215b**
solar energy · · · · · · · · · **2:216a–215b**
vulnerability · · · · · · · · · **2:214b–215a**
Energy vulnerability · · · · · · · **2:214b–215a**
Engagement · · · · · · · · · · · · · · · **5:4b**
Engakuji · · · · · · · 円覚寺 1:*191a*; **2:217a;**
4:120b; 7:76a
Engakukyō · · · · · · · 円覚経 · · · · **6:247b**
Engawa · · · · · · · · · · · · · · · · · · **1:82a**
Engi · · · · · · · · · · · 縁起 · · · · · **1:177a;**
2:217a–217b
Engi Kyaku · · · · · · · 延喜格 · · · · **6:332a**
Engi Kyakushiki. See **Engi Shiki**
Engi Reform (902)
· · · · · · · · · 延喜の改革 · · · · **2:57a, 104b**
Engi Shiki · · · · · 延喜式 · **2:217b; 7:96a**
background · · · · · · · · · · · · · **2:217b**
Daigo, Emperor · · · · · · · · · · · **2:57a**
daijōsai · · · · · · · · · · · · · **2:59a–59b**
harae · · · · · · · · · · · · · · · · · **3:101a**
ritsuryō system · · · · · · · · · · · **6:332a**
Shintō · · · · · · · · · · · · **7:126b, 138b**
Engi Tenryaku no chi
· · · · · · · 延喜・天暦の治 · · **2:217b–218a**
Shin kokinshū · · · · · · · · · · · **7:120a**
England and Japan. See **United**
Kingdom and Japan
English ivy · · · · · · · · · · · · · · · **8:320a**
English Peninsular and Oriental
Navigation Company (P & O) · **3:362b**
Engo · · · · · · · · · · · · · · · · · · · **8:203b**
Eniwa · · · · · · · · · 恵庭 · · · · · · **2:218a**

Eniwa case · · · · · · · · · · · · · · **2:218a**
judicial review · · · · · · · · · · · · **4:79b**
Enkai · · · · · · · · · · · · · · · · · · **2:218a**
Enkiridera · · · · · · 縁切寺 · · · · · **4:115b**
Enkō sugi · · · · · · · · · · · · · · · · **7:257b**
Enkū · · · · · · · · · · 円空 · **1:194a, 199b;**
2:218a–218b
Enkyoku · · · · · · · · 宴曲 · · · · · · **2:218b**
Enlightenment · · · · · · · · · · · · · **7:28b**
Enlightenment Faction · · · · · · · **4:101b**
Ennen · · · · · · · · · · 延年 · · · · **2:74a,**
218b–219a, 259a, 297b
furyū · · · · · · · · **2:218b–219a, 373b**
kaiko · · · · · · · · · · · · · · · · · · **2:218b**
renji · · · · · · · · · · · · · · · · · · **2:219a**
Enni · · · · · · · · · · · 円爾 · **2:219a; 7:80b**
Enni Ben'en. 円爾弁円 See **Enni**
Ennichi · · · · · · · · · · · · · · **2:219a; 7:250a**
Ennin · · · · · · · · · · 円仁 · · · · · **2:219a**
raigōzu · · · · · · · · · · · · · · · · **6:277a**
Risshakuji · · · · · · · · · **6:320b–321a**
wasan · · · · · · · · · · · · · · · · · **8:231a**
Ennin's Diary: The Record of a
Pilgrimage
to China in Search of the Law · · **6:289a**
Ennin's Travels in T'ang China · · **6:289a**
En no Gyōja · · · · · · · 役行者 · **2:219a–219b;**
7:67a
En no Ozunu · · · · · 役小角 · · · · · **5:295b**
Ennō Zenji · · · · · 円応禅師 · · · · **4:1b–2a**
Enoken · · · · · · · · · エノケン · · · · **2:219b**
Enola Gay · · · · · · · · · · · · · · **1:176a**
Enomoto Ken'ichi
· · · · · · · · · 榎本健一 · · · · **2:219b**
Furukawa Roppa · · · · · · · · · · **2:373b**
Enomoto Kikaku. See **Takarai Kikaku**
Enomoto Takeaki 榎本武揚 · **1:165a, 167b;**
2:219b–220a
French-Japanese relations · · · · · · **2:331b**
Goryōkaku, Battle of · · · · · · · · · **3:47a**
Kaigun Denshūjo · · · · · · · · · · **4:110a**
Enoshima · · · · · · · 江ノ島 · **2:220a, 345b;**
7:88a
"Enrai no kyakutachi"
· · · · · · · · · 遠来の客達 · · · · **7:228b**
"Enrich the Country and Strengthen
the Military" · · · · **1:86a; 2:360b–361a**
Enryakuji · · · · · · · 延暦寺 · **1:178b, 182b;**
2:220a–221a, 220b, 221a; 4:138a, 163a;
6:149b; 7:91a
monasticism · · · · · · · · · **5:237b–238a**
Tendai sect · · · · · · · · · · · · · · **8:4a**
Enryakuji, burning of
· · · · · · · · 延暦寺焼き打ち · · · · **2:221a**
Enryakuji community · · · · · · · · **2:187a**
Enryo · · · · · · · · · · · · · · · · · · **2:221a**
En school · · · · · · · 円派 · · · · · **2:221a**
founder · · · · · · · · · · · · · · · · **1:303b**
En Seigai · · · · · · · 袁世凱 · · · **8:354a–354b**
Ensuikō Sugar Refining Co, Ltd
· · · · · · · · · · · · · · · · · · · **2:221a–221b**
Entairyaku · · · · · · · 園太暦 · · · · **2:221b**
Enterprise · · · · · · · · · · · · · · **7:252b**
Enterprise groups · · · · **1:139a; 2:221b**
one-set principle · · · · · · · · · · **6:106a**
Enterprise Incident · · · · · · **2:221b–222a**
Enterprise unions. See **Labor unions**
Entō · · · · · · · · · · · 遠島 · · · · · **2:222a**
Entrance examinations · **2:41b, 222a–224a;**
4:83b–84a; 7:215a
children of returnees · · · · · · · · **2:182a**
research · · · · · · · · · · · · · · · · **2:181a**
universities and colleges · · · · · · **8:170b**
Entrepreneurs
Fujita Denzaburō · · · · · · · · · · **2:346a**
Fujiyama Raita · · · · · · · · · · · · **2:359a**
Furukawa Ichibei · · · · · · · · · **2:372b–373a**
Godai Tomoatsu · · · · · · · · · · · **3:39a–39b**

Gotō Keita · · · · · · · · · · · · · · · · **3**:53a
Gunji Shigetada · · · · · · · · · · · · **3**:68b
Hattori Kintarō · · · · · · · · · · · · **3**:113b
Ibuka Masaru · · · · · · · · · · · · · · **3**:254a
Idemitsu Sazō · · · · · · · · · · · · · · **3**:259a
Iwasaki Yatarō · · · · · · · · · · · · · **3**:362a
Kaneko Naokichi · · · · · · · · · · · · **4**:139a
Mitsunaga Hoshio · · · · · · · · · · · **5**:214a
Mori Kaku · · · · · · · · · · · · · · · · **5**:249b
Ōhara Magosaburō · · · · · · · · · · **6**:73b
Ōkura Kihachirō · · · · · · · · · · · · **6**:98a
Shibusawa Eiichi · · · · · · · · **7**:86a–86b
Takenouchi Tsuna · · · · · · · · · · · **7**:325a
Environment Agency · · · · **1**:219a; **2**:224a
   standards · · · · · · · · · · · · · · · **2**:226a
Environmental conservation · · **1**:359a–360a
Environmental education · · · · · · · · **2**:224a
Environmental law · · · · · · · · **2**:224a–225b
   courts · · · · · · · · · · · · · · · · · **2**:225b
   statutory framework · · · · · · **2**:224b–225b
Environmental movements · · · · · · · **1**:315a
Environmental Pollution
   Countermeasures Council · · · · · · **6**:217b
Environmental quality · · · · · · **2**:225b–229a
   antipollution measures
      expenditures and personnel **2**:228b–229a
      research, technology, and planning
         · · · · · · · · · · · · · · · · · **2**:229a
      assessment · · · · · · · · · · · · **2**:229a
   natural · · · · · · · · · · · · · · · · **2**:228a
   pollution · · · · · · · · · · · · · **2**:226a–228a
      air · · · · · · · · · · · · · · · **2**:227b–228a
      exhaust gas regulation · · · · · **2**:236a–236b
      forms · · · · · · · · · · · · · · · **2**:228a
      public health · · · · · · · · · **2**:226a–227b
   protection legislation and
      administration · · · · · · · · **2**:228a–228b
   women in · · · · · · · · · · · · · · · **8**:263b
Environmental right · · · · · · · **2**:229a–229b
   civil liberties · · · · · · · · · · · · **1**:318a
En'ya Hangan Takasada
         塩谷判官高貞 · · · · · **4**:275a
Enza · · · · · · · · · · 縁坐 **2**:229b; **7**:249b
Enzan · · · · · · · · · · · · 塩山 **2**:229b
Epictetus' *Discourses* · · · · · · · · · **4**:233a
Epidemiologists
   Futaki Kenzō · · · · · · · · · · · · **2**:376a
Episōdo · · · · · · エピソード · · · **4**:169a
Epistolary style · · · · · · · · · · **7**:230a–231b
Equality of the sexes under the law
         · · · · · · · · · · · · · **2**:229b–230a
   marriage law · · · · · · · · · · · · **5**:118a
Equality under the law · · · · · **2**:230a–230b
Equal opportunity in education · · · **2**:230b
Equestrianism. *See* **Horsemanship**
Equity market · · · · · · · · · · · · · **1**:243a
Era · · · · · · · · · · · · · · · · · **4**:203b–204a
Era names · · · · · · · · · · · · · · · **5**:360a
"Eriko to tomo ni"
   ("Together with Eriko")
      · · · · · · · · · えり子とともに · · **8**:125a
Erimomisaki · · · · · · · 襟裳岬 **2**:230b
Erisen. 撰銭   *See* **Erizeni**
Erithacus akahige · · · · · · · · · · **4**:264b
Erizeni · · · · · · · · · · · 撰銭 **2**:230b
EROA · · · · · · · · · · **2**:155a, 158a–158b
Ero guro nansensu bungaku
   Shinkō Geijutsu Ha · · · · · · · · · **7**:119b
Eroshenko, Vasilii Iakovlevich
         · · · · · · · · · · · · · **2**:230b–231a
Erosion control · · · · · · · · · · · · · **2**:72b
Erotic art. *See* **Shunga**
Eruption Smoke (Fun'en) · · · · · · · **6**:*156b*
Esaki Reona · · 江崎玲於奈 **2**:231a
Esashi · · · · · · · · · · · 江差 **2**:231a
"Escalator schools" · · · · · · · · · · **2**:222b
Eschatology · · · · · · · · **2**:101b, 231a
   Rinzai sect · · · · · · · · · · · · · **6**:319a

Shinran · · · · · · · · · · · · · · · · · **7**:123a
Eshi no sōshi · · · · 絵師草紙 **2**:199b
Esoteric Buddhism · · · **1**:185a, 187b–189a;
                        2:231a–231b; **7**:15b
   architecture · · · · · · · · · · · · **1**:188a
   art · · · · · · · · · · · · · · · · **1**:187b–189a
   Dainichi ("Great Sun") · · · · · · · · **2**:64b
   Goma ceremony · · · · · · · · **1**:188a, 195b
   inzō · · · · · · · · · · · · · · · · · **3**:328a
   Kannon, Eleven-Headed · · · **1**:187b, 189a
   Kongōkai · · · · · · · · · · · · · · **4**:269b
   Kūkai · · · · · · · · · · · · · · · · **4**:304a
   prayer · · · · · · · · · · · · · · · · **6**:233a
   ritual implements · · · · · · · · · · **1**:196a
   Ryōbu Shintō · · · · · · · · · **1**:187b–188a
   Saichō · · · · · · · · · · · · · **6**:365a–366b
   Shingon sect · · · · · · · · · · **7**:113b–115a
   Shintō · · · · · · · · · · · · · · · · **7**:127a
   statues, wood · · · · · · · · · · · · **1**:189a
   symbols · · · · · · · · · · · · · **5**:99b–100b
Esperanto · · · · · · · · · · · · · · · **2**:231b
Essayists
   Baba Kochō · · · · · · · · · · · · · · **1**:129a
   Hirata Tokuboku · · · · · · · · · · · **3**:145b
   Kamo no Chōmei · · · · · · · · **4**:128b–129a
   Sei Shōnagon · · · · · · · · · · **7**:52a–54a
   Terada Torahiko · · · · · · · · · · · **8**:11a
   Yoshida Kenkō · · · · · · · · · **8**:341a–342b
Essays · · · · · · · · · **3**:77a–78a; **8**:106a
Essentials of Civil Law · · · · · · · · · **8**:147a
Esso Standard Oil Co, Ltd · · · · · · **2**:231b
   Tōa Nenryō Kōgyō · · · · · · · · · · **8**:30b
Estate stewards · · · · **4**:62b–63b; **7**:183a
Esugoroku · · · · · · · · · · · · · · · · **7**:259a
Eta Funayama Tomb
         江田船山古墳 · · · · **2**:231b
   Tamana · · · · · · · · · · · · · · · · **7**:332a
Etajima · · · · · · · · · · 江田島 **2**:231b
Eta (outcasts) · · · · · · · · · · · · · · **8**:178b
   shi-nō-kō-shō · · · · · · · · · · · · **7**:122b
Etchan · · · · · · · · 悦ちゃん **7**:148b
Etching, modern · · · · · · · · · · · · **5**:233b
Ethics, East and West · · · · · · **2**:232a–232b
   Confucianism · · · · · · · · · · **1**:352b–358b
   corporate culture · · · · · · · · **2**:26b–27a
   vs etiquette · · · · · · · · · · · · · **2**:232b
   evil · · · · · · · · · · · · · · · · · · **2**:236a
   religious codes · · · · · · · · · · · **6**:290a
   townsmen · · · · · · · · · · · **1**:302b–303a
   utilitarian · · · · · · · · · · · · · · **2**:27a
Ethnographical museums · · · · · **5**:278a–278b
Ethnologists
   Iha Fuyū · · · · · · · · · · · · · · · **3**:262a
   Minakata Kumakusu · · · · · · · · · **5**:176a
Etiquette · · · · · · · · · · · · **2**:232b–234a
   behavior · · · · · · · · · · · · · · · **2**:233a
   vs ethics · · · · · · · · · · · · · · · **2**:232b
   military · · · · · · · · · · · · · · · · **6**:69a
   ojigi · · · · · · · · · · · · · · · · · · **6**:76a
   rei · · · · · · · · · · · · · · · · · · · **6**:288b
   social organization · · · · · · · · · **2**:233b
   symbolic communication · · · · **2**:233b–234a
   tatemae-honne, giri-ninjō, and
      omote-ura · · · · · · · · · · · **2**:233a–233b
Eto. 干支   *See* **Jikkan jūnishi**
Etō Jun · · · · · · · · · · 江藤淳 **2**:234a
Etorofu · · · · · · · · · · 択捉 **2**:234a
   Russia · · · · · · · · · · · · · · · · **6**:340b
Etō Shimpei · · · · 江藤新平 **1**:34b;
                        2:234a–234b
   Civil Code · · · · · · · · · · · · · · **2**:319a
   Freedom and People's Rights Movement
         · · · · · · · · · · · · · · · · · **2**:334a
   Itagaki Taisuke · · · · · · · · · · · **3**:349a
   Saga Rebellion · · · · · · · · · **6**:364b–365a
Eugenic Protection Council · · · · · · · **2**:234b
Eugenic Protection Law **1**:5a; **2**:48a, 234b,
                        247b; **6**:224a

Eugenics movement · · · · · · · · · · · **2**:234b
Eulalia · · · · · · · · · · · · · · · · · **7**:279a
Eulenberg, Ambassador Graf Fritz zu
         · · · · · · · · · · · · · · · · · **3**:26b
Eulenburg, Friedrich Albert · · · · **1**:167a;
                        2:234b–235a
European Atomic Energy Community
   (EURATOM) · · · · · · · · · · · · **2**:235a
European Coal and Steel Community
   (ECSC) · · · · · · · · · · · · · · · **2**:235a
European Community and Japan
         · · · · · · · · · · · · · **2**:235a–235b
European Depositary Receipts · · · **2**:235b
European Economic Community (EEC)
         · · · · · · · · · · · · **2**:235a; **8**:164a
Euthanasia · · · · · · · · · · · **2**:235b–236a
   dying with dignity · · · · · · · **2**:235b–236b
   legislation · · · · · · · · · · · · · · **2**:236a
Evil · · · · · · · · · · · · · · · · · · **2**:236a
Evolution · · · · · · · · · · · · · · **4**:33b–34a
Ewing, James Alfred
   earth sciences · · · · · · · · · · · · **2**:140b
Excavations · · · · · · · · · · · · · **1**:78a–78b
Exceptional Provisions to the
   Copyright Law · · · · · · · · · · · · **8**:98a
Excessive Economic Power
   Decentralization Law · · · · · · · · · **5**:303a
Exchange of Sakhalin for the
   Kuril Islands, Treaty of · · · · **6**:371a; **8**:13b
Exclusionism · · · · · · · · · · · · · · **2**:200a
Execution of judgment · · · · · · · · · **4**:333a
Executive branch of government
         · · · · · · · · · · · · · **3**:55b–56a
Exhaust gas regulation · · · · · · **2**:236a–236b
Exile · · · · · · · · · · · · · · · · · · **6**:339b
Existentialism · · · · · · · · · · · · **2**:236b
Exorcism · · · · · · **2**:236b–237a; **6**:295b; **7**:71b
Exoteric Buddhism · · · · · · · · **1**:195b–196a
Expansionism · · · · · · · · · · · · **3**:320b–321a
Ex parte Endo (323 US 283) · · · · · · **4**:18a
Expense accounts · · · · · · · · **2**:237a–237b
   taxes · · · · · · · · · · · · · · · · · **7**:353a
Explorers
   Kawaguchi Ekai · · · · · · · · · · · **4**:177b
   Kondō Jūzō · · · · · · · · · · · **4**:269a–269b
   Mamiya Rinzō · · · · · · · · · · **5**:88b–89a
   Matsuura Takeshirō · · · · · · · · · **5**:141b
   Mogami Tokunai · · · · · · · · · · · **5**:233b
   Okamoto Kansuke · · · · · · · · · · **6**:80a
   Shirase Nobu · · · · · · · · · · · · · **7**:147a
   Uemura Naomi · · · · · · · · · · · · **8**:128a
Export-Import Bank of Japan · · · · **1**:139b;
                        2:237b; **6**:190a
   China · · · · · · · · · · · · · · · · · **1**:290b
   fiscal system · · · · · · · · · · · · · **2**:281b
   foreign aid policy · · · · · · · · · · **2**:310a
   import financing · · · · · · · · · · · **2**:326a
   reorganization · · · · · · · · · · · · **2**:321b
Export Insurance Law · · · · · · · · · · **6**:190a
Exports
   arms · · · · · · · · · · · · · · · **1**:90a–90b
   computers · · · · · · · · · · · · · · **1**:344b
   oil · · · · · · · · · · · · · · · · **1**:71b–72a
   steel · · · · · · · · · · · · · · · **3**:335b–336a
Exposition of the Administrative Laws
         · · · · · · · · · · · · · · · · · **6**:352b
Expo '70 · · · · · · **2**:237b–238a; **7**:264b
Expressways · · · · · · · · · · · · · · **2**:238a
   roads · · · · · · · · · · · · · · · · · **6**:332b
   urban life · · · · · · · · · · · · · · **8**:178b
"Expulsion Ordinance"
   Peace Preservation Law of 1887 · · · · **6**:167b
Extended family · · · · · · · · · · · · · **7**:213a
   honke and bunke · · · · · · · · · · · **3**:223a
Extracurricular activities · · · · · · · · · **7**:35b
Extradition · · · · · · · · · · · · · · **2**:238a
Extraordinary Council on Education
         · · · · · · · · · · · · · · · · · **6**:318b

Extraterritoriality, principle of ······ **7**:78a
Eyebrow paint (mayuzumi) ····· **2**:38a-38b
Ezaki Glico Co, Ltd ········ **2**:238a-238b
Ezo　　蝦夷　········· **1**:211b;
　　　　　　　　　　2:238b; **7**:263a
　aborigines ················· **2**:238b
　development ················ **4**:113a
　military campaigns against ····· **2**:370b
　northern regions ············ **2**:238b
　　Russo-Japanese frontier ······· **2**:238b
　　settlement ··············· **2**:238b
　saku (stockades; palisades) ····· **7**:3a
　samurai ··················· **7**:7b
　shōgun ··················· **7**:160a
　suppression ················ **4**:189a
　war against ················ **7**:294b
Ezo Mountains ·蝦夷山系· **2**:239a-239b
　Ishikari Mountains ··········· **3**:342a

F

Fabian ··················· **2**:241a
　Hayashi Razan ·············· **3**:117b
"**Face**" ··················· **4**:155a
Face of Another, The ········· **1**:3a
Facial powder (oshiroi) ········· **2**:38a
Facing Two Ways ············ **4**:169b
Factionalism ················ **3**:315a
Factions. *See* **Batsu**
Factories
　government-operated, Meiji period
　·························· **3**:56a-56b
　industrial zones ············· **3**:303a
Factory Law of 1911 · **2**:241a-241b; **4**:351a,
　　　　　　　　　357b-358a; **7**:209a
　conditions of factory workers ···· **7**:164a
　industrial injuries ············ **3**:292a
　job safety regulations ········· **2**:241b
　Katsura Tarō ··············· **2**:241b
　minimum working age ········· **2**:241b
　women ···················· **8**:264b
　worker's compensation ········ **8**:270a
　work hours ················ **8**:270a
Factory workers, labor conditions · **7**:164a
Fa-hsiang Tsung ········· **3**:237a-237b
Fairies and celestial beings · **5**:295a-295b
Fair Trade Commission
　(Kōsei Torihiki Iinkai) ··· **3**:296a; **4**:378b
　antimonopoly law ············ **1**:65b
　antimonopoly proceedings ······ **1**:67b
　industrial organization ······ **3**:293b, 296a
　public employees ············ **6**:264b
"**Falcon**" (fighter plane) ······· **3**:114b
Falconry ················· **2**:241b
Familism ·················· **7**:213b
Family ··················· **2**:241b-245b
　average, living conditions of · **7**:243b-244a
　child rearing and education · **1**:277a-278b;
　　　　　　　　　　　　2:244b-245a
　　entrance examinations ······· **2**:245a
　　father's role ·············· **2**:244b
　　mother's role ·········· **2**:244b-245a
　contemporary ··········· **2**:243a-245b
　cyclic variations ·········· **2**:242a-242b
　　adoption ················ **2**:242a
　　primogeniture ············· **2**:242a
　dating and marriage planning **2**:243b-244a
　　marriage age ·············· **2**:244a
　divorce ··············· **2**:121b-122b

　education at home ··········· **2**:181b
　filial piety ············· **2**:245a, 267a
　functions ·············· **2**:242b-243a
　　oyabun-kobun ············· **2**:243a
　genealogy ·············· **3**:17b-18a
　grandparents ············ **2**:245a-245b
　　retirement ··············· **2**:245b
　housewives ············· **3**:241a-242a
　husband ·················· **3**:242a
　husband-wife relationships **2**:244a-244b
　　division of labor ··········· **2**:244a
　　divorce ················· **2**:244b
　　emotional intimacy ········· **2**:244b
　marriage ·············· **7**:214b-215a
　　age ···················· **2**:44a
　　planning ············· **2**:243b-244a
　parental relationships ······ **1**:277b-278a
　religion ··················· **6**:291a
　ritsuryō system ·········· **6**:324b-325a
　"ritual parents" ············· **1**:277a
　roles ···················· **2**:242b
　terminology ············ **2**:241b-242a
　　ie ····················· **2**:242a
　　kazoku ·················· **2**:242a
　　setai ··················· **2**:242a
　traditional ············· **2**:241b-243a
　training and discipline ····· **1**:277b-278a
　typical life ················ **2**:243b
　　leisure-time activities ······· **2**:243b
　　standard of living ·········· **2**:243b
　women working ············· **2**:245a
　yorioya and yoriko ·········· **8**:338b
Family court ······· **2**:245b-246b; **7**:277a
　domestic cases ············· **2**:246a
　　conciliation procedure ······· **2**:246a
　　determination procedures ····· **2**:246a
　history and concept ········ **2**:245b-246a
　　probation officers ·········· **2**:246a
　　structure ············· **2**:245b-246a
　juvenile cases ··········· **2**:246a-246b
　　hearings ················· **2**:246b
　juvenile crime ·············· **4**:87a
　juvenile law ··············· **4**:87b
　juvenile reformatories ········· **4**:87b
　penal system ··············· **6**:172a
　present and future ··········· **2**:246b
　probation officers ··········· **2**:246a
Family courts ········· **2**:45b; **4**:80b, 81b
Family law. *See* **Shinzoku Hō**
Family names ··········· **5**:324b-325a
Family planning ····· **2**:246b-247b; **8**:261a
　abortion ··········· **1**:5a; **2**:247a-247b
　　Eugenic Protection Law ······ **2**:247b
　birth rate ·············· **2**:246b-247a
　contraception ··········· **2**:247a-247b
　　Ogino Kyūsaku ············ **2**:247a
　movement ············· **2**:246b-247a
　　Katō Shizue ··········· **4**:169a-169b
　　Margaret Sanger ··········· **2**:246b
　　zero population growth ······· **2**:247a
　role of government and other
　　organizations ············· **2**:247b
Family Planning Research Institute
　·························· **2**:247b
Family Registers. *See* **Household
Registers**
Family Registration Law
　(Koseki Hō) ······· **4**:33a, 60b; **8**:91b
Family Registration Law Enforcement
　Regulations (Koseki Hō Sekō Kisoku)
　·························· **8**:91b
Family-state ················ **4**:185b
Family succession system ······· **6**:324a
Famines ··················· **7**:381a
Fans ················· **2**:247b-248a
　construction ············ **2**:247b-248a
　symbols of office ··········· **2**:248a
　types ···················· **2**:248a

Far East Command ··········· **2**:248a
　MacArthur, General Douglas ····· **2**:248a;
　　　　　　　　　　　　5:77a-78a
　Ridgway, Matthew ······ **2**:248a; **6**:311b
Far Eastern Commission (FEC) · **1**:237b;
　　　　　　　　　　　　2:248a
　Allied Council for Japan ···· **1**:48a; **2**:248a
　Australia ·············· **1**:117a-117b
　Canada ·················· **1**:237b
　Occupation ················ **6**:51b
　Potsdam Declaration ·········· **2**:248a
　reparations for Southeast Asia ··· **6**:302b
　Russia and Japan ············ **6**:343b
　San Francisco Peace Treaty · **2**:248a; **7**:10b
　Sansom, George Bailey ········· **7**:17a
　SCAP ···················· **7**:32b
　strike report ··············· **7**:250b
　United Kingdom ············· **8**:153a
Far Eastern Conference ········· **8**:37a
Far Eastern Republic ····· **2**:248b; **3**:328a
　Ioffe, Adolf Abramovich ······· **2**:248b
　Russia and Japan ············ **6**:343a
Far East Network (FEN) ···· **2**:248b-249a
　Radio Law ················ **2**:249a
Far East Society ············· **8**:37a
Farewell gifts ············· **2**:249a
Farmers
　bakuhan system ········· **1**:131b-132a
　hyakushō ············· **3**:249a-249b
　landholding ··············· **4**:194b
　rōnō ···················· **6**:337b
　as social class ·············· **1**:323a
　See also **Agriculture**
Farmers' Movement ·········· **2**:249a
Farm households ············· **1**:26a
Farmhouses ············ **5**:192-193b
Farming
　equipment
　　sembakoki ··············· **7**:61a
　　threshers ················ **7**:61a
　mechanization ·············· **1**:25a
　postwar changes ·········· **1**:24b-26a
　riots ···················· **8**:124a
　storage facilities ············ **7**:248a
Farming techniques · **1**:28a-32a; **7**:178a
　agricultural chemicals ········· **1**:30b
　agricultural implements ····· **1**:30a-30b
　animal husbandry ········· **1**:29b-30a
　dry field farming ········· **1**:29a-29b
　fertilizers ················· **1**:30b
　horticulture ················ **1**:30a
　insect pests ················ **1**:30b
　irrigation ················· **1**:29b
　land improvements ··········· **1**:29b
　new varieties ··············· **1**:30a
　plant diseases ·············· **1**:30b
　rice planting ············ **1**:28b-29a
Farmland. *See* **Agriculture**
FAS Association ············· **3**:151b
Fascism ············ **2**:111b; **6**:204a
Faulds, Henry ·········· **2**:249a-249b
　Morse, Edward S. ············ **2**:249b
Faxiang Zong ············ **3**:237a-237b
February First Strike. *See* **General Strike
of 1947**
February 26th Incident 二・二六事件
　·················· **2**:249b-250b; **8**:344a
　Araki Sadao ··············· **2**:250a
　Chichibu, Prince ············· **2**:250a
　Hayashi Senjūrō ············· **3**:117b
　Hirohito, Emperor ······· **2**:249b; **3**:147a
　Hirota Kōki ··············· **2**:250a
　Ishiwara Kanji ·············· **3**:345b
　Kawai Eijirō ··············· **4**:178a
　Kita Ikki ············ **2**:250a; **4**:226a
　Kōno Hisashi ··············· **2**:250a
　Makino Nobuaki ············· **2**:249b
　Mazaki Jinzaburō ············ **2**:250a

Mishima Yukio ············· **2**:250b
Nagata Tetsuzan ············· **2**:250a
Nishida Mitsugi ············· **2**:250a
Nonaka Shirō ············· **2**:250a
Okada Keisuke ············· **2**:249b
Saitō Makoto ············· **2**:249b
Shōwa Depression ············· **7**:174a
Shōwa Restoration ······· **7**:176b-177a
Suzuki Kantarō ············· **2**:249b
Takahashi Korekiyo ····· **2**:249b; **7**:312a
Takami Jun ············· **2**:250b
Takeda Taijun ············· **2**:250b
Tatekawa Yoshitsugu ············· **7**:349a
Terauchi Hisaichi ············· **8**:12a
Watanabe Jōtarō ····· **2**:249b; **8**:235b
World War II ············· **8**:271b
Young Officers Movement ········· **2**:250a
FEC. *See* **Far East Command; Far Eastern Commission**
Federation of Economic Organizations (Keidanren) ········· **4**:188a-188b; **6**:237b
Federation of Independent Unions of Japan (Chūritsu Rōren) ···· **1**:313b-314a; **4**:188b; **7**:189b
Federation of Youth Groups of Japan ················· **2**:66b
Feminine language ········· **2**:250b-251b
asobase-kotoba ············· **2**:251a
femininity expression ············· **2**:250b
nyōbō kotoba ········· **2**:250b; **6**:45a-45b
patterns ············· **2**:251a-251b
Sei Shōnagon ············· **2**:250b
women's social status ········· **2**:250b-251b
Feminism ············· **8**:260b
organizations representing Seitōsha ················· **7**:54a-54b
Feminists
Fukuda Hideko ············· **2**:362a-362b
Hiratsuka Raichō ············· **3**:146a
Ichikawa Fusae ············· **3**:257a
Itō Noe ············· **3**:355a
Kaneko, Josephine Conger ········· **4**:138a
Kanno Suga ············· **4**:145a-145b
Katō Shizue ············· **4**:169a
Kawasaki Natsu ············· **4**:184a
Kishida Toshiko ············· **5**:313b-314a
Kozai Shikin ············· **4**:300a
Kubushiro Ochimi ············· **4**:301b
Oku Mumeo ············· **6**:96b
Sakai Magara ············· **7**:57a
Sasaki Toyoju ············· **7**:23b
Takamure Itsue ············· **7**:316b
Tanno Setsu ············· **7**:344a
Tatewaki Sadayo ············· **7**:349b
Yamada Waka ············· **8**:289b
Yamakawa Kikue ············· **8**:297a
Yamataka Shigeri ············· **8**:307b
FEN. *See* **Far East Network**
Fencing ············· **3**:253a; **4**:195b
Fenimore Cooper ············· **1**:175a
Fenollosa, Ernest Francisco **2**:251b-252a, 311a
art preservation ············· **2**:252a
Bigelow, William Sturgis ············· **1**:54b
career ············· **2**:251b-252a
Kanō Hōgai ············· **4**:147a
Kiyozawa Manshi ············· **4**:233a
works ············· **2**:252a
Fenton, John William ············· **5**:286a
Ferdinand, Crown Prince Franz ················· **1**:120a
Fern frond design ········· **1**:174a; **2**:252a
Kamegaoka site ············· **4**:125a
Ōzuka tomb ············· **6**:141a
Ferns [(shida) order Filicales] ····· **2**:252a
Fertility rites ············· **2**:86a; **6**:290a
Fertilizers ············· **1**:30b
rice ············· **6**:309a

Fesca, Max ············· **2**:252a
Festival of Hōkoku Shrine ········· **4**:150a
Festivals ········· **2**:252b-262a; **7**:71b; **8**:183a
Ae no Koto ············· **2**:259a
Aoi ············· **1**:68a; **2**:253a
Atami ············· **1**:107b
Bon Festival ············· **1**:160b
Boys' Day ············· **1**:279a
Children's Day ········· **1**:279a-279b; **2**:261a
Chrysanthemum Festival ············· **1**:310a
dashi ············· **2**:78a
Dazaifu Shrine ············· **2**:79b
dealing with sex ············· **7**:74a
doll ········· **1**:277b, 279b; **2**:127b-128a
ennichi ············· **8**:322b
folk performing arts ········· **2**:296b-298a
Gion ············· **3**:33b-34a
Hakata Dontaku ············· **3**:85a
hanagasa ············· **8**:290b
hana matsuri ············· **3**:94a
hari kuyō observance ············· **2**:260b
hatsumōde ············· **2**:259b
hatsuuma ············· **3**:113b
Hi Matsuri ············· **2**:259a
Hiratsuka ············· **7**:335a
horse (Chaguchagu Umakko) ········· **1**:266a
iris ············· **1**:279a
Japanese cooking ············· **2**:22a
Jidai Matsuri ············· **2**:258b; **4**:53a
kagura ············· **4**:106a-107b
kakizome ············· **2**:259b
kamakura ············· **2**:252b
Kamakura Matsuri ············· **2**:252b
Kanda ············· **4**:137a
Kantō ············· **2**:255a
kawabiraki ············· **4**:177a
kites ············· **4**:229b-231b
list of ············· **2**:256a-257b
masks ············· **5**:126b-127a
matsuri ············· **2**:252b-258a
communion ············· **2**:254b-255b
deity ············· **2**:254a
essentials ············· **2**:254a-255b
Gion Festival ············· **2**:255b
group ············· **2**:255b
hare and ke ············· **2**:253b-254a
modern society ············· **2**:258a
offerings ············· **2**:254b
purificatory asceticism ······ **2**:254a-254b
seasons ············· **2**:254a
village and city festivals ········· **2**:255b
Mitaue Matsuri ············· **1**:103b
Momo no Sekku (Peach Festival) ··· **7**:58a
mura matsuri ············· **6**:205a
Nanakusa Sekku (Seven Herb Festival) ················· **7**:58a
National Sports Festival ············· **5**:348a
nebuta ············· **1**:69b; **2**:255a
Nenchū gyōji ········· **2**:252b-253a, 258a-262a
annual events ············· **2**:262b
Bon Festival ············· **1**:160b
Boys' Day ············· **1**:279a
Children's Day ············· **1**:279a-279b
Chrysanthemum Festival · **1**:310a; **2**:260b
hana matsuri ············· **2**:260a; **3**:94a
hari kuyō ············· **2**:260b
hatsumōde ············· **2**:259b
hatsuuma ············· **2**:260a
higan ············· **2**:260a
kakizome ············· **2**:259b
Momo no Sekku (Peach Festival) ··**7**:58a
Nanakusa Sekku (Seven Herb Festival) ················· **7**:58a
National Sports Festival ········· **5**:348a
New Year ············· **5**:371b-372a
post-Heian period ············· **2**:260b-262a
pre-Heian antecedents ····· **2**:258b-259b
sekku ············· **2**:260a

setsubun ············· **2**:259a-259b, *260b*
shichigosan ············· **2**:261b, 262a
Shōbu no Sekku ············· **7**:58b
sources ············· **2**:258a-258b
tanabata ············· **2**:260b
tōrō nagashi ············· **2**:261a
toshi no ichi (year-end fair) ········· **2**:262a
tsukimi (moon viewing) ············· **2**:261b
New Year ············· **5**:371b-372a
Nomaoi Matsuri ············· **2**:254b
Okunchi ············· **2**:258b
Peiron ············· **1**:37b
religion ············· **6**:290a
rice ············· **1**:103b; **6**:309b
Rice-Transplanting Festival ············· **2**:254b
Sanja Festival (Sanja Matsuri) ····· **2**:253a; **7**:11b
Sannō Festival (Sannō Matsuri) ····· **7**:15a
Sendai ············· **7**:335a
setsubun ············· **2**:260b
shichigosan ············· **2**:261b
Shintō rites ············· **7**:139a
Shōbu no Sekku ············· **7**:58b
Snow Festival (Yuki Matsuri) ····· **2**:252b
Sōma Nomaoi ············· **7**:226b
Takayama ············· **7**:320a
Tango ············· **1**:279a
tōrō nagashi ············· **2**:261a
toshi no ichi (year-end fair) ············· **2**:262a
tsukimi (moon viewing) ············· **2**:261b
Yamaguchi Gion ············· **8**:294a
Fēton gō Jiken
·······フェートン号事件 ······· **6**:182a
Feudal age
historiography ············· **3**:153b-154b
periodization ············· **6**:176b
Feudalism ········· **2**:263a-267a; **7**:218a
abolition ············· **3**:192a-194b
bushidō ("the Way of the warrior") ················· **1**:221b-223b
decline: Edo period ············· **2**:266a-267a
bakuhan system ············· **1**:131a
bureaucracy ············· **2**:266b
daimyō vassalage ············· **2**:266a-266b
economic growth ············· **2**:266b-267a
Sankin Kōtai system ············· **2**:266b
urbanization ············· **2**:266b
gains ············· **4**:63a
mature: late Muromachi and Azuchi-Momoyama periods · **2**:265a-266a
daimyō ············· **2**:265a-266a
fief holders ············· **2**:265b
instability ············· **2**:266a
oath of allegiance ············· **2**:265b
Sengoku period ············· **2**:265a
vassalage ············· **2**:265b-266a
problems of definition ············· **2**:263a-263b
characteristics ············· **2**:263b
Japanese ············· **2**:263a-263b
Marxist ············· **2**:263a
Western ············· **2**:263a
protofeudalism: Kamakura period ················· **2**:264a-264b
Carolingian ············· **2**:264b
go-on ("favor") ············· **2**:264a
government centralization ············· **2**:264a
hōkō ("service") ············· **2**:264a
limited character ············· **2**:264b
rise of warrior class ············· **2**:263b-264a
alliances ············· **2**:264a
hereditary aspect ············· **2**:263b-264a
origins ············· **2**:263b
warfare ············· **2**:264a
transition to: early Muromachi period ················· **2**:264b-265a
gokenin system ············· **2**:264b
kokujin ············· **2**:265a
shugo rebellion ············· **2**:265a

warrior government ············· **8**:228b
Fiction
 Edo period ········ **3**:28a-29a; **5**:48b-49b
 modern ··········· **5**:50b-56a; **6**:220b-221b
 pre-modern ········· **5**:14a, 245b-246b
Fiction literary groups ······· **5**:18b-19b
Fidelity and good faith, principle of
 ······························· **6**:245b
Fidelity (shin) ················· **4**:141b
Fields Prize ··········· **3**:147b; **7**:311a
Figure painting ················ **6**:158b
Figurines, clay ············· **4**:74a-74b
Filial piety ······ **2**:245a-245b, 267a; **6**:163a
 religion ····················· **6**:291a
 censorship ·················· **2**:338b
Film, Japanese ·············· **2**:267a-276a
 actors and actresses
  Aratama Michiyo ··········· **2**:273a
  Asaoka Ruriko ·············· **2**:275a
  Atsumi Kiyoshi ········ **1**:115b; **2**:275a
  Fuji Tatsuya ··············· **2**:275a
  Funakoshi Eiji ············· **2**:273a
  Hanayagi Shōtarō ··········· **3**:95a
  Hara Setsuko ····· **2**:271a; **3**:102a-102b
  Hasegawa Kazuo ············· **3**:107a
  Hayakawa Sesshū ············ **3**:115a
  Hidari Sachiko ···· **2**:274b; **3**:130a-130b
  Ichikawa Utaemon ··········· **3**:258a
  Inoue Masao ················ **2**:268b
  Iwashita Shima ············· **2**:274b
  Katsu Shintarō ············· **4**:174b
  Kazami Akiko ·········· **2**:269a, 270b
  Matsuda Eiko ··············· **2**:275a
  Mifune Toshirō ·········· **2**:270b-271a;
   5:168a-168b
  Mikuni Rentarō ········ **5**:172b-173a
  Mochizuki Yūko ············· **5**:228b
  Mori Masayuki ············· **2**:272b
  Nakadai Tatsuya ············ **2**:273a
  Nakamura Kichiemon ········· **2**:274b
  Okada Eiji ················· **6**:78a
  Ōkōchi Denjirō ······· **2**:268b; **6**:93a
  Otowa Nobuko ··············· **6**:133b
  Ryū Chishū ·········· **2**:271a; **6**:353b
  Saitō Tatsuo ··············· **2**:269a
  Shimura Takashi ············ **7**:108b
  Takakura Ken ··············· **7**:314a
  Takamine Hideko ······· **2**:272b; **7**:315a
  Tanaka Kinuyo ········· **2**:270b; **7**:337a
  Wakao Ayako ················ **8**:218b
  Yamaguchi Yoshiko ·········· **8**:295b
  Yamamoto Fujiko ············ **8**:297b
  Yorozuya Kinnosuke ········· **8**:339b
 Ai no korīda (Realm of the Senses) · **2**:275a
 benshi and storytelling cinema
  ···························· **2**:267b-268a
   editing techniques ········· **2**:268a
   live performances ·········· **2**:267b
   vocal styles ··············· **2**:267b
 censorship ············ **2**:271b, 338b
  compliance ················ **2**:271b
  military themes ············ **2**:271b
 Chūji tabi nikki (Chūji's Travel Diary)
  ····························· **2**:268b
 companies
  Daiei Co, Ltd ········ **2**:56b, 271b-272a
  Nikkatsu Corporation **2**:267b-268a, 270b;
   6:1a-1b
  Shin Tōhō Co, Ltd ······ **2**:271b, 273b
  Shōchiku Co, Ltd ······ **2**:268a, 269b
  Tōei Co, Ltd ··· **2**:272a, 273a-273b, 274b;
   8:35a
  Tōhō Co, Ltd ········· **2**:270b; **8**:36b
 directors
  Fukasaku Kinji ············· **2**:359b
  Gosho Heinosuke ············ **3**:50a
  Hani Susumu ············ **3**:97a-97b
  Ichikawa Kon ·········· **3**:257b-258a

Imai Tadashi ················ **3**:273a
Imamura Shōhei ·········· **3**:273b-274a
Inagaki Hiroshi ············· **3**:282a
Itami Mansaku ··············· **3**:351b
Itō Daisuke ············· **3**:351b-352a
Kinoshita Keisuke ··········· **4**:215b
Kinugasa Teinosuke ······· **4**:218b-219a
Kobayashi Masaki ······ **4**:237a; **8**:300b
Kumai Kei ·················· **4**:305b
Kumashiro Tatsumi ··········· **4**:307a
Makino Masahiro ············· **5**:86b
Makino Shōzō ··············· **5**:87a
Matsuyama Zenzō ········ **5**:141b-142a
Mizoguchi Kenji ········· **5**:225a-225b
Murata Minoru ·············· **5**:269b
Naruse Mikio ··········· **5**:335a-335b
Ōshima Nagisa ·········· **6**:125b-126a
Ozu Yasujirō ··········· **6**:141a-142b
Shimazu Yasujirō ············ **7**:102b
Shinoda Masahiro ········ **7**:122a-122b
Tasaka Tomotaka ············· **7**:347b
Teshigahara Hiroshi ·········· **8**:15a
Toyoda Shirō ············ **8**:90a-90b
Uchida Tomu ················ **8**:124a
Yamada Yōji ············ **8**:289b-290a
Yamamoto Kajirō ············· **8**:298b
Yamamoto Satsuo ············· **8**:299a
Yamanaka Sadao ·············· **8**:300b
Yoshimura Kōzaburō ·········· **8**:348a
documentary ············ **2**:275b-276a
early history ··········· **2**:267a-267b
 importance ················ **2**:267a
early postwar era ········ **2**:271b-272a
 communist purge ··········· **2**:271b
 labor unions ·············· **2**:271b
 Occupation film policy ······ **2**:271b
 theaters ··················· **2**:272a
first gendaigeki ········· **2**:268b-269a
 comedies ·················· **2**:269a
 influences ················· **2**:268b
genres
 chambara ·········· **2**:271a, 274b
 geidō-mono ················ **2**:271a
 gendaigeki ····· **2**:267b, 269b, 271b
 haha-mono ················· **2**:269b
 hōmu dorama ··············· **2**:269b
 jidaigeki · **2**:267b-268a, 269b, 271b, 274a
 kaidan jidaigeki ··········· **2**:273a
 Meiji-mono ················ **2**:269b
 merodorama ················ **2**:269b
 pinku ····················· **2**:275a
 rensageki ················· **2**:267b
 roman poruno ·············· **2**:275a
 shimpa ············· **2**:267b, 268b
 shōshimin geki ············· **2**:270a
 taiyōzoku ················· **2**:273b
 torimonochō ··············· **2**:271b
 tsuma-mono ················ **2**:269b
 yakuza ···················· **2**:343a
Hadaka no shima ············· **3**:75a
Kurutta ippeiji (A Page Out of Place) **2**:268b
late 1920s and early 1930s ··· **2**:269b-270a
mainstream ················· **2**:269b
 characteristics ············ **2**:269b
 genres ···················· **2**:269b
 motif ····················· **2**:269b
 rival productions ·········· **2**:269b
 series and remakes ········· **2**:269b
new wave ··············· **2**:273b-274a
 literary sources ··········· **2**:274a
 television ················· **2**:273b
 thematic changes ········ **2**:273b-274a
Nijūshi no hitomi (Twenty-Four Eyes)
 ····························· **2**:272b
1970s ····················· **2**:275b
 independent film making ····· **2**:275b
 largest grossing film ······· **2**:275b

Ningen no jōken (The Human Condition)
 ····························· **2**:273a
Nippon konchūki (The Insect Woman)
 ····························· **2**:274b
Nobi (Fires on the Plain) ······· **2**:273a
obscenity cases ·············· **1**:255a
Otoko wa tsurai yo; Torajirō wasurenagusa
 (*Hard to Be a Man; Tora's Forget-me-not*)
 ····························· **2**:275a
producers
 Kido Shirō ················· **4**:202a
 Makino Shōzō ··············· **5**:87a
 Nagata Masaichi ········ **5**:306b-307a
radio drama ················· **6**:275b
reformation of early 1920s ···· **2**:268a-268b
 female impersonators ········ **2**:268a
 film criticism ············· **2**:268a
 manzai ···················· **2**:268a
 popular cultural influence ··· **2**:268a
retrenchment and 1960s ····· **2**:274a-274b
 anti-heroes ················ **2**:274a
 minorities as theme ········· **2**:274a
Saikaku ichidai onna (The Life of Oharu)
 ····························· **2**:270b
screenwriters
 Hashimoto Shinobu ·········· **3**:110b
 Hisaita Eijirō ············· **3**:151b
 Itami Mansaku ·············· **3**:351b
 Matsuyama Zenzō ········ **5**:141b-142a
 Mizuki Yōko ··············· **5**:226a
 Noda Kōgo ················· **6**:30b
 Tanaka Sumie ··············· **7**:339b
 Terayama Shūji ········· **8**:12b-13a
 Yasumi Toshio ·············· **8**:319b
 Yoda Yoshikata ············· **8**:326b
Shichinin no samurai (Seven Samurai)
 ····························· **2**:271a
Shinjū Ten no Amijima (Love Suicide at
Amijima; Double Suicide) ···· **2**:274b
talkie ················· **2**:270a-271b
 fantasy films ·········· **2**:270b-271a
 literary influences ········· **2**:270b
 output ··············· **2**:271a-271b
 realism ··············· **2**:270a-270b
television age ··········· **2**:274b-275a
 movie attendance ··········· **2**:275b
 sexual themes ·············· **2**:275a
Third Golden Age ········ **2**:272a-273b
 comedy ··············· **2**:272b-273a
 creativity ················· **2**:272a
 monster movies ············· **2**:273b
 Motion Picture Code Committee · **2**:280b
 Rashōmon ················· **2**:272a
 sexual themes ·············· **2**:273b
 violence as theme ········ **2**:273a-273b
 war as theme ··········· **2**:272a-272b
Tōkyō monogatari (Tōkyō Story) ····· **2**:271a
Tsuchi (Earth) ············ **2**:269a
Tsuchi to heitai (Mud and Soldiers) · **2**:270b
Ukigumo (Floating Clouds) ···· **2**:272b
Umarete wa mita keredo (I Was Born,
But . . .) ················ **2**:269a
Film libraries ·············· **2**:276a
Finance ··············· **2**:276a-276b
 capital markets ········· **2**:276a-276b
 corporate ············· **2**:28b-29b
 cost accounting standards ··········· **2**:38b
 dividends ············· **2**:120b-121a
 financial intermediaries ····· **2**:276a-276b
 government bonds ············· **3**:54b
 household ·············· **2**:18b-20a
 insurance, miscellaneous ···· **3**:316a
 insurance system ········· **3**:316b-317a
 interest rate structure ···· **3**:317b-318a
 iron and steel industry ········ **3**:335b
 loans ··········· **3**:56b-57a; **6**:16a
 museums ·············· **5**:280b-280b
 national budget ·········· **1**:204b-206a

reserve funds ·················· **7:**87a-87b
Finance, local government ··· **2:**276b-277a
  budgets ·························· **2:**276b
  equalization grants ············ **2:**276b-277a
  revenues ························ **2:**276b
  taxes ························· **7:**353b
Finance law ········· **1:**160a; **2:**6b, 276b
  Public Accounts law ··········· **2:**276b
  Tax Allocation to Local Governments
  law ····························· **2:**276b
  Tax law ························· **2:**276b
**Financial Accounting Standard on
Consolidated Financial Statements**
  ·································· **2:**278a
Financial aid for students ··· **2:**179b-180a,
                                          277a
  scholarship loans ·············· **2:**277a
Financial circles ··········· **8:**366b-367a
Financial Crisis of 1927 ··· **2:**277a-277b
  French-Japanese relations ······ **2:**332b
  Inoue Junnosuke ············· **3:**309b-310a
  Itō Miyoji ····················· **3:**355a
  Suzuki Shōten ················· **4:**139a
  Taiwan Ginkō ················· **7:**309b
  Takahashi Korekiyo ············ **7:**312b
  Tanaka Giichi ············· **7:**336a-336b
Financial depression of 1930 **7:**173b-174a
Financial reporting ········· **2:**277b-278a
  cultural influences ············ **2:**277b
    directors' function ·········· **2:**277b
    stockholders ················ **2:**277b
  legal influences ·············· **2:**277b-278a
    Commercial Code ············ **2:**277b-278a
    Securities Exchange Law ··· **2:**277b-278a
  western influences and consolidated
  statements ····················· **2:**278a
Financial statements ········ **2:**278a
  interim ························· **2:**278b
  limited liability company ········ **5:**10a
  periodic ························ **2:**278b
Financial System Research Committee
  ·································· **2:**278b
Fine arts exhibitions ········ **1:**215b
Fines, nonpenal ········· **2:**49a; **6:**35a-35b
Finger pressure treatment. *See* **Shiatsu**
Fingerprints ················· **2:**249b
Firearms ····················· **1:**89b
  hinawajū ······················ **3:**140a
  introduction of ··········· **2:**279a-279b
**Firearms and Sword Possession Control
Law** ························ **2:**278b-279a
  licensing criteria ·············· **2:**279a
Fire Defense Agency ········· **2:**280a
Fire Defense College ········ **2:**280a
Fire Defense Research Institute ··· **2:**280a
Fire defense system ········ **2:**279a-280a
  history ························· **2:**279b
  operations ····················· **2:**279b
    fire prevention ·············· **2:**279b
    preservation of order ········ **2:**279b
    rescue and ambulance operations **2:**279b
  organization and system ······· **2:**279b
Fire fighters ············· **3:**137b-138a
Fireflies [(hotaru) family Lampyridae]
  ·································· **2:**280a-280b
Firefly viewing ·············· **2:**280b
Firemen's uniforms, traditional
  ·································· **2:**280b-281a
Fire Services Law ··········· **2:**280a
Fireworks ···················· **2:**281a
Firipin Oki Kaisen
  フィリピン沖海戦 ········ **4:**383a
Fiscal investment and loan program
  ·································· **8:**367b
Fiscal system ·············· **2:**281a-281b
  government-affiliated agencies ····· **2:**281b
  national government accounts **2:**281a-281b

Fish. *See* **Animals**
Fish and shellfish farming ··· **2:**281b-282b
  farming ····················· **2:**281b-282b
    techniques ·················· **2:**282b
  freshwater fish culture ······· **2:**281b-282a
    carp ······················· **2:**281b
    production ·················· **2:**281b-282a
    tilapia ····················· **2:**281b
  method of culture ············ **2:**282a-282b
    disease ···················· **2:**282a-282b
    feeding ···················· **2:**282a-282b
    oxygen requirements ········ **2:**282a
    rare species ················ **1:**60b-61a
  saltwater fish culture ········ **2:**282a
    nori ······················· **2:**282a
    production ·················· **2:**282a
    seaweed ···················· **2:**282a
Fisheries Preservation and Control Act
  ·································· **2:**283a
Fishery agreements ····· **2:**282b-283a, 285b
  bilateral ·················· **2:**282b-283a
  Korean ····················· **4:**284b-285a
  multilateral ················· **2:**282b
  Russo-Japanese ············ **6:**344a, 345b
  200-mile fishing zone ········ **2:**283a
Fishery Convention ·········· **7:**238a
  Russo-Japanese fisheries ····· **6:**345a-345b
Fishery zones ·············· **2:**283a-283b
  Russo-Japanese fisheries ······ **6:**345b
Fishes ···················· **1:**60b-61a
  abalones ····················· **1:**1a-1b
  anglerfishes ·················· **1:**56b
  ayu ························· **1:**125b
  bonito ····················· **1:**160b-161a
  carp ························· **1:**244a
  catfishes ···················· **1:**249b
  crucian carp ················· **2:**52a
  eel, Japanese ················ **2:**184a
  globefishes ················· **3:**36b-37a
  gobies ······················ **3:**38b
  goldfish ····················· **3:**43b
  herring ····················· **3:**128a
  mackerel ····················· **5:**79a
  octopuses ·················· **6:**60a-60b
  salmons ······················ **7:**5b
  samma ······················ **7:**6b-7a
  sardines ····················· **7:**21b
  sea bream ···················· **7:**45a
  tuna ························· **8:**120a
  whitebait ···················· **8:**251a
  yellowtail ··················· **8:**323b
Fish farming. *See* **Fish and shellfish
farming**
Fish finders ················· **2:**286a
Fishing ················· **2:**283b-284a
Fishing industry ·········· **2:**284a-287b
  ama ························· **1:**48a
  companies
    Hōkō Fishing Co, Ltd ········· **3:**214b
    Kyokuyō Co, Ltd ············· **4:**332b
    Nichiro Gyogyō Kaisha, Ltd ····· **5:**378a
    Nippon Suisan Kaisha, Ltd ······ **6:**13a
    Taiyō Fishing Co, Ltd ····· **7:**309b-310a
  conclusion ···················· **2:**287b
  future prospects ············ **2:**285a-285b
  modernization ················ **2:**286a-286b
    equipment ·················· **2:**286a-286b
    fish finders ················· **2:**286a
    other devices ··············· **2:**286a
  offshore fishing grounds ······· **2:**284a
  principal fisheries ·········· **2:**285b-286a
    northern sea operations ······· **2:**285b
    Pacific saury net ············ **2:**285b
    purse seining ··············· **2:**285b
    set net ···················· **2:**286a
    skipjack pole-and-line ········ **2:**286a
    squid ······················ **2:**286a
    trawlnet ···················· **2:**285b

  tuna longline ············ **2:**285b-286a
    production ·················· **2:**284a
  state of industry ············· **2:**284a
    aquiculture ················· **2:**284a
    companies ·················· **2:**284a
    employees ·················· **2:**284a
  traditional Japanese fisheries · **2:**286b-287b
    angling ···················· **2:**287a
    ayu ························ **2:**287b
    cormorant fishing ········ **2:**26a, 287b
    eels ······················· **2:**287b
    octopuses ·················· **2:**287a
    pearls ····················· **2:**287a
    sea cucumbers ·············· **2:**287a
  types ······················ **2:**284a-285a
    drift netting ················ **2:**284b
    longline angling ············· **2:**284b
    mackerel ··················· **2:**284b
    offshore ··················· **2:**284a
    pelagic ···················· **2:**284b
    pollack ···················· **2:**285a
    purse seining ··············· **2:**284b
    sardines ··················· **2:**284b
    squid and cuttlefish ········· **2:**284b
    whaling ···················· **2:**284b
Fishing tackle ·············· **7:**105b
Fish weir ·················· **2:**287b
Five Amakusa Bridges ········ **8:**174a
Five Commissioners (Gobugyō) ··· **1:**95b
"Five government enterprises" ··· **6:**264b
Five Great Elders (Gotairō) ···· **8:**95b-96a
Five Highways, The ········· **3:**41a-41b
Five Kings of Wa 倭の五王 ········ **2:**161a,
                                      287a-288b
  lineage ···················· **2:**287b-288a
  tomb mounds ················· **1:**79a
"Five-man groups" ········· **3:**45a-45b
**Five Men of the Pear Chamber
(Nashitsubo no Gonin)** ······· **5:**179a
Five Peaks of Aso ··········· **1:**103a
Five-Power Treaty
  Washington Naval Treaty of 1922 **8:**235b
Five Regents' Houses ······· **3:**48a-48b
Five Temples. *See* **Gozan**
Five Wisdom Kings ··········· **1:**200b
Flag, national ··············· **5:**339a
Flags and banners ··········· **2:**288a
Flexed Burials. *See* **Prehistoric burials**
Floats ····················· **7:**15a
Flood control ·············· **2:**72a-72b
Floor mat ··················· **7:**348a
Flora Japonica ··············· **4:**316b
Florenz, Karl ··········· **3:**27b; **4:**42b
Flower arrangement ········ **2:**288a-292a
  Adachi Chōka ················ **2:**291a
  chabana (tea-ceremony) ·········· **2:**289a
  design ······················ **2:**88a
  fūryū ······················· **2:**374b
  iemoto ······················ **3:**260b
  Ikenobō Sengyō ·············· **2:**288b
  leisure-time activity ·········· **4:**382a
  modern ikebana
    abroad ···················· **2:**292a
    avant-garde ············ **2:**291b, 292b
    free-style ················ **2:**291a-291b
    moribana ·················· **2:**290b-291a
    schools ···················· **2:**291b
    today ···················· **2:**291b-292a
  modern (free style) nageire ······ **2:**291a
  moribana-style ················ **2:**291a
  Ohara Hōun ·················· **2:**291a
  religion ····················· **6:**292a
  rikka-style ·················· **2:**288b
    contemporary ··············· **2:**293a
  shōka-style ·················· **2:**290b
    contemporary ··············· **2:**293a
  Teshigahara Hiroshi ············ **2:**292b
  Teshigahara Sōfū ·············· **2:**290a

traditional ikebana ·········· 2:288a-290a
  historical development ····· 2:288a-288b
  modern ························· 2:290a-290b
  nageire ······················ 2:289b-290a
  rikka ························· 2:288b-289b
  schools ························· 2:288b
  shōka ···························· 2:290a
"Flower divination" ·············· 6:191b
Flower Festivals ··············· 3:94a-94b
Flowering hazel ··················· 8:81b
Flowers
  chrysanthemums [(kiku) *Chrysanthemum*
  morifolium] ················· 1:310a-311a
  day lilies [(kisuge) *Hemerocallis thunbergii*]
  ··························· 2:78b-79a
  gardenia [(kuchinashi) *Gardenia jasminoides*]
  ································· 3:8a
  gentians [(rindō) *Gentiana scabra* var.
  buergeri] ···················· 3:24a
  hirugao [(bindweed) *Calystegia japonica*]
  ··························· 3:151a
  irises ························ 3:331b-332a
  kikyō [(balloonflower) *Platycodon*
  grandiflorum] ··················· 4:207b
  morning glories [(asagao) *Pharbitis*] · 5:255a
  peonies [(botan; shakuyaku) *Ranunculaceae*]
  ··························· 6:173b
  roses ························· 6:339a
  shimotsuke (*Spiraea japonica*) ·· 7:106b-107a
  violets [(sumire) *Violaceae*] ··· 8:192a-192b.
  See also **Plants**
Flower viewing ·············· 3:94a, *94b*
Flower-viewing party ············· 6:191b
Flow of funds ··············· 2:292b-293b
  corporate deficits ··············· 2:292b
  development ···················· 2:292b
  double-entry bookkeeping ·········· 2:292b
  personal sector ················· 2:292b
Flute Player on a Buffalo ·········· 6:77b
Flying Granary, The ··············· 7:93a
Flying squirrels ··············· 2:293b
Folding-screen panel ············· 7:*169b*
Folk crafts ··············· 2:293b-296a
  classification ·············· 2:295b-296a
    ceramics ··············· 2:*294b*, 295b
    metalwork ················· 2:295b
    paper ···················· 2:296a
    textiles ········· 2:295a, 295b-296a; 8:19b
    typography ················· 2:296a
    wood and bamboo ······· 2:*294b*, 295b
  Hamada Shōji ··················· 3:89b
  history of tradition ·········· 2:295a-295b
    decline ················ 2:295a-295b
  Japan Folk-Craft Museum ·········· 4:46a
  Kawai Kanjirō ················· 4:178b
  Leach, Bernard Howell ············ 4:372b
  mingu ························· 5:184a
  Munakata Shikō ······ 5:532b, *233a*, 264b
  museums ························ 5:278a
  traditional
    makers ···················· 7:165a
  Yanagi Muneyoshi ··· 2:293b-295a; 8:314a
Folk culture. *See* Folklore
Folk dances. *See* **Dance, traditional**
Folklore
  ghosts ························· 3:30a
  Kintarō (Golden Boy) ············· 4:218b
  New Year
    Ōtoshi no kyaku ·············· 6:133b
Folklore studies ······· 2:296a-296b, 302a
  contemporary status ·············· 2:296b
  historical development ········ 2:296a-296b
  literary-philosophical approach ····· 2:296b
  local history ··············· 5:71a-71b
  Orikuchi Shinobu ··············· 2:296b
  scholars ······················ 7:256b
  Shibusawa Keizō ················· 7:86b
  Yanagi Muneyoshi ··············· 2:296b

Folk performing arts ········· 2:296b-298a
  dengaku ························ 2:*298b*
  festival context ············· 2:297b-298a
  furyū ························· 2:*299a*
  general characteristics ······· 2:297a-297b
    agricultural nature ············ 2:297a
    processions ············· 2:297a-297b
    purification ················· 2:297a
    seasonal nature ··············· 2:297b
  Honda classification ·············· 2:297b
  kadozuke ······················ 4:101a
  kagura ························ 2:*297a*
  Kuromaru odori (dance) ·········· 2:*299a*
  nembutsu odori ················· 5:360a
  rain dances ···················· 6:280b
  range and diversity ·········· 2:296b-297a
  rice ·························· 6:309a
Folk religion ··· 2:298a-300b; 6:291a; 7:76a
  characteristics ·············· 2:298a-298b
  historical development ············ 2:298b
  modern ···················· 2:299b-300b
    nationalism ················· 2:299b
    new religions ················ 2:300a
    revival ····················· 2:300a
  patterns ················· 2:298b-299b
    rites of passage ··············· 2:299b
    seasonal ···················· 2:*299a*
Folk Shintō ····· 民間神道 ······· 2:300b
  dimensions ···················· 2:300b
  matsuri ······················ 2:253a
Folk song ················ 2:300b-301a
  instrumental accompaniment ········ 2:301a
  musical structure ················ 2:301a
  Ryōjin hishō ··················· 6:351b
  ryūkōka ······················ 6:354a
  study and collection ·········· 2:301b-302a
  types ···················· 2:301a-301b
    historical ·················· 2:301b
    regional ················· 2:301a-301b
Folktales ················· 2:302a-304a
  "Ash Scatterer" ················· 2:303a
  Bumbuku chagama ··········· 1:207a-207b
  diffusion routes to Japan ······ 2:303b-304a
  foxes ························· 2:330a
  Hamamatsu Chūnagon monogatari · 3:90b-91a
  Hanasaka jijii ··················· 3:94b
  history of study ············· 2:302a-302b
  interrelationship between oral and written
    literature ················ 2:302b-304a
  Issumbōshi ··················· 3:348b
  Itō Einosuke ··················· 3:352a
  "Kachikachi mountain" ······· 2:303a-303b
  monkeys ···················· 5:245a-245b
  oni ·························· 6:106a
  "Peach Boy" ··················· 2:302b
  publication ················ 2:302a-302b
  "Sarukani kassen" ("The Battle between
  the Monkey and the Crab") ······· 7:22b
  Shitakiri suzume ("Tongue-cut Sparrow)
  ···················· 2:303a; 7:149b
  type and motif ················· 2:302b
  Uji shūi monogatari ·············· 8:137b
  Urashima Tarō ················· 8:175b
  "Urikohime" ("The Melon Princess")
  ··························· 8:181a
  "Wen Removed" ············· 2:302b-303a
  writing style ·············· 4:132a-132b
  Yoru no nezame ("Nights of Fitful
  Waking") ···················· 8:339a
  Yuriwaka legend ················· 8:358a
Fontanesi, Antonio ··············· 2:304a
  Asai Chū ················· 1:93b; 2:304a
  Yamamoto Hōsui ··········· 2:304a; 8:298a
Food additives and contamination
  ···················· 2:304a-304b
  consumer reaction ··············· 2:304b
  fish contamination ··············· 2:304b
  Kanemi Oil Poisoning Incident ····· 2:304b

  Minamata disease ··············· 2:304a
  Morinaga Powdered Milk Incident · 2:304a
  political issue ·················· 2:304b
Food and eating ············· 2:304b-307a
  consumer expenditure · 2:17a; 7:244a-245a
    household ··················· 2:19a
  contemporary ·············· 2:306b-307a
    changes in eating habits ········· 2:307a
    eating customs ············ 2:306a-307a
    seasoning and cooking ·········· 2:306a
    staple foods and side dishes ····· 2:306b
  cooking ···················· 2:20b-25b
  history of Japanese ·········· 2:304b-306b
    Azuchi-Momoyama period ······· 2:306a
    Chinese influence ·········· 2:304b-305a
    Edo period ··············· 2:306a-306b
    Heian period ················· 2:305b
    Jōmon period ················· 2:305a
    Kamakura period ·············· 2:305b
    Kofun and Nara periods ········· 2:305b
    Korean influences ············· 2:305a
    modern period ············ 2:306a-306b
    Muromachi period ········· 2:305b-306a
    Western influences ············ 2:305a
    Yayoi period ················· 2:305a
  instant ························ 3:315b
Food May Day ············· 4:358a; 7:165a
Food processing industry ········· 2:307a
Food products industries
  Ajinomoto Co, Inc ············· 1:38b-39a
  Calpis Food Industry Co, Ltd (Karupisu
  Shokuhin Kōgyō) ·············· 1:236b
  House Food Industrial Co, Ltd ····· 3:240a
  Itō Ham Provisions Co, Ltd ······· 3:352a
  Marudai Food Co, Ltd ··········· 5:120b
  Nippon Flour Mills Co, Ltd ········· 6:9b
  Nippon Reizō ················ 6:11b-12a
  Nisshin Flour Milling Co, Ltd · 6:20b-21a
  Nissin Food Products Co, Ltd ······ 6:21b
  Q. P. Corporation ··············· 6:273a
  Snow Brand Food Co, Ltd ········· 7:206b
  Tōyō Seikan Kaisha, Ltd ·········· 8:92b
  Tōyō Suisan Kaisha, Ltd ·········· 8:93a
Food Sanitation Law ·········· 2:307a-307b
Foodstuff Control Law ··········· 6:310a
Foodstuff Control Special Account
  ··························· 2:307b
  rice surplus ···················· 2:307b
  transfers to ···················· 1:205b
Food supply ··················· 2:308a
  improvement measures ············ 2:308a
  rice ·························· 2:308a
  self-sufficiency ················· 2:308a
  wheat ························· 2:308a
Fool's Dance ··················· 1:124a
Footgear, traditional ············· 2:308a
  rain ·························· 6:280b
Footprints in the Snow ············· 8:59b
Forbidden Room, The ············· 5:198a
Forceful appeals ················· 3:50a
Ford, Gerald ···················· 4:18a
Foreign aid policy ············ 2:308a-310a
  administration ·················· 2:309b
  changes ················· 2:308b-309b
    developing nations ········· 2:309a-309b
    economic interests ············ 2:309a
    emphases ··················· 2:309b
    geographic distribution ········· 2:309b
    political aspects ·············· 2:309b
  international comparisons ···· 2:308a-308b
  Overseas Economic Cooperation Fund
  ··························· 6:136a
Foreign concessions, 19th century. *See*
  Kyoryūchi
Foreign currency reserves ········· 2:310a
Foreign employees of the Meiji period
  ··················· 2:310b-311b
  Bälz, Erwin von ················· 1:135b

Boissonade de Fontarabie, Gustave Emile ·········· **1**:160a; **2**:311a
Bousquet, Georges Hilaire ········· **2**:166a
Brinkley, Frank ··········· **1**:170b; **2**:311a
Brunton, Richard Henry · **1**:1:175b; **2**:311b
Capron, Horace ··········· **1**:243b; **2**:311a
Chamberlain, Basil Hall ····· **1**:266a–266b; **2**:311a–311b
Chiossone, Edoardo ······· **1**:296b; **2**:311b
Clark, Edward Warren ··· **1**:1:321b; **2**:311a
Clark, William Smith ······ **1**:321b; **2**:311b
Denison, Henry Willard ··· **2**:86b; **2**:311a
Du Bousquet, Albert Charles · **2**:134a–134b
Fenollosa, Ernest Francisco ··· **2**:251b–252a
Griffis, William Elliot ···· **2**:311a; **3**:62b
Mayet, Paul ··········· **5**:142b
Morse, Edward Sylvester ··· **2**:311a; **5**:256a
Mosse, Albert ·········· **5**:256a–256b
Murray, David ········· **2**:311a; **5**:275a
Roesler, Karl Friedrich Hermann ·· **2**:311a; **6**:334a
Verbeck, Guido Herman Fridolin · **2**:311a; **8**:189b–190a
Foreigners, attitudes toward · **2**:311b–313a
Dejima ·············· **2**:83a–83b
East and West in Japanese culture · **2**:312a
Japan's modern History and the West
nationalistic factors ··············· **2**:312a
political factors ··············· **2**:311b
Japan's modern history and West ················· **2**:311b–312a
konketsuji ··············· **4**:271a–271b
Whites and Blacks ········ **2**:312a–313a
discontinuity with Japanese ···· **2**:312a
negative feeling toward ···· **2**:312b–313a
positive feelings toward ········ **2**:313a
Foreigners in Japan ········· **2**:313a–314a
adjustment problems ······· **2**:313b–314a
Alien Registration Law ············· **2**:313a
ethnic discrimination ········· **2**:314a
historical roles ············· **2**:313a
konketsuji ··············· **4**:271a–271b
legal status ············· **2**:314a
sex discrimination ············ **2**:313b
national differences ········ **2**:313a–313b
demographic factors ········· **2**:313b
sex ratio ············· **2**:313a–313b
percentage of population ········ **2**:313a
Foreign Exchange and Foreign Trade Control Law ···· **1**:13b; **2**:314a–314b, 320b
prewar ··············· **2**:314a
trade controls ············ **2**:314b
Foreign exchange control ···· **2**:314b–316b
background ············· **2**:314b
postwar ··············· **2**:314b
prewar ··············· **2**:314b
budget ··············· **2**:315b
capital control ············ **2**:315b
direct and portfolio investments · **2**:315b
yen base system ············ **2**:315b
evolution of system ······· **2**:316a–316b
liberalization ············· **2**:316a
Foreign Trade Control Law ······· **2**:314b
enforcement ············ **2**:315a
objective ··············· **2**:315a
Investment Law ············ **2**:315a
coverage ··············· **2**:315a
modern economy ··········· **2**:163a
standard settlement ········· **2**:315a
tariffs ··············· **7**:346b–347a
technology imports ········· **2**:315b–316a
contract categories ········· **2**:316a
Foreign Exchange Control Law of 1980 ················ **2**:315b–316a, 320a
monetary policy ··········· **5**:240b
Foreign exchange quotas ······ **2**:325a
Foreign Investment Council ···· **2**:316b
foreign exchange control ······· **2**:316b

foreign investment in Japan ······· **2**:316b
Organization for Economic Cooperation and Development (OECD) ······· **2**:316b
technology transfer ········· **7**:374b
Foreign investment in Japan
guidelines for foreign firms ·· **2**:316b–319a
foreign executives ·········· **2**:318a–318b
image ··············· **2**:317b
Japanese interdependency ·· **2**:317b–318a
Japanese personnel ········ **2**:318a
perceptions of the Japanese ····· **2**:317b
history ··············· **2**:316b–317a
after World War II ········· **2**:317a
relaxation of restrictions ······· **2**:317a
Foreign Investment Law. *See* **Foreign exchange control**
Foreign Investment Law ···· **2**:314a–314b, 320b; **6**:180a
technology transfer ··········· **7**:374b
Foreign language training in the schools ··········· **2**:318b; **7**:35b
Foreign law, study of ······· **2**:318a–319a
Civil Code ············· **2**:319a
foreign scholars ··········· **2**:319a
modernization ··········· **2**:318a–319a
Foreign Mission Society of Paris (MEP) ················ **1**:249a
Foreign museums ········· **5**:280b
Foreign relations. *See* **International relations**; *specific country*
Foreign ships, decree concerning **7**:125b
Foreign students in Japan · **2**:319a–319b
Foreign trade ··· **2**:319b–324b; **8**:161a–164b
Ansei commercial treaties ·········· **1**:63a
Azuchi-Momoyama history ······· **3**:184b
balance-of-payments ········ **2**:324a–324b
deficits ··············· **2**:324a
before 1600 ············· **2**:148a
Brazil ··············· **1**:167a–169a
postwar ··············· **1**:168a–168b
prewar ··············· **1**:167b–169a
commodity composition of exports ················ **2**:321b–322a
developing countries ········ **2**:322a
home market expansion ···· **2**:321b–322a
definition ············· **2**:319b
Dutch ··············· **2**:135b–136a
early modern ··········· **2**:151a–151b
economic rehabilitation ········ **2**:320a–320b
Greater East Asia Coprosperity Sphere ················ **2**:320a
Edo period ············· **2**:150a
export performance ········· **2**:321b
annual rate ············ **2**:321b
percentage of world total ······· **2**:321b
export promotion ········· **2**:320b–321a
Export-Import Bank of Japan ··· **2**:321a
import licenses ··········· **2**:320b–321a
Ministry of International Trade and Industry ············· **2**:320b
geographical distribution ···· **2**:322a–322b
horizontal trade relations ···· **2**:322b
Harris Treaty ············ **2**:319b
import dependence ········ **2**:322b–323a
raw materials ············ **2**:322b
import liberalization ········· **2**:323a–324a
industrial structure ········· **2**:323b
International Monetary Fund ···· **2**:323b
interwar period ··········· **2**:320a
Depression effects ········· **2**:320a
protective policies ········· **2**:320a
role of colonies ··········· **2**:320a
iron and steel industry ········ **3**:335b–336a
Italy ··············· **3**:351a
Iwakura mission ·········· **3**:359b
modern era, advent of (1868 to World War I) ············· **2**:319b–320a
dualistic pattern ········· **2**:319b

Taiping Rebellion ············· **2**:319b
tariff autonomy ··········· **2**:320a
Unequal Treaties ·········· **2**:320a
multinational enterprises ····· **5**:263a–264a
postwar protectionism ········· **2**:320b
Foreign Exchange and Foreign Trade Control Law ··········· **2**:320b
tariff levels ············· **2**:320b
trading partners ············ **2**:320b
post-World War II ··········· **2**:157a
regulations limiting ·········· **7**:171a
Thailand ············· **8**:20b
trading companies ··········· **2**:324a
Foreign trade, government policy on ················ **2**:324b–326b
administrative guidance ········· **2**:326a
balance-of-payments ········· **2**:324b
cartels ··············· **2**:325a
export quality checks ········· **2**:325a
foreign exchange quotas ········· **2**:325a
Greater East Asia Coprosperity Sphere ················ **2**:325a
history ··············· **2**:324b
importance ············· **2**:324b
industrialization ··········· **2**:325b
liberalization ············· **2**:325b–326b
linkage system ············ **2**:325b
Ministry of International Trade and Industry (MITI) ············· **2**:325a
national seclusion ··········· **2**:324b
protectionist ············· **2**:325a
research and development ········ **2**:325a
tariffs ··············· **2**:325a
Forestry ············· **2**:326b–327a
forest conditions ··········· **2**:326b
species ··············· **2**:326b
total forest area ··········· **2**:326b
history of wood utilization ······· **2**:327a
construction ············ **2**:327a
fuel ··············· **2**:327a
Tōkyō Earthquake of 1923 ······· **2**:327a
operations ············· **2**:326b–327a
national forests ··········· **2**:326b–327a
private ··············· **2**:327a
profit-sharing ············ **2**:326b–327a
supply and demand of wood ····· **2**:326b
Formosa. *See* **Taiwan**
Formulary of Adjudications ····· **3**:47b–48a
Fortune-telling ··········· **6**:101b
ommyōdō ············· **6**:103a
Forty-Seven Rōnin Incident 赤穂事件 **2**:327a–328a; **7**:28a; **8**:293a
Akō ··············· **1**:44b
background ············· **2**:327a–327b
Confucian scholars' opinions ······ **2**:327b
Muro Kyūsō ············· **2**:327b
Ogyū Sorai ············· **2**:327b
Satō Naotaka ············· **7**:28a
Yamagata Daini ············ **8**:293a
dramatic portrayal ··········· **2**:269b
katakiuchi ············· **4**:165a
Kanadehon chūshingura ········· **4**:96a
public reaction ············ **2**:327b–328a
dramatic portrayals ········· **2**:328a
Tokugawa Tsunayoshi ········ **2**:328a
shogunate's dilemma ········· **2**:327b
vendetta ··············· **2**:327b
Kira Yoshinaka ············ **4**:220a
Ōishi Yoshio ············· **2**:327b
Fossa Magna ··· **2**:328a, 345a; **4**:8b
earthquakes ············ **2**:139a–139b, 141a
Naumann, Edmund ·········· **5**:358a
Fossils ··············· **2**:328a–329b
characteristics ············ **2**:328b–329b
cenozoic ··············· **2**:329a
cretaceous ············· **2**:329a
jurassic ··············· **2**:328b
mesozoic ··············· **2**:328b–329a

neogene · · · · · · · · · · · · · · · · · · 2:329a
paleogene · · · · · · · · · · · · · · · · · 2:329a
paleozoic · · · · · · · · · · · · · · · · · 2:328b
pleistocene · · · · · · · · · · · · · · · · 2:329a
triassic · · · · · · · · · · · · · · · · · · 2:328b
Foster child · · · · · · · · · · · · · · · · · · 8:338a
Foster family program · · · · · · · · · · 7:26b
Foster parent · · · · · · · · · · · · · · · · · 8:338b
Foujita, Léonard · · · · · · · · · · · · · · 2:347a
Foundlings · · · · · · · · · · · · · · · · · · · 1:15b
Fountains, legends · · · · · · · · · · · · · 5:295a
Four Books and Five Classics · · · · 2:329b
Four Elegant Pastimes, The · · · · · · · 4:146a
442nd Regimental Combat Team
· · · · · · · · · · · · · · · · · 2:329b-330a; 4:15a
Four Great Kings · · · · · · · · · · · · · · 7:298a
"Four Great Surnames" · · · · · · · · · · 7:292a
Four Guardian Kings of Classical Poetry
(Waka Shitennō) · · · · · · · · · · · · · 8:73b
Four Monk-Writers · · · · · · · · · · · · · · 4:1b
Four Pleasures · · · · · · · · · · · · · · · · 4:110b
Four-Power Treaty of 1921 · · · · · · 2:330a
Anglo-Japanese Alliance · · · · 1:57a; 8:152a
United States · · · · · · · · · · · · · · 8:157a
Washington Conference · · · · · · · · 8:234b
"Four S's" · · · · · · · · · · · · · · · · 7:316a-316b
Fowl. *See* Chicken, Japanese
Foxes [(kitsune) *Vulpes vulpes*] · · · 2:330a
hondokitsune · · · · · · · · · · · · · · · 2:330a
Inari, symbol of · · · · · · · · · · · · · · 3:283a
Kitakitsune · · · · · · · · · · · · · · · · · 2:330a
legends · · · · · · · · · · · · · · · · · · · 2:330a
mythology · · · · · · · · · · · · · · · · · 5:296b
Foxtrot · 6:354b
"Framework Agreement for Economic
Cooperation between Japan and
Canada" · · · · · · · · · · · · · · · · · · 1:238a
France and Japan · · · · · · · · · · · 2:330a-333a
closed Japan · · · · · · · · · · · · · 2:330b-331a
Dutch influence · · · · · · · · · · 2:330b-331a
Kanagawa Treaty · · · · · · · · · · · · 2:331a
Edo period (latter part) · · · · · · 2:331a-331b
first French consul-general · · · · · · 2:331a
foreign trade agreements · · · · · · · 2:331b
Japanese delegations to France
· · · · · · · · · · · · · · · · · · · 2:331a-331b
first contact · · · · · · · · · · · · · · · · · 2:330a
Japanese expansion · · · · · · · · 2:332a-333a
cultural agreements · · · · · · · · · · 2:333a
diplomatic agreements · · · · · 2:332a-332b
economic agreements · · · · · · · · · 2:332b
Financial Crisis of 1927 · · · · · · · · 2:332b
Indochina · · · · · · · · · · · · 2:333a; 3:290b
Sino-Japanese War · · · · · · · · · · · 2:332b
Japanese studies · · · · · · · · · · · · 4:42a-42b
Meiji period · · · · · · · · · · · · · · 2:331b-332a
Boshin Civil War · · · · · · · · · · · · 2:331b
Constitution · · · · · · · · · · · · · · · 2:332a
educational system · · · · · · · · · · · 2:332a
Freedom and People's Rights
Movement · · · · · · · · · · · · · · · 2:332a
French political thought · · · · 2:331b-332a,
2:335b
military cooperation · · · · · · · 2:331b-332a
post-World War II · · · · · · · · · · · · · 2:333a
France Bed Co, Ltd · · · · · · · · · · · · 2:333b
Franciscans · · · · · · · · · · · · · · · · · 2:333b
Franco-Japanese Agreement of 1907
· 2:332b, 333b
**Franco-Japanese Treaty on Trade and
Navigation** · · · · · · · · · · · · · · · · 2:332a
*Franz Xaveri Sein Leben und Seiner Zeit
(Francis Xavier: His Life and Times)*
· 8:281a
Fraternal associations (kō) · · · · · · 4:234a
Free Artists Association · · · · · · · · · 8:294b
Freedom and People's Rights Movement
· 2:1b, 333b-337a; 7:92b, 99a, 251a; 8:291b

Akita Incident · · · · · · · · · · · · · · · · 1:42b
Baba Tatsui · · · · · · · · · · · · · · · · · 1:129a
background · · · · · · · · · · · · · · 2:333b-334a
Korean debate · · · · · · · · · · · · · · 2:334a
leadership · · · · · · · · · · · · · · · · · 2:334a
Chichibu Incident · · · · · · · · · · · · · 1:271b
Daidō Danketsu Movement · · · · · · 2:56a
Dajōkan (Grand Council of State) · · · 2:70b
early organization · · · · · · · · · 2:334a-334b
Aikoku Kōtō · · · · · · · · · · · · · · · · 1:34b
Aikokusha · · · · · · · · · · · · · · · · 2:334b
elitist nature · · · · · · · · · · · · · · · · 2:334a
Ōsaka Conference of 1875 · · · · · · 2:334b
Risshisha · · · · · · · · · · · · · · · · · 2:334a
eclipse · 2:336a
Constitution · · · · · · · · · · · · · · · 2:336a
Daidō Danketsu Movement · · · · · · 2:336a
Ōsaka Incident · · · · · · · · · · · · · · 2:336a
Peace Preservation Law of 1887 · · 2:336a
France and Japan · · · · · · · · · · · · · 2:332a
freedom of speech · · · · · · · · · · · · 2:338b
Fukuda Hideko's involvement · · · · · 2:362a
Fukushima Incident · · · · · · · 2:335a, 366a
Furusawa Shigeru · · · · · · · · · · · · · 2:373a
fundamental liberties · · · · · · · · · · 2:369a
Gakumon no susume · · · · · · · · · · · · 3:4b
Gumma Incident · · · · · · · · · · · · · · 3:67b
ideology · · · · · · · · · · · · · · · · 2:335b-336a
European influence · · · · · · · · 2:335b-336a
natural rights · · · · · · · · · · · 2:335b-336a
Iida Incident · · · · · · · · · · · · · · · · · 3:262b
Inoue Kaoru · · · · · · · · · · · · · · · · · 3:310b
interpretations · · · · · · · · · · · · 2:336a-337a
authoritarianism · · · · · · · · · · · · 2:336a
individualism · · · · · · · · · · · · · · · 2:336b
regionalism · · · · · · · · · · · · · 2:336a-336b
Itagaki Taisuke and · · · · · · · · · · · · 3:349a
Kabasan Incident · · · · · · · · · · · · · · 4:89a
Kawakami Otojirō · · · · · · · · · · · · · 4:181a
Kishida Toshiko · · · · · · · · · · · · · · 4:223a
Kitamura Tōkoku · · · · · · · · · · · · · 4:227b
kōgi seitai ron used by · · · · · · · · · · 4:249a
Kokumin no tomo reflected · · · · · · · 4:261a
local societies · · · · · · · · · · · · 2:334b-335a
League for Establishing a National
Assembly · · · · · · · · · · · · · · · · 2:335a
non-elitist nature · · · · · · · · · · 2:334b-335a
military expansion criticism · · · · · · 2:361a
modern philosophy · · · · · · · · · · · · 5:229b
naichi zakkyo · · · · · · · · · · · · · 5:309b-310a
Nakae Chōmin · · · · · · · · · · · · 5:311b-312a
Nakajima Nobuyuki · · · · · · · · · 5:313b-314a
nationalism · · · · · · · · · · · · · · · · · 5:342b
news agencies · · · · · · · · · · · · · · · 5:396a
Ōi Kentarō · · · · · · · · · · · · · · · · · · 6:75a
opposition · · · · · · · · · · · · · · · · · · 2:361b
Ōsaka Incident · · · · · · · · · · · · · · · 6:121a
Peace Preservation Law of 1887 · · · 6:167b
Political Crisis of 1881 · · · · · · · · · · 6:202b
Press Ordinance of 1875 · · · · · · · · 6:236a
Proletarian literature movement · · · 6:254b
Publication Ordinance of 1869 · · · · 6:262b
rise of parties · · · · · · · · · · · · 2:335a-335b
Jiyūtō · 2:335b
Minto · 2:335b
organization · · · · · · · · · · · · · · · · 2:335b
Rikken Kaishintō · · · · · · · · · · · · · 2:335b
socioeconomic composition · · · · · · 2:335b
Risshisha · · · · · · · · · · · · · · · · · · · 6:321a
Sandai Jiken Kempaku Movement
(Movement to Memorialize Three
Important Items) · · · · · · · · · · · · · 7:9b
Sanshimpō ("Three New Laws") · · · 7:16b
seiji shōsetsu · · · · · · · · · · · · · · · · · 7:50b
shimpa · 7:107b
shizoku · 7:152a
Tanaka Shōzō · · · · · · · · · · · · 7:338b-339b
Taoka Reiun · · · · · · · · · · · · · · · · · 7:346a

Tarui Tōkichi · · · · · · · · · · · · · · · · · 7:347a
Tōyama Mitsuru · · · · · · · · · · · · · · · 8:88a
Ueki Emori · · · · · · · · · · · · · · · · · · 8:127a
Unequal Treaties revision · · · · · · · · 8:149a
women in · · · · · · · · · · · · · · · · · · · 8:260b
women's suffrage · · · · · · · · · · · · · · 8:268b
Yokohama mainichi shimbun · · · · · · · 8:330a
Freedom injuristic acts, principle of 4:86a
Freedom of assembly · · · · · · · · · · · 2:337a
constitutional guarantee · · · · · · · · 2:369b
Public Order and Police Law of 1900
· 2:337a
Tōkyō ordinance decision (20 July 1960)
· 8:68b
Freedom of association · · · · · 2:337a-337b
constitutional guarantee · · · · · · · · 2:369b
Peace Preservation Law of 1925 · 2:337b
Public Order and Police Law of 1900
· 2:337b
Subversive Activities Prevention Law
· 2:337b
Freedom of contract · · · · · · · 2:337b; 4:86a
Freedom of religious faith · · · · 2:337a-338a;
4:372a
constitutional guarantee · · · · · · · · 2:369b
legal interpretations · · · · · · · · 2:337b-338a
separation of state and religion
· 2:337b-338a
Freedom of speech · · · · · · · 1:254b; 2:338a
constitutional guarantee · · · · · · · · 2:369b
freedom of the press · · · · · · · · · · · 2:338a
obscenity · · · · · · · · · · · · 2:338a; 6:49b-50a
Peace Preservation Law of 1925 · · · 2:338a
Press Law of 1909 · · · · · · · · · · · · · 2:338a
Publication Law of 1893 · · · · · · · · · 2:338a
Freedom of speech, regulation of
· · · · · · · · · · · · · 1:251b-255a; 2:338a-338b
Edo period · · · · · · · · · · · · · · · · · · 2:338b
Meiji and Taishō periods · · · 2:338b-339a
censorship system · · · · · · · · · · · · 2:338b
films · · · · · · · · · · · · · · · · · · 2:338b-339a
newspapers · · · · · · · · 2:338b-339a; 6:236a
publication · · · · · · · · · · · · · · · · · 6:262b
radio broadcasting · · · · · · · · · · · · 2:339a
Shōwa period · · · · · · · · · · · · · · · · 2:339a
censorship repeal · · · · · · · · · · · · 2:339a
Freedom of the press · 2:338a, 339a-339b;
6:236a, 267b
constitutional guarantee · · · · · · · · 2:369b
privacy, right to · · · · · · · · · · · · · · 6:249b
restrictions · · · · · · · · · · · · · · 2:339a-339b
Free markets · · · · · · · · · · · · · · · · · 6:282b
Free Thai Movement (FTM) · · · · · · · 2:339b;
6:238b; 7:65b; 8:20b
Fregat Pallada (Frigate *Pallas*) · · · · 3:45a;
6:270b
Friends · 1:3b
Friendship and Commerce, Treaty of
(between Russia and Japan) · · · · · 6:341b
Friendship Association · · · · · · · · · · 8:354a
Friends of Constitutional Government
Party · · · · · · · · · · · · · · · · · 6:315a-315b
Fringed pink [(kawara nadeshiko)
Dianthus superbus] · · · · · · · · · · · 2:339b
Fröbel, Friedrich Wilhelm August · 2:339b
Frogs [(kaeru) order Anura] · 2:339b-340a
Frois, Luis · · · · · · · · · · · · · 1:96b; 2:340a
Fruit. *See specific fruit*
Fruit trees production · · · · · · · · 1:27a-27b
Fūbaika · · · · · · · · · · · · 風媒花 · · · · · · 7:323b
Fucan Fabian. *See* Fabian
Fuchi · · · · · · · · · · · · · · 扶持 · · · · · · 2:340a
Fuchimai · · · · · · · · · · · · 扶持米 · · · · · · 2:340a
Fuchū (central Honshū)
· · · · · · · · · · · · · · · · · 府中 · · · · · · 2:340a
Fuchū (western Honshū)
· · · · · · · · · · · · · · · · · 府中 · · · · · · 2:340a

Fudai ·········· 譜代 ······ 1:131b;
　2:340b; 3:186b; 5:308b; 8:56b–57a
　daimyō ································ 2:340b
　peasants ····························· 2:340b
　rōjū ································· 6:334a
Fudasashi ······· 札差 · 2:340b–341a
　chōnin ····························· 1:302a
　functions ·························· 2:340b
　Kansei Reforms ················· 4:152b
　monopoly associations ········· 2:340b
　origins ····························· 2:340b
　Fude (brush) ······················ 1:232b
Fude no susabi 筆のすさび ···· 4:152a
Fudō ··············· 不動 ········ 4:98b
Fudōchō ········· 不同調 ······· 4:130b
Fudoki ·········· 風土記 1:151b; 2:296a,
　341a–341b; 7:76a; 8:175b
　Bungo ····························· 2:341b
　geography ························· 6:288a
　Harima ····························· 2:341b
　Hitachi ····························· 2:341a
　Hizen ······························ 2:341b
　Izumo ······························ 2:341a
　mythology ························· 5:292a
　religious symbolism ············· 6:295b
　thought and culture ············· 8:25b
　uses ································ 2:341a
Fudoki texts ···················· 4:20b
Fudō Myōō ······ 不動明王 4:147a; 6:151a
Fuefuki dōji ····· 笛吹童子 ····· 8:339a
Fuefukigawa ······ 笛吹川 · 2:341b, 343b;
　4:122b
Fuel Research Institute ··········· 6:305b
Fuels. See Energy, sources
Fūgai Ekun ····· 風外慧薫 · 2:341b
Fugaku sanjūrokkei (Thirty-six Views of
　Mt Fuji) ···· 富嶽三十六景 ···· 3:215a
Fūgashū (Collection of
　Elegance) ········· 風雅集 2:186a; 8:213b,
　214b
Fugitive Criminal Extradition Law · 2:238a
Fugu ······························ 3:36b–37a
Fuhito ··············· 史 ········ 4:89a
Fuji ·············· 富士 · 2:341b; 7:48a
Fuji. See Wisteria, Japanese
Fuji, Mount. 富士山　　See Fujisan
Fujian (Fukien) People's Government
　········· 福建人民政府 · 2:341b–342a
Fuji Bank, Ltd ·········· 1:168a; 2:342a
Fujieda ············ 藤枝 ····· 2:342a
Fujieda Shizuo ··· 藤枝静男 · 2:342a
Fuji Electric Co, Ltd · 2:342a–342b, 347a,
　372b
Fuji Five Lakes · 富士五湖 · 2:342b, 345a,
　359b; 4:177b
Fujigawa, Battle of
　············ 富士川の戦 · 2:342b
　Azuma kagami ·················· 2:342b
　Minamoto no Yoritomo ········· 5:181b
　Taira-Minamoto War ············ 7:300a
**Fuji-Hakone-Izu National
　Park**
　···· 富士箱根伊豆国立公園 · 1:49b, 107b;
　2:342b–343a; 4:135a
Fuji Heavy Industries, Ltd · 2:343a; 5:313b
　Nissan Motor Co, Ltd Affiliation · 2:343a
　passenger car production ········· 1:122a
Fujiidera ·········· 藤井寺 ···· 2:343a
Fujii Heigo ······ 藤井丙午 · 2:343a
Fujii Kenjirō ··· 藤井健次郎 · 2:343a
Fuji Junko ····· 藤純子 · 2:343a–343b
Fujikawa ········ 富士川 · 2:341b, 343b;
　4:122b
Fujikawa Yū ···· 富士川游 · 2:343b
Fuji Kōsan Co, Ltd ·············· 2:343b
Fujikoshi ··························· 5:299b
Fujikura, Ltd ···················· 2:343b
Fujimi ············ 富士見 ····· 2:343b

Fujimori Seikichi 藤森成吉 ···· 2:343b
Shin Nihon bungaku ············· 7:122a
Fujimoto Kizan ··· 藤本箕山 · 7:95b–96a
Fujin bungei ···· 婦人文芸 ···· 4:126a
Fujin kōron ···· 婦人公論 2:344a; 7:100a
Fujin Kyōfūkai ·婦人矯風会 · 4:324b
Fujin no tomo · 婦人之友 · 2:344a
Fujinomiya ········ 富士宮 ···· 2:344a
Fujin Sanseiken Undō
　········· 婦人参政権運動 · 8:169a
Fuji Oil Co, Ltd ·················· 2:344a
Fujioka ············ 藤岡 ······ 2:344a
Fujioka Sakutarō
　········· 藤岡作太郎 · 2:344a–344b
Fuji Photo Film Co, Ltd ··· 2:344b, 359a
Fujisan ············ 富士山 · 2:344b,
　344b–345b, 347b; 4:177b
　height ····························· 2:344b
　plants, animals, and man ········· 2:345a
　religious faith and climbing · · 2:345a–345b
　religious symbolism ·············· 6:295b
　scale and location ········· 2:344a–345a
Fujisan Hongū Sengen
　Jinja 富士山本宮浅間神社 ····· 7:64a
Fujisawa ··········· 藤沢 2:345b; 4:135a
Fujisawa Pharmaceutical Co, Ltd · 2:345b
Fujisawa Takeo · 藤沢桓夫 · 2:345b
Fujishima Takeji ·藤島武二 · 2:345b–346a
　Kokusen (Black Fan) ············ 2:346b
Fuji Spinning Co, Ltd ············· 2:346a
Fujita Art Museum ······· 2:346a; 5:277a
Fujita Corporation ··············· 2:346a
Fujita Denzaburō
　········· 藤田伝三郎 · 2:346a–346b
　museums ·························· 5:277a
Fujita Gorō ········ 藤田五郎 · 3:46b
Fujitani Mitsue 富士谷御杖 · 2:346b; 5:17b
Fujitani Nariakira
　········· 富士谷成章 · 2:346b–347a;
　5:17a; 7:281a
Fujita Tōko ····· 藤田東湖 · 2:347a
　Fujita Yūkoku ···················· 2:347a
Fujita Tsuguharu 藤田嗣治 · 2:347a
Fujita Tsuguji ···· 藤田嗣治 · 2:347a
Fuji Tatsuya ······· 藤竜也 · 2:275a
Fujita Yūkoku ··· 藤田幽谷 · 2:347a–347b
　Fujita Tōko ······················· 2:347a
Fuji Telecasting Co, Ltd · 1:173a; 2:347b;
　7:14a
Fuji Tradition ······················ 7:303b
Fujitsū, Ltd ············· 2:342b, 347b
Fuji Volcanic Zone
　·········· 富士火山帯 · 2:345a, 347b
Fujiwara culture 藤原文化 · 2:347b–348a
Fujiwara family ···· 藤原氏 1:190b; 2:166a,
　348a–348b; 7:7b, 19b, 45b,
　74a, 166a, 256b
　alliances ·························· 2:264a
　Asukai Masatsune ················ 1:106a
　branch families ········· 2:348a, 350b–351a
　Buddhist sculptors ··············· 1:199b
　decline ···························· 2:348b
　　insei ···························· 3:314b
　founder ···························· 2:351a
　founding ··························· 2:348a
　Fujiwara culture ················· 2:347b
　Fujiwara no Fuhito ··············· 2:350b
　Fujiwara no Michinaga ··········· 2:352a
　Fujiwara no Yoshifusa ··········· 2:358a
　Gosekke (Five Regents' Houses) 3:48a–48b
　Ichijō, Emperor ············ 3:255b–256a
　Jien ······························ 4:53b
　Konoe family ····················· 4:272b
　libraries ·························· 5:1a
　Murasaki Shikibu ················· 5:267b
　narrative histories ··············· 3:153a
　power ····························· 2:352b
　regency government ·············· 6:286a

　regents ··························· 2:348b
　rule ···················· 2:204a–204b
　Tōshi kaden ···················· 8:83a
　women in ························· 8:258b
Fujiwara Foundation of Science · · 2:348b
Fujiwara Ginijrō 藤原銀次郎 · 2:348b
Fujiwara Iwaichi 藤原岩市 2:348b; 3:289b
Fujiwara Kei ······ 藤原啓 · 1:260b
Fujiwara Kikan 藤原機関 · 2:348b, 350a
Fujiwarakyō ······ 藤原京 1:182a; 2:350a
　excavations ······················ 1:79b
　mokkan ················· 5:234a, *234b*
Fujiwara no Akihira
　········· 藤原明衡 · 2:350a; 5:37b
　literature ························· 1:293a
　Meigō ōrai ·············· 5:152b–153a
Fujiwara no Akisuke
　········· 藤原顕輔 · 2:350a; 5:38a
　Fujiwara no Kiyosuke ············· 2:352b
　Kenshō ··························· 4:198b
　Shika wakashū ············ 7:95a–95b
Fujiwara no Fuhito
　········· 藤原不比等 · 2:348a, 350b
　Kaifūsō ························· 4:109a
　Taihō Code ······················ 7:295b
　Yōrō Code ······················· 8:339a
Fujiwara no Fujifusa
　················ 藤原藤房 · 2:350b
Fujiwara no Fuyutsugu
　················ 藤原冬嗣 · 2:350b
Fujiwara no Hidehira 藤原秀衡 · 2:350b
Fujiwara no Hidesato
　················ 藤原秀郷 · 2:350b
Fujiwara no Hirotsugu, Rebellion of
　········· 藤原広嗣の乱 · 2:351a; 7:91a
Fujiwara no Ietaka
　················ 藤原家隆 · 2:351a; 5:41a
　Shin kokinshū ·················· 7:119b
Fujiwara no Kamatari
　················ 藤原鎌足 · 2:348a,
　351a–351b
　naidaijin ·················· 5:310a–310b
　Taika Reform ···················· 7:295b
　Tōshi kaden ···················· 8:83a
　Yamashinadera established ········ 4:243b
Fujiwara no Kaneie
　················ 藤原兼家 · 2:351b
　regency ··························· 2:352b
Fujiwara no Kanemichi
　················ 藤原兼通 · 2:351b; 7:26a
Fujiwara no Kanesuke
　················ 藤原兼輔 · 2:351b; 7:13a
Fujiwara no Kanezane
　················ 藤原兼実 · 4:303b
Fujiwara no Kintō
　················ 藤原公任 · 1:18a; 2:258a,
　352a–353b; 5:14a; 8:210a
　critical influence ················· 2:352a
　Sanjūrokkasen (The Thirty-Six Poetic
　Geniuses) ······················· 7:12b
　Shūi wakashū ··················· 7:184b
　Wakan rōeishū ················· 8:218a
Fujiwara no Kiyohira. 藤原清衡
　See Ōshū Fujiwara family
Fujiwara no Kiyokawa
　················ 藤原清河 · 2:352a–352b
Fujiwara no Kiyosuke
　················ 藤原清輔 · 2:352b
Fujiwara no Korechika
　················ 藤原伊周 · 2:352b; 7:53a
　Fujiwara no Michinaga ····· 2:352b–353a
Fujiwara no Kōzei
　················ 藤原行成 · 1:234a–234b;
　2:358b
Fujiwara no Ietaka 藤原家隆 · 3:51a–52a
Fujiwara no Masatsune
　················ 藤原雅経 · 1:137a

Fujiwara no Michinaga
　　　藤原道長 ······ 2:348b,
　　　352b–353a; 5:34a–34b; 7:53b
　Byōdōin temple ·········· 1:227a
　Fujiwara no Kintō ········ 2:352a
　Fujiwara no Korechika ····· 2:352b
　Fujiwara no Yorimichi ····· 2:357b–358a
　Kagerō nikki ············ 4:104a
　Midō Kampaku ki ········ 5:167a
　regency ····· 2:351b, 352b, 6:286b
　Sanjō, Emperor ··········· 7:12a
Fujiwara no Michinori
　　　藤原通憲 ······· 2:353a
Fujiwara no Michitoshi
　　　藤原通俊 · 2:353a–353b;
　　　　　　　　　5:38a
Fujiwara no Michitsuna no Haha.
　藤原道綱母　　*See* **Kagerō nikki**
Fujiwara no Mitsuyoshi 藤原光能　6:227a
Fujiwara no Motohira.
　藤原基衡　*See* **Ōshū Fujiwara family**
Fujiwara no Mototoshi
　　　藤原基俊 · 2:353b; 5:15a,
　　　　　　38b; 7:68a; 8:211a
Fujiwara no Mototsune. 藤原基経
　　　See **Akō Incident of 887**
　Fujiwara no Toshinari ········· 2:357a
Fujiwara no Nakamaro
　　　藤原仲麻呂 ······ 2:353b
Fujiwara no Nobuzane
　　　藤原信実 ····· 2:353b–354a
　Fujiwara no Takanobu ······· 2:355b
Fujiwara no Norinaga
　　　藤原教長 ········· 1:137a
Fujiwara no Sadaie
　　　藤原定家 · 1:5b; 2:348b,
　　　351b, 354a–355a; 4:*133b*; 5:14b, 42a; 7:61b,
　　　　　　　　96b
　Fujiwara no Takanobu ········ 2:355b
　Fujiwara no Tameie ········· 2:355b
　Fujiwara no Toshinari ········ 2:356b
　Fujiwara no Toshinari no Musume 2:357b
　Go-Toba, Emperor ······· 3:51b–52a
　heirs ················· 4:254a
　Jakuren ················ 4:1b
　Lady Daibu ············· 4:197b
　life ·············· 2:354a–354b
　orthographic studies ······· 4:133b
　poetry and poetic ideals ···· 2:354b–355a
　Shinkei ················ 7:119a
　Shin kokinshū ············ 7:119b
　Teika kanazukai ·········· 4:133b
　treatises and criticism ····· 2:354b–355a
Fujiwara no Sadanaga
　　　藤原定長 ··········· 4:1b
Fujiwara no Sanekata
　　　藤原実方 ········· 7:53b
Fujiwara no Sari. 藤原佐理
　　　See **Fujiwara no Sukemasa**
Fujiwara no Shōshi.　*See* **Jōtō Mon'in**
Fujiwara no Shunzei
　　　藤原俊成 · 2:355a, 356b;
　　　　　　5:39a; 8:211b, 355b
　　　See **Fujiwara no Toshinari**
Fujiwara no Sukemasa
　　　藤原佐理 1:234a; 2:355a
Fujiwara no Sumitomo
　　　藤原純友 ··· 2:355a–355b
Fujiwara no Tadamichi. 藤原忠通
　　　See **Hōgen Disturbance**
Fujiwara no Takanobu
　　　藤原隆信 2:355b; 5:*181a*;
　　　　　　　　6:227a
　Fujiwara no Nobuzane ······· 2:353b
　Jingoji ················ 4:58b
　Sei Shōnagon ········· 7:53a–53b

Fujiwara no Tameie
　　　藤原為家 · 1:5b; 2:348b,
　　　354a, 355a, 355b–356b; 8:213b
Fujiwara no Teika
　　　藤原定家 2:354a; 8:211b,
　　　See **Fujiwara no Sadaie**
Fujiwara no Teishi
　　　藤原定子 ········· 2:356b
　Fujiwara no Korechika ······· 2:352b
Fujiwara no Toshinari
　　　藤原俊成 1:181a; 2:348b,
　　　354a, 356b–357b; 4:128b; 5:39, 42a;
　　　　　　7:96b; 8:211b, 355b
　Fujiwara no Ietaka ········· 2:351a
　Fujiwara no Mototoshi ······· 2:353b
　Fujiwara no Tameie ········· 2:355b
　Go-Toba, Emperor ······· 3:51a–52b
　Jakuren ················· 4:1b
　Kamo no Chōmei ·········· 4:128b
　life ·················· 2:356b
　poetic career ·········· 2:356b–357a
　poetic ideals ············· 5:14b
　poetic ideals and principles · 2:357a–357b
　poetry ················ 2:357a
　Senzai wakashū ········· 7:68a–68b
　Shinkei ················ 7:119a
Fujiwara no Toshinari no Musume 2:357b
　Shin kokinshū ············ 7:120a
Fujiwara no Tsugikage
　　　藤原継蔭 ········· 3:336b
Fujiwara no Yasuhira. 藤原泰衡
　See **Ōshū Fujiwara family**
Fujiwara no Yorimichi
　　　藤原頼通 ··· 2:357b–358a
　Byōdōin temple ·········· 1:227a
　regency ········· 2:353a, 6:286b
Fujiwara no Yorinaga. 藤原頼長
　　　See **Hōgen Disturbance**
Fujiwara no Yoshifusa
　　　藤原良房 · 2:348a, 358a
　kampaku ··············· 4:130a
　Jōwa conspiracy ·········· 4:78a
　sesshō ················ 7:69b
Fujiwara no Yoshitsune
　　　藤原良経 · 2:358a–358b;
　　　　　　　　5:40b
　posthumous portraits ······· 4:147b
　Shin kokinshū ··········· 7:119b
Fujiwara no Yukinari
　　　藤原行成 1:234a; 2:358b
　Fujiwara no Sukemasa ······· 2:355b
　Gonki ················ 3:45b
　Sei Shōnagon ········· 7:53a–53b
Fujiwara Regency Government ···· 2:69b
Fujiwara Seika · 藤原惺窩 · 2:358b–359a
　education ·············· 2:173a
　Hayashi Razan ··········· 3:117a
Fujiwara Technological University 2:348b
Fuji Xerox Co, Ltd · 2:344b, 359a; 6:311b
Fujiya Confectionery Co Ltd ····· 2:359a
Fujiyama Aiichirō
　　　藤山愛一郎 ······· 2:359a
Fujiyama Raita · 藤山雷太 · 2:66b, 359a
　Fujiyama Aiichirō ·········· 2:359a
Fuji Yoshida ···· 富士吉田 · 2:359a–359b
Fuju Fuse sect 不受不施派 · 2:359b;
　　　　　5:375a–377b; 8:12b
Fukagawa ··········· 深川 · 2:359b
Fukai Shidōken den 深井志道軒伝 4:256a
Fukan zazengi 普勧坐禅儀 · 2:123b
Fukasaku Kinji ·· 深作欣二 · 2:275b, 359b
Fukaya ············ 深谷 · 2:359b
Fukazawa Shichirō
　　　深沢七郎 2:360a; 7:100a
Fukeizai.　*See* **Lese majesty**
Fuke sect ·········· 普化宗 · 7:75b
Fuki [(butterbur) *Petasites japonicus*]
　　　·················· 2:360a

Fukiagehama ····· 吹上浜 · 2:360a
Fukidera ········ 富貴寺 · 2:360a
Fukien People's Government, *See* **Fujian (Fukien) People's Government**
Fukin and fugin
　　　夫金, 夫銀 · 2:360a–360b
Fukinuki yatai ············ 2:360b
　Genji monogatari emaki ······· 3:20b
Fukken Jimmin Seifu
　　　福建人民政府 · 2:341b–342a
Fukkisō *(Pachysandra terminalis)* · 2:360b
Fukko Shintō ···· 復古神道 · 6:306a–306b
Fukko Yamato-e school
　　　復古大和絵派 ····· 2:360b
Fuko ············ 封戸 · 2:360b
Fukoku kyōhei · 富国強兵 · 1:86a;
　　　　　　　2:360b–361a
Fuku ·········· 4:163b, 321b
Fukuba Bisei ··· 福羽美静 · 2:361a–361b
Fukuba Hayato · 福羽逸人 · 2:361b
Fukuba Yoshishizu.　*See* **Fukuba Bisei**
Fukubiki ················ 2:361b
Fukuchi Gen'ichirō
　　　福地源一郎 ······ 2:361b
　Rikken Teiseitō ··········· 6:315b
Fukuchiyama ······ 福知山 · 2:361b
Fukuda Doctrine of 1977 ·· 7:196b, 236a;
　　　　　　　　　8:192a
Fukuda Eisuke ··· 福田英助 · 5:219b
Fukuda Gyōkai · 福田行誡 · 2:361b–362a
Fukuda Heihachirō
　　　福田平八郎 ······ 2:362a
Fukuda Hideko ·· 福田英子 · 2:362a–362b;
　　　　　　7:54a, 56a
Fukuda Shōji.　*See* **Shōji Kaoru**
Fukuda Takeo · 福田赳夫 · 2:362b
　foreign aid policy ········· 2:309b
Fukuda Tokuzō · 福田徳三 · 2:362b
　Reimeikai ·············· 6:288b
Fukuda Tsuneari 福田恆存 · 2:362b; 5:13b
　Shingeki ·············· 7:112a
Fukue ············ 福江 · 2:362b
Fukuejima ········ 福江島 · 2:363a
Fukugen Movement (Restoration of the Original Teachings)
　Tenrikyō ·············· 8:9a
Fukuharakyō ····· 福原京 · 2:363a
Fukui ············ 福井 · 2:363a–363b
Fukui Cave ···· 福井洞穴 · 2:363b; 4:75a
Fukui Ken'ichi ··· 福井謙一 · 2:363b
Fukuin shūhō ···· 福音週報 · 8:127b
Fukui Plain ····· 福井平野 · 2:363b
Fukui Prefecture · 福井県 · 2:364a
Fukūkenjaku Kannon 不空羂索観音
　　　········· 1:*187a*; 4:253a
Fukumoto Kazuo 福本和夫 · 2:364a
　Japan Communist Party ······· 4:11b
Fukunaga Takehiko
　　　福永武彦 · 2:364a–364b
Fuku no kami ······ 福ノ神 · 4:*325a*, 327a
Fukuoka ········· 福岡 · 2:364b, 365a
Fukuoka nichinichi
　shimbun · 福岡日日新聞 · 4:207b
Fukuoka Plain ···· 福岡平野 · 2:364b
Fukuoka Prefecture 福岡県 · 2:364b–365b
Fukuoka Takachika
　　　福岡孝弟 · 2:365b; 7:54a,
　　　　　　　　55a
Fukuroda Falls ···· 袋田滝 · 2:365b
Fukuroi ·········· 袋井 · 2:365b
Fukurokuju ············· 5:296a
Fukurotoji ············· 1:153b
Fukushi Kōjirō 福士幸次郎 · 2:365b–366a
Fukushima ········ 福島 · 2:366a
Fukushima Basin 福島盆地 · 2:366a
Fukushima Incident
　　　福島事件 · 2:335b, 366a
　cause ················ 2:366a

effects. · **2:**366a
Kabasan Incident · · · · · · · · · · · · **4:**89a
Kōno Hironaka · · · · · · · · · · · · · · **4:**274a
Fukushima Kazuo
　　　　　福島和夫 · · · · · · · · · **2:**366b
Fukushima Masanori
　　　　　福島正則 · · · · · · · · · **2:**366b
Fukushima Prefecture
　　　　　福島県 · **2:**366b-367a
Fukushima Yasumasa
　　　　　福島安正 · · · · · · · · · **2:**367a
Fukutoshin · · · · · · · · · · · · · · · · · · **8:**181a
Fuku warai · · · · · · · · · · · · · · · · **2:**367a-367b
Fukuyama · · · · · · · 福山 · · · · · **2:**367b
Fukuzawa Yukichi
　　　　福沢諭吉 · · · · **1:**8a, 16b,
　　155a; **2:**367a, 367b-368a; **4:**384b; **7:**338b
　Bummeiron no gairyaku · · · · · · **1:**207b
　Freedom and People's Rights Movement
　　· **2:**335a
　French-Japanese relations · · · · · **2:**331a
　Gakumon no susume · · · · · · · · · **3:**4a
　historiography · · · · · · · · · · · · · · **3:**156a
　Kaehwap'a · · · · · · · · · · · · · · · · · **4:**101b
　Keiō University · · · · · · · · · · · · · **4:**189a
　Koizumi Shinzō, specialist · · · · · **4:**251a
　Kōjunsha · · · · · · · · · · · · · · · · · · **4:**252b
　Korean enlightenment · · · · · · · · **4:**280b
　Meirokusha · · · · · · · · · · · · · · · · **5:**161a
　nephew · · · · · · · · · · · · · · · · **5:**314a-314b
　Seiyō jijō · · · · · · · · · · · · · · · · · · **7:**54b
　westernization · · · · · · · · **2:**311b; **4:**387a
　works · · · · · · · · · · · · · · · · **2:**367b-368a
Fulbright, William · · · · · · · · · · · · **4:**50a
Fulbright Commission · · · · · · · **4:**50a-50b
Fulbright scholars · · · · · · · · · · · · **4:**50a
Fumai. 夫米　　*See* **Fukin and fugin**
Fumie. 踏絵 · · · · · · · · · · · · · · · · **2:**368a
Funa. *See* **Crucian carp**
Funabashi · · · · · · 船橋 · · · **2:**368a-368b
Funa Benkei · · · · 船弁慶 · **4:**154b, 326a
Funadama · · · · · · · · · · · · · · · · · · **2:**368b
Funahashi Seiichi
　　　　　舟橋聖一 **2:**368b; **7:**103b
　fūzoku shōsetsu · · · · · · · · · · · · · **2:**378b
　Shinkō Geijutsu Ha · · · · · · · · · · **7:**119b
Funakoshi Eiji · 船越英二 · · · · · **2:**273a
Fundamental labor rights · · · · **2:**369a;
　　　　　　　　　　　6:312a-312b
　collective bargaining · · · · · · · · · **1:**334b
Fundamental Law of Education
　Occupation · · · · · · · · · · · · · · · · **6:**53a
Fundamental liberties · · · **2:**369a-369b
　absolute guarantee · · · · · · · · · · · **2:**369a
　Western concepts · · · · · · · · · · · · **2:**369a
Fundoshi · · · · · · · · · · · · · · · · · · · **2:**369b
Funeral goods. *See* **Funerary sculptures**
Funerals · · · · · · · · · · · · · · · **2:**369b-370a
　commemorative rites and services
　　· **2:**370a-370b
　　hōyō · · · · · · · · · · · · · · · · · · · **2:**370b
　　kōdengaeshi · · · · · · · · · · · · · · **2:**370b
　customs · · · · · · · · · · · · · · · · · · · **2:**105a
　post-funerary rites · · · · · · · · · · · **2:**307a
　　kichū · · · · · · · · · · · · · · · · · · · **2:**370a
　　mochū · · · · · · · · · · · · · · · · · · · **2:**370a
　rites and services · · · · · · · · · · · · **2:**370a
　　ihai · · · · · · · · · · · · · **2:**369a, 370a
　　incense money · · · · · · · · · · · · **2:**370a
　　mikoto · · · · · · · · · · · · · · · · · · **2:**370a
　　mourning period · · · · · · · · · · · **2:**370a
　　oharai · · · · · · · · · · · · · · · · · · **2:**370a
　　sakaki · · · · · · · · · · · · · · · · · · · **2:**370a
　　senreisai · · · · · · · · · · · · · · · · · **2:**370a
　　shimenawa · · · · · · · · · · · · · · · **2:**370a
　　shinobite · · · · · · · · · · · · · · · · **2:**370a
　　tamagushi · · · · · · · · · · · · · · · · **2:**370a
　　wake · **2:**370a

Funerary sculptures · · · · · **1:**75b, 77a
Fun'ya no Watamaro
　　　　　文室綿麻呂 · · · · · · · **2:**370b
Furandoru no fuyu
　　　　　フランドルの冬 · · · · **4:**102b
Furano · · · · · · · · 富良野 · · · · · **2:**370b
Furano Basin · · · 富良野盆地 · · **2:**370b
Fūren, Lake · · · · · 風蓮湖 · · · · **2:**370b
Fūren Shōnyūdō
　　　　　風連鍾乳洞 · · · · · · · **2:**370b
Fūrin. *See* **Wind-bells**
Furisode Fire. *See* **Meireki Fire**
Furniture, traditional · · · **2:**370b-371b
　cabinets · · · · · · · · · · · · · · · · · · · **2:**371b
　chabudai · · · · · · · · · · · · · · · · · · **2:***371a*
　chairs · **2:**371b
　charcoal braziers · · · · · · · · · · · · **2:**371b
　chests · **2:**371a
　continuing use · · · · · · · · · · · · · · **2:**371a
　decoration · · · · · · · · · · · · · · · · · **2:**371b
　desks · **2:**371a
　earliest examples · · · · · · · · · · · · **2:**370b
　lamps · **2:**371b
　materials · · · · · · · · · · · · · · · · · · **2:**371b
　screens · **2:**371a
　tables · **2:**371a
　tansu · **2:***371a*
　towel racks · · · · · · · · · · · · · · · · · **2:**371b
Furoshiki · · · · · **1:**146b; **2:**295b, 371b
Furugaki Tetsurō 古垣鉄郎 · · **2:**371b
Furuhashi Hironoshin
　　　　　古橋広之進 · · · · · · · **2:**371b
Furuhata Tanemoto
　　　　　古畑種基 · **2:**371b-372a
Furuichi Kimitake
　　　　　古市公威 · · · · · · · · · **2:**372a
Furui Yoshikichi · 古井由吉 · · **2:**372a
Furukawa (city) · · · 古川 · · · · **2:**372a
Furukawa (industrial
　combine) · · · · · · · 古河 · · · · · **2:**372a
　government enterprise sales · · · · **4:**138a
　mining · **2:**31b
Furukawa Co, Ltd. · · · · **1:**92b; **2:**372b
Furukawa Electric Co, Ltd · · · **1:**92b;
　　　　　　　　　2:342a-342b, 372b
　Yokohama Rubber Co, Ltd · · · · **8:**330b
Furukawa Ichibei
　　　　　古河市兵衛 · · · · · · · **2:**372b
Furukawa Roppa
　　　　　古川緑波 · · · · · · · · · **2:**373a
Furuno Inosuke
　　　　　古野伊之助 · · · · · · · **2:**373a
Furuoka Hideto · · · · · · · · · · · · · · · **3:**3b
Furusawa Shigeru · 古沢滋 · · **2:**373a-373b
Furusawa Uruo · · · · 古沢滋 · · · **2:**373a
Furuta Oribe · · · 古田織部 · **2:**373b; **7:**361a
Furuta Shigenari · 古田重然 · · · **2:**373b
Furuyama Komao
　　　　　古山高麗雄 · · · · · · · **2:**373b
Furuyama Moromasa
　　　　　古山師政 · · · · · · · · · **2:**373b
Furyoki (Prisoner of War)
　　　　　俘虜記 · · · · · · · · · · · **6:**113b
Furyū (dance) · · · · 風流 · · **2:**74a, 255b,
　　373b-374a; **3:**183a-184b; **4:**326a; **6:**23b
　creative spirit · · · · · · · · · · · · · · · **2:**373b
　folk performing arts · · · · · · · · · · **2:**297b
　folk song · · · · · · · · · · · · · · · · · · **2:**301a
　subtypes · · · · · · · · · · · · · · · **2:**373b-374a
Fūryū (refinement of taste)
　　　　　風流 · · · **2:**374a-374b
Fūryū Fukagawa uta 風流深川唄 **7:**108a
Fūryū mijinzō · 風流微塵蔵 · · · **4:**242b
Fūryū monji · · · · · · · · · · · · · · · · **2:**374b
Fūryū mutan Incident. 風流夢譚事件
　　　See **Shimanaka Incident**
Fūryū Shidōken den
　　　　　風流志道軒伝 **3:**142a; **4:**256a

Fūryū yomo byōbu
　　　　　風流四方屏風 · · · · · **8:**78b
Fusain Society (Fyūzankai) · · · · **6:**156a
*Fusang youji (Fu-sang yu-chi; A Record
　of Travels in Japan)* · · · · · · · · **8:**222b
Fusen Jōyaku · · · 不戦条約 · · · · **4:**191a
Fusen Kakutoku Dōmei
　(Women's Suffrage
　League) · · 婦選獲得同盟 · · **2:**374b;
　　　　　　　　　8:260b, 268b
　Ichikawa Fusae · · · · · · · · · · · · · **3:**257b
Fuseya Soteki · 伏屋素狄 · · **2:**374b-375a
Fushi · **4:**77a
Fushimi, Emperor
　　　　　伏見天皇 · · · · · · · · · **2:**375a
　calligraphy · · · · · · · · · · · · · · · · · **1:**235a
　Go-Uda, Emperor · · · · · · · · · · · · **4:**125b
　Gyokuyō wakashū · · · · · · · · · · · **3:**71b
Fushimi Castle · · · 伏見城 **1:**126b; **2:**375a;
　　　　　　　　　　　　　　3:178a
　Nanzenji · · · · · · · · · · · · · · · · · · · **5:**330b
Fushimi Inari Shrine
　　　　　伏見稲荷大社 **2:**357a; **3:**283a;
　　　　　　　　　　　　　7:126b
Fushin bugyō
　Kobori Enshū · · · · · · · · · · · · · · · **4:**238b
Fūshinjō · · · · · · · 風信帖 · · · · · **1:**234a
Fusō ryakki · · · · · 扶桑略記 · · **1:**76a; **3:**153a
Fusō shūyō shū
　　　　　扶桑拾葉集 · · · · · · · **8:**105a
Fussa · · · · · · · · · · 福生 · · · · · · **2:**375a
Fusuma (kimono-like coverage) · · **1:**148b
Fusuma (sliding door) · · · · · · · · · **1:**82b
Fusuma-e · · · · · · · · · · · · · · · · · · · **7:**42a
Fusumashōji · · · · · · · · · · · · · · · · · **7:**41b
Futabatei Shimei
　　　　　二葉亭四迷 · · **2:**375a-376a;
　　　　　　　　　　　7:81a, 103b
　Futabatei Shimei ron · · · · **5:**315a-315b
　gembun itchi · · · · · · · · · · · · · · · · **3:**16b
　personal life · · · · · · · · · · · · **2:**375a-375b
　Russian literature translations **2:**375a-375b
Futabu Industries, Ltd
　Toyota Motor Co, Ltd · · · · · · · · · **8:**93b
Futagawa Buntarō
　　　　　二川文太郎 · · · · · · · **2:**268a
Futagawa Dam · 二川ダム · · · · **1:**83a
Futagawa ware · · · 二川焼 · · · · · **2:**295b
Fūtai · **4:**116a
Futaki Kenzō 二木謙三 · · · · · · **2:**376a
Futamigaura · · · 二見浦 · **2:**376a, *376b*
Futamunerō · · · · · · · · · · · · · · · · · · **7:**111a
Futarasan. 二荒山　*See* **Nantaisan**
Futarayama Shrine
　　　　　二荒山神社 · · · · · · · **2:**376a
Futari (or Ninin) daimyō
　　　　　二人大名 · · · · · · · · · **4:**327a
Futasujimichi · · · 二筋道 · · · · · **7:**108a
*Futatsu chōchō kuruwa
　no nikki* 双蝶蝶曲輪日記 · · · · **4:**95b
*Fūten rōjin nikki (Diary of
　a Mad Old Man)*
　　　　　瘋癲老人日記 **6:**230a; **7:**343a
Futofude (thick brush) · · **1:***233a*, 233b
Futokoro nikki
　　　　　ふところ日記 · · · · · · **4:**180a
Futon. *See* **Bedding**
Futon (quilt) · · · · · 蒲団 · · · · · **7:**358b
Futsunomitama no Ōkami
　　　　　布都御魂大神 · · · · · **3:**348a
**Futsū Senkyo Kisei
　Dōmeikai**
　　　　　普通選挙期成同盟会 **2:**376a-377b
Futsū Senkyo Undō. *See* **Universal
　Manhood Suffrage Movement**
Futtsu · · · · · · · · 富津 · · · · · · · **2:**376b
Fuwa · · · · · · · · · · 不破 · · · · · · · **4:**98b

Fuwa no Seki. 不破関　*See* **Sekisho**
Fuyu and funyū　不輸不入 ···· 2:376b
Fuyuhikoshū　　冬彦集 ···· 8:11a
Fuyu kodachi　　冬木立 ···· 6:297b
Fuyukusa　ふゆくさ ···· 8:112a
Fuyu no yado　冬の宿 ···· 1:4b
Fuzambō ···· 2:376b-377a
Fūzokuga ···· 2:377a-378a
　emergence ···· 2:377b
　Kambun ···· 2:378a
　Kan'ei ···· 2:377b-378a
　Keichō ···· 2:377b
　painting subjects ···· 6:158b
　precursors ···· 2:377b
Fūzoku shōsetsu ···· 2:378a-378b;
　　5:315a-315b; 6:221b
　literary status ···· 2:378a
　postwar changes ···· 2:378b

G

Ga ···· 蛾 ···· 4:138b
Gagaku ···· 雅楽　1:157a, 159b;
　　3:1a-2b, *2b*; 6:298b
　bugaku ···· 3:1b
　history ···· 3:1a-1b
　instruments ···· 3:1b-2a
　repertoire ···· 3:1a
　theory and formal structure ···· 3:2a-2b
　tsuzumi ···· 8:119b
Gagaku court music ···· 5:15b
Gagen shūran ··· 雅言集覧 ···· 3:3a
Gago onjō kō ·· 雅語音声考 ···· 7:281a
Gaiban tsūsho ··· 外蕃通書 ···· 4:269b
Gaijin ···· 2:314a
Gaikoku bugyō ··· 外国奉行 ···· 3:3a
Gaikoku hōjin ···· 外国法人 ···· 3:3a
Gaikokujin gakkō ···· 3:3a
Gaikokusen Uchiharai Rei
　　外国船打払令 ···· 3:3a-3b;
　　7:125b
Gaimushō ········· 外務省 ···· 5:188a-189b
Gaki-zōshi ····· 餓鬼草紙 ···· 1:190b, *191a*
Gakkai. *See* **Learned societies**
Gakken Co, Ltd ···· 3:3b
Gakkiron ···· 楽毅論 ···· 1:232a
Gakkō ···· 1:*187a*, 198a
Gakkō Kyōiku Hō
　　学校教育法 ···· 7:36a
Gakkōrei ···· 学校令 ···· 7:36b
Gakubatsu (academic
　clique) ···· 学閥　1:147a;
　　3:3b-4a; 6:205b
Gakudō ···· 咢堂 ···· 6:140a
Gakukan'in ···· 2:77a
Gakumon no susume
　　学問ノスヽメ 1:207b; 2:183a,
　　368a; 3:4a-4b
Gakuō Zōkyū ···· 岳翁蔵丘 ···· 3:4b-5a
Gakureki shakai ···· 3:5a
Gakuren Incident 学連事件 ···· 4:339a
Gakusei ···· 学制 ···· 2:182b-183a
Gakushūin University ···· 1:5a; 3:5a
　Konoe Atsumaro ···· 4:272b
Gakushū shidō yōryō ···· 7:34a
Gakusō ···· 楽箏 ···· 3:2a; 4:297a
Gakusoku ···· 学則 ···· 6:72b
Galilean theory ···· 5:356a
Gamagōri ···· 蒲郡 ···· 3:5a

Gambaru ···· 3:5a
Gambler (yakuza) ···· 8:286b
Gambling ···· 3:5b-6a
　cockfighting ···· 1:333b-334a
　hanafuda ···· 3:93a-93b
　mah-jongg ···· 3:6a
　pachinko ···· 3:6a
　playing cards ···· 6:192a
　professional ···· 3:5b
　urban life ···· 8:177b
　Western influence ···· 3:5b
Games ···· 3:6a
　bean bag (otedama) ···· 1:148a
　children's ···· 4:105a; 5:359b
　　iroha karuta ···· 3:332a
　dogfighting ···· 2:124a-124b
　Edo period ···· 4:108a
　fireworks ···· 2:281a
　foreign influences ···· 7:195a
　fukubiki ···· 2:361b
　fuku warai ···· 2:367a
　go ···· 3:37b-38a
　hanafuda ···· 3:93a-93b
　Heian period ···· 4:108a
　indoor ···· 4:381a-381b
　injiuchi ···· 3:305b
　jūroku musashi ···· 4:86a
　Kagome Kagome ···· 4:105a
　Kai-awase ···· 4:108a
　kemari (kickball) ···· 1:106b
　mah-jongg ···· 5:84a
　menko ···· 5:162b
　outdoor ···· 4:381a-381b
　pachinko ···· 6:143a
　playing cards ···· 3:6a; 6:192a
　renju ···· 6:300a
　shōgi ···· 7:158b-159b
　sugoroku ···· 7:259a
　sumō wrestling ···· 7:270b-271a
　word ···· 8:269b-270a
Gamō Katahide ··· 蒲生賢秀 ···· 3:6b
Gamō Kumpei ··· 蒲生君平 1:76b; 3:6a-6b
Gamō Masuhide ··· 蒲生賦秀 ···· 3:6b
Gamō Ujisato ··· 蒲生氏郷 ···· 3:6b
Gan ···· 3:13b
Gangōji ···· 元興寺 3:6b-7a; 7:16b
　Kanroku ···· 4:151b
Gangster (yakuza) ···· 8:286b
Ganjin ···· 鑑真 ···· 3:7a-7b;
　　5:237a
　Buddhist sculpture ···· 3:*7a*
　China ···· 1:282b
　Ritsu sect ···· 6:332a
　statue of ···· 3:*7a*
　Tōshōdaiji ···· 8:83b
Gankake ···· 3:7b
Ganku ···· 岸駒 ···· 3:7b-8a
Gankutsuō ···· 巌窟王 ···· 4:316a
Gannen-mono ···· 4:13b
Gan (The Mistress) ··· 雁 ···· 8:90b
Garabō ···· 3:8a
Garakuta bunko
　　我楽多文庫 ···· 4:198b;
　　6:139b; 8:288b
Garan ···· 1:182a
Garashiya Hosokawa fujin
　　がらしあ・細川夫人 ···· 7:339b
Gara Spinning ···· 3:8a
Garasu ···· 3:35b
Garbhadhātu ···· 7:310a
''Garden Guard'' ···· 6:22b
Gardenia [(kuchinashi) *Gardenia*
　jasminoides f.
　grandiflora)] ···· 3:8a
Gardens ···· 3:8a-11b
　Byōdōin ···· 1:227a-227b
　designers
　　Kobori Enshū ···· 3:9b; 4:238b

　Musō Soseki ···· 3:10a; 5:287b
　Hama Detached Palace Garden ···· 3:90a
　history ···· 3:8b-10a
　Katsura Detached Palace 3:*9b*; 4:172b-173a
　Kenrokuen ···· 3:*9a*; 4:198b
　Kinkakuji ···· 4:213a
　Kōrakuen ···· 4:276a, *276b*
　Ritsurin Park ···· 6:321b-322a, *322b*
　Ryōanji ···· 3:*8b*; 6:347b
　scenic composition ···· 3:11a-11b
　Shugakuin Detached Palace ···· 7:181b-182a
　space ···· 3:10b-11a
　styles ···· 3:10a-11b
　　funa asobi ···· 3:10b-11a
　　kaiyū ···· 3:10a-11a
　　kanshō ···· 3:10b-11a
　　rock and sand garden (kare sansui) ··· 3:9b
　　shūyū ···· 3:10b-11a
　　tea garden (roji niwa) ···· 3:9b
　technique and composition ···· 3:10b
GARIOA ···· 2:155a, 158a-158b; 7:253a
GARIOA-EROA ···· 3:11b-12a
Garment industry ···· 3:12a
　Kashiyama & Co, Ltd ···· 4:163a
　Renown, Inc ···· 6:300b
　Wacoal Corporation ···· 8:197b
Gasan ···· 4:116a
Gas industries
　Nippon Sanso ···· 6:12a
　Ōsaka Gas Co, Ltd ···· 6:121a
　Teisan ···· 7:376b
　Tōkyō Gas Co, Ltd ···· 8:67a
Gassan ···· 月山 ···· 1:136b
　　3:13a
Gasshō-zukuri ···· 5:*192b*
Gates ···· 3:12a-13a
　chūmon (inner gate) ···· 3:*12b*
　city ···· 3:12b
　domestic ···· 3:13a
　fortifications ···· 3:12a
　karamon ···· 3:*12b*, 13a
　nagayamon (rowhouses) ···· 3:13a
　temple ···· 3:12a-12b
　yakuimon ···· 3:13a
Gāthā ···· 3:58a
GATT. *See* **General Agreement on Tariff
　and Trade**
Gauffrage (blind printing) ···· 8:142a
Gaun nikkenroku
　　臥雲日件録 ···· 3:13b
Gaun Tatsumune 臥雲辰致 ···· 3:8a
Gauzes (ra and sha) ···· 8:17b
Gay life ···· 8:177b-178a
Gazoku setchū ···· 4:243a
Geba ···· 7:252b
Gebaruto ···· 7:252b
Gedatsu ···· 解脱 ···· 4:98b
Geese [(gan; kari) family Anatidae] 3:13b
Geiami ···· 芸阿弥 · 1:52b; 3:14a
　works ···· 1:52b
Geibikei ···· 猊鼻渓 ···· 3:14a
Geidō-mono ···· 2:271a
Geijutsu ha sengen
　Shinkō Geijutsu Ha ···· 7:119b
Geijutsusai Taishō (National Art Festival
　Grand Prize) ···· 8:289a
Geisha ···· 3:14a-15b; 6:257a
　dance, traditional ···· 2:75b
　fees ···· 3:15a
　history ···· 3:15a-15b
　Morgan, Yuki ···· 5:248b
　organization ···· 3:14b-15a
　profession ···· 3:14a-14b
　ryūkōka ···· 6:354a
　shimpa ···· 7:108a
　Shindō Kaneto ···· 7:111a
　tattoos ···· 7:350b
　training ···· 3:14b

geisha houses · · · · · · · · · · · · · · · 3:14b
   traditional arts · · · · · · · · · · · · · 3:14b
   urban life · · · · · · · · · · · · · · · · · · 8:177b
Geiyo Islands 芸予諸島 · · · · · 3:15b
   Innoshima · · · · · · · · · · · · · · · · · · 3:308b
   Ōkunojima · · · · · · · · · · · · · · · · 6:97b-98a
Gejijō · · · · · · · · · · · 下知状 · · · · · 3:15b
Gekika jiken · · · · · · 1:271b; 2:335b; 4:89a
Geki nikki · · · · · · 外記日記 · · · · · 3:219a
Gekken · · · · · · · · · · · · · · · · · · · 4:195b
Gekokujō · · · · · · · · 下剋上 · · · 3:15b-16a
   bushidō · · · · · · · · · · · · · · · · · · · 1:222a
   gōson system · · · · · 3:50a-51a, 173a
   Sengoku period · · · · · · · · · · · · · 7:64b
Gembaku no ko
   Shindō Kaneto · · · · · · · · · 7:111a-111b
Gembakushō · · · · 原爆症 · · 1:111b-114a
Gembikei · · · · · · · · 厳美渓 · · · · · 3:16a
Gembō · · · · · · · · · · · 玄昉 · · · · · · 3:16a
Gembudō · · · · · · · · 玄武洞 · · · · · 3:16b
Gembun itchi · · · 言文一致 · · · · · 3:16b
   Futabatei Shimei · · · · · · · · · · · · 2:375b
   Japanese language reform · · · · · · · 4:30a
   Ken'yūsha · · · · · · · · · · · · · · · · · 4:199a
   Yamada Bimyō · · · · · · · · · · · · · 8:288b
Gembun itchiron gairyaku
        言文一致論概略 · · · · · 8:288b
Gemmei, Emperor 元明天皇 · · 2:350a
Gemmu monogatari 幻夢物語 · · 6:130a
Gempei jōsuiki. See **Gempei seisuiki**
Gempei no Sōran
        源平の争乱 · · 7:299b-300b
Gempei seisuiki
      · · · · 源平盛衰記 · 1:294a; 3:16b;
                      5:44a, 246a
Gempei War. See **Taira- Minamoto War**
Gempuku · · · · · · · 3:17a; 5:325a-326a
Gendaigeki · · · · · · 2:267b, 269b, 271b
Gendai Haiyū Kyōkai · · · · · · · · 8:289a
Gendaijin no kenkyū
      現代人の研究 · · · · · 4:125b
Gendai kanazukai · · · · · · · · · · · 4:134b
Gendai Nihon bungaku
   zenshū 現代日本文学全集 1:276b; 2:212b
Genda Minoru · · · · 源田実 · · 3:17a-17b
Gendarme force in Korea · · · · · · 4:282a
Gen'e · · · · · · · · · · · · 玄恵 · · · · · · 3:17b
Genealogy · · · · · · · · · · · · · · · 3:17b-18a
   charting · · · · · · · · · · · · · · · 3:17b-18a
   compilations · · · · · · · · · · · · 3:17b-18a
   imperial · · · · · · · · · · · · · · · · · · 3:152b
   medieval tables · · · · · · · · · · · · 7:227a
   noble families of Heian period · · · 7:124b
   Sompi bummyaku · · · · · · · · · · · · 3:17a
Gene marker · · · · · · · · · · · · 4:35b-36b
General accounts · · · · · · · 2:281a-281b
General Agreement on Tariffs and Trade
   (GATT) 1:117b; 2:320b; 3:13a-13b; 8:324a
   tariffs · · · · · · · · · · · · · · · 7:346b-347a
   United Kingdom · · · · · · · · · · · · 8:153a
   United States · · · · · · · · · · · · · · 8:161a
General clause · · · · · · · · · · · · · · 3:18a
General Corporation · · · · · · · · · · 3:18a
General Council of Trade Unions of
   Japan · 4:188b; 6:212b; 7:188b, 223b-224a
General Electric · · · · · · · · · · · · · 2:317a
General Federation of Korean Residents
   · 4:286b
General Headquarters (GHQ) · · · · · 3:30a
Generally Accepted Accounting
   Principles (GAAP) · · · · · · · · · · · 1:8b
General Sekiyu · · · · · · · · · · · 3:18a-18b
General Strike of 1947 · · · · · 3:18b; 4:351b
   communist influence · · · · · · · · · · 3:18b
   Occupation Purge · · · · · · · · · · · · 6:58b
   Sambetsu Kaigi (Congress of Industrial
   Labor Unions of Japan) · · · · · · · · · 7:6a

General trading companies · · · · · 2:324a;
                3:18b-20a; 7:268a
   C. Itoh & Co, Ltd · · · · · · · · · · · · 1:316a
   functions and characteristics · · · 3:19a-19b
      financial · · · · · · · · · · · · · · · · · 3:19a
      personnel · · · · · · · · · · · · · 3:19a-19b
   future · · · · · · · · · · · · · · · · · 3:19b-20a
   Japanese business in U.S. · · · · · · · 4:22b
   Kanematsu-Gōshō, Ltd · · · · · · · · · 4:139a
   keiretsu · · · · · · · · · · · · · · · · · · 4:189b
   Marubeni Corporation · · · · · · · · · 5:120b
   Mitsubishi Corporation · · · · · · · · · 5:207a
   Mitsui & Co, Ltd · · · · · · · 5:210b-211a
   multinational enterprises · · · · · · · 5:263a
   Nisshō-Iwai Co, Ltd · · · · · · · 6:21a-21b
   origins · · · · · · · · · · · · · · · · 3:18b-19a
      zaibatsu vs non-zaibatsu · · · · · · · 3:19a
   strategy and competition · · · · · · · 3:19b
      international · · · · · · · · · · · · · · · 3:19a
   Sumitomo Corporation · · · · · · · · 7:268a
   Toyō Menka Kaisha, Ltd · · · · · · · · 8:92a
Geneticists
   Kihara Hitoshi · · · · · · · · · · · · · · 4:204b
   Kimura Motoo · · · · · · · · · · · · · · 4:211b
   Toyama Kametarō · · · · · · · · · · · · 8:88a
Genetics · · · · · · · · · · · · · · · · · · 1:156a
Geneva Naval Conference of 1927 · 3:20a
Geneva Whaling Control Convention
   of 1931 · · · · · · · · · · · · · · · · · 6:250b
Gengenshū · · · · · · · 元元集 · · · · · 4:224b
Gengō. 元号   See **Nengō**
Gengo · · · · · · · · · · · 玄語 · · · · · 5:214b
Gengyo shishu ron
      言語四種論 · 4:31b; 7:281a
Genin · · · · · · · · · · · 下人 · · 3:20a; 7:62a
Genji   源氏
   Murakami · · · · · · · · · · · · · 5:177b-178a
   Seiwa · · · · · · · · · · · · · · · 5:178a-178b
   See **Minamoto family**
Genji Keita · · · · · 源氏鶏太 · 2:274a; 3:20a
*Genji monogatari.*源氏物語 *See* **Tale of Genji**
Genji monogatari emaki
      源氏物語絵巻 · · · 3:20a-21a
Genji monogatari
   shinshaku 源氏物語新釈 · · · · · 4:129a
Genjitsu · · · · · · · · · 現実 · · · · · · 4:125a
Genka · · · · · · · · · · · 幻化 · · · · · · 8:147b
Genkai · · · · · · · · · · 言海 · · · · · · 2:57a
   Ōtsuki Fumihiko · · · · · · · · · · · · 6:134b
Genkainada · · · · · · 玄海灘 · · · · · 4:211a
Genkai Sea · · · · · · 玄界灘 · · · · · 3:21a
Genkan (entry hall) · · · · · · · · · · 7:162b
Genkan (musical instrument) · · · · · 7:195a
Genkō Incident · · · 元弘の変 · · · 3:21a
   Ashikaga Takauji · · · · · · · · · · · · 1:100a
   Kemmu restoration · · · · · · · · · · · 4:192a
   Kikuchi Taketoki · · · · · · · · · · · · 4:206b
   Kōgon, Emperor · · · · · · · · · · · · · 4:249a
   Kojima Takanori · · · · · · · · · · · · 4:252a
   Kusunoki Masashige · · · · · · · · · · 4:321a
Genkō shakusho 元亨釈書 · · 1:294b;
              3:21a-21b; 4:252b
Genkun · · · · · · · · · · · · · · · · · · · 3:21b
Genre painting · · · 2:377a-378a; 6:153b, *155a*
Genrin, Yamaoka 山岡元隣 · · · · 3:77b
Genrō · · · · · · · · · · · 元老 · · · 3:21b-22a
   influence on government · · · · 3:197a-198a
   members
      Inoue Kaoru · · · · · · · · · · 3:310a-310b
      Itō Hirobumi · · · · · · · · · · 3:352a-353a
      Katsura Tarō · · · · · · · · · · 4:173b-174a
      Kuroda Kiyotaka · · · · · · · · 4:314a-314b
      Matsukata Masayoshi · · · · · 5:134b-136a
      Ōyama Iwao · · · · · · · · · · 6:138a-138b
      Saigō Tsugumichi · · · · · · · · · · · · 6:367a
      Saionji Kimmochi · · · · · · · · 6:371b-372b
      Yamagata Aritomo · · · · · · · 8:290b-292a

   political system · · · · · · · · 6:214a, 216b
   prime minister and cabinet · · 6:241b-242b
Genrōin · · · · · · · · · 元老院 · · · · · 3:22a
   early Meiji Dajōkan · · · · · · · · · · · 2:70b
   Meiji Constitution · · · · · · · · · · · · 2:1b
   Ōsaka Conference of 1875 · · · · · · 6:121a
   shigi kempō · · · · · · · · · · · · · · · · 7:92b
Genroku era · · · · · · 元禄時代 · · 1:211b;
              3:22a-23a, 191a
   arts and crafts · · · · · · · · · · · · · · 3:23a
   education · · · · · · · · · · · · · · · · · · 3:22b
   Forty-Seven Rōnin Incident · · · · · 2:328a
   historical accounts · · · · · · · · · · · 4:102a
   kabuki · · · · · · · · · · · · · · · · · · · 4:90b
   literature · · · · · · · · 3:22b-23a; 4:102a
   periodization · · · · · · · · · · · · · · 6:175a
   puppet theater · · · · · · · · · · · · · · 3:22b
   scholars · · · · · · · · · · · · · · · · · · 3:23a
   textiles · · · · · · · · · · · · · · · · · · · 8:19a
   Tokugawa Tsunayoshi · · · · · · · · · 8:56a
Genroku literature
        元禄文学 · 5:46b-47b
   Bashō · · · · · 1:144a-145b; 5:46b-47a
   Chikamatsu Monzaemon · 1:275a-276b;
                      5:47a
   Saikaku · · · · · 5:47a; 6:369b-370b
Gensen · · · · · · · · · 言泉 · · · 3:23a-23b
Gense shugi · · · · · · · · · · · · · · · · 8:24b
Genshi, josei wa taiyō de atta · · · · · 7:339b
Genshin · · · · · · · · · 源信 · · · · · · 3:23b
   beliefs · · · · · · · · · · · · · · · · · · · 3:23b
   nembutsu · · · · · · · · · · · · · · 4:67a-67b
   raigōzu · · · · · · · · · · · · · · · · · · 6:277a
   Sanzen'in · · · · · · · · · · · · · · · · · 7:19b
   wasan · · · · · · · · · · · · · · · · · · · 8:231a
   works · 3:23b
Gensuikin. See **Atomic weapons,**
   movement to ban
Gensuikyō. See **Atomic weapons,**
   movement to ban
Gentians [(rindō) family Gentianaceae)]
   · 3:24a
Gentlemen's Agreement of 1907
   · · · · · · · · · · · · · · 3:24a-24b; 8:156a
   Japanese Americans · · · · · · · · · · 4:14a
   Japanese Associations of America · · 4:22a
   Okinawa · · · · · · · · · · · · · · · · · · 6:87b
   Roosevelt, Theodore · · · · · · · · · · 6:339a
   segregation of Japanese schoolchildren in
   the United States · · · · · · · · · · · · 7:49a
   United States Immigration Acts of 1924,
   1952, and 1965 · · · · · · · · · · · · · 8:164b
Gen'yōsha · · · · · · · 玄洋社 · · 3:24b-25a
   Amur River Society · · · · · · · · · · · 1:53b
   nationalism · · · · · · · · · · · · 5:342b-343a
   tactics · · · · · · · · · · · · · · · 3:24b-25a
   tairiku rōnin · · · · · · · · · · · · · · · 7:302b
   Tōyama Mitsuru · · · · · · · · · · · · · 8:88a
   Uchida Ryōhei · · · · · · · · · · · · · 8:124a
   ultranationalism · · · · · · · · · · · · 8:145b
Genzammi Yorimasa. 源三位頼政
    See **Minamoto no Yorimasa**
Genzu mandara
   Ryōbu Mandara · · · · · · · · · · · · · 6:348a
Geographers
   Iizuka Kōji · · · · · · · · · · · · · · · · 3:264a
   Inō Tadataka · · · · · · · · · · · · · · · 3:309a
   Kiuchi Shinzō · · · · · · · · · · · · · · 4:231b
   Nagakubo Sekisui · · · · · · · · 5:301b-302a
   Nishikawa Joken · · · · · · · · · · · · · 6:17a
   Ogawa Takuji · · · · · · · · · · · · · · 6:70a
   Shiga Shigetaka · · · · · · · · · · · · · 7:91b
   Tada Fumio · · · · · · · · · · · · · · · · 7:293b
   Takahashi Kageyasu · · · · · · · · · · 7:312a
   Yamamura Saisuke · · · · · · · · · · · 8:300a
   Yamazaki Naomasa · · · · · · · · · · · 8:313a
Geographical names · · · · · · 5:326a-326b
Geographic Survey Institute · · · · · 3:25a

maps ········· 5:112a
National Atlas of Japan ········· 5:336b
Geographies, regional ········· 6:288a
Geography ········· 3:25a-26a
organizations ········· 3:25b-26a
regional ········· 6:288a
school education ········· 3:25b
studies ········· 3:25a-25b
foreign influence ········· 3:25a-25b
Nishikawa Joken ········· 3:25b
Geography in Japan ········· 3:26a
Geological Society of Japan ····· 2:329b
Geological structure ········· 4:8a-9b
crustal movement ········· 4:8b-9a
history of Japanese Islands ····· 4:9a-9b
Northeastern and Southwestern Japan 4:8b
topography ········· 4:8b
Geological Survey of Japan · 1:21b; 3:26a
Naumann, Edmund ········· 5:358a
Geologische Arbeiten in Japan ···· 5:358a
Geologists
Naumann, Edmund ········· 5:358a
Ogawa Takuji ········· 6:70a
Yabe Hisakatsu ········· 8:283a
Geology ········· 2:141a
Geomancy ········· 4:163a
Geophysicists
Tanakadate Aikitsu ········· 7:336a
German Academic Exchange Service
········· 3:28a
Germany and Japan ········· 3:26a-28a
Anti-Comintern Pact ········· 1:65a-65b
Edo period ········· 3:26a-26b
interwar period ········· 3:27a-27b
economic ········· 3:27a-27b
political ········· 3:27b
Japanese studies ········· 4:42b-43a
Jiaozhou concession ········· 4:53a
late 1860s to World War I ····· 3:26b-27a
medicine, influence on ······ 5:147a-147b
Russia and Japan ········· 6:342a
Tripartite Pact ········· 8:107a
World War II to present ····· 3:27b-28a
economic ········· 3:27b-28a
Gero 下呂 ········· 3:28a
Gesaku 戯作 ····· 3:28a-29a;
5:48b; 7:103a
early ········· 3:28b
gōkan ········· 4:42a-42b
kibyōshi ········· 4:201b
kokkeibon ········· 4:256a
late ········· 3:28b-29a
ninjōbon ········· 6:5b-6a
rise ········· 3:28b
sharebon ········· 7:79b-80a
tradition and modern literature ···· 3:29a
writers ········· 3:29b
yomihon ········· 8:336a
*Geschichte des Wahlrechts zum
englischen Parlament* ········· 6:312a
Gesshō 月照 ········· 3:29a
Gestures ········· 3:29a-30a
significance ········· 3:29b
types ········· 3:29a-30a
Gesu 下司 ········· 4:63a
Geta ········· 3:30a
footgear, traditional ········· 2:308a
Gewalt ········· 7:252b
Gezairoku 戯財録 ········· 5:16b
Ghost of Tomomori, The ········· 8:184a
Ghosts ····· 1:130b; 3:30a; 8:357a
Ghost Story of Tōkaidō Yotsuya
········· 8:41b-42a
GHQ ········· 3:30a
Gi ········· 4:141b
Gidayū-bushi · 義太夫節 · 2:301a;
3:30a-30b; 4:99a
jōruri ········· 4:77a

Gidō Shūshin 義堂周信 ···· 3:30b
Gift giving ········· 2:17b; 3:30b
chūgen ········· 1:312a
condolence ········· 3:30b
etiquette ········· 2:232b-234a
kaeshi ········· 1:102a
miyage ········· 5:217a
occasions ········· 3:30b
otoshidama ········· 6:133a
seibo ········· 7:49a
shūgi ········· 7:183a
significance ········· 3:30b
Gifu 岐阜 ········· 3:31a
Gifu Castle 岐阜城 ········· 3:31a
Gifu Prefecture 岐阜県 ···· 3:31a-31b
Gifu-Yōrō Prefectural Park
岐阜養老県立公園 ········· 8:338b
Gigaku 伎楽 ········· 2:297b;
3:31b-32a; 7:148b, 195a
dance, traditional ········· 2:73b-74a
masks ········· 5:125b-126a
Gigaku mask ········· 5:125a
Gigen yōki shū 戯言養気集 ···· 6:282a
Giin Shōgen Hō ········· 4:262a
Gijō (officials) 議定 ········· 7:16b
Gijutsu dōnyū ········· 3:32a-32b
Gijutsu iten. *See* **Technology transfer**
Gijutsu kakushin. *See* **Technological
innovation**
Gikai Deiri Kishadan (Diet Journalists
Club) ········· 6:236a
Gikeiki 義経記 · 3:32b; 7:152b
summary ········· 3:32b
Giko monogatari (pseudoclassical tales)
擬古物語 · 3:32b-33a;
5:246a
Gila River Relocation Center ···· 3:33a
Gimbura ········· 7:250a
Ginkakuji 銀閣寺 · 3:33a-33b;
4:336a
paintings ········· 4:147b
structure ········· 3:33a
tea ceremony ········· 7:361a
Ginkgo [(ichō) *Gingko biloba*] ···· 3:33b
Gin no saji (The Silver
Spoon) 銀の匙 · 5:314a
Ginowan 宜野湾 ········· 3:33b
Ginsekai 銀世界 ········· 8:143a
Ginseng ········· 7:334b
Ginza 銀座 ········· 8:63a
Ginzan Hot Spring
銀山温泉 ········· 3:33b
Giōji 祇王寺 ········· 3:33b
Gion Festival 祇園祭 · 2:255b;
3:33b-34a; 4:336a, 336b; 8:316b
dashi ········· 2:78a
depiction in art ········· 2:377b
floats ········· 3:34a
fūryū ········· 2:374a
Gion Nankai 祇園南海 · 1:211a; 3:34a
Gion no shimai (Sister of
the Gion) 祇園の姉妹 · 8:289a
Gion Shrine 祇園社 ···· 4:59b
Girard case ········· 3:34a-34b
United States-Japan security treaties
········· 8:167b
Girard, P.S.B. ········· 4:32a
Girard, William S. ········· 3:34a-34b
Giri (obligation) ········· 1:149b
Giri and ninjō (obligation and human
feeling) ····· 2:232a; 3:34b; 6:206a
Chikamatsu Monzaemon ···· 1:276a
etiquette ········· 2:233a
gakubatsu ········· 3:4a
groups ········· 3:63a
literary criticism, premodern ···· 5:16b
on ········· 6:105a
political culture ········· 6:206a

Giri ninjō i ro ha ni ho he to hen · 4:157b
Girl Scouts ········· 3:34b
Girls' Festival. *See* **Doll Festival**
Girls' high schools ····· 4:297a-297b
Gisaku. *See* **Gesaku**
Giseigo ········· 6:110b
Gishi wajinden. 魏志倭人伝
See **Wei zhi (Wei chih)**
Gissha ········· 3:35a; 6:301a
Kasuga gongen genki ········· 3:35a
Gitaigo ········· 6:110b
Giwadan no Ran
義和団の乱 · 1:166a-166b
Glass ········· 3:35b-36b
Edo period (1600-1868) ···· 3:36a-36b
Heian period (794-1185) ········· 3:36a
Kamakura, Muromachi, and
Azuchi-Momoyama periods (1185-1600)
········· 3:36a
Kofun period (ca 300-710) ········· 3:35b
Meiji period (1868-1912) to present · 3:36b
Nara period (710-794) ········· 3:35b-36a
Satsuma cut glass ········· 3:35a
Yayoi period (ca 300 BC-ca AD 300) 3:35b
Glass industry ········· 3:36b
Glazes ········· 1:265a-265b
Globefishes [(fugu) family
Tetraodontidae] ········· 3:36b-37a
Glover, Thomas Blake ········· 3:36b-37a
Glycine max ········· 7:239a
Gneist, Rudolf von ····· 2:2b; 3:37b, 194a
Go (game) ····· 3:37b-38a; 6:300a
basic rules ········· 3:37b-38a
equipment ········· 3:38a
grandmaster, title of ········· 3:222b
history ········· 3:38a
schools ········· 3:38a
Nihon Kiin ········· 5:380b
professional and international ······· 3:38a
rankings ········· 3:38a
Gō (village) 郷 ········· 3:38b
Goban Tadanobu
Onoe Matsunosuke ········· 6:109b
Go-betweens (Nakōdo) ··· 5:4b; 320b-321a
Gobies [(haze) family Gobiidae] ···· 3:38b
Goble, Jonathan ········· 1:142a
Gobō 御坊 ········· 3:38b
Gobō no Keiji 五榜の掲示 ···· 3:38b
Gobuji chūshingura
御無事忠臣蔵 ···· 8:183b
Gobusho 五部書 ···· 3:38b-39a;
8:236b
Gochi Kokubunji
五智国分寺 ···· 4:69a
········· 7:66a
Go-Daigo, Emperor
後醍醐天皇 · 1:99a; 3:39a;
7:66a, 84a
Ashikaga Takauji ···· 1:100a-100b; 3:172b
Fujiwara no Fujifusa ········· 2:350b
Gen'e ········· 3:17b
Genkō Incident ········· 3:21a; 4:206b
Kanenaga, Prince ········· 4:139b
Kemmu nenchū gyōji ········· 4:191b
Kemmu Restoration ········· 4:191b
Kimbusenji ········· 4:208a
Kitabatake Akiie ········· 4:224a
Kojima Takanori's support ········· 4:252a
Nakasendai Rebellion ········· 5:317b
Northern and Southern Courts ······ 6:39a
rule ········· 2:204b
warrior government ········· 8:229a
Godaiō ki. See **Godai teiō monogatari**
Godai teiō monogatari
五代帝王物語 ········· 3:39a
historiography ········· 3:154a
Godai Tomoatsu · 五代友厚 · 3:39a-39b;
7:52a

diplomat ·················· **3**:39a–39b
economic development ······· **3**:39a–39b
Kaigun Denshūjo ············· **4**:110a
Gods. *See* **Kami**
Godzilla ····················· **2**:273b
Gofu ························· **3**:39b
Gofuchinin tomura ············ **4**:112b
Go-Fukakusa, Emperor 後深草天皇 **3**:39b
Fushimi, Emperor ·········· **2**:375b
Kameyama, Emperor ········ **4**:125b
Northern and Southern Courts · **6**:39a
succession ················ **4**:192a
Gōgai ························ **3**:40a
Gōgaku ······················ **3**:40a
Gogaku shinsho (New
Book on Linguistics)
············· 語学新書 ····· **8**:243a
Gōgawa. 江川 *See* **Gōnokawa**
Go Haifu ···· 呉佩孚 ······· **8**:279b
Go-Hanazono, Emperor
············· 後花園天皇 ·· **3**:40a; **7**:9b
Gohei ···· **3**:40a; **4**:195a; **7**:249b, 272b
origami ····················· **6**:116b
Gohonzon ···················· **7**:225a
Go-Horikawa, Emperor 後堀河天皇 **4**:72a
Gohō shinan (A Guide to
Grammar) ····· 語法指南 ··· **6**:134b
Goichigo Jiken
············· 五・一五事件 · **5**:142b–143a
Go-Ichijō, Emperor
············· 後一条天皇 ··· **3**:40a–40b
Fujiwara no Yorimichi ······· **2**:357b
regency ···················· **2**:353a
Goikō ········· 語意考 ···· **4**:129b
Gōi shinjū ·················· **7**:262a
Gojira (Godzilla) ·· ゴジラ ·· **8**:111a
Gojō ········· 五條 ······ **3**:40b
Gojūon ('50-sound') chart ····· **8**:221b
Gojūon zu ················ **3**:40b–41a
siddham ···················· **7**:192b
Gokaidō ····· 五街道 ··· **3**:41a–41b
centralized government ······ **3**:41b
ekisei ······················ **2**:188b
history ···················· **3**:41a–41b
Kōshū Kaidō ················ **3**:41b
Nakasendō ················· **5**:318a
Nikkō Kaidō ················ **3**:41b
Ōshū Kaidō ················ **3**:41b
sankin kōtai ················ **7**:14a
sekisho ···················· **7**:57a
sukegō ····················· **7**:265a
Tōkaidō ···················· **8**:40b
Gokajō no Goseimon. *See* **Charter Oath**
Go-Kameyama, Emperor
············· 後亀山天皇 ··· **3**:41b–42a;
············· **4**:319b; **5**:49a
Gōkan ········ 合巻 ····· **3**:42a–42b;
············· **7**:18a
Jippensha Ikku ············· **4**:61a
kabuki influence ············ **3**:42a–42b
Shikitei Samba ············· **7**:96b–97b
Tamenaga Shunsei ·········· **7**:333b–334a
writers ···················· **3**:42a–42b
Gokanoshō ···· 五家荘 ··· **3**:42b
Gokasegawa ··············· **3**:42b
Gokasho shōnin
············· 五箇所商人 ··· **3**:42b
Gokasho Shōnin Kaisho
············· 五箇所商人会所 · **5**:304a
Gōkawa. *See* **Gōnokawa**
Gokayama ···· 五箇山 ··· **3**:42b
Gokenin ···· 御家人 ····· **1**:131b;
············· **2**:264a–264b; **3**:42b; **4**:122a, 196b; **7**:183a
ienoko and rōtō ············· **3**:261a
kobushin ··················· **4**:239a
protection ·················· **3**:42b
Shōheikō ··················· **7**:162a
yoriki and dōshin ··········· **8**:338b

Goken Sampa Naikaku
············· 護憲三派内閣 · **3**:43a
Goken Undō. *See* **Movement to Protect
Constitutional Government**
Gōke shidai ··· 江家次第 ·· **3**:43a
Goki Shichidō · 五畿七道 ·· **3**:43a
Gokō gomin ··· 五公五民 ·· **3**:43a
Gokokuji ····· 護国寺 ···· **3**:43a
Go-Komatsu, Emperor
············· 後小松天皇 ·· **3**:43b; **6**:39a;
············· **8**:356a
Gokuchū jūhachinen (Eighteen Years in
Jail) ·········· 獄中十八年 · **8**:44b
Gokurakubō ····· 極楽坊 ·· **3**:6b–7a
Gokuraku Jōdo kubon ōjō gi
············· 極楽浄土九品往生義 · **6**:351b
Gokyō (Defending the Faith) ······ **8**:296a
Go-Kyōgoku Yoshitsune
············· 後京極良経 ·· **2**:358a
Gold beetle [(koganemushi) *Minela
splendens*] ·················· **3**:43b
Golden Pavilion ·············· **4**:212b
Goldfish [(kingyo) *Carassius auratus*]
··························· **3**:43b
Goldmines ·········· **3**:365a; **6**:363a
Goldmining ··········· **3**:184b–185a
Gold standard, return to ······· **7**:173b
Golf ························ **3**:43b
Golovnin, Vasilii Mikhailovich · **3**:43b–44a
capture by Japanese ·········· **3**:44a
memoirs ···················· **3**:44a
Goma ······················· **3**:127b
Goma ceremony ·············· **1**:188a
Gomi Yasusuke · 五味康祐 · **3**:44b; **7**:85a
Go-Mizunoo, Emperor
············· 後水尾天皇 ·· **3**:44b; **7**:255a,
············· 270a
Katsura Detached Palace ····· **4**:172b
Shie Incident ··············· **7**:89b
Gomoku narabe. *See* **Renju**
Gonaisho ···· 御内書 ···· **3**:44b
Goncharov, Ivan Aleksandrovich
··························· **3**:44b–45a
Gondō Nariaki. *See* **Gondō Seikyō**
Gondō Seikyō · 権藤成卿 ·· **3**:45a
Gongan ······················ **4**:234a
Gonge ················ **1**:122b–123a
Gongen. *See* **Avatar**
Goningumi (five-family
associations) ··· 五人組 ··· **3**:45a–45b;
············· **6**:198a
function ···················· **3**:45a–45b
gōson system ··············· **3**:50a–51a
model ······················ **3**:45a
registers ··················· **3**:45b
tonarigumi ·················· **8**:74a
Gonjinshū ····· 言塵集 ···· **3**:272a
Gonki ········ 権記 ······ **3**:45b
Gōnō ········ 豪農 ······ **2**:335a;
············· **3**:45b–46a
Gōnokawa ···· 江川 ····· **3**:46a
Gonorrhea ··················· **8**:189b
Gonrei ········· 権令 ······ **4**:197b
"Good-for-nothing" ··········· **8**:286b
Good luck charms ············ **3**:91a
Goodman, Mary Ellen ········· **4**:39b
Go on ········ 呉音 ····· **3**:46a
on readings ················· **6**:112b
Gorer, Geoffrey ·············· **4**:38a
Gorges
Chōmonkyō ············ **1**:5a, 300a
Dangyokei ················· **2**:76b
Dorokyō ··················· **2**:131b
Enakyō ···················· **2**:213a
Geibikei ···················· **3**:14a
Gembikei ··················· **3**:16a
Iyadani ···················· **3**:364a
Kurobe Kyōkoku ············ **4**:314a

Nagatoro ··················· **5**:307b
Nakatsu Keikoku ············ **5**:318b
Nakatsukyō ················· **5**:318b
Nakayama Shichiri ·········· **5**:319a
Nezamenotoko ·············· **5**:373b
Ōboke ····················· **6**:49b
Omogokei ·················· **6**:103a
Shōsenkyō ·················· **7**:167b
Sōunkyō ···················· **7**:234b
Taishakukyō ················ **7**:303b
Takachihokyō ··············· **7**:310b
Tenninkyō ·················· **8**:7b
Yabakei ················ **8**:283a, 297a
Gorintō ····· 五輪塔 ···· **3**:46a
Gōri system ·· 郷里制 ··· **3**:46a–46b
gō ························· **3**:38b
ritsuryō system ············· **6**:325b
Goroku ······ 語録 ······ **3**:46b
Goryō ······· **3**:46b–47a; **4**:126a
festivals ··················· **3**:147a
Goryōkaku ···· 五稜郭 ·· **3**:85a; **7**:160a
Goryōkaku, Battle of
············· 五稜郭の戦 · **1**:165a; **3**:47a
Go-Saga, Emperor 後嵯峨天皇 · **3**:47a
Fujiwara no Tameie ········· **2**:356a
Kameyama, Emperor ········ **4**:125b
succession ················· **4**:192a
Go-Sanjō, Emperor 後三条天皇 · **3**:47a
Fujiwara family ············· **2**:348b
Fujiwara no Yorimichi ······· **2**:357b
insei ······················ **3**:314b
Kiroku Shōen Kenkeijo ······ **4**:222a
Gosanjū Jiken
············· 五・三〇事件 · **5**:143b
Gosanke ····· 御三家 ···· **3**:47b; **1**:86b
shimpan ··················· **7**:108a
Gosankyō ···· 御三卿 ···· **3**:47b
shimpan ··················· **7**:108a
Gosannen kassen ekotoba
············· 後三年合戦絵詞 · **4**:369a
Gosannen no Eki
············· 後三年の役 · **4**:368b–369a
Gose ········ 御所 ······ **3**:47b
Gosechi no mai · 五節舞 ·· **3**:47b
Goseda Hōryū · 五姓田芳柳 · **8**:298a
Goseibai Shikimoku
············· 御成敗式目 ·· **1**:212a;
············· **3**:47b–48a; **4**:377a; **7**:96a
Daibon Sankajō ············· **2**:55b
Hōjō Yasutoki ·············· **3**:212a
nenki ······················ **5**:361b
Gō Seinosuke · 郷誠之助 ·· **3**:48a
Gosekke ····· 五摂家 ···· **3**:48a–48b
Fujiwara family ······· **2**:348b, 349a–349b
kampaku ··················· **4**:130a
Konoe family ··············· **4**:272b
Kujō family ················· **4**:303b
Sanjō Sanetomi ············· **7**:12b
Gosekku ······· 五節句 ···· **2**:299a
Gosen ······· 五泉 ·· **3**:48b; **7**:62a
Gosenshū. See **Gosen wakashū**
waka ······················ **8**:204a
Gosen wakashū
············· 後撰和歌集 · **3**:48b; **4**:132b;
············· **5**:33a; **6**:105a
poets ······················ **3**:48b
Gosetsu
ink painting ················ **3**:306b
Gōshi ········ 郷士 ·· **3**:48a–49a
functions ·················· **3**:49a
Gōshidai ······ 江次第 ···· **3**:43a
Goshikinuma 五色沼 · **1**:137a; **3**:49a
Goshintai ················· **3**:49a–49b
origin ····················· **3**:49a
Go-Shirakawa, Emperor
············· 後白河天皇 · **3**:49b; **7**:13a,
············· 68a, 96b, 279b
Hōgen Disturbance ··········· **3**:209a

insei ············· 3:315a
Ryōjin hishō ········· 6:352a
Taira-Minamoto war ········ 7:299b, 300b
Goshi Undō ··· 五・四運動 ·· 5:143a–143b
Goshkevich, Iosif Antonovich · 3:49b–50a
Goshogawara · 五所川原 ······· 3:50a
Gosho Heinosuke
········· 五所平之助 · 2:269a, 270a,
272a; 3:50a; 7:102b
Gōshō hensō ···· 迎接変相 · 6:276b–277b
Gōshō mandara 迎接曼荼羅 · 6:276b–277b
Gosho ningyō ················ 2:128b
Goshūishū ······· 後拾遺集 2:353a; 8:210a
Goshun. 呉春 *See* **Matsumura Goshun**
Gōso ············· 強訴 ····· 3:50a
Gōson system ······ 郷村制 ·· 3:50a–51a
dissolution ················ 3:51a
responsibilities ·············· 3:50b–51a
social stratification ·········· 3:50b
Gossha ··········· ごっしゃ ·· 4:119a
Gosu ···················· 4:179a
Gotemba ·········· 御殿場 ··· 3:51a
Gotō Art Museum · 3:51a; 5:276b; 8:341a
Go-Toba, Emperor
········· 後鳥羽天皇 · 1:40a; 2:355b,
357b, 358a; 3:51a–52b; 5:14b; 6:297a; 7:13a,
96b
abdication and exile ········· 3:52b
Bureau of Poetry ············ 3:52a
calligraphy ················· 1:235a
imperial poetry anthologies ···· 2:354a
Jien ··················· 4:53b–54a
Jōkyū Disturbance ··········· 4:192a
Lady Daibu ················· 4:197b
patron of arts ·············· 3:51a–52b
poet ··················· 3:51b–52a
works ················· 3:52a–52b
portraits ·················· 2:353b
Shin kokinshū ············· 7:119b
waka ··················· 8:212a–212b
Go-Toba In-bon
·········· 後鳥羽院本 ···· 4:161b
*Go-Toba In Kumano
gyokō ki*
····· 後鳥羽院熊野御幸記 ··· 8:105b
Go-Toba no in gokuden
·········· 後鳥羽院御口伝 ·· 3:52b
Gotō Chūgai ····· 後藤宙外 ··· 3:52b
Gotō Fumio ······ 後藤文夫 ·· 3:52b
Gotō Islands ···· 五島列島 · 2:363a;
3:52b–53a
Gotō Katsu ········ 後藤潤 ··· 3:53a
Gotō Keita ····· 五島慶太 ··· 3:53a
Gotō Konzan ··· 後藤艮山 · 3:53a, 239a
Kagawa Shūtoku ············ 4:103b
Gotō Mitsutsugu 後藤光次 · 3:53a; 7:274b
Gotō Ryūnosuke
·········· 後藤隆之助 ···· 3:53b
Gotō Shimpei ··· 後藤新平 · 3:53b–54a
foreign affairs ·············· 3:53b–54a
Gotō Shōjirō ··· 後藤象二郎 · 1:34b; 2:56a,
336a; 3:54a; 7:23a
Freedom and People's Rights
Movement ··············· 2:333b–334a
Fukuoka Takachika ·········· 2:365b
Itagaki Taisuke ············· 3:349b
Jiyūtō ·················· 4:65a–65b
Gotō Shōzaburō. *See* **Gotō Mitsutsugu**
Gotō Shuichi ····· 後藤守一 · 1:77b;
3:54a–54b
Gotō Tokujō ···· 後藤徳乗 ··· 3:53a
Gōtsu ············ 江津 ····· 3:54b
Go-Uda, Emperor
·········· 後宇多天皇 ···· 3:54b
Emperor Fushimi ············ 2:375a
Kameyama, Emperor ········· 4:125b

Government: [Premodern (to 1868)]
insei ("cloister government") ···· 3:166b;
3:314b–315a
regency government ········· 3:166a–166b;
6:286a–288a
ritsuryō system · 3:162b–166a; 6:322a–332a
emperor ················· 2:203b–204a
warrior government ········· 8:228b–230a
Kamakura shogunate · 3:169a–171a, 172a;
4:121b–122b
Muromachi shogunate ····· 3:172a–175a;
5:271b–274a
Shokuhō seiken ("Oda-Toyotomi
regime") · 3:177a–180b; 7:164b–165a
Tokugawa shogunate · 3:185b–189b,
192a–192b; 8:52b–56a
bakuhan system ·········· 1:131a–133a
Yamato court ··· 3:160a–162b; 8:308b–309a
emperor ················· 2:203a–203b
Government: [Modern (1868–1945)]
early Meiji
Dajōkan system ··········· 2:70a–70b
political system ··········· 6:213b–214b
under Meiji Constitution
cabinet ··············· 6:240b–242a
emperor ·············· 2:205b–207a
genrō ················· 3:21b–22a
Great Court of Cassation ···· 3:60b
Imperial Diet ··········· 3:275b–277a
Meiji Constitution ········ 2:1a–3b
Privy Council ·········· 6:252b–253a
Government [Contemporary
(1945–present)]
Constitution of 1947 ···· 2:3b–7a, 9b–13a
Diet
House of Councilors ······· 2:188a–188b
House of Representatives ···· 2:188a–188b
Executive ·············· 3:55b–56a
Prime Minister and cabinet · 6:240b–244a
Judiciary ·············· 4:80b–81b
constitutional rights ······ 2:337a–339a,
369a–369b
supreme court ··········· 7:277a–277b
Government, executive branch 3:55b–56a
Government agricultural policy. *See*
Agriculture
Government and Relief in Occupied
Areas-Economic Rehabilitation in
Occupied Areas (GARIOA-EROA)
····················· 3:11b–12a
Government bonds ··········· 3:54b
Government compensation ··· 3:54b–55b
Government educational policy. *See*
Education
Government-General of Korea ····· 4:283a
Government grants-in-aid ······ 3:56a
taxes ··················· 7:353b
**Government-operated factories, Meiji
period** ··········· 2:361a; 3:56a–56b
sale ····················· 4:138a
Government school ············ 4:140a
Governors and mayors ········ 3:56b
election ·················· 3:56b
Gowland, William ············· 1:77a
Goyō eshi ················· 7:270b
Goyōkin ·················· 3:56b–57a
Goyō shōnin ····· 御用商人 · 3:57a; 5:209b;
7:267a
goyōkin ················· 3:56b–57a
Goza ····················· 4:160b
Gozan ··········· 五山 ··· 2:358b;
3:57a–58a; 4:120b
decline ················· 3:57b–58a
descriptions ·············· 4:302a
formation ················ 3:57a–57b
ink painting ·············· 3:306a
Nanzenji ················ 5:330a–330b

political and economic background · 3:57b
religious and cultural factors ···· 3:57b
literature ················· 3:58a–59a
Gozan editions ····· 五山版 ··· 1:152b
Gozan literature · 五山文学 · 1:150b, 294b;
3:57b, 58a–59a
Betsugen Enshi ············· 1:150b
Chūgan Engetsu ············ 1:311b
development and change ······ 3:58b
Gidō Shūshin ·············· 3:30b
Gozan monasteries ·········· 3:58a
Issan Ichinei ··············· 3:348b
Kokan Shiren ·············· 4:252b
Kyōshi ··················· 1:295b
outstanding figures ·········· 3:58b
poetry and prose in Chinese · 6:194b–195a
quality ·················· 3:58a–59a
scholarship ··············· 3:58b–59a
Sesson Yūbai ·············· 7:70b
Zekkai Chūshin ············· 8:369b
zen ····················· 8:370b
Goze ············· 瞽女 · 3:59a; 5:45a;
7:250a
Gozen gikeiki · 御前義経記 ····· 6:20a
Gozen kaigi ··· 御前会議 ··· 3:59a–59b
Graduate schools ········ 3:59b; 8:171a
Graffiti ·················· 3:59b–60a
Daidairon ················ 3:59a
political ·················· 3:59b–60a
Grain embargo controversy ··· 3:60a–60b;
4:281a
Grammar ················· 4:24b–27b
Grand chamberlain ············ 7:207b
Grand Council of State · 2:69a–70b; 4:187b
Grand Order of the Chrysanthemum
····················· 8:297b
Grant, Ulysses Simpson ··· 3:60b, 359a
Grants-in-aid ··············· 3:56a
Grapefruit ················ 6:112a
Grapes ·················· 3:60b
Grape Society, The (Budō no Kai) 8:299b
Grave goods. *See* **Beads, ancient; Ear
ornaments, ancient; Funerary
sculptures**
Great Court of Cassation (Daishin'in)
····· 2:13b; 3:60b, 135a; 4:383a; 7:277a
"Great East Academy" ·· 2:67b–68a
Great East Asia Conference ····· 3:321b
Great elder ·············· 7:302b–303a
Greater East Asia Conference ····· 8:20b
Greater East Asia Coprosperity Sphere
·· 2:320a, 325a; 3:60b–62a; 7:235a; 8:273b
Asia Development Board ······· 1:102b
background ·············· 3:60b–61a
Japanese expansionism ····· 3:61a–61b
conference ·············· 3:61b–62a
participants ·············· 3:61b
international relations ······· 3:321b–324a
Konoe Fumimaro ·········· 4:273a
ministry ················· 3:61b
"Greater East Asia War" ······· 3:61b
Greater Japan Production Party ···· 3:25a
Great Fish Panic of 1973 ········ 2:304b
Great Japan Agricultural Association
····················· 7:109a
Great Japan Association (Dai Nihon
Kyōkai) ·················· 8:91a
Great Japan National Essence Society
····················· 2:66a
Great Japan Production Party ····· 7:108a
Great Japan Women's Society ····· 2:65b
Great Learning for Women, The ··· 6:108a
Great Mirror, The ············ 6:79a
Great Mirror of the Erotic Way, The
····················· 7:95b–96a
Green, Thomas Hill ············ 4:178a
Green Breeze Society ··········· 6:352a
Green Tuff zone ·············· 4:9b

Greeting cards ················· 5:372b
Gregorian chant ··············· 5:283b
Grew, Joseph Clark ···· 3:62a-62b; 7:246b
　World War II ················· 3:62a
Grid-pattern city ·············· 1:245b
Grievance procedure ········· 3:62b
　labor unions ················· 4:348a
Griffis, William Elliot ··· 2:311a; 3:62b
Grillo, Pompeo ················ 3:350b
Groom, Arthur H. ·············· 3:43b
Gross domestic product ···· 2:145b-146b
Gross national product (GNP)
　······ 2:145a-145b, 159a-159b, 161b-162a,
　　　　　　　　　　　163a-165b
　capital formation ········· 1:240a-242a
　defense industry ·············· 2:82a
　land problem ················· 4:363b
　monetary policy ·············· 5:241a
　national income ·········· 5:339a-341b
Ground Self Defense Forces ··· 7:60a-60b
Group consciousness ··········· 3:260a
Group hiring ··············· 3:62b-63a
Group responsibility ··········· 6:301a
Groups ···················· 3:63a-63b
　batsu-type ··················· 1:146b
　family ·················· 2:241b-245b
　motivation ···················· 3:63a
　murahachibu (ostracized household)
　······························ 5:266a
　occupational
　　hereditary (be) ············· 1:147b
　paternalism ··················· 6:165a
　ranking system ················ 3:63a
Group travel ·········· 3:63b; 8:104b
Growth industries ··········· 3:63b
Guadalcanal ·········· 3:63b; 8:275a
Guam ···················· 3:63b-64a
Guandong (Kwantung)
　Army ··········· 関東軍　3:64a-64b;
　　　　　　　　　　　　　7:89a
　activists ················· 3:64a-64b
　Doihara-Qin (Doihara-Ch'in) Agreement
　······························ 2:126b
　Guandong (Kwantung) Territory 3:64b-65a
　Honjō Shigeru ················ 3:223b
　Ishiwara Kanji ··············· 3:345b
　Manchukuo ················ 5:96a-97b
　Manuchurian Incident ······· 5:97b-99a
　Mutō Akira ··················· 5:288a
　post-World War I ·············· 3:200a
　Shanghai Incident ············· 7:77b
　Soviet Union vs. ········· 3:64a-64b
　Tanggu (Tangku) Truce ···· 7:340b-341a
　Tatekawa Yoshitsugu ·········· 7:349a
Guandong (Kwantung) Territory
　···························· 3:64b-65a
　administration ················ 3:64b
　Twenty-One Demands ··········· 8:120b
Guanjing xuanyi ················ 4:67b
Guanyin ·················· 4:144b-145a
Guan Yu (Kuan Yü). ············· 4:154a
Guardian ················· 4:253b-254a
Gubijinsō ············· 虞美人草　5:350a
Guest room ···················· 6:124b
Guidebooks ···················· 8:41b
Guideline for Peoples' Action ··· 4:260b
Gukanshō ······· 愚管抄　2:101b, 102b;
　　　　　　　　　　　　3:65a-65b
　historiography ················ 3:153b
　Jien ························· 4:53b
　secular concerns ·············· 3:65a
　theological principles ······ 3:65a-65b
Gullion, Allen ················· 4:17b
Gulls [(kamome) family Laridae] ·· 3:65b
Gumbatsu ··········· 軍閥　3:65b-67a
　Imperial Way vs Control factions · 3:66b
　Satsuma ················· 3:65b-67a
Gumbu ················ 軍部　3:67a-67b

Gumbu daijin gen'eki
　bukan sei
　····· 軍部大臣現役武官制 ········· 3:67b
Gumma Incident 群馬事件 ····· 3:67b-68a
Gumma Prefecture 群馬県 ········ 3:68a
Gun. 郡　　　See **Kokugun system**
Gunchūjō ··········· 軍忠状 ···· 3:68a
Gundai ············· 郡代 ······· 3:68a
　kanjō bugyō ·················· 4:144a
Gundan ············· 軍談 ······· 3:68b
Gunji ·············· 郡司 ······· 3:68b
Gunjin Chokuyu 軍人勅諭 ···· 3:279b-280a
Gunji Shigetada 郡司成忠 ········ 3:68b
Gunka ····························· 3:69a
　Mikado, The ·················· 3:69a
　ryūkōka ····················· 6:354a
Gunki monogatari
　········ 軍記物語 1:294a; 2:101b;
　　　　　　　　　3:69a-69b; 5:39b, 246a
　development ··············· 3:69a-69b
　Gikeiki ······················ 3:32b
　Heiji monogatari ·············· 3:123b
　Heike monogatari ·········· 3:124a-125a
　Hōgen monogatari ············· 3:209b
　influence ····················· 3:69b
　kōdan tradition ··············· 4:241b
　Shōmonki ····················· 7:165b
　Soga monogatari ·············· 7:221a
　Taiheiki ····················· 7:295a
Gunnery ······················ 3:283b
Gunpowder ···················· 7:106b
Gunreibu ·············· 軍令部 ····· 5:358b
Guns ························· 3:140a
Gunseki yōran ········ 群籍要覧 ···· 1:154a
Gunsho ichiran ······· 群書一覧 ···· 1:154a
Gunsho kaidai ········ 群書解題 ···· 1:154b
Gunsho ruijū 群書類従 1:154b; 3:69b;
　　　　　　　　　　　　7:294b
　Hanawa Hokiichi ·············· 3:95a
　historiography ················ 3:155b
　Kuroita Katsumi ·············· 4:316a
Guntai nikki ······ 軍隊日記 ······· 4:318b
Gun'yaku ············ 軍役 ··· 3:69b-70a
Gunze, Ltd ····················· 3:70a
Guomindang [(Kuomintang (KMT)]
　·········· 1:270b; 2:59a; 3:128b
Guo Moruo (Kuo Mo-jo) ···· 3:70a-70b
　works ························· 3:70a
Guo Songling (Kuo Sung-ling) ···· 3:70b
Gurin. 愚林　　　See **Chūyūki**
Gusai ············· 救済 ········ 3:70b
　Shinkei ······················ 7:119a
Gushikawa ·········· 具志川 ······ 3:70b
Gūzō saikō (Resurrecting
　Idols) ·········· 偶像再興 ······· 8:237b
Gymnastics ················ 3:70b-71a
Gyōda ············· 行田 ········ 3:71a
Gyōdō mask ··········· 5:126a, 126b
Gyōgi ·········· 行基　1:159b; 3:71a
　education ····················· 2:172a
　monasticism ·················· 5:237a
Gyōji ryōri cuisine
　·············· 行事料理法 ········ 2:22a
Gyojū gaigen (An Outline
　on the Subduing of
　Foreigners) ······ 馭戎慨言 ····· 8:306a
Gyōki. 行基　　　See **Gyōgi**
Gyokudō. 玉堂　　See **Uragami Gyokudō**
Gyokudō Art Museum ·· 3:71a; 4:178b
Gyokudō Kinshi. See **Uragami Gyokudō**
Gyokuen Bompō 玉畹梵芳 ···· 3:70a-70b
Gyokugan ····················· 3:71b
Gyokukai ············· 玉海 ········ 3:71b
Gyokusai ("total sacrifice") ····· 1:116a
Gyokusen School ··············· 3:336a
Gyokuyō ············ 玉葉 ······· 3:71b
　Kujō Kanezane's diary ········ 4:303b
　　　　　　　　　　　8:213b, 214b

Gyokuyō wakashū
　············· 玉葉和歌集　3:71b-72b;
　　　　　　　　　　4:329b; 7:302a
　Eifuku Mon'in ················ 2:186a
　poets ····················· 3:71b-72a
　structure ····················· 3:72a
　styles ···················· 3:71b-72a
Gyōkyō ············· 行教 ······· 3:363a
Gyōmin Kyōsantō
　(Awakened People's
　Communist Party)
　·············· 暁民共産党 ······· 6:210b
Gyomotsu sekki 御物石器 ········· 7:248a
Gyōnen ············· 凝然 ······· 3:72b
Gyō no tetsugaku
　(Philosophy of Spiritual
　Discipline) ········ 行の哲学 ····· 4:204b
Gyōsai. See **Kawanabe Gyōsai**
Gyōsai gadan ··· 暁斎画談 ········· 4:182a
Gyōsai manga shinseki
　·········· 暁斎漫画真蹟 ········· 4:182a
Gyōsei Kanri Chō
　·············· 行政管理庁 ········ 1:14a
Gyōsei shidō ················ 1:12a-13a
Gyōsho ("running-style" script) · 1:233b;
　　　　　　　　　　　　7:171a
Gyōshōnin ····················· 7:250b
Gyōzui ······················ 3:72b
Gyūnabe ······················ 7:265b

H

Habachi (sawflies) ············· 1:149a
Habaki ························ 4:323b
Habatsu (cliques) ··· 派閥　1:147a; 3:73a;
　　　　　　　　　　6:205b; 7:62b
Habeas Corpus Law ······ 2:6b; 3:73a
Habikino ············ 羽曳野 ····· 3:73a
Habōhō. See **Subversive Activities**
　Prevention Law
Haboku ············· 破墨 ··· 3:73a-73b
　artists ······················· 3:73b
　ink painting technique ········ 3:305b
Haboku landscape ··············· 7:69a
Habomai Islands 歯舞諸島 ······· 3:73b
　Soviet-Japanese relations ······ 7:10b
Hachi ························· 1:149a
Hachigyaku ·············· 八虐　3:73b
Hachihachi Kantai
　·············· 八八艦隊　1:87b; 3:73b
　Nagato ······················ 5:307a
Hachiichi sengen 八一宣言 ········· 1:116b
Hachijōjima ·········· 八丈島 ····· 3:74a
Hachijō susuki ················· 7:279a
Hachiku (Phyllostachys nigra var.
　henonis) ···················· 1:136a
Hachimaki ········· 2:253b; 3:74a
　morning glory fair ············· 3:74b
　tasuki ······················· 7:348a
Hachiman ········ 八幡　3:74a-74b;
　　　　　　　　　　　7:134b, 136a
　Iwashimizu Hachiman Shrine ···· 3:363a
　religious symbolism ············ 6:295b
　theories of origin ·········· 3:74a-74b
Hachimantai ········ 八幡平 ····· 3:74b
Hachimonjiya-bon
　············ 八文字屋本 ·· 3:74b; 8:144b

Hachimonjiya Jishō
·················· 八文字屋自笑 · 2:188a; 5:16b, 48b
Hachinohe ············ 八戸 ·········3:74b
Hachiōji ············· 八王子 ·········3:74b
silk weaving ·············2:296a
Hachirōgata ········· 八郎潟 ·········3:74b
Hachisu no tsuyu
Ryōkan ····················6:352a
Hadairo no tsuki · 肌色の月 ·········3:151b
Ha Daiusu ········ 破提宇子 ·········2:241a
Hadaka no shima · 裸の島 ·········3:75a
Shindō Kaneto ···········7:111b
Hadano ················ 秦野 ·········3:75a
Haedong chegukki ··············8:325a
"Haedong jegukki" ··············4:278a
Haerbin ·····················3:103b
Ha-erh-pin ···················3:103b
Hagakure ········ 葉隠 · 1:222b, 223b; 3:75a-75b
Haga Yaichi ····· 芳賀矢一 ·········3:75b
Gensen ···················3:23a-23b
Hagerty Incident ···············3:75b
Hagi (city) ············ 萩 ·········3:75b
Hagi [(Japanese bush clover) Lespedeza bicolor var. japonica] ···3:75b-76a
types ·····················3:75b
Haginoya ········ 萩の舎 ·········3:136a
Hagi Rebellion of 1876
··········· 萩の乱 · 3:76a; 5:79b; 7:152a
chitsuroku shobun ··········1:298a
Hagiwara Kyōjirō 萩原恭次郎 ·········3:76a
Hagiwara Sakutarō
············· 萩原朔太郎 ···3:76a-76b
"voluptuous grave" ··········5:57a
Western influence ··········3:76a
works ···················3:75b-76a
Hagiwara Yūsuke 萩原雄祐 ·········3:76b
Hagi ware ········ 萩焼 ···3:76b-77a
collections ··············3:77a
glazes ···················3:76b
tea ceremony ············7:363b
Hagi-yaki Tōgei Kaikan ·········3:77a
Hagnenauer, Charles ·········4:42b
Hagoita ·····················3:77a
Hagoita ichi ·················3:77a
Hagoromo ······ 羽衣 · 2:73a; 5:295a
Hagoromo Falls ·羽衣ノ滝 ·········8:7b
Hagoromo legend ········ 羽衣 ·········3:77a
Nō ·······················6:28b
prototypes ··············2:341a
Hagurosan ······ 羽黒山 · 1:136b-137a; 3:77a
Haha (The Mother) ····· 母 ·········8:117a
Haibun ·····················1:295b; 3:77a-78a; 6:297b-298a
anthologies ··············3:77b-78a
Bashō ·············· 1:144a; 3:77b
categories ··············3:78a
characteristics ············3:77a-77b
decline ··················3:78a
early ····················3:77b
Issa ·····················3:348a
Yokoi Yayū ··············8:331b
Haibutsu kishaku 廃仏毀釈 ·········3:78a
Haifū yanagidaru
············· 誹風柳多留 ·········4:157a
Haigon ·····················3:78b
Haihan chiken ··· 廃藩置県 · 6:233b-235a
Haikai ············ 俳諧 6:296b-300a; 7:208a
compared to renga ·········3:78b
criticism ················5:16a
haiku, hokku, haikai
distinction between ·········3:78b
literary groups ············5:18a
Haikai gosan · 俳諧五山 ·········7:140a
Haikai jūron · 俳諧十論 · 4:102b

Haikai jūsanjō · 俳諧十三条 ·········6:126a
Haikaishi ········ 俳諧師 ·········7:311b
Haikai shichibushū
················· 俳諧七部集 · 3:78a; 4:102b
Haiku ·········· 俳句 ·········3:78a-82a
abroad ··················3:80b
cicadas as symbols ·········1:315a
development (premodern) ·····3:78b-79b
decline ················3:79a
Matsunaga Teitoku ·······3:78b-79b
notable poets ···········3:79a
haibun ··················3:77b
hokku, and haikai ·········3:78b
modern ··················3:79b-80b
factions ···············3:80a
magazines ·············3:80a
Masaoka Shiki's reform · 3:79b; 5:123b
moon viewing ············5:248a
principles ···············3:80b-82a
seasons depicted ·········1:325b-326b
travel diaries ············8:105b
writing in English ·········3:80b-82a
metrical pattern ·········3:81a
seasonal theme principle ····3:81a-82a
subjects ··············3:80b
technique of cutting ·······3:81a-81b
Haiku contests ···············5:15a
Haiku literary groups (modern) ·····5:20a
Haiku paintings ···············4:201a
Haiku poets
Arakida Moritake ··········1:73b
Awano Seiho ···········1:124b
Bashō ··········· 1:144a-145b, 224b-225a
Buson ··················1:224b-225a
Hattori Ransetsu ··········3:114a
Hattori Tohō ············3:114a
Hōjō Dansui ············3:210b
Iida Dakotsu ············3:262a
Ikenishi Gonsui ·········3:266b
Ishida Hakyō ············3:340a
Ishida Mitoku ···········3:340a
Issa ·············· 1:224b; 3:348b
Kagami Shikō ············4:102b
Kaga no Chiyo ···········4:102b
Katō Kyōtai ············4:168b-169a
Katō Shūson ············4:169b
Kawabata Bōsha ·········4:175b
Kawahigashi Hekigotō ······4:178a
Kawai Sora ···········4:179a
Kaya Shirao ············4:185a
Kitamura Kigin ···········4:227a
Kitao Shigemasa ·········4:228a-228b
Konishi Raizan ···········4:270a
Kubota Mantarō ·········4:301a-301b
Masaoka Shiki ···········5:123b-124a
Matsue Shigeyori ·········5:133a
Matsumura Goshun ·······5:138a
Matsunaga Teitoku ·······5:138b-139a
Miura Chora ············5:215a
Mizuhara Shūōshi ·········5:225b
Morikawa Kyoroku ·······5:250a
Mukai Kyorai ···········5:262a
Murakami Kijō ···········5:266a-266b
Naitō Jōsō ··············5:311a
Nakamura Kusatao ·······5:315a
Nakarai Bokuyō ·········5:317b
Nonoguchi Ryūho ·········6:34b-35a
Nozawa Bonchō ·········6:42a
Ochi Etsujin ············6:59b
Ogiwara Seisensui ·········6:70b
Okanishi Ichū ···········6:80b
Ōshima Ryōta ···········6:126a
Ōsuga Otsuji ············6:127a
Ozaki Hōsai ············6:139a
Satō Nempuku ···········7:28a
Sugiyama Sampū ·········7:259a
Takahama Kyoshi ·········7:311a-311b
Takai Kitō ··············7:313b-314a

Takano Sujū ············7:317a-317b
Takarai Kikaku ···········7:318a
Takebe Ayatari ··········7:321a-321b
Takii Kōsaku ············7:326b
Taneda Santōka ·········7:340a
Tan Taigi ··············7:344b-345a
Uejima Onitsura ·········8:127a
Yamaguchi Seishi ·········8:295a-295b
Yamaguchi Sodō ·········8:295b
Yamazaki Sōkan ·········8:331a
Yasuhara Teishitsu ·······8:318b
Yokoi Yayū ············8:331b
Hairstyles ····· 2:38a; 3:82a-83b; 4:127b
aristocratic ··············3:82a
Chinese influence ·········3:82b
clothing ················1:332b
combs ··················1:337a
Heian period (794-1185) ·····3:82b
kanzashi ················4:154b
samurai ················3:82b-83b
Tokugawa shogunate (1603-1868) ·3:83a
Western influence ·········3:83a
Haishō hitosuji 廃娼ひとすじ ·········4:301a
Haitoku no mesu
················ 背徳のメス ·········4:316b
Haitōrei ········ 廃刀令 · 1:89a; 3:83b
Dampatsurei ············2:72a
Haiya-bushi ······ ハイヤ節 ·········2:301b
Haiyūza ···················7:113b
Haji (shame) ···············3:83b-84a
Hajibe ············ 土師部 ·········1:147b
Haji Seiji ········ 土師清二 ·········3:84a
Haji ware ········ 土師器 1:258a; 2:305b; 3:84a-84b; 7:30b, 256a
archaeological dating ·······3:84b
characteristics ············3:84a-84b
functions ···············3:84a-84b
jar ·····················3:84b
kofun deposits ···········4:245b
rokuro ··················6:335b
typological studies ·········1:79a
Hakamada Satomi
················ 袴田里見 ·········4:11b
Hakamagoshi ······ 袴腰 ·········1:183a
Hakase ·············3:84b; 4:140a
Hakata. 博多 See Fukuoka
Hakata Dontaku
··········· 博多どんたく ·········3:85a
Hakata merchants
··········· 博多商人 ·········3:85a
tally trade ··············7:331b-332a
Hakata Station film decision ·3:85a-85b
"Hakidame" ········ 塵溜 ·········4:179b
Hakkōdasan ······ 八甲田山 ·········3:85b
Hakkō Hikka Incident
············· 白虹筆禍事件 ·········6:120a
Hakkō ichiu ······ 八紘一宇 ·········3:85b
Hakoda Rokusuke
················ 箱田六輔 ·········8:88a
Hakodate ········ 函館 ·········3:85b
Goryōkaku ··············3:85a
Hakodate bugyō ·箱館奉行 ·········3:86a
Hakodate Dock Co, Ltd ·········3:86a
Hakone ············ 箱根 ·········3:86a
Hakone Canal · 箱根用水 ·········3:86a
Hakone Museum of Art · 3:86a-86b; 7:56a
Hakone no Seki · 箱根関 · 3:86b; 7:57a
Hakone Open-Air Museum · 3:87a; 5:279b
Hakone Pass ···· 箱根峠 ·········3:87a
Hakoneyama ···· 箱根山 · 2:347b; 3:87a; 8:194a
Hakoniwa ·················3:87a
Hako otoko ········ 箱男 ·········1:3a
Hakozaki Shrine · 宮崎宮 ·········3:87a
Hakuba ············ 白馬 ·········3:87a
Hakubakai (White Horse
Society) ········· 白馬会 · 2:345b; 3:87a-87b; 8:328a

Hakubakai exhibition ······················ 1:69a
Hakubunkan ····························· 3:87b
  children's literature ··················· 1:279b
  Ōhashi Sahei ·························· 6:73b
  Ozaki Kōyō ······················· 4:198b-199a
Hakubyōga ················ 白描画 ····· 3:87b
  precedents ···························· 3:87b
Hakugō shugi (White Australia) ··· 1:119a
Hakuhō culture ····· 白鳳文化 ···· 3:87b-88a
Hakuhōdō ······························ 1:17a
Hakuhōdō, Inc ······················· 3:88a
  founder ····························· 7:56b
  Seki Hironao ························· 7:56b
Hakuhō period ························· 6:175b
Hakui ······················ 羽咋 ····· 3:88a
Hakuin ·············· 白隠 ·1:179b, 193a,
                   194a; 3:88a-88b; 7:89b
  calligraphy ·························· 3:88b
  paintings ···························· 3:88b
  Rinzai sect ·························· 6:320a
  teachings ···························· 3:88a
  writings ····························· 3:88a
Hakurai ····························· 3:88b
Hakusan ···················· 白山 ···· 3:88b
Hakusan National Park
         ·········· 白山国立公園 ······ 2:364a;
                              3:88b-89a
Hakusan Volcanic Zone
            ········ 白山火山帯 ········· 3:89a
Hakushaku fujin (The
  Countess) ······ 伯爵夫人 ······· 6:221a
Hakusho ····························· 8:251b
Hakusōrei ················ 薄葬令 ····· 7:296b
Hakusukinoe, Battle of
          ········· 白村江の戦 ··· 1:4a; 3:89a;
                            7:260a, 263a
  Paekche ···························· 6:146b
  Taika Reform ······················· 7:296a
  Yamato's foreign relations ········· 4:277a
Hakuyōkyū ·············· 白羊宮 ····· 7:279b
Halberd heads ························ 1:175a
Hall, John W. ················ 4:41b; 5:228b
Hamada ················ 浜田 ·· 3:89a; 7:101a
Hamada Hikozō ··· 浜田彦蔵 ···· 3:89a-89b
Hamada Kōsaku ··· 浜田耕作 ·· 1:77a; 3:89b
Hamada Shōji ····· 浜田庄司 ·· 2:294a; 3:89b
Hamada Yahyōe
       ·········· 浜田弥兵衛 ······ 3:89b-90a;
                              7:255b
Hama Detached Palace
  Garden ······· 浜離宮庭園 ······· 3:90a
Hamaguchi Osachi
         ········· 浜口雄幸 ··· 3:90a; 7:88b
Hamaguchi Osachi cabinet
  Dan Takuma ························· 2:77b
  Nakano Seigō ··············· 5:316a-316b
Hamaguchi Yūkō. 浜口雄幸.
       See **Hamaguchi Osachi**
Hamaguri Gomon Incident
         ······· 蛤御門の変 ·· 3:90a; 5:317b
  Kido Takayoshi ····················· 4:202b
  Shimonoseki Bombardment ········ 7:106a
  Shinsengumi ························ 7:124b
Hamakita ················ 浜北 ····· 3:90b
Hamamatsu ·············· 浜松 ····· 3:90b
  Nippon Gakki Company ············· 3:90b
Hamamatsu Chūnagon
  monogatari
       ······· 浜松中納言物語 ···· 3:90b-91a;
                              7:257b
  theme ······························ 3:90b
Hamana, Lake ···· 浜名湖 ······ 3:91a
Hamao Arata ····· 浜尾新 ······ 3:91a
Hamaya and Hamayumi ·········· 3:91a
Hamayū (*Chrinum asiaticum* var.
  japonicum) ························ 3:91a
Hamayumi ···························· 3:91a

Hamba seido ······················· 3:91b
  conditions ··························· 3:91b
Hambatsu (domain clique)
            ·········· 藩閥 ········ 1:147b;
                        3:91b-92a; 4:340a
  influence on government ······ 3:91b-92a
  use ································· 3:92a
Hambun hiraita mado
            ······· 半分開いた窓 ····· 6:112a
Hamlet ······························ 7:112b
Hammotsu ·············· 判物 ·· 2:100a-100b
Hampon ······························ 2:295b
Han (domain) ············ 藩 ······ 3:92b
  common features ···················· 3:92b
  productivity ·························· 3:92b
  size ································· 3:92b
"Hana" ···················· 鼻 ······ 1:45a
Hanabachi (bees) ····················· 1:149a
Hanabatake Kyōjō
            ·········· 花畑教場 ······ 3:265b
Hanabusa Itchō ···· 英一蝶 ···· 3:92b-93a
Hanabusazōshi (A
  Garland of Tales) 英草紙 ········· 8:336b
Hanada Kiyoteru 花田清輝 ·· 3:93a; 5:13b
Hanafuda ········· 3:93a-93b; 6:192a
  origin ··························· 3:93a-93b
Hanagatami ·············· 花筐 ····· 2:76b
Hanagoi (carp) ······················· 1:244a
Hanagoyomi hasshōjin
            ·········· 花暦八笑人 ····· 6:359a
Hanaike ······························ 1:136a
Hanai Takuzō ······ 花井卓蔵 ····· 3:94a
Hanakago ···························· 1:136a
Hana Karuta ···················· 3:5b, 93a
Hanako, Princess ···· 華子妃 ······ 3:277a
Hanamaki ··············· 花巻 ····· 3:94a
Hana Matsuri ····· 花祭 ·· 2:260a; 3:94a
  yudate rites ·························· 4:107b
Hanami ············ 3:94a-94b; 4:381a
  flower viewing (Ueno Park) ········· 3:94b
Hanamichi 4:91a, 93a-94a, 95a, 95b; 7:272a
Hanamori ················ 花守 ····· 8:334a
Hana no byakkotai
            ········ 花の白虎隊 ······ 4:174b
Hana no sugao 花の素顔 ········ 6:78a
Hanaoka Seishū 華岡青洲 ········ 3:94b
Hanasaka jijii ······ 花咲爺 ······ 3:94b
Hana saku minato
            ·········· 花咲く港 ······ 4:207a
Hanasanjin ········ 鼻山人 ···· 3:94b-95a
Hanashi (stories) ····················· 6:282a
Hanashōbu ··························· 4:22b
Hanawa Hokiichi 塙保己一 ·· 1:154a; 3:95a
  Gunsho ruijū ······················ 3:69b
  historiography ······················ 3:155b
Hanayagiryū ········· 花柳流 ······ 2:74b
Hanayagi Shigeka 花柳茂香 ········ 2:74b
Hanayagi Shōtarō
            ········ 花柳章太郎 ······ 3:95a
  shimpa ····························· 7:108a
Hanayagi Suzushi
            ········ 花柳寿々紫 ······ 2:76a
Hanazono, Emperor
            ·········· 花園天皇 ······ 5:291a
Hanazono Tennō shinki
            ········ 花園天皇辰記 ······ 3:95a
Handa ················· 半田 ····· 3:95a
Handen shūju system
            ········· 班田収授法 ···· 2:104a;
    3:95a-96a, 162b; 4:76a; 7:89a-89b, 296a
  abandonment of land ··············· 1:303b
  breakdown ······················ 3:95b-96a
  Chinese model ··················· 3:95a-95b
  economy ···························· 2:147a
  keichō ······························ 4:187b
  ko (household) unit ············ 4:233b-234a
  process ······························ 3:95b
  regulations ·························· 3:95b

ritsuryō system ······················ 6:326a
  ryōshu ····························· 6:353a
  shōen ······························ 7:155b
Handicapped
  aid ································ 7:212a
  discrimination ······················ 5:195b
  schools ····························· 7:241b
Handicraft industry ·················· 2:150a
  taxes ······························ 7:239b
Handscrolls (emakimono) ····· 2:198a-200a
  format ························· 2:198a-199a
  history ························· 2:199a-200a
  painting ···························· 6:150a
Han dynasty ························· 4:55b
Haneda Airport ······················ 5:371a
Han'ei sembai ····· 藩営専売 ·· 3:96a-96b
  Kaiho Seiryō ························ 4:110a
Hanetsuki ··················· 3:77a, 96b
Hanging scroll ······················· 4:116a
"Hangman, The" (Maedakō Hiroichirō)
            ······························ 5:80a
Han'gŭl ············· 3:96b; 4:289b, 291a
Hani Gorō ·········· 羽仁五郎 ····· 3:96b
Hani Motoko ··· 羽仁もと子 ····· 2:344a;
                              3:96b-97a
  publications ························· 3:96b
  Shin Kyōiku Undō ··················· 7:121a
Hani Susumu ······· 羽仁進 ····· 2:274a;
                              3:97a-97b
  documentary techniques ········ 3:97a-97b
  films ··························· 3:97a-97b
Haniwa ········· 埴輪 ·· 1:75b, 77a,
  147b, 197a-197b, 257b; 3:97b-98a, 98b, 99a;
                              7:143a
  chokkomon ·························· 1:299b
  falconry ···························· 2:241b
  kofun ······························ 4:244b
  origins ························· 3:98a; 4:84b
  placement patterns ············· 3:97b-98a
  ritual function ······················ 3:98a
  surface detail ······················ 3:97b
Haniya Yutaka · 埴谷雄高 · 3:98a-98b
Hankanfu ············ 藩翰譜 ····· 1:72b;
                              3:98b-99a
Hanko. *See* **Seals**
Hankyū Corporation ··· 3:99a-99b; 4:188b
Hankyū Department Stores, Inc ···· 3:99b
Hankyū Electric Railway Co ········· 4:188b
Hannō ················· 飯能 ····· 3:99b
Han pronunciation ··················· 4:148a
Hanren ····························· 4:123b
Hansatsu ·············· 藩札 ····· 3:99b;
                              5:242a-242b
  economy ···························· 2:150a
Hanshan (Han-shan) and Shide
  (Shih-te). *See* **Kanzan and Jittoku**
Hansharo ············· 反射炉 ····· 3:99b
Hanshi ····························· 4:196a
Hanshichi torimonochō
            ········ 半七捕物帳 ······ 6:80b
Hanshin Industrial Zone ·· 3:100a; 8:326b
  Ōsaka ····························· 6:120a
Han shu (History of the Former Han
  Dynasty) ··························· 8:197a
Hansŏng ····························· 6:146a
Hansŏng sunbo ···················· 4:280b
Hanwa Co, Ltd ···················· 3:100a
Hanwen ····························· 4:123b
Hanyū ················· 羽生 ····· 3:100a
Hanzei ················· 半済 ····· 3:100a
  Ashikaga Yoshimitsu ················ 1:101b
  Kaei sandai ki ····················· 4:101b
  Muromachi shogunate ··············· 5:272a
  shōen ······························ 7:158a
Hara ···························· 3:100a-100b
Harada Magoshichirō
       ········ 原田孫七郎 3:100b; 4:369a
Harada Naojirō 原田直次郎 ···· 3:100b

Harada Yoshito ·· 原田淑人 ······· 3:100b
Harae ····················· 3:100b-101b
　　atonement ··················· 3:100b
　　offerings ···················· 3:100b
　　purification rite ········· 3:100b-101a
　　variant forms ··········· 3:101a-101b
Haragei ························· 3:100a
Hara Katsurō········· 原勝郎 ···· 3:156b
Hara Kei. 原敬　　See Hara Takashi
Harakiri ··· 3:101b-102a; 4:84b; 7:68b, 261a
　　ritual ······················ 3:101b
　　Seppuku ····················· 7:68b
Haramachi ·············· 原町 ···· 3:102a
Hara Martinho · 原マルチノ ······ 3:102a
Hara Setsuko ······· 原節子···· 2:271a;
　　　　　　　　　　　　3:102a-102b
Hara Takashi ········· 原敬 3:102b-103b,
　　　　　　　　　　　　　　198a
　　historical significance ········ 3:102b
　　party leader ················· 3:102b
　　Rikken Seiyūkai ········ 6:315a-315b
　　Shandong (Shantung) Question ····· 7:77b
　　suffrage ····················· 3:103a
Hara Tamiki ·········· 原民喜 ··· 3:103b
Hara Yasusaburō 原安三郎 ······ 3:103b
Harbin ························· 3:103b
Hare ···· 2:253b-254a; 4:186a; 6:362a-362b
Hare of Inaba ·················· 5:293b
Hares. See Rabbits
Hari ···························· 1:10b
Haribako ······················· 3:103b
Hari kuyō ············ 針供養 ··· 3:104a
Hari kuyō observance ············ 2:260b
Harima industrial area ··········· 3:146b
Harima Plain ·· 播磨平野 ······· 3:139a
Harima school ······ 播磨節 ····· 4:77a
Harima Sea ·········· 播磨灘 ···· 3:104a
Haring, Douglas ················· 4:38b
Harinoki Pass ·· 針ノ木峠 ······ 3:104a
Harivarman ····················· 4:71a
Harquebus ······················ 3:140a
Harriman, E. H. ················· 4:268a
Harris, Merriman Colbert ······· 3:104a
Harris, Thomas Lake · 1:73a; 3:104a-104b;
　　　　　　　　　　　　5:306b
Harris, Townsend · 3:104b-105a; 7:104b
　　Harris Treaty ················ 3:105a
　　Heusken, Henry C. J. ········· 3:128b
　　Opening of Japan ············· 5:155b
Harris Treaty ········· 2:319b; 3:105a
　　fumie prohibition ············ 2:368a
　　Ii Naosuke ·················· 3:263b
　　Inoue Kiyonao ··············· 3:310b
　　Iwakura Tomomi and ·········· 3:360a
　　Iwase Tadanari ·············· 3:363a
　　Kanrin maru ················· 4:151b
　　Kawaji Toshiakira ············ 4:179b
　　Kōmei, Emperor ·············· 4:266a
　　Muragaki Norimasa ··········· 5:265b
　　Nakahama Manjirō ········· 5:313a-313b
　　national flag ················ 5:339a
　　provisions ·················· 3:105a
　　shogunal succession ·········· 5:156a
　　Tokugawa Nariaki ············· 8:52a
　　United States ················ 8:154b
　　Yokohama ··················· 8:329b
Hart, H.L.A. ···················· 4:85b
Hartmann, Carl Sadakichi ··· 3:105a-105b
Haru ichiban ····················· 4:8a
Haru Koma ····················· 7:250a
Haruma Wage · 波留麻和解 3:105b; 8:242b
　　Inamura Sampaku ············· 3:282b
Haruna, Lake ······· 榛名湖 ···· 3:105b
Harunasan ·········· 榛名山 3:106a; 7:86a
Harunobu ··········· 春信 3:106a-106b;
　　　　　　　　　　　　5:18a; 7:84a
　　pictorial calendars ········ 3:106a-106b
　　techniques ·················· 3:106a

works ···················· 3:106a
Haru no shiro ······· 春の城 ···· 1:21a
Harusame monogatari
　(Tales of the Spring
　Rain) ··········· 春雨物語 · 5:48b; 8:126b
"Haru wa basha ni notte" (Spring,
　Riding in a Carriage)
　　　　　　　春は馬車に乗つて ···· 8:332a
Harvard Journal of Asiatic Studies 2:196b
Harvard-Yenching Institute ······· 2:196b
Harvest rites ···················· 1:23a
Hase ················· 初瀬 ···· 3:106b
Hasebe Kotondo
　　　　　　　長谷部言人 · 3:106b; 4:74a
　　physical characteristics of Japanese
　　people ······················ 4:35a
Hasedera ··········· 長谷寺 ·· 3:106b-107a
　　Shingon sect ················ 7:115a
Hasegawa Kazuo
　　　　　　　　長谷川一夫 ···· 3:107a
Hasegawa Kiyoshi 長谷川清 ···· 3:107a
Hasegawa Nyozekan
　　　　　　長谷川如是閑 1:155b; 3:107a
Hasegawa Roka
　　　　　　　長谷川路可 ··· 3:107a-107b
Hasegawa school
　　　　　　　長谷川派 3:107b; 4:146a
　　founding ················· 3:108b-109a
　　Kanō school rivalry ·········· 4:147b
Hasegawa Shin ··· 長谷川伸 · 3:107b-108a
　　"Kutsukake Tokijirō" ········· 7:121a
　　literary genre ··············· 3:107b
　　"Mabuta no haha" ············ 7:121a
　　"Seki no Yatappe" ··········· 7:121a
　　shin kabuki ················· 4:92a
　　Shinkokugeki ················ 7:121a
　　themes used ················· 3:108a
Hasegawa Shirō
　　　　　　　長谷川四郎 ···· 3:108a
Hasegawa Tai ··· 長谷川泰 ···· 3:108a
Hasegawa Tatsunosuke
　　　　　　　長谷川辰之助 ···· 2:375b
Hasegawa Tenkei
　　　　　　長谷川天渓 · 3:108a-108b;
　　　　　　　　　　　　5:13a
Hasegawa Tōhaku · 長谷川等伯 · 3:108b, 182a,
　　　　　　307a; 7:41a-41b, 42b, 70a
　　Hasegawa school ············· 3:107b
　　ink painting ················· 3:108b
　　Pine Trees ·················· 3:108b
　　works ······················ 3:108b
Hasekura Tsunenaga
　　　　　　　支倉常長 ···· 3:109a
　　French-Japanese relations ····· 2:330a
　　Vatican expedition ··········· 4:369a
Hashiguchi Goyō 橋口五葉 · 3:109a-109b
Hashikuiiwa ········ 橋杭岩 ···· 3:109b
Hashima (city) ······ 羽島 ····· 3:109b
Hashima (island) ···· 端島 ····· 3:109b
Hashimoto ·········· 橋本 ····· 3:109b
Hashimoto Gahō 橋本雅邦 ···· 3:109b
　　Shimomura Kanzan ······· 7:105a-105b
　　works ······················ 3:109b
Hashimoto Kansetsu
　　　　　　　橋本関雪 ···· 3:110a
Hashimoto Kingorō
　　　　　　　橋本欣五郎 ···· 3:110a
　　Sakurakai (Cherry Blossom Society) ·· 7:5a
Hashimoto Sanai 橋本左内 · 3:110a-110b;
　　　　　　　　　　　　7:3b
　　Ansei purge ················· 1:63b
　　fukoku kyōhei ··············· 2:360b
Hashimoto Shinkichi
　　　　　　　橋本進吉 ···· 3:110b
　　orthographic studies ·········· 4:134b
Hashimoto Shinobu
　　　　　　　橋本忍 ···· 3:110b

Hashimoto Toshio
　　　　　　　橋本敏雄 ···· 1:124b
Hashira-e (pillar prints)
　　　　　　　　　　柱絵 ···· 8:141a
Hassōan ·········· 八窓庵 ····· 5:333a
Hasu ························ 5:73b-74a
Hasuda ············· 蓮田 ····· 3:111a
Hata. See Flags and banners
Hata family ········ 秦氏 ····· 3:111a
　　Aya family ·················· 1:125b
　　Inari ······················ 3:283a
　　kikajin ····················· 4:205b
　　Kōryūji built for ············ 4:294a
　　Nagaokakyō ················· 5:303b
Hatakebiraki ···················· 7:109b
Hatakenaoshi shinkai ············ 7:109b
Hatakeyama family 畠山氏 · 3:111a; 7:83b
　　kanrei ····················· 4:151a
Hatakeyama Kinenkan ······· 3:111a-111b
Hatakeyama Kizan
　　　　　　　　　畠山箕山 ·· 7:95b-96a
Hatakeyama Masanaga
　　　　　　　　　畠山政長 ··· 8:303a
Hatakeyama Museum 3:111a-111b; 5:276b
Hatakeyama Shigetada
　　　　　　　　　畠山重忠 ···· 3:111b
Hatakeyama Yoshinari
　　　　　　　　　畠山義就 ··· 8:303b
Hatakeyama Zekan
　　　　　　　　　畠山是閑 ··· 2:144a
Hatamoto ··········· 旗本 · 1:131b;
　　　　　　　2:340b; 3:111b-112a
　　decline ·················· 3:111b-112a
　　genealogies ················· 4:138a
　　heirs ······················ 3:111b
　　kanjō gimmiyaku ············· 4:144a
　　kobushin ···················· 4:239a
　　registers ··················· 1:206a
　　ryōshu ····················· 6:353a
　　Shōheikō ···················· 7:162a
　　status ······················ 3:111b
Hatamoto ryō ··················· 8:10a
Hatamoto yakko ···· 旗本奴 ···· 3:112a
　　behavior ··················· 3:112a
Hatanagi Daiichi Dam 畑薙第1ダム · 2:73b
Hatano Kanji · 波多野完治 ··· 3:112a
Hata no Kimi Irogu
　　　　　　　秦公伊呂具 ···· 3:283a
Hatano Seiichi 波多野精一 ···· 3:112b
Hata Sahachirō · 秦佐八郎 ···· 3:112b
Hata Toyokichi ·· 秦豊吉 ····· 3:112b
Hatogaya ··········· 鳩ケ谷 ···· 3:112b
Hatoyama Haruko
　　　　　　　　鳩山春子 ···· 3:112b
Hatoyama Hideo · 鳩山秀夫 ··· 3:112b-113a
Hatoyama Ichirō · 鳩山一郎 · 1:97b; 3:113a;
　　　　　　　　4:386a; 7:92a
　　founding Liberal Party (Jiyūtō) ··· 4:387b
　　Liberal Democratic Party ······ 4:386a
　　Nihon Jiyūtō (Japan Liberal Party) ·· 4:65b
　　Nihon Minshutō (Japan Democratic Party)
　　　　　　　　　　　　5:381a
　　Prime minister ··············· 3:113a
Hatoyama Kazuo 鳩山和夫 ···· 3:113a
Hatsuboku ·········· 溌墨 ····· 3:305b
Hatsukaichi ········· 廿日市 ···· 3:113b
Hatsukari ··········· 初雁 ····· 1:237a
Hatsumōde ······················ 2:259b
Hatsuse. 初瀬　　See Hase
Hatsushima ··········· 初島 ···· 3:113b
Hatsusugata ········· 初姿 ····· 4:296a
Hatsuuma ··· 初午 2:260a; 3:113b
Hatta, Mohammad ······· 3:113b; 7:253b
Hattori Dohō ········ 服部土芳 ·· 3:114a
Hattori Kintarō 服部金太郎 · 3:113b; 4:200b
Hattori Nankaku ·· 服部南郭 · 3:113b-114a
Hattori Ransetsu · 服部嵐雪 ···· 3:114a
Hattori Shirō ······ 服部四郎 ··· 3:114a

Japanese language studies · · · · · · · · · **4**:31b
orthographic studies · · · · · · · · · **4**:134b
Hattori Shisō ·服部之総· · · · **3**:114a
Shinjinkai · · · · · · · · · · · **7**:115b
Hattori Tohō ·服部土芳· **3**:114a; **5**:16a
Hausknecht, Emile · · · · · · **3**:114a–114b
Hauta ·端唄· · · · · · · · · · **4**:64b
Hawaii
Japanese immigration · · · · · · **2**:200b; **4**:13b
Japanese labor disputes · · · · · · · **3**:53a
Hawai-Marē oki Kaisen
(The War at Sea from
Hawaii to Malaya)
· · · ·ハワイ・マレー沖海戦 · · · · · **8**:111a
Hawks and eagles · · · · · · · **3**:114b
Hayabusa ·隼· · · · · · · · · **3**:114b
Hayachinesan ·早池峰山· · · · **3**:114b
Hayagawari · · · · · · · · · · **4**:94a
Hayaishi Osamu ·早石修· · · · **3**:114b
Hayakawa Sesshū
·早川雪洲 **3**:115a; **4**:127b
Hayama ·葉山· · · · · · · · · **3**:115a
Hayama Yoshiki ·葉山嘉樹· **3**:115a–115b
Bungei sensen · · · · · · · · · **1**:209b
labor activities · · · · · · · · **3**:115a–115b
proletarian literature movement · **6**:255a
work · · · · · · · · · · · · · **3**:115a–115b
Hayami Gyoshū ·速水御舟· · · · **3**:115b
Hayariuta · · · ·はやり唄· · · · **4**:296a
Hayashi · · · · · · · · · **3**:115b; **4**:99a
Hayashi Akira. *See* **Hayashi Fukusai**
Hayashi Fubō · · · ·林不忘· · · · **3**:116a
Hayashi Fukusai ·林復斎· · · · **3**:116a
Hayashi Fumiko ·林芙美子· **2**:274a;
3:116a–116b; **7**:25a
childhood · · · · · · · · · · **3**:116a–116b
poetry · · · · · · · · · · · · **3**:116a
works · · · · · · · · · · · · **3**:116a–116b
Hayashi Fusao · · · ·林房雄 **3**:116b; **7**:103b
Shinjinkai · · · · · · · · · · · **7**:115b
Hayashi Gahō · · · ·林鵞峰 **1**:154a; **3**:116b;
8:295b
historiography · · · · · · · · · **3**:154a
Hayashi Hōkō · · · ·林鳳岡· · · · **3**:116b
Hayashi Jussai · · · ·林述斎· **3**:116b–117a;
7:27a
Hayashikane Shōten. *See* **Taiyō Fishery
Co, Ltd**
Hayashi Razan · · · ·林羅山 **2**:241a; **3**:117a;
5:16b; **7**:274b; **8**:290a
Fujiwara Seika · · · · · · · · · **2**:358b
historiography · · · · · · · · · **3**:154b
Kan'ei shoka keizu den · · · · · **4**:138a
promotion of Zhu Xi Neo-Confucianism
· · · · · · · · · · · · · · · · **3**:117a
Tokugawa shogunate service · · · · · **3**:117a
works · · · · · · · · · · · · · **3**:117a
Hayashi Senjūrō ·林銑十郎· **3**:117b–118a;
7:28a
Hayashi Senjūrō cabinet · · · · · · · **8**:337a
Hayashi Shihei · · · ·林子平· · · · **3**:118a
naval defense · · · · · · · · · · **3**:118a
Hayashi Tadasu · · · ·林董· · · · **3**:118a
Hayashi Yūzō · · · ·林有造· **3**:118a–118b
Hayashizaki Jinsuke
Shigenobu ·林崎甚助重信· · · · **3**:253a
Hayato · · · · · · ·隼人· · · · **3**:118b
dialects · · · · · · · · · · · · **2**:91b
Kagoshima Prefecture · · · · · · **4**:105b
Hayatozuka ·隼人塚· · · · · · · **3**:118b
Hazama-Gumi, Ltd · · · · · · · **3**:118b
Hazama Shigetomi ·間重富· · · · **3**:309a
Haze (gobies) · · · · · · · · · · **3**:38b
Headgear · · · · · · · · · · · **3**:118b–119b
categories · · · · · · · · · · · **3**:118b
ceremonial · · · · · · · · · · · **3**:118b
functional · · · · · · · · · · · **3**:119a
Western influence · · · · · · · **3**:119a–119b

Headquarters for Pacification and
Defense · · · · · · · · · · · · **1**:296a
Health and Welfare, Ministry of · · · **7**:206a
Health care system · · · · · · **3**:119b–120b
health care activity · · · · · · · **3**:120a
medical education system · · · · · **3**:120a
medical facilities · · · · · · · **3**:120a–120b
medical services · · · · · · · · · **3**:120a
National Health Administration
· · · · · · · · · · · · · · · · **3**:119b–120a
personnel · · · · · · · · · · · **3**:120a
present conditions and priorities for
future · · · · · · · · · · · · · **3**:120b
Western influence · · · · · · · · **3**:119b
Health Insurance Law (Kenkō Hoken
Hō) · · · · · · · · · · · **5**:144b; **8**:270a
Health insurance system · · · · · · · **4**:47a
Hearken to the Ocean's Voice! · · · · **4**:206a
Hearn, Lafcadio · · · · **2**:41b; **3**:120b–121a
works · · · · · · · · · · · · **3**:120b–121a
Hearst, William Randolph · · · · · · **8**:323a
"Heart Learning" · · · · · · · · · **7**:111b–112a
Heart Mountain Relocation Center **3**:121a
Heaven · · · · · · · · **2**:80b; **3**:121a–121b
Heban shi shinrigaku
·奚般氏心理学· · · · · · · · **6**:260b
Hebei-Chahar (Hopeh-Chahar) Political
Council. *See* **Ji-Cha (Chi-Ch'a)
Autonomous Political Council**
Hebi · · · · · · · · · · · · · · · **7**:206b
Hebi Hime sama (Snake
Princess) · · · · · · ·蛇姫様· · · · **8**:289a
Heco, Joseph · · · · · · · · · · · **3**:89a
Heda Museum of Shipbuilding and Folk
Arts · · · · · · · · · · · · · **6**:270b
Hedonism in art · · · · · · · · · · **2**:378a
Hegurajima · · · · · ·舳倉島· · · · **3**:121b
Heianchō bumpō shi
(History of Heian Period
Grammar) ·平安朝文法史· · · · **8**:290a
Heian history. *See* **History of Japan**
Heian ibun (Documentary
Remains of the Heian
Period) · · · · · · · ·平安遺文· · · · **2**:104b
Heiankyō · · · · · · · · ·平安京· · · · **2**:350a;
3:121b–122b;
4:128a–128b, 334b; **5**:303b
administration · · · · · · · · · **3**:122a
crime · · · · · · · · · · · · · **3**:122a
design · · · · · · · · · · · · **3**:121b–122b
inhabitants · · · · · · · · · · · **3**:122a
urban life · · · · · · · · · **8**:176a 177a
urban planning · · · · · · · · · **8**:179b
Heian literature. *See* **Literature**
Heian period · · · · · ·平安時代· · · · **3**:122b
Heian Shrine · · · · ·平安神宮 **3**:122b; **4**:336a
Heibonsha, Ltd, Publishers · · · · **3**:122b
founder · · · · · · · · · · · · **7**:105b
Heichū monogatari
·平仲物語· **3**:122b–123a;
5:246a
kakekotoba · · · · · · · · · · · **4**:115b
monogatari bungaku · · · · · · · **5**:246a
Heifuku Kumiuchi · · · · · · · · · **4**:82a
Heigenji · · · · · · · · ·平間寺· · · · **4**:183a
Heiji Disturbance 平治の乱 · **3**:123a; **7**:96b
Fujiwara no Michinori, death of · · ·**2**:353a
Go-Shirakawa, Emperor · · · · · · · **3**:49a
Minamoto no Yorimasa · · · · · · **5**:180b
Minamoto no Yoshitomo · · · · · · **5**:182b
samurai · · · · · · · · · · · · · **7**:7b
Taira-Minamoto War · · · · · · · **7**:299b
Taira no Kiyomori · · · · · · · · **7**:301a
Taira no Shigemori · · · · · · · · **7**:302a
warrior government · · · · · · · · **8**:229a
Heiji monogatari 平治物語 · · · · **3**:69a,
123a–123b; **5**:43b, 246a
gunki monogatari · · · · · · · · **3**:69a–69b

Heiji monogatari ekotoba (Tale of Heiji
scrolls) · · · · ·平治物語絵詞· · · · **6**:*152a*
Heiji monogatari emaki
· · · · · · ·平治物語絵巻 **1**:137a; **3**:123b
episodes illustrated · · · · · · · **3**:123b
styles · · · · · · · · · · · · · **3**:123b
Heiji no Ran. *See* **Heiji Disturbance**
Heijōkyō · · · · · · · · ·平城京 **2**:350a; **3**:124a;
5:303b
artifacts · · · · · · · · · · · · **3**:124a
design · · · · · · · · · · · · · **3**:124a
Kizugawa and · · · · · · · · · · **4**:233b
Nara National Research Institute of
Cultural Properties · · · · · · **5**:333a–333b
temples · · · · · · · · · · · · **3**:124a
urban life · · · · · · · · · · **8**:176a, 177a
urban planning · · · · · · · · · **8**:179b
Heijō Palace site ·平城宮址· · · · **5**:334a
Heike monogatari
· · · · · · ·平家物語· · · · **1**:40a, 294a;
2:101b, 241a; **3**:124a–125a; **5**:43b, 246a;
7:270a, 299a
gunki monogatari · · · · · · · · **3**:69a–69b
Buddhist doctrine · · · · · · · · **3**:125a
chanting · · · · · · · · · · · · **3**:125a
biwa hōshi · · · · · · · · · · · **1**:157b
heikyoku · · · · · · · · · · · · **3**:125a
episodes · · · · · · · · · · · · **3**:124b
Giōji · · · · · · · · · · · · · · **3**:33b
gunki monogatari · · · · · · · · **3**:69a–69b
historiography · · · · · · · · · **3**:154a
Jakkōin · · · · · · · · · · · · · **4**:1a
Jesuit mission press · · · · · · · **4**:52a
Nō · · · · · · · · · · · · · · · **6**:26a
ochiudo legends · · · · · · · · · **6**:60a
otogi-zōshi · · · · · · · · · · · **6**:130a
Taira no Kiyomori · · · · · · · · **7**:301a
Tomoe Gozen · · · · · · · · · · **8**:73a
travel diaries · · · · · · · · · · **8**:105a
Heikyoku · · · · · · · · ·平曲 **2**:301a; **3**:125a
Nasu no Yoichi · · · · · · · · · **5**:336a
repertoire · · · · · · · · · · · **3**:125a
Heimin · · · · · · · · · · ·平民 **3**:125b; **7**:151a
shi-nō-kō-sho · · · · · · · · · · **7**:122b
Heiminsha · · · · · · · ·平民社 **1**:72a; **3**:125b
Fukuda Hideko · · · · · · · · · **2**:362a
Ishikawa Sanshirō · · · · · · · · **3**:344a
Kōtoku Shūsui · · · · · · · **3**:125b; **4**:279b
newspapers · · · · · · · · · · · **3**:125b
Russo-Japanese War · · · · · · · **6**:347a
Sakai Toshihiko · · · · · · · · · **6**:377a
Heimin shimbun ·平民新聞· **1**:2a; **3**:125b;
8:296b
pacifism · · · · · · · · · · · · **6**:144a
Russo-Japanese War · · · · · · · **6**:346b
suspension · · · · · · · · · · · **1**:252b
Heimin shugi · · · · · · · · · · · **8**:60b
Heimon · · · · · · · · · · · · · **3**:126a
Heinō bunri · · · · · ·兵農分離 **3**:187b; **4**:194a;
7:285a
Heirs, adopted · · · · · · · · · · · **1**:14b
Heishi. 平氏 *See* **Taira family**
Heiwa (Peace) · · · · · · ·平和· · · · **4**:174b
Heiwa Mondai Danwa Kai
(Discussion Committee
on the Problems of War)
· · · · · · · · · · · · · · · · **6**:144a, 145b
Heizei, Emperor. 平城天皇 *See*
Kusuko Incident
Hekian · · · · · · · · · · · · · · **4**:133b
Hekigotō kushū
· · · · · · · · ·碧梧桐句集· · · · **4**:178a
Hekinan · · · · · · · · ·碧南· · · · **3**:126a
Hekisho · · · · · · · · · ·壁書· · · · **4**:90a
Hekizan nichiroku
· · · · · · · · · ·碧山日録· · · · **3**:126a
Hell · · · · · · · · · · **2**:80b; **3**:126a
Emma · · · · · · · · · · · · · · **2**:201b

Hemeden ··········· 変目伝 ······· **3**:151a
Hemp ·································· **1**:91b
Henderson, Harold G ····· **3**:126a-126b
Henjō ············ 遍昭 · **3**:126b; **7**:13a
   Kokinshū ······················· **4**:245b
   Rokkasen ······················ **6**:334b
Hennen kiryaku ·· 編年紀略 ····· **5**:381a
Hentai kambun ··· 変体漢文 · **3**:126b-127a;
                      7:230a
   characteristics ················· **3**:127a
   styles ·························· **3**:126b
   used in *Kojiki* ················ **4**:251a
Hepburn, James Curtis ····· **1**:150b, 171a,
         308a; **3**:127a-127b
Hepburn system ················ **6**:335b
Herbicides ······················ **6**:309a
Herbs and spices ····· **2**:306b; **3**:127b
Hermit, The ···················· **3**:328a
Heroic tales ·············· **5**:296a-296b
Heroin abuse ··················· **2**:134a
Herons [(sagi) family Ardeidae]
                      3:127b-128a
Hero worship ········ **3**:128a; **8**:311a-311b
   characteristics ················· **3**:128a
   ochiudo legends ················· **6**:60a
Herring [(nishin) *Clupea pallasi*] ·· **2**:285b;
                       3:128a
Hetsumiya Shrine
      ········· 辺津宮 ··· **5**:264b-265a
Hettsui ························· **4**:120b
He-Umezu (Ho-Umezu)
  Agreement
       梅津—何応欽協定 **2**:126b; **3**:128b
   He Yingqin (Ho Ying-ch'in) ······· **3**:128b
   Umezu Yoshijirō ················ **8**:147b
Heusken, Henry C.J. ············ **3**:128b
   Harris, Townsend ··············· **3**:104a
Heya (sumō) ·············· **7**:272b-273a
He Yingqin (Ho Ying-ch'in) ······· **3**:128b
Hiai no kōchō · 悲哀の高調 ······· **8**:116a
Hibachi ······· **1**:267a; **2**:371b; **3**:128b-129a
Hibakusha ······· 被爆者 · **1**:111a, 114b
Hibakusha Special Welfare Law ··· **1**:110b
Hibara, Lake ······· 檜原湖 ····· **3**:129a
Hibari ························· **4**:368b
Hibi Ōsuke ······· 日比翁助 ····· **3**:129a
Hibiya Incendiary Incident ·· **3**:129a-129b;
                      4:274a
   Taishō democracy ··············· **7**:304b
Hibiya Park ······ 日比谷公園 · **3**:129b
Hibiya Yakiuchi Jiken. 日比谷焼打事件
   See **Hibiya Incendiary Incident**
Hiburishima ········· 日振島 · **3**:129b
Hichiriki ······················· **3**:129b
   gagaku ·························· **3**:1b
   kagura uta ····················· **4**:108a
Hida Folklore Village ·········· **3**:129b
Hidaka Mountains
        ··· 日高山脈 · **3**:130a; **4**:9b
Hida-Kisogawa
   Quasi-National Park
    飛驒木曽川国定公園 ··· **5**:319a
Hida Mountains · 飛驒山脈 ··· **3**:130a
Hidari Jingorō ··· 左甚五郎 · **3**:130a
Hidari Sachiko ··· 左幸子 · **2**:274b;
                   3:130a-130b
   director ························ **3**:130b
   films ··························· **3**:130a
Hiden'in ········· 悲田院 · **3**:130b; **7**:74a
   Kōfukuji building ··············· **4**:243b
   Kōmyō, Empress ················ **4**:268b
   seyakuin ························ **7**:74a
Hie
   Shintō ························· **7**:126b
Hieda no Are ··· 稗田阿礼 · **3**:130b;
                      6:112a

kataribe ······················· **4**:166b
Kojiki ··························· **4**:251a
Hieizan ········· 比叡山 **2**:220a; **3**:130b;
                     7:333a
Hie Shrine ······· 日吉大社, 日枝神社
  ·· **3**:130b-131a; **4**:137a; **6**:133b; **7**:91a, 180a
   annual festival ················· **3**:131b
   jinnin ························· **4**:59b
   religious symbolism ············· **6**:295b
   Sannō Festival ················· **7**:15a
   Shintō architecture ············· **7**:133b
Hifuryaku ········· 秘府略 ····· **1**:151b
Higaki kaisen
  (lozenge-fenced cargo
  ship) ········ 菱垣廻船 **4**:112b; **7**:144b
Higambana [(herb) *Lycoris radiata*]
                      3:131a
Higambana (Equinox
  Flower) ··········· 彼岸花 ····· **6**:141b
Higamu ·························· **7**:275b
Higan ············ 彼岸 ·· **2**:22a, 260a;
          3:131a-131b; **7**:276a
Higashi Ajia bunkaken
Higashi Hiroshima ·· 東広島 ······· **3**:131b
Higashi Honganji 東本願寺 · **3**:131b-132a
   architecture ··················· **3**:131b-132a
Higashikuni Naruhiko
  ·············· 東久邇稔彦 · **2**:3b; **3**:132a;
                    7:92a
Higashi Kurume · 東久留米 · **3**:132a
Higashi Matsuura
  Peninsula ····· 東松浦半島 · **3**:132a
Higashi Matsuyama 東松山 · **3**:132a
Higashi Murayama 東村山 · **3**:132a
Higashine ············ 東根 · **3**:132a
Higashi Nihon ······· 東日本 · **2**:142b
Higashi Ōsaka ···· 東大阪 · **3**:132a-132b
Higashi Shinakai · 東シナ海 · **2**:142a
Higashiyama culture
  ············ 東山文化 **1**:101a; **3**:132a
Higashi Yamato ··· 東大和 · **3**:132a
Higashiyama Zoological Gardens · **8**:379b
Higeki kigeki ···· 悲劇喜劇 · **3**:132b
High courts ········· **3**:138a; **4**:80b-81a, 190a
High Energy Physics, National
  Laboratory
  for ··························· **3**:133
Higher education ······· **3**:133a-135a
   and culture ···················· **3**:134a-135a
   development ···················· **3**:133a-133b
     government institutions ········· **3**:133a
     Imperial University ············· **3**:133a
     post-World War II ·············· **3**:133b
     private institutions ············· **3**:133a
   finance ························ **3**:134a
   multilayered multisector structure · **3**:133b
     private vs public sector ········· **3**:133b-134a
   types of schools ················ **3**:133b
Higher Girls' School Order in 1899 **8**:260a
Higher schools ················· **3**:135a
Highlands
   Ebino Kōgen ··················· **2**:143b
   Hachimantai ··················· **3**:74b
   Hiruzen Kōgen ················· **3**:151b
   Kirigamine ····················· **4**:220b
   Konsen ························· **4**:275b
   Kujū Kōgen ···················· **4**:303b
   Midagahara ···················· **5**:166b
   Nasu Kōgen ···················· **5**:335b-336a
   Sengokuhara ··················· **7**:64b
   Senjōgahara ···················· **7**:65b
   Shiga Kōgen ··················· **7**:89b
   Sugadaira ······················ **7**:256b
   Tateshina Kōgen ················ **7**:349a
High schools (Kōtō gakkō) ······· **2**:195b
High Treason Incident of 1910 ····· **1**:2a;
  2:241b; **3**:135a-136a; **4**:345a; **6**:127b;
         7:241b, 281a; **8**:296b

Futsū Senkyo Kisei Dōmeikai
  dissolution ···················· **2**:376b
  impact on intelligentsia ········· **3**:133b-134a
  Kanno Suga ···················· **4**:145b
  Kōtoku Shūsui ·················· **4**:297b
  prosecution's case ·············· **3**:135a-135b
  Red Flag Incident ··············· **6**:285b
  sentences ······················ **3**:135a-135b
  Uemura Masahisa ··············· **8**:128a
  Universal Manhood Suffrage Movement
                   8:169a
Highways ························· **6**:332b
Higuchi Ichiyō ····· 樋口一葉 · **3**:136a-136b;
                   5:11b
   early career ···················· **3**:136a-136b
   later career and death ··········· **3**:136b
   works ·························· **3**:136a-136b
   youthful literary interests ········ **3**:136a
Higuma (*Ursus arctos*) ··········· **1**:148a
Higurashi suzuri ··· 日暮硯 · **6**:106a
Hihyō ············ 批評 ···· **8**:298b
Hiikawa ············ 斐伊川 · **3**:136b
Hijikawa ············ 肱川 · **3**:136b
Hijiki [(alga) *Hizikia fusiformis*] ···· **3**:136b
Hijiri ············ **3**:136b-137a; **4**:299a
   nembutsu ······················ **4**:67a
   oshi ··························· **6**:124b
"Hikage no hana"
           ひかげの花 ····· **7**:176a
Hikaku Sangensoku ··········· **3**:137a-137b
   national defense ················ **5**:336b-338a
Hikan ············ 被官 · **3**:137b
Hikari ············ 光 · **3**:137b
Hikari to sono kaichō
  (Light and Its Harmony)
         光とその諧調 ····· **6**:186a
Hikawa Shrine ··· 氷川神社 · **3**:137b
Hikeshi ············ 火消 · **3**:137a,
             137b-138a
   fireman's uniforms, traditional
               2:280b-281a
Hikiate ························ **4**:117a
Hikidemono ···················· **3**:138a
Hikiita. *See* **Naruko**
Hikimawashi ····· 引回し · **3**:138a
Hikime Kagibana 引目鉤鼻 · **3**:20b
Hikitsuke ········· 引付 · **3**:138a; **4**:122a
Hikitsukeshū ····· 引付衆 · **4**:122a
Hiki Yoshikazu · 比企能員 · **3**:138a-138b
   assassination ··················· **1**:51a
Hikone ············ 彦根 · **3**:138b
Hikone byōbu · 彦根屏風 · **2**:377a, 378a
Hikone domain ··· 彦根藩 · **3**:263a
Hikosan ········· 英彦山 · **3**:138b
Hikoshima ········· 彦島 · **3**:138b
Hikyaku ············ 飛脚 · **3**:138b-139a
   postal service ·················· **6**:229a
Hill, James Jerome ············· **3**:139a
Hill-on-the-plain castle (hirayamajiro)
                  1:247b
Hills
   Iimoriyama ····················· **3**:262b
   Kasugayama ···················· **4**:164a
   Kiyosumiyama ·················· **4**:232b-233a
   Kunōzan ······················· **4**:310b
   Kuramayama ···················· **4**:311b
   Miwayama ······················ **5**:216b
   Myōkensan ····················· **5**:290b
   Nokogiriyama ··················· **6**:32b
   Ogurayama ····················· **6**:71b
   Ōsakayama ····················· **6**:123a-123b
   Senjōsan ······················· **7**:66a
   Shigisan ······················· **7**:92b
   Shiroyama ······················ **7**:148a
   Tama ·························· **7**:332b
   Tennōzan ······················ **8**:8b
   Togakushi Kōgen ················ **8**:35b
   Tōnomine ······················ **8**:75a

Yamato Sanzan ·········· 8:310b
Himachi and tsukimachi ····· 3:139a
Hi Matsuri (Kurama Fire
Festival) ···· 火祭 2:259a; 4:311b
Himebachi *(ichneumons)* ····· 1:149a
Himeji ···· 姫路 ········· 3:139a
Himeji Castle ·· 姫路城 1:247a; 3:139a
Himeji Plain ·· 姫路平野 ····· 3:139a
Himemasu ·················· 4:321b
Himeyuri Butai 姫百合部隊 ···· 3:139b
Himi ···· 氷見 ············ 3:139b
Himiko ····· 卑弥呼 3:139b-140a,
160b; 8:305a-305b
Wei China ·········· 3:139b-140a
Wei zhi (Wei chih) ········ 8:240a
*Himitsu mandara jūjūshin
ron* · 秘密曼荼羅十住心論 ···· 4:83b
Himmin shinri no kenkyū
···· 貧民心理の研究 ····· 4:104a
Hinagu Hot Spring
··· 日奈久温泉 ····· 8:320a
Hina Matsuri ···· 雛祭 ·· 2:127b-128a
Hinatsu Kōnosuke
·········· 日夏耿之介 ··· 3:140a
Hinawajū ···· 火縄銃 ········· 3:140a
Hinin ···· 非人 ·· 3:140a; 7:62a
shi-nō-kō-shō ············ 7:122b
Hino ···· 日野 ············ 3:140b
Hino Ashihei ·· 火野葦平 3:140b; 7:103b
Hino family ··· 日野氏 ····· 3:140b
*Hi no hashira (Pillar of
Fire)* ········ 火の柱 ··· 6:254a
Hinoki ·············· 2:53b-54a
Hinomaru. ***See* National flag**
Hino micro-mixing system ······· 3:140b
Hinomisaki ·· 日御碕 ·········· 3:140b
Hino Motors, Ltd ······· 3:140b-141a
automotive industry ········· 1:121b
Hino Tomiko ·· 日野富子 ······ 3:141a
Hinoyama Park 火の山公園 ····· 7:105b
Hinuma ········ 涸沼 ······· 3:141a
Hirabayashi Hatsunosuke
·········· 平林初之輔 ··· 3:141a
Hirabayashi Taiko
········· 平林たい子 · 3:141a-141b
proletarian literature movement ··· 6:255a
Hirabayashi v US (320 US 81) ····· 4:18a
Hirado ···· 平戸 3:141b; 7:256b
Dutch East India Company ·· 2:330a
Hiradoshima ·· 平戸島 ····· 3:141b
Hirafuku Hyakusui
········· 平福百穂 · 3:141b-142a
Kaburagi Kiyokata ········· 4:100b
Hiraga Gennai ··· 平賀源内 ··· 1:225a;
3:142a-142b
gesaku ················· 3:28b
herbal medicine ··········· 3:142a
kokkeibon ················ 4:256a
Nakagawa Jun'an ········· 5:313a
pseudonyms ·············· 3:142a
Satake Shozan ············· 7:25b
sharebon ················ 7:80a
Shikitei Samba ············ 7:97a
taketombo ················ 7:325b
works ·············· 3:142a-142b
Hiraga Motoyoshi
·········· 平賀元義 ··· 3:142b
Hiragana ·· 1:153b; 4:131b; 6:248b; 7:163a
Hiraga Renkichi · 平賀練吉 ··· 3:142b
Hiraga Yuzuru · 平賀譲 ····· 3:142b
Hiragushi Denchū
·········· 平櫛田中 ··· 3:142b-143a
Hiraide site ·· 平出遺跡 ····· 3:143a
Hiraizumi ···· 平泉 ········· 3:143a
Ōshū Fujiwara family ··· 6:126a-127a
urbanization ·············· 8:176a
Hirakata ···· 枚方 ········· 3:143a
Hira maki-e ···· 平蒔絵 · 4:240b, 360b

Hira Mountains 比良山地 ··· 3:143a
Hirano Ken ··· 平野謙 · 3:143b; 5:13b,
316b-317a
Hirano Kuniomi · 平野国臣 ··· 3:143b
Hirano Yoshitarō
·········· 平野義太郎 ··· 3:143b
Hiranuma Kiichirō
·········· 平沼騏一郎 ··· 3:143b-144a
Ministry of Justice ········· 3:143b
National Spiritual Mobilization
Movement ·············· 5:347a
prime minister ············ 3:144a
right wing philosophy ····· 3:143b
Hiranuma Kiichirō cabinet
Arita Hachirō ············· 1:85a
Yonai Mitsumasa ·········· 8:337a
Hiranuma Ryōzō · 平沼亮三 ··· 3:144b
Hirao ················· 4:308a
Hiraodai ···· 平尾台 ········· 3:144b
Hiraoka Kōtarō 平岡浩太郎 ··· 8:88a
Hirara ······ 平良 ········· 3:144b
Hirasawa Tsunetomi. 平沢常富
See **Hōseidō Kisanji**
Hirase Sakugorō
·········· 平瀬作五郎 ··· 3:144b-145a
Koishikawa Botanic Garden ·· 4:250a
Hirashimizu ware 平清水焼 ··· 3:145a
decoration ··············· 3:145a
Hirata ···· 平田 ·········· 3:145a
Hirata Atsutane ·· 平田篤胤 ·· 1:211b;
3:145a-145b; 5:17b; 7:28b, 94b, 264a
Kokugaku ············ 4:257b-258b
works ·············· 3:145a-145b
Hirata Gōyō ····· 平田郷陽 2:130b; 3:145b
Hirata Tokuboku 平田禿木 ··· 3:145b
Hirata Tōsuke ·· 平田東助 · 1:21b; 3:145b
Hiratsuka ···· 平塚 3:146a; 4:135a;
7:335a
Hiratsuka Raichō
·········· 平塚雷鳥 1:155b; 3:146a;
7:54b
Fujin kōron publication ····· 2:344a
Ichikawa Fusae ············ 3:257a
photo ··················· 3:146b
Seitōsha ················ 7:54b
Shin Fujin Kyōkai ········· 7:111b
social concerns ············ 3:146a
Hiratsuka Tsunejirō
·········· 平塚常次郎 ··· 3:146a
Hiratsuka Un'ichi
·········· 平塚運一 ··· 3:146b
modern prints ············· 5:232b
Hirayama Teruo 平山輝雄 ··· 4:31a
Hirayu Hot Spring
·········· 平湯温泉 ··· 1:5a; 3:146b
Hiro, Prince ····· 浩宮 3:147b, 277a
Hiroba no kodoku (Alone
in the Marketplace)
········· 広場の孤独 3:240a; 6:231a
Hirohata ···· 広畑 ········· 3:146b
Hirohito, Emperor 天皇, 裕仁 2:207a-207b;
3:147a, 147b; 277a
February 26th Incident ····· 2:249b
politics ·················· 3:147a
renunciation of divinity by emperor
···················· 2:209a
Sakuradamon Incident ······· 7:4b
Hirohito, Prince Regent ····· 8:76a
Hiroi Isamu ··· 広井勇 ····· 3:147b
Hiroioya ················· 7:279b
Hironaka Heisuke
·········· 広中平祐 ··· 3:147b
Hirosaki ···· 弘前 ········· 3:147b
Hirose ··················· 7:126b
Hirose Saihei · 広瀬宰平 · 3:147b; 7:267a
Hirose Shrine ·· 広瀬神社 · 3:147b-148a
Tatsuta Shrine ············ 7:350a
Hirose Takeo ··· 広瀬武夫 ··· 3:148a

Hirose Tansō ···· 広瀬淡窓 3:148a; 4:233a;
7:94b
Hiroshige ····· 広重 · 1:211b, 300b;
3:148a-149b; 8:144b
illustrations ·········· 3:148a-148b
kachōga prints ··········· 3:148b
landscapes ·········· 3:148a-148b
Shōno (Rain at Shōno) ···· 3:148b
Tōkaidō gojūsantsugi (Fifty-three Stations
of the Tōkaidō) ········· 3:148b
Hiroshige II ·· 広重(二代) ··· 3:149a
Hiroshige III ·· 広重(三代) ··· 3:149a
Hiroshige IV ·· 広重(四代) ··· 3:149a-149b
Hiroshima ········ 広島 1:108b; 3:149b;
8:276a
atomic bomb ·············· 3:149b
atomic bomb related diseases 1:111b-112a
Chūgoku region ············ 1:312a
Peace Memorial Park cenotaph ··· 3:149a
peace movement ······· 6:166a-166b
Shindō Kaneto ············ 7:111b
Hiroshima Bay ·· 広島湾 ··· 3:149b
Hiroshima Maidens programs ····· 1:111a
Hiroshima Peace Center ········ 7:340b
Hiroshima Plain 広島平野 ··· 3:149b
Hiroshima Prefectural Women War
Victims (1948) ··········· 1:111a
Hiroshima Prefecture
·········· 広島県 ··· 3:149b-150a
Hiroshima University ······· 3:150a
Hirota ··················· 7:126b
Hirota-Karakhan fishing agreements
···················· 3:150a
Hirota Kōki ···· 広田弘毅 · 3:150a-150b;
7:28a; 8:225a
February 26th Incident ····· 2:250a
military policies ··········· 3:150b
Hirota Kōki cabinet
Arita Hachirō ············· 1:85a
Nagano Osami ············ 5:302b
Hirota Shrine ··· 広田神社 ··· 3:150b
Hirotsu Kazuo ·· 広津和郎 3:151a; 5:13a
Hirotsu Ryūrō ·· 広津柳浪 ··· 3:151a
Ken'yūsha ················ 4:199a
Shinshōsetsu ············ 7:125b
"tragic novels" ············ 3:151a
Hiru ···················· 4:374b
Hirugao [(bindweed) *Calystegia
japonica*] ············ 3:151a
Hiruzen Kōgen · 蒜山高原 ··· 3:151b
Hisago ················ 3:151b
Hisai ················· 3:151b
Hisaita Eijirō · 久板栄二郎 ··· 3:151b
Hisamatsu Sen'ichi 久松潜一
Kokutai no hongi, prepared draft ···· 4:264a
Hisamatsu Shin'ichi
·········· 久松真一 ··· 3:151b
Hisao Jūran ··· 久生十蘭 ··· 3:151b
Hishi ··················· 1:153b
Hishida Shunsō 菱田春草 · 3:151b-152a;
6:157a
style ··················· 3:152a
Hishikawa Moronobu
·········· 菱川師宣 ··· 5:255b-256a;
6:155b; 8:138b
Hishizashi stitches ··········· 7:24b
Historians. *See* **Discipline of Japanese
history: a guide to research**
Historical documents. *See* **Diplomatics**
Historical Materials of Great Japan · 2:65b
Historical periods. *See* **Periodization**
Historical scholarship ····· 2:101a-116b
diplomatics. *See* **Diplomatics**
history, views of ······ 2:101a-102b
Confucian ·············· 2:102a
laws of history ········· 2:101b-102a
loyalty, theory of ········· 2:102a
modern period ········· 2:102a-102b

myth and history · · · · · · · · · 2:101a–101b
　as story · · · · · · · · · · · · · · · · · · 2:101b
　local · 5:71a–71b
medieval and early modern · · · 2:106–110a
　Azuchi-Momoyama and Edo periods
　· 2:108a–109b
　Kamakura period · · · · · · · · · 2:106b–107a
　Muromachi period · · · · · · · · 2:107b–108a
modern and contemporary · · · 2:110a–112b
　modern Japan · · · · · · · · · · · 2:110a–111a
　research areas · · · · · · · · · · · 2:111a–112b
prehistory and ancient history
　· 2:102b–106b
　arts · · · · · · · · · · · · · · · · · · 2:150a–150b
　documentary sources · · · · · · 2:104b–105a
　fifth century and earlier · · · · · · 2:103a–103b
　ninth to eleventh centuries · · · · · 2:104b
　religion · · · · · · · · · · · · · · · · · · 2:105a
　seventh and eighth centuries
　· 2:104a–104b
　sixth century · · · · · · · · · · · 2:103b–104a
source materials · · · · · · · · · · · · 2:115a–116a
　ancient period · · · · · · · · · · · · · 2:115b
　early modern period · · · · · · · · · · 2:116a
　general · · · · · · · · · · · · · · · 2:115a–115b
　medieval period · · · · · · · · · · · · · 2:116a
　modern and contemporary periods
　· 2:116a–116b
Historical tales (rekishi monogatari)
　· 5:246a
*Historik: ein Organo geschichtlichen
Denkens und Forschens* · · · · · · · · 6:312a
　publications · · · · · · · · · · · · · · · 3:156b
**Historiographical Institute, Tokyo
University** · · · · · · · · · · · · 2:65a; 3:152a
　Dajōkan (Grand Council of State) · · · 2:70b
　publications · · · · · · · · · · · · · · · 3:156b
Historiography · · · · · · · · · · 3:152a–158a
　aristocratic age · · · · · · · · · 3:152a–153b
　　official histories · · · · · · · · 3:152a–153b
　　unofficial histories · · · · · · · 3:152a–153b
　Edo period · · · · · · · · · · · · · 3:154b–156a
　　beginnings of modern · · · · · · · · 3:155a
　　critical historical scholarship · · · · · 3:155b
　　Japanese classicists · · · · · · · · · 3:155a
　　new national histories · · · · · · · · 3:154b
　feudal age · · · · · · · · · · · · · 3:153b–154b
　　contemporary affairs · · · · · · · · 3:154a
　　critical approach · · · · · · · · 3:153b–154b
　　Gukanshō · · · · · · · · · · · · · · 3:65a–65b
　　popular literature · · · · · · · 3:153b–154a
　　traditional writing · · · · · · · · · · 3:154a
　modern period · · · · · · · · · · 3:156a–157b
　　new academic tradition · · · · · · · 3:156a
　　perspectives and interests · · · 3:156b–157b
　　scholarship · · · · · · · · · · · · · · 3:156a
　recent trends · · · · · · · · · · · · · · 3:157b
　　Marxist influence · · · · · · · · 3:157b–158a
　　Western influence · · · · · · · 3:156a–157b
　specialization · · · · · · · · · · · 3:156b–157a
　　cultural · · · · · · · · · · · · · 3:156b–157a
　　historical materialism · · · · · 3:156a–156b
　　socioeconomic · · · · · · · · · · 3:156a–157b
History of Great Japan · 2:65a–65b; 7:164a
History of Japan · · · · · 2:101b; 3:158a–206a;
　· 4:101b
　Asuka · · · · · · · · · · · · · · · · 3:161b–163b
　　Buddhism and Soga family · 3:162a–162b
　　Fujiwara capital · · · · · · · · 3:163a–163b
　　Korea · · · · · · · · · · · · · · · 3:162a–162b
　　Taika Reforms · · · · · 3:162b; 7:295a–297a
　　Temmu · · · · · · · · · · · · · · 3:162b–163a
　　Yamato court · 3:161b–162a; 8:308b–309a
　Azuchi-Momoyama · · · · · · · · 3:177b–185b
　　culture · · · · · · · · · · · · · · 3:180b–181a
　　institutional developments · 3:178b–180b
　　international dimension · · · · 3:184b–185b
　　periodization · · · · · · · · · · 3:177b–178b

Shokuhō seiken · · · · · · · · · · · 7:164b–165a
Edo · · · · · · · · · · · · · · · · · · 3:185b–192b
　bakuhan state · · · · · · · · · · 3:188b–189b
　bakuhan system, administration
　· 3:187a–187b
　bakuhan system, social structure
　· · · · · · · · · · · · · · · 1:131a–133a; 3:187b–188b
　bakumatsu · · · · · · · · · · · · · 3:192a–192b
　economy and culture · · · · · · 3:189b–191a
　intellectual ferment · · · · · · · 3:191a–192a
　seclusion · · · · · · · · · 3:188b; 5:346b–347a
　Tokugawa power structure · 3:186a–186b
　Tokugawa regime · · · · · · · · 3:186a–187a
　Tokugawa shogunate · · · · · · · 8:52b–56a
Heian · · · · · · · · · · · · · · · · · 3:165a–169b
　art · · · · · · · · · · · · · · · · · · 3:169a–169b
　cultural life · · · · · · · · · · · · · · · 3:168a
　institutions · · · · · · · · · · · · 3:165b–166a
　landholding system · · · · · · · 3:166b–168a
　literature · · · · · · · · · · · · · · 3:168b–169a
　Nara, Nagaoka, Kyōto · · · · 3:121b–122b,
　· 165a–165b
　politics and government · · · · 3:166a–166b
　regency government · · · · · · · 6:286a–290a
　religion · · · · · · · · · · · · · · · 3:168a–168b
Kamakura · · · · · · · · · · · · · · · 3:169b–172a
　arts · · · · · · · · · · · · · · · · · · 3:171b–172a
　background · · · · · · · · · · · · · · · 3:170a
　Buddhism · · · · · · · · · · · · · 3:171a–171b
　constitution of military class 3:170a–170b
　economy · · · · · · · · · · · · · · · · · 3:171a
　Hōjō Regency · · · · · 3:170b–171a; 7:97
　life of warrior · · · · · · · · · · · · · · 3:170b
　Mongol invasions · · · 3:171a; 5:243b–245a
　shogunate · · · · · · · · · 3:172a; 4:121b–122b
Meiji · · · · · · · · · · · · · · · · · · 3:192b–197b
　abolition of feudalism · · · · · 3:193a–194b
　constitutional government · 3:195b–196b
　institution building · · · · · · · 3:194b–195b
　Meiji Constitution · · · · · · · · · · · 2:1a–3b
　Meiji Restoration · · · · · · · · 5:155a–160a
　role of emperor · · · · · · · · · 3:192b–193a
　Russo-Japanese War · · · · · · 3:196b–197a;
　· 6:345b–347a
　Sino-Japanese War of 1894–1895
　· 7:197b–198a
Muromachi · · · · · · · · · · · · · · 3:172a–177b
　central government · · · · · · · 3:173a–174b
　economic and social developments
　· 3:175a–176b
　interpretations · · · · · · · · · · · · · 3:173a
　local rule · · · · · · · · · · · · · · 3:174b–175a
　Muromachi shogunate · · · · · 5:271b–274a
　Northern and Southern Courts 6:39a–40a
　religion and culture · · · · · · · 3:176b–177b
　Sengoku period · · · · · · · · · · 7:64a–64b
Nara · · · · · · · · · · · · · · · · · · 3:163b–165a
　end of period · · · · · · · · · · · 3:164b–165a
　Heijōkyō · · · · · · · · · · · · · · · · · 3:124a
　ritsuryō system · · · · · · · · · · 3:163b–164a;
　· 6:322a–332a
　Tempyō culture · · · · · · · · · · 3:164a–164b
postwar · · · · · · · · · · · · · · · · 3:203a–206a
　Constitution of 1947 · · · · · · · · · 2:3b–7a
　economic development · · · · · · · · 3:205b
　economic growth · · · · · · · · · 3:203a–203b
　educational system · · · · · · · · · · 3:204a
　end of era · · · · · · · · · · · · · 3:205b–206a
　foreign affairs · · · · · · · · · · · · · · 3:205a
　political system · · · · · · · · · 3:204a–205a;
　· 6:213b–217a
　social changes · · · · · · · · · · 3:203b–204a
prehistory · · · · · · · · · · · · · · · 3:158a–160a
　Jōmon period · · · · · · 3:158b–159b; 4:72a–74a
　Paleolithic period · · · · · · · · 3:158a–158b;
　· 6:159b–160a
　Yayoi period · · · 3:159b–160a; 8:321a–322a
　protohistory · · · · · · · · · · · · 3:160a–161b

early and middle Kofun period
　· · · · · · · · · · · · · 3:160b–161b; 4:244a–246a
late Yayoi period · · · · · · · · · · · · 3:160b
Taishō and early Shōwa · · · · · 3:197b–203a
　bureaucratic government · · · · · · · 3:200b
　change in leadership · · · · · · · 3:197b–199a
　China War · 3:201a–202a; 7:199a–202a
　economic recovery · · · · · · · · · · 3:201a
　Pacific War · · · 3:202a–203a; 8:271b–278b
　wartime boom and postwar
　depression · · · · 3:199b–200a; 8:270b–271b
　wartime political structure · · · · · 3:202a
　World War I and postwar foreign
　policy · · · · · · · · · · · · · · · · · · · 3:199a
　years of crisis · · · · · · · · · · · 3:200a–200b
History of Japanese Religion · · · · · · · 1:56b
Hita (city) · · · · · · · · · · · · 日田 · · · · 3:206a
Hita Basin · · · · · · · 日田盆地 · · 3:206a–206b
Hitachi, Prince · · · · · · 常陸宮 · · · · 3:207b
Hitachi (city) · · · · · · · · 日立 · · · · 3:206b
Hitachibō Kaison
　· · · · · · · · · · · 常陸坊海尊 · · · · · · 1:42a
Hitachi Cable, Ltd · · · · · · · · · · · 3:206b
Hitachi Chemical Co, Ltd · · · · · 3:206b
Hitachi Corporation
　Tōshiba Corporation · · · · · · · · · · 8:82b
Hitachi Ltd · · · · · · · · · · · · · 3:206b–207a
　in *Pak Chong-sŏk v. Hitachi, Ltd* · · · 4:291b
Hitachi Metals Ltd · · · · · · · · · · · 3:207a
Hitachi Ōta · · · · · · · 常陸太田 · · · · 3:207a
**Hitachi Plant Engineering &
Construction Co, Ltd** · · · · · · · · 3:207a
Hitachi Sales Corporation · · · · · · 3:207b
Hitachi Zōsen Corporation · · · · · 3:207b
Hitler, Adolf · · · · · · · · · · · · · · · 8:272b
Hitobashira · · · · · · · · · · · · · · · · 3:207b
Hitodama · · · · · · · · · · · · · · · · · 3:207b
Hitoegusa (seaweed) · · · · · · · · · · · 7:47a
Hitogaeshi · · · · · · · · 人返し · · 3:207b–208a
Hitogata · · · · · · · · · · · · · · · · · · · 4:166b
Hitojichi · · · · · · · · · · · 人質 · · · · 3:208a
Hitomi Kinue · · · · 人見絹枝 · · · · 3:208a
Hito no Michi Kyōdan
　· · · · · · · · · · ひとのみち教団 · · · · · · 6:192b
Hitori musuko (The Only
Son) · · · · · · · · 一人息子 · · · · 6:141b
Hitorishizuka (*Chloranthus japonicus*)
　· 3:208a
Hitō Shōgō Sakusen
　· · · · · · · · · · 比島捷号作戦 · · · · · · 6:115a
Hitosuji no michi
　· · · · · · · · · ひとすじの道 · · · · · 4:169b
Hitotsubashi University 3:133a, 208a–208b
Hitotsume kozō · · · · · · · · · · · · · 3:208b
Hitoyogiri · · · · · · · · · · · · · · 3:208b; 7:75b
Hitoyoshi (city) · · · · · · · 人吉 · · · · 3:208b
Hitoyoshi Basin · · · 人吉盆地 · · · · 3:208b
Hitsuji no uta · · · · · · · · 羊の歌 · · · · 4:169b
Hittōsha · · · · · · · · · · · · · · · · · · · 3:240a
Hiuchigadake · · · · · · 燧ケ岳 2:366b; 3:208b
Hiyuka poems · · · · · · · · · · · · · · · · 5:105b
Hizakurige series · · · · · · · · · · · 4:61a–61b
Hizōhōyaku · · · · · · · 秘蔵宝鑰 · · · · 4:83b
Hō · 2:91b
Hoan Jōrei · · · · · · · · · 保安条例 · · · · 6:167b
Hoantai · 5:346a
Hoashi Banri · · · · · 帆足万里 · · 3:208b–209a
Ho Chi Minh · · · · · · · · · · · · · · · · 2:333a
Hōchi shimbun · · · 報知新聞 3:209a; 8:355a
Hoderi no Mikoto · · · 火照命 · 5:294b–295a
Hodosan · · · · · · · · · · 宝登山 · · · · 3:209a
Hoes · 4:322a
Hoffman, Hermann · · · · · · · · · · · · 7:229a
Hoffman, Johann Joseph · · · · · · · 3:209a
Hōfu · · · · · · · · · · · · · 防府 · · · · · 3:209a
Hōgen · · · · · · · · · · · · 法眼 · · · · · 7:270a
**Hōgen Disturbance of
1156** · · · · · · · 保元の乱 · · · 3:209a–209b

Fujiwara family ············ **2:**348b
Go-Shirakawa, Emperor ····· **3:**49b
insei ······················· **3:**315a
Minamoto no Yorimasa ····· **5:**180b
samurai ····················· ＇**7:**7b
Taiki ······················· **7:**297b
Taira family ················ **7:**299a
Taira-Minamoto War ········· **7:**299b
Taira no Kiyomori ·········· **7:**301a
Taira no Shigemori ········· **7:**302a
Taira no Tadamori ·········· **7:**302a
Toba, Emperor ·············· **8:**31b
warrior government ········· **8:**229a
Hōgen monogatari
··················· 保元物語 ··· **3:**69a-69b,
　　　　　　　　　209b; **5:**43b, 246a
Heiji monogatari ··········· **3:**123b
texts ······················ **3:**209b
Hōgen no Ran. See **Hōgen Disturbance**
Hōgen to kaishaku
··············· 方言と解釈 ······ **7:**259a
Hōgo. See **Goroku**
Hōhei kōshō ····· 砲兵工廠 ··· **3:**210a
Hohnen Oil Co, Ltd ········· **3:**210a
Hōitsu. 抱一　See **Sakai Hōitsu**
Hōji Conflict ···· 宝治合戦 ··· **3:**210a-210b
Hōjin ····················· **3:**210b
tax law ···················· **7:**355a-358b
Hōjō ·················· 北条 ··· **3:**210b
Hōjō Dansui 北条団水 ··· **3:**210b-211a
Hōjō family ···· 北条氏 ··· **3:**211a; **7:**58a,
　　　　　　　　　　　　　　70a
Hōjō Masako ··············· **4:**122a
Hōjō Sōun ·················· **4:**118b
Kamakura shogunate ········ **4:**122a
Mongol invasions of Japan ·· **5:**244a
museums ··················· **5:**277a
Nakasendai Rebellion ······· **5:**317b
rule ······················· **2:**204b
Samurai-dokoro (Board of Retainers) **7:**8b
shikken ···················· **7:**97b
Taira no Yoritsuna ········· **7:**302b
Uesugi Kenshin ············· **8:**129b-130a
warrior government ········· **8:**229a
Hōjō godai ki 北条五代記 **2:**279a; **3:**211a;
　　　　　　　　　　　　　4:187b
Hōjō Hideji ···· 北条秀司 ··· **3:**211a-211b
"Ōshō" ····················· **7:**121a
Hōjōki (An Account of My
Hut) ················ 方丈記 ··· **4:**129a; **5:**43b
Hojokin ···················· **3:**56a
Hōjō Masako ···· 北条政子 ··· **3:**211b
Eisai ······················ **2:**187a
Jōkyū Disturbance ········· **4:**72a
Minamoto no Yoriie ········ **4:**122a
Minamoto no Yoritomo ····· **4:**181a
Hōjō no umi (The Sea of
Fertility) ········· 豊饒の海 ··· **6:**231b
Hōjō Sanetoki. See **Kanazawa Bunko**
Hōjō Sōun ····· 北条早雲 ·· **3:**211a, 211b;
　　　　　　　　　　　　　　7:64b
Sōunji Dono Nijūikkajō ·········· **4:**118b
Hōjō Takatoki ·· 北条高時 ·· **3:**172a, 211b;
　　　　　　　　　　　　　　5:317b
Hōjō Tamio ···· 北条民雄 ·· **3:**211b-212a
Hōjō Tokimasa ·· 北条時政 ·· **3:**211a, 212a;
　　　　　　　　　　　　4:181a; **7:**97b
Hōjō Tokimune ·· 北条時宗 ·· **3:**171a, 212a
Hōjō Tokiyori ·· 北条時頼 ·· **1:**11a; **3:**212a;
　　　　　　　　　　　　7:58a, 80b
Hōjō Tokiyuki ···· 北条時行 ··· **5:**317b
Hōjō Yasutoki ·· 北条泰時 ·· **3:**212a-212b;
　　　　　　　　　　　　7:85b, 97b
Jōkyū Disturbance ········· **4:**72a
Hōjō Yoshitoki 北条義時 ·· **3:**212a-212b
Hōjō Sanetoki ············· **4:**136a
Jōkyū Disturbance ········· **4:**72a
Hōka ················ 放下 ··· **3:**212b

Hōkaiji ········· 法界寺 ··· **3:**212b
Hōkan ············ 幇間 ··· **3:**342b
Hokekyō ··········· 法華経 ··· **5:**74a
Hōken seido ······ 封建制度 ·· **2:**263a
Hōken taiki ······ 保建大記 ·· **4:**313b
Hokkaidō ········ 北海道 ··· **3:**212b-213a;
　　　　　　　　　　　　　　4:7a
area ······················· **4:**2b
capital ····················· **7:**20a
population density ········· **4:**2b, 7a
Russia ····················· **6:**340b
Hokkaidō Colonization
Office (Kaitakushi)
············· 開拓使 **1:**243b; **4:**113a;
　　　　　　　　　　　　　　5:299a＇
Hokkaidō Colonization Office Scandal
of 1881 ········· **3:**213a-213b; **4:**113a
Hokkaidō Development Agency · **1:**219a;
　　　　　　　　　　　　3:213a-214b
Hokkaidō Electric Power Co, Inc · **3:**214a
Hokkaidō Kaihatsu Hō
····························· **3:**213b-214a
Hokkaidō shimbun
··············· 北海道新聞 ··· **3:**214a
Hokkaidō Takushoku Bank, Ltd · **1:**139a;
　　　　　　　　　　　　　　3:214a
Hokkaidō University ········· **3:**214a
Hokkatei ·········· 北花亭 ··· **4:**189b
Hokke gengi shakusen
············· 法華玄義釈選 ··· **6:**248a
Hokke gisho (Commentary on the Lotus
Sutra) ········· 法華義疏 ··· **1:**234b
Hokkeji ········· 法華寺 ·· **3:**214a-214b
Kōmyō, Empress ·········· **4:**268b
Hokkekyō ········ 法華経 ·· **1:**180b
Hokke metsuzai no tera
············· 法華滅罪之寺 ··· **4:**257a
Hokku ····················· **3:**78b
Hokkyō ············ 法橋 ··· **7:**270a
Kōrin's award ············· **4:**293a
Hōkō Fishing Co, Ltd ·· **2:**284a; **3:**214b
Hōkōji. 法興寺　See **Asukadera**
Hōkōnin ··················· **2:**211b-212b
Hokubei yūzeiki (A
Stumping Tour of North
America) ······ 北米遊説記 ··· **8:**117a
Hokuetsu Paper Mills, Ltd ···· **3:**214b
Hokuetsu seppu (Annals
of Snow in the Hokuetsu
Region) ········ 北越雪譜 ··· **3:**214b
Hokuman Tetsudō
············· 北満鉄道 ··· **1:**292a-292b
Hokumen no bushi
············· 北面の武士 ·· **3:**214b-215a
Shirakawa, Emperor ······· **7:**146b
takiguchi no bushi ········· **7:**326b
Hokuriku ·········· 北陸 ··· **7:**46a
Hokuriku Electric Power Co, Inc · **3:**215a
Hokuriku Industrial Zone ·· **8:**87b
Hokusai ·········· 北斎 ·· **1:**170a, 211b;
　　3:215a-216a; **5:**101a; **7:**17b, 79a; **8:**143b
Fugaku sanjūrokkei (Thirty-six Views of
Mt Fuji) ····················· **3:**215a
Mt Fuji Viewed Through Waves Off the
Coast of Kanagawa ··········· **3:**215a
Hokusai manga 北斎漫画 ··· **8:**143b
Hokushin Jihen 北清事変 ··· **1:**166a-166b
Hokutei ··········· 北亭 ··· **4:**189b
Holding companies ·· **2:**31b; **3:**216a
Antimonopoly Law ········ **3:**216a
Holidays ·················· **3:**216b
national. See **Festivals**
Holy Orthodox Church ··· **1:**308a; **3:**216b
Holy Spirit Association for the
Unification of World Christianity
····························· **3:**216b-217a
Hombyakushō ······ 本百姓 ··· **3:**217a
gōson system ············· **3:**50b-51a

shinden kaihatsu ·········· **7:**110a
Home economics
school curriculum ········· **7:**35a
Home life
family. See Family life
lifestyles ·················· **5:**7b
Home Ministry (Naimushō) · **3:**217a-217b;
　　　　　　　　　　　　　　6:198a
fukoku kyōhei leadership ··· **2:**361a
Ōkubo Toshimichi ········· **6:**94b
urban planning ············ **8:**180a
Homma Art Museum ········· **5:**276b
Homma Kazuo ······ 本間一夫 ·· **4:**10b
Hommonji ········ 本門寺 ··· **3:**217b
Hommon sect　　本門宗
Taisekiji ··················· **7:**303b
Homosexuality ·········· **3:**217b-218a
legal history ··············· **3:**218a
Hōmushō ········ 法務省 ··· **5:**191b
Homutawake no Mikoto
··············· 誉田別尊 ··· **6:**76b
Hon'ami Kōetsu
········· 本阿弥光悦 **1:**153a, 166b,
　193b, *235a*, 236a; **3:**182a, *218b*, 218b-219a
Furuta Oribe ·············· **2:**373b
rimpa ····················· **3:**317b
Honchō gashi ···· 本朝画史 ·· **4:**148b, 150a
Honchō jinja kō
··············· 本朝神社考 ··· **7:**128b
Honchō monzui 本朝文粋 **1:**293a; **2:**350a;
　　　　　　　　　　3:219a; **5:**37a
Honchō seiki ···· 本朝世紀 **2:**353a; **3:**219a
Honchō shojaku
mokuroku 本朝書籍目録 **1:**154a; **3:**219a
Honchō tsugan (Speculum
of Japan) ····· 本朝通鑑 **3:**154b; **7:**191a;
　　　　　　　　　　　　　　8:49a
Honda Kōtarō 本多光太郎 ·· **3:**219a
Honda Motor Co, Ltd ·· **3:**219a-219b
Honda Sōichirō ··········· **3:**219b
passenger car production ··· **1:**122a
Honda Sado no Kami
Masanobu
··········· 本多佐渡守正信 ··· **3:**226b
Honda Seiroku ·· 本多静六 ·· **3:**219b
Honda Shūgo ···· 本多秋五 ·· **3:**219b
Honda Sōichirō
··············· 本田宗一郎 ··· **3:**219b
Honda Toshiaki 本多利明 ·· **3:**219b-220a
Honda Yasuji ··· 本田安次 **2:**297b, 374a
Honden (main hall) ········ **4:***297a*
Hondo ············ 本渡 ··· **3:**220a
Hōnen ············ 法然 ·· **3:**220a-220b
Hōnen shōnin eden ··········· **3:***220b*
Jōdo sect ·················· **4:**67a-68a
raigōzu ···················· **6:**277a
Senchakushū (Senchaku hongan nembutsu
shū) ·················· **7:**63a, 123a
Shinran ···················· **7:**122b
Hōnen shōnin eden
············· 法然上人絵伝 ··· **7:**42b
Honest John Incident ···· **3:**220b-221a
Honeysuckle, Japanese [(nindō)
Lonicera japonica] ········· **3:**221a
Hongaku ·········· 本覚 ·· **3:**221a; **7:**5a,
　　　　　　　　　　　　　　114a
Honganji ········ 本願寺 ··· **3:**221a-222b
division ···················· **3:**221b-222b
history ····················· **4:**68a
Oda Nobunaga vs ·· **3:**222a-222b; **6:**63a
Ōtani University ··········· **6:**129a
political and military power · **3:**221b-222b
Rennyo ···················· **3:**221b; **6:**300a
Shinran ···················· **7:**123b
Hongawara-buki ··········· **6:**337b
Hon'imbō ········ 本因坊 ··· **3:**222b
Honjibutsu ······ 本地仏 ·· **3:**222b-223a
Honjin (daimyō inns) 本陣 **3:**223a; **6:**229b

Honjin satsujin jiken
　　　　　本陣殺人事件 ····· **8**:333b
Honji suijaku 本地垂迹 **3**:223a; **7**:80b
Honjō (northern Honshū)
　　　　　本荘 ·········· **3**:223a
Honjō (central Honshū) 本庄 **3**:223a
Honjō Mutsuo 本庄陸男 ··· **3**:223b
Honjō Shigeru 本庄繁 ····· **3**:223b
Honkadori 本歌取 **2**:357a; **3**:223b;
　　　　　　　　　　　　　　5:42b
Honke and bunke **3**:223b-224a; **4**:218a
Honke and ryōke
　　　　　本家, 領家 **3**:224a; **7**:156b
Honke-gaeri ············ **4**:151a
Honkyōgen 本狂言 ········ **4**:326b
Honkyoku ·············· **7**:75b
Honne ················· **6**:204b
Honnōji Incident of 1582
　　　　　本能寺の変 ····· **3**:224a
　Akechi Mitsuhide ····· **1**:41a
　Oda Nobunaga ········ **6**:64b
　Shinchō kō ki ········ **7**:109b
　Tsutsui Junkei ········ **8**:118b
Hōnoki (*Magnolia obovata*) · **3**:224a-224b
Honor ················· **3**:224b
Honorific language ··· **3**:224b-226a
　diplomatics ··········· **2**:97b
　speech style ·········· **3**:225a
　third person reference ·· **3**:226a
　types ··············· **3**:225a-226a
　world perspective ····· **3**:226a
Honors system ········· **2**:187b
Hō no shihai to saiban
　　　　　法の支配と裁判 ··· **7**:337b
Honryō ando. 本領安堵
　　　　　See
Honsaroku 本佐録 ······· **3**:226b
Honshū 本州 ··········· **3**:226b
　area ················· **4**:2b
　dialects ············· **2**:91b-92a
　electric power ········ **2**:191b
　population density ····· **4**:2b, 7a
Honshū Paper Co, Ltd ··· **3**:226b
Honto mononari 本途物成 **3**:226b-227a;
　　　　　　　　4:267b; **5**:360b
Honzen ryōri 本膳料理 **2**:21b, 305a,
　　　　　　　　　　　　　306a
Honzōgaku 本草学 ······ **1**:155b
　Abe Shōō ············ **1**:4b
　Iinuma Yokusai ······· **3**:263b
　Inō Jakusui ·········· **3**:308a
　Itō Keisuke ·········· **3**:354b
　Iwasaki Kan'en ······· **3**:361b
　Matsuoka Joan ······· **5**:139a
　Ono Ranzan ·········· **6**:111b
　Tamura Ransui ······· **7**:334b
Honzō kōmoku keimō
　　　　　本草綱目啓蒙 ···· **6**:111b
Honzō wamyō ··· 本草和名 **4**:50b, 374b;
　　　　　　　　　　　　　7:179b
Hōō ·············· 法皇 **3**:227a
Hoori no Mikoto 火遠理命 **5**:294b-295a
Hoover-Stimson Doctrine ·· **6**:35b
Hōōzan 鳳凰山 ········· **3**:227a
Hopeh-Chahar Political Council. *See*
　**Ji-Cha (Chi-Ch'a) Autonomous
　Political Council**
Hoppō Bunka Museum ···· **5**:276b
Horagai ··············· **3**:227a
Hōraichiku (*Bambusa nana* var.
　normalis) ··········· **1**:136a
Hōraijisan ········ 鳳来寺山 **3**:227a
Hōreki Incident 宝暦事件 **3**:227a-227b
Horie Ken'ichi 堀江謙一 ·· **3**:227b
Horie Shigeo 堀江薫雄 ··· **3**:227b
Horiguchi Daigaku
　　　　　堀口大学 ········ **3**:227b
Horiguchi Sutemi 堀口捨巳 **1**:81a; **3**:227b
Hori Hidemasa ···· 堀秀政 **3**:227b-228a

Hori Hidenari ····· 堀秀成 **1**:104a
Horikawa hyakushu
　　　　　堀河百首 ········ **5**:38a
Hori Keizan 堀景山 **4**:258a; **5**:257b
Horikoshi Jirō 堀越二郎 ·· **3**:228a
Horikoshi Kubō 堀越公方 **3**:228a; **7**:64b
Hori Kyūsaku 堀久作 ···· **3**:228a
Horimono. *See* **Tattoos**
Hori Ryūjo 堀柳女 ······· **3**:228a
Horishi
　tattoos ·············· **7**:350a
Hori Tatsuo ······ 堀辰雄 **3**:228a
Hōritsu ··············· **3**:228a-228b
*Hōritsu shakaigaku no
　shomondai*
　　　　　法律社会学の諸問題 ··· **4**:112a
Horiuchi Masakazu
　　　　　堀内正和 ········ **3**:228b
Horn, musical ·········· **3**:227a
Hōroku ··············· **3**:228b
Horsecars ············· **3**:228b
Horse chestnut, Japanese [(tochinoki)
　Aesculus turbinata] · **2**:326b; **3**:228b-229a
Horsemanship ·········· **3**:229a
　martial arts ·········· **1**:206a
Horseracing at the Kamo Festival · **4**:320b
Horse-rider theory ··· **1**:78b; **2**:103b;
　　　　　　3:229a-231a; **4**:276b
　criticism and revisions ·· **3**:230b
　Egami Namio ········ **3**:229b-230a
　historical perspective ·· **3**:230a-230b
　1948 Symposium on Japanese
　origins ············· **3**:229b-230a
　Oka Masao ·········· **3**:229b
　origin of Japanese people ·· **4**:34a
　physical characteristics of Japanese
　people ·············· **4**:35a
Horses (*uma*) ·········· **3**:231a
　breeding ············· **7**:116a
Horseshoe crab [(kabutogani)
　Tachypleus tridentatus] ··· **3**:231a;
　　　　　　　　　　5:352a-352b
Horse trappings, ancient ··· **1**:78a;
　　　　　　　3:231a-231b
　of kofun ············· **4**:245a
Horticulture ······· **1**:30a; **3**:231b
　bonsai ·············· **1**:161b-163a
　modern and contemporary ···· **3**:231b
　mosses ·············· **5**:256b
Hōryūji ········ 法隆寺 **1**:178a, 182a,
　185a; **3**:231b-233b; **4**:145a; **7**:13b, 42a, 85a,
　　　　　　　　　　　　　264a
　founding ············· **3**:232a
　gates ··············· **3**:12a
　graffiti ·············· **3**:59b
　images ·············· **3**:232a
　main hall (kondō) ····· *3*:232*b*
　pagoda ·············· *3*:232*b*
　rebuilding controversy ·· **1**:79b
　textiles ············· **8**:17a
treasures of
　　　　　　　　　　3:233b-234b
**Hōryūji Great Treasure
　House** · 法隆寺大宝蔵殿 **3**:233b
　treasures of
　　　　　　　　　　3:233*a*,
　　　　　　　　233b-234b
　Kanchōban ·········· **3**:233*a*
　Queen Māya figurines ·· **3**:233*a*
Hōsa Bunko 蓬左文庫 ···· **3**:234a
Hōseidō Kisanji
　　　　　朋誠堂喜三二 ···· **3**:234a
Hōsei University ········ **3**:234b-235a
"Hōsenka" 鳳仙花 ······· **4**:183a
Hōshakaigaku kōza
　　　　　法社会学講座 ····· **4**:184a
Hoshina Masayuki
　　　　　保科正之 ·· **3**:235a; **7**:81a

Hoshino site ····· 星野遺跡 **3**:235a
Hoshi Ryō. 星良 *See* **Sōma Kokkō**
Hoshi Shin'ichi ···· 星新一 **3**:235a
　science fiction ······· **7**:38b-39a
Hoshi Tōru ·········· 星亨 **2**:56a;
　　　　　　　　　　3:235a-235b
　Sandai Jiken Kempaku Movement
　(Movement to Memorialize Three
　Important Items) ····· **7**:9b
Hōshō ················ **5**:144a-144b
Hōshō Fusao 宝生英雄 ··· **6**:24*b*
Hōshō Kan 宝生閑 ······ **6**:26*b*
Hōshō school 宝生流 ····· **3**:235b
Hōshosen 奉書船 ········ **3**:235b
　National Seclusion ···· **5**:347a
Hōshō Shūzai 宝所周財 ·· **3**:33a
Hōshō Yaichi 宝生弥一 ·· **6**:26*b*
Hōsō Bunka Shō (Broadcasting Prize)
　　　　　　　　　　8:299b
Hosoda Eishi ···· 細田栄之 **3**:235b
Hōsō Daigaku ········· **1**:171a-171b
Hosoda Tokitomi. *See* **Hosoda Eishi**
Hosofude ·········· **1**:*233a*, 233b
Hōsōhō. *See* **Broadcasting Law**
Hosoi Heishū 細井平洲 **3**:235b-236a;
　　　　　　　　　　　　　7:71a
Hosoi Kōtaku 細井広沢 ·· **3**:236a
Hosoi Wakizō 細井和喜蔵 **4**:71b
Hosokawa family 細川氏 **3**:236a; **7**:83b
　kanrei ··············· **4**:151a
Hosokawa Fujitaka. 細川藤孝
　　　　See **Hosokawa Yūsai**
Hosokawa Gracia
　　　　　細川ガラシア ·· **3**:236a-236b
Hosokawa Karoku
　　　　　細川嘉六 ········ **3**:236b
Hosokawa Katsumoto
　　　　　細川勝元 **3**:236b; **6**:107a
Hosokawa Sansai. 細川三斎 *See*
　Hosokawa Tadaoki
Hosokawa Tadaoki
　　　　　細川忠興 **3**:236a-237a
Hosokawa Tama 細川玉 **3**:236a-236b
Hosokawa Yūsai 細川幽斎 **3**:236a, 237a;
　　　　　　　　　　　　　8:215b
　Kokin denju ········· **4**:254a
Hospitals ············· **3**:120a
Hosshinshū 発心集 ······· **4**:129a
Hossō School ·········· **1**:312b
Hossō sect 法相宗 **1**:106a, 178b;
　　　　　　　　3:237a-237b
　Dōshō ·············· **2**:132a
　headquarters ········· **5**:332a
Hossō shiyō sho
　　　　　法曹至要抄 ······ **4**:376b
Hostages ············· **3**:208a
Host-guest relationship ·· **2**:233b
Hotakadake 穂高岳 **3**:237b; **4**:127a
Hotakayama 武尊山 ····· **3**:237b
Hotaru ··············· **2**:280a-280b
Hotarugari. *See* **Firefly viewing**
Hotarugusa (The
　Dayflower) ···· 螢草 **6**:221b
Hotei ················ **5**:296a
Hoteichiku (*Phyllostachys bambusoides*
　var. *aurea*) ········ **1**:135b-136a
Hotels
　Hotel Ōkura ········· **7**:341b
　Imperial Hotel ······· **3**:277b
Hōten Kaisen ········· **5**:262b
Hōtetsugaku ··········· **4**:85a-85b
Hotoke. *See* **Buddha**
*Hō to shūkyō to shakai
　seikatsu*
　　　　　法と宗教と社会生活 ·· **7**:337b
Hototogisu ···· ホトトギス **3**:237b; **4**:178a;
　　　　　　　　5:20a; **8**:295a
　haiku ··············· **3**:79b-80a

Masaoka Shiki · · · · · · · · · · · · · · 5:123b
Natsume Sōseki · · · · · · · · · · · · 5:350a
Satō Nempuku · · · · · · · · · · · · · · · 7:28a
Takahama Kyoshi · · · · · · · · · · · 7:311a
Hototogisu [(little cuckoo)
   Cuculus poliocephalus]
· 1:223a

Hototogisu (Namiko)
   · · · · · · · · 不如帰(浪子) · **6**:221a; **8**:59b
Hototogisu [(toad lily)
   Tricyrtis hirta] · · · · · · · · · · · 3:237b
Hot Spring Law · · · · · · · · · · · · · 3:239a
Hot springs · · · · · 3:238a–239b; 7:191b
   Akakura · · · · · · · · · · · · · · 1:40a; 8:293b
   Arima · 1:83b
   Asama · 1:95b
   Asamushi · · · · · · · · · · · · · · · · · · · 1:95b
   Atagawa · · · · · · · · · · · · · · · · · · · 1:107b
   Atami · 1:107b
   Awara · · · · · · · · · · · · · · · · 1:124b–125a
   Azusagawa · · · · · · · · · · · · · · · · · 1:127b
   balneotherapy in Japan · · · · · · 3:239a–239b
      history · · · · · · · · · · · · · · · · · · 3:239a
      present conditions · · · · · · 3:239a–239b
   Beppu · 1:150a
   Dake · · · · · · · · · · · · · · · · · · · 2:70b–72a
   definition · · · · · · · · · · · · · · · · · 3:238a
   distribution · · · · · · · · · · · · · · · 3:238a
      in Japan · · · · · · · · · · · · · · · · 3:238a
      world · · · · · · · · · · · · · · · · · · · 3:238a
   Dōgo · 2:126a
   geothermal electrical generation
· 3:238b–239a
   Ginzan · · · · · · · · · · · · · 3:33b; 8:293b
   Higashine · · · · · · · · · · · · · · · · · 8:293b
   Hirayu · · · · · · · · · · · · · · · 1:5a; 3:146b
   Iizaka · 3:264a
   Isobe · 1:62b
   Japanese attitude · · · · · · · 3:238a–238b
   Kaminoyama · · · · · · · · · · · · · · · 8:293b
   Kami Suwa · · · · · · · · · · · · · · · · 4:127b
   Katsuura · · · · · · · · · · · · · · · · · · 5:300a
   Kawaji · 4:179a
   Kinugawa · · · · · · · · · · · · · · · · · 4:219a
   Kusatsu · · · · · · · · · · · · · · · · · · · 4:319b
   Manza · 5:111a
   Masutomi · · · · · · · · · · · · · · · · · 5:130a
   Ōwakudani · · · · · · · · · · · · · · · · 6:136b
   Sakunami · · · · · · · · · · · · · · · · · · · 7:4a
   Shima · 7:99a
   Shirahone · · · · · · · · · · · · · · · · · 7:145a
   Sukayu · 7:265a
   Tamatsukuri · · · · · · · · · · · 7:332b–333a
   Tawarayama · · · · · · · · · · · · · · · 7:351b
   Tōgatta · 8:36a
   Tsubaki · · · · · · · · · · · · · · · · · · · 8:109b
   Uchinomaki · · · · · · · · · · · · · · · 1:102b
   utilization · · · · · · · · · · · · · · · · · 3:238b
   water volume and radiation · · · · · · 3:238a
   Yamanaka · · · · · · · · · · · · · · · · · 8:300b
   Yuda · 8:294a
   Yudanaka · · · · · · · · · · · · · · · · · 8:355a
   Yugashima · · · · · · · · · · · 1:49b; 8:355a
   Yukawa · · · · · · · · · · · · · · · · · · · 5:300a
   Yumoto · · · · · · · · · · · · · · · · · · · 8:295a
   Yunoyama · · · · · · · · · · · · · · · · · 8:357a
   Zaō · · · · · · · · · · · · · · · · · · 8:293b, 367b
Hotta Masatoshi ·堀田正俊· 3:239a
Hotta Masayoshi ·堀田正睦· 3:239b
Hotta Shōzō ·堀田庄三· · · · 3:239b
Hotta Yoshie ·堀田善衛· 3:239b–240a
Hou Han shu (History of the Later Han
   Dynasty) · 6:258b; 7:264a; 8:232b
Ho-Umezu Agreement. *See* **He-Umezu
   (Ho-Umezo) Agreement**
House, Edward Howard · · · · · 3:240a

House arrest · · · · · · · · · · · · · · · 3:126a
House codes. *See* **Kakun**
"House elders" · · · · · · · · · · · · · · 4:160a
House Food Industrial Co, Ltd · · · 3:240a
Household · · · · · · · · · 3:259a–260b; 7:213a
   contemporary standard of living
· 7:243b–245a
      importance · · · · · · · · · · · · · · 7:212a
      paternalism · · · · · · · · · · · · · 6:165a
   See also **Ie**
Household furnishings · · · · · · 1:148b; 5:8a
Household-Precept Letter Writer · 7:376a
Household precepts · · · 4:118a–119a; 7:234b
Household registers · · · 3:240a–241a; 5:321a
   history · · · · · · · · · · · · · · · · 3:240b–241a
   minority rights · · · · · · · · · · · · 5:195b
   ryōmin · 6:352a
   social classes
      heimin · · · · · · · · · · · · · · · · · 3:125b
Housemen · · · · · · · · · · · · · · 3:42b; 4:196b
House name (yagō) · · · · · · · · · · · 8:284a
House of Councillors · 2:189a–189b; 6:214b
   Diet member legislation · · · · · · · 2:96b
   Ryokufūkai · · · · · · · · · · · · · · · · 6:352a
   Tanaka Kōtarō · · · · · · · · · · · · · 7:337b
House of Ono · · · · · · · · · · · · · · · 6:110a
House of Peers · · · 3:241a; 6:171a; 7:304a
   factions · · · · · · · · · · · · · · · · · · · 3:276b
House of Representatives · · · 2:188b–189b,
                          190a; 3:276a; 6:214b
   Diet member legislation · · · · · · · 2:96b
House of Representatives Members
   Election Law · · · · · · · · · · · · · 6:212a
House of the Sleeping Beauties · 4:176b
Housewives · · · · · · · · · · · · 3:241a–242a
   nature of job · · · · · · · · · · · · · · 3:241b
   preparation · · · · · · · · · · · 3:241b–242a
   relations with husbands · · · · · · 3:242a
Housewives Association (Shufuren)
· 8:263b

Housing
   apartments · · · · · · · · · · · · · · · · · · 5:6a
   construction · · · · · · · · · · · · · · · · · 5:6a
   consumer expenditure · · · · · · · · 2:17a
   exterior · · · · · · · · · · · · · · · · · · · 3:243a
   history · · · · · · · · · · · · · · · 3:242b–244b
      ancient religious influence · 3:243a–243b
      architecture · · · · · · · · · · · · · 3:244a
      modern · · · · · · · · · · · · · 3:244a–245b
      prehistoric dwellings · · · · · · 3:243a
      residential styles emergence of
· 3:243b–244a
   interior · · · · · · · · · · · · · · · · · · · 3:242b
   lifestyles · 5:6a
   minka · · · · · · · · · · · · · · · · · 5:192a–194a
   modern · · · · · · · · · · · · · · · 3:244a–245b
      changes in design · · · · · · 3:244b–245a
      danchi · · · · · · · · · · · · · · · · · 3:245a
      multiunit dwellings · · · · · 3:245a–245b
   problems · · · · · · · · · · · · · 3:245b–246b
   quality · · · · · · · · · · · · · · · · · · · 7:245a
   rents · 4:363b
   Yayoi · · · · · · · · · · · · · · · · · 8:321a–322a
**Housing and Urban Development
   Corporation** · · · · · · · · · · 3:321b–322a
Housing Construction Planning Law
· 3:246a
Housing developers · · · · · · · · · 3:242b
Housing Loan Corporation · · · · 3:244b
   fiscal system · · · · · · · · · · · · · · · 2:281b
Howling at the Moon · · · · · · · · · 3:76a
Hōya · · · · · · · · · · 保谷 2:305b; 3:246b
Ho Ying-ch'in. *See* **He Yingqin (Ho
   Ying-ch'in)**
Hōyō kazoku · · · · 抱擁家族 4:252a
Hōza · 6:321b
Hōzan Tankai. 宝山湛海 *See* **Tankai**
Hozugawa · · · · · 保津川 · · · · 3:246b

Hōzuki [(ground cherry) *Physalis
   alkekengi*] · · · · · · · · · · · · · · · 3:246b
   noisemaking toy · · · · · · · · · · · 3:246b
   plant · 3:246b
Hōzuki ichi · · · · · · · · · · · · · · · 3:247a
Hozumi Nobushige
   穂積陳重 2:319a; 3:247a
Hozumi Shigetō
   穂積重遠 · · · · · · · · · · · · · · · 3:247a
   Nakagawa Zennosuke · · · · · · · 5:313a
Hozumi Yatsuka 穂積八束 · 3:247a
   Ernest Francisco Fenollosa · · · 2:251b
Hsien-jen · · · · · · · · · · · · · · · · · · · 7:67a
Hsin-min Hui. *See* **Xinmin Hui
   (Hsin-min Hui)**
Hsu, Francis L.K. · · · · · · · · · · · · 4:38b
Huang Xing (Huang Hsing) · · · 3:247b
Huang Zunxian (Huang Tsun-hsien)
· 3:247b; 4:141a
Huiguo · 6:348a
Huike (Hui-k'o) Severing His Arm · 8:371a
Hukbalahap · · · · · · · · · · · · · · · · 3:247b
Hukbo ng Bayan Laban sa Hapon
   (People's Anti-Japanese Army) · 3:247b
"Huks, the" · · · · · · · · · · · · · · · · · 3:247b
Hull, Cordell · · · · · · · · · · 3:247b–248a
   Hull note · · · · · · · · · · · · · · · · · 3:321a
Human rights · · · · · · · · · · · · · · · 4:379b
   government compensation · · · · 3:54b–55a
   protection of civil liberties · · · · 1:317b
Hundred Days' Reform · · · · · · · 4:141a
Hundred-Poem Sequences · · · · · · 3:52a
Hundred Regiment Offensive · · · 3:248a
Hungary · · · · · · · · · · · · · · · · · · · 2:142b
Hŭngsŏn'gun. *See* **Taewŏn'gun**
Hunting · · · · · · · · · · · · · · · 3:248a–248b
   falconry · · · · · · · · · · · · · · · · · · 2:241b
   policy · · · · · · · · · · · · · · · · 3:248a–248b
   use of hawks · · · · · · · · · · · · · · 3:114b
Hunting and gathering economy · · 4:72a
Husband · · · · · · · · · 2:244a–244b; 3:242a
Husi san xiao · · · · · · · · · · · · · · · 4:253b
Hu-ssu san hsiao · · · · · · · · · · · · 4:253b
Hyakudan Taisen 百団大戦 · 3:248a
Hyakuichi shinron (New
   Theory of the Hundred
   and One) · · · ·百一新論 · · 6:14a
Hyakumantō darani
   ("mantras of the million
   stupas") · · ·百万塔陀羅尼 1:152a; 6:247b
Hyakunin isshu · 百人一首 · 1:4a; 2:354b;
      3:248b–249a; 4:161b; 7:61b; 8:184a
   Hon'ami Kōetsu · · · · · · · · · · · · 1:235a
   Ōeyama · 6:67b
   uta karuta · · · · · · · · · · · · · · · · 3:248b
Hyakurenshō · · · · ·百練抄 · 3:249a
   historiography · · · · · · · · · · · · · 3:154a
Hyakushō · · · 3:249a–249b; 4:194b; 5:360b
Hyakushōdai · · · 百姓代 4:55a; 5:270a
Hyakushō ikki · · · 百姓一揆 · 3:192a,
                  249b–250b, 269a;
            7:5a, 345b; 8:293a, 337b
   Marxist vs non-Marxist
      interpretations · · · · · · · · · 3:250a–250b
   phases · · · · · · · · · · · · · · · · · · · 3:269a
Hyakushōuke · · · · 百姓請 · 3:250b
Hydrangea, Japanese [(ajisai)
   *Hydrangea
   macrophylla* var. *otaksa*] · · · · · · · 3:251a
Hydroelectric power · · · · · · · 2:190b–192a;
                        5:353a–353b
   dams · · · · · · · · · · · · · · · · · · 2:72a–72b
Hyō, Lake · · · · · · · 瓢湖 · · · 3:252a
Hyōe · · · · · · · · · · · · · 兵衛 · · · 2:184a
Hyōgikai · · · · · · · · · · · · · 4:11a; 7:344a
Hyōgo Prefecture ·兵庫県· 3:251b
Hyōgo Shipyards
   · · · · · · · · · · · 兵庫造船所 · · · 3:252a
Hyōjōsho (Judicial Council) 評定所 8:53a

Hyōjōshū ·········· 評定衆 **3**:252a; **4**:122a; **7**:97b
  keishi ·············· **4**:190a
Hyōjun system ············· **6**:335b
Hyŏn Chun-Gŭk ············ **4**:287a
Hyŏn Chun-hyŏk ··········· **4**:208b
Hyōrōmai ····· 兵糧米 · **3**:252a–252b
Hyōsō ··················· **4**:116a
Hyōtan ·················· **3**:151b
Hypothec ················· **3**:252b
Hyūga ·············· 日向 · **3**:252b

I

Iai ······················· **3**:253a
Iaidō ·············· 居合道 · **3**:253a
Ianfu ···················· **4**:159b
Ibara ··············· 井原 · **3**:253a
Ibaraki ············· 茨城 · **3**:253a
Ibaraki Prefecture ··· 茨城県 · **3**:253a
  industrial development ······ **3**:253a
  tourist attractions ··········· **3**:253b
Ibaraki Satellite Communication station
  ························· **7**:311a
Iba site ········· 伊場遺跡 · **3**:253b
Ibigawa ·········· 揖斐川 **3**:253b; **5**:303b
IBM Japan, Ltd ············ **3**:253b
  computer industry ·········· **1**:345a
  United States economic relations
  (1945–1973) ·············· **8**:162a
IBRD ·············· **3**:253b–254a
Ibuka Masaru ······ 井深大 · **3**:254a
Ibuse Masuji ····· 井伏鱒二 · **3**:254a–255a;
  ················ **5**:55b–56a; **7**:119b
  awards ·················· **3**:254b
  works of ············· **3**:254b–255a
Ibusuki ············· 指宿 · **3**:255a
Ichi ················· 市 · **5**:114b–115a
Ichiba ············· 市場 · **5**:114b–115a
Ichiba machi ······· 市場町 · **5**:115a–115b
Ichibō ·············· 一房 · **4**:62a
Ichibukin ·········· 一分金 · **5**:242a–242b
Ichidai toshiyori ·········· **7**:274a
Ichien chigyō ····· 一円知行 **1**:274a; **3**:255a
  shōen ··················· **7**:157a
Ichigo ichie ········· 一期一会 · **1**:52b
Ichigō Sakusen ··········· **6**:115a
Ichihara ··········· 市原 · **3**:255b
Ichii [(Japanese yew) *Taxus cuspidata*]
  ······················· **3**:255b
Ichijitsu shintō ki
  ············· 一実神道記 · **3**:255b
Ichijō, Emperor ··· 一条天皇 · **3**:255b–256a;
  ························· **7**:52b
  Fujiwara no Kaneie ········· **2**:351b
  Fujiwara no Korechika ······ **2**:352b
  Fujiwara no Teishi ·········· **2**:356b
  regency ·················· **2**:356b
  Sei Shōnagon ·············· **7**:52b
Ichijō family. ··· 一条家 · *See* **Gosekke**
Ichijō Kaneyoshi 一条兼良 · **3**:256a
  handbook on statecraft ······ **1**:207b
  poet and critic ············· **3**:256a
  politician ················· **3**:256a
  scholar ·················· **3**:256a
  works ··················· **3**:256a
Ichijō Norifusa ···· 一条教房 · **3**:256b
Ichijō Sanetsune 一条実経 · **3**:256b

Ichijō Tsunetsugu
  ············· 一条経嗣 · **3**:256b
Ichikawa ············ 市川 · **3**:256b
Ichikawa Beian 市河米庵 · **3**:256b–257a
  Chinese influence ··········· **3**:256b
Ichikawa Danjūrō
  ············· 市川団十郎 · **3**:257a; **5**:49b
  debut ··················· **4**:91a
  jōruri ··················· **4**:77a
  kabuki jūhachiban ·········· **4**:97b
  style ···················· **3**:257a
Ichikawa Danjūrō XI ········ **4**:90b
Ichikawa Fusae · 市川房枝 · **3**:257a
  Fusen Kakutoku Dōmei ······ **2**:374b
  politician ················· **3**:257a
  Shin Fujin Kyōkai ·········· **7**:111b
  work for women's rights ····· **3**:257b
Ichikawa Gakusan 市川岳山 · **6**:116b
Ichikawa Kon ······ 市川崑 · **2**:272a, 273a,
  ················ **274a**; **3**:257b–258a
  films ···················· **3**:257b
  Shindō Kaneto ············· **7**:111a
  style ···················· **3**:257b
Ichikawa Shōichi 市川正一 · **3**:258a
Ichikawa Utaemon
  ············ 市川右太衛門 · **2**:269b; **3**:258a
Ichikishima Hime no Mikoto
  ·············· 市杵島姫命 · **3**:357a
Ichimon ··········· **7**:108a, 273b
Ichimonji ················ **4**:116a
Ichimura Kiyoshi ·· 市村清 · **3**:258a
Ichimura Sanjirō
  ············· 市村瓚次郎 · **3**:258a
Ichinen yūhan (A Year
  and a Half) ····· 一年有半 · **5**:311b–312a
Ichinomiya ········· 一宮 · **3**:258a
Ichinoseki ········· 一関 · **3**:258b
Ichi no Shōnin ··· 市の聖人 · **7**:166b
Ichinotani, Battle of 一谷の戦
  Taira no Munemori ·········· **7**:301b
  Taira no Shigehira ·········· **7**:302a
  Taira no Tadanori ·········· **7**:302a
  Taira no Tomomori ·········· **7**:302b
"Ichioku sōhakuchika" ········ **6**:138b
Ichirinsō (*Anemone nikoensis*) ·· **3**:258b
Ichirizuka ········· 一里塚 · **3**:258b
Ichiyō joshi no haka
  ············· 一葉女史の墓 · **4**:100b
Ichizoku ················· **7**:108a
Ichizoku rōtō ········ 一族郎党 · **3**:260b
Ichō ···················· **3**:33b
Icons ···················· **7**:67b
Idealism vs pragmatism ······· **6**:232b
Ideals of the East, The ······ **5**:12a; **6**:79b;
  ························· **7**:294b
Idemitsu Art Gallery ········ **3**:258b
Idemitsu Kōsan Co, Ltd ·· **3**:258b–259a
Idemitsu Sazō ··· 出光佐三 · **3**:259a
  Idemitsu Art Gallery ········ **3**:258b
  Idemitsu Kōsan Co, Ltd ····· **3**:258b
Ideographs ············· **4**:141b–143b
Ideological "conversion." *See* **Tenkō**
Idioms ················ **3**:303b–304a
Idiophones ················ **5**:282b
Idojiri Archaeological Hall ···· **3**:259a
Ie (household) ·· **2**:241b–242a; **3**:259a–260b;
  ························· **4**:217b
  composition ··············· **3**:259a
  concept ··············· **3**:259a–260b
  in group consciousness ······ **3**:260a
  functional meaning and its decline · **3**:260a
    economic factors ········· **3**:260a
    samurai status ··········· **3**:260a
  industry ·················· **3**:260a
  principle of succession ···· **3**:259b–260a
    adoption ·············· **3**:259b
    inheritance ············· **3**:259b
  rice culture ··············· **6**:309b

  sibling relationships ········ **3**:259b
Iejima ············· 伊江島 · **3**:260b
Iemoto ·········· **2**:291b; **3**:260b
  disciples ················· **3**:260b
  ie pattern ················ **3**:260b
Ienaga Saburō ··· 家永三郎 · **3**:261a; **4**:67b
Ienaga textbook review case ·· **3**:261a
Ie no hikari ······· 家の光 · **3**:261a
Ienoko and rōtō
  ············· 家子, 郎党 · **3**:261a; **7**:7a
Iesu no Mitama Kyōkai
  Kyōdan
  ···· イエス之御霊会教団 ···· **7**:242b
Iesu no shōgai
  ············· イエスの生涯 · **2**:214a
Ietsukasa ··········· 家司 · **4**:190a
Igai ················ 意外 · **4**:181a
Igakujo ············ 医学所 · **3**:261a
  Koishikawa Yōjōsho ········ **4**:250b
Igarashi Chikara · 五十嵐力 · **3**:261b
Iga ware ·········· 伊賀焼 · **2**:295b;
  ················· **3**:261b; **7**:256a
  characteristics ············· **3**:261b
  production ················ **3**:261b
Igaya Chiharu ··· 猪谷千春 · **3**:262a
Igo. 囲碁 *See* **Go**
Igusa ···················· **7**:266a
Iha Fuyū ········· 伊波普猷 · **3**:262a
Ihara Saikaku. 井原西鶴 *See* **Saikaku**
Iha shell mound · 伊波貝塚 · **3**:262a
Ii ························ **6**:288b
Iida ··············· 飯田 · **3**:262a
Iida Dakotsu ······ 飯田蛇笏 · **3**:262a
Iida Incident ······ 飯田事件 · **3**:262b
Iimoriyama ········ 飯盛山 · **1**:38b; **3**:262b
Ii Naomasa ······· 井伊直政 · **3**:262b; **7**:56b
Ii Naosuke ········ 井伊直弼 · **3**:263a–263b;
  ······ **4**:179b; **5**:156a; **7**:4b, 102a–102b
  Ansei Purge ·········· **1**:63b; **3**:263b
  Harris Treaty ·············· **3**:105a
  Meiji Restoration ··········· **5**:156a
  Movement for Union of Court and
  shogunate ·············· **5**:260a–260b
  Sakurada mongai Incident ···· **1**:84a; **7**:4b
Iinuma Yokusai ··· 飯沼慾斎 · **3**:263b
Iiyama ············· 飯山 · **3**:263b–264a
Ii Yōhō ··········· 伊井蓉峰 · **3**:264a
Iizaka Hot Spring 飯坂温泉 · **3**:264a
Iizawa Tadasu ···· 飯沢匡 · **3**:264a
  radio drama ··············· **6**:275b
Iizuka ············· 飯塚 · **3**:264a
Iizuka Kōji ········ 飯塚浩二 · **3**:264a
I-jan ·················· **3**:357a–357b
Ijūin family ······· 伊集院氏 · **3**:264b
Ika ···················· **7**:243a–243b
Ikaho ············· 伊香保 · **3**:264b
Ikai ················ 位階 · **2**:39b–41a
Ikaruga ············ 斑鳩 · **3**:264b
Ikarugadera ·········· 斑鳩寺 · **3**:231b
Ikaruga no Miya ··· 斑鳩宮 · **3**:264b
Ikat ·················· **4**:164a–165a
Ikawa Dam ········· 井川ダム · **2**:73b
Ikazuchi Kai ···· いかづち会 · **5**:19b
Ikebana ·········· **2**:288a–292a
Ikebana International ········ **2**:292a
Ikebe Sanzan ···· 池辺三山 · **3**:264b
Ikeda (city) ········· 池田 · **3**:264b–265a
Ikeda (town) ········ 池田 · **3**:265a
Ikeda, Lake ········ 池田湖 · **3**:265b
Ikeda Daisaku ···· 池田大作 · **3**:265a
Ikeda-Diefenbaker communique · **1**:238a
Ikeda Hayato ···· 池田勇人 **2**:333a; **3**:265a;
  ························· **7**:275b
  Income-Doubling ··········· **3**:287a
  Japanese self-defense ········ **3**:265a
  Kōno Ichirō ··············· **4**:274a
  normalization with Korea ····· **4**:285a
  prime minister ············· **3**:265b

Sakurada Takeshi ·················· **7**:4b
Satō Eisaku ····················· **7**:26a
Ikeda-Kennedy Agreements ······ **3**:265a;
                                 8:160a
Ikeda Kikunae ·池田菊苗· **1**:39a, 268a;
                                 3:265b
Ikeda Mitsumasa 池田光政 **1**:158a; **3**:265b
  Confucianism ·················· **3**:265b
Ikeda Museum of Twentieth-Century Art
  ······························ **5**:279b
Ikeda Nagaoki ·池田長発· **3**:265b-266a
Ikeda-Robertson Talks ·········· **3**:266a
Ikeda Shigeaki ·池田成彬 ········ **3**:266a
Ikeda Terumasa ·池田輝政 ·**3**:266a; **7**:56b
Ikeda Yaemon
  ·········· 池田八右衛門 ······· **6**:359a
Ikedaya Incident
  ··········池田屋騒動 ··· **3**:266a-266b
  Kondō Isami ·················· **4**:269a
  Shinsengumi ·················· **7**:124b
Ikeda Yoshinobu 池田義信 ········ **4**:189b
Ikegai Shōtarō 池貝庄太郎 ······ **3**:266b
Ikejima Shimpei 池島信平 ······· **3**:266b
Ikenishi Gonsui ·池西言水 ······· **3**:266b
Ike no Gyokuran ·池玉瀾 **1**:211a; **3**:266b
Ike no mokuzu ·池の藻屑 ········· **1**:73b
Ikeno Seiichirō 池野成一郎 ······ **3**:266b
Ike no Taiga ······ 池大雅·**1**:193b, 210b,
  211a, 225a; **3**:267a-267b; **7**:17b
  as calligrapher ················ **3**:267b
  influences ···················· **3**:267a
  Sanzui jimbutsu zu ············ **3**:267a
  techniques ··················· **3**:267a
Ike no Zenni ·······池禅尼 ······ **3**:267b
Iki (island) ········壱岐 ········ **3**:267b
Iki and sui (ideals) ······· **3**:267b-268a
  iki ·························· **3**:268a
  sui ···················· **3**:267b-268a
Ikigai ························· **3**:268a
Ikigami ······················ **3**:268a
Iki no Hakatoko ·伊吉博徳· **3**:268b
Iki no Muraji Hakatoko no
  fumi ·········伊吉連博徳書 ··· **3**:268b
  kokiroku ····················· **4**:255a
Ikiru ·············生きる **2**:272a; **3**:268b
  Shimura Takashi ··············· **7**:108a
Ikiteiru heitai
  ·············生きてゐる兵隊 ···· **7**:176b
Ikite iru Yuda (The Living
  Judas) ·生きているユダ **6**:139a
Ikkai Gyojin. *See* **Soganoya Gorō**
Ikka shinjū ··················· **7**:262a
Ikki ·················一揆 ······ **3**:268b
  kokujin ······················ **4**:260a
  types ···················· **3**:268b-269a
Ikkō ikki ··········一向一揆 ···· **3**:269b
Ikkoku Ichijō Rei
  ·············一国一城令 ······ **3**:269b
Ikkōshū. *See* **Jōdo Shin sect**
Ikko sono ta ·一個その他 **5**:301b
Ikkyū ················一休 **1**:294b;
                               3:269b-270b
  portrait ······················ **3**:270b
  works ························· **3**:270a
Ikkyū Sōjun ·····一休宗純 **1**:192a;
                               3:269b-270b
  portrait painting ··············· **6**:227b
Ikoku nikki ······· 異国日記 **3**:270b; **7**:255a
Ikokusen Uchiharai Rei. 異国船打払令
  See **Gaikokusen Uchiharai Rei**
Ikoma ·············生駒 ······ **3**:270b
Ikomayama ········生駒山 ····· **3**:270b
Ikudama manku ·生玉万句 ··· **2**:77b
Ikukunitama Shrine
  ·············生国魂神社 ··· **3**:270b-271a
Ikumatsu ·············幾松 ···· **4**:202b
Ikuno Disturbance
  ··············生野の変 ····· **3**:271a

Tenchūgumi Rebellion ·········· **8**:4a
Ikuno Silver Mine生野銀山 ···· **3**:271a
Ikushima Shingorō
  ·············生島新五郎 ···· **2**:188a
Ikuta Chōkō ······生田長江 **3**:271a; **7**:54b
Ikuta Kengyō ·····生田検校 ···· **4**:64b
Ikuta Shungetsu ·生田春月 ···· **3**:271a
Iku Tatsufu ·······郁達夫 ···· **8**:355a
Ikuta Yorozu, Rebellion of
  ·············生田万の乱 ····· **3**:271a
IL ·················イル ····· **4**:139a
Ilchin-hoe ····················· **4**:282a
Illegitimacy ···················· **6**:163a
Illumination painting ············ **6**:150a
Illustrated Sutra of Cause and Effect
  (E inga kyō) ················ **6**:*149a*
Illustration, book ············· **1**:163b-164a
Imabari ···········今治 ······ **3**:271a
Imado shinjū ·····今戸心中 **3**:151a; **4**:199b
Imagawa family ···今川氏 ·**3**:271b; **7**:84a,
                                274b
Imagawa Kana Mokuroku
  ··········今川仮名目録 ····· **3**:271b
  Imagawa Yoshimoto ············ **3**:272a
  Shingen Kahō ················· **7**:113a
Imagawa Sadayo
  ··········今川貞世 **3**:272a; **4**:140a;
                                8:215a
  military career ················ **3**:272a
  poetic activities ··············· **3**:272a
  poetic diction ················· **3**:272a
Imagawa Ujichika 今川氏親 ····· **3**:271b
Imagawa Yoshimoto
  ·············今川義元 ····· **3**:272b
Imaichi ···········今市 ··· **3**:272b-273a
Imai Sōkyū ·······今井宗久 **3**:181a, 273a;
                                7:67a
Imai Tadashi ······今井正·**2**:272a-272b;
                                3:273a
  film-making style ·············· **3**:273a
  Shindō Kaneto ················ **7**:111a
  works ························· **3**:273a
Imakagami ········今鏡 **3**:273b; **5**:39b
Imaki no tehito 今来の才伎 **4**:205b
Ima monogatari ····今物語 ···· **3**:69b
Imamukashi ayatsuri
  nendaiki ·今昔操年代記 ····· **6**:20a
Imamura Arao ·今村荒男 ··· **3**:273b
Imamura Shikō ·今村紫紅 **3**:273b; **6**:*158b*
Imamura Shōhei 今村昌平 ·**2**:273b-274a,
  275b; **3**:273b-274a
  film protagonists ·············· **3**:273b
  films ························· **3**:274a
  methods ····················· **3**:274a
Imanishi Kinji ·今西錦司 **3**:274a; **6**:240a
  monkeys ····················· **1**:156a
Imari ·············伊万里 ···· **3**:274a
Imari ware. *See* **Arita ware**
Imari ware jar ················· **1**:*260b*
Imbanuma ········印旛沼 ·**3**:274b; **7**:4a
  Tanuma Okitsugu ·········· **7**:345a-346a
Imbe ·········忌部, 斎部 ····· **1**:147b
Imbe Family ·忌部氏, 斎部氏 ···· **3**:274b
Imbe no Hironari 斎部広成 ····· **1**:116a
IMF
  Japan's membership ············ **3**:274b
  yen exchange system ··········· **3**:274b
IMF-JC (International Metalworkers
  Federation-Japan Council) **3**:274b-275a;
                                4:360a
  Jidōsha Sōren ················ **4**:53b
Imiki ·············忌寸 ····· **4**:89a
Imikotoba ····················· **7**:291b
Immediate acquisition ··········· **7**:68a
Immigrants. *See* **Kikajin**
Immigration
  Australia ·········· **1**:116b-117a, 119a
  Brazil ················· **1**:169a-169b

  Hiraga Renkichi ··············· **3**:142b
  Wako Shungorō ··············· **8**:221b
  Canada ······················ **1**:238b
  Hawaii
    Irwin, Robert Walker ·········· **3**:336a
  United States Immigration Acts of
    1924, 1952, and 1965 ···· **8**:164b-165a
Immigration control. *See* **Emigration**
  and immigration control
Immigration Control Law ········· **2**:313b
Immigration Control Order (1924) ·· **1**:47b
Immigration Exclusion Act (1924) ·· **4**:13a
Immortality ········· **1**:20a; **2**:80b-81a
Imochibyō ····················· **6**:310a
Imohori chōja ····芋掘長者 ···· **7**:269b
Imo Mutiny ····· **2**:361a; **3**:275a; **4**:280a
  draft notification slips ·········· **7**:167b
  Kaehwap'a ···················· **4**:101b
  Taewŏn'gun ·················· **7**:294a
Imori [newt (*Triturus pyrrhogaster*)]
  ···························· **3**:275a
Imoseyama onna teikin
  ··········妹背山婦女庭訓 ····· **1**:274b
Imo to sekagami
  ··········妹と背かゞみ ····· **8**:110b
Impāru Sakusen ·············· **3**:281b
Impeachment ······· **3**:275a; **6**:242b
  grounds ······················ **3**:275b
Imperial Academy Prize ········ **7**:315b
Imperial anthologies 2:354a; **3**:275b; **7**:94b
  Chinese poetry
    Bunka shūreishū ······· **1**:211b-212a
    Keikokushū ··············· **4**:189a
    Ryōunshū ······· **4**:109a, 189a; **5**:29a
  waka
    Fūgashū ·················· **3**:275b
    Go shūishū ················ **2**:353a
    Gyokuyō wakashū ··········· **3**:71b
    Kin'yō wakashū ········ **4**:219a-219b
    Kokinshū ············ **4**:254b-255a
    Senzai wakashū ············· **7**:68a
    Shika wakashū ·············· **7**:95a
    Shin chokusenshū ··········· **2**:354a
    Shin kokinshū ········· **7**:119b-120b
    Shin shūishū ··············· **8**:73b
    Shin zoku kokinshū ·· **7**:170b; **8**:204a
    Shūi wakashū ··············· **7**:184b
Imperial Art Academy ·········· **4**:178b
Imperial authority ··············· **3**:152b
Imperial conferences ········· **3**:59a-59b
Imperial Diet ······· **3**:275b-277a; **6**:214a
  armed forces ·················· **8**:85a
  Genrōin ······················ **3**:22a
  history: Meiji period ············ **3**:276b
    political parties & factions ····· **3**:276b
  history: Shōwa period ······· **3**:276b-277a
  history: Taishō period ··········· **3**:276b
  Itō Hirobumi ·················· **3**:353a
  Meiji, Emperor ················ **5**:153a
  Meiji Constitution **2**:2b, 8a, 8b, 9a; **3**:195b
  operation ····················· **3**:276a
    sessions ··················· **3**:276a
  organization ·················· **3**:276a
    House of Peers ········· **3**:241a, 267a
    House of Representatives ······ **3**:276a
    powers ···················· **3**:276a
  Taishō, Emperor ··············· **2**:207a
  Taishō democracy ·············· **7**:304a
  Universal Manhood Suffrage Movement
    ························· **8**:169a
Imperial edict ················ **3**:277a
  rinji ························· **6**:318a
  semmyō ······················ **7**:62a-62b
  senji ························· **7**:65b
Imperial family ··············· **3**:277*a*
  Fujiwara family ········ **2**:348a, 350a
  Shintō rituals surrounding ······ **7**:126b

See also **Imperial household**
Imperial Fine Arts Academy (Teikoku Bijutsuin) ·············· **8**:318b
Imperial Guard, Office of ········ **2**:184a
Imperial Headquarters ·········· **2**:58b
　independence ············· **1**:86b–87a
Imperial Hotel ············· **3**:277b; **8**:279a
　Raymond, Antonin ············ **6**:284b
Imperial household ·············· **3**:277b
Imperial Household Agency ···· **1**:218b; **3**:277b–278a; **6**:214a
Imperial Household Council ······ **2**:377b
Imperial Household Law ··· **2**:6b, 8a, 206a; **3**:278a; **7**:69b
　commentary ················ **4**:192b
　Daijōsai ················· **2**:59a–59b
　Itō Hirobumi ··············· **3**:353a
　kōgō defined ··············· **4**:249a
Imperialism ·············· **4**:387a; **7**:198b
Imperial Japanese Army ········ **3**:278a
　Nakano School ·············· **5**:316a
Imperial Japanese Navy ········ **3**:278a
　Naval Academy ··········· **5**:358a–358b
　Naval General Staff Office ····· **5**:358b
Imperial Law of the Houses ····· **2**:95a
Imperial legitimacy, historical debate ················· **5**:323b–324a
"Imperial loyalists" ··········· **2**:205a
Imperial Military Reservists' Association ············· **3**:278a; **5**:174a
　Imperial Rule Assistance Association ··············· **3**:280b
　Tanaka Giichi ··········· **7**:336a–336b
Imperial Mirror ·············· **4**:148b
Imperial National Defense Policy ··· **1**:87b
Imperial New Year's Poetry Reading ···················· **3**:278b
Imperial ordinance ············ **3**:278b
　Imperial Diet ··············· **3**:276a
Imperial Palace ·············· **8**:61a
Imperial Palace Music Department ·· **3**:1b
Imperial Party ················ **7**:376b
Imperial police ··············· **4**:185a
Imperial Prize of the Japan Academy ···················· **4**:9b
　Ogura Shimpei (1935) ·········· **6**:71b
　Tawara Sunao (1914) ·········· **7**:351a
Imperial regalia **1**:51b; **3**:278b–279a; **7**:278b
　death of Tokiko ·············· **1**:67b
　Ise Shrine ················· **3**:338a
　Kusanagi no Tsurugi ("grass-cutting" sword) ············· **1**:115b–116a
　legend ··················· **3**:278a
　magatama ················· **1**:147b
　mythology ················· **5**:293b
　Shintō ··················· **7**:126a
　Shintō art ················· **7**:135a
　Taira-Minamoto War ·········· **7**:300b
Imperial Rescript on Education of 1890 · **1**:165b, 252b; **2**:175a; **3**:195b, 279a–279b; **6**:192b; **8**:28b, 291b
　basis ···················· **3**:279a
　Confucianism ·············· **1**:358a
　historical background ········· **3**:279a
　Inoue Kowashi ·············· **3**:311a
　kokutai ··················· **4**:263a
　modern philosophy ··········· **5**:229b
　Motoda Nagazane ············ **5**:257a
　nationalism ················ **5**:342b
　policy ··················· **2**:182a
　principles ·············· **2**:183a–183b
　religion ·················· **6**:293b
Imperial rescripts ············· **1**:165b
Imperial Rescript to Soldiers and Sailors ······ **3**:279b–280a; **5**:173b; **7**:65b; **8**:291b
　political circumstances ········· **3**:280a
　precedents ············· **3**:279b–280a
　principles of conduct ······· **3**:279b–280a

Takehashi Insurrection ········· **7**:324a
Imperial Rule Assistance Association (IRAA) ···· **1**:40a, 84a; **2**:94b; **3**:280a–281a; **6**:207a; **6**:211b; **8**:277b
　China War ················· **3**:202a
　cultural section ············· **7**:176b
　Gotō Ryūnosuke ············· **3**:53b
　Kawakami Jōtarō ············· **4**:181a
　Konoe Fumimaro ············· **4**:273a
　local level ················ **3**:280b
　Nagai Ryūtarō ·············· **5**:301b
　Nakano Seigō ··········· **5**:316a–316b
　New Order Movement ········· **5**:366a
　Occupation Purge ············ **6**:58a
　"reformists" vs *"Japanists"* ···· **3**:280a
　Rikken Seiyūkai ············· **6**:315b
　Tōjō Hideki ················ **8**:39b
Imperial Shintō ·············· **2**:300b
Imperial Theater ··········· **2**:75b–76b
Imperial universities ··········· **3**:281a
　higher schools ·············· **3**:135a
　privileges ················· **3**:281b
　research and development ··· **6**:303b–305b
　systematizing higher education ·· **3**:133a
Imperial Universities Athletic Association ················ **7**:242b
Imperial University Order ········ **8**:170a
Imperial Veterans Association ···· **3**:278a
Imperial Way faction ····· **1**:74a; **4**:243a
Imphal Campaign ············· **3**:281b
　United Kingdom ············· **8**:152b
Important Cultural Properties. *See* **National Treasures**
Important Intangible Cultural Assets. *See* **Living National Treasures**
Imports. *See* **Foreign trade;** *and specific country*
Imprisonment ··············· **6**:172b
Imprisonment of the Companions of Barbarian Studies ·········· **1**:141b
In. *See* **Seals**
Ina ·················· 伊那 ···· **3**:281b
Ina Basin ·············· 伊那盆地 ·· **3**:281b
Inada Ryōkichi ·········· 稲田龍吉 ·· **3**:282a
Inagaki Hiroshi ···· 稲垣浩 ··· **2**:269b–270a, 271a; **3**:282a
Inagaki Taruho ········ 稲垣足穂 ··· **3**:282b
　works ··················· **3**:282a
Inagi ················· 稲城 ··· **3**:282b
Inago ·················· **5**:72a
Inaka kyōshi ·········· 田舎教師 ··· **7**:359a
Inamura Junzō ········· 稲村順三 ··· **4**:48b
Inamura-Morito dispute ········ **4**:48b
Inamura Sampaku 稲村三伯 ··· **3**:282a
　Haruma wage ············· **3**:105a
Inari ········· 稲荷 · **3**:282b–283a, 375a
　Hatsuuma ················· **3**:113b
　origins ·················· **3**:283a
　symbol ··················· **3**:283a
Inariyama tomb 稲荷山古墳 ··· **1**:79a; 233b; **3**:283a
Ina Tadatsugu ········ 伊奈忠次 ··· **3**:283b
Inatomi Naoie ········· 稲富直家 ··· **3**:283b
　Inatomi school of gunnery ····· **3**:283b
Inawashiro, Lake 猪苗代湖 **1**:137a; **3**:283b
Inawashiro Kensai 猪苗代兼載 ··· **3**:283b
　Shinsen tsukubashū ········· **7**:124b
Inayama Yoshihiro 稲山嘉寛 ··· **3**:284a
Inazawa ·············· 稲沢 ··· **3**:284a
Incantations, prayer ··········· **6**:233a
Incarceration ············· **2**:48b–49a
　wartime ················ **4**:17a–17b

Incense ceremony ··········· **3**:284a–285a
　history ··················· **3**:284b
　various ceremonies ········· **3**:284b–285a
"Incident of the Bell Inscription" ·· **7**:165b
Income, national ·········· **5**:339b–341b
　complementary structure and economic growth ········· **5**:340a–340b
　consumption behavior ········ **2**:18a–20b
　disposable ·············· **2**:18a–20b
　public sector ············ **5**:340b–341a
　savings behavior ········· **2**:18a–20b
　size and structure ········ **5**:339b–340a
　transfer payments ········ **5**:341a–341b
　wealth ················· **5**:349a–349b
Income distribution ···· **3**:285b–287a; **7**:216b
　factors of ················ **3**:286a
　international comparisons ···· **3**:285b–287a
　　economic ················ **3**:286a
　　historical ·············· **3**:286a
　　social ············· **3**:286b–287a
　　statistical ·············· **3**:286a
　life-cycle differences ····· **3**:286a–287a
　modern ·················· **2**:165a
　prewar and postwar patterns ····· **3**:285b
　urban/rural differentials ······· **3**:285b
　taxes ················ **7**:353b–354a
Income-Doubling Plan ···· **3**:287a; **8**:180a
　technological development ······ **7**:370a
Income per capita ·········· **2**:16b–17a
Incomes policy ·············· **3**:287b
　industrial policy ············ **3**:296b
Income Tax Law ············· **2**:276b
　tax accounting ············· **7**:352a
Increase Production and Promote Industry ················· **7**:165b
Indebtedness ··············· **6**:105a
Indebtedness, certificate of ······ **2**:81a
Independence Club ········ **3**:287b; **6**:307b
　anti-Russian activities ········· **4**:281b
Independence Party ··········· **4**:101b
Independent act ·············· **4**:86a
Independent movie productions ·················· **3**:287b–288a
India
　Bose, Rash Behari ········ **1**:164a–164b
　military commanders ········· **7**:197a
　nationalist leaders
　　Bose, Subhas Chandra ······ **1**:164b–165a
　religion ············· **6**:290a–293b
　Ryōbu Mandara ············· **6**:347b
India and Japan ·········· **3**:288a–289b
　British India ·············· **3**:288a
　early attitude ·············· **3**:288a
　early Buddhist influences ······ **3**:288a
　postwar cultural relations ······ **3**:289a
　postwar economic relations ····· **3**:289a
　postwar political relations ··· **3**:288b–289a
Indian National Army (INA) ···· **1**:164b; **2**:348b; **3**:289a–290a; **6**:260a; **7**:197a
Indian Ocean Fisheries Commission ················ **2**:283a
Indian-Pacific Ocean Fisheries Commission ·············· **2**:283a
Indigents' Party ········· **1**:272a; **4**:267a
Indigo ········· **2**:136a, 296a; **3**:290a; **7**:24a
　vat-dye method ············· **3**:290a
Individual autonomy, principle of ··· **4**:86a
Indochina
　French-Japanese relations ······ **2**:333a
　Japanese occupation ········· **3**:290b
Indonesia and Japan ········ **3**:290b–291a
　immigration ··············· **3**:290b
　World War II ··········· **3**:290b–291a
Indonesian Pembela Tanah Air ···· **6**:179b
Industrial Bank of Japan, Ltd ···· **1**:139a; **3**:291a; **5**:319a–319b; **8**:357b
Industrial complexes ········· **3**:291b

Industrial design. *See* Design
Industrial funds ·············· 3:291b-292a
lending rates ·················· 3:291b
sources ························· 3:291b
Industrial injuries ············· 3:292a
Industrial insurance ············· 3:317a
Industrial Investment Special Account
···························· 1:139b
Industrialization
class structure ················ 1:323a
"closed" employment systems
························· 4:344a-344b
company welfare system ········· 1:342b
crime rate ···················· 7:209a
dekasegi ···················· 2:83b-84a
early modern economy ····· 2:151a-153b
effect on today's society ··· 7:213a-218b
labor ························ 4:343a
modern employment system ····· 2:210b
Shibusawa Eiichi ············· 7:86a-86b
social welfare as outgrowth ······· 7:211a
Industrial organization ···· 3:292a-296b
capital concentration ····· 3:293b-294a
contemporary ····· 2:162b-163a; 3:296a
historical background ·········· 3:292a
modern vs traditional ········ 3:292a
post-World War II ·········· 3:292b
history of economic concentration
························ 3:292b-293b
cartels ···················· 3:293a
zaibatsu ·················· 3:292b
importance of groups ·········· 3:295a
intercorporate stockholding ····· 3:295a
shihon keiretsu ············· 3:295b
industrial policy ·············· 3:296a
market concentration ····· 3:294a-295a
low vs high ················ 3:294a
role of legal cartels ····· 3:295b-296a
types ······················ 3:296a
Industrial Patriotic Association ···· 4:345b
Industrial plants, production ······ 1:27b
Industrial policy ········· 3:296b-297a
categories ··············· 3:296b-297a
means of implementation ······ 3:297a
Industrial property ··········· 3:297a
classes ····················· 3:297a
registration ················· 3:297a
rights ······················ 3:297a
Industrial relocation policy ······· 3:297b
goals ······················ 3:297b
Industrial Relocation Promotion Law
of 1972 ···················· 3:297b
Industrial reorganization ······· 3:298a
Industrial revolution in Japan ····· 3:298a;
7:198b
Industrial robots ········· 3:298b-299b
economic and social role ······· 3:299a
government programs to faster use 3:299b
growth of robot industry ··· 3:298b-299a
development ··············· 3:298b
exports ················ 3:298b-299a
types and primary uses of ······ 3:299a
Industrial Standard, Japanese (JIS)
························· 4:61b-62a
Industrial Standardization Law of 1949
··················· 4:61b-62a; 6:273b
Industrial structure ········· 3:299b-302a
changes in manufacturing ··· 3:300b-301b
conclusion ··················· 3:302a
economic sectors ············· 3:299b
industrial policy ·············· 3:296b
Japan's historical experience · 3:299b-300b
national income ·········· 5:339b-341b
relationship to foreign trade
structure ·············· 3:301b-302a
Industrial Structure Council 1:12a; 3:302a
economic planning ············ 2:167a
functions and council reports ····· 3:302b

organization and membership ····· 3:302a
Industrial waste ·············· 3:302b
contamination ··············· 3:302b
disposal ···················· 3:302b
Industrial zones ·············· 3:303a
Industries
chemical ···················· 1:267b
commodities ················· 3:313a
computer ···················· 1:344a
Japanese market share ······ 1:344a
construction ················· 2:14a
construction machinery ········ 2:14a
copper ······················ 2:372a
declining ···················· 2:81b
development
industrial robots ·········· 3:298b
electrical equipment ····· 2:342a, 372a
energy ················ 2:214a-214b
fish and shellfish farming ··· 2:281b-282b
fishing ················· 2:284a-287b
food processing ·············· 2:307a
garment ····················· 3:12a
glass ······················· 3:36b
government-operated factories ·· 3:56a-56b
government promotion of ········ 7:165b
growth ······················ 3:63b
input-output analysis ·········· 3:313a
internal organization ··········· 3:318a
iron ··················· 3:333b-336a
knowledge-intensive ··········· 3:63b
machine tool ················· 5:78b
mining ················· 5:184b-185a
modern vs traditional ··········· 3:19a
monopoly and oligopoly ···· 5:247a-247b
nonferrous metals ············· 6:34b
petrochemical ················ 6:180a
pharmaceutical ··············· 6:182a
precision machinery ··········· 6:233b
primary industries ············· 6:239b
public corporations ············ 6:263a
public utilities ··············· 6:266b
public utility rates ············· 6:266b
publishing ··················· 6:267a
secondary ··················· 7:47b
service ····················· 3:313a
sewing machines ·············· 4:2a
shipbuilding ············ 7:141b-143a
silk production ··············· 7:194a
steel ·················· 3:333b-336a
subcontractors ··············· 2:14a
tertiary industries ········· 8:14b-15a
textile ················· 8:16a-16b
whaling ················ 8:249b-250b
Infancy ······················ 5:4a
Infanticide ··············· 2:246b; 6:224a
Inflation
Dodge line ·················· 2:122b
land reform ················· 4:365a
Political Crisis of 1881 ········· 6:202b
Inflation and price stability ······· 3:303a
economic indicators ··········· 3:303a
input-output analysis ·········· 3:313a
types of inflation ············· 3:303a
Inga ························· 3:303b
Ingaōhō ····················· 4:93b
Ingen ·············· 隱元 1:179b; 3:303b
Itsunen ····················· 3:357a
Ingo ······················ 3:303b-304a
Inheritance ··············· 1:14b; 6:244a
adoption ················· 1:15a-15b
land ······················ 7:232a
principle of succession ·········· 3:259b
Inheritance law ···· 3:304a-305b; 4:379a
history of inheritance system ····· 3:304a
Edo period (1600-1868) ······ 3:304a
Meiji period (1868-1912) ······ 3:304a
summary of present ········ 3:304a-305b
acceptance and renunciation ····· 3:304b

administration of estate ········ 3:305a
disinheritance ··············· 3:304b
disqualification ·············· 3:304b
order of inheritance ··········· 3:304b
partition of estates ············ 3:305a
principle ··················· 3:304a
secured portions ············· 3:305a
shares ················· 3:304b-305a
In Hōkichi ·········· 伊奉吉 8:357b-358a
Injiuchi ·············· 3:305b; 8:325b
Injū ·················· 陰獣 2:170b
"Ink-flow" ··················· 7:266b
"Inki na tanoshimi"
············· 陰気な愉しみ ······ 8:319b
Ink line painting (hakubyōga) ····· 3:87b
Ink painters. *See* Painters, ink
Ink painting (suibokuga) ········· 1:192a;
3:305b-307b; 6:150b
China ····················· 1:283a
Hasegawa Tōhaku ············ 3:307a
Higashiyama culture ··········· 3:132b
history ················· 3:306a-307a
rise ····················· 3:306a
Kanō school ············ 4:149a, 150a
Kaō Ninga ················· 3:305a
Rimpa ···················· 6:317b
Sesshū Tōyō ············· 7:69b-70a
Ama no Hashidate ········· 6:152a
Haboku Landscape ········· 7:68a
Landscape of the Four Seasons · 3:306b
Shūbun ················ 3:180b-181a
subjects ··················· 3:306a
Inkyo ·················· 3:307b-308a
ideals ····················· 3:307b
kanreki ···················· 4:151a
social class ················· 3:307b
Inland Sea · 瀬戸内海 3:308a, 308b; 7:97b
Awajishima ············· 1:124a-124b
Inland Sea Industrial Region ····· 3:308a
Inland Sea National Park
·········· 瀬戸内海国立公園 1:124b; 4:103b
Okayama Prefecture ··········· 6:83a
"Innate Buddhahood" ··········· 8:27a
Inner minister ············ 5:310a-310b
Inner Mongolia, Russo-Japanese
agreements of 1907-1916 ······ 6:344b
Innoshima (city) ·········· 因島 3:308b
Innoshima (island) ··· 因島 3:308b
Inns ······················· 3:308b
"Inochi no Shoya"
············· いのちの初夜 ······ 7:176a
Inō Jakusui ·········· 稲生若水 3:308b
Kaibara Ekiken ·············· 4:108b
Inokuchi Ariya ···· 井口在屋 3:309a
Inō maps ············· 伊能図 3:309a
Inomata Tsunao
············· 猪俣津南雄 3:309a
Inoshishi ···················· 8:253a
Inō Tadataka ··· 伊能忠敬 2:65a; 3:309a;
7:31b
Inoue Enryō ········· 井上円了 3:309b
Fenollosa, Ernest Francisco ····· 2:251b
Inoue Hisashi · 井上ひさし 3:309b
Inoue Junnosuke
············· 井上準之助 3:309b-310a
assassination ················ 4:373a
Inoue Kaoru ········· 井上馨 ·1:160a; 2:56a;
3:310a; 5:314a-314b; 7:9b, 29a, 86a
diplomat ··················· 3:310a
financial policies ············· 3:310a
foreign minister ·············· 3:310b
Fujita Denzaburō ············· 2:346a
genrō ····················· 3:310b
Hara Takashi ················ 3:102b
Kanghwa, Treaty of ··········· 4:140b
naichi zakkyo ··········· 5:309a-310a
Treaty of Seoul ·············· 4:280b
Inoue Kiyonao ··· 井上清直 3:310b-311a

Inoue Kowashi ···· 井上毅 **2**:2b, 332a;
　　3:311a
　　Imperial Rescript on Education ···· **3**:279a
　　Meiji Constitution ···················· **2**:2b
　　Minister of Education ··············· **2**:176a
　　natural science ······················ **5**:356b
Inoue Masao ···· 井上正夫 ········· **2**:268b
Inoue Mitsuharu 井上光晴 ········ **3**:311a
Inoue Mitsusada 井上光貞 ········ **4**:261b
Inoue Nisshō 井上日召 **3**:311a; **7**:108a
Inoue Tetsujirō 井上哲次郎 **1**:223a; **3**:311a;
　　7:270b
　　Fenollosa, Ernest Francisco ········ **2**:251b
Inoue Yasushi ···· 井上靖 **1**:164a, 207a;
　　3:311b; **7**:103b
　　awards ······························· **3**:311b
　　works ······························· **3**:311b
I-novel ·········· **3**:312a; **7**:175b–176a
　　bundan ······························· **1**:208b
　　criticism ···························· **3**:312a
　　evolution ···························· **3**:312a
　　modern ··························· **5**:54a–54b
　　postwar literature ············· **6**:230b–231a
Input-output analysis ········ **3**:312b–313a
　　commodities and services industries
　　·································· **3**:313a
　　Japan vs West Germany ············· **3**:312b
　　relative price changes ········ **3**:312b–313a
　　"skyline" of Japanese industry ···· **3**:312b
Inrō ·············· 印籠 **1**:166b; **3**:313b
　　construction ······················· **3**:313b
　　functions ·························· **3**:313b
　　netsuke ···························· **3**:313a
　　Yamada Jōka ······················· **3**:313a
Inryōken nichiroku
　　蔭涼軒日録 ···· **4**:147b
Insai Hakusui 淫斎白水 ········· **4**:189b
Insanity ··························· **5**:162b
**Insatsu Kōgyō Kai (Japan Printers'
Associations)** ···················· **6**:246b
In school ························· **3**:313b
　　Inson ······························· **3**:315a
Inscriptions ·············· **3**:313b–314a
　　calligraphy ························· **1**:233b
　　historical sources ················· **3**:314a
　　methods ···························· **3**:313b
　　studies ···························· **3**:314a
Insect Book (Ehon mushi erami) ···· **8**:142a
Insecticides ····················· **6**:309a
Insects ····························· **1**:61a
　　ants ······························ **1**:67b–68a
　　bees and wasps ···················· **1**:149a
　　butterflies ··················· **1**:225b–226a
　　cicadas ···························· **1**:315a
　　crickets ························ **2**:43b–44a
　　dragonflies ························ **2**:133b
　　fireflies ·························· **2**:280a
　　gold beetle ························ **3**:43b
　　Japanese beetle ···················· **4**:22a
　　kirigirisu ························· **4**:220b
　　plant hopper ······················ **6**:190a
　　spiders ···························· **7**:242b
Insei ············ 院政 **3**:314b–315a;
　　7:69b
　　factional strife ··················· **3**:315a
　　interpretation ···················· **3**:315a
　　Kōgon headed ······················ **4**:249a
　　political structure ················ **3**:314b
　　reassertion of Imperial Rule ······· **3**:314b
　　after Shirakawa ···················· **3**:315a
　　Shirakawa and the establishment
　　·························· **3**:314b–315a
Inshō ·························· **7**:45b–46a
Insignias ···················· **2**:42a–43b
Inson ············ 院尊 **1**:199b; **3**:315a
Inspectors general *(ōmetsuke)* ···· **6**:101a
Installment Sales Law ············· **3**:315b
　　freedom of contract ··············· **2**:337b

　　provisions ························· **3**:315b
Instant foods ··················· **3**:315b
Institute for Infectious Diseases ··· **4**:229a;
　　6:305b
Institute for the Investigation of
Barbarian Books ··············· **1**:141b–142a
Institute of Asian Economic Affairs **3**:319b
Institute of Japanese Culture and
Classics ···························· **4**:259b
**Institute of Oriental Culture, Tōkyō
University** ······················· **3**:315b
Institute of Pacific Relations · **3**:315b–316a
**Institute of Physical and Chemical
Research** ··· **1**:268a; **3**:316a, 372a; **4**:207a;
　　6:303b, 305b, 311b
　　Ikeda Kikunae ····················· **3**:265b
　　natural science ···················· **5**:356b
　　Ōkōchi Masatoshi ··················· **6**:93a
　　technology, modern ················· **7**:372b
Institute of Statistical Mathematics
　　·························· **4**:116b; **6**:261a
Institut Franco-Japonaise ··········· **2**:332b
Insurance
　　casualty ····················· **3**:316a–316b
　　life ·································· **5**:5b
　　medical ···························· **3**:120a
　　medical and health ··········· **5**:144b–145b
　　miscellaneous ················· **3**:316a–316b
　　unemployment ······················ **8**:148a
Insurance Business Law (Hokengyō
Hō) ································· **8**:316a
Insurance companies
　　Dai-Ichi Mutual Life Ins Co ···· **2**:58b–59a
　　Meiji Mutual Life Insurance Co ··· **5**:154b
　　mutual company ···················· **5**:289b
　　Nippon Life Insurance Co ···· **2**:58b; **6**:10b
　　Sumitomo Mutual Life Insurance Co
　　·································· **7**:269b
　　Taishō Marine & Fire Insurance Co, Ltd
　　·································· **7**:305b
　　Tokio Marine & Fire Insurance Co., Ltd
　　·································· **8**:43a
　　Yasuda Fire & Marine Insurance Co,
Ltd ····························· **8**:317b–318a
Insurance system ··········· **3**:316b–317a
　　government ························· **3**:317a
　　history ···························· **3**:316b
　　private insurance companies ·· **3**:316b–317a
Intangible property rights ···· **3**:317a–317b
Intendants ·············· **2**:60a; **8**:292b
Interdependent origination ··· **2**:217a–217b
Interest groups ···················· **6**:236b
Interest Limitation Law ··········· **3**:317b
Interest rate structure ······· **3**:317b–318a
　　corporate finance ·················· **2**:29a
　　discount rate ····················· **3**:317b
　　monetary policy ··················· **5**:239b
　　prime lending rate ················· **3**:317b
"Interference by Demons"
Shimomura Kanzan ··············· **7**:105b
Inter-Governmental Group on Indonesia
(IGGI) ····························· **3**:291a
Interim Measure Law concerning Fishing
Zones ······························ **2**:283b
Interim Treaty for the Preservation of Fur
Seals in the North Pacific Ocean **2**:283b
Intermediaries ····················· **2**:233a
**Internal organization of Japanese
companies** ···················· **3**:318a–318b
　　decision-makeup ··················· **3**:318a
　　impact of technological progress ··· **3**:318a
　　research and development ··········· **3**:318a
International Accounting Standards
Committee (1973) ····················· **1**:8b
International Air Transport Association,
(IATA) ····························· **4**:10a
International Bank for Reconstruction
and Development (BRD) ···· **3**:253b–254a

International Banking Consortium
for China ····················· **7**:297a–297b
International Christian University · **3**:318b
International Commerce ·············· **4**:11a
International communications
　·································· **3**:318b–319a
　　business communications ·········· **3**:319a
　　news agencies
　　　foreign ························· **3**:319a
　　　Japanese ························· **3**:318b
　　television relay ·················· **3**:319a
International Confederation of Free
Trade Unions (ICFTU) · **4**:347a; **7**:223b
International Convention for the
Regulation
of Whaling of 1946 ············· **8**:250b
International Court of Justice ···· **7**:337b
International crimes ·············· **3**:319a
International Criminal Police
Organization ····················· **3**:319a
International cultural exchange ··· **3**:319a
　　government involvement ··········· **3**:319b
　　organizations ···················· **3**:319b
　　programs ························· **3**:319b
International Energy Agency ······· **2**:215b
International Federation for the
Promotion
of Sister Cities ··············· **7**:202a
International Finance Bureau ······ **5**:188a
**International friendship
organizations** ·············· **3**:319b–320a
　　diplomacy ························· **3**:320a
　　economy ·························· **3**:319b
International Geographical Union · **7**:293b
International Geophysical Year ···· **7**:240a
International Jūdō Federation ······ **4**:82b
International Kendō Federation ··· **4**:196a
International Labor Organization (ILO)
　·········· **4**:344b, 351a, 373a; **4**:178b; **7**:209a
　　occupational structure ············ **6**:55b
International Latitude Observation
Project Center ··················· **1**:104a
International law, private ····· **6**:250a–252b
　　choice-of-law rules ··········· **6**:250a–251b
　　　adoption ················· **6**:251a–251b
　　　decree of legal death ··········· **6**:250b
　　　inheritance ···················· **6**:251b
　　　legal acts and contracts ········ **6**:250b
　　　legal capacity ················· **6**:250b
　　　legal incompetency ············· **6**:250b
　　　legitimacy ····················· **6**:251a
　　　marriage and divorce ··········· **6**:251a
　　　national law determination ······ **6**:251b
　　　obligations ···················· **6**:251a
　　　parent-child relationship, rights and
　　　duties ························· **6**:251b
　　　paternity ····················· **6**:251a
　　　property rights ············ **6**:250b–251a
　　　renvoi ························· **6**:251b
　　civil procedure ··············· **6**:251b–252a
　　　foreign judgments ··············· **6**:252a
　　　jurisdiction over foreigners · **6**:251b–252a
　　　standing to sue ················· **6**:251b
International Metalworkers'
Federation-Japan Council (IMF-JC)
　·············· **3**:274b; **4**:348a; **7**:189b
International Military Tribunal for the Far
East ······························· **8**:223b
International Monetary Fund (IMF) **2**:310a;
　　3:13b, 274b; **8**:324a
　　import liberalization ············· **2**:323b
　　United States ···················· **8**:161a
International Origami Association · **6**:118b
International Planned Parenthood
Federation (IPPF) ················· **2**:247b
International Polar Motion Observation
Project Center ··················· **1**:104a
International relations ········ **3**:320a–325b

economic issues ··········· 3:325a
evolving relations with the United States
··············· 3:325a
expansion on the Asian mainland ·· 3:320b
future prospects ············ 3:325b
incursions in Manchuria and China 3:321b
Japan as a major power ······ 3:320b-321a
Japan in the cold war ········ 3:324a-324b
occupation period ············ 3:324a
opening of Japan ············ 3:320a
selected indicators of Japan's foreign
relations ··········· 3:322a-323b
territorial issues and treaty revision 3:320b
toward a more independent diplomacy
··············· 3:324b-325a
World War I and its aftermath ··· 3:321a
World War II and the Greater East Asia
Coprosperity Sphere ······· 3:321b-324a
See also each country
International trade. See Foreign trade
International Travel Inns ········· 3:308b
International Treaty concerning Fishing
on the High Seas in the North Pacific
Ocean ················· 2:282a
International Treaty for the Preservation
of Tuna in the Northwest Atlantic
Ocean ················· 2:282a
International Tribunal of the Far East
··············· 8:36b, 223b
International Whaling Commission 8:249b
International Whaling Control Treaty
··············· 2:282b; 8:250a
International Whaling Convention
of 1937 ··············· 8:250b
Internists. See Medicine, internists
Interrogation (jimmon) ········· 2:49b
Into a Black Sun ············ 4:111b
Intoku taiheiki· 陰徳太平記 ···· 6:132b
Intoxication ··············· 2:48a
Inu ················· 2:124b-126a
Inubōzaki ········ 犬吠埼 ···· 3:325b
Inu hariko ········· 3:325b; 8:96b
Inuiyama ·········· 乾山 ···· 4:199b
Inu jinin ········· 犬神人 ···· 4:59b
Inukai Tsuyoshi ···· 犬養毅 · 3:326a-326b;
4:384b; 5:316a-316b; 7:4b, 78a, 276b
assassination (May 15th Incident) · 4:373a;
5:142b
cabinet ················· 1:74a
goals ················· 3:326a
Kakushin Kurabu ············ 4:120a
support of Sun Yat-Sen
Inuoumono ········ 犬追物 3:326b; 4:160b
Inu tsukubashū ·犬筑波集 ···· 7:140a
Inuyama ·········· 犬山 ···· 3:326b
Invasions of Korea in 1592 and 1597
··············· 3:326b-327b
Bunroku Campaign ········· 3:326b-327a
causes ················· 3:326b
Chinese involvement ······· 3:326b-327a
difficulties ·············· 3:327b
Fujiwara Seika ············ 2:358b
Fukushima Masanori ·········· 2:366b
Keichō Campaign ············ 3:327a
Korean-Japanese relations ······ 4:140b
Korean potters ············ 6:320b
national flag ············ 5:339a
National Seclusion ··········· 5:347a
peace negotiations ··········· 3:327a
supply base ············· 4:127b
Tōdō Takatora ············ 8:34b
Ukita Hideie ············· 8:137b
waegwan ··············· 8:198a
Investments
character of Japanese ········ 5:263b
foreign ··············· 2:29a-30b
monetary policy ··········· 5:240b
industrial funds ············ 3:291b

monetary policy ··········· 5:239b-240a
savings ·············· 2:160b-161a
Investment trusts ············ 3:327b-328a
In-yō (Chinese: yin-yang) ········· 5:151a
Inzō ·············· 印相 ···· 3:328a
Iodochlorhydroxyquin ··········· 7:206a
Ioffe (Joffe), Adolf Abramovich ·· 2:248b;
3:328a
Iō Islands ········· 硫黄列島 ···· 3:328a
Iōjima ·········· 硫黄島 3:328b; 4:207a;
8:276a
4:207a; 8:276a
Iōjima (Iwojima), Battle of ········· 3:328a
Ionushi ········· いほぬし ···· 3:328b
"Ippeisotsu" ········ 一兵卒 ···· 7:358b
Ippen ·············· 一遍 3:328b-329b
Ippen shōnin eden ··········· 3:329a
Ji sect ················· 4:62a
studies ··············· 3:328b-329a
travels ················· 3:329a
Ippen shōnin eden
(Pictorial Biography of
the Monk Ippen)
············· 一遍上人絵伝 · 3:329b; 8:29b
Ippitsuan Kakō 一筆庵可候 ······ 4:189b
Ippitsusai Bunchō
············ 一筆斎文調 ···· 3:329b
Ippon-gatana dohyōiri
············ 一本刀土俵入 3:108a; 4:166a
IPR ················· 3:315b-316a
Iragomisaki ······ 伊良湖岬 ···· 3:329b
Irako Seihaku ·伊良子清白 ···· 3:329b
Iran Committee ············ 4:188a
Irejichi ················· 7:87a
Irezumi ·········· 入墨 ···· 8:73a
Iriai ············· 入会 3:329b-331a
fertilizers ·············· 3:330b
legal battles over ··········· 3:330b
Meiji government ············ 3:331b
tomeyama ··············· 8:70b
types ················· 3:330a
Iriaiken no kaitai
············ 入会権の解体 ···· 4:184b
Iriai no kenkyū 入会の研究 ······ 4:111b
Irie Takako ······ 入江たか子 ···· 3:331a
Iriomotejima ······· 西表島 ···· 3:331a
Iriomote National Park
············ 西表国立公園 ···· 3:331a
Irises (family Iridaceae) ······ 3:331b-332a
cultivation ··············· 3:331b
introduction to West ··········· 3:331b
Iris Screens ············ 6:154a-154b
Irodorareru kuchibiru
(Painted Lips)彩られる唇 ······ 8:90b
Irogoi (carp) ············· 1:244a
Iroha jirui shō ·色葉字類抄 · 2:93b; 3:332a
Iroha karuta ······ 3:332a, 332b; 6:192a
Iroha poem ············ 3:332a-332b
Irohazaka ········ いろは坂 ···· 3:332b
Iron age ········· 鉄器時代 ···· 3:332b-333a
Iron and steel ············ 3:333a-333b
Iron and steel industry · 3:333a, 333a-336a
companies
Kawasaki Steel Corporation ··· 4:184a
Kōbe Steel, Ltd ·········· 4:238a
Nippon Kōkan ·········· 6:10a-10b
Nippon Steel Corporation ···· 6:12b-13a
Sumitomo Metal Industries, Ltd · 7:269a
economic independence ········ 2:165b
economic planning ··········· 2:165b
exports ·············· 3:335b-336a
facilities and technology ········· 3:335b
finance ················· 3:335b
labor and industrial relations ······ 3:335a
Meiji period ············· 2:153a
modern ················· 3:333b
origins ·············· 3:333b-334a
English furnaces ··········· 3:333b

government involvement ··· 3:333b-334a
postwar recovery and growth 3:334a-334b
competition ············ 3:334b
rationalization programs ······ 3:334b
problems and prospects ········· 3:336a
raw material supply ··········· 3:335a
structure ·············· 3:334b-335a
swords ·············· 3:333a-333b
tatara-buki ········ 3:333a; 7:348a-348b
wage bargaining ··········· 7:189b
Irori tan ········· 囲炉裡譚 ···· 7:292a
Irōzaki ············· 石廊崎 ···· 3:336a
Irozange (Confession)
············ 色ざんげ ···· 8:173a
Irregular Militia ············ 4:204b
Irrigation
dams ················· 2:72b
ritsuryō system ············ 6:329a
techniques ··············· 1:29b
Iruma ·············· 入間 ···· 3:336a
Iruman ················· 1:145b
Irwin, Robert Walker ··········· 3:336a
Japanese American ··········· 4:13b
Irwin, Sophia A. ············ 3:336a
Irwin Convention ············ 4:13b
Irwin School ············· 3:336b
Isahaya ············· 諫早 ···· 3:336b
Isamu Noguchi
············ イサムノグチ ···· 8:295b
Isanatori ········· いさなとり ···· 4:242b
Isa Tomomune ····伊佐朝宗 ···· 2:78a
Isawa (city) ········· 石和 ···· 3:336b
Ise (city) ············ 伊勢 ···· 3:336b
Ise (poet) ············ 伊勢 ···· 3:336b
Kokinshū ··············· 4:254b
Sanjūrokkasen ············· 7:13a
Ise Bay ·········· 伊勢湾 ···· 3:336b-337a
Isehara ············· 伊勢原 ···· 3:337a
Ise kagura ········ 伊勢神楽 ···· 4:107b
Iseki ·············· 伊勢記 ···· 4:128b
Iseki & Co, Ltd ············· 3:337a
Ise monogatari ··· 伊勢物語 · 1:85b; 3:337a;
4:129b; 5:245b; 8:118b
commentaries ········· 3:337a; 4:188a
influence ··············· 3:337b
manuscripts ··············· 3:337a
monogatari bungaku ·········· 5:245b
parody ················· 4:136b
waka ·············· 8:208b, 212a
Isenoumi Prefecture
Natural Park
············ 伊勢海県立自然公園 ···· 1:45a
Ise Plain ·········· 伊勢平野 ···· 3:337b
Ise Province ········ 伊勢国 ···· 3:337b
Ise Rebellion ······ 伊勢暴動 ···· 3:337b-338a
Ise Sadamichi····伊勢貞陸 ···· 8:303b
Isesaki ············· 伊勢崎 ···· 3:338a
Ise-Shima National Park
············ 伊勢志摩国立公園 ···· 1:21b; 3:338a
Ise Shrine ········ 伊勢神宮 · 2:248a, 300b;
3:338a-339a;
7:80b, 180a, 248a, 250a
Amaterasu Ōmikami ······ 1:51a; 4:144a
architecture ··············· 3:338a
cult of ················· 3:338b
"eejanaika" ··············· 2:184a
"emperor art"
Taut, Bruno ········· 7:351a-351b
inner shrine ··············· 3:338a
Inner Shrine, main building ······ 3:338b
kamikaze ················· 4:126b
okage mairi ··············· 6:79a
outer shrine ··············· 3:338b
rites ················· 3:338a
Ryōbu Shintō ············· 6:351a
sacred fire ··············· 2:53b
Shintō ················· 7:126a
Shintō architecture ··········· 7:132b

Shintō rites · 7:137b
tama · 7:332a
Usa Hachiman Shrine · 8:181b
Isetan Co, Ltd · 3:339a
I-shan I-ning · 3:348b
Ishibashi Ningetsu
石橋忍月 · 3:339a; 5:13a; 7:125b
Ishibashi Shian · 石橋思案 · 4:198b
Ishibashi Shōjirō
石橋正二郎 1:170b; 3:339a
Western-art museums · 5:279a
Ishibashi Tanzan 石橋湛山 · 3:339b; 7:92a
Ishibashiyama, Battle of
石橋山の戦 · 2:342b
Kajiwara Kagetoki · 4:114b
Minamoto no Yoritomo · 5:181a
Sasaki Takatsuna · 7:23a
Taira-Minamoto War · 7:300a
Ishibatsuki · 4:195a
Ishibutai tomb · 石舞台古墳 · 3:*339a*, 339b
Ishida Baigan · 石田梅岩 · 3:339b-340a
doctrines · 3:340a
Shingaku · 7:111b
Teshima Toan · 4:120a
works · 3:340a
Ishida Eiichirō · 石田英一郎 2:312a; 3:340a
Ishida Hakyō · 石田波郷 · 3:340a
Ishida Mitoku · 石田未得 · 3:340a; 5:48a
Ishida Mitsunari · 石田三成 · 3:340a; 7:9a, 99a
Sekigahara, Battle of · 7:56b
Ishida Taizō · 石田退三 · 3:340b
Ishi-dōrō lanterns · 4:367b-368a
Ishigaki · 石垣 · 3:340b
Ishigakijima · 石垣島 · 3:340b
Ishiguro Munemaro
石黒宗麿 · 3:340b-341a
glazes · 3:340b
Ishiguro Tadaatsu
石黒忠篤 · 3:341a
Ishihara Kanji · 石原莞爾 · 3:345b-346a
Ishihara Shinobu
石原忍 · 3:341a
Ishihara Shintarō
1:209a; 2:273b;
石原慎太郎 · 3:341a
Ishii Baku · 石井漠 · 2:75b
Ishii Hakutei · 石井柏亭 · 3:146b
Ishii Kikujirō · 石井菊次郎 3:341a; 4:366b; 7:88a
League of Nations · 4:373a
Ishii-Lansing Kyōtei
石井－ランシング協定 · 4:366b-367b
Ishii Mitsujirō · 石井光次郎 · 3:341b
Ishii Ryōsuke · 石井良助 · 3:341b
Ishii Teabowl Art Museum · 3:77a
Ishikari Coalfield 石狩炭田 · 1:39a; 3:341b
Ishikaridake · 石狩岳 · 3:341b
Ishikarigawa · 石狩川 · 3:342a
Ishikari Mountains
石狩山脈 · 3:342a
Ishikari Plain · 石狩平野 3:342a; 7:20a
Ishikawa · 石川 · 3:342a
Ishikawa Chiyomatsu
石川千代松 1:156a; 3:342a
Ishikawa Ichirō · 石川一郎 · 3:342a
**Ishikawajima-Harima Heavy Industries
Co, Ltd** · 3:342b; 4:139a, 183b
defense industry · 2:82b
Dokō Toshio · 2:127b
history · 3:342b
Mutsu · 5:288a
Suzuki shōten subsidiary · 4:238a
Ishikawa Jōzan · 石川丈山 · 3:342b
Ishikawa Jun · 石川淳 · 3:342b-343b
critiques · 3:343a
lifestyle · 3:343a
novels · 3:343a

translations · 3:342b
Ishikawa Masamochi
石川雅望 · 2:303b; 3:343b; 7:95a
Gagen shūran · 3:3a
Ishikawa Prefectural Art Museum · 4:198a
Ishikawa Prefecture
石川県 · 3:344a
industries · 3:344a
tourist attractions · 3:344a
Ishikawa Sanshirō
石川三四郎 · 3:344a; 7:56a
Fukuda Hideko · 2:362b
works · 3:344a
Ishikawa Tairō · 石川大浪 · 3:344a
Ishikawa Takeyoshi
石川武美 · 3:344b
Ishikawa Takuboku
石川啄木 · 3:344b-345a; 5:12b, 290b; 7:253b
influence · 3:345a
works · 3:344b
Ishikawa Tatsuzō 石川達三 · 3:345a; 7:103b
fūzoku shōsetsu · 2:378b
Ishikawa Toyonobu
石川豊信 · 3:345a
Ishimoto Yasuhiro 石元泰博 · 6:*186b*
Ishin denshin · 3:29b
Ishinomaki · 石巻 · 3:345a
Ishioka · 石岡 · 3:345a
Ishisaji · 7:247b
Ishiwara Jun · 石原純 · 3:345a
Ishiwara Kanji · 石原莞爾 · 3:345b-346a
China policy · 3:345b-346a
in Manchuria · 3:345b
political machinations · 3:345b
theory of war · 3:345b
Ishiwara Ken · 石原謙 · 3:346a
Ishiyamadera · 石山寺 · 3:346a; 7:91a
art treasures · 3:346b
patrons · 3:346b
Ishiyama Honganji
石山本願寺 · 3:221a-222b, 346b-347a
Oda Nobunaga vs · 3:179a
Ōsaka Castle · 6:120a
screen paintings · 4:148a
Ishizaka Kimishige
石坂君茂 · 3:347a
Ishizaka Taizō · 石坂泰三 · 3:347a
Ishizaka Yōjirō 石坂洋次郎 2:270b; 3:347a; 7:103b
fūzoku shōsetsu · 2:378b
Ishizara · 7:247b
**Ishizuchi Quasi-National
Park** · 石鎚国定公園 · 2:185a-185b
Ishizuchisan · 石鎚山 · 3:347a; 7:97b
Ishizuka Tatsumaro
石塚龍麿 · 3:347a
orthographic studies · 4:134a
Ishō nihonden · 異称日本伝 · 3:347b
Ishō ningyō · 2:*129a*
Islam · 8:70b
Island, The · 3:75a; 7:111b
Islands
Amakusa · 1:50a
Amami · 1:50a
Aoshima · 1:70b
Awajishima · 1:124a-124b
Bentenjima · 1:150a; 4:2b
Birōjima · 1:156b
Chichijima · 1:272a-272b
Chikubushima · 1:276b
Dejima · 2:83a-83b
Dōgashima · 2:123a
Enoshima · 2:220a
Etorofu · 2:234a
Fukuejima · 2:363a

Geiyo · 3:15b
geological structure · 4:9a-9b
Gotō · 3:52b-53a
Habomai · 3:73b
Hachijōjima · 3:74a
Hashima · 3:109b
Hatsushima · 3:113b
Hegurajima · 3:121b
Hiburishima · 3:129b
Hikoshima · 3:138b
Hiradoshima · 3:141b
Hokkaidō · 3:212b-213a
Honshū · 3:226b
Iejima · 3:260b
Iki · 3:267b
Innoshima · 3:308b
Iō · 3:328b
Iōjima · 3:328b
Iriomotejima · 3:331a
Ishigakijima · 3:340b
Itsukushima · 3:357a
Izu Islands · 3:365a
Jōgashima · 4:69a
Kakuijima · 4:118a
Kashikojima · 4:162a
Kerama · 4:200a
Kikaishima · 4:205a
Kinkazan · 4:213a
Kōjima · 4:251b
Koshikijima · 4:295b
Kumejima · 4:307b
Kunashiri · 4:308b
Kurahashijima · 4:311a
Kuril · 4:313a
Kyūshū · 4:341a
Matsushima · 5:140a
Megijima · 5:152a
Minami Daitōjima · 5:176b
Minami Torishima · 4:2b; 5:176b
Mishima · 5:199a
Miyakejima · 5:218a
Miyako · 5:219b
Miyakojima · 5:219b
Naoshima · 5:331b
Nōmijima · 6:33b-34a
Ogasawara · 4:2b; 6:68b
Oki · 6:84a-85b
Okinawa · 4:2b
Okinoerabujima · 6:92a
Okinoshima · 6:92b
Okinotorishima · 4:2b; 6:93a
Ōkunojima · 6:97b-98a
Okushiri · 6:98b
Ōmishima · 6:102a
Ōshima (Izu Ōshima) · 6:125a
Ōshima (Inland Sea) · 6:125b
Rebun · 6:284b
Rishiri · 6:320b
Sado · 6:362b-363b
Sakhalin · 7:1b-2a
Sakishima · 7:3a
Sakurajima · 7:4b
Satsunan Islands · 7:30b
Senkaku · 7:66a
Sensuijima · 7:67b
Shikanoshima · 7:94b
Shikoku · 7:97b
Shikotan · 7:98a
Shisakajima · 7:148a
Shōdoshima · 7:155a
Taketomijima · 7:325b
Tanegashima · 7:340a
Tobishima · 8:32b
Tokara · 8:42b
Tokunoshima · 8:58a
Torishima · 8:80b
Toshima · 8:83a
Tsushima · 8:117b-118a, 325b

Yaeyama · · · · · · · · · · · · · · · 8:283b
Yakushima · · · · · · · · · · · · · · 8:286b
Yonagunijima · · · · · · · · · · 4:2b; 8:337a
Yoronjima · · · · · · · · · · · · · · 8:339a
Isoda Kōichi · · · · · · · 磯田光一 · 3:347a
Isoda Koryūsai 磯田湖龍斎 · · · · · 3:347b
Isoda Kyūjirō · 磯田久次郎 · · · · · 4:171b
Isoho monogatari
· · · · · · · · · · 伊曽保物語 · 3:347b; 4:52a,
136b; 5:46a
Isonokami no Yakatsugu
· · · · · · · · · · · · · · 石上宅嗣 · 3:347b
Kaifūsō · · · · · · · · · · · · · · · · 4:109a
Untei · · · · · · · · · · · · · · · · · 8:174a
Isonokami Shrine石上神宮 3:348a; 7:126b
Isozaki Arata · · · · · · · 磯崎新 · · 3:348a
Israel · · · · · · · · · · · · · · · · · 4:43b
Issa · · · · · · · · · · · · · 一茶 · 1:182a; 3:79b,
348a; 5:16a; 7:5b
style · · · · · · · · · · · · · · · · · 3:348b
works · · · · · · · · · · · · · · · · · 3:348a
Issai-kyō · · · · · · · · · · · 1:187b; 4:136a,
299b
Issan Ichinei · · · · · · 一山一寧 · 3:348b; 7:70b
Gozan literature · · · · · · · · · · 3:58a-59a
Issei · · · · · · 4:12b-13b, 14b-15a; 6:179a
Gentlemen's Agreement · · · · · · 4:22a
major organizations · · · · · · · · 4:22a
political involvement · · · · · · · 4:15b
United States Immigration Acts of 1924,
1952, and 1965 · · · · · · · · · · 8:165a
voting · · · · · · · · · · · · · · · · 4:15b
World War II incarceration · · · · 4:17a-17b
Issekikai (political group) · · · · · 8:39b
Isshin Tasuke · · · 一心太助 · · · 8:339a
Issuikai · · · · · · · · · · · 一水会 · · 8:318b
Issumbōshi · · · · · · · 一寸法師 3:348b; 5:296a
folk tales · · · · · · · · · · · · · 2:302b
Isuzu Motors, Ltd · · · · · · · · · · 3:348b
Diesel Kiki Co, Ltd · · · · · · · · · 2:94a
Itabashi Ward · · · · · 板橋区 · · 3:349a
Itadori [(Japanese knotweed)
Polygonum cuspidatum] · · · · · · · 3:349a
Itagaki Seishirō
· · · · · · · · · · · · · 板垣征四郎 · 3:349a
Itagaki Taisuke · 板垣退助 · 1:271b; 2:56a;
3:349a-350a
Aikoku Kōtō · · · · · · · · · · · · · 1:34b
Aikokusha · · · · · · · · · · · · · · 2:366a
Freedom and People's Rights
Movement · · · · · · · 2:334a-334b, 373a
hambatsu · · · · · · · · · · · · · · · 3:91b
Hayashi Yūzō · · · · · · · · · · · · 3:118a
Jiyūtō · · · · · · · · · · · · · · · 4:65a-66a
Kenseitō · · · · · · · · · · · · · · · 4:198b
Kōno Hironaka · · · · · · · · · · · 4:273b
popular rights advocacy · · · · · · 3:349b
rise in power · · · · · · · · · · · · 3:349b
Sandai Jiken Kempaku Movement
(Movement to Memorialize Three
Important Items) · · · · · · · · · · 7:9b
Seikanron issue · · · · · · · · · · · 7:50b
Itaguwa · · · · · · · · · · · · · · · · 4:322a
Itai itai disease
· · · · · · · · · · イタイイタイ病 · 2:226b; 4:61a;
5:185b; 6:218b
Itako · · · · · · · · · · · · · 潮来 · · 3:350a
Itakura Katsukiyo板倉勝静 · · · · · 3:350a
Itakura Katsushige · 板倉勝重
· · · · · · · · · · 1:301b; 3:350a; 4:338b
Italy and Japan · · · · · · · · · · 3:350b-351a
Anti-Comintern Pact · · · · · · · · 1:65a
Catholic missionaries · · · · · · · 3:350b
cultural exchange after 1868 · 3:350b-351a
arts · · · · · · · · · · · · · · · · · 3:350b
technology · · · · · · · · · · · · · 3:350b
Japanese studies · · · · · · · · · · 4:43a
relations after World War II · · · · 3:351a

Itamae · · · · · · · · · · · · · · · · 2:25b
Itami · · · · · · · · · · · · · 伊丹 · · 3:351b
Itami Mansaku · · 伊丹万作 · 2:270a, 271a;
3:351b
Itaya Hazan · · · · · 板谷波山 · · 3:351b
Itchakushu-han · · · · · · · · · · · · 1:203a
Itō · · · · · · · · · · · · · · 伊東 · · 3:351b
Itō, Mancio · · · · · 伊東満所 · · 3:355a
French-Japanese relations · · · · · 2:330a
Ito Castle · · · · · · · · 怡土城 · · 3:354b
Itō Chūta · · · · · · · 伊東忠太 · · 1:80b
Itō Daisuke · · · · · 伊藤大輔 · 2:268b;
3:351b-352a
Itō Eiga Kenkyūjo · · · · · · · · · · 3:351b
Itō Einosuke · · · · 伊藤永之介 · · 3:352a
Itō Gemboku · · · · 伊東玄朴 · 3:352a; 7:16a
Itō Ham Provisions Co, Ltd · · · · · 3:352a
Itō Hirobumi · · · · · 伊藤博文 · 1:11b, 86b,
120a;
2:334a; 3:352a, 352b, 353a-353b; 4:198b
241a; 7:29a, 51a, 105a, 255b
Anglo-Japanese Alliance · · · · · · 1:56b
assassination · · · · · · · · 1:55a; 4:282b
diplomat · · · · · · · · · · · · · · 3:353a
early career · · · · · · · · · · · 3:353b-354a
genrō · · · · · · · · · · · · · · · · · 3:21b
Gneist, Rudolf von · · · · · · · · · 3:37b
hambatsu · · · · · · · · · · · · · · · 3:91b
Imperial Diet · · · · · · · · · · · · 3:276a
Inoue Kaoru · · · · · · · · · · · · · 3:310a
Inoue Kowashi · · · · · · · · · · · · 3:311a
Itō Miyoji · · · · · · · · · · · · · · 3:355a
Jiyūtō · · · · · · · · · · · · · · · · 4:65b
Kaneko Kentarō · · · · · · · · · · · 4:138b
Kojong abdicated throne · · · · · · 4:252b
Korea · · · · · · · · · · · · · 4:280b, 282a
last years · · · · · · · · · · · · · · 3:353a
Li Hongzhang · · · · · · · · · · · · 5:9b
Meiji Constitution · · · · · · · · · · 2:1b
nationalism · · · · · · · · · · · · · 5:342b
party politics · · · · · · · · · · · · 3:353a
prime minister · · · · · · · · · · · 6:243a
Rikken Seiyūkai · · · · · · · · · · · 6:315a
Treaty of Shimonoseki · · · · · · · 7:106a
youth · · · · · · · · · · · · · · · · 3:353a
Itoigawa · · · · · · · · · 糸魚川 · · 3:352b
Itoigawa-Shizuoka
tectonic line
· · · · · 糸魚川−静岡構造線 · · · · 4:8b
Itō Jakuchū · · · · · 伊藤若冲 · 3:353b-354a
religious scrolls · · · · · · · · · · · 3:353b
Itō Jinsai · · · · · · · 伊藤仁斎 1:357a; 3:354a;
4:58a, 247b; 7:94b
Confucian teachings · · · · · · · 1:355b-357b
Kagawa Shūtoku · · · · · · · · · · · 4:103b
Kogaku proponent · · · · · · · · · 4:246b
Kogidō founded and directed by · · 4:248b
Kogigaku · · · · · · · · · · · · · · · 3:354a
works · · · · · · · · · · · · · · · · · 3:354a
Itojō · · · · · · · · · · · · 怡土城 · · 3:354b
Itokawa Hideo · · · · 糸川英夫 · · 3:354b
Itō Keiichi · · · · · · · 伊藤圭一 · · 3:354b
Itō Keisuke · · · · · · 伊藤圭介 · 1:76b; 3:354b
Itokoku · · · · · · · · · · 伊都国 · · 3:354b
Itoman · · · · · · · · · · · 糸満 · · 3:354b
Itōman & Co, Ltd · · · · · · · · · · 3:355a
Itō Michio · · · · · · · 伊藤道郎 · · 2:75b
Itō Miyoji · · · · · · · 伊東巳代治 · 2:2b; 3:355a
Kaneko Kentarō · · · · · · · · · · · 4:138b
Meiji Constitution drafting · · · · · 2:2b
Itō Noe · · · · · · · · · 伊藤野枝 · 3:355a; 7:57a
Kamichika Ichiko · · · · · · · · · · 4:126a
murder · · · · · · · · · · · · 4:125a; 6:128a
Ōsugi Sakae · · · · · · · · · · · · · 6:127b
Seitōsha · · · · · · · · · · · · · · · 7:54b
Itō Sachio · · · · · · 伊藤左千夫 · 1:74b; 3:355a

Nagatsuka Takashi · · · · · · · · · 5:307b
Itō Sei · · · · · · · · · · 伊藤整 · 3:355b-356a;
5:275b
awards · · · · · · · · · · · · · · 3:355b-356a
critical essays · · · · · · · · · · · 3:355b
new psychological literature · · · · 3:355b
novels · · · · · · · · · · · · · · · 3:355b-356a
Shinchō · · · · · · · · · · · · · · · 7:109a
Itō Shinsui · · · · · · · 伊東深水 · · 3:356a
Kaburagi Kiyokata · · · · · · · · · · 4:100b
Itō Shizuo · · · · · · · 伊東静雄 · · 3:356a
Itō Sukechika · · · · · 伊東祐親 · · 3:356a
Itō Sukeyuki · · · · · · 伊東祐之 · · 8:287a
Itō Tōgai · · · · · · · · 伊藤東涯 · · 3:356a
Itowappu · · · · · · · · 糸割符 · · 3:356b;
5:323a-323b
National Seclusion · · · · · · · · 5:346b-347a
Itō-Yōkadō Co, Ltd · · · · · · · · · 3:356b
Itsukaichi · · · · · · · · 五日市 · · 3:356b
Itsuki Hiroyuki · · · · 五木寛之 · 3:356b-357a
fūzoku shōsetsu · · · · · · · · · · 2:378b
Itsukushima · · · · · · · 厳島 · · · 3:357a
Itsukushima Shrine
· · · · · · · · · · · 厳島神社 · · 1:187b;
3:357a; 5:277b; 7:232b
Itsunen · · · · · · · · · · 逸然 · · · 3:357a
Itsu no Kotowaki · 稜威言別 · · 7:292b
Itsuō Art Museum · · · · · · · · · · 3:357b
Ittsui otoko hayari no
Utagawa (Two Stars
of the Utagawa School)
· · · · · · · · · · 一対男時花歌川 · 8:184b
Iva Toguri D'Aquino · · · · · · · · · 4:15a
Tōkyō Rose · · · · · · · · · · · · · 8:68b
IVR · · · · · · · · · · · · · · · · · · 4:85b
Iwafune no ki · · · · · · 磐舟柵 · · 3:357b
Iwafune no saku · · 磐舟柵 · · 3:357b
Iwai · · · · · · · · · · · · 岩井 · · · 3:357b
Iwai, Rebellion of 磐井の乱 · 3:357b-358a
Iwai Akira · · · · · · · 岩井章 · · · 3:357b
Iwajuku site · · · · · · 岩宿遺跡 · 1:38a, 76a;
3:358a
Iwaki · · · · · · · · · · 磐城 2:367a; 3:358a
Iwakigawa · · · · · · · 岩木川 · · 3:358a
Iwakisan · · · · · · · · · 岩木山 · · 3:358a
Iwakuni · · · · · · · · · · 岩国 · · · 3:358a
Iwakura · · · · · · · · · · 岩倉 3:358b; 7:248b
Iwakura mission of 1871
· · · · · · · · · · 岩倉遣外使節 · 1:119b-120a;
2:311a; 3:358b-360a; 7:50b, 270b
Bacon, Alice Mabel · · · · · · · · · 1:129b
Hayashi Tadasu · · · · · · · · · · · 3:118a
influence on Japanese policies · · · 3:359b
Itō Hirobumi · · · · · · · · · · · · 3:352a
Iwakura Tomomi · · · · · · · · · · · 3:360a
Kido Takayoshi · · · · · · · · · · · 4:203a
Kume Kunitake · · · · · · · · · · · 4:307b
Nagayo Sensai · · · · · · · · · · · · 6:164a
Parkes, Sir Harry Smith · · · · · · 5:308a
purpose · · · · · · · · · · · · · 3:358b-359a
reception · · · · · · · · · · · · · · 3:359a
route map · · · · · · · · · · · · · · 3:358b
Sasaki Takayuki · · · · · · · · · · · 7:23b
Seikanron · · · · · · · · · · · · · · 7:50b
shogunate missions to the West · · 7:161b
Tanabe Taichi · · · · · · · · · · · · 7:335a
Tanaka Fujimaro · · · · · · · · · · 7:336a
tour · · · · · · · · · · · · · · · · 3:358b-359a
Tsuda Umeko · · · · · · · · · · · · 8:112b
Unequal Treaties revision · · · · · 8:148b
Verbeck, Guido Herman Fridolin · · 8:190a
Iwakura Tomomi 岩倉具視 · 3:360a; 7:29a
Iwakura mission · · · · · · · · · 3:358b-360a
Meiji Restoration · · · · · · · · · · 3:360a
Sanjō Sanetomi · · · · · · · · · · · 7:12b
Iwakuro Hideo · · · · 岩畔豪雄 · · 7:197a
Iwami Silver Mine
· · · · · · · · · · · 石見銀山 3:360a; 4:127b

Iwamizawa ········ 岩見沢 ······· 3:360b
Iwamoto Yoshiharu

·········· 巌本善治 1:208b; 3:360b
Iwanaga News Agency ········ 3:360b
Iwanaga Yūkichi 岩永裕吉 ······ 3:360b
  Furuno Inosuke ············· 2:373a
Iwanami Bunko ·岩波文庫· 3:360b-361a
Iwanami Shigeo ·岩波茂雄· 3:360b
Iwanami Shoten Publishers ·3:360b-361a;
    7:55b
  publications ············· 3:360b-361a
  series ····················· 3:361a
Iwanari Tomomichi

············· 岩成友通 ···· 5:224a
Iwano Hōmei 岩野泡鳴 3:361a; 7:54b
  critiques ···················· 3:361a
  novels ······················ 3:361b
  plays ······················· 3:361a
  poetry ······················ 3:361a
  Shinshichō ················· 7:124b
  Shinshōsetsu ··············· 7:125b
Iwanuma ···················· 岩沼 ·· 3:361b
Iwasaki Kan'en · 岩崎灌園 · 3:361b
Iwasaki Koyata 岩崎小弥太 · 3:361b-362a;
    7:50b
Iwasaki Yanosuke

··············· 岩崎弥之助 ··· 7:50b
Iwasaki Yatarō 岩崎弥太郎 · 3:362a; 7:52a
  Kaiseikan of Tosa ··········· 3:362a
  Mitsubishi ················· 5:205b
  Shinagawa Yajirō ·········· 7:109a
  shipping business ·········· 3:362a
  tactics ···················· 3:362a
  Taiwan Expedition ·········· 3:362b
Iwasa Matabei ·岩佐又兵衛· 3:362b-363a
  works ······················ 3:363a
I was Born, But ········· 8:146a-146b
Iwase Tadanari · 岩瀬忠震 ·· 3:363a
Iwase "thousand-mound" tomb cluster

············ 岩橋千塚古墳群 ·· 3:363a
Iwashi ······················· 7:21b
Iwashimizu Hachiman
  Shrine ·· 石清水八幡宮 · 3:74a-74b,
    363a; 4:164a; 7:126b
  Shintō architecture ········ 7:133b
Iwashimizu monogatari
  (Tale of Iwashimizu)

············ 石清水物語 ·· 5:246a
Iwashimotsuke ··············· 7:107a
Iwashita Shima ·岩下志麻· 2:274b
Iwashita Sōichi · 岩下壮一 · 3:363a-363b
Iwata ······················ 磐田 ·· 3:363b
Iwatahara ············· 磐田原 ·· 3:363b
Iwata Sentarō · 岩田専太郎 · 1:163a
Iwata Toyoo. *See* **Shishi Bunroku**
Iwate Prefecture ··· 岩手県 ·· 3:363b
  tourist attractions ········· 3:363b
Iwatesan ············· 岩手山 ·· 3:363b
Iwatsuki ············· 岩槻 ·· 3:364a
Iwayagawachi kiln

············ 岩谷川内窯 ·· 5:299a
Iwaya Sazanami · 巌谷小波 1:164a; 3:364a
  children's literature ········ 1:279b
  Ken'yūsha ················· 4:199a
Iwojima. 硫黄島   *See* **Iōjima**
Iyadani ····· 祖谷渓 · 3:364a; 7:97b
Iyo ························· 伊予 ·· 3:364a
Iyo Mishima ···· 伊予三島 ·· 3:364b
Izanagi and Izanami

········· 伊弉諾, 伊弉冉 · 2:302b, 376a;
  3:364b-365a; 4:125b; 5:292b-293a
  leech baby ················· 4:374b
Izanagi no Mikoto

············· 伊弉諾尊 · 3:364b-365a
Izanami no Mikoto

············· 伊弉冉尊 · 3:364b-365a
Izawajō ········ 胆沢城 3:365a; 6:379a;
    7:3a

Izawa Shūji ····· 伊沢修二 ·· 3:365a
Izayoi nikki (Diary of the
  Waning Moon)

············ 十六夜日記 ··· 1:5b-6a;
    6:2b; 8:105a-105b
Izu Dancer, The ·············· 4:175b
Izu Gold Mine ····· 伊豆金山 ·· 3:365a
  Ōkubo Nagayasu ············ 6:93b
Izuhara port ········· 厳原港 ·· 8:117a
Izui Hisanosuke

············· 泉井久之助 ·· 4:20a
Izu Islands ···· 伊豆諸島 2:342b; 3:365a
  Hachijōjima ················ 3:74a
  Ōshima ··················· 6:125a
Izumi (northern Honshū)

·························· 泉 ·· 3:365a
Izumi (central Honshū)

··············· 和泉 ·· 3:365a
Izumi (Kyūshū) ····· 出水 · 3:365a-365b
Izumi Kyōka ···· 泉鏡花 3:365b; 7:103b
  Ken'yūsha ················· 4:199a
  shimpa ···················· 7:108a
  Shinshōsetsu ··············· 7:125b
  style ······················ 3:365b
  works ······················ 3:365b
  Yashagaike ················ 7:122b
Izumi Motohide ···· 和泉元秀 · 4:327a
Izumi Mountains ·和泉山脈· 3:366a
Izumi Ōtsu ········· 泉大津 ·· 3:366a
Izumi Sano ········· 泉佐野 ·· 3:366a
Izumi school ···· 和泉流 3:366a; 4:325b
Izumi Seiichi ········ 泉靖一 ·· 3:366a
Izumi Shikibu ···· 和泉式部 · 3:366a; 5:34b;
    7:52b, 95a
  poetry ····················· 3:366a
  Shin kokinshū ·············· 7:120a
Izumo ············· 出雲 · 3:367a; 7:101a
Izumo cycle of mythology ·· 5:293b-295a
Izumo kagura ····· 出雲神楽 ·· 4:107b
Izumo no Okuni 出雲阿国 · 3:367a; 6:97a
Izumo Plain ···· 出雲平野 · 3:366b, 367a
Izumo Province ····· 出雲国 ·· 3:367a
Izumo Shrine ···· 出雲大社 · 3:367a; 7:100b
  architecture ··············· 3:367b
  festivals ··················· 3:367b
  Lake Shinji ················· 7:115a
  main building ··············· 3:367a
  mythic origins ·············· 3:367b
  Ōkuninushi no Mikoto ······· 6:97b
  Shintō ····················· 7:126a
  Shintō architecture ········· 7:133a
  Taisha ····················· 7:303b
Izu Nagaoka ···· 伊豆長岡 ·· 3:367b
Izu no odoriko 伊豆の踊子 · 1:49b; 4:175b
Izu Ōshima ······· 伊豆大島 ·· 6:125a
Izu Ōshima volcano 伊豆大島火山 · 8:194b
Izu Peninsula ·· 伊豆半島 2:342b; 3:367b
Izura ······················ 五浦 ·· 3:367b
Izu Shrine ········· 伊豆神社 ···· 7:206b

J

JACL ························ 4:12b-13a
Jagatara-bumi

·········· ジャガタラ文 ·· 4:1a
Jaguaré Fertilizer Company ······ 5:317b
Jahana Noboru ···· 謝花昇 ···· 4:1a
Jaimini ········· 闍威弥尼 ········ 1:69a

Jakkōin ··············· 寂光院 ·· 4:1a
  origins ····················· 4:1a
Jakuchū. 若冲 *See* **Itō Jakuchū**
Jakugon ··············· 寂厳 ·· 4:1a-1b
Jakuren ··············· 寂蓮 · 4:1b; 5:41a
  Fujiwara no Ietaka ·········· 2:351a
  Kenshō ···················· 4:198b
  Shin kokinshū ·············· 7:119b
Jakushitsu Genkō

·········· 寂室元光 ·· 4:1b-2a
JAL (Japan Air Lines Co, Ltd) ···· 4:10a
JALPAK ····················· 4:10a
JALTOS ····················· 4:10a
Janes, Leroy Lansing ········· 4:2a
Jan Joosten, Lodenstijn ···· 4:2a; 5:3b
Janken. *See* **Ken**
Janome Sewing Machine Co, Ltd ·· 4:2a
Jansen, Marius B. ··········· 5:228a
Japan ······· 4:2b-9b; 6:135a, 288a
  geological structure ········· 4:8a-9b
    crustal movement ·········· 4:8b-9a
    history of islands ·········· 4:9a-9b
    northeastern and southwestern · 4:8b
    topography ················· 4:8b
  maps ····················· *4:3a-6b*
  natural features ············ 4:7b-8a
    climate ·· 1:325a-328b; 4:7b-8a
    life and nature ············· 4:8a
    topography ················· 4:7b
  territory and administrative divisions

    ························ 4:2b-7b
    changes in ················· 4:7a
    formation of country ········ 4:7a
    modern administrative system · 4:7a-7b
    population · 4:2b-7a; 6:222a-225b
    territory of Japan · 4:2b; 8:13b-14b
  See also **Prefectures**
Japan, Past and Present ········· 6:289a
Japan: The Story of a Nation ······ 6:289a
Japan Academy ····· 4:9b; 7:3b; 8:289b
Japan Advertiser ······· 4:9b; 7:229b
Japan Advertisers Association ···· 4:9b
Japan Advertising Artists Club (JAAC)

··························· 2:89b
Japan Advertising Review
  Organization ·········· 4:9b-10a
Japan Air Lines Co, Ltd (JAL) ···· 1:48a;
    4:10a; 8:102b
Japan Air Lines Development Co ··· 4:10a
Japan Air Lines Law ············ 4:10a
Japan Alpine Club ····· 5:259b; 8:249a
Japan Amateur Sports Association 4:10a,
    82; 7:243a
  founding ··················· 4:147a
  Kishi Seiichi ··············· 4:223b
  National Sports Festival ······ 5:348a
Japan Amateur Wrestling Association

··························· 8:279a
Japan-American Institute of Management
  Science (JAIM) ·············· 2:347b
Japan-American Student Conference

·························· 4:10a-10b
Japan Art Academy ············ 4:10b
  Kitamura Rokurō ············ 4:227a
  Kosugi Tengai elected to ······ 4:296a
  Takii Kōsaku ··············· 7:326b
  Tanaka Chikao ·············· 7:335b
Japan Art Academy (Nihon Geijutsuin)

··························· 6:158a
Japan Art Academy Literary Prize
  Ikko sono ta (1965) ·········· 5:301b
Japan Art Academy Prize
  Yamamoto Kenkichi (1966) ···· 8:298b
Japan Art Association ··········· 7:359a
Japan Association for Legal Philosophy

··························· 4:85b
Japan Association of National
  Universities ················ 4:10b

Japan Association of Tax Accounting
·················· 7:351b
Japan Atomic Power Company · 4:10b
Japan-Australia Business Cooperation Committee ············· 1:118b-119a
Japan Book Publishers Association
·················· 4:10b
Japan Braille Library ········· 4:10b-11a
Japan Broadcasting Association ··· 1:11a
Japan Broadcasting Corporation. *See* **NHK**
Japan Buddhist Federation. *See* **Zen Nihon Bukkyō Kai**
Japan Center for Area Research and Development ··············· 4:11a
Japan Chamber of Commerce and Industry ······ 1:11a; 4:11a, 188a; 6:237b
collective bargaining ··········· 4:348b
international friendship organizations
·················· 3:320a
Nagano Shigeo ················· 5:303a
Japan Chemical Society ·········· 4:373b
Japan-China Cultural Association · 7:323b
Japan Chronicle ················ 4:49b
Japan Commercial Arbitration Association ················· 2:118b
Japan Committee for Economic Development (Keizai Dōyū Kai) · 4:11a, 188a, 348b; 5:319a-319b; 6:238a; 8:367a
Japan Communist Party · 2:7a; 4:11a-12a; 6:210b; 7:25a, 215b, 251b, 264b; 8:296b
Akahata ···················· 1:39b
Akamatsu Katsumaro ············ 1:40a
Arahata Kanson ··············· 1:72a
campaign to destroy ··········· 7:242a
Diet ······················· 2:95a
Fukumoto Kazuo ······· 2:364a; 4:180b
history
postwar ··············· 4:11b-12a
through 1945 ··········· 4:11a-11b
Ichikawa Shōichi ·············· 3:258a
Inoue Mitsuharu ··············· 3:311a
Japan Socialist Party ··········· 4:48b
labor reforms ················ 4:358a
March 15th Incident ··········· 5:112b
Minsei ···················· 5:197a
Miyamoto Kenji ··············· 5:220a
Miyamoto Yuriko ·············· 5:220b
Mizuno Shigeo ················ 5:226b
modern philosophy ············ 5:231b
national defense ··········· 5:336b-338b
National Railway Workers' Union · 7:107a
Nosaka Sanzō ················· 8:315b
Occupation ·················· 6:54a
party strength ················ 4:12a
peace movement ·············· 6:166b
Peace Preservation Law of 1925 ···· 6:168b
Planning Board Incident ········· 6:189b
postwar activity ·········· 3:204b-205a
Red Purge ··················· 6:285b
Sakai Toshihiko ··············· 6:377a
Sambetsu Kaigi (Congress of Industrial Labor Unions of Japan) ········· 7:7a
Shiga Yoshio and ·············· 7:91b
Shinjinkai ··················· 7:115b
Taira Incident ················ 7:299b
Tanno Setsu ·················· 7:344a
Tokuda Kyūichi ················ 8:44b
Watanabe Masanosuke ·········· 8:236a
Yamakawa Hitoshi ············· 8:296b
Japan Confederation of A- and H-bomb Sufferers Organizations ········· 1:111a
Japan Council against Atomic and Hydrogen Bombs ·············· 6:166a
Japan Creative Tours Co ········· 4:10a
Japan Current. *See* **Kuroshio**
Japan Democratic Party (Nihon Minshutō) ········· 4:384b; 5:381a

Japan Design Promotion Organization (JIDPO) ················· 2:90a
Japan Development Bank · 1:139b; 4:12b; 5:319a-319b; 6:263b
fiscal system ················· 2:281b
Japan Development Bank Law ···· 4:12b
Japan Electronic Industry Development Association ················ 2:193b
Japan Emigration Promotion Company
·················· 2:201a
Japan Emigration Service (JEMIS) 2:201a
Japanese, The ··············· 6:289a
"Japanese Adam Smith, The" ···· 7:294b
Japanese Agricultural Standard ··· 4:50b
Japanese Alps ·········· 4:12b, 224a
Akaishi Mountain range ········ 1:39b
Chūbu region ················ 1:311a
mountaineering ·············· 5:259b
Japanese American Bar Association
·················· 4:14b
Japanese American Citizens League (JACL) ·········· 4:12b-13a, 15a
voter registration ············· 4:15b
Japanese American Claims Act of 1948 ·········· 4:13a, 17b
Japanese American Relations Committee ·················· 1:47b
Japanese Americans ······ 4:13a-16a
cultural changes and adaptation ····· 4:15b
current issues ················ 4:15b
evacuation during World War II 4:14a-14b
442nd Regimental Combat Team · 2:329b
Gentlemen's Agreement ········· 3:24b
Hawaii ················· 4:16a-17a
cultural continuity and change 4:16b-17a
immigration history ·········· 4:16a
occupational trends and economic standing ················· 4:16b
political participation ········· 4:16b
immigration background ······ 4:13b-14a
as *inu* ··················· 4:13a
Japanese American Citizens League
·················· 4:12b-13a
Japan's ················· 4:15a-15b
military service ··········· 4:15a, 18a
organizations ············ 4:14b-15a
political involvement ·········· 4:15b
Topaz Relocation Center ······· 8:75b
War Relocation Authority (WRA) · 8:228b
wartime relocation centers ····· 1:48b
wartime relocation of ····· 4:13a, 14a-14b, 17a-18a; 8:158b
aftermath ················· 4:18a
evacuation and relocation ····· 4:17b-18a
genesis of evacuation ········ 4:17a-17b
Rohwer Relocation Center ····· 6:334a
Japanese andromeda ··········· 1:97a
Japanese angelica tree ·········· 7:346a
Japanese Asian Solidarity Committee
·················· 1:19b
Japanese Association of International Law ····················· 8:289b
Japanese Association of Medical Sciences ··················· 4:374a
Japanese Associations of America
·················· 4:22a-22b
Japanese American Citizens League · 4:22b
Japanese American Organizations
·················· 4:14b-15a
Japanese beauty-berry ·········· 5:269b
Japanese beetle [(manekogane) *Popillia japonica*] ················· 4:22b
Japanese box ·············· 8:113a-113b
Japanese bush clover ········ 3:75b-76a
Japanese business in America 4:22b-23a
basic resources ············ 4:22b-23a
conclusions ················· 4:23a
manufacturing ··············· 4:23a

sales and distribution ·········· 4:23a
service industries ············· 4:22b
Japanese cedar ··············· 7:257b
Japanese Chronological Tables ···· 1:231b
Japanese Cities, A Geographical Approach ················· 4:23b
Japanese Confederation of Labor 2:130a; 7:189a
peace movement ·············· 6:166b
Japanese Culture Research Institute 1:2b
Japanese Culture Society of Brazil 5:317b
(Sociedade Brasileira de Cultura) · 8:298b
Japanese Exclusion Act of 1924 ·· 8:157b
United States ················ 8:157a
Japanese Fair Trade Commission · 6:268b
Japanese Folklore Studies ······· 6:118b
Japanese Gospel Society of San Francisco ·················· 4:14b
Japanese hop ················· 4:135b
Japanese Industrial Standard ·· 4:61b-62a
Japanese Institute of Certified Public Accountants (JICPA) ··········· 1:8b
Japanese knotweed ············ 3:349a
Japanese-Korean Treaty of Alliance
·················· 4:281a
Japanese labor movement ······· 6:129a
Japanese language ·········· 4:23b-29b
accent in. *See* **Accent in Japanese language**
alleged difficulty ············· 4:28a
Altaic languages ·········· 4:18b-20b
comparative method ········· 4:19a-20b
conclusions ················· 4:20a
classical. *See* **Classical Japanese**
classical standard ············· 4:30a
colloquial standard ············ 4:30a
dialects ············· 2:91b-92a; 4:23b-24a
dialects and speech of Tōkyō ··· 4:23b-24a
dictionaries ··············· 2:93a-94a
feminine. *See* **Feminine language**
as foreign language ········· 4:21a-22a
pre-World War II ··········· 4:21a
World War II ·············· 4:21a
post-World War II ········· 4:21a-22a
genetic relationships ·········· 4:23b
gojūon zu ··············· 3:40b-41a
grammar ················· 4:24b-27a
adjectives ·············· 4:26a-26b
copula ················· 4:26a-26b
levels of speech ············ 4:26b
modern ················ 4:24b-27a
nouns ················· 4:24b-25a
sentence ··············· 4:26b-27a
verbs ·················· 4:24a-26a
vocabulary ··············· 4:27a
Hawaii ···················· 4:17a
history ·················· 4:28b-29b
honorific. *See* **Honorific language**
hyōjungo ·················· 4:23b
kana. *See* **Kana**
kanji. *See* **Kanji**
Korean language ·········· 4:289b-291a
Malayo-Polynesian languages ·· 4:20a-21a
masculine. *See* **Masculine language**
medieval ·················· 7:165b-166a
morphology ················· 4:19b
onomatopoeia. *See* **Onomatopoeia**
phonology ················ 4:24a-24b
consonants ·············· 4:24a-24b
of the standard ··········· 4:24a-24b
stress accent ·············· 4:24b
syllable ················ 4:24a-24b
vowels ················· 4:24a-24b
process theory ··············· 8:42b
reforms ················· 4:29b-30b
first period (1868-1900) ···· 4:29b-30a
second period (1900-1960) ··· 4:30a-30b
third period (1960-present) ···· 4:30b

future · 4:30b
romanization of · · · · · · · · · · · · · 6:335b–336b
school curriculum · · · · · · · · · · · · · · · · 7:34b
speech of Tōkyō · · · · · · · · · · · · · · · 4:23b–24a
studies, history of · · · · · · · · · 4:30b–32a
vernacular. *See* **Gembun itchi**
writing
jōyō kanji · · · · · · · · · · · · · · · · · · · 4:27b
kana · 4:27b–28a
kun readings · · · · · · · · · · · · · · · 4:27b–28a
on readings · · · · · · · · · · · · · · · 4:27b–28a
writing system · · · · · · · · · · · · · · 4:27a–28a
Japanese language studies · · · · 4:21a–22a
Japanese laurel · · · · · · · · · · · · · · · · · 1:68b
Japanese literature and Christianity
· 4:32a–32b
Japanese Literature Patriotic Association
· 7:316a
Japanese National Commission for
UNESCO. *See* **UNESCO activities in
Japan**
Japanese nationalism · · · · · · · · · · · · 7:320a
Japanese nationality · · · 2:313b; 4:32b–33a
acquisition · · · · · · · · · · · · · · · · 4:32b–33a
konketsuji · · · · · · · · · · · · · · · · · · · 4:271b
of Koreans in Japan · · · · · · · · · · · · 4:291b
loss · 4:33a
naturalization · · · · · · · · · · · · · · · · 5:351b
Japanese National Railways (JNR)
· · · · · · · · · 4:33b; 6:278a; 7:14b; 8:99a–99b
background · · · · · · · · · · · · · · · · · · · 4:33b
fiscal system · · · · · · · · · · · · · · · · · 2:281b
Kōrōkyō membership · · · · · · · · · · · 4:294a
organization and scale of operation · 4:33b
problems and plans · · · · · · · · · · · · 4:33b
Shinkansen · · · · · · · · · · · · · · · 7:116b–119a
Teito Rapid Transit Authority · · · · 7:377a
Yamanote Line · · · · · · · · · · · · · · · · 8:302a
Japanese National Railways Labor
Union · 4:84a
Japanese Newspaper Association · · 4:79a
Japanese Olympic committee · · · · · 7:310a
Japanese people
origins · · · · · · · · · · · · · · · · · · 4:33b–35a
formation of the Yamato · · · · · · · · 4:34b
Jōmon hunters and Yayoi cultivators
· 4:34a–34b
modern man · · · · · · · · · · · · · · · · · · 4:34a
time depth and early man · · · · 4:33b–34a
physical characteristics · · · · · · · · 4:35a–38a
abnormal hemoglobins · · · · · · · · · · 4:36b
adaptation · · · · · · · · · · · · · · · 4:37a–37b
blood group antigens · · · · · · · · 4:35b–36a
color blindness · · · · · · · · · · · · · · · · 4:36b
descriptive traits · · · · · · · · · · · · · · 4:35a
earwax · 4:35b
fingerprints · · · · · · · · · · · · · · · · · · 4:35b
gamma globulins · · · · · · · · · · · 4:36a–36b
glandular secretions · · · · · · · · · 4:36b–37a
hair follicles · · · · · · · · · · · · · · · · · 4:35b
mate selection and inbreeding · · · · 4:38a
morphological types · · · · · · · · · 4:35a–35b
red cell enzymes · · · · · · · · · · · · · · 4:36a
regional variability · · · · · · · · · · · · 4:35b
secular trend increases · · · · · · · 4:37b–38a
serological gene markers · · · · · · · · 4:35b
serum proteins · · · · · · · · · · · · · · · 4:36a
virus studies · · · · · · · · · · · · · · · · · 4:36b
psychology of · · · · · · · · · · · · · 4:38a–40b
achievement orientation · · · · · · · · · 4:39b
compulsive personality theory · · · · 4:38b
early national character studies
· 4:38a–39a
modal personality-conceptual
problems · · · · · · · · · · · · · · · 4:39a–40b
psychological reductionism · · · · · · · 4:39a
reaction formation · · · · · · · · · · · · · 4:38b
rituals · 4:38b

Japanese pittosporum · · · · · · · · · 8:32a–32b
Japanese Political League of Small and
Medium Enterprises · · · · · · · · · · · 6:238a
Japanese privet · · · · · · · · · · · · · · · · 5:374a
Japanese Psychological Association
(Nihon Shinri Gakkai) · · · · · · · · · 6:260b
Japanese Red Cross Society · · · · · · 4:40b
Sano Tsunetami · · · · · · · · · · · · · · 7:16a
Japanese robin · · · · · · · · · · · · · · · · 4:264b
Japanese Romantic School · · · · · · · 5:381b
Japanese sago palm · · · · · · · · · · · · 7:233a
Japanese scabiosa · · · · · · · · · · · · · 5:138b
Japanese serow · · · · · · · · · · · · · · · 4:129b
Japanese snowbell · · · · · · · · · · · · · 2:184b
Japanese society, interpretations of
· 7:217b–218a
Japanese Society for Science of Design
(JSSD) · 2:90a
Japanese Society for the Study of
Wooden Documents · · · · · · · · · · · 1:80a
Japanese spaniel (chin) · · · · · · · 4:40b–41a
Japanese spicebush · · · · · · · · · · · · 4:316b
Japanese spirit, Chinese learning · 8:221a
Japanese spirit, Western learning
· 8:221a–221b
Japanese studies abroad · · · · · · 4:41a–45a
Japanese as foreign language · · · · · · 4:45a
multidisciplinary approach · · · · 4:41b–42a
Japanese Studies in the United States
· 4:41b
*Japanese Studies in the Universities and
Colleges of the United States* · 4:41b
Japanese-style painting · · · · · 5:379a–380a;
6:154a, 155a
Japanese-style Painting Society · 4:175b;
8:13a
Japanese Tax Law Review Commission
· 7:355a–358a
Japanese terrier (Nippon teriya) · 4:45a
Japanese Utility-Model Law of 1905
· 8:187a
Japanese yew · · · · · · · · · · · · · · · · 3:255b
Japan Esperanto Association · · · · · 2:231b
Japan Esperanto Institute · · · · · · · 2:231b
Japan Euthanasia Association · · · · 2:236a
Japan External Trade Organization. *See*
JETRO
Japan Fabian Society
founding · 1:2a
Kimura Ki · · · · · · · · · · · · · · · · · · 4:211a
Japan Family Planning Association
· 2:247b
Japan Family Planning Federation 2:247b
Japan Farmers' Union · · · · · · · · · · · 1:84a
Japan Federation of Bar Associations
· 4:45b
civil liberties · · · · · · · · · · · · · · · 1:318a
Japan Federation of Employers'
Associations. *See* **Nikkeiren**
Japan Federation of Engineering
Societies · 4:374a
Japan Federation of Japanese Overseas
Associations · · · · · · · · · · · · · · · · 2:201a
Japan Federation of Labor · · · · · · · · 1:2a;
7:219a–219b
Japan Federation of Labor Unions 6:212b
Japan Federation of Proletarian
Literature · · · · · · · · · · · · · · · · · · 7:175a
Japan Federation of Religions · · · · 4:45b
Japan Federation of Tax Agents
Associations · · · · · · · · · · · · · · · · · · 1:9a
Japan Federation of Textile Industry
Workers Unions · · · · · · · · · · · · · · 8:376b
Japan Fine Arts Academy (Nihon
Bijutsuin) · · · · · · · · · 1:154b; 4:45b–46a
modern painting · · · · · · · · · · · · · · 6:156a
Okakura Kakuzō · · · · · · · · · · · · · · 6:79b
Rimpa · 6:318a

Shimomura Kanzan · · · · · · · · · · · · 7:105b
Yokoyama Taikan · · · · · · · · · · · · · 8:334b
Japan Fine Arts Association · · · · · · 4:175b
Japan Fisheries Agency · · · · · · · · · · 2:304b
Japan Folk-Craft Museum · · · · · · · 4:46a
Japan Folk Craft Society · · · · · · · · 2:294b
Japan Folklore Institute · · · · · · · · · 2:296b
Japan Foundation · · · · · · · · 3:341a; 4:46a
Malaysia · 5:88b
Japan Foundation Library · · · · · · · 4:46a
Japan Graphic Designers Association
· 2:89b
Japan Greening Center · · · · · · · · · · 4:11a
Japan Handicrafts Association · · · · 3:341a
Japan Herald · · · · · · · · · · · · · · · · · 4:46a
Japan Highway Public Corporation
· 4:46a–46b
expressways · · · · · · · · · · · · · · · · · 2:238a
roads · 6:332b
Japan Historical Geography Society
(Nihon Rekishi Chiri Kenkyū kai) 4:228b
Japan Housewives Association. *See*
Shufuren
Japan Housing Corporation. *See*
**Housing and Urban Development
Corporation**
Japan-Hungary Cultural Agreement
· 2:142a
Japan Imperial Table
Tennis Association · · · · · · · · · · · 7:291b
Japan Imperial Volleyball Association
(Japan Volleyball Association) · · · 8:195b
Japan Incorporated · · · · · · · · · 4:46b–47a
Ministry of International Trade and
Industry · · · · · · · · · · · · · · · · · · 5:190a
Japan Industrial Council (Nihon Sangyō
Kyōgikai) · · · · · · · · · · · · · · · · · 4:188a
Japan Industrial Designers Association
· 2:89b
Japan Industrial Robots Association
· 3:298b
Japan Information Center for Science
and Technology · · · · · · · · · · · · · · 7:38a
Japan International Cooperation Agency
· 4:47a
foreign aid policy · · · · · · · · · · · · · 2:310a
international friendship organizations
· 3:319b
Overseas Economic Cooperation Fund
· 4:47a
Japanism. *See* **Nihon shugi**
Japan Labor Council · · · · · · · · · · · · 7:189a
Japan Labor-Farmer Party. *See* **Nihon
Rōnōtō**
Japan Liberal Party · · · · · · · · 4:274a; 6:211b
Japan Line, Ltd · · · · · · · · · · · · · · · 4:47a
Japan Literati Painting Association
· 7:344b
Japan Magazine Publishers Association
· 4:47a
Japan Mail · · · · · · · · · · · · · · · · · · · 4:49b
Japan Mathematical Society · · · · · · 4:373b
Japan Medical Association (Nihon Ishi-
kai) · · · · · · · 4:47a–47b; 6:237a, 238a;
8:263a
Japan Metals & Chemicals Co, Ltd 4:47b
Japan Monopoly Corporation · · · · · 6:263b
Japan Mountaineering Association 5:259b
Japan National Oil Corporation (JNOC)
· 6:182a
**Japan Newspaper Publishers and
Editors Association** · · · · · · · · · · 4:47b
Japan Opera Association · · · · · · · · 8:289a
**Japan Overseas Cooperation
Volunteers** · · · · · · · · · · · · 1:19b; 4:47b
Japan Painting Association (Nihon Kaiga
Kyōkai)
Uemura Shōen · · · · · · · · · · · · · · · 8:128a

Japan Peasant Union (Nihon Nōmin Kumiai) ············ 4:363a
Japan P. E. N. Club ········ 4:47b–48a
Japan Petroleum Exploration Co, Ltd ············ 6:181b
Japan Physics Society ········ 4:373b
Japan Productivity Center ··· 1:11a; 4:48a
collective bargaining ······ 4:348a
Japan Proletarian Arts League (Nihon Puroretaria Geijutsu Remmei) ············ 6:255a
Japan Proletarian Literary Arts League (Nihon Puroretaria Bungei Remmei) ············ 6:254b–255a
Japan Proletarian Party ·········· 5:381a
Japan Pulp & Paper Co, Ltd ···· 4:48a
Japan Punch ············ 8:254b
Japan Railway Company ········ 5:384a
Japan Reform Party ············ 1:40b
Japan Research Council on Economics Education ············ 4:11a
Japan Review ············ 5:380a
Japan Robot Leasing Corporation 3:299b
Japan Science Council ············ 4:256a
Japan Securities Finance Co, Ltd ··· 4:48a
Japan Shōgi Federation ······ 7:158b–159a
Japan-Singapore Association ····· 7:196b
Japan Socialist League. *See* **Nihon Shakai Shugi Dōmei**
Japan Socialist Party
postwar ·· 1:2b; 2:7a; 4:48a–49a, 285b; 6:211b–212a; 7:215b
Arahata Kanson ·········· 1:72a–72b
Asanuma Inejirō ············ 1:96a
Asukata Ichio ············ 1:107b
ban-the-bomb movement ··· 1:114b–115a
Democratic Socialist Party ···· 2:85a–85b
Den Hideo ············ 2:86b
Diet ············ 2:96b
Eda Saburō ············ 2:168b
Katayama Tetsu ············ 4:167a
labor unions ············ 4:347a
Narita Tomomi ············ 5:334b
national bureaucracy ············ 1:220b
national defense ············ 5:336b–338b
Occupation ············ 6:54a
Ōuchi Hyōe ············ 6:135a
peace movement ············ 6:166b
Planning Board Incident ······ 6:189b
postwar power ············ 3:204b
pressure groups ·········· 6:236b, 238a
Sasaki Kōzō ············ 7:22b–23a
United Social Democratic Party 8:154b
Sakisaka Itsurō ············ 7:3a
pre–World War II ····· 4:48a; 6:210b
Heimin shimbun ············ 3:125b
Katayama Sen ············ 4:167a
Kōtoku Shūsui ············ 6:298a
Nishikawa Mitsujirō ············ 6:17a
Sakai Toshihiko ············ 6:377a
Tazoe Tetsuji ············ 7:359b
Japan Society for the Promotion of Science ··· 4:49a–49b; 6:303b
Japan Society for the Study of Education ············ 2:181a
Japan Society in London ········ 6:188a
Japan Sociological Society ······ 8:34b
Japan-Soviet Committee ········ 4:188a
Japan State Socialist Party ····· 1:40b
Japan Statutory Auditors Association ············ 1:9a
Japan Steel Works, Ltd ············ 4:49b
Japan Sumō Association ········ 7:271b
Japan Symphony Orchestra ····· 5:287a
Japan Synthetic Rubber Co, Ltd ··· 4:49b
Japan Teachers' Union. *See* **Nikkyōso**
Japan Times ············ 4:49b–50a
Japan Times and Mail ············ 6:343a

Japan Tobacco and Salt Public Corporation ············ 4:50a; 7:14b
Kōrōkyō membership ············ 4:294a
Japan Travel Bureau, Inc ········ 4:50a
railways ············ 6:280a
Japan-United States Educational Commission ············ 4:50a–50b
Japan-United States Extradition Treaty ············ 2:238a
Japan Upper Secondary School Teachers' Union ············ 7:366b
Japan-U.S.-Canada Fishery Agreement ············ 2:285a
Japan-U.S.S.R. Fishery Agreement ············ 2:285b
Japan Women's College ········ 8:267b
Japan Women's University ···· 4:50b; 7:54a
founder ············ 5:335a
Japan Wool Textile Co, Ltd ···· 4:50b
Japan Wrestling Association ····· 8:279a
Japan Yearbook ············ 4:44a
Japan Youth Painting Society (after 1897 the Japanese-Style Painting Society, Nihonga Kai) ············ 8:13a
Japan Zoological Society ········ 4:373b
JAPEX. *See* Japan Petroleum Exploration Co, Ltd
JAS (Japanese Agricultural Standard) ············ 4:50b
Jashūmon (Heathen Gate) 邪宗門 ············ 8:13a
Jayanagi 蛇柳 ············ 4:99a
Jazz ············ 1:44b
Jellyfish (kurage) ············ 1:149a
JEMIS (Japan Emigration Service) 2:201a
Jerome Relocation Center ····· 4:50b–51a
Jesuit mission press キリシタン版 4:51a, 119b; 5:322a–323a; 6:248a; 8:248b
Doctrina Christan ······ 4:52a, 52b
Korean moveable type ······ 4:279a
Jesuits 1:306b; 4:51a–51b; 6:334a
mission to Europe of 1582 ······ 5:203a
namban art ············ 5:322a–323a
Ōmura Sumitada ············ 6:104b
Ōtomo Sōrin ············ 6:132b
romanization of Japanese ······ 6:336a
JETRO (Japan External Trade Organization) ··· 1:120a; 1:168b; 2:321a; 4:52a; 7:257b
Ministry of International Trade and Industry ············ 5:191a
Jewelry
bracelets, ancient ············ 1:167a
JGC Corporation ············ 4:52b
Jiaozhou (Kiaochow) concession ···· 4:53a
Ji-Cha (Chi-Ch'a) Autonomous Political Council ············ 4:53a; 6:260a
Jichikai (self-governing associations) 自治会 7:252a–252b; 8:375a
Jichin 慈鎮 ···· 4:53b–54a
Jichinsai ············ 4:195a
Jichirō (All Japan Prefectural and Municipal Workers' Union) 自治労 4:53a; 4:348b; 6:238a
Jichishō. 自治省 *See* **Ministry of Home Affairs**
Jidai Festival 時代祭 2:258b; 4:53a, 336a
Heian Shrine ············ 3:122b
Jidai fudō uta-awase 時代不同歌合 ············ 4:161a
Jidaigeki (period drama) ···· 2:267b–268a, 269b, 271b, 274a; 7:31a

Jidai-mono (historical plays) 時代物 4:91a, 93a–94a; 5:234b
acting style ············ 4:94a
costume, wig and makeup ···· 4:95b
dialogue ············ 4:94a
Jidan ············ 4:53b
Jidong Fanggong Zizhi Zhengfu ·· 2:142b
Jidōsha Sōren ············ 4:53b
Jieikan ············ 7:58b, 60b
Jieitai. *See* **Self Defense Forces**
Jien 慈円 ············ 4:53b–54a
Fujiwara no Tameie ············ 2:356a
Fujiwara no Yoshitsune ······ 2:358a
Gukanshō ············ 3:65a–65b
historical principles ············ 3:153b
Shin kokinshū ············ 7:120a
Jigabachi (sand wasps) ············ 1:149a
Jige (groundlings) 地下 2:40a; 4:54a
Jigenin 地下人 ········ 4:54a
Jigeuke 地下請 ········ 3:250b
Jigoku. *See* **Hell**
Jigokumon 地獄門 ········ 2:56b
Daiei Co, Ltd ············ 2:56b
Jigoku-zōshi 地獄草紙 ··· 1:190b; 4:54a–54b; 5:333a
Jihon ············ 3:255b
Jiji Press ············ 4:54b
directorship ············ 2:373a
international communications ··· 3:318b
Jiji shimpō 時事新報 1:16b; 2:367b; 4:54b, 206b; 5:314a–314b
Sankei shimbun ············ 7:13b
Jiji Tsūshinsha ············ 4:54b
Jikaku ni okeru chokkan to hansei (Intuition and Reflection in Self-consciousness) 自覚に於ける直観と反省 ············ 6:15a
Jikan (vice-ministers) ··· 8:191a–191b
"Jikan" (Time) 時間 ········ 8:332b
Jikata 地方 ········ 4:54b–55a
Jikata hanrei roku 地方凡例録 ··· 4:55a–55b
Jikata sanchō 地方三帳 ····· 4:55a
Jikatasho 地方書 ········ 4:55a
Jikatatori 地方取 ········ 4:55a
Jikei University School of Medicine ············ 7:311a
Jikifu 食封 ········ 4:55b
Jikiso 直訴 ········ 4:55b
Jikkan ············ 1:232a
Jikkan jūnishi 十干十二支 4:55b–57a
calendar, dates, and time ·· 1:232a–232b
kanreki ············ 4:151a
kigen ············ 4:204a
kōshin ············ 4:57a
periodization ············ 6:174b–175a
Jikken shitsu (The Laboratory) 実験室 ····· 8:289b
Jikkinshō 十訓抄 4:57a; 7:72a
Jikkoku Pass 十国峠 ····· 4:57a
Jikkunshō 十訓抄 ····· 4:57a
Jimbō Kaku 神保格 ····· 4:31b
Jimbutsuga (figure painting) 1:156a; 7:17b
Jimmeiyō kanji beppyō (A Supplementary Table of Chinese Characters for Use in Personal Names) ············ 8:91b
Jimmeiyō kanji tsuika hyō (Table of Additional Characters for Use in Personal Names) ············ 8:91b
Jimmin bunko 人民文庫 ···· 7:176b
Jimmin Sensen Jiken. 人民戦線事件 *See* **Popular Front Incident**
Jimmu, Emperor 神武天皇 4:57a–57b; 7:264b
folktales ············ 2:302b
hakkō ichiu ············ 3:85b

imperial era · · · · · · · · · · · · · · 4:203b
Kigensetsu controversy · · · · · · · · 4:204a
Kojiki · · · · · · · · · · · · · · · · · 5:27b
Nihon shoki · · · · · · · · · · · · · · 5:384a
Jimoku · · · · · · · 除目 · 4:57b–58a
Jimpūren Rebellion
· · · · · · · · 神風連の乱 · 4:58a; 7:152a
chitsuroku shobun · · · · · · · · · · 1:298a
Jin · · · · · · · · · · · · · 3:354a; 4:141b
Itō Jinsai's concept · · · · · · · · · 4:247b
Jinaichō · · · · · · · 寺内町 · · 4:58a
Jinan (Tsinan) Incident · · · · · · · 4:373b
Jindaiji · · · · · · · 深大寺 · · 4:58a
Jindai moji · · · 神代文字 · · 4:58a
Jing · · · · · 7:263b; 8:119a–119b
Jingi · · · · · · · · · 仁義 · 4:58a–58b
Jingikan. 神祇官 *See* **Dajōkan**
Jingō, Empress. 神功皇后*See* **Jingū,**
Empress
Jingoji · · · · · · 神護寺 · 2:355b; 4:58b
Shinshōji · · · · · · · · · · · · · · 7:125a
Jingo Jihen · · · · · 壬午事変 · 3:275a
Jingōki. 塵劫記 *See* **Yoshida**
Mitsuyoshi
Jingū, Empress · 神功皇后 · 4:59a; 8:286b
Hirota Shrine · · · · · · · · · · · · 3:150b
Ōjin, Emperor · · · · · · · · · · · · 6:76b
Jingū Bunko · · · · · · · · · · · 4:58b–59a
Jingūreki (Ise Shrine Calendar) · · · 1:*231a*
Jinin. 神人 *See* **Jinnin**
Jinja. *See* **Shrines**
Jinja Honchō · · · · 神社本庁 · 7:139b
Jinja Shintō · · · · 神社神道 · 7:180b
Jinjiin. 人事院 *See* **National Personnel**
Authority
Jinkaishū · · · · · · · · 塵芥集 · 4:59a
Date family · · · · · · · · · · · · · 2:78a
Jinken shinsetsu · 人権新説 · 4:168b
Jinken yōgo · · · · · · · · · · · 1:317b–318a
Jinkōki · · · · · · · · · 塵劫記 · 8:231b
Jinku · · · · · · · · 甚句 2:301b; 7:272b
Jinnin · · · · · · · · · · 神人 · 4:59b
Jinnō shōtō ki · 神皇正統記 · 1:67b;
2:101b–102a; 4:59b–60a
historiography · · · · · · · · · · · · 3:153b
Nambokuchō seijun ron · · · · · · 5:323b
Jinrikisha. *See* **Rickshaw**
Jinsei gekijō · · · 人生劇場 · 6:140a
Jinsei sampō setsu
(Theory of the Three
Human Treasures)
· · · · · · · · 人生三宝説 · · 6:14a
Jinshin Disturbance (672)
· · · · · · · · 壬申の乱 · · 2:103a;
4:60a–60b; 8:285b
handen shūju system · · · · · · · · 3:96a
poetry · · · · · · · · · · · · · · · · 4:117a
Taika Reform · · · · · · · · · · · · 7:296b
toneri · · · · · · · · · · · · · · · · 8:74b
Jinshin Koseki · 壬申戸籍 · 4:60b–61a
Jinshin no Ran. 壬申の乱 *See* **Jinshin**
Disturbance
Jinzūgawa · · · · · 神通川 · · 4:61a
Jion kanazukai · · · · · · · · · · · 4:134a
Jippensha Ikku 十返舎一九 1:211b; 2:378a;
3:42a; 5:49a; 4:61a–61b; 7:97a
kokkeibon · · · · · · · · · · · · · · 4:256a
Ji Qiao Tian
Tanabata Festival · · · · · · · 7:334b–335a
Jiraigen · · · · · · · · 地雷原 · 7:334b
Jiriki. *See* **Tariki**
JIS (Japanese Industrial Standard)
· · · · · · · · · · · · · · · · · · 4:61b–62a
Ji sect · · · · · · · · 時宗 3:177a; 4:62a;
8:356a
Ippen · · · · · · · · · · · · · 3:328b–329b
nembutsu · · · · · · · · · · · · · · 5:359b
temples · · · · · · · · · · · · · · · 2:345b

Jisha bugyō · · · · 寺社奉行 · · 4:62b; 7:6a
Jishi · · · · · · · · · · · 地子 · 4:62b
Jishimban and tsujiban
· · · · · · · · · · 自身番と辻番 · 4:62b
Jishoiron · · · · · · · · · · · · 8:28a, 335b
Jishōji. 慈照寺 *See* **Ginkakuji**
Jishū · · · · · · · · · · 時宗 · 4:62a
Jissatsu · · · · · · · · 十刹 · 3:57a
Jisshinshi (real parent-child
relationships) · · · · · · · · · · · 6:162a
Jitō, Empress · · · · 持統天皇 · 4:63b–64a;
8:285b
court · · · · · · · · · · · · · · · · 2:350a
Kakinomoto no Hitomaro · · · · · · 4:117a
Naniwakyō · · · · · · · · · · · · · 5:328b
Jitō · · · · · · · · · · · 地頭 · 4:62b–63b
appointment · · · · · · · · · · · · 4:121b
corvée labor · · · · · · · · · · · · 1:226b
dismissal · · · · · · · · · · · · · · 4:108b
economy · · · · · · · · · · · · · · 2:147b
governmental functions · · · · · · 2:264a–264b
kokujin · · · · · · · · · · · · · · · 4:260a
shitaji chūbun · · · · · · · · · · · 7:149b
shōen · · · · · · · · · · · · · · · · 7:157a
Jitsugakutō (Practical
Party) · · · · · · · · · · 実学党 · 8:331a
Jitsugyō Dōshikai
· · · · · · · · · · 実業同志会 · 4:64a
Jitsugyō no shisō
· · · · · · · · · · 実業の思想 · 6:93a
Jitsugyō semmon gakkō · · · · · · · 7:62a
Jitsuin · · · · · · · · · · · · · · · 4:156a
Jitsuin ("true seals") · · · · · · · · 7:46a
Jitsuroku · · · · · · · · · · · · · · 6:316a
Jitsurokumono · · 実録物 · 4:64a
Jitte · · · · · · · · · · · · · · · 4:64a
Jiun Onkō · · · · 慈雲飲光 · 4:64a–64b
Jiun Sonja. 慈雲尊者 *See* **Jiun Onkō**
Jiuta · · · · · · · · · · 地唄 · 4:64a–65a
Jiutamai · · · · · · · 地唄舞 · 4:65a
· · · · · · · · · · · · · · · · · · · 7:148b
Jiyū gakkō (Freedom
School) · · · · · · · 自由学校 6:221b; 7:148b
Jiyū Gakuen · · · · · · · · · · 3:96b; 7:121b
Jiyū Gekijō (Free Theater)
Pan no Kai · · · · · · · · · · · · · 6:161b
shingeki · · · · · · · · · · · · · · · 7:112b
Jiyūkei · · · · · · · · · 自由刑 · 7:140b
Jiyū Minken Undō. 自由民権運動 *See*
Freedom and People's Rights
Movement
Jiyū Minshutō. 自由民主党 *See* **Liberal**
Democratic Party
Jiyū shimbun · · · · 自由新聞 · 4:65a
Jiyū Shisō (Free thought)
· · · · · · · · · · · 自由思想 · 4:145b
Jiyūtō (Liberal Party)
· · · · · · · · · · · · 自由党 · · 1:34b;
4:65a–65b; 6:207a; 7:66b, 255b
Baba Tatsui · · · · · · · · · · · · · 1:129a
Chichibu Incident · · · · · · · · · 1:271b
dissolution · · · · · · · · · · · · · 2:336a
establishment · · · · · · · · · · · 2:335a
Freedom and People's Rights Movement
· · · · · · · · · · · · · · · · 2:333b–336a
Furusawa Shigeru and · · · · · · · 2:373b
Imperial Diet · · · · · · · · · · · · 3:276b
Itagaki Taisuke · · · · · · · · · · · 3:349a
Kishida Toshiko · · · · · · · · · · 4:223a
Korean contact · · · · · · · · · · · 4:280b
local affiliates · · · · · · · · · · · 2:366a
predecessor · · · · · · · · · · · · · 4:372b
Rikken Teiseitō · · · · · · · · · · · 6:315b
Shimpotō · · · · · · · · · · · · · · 7:108a
Takenouchi Tsuna · · · · · · · · · 7:325a
Ueki Emori · · · · · · · · · · · · · 8:127b

Jiyūtō (post-World War II). *See* **Liberal**
Party
Jiyūtō shi · · · · · 自由党史 · 4:65b–66a
Jizaikagi · · · · · · · · · · 2:371b; 4:66a
open hearth (irori) · · · · · · · · · 4:*66b*
Jizamurai · · · · · · 地侍 · 2:265a; 4:66a
Jizō · · 1:159b, *201a*; 4:66a, *66b*, 144b; 5:43b
JMPA (Japan Magazine Publishers
Association) · · · · · · · · · · · · 4:47a
Jōban Coalfield · · 常磐炭田 · 4:66a
Job placement · · · · · · · · · · · 2:210a
Job tenure · · · · · · · · · · · · 4:356b–357b
Jōchi Daigaku · · · · · · · · · · · 7:229a
Jōchō · · · · · · · · 定朝 · 1:199b, *201a*,
227b; 4:66a–66b
In school · · · · · · · · · · · · · · 3:313b
Jōdai · · · · · · · · · · 城代 · 4:66b
Jōdai kanazukai · · · · · · · · · · · 4:134a
Jōdogahama · · · · 浄土ケ浜 · 4:67a
Jōdoji · · · · · · · · · · · 浄土寺 · 6:108b
Jōdo mandara-zu
· · · · · · · · · 浄土曼荼羅図 · 5:333a
Jōdo sect · · · · · · · 浄土宗 · 4:67a–68a;
7:63a
Azuchi Disputation · · · · · · · 1:126b–127a
Byōdōin temple · · · · · · · · · · · 1:227b
doctrinal basis · · · · · · · · · · · 4:67a
Fujiwara culture · · · · · · · · · · 2:347b
Fukuda Gyōkai · · · · · · · · · 2:361b–362a
Hōnen · · · · · · · · · · · · · · · · 3:220a
Japanese foundation · · · · · · · 4:67b–68a
lineage · · · · · · · · · · · · · · · 4:67a
painting · · · · · · · · · · · · · · · 6:149b
pure land faith · · · · · · · · · · · 4:67a–67b
tariki · · · · · · · · · · · · · · · · 7:347a
Jōdo Shin sect · 浄土真宗 · 3:177a; 4:62a,
68a–69a; 6:300a; 7:84b
doctrines · · · · · · · · · · · · · · 4:68b
historical developments · · · · · · 4:68a
Ikkō ikki · · · · · · · · · · · · · · 3:269b
Kiyozawa Manshi · · · · · · · · · · 4:233a
mandalas · · · · · · · · · · · · · · 5:100b
naikan therapy · · · · · · · · · 5:310b–311a
popularization of Buddhism · · · · 3:171a
Shimaji Mokurai · · · · · · · · · · 7:99b
Shimazu Yoshihiro
1597 prohibition · · · · · · · · · 7:102b
shinjin · · · · · · · · · · · · · · · 4:68b
Shinran · · · · · · · · · · · · · · · 7:122b
Temmon Hokke Rebellion · · · · · 7:381b
Toyotomi Hideyoshi · · · · · · · · 8:95a
vow
tariki · · · · · · · · · · · · · · · · 7:347a
Jōdo Shinshū · · · · 浄土真宗 · 4:68a–69a
Jōdo sugoroku · · · · 浄土双六 · 7:259a
Jōdo wasan · · · · · 浄土和讃 · 8:231b
Jōei Shikimoku. 貞永式目 *See* **Goseibai**
Shikimoku
Jōetsu · · · · · · · · · 上越 · · 4:69a
Joffe, Adolf Abramovich · · · · · · 3:328a
Jogaku shinshi · · · 女学新誌 · 4:69a
Jogaku zasshi · · · 女学雑誌 · 1:208b; 4:69a;
7:23b
Iwamoto Yoshiharu · · · · · · · · · 3:360b
Jōganjigawa · · · · 常願寺川 · 4:69a
Jōgashima · · · · · · 城ヶ島 · 4:69a
Jōgū Shōtoku Hōōtei
setsu · · 上宮聖徳法王帝説 · 4:69a; 7:376a
Jōha · · · · · · · · · · · 紹巴 · 6:299b
Jōhana-nuri · · · · · · 城端塗 · 8:181a
Jōhei and Tengyō Rebellions.
承平・天慶の乱 *See* **Fujiwara no**
Sumitomo; Taira no
Masakado
Jōheisō · · · · · · · · 常平倉 · 4:69b
Jōhikeshi · · · · · · 定火消 · 3:137a
John Gabriel Borkman
shingeki · · · · · · · · · · · · · · · 7:112b

Johnston, Percy H. ·············· 4:69b
Johnston Report ·············· 4:69b
Jōin ························· 4:69b
Joint acts ···················· 4:86a
Joint Council of Fellow Activists on
  the Peace Question ····· 3:129a-129b
Joint Staff College ··········· 4:69b
Joint Staff Council 2:82a; 4:69b-70a; 7:59a
Joint-stock company ····· 2:31b-32a, 37b;
            4:70a-71a; 7:247a
  articles of association ······· 2:37b
  vs. limited liability company ··· 5:10a
Joint ventures ········ 4:71a; 6:164b
  multinational enterprises ····· 5:263b
Jōjitsuron (Satyasiddhi)
  ··············· 成実論 · 1:178b; 4:71a,
            132b; 5:332b
Jōjitsu school ···· 成実宗 ···· 1:178b;
            4:71a-71b
Jojōshi ········ 抒情詩 ··· 4:309a
Jōka machi. *See* **Castle towns**
Jōkō ············ 上皇 ···· 4:71b
Jokō aishi (The Tragic
  History of Women
  Workers) ····· 女工哀史 · 4:71b; 8:264a
Jō komononari · 定小物成 ···· 4:267b
Jokotoba ·················· 4:71b-72a
  waka ····················· 8:203a
Jokō to kekkaku (Women
  Workers and
  Tuberculosis) 女工と結核 ··· 8:264a
Jōkyū Disturbance (1221)
  ············· 承久の乱 · 2:107a; 4:72a
  Fujiwara no Tameie ········ 2:355b
  Goseibai Shikimoku ····· 3:47b-48a
  Go-Toba, Emperor ······ 3:51a-52b
  jitō appointments ········· 4:122a
  Kaidōki ················· 4:108a
  Kamakura shogunate ····· 4:122a
  Shin kokinshū ············ 7:120a
  shōen ···················· 7:157b
  Takeda family ··········· 7:322a
  thought and culture ······· 8:26b
  Tsuchimikado, Emperor ····· 8:112a
Jomei, Emperor · 舒明天皇 · 2:55a; 8:303a
Jōmen ········· 定免 · 4:72a; 4:331b
  nengu ··················· 5:360b
Jōmō Kyōkai geppō
  ········· 上毛教会月報 ····· 4:162b
Jōmon culture ··· 縄文文化 · 3:158b-159b;
            4:72a-74a; 7:178b-179a
  artifacts ················· 4:153b
  economy ················· 2:147a
  final ·················· 4:73b-74a
  housing ·················· 3:243a
  late ···················· 4:73a-73b
  middle ··················· 4:72b
  origin of ················· 4:276b
Jōmon figurines ····· 4:74a-74b, 74b
  Kamegaoka site ··········· 4:125a
  Shintō ··················· 7:125b
Jōmon peoples, diet of ········ 7:83a
Jōmon period ···· 縄文時代 ···· 4:75a
  archaeological remains ···· 4:34a-34b
  culture ················· 4:72a-74a
  figurines ··············· 4:74a-74b
  pottery ················· 4:75a-75b
  religion ················· 7:125b
  stone tools ··············· 7:247b
Jōmon pottery 縄文式土器 · 1:76a, 256b;
            4:75a-75b
  lacquer use ··············· 4:361a
Jonidan ············· 7:272a, 273a
Jonokuchi ··········· 7:272a, 273a
Jon Shirubā
  ······················· 4:157b
Jōrei ············· 5:71b; 7:56a

Jōri ·········· 条理 · 4:75b, 247a;
            5:214b-215a
Jōri system ······ 条里制 · 2:104a;
            4:75b-76a; 7:296a
  handen shūju system ········ 3:95b
  Haorigata method ·········· 4:75b
  Nagachigata method ········· 4:75b
  ri ······················ 6:308a
  Temmu, Emperor ····· 7:381b-382b
Jōruri ········ 浄瑠璃 · 2:267b;
            4:76a-77b; 5:45a; 7:249b
  bun'ya-bushi ·············· 4:77a
  criticism ················· 5:16a
  dan-mono shū ············· 4:77a
  development ··········· 4:76b-77a
  Gidayū-bushi ·········· 4:77a-77b
  Jippensha Ikku ············· 4:61a
  kabuki adaptations ········· 4:91a
  kiyomoto-bushi ············ 4:77a
  ningyō ··················· 4:77a
  origin ··················· 4:76b
  sekkyō ··················· 4:77a
  Takemoto Gidayū I ········ 7:324b
  tokiwazu-bushi ············ 4:77a
  See also **Bunraku**
Jōruri hime monogatari
  (*Jōruri Hime*)
  ······· 浄瑠璃姫物語 · 3:184a; 4:76b
Jōruriji ········ 浄瑠璃寺 ···· 4:77a
Joseigo ··················· 2:250b
Josetsu ········· 如拙 · 4:77b-78a;
            7:70a
Catching a Catfish With a Gourd (Hyōnenzu)
  ······················· 4:78b
  screen painting ············ 7:42b
Jōshi ····················· 7:262a
Joshi Eigaku Juku (Tsuda College)

**Jōshin'etsu Kōgen
National Park**
  ······· 上信越高原国立公園 · 1:95b; 4:78a
Joshi Rōdo Teishintai
  (Volunteer Labor Corp)
  ··········· 女子労働挺身隊 · 8:261a
Josūshi ··················· 2:39a
JOTF (Kyokutō Hōsō) ········ 4:332b
Jōtō Mon'in ····· 上東門院 ···· 4:78a
Jōun ············ 浄雲 · 4:76b-77a
Journalists
  American
    House, Edward Howard ····· 3:240a
    Vaughn, Miles W. ········ 8:189a
  Anglo-Irish
    Brinkley, Frank ····· 1:170b-171a
  British
    Black, John Reddie ········· 1:158b
    Murdoch, James ·········· 5:270b
  Chinese
    Dai Jitao (Tai Chi-t'ao) ····· 2:59a
    Wang Tao (Wang T'ao) ··· 8:222b
    Zou Taofen (Tsou T'ao-fen) · 8:380a
  Japanese
    Abe Shinnosuke ··········· 1:4b
    Akiyama Teisuke ··········· 1:44a
    Arahata Kanson ······· 1:72a-72b
    Baba Tsunego ······· 1:129a-129b
    Fukuchi Gen'ichirō ········ 2:361b
    Furugaki Tetsurō ·········· 2:371b
    Furuno Inosuke ··········· 2:373a
    Hani Motoko ········· 3:96b-97b
    Hasegawa Nyozekan ······· 3:107a
    Hosokawa Karoku ········· 3:236b
    Ikebe Sanzan ············· 3:264b
    Ishibashi Tanzan ·········· 3:339b
    Iwanaga Yūkichi ·········· 3:360b
    Kanagaki Robun ··········· 4:135a
    Kaneko, Josephine Conger ··· 4:138a
    Kikutake Sunao ··········· 4:207b

    Kiryū Yūyū ·············· 4:222a
    Kishida Ginkō ············ 4:222b
    Kiyosawa Kiyoshi ·········· 4:232b
    Komatsubara Eitarō ········ 4:265b
    Kuga Katsunan ··········· 4:302a
    Kurimoto Joun ······· 4:313a-313b
    Maeda Yoshinori ··········· 5:81b
    Miura Saku ·············· 5:216a
    Miyatake Gaikotsu ········· 5:221a
    Motoyama Hikoichi ········· 5:259a
    Murayama Ryōhei ····· 5:270a-270b
    Nakano Seigō ········ 5:316a-316b
    Narushima Ryūhoku ········ 5:335b
    Numa Morikazu ············ 6:44b
    Ogata Taketora ······· 6:69a-69b
    Oka Shigeki ·············· 6:81a
    Ozaki Hotsumi ············ 6:139b
    Seki Hironao ············· 7:56b
    Shimada Saburō ··········· 7:99a
    Suehiro Tetchō ············ 7:255b
    Sugimura Sojinkan ········· 7:258a
    Taoka Reiun ············· 7:346a
    Torii Sosen ········· 8:79b-80a
    Ueno Riichi ············· 8:129a
    Yamaji Aizan ············ 8:296a
    Yanagawa Shunsan ········· 8:313b
  Mexican
    Tablada, José Juan ········· 7:291a
Jōwa Conspiracy 承和の変 ···· 4:78a
  Fujiwara no Yoshifusa ······ 2:358a
Jōyaku kaisei. *See* **Unequal Treaties,
  revision of**
Joya no kane ················ 5:371a
Jōyō ············· 城陽 ···· 4:78b
Jōyō kanji ········· 4:30b, 78b-79a
  Japanese language reform ···· 4:30b
  Japanese writing ··········· 4:27b
Jōyō kanji hyō ········· 4:78b-79a
Jōyuishiki ron · 成唯識論 ···· 6:247b
Jōzankei Hot Spring
  ········ 定山渓温泉 · 4:79a; 7:98a
JSC (Science Council of Japan) ···· 7:38a
JSP (Japan Socialist Party) ···· 4:48a-49a
JTB (Japan Travel Bureau, Inc) ···· 4:50a
J-turn phenomenon ·········· 8:176b
Jūbako ·················· 4:79a
Judaism, tolerance in Japanese religion
  ······················· 8:70b
Judges ················ 4:79a-79b
  impeachment ············· 3:275a
  responsibilities
    civil cases ··········· 1:320a-320b
Judicial Committee of the House of
  Councillors ··············· 4:81a
Judicial precedents ········ 4:79b
Judicial review · 2:13a; 4:79b-80a; 7:275a
  administrative law ·········· 1:13a
  fundamental liberties and ···· 2:369b
  introduction ············· 4:378a
Judicial scrivener ······· 4:80a-80b
Judicial system ········ 4:80b-81a
  Administrative Court ··· 1:11b-12a, 13a
  administrative litigation ····· 1:13b
  bail ··················· 1:130a
  judges ················ 4:79a-79b
  Supreme Court ············ 7:277b
Judiciary ·················· 6:215a
  constitutional litigation ···· 2:13a-13b
  source of information on ····· 7:181b
Jūdō ······ 柔道 · 1:34a; 4:82a-83a, *83a*
  competition techniques ···· 4:82b-83a
  expansion ················ 4:82b
  history and development ···· 4:82a-82b
  Ippon ················· 4:82b-83a
  kangeiko ················· 4:140b
  Kōdōkan ················· 4:243a
  ranks ··················· 4:83a
  schools ················· 4:147a

swordplay vs ·········· **5**:119a
Jūgatsu Jiken ··· 十月事件 ··· **6**:60a
Jūgatsukai ·········· 十月会 ··· **5**:19b
Jūgoya ·········· 十五夜 ··· **5**:248a
Jūgoya festivities ·········· **1**:23a
Jūhachi Daitsū · 十八大通 ··· **4**:83a
Jūichigatsu Jiken
 ·········· 十一月事件 ···· **6**:41b–42a
Jūichikai (Society of
 Eleven) ·········· 十一会 ··· **8**:327a
Jui ippon ·········· 儒医一本 ··· **4**:103a
Jūjiro ·········· 十字路 ··· **2**:269a
 Kinugasa Teinosuke ··· **4**:218b
Jūjō Paper Co, Ltd ··· **4**:83a–83b
Jūjūshin ron ··· 十住心論 ··· **4**:83b
 Kūkai ·········· **4**:304a
Jūjutsu. See **Jūdō**
Juka bijin ·········· 樹下美人 ··· **4**:83b
Jukaie ·········· 授戒会 ··· **7**:234a
*Jūkan kaishū shōkai
 shingo* 重刊改修健解新語 ··· **7**:163a
Jūkei seifu ·········· 重慶政府 ··· **1**:300b
Juki sampō ·········· 拾璣算法 ··· **8**:231b
Juku ·········· **4**:83b–84a
 cram schools ·········· **2**:41b
Jumbungaku ·········· **3**:312a
 Toyoda Shirō ·········· **8**:90b
Jūmin soshō ·········· **4**:84a
Jumpō tōsō ·········· **4**:84a; **7**:250a
Jūnidan ·········· 十二段 ··· **4**:76b
Jūnidan sōshi · 十二段草子 ··· **4**:76b
Jūnikyū Undō ·········· **2**:81a–81b
Junior colleges ··· **4**:84a–84b; **8**:170b
Junior Pilot Training Corps (Yokaren)
 ·········· **8**:329a
Jūnishi ·········· 十二支 ··· **1**:232a
Junnin, Emperor · 淳仁天皇 ··· **4**:253b
Junrei monogatari
 ·········· 巡礼物語 ··· **4**:187a
Junshi ·········· **4**:84b–85a
 Nogi Maresuke ·········· **6**:31a
Junsō ·········· **4**:84b
Junsui haiku ··· 純粋俳句 ··· **8**:298b
Jun tian ·········· **3**:95b
Juntoku, Emperor 順徳天皇 ··· **4**:85a
 Fujiwara no Sadaie ·········· **2**:354b
 Fujiwara no Tameie ·········· **2**:355b
 Jōkyū Disturbance ·········· **4**:72a
Juntoku In Mishō
 ·········· 順徳院御抄 ··· **4**:210b
Jūō-gyō ·········· 十王経 ··· **1**:20a
Juridical Foundation Hikari Association
 ·········· **6**:220a
Juridical Persons Tax Law · **7**:355a–358b
Jurisprudence ·········· **4**:85a–85b
Juristic act ·········· **2**:20a; **4**:86a
 general clause ·········· **3**:18a
 kōjo ryōzoku ·········· **4**:252b
Juristic person. See **Hōjin**
Jurōjin ·········· 寿老人 ··· **5**:296a
Jūroku musashi ·········· **4**:86a
Jurong Industrial Complex ··· **7**:196b
Jūron ibenshō · 十論為辯抄 ··· **4**:102b
Jūryō ·········· **7**:272a, 273a
Jury system ·········· **4**:81b
Jūsan, Lake ·········· 十三湖 ··· **4**:86a
Jusco Co, Ltd ·········· **4**:86a–86b
Jushi ·········· **4**:325a
Jūshichijō no Kempō. 十七条の憲法
 See **Seventeen-Article Constitution**
Jūshin ·········· **4**:86b
Jus sanguinis ·········· **4**:32b
Jus soli ·········· **4**:32b
Juvenile crime ·········· **4**:86b–87a
Juvenile delinquency ·········· **2**:44b
 penalties ·········· **2**:45b
Juvenile labor ·········· **4**:87a
Juvenile Law ··· **2**:246a; **4**:87a–87b; **6**:172a

juvenile crime ·········· **4**:86b
Juvenile Law of 1948 ·········· **2**:51b
**Juvenile reformatories and classification
centers** ·········· **4**:87b
**Juvenile workers, protective legislation
for** ·········· **4**:87b–88a
Jūyokkakai ·········· 十四日会 ··· **5**:281a
Jūyō Sangyō Tōsei Hō. See **Law
concerning the Control of Important
Industries**
Juzu ·········· **1**:197a

K

Kabane ·········· 姓 ··· **5**:324b
 ason ·········· **1**:103a
 uji-kabane system ·········· **8**:131b
 Yakusa no Kabane ·········· **4**:89a
Kabasan Incident
 ·········· 加波山事件 ···· **4**:89a–89b
 Freedom and People's Rights Movement
 ·········· **2**:335b; **4**:89a
 Mishima Michitsune ·········· **4**:89a
Kabayama Sukenori
 ·········· 樺山資紀 ··· **4**:89b–90a
Kabegaki ·········· 壁書 ··· **4**:90a
 domainal codes ·········· **4**:90a
 Kemmu irai tsuika hō ·········· **4**:90a
 Ōuchike Kabegaki ·········· **6**:135b
 Ruijū fusen shō ·········· **4**:90a
 sata mirensho definition ·········· **4**:90a
 Tokusei edicts ·········· **4**:90a
Kabi (Mold) ·········· 黴 ··· **8**:45a
Kabo Reform ···· 甲申政変 ··· **4**:90a
Kabu ·········· **4**:100a
Kabufuda ·········· 株札 ··· **4**:100a
Kabuki ·········· 歌舞伎 ··· **2**:74b;
 4:90a–97b, 336b; **5**:46a; **7**:31a, 43a, 97a,
 249b; **8**:21a–23a
 acting families ·········· **4**:94a–95a
 acting roles ·········· **4**:94a
 acting style ·········· **4**:94a
 actor-centered theater ·········· **4**:94a–94b
 Aoto-zōshi hana no nishiki-e ·········· **4**:95a
 Bandō Tamasaburō ·········· **4**:91a
 costume, wig, and makeup ··· **4**:95b; **8**:24a
  Kumadori ·········· **4**:95b
 dance, traditional ·········· **2**:73b
 dialogue ·········· **4**:94a
 Edo period ·········· **4**:92a
  late ·········· **5**:49b–50a
 fashion ·········· **1**:332b
 folk versions ·········· **2**:296b
 formalized behavior ·········· **4**:93b
 furyū influence ·········· **2**:374a
 future ·········· **4**:95b–96a
 fūzokuga ·········· **2**:378a
 Genroku era ·········· **4**:91a
 hanamichi ·········· **4**:95a
 Ichikawa Danjūrō ·········· **3**:257a
 Ichikawa Danjūrō XI ·········· **4**:90b
 jōruri ·········· **4**:77a
 kakubei-jishi ·········· **4**:118a
 Kanjinchō ·········· **4**:92a
 Kanze Nobumitsu ·········· **4**:154b
 Kataoka Takao ·········· **4**:91a
 Kyōganoko musume Dōjōji ·········· **4**:93a
 ma, use of ·········· **5**:77a
 Matsumoto Kōshirō VIII ·········· **4**:94b

Meiboku sendai hagi ·········· **4**:94b
 Mokuami and the Meiji period ·········· **4**:92a
 Morita Kan'ya ·········· **5**:253b
 music and dance. *See* **Kabuki music**
 nagauta ·········· **5**:307b
 Nakamura Kanzaburō XVII ·········· **4**:94b
 Nakamura Utaemon ·········· **5**:315b
 Nakamura Utaemon VI ·········· **4**:93a, 94b
 Okuni ·········· **6**:97a
 onnagata ·········· **6**:108a
 Onnagoroshi abura no jigoku ·········· **4**:91a
 Onoe Kikugorō ·········· **6**:109a
 Onoe Matsunosuke ·········· **6**:109b
 Onoe Shōroku ·········· **4**:92b
 origin ·········· **3**:184a–184b; **4**:90b
 Ōsaka school ·········· **6**:123a
 other traditional dramas ·········· **4**:92b
 performances ·········· **4**:93b–94a
 plays ·········· **4**:93a
 post-Meiji ·········· **4**:92a
 post-World War II ·········· **4**:92a–92b
 puppet theater ·········· **4**:91b, 93a
 Sakata Tōjūrō I ·········· **6**:379b
 San'yūtei Enchō ·········· **7**:19b
 Sawamura Sōjūrō ·········· **7**:31a
 Shibaraku ·········· **4**:92b
 shimpa ·········· **7**:107b
 shingeki ·········· **7**:112a
 Shinkokugeki ·········· **7**:121a
 Shinoda Masahiro ·········· **7**:122b
 after 1652 ·········· **4**:90b–91a
 social position of actors ·········· **4**:95a–95b
 stage ·········· **4**:95b
 stage assistants ·········· **4**:94a
 staging ·········· **4**:93b
 Sukeroku yukari no edo-zakura ·········· **4**:90b
 Takeda Izumo ·········· **7**:322b
 tattoos ·········· **7**:350b
 Tokugawa thought ·········· **4**:93b
 Tōkyō ·········· **8**:63b
 Torii school ·········· **8**:79a
 tsuzumi ·········· **8**:119b
Kabuki Jūhachiban
 ·········· 歌舞伎十八番 ··· **1**:213b;
 4:97b–99a
 Ichikawa Danjūrō ·········· **3**:257a; **4**:97b
Kabukimono ····· 歌舞伎者 ··· **4**:332b
Kabuki music ·········· **4**:91b–92a, 99a–100a
 early history ·········· **4**:99a
 form ·········· **4**:99b–100a
 functions ·········· **4**:99b
 Nagauta school ·········· **4**:91b
 performance practice ·········· **4**:99a
 traditional ·········· **5**:285a
 types ·········· **4**:99a
Kabuki theater
 Okuni ·········· **6**:97a
 puppet theater influence ·········· **1**:215a
Kabunakama ·········· 株仲間 ··· **2**:147b–148a;
 4:100a
 apprentice system ·········· **1**:71a
 dissolution ·········· **4**:100a
 fudasashi ·········· **2**:340b
 increase ·········· **4**:100a
 kokuso used against ·········· **4**:262b
 membership ·········· **4**:100a
 monopoly status ·········· **1**:132b
 opposition ·········· **2**:149b
 premodern economy ·········· **2**:149b
 Tanuma Okitsugu ·········· **7**:345a–346a
Kaburagi Kiyokata
 ·········· 鏑木清方 · **4**:100a–100b
Kaburaya ·········· **4**:160b
Kabushiki kaisha. See **Joint-stock
company**
*Kabushiki kaisha keizai
 ron* ····· 株式会社経済論 ··· **8**:127a
Kabutogani ·········· **3**:231a

Kachikachi Mountain
· 4:100b
Kachikachi yama
· · · · · · · · · · · · · かちかち山 2:303a; 4:100b
Kachikoshi · · · · · · · · · · · · · · · · · 7:273a
Kachō · 1:14b
Kachōga · · · · · · · · · 花鳥画 · 1:156a–156b;
7:17b
subjects · · · · · · · · · · · · · · · · · · · 6:158b
Kadankai · · · · · · · · · · · · · · · · · · · 5:19b
Kada no Arimaro 荷田在満 4:100b
Kada no Azumamaro · · · · · · · · · 4:100b
Kada no Azumamaro
· · · · · · · · · · · · · · 荷田春満 · 1:154a;
4:100b–101a
Kada no Arimaro · · · · · · · · · · · · 4:100b
Kamo no Mabuchi · · · · · · · · · 4:100b, 129a
Kokugaku · · · · · · · · · · · · · · · · · 4:257b
Man'yōshū scholarship · · · · · · 5:110b
Kada zenshū · · · · · · 荷田全集 · 4:101a
Kadena · · · · · · · · · · · 嘉手納 · 4:101a
Kades, Charles Louis · · · · · · · 4:101a
Kadokawa Gen'yoshi
· · · · · · · · · · · · · · · · · · 角川源義 · 4:101a
Kadokawa Publishing Co, Ltd · 4:101a;
6:268a
Kadoma · · · · · · · · · · · · 門真 · 4:101a
Kadomatsu · · · · · · · · · · · · · · · · · 5:371a
Kadoya Shichirobei
· · · · · · · · · · · · · · 角屋七郎兵衛 · 4:101a
Kadozuke · · · · · · · · · · · · · 4:101a–101b
Kaede · · · · · · · · · · · · 4:64b; 5:111b–112a
Kaedegawa Shiin
· · · · · · · · · · · · · · · 楓川市隠 · 4:189b
Kaehwap'a (Enlightenment Faction)
· · · · · · · · · · · · · · · · · · · 4:101b, 280b
Fukuzawa Yukichi · · · · · · · · · · 4:101b
Kapsin Political Coup · · · · · · · · 4:156b
Kim Ok-kyun · · · · · · · · 4:101b, 209a
Pak Yǒng-Hyo · · · · · · · 4:101b; 6:159b
Sugup'a · · · · · · · · · · · · · · · · · · · 4:101b
Kaei sandai ki 花営三代記 · 4:101b
Kaempfer, Engelbert · · 1:237a, 269b;
4:101b–102a
German-Japanese relations · · · · 3:26a
History of Japan · · · · · · · · 4:101b–102a
sazanka · · · · · · · · · · · · · · · · · · · 7:32a
Shizuki Tadao · · · · · · · · · · · · · 4:102a
Kaerazaru natsu
· · · · · · · · · · · · · · · 帰らざる夏 · 4:102b
Kaeriten · · · · · · · · · · · · · · · · · · 4:124a
Kaeriyama Norimasa
· · · · · · · · · · · · · · · 帰山教正 · 2:268a
Kaeru · · · · · · · · · · · · · · · · 2:339b–340a
Kaesen · · · · · · · · · · · · · · 替銭 · 4:102a
Kaeshi · · · · · · · · · · · · · · · · · · 4:102a
gift giving · · · · · · · · · · · · · · · · · 3:31a
Kaezeni · · · · · · · · · · · · · · 替銭 · 4:102a
Kaezeniya · · · · · · · · · · · 替銭屋 · 4:102a
Kaga · · · · · · · · · · · · 加賀 · 4:102a–102b
Kaga Bunko Collection · · · · · · · 8:67b
Kagaku Gijutsu Chō
· · · · · · · · · · · · · · · 科学技術庁 · 7:37b–38a
Kagaku Gijutsu Kaigi · · · · · · · · 7:38a
Kagakukai · · · · · · · · · · · 歌学会 · 5:19b
Kagakuron (On Science) · 科学論 · 8:81b
Kagaku teiyō · · · · 歌学提要 · 4:103a
Kagami Kenkichi 各務鎌吉 · 4:102b
Kagami Shikō · 各務支考 · 4:102b; 5:16a;
6:299b
Kaga no Chiyo · 加賀千代 · 4:102b
Kaga no Jō · · · · · · · 加賀掾 · 4:77a
Kaga Otohiko · · · 加賀乙彦 · 4:102b
Kagawa Gen'etsu 賀川玄悦 · 4:102b
Kagawa Kageki · 香川景樹 · 4:102b–103a;
5:17a, 48a
Kamo no Mabuchi · · · · · · · · · · 4:103a
Ki no Tsurayuki · · · · · · · · · · · · 4:103a

Masaoka Shiki · · · · · · · · · · · · · · 4:103a
Ozawa Roan · · · · · · · · · · · · · · · 4:103a
Kagawa Prefecture 香川県 · 4:103a–103b
history · 4:103b
Sanuki Mountains · · · · · · · · · · · 4:103a
tourist attractions · · · · · · · · · · · 4:103b
Kagawa Shūtoku 香川修徳 · 3:239a; 4:103b
Gotō Konzan · · · · · · · · · · · · · · · 4:103b
Itō Jinsai · · · · · · · · · · · · · · · · · · 4:103b
Kagawa Toyohiko
· · · · · · · · · · · · · · · · 賀川豊彦 · 1:84a;
4:103b–104a
Kaizō · 4:113b
labor movement activities · · · · · 4:104a
pacifism · · · · · · · · · · · · · · · · · · 6:144a
social gospel · · · · · · · · · · · · · · · 4:103b
Kagayakeru yami 輝ける闇 · 4:111b
Kageki Shakai Undō Torishimari Hōan
· · · · · · · · · · · · · · · · · · · 2:133a–133b
Kagekiyo · · · · · · · · · · · 景清 · 4:98b
Kagemusha · · · · · · · 影武者 · 8:36b
Kagerō · · · · · · · · · · かげろう · 7:111b
Kagerō nikki · · · 蜻蛉日記 · 4:104a–104b;
6:2a; 7:257b
Fujiwara no Michitsuna no Haha · 4:104a
Kageyama Hideko
· · · · · · · · · · · · · · · 景山英子 · 2:362a
Kageyu · · · · · · · · · · · · · 勘解由 · 4:104b
Kageyujō · · · · · · · · · · 勘解由状 · 4:104b
Kageyushi · · · · · · · 勘解由使 · 4:104b
Kagi (The Key) · · · · · · 鍵 6:230a; 7:343a
Kago (baskets) · · · · · · · · · · · 4:104b–105a
Kago (conveyance) · · · · · · · · · · 4:104b
Kagome Co, Ltd · · · · · · · · · · 4:105a
Kagome kagome
· · · · · · · · · · · · · かごめかごめ · 4:105a
Kagoshima · · · · · · · 鹿児島 · 4:105a, 105a,
105b, 221b
Kagoshima Bay 鹿児島湾 · 4:105b
Kagoshima Bombardment
· · · · · · · · · · · · · · 薩英戦争 · 1:86a; 4:105b;
8:253b
Kagoshima Juzō
· · · · · · · · · · · · · · 鹿児島寿蔵 · 4:105b
Kagoshima Prefecture
· · · · · · · · · · · · · · 鹿児島県 · 4:105b–106a;
7:30a
economy · · · · · · · · · · · · · · · · · · 4:106a
geography · · · · · · · · · · · · · · · · · 4:105b
history · · · · · · · · · · · · · · · · · 4:105b–106a
tourist attractions · · · · · · · · · · · 4:106a
Kagura · · · · · · · · 神楽 · 2:255b, 297a,
297b; 4:106a–108a; 7:148b
dance, traditional · · · · · · · · · · · 2:73b
forms · · · · · · · · · · · · · · · · · 4:107a–108a
ise · 4:107b
izumo · 4:107b
mikagura · · · · · · · · · · · · · · · · · 4:107a
miko · 4:107b
minkan · · · · · · · · · · · · · · · · · · · 4:107b
sato · 4:107b
shishi · 4:107b
gagaku · · · · · · · · · · · · · · · · · · · 3:1a
importance · · · · · · · · · · · 2:137a–138a
kannamesai · · · · · · · · · · · · · · · 4:144b
nature · · · · · · · · · · · · · · · 4:106b–107a
Shintō rites · · · · · · · · · · · · · · · · 7:139b
Kagurabue · · · · · · · · · · · · · · · · · 4:108a
Kagura uta · · · · · · 神楽歌 · 4:108a
accession ceremony performance · 4:108a
gagaku style · · · · · · · · · · · · · · · 4:108a
modern performances · · · · · · · · 4:108a
parts · 4:108a
Kahō · · · · · · · · · · · · · · · 家法 · 4:119a
Kahokugata · · · · · · · · · 河北潟 · 4:108a
Kai · · · · · · · · · · · · · · · 花彙 · 6:111b
Kai-awase · · · · · 貝合せ · 4:108a; 7:82a
Kaibara Ekiken 貝原益軒 · 4:108a–108b

Onna daigaku · · · · · 4:108b; 6:108a
Yōjōkun · · · · · · · · · · · · · · · · · · 8:328b
Kaibun (palindromes) · · · · · · · · 8:270a
Kaichōon · · · · · · · 海潮音 · 8:127a
Kaidan jidaigeki · · · · · · · · · · · · 2:273a
Kaidō · · · · · · · · · · · · · · · · · · 4:108b
Gokaidō · · · · · · · · · · · · · · · · · · 4:108b
post-station towns · · · · · · · · · · 4:108b
Kaidōki · · · · · · · · 海道記 · 1:294a; 4:108b,
128b; 8:104b–105a
Kaieki · · · · · · · · · · · 改易 · 4:108b–109a
Kaientai · · · · · · · 海援隊 · 4:109a;
5:313b–314a
Sakamoto Ryōma · · · · · · · · · · · 4:109a
Kaifūsō · · · · · · · · 懐風藻 · 1:180b;
2:350b; 4:109a; 5:26a; 6:193a
authorship · · · · · · · · · · · · · · · · 4:109a
Chinese literary influence · 1:293a; 4:109a
Kōbun, Emperor · · · · · · · · · · · 4:239a
Ōmi no Mifune · · · · · · · · · · · · · 6:102a
poetic style · · · · · · · · · · · · · · · · 4:109a
Kaigai Ijū Shinkō Kabushiki Kaisha
· 2:201a
Kaigai Tokō Kinshi Rei
· · · · · · · · · 海外渡航禁止令 · 4:109b
Kaigata Hot Spring 海潟温泉 · 7:347b
Kaigenrei · · · · · · · · · · · · · · · · · 5:120a
Kaigetsudō Ando 懐月堂安度 · 4:109b
Kaigetsudō school
· · · · · · · · · · · · 懐月堂派 4:109b; 8:140a,
140b
Kaigo Tokiomi · 海後宗臣 · 4:109b
Imperial Rescript on Education · 4:109b
Kaigun · · · · · · · · · 海軍 · 7:148b, 263a
Kaigun Denshūjo 海軍伝習所 · 4:110a
Enomoto Takeaki · · · · · · · · · · · 4:110a
Godai Tomoatsu · · · · · · · · · · · 4:110a
Katsu Kaishū · · · · · · · · · · · · · · 4:110a
Kimura Yoshitake · · · · · · · · · · 4:211b
Sano Tsunetami · · · · · · · · · · · · 4:110a
Kaigun Heigakkō. *See* Naval Academy
Kaigun Kōshō · · 海軍工廠 · 8:334a
Kaigunshō · · · · · · · 海軍省 · 5:358b
Kaihaku Goshi Shinrei. 海舶互市新例
See **Shōtoku Nagasaki Shinrei**
Kaihō school · · · 海北派 · 4:110a, 146a
Kaihō Yūshō · · · · · · · 4:110a, 110b–111a
Kanō school rivalry · · · · · · · · · · 4:150a
style · 4:110a
Kaiho Seiryō · 海保青陵 · 4:110a–110b
domainal monopoly advocacy · · 4:110a
Kaihō Yūshō · 海北友松 · 4:110a–111a;
7:42b
Clouds and Dragons · · · · · · 4:110a–110b
Kaijin nijūmensō
· · · · · · · · · · · · 怪人二十面相 · 7:166b
Kaijō geijutsu · · · 会場芸術 · 4:175b
Kaikaha · · · · · · · · · 開化派 · 4:101b
Kaikei · · · · · · · · · · 快慶 · 1:199a, 201a;
4:111a
Kaikei Kensa In · · · · · · · · · · · · 1:159a
Kaikō · · · · · · · · · · 歌意考 4:129b; 7:196a
Kaikō Ken · · · · · · 開高健 · 1:209a;
4:111a–111b; 7:85a
Kaikoku. 開国 *See* **Opening of Japan**
Kaikoku heidan (Military
Discussion of a Maritime
Country) · · · · · · · · 海国兵談 · 8:243a
Kaikoma · · · · · · · · · 甲斐駒 · 4:265a
Kai Komagatake
· · · · · · · · · · · · · · 甲斐駒ケ岳 · 4:265a
Kaikō Takeshi. 開高健 *See* **Kaikō Ken**
Kaikyū oyobi daisan
shikan · 階級及び第三史観 · 7:319b
Kaimondake · · · 開聞岳 · 4:105b, 111b
Kainan · · · · · · · · · · · 海南 · 4:111b
Kainan Gisha · · · 海南義社 · 4:166a
Kainan Jiyūtō · 海南自由党 · 6:321a

Kain no matsuei
········ カインの末裔 ·····1:84b
Kainō Michitaka 戒能通孝 ·4:111b–112a
　civil rights ·············4:112a
　early research ············4:112a
　war crimes trials ··········4:112a
Kaionji Chōgorō
········ 海音寺潮五郎 ···4:112a
Kairaishi ki (Account of
　Kairaishi) 傀儡子記 ·····6:269b
Kairakuen ·········偕楽園 ·4:112a, 198a
Kairō ni te 廻廊にて ·······8:113b
Kaisaku bugyō 改作奉行 ···4:112b
Kaisakuhō ·······改作法 ·4:112a–112b
　administrators ············4:112b
　effects ················4:112a
　Maeda family ············4:112a
　peasants' tax burden ······4:112b
　tax rate ···············4:112b
Kaiseijo 開成所 ··········1:142a
Kaiseikan 開成館 ·········3:362a
Kaiseki gairon · 解析概論 ·····7:311a
Kaiseki ryōri · 会席料理 ·2:22a, 305a
Kaisen ···········廻船 ·4:112b–113a
　higaki ·················4:112b
　kitamaebune ············4:112b
　ports ·················4:112b
　sea routes ·············4:112b–113a
　sengokubune ············4:112b
　steamboat replacements ····4:113a
　taru ·················4:113a
Kaisen shikimoku 廻船式目 ···4:112b
Kaishi ······4:113a; 6:362b, 363a
Kaishiki ······2:25b; 6:362b, 363a
Kaishin shimbun 改進新聞 ···1:155a
Kaishintō. 改進党 *See* **Rikken Kaishintō**
Kai Shirane. *See* **Shirane Sanzan**
Kaisho ······4:142a–142b; 7:171a, 172b
Kaitai shinsho · 解体新書 · 4:173a; 5:82a;
　　6:65a; 7:258b; 8:242a
Kaitakushi ·········開拓使 ·4:113a
　budget ················4:113a
　Hokkaidō Colonization Office ·4:113a
　Kuroda Kiyotaka ·········4:113a
　militia system ···········4:113a
Kaitakushi Kan'yūbutsu
　Haraisage Jiken
· 開拓使官有物払下げ事件 ·3:213a–213b
Kaitakushi Scandal of 1881. *See*
**Hokkaidō Colonization Office Scandal
　of 1881**
Kaitei Ritsurei · 改定律例 ·4:113b
　Shinritsu Kōryō ··········7:124a
Kaiten ············回天 ·4:113b
Kaito ·················4:308a
Kaitokudō ··········懐徳堂 ·4:113b
　curriculum ·············4:113b
　Miyake Sekian ···········4:113b
　Nakai Riken ············5:313b
Kaitoku Shoin. 懐徳書院
　See **Kaitokudō**
Kai tsūshō kō (Study of
　Commercial Intercourse
　with the Chinese and
　Other Foreigners)
········ 華夷通商考 · 8:241b, 242a
Kaizei Yakusho · 改税約書 ·4:113b
　import tariff reduction ·····4:113b
　shogunate trade control ····4:113b
Kaizō (Reconstruction)
········ 改造 · 4:113b–114a;
　　6:267b; 7:309a; 8:297a
　censorship ·············1:253a
　Chūō Kōron ············4:114a
　Yamamoto Sanehiko ·······4:113b
　Yokohama Incident ········8:330a
Kaizōsha ···············8:298b
Kaizuka (city) ·····貝塚 ·4:114a

Kaizuka. *See* **Shell mounds**
Kajii Motojirō · 梶井基次郎 ·4:114a–114b
Kajikisen (facsimiles)
········ 加治木銭 ·····4:239a
Kajima Corporation ·····4:114b
　Taisei Corporation ·······7:303a
Kajimaya ·······加島屋 ·4:114b
　daimyō loans ············4:114b
　Dōjima Rice Market activities ·4:114b
Kaji shōzoku ·······2:280b–281a
Kajiwara Kagetoki
········ 梶原景時 ·4:114b; 7:80b
　Minamoto no Yoriie ·······4:114b
　Minamoto no Yoritomo rescue ·4:114b
　Minamoto no Yoshitsune ····4:114b
　Taira-Minamoto War ······4:114b
Kajiwara Shōzen 梶原性全 ·4:114b–115a
　Ban'ampō ·············4:114b–115a
　Ton'ishō ··············4:114b
Kajiya ················7:206a
Kajiyama Toshiyuki
········ 梶山季之 ·····4:115a
Kakamigahara ······各務原 ·4:115a
Kakari ················4:191a
Kakari-musubi ···········4:115a
Kakashi ···············4:115a
Kake ·················1:273a
Kakebuton ··············1:148b
Kakegawa ··········掛川 ·4:115a
Kakei Katsuhiko · 筧克彦 ·4:115a–115b
　Dai Nippon teikoku kempō no kompongi 4:115b
　Hirata Atsutane ··········4:115b
　Kami nagara no michi ·····4:115b
　Koshintō taigi ··········4:115b
　Minobe Tatsukichi ········4:115b
　Motoori Norinaga ·········4:115b
Kakeizu ·········家系図 ·3:17b
Kakekomidera ···········4:115b
Kakekotoba (pivot words)
········ 掛詞 ·······4:115b
　word games ············8:269b
Kakemono ······4:116a, 116b
Kakemonokake ············4:116a
Kakeya ·····掛屋 2:340b; 4:116a
　daimyō loans ·······2:64b; 4:116a
　Kōnoike family ·······4:116a, 274a
Kakeya Sōichi · 掛谷宗一 ·4:116a
Kakibe ·········部曲 ·1:147b
Kakiemon ware
········ 柿右衛門手 · 1:85a–85b,
　　　　　　260a; 4:116b
　Edo period ·············1:263b
　foreign imitations ·······4:116b
　jar ··················1:261a
　Sakaida Kizaemon ········4:116b
　typical forms ···········4:116b
Kaki futatsu 柿二つ ·······7:311b
Kakihan ·········書判 ·4:155b
Kakiire ···············7:87a
　main suit ··············4:117a
　money suit ·············4:117a
Kaki no ki no aru ie 柿の木のある家
········ ··············8:110a
Kakinomoto no Hitomaro
········ 柿本人麻呂 ·····1:299b;
　4:117a–117b; 5:13a, 104b; 7:13a; 8:287b
　chōka ·················4:117a
　Jinshin Disturbance of 672 ··4:117a
　Man'yōshū ······4:117a; 5:107b
　Shin kokinshū ··········7:120a
　style ·················4:117a
Kakitsubata. *See* **Irises**
Kakitsubata gunraku
········ カキツバタ群落 ·····7:339a
Kakitsu Incident · 嘉吉の乱 ·1:40b
Kakiuchi ·········垣内 ·4:119b
Kakizaki family · 蠣崎氏 ·2:238b
Kakizome ···············2:259b

Kakogawa (city) ·····加古川 ·4:117b
Kakogawa (river) ·····加古川 ·4:117b
Kako genzai inga kyō emaki.
過去現在因果経絵巻 *See* **E inga kyō**
Kakoimai ············囲米 ·4:117b
Kaku ·················4:131a
Kakuban ·········覚鑁 ·4:117b–118a
　Dai Dembōin ············4:118a
　Kūkai ················4:304a
　Pure Land worship ·······6:270a
　Shingon sect ············7:115a
Kakubei-jishi ·······4:118a, 118b
Kakubetsu chigyō
········ 格別知行 ·····3:255b
Kakuda ···········角田 ·4:118a
Kakudai ···············4:308a
Kakuijima ·······鹿久居島 ·4:118a
Kakujō ··············2:187b
Kaku Matsujaku · 郭沫若 ·3:70a–70b
Kakun ···········家訓 ·4:118a–119a
　Asakura Takakage Jōjō ····4:118b
　Asakura Toshikage, 17-Article
　　Code of ·············1:94b–95a
　Gokurakuji Dono Goshōsoku ·4:118b
　kabegaki ···············4:90a
　Kibi no Makibi ···········4:118a
　Kōnoike constitution ······4:274b
　Mōri Motonari ···········4:118b
　okibumi similarity ········4:118b
　Rokuhara Dono Gokakun ···4:118b
　Shingen Kahō ············7:113b
　Sōunji Dono Nijūikkajō ·····4:118b
Kakunodate ··········角館 ·4:119a
Kakure Kirishitan ·····4:119a–120a
　Francis Xavier ···········8:281a
　fumie ·················2:368a
　lay leadership ··········4:119a–119b
　orashio ················4:119b
　persecution ·············6:118a
　sacraments ·············4:119b
　Taketa ················7:325b
Kakushiaji ··············2:25b
Kakushin Kurabu
········ 革新倶楽部 ·····4:120a
　dissolution ·············4:120a
　goals ·················4:120a
　Inukai Tsuyoshi ······3:326a; 4:120a
　Kenseikai ···········4:120a, 198a
　Kiyoura Keigo ···········4:233a
　movement to protect constitutional
　　government ···········4:120a
　Ozaki Yukio ············4:120a
　Rikken Kokumintō ········4:120a
　support ················4:120a
Kakushin Ni ·······覚信尼 ·4:68a
Kakushi toride no san akunin
　Shimura Takashi ··········7:108a
Kaku Shōrei ·······郭松齢 ·3:70b
Kakushu gakkō ···········5:198b
Kakuyū. *See* **Toba Sōjō**
Kakuzenshō ·······覚禅鈔 ·4:120a
　Buddhist sculpture ·······1:203b
Kakyō hyōshiki · 歌経標式 ·8:209a
Kama
Kama and kamado (rice pot and hearth)
········ ··············2:25a
Kamada Ryōō · 鎌田柳泓 ·4:120a
Kamado ······4:120a–120b; 5:193a
　cultural significance ·······4:120a
　history ················4:120b
　types ·················4:120b
Kamadogami ·············4:120b
Kamagaya ·······鎌ケ谷 ·4:120b
Kamahige ·········鎌髭 ·4:99a
Kamaishi ·········釜石 ·4:120b
Kamaishi Iron Mine ·······3:333a
Kamakura ·········鎌倉 2:252b; 4:120b,
　　　　　　135a; 7:161a

Daibutsu · · · · · · · · · · · · · · · **4**:120b
Engakuji · · · · · · · · · · · · · · · · **4**:120b
Gozan · · · · · · · · · · · · · · · · · · · **4**:120b
Kenchōji · · · · · · · · · · · · · · · · **4**:120b
Minamoto no Yoritomo · · · · **4**:120b
Tōkeiji · · · · · · · · · · · · · · · · · · **4**:120b
Tsurugaoka Hachiman Shrine · · · · · **4**:*120b*
urbanization · · · · · · · · · · · · · · **8**:176a
Kamakura bakufu. See **Kamakura shogunate**
Kamakura-bori · · 鎌倉彫 **2**:295a; **4**:121a
Kamakura Daibutsu 鎌倉大仏 · · · **2**:55a
Kamakurafu 鎌倉府 · · · · · · · **5**:272b
Kamakura Gozan 鎌倉五山 See **Gozan**
Kamakura history. See **History of Japan**
Kamakura Matsuri · · · · · · · · **2**:252b
Kamakura National Treasure House · **5**:276b
Kamakura ōzōshi 鎌倉大草紙 · · · · · · · · · · · · · **4**:121a
Kantō Kanrei · · · · · · · · · · · · · **4**:121a
Kūbo · **4**:121a
Taiheiki · · · · · · · · · · · · · · · · · **4**:121a
Kamakura period 鎌倉時代 · · · **4**:121b
Kamakura shogunate 鎌倉幕府 · · **4**:121b-122a
Azuma kagami · · · · · · · · · · · · **1**:127a
character · · · · · · · · · · · · · · · · · **4**:122a
Jōkyū Disturbance of 1221 · · **4**:122a
lord-vassal relationship · · · · **4**:122a
shiki · · · · · · · · · · · · · · · · · · · **4**:122a
Council of State · · · · · · · · · · **3**:252a
decrees (tokusei) · · · · · · · · · · **8**:58b
development · · · · · · · · · **4**:122a-122b
exchange economy · · · · · · · · **4**:122a
Goseibai shikimoku · · **3**:47b; **5**:101b
Hōjō family · · · · · · · · · · · · · · **4**:122a
mandokoro · · · · · · · · · · · · · · **4**:122a
Minamoto no Sanetomo · · · · **4**:122a
Minamoto no Yoriie · · · · · · · **4**:122a
monchūjo · · · · · · · · · · · · · · · **4**:122a
Mongol invasions · · · · · · · · · **4**:122a
overthrow · · · · · · · · · · · · · · · **4**:122a
political change · · · · · · · · · · · **4**:122a
samurai-dokoro · · · · · · · · · · **4**:122a
toimaru · · · · · · · · · · · · · · · · · **4**:122b
education · · · · · · · · · · · · · · · · · **2**:172b
establishment · · · · · · · · · · · · · **4**:122a
jitō appointments · · · · · · · · · **4**:122a
Minamoto no Yoritomo · · · · **4**:122a
shugo appointments · · · · · · · **4**:122a
Taira family defeat · · · · · · · · **4**:122a
Go-Daigo, Emperor · · · · · · · · **3**:39a
inheritance of land · · · · · · · · · **7**:232a
Kameyama, Emperor · · · · · · · · **4**:125b
kokushi's status during · · · · · · **4**:262b
Korean court, relations between · · · **4**:276a
military governors · · · · · · · · · **7**:220a
Minamoto family · · · · · · · · · · **5**:178a
Minamoto no Yoriie · · · · · · · · **5**:180b
Minamoto no Yoritomo · · · · · **5**:181a-182a
Mongol invasions of Japan · · · **5**:243b
nenki · **5**:361b
samurai · · · · · · · · · · · · · · · · · · **7**:8a
sekke shōgun · · · · · · · · · · · · **7**:57b-58a
shikken (shogunal regent) · · · · **7**:97b
trade · **2**:148a
yoriai · **8**:338a
Kamanashigawa 釜無川 · **2**:341b, 343b; **4**:122b
Kamasu · · · · · · · · · · · · · · · · · · **4**:123a
Kamba Falls · · · · · 神庭滝 · **4**:123a
Kamban · · · · · · · · · · · · · · · · · · **7**:193b
Kambara Ariake 蒲原有明 · **4**:123a
Shinshichō · · · · · · · · · · · · · · · **7**:124b
Kambayashi Akatsuki · · · · · · · · · · · · · · · · · 上林暁 · **4**:123a

Kambun · · · · · · · **1**:293a-293b; **2**:97b; **4**:31a, 123a-124b; **7**:34b, 62a
Kambun Master · · · · · · · · · · **4**:124b
Kame · · · · · · · · · · · · · · · · **8**:120a-120b
Kameda Bōsai · 亀田鵬斎 · · · · **2**:347a; **4**:124b-125a
Kamegaoka site · · · · · · · · 亀ケ岡遺跡 · **4**:74a, 75b, 125a
beads · · · · · · · · · · · · · · · · · · · **4**:125a
bone articles · · · · · · · · · · · · · · **4**:125a
fern frond designs · · · · · · · · · **4**:125a
Jōmon figurines · · · · · · · · · · · **4**:125a
stone tools · · · · · · · · · · · · · · · **4**:125a
Kameido Incident · · · · · · · · · · · · · · · · · 亀戸事件 · **4**:125a
Tanno Setsu · · · · · · · · · · · · · · **7**:344a
Tōkyō Earthquake of 1923 · · · · **8**:66b
Kamei Katsuichirō · · · · · · · · · · · · 亀井勝一郎 · **4**:125a-125b; **5**:13a
Nihon Rōmanha · · · · · · · **4**:125a; **5**:381b
Proletarian literature movement involvement · · · · · · · · · · · · · · **4**:125a
Shinjinkai · · · · · · · · **4**:125a; **7**:115b
Yasuda Yojūrō · · · · · · · · · · · · **4**:125a
Kamei Nammei · 亀井南冥 · · · · · **1**:76b
Kamen no kokuhaku (Confessions of a Mask) 仮面の告白 · · · · · · · · **6**:231a
Kameoka · · · · · · · · · · · · 亀岡 · **4**:125b
Akechi Mitsuhide rule · · · · · · **4**:125b
post-station · · · · · · · · · · · · · · **4**:125b
Kameyama (city) · · · 亀山 · · **4**:125b
Kameyama, Emperor 亀山天皇 · · · · · · · · · · · · · · · · · **4**:125b
Emperor Fushimi · · · · · · · · · · **4**:125b
Emperor Go-Fukakusa · · · · · · **4**:125b
Emperor Go-Saga · · · · · · · · · **4**:125b
Emperor Go-Uda · · · · · · · · · · **4**:125b
Northern and Southern Courts · · **6**:39a
succession · · · · · · · · · · · · · · · **4**:192a
Kami · · · · · · · **1**:62a, 122b-123a; **2**:236b-237a; **4**:125b-126a; **7**:263a, 361b
earthly divinities · · · · · · · · · · **4**:125b
exorcism · · · · · · · · · · · · · · · · **4**:126a
heavenly divinities · · · · · · · · · **4**:125b
High Celestial Plain · · · · · · · · **4**:126a
kagura · · · · · · · · · · · · · · · · · · · **4**:106b
kites · · · · · · · · · · · · · **4**:229b-231b
manifestation · · · · · · · · · · · · · **4**:126a
mountains, worship of · · · · **5**:259b-260a
religion and society · · · · · · · · · **6**:293b
in Shinto art · · · · · · · · · · · · · **7**:134b
tatari · **7**:257a
thought and culture · · · · · · · **8**:25a-26a
vengeful spirits · · · · · · · · · · **3**:46b-47a
worship · · · · · · · · · · · · · **7**:179b-180a
See also Deities
Kamichika case · · · · · · · · · · · **6**:250a
Kamichika Ichiko 神近市子 **4**:126a; **6**:250a
Hikage Teahouse Incident · · · · **4**:126a
Kamichika Ichiko jiden: Waga ai waga tatakai · · · · · · · · · · · · · · · · · · **4**:126a
Ōsugi Sakae · · · · · · · · · · · · · · **4**:126a
Seitōsha membership · · · · · · · **4**:126a
Kamidana ("god shelf"). See **Shintō family altars**
Kami Fukuoka · · · · · · · 上福岡 · **4**:126a
Kami fūsen. See **Paper balloons**
Kamigata · · · · · · · · · · · · 上方 · **4**:151b
Kamigumi Co, Ltd · · · · · · · · · **4**:126b
Kamikakushi · · · · · · · · · · · · · · **4**:126b
Kamikawa Basin 上川盆地 · **4**:*126b*
Kamikaze · · · · · · · · · · · 神風 · **1**:123b; **4**:126b; **7**:262a-262b
literary usage · · · · · · · · · · · · · **4**:126b
Mongol armada destruction · · · · · **4**:126b

Kamikaze Special Attack Force 神風特別攻撃隊 **4**:127a; **8**:276a
effectiveness · · · · · · · · · · · · · · **4**:127a
suicide weapons · · · · · · · · · · **4**:127a
Kamikōchi · · · · · · · · · 上高地 · **4**:*127a*
Yakedake volcano · · · · · · · · · **8**:285a
Kami no Hakubutsukan · · · · · · **6**:162a
Kaminoyama · · · · · · · · 上山 · **4**:127a
Kamiokuri · · · · · · · · · · · · · · · · **1**:155a
Kami Shiiba Dam 上椎葉ダム · · **2**:73a
Kami Suwa Hot Spring 上諏訪温泉 · · · · · · · · · · · · · · · · · · · **4**:127b
Kami tobi (paper hawk kite) · · **4**:229b
Kami to hito no aida 神と人の間 · · · · · · · · · · · **7**:342b
Kamitsukasa Shōken 上司小剣 · · · · · · · · · · · · · **4**:127b
Kamiyama Sōjin 上山草人 · · **4**:127b
Ai yo jinrui to tomo ni are · · · · **4**:127b
Shingeki movement · · · · · · · · **4**:127b
Thief of Baghdad, The · · · · · · **4**:127b
Kamiya Sōtan · 神谷宗湛 · **4**:127b; **7**:99a
Kamiya Sōtan nikki · · · · · · · · **4**:127b
Kobayakawa Hideaki · · · · · · · **4**:127b
Shimai Sōshitsu · · · · · · · · · · · **4**:127b
Toyotomi Hideyoshi · · · · · · · · **4**:127b
Kamiya Ten'yū 神谷天遊 · · · · · · **8**:297a
Kamiyui · · · · · · · · · · · · · · · · · · **4**:127b
Dampatsurei law · · · · · · · · · · **4**:127b
hairstyles · · · · · · · · · · · · · · · · **4**:127b
Ukiyodoko descriptions · · · · · · **4**:127b
Kammon Bridge · · · 関門橋 · **7**:*106b*
Shimonoseki · · · · · · · · · · · · · · **7**:105b
Kammon gyoki · 看聞御記 · **4**:127b-128a
Kammon nikki 看聞日記 · **4**:127b
Kammon Strait · 関門海峡 · **4**:128a
Shimonoseki · · · · · · · · · · · · · · **7**:105b
Kammon Tunnels · · · · · · · · · · **7**:105b
Kammu, Emperor 桓武天皇 · **4**:128a; **7**:62b
Heiankyō · · · · · · · · · · · · · · · · **3**:121a
Kūkai · **4**:128a
monasticism · · · · · · · · · · · · · · **5**:237b
Saichō · · · · · · · · · · · · · · · · · · · **4**:128a
Kammuri · · · · · · · · · · · · · · · · · **3**:119a
Kammuriyama · · · · · · · · 冠山 · **4**:128a
Kamo (city) · · · · · · · · · 加茂 · **4**:128a
Kamo. See **Wild ducks**
Kamochi Masazumi · · · · · · · · · · · · 鹿持雅澄 · **4**:128a
Man'yōshū scholarship · · · · · · **5**:110b
Kamogawa (city) · · · 鴨川 · **4**:128a
Kamogawa (river) · 賀茂川 · **4**:128a-128b, 338a
Kamon · · · · · · · · · · · 家門 · **7**:108a
Kamo no Chōmei · 鴨長明 · **1**:181b, 294a; **4**:128b-129a; **5**:14b, 43b; **7**:72a
elderly recluse · · · · · · · · · **4**:128b-129a
Hōjōki · · · · · · · · · · · · · **4**:129a; **5**:43b
poet and literary critic · · · · · · · **4**:129a
mujō · · · · · · · · · · · · · · **4**:129a; **5**:262a
yūgen advocacy · · · · · **4**:128b; **8**:355b
Tosa Mitsuhide · · · · · · · · · · · **4**:*128b*
Kamo no Chōmei shū 鴨長明集 · **4**:128b
Kamo no kurabeuma 賀茂競馬 · · **4**:129a
depiction in art · · · · · · · · · · · · **2**:377b
Kamo no Mabuchi 賀茂真淵 · **1**:154a; **4**:129a-129b; **5**:17a
chōka revival · · · · · · · · · · · · · **4**:129a
Genji monogatari shinshaku · · · **4**:129b
Ise monogatari commentaries · · · **4**:129b
Kada no Arimaro · · · · · · · · · · **4**:100a
Kada no Azumamaro · · · · **4**:100b, 129b
Kagawa Kageki · · · · · · · · · · · **4**:103a
Kanjikō · · · · · · · · · · · · · · · · · · **4**:129b
Katō Chikage · · · · · · · · · · · · · **4**:129b

Katori Nahiko · · · · · · · · · · · · 4:129b
Keichū · · · · · · · · · · · · · · · 4:129a
Kokugaku commentaries · · · · · · 4:257b
Man'yōshū commentaries · · · · · 4:129a-129b
Man'yōshū scholarship · · · · · · 5:110b
Motoori Norinaga · · · · · · · · · 4:129b
Murata Harumi · · · · · · · · · · · 4:129b
Niimanabi · · · · · · · · · · · · · · 4:129b
poetic style · · · · · · · · · · · · · 4:129b
Tale of Genji commentaries · · · · 4:129b
Tayasu Munetake · · · · · · · · · · 4:129b
Tokugawa Yoshimune · · · · · · · 4:129b
Kamoshika [(Japanese serow)
Capricornis crispus] · · · · · · · 4:129b
Kamo Shrines · · · 賀茂神社 4:128a, 130a,
                                    336b; 7:180a
Aoi Festival · · · · · · · · · 1:68a; 4:130a
horse race · · · · · · · · · · · · · · 4:129a
Kamo no Chōmei · · · · · · · · · · 4:128b
origins · · · · · · · · · · · · · · · · 4:130a
Kampaku · · · · · · · · · · · · · 関白 2:204a-204b,
              348a, 351b; 4:130a; 7:69b
Fujiwara no Yoshifusa · · · · · · · 4:130a
Gosekke family · · · · · · · · · · · 4:130a
Ichijō Norifusa · · · · · · · · · · · 3:256b
Ichijō Sanetsune · · · · · · · · · · 3:256b
Ichijō Tsunetsugu · · · · · · · · · 3:256b
Kujō family eligible for · · · · · · 4:303b
political power · · · · · · · · · · · 4:130a
regency government · · · · · · · · 4:130a
Toyotomi Hidetsugu · · · · · · · · 4:130a
Toyotomi Hideyoshi · · · · · · · · 4:130a
**Kampan Batabiya
  shimbun**
         · · 官板バタビヤ新聞 · · · 4:130a
Kampan kaigai shimbun
         · · · · · 官板海外新聞 · · · 4:130a
Kampō. *See* **Official Gazette**
Kampō (medicine) · · · · · · · · 5:150b-151b
characteristics · · · · · · · · · · · 5:151a
examination methods · · · · · · · 5:151b
schools · · · · · · · 5:146a-146b, 150b-151a
Kampu · · · · · · · · · · · · 官符 4:130a-130b
dajōkam-pu · · · · · · · · · · · · · 4:130a
Kampūzan · · · · · · · · · 寒風山 4:130b
Kamu · · · · · · · · · · · · · · · 4:106b
Kamuikotan · · · · · · · 神居古潭 4:130b
Kamura Isota · · · · · · · 嘉村礒多 4:130b
Shinkō Geijutsu Ha · · · · · · · · 7:119b
Kamurikiyama 冠着山
  Obasuteyama · · · · · · · · · · · 6:48a-48b
Kamu Yamato Iware Hiko no Mikoto
         神日本磐余彦尊 4:57a-57b
Kan · · · · · · · · · · · · · · · · 4:130b-131a
aspects · · · · · · · · · · · · · · · 4:130b
kaku · · · · · · · · · · · · · · · · · 4:131a
kotsu · · · · · · · · · · · · · · · · · 4:131a
Kuroda Ryō · · · · · · · · · · · · · 4:130b
Kana · · · · · · · · · · · · 仮名 1:151b, 153b,
      233a; 2:348a; 4:131a-135a; 6:248b; 7:34b
Gojūon zu · · · · · · · · · · · · · 3:40b-41a
hiragana · · · · · · · · · · · · · · · 4:132b
  Kokin wakashū · · · · · · · · · 4:132b
  onnade · · · · · · · · · · · · · · · 4:132b
  Tosa nikki · · · · · · · · · · · · 4:133b
  use by women · · · · · · · · · · 4:132b
ideographs · · · · · · · · · · · · · 4:141b-143b
Japanese language · · · · · · · · · 4:27a-28a
Japanese language reform · · · · · 4:30a
kambun · · · · · · · · · · · · · · · 4:124a
kaō · · · · · · · · · · · · · · · · · · 4:155b
katakana · · · · · · · · · · · · · · · 4:132a-133a
  earliest examples · · · · · · · · · 4:132b-133a
  Gosen wakashū · · · · · · · · · 4:132b
  Kanamajiri bun · · · · · · · · · · 4:132b
  Konjaku monogatari · · · · · · · 4:132b
  mnemonic function · · · · · · · · 4:132a-132b
  Tōdaiji fujumon kō · · · · · · · 4:132b

variant symbols · · · · · · · · · · 4:133a
man'yōgana · · · · · · 4:131b-132b, *133a*;
                          5:109a-109b
  characters · · · · · · · · · · · · · 4:131b-132a
  gisho reading · · · · · · · · · · · 4:131b
  kun reading · · · · · · · · · · · · 4:132a
  Man'yōshū writing system · · · 4:131b
  on reading · · · · · · · · · · · · · 4:132a
  syllables · · · · · · · · · · · · · · 4:131b
orthography · · · · · · · · · · · · · 4:132b-135a
  Fujiwara no Teika (sadaie) · · · 2:354a-355a
  gendai · · · · · · · · · · · · · · · 4:134b-135a
  jion · · · · · · · · · · · · · · · · · 4:134a
  jōdai · · · · · · · · · · · · · · · · 4:134a-134b
  Keichū · · · · · · · · · · · · · · · 4:187b-188a
  Monnō · · · · · · · · · · · 4:134a; 5:245b
  Motoori Norinaga · · · 4:134a; 5:257a-258b
  rekishiteki · · · · · · · · · · · · · 4:133a-134a
  Teika · · · · · · · · · · · · · · · · 4:133a-133b
Ryūkyū dialects · · · · · · · · · · 6:355b
sōgana · · · · · · · · · · · · · · · · 4:132a
studies · · · · · · · · · · · · · · · · 4:31a-31b
"Kanadehon
  chūshingura"
         仮名手本忠臣蔵 · 1:*212b*; 4:61a,
                                    93b
Shinkokugeki · · · · · · · · · · · · 7:121a
Kanagaki Robun
         · · · · 仮名垣魯文 4:135a; 7:103a
  Agura nabe · · · · · · · · · · · · 4:135a
  fūzoku shōsetsu · · · · · · · · · 2:378b
  Seiyō dōchū hizakurige · · · · · 4:135a
**Kanagawa Prefectural Museum of
  Modern Art** · · · · · · · · · · · 4:135a
Kanagawa Prefecture
         神奈川県 4:135a; 8:355a
  Fuji-Hakone-Izu National Park · · · 4:135a
  Kamakura · · · · · · · · · · · · · 4:135a
  Kawasaki · · · · · · · · · · · · · 4:135a
  Tōkyō Earthquake of 1923 · · · · 4:135a
  Yokohama · · · · · · · · · · · · · 4:135a
Kanagawa shimbun
         神奈川新聞 · · · · 4:211a
Kanagawa Treaty
         神奈川条約 · 1:3b; 2:331a;
              4:135a-135b; 7:104b; 8:329a
  Kawaji Toshiakira · · · · · · · · · 4:179b
  Kōmei, Emperor · · · · · · · · · · 4:266a
  National Seclusion termination · · 4:135b
  Perry, Matthew Calbraith · · · · 4:135a-135b;
                                    6:177b
  United States · · · · · · · · · · · 8:154b
Kanai Akira · · · · · · · · 金井章 6:*24b*
Kanai Noburu · · · · · · 金井延 4:135b
  Ernest Francisco Fenollosa · · · 2:251b
  Shakai keizaigaku · · · · · · · · 4:135b
  Shakai mondai · · · · · · · · · · 4:135b
  Shichihakase Jiken · · · · · · · · 4:135b
Kanamajiri bun · · · · · · · · · · · 4:132b
Kan'ami · · · · · · · · 観阿弥 4:135b; 5:43a;
                                    6:24a
  Kanze school · · · · · · · · · 4:135b, 155a
  Zeami · · · · · · · · · · · 4:135b; 8:369a
Kan'ami Kiyotsugu
         観阿弥清次 · · · · 4:135b
Kanamori Tokujirō
         · · · · · 金森徳次郎 · 2:4a; 4:135b
  constitution · · · · · · · · · · · · 4:135b
  Minobe Tatsukichi · · · · · · · · 4:135b
  National Diet Library · · · · · · · 4:135b
  Yoshida Shigeru cabinet · · · · · 4:135b
Kanamugura [(Japanese hop) *Humulus
  japonicus*] · · · · · · · · · · · · · 4:135b
Kanashiki chichi · 哀しき父 · · · 4:160b
Kanashimi no daika
  (Prince in Sadness)
         · · · · · 悲しみの代価 · · · · · · 8:332b
Kanaya · · · · · · · · · · 金谷 4:136a

post-station · · · · · · · · · · · · · 4:136a
tea cultivation · · · · · · · · · · · 4:136a
Kanazawa · · · · · · · · 金沢 4:136a
Kanazawa Bunko 金沢文庫 1:151b; 4:136a
  Hōjō Sanetoki · · · · · · · · · 4:118b, 136a
Kanazawa Plain · 金沢平野 · · · 4:136a
Kana-zōshi · · · · · · 仮名草紙 · 1:94a; 3:347b;
              4:136b; 5:46a; 8:144a
Kanazukai · · · · · · · · · · · · · · 4:132b-133a
*Kanazukai oyobi kana jitai enkaku
  shiryō* · · · · · · · · · · · · · · · · 6:138b
Kanchiku (*Chimonobambusa
  marmorea*) · · · · · · · · · · · · · 1:136a
Kanchōban · · · · · · · 灌頂幡 · · · 3:*233a*
Kanchōrō Kakai
         観潮楼歌会 · · · 5:19b
Kanchūki · · · · · · · 勘仲記 · 4:136b-137a
  Mongol invasions · · · · · · · · · 4:137a
  shōen disputes · · · · · · · · · · 4:137a
Kanda Akiko · · · · · · · · · · · · 2:76a
Kanda Aqueduct 神田上水 · · · 4:137a
  Tamagawa Aqueduct · · · · · · · 7:332b
Kandachime · · · · · · · · 上達部 · 4:302b
Kanda Festival · · · 神田祭 4:137a; 7:15a
  dashi · · · · · · · · · · · · · · · · 4:137a
  Kanda Shrine · · · · · · · · · · · 4:137a
  mikoshi · · · · · · · · · · · · · · · 4:137a
  shogunal patronage · · · · · · · · 4:137a
Kandaka · · · · · · · · 貫高 · · · 4:137a
  eidaka · · · · · · · · · · · · · · · 4:137a
  eirakusen · · · · · · · · · · · · · 4:137a
  Kammon · · · · · · · · · · · · · · 4:137a
  replaced by kokudaka · · · · · · 4:257b
  replacement · · · · · · · · · · · · 4:137a
Kanda Kōhei. *See* Kanda Takahira
Kanda Shrine · · · 神田明神 4:137a
  Kanda Festival · · · · · · · · · · 4:137a
  Ōkuninushi no Mikoto · · · · · · 6:97b
  Taira no Masakado · · · · · · · · 4:137a
Kanda Takahira · 神田孝平 · 4:137a-137b
Kanden (official fields)
         官田 · · · · 2:104b
Kanebō, Ltd · · · · · · · · · · · 4:137b
Kaneda Masaichi 金田正一 · · · 4:137b
Kanegafuchi Bōseki · · · · · · · 4:64a
Kanegafuchi Chemical Industry Co, Ltd
                                    4:137b
Kan'ei House Genealogies · · · 4:138a
Kan'eiji · · · · · · · · 寛永寺 · 4:137b-138a,
                                    163a
  Tenkai · · · · · · · · · · · · · · · 4:138a
  Tokugawa Iemitsu · · · · · · · · 8:48a
Kan'ei jigyō haraisage
         官営事業払下げ · · · 4:138a
  Furukawa · · · · · · · · · · · · · 4:138a
  government-operated factories · 3:56a-56b;
                                    4:138a
  Mitsubishi · · · · · · · · · · · · · 4:138a
  Mitsui · · · · · · · · · · · · · · · · 4:138a
  seishō · · · · · · · · · · · · · · · 4:138a
  zaibatsu · · · · · · · · · · · · · · 4:138a
Kan'ei kōjō · · · 官営工場 · 3:56a-56b
"**Kan'ei Sampitsu**"
         寛永三筆 1:*236b*; 4:273b
Kan'ei shoka keizu den
         寛永諸家系図伝 · 4:138a
  Fujiwara · · · · · · · · · · · · · · 4:138a
  Hayashi Razan · · · · · · · · · · 4:138a
  Minamoto · · · · · · · · · · · · · 4:138a
  miscellaneous · · · · · · · · · · · 4:138a
  Taira · · · · · · · · · · · · · · · · 4:138a
Kan'ei tsūhō · · · 寛永通宝 · 5:242a-242b
Kaneko, Josephine Conger · 4:138a-138b
Kaneko Fumiko · 金子文子 · · · 6:159a
Kaneko Kentarō
         金子堅太郎 · 2:2b; 4:138b
  diplomatic career · · · · · · · · · 4:138b
  drafting of Meiji Constitution · · · 4:138b

Inoue Kowashi ·············· **4**:138b
Itō Hirobumi ·············· **4**:138b
Itō Miyoji ·················· **4**:138b
Kaneko Mitsuharu
·············· 金子光晴 **4**:138b-139a
antiwar poems ··········· **4**:138b; **5**:57b
Kaneko Naokichi 金子直吉 ··· **4**:139a
Ishikawajima-Harima Heavy
Industries Co, Ltd ······· **4**:139a
Kōbe Steel, Ltd ·········· **4**:139a
Suzuki Shōten ··········· **4**:139a
Teijin, Ltd ··············· **4**:139a
Kanematsu-Gōshō, Ltd ··· **4**:139a-139b
Kanemi kyō ki ·· 兼見卿記 ·· **4**:139b
Oda Nobunaga ·········· **4**:139b
Toyotomi Hideyoshi ····· **4**:139b
Kanemi Oil Poisoning Incident · **2**:304b;
4:139b
Kanegafuchi Chemical ··· **4**:139b
Kanemi Sōko Co ········· **4**:139b
legal aspects ············ **4**:139b
Kanenaga, Prince
·········· 懐良親王 · **4**:139b-140a
Emperor Go-Daigo ····· **4**:139b-140a
Imagawa Sadayo ········ **4**:140a
Kanenaka ki · 兼仲記 ···· **4**:136b
Kanenaka Kyō ki 兼仲卿記 · **4**:136b
Kanesawa Bunko.金沢文庫 *See*
Kanazawa Bunko
Kanesawa Sanetoki. 金沢実時
See **Kanazawa Bunko**
Kaneshige Tōyō ·金重陶陽 **1**:158a; **4**:140a
bizen ware ·············· **4**:140a
Living National Treasure ··· **4**:140a
Tea ceremony vessels ····· **4**:140a
Kanga ········· 漢画 ········ **4**:157a
Kangaku
Daigaku ················· **4**:140a
Daigakuryō ·············· **4**:140a
Fujiwara no Fuyutsugu ··· **4**:140a
Kangakuin ·········· 勧学院 **4**:140a; **2**:350b;
4:140a
Kangeiko ·············· **4**:140a-140b
Kanghwa, Treaty of ··· **4**:140b-141a, 279a;
7:7a, 197b; **8**:325b
Inoue Kaoru ············· **4**:140b
Kanghwa Incident ······· **4**:140b
Kuroda Kiyotaka ········ **4**:140b
relations with China ····· **1**:286b
Sino-Japanese War of 1894-1895 · **4**:140b
Taewŏn'gun rule ········ **4**:140b
terms ··················· **4**:140b
waegwan ················ **8**:198a
Kanginshū ············ 閑吟集 **2**:301b; **4**:141a;
7:64b
musical structure ········ **4**:141a
themes ·················· **4**:141a
Kango ·············· 敢語 **5**:214b
Kangō bōeki · 勘合貿易 · **7**:331b-332a
Kang Youwei (K'ang Yu-wei)
·············· **4**:140a-140b, 384a
Huang Zunxian ·········· **4**:141a
Hundred Days' Reform ··· **4**:141a
Miyazaki Tōten ·········· **4**:141b
Ōkuma Shigenobu ······· **4**:141a
Prince Konoe Atsumaro ··· **4**:141a
Treaty of Shimonoseki rejection ··· **4**:141a
Wang Tao ··············· **4**:141a
Kan Hasshū ···· 関八州 · **4**:141a
Kani ·················· **2**:41a-41b
Kan'i jūnikai ·· 官位十二階 · **2**:39b; **4**:141b;
7:264a
chi ······················ **4**:141b
gi ······················· **4**:141b
jin ······················ **4**:141b
rei ······················ **4**:141b
ritsuryō system ·········· **6**:322a
shin ····················· **4**:141b

toku ····················· **4**:141b
Kani kōsen (The Cannery
Boat) ············· 蟹工船 · **7**:175b
Kan'in, House of ·· 閑院宮 · **4**:141b
Arai Hakuseki ··········· **4**:141b
commoner status ········ **4**:141b
Kani yamabushi ··· 蟹山伏 · **4**:327b
Kanji ············· **4**:141b-143b; **7**:170b
Ashide style ············ **1**:97b
calligraphy ············· **1**:233a
character styles ········· **4**:142b-143a
clerical ················· **4**:143b
greater seal ············· **4**:143b
gyōsho ·················· **4**:143b
kaisho ·················· **4**:143b
kimbun ················· **4**:143b
lesser seal ·············· **4**:143b
oracle bone ············· **4**:142b-143a
sekibun ················· **4**:143b
sōsho ··················· **4**:143b
tadpole ················· **4**:143b
zokuji ·················· **4**:143b
go on ··················· **3**:46a
kan on ·················· **4**:148a
kun readings ············ **4**:310b
on and kun readings
go on ··················· **4**:143b
jukuji kun ·············· **4**:143b
kan on ·················· **4**:143a-143b
tō on ··················· **4**:143a-143b
script style ············· **7**:170a
Shinsen jikyō ·········· **7**:124b
styles ··················· **7**:170a
tō on ··················· **8**:75b
types of Chinese characters · **4**:142a-142b
borrowing ·············· **4**:142b
combined meanings ····· **4**:142a
diagrammatic ··········· **4**:142a
dictionary arrangement ·· **4**:142b
domestic ················ **4**:142b
extension ··············· **4**:142b
numbers ················ **4**:142b
pictographs ············· **4**:142a
Kanjiki ··············· **4**:143b
Kanjikō ·········· 冠辞考 · **4**:129b
Kanjin ··············· **3**:137a
Kanjinchō ········ 勧進帳 · **4**:94b, 98a
Kanjō ···· 灌頂 **1**:179a; **4**:117b
Kanjō bugyō ···· 勘定奉行 · **4**:143b-144a;
7:6a
daikan ·················· **4**:144a
gundai ·················· **4**:144a
kattegakari ············· **4**:144a
kattekata ··············· **4**:144a
kujikata ················ **4**:144a
Rōjū ···················· **4**:144a
tenryō ·················· **4**:144a
Tokugawa Yoshimune ··· **4**:144a
Kanjō gimmiyaku
·············· 勘定吟味役 · **4**:144a
Kanjō Jōyaku · 漢城条約 · **7**:68b
Kanjō rekimei · 灌頂歴名 · **4**:58b
Kankakei ·········· 寒霞渓 · **4**:144a
Kanken ············· 観賢 · **2**:57b
Kanko ··············· 官戸 · **7**:62a
Kankoku Tōkanfu
·············· 韓国統監府 · **6**:306a
Kankō maru ···· 観光丸 · **4**:110a
Kanku kidōtai ··········· **6**:320b
Kankyōchō ······· 環境庁 · **2**:224a
Kannamesai ····· 神嘗祭 · **4**:144a-144b
Daijōsai ················ **2**:59a-59b
Engi shiki description ·· **4**:144a
Shintō rites ············· **7**:138b-139b
Taihō Code description ·· **4**:144a
Kannen shōsetsu ········ **4**:179b, 199a
Kannō Disturbance
·············· 観応の擾乱 · **4**:144b

Ashikaga Tadayoshi ····· **1**:100a; **4**:144b
Ashikaga Takauji ········ **1**:100b; **4**:144b
Kō no Moronao ········· **4**:144b
Kan no kenkyū · 勘の研究 · **4**:131a
Kannon ········ **1**:122b-123a, 159b; **2**:376b;
4:144b-145a; **5**:43b; **7**:20a, 67b
Amida ·················· **4**:144b
Byōdōin temple ········· **1**:227a
Daianji ················· **2**:55a-55b
Daigoji ················· **2**:57a
Daitokuji ··············· **2**:68b
feminine representation ··· **4**:144b-145a
Hall of Dreams (Yumedono) ·· **4**:*145a*
Ishiyamadera ··········· **3**:346a
Lotus Sutra depiction ··· **4**:144b
miracles ················ **4**:144b
Nanzenji ················ **5**:330b
Omizutori ·············· **6**:102b
pilgrimages ············· **4**:144b
Pure Land Buddhism ···· **4**:144b
ritual implements ······· **1**:196a
Takasaki ················ **7**:318b
Kannon, Eleven-Headed ··· **1**:187b, 189a
Kannonji Castle ·· 観音寺城 · **1**:126b
Kannon Riding on a Dragon ··· **8**:328a
Kanno Suga ···· 管野スガ · **4**:145a-145b
Arahata Kanson ········· **1**:72a; **4**:145b
High Treason Incident of 1910 ··· **3**:135a;
4:145b
Jiyū shisō ············· **4**:145b
Kōtoku Shūsui ·········· **4**:145b
Kyōfūkai membership ··· **4**:145a
Red Flag Incident of 1908 ····· **4**:145b
"Shide no michikusa" ···· **4**:145b
Kannoura ········· 甲浦 · **4**:145b
Kan no Wa no Na no
kokuō no in
·············· 漢委奴国王印 · **1**:76b; **4**:*145a*,
145b; **5**:321b
Kannushi ·········· **4**:145b-146a; **6**:238b-239a
Edo period ·············· **4**:145b
gūji ···················· **4**:146a
hafuri ·················· **7**:138b
Heian period ············ **4**:145b
hereditary nature ······· **4**:145b
miyaza ·················· **5**:221a
negi ···················· **6**:239a
Kanō Einō ······· 狩野永納 · **4**:148b
Kanō Eitoku ···· 狩野永徳 **1**:157b; **2**:*377a*;
4:146a-146b; **7**:42b
Azuchi Castle paintings ··· **4**:146a
Azuchi-Momoyama history ··· **3**:177b
Birds and Flowers ······ **4**:146a
Chao Fu ··············· **4**:146a
Chinese Lions (Karajishi zu) ··· **4**:*146a-146b*
Chinese Mythical Lions ··· **4**:146b
Cypress Trees ·········· **4**:146b
developed style ········· **4**:146b
early style ·············· **4**:146a
Four Elegant Pastimes, The ··· **4**:146a
fūzokuga ················ **2**:377b
Kaihō Yūshō ············ **4**:110b
Kanō Motonobu ········· **4**:146a
Nanzenji ················ **5**:330b
Ōsaka Castle paintings ··· **4**:146a
Scenes in and around Kyōto ··· **4**:146a
Uesugi Kenshin ········· **4**:146a
yamato-e style ·········· **4**:146a
Kanoe saru ············· **4**:295b
Kanogawa ······· 狩野川 · **4**:146b
Kanō Hōgai ···· 狩野芳崖 · **4**:146b-147a;
6:*378b*
Deva Seizing a Demon ··· **4**:147a
Ernest F. Fenollosa ······ **4**:147a
Hashimoto Gahō ········ **4**:147a
Kanō Tan'yū ············ **4**:146b-147a
Merciful Mother Kannon ··· **4**:147a
Okakura Kakuzō ········· **4**:147a

Sakuma Shōzan ·············· 4:146b
Sesshū Tōyō ··············· 4:146b
Sesson Shūkei ·············· 4:146b
Shimazu family ············· 4:146b
Shimomura Kanzan ······ 7:105a-105b
Kanō Jigorō ··· 嘉納治五郎 · **4:82a-83a,**
147a; 7:270b
Ernest Francisco Fenollosa ··· 2:251b
Japan Amateur Sports Association
leadership ················· 4:147a
jūdō activities ·············· 4:147a
Kōdōkan established by ······ 4:243a
Kanō Kōkichi ··· 狩野亨吉 ··· 4:147a
Andō Shōeki ··············· 1:155b
Shizuki Tadao ·············· 7:152b
Kanō Masanobu · 狩野正信 · 4:147a-147b;
7:42b
Admiring Lotus Blossoms ······· 4:147b
Ashikaga Yoshimasa ········· 4:147b
Bamboo and White Crane ······ 4:147b
Eight Views of Xiao and Xing, The · 4:147b
Fujiwara no Yoshitsune ······· 4:147b
Inryōken nichiroku ··········· 4:147b
Kanō school ··············· 4:147a
Oguri Sōtan ··············· 4:147b
Shūbun ··················· 4:147b
Kanō Mitsunobu · 狩野光信 · 4:147b
Azuchi Castle paintings ······· 4:147b
Hasegawa school rivalry ······· 4:147b
Kanō Eitoku ··············· 4:147b
Nanzenji ·················· 5:330b
Ōsaka Castle paintings ······· 4:147b
Toyotomi Hideyoshi ········· 4:147b
Kanō Motohide · 狩野元秀 ··· 6:62a
Kanō Motonobu · 狩野元信 · 1:156a, 192b;
4:147a, 147b-148a; 7:42b
bird-and-flower painting ······· 4:148a
Daitokuji temple paintings ····· 4:148a
fusuma-e ·················· 4:148a
ink painting ··············· 4:148a
Kaihō Yūshō ·············· 4:110b
Kanō Eitoku ··············· 4:148a
Kanō Masanobu ············ 4:147b
Myōshinji temple paintings ···· 4:148a
Nanzenji ·················· 5:330b
sansuiga (landscape painting) ··· 7:17b
shogunal patronage ·········· 4:148a
yamato-e painting style ······· 4:148a
Kan on ··················· 4:148a
go on ···················· 3:46a
on readings ··············· 6:112b
Kanō Naganobu ·狩野長信 · 6:155a
Kan'onji ········ 観音寺 ··· 4:148b
Kanō Sakujirō · 加能作次郎 · 4:148b
Kanō Sanraku ··· 狩野山楽 · 2:57b; 3:181b;
4:148b; 6:153a; 7:42b
Battle of the Carriages ········ 4:148b
Birds of Prey ············· 4:148b
Imperial Mirror ············ 4:148b
Kanō Eitoku ··············· 4:148b
Kanō Mitsunobu ············ 4:148b
Kanō school of painting ······· 4:148b
Nanzenji ·················· 5:330b
Kanō Sansetsu · 狩野山雪 · 4:148b-149a
Honchō gashi ············· 4:148b
Kanō Sanraku ············· 4:148b
Kanō school ··············· 4:148b
Winter Seascape with Birds ···· 4:148b
Kanō school ····· 狩野派 · **4:149a-150b;**
7:84a, 270a
art historical significance ······ 4:150b
Hashimoto Gahō ··········· 4:150b
heterodox tradition ········· 4:150b
Kanō Hōgai ··············· 4:150b
Printing Appreciation Society ··· 4:150b
bunjin artists ·············· 1:210b
"Eight Views" themes ········ 7:167b
fūzokuga ·················· 2:377b

Hashimoto Gahō ··········· 4:178b
history ··················· 4:149a
ink painting ··············· 4:149a
Kanō Eitoku ··············· 4:149a
Kanō Masanobu ············ 4:149a
Kanō Motonobu ············ 4:149a
Kanō Sanraku ············· 4:149a
Kanō Tan'yū ·············· 4:149a
screen and wall painting ······ 4:149a
Shōkokuji ················· 4:149a
Shūbun ··················· 4:149a
yamato-e style ············· 4:149a
impact on screen and wall painting · 7:43a
ink painting ··············· 4:150a
suiboku ··················· 4:150a
Tan'yū copies ············· 4:150a
Kanō Eitoku ··············· 4:146a
Kanō lineage ·············· 4:149a
Kajibashi branch ··········· 4:149b
Kanō Mitsunobu ············ 4:149b
Kanō Sansetsu ············· 4:149b
Kanō Tan'yū ·············· 4:149b
Kobikichō branch ··········· 4:149b
machieshi ················· 4:149b
okueshi ··················· 4:149b
omoteeshi ················· 4:149b
studio system ············· 4:149b
Kanō Masanobu ············ 4:147a
kara-e-mekiki painters ······· 5:305b
namban screens ········· 5:322a-323a
painting ·············· 6:151b, 153a
screen painting ········· 4:150a-150b
Birds and Flowers of the Four Seasons
·············· 4:150b
Cypress Trees ············· 4:150b
heroic style ··············· 4:150b
Kanō Eitoku ··············· 4:150b
Kanō Mitsunobu ············ 4:150b
Kanō Sanraku ············· 4:150b
military patronage ·········· 4:150a
seals ···················· 6:281b
Shimomura Kanzan ·········· 7:105b
style ···················· 4:110a
stylistic and thematic range ·· 4:149b-150a
Battle of the Carriages ······· 4:149b
Craftsmen of Various Trades ··· 4:150a
ema ····················· 4:149b
emakimono ················ 4:149b
Festival of Hōkoku Shrine ····· 4:150a
Hanabusa Itchō ············ 4:150a
kakemono ················· 4:149b
kanga ···················· 4:150a
Maple Viewing at Takao ······ 4:150a
Merrymaking under the Cherry Blossoms
·············· 4:150a
Rakuchū rakugai zu ········· 4:149b
Seiryōji engi emaki ·········· 4:149b
Tōshōgu engi emaki ········· 4:149b
yamato-e ················· 4:149b
Takahashi Yuichi ··········· 7:313b
Tatebayashi Kagei ··········· 7:349a
Terazaki Kōgyō ············· 8:13a
Western-style pictures ········ 8:248b
Kanō Shōsen'in
··········· 狩野勝川院 · 4:146b
Kanō Tan'yū ···· 狩野探幽 ······· 1:193b;
4:150b-151a; 7:43a; 8:49a
art connoisseurship ·········· 4:151a
Edo Castle paintings ········· 4:151a
hōgen title ··············· 4:151a
Kanō Eitoku ··············· 4:150b
Nagoya Castle paintings ······ 4:151a
Nanzenji ·················· 5:330b
Nanzenji temple paintings ····· 4:151a
Nijō Castle paintings ········ 4:151a
Tokugawa official painter ····· 4:151a
Tōshōgu engi ············· 4:151a
Tōshōgu paintings ··········· 4:151a

yamato-e painting style ······· 4:151a
Kanoya ········· 鹿屋 · 4:106a, 151a
Kanrai ·········· 寒雷 ···· 4:169b
Kanrei ········· 管領 · 4:151a; 7:64b,
83b
Hatakeyama family ·········· 4:151a
Hosokawa family ··········· 4:151a
proclamations ············· 4:90a
Shiba family ·············· 4:151a
shitsuji ·················· 4:151a
Kanrei kabegaki · 管領壁書 ···· 4:90a
Kanreki ················· 4:151a
inkyo status ·············· 4:151a
jikkan jūnishi ············· 4:57a
Kanrin maru (warship)
·············· 咸臨丸 · 1:175a-175b;
2:367b; 4:151b; 8:154b
Admiral Kimura Yoshitake ····· 4:151b
Captain Katsu Kaishū ········ 4:151b
Kimura Yoshitake ··········· 4:211b
national flag ·············· 5:339a
Kanroku ········ 観勒 · 4:151b
calendrical science ·········· 4:151b
Empress Suiko ············· 4:151b
Gangōji temple lectures ······ 4:151b
Kanryō ··········· 管領 · 4:151a
Kansai ····· 関西 2:364a; 4:151b
Chūgoku region ············ 4:151b
Kantō ··················· 4:151b
Kinki region ·············· 4:151b
Kansai Electric Power Co, Inc ··· 1:97a,
311; 4:151b-152a
Kurobe Dam No. 4 hydroelectric plant
·············· 4:151b
nuclear power development ····· 4:151b
Tōkyō Electric Power Co, Inc ··· 4:151b
Kansai Fine Arts Academy (Kansai
Bijutsuin) ··········· 7:326a; 8:328a
Kansai Paint Co, Ltd ········ 4:152a
Kansai region ··· 関西地方 · 4:153b
Kansatsushi ······· 監察使 · 4:104b
Kan Sazan ········ 菅茶山 1:295a; 4:152a;
7:94b
Kansei Calendar
Takahashi Yoshitoki ········· 7:313b
Kansei chōshū shoka fu
·········· 寛政重修諸家譜 · 4:152a
Hayashi Jussai ············· 4:152a
Kan'ei shoka keizu den supplement · 4:152a
Yashiro Hirokata ··········· 4:152a
Kansei Gakuin University ····· 4:152a
Kansei Reforms
········· 寛政の改革 · 1:157a, 211b;
3:189b; 4:152a-152b; 7:87a, 95a
administrative efficiency ······· 4:152b
Ban on Heterodoxy ·········· 4:152b
censorship ················· 1:252a
conservatism ·············· 4:152b
Decree of the Cancellation of Debts · 4:152b
economic ················· 4:152b
fudasashi ··········· 2:340b; 4:152b
gesaku ··················· 3:28b
hitogaeshi ·········· 2:207b-208a
kabunakama dissolution ······· 4:100a
Kameda Bōsai ············· 4:124b
Koikawa Harumachi's satire ···· 4:250a
Matsudaira Sadanobu ········ 4:152a
Neo-Confucianism ·········· 1:356a
Rōjū ···················· 4:152b
rural reconstruction ········· 4:152b
sharebon ················· 7:80a
Shōheikō ················· 7:162a
sobayōnin ················ 4:152b
social atmosphere ··········· 4:157a
Tokugawa Ienari ··········· 8:48a
Tokugawa shogunate ········· 8:55b
Kansha ··················· 7:96a

Kanshi. *See* **Poetry and prose in Chinese**
Kanshibun ···················· **6**:193b
Kan Shinsui ····· 菅晋帥 ······· **4**:152a
Kan susuki ···················· **7**:279a
Kantan ········· 邯鄲 ······· **4**:201b
Kantei style ····· 勘亭流 ···· **4**:153a
　kabuki ····················· **4**:153a
　sumō wrestling ············· **4**:153a
Kantō ·········· 関東 **2**:255a; **4**:153a
　Tanabata Festival ·········· **4**:153a
Kantō Auto Works, Ltd ···· **4**:153a
　Toyota Motor Co, Ltd ··· **4**:153a; **8**:93b
Kantō Daishinsai. 関東大震災 *See* **Tōkyō Earthquake of 1923**
Kantō Earthquake. *See* **Tōkyō Earthquake of 1923**
Kantō Electrical Construction Co, Ltd
　······························· **4**:153a
　Tōkyō Electric Power Co, Inc ·· **4**:153a
Kantōgun. 関東軍 *See* **Guandong (Kwantung) Army**
Kantō kanrei ····· 関東管領 ·· **4**:121a, 153a
　Muromachi shogunate ······ **4**:153a
　Uesugi family ·············· **4**:153a
Kantō loam ········ **1**:38a; **4**:153a–153b
　Iwajuku site ·············· **3**:358a
　Jōmon culture artifacts ····· **4**:153b
　Kantō Plain ············ **4**:153a–153b
　paleolithic culture artifacts ·· **4**:153b
Kantō Mountains 関東山地 **1**:272a; **4**:153b
　Kimpusan ················· **4**:153b
　Kobushigadake ············· **4**:153b
Kantō Oxygen ··············· **3**:342a
Kantō Plain ····· 関東平野 ··· **4**:153b
Kantō region ····· 関東地方 ··· **4**:141b, 153b–154a
　agricultural production ····· **4**:153a
　border ···················· **4**:154b
　frontier status ············ **4**:153b
　Keihin Industrial Zone ····· **4**:154a
　Tokugawa shogunate ······· **4**:153b
　Tōkyō ···················· **4**:153b
　Tonegawa ················· **4**:153b
Kantōshū. 関東州 *See* **Guandong (Kwantung) Territory**
Kantsubaki (*Camellia hiemalis*) ···· **1**:237a
Kan U ······· 関羽 ··· **4**:98b, 154a
　deification ··············· **4**:154a
　pictorial depiction ········· **4**:154a
Kanuchibe ········· 鍛冶部 ···· **1**:147a
Kanuma ········· 鹿沼 ····· **4**:154a
　post-station towns ········· **4**:154a
　Tokugawa Ieyasu mausoleum ··· **4**:154a
Kanwa jiten ····· 漢和辞典 ··· **2**:93b–94a
Kan'yagami ······· 紙屋紙 ···· **8**:233a
Kan'ya no shikishi
　··············· 紙屋色紙 ···· **8**:233a
Kanzaki Paper Mfg Co, Ltd ·· **4**:154a
　Occupation monopoly policy ·· **4**:154a
　Ōji Paper Co, Ltd affiliation ·· **4**:154a
Kanzan ········· 寒山 ······ **3**:305a
　See also **Kanzan and Jittoku**
Kanzan and Jittoku
　··············· 寒山拾得 ···· **4**:154a
　ink painting subjects ······· **4**:154a
　Zen spirit ················· **4**:154a
Kanzanchiku (*Pleioblastus hindsii*) **1**:136a
Kanzanji ········ 寒山寺 ····· **4**:154b
Kanzanji temple ············· **4**:154b
Kanzashi ················· **4**:154b
　hairstyles ················· **3**:83a
Kanzei. *See* **Tariffs**
Kanze Motokiyo. 観世元清 *See* **Zeami**
Kanze Motomasa 観世元雅 ·· **4**:154b
　Kanze school ·············· **4**:155a
Kanze Nobumitsu
　················ 観世信光 ···· **4**:154b

Kanze school ··············· **4**:155a
Kanze school ····· 観世流 ··· **4**:155a
　Nō ······················· **6**:24a
　Yūzaki troupe ············· **4**:135b
Kanze-yori ·················· **4**:299b
Kao (face) ·················· **4**:155a
Kaō (monograms) ···· 花押 ·· **4**:155a–155b; 155–156a; **7**:45b
　diplomatics ··········· **2**:98a; **4**:156a
　Edo period ············ **4**:155b–156a
　Heian period ·············· **4**:155b
　jitsuin ···················· **4**:156a
　kakihan ··················· **4**:155b
　Kamakura period ·········· **4**:155b
　Meiji Restoration ·········· **4**:156a
　Muromachi period ········· **4**:155b
　seals ····················· **6**:281b
　Sengoku period ············ **4**:155b
　Zen Buddhist ············· **4**:155b
Kaō Corporation ··········· **4**:156a
Ka Ōkin ········· 何応欽 ···· **3**:128b
Kaō Ninga ······· 可翁仁賀 ·· **3**:305a; **4**:156a–156b
　Koga bikō ················ **4**:156a
　Takuma school ············ **4**:156a
Kappa ········· 河童 **4**:156b; **7**:263b
　Akutagawa Ryūnosuke ····· **1**:45b
　bakemono ················· **1**:130b
"**Kappan'ya no hanashi**"
　················ 活版屋の話 ··· **5**:301b
　Ogawa Usen ··············· **6**:70a
Kapsan Faction ·············· **4**:208b
Kapsin Political Coup (1884) **4**:156b–157a, 280b
　fukoku kyōhei ············· **2**:361a
　Kaehwap'a ··········· **4**:101b, 156b
　Kim Ok-kyun ············· **4**:156b
　Pak Yŏng-hyo ············· **4**:156b
　Sugup'a ·················· **4**:156b
　Tianjin Convention ···· **4**:157a; **8**:29b
　Treaty of Seoul ······· **4**:157a; **7**:68b
Kara-e (Chinese-style painting) ·········· 唐絵 **4**:157a; **7**:42a
　Heian period ·············· **4**:157a
　Kanga ···················· **4**:157a
　Tang dynasty ·············· **4**:157a
　yamato-e contrast ·········· **4**:157a
Kara-e-mekiki painters ········ **5**:305b
Karafuto. 樺太 *See* **Sakhalin**
Karafuto-Chishima Kōkan Jōyaku. *See* **St. Petersburg, Treaty of**
Karagoromo Kisshū
　··············· 唐衣橘洲 ···· **4**:157a
　Kyōka poetry ········· **4**:157a, 332a
Karaguwa ··················· **4**:322a
Karai Hachiemon
　··············· 柄井八右衛門 ·· **4**:157a
Karai Senryū ··· 柄井川柳 · **4**:157a–157b; **8**:368a
Kara Jūrō ······· 唐十郎 ···· **4**:157b
Karakami (kagura uta) ········ **4**:108a
Karakhan, Lev Mikhailovich ·· **4**:157b
Karaki Junzō ····· 唐木順三 ··· **5**:13b
Karako site ····· 唐古遺跡 **4**:157b; **7**:265b
　bone articles ·············· **4**:157b
　bronze bell molds ·········· **4**:157b
　excavation ················ **1**:77b
　pit houses ················· **4**:157b
　rokuro ···················· **6**:335b
　stone tools ················ **4**:157b
　Yayoi pottery ············· **4**:157b
Karamatsu. *See* **Larch, Japanese**
Karamete (castle entrance) ·········· 搦手 ·· **1**:248a
Karamon (gate) ········· **3**:12b, 13a
Kara-ori ·················· **4**:158a
Karasu ················· **2**:51b–52a

Karasumaru Mitsuhiro
　············· 烏丸光広 · **4**:158a; **5**:48a
Karate ········· 空手 · **4**:158a–159a
　modern development ······· **4**:158b
　　clubs ··················· **4**:158b
　　federation of organizations ·· **4**:158b
　　Funakoshi Gichin ········· **4**:158b
　　schools ················· **4**:158b
　　styles ·················· **4**:158b
　origins ·············· **4**:158a–158b
　　legendary ··············· **4**:158a
　　Okinawa ················ **4**:158b
　　quanfa ·················· **4**:158a
　　Ryūkyū Islands ··········· **4**:158b
　　Shōrinji kempō ··········· **4**:158a
　　tōde ···················· **4**:158b
　technique and contests ····· **4**:159a
　　form competitions ········ **4**:159a
　　practice methods ········· **4**:159a
　　sparring matches ········· **4**:159a
Karatedō ··················· **4**:158b
Karatsu ········· 唐津 ····· **4**:159a
　Karatsu ware ············· **4**:159a
　Niji no Matsubara ········· **4**:159a
Karatsu ware ···· 唐津焼 · **1**:260b, 263b; **2**:295b; **4**:159a–159b
　Agano ware ··············· **1**:20b
　first written record ········ **4**:159b
　Furuta Oribe ·············· **4**:159b
　kilns ····················· **4**:159b
　Korean pottery techniques ·· **4**:159b
　Korean style ·············· **4**:159a
　museums ················· **5**:279b
　Nakazato Tarōemon XII ···· **4**:159b
　plain ····················· **4**:159a
　Sen no Rikyū ············· **4**:159b
　Takatori ware ············· **7**:320a
　Tea ceremony ····· **4**:159a–159b; **7**:363b
　underglazed ··············· **4**:159a
Karayō ············ 唐様 ····· **1**:236a
Karayuki san ············ **4**:159b–160a
　film
　　Imamura Shōhei ·········· **3**:274a
　　Indonesia and Japan ······ **3**:290b
　　Manchurian Incident of 1931 **4**:159b
　　military prostitution ······ **4**:159b
"**Kareki no aru fūkei**"
　················ 枯木のある風景 **7**:176a; **8**:173b
Kare no kokyō ·· 彼の故郷 ··· **6**:69b
Kari ······················· **3**:13b
Kariage ············ 借上 ···· **4**:161b
Karikachi Pass ··· 狩勝峠 ··· **4**:160a
Kariya ········· 刈谷 ······ **4**:160a
Karlgren, Bernhard ········· **4**:160a
　Chinese phonology studies ·· **4**:160a
　Museum of Far Eastern Antiquities Bulletin, The ········· **4**:160a
Karmic evil ················· **4**:68b
Karō ············ 家老 ····· **4**:160a
　administrative responsibilities **4**:160a
　toshiyori ················· **4**:160a
Karuizawa ······ 軽井沢 ···· **4**:160b
　Onioshidashi ·············· **4**:160b
　Shiraito Falls ············· **4**:160b
Karurusu Hot Spring ········ **4**:160b
Karuta. *See* **Playing cards**
Karyūkai ··················· **3**:14a
Kasa ······················ **3**:119a
Kasabuta Shikibu kō かさぶた式部考 **1**:42a
Kasagake ········ 笠懸 ····· **4**:160b
　Kaburaya ················· **4**:160b
　Kamakura period ·········· **4**:160b
　Muromachi period ········· **4**:160b
Kasagi Mountains
　··············· 笠置山地 ···· **5**:332a
Kasai ··················· **4**:160b
Kasai Zenzō ····· 葛西善蔵 ·· **4**:160b

I-novel · · · · · · · · · · · · · · 3:312a; 4:160a
Kasa jizō · · · · · · · 笠地蔵 **4:**160b
Kasama · · · · · · · 笠間 **4:**161a
Kasaneori · · · · · · · · · · **6:**118a
Kasa no Kanamura 笠金村 **4:**161a; **8:**206b
Man'yōshū · · · · · · · · **4:**161a
poems in *Man'yōshū* · · **5:**107b
Kasaoka · · · · · · · 笠岡 **4:**161a
Kasaya Yukio · · · · 笠谷幸生 **4:**161a
Sapporo Winter Olympic Games · · · **7:**20b
Kaseda · · · · · · · 加世田 **4:**161a
Kasen-e · · · · · · · 歌仙絵 **4:**161a-161b
Agedatami-bon · · · · · · **4:**161b
Buson · · · · · · · · **4:**161b
formats · · · · · · · **4:**161b
Fujiwara no Nobuzane · · · · · · · **4:**161b
Go-Toba In-bon · · · · · · **4:**161b
hyakunin isshu · · · · · · **4:**161b
Jidai fudō uta-awase · · · · **4:**161b
Kakinomoto no Hitomaro · · · · **4:**161b
Kōrin · · · · · · · · **4:**161b
Narikane-bon · · · · · · **4:**161b
Sanjūrokunin sen · · · · **4:**161b
Satake-bon · · · · · · **4:**161b
yamato-e theme · · · · · · **4:**161a
Kasen koi no bu (Selected Poems on Love)
· · · · · · · 歌撰恋の部 · · · · · · **8:**186b
Kashi · · · · · · · · · · **6:**47a
Kashiage · · · · · · 借上 **4:**122b, 161b
Kashihara · · · · · · 橿原 **4:**162a
Fujiwarakyō site · · · · **4:**162a
Jimmu enthronement · · · · **4:**162a
Kashihara Shrine 橿原神宮 · · · · **4:**162a
Kashihon'ya Library
Tamenaga Shunsei · · · **7:**333b-334a
Kashii Shrine · · · · 香椎宮 **4:**162a
imperial patronage · · · · **4:**162a
Kashii-zukuri style · · · · **4:**162a
Kashii-zukuri · · · · 香椎造 **4:**162a
Kashikojima · · · · 賢島 **4:**162a
Kashima (city) · · · · 鹿島 **4:**162a
Kashima (town) · · · · 鹿島 **4:**162a
Kashima Sea · · · · 鹿島灘 **2:**285b; **4:**162a
Kashima Shrine · · 鹿島神宮 **4:**162b
festival · · · · · · · **4:**162a
Takemikazuchi no Mikoto · · · · **4:**162a
Kashima Yarigatake
· · · · · · 鹿島槍ケ岳 · · · **4:**162b
Kashindan · · · · · · 家臣団 · · · **1:**131b
Kashin (Good News) · 嘉信 **8:**315b
Kashiwa · · · · · · 柏 **4:**162b
Kashiwabara Hyōzō
· · · · · · 柏原兵三 **4:**162b
Kashiwadebe · · · · · 膳部 **1:**147b
Kashiwagi Gien · 柏木義円 · · · · **4:**162b
Kashiwagi Yoshimaru
· · · · · · 柏木義円 **4:**162b
Ashio Copper Mine Incident involvement · · · · · · **4:**162b
Jōmō kyōkai geppō · · · · **4:**162b
Niijima Jō · · · · · · **4:**162b
Kashiwara · · · · · 柏原 · · **4:**162b-163a
Kashiwazaki · · · · 柏崎 **4:**163a
Kashiyama & Co, Ltd · · · · **4:**163a
Kasho · · · · · · 過書 **4:**163a
firearms · · · · · · · **4:**163a
tegata · · · · · · · **4:**163a
women · · · · · · · **4:**163a
Kasho-bune · · · · 過書船 **4:**163a
Kashōki · · · · · · 可笑記 **4:**136b
Kasō · · · · · · · 家相 **4:**163a
Kimon · · · · · · · **4:**163a
Ommyōryō · · · · · · **4:**163a
Kasori shell mounds
· · · · · · 加曽利貝塚 **4:**163b
bone articles · · · · · · **4:**163b
Jōmon pottery · · · · · · **4:**163b

pit houses · · · · · · · **4:**163b
stone tools · · · · · · · **4:**163b
Kasō Sōdon · · · · 華叟宗曇 **3:**269b
Kassen Togamegoto
· · · · · · 合戦咎事 **4:**196b
Kasshi Reform 甲子の改革 **7:**296b
Kasuga · · · · · · 春日 **4:**163b; **7:**136a
Occupation military base · · · · **4:**163b
Shintō · · · · · · · **7:**126b
Suku site · · · · · · · **4:**163b
Kasuga gongen genki 春日権現験記 **3:**35a
Kasugai · · · · · · 春日井 **4:**163b
Kasuga Ikkō · · · · 春日一幸 · **4:**163b; **7:**23a
Kasuga mandara
· · · · · · 春日曼荼羅 **4:**164a; **5:**100a
Kasuga no Tsubone
· · · · · · 春日局 **4:**163b
Akechi Mitsuhide · · · · **4:**163b
Ōoku · · · · · · · **4:**163b
Tokugawa Iemitsu · · · · **4:**163b; **8:**48a
Kasuga Shrine · · 春日大社 · **4:**163b-164b, 169a, 368a; **5:**331a
architectural style · · · · **4:**164a
branch shrines · · · · **4:**164a
festival · · · · · · · **4:**164a
Kasuga mandara · · · · **5:**100a
Kōfukuji · · · · · · · **4:**243b
sacred symbol · · · · · · **4:**163b
Shintō architecture · · · · **7:**132a
Kasugayama · · · · 春日山 **4:**164a
Kasukabe · · · · · 春日部 **4:**164a
Kasumigaseki · · · · 霞が関 **8:**62b
Kasumigaura · · · · 霞ケ浦 · **4:**164a, 164b
Kasuri · · **2:**295b; **4:**164a-165a, 312a, 318b; **8:**19b
cottage industry · · · · **4:**164b
e-dai · · · · · · · · **4:**164b
e-gasuri · · · · · · · **4:**164b
kosode · · · · · · · **4:**164a
local textile areas · · · · **4:**164b
Nō costumes · · · · · · **4:**164a
patterns · · · · · · · **4:**164b
weaving development · · · · **4:**164a-164b
Kata · · · · · · · · **4:**196a
Katagami Noboru · 片上伸 **4:**165a
Katagami Tengen 片上天弦 **4:**165a
Katagi · · · · · · · **4:**165a
Katagimono · · · · 気質物 **2:**188a; **8:**144b
Katagiri Katsumoto
· · · · · · 片桐且元 **4:**165a
Battle of Shizugatake · · · · **4:**165a
daimyō status · · · · · · **4:**165a
Kimura Shigenari · · · · **4:**165a
Ono Harunaga · · · · · · **4:**165a
Shōmei Incident · · · · **4:**165a
Tokugawa Ieyashu · · · · **4:**165a
Toyotomi Hideyoshi · · · · **4:**165a
Toyotomi Hidiyori · · · · **4:**165a
Katakago · · · · · · 堅香子 **4:**165b
Katakana. *See* **Kana**
Katakiuchi · · · · · **4:**165a-165b
archetype of practice · · · · **4:**165b
dramatic subject · · · · **4:**165b
Edo period · · · · · · **4:**165b
Forty-Seven Rōnin Incident · · · · **2:**327a
justification · · · · · · **4:**165a-165b
prohibition · · · · · · **4:**165b
rules · · · · · · · · **4:**165b
Soga brothers · · · · · · **4:**165b
Katakuri [(trout lily) *Erythronium japonicum*] · · · · **4:**165b
Katakuriko · · · · 片栗粉 **4:**165b
Katamewaza · · · · · · **4:**82b
Katamino · · · · · · **7:**249a
Katanagari. 刀狩 *See* **Sword hunt**
Katano · · · · · · 交野 **4:**166a
Kataoka Chiezō
· · · · · · 片岡千恵蔵 · · · · **4:**166a

Kataoka Kenkichi
· · · · · · 片岡健吉 **4:**166a
Aikokusha formation · · · · **4:**166a
Freedom and People's Rights Movement · **2:**334b; **4:**166a
Itagaki Taisuke · · · · · · **4:**166a
Jiyūtō formation · · · · **4:**166a
League for Establishing a National Assembly representation · · · · **4:**166a
Risshisha formation · · · · **4:**166a
Sandai Jiken Kempaku Movement (Movement to Memorialize Three Important Items) · · · · **7:**9b
Kataoka Takao · 片岡孝夫 **4:**91a
Kataoka Teppei · 片岡鉄兵 **4:**166a-166b; **7:**175a
Bungei jidai · · · · · · **4:**166b
fūzoku shōsetsu · · · · **2:**378b
Proletarian literature movement involvement · · · · · · **4:**166b
Shinkankaku school · **4:**166b; **7:**116a-116b
Kataribe · · · · · · 語部 **4:**166b
ceremonial role · · · · **4:**166b
Engi shiki · · · · · · **4:**166b
forerunner · · · · · · **4:**166b
Hieda no Are · · · · · · **3:**130b
Katari-mono · · · · 語り物 **4:**93a
Katashiro · · · · · · **4:**166b
Doll Festival · · · · · · **2:**128a
mamako nagare rite · · · · **5:**308b
nagoshi · · · · · · · **5:**308b
Nagoshi observance · · · · **4:**166b
origami · · · · · · · **6:**116b
Snake Day exorcism · · · · **4:**166b
Katatagae · · · · · · **4:**166b
"Kataude" · · · · · · 片腕 **4:**176b
Katauta
Takebe Ayatari · · · · **7:**321a
waka · · · · · · · · **8:**202b
Katayama Sen · · 片山潜 **4:**166b-167a, 382b; **7:**74a-74b
antiwar activities · · · · **4:**167a
Bolshevism · · · · · · **4:**167a
expatriation · · · · · · **4:**167a
Futsū Senkyo Kisei Dōmeikai · · · **2:**376b
Kōtoku Shūsui · · · · **4:**167a
labor movement · · · · **4:**167a
Rōdō sekai editorship · · · · **4:**167a
trade union movement · · · · **4:**167a
"Katayama's Formula" · · · · **1:**268b
Katayama Tetsu · · 片山哲 **4:**167a-167b; **7:**74b
Abe Isoo · · · · · · · **4:**167a
coalition cabinet · · · · **4:**167a
Democratic Socialist Party formation
· · · · · · **4:**167b
Japan Socialist Party · · **4:**48b, 167b
Shakai Minshūtō membership · · · · **4:**167a
Shakai Taishūtō membership · · · · **4:**167a
Katayama Tōkuma
· · · · · · 片山東熊 · · · · **1:**80b
Katazome · · · · · · **4:**167b; **8:**19b
bokashi · · · · · · · **4:**167b
kimono · · · · · · · **4:**167b
komon · · · · · · · **4:**167b
kōzo · · · · · · · · **4:**167b
patterns · · · · · · · **4:**167b
technical development · · · · **4:**167b
Katei shōsetsu · · · · · · **4:**199b
Katō case · · · · · · **6:**250a
Katō Chikage · · 加藤千蔭 **4:**167b
Kamo no Mabuchi · · · · **4:**129b, 167b
Man'yōshū scholarship · · · · **5:**110b
Katō Gen'ichi · · 加藤元一 **4:**167b
Katō Hajime · · 加藤土師萌 **1:**261a, 262b; **4:**168a
Living National Treasure · · · · **4:**168a
Mino ware · · · · · · **4:**168a

Seto ware ··········· **4**:168a
Katō Hiroharu ·· 加藤寛治 ······· **4**:168a
  London Naval Conference ······· **4**:168a
  militarism ··················· **4**:168a
  Washington Conference of 1921-22 **4**:168a
Katō Hiroyuki ·· 加藤弘之 ·· **4**:168a-168b
  Freedom and People's Rights Movement
    opposition ··············· **4**:168a
  Kaiseijo position ············· **4**:168a
  Meirokusha membership ········· **4**:168a
  Sakuma Shōzan ··············· **7**:3b
  Social Darwinism ········ **4**:168a-168b
  Western Learning ············· **4**:168a
Katō Kanji. 加藤寛治 *See* **Katō Hiroharu**
Katō Kiyomasa ·· 加藤清正 ·· **4**:168b, 305b
  Battle of Sekigahara ·········· **4**:168b
  Battle of Shizugatake ········· **4**:168b
  invasions of Korea ········ **3**:327a; **4**:168b
  Konishi Yukinaga ············· **4**:168b
  Tokugawa Ieyasu ············· **4**:168b
  Toyotomi Hideyori ··········· **4**:168b
  Toyotomi Hideyoshi ·········· **4**:168b
Katō Kōmei.   加藤高明   *See* **Katō**
  Takaaki
  Katoku ···················· **3**:304a
Katō Kyōtai ······· 加藤暁台 ·· **1**:225a;
                            4:168b-169a
  Buson ················· **4**:168b-169a
Katō Michio ······ 加藤道夫 ···· **4**:169a
  shingeki ·················· **7**:113a
Katorikku daijiten ··············· **1**:250b
Katori Nahiko ·· 楫取魚彦 ···· **4**:169a
  Kamo no Mabuchi ······· **4**:129b, 169a
Katori Shrine ··· 香取神宮 ·· **4**:162b, 169a;
                                  7:31b
  festival ··················· **4**:169a
  Fujiwara family patronage ······ **4**:169a
Katō Sawao ······· 加藤沢男 ···· **4**:169a
Katō Shizue ···· 加藤シヅエ · **4**:169a-169b
  Facing Two Ways ············· **4**:169b
  family planning activities ······ **4**:169a
  Hitosuji no michi ············· **4**:169b
  Japan Socialist Party membership **4**:169a
  Margaret Sanger ············· **4**:169a
Katō Shūichi ···· 加藤周一 ···· **4**:169b
Katō Shūson ···· 加藤楸邨 ···· **4**:169b
Katō Takaaki ···· 加藤高明 ····· **4**:198a;
    4:169b-170b; **7**:270b
  Goken Sampa Naikaku ········· **3**:43a
  Inukai Tsuyoshi ············· **4**:120a
  Iwasaki Yatarō ············· **4**:169b
  Kenseikai ················· **4**:198a
  premiership ········· **4**:170a-170b
    movement to protect constitutional
      government ············· **4**:170a
    Peace Preservation Law of 1925 · **4**:170a
  public life ················· **4**:169b
    Katsura Tarō cabinet ········· **4**:170a
    Rikken Dōshikai leadership ····· **4**:170a
    Saionji Kimmochi cabinet ······ **4**:170a
    Twenty-One Demands ········· **4**:170a
  Shidehara Kijūrō ············· **7**:88b
Katō Takeo ······· 加藤武男 ···· **4**:170b
  Iwasaki Koyata ············· **4**:170b
  Mitsubishi directorship ······· **4**:170b
  Shinkō Geijutsu Ha ·········· **7**:119b
Katō Tōkurō ··· 加藤唐九郎 ··· **4**:170b
Katō Tomosaburō
                加藤友三郎 ···· **4**:170b
  Battle of Tsushima ··········· **4**:170b
  on Japanese-American relations ··· **1**:57a
  Washington Conference delegation **4**:170b
Katō Works Co, Ltd ······· **4**:170b-171a
Katsu Awa. 勝安芳 *See* **Katsu Kaishū**
Katsugo danzoku fu
              活語断続譜 ······· **7**:281a
Katsugo shinan ·· 活語指南 ······· **8**:39b

Katsu Kaishū ······ 勝海舟 ······· **1**:165a;
         4:171a-171b; **7**:3b, 263b
  Kaigun Denshūjo ········ **4**:110a, 171a
  Kanrin maru ··········· **4**:151b, 171a
  Kimura Yoshitake ············· **4**:211b
  Saigō Takamori ············· **4**:171a
  Tokugawa shogunate negotiator ·· **4**:171a
  Tokugawa Yoshinobu ········· **4**:171a
Katsukawa school 勝川派 ···· **4**:171b
  Katsukawa Shunshō ··········· **4**:171b
  nigao-e ··················· **4**:171b
  yakusha-e ················· **4**:171b
Katsukawa Shun'ei
          勝川春英 · **4**:171b; **7**:79a;
                         8:141b
  kabuki actor portraits ········· **4**:171b
  Katsukawa Shunshō ··········· **4**:171b
  Sharaku ··················· **4**:171b
  sumō wrestler portraits ········ **4**:171b
  Utagawa Kunimasa ············ **4**:171b
  Utagawa Toyokuni ············ **4**:171b
Katsukawa Shunshō
          勝川春章 · **4**:171b-172a;
                         8:141a
  kabuki actor portraits ········ **4**:171b-172a
  pupils ···················· **4**:172a
  sumō wrestler portraits ······ **4**:171b-172a
Katsuki Yasuji ·· 勝木保次 ···· **4**:172a
Katsumoto Seiichirō
          勝本清一郎 ····· **4**:172a
Katsunuma ········ 勝沼 ······· **4**:172a
Katsunuma Seizō 勝沼精蔵 ··· **4**:172a
Katsuo. *See* **Bonito**
Katsuo no eboshi ··············· **4**:50b
Katsurada Fujio
          桂田富士郎 ····· **4**:172a
Katsura Detached Palace
          桂離宮 ········ **3**:9b;
    4:172b-173a, *172b*, 336a; **7**:*265a*, 266a
  "emperor art"
    Taut, Bruno ·········· **7**:351a-351b
  gardens ··················· **3**:10a
  shoin-zukuri architecture ······ **4**:172b
  sukiya-zukuri architecture ······ **4**:172b
  tea gardens
    Kobori Enshū ············· **4**:238a
    Toshitada, Prince ··········· **4**:172b
Katsuragawa ········· 桂川 · **4**:128a-128b,
                        173a, 338a
Katsuragawa Hoshū
          桂川甫周 **4**:173a; **7**:258b
  Daikokuya Kōdayū ··········· **2**:60b
  Hokusa bunryuaku ··········· **4**:173a
  Izak Titsingh ··············· **4**:173a
  Kaitai shinsho ·············· **4**:173a
  Maeno Ryōtaku ············· **4**:173a
  Roshia shi ················ **4**:173a
  Sugita Gempaku ············· **4**:173a
  Thunberg, Peter ············· **4**:173a
Katsuragi, Prince. 葛城王
  See **Tachibana no Moroe**
Katsurahama ······· 桂浜 ····· **4**:173a
Katsura Kogorō. 桂小五郎 *See* **Kido**
  Takayoshi
Katsura-Taft Agreement
  (1905) ··· 桂-タフト協定 · **4**:173a-173b;
                         8:156a
  Korea and Japan ············· **4**:282a
  Korea's annexation ··········· **4**:287b
Katsura Tarō ···· 桂太郎 · **1**:86b, 165b;
    2:241b; **3**:198a; **4**:173b-174a; **7**:88a
  Anglo-Japanese Alliance ·· **1**:56b; **4**:173b
  Hara Takashi ·········· **3**:103a; **4**:173b
  Hibiya Incendiary Incident ····· **3**:129a
  High Treason Incident of 1910 ··· **4**:174a
  Kiyoura Keigo ············· **4**:233a
  Kodama Gentarō cabinet ······· **4**:241a

  Korea annexation ············ **4**:173b
  Movement to Protect Constitutional
    Government ··············· **4**:174a
  Ōyama Iwao ················ **4**:173b
  Rikken Dōshikai ······· **4**:173b; **6**:314b
  Rikken Seiyūkai ············· **4**:173b
  Russo-Japanese War ·········· **4**:173b
  Saionji Kimmochi ············ **4**:173b
  Sino-Japanese War of 1894-1895 · **4**:173b
  Taishō political crisis ···· **4**:174a; **7**:305b
  Tokutomi Sohō ············· **4**:174a
  Treaty of Portsmouth ········· **4**:174a
  Yamagata Aritomo ··········· **4**:173b
Katsura tree [(katsura) *Cercidiphyllum*
  japonicum] ··············· **4**:174a-174b
Katsureki-mono ·· 活歴物 ······· **5**:234b
Katsu Rintaro. 勝麟太郎
          See **Katsu Kaishū**
Katsushika Hokusai. 葛飾北斎 *See*
  Hokusai
Katsushika Ward · 葛飾区 ···· **4**:174b
Katsu Shintarō · 勝新太郎 **2**:274b; **4**:174b
Katsuta ············ 勝田 ····· **4**:174b
Katsuura ········· 勝浦 ····· **4**:174b
Katsuyama ········ 勝山 ····· **4**:175a
Kattegakari rōjū
  (councillors) 勝手掛老中 ····· **4**:331a
Katydid ···················· **4**:220b
Kauffman, James Lee ········· **4**:175a
Kawabata Bōsha 川端茅舎 ···· **4**:175a
Kawabata Gyokushō
          川端玉章 · **4**:175a-175b
  bunjinga ·················· **4**:175a
  Charles Wirgman ············ **4**:175a
  Hirafuku Hyakusui ··········· **4**:175b
  Mitsui family commissions ····· **4**:175b
Kawabata Nobukazu
          川端信一 ······· **4**:175a
Kawabata Ryūshi 川端龍子 ···· **4**:175b
Kawabata Shōtarō
          川端昇太郎 ····· **4**:175b
Kawabata Yasunari
          川端康成 **2**:274a; **4**:*175a*,
          175b-177a; **5**:13a; **7**:103b
  Bungeijidai ··············· **1**:209a
  death ···················· **4**:176b
  early years ················ **4**:175a
  "Izu no odoriko" ············ **4**:175a
  last years ··········· **4**:176b-177a
  Nemureru bijo ············· **4**:176b
  postwar years ········· **4**:176a-176b
  Nobel prize (1969) ··········· **4**:176b
  Sembazuru ················ **4**:176b
  Yama no oto ··············· **4**:176b
  Shinkankaku school · **4**:175b; **7**:116a-116b,
                      175a-175b
  war years ················· **4**:176a
  Yukiguni ················· **4**:176a
Kawabiraki ··············· **4**:177a
Kawachi Nagano 河内長野 ···· **4**:177a
Kawagoe ········· 川越 ····· **4**:177b
Kawaguchi ······· 川口 **2**:345a; **4**:177b
Kawaguchi, Lake ·河口湖 ···· **4**:177b
Kawaguchi Ekai 河口慧海 ···· **4**:177b
  Chibetto ryokōki ··········· **4**:177a
  Inoue Enryō ··············· **4**:177a
Kawaguchi Matsutarō
         ·川口松太郎 **2**:274a; **4**:177b
  fūzoku shōsetsu ············· **2**:378b
Kawahara Keiga 川原慶賀 · **4**:177b-178a;
                        5:306a
  Dejima ·············· **4**:177b-178a
  Hendrick Doeff portrait ······· **4**:178a
  Ishizaki Yūshi ·········· **4**:177b-178a
  Philipp von Siebold ····· **4**:178a; **7**:192b
  yamato-e ·················· **4**:178a
Kawahigashi Hekigotō
          河東碧梧桐 ····· **4**:178a

haiku · · · · · · · · · · · · · · · · · 3:79b
Hototogisu · · · · · · · · · · · 3:237b; 4:178a
Kawai Eijirō · · · 河合栄治郎 · · · 4:178a–178b
fascism opposition · · · · · · · · · 4:178b
idealist socialism · · · · · · · · · · 4:178b
labor reform advocacy · · · · · · · 4:178b
Publication Law of 1893 violation · 4:178b
Kawai Gyokudō · 川合玉堂 · · · 4:178b
Gyokudō Art Museum · · · 3:71a; 4:178b
Hashimoto Gahō · · · · · · · · · · 4:178b
Kōno Bairei · · · · · · · · · · · · 4:178b
Kawai Kanjirō · 河井寛次郎 · · 2:294a;
4:178b–179a
Kawai Matahei · 河井又平 · · · 4:179a
Kawai Michi · · · · · · 河井道 · · · 4:179a
Nitobe Inazō · · · · · · · · · · · · 4:179a
Tsuda Umeko · · · · · · · · · · · · 4:179a
Uemura Masahisa · · · · · · · · · · 4:179a
Young Women's Christian Association
· · · · · · · · · · · · · · · · · · 4:179a
Kawai Musical Instruments Mfg Co, Ltd
· · · · · · · · · · · · · · · · · · 4:179a
Kawai Sora · · · · · · 河合曽良 · 1:144b; 4:179a
Kawai Suimei · 河井酔茗 · 4:179a–179b
Kawai Tsugunosuke
· · · · · · · · · 河井継之助 · · · 4:179b
National Seclusion opposition · · · 4:179b
Sakuma Shōzan · · · · · · · · · · · 4:179b
Kawaji Hot Spring
· · · · · · · · · · · · · 川治温泉 · · 4:179b
Kawaji Ryūkō · 川路柳虹 · · · 4:179b
Kawaji Toshiakira
· · · · · · · · · · · · · 川路聖謨 · · 4:179b
Egawa Tarōzaemon · · · · · · · · · 4:179b
Evfimii Vasil'evich Putiatin · · · · · 4:179b
Fujita Tōko · · · · · · · · · · · · 4:179b
Hotta Masayoshi · · · · · · · · · · 4:179b
Inoue Kiyonao · · · · · · · · · · · 4:179b
Satō Issai · · · · · · · · · · · · · 4:179b
Watanabe Kazan · · · · · · · · · · 4:179b
Kawakami Bizan · 川上眉山 · · · 1:209b;
4:179b–180a
Futokoro nikki · · · · · · · · · · · 4:180a
haibun · · · · · · · · · · · · 3:78a; 4:180a
Harin · · · · · · · · · · · · · · · · 4:180a
Kannen shōsetsu · · · · · · · · 4:179b–180a
Kannon iwa · · · · · · · · · · · · 4:180a
Ken'yūsha · · · · · · · · · · 4:180a, 199a
naturalism influence · · · · · · · · 4:180a
Ozaki Kōyō · · · · · · · · · · · · 4:180a
"Sodezukin" · · · · · · · · · · · · 4:180a
Yamada Bimyō · · · · · · · · · · · 4:180a
Kawakami Gen'ichi
· · · · · · · · · · · · · 川上源一 · · 4:180b
Yamaha Motor Co, Ltd · · · · · · · 4:180b
Yamaha Music Foundation · · · · · 4:180b
Kawakami Hajime · 河上肇 · 1:155a;
4:180b–181a; 7:251a
Kawakami Jōtarō
· · · · · · · · · · · · · 川上丈太郎 · · 4:181a
Kawakami Otojirō
· · · · · · · · · 川上音二郎 · · · 4:181a–181b
Freedom and People's Rights Movement's
activities · · · · · · · · · · · · · 4:181a
Igai · · · · · · · · · · · · · · · · · 4:181a
Kawakami Sadayakko · · · · · · · · 4:181b
Oppekepē-bushi · · · · · · · · · · 4:181a
shimpa · · · · · · · · · · · · · · · 7:107b
shimpa theatrical tradition · · · · · 4:181a
Kawakami Sadayakko. 川上貞奴 *See*
Kawakami Otojirō
Kawakami Sōroku
· · · · · · · · · · · · 川上操六 · · · 4:181b
Kawakami Tetsutarō
· · · · · · · · · 河上徹太郎 · 4:181b; 5:13a
Kawakami Tōgai · 川上冬崖 4:181b; 8:327a
Kawamoto Kōmin
· · · · · · · · · · · · · 川本幸民 · · · 4:181b

Bansho Shirabesho · · · · · · · · · 4:181b
Kikai kanran kōgi · · · · · · · · · 4:181b
Shimazu Nariakira · · · · · · · · · 4:181b
Kawamura Zuiken
· · · · · · · · · · · 河村瑞賢 · 1:38b; 4:182a
rice tax transport · · · · · · · · · · 4:112b
Kawanabe Gyōsai
· · · · · · · · · · · · · 河鍋暁斎 · · 4:182a
Josiah Conder · · · · · · · · · · · 4:182a
Kanō school · · · · · · · · · · · · 4:182a
Toba Sōjō · · · · · · · · · · · · · 4:182a
Utagawa Kuniyoshi · · · · · · · · · 4:182a
Kawanabe Nobuyuki
· · · · · · · · · · · · · 河鍋陳之 · · 4:182a
Kawanakajima, Battles of
· · · · · · · · 川中島の合戦 · · 4:182a
military chronicles · · · · · · · · · 4:182a
site · · · · · · · · · · · · · · · · · 5:302a
Takeda Shingen · · · · · 4:182a; 7:323a
Uesugi Kenshin · · · · · 4:182a; 8:129b
Kawanishi · · · · · · · · 川西 · · 4:182a
Kawanoe · · · · · · · 川之江 · 4:182a–182b
Kawaraban · · · · · · · 瓦版 · · 4:182a
newspapers · · · · · · · · · · · · · 5:369a
Kawaradera remains
· · · · · · · · · · · · · 川原寺址 · · 4:182b
Kawaramono · · · · · 河原者 · 4:182b–183a;
7:12a
acting profession association · · · · 4:95b
discriminatory policy · · · · 4:182b–183a
entertainers · · · · · · · · · · · · 4:182b
Kawara nadeshiko · · · · · · · · · 2:339b
Kawari-e origami · · · · · · · · · · 6:118a
Kawasaki · · · · · · · · 川崎 · 4:135a, 183,
183a
Kawasaki Daishi · · · · · · · · · · 4:183a
Keihin Industrial Zone · · · · · · · 4:183a
Kawasaki Aircraft Co, Ltd · · · · · 4:183b
Kawasaki asthma 川崎喘息 · · 4:183b
Kawasaki Car Manufacturing Co, Ltd
· · · · · · · · · · · · · · · · · · 4:183b
Kawasaki Chōtarō
· · · · · · · · · · · · · 川崎長太郎 · · 4:183b
Aka to kuro · · · · · · · · · · · · 4:183b
Kikuchi Kan · · · · · · · · · · · · 4:183b
Kawasaki Daishi · 川崎大師 · 4:183a–183b
festivals · · · · · · · · · · · · · · 4:183b
Hirama Kanenori · · · · · · · · · · 4:183b
Kūkai · · · · · · · · · · · · · · · · 4:183b
Kawasaki disease · 川崎病 · · 4:183b
Kawasaki Heavy Industries, Ltd
· · · · · · · · · · · · · · · 4:183b–184a
aviation · · · · · · · · · · · · · · 1:124a
defense industry · · · · · · · · · · 2:82b
Kawasaki Kisen Kaisha, Ltd · · · · 4:183b
Kawasaki Steel Corporation · · · · 4:183b
original technologies · · · · · · · · 4:183b
overseas markets · · · · · · · · · · 4:183b
Kawasaki Hyōgo Shipyard · · · · · 4:183b
Kawasaki Kisen Kaisha, Ltd · 4:183b–184a
Kawasaki Heavy Industries, Ltd · · 4:183b
Kawasaki Steel Corporation · · · · 4:183b
Kawasaki Natsu · 河崎なつ · · 4:184a
Fusen Kakutoku Dōmei · · · 2:374b; 4:184a
Miyamoto Yuriko · · · · · · · · · · 4:184a
Tatewaki Sadayo · · · · · · · · · · 4:184a
Kawasaki Shipbuilding Co · · · · · 4:184a
Kawasaki Shipyard Co · · · · · · · 4:183b
Kawasaki Steel Corporation · · 4:184a
Chiba steel mill · · · · · · · · · · 4:184a
Kawasaki Heavy Industries, Ltd · · 4:184a
Kawasaki Tsukiji Shipyard · · · · · 4:183b
Kawase kaisha · · 為替会社 · 1:138a;
4:184a–184b
Mitsui · · · · · · · · · · · · · · · 4:184a
Ono-Gumi · · · · · · · · · · · · · 4:184a
technological development · · · · · 7:369a
Kawashi · · · · · · · · · · 為替 · 4:102a

Kawashima Takeyoshi
· · · · · · · · · · · · · 川島武宜 · · 4:184b
Kawashima Yūzō 川島雄三 · · 2:273a
Kawashō Corporation · · · · · 4:184b
Kawasumi Hiroshi · 河角広 · · 2:139a
Kawatake Mokuami. 河竹黙阿弥
See **Mokuami**
Kawate Bunjirō 川手文治郎 · · 4:271b
Kawauso [(otter) *Lutra lutra*] · · 4:184b
Kawazu, Seven Falls of · · · · · 4:184b
Kaya (Korea) · · · · · · 伽耶 · 4:185a, 195a,
276a; 7:2a
Iwai, Rebellion of · · · · · · · · · 3:357b
Keitai, Emperor · · · · · · · · · · 4:190b
Mimana · · · · · · · · · · · · · · 4:276a
Kaya (mosquito net) · · · · · · · 1:148b
Kayaba Industry Co, Ltd · · · · 4:185a
Kayabuki · · · · · · · · · · · · · · 7:249b
Kayari · · · · · · · · · · · · · · 4:185a
Kaya Seiji · · · · · · 茅誠司 · · 4:185a
Kaya Shirao · · · · · 加舎白雄 · 4:185a
Kayōkyoku (popular
music) · · · · · · · · · · 歌謡曲 · · 4:248a
Kazami Akiko · · · · 風見章子 · 2:269a
Kazan, Emperor · 花山天皇 · · 4:185a
abdication · · · · · · · · · 2:351b; 4:185a
Fujiwara no Kaneie · · · · · · · · · 4:185a
Fujiwara no Korechika · · · · · · · 2:352b
imperial poetry anthology · · · · · 2:352a
Kazarinashi · · 加佐里那止 · · 4:185a
Kaze ni soyogu ashi (Like
a Reed Shaken in the
Wind) · · · · · 風にそよぐ葦 · 8:330a
"Kaze tachinu" · 風立ちぬ · 7:176a
Kazo · · · · · · · · · · 加須 · · 4:185b
Kazoku. 華族 *See* **Peerage**
Kazoku (Where Spring
Comes Late) · · · · · 家族 · · 8:290a
Kazoku kaigi (Family
Conference) · · · · 家族会議 7:176a; 8:333a
Kazoku kokka · · · · · · · · · · · 4:185b
Kazu, Princess · · · 和宮 · · 4:185b
Kazuken · · · · · · · · · · · · · · 4:193a
Kazuno · · · · · · · · · 鹿角 · · 4:185b
KDD (International Telegram and
Telephone Public Corporation) · 4:261b
Ke · · · · · · · · · 2:253b–254a; 6:362a–362b
Kebiishi · · · · · · · 検非違使 · · 4:185b
police system · · · · · · · · · · · · 6:2a
ryōge no kan · · · · · · · · · · · · 6:351b
Kebukigusa · · · · · · · 毛吹草 · 6:258b
Keenan, Joseph Berry · · · · 4:185b–186a
Kegare · · · · · · · · · · · · · 4:186a–186b
categories · · · · · · · · · · · · · 4:186a
taboo · · · · · · · · · · · · · · · · 7:291b
tsumi · · · · · · · · · · · · 8:115a–115b
Kegon · · · · · · · · · · 華厳 · · 4:175a
Kegon Falls · · · · · · 華厳滝 · · 4:186b
Kegonkyō · · · · · · · 華厳経 · · 4:186b
Kegon sect · · · · · 華厳宗 1:178b; 4:186b
Dōsen · · · · · · · · · · · 2:131b; 4:186b
Gangōji · · · · · · · · · · · · · · · 3:6b
Gyōnen · · · · · · · · · · · 3:72b; 4:186b
headquarters · · · · · · · · · · · · 5:332b
Kōzanji · · · · · · · · · · · · · · · 4:300a
Rōben · · · · · · · · · · · · · · · · 6:333a
Kehi Shrine · · · · · 気比神宮 · · 4:186b
Shintō · · · · · · · · · · · · · · · 7:126b
Keian Genju · · · · 桂庵玄樹 · 4:186b–187a
Gozan training · · · · · · · · · · · 4:187a
Kenninji · · · · · · · · · · · · · · 4:187a
Keian Incident (1651)
· · · · · · · · · · · · · 慶安事件 · · 4:187a
Abe Tadaaki · · · · · · · · · · · · · 1:4b
literary portrayal · · · · · · · · · · 4:187a
Marubashi Chūya · · · · · 4:187a; 5:120a
Matsudaira Nobutsuna · · · · · · · 4:187a
Sumpu burning · · · · · · · · · · · 4:187a

Tokugawa Iemitsu ··············· **4**:187a
Tokugawa Ietsuna ··········· **4**:187a; **8**:49a
Yui Shōsetsu ··················· **4**:187a
Keian no Ofuregaki
·········慶安の御触書 **1**:131b; **4**:187a;
8:266a
Keian taiheiki · 慶安太平記 ···· **4**:187a
Keibatsu ········· **1**:147a; **4**:187a–187b
Keichō ···············計帳 ···· **4**:187b
Keichō Campaign (1597–98) ······ **3**:327a
Keichō kemmon shū
·········慶長見聞集 ···· **4**:187b
Keichō koban 慶長小判 ·· **4**:234b; **5**:242*a*
Keichū ···············契沖 ···· **1**:154a;
4:187b–188a; **5**:17a; **7**:105a
historiography ··············· **3**:155a
Japanese language studies ······· **4**:31a
Kamo no Mabuchi ······ **4**:129a, 188a
kana research ··················· **4**:187b
Kokugaku forerunner ········· **4**:257a
Man'yōshū scholarship ····· **5**:110a–110b
orthographic studies ·········· **4**:133b
Waji shōran shō ······· **4**:188a; **8**:201a
Keidanren ···········経団連 ···· **4**:188a–188b
Dokō Toshio ··················· **2**:127b
functions ·················· **4**:188a–188b
Ishikawa Ichirō ··············· **3**:342a
Ishizaka Taizō ··············· **3**:347a
leadership effectiveness ········· **4**:188a
oil crisis of 1973 ··············· **4**:188b
political influence ··············· **4**:188b
Uemura Kōgorō ······· **4**:188b; **8**:127b
Keiei keizaigaku sōron
·········経営経済学総論 ···· **8**:127a
Keien isshi · 桂園一枝 ···· **4**:103a
Keien school · 桂園派 ···· **8**:216a
Keifugaku. 系譜学 ······· *See* **Genealogy**
Keigo. *See* **Honorific language**
Keihan Electric Railway Co, Ltd ·· **4**:188b
**Keihin Electric Express Railway Co,
Ltd** ····················· **4**:188b
Keihin Industrial Zone
·········京浜工業地帯 ·· **4**:154a, 183a,
188b–189a; **8**:329b
Ōta Ward ··················· **6**:129b
Shinagawa Ward ··············· **7**:108b
Keiji soshōhō kōgi
·········刑事訴訟法講義 ···· **6**:111b
Keijō nippō ·······京城日報 ···· **4**:283a
Keijo Shūrin · 景徐周麟 ···· **4**:147a
Keikō, Emperor · 景行天皇 ···· **4**:189a
Yamatotakeru, Prince ··········· **8**:311a
Keikō film ················ **2**:269b–270a
Keikokushū ·······経国集 **1**:293a; **4**:189a;
5:29b
Keiō University ··········· **3**:133a; **4**:189a
Keiō University Hiyoshi Dormitory · **7**:341b
Keiran jūyō shū
·········渓嵐拾葉集 ···· **7**:127b
Keiretsu ···· **4**:47a, 189a–189b; **7**:266b–267a
general trading companies ······· **4**:189b
kigyō ··························· **4**:189a
kin'yū ··························· **4**:189a
modern economy ··············· **2**:163a
ownership ties ··············· **4**:189b
shihon ··························· **4**:189a
zaibatsu subsidiaries ··········· **4**:189a
Keirin Gakumei (Statecraft Study
Association) ··················· **8**:130b
Keisai ···········渓斎 ···· **4**:189b
Keisai Eisen ···渓斎英泉 · **4**:189b–190a
erotica ··························· **4**:189b
Mumeiō zuihitsu ··············· **4**:189b
surimono ······················· **4**:189b
Keisatsu Yobitai. *See* **National Police
Reserve**
Kei school ··················· **4**:190a
Keisei ehon ·傾城絵本 ···· **8**:78b

Keisei Electric Railway Co, Ltd ··· **4**:190a
Keisei irojamisen
(Courtesan Samisen of
Love) ······傾城色三味線 ······· **8**:144a
Keisen Jogakuen ··············· **4**:179a
Keishi ···············家司 ···· **4**:190a
Keishichō ·······警視庁 ···· **8**:67b–68a
Keishinshi (stepparent-child
relationships) ··············· **6**:162b
Keishū Bungaku Kai
·········閨秀文学会 ···· **7**:54b
Keitai, Emperor · 継体天皇 · **4**:190a–190b
Emperor Jimmu ··············· **4**:57b
Emperor Ōjin ············· **4**:190a–190b
Nihon shoki ··················· **4**:190a
Ōtomo no Kanamura ··········· **4**:190a
Keiyaku ··························· **4**:308a
Keiyakuhō ·······契約法 ···· **7**:255b
Keiyō Industrial Region
·········京葉工業地帯 ······· **8**:339b
Keizai Antei Hombu ··········· **2**:168a
Keizai Dōyū Kai. 経済同友会 *See* **Japan
Committee for Economic Development**
Keizai hakusho ··············· **8**:251b
Keizai hyōron ·······経済評論 ···· **4**:300a
Keizai Jissō Hōkokusho
(Report on Actual
Economic Conditions)
·········経済実相報告書 ···· **8**:251b
Keizai kanchō ··················· **4**:190b
Economic Planning Agency ····· **4**:190b
Ministry of Construction ······· **4**:190b
Ministry of Finance ··········· **4**:190b
Ministry of Foreign Affairs ····· **4**:190b
Ministry of International Trade and
Industry ··················· **4**:190b
Ministry of Transport ··········· **4**:190b
Keizai Kikaku Chō. 経済企画庁 *See*
Economic Planning Agency
Keizai rinri no kōzō
·········経済倫理の構造 ···· **7**:258a
Keizai sanron (Essays on
Economics) ·······経済纂論 ···· **6**:126a
Keizai shinkaron
·········経済進化論 ···· **7**:359a
Keizai shōgaku · 経済小学 ···· **4**:137b
*Keizai tetsugaku no kihon
mondai*
·········経済哲学の基本問題 ···· **7**:258a
Keizai zasshi ·······経済雑誌 ···· **4**:316a
Keizan Jōkin ·······瑩山紹瑾 ···· **4**:190b
Keizan oshō shingi
·········瑩山和尚清規 ···· **4**:190b
Keizu ···············系図 ···· **3**:17a
Kellner, Oscar ··············· **4**:190b–191a
Kellogg-Briand Pact (1928) **4**:191a; **8**:272b
Tanaka Giichi ············· **7**:336a–336b
war crimes trials ··············· **8**:224b
Kelsen, Hans ··················· **4**:375a
Kelsenists ······················· **4**:375a
Keman ··························· **1**:196*b*
Kemari ···············蹴鞠 · **4**:191a, 381a
Asukai Masatsune ··············· **1**:106b
leisure-time activities ··········· **4**:381a
Kembun gunshō ·見聞軍抄 ···· **4**:187b
Kembunshū ·······見聞集 ···· **4**:187b
Kemi ···············検見 ·· **4**:191a–191b
inspection methods ········· **4**:191a–191b
Land Tax Reform of 1873–1881 ·· **4**:191b
tax-adjustment methods ····· **4**:191a–191b
Kemmi ···············検見 ·· **4**:191a–191b
Kemminshi ·······遣明使 ···· **7**:144a
Kemmu irai tsuika hō
·········建武以来追加法 ···· **4**:90a
Kemmu nenchū gyōji
·········建武年中行事 ···· **4**:191b
Kemmu nenkan ki
·········建武年間記 ···· **4**:191b

Kemmu Restoration
·········建武中興 ···· **3**:172a;
4:191b–192b; **7**:66a
Ashikaga Takauji ····· **1**:100a; **4**:191b–192b
court ceremonies ··············· **4**:191b
failure ··················· **4**:139b, 192b
Fujiwara no Fujifusa ··········· **2**:350b
Go-Daigo, Emperor · **3**:39a; **4**:191b–192b
Go-Fukakusa, Emperor ········· **4**:192a
historical assessment ··········· **4**:192b
Hōjō family ········· **3**:211a; **4**:192b
imperial restoration concept ····· **4**:191b
Jinnō shōtōki ··············· **4**:59b–60a
Kamakura shogunate ··········· **4**:192a
Kameyama, Emperor ··········· **4**:192b
Kōgon's abdication ··············· **4**:249a
Kusunoki Masashige ··········· **4**:192b
Nawa Nagatoshi ··············· **5**:353b
Nitta Yoshisada ··············· **4**:192a
restoration ··················· **4**:192a
rinji ······························· **6**:318a
Sasaki Takauji ··················· **7**:23b
shōen ··························· **7**:158a
warrior government ············· **8**:229b
Kemmu Restoration government
Nakasendai Rebellion ··········· **5**:317b
Kemmu Shikimoku
·········建武式目 ···· **4**:192b, 377a;
7:73b, 96a
dosō ··························· **2**:132a
Sasaki Takauji ··················· **7**:23b
supplementary articles ··········· **4**:90a
Kempei. *See* **Military police** (pre-World
War II)
Kempeitai in Korea ··············· **4**:282a
Kempō Chōsakai. *See* **Commission on
the Constitution**
Kempō gige ·······憲法義解 ·· **4**:192b–193a
Kempō Mondai Kenkyūkai. *See*
Constitutional Problems Study Group
Kempō satsuyō · 憲法撮要 ···· **4**:193a
Hozumi Yatsuka ··············· **4**:193a
Minobe Tatsukichi ··············· **4**:193a
Uesugi Shinkichi ··············· **4**:193a
Ken ···············拳 ···· **4**:193a;
8:239b, 240a
standardization ··················· **1**:82b
Kenchi ···············検地 ·· **4**:193a–195a
Chōsokabe family ··············· **4**:193a
cultivator class ············· **4**:194a–194b
Edo period ····················· **4**:193a
heinō bunri ··················· **4**:194a
Hōjō family ··················· **4**:193b
Imagawa family ··············· **4**:193b
Ishida Mitsunari ··············· **4**:193b
kokudaka ······················· **4**:194a
land registration ··············· **4**:194a
Land Tax Reform of 1873–1881 ·· **4**:195a
Mōri family ··················· **4**:193b
Muromachi period ··············· **4**:193a
national implementation ········· **4**:193b
Oda Nobunaga ··············· **4**:193b
samurai ··················· **4**:194a–194b
sashidashi ····················· **4**:193a
sengoku daimyō ············· **4**:193a–193b
Shimazu family ··············· **4**:193b
social results ············· **4**:194b–195a
standard measures ········· **4**:193b–194a
Taikō ··················· **4**:193b–195a
Takeda family ··················· **4**:193b
Tokugawa family ··············· **4**:193b
Toyotomi Hideyoshi ··········· **4**:193b
yield measurements ············· **4**:194a
Kenchichō (land register)
·········検地帳 ···· **4**:194b
Kenchiku girei ··················· **4**:195a
chōna hajime ··················· **4**:195a
ishibatsuki ····················· **4**:195a

jichinsai · 4:195a
koyairi · 4:195a
muneage · 4:195a
omoto · 4:195a
shimenawa · · · · · · · · · · · · · · · · · · · 4:195a
shinchiku iwai · · · · · · · · · · · · · · · 4:195a
tatemae · 4:195a
tōryō okuri · · · · · · · · · · · · · · · · · · 4:195a
yautsuri · 4:195a
Kenchōji · · · · · · · · · · · 建長寺 · · · · · · 4:120b,
195a-195b
Kenchōji-bune · · 建長寺船 · · · · · · 4:195b
Kenchū · · · · · · · · · · · · · · 検注 · · · · · · · 4:193a
Kenchūchō · · · · · · · · · · 検注帳
ōtabumi · 6:128a
Kendan · · · · · · · · · · · · · 検断 · · · · · · 4:195b
jitō · 4:195b
shugo · 4:195b
Kendan sata · · · · · · · · · · 検断沙汰 · · · · 4:195b
Kendō 剣道 · · · · 4:195b-196a, 196b
All Japan Kendō Federation · · · · 4:196a
grades · 4:196a
International Kendō Federation · · · 4:196a
kangeiko · 4:140b
matches · 4:196a
naginata · · · · · · · · · · · · · · · · · · 5:308a-308b
school curriculum · · · · · · · · · · · · · 4:196a
schools · 4:196a
training · 4:196a
Ken'eki · 6:274a
Ken'etsu Seido Kaisei Kisei Dōmei
(Organization
for the Revision of the Censorship
System) · 1:253a
Kengiroku · · · · · · · · 顕偽録 · · · · · · 7:186a
Kenin · · · · · · · · · · · · · · 家人 · · 4:196b; 7:7b,
62a
Kenjichi · 7:87a
Kenjinkai (group of persons born in
the same prefecture) · · · · · 4:14b; 6:205a
Kenji sannen ki 建治三年記 · · · · 4:255b
Kenjutsu · · · · · · · · 剣術 3:253a; 4:195b
Kenka ryōseibai
喧嘩両成敗 · · · · 4:196b
Kujikata Osadamegaki · · · · · · · · 4:196b
Sengoku daimyō · · · · · · · · · · · · · 4:196b
Kenkoku Kinembi
建国記念日 · · · · 4:204a
Kenkyō ruiten · · · · 憲教類典 · · · · 4:269b
Kennaiki · · · · · · · · · · 建内記 · · 4:196b-197a
Kennedy, John F. · · · · · · · · · · · · · 3:265a
Ikeda Hayato · · · · · · · · · · · · · · · · 4:285a
Kennedy Round talks · · · · · · · · · 8:161b
tariffs · · · · · · · · · · · · · · · · · · 7:346b-347a
Kenninji · · · · · · · · · · · 建仁寺 · · 4:197a-197b
paintings · 4:110b
Kennyo Kōsa · · · · · 顕如光佐 · · · · 3:346b
Kenrei Mon'in · · · · · · 県令 · · · · · · 4:197b
Kenrei Mon'in · · · · 建礼門院 · · · · · · 4:1a
Kenrei Mon'in Ukyō no
Daibu shū
· · · · · · 建礼門院右京大夫集 · · 4:197b-198a;
5:40a
Kenrikin. See **Key money**
Kenri ran'yō no kenkyū
· · · · · · · · · · 権利濫用の研究 · · · · · · 7:255b
Kenri shingai ron
· · · · · · · · · · · 権利侵害論 · · · · · · 7:255b
Kenrokuen · · · · · · · 兼六園 · · 3:9a; 4:136a,
198a
Kenryaku gyoki · · 建暦御記 · · · · 4:210b
Kensatsukan (public prosecutors) · · 6:266a
Kensei Hontō (True
Constitutional Party)
· · · · · · · · · · · · · · 憲政本党 4:198a; 6:210a
Kenseitō · 4:198b
Ōkuma Shigenobu · · · · · 4:198a; 6:96a
Rikken Kokumintō · · · · · · · · · · · 6:314b

Rikken Seiyūkai alliance · · · · · · · · 4:198a
Kenseikai (Constitutional
Association) · · · · · · · · 憲政会 · · · · 4:198a;
5:316a-316b; 6:210a; 7:55a, 66b
Kakushin Kurabu · · · · · · · · · · · · 4:120a
Katō Takaaki · · · · · · · · · · · · · · · · 4:198a
Kiyoura Keigo · · · · · · · · · · · · · · · 4:233a
Peace Preservation Law of 1925 · · · 4:198a
Rikken Minseitō · · · · · · · · 4:198a; 6:315a
Rikken Seiyūkai alliance · · · · · · · · 4:198a
Tanaka Giichi · · · · · · · · · · · · · · · · 4:198a
Universal Manhood Suffrage Movement
· 8:169b
Wakatsuki Reijirō · · · · · · · · · · · · 4:198a
Kenseitō (Constitutional
Party) · · · · · · · · · · · · · 憲政党 · · · · 3:196b;
4:198a-198b 6:210a
hambatsu · 3:92a
Itagaki Taisuke · · · · · · · · · 3:350a; 4:198b
Itō Hirobumi · · · · · · · · · · · · · · · · · 3:353a
Ozaki Yukio · · · · · · · · · · · · · · · · · 4:198b
Rikken Seiyūkai · · · · · · · · 4:198b; 6:315a
Shimpotō · 7:108b
Kensei Yōgo Undō. See **Movement to**
Protect Constitutional Government
Kensetsushō. 建設省
See **Ministry of Construction**
Kenshō · · · · · · · · · · · · · · 顕昭 · 4:198b; 5:15a
Jakuren · · · · · · · · · · · · · · · · 4:1b, 198b
Kenshōin · · · · · · · · · · · 見性院 · · · · · 8:302a
Kenshō In Naifu ki
· · · · · · · · · · · · · 建聖院内府記 · · · · 4:196b
Kentōshi. 遣唐使 *See* **Sui and**
Tang (T'ang) China, embassies to
Kenuki · · · · · · · · · · · · · · 毛抜 · · · 4:98a-98b
Ken'yakurei · · · · · · · · 倹約令 · · · · 4:198b
Ken'yūsha · · · · · · · · · 硯友社 1:163b, 208a;
4:198b-199b; 5:18b, 7:358b
evolution · · · · · · · · · · · · · · · 4:198b-199a
Garakuta bunko · · · · · · · · · 4:198b; 5:22a
Ozaki Kōyō · · · · · · · · · · · · · 4:199b; 6:139b
significance · · · · · · · · · · · · · · · · · · 4:199b
Yamada Bimyō · · · · · · · · · · 4:198b; 8:288b
Kenzan · · · · · · · · · · · · · 乾山 · · · · · 2:346a;
4:199b-200a, 337a
Hon'ami Kōetsu · · · · · · · · · · · · · 4:199b
Kōrin's collaborations · · · · · · · · · 4:293a
Nonomura Ninsei · · · · · · · · 4:199b; 6:35a
plate by · *1:262b*
Raku ware · · · · · · · · · · · · · · · · · · · 4:199b
teabowl by · · · · · · · · · · · · · · · · · · · *4:199a*
Kenzō. See **Takada Kenzō**
Kenzuishi. 遣隋使 *See* **Sui and**
Tang (T'ang) China, embassies to
Kenzuishi and kentōshi
遣隋使, 遣唐使 · · 7:259b-261a
Keppan · · · · · · · · · · · · · 血判 · · · · · · 4:200a
Kerama Islands
慶良間列島 · · · · 4:200a
Kesaku. See **Gesaku**
Kesatuan Melayu Muda (KMM) · · · 2:348b
Kesennuma · · · · · · · · · 気仙沼 · · · · 4:200a
Keshin · · · · · · · · · · · · · · · · · · · 1:122b-123a
Keshōjio · 2:25b
Keshōmawashi · · · · · · · · · · · · · · · 7:272a
Kessen no ōzora e
(Toward a Decisive
Battle in the Sky)
· · · · · · · · · · 決戦の大空へ · · · · 8:319b
Ketsumeidan
Inoue Nisshō · · · · · · · · · · · · · · · · 3:311a
Ketsumeidan Jiken. 血盟団事件 *See*
League of Blood Incident
Ketsuzei ikki · · · · 血税一揆 · · 4:200a-200b
Keyaki · 8:369b
Key money · · · · · · · · · · · · · · · · · · 4:200b

K. Hattori & Co, Ltd · · · · · 3:113b; 4:200b
Khubilai Khan · · · · · · 忽必烈汗 · · · 3:171a;
5:243b-245a
Khvostov, Nikolai Aleksandrovich · · 6:341a
Ki · · · · · · · · · · · · · · · · · · 気 · 4:200b-201a;
7:190a-190b
Kiaochow concession. *See* **Jiaozhou**
(Kiaochow) concession
Kibachi (horntails) · · · · · · · · · · · · · 1:149a
Ki Baitei · · · · · · · · · · · 紀梅亭 1:211a; 4:201a
Kiba minzoku setsu · · · · · · · · 3:229a-231a
Kibei · 4:14b
Kibi Daijin nittō ekotoba
· · · · · · · · · · · · 吉備大臣入唐絵詞 · · 4:201b
Kibi Kōgen · · · · · · · · · 吉備高原 · 4:128a, 201a
Kibi no Makibi · · · · · · 吉備真備 · 4:201a-201b
Abe no Nakamaro · · · · · · · · · · · · 4:201a
Fujiwara no Hirotsugu, Rebellion of
· 2:351a
Fujiwara no Nakamaro · · · · · · · · 4:201a
Gembō · · · · · · · · · · · · · · · · 3:16a; 4:201a
kakun · 4:118a
ritsuryō system · · · · · · · · · · · · · · · 6:331b
Sui and Tang (T'ang) China, embassies to
· 7:260a
Tachibana no Moroe · · · · · · · · · · 4:201a
Kibune Shrine · · · · · · 貴船神社 · · 4:201b
Kibuneyama · · · · · · · · 貴船山 · · · · 4:201b
Kibutsu poetry · · · · · · · · · · · · · · · · 5:106a
Kibyōshi · · · · · · · · · · · · 黄表紙 · · · 4:61a,
201b-202a; 5:49a; 7:18a, 96b; 8:141b
format · 4:201b
Hōseidō Kisanji · · · · · · · · · 3:234b; 4:202a
Koikawa Harumachi · · · · · · · · · · 4:250a
Shikatsube Magao · · · · · · · · · · · · 7:95a
Kichigai buraku shūyū
kikō 気違い部落周遊紀行 · · 4:202a
Kichijō Kekae ceremony · · · · · · · · 8:286a
Kichijōten · · · · · · · · 吉祥天 · 1:185a; 4:77b
Kichi mondai · · · · · · · · · · · · · 8:167b-168b
Kidai · 3:81b
Kida Minoru · · · · · · · きだみのる · · 4:202a
Kido Jun'ichirō 木戸準一郎 · · · · · · 4:203a
Kido Kanji · · · · · · · · · 木戸貫治 · · · 4:203a
Kido Kōichi · · · · · · · · 木戸幸一 · · · 4:202a
Konoe Fumimaro cabinet · · · · · · 4:202a
lord keeper of the privy seal · 5:310a-310b
war crimes conviction · · · · · · · · · 4:202a
Kido Kōin. 木戸孝允 *See* **Kido Takayoshi**
Kido nikki · · · · · · · · · 木戸日記 · · · 4:202a
Kido Shirō · · · · · · · · · 城戸四郎 · · · 4:202a
Kidōtai · · · · · · · · · · · · · · · · · · · 6:320a-320b
Kido Takayoshi · · · 木戸孝允 · 4:202b-203a;
7:29b, 51a
cabinet critic · · · · · · · · · · · · · 4:203a-203b
Assembly of Prefectural Governors
· 4:203a
Land Tax Reform of 1873-1881 · · 4:203a
Chōshū samurai · · · · · · · · · · · · · · 4:202b
Egawa Tarōzaemon · · · · · · · · · · · 4:202b
Western Learning · · · · · · · · · · · · · 4:202b
Yoshida Shōin · · · · · · · · · · · · · · · 4:202b
Meiji councillor · · · · · · · · · · · · · · 4:203a
Charter Oath · · · · · · · · · · · 1:267a; 4:203a
Iwakura mission · · · · · · · · · · · · · · 4:203a
modernization policies · · · · · · · · · 4:203a
Restoration activist · · · · · · · · · · · 4:202b
Coup d'Etat of 30 September 1863
· 4:202b
Hamaguri Gomon Incident · · · · · 4:202b
Sakamoto Ryōma · · · · · · · · · · · · · 4:203a
Shinagawa Yajirō · · · · · · · · · · · · · 7:109a
Kienrei · · · · · · · · · · · · · 棄捐令 · · · · 4:203b
Ki family · · · · · · · · · · · 紀氏 · · · · · · 4:203b
Kiga kaikyō (The Straits of
Starvation) · · · · · · · · · 飢餓海峡 · · · 8:89a
Uchida Tomu · · · · · · · · · · · · · · · · 8:124a
Kiganjo · 4:195b

Kigen ·········紀元 ······ 1:232a; 4:203b–204a
  Emperor Jimmu ······ 4:57a, 203b
  Kigensetsu ······ 4:204a
  periodization ······ 6:175a
  Tokugawa Nariaki ······ 4:204a
Kigensetsu ···· 紀元節 ······ 4:204a
Kigensetsu controversy ······ 4:204a
Kiguchi Kohei ····木口小平 ······ 4:204a
Kihara Hitoshi ····木原均 1:156a; 4:204b
Kihara Institute for Biological Research
  ······ 4:204b
Kiheitai ······ 奇兵隊 ···· 1:86a; 4:204b
  Boshin Civil War ······ 4:204b
  Ikuno Disturbance ······ 3:271a
  Shimonoseki Bombardment ······ 4:204b
  Takasugi Shinsaku ···· 4:204b; 7:319a–319b
  Yamagata Aritomo ······ 4:204b
Kihira Masami ···· 紀平正美 ······ 4:204b
Kihira Tadayoshi 紀平正美 ······ 4:204b
Kii Channel ····紀伊水道 ······ 4:204b
Kii Mountains ····紀伊山地 ······ 4:204b
Kii Ōshima ····紀伊大島 ······ 6:125a
Kii Peninsula ····紀伊半島 ······ 4:205a
Kiji. See **Pheasants**
Kijibiki ······ 4:205a
Kijishi ······ 4:205a
Kijiya ······ 4:205a
  rokuro ······ 6:335b
Kikai kanran (Beholding the Waves in the Sea of Ether) ···· 気海観瀾 ······ 8:242b
Kikai kanran kōgi
  ····気海観瀾広義 ······ 4:181b
"Kikai" (Machine) ····機械 ······ 8:332b
Kikaishima ····喜界島 ······ 4:205a
Kikajin ······帰化人 ······ 1:147b; 4:205a–205b, 338a; 7:256a
  Aya family ······ 4:205b
  Buddhism introduction ······ 4:205b
  court rank ······ 4:205b
  Hata family ······ 4:205b
  periods of arrival ······ 4:205b
  Sakanoue family ······ 4:205b
  Shiba Tatto ······ 4:205b
  titles ······ 4:89a
  Wani ······ 4:205b
  Yamato court ······ 4:277a
  Yuzuki no Kimi ······ 4:205a
Kikakuin Jiken ·企画院事件 ······ 6:189b
Kikawada Kazutaka
  ····木川田一隆 ····2:167b; 4:205b
Kike wadatsumi no koe
  ····きけわだつみのこえ ······ 4:206a
Kikikata ······聞方 ······ 4:119b
Kikkōchiku ······ 1:135b
Kikkōman Corporation ······ 4:206a
  Kikkōman Foods, Inc ······ 4:206a
  Kikkōman International, Inc ······ 4:206a
  Kikkōman Trading Europe, GmbH · 4:206a
Kikō ······ 8:104b–106a
Kiku ······ 1:310a–311a
Kikuchi ······菊池 ······ 4:206a
Kikuchi Dairoku 菊池大麓 ······ 4:206a
Kikuchi family ····菊池氏 ···4:206a–206b
Kikuchi Hiroshi ····菊池寛 ······ 4:206b
Kikuchi Kan ····菊池寛 ···· 4:206b–207a; 7:81a, 103b, 109a, 125a, 126b
  Bungei Shunjū ····1:209b–210a; 4:206b
  fūzoku shōsetsu ······ 2:378b
  literary prizes ···· 4:206b–207a; 5:24b
  radio drama ······ 6:275a
  sponsorship of Furukawa Roppa ··· 2:373a
  Yamamoto Yūzō ······ 4:206b
Kikuchi Seishi 菊池正士 ······ 4:207a
Kikuchi Taisuke ·菊池太輔 ···· 7:96b–97b

Kiku gashira kōmori (*Rhinolophus ferrumequinum*) ······ 1:146b
Kikumura Itaru ····菊村到 ······ 4:207a
Kiku no Sekku. 菊の節句
  See **Chrysanthemum Festival**
Kikuta Kazuo ····菊田一夫 ···· 4:207a–207b
  dramatic serials ······ 4:207a
  Furukawa Roppa ···· 2:373a; 4:207a
  plays ······ 4:207a
  radio drama ······ 6:275b
Kikutake Kiyonori
  ······菊竹清訓 ······ 4:207b
Kikutake Sunao 菊竹淳 ······ 4:207b
Kikuta Noboru ····菊田登 ······ 1:15b
Kikyō [(balloonflower) *Platycodon grandiflorum*] ······ 4:207b
Kikyō (Homecoming) ·帰郷 ······ 6:221b
Kilns ······ 1:256a–265b; 7:91a
Kimbusenji ······金峰山寺 ···· 4:207b–208a
Kimbusen Shugen Honshū
  ······金峰山修験本宗 ······ 4:207b
Kim Ch'angam ······ 4:208a
Kim Ch'angsu ······ 4:208a
Kim Dae-jung ······ 4:211a
Kim Gu ······ 4:208a
Kimi ······君 ···· 4:89a, 310a
Kimigayo (His Majesty's Reign) ······君が代 ······ 5:336a
Kimiidera ······紀三井寺 ······ 4:208a
Kim Il-sŏng ······ 4:208b
  Japanese imperialism ······ 4:284a
  Kapsan faction ······ 4:208b
  Korean People's Liberation Army · 4:208b
  premiership ······ 4:208b
Kimi no na wa (What's Your Name?) ····君の名は ······ 6:275b
Kimi Pass ······紀見峠 ······ 4:208b
Kimitsu ······君津 ······ 4:208b
Kim Jong-p'il ······ 4:211a, 285a
Kimmeichiku (*Phyllostachys bambusoides var. castillonis*) ······ 1:135b
Kimmei, Emperor 欽明天皇 4:208b; 7:264a
Kimmon Incident. 禁門の変
  See **Hamaguri Gomon Incident**
Kim-Ōhira Memorandum ······ 4:288a
Kimoiri. See **Shōya**
Kim Ok-kyun ······ 4:209a
  assassination of ······ 4:281a
  Fukuzawa Yukichi ······ 4:209a
  Independence Party ······ 4:209a
  Japanese visit ······ 4:280b
  Kaehwap'a ······ 4:101b, 209a
  Kapsin Political Coup ······ 4:156b, 209a
Kimon ······ 4:163a
Kimono ······着物 1:329a; 4:209a, 209b, 210a–210b; 7:272b; 8:358b
  atsuita ······ 1:115b
  caring ······ 4:210b
  dyes and dye colors ······ 2:136b
  how to wear ······ 4:210a
  kara-ori ······ 4:158a
  kosode predecessor ·1:332b; 2:90b; 4:209a
  men's ······ 4:209b
  ro and sha ······ 6:333a
  sarasa (calico; batik) silk ······ 7:21a
  style and tailoring ······ 4:210a
  tasuki ······ 7:348a
  textiles, care and preservation of ·· 8:20a
  women's ······ 4:209b–210a
Kimpira ······金平 ······ 4:77a
Kimpishō ······禁秘抄 ······ 4:210b
Kimpokusan ······金北山 ······ 4:210b
Kimpusan ······金峰山 1:272a; 4:153b, 211a
Kim Sŏng-ju ······ 4:208b
Kim Tae-jung ······ 4:211a
  Japanese-Korean relations ······ 4:286a

Kim Tal-su ······ 4:211a
Kimura Hisashi ····木村栄 ······ 4:211a
Kimura Ihei ····木村伊兵衛 ······ 6:185a
Kimura Kaishū. 木村芥舟 See **Kimura Yoshitake**
Kimura Ki ····木村毅 ···· 4:211a–211b
Kimura Motoo ····木村資生 ······ 4:211b
Kimura Shigenari 木村重成 ······ 4:211b
  Tōdō Takatora ······ 4:211b
  Tokugawa Hidetada ······ 4:211b
  Tokugawa Ieyasu ······ 4:211b
  Toyotomi Hideyori ······ 4:211b
  Uesugi Kagekatsu ······ 4:211b
Kimura Toshio 木村俊夫
  visit to Africa ······ 1:19b
Kimura Yoshitake
  ······ 木村喜毅 ······ 4:211b
  Kanrin maru ······ 4:151b, 211b
  Katsu Kaishū ······ 4:211b
Kin ······ 7:87b
Kinai ······畿内 ···· 4:211b–212a
Kin Bay ······金武湾 ······ 4:212a
Kinchū Narabi ni Kuge Shohatto
  ······禁中並公家諸法度 ······ 3:186b; 4:212a
  Tokugawa shogunate ······ 8:53a–53b
Kindai bungaku 近代文学 4:212a; 6:230b
Kindai bungaku nōto
  ······近代文学ノート ······ 4:172a
Kindai Bungaku Kondan Kai ······ 5:19b
Kindaichi Haruhiko
  ······金田一春彦 ······ 4:31b
Kindaichi Kyōsuke
  ······金田一京助 ···· 1:36b; 4:212a
Kin Daichū ······金大中 ······ 4:211a
Kindai Eiga Kyōkai ······ 2:275b
Kindai kaiga ····近代絵画 ······ 5:13a
Kindai keizaigaku shi
  ······近代経済学史 ······ 7:258a
Kindai ōshū keizaishi josetsu (Introduction to Modern European Economic History)
  ······近代欧州経済史序説 ······ 6:134a
Kindai seikatsu ····近代生活 ······ 7:175b
Kindai shisō (Modern Thought) ····近代思想 ······ 1:72a
  Ōsugi Sakae ······ 6:127b
Kindergarten Order (Yōchien Rei) 6:235b
Kindergartens. See **Preschool education**
Kinema Jumpō Prize
  Tanaka Kinuyo ······ 7:337a
King of Chūzan ····中山王 ······ 1:314b
Kingu ······キング ······ 4:212b
Kingu Prize ······ 4:242a
Kingyo ······ 3:43b
Kin Gyokukin ····金玉均 ······ 4:209a
Kingyotsubaki ······ 1:237a
Kinkafu ······琴歌譜 ······ 4:297a
  early Japanese songs ······ 2:138a
Kinkai wakashū
  ······金槐和歌集 ······ 4:212b
  Minamoto no Sanetomo ···· 4:122a, 212b; 5:179a
Kinkakuji ······金閣寺 ······ 4:213a, 336a–336b
  Golden Pavilion ······ *4:212b*
Kinkazan ······金華山 ···· 4:213a; 7:16a
Kinki Electrical Construction Co, Inc
  ······ 4:213a
Kinki kakumei 錦旗革命
  October Incident ······ 6:60a
Kinkikan Incident
  ······錦輝館事件 ······ 6:285a–285b
Kinki Nippon Railway Co, Ltd ···· 4:213b
  Nagoya Railroad Co, Ltd ······ 5:309b

Kinkin sensei eiga no yume (Mr. Glitter n' Gold's Dream of Splendor)
　　　金々先生栄花夢 · 4:201b, 250a
Kinki region 　近畿地方 · 4:151b, 213b
　parks · · · · · · · · · · · · · · 4:213b
　urban planning · · · · · · · 8:179b
Kinki Region Development Law · 4:213b
Kinki shoga 　琴棋書画 · 4:213b–214a
Kinko (cucumber) · · · · · · 7:45a
Kinkō Bay · · · · · · · 錦江湾 · 4:105b
Kinkō bunseki no kihon mondai (Basic Problems of Equilibrium Analysis)
　　　均衡分析の基本問題 · · · 8:319a
Kinkyōrei · · · · 禁教令 · 1:64b–65a
Kin Kyū · · · · · · · · 金九 · 4:208a
Kin Nissei · · · 金日成 · 4:208a–208b
Kinnōka · · · · · · 勤皇家 · 2:205a
Ki no Kaion · · · · 紀海音 · 4:214a
　jōruri plays · · · · · · · · · · · 4:77a
　Kyūemon and Matsuyama romance 4:93b
Kinokawa · · · · · · · 紀ノ川 · 4:214a
Kinoko · · · · · · · · 5:282a–282b
Kinokuniya Bunzaemon
　　　紀国屋文左衛門 · · · 4:214a
　chōnin · · · · · · · · · · · · · 1:302a
Kinosaki · · · · · · · · 城崎 · 4:214a; 7:11b
Kinoshita Chōshōshi
　　　木下長嘯子 4:214b; 7:105a;
　　　　　　　　　　　 8:215b
Kinoshita Jun'an 　木下順庵 · · · · · · 4:214b
　Amenomori Hōshū · · · · · · 4:214b
　Arai Hakuseki · · · · · · · · 4:214b
　Kaibara Ekiken · · · · · · · 4:108b
　Maeda Tsunanori · · · · · · 4:214b
　Matsunaga Sekigo · · · · · · 4:214b
　Miyake Kanran · · · · · · · 4:214b
　Muro Kyūsō · · · · · · · · · 4:214b
　Tokugawa Tsunayoshi · · · · 4:214b
Kinoshita Junji · 木下順二 · 2:76b;
　　　　 4:214b–215b; 5:59b
　Shingeki · · · · · · · · · · 7:112a, 113a
　Yamamoto Yasue · · · · · 4:214b; 8:299b
Kinoshita Keisuke
　　　木下恵介 · 2:272a–272b,
　　　　 273b–274a; 4:215b
　Shindō Kaneto · · · · · · · 7:111a
Kinoshita Mokutarō
　　　木下杢太郎 4:215b; 7:253b
Kinoshita Naoe · 木下尚江 · 1:155a;
　　　　 4:215b–216a; 7:74a–74b
　Futsū Senkyo Kisei Dōmeikai · · · · · · 2:376a
　pacifism · · · · · 4:215b–216a; 6:143b
Kinoshita Rigen · 木下利玄 · 4:216a
Kinoshita Takafumi
　　　木下幸文 · · · 4:216a
Kinoshita Takeji · 木下竹次 · 7:36a
Ki no Tomonori · 紀友則 · 4:216a–216b;
　　　　 7:13a
　Kokinshū · · · · · · · · · · · 4:254b
Ki no Tsurayuki · · · · 紀貫之 · · · 1:18a, 85b;
　2:301b; 4:216b–217a; 5:14a; 6:113b, 299a;
　　　　 7:13a, 42b; 8:287b
　court poet · · · · · · · · · · · 4:216a
　imperial poetry anthology · · · · 4:216b
　Kagawa Kageki · · · · · · · 4:103a
　Kokinshū · · · · · · · · · · · 4:254b
　poetic style · · · · · · · · · · 2:352a
　Shin kokinshū · · · · · · · · 7:120a
　Tosa nikki · · · · · · · · · 4:216b
Kinō wa kyō no monogatari
　　　きのふはけふの物語 · · · 6:282a
Kinran and ginran · · · · 4:217a
Kinrō Kokumintō
　　　勤労国民党 · · · · · · 1:2b
Kinroku kōsai · 金禄公債 · 4:217a
Kinsaku · · · · · · · · · · · · 1:144a

Kinsei kijin den
　　　近世崎人伝 · · · · · · · 4:217a
Kinsei Nihon kokumin shi (A History of Early Modern Japan)
　　　近世日本国民史 · · · · · 8:60a
Kinsekibun 　金石文 · 3:313b–314a
Kinshi Kunshō · 金鵄勲章 · 4:217a
Kinship · · · · · · · · 4:217a–218b
　affines · · · · · · · · · · · · · 4:217b
　bilateral pattern · · · · · · · 4:217a
　cognates · · · · · · · · · · · · 4:217b
　composition of shinrui · · · · · 4:217b
　　head of household · · · · · 4:217b
　　socioeconomic obligation · · 4:217b
　Confucian influence · · · · · · 1:353b
　consanguinity · · · · 1:358b–359a
　dominant tendency of male side
　　　　 4:217b–218a
　　dōzoku · · · · · · · · · · · 4:218a
　　surnames · · · · · · · · · · 4:218a
　　virilocal marriage · · · · · · 4:217b
　honke and bunke · · · 3:223b–224a
　ie · · · · · · · · · · · · · · 3:260a
　importance of women in network
　　　　 4:218a–218b
　terminology · · · · · · · · · · 4:217a
Kinshō-Mataichi Corporation · · 4:218b
Kintarō · · · · · · · 金太郎 · 4:218b
Kintōshū · · · · · · · 公任集 · 8:188a
Kinu · · · · · · · · · · · · 7:194a
Kinugasa Teinosuke
　　　衣笠貞之助 · 2:56b, 269a,
　　　　 271a, 273b; 4:218b–219a
　Jigokumon · · · · · · · · · 4:219a
　Jūjiro · · · · · · · · · · · 4:218b
　Kawabata Yasunari · · · · · 4:218b
　Kurutta ippeiji · · · · · · 4:218b
　onnagata · · · · · · · · · · · 4:218b
Kinugawa · · · · · · 鬼怒川 · 4:219a
　Shimotsuma · · · · · · · · · 7:107a
Kinugawa Hot Spring
　　　鬼怒川温泉 · · · · · 4:219a
Kinunuibe · · · · · · 衣縫部 · 1:147b
Kinuta · · · · · · · · 砧 · 7:293a
Kin'yōshū · · · · · · 金葉集 · 4:219a–219b
Kin'yō wakashū
　　　金葉和歌集 2:350a; 3:275b;
　　　　 5:38a, 179b; 7:95a
　major poets · · · · · · 4:219a–219b
　Minamoto no Toshiyori · · · · 4:219a–219b;
　　　　 5:179b
Kin'yū keiretsu · · · · · · 4:189a
Kinza, ginza, and zeniza
　　　金座, 銀座, 銭座 · 4:219b–220a
　Gotō family · · · · · · 4:219b–220a
　ōban · · · · · · · · · · · · · 6:48a
　Tokugawa Ieyasu · · · · 4:219b–220a
Kioku to genzai 記憶と現在 · 6:113b
Kira Yoshinaka · 吉良義央 · 4:220a
　Forty-Seven Rōnin Incident · · 2:327a
Kiri. *See* **Paulownia**
Kiribi · · · · · · · · · · · · 4:220a
Kirigamine · · · · · 霧ケ峰 · 4:127b, 220b
Kirigirisu [(katydid) *Gampsocleis buergeri*] · · · · · · · · · · · 4:220b
Kirikane · · · · · · · 切金 · 4:220b–221a
Kirimai · · · · · · · 切米 · 4:221a
Kirin · · · · · · · · 麒麟 · 7:342b
Kirin Brewery Co, Ltd · · · · 4:221a
Kiri no naka · · · · · 霧の中 · 7:334a
Kirino Toshiaki · 桐野利秋 · 7:51a
Kirishima Volcanic Zone
　　　霧島火山帯 · · · · · · 4:221a
Kirishima-Yaku National Park 　霧島屋久国立公園 · 4:105a, 106a, 221a–221b; 5:304a

Kirishimayama · · · · 霧島山 · 4:105b, 221b
Kirishitan. *See* **Kakure Kirishitan**
Kirishitan-ban. 　切支丹版 *See* **Jesuit mission press**
Kirishitan daimyō. *See* **Christian daimyo**
Kirishitan monogatari
　　　切支丹物語 2:241a; 4:221b
Kirishitan Yashiki
　　　切支丹屋敷 · 4:221b–222a
Kirisute gomen · 切捨御免 · 4:222a
Kirisutoki · · 契利斯督記 · 7:186a
Kirisutokyō no gaidoku
　　　キリスト教の害毒 · · · · 4:168b
Kiritake Monjūrō II
　　　桐竹紋十郎(二代) · · · 4:222a
Kiritsunagi origami · · · · · 6:118a
Kiroku Shōen Kenkeijo
　　　記録荘園券契所 · · · 4:222a
Kirokutai · · · · · · · · 3:126b–127a
Kiryoka (travel poems)
　　　羇旅歌 · · · · · · · 8:104b
Kiryū · · · · · · · · 桐生 · 4:222a
　silk weaving · · · · · · · · · 2:296a
Kiryū Yūyū · · · 桐生悠々 · 4:222a
Kisaku. *See* **Gesaku**
Kisarazu · · · · · · · 木更津 · 4:222b
Kisatsu Seimu Iinkai
　　　冀察政務委員会 · · · · 4:53a
Kisegawa · · · · · · 黄瀬川 · 4:222b
Kisen
　Kokinshū · · · · · · · · · · 4:254b
Kisen Shūshō · 亀泉集証 · 4:147b
Kishibojin · · · · · 鬼子母神 · 4:222b
Kishida Ginkō · · 岸田吟香 · 4:222b
Kishida Kunio · · 岸田国士 · 4:222b
　fūzoku shōsetsu · · · · · · · 2:378b
　shingeki · · · · · · · · · · · 7:113a
Kishida Ryūsei · 岸田劉生 · 4:223a
　Kishida Ginkō · · · · · · · · 4:223a
　Kuroda Kiyoteru · · · · · · · 4:223a
　modern painting · · · · · · · 6:156a
　Mushanokōji Saneatsu · · · · 4:223a
Kishida Toshiko · 岸田俊子 · 4:223a; 7:54a
　Fukuda Hideko · · · · · · · 2:362a
Kishi-Eisenhower joint declaration 8:160b
Kishi Nobusuke · · 岸信介 2:333a; 3:289a;
　　　　 4:223a–223b; 7:275b
　Fujiyama Aiichirō · · · · · · 2:359a
　national defense · · · · 5:336b–338b
　United States-Japan security treaties
　　　　 8:166b
Kishi school · · · · · · 岸派 · 3:7b–8a
Kishi Seiichi · · · · 岸清一 · 4:223b
Kishiwada · · · · · · 岸和田 · 4:223b
Kishō-bori
　tattoos · · · · · · · · · · · · 7:350a
Kishōchō · · · · · · · 気象庁 · 5:165a
Kishōgaku · · · · · · 気象学 · 6:78b
Kishōgaku kōwa
　　　気象学講話 · · · · · · 6:78b
Kiska · · · · · · · · · · · · 4:223b
Kisodani · · · · · · · 木曽谷 · 4:223b
Kiso Fukushima · 木曽福島 · 4:223b–224a
Kisogawa · · · · · · 木曽川 4:224a; 5:303b
Kiso Kaidō rokujūkutsugi (69 Stations of the Kiso Kaidō Road)
　　　木曽街道六十九次 · · · 4:190a
Kisokoma · · · · · · · 木曽駒 · 4:265a
Kiso Komagatake
　　　木曽駒ケ岳 · · · · · 4:265a
Kiso Mountains · 木曽山脈 · 4:224a–224b
Kiso Ontake · · · · · 木曽御岳 · 6:112b
Kiso Yoshinaka. 　木曽義仲
　See **Minamoto no Yoshinaka**
Kissaten · · · · · · · · · · 1:334a–334b
Kissa yōjō ki · 喫茶養生記 · 2:187a
Kisuge · · · · · · · · · · · · 2:78b–79a

Kitabatake Akiie · 北畠顕家 · · · · · · · 4:224a
  Kō no Moronao destroyed · · · · · · · 4:275a
Kitabatake Chikafusa
  · · · · · · · · · · · · 北畠親房　4:224a; 7:164b
  historiography · · · · · · · · · · · · · · 3:153b
Kitabatake family · · · · · 北畠氏 · · 4:224b
Kita Chishima ainugo
  · · · · · · · · · 北千島アイヌ語 · · · · 1:36b
Kita Daitōjima · · · 北大東島 · · · · 4:224b
Kitadake · · · · · · · · · · 北岳 · · · · · · 4:224b
  Shirane Sanzan · · · · · · · · · · · · · 7:147a
Kitagata, Lake · · · · 北潟湖 · · · · · 1:125a
Kitagawa Fuyuhiko
  · · · · · · · · · · · · · 北川冬彦 · · · · · 4:224b
  Kajii Motojirō · · · · · · · · · · · · · · 4:114a
Kitagawa Morisada. 喜田川守貞
  See **Morisada mankō**
Kitagawa school 喜多川派 · 4:224b-225a
Kitagawa Utamaro. 喜多川歌麿
  See **Utamaro**
Kitahara Hakushū 北原白秋 · 4:225a;
                     7:253b; 8:341a
  "Jōgashima no ame" · · · · · · · · · 4:69a
Kitahara Takeo · 北原武夫 · 4:225a-225b
Kitahara Tasaku · · 北原多作 · · · 4:225b
Kita Ibaraki · · · · · · 北茨城 3:367b; 4:225b
Kita Ikki · · · · · · · · 北一輝 · 4:225b-226a
  February 26th Incident · · · · · · · 2:250a
Kitakami (city) · · · · 北上 · · · · · · 4:226a
Kitakami Basin · · 北上盆地 · · · · 4:226a
Kitakamigawa · · · · 北上川 · · · · · 4:226a
Kitakami Mountains
  · · · · · · · · · · · · · 北上山地 · 4:226a-226b
Kitakata · · · · · · · · 喜多方 · · · · · 4:226b
Kita Kyūshū · · · · 北九州 · 2:364b-365a;
                             4:226b
Kita Kyūshū Municipal Art Museum
  · 5:279a
Kitamaebune · · · · 北前船 · · · · · 4:112b
Kitami · · · · · · · · · · 北見 · · · · · · 4:226b
Kitami Mountains 北見山地 · · · 4:226b
Kitamori Kazō · · 北森嘉蔵 · · · · 4:227a
Kita Morio · · · · · 北杜夫 · · · · · · 4:227a
Kitamoto · · · · · · · · 北本 · · · · · · 4:227a
Kitamura Kigin · · 北村季吟 · · · · 4:227a
  Man'yōshū scholarship · · · · · · · 5:110b
Kitamura Kusuo
  · · · · · · · · · 北村久寿雄 · · · · · 4:227a
Kitamura Rokurō
  · · · · · · · · · · 喜多村緑郎 · · · · 4:227a
  shimpa · · · · · · · · · · · · · · · · · · 7:107b
Kitamura Sayo · 北村サヨ · 4:227b; 7:76b
Kitamura Seibō · · 北村西望 · · · 5:304b
Kitamura Tōkoku 北村透谷 · 4:227b-228a;
                           5:11b
  Bungakukai · · · · · · · · · · · · · · 1:208b
  pacifism · · · · · · · · · · · · · 6:143b-144a
Kitano　　　　　　　北野
  Shintō · · · · · · · · · · · · · · · · · · · 7:126b
Kitano Shrine · 北野天満宮 4:228a; 7:257a
  Takayama Sōzei · · · · · · · · · · · · 7:320a
  temmangū · · · · · · · · · · · · · · · · 7:381a
Kitano Tenjin engi
  · · · · · · · · · 北野天神縁起 · 4:228a; 7:136b
Kitaōji Rosanjin
  · · · · · · · · · 北大路魯山人 · · 4:228a-228b
Kitao Masanobu · 北尾政演 · · · · 7:18a
Kitao Shigemasa 北尾重政 · · · · 4:228b
  Santō Kyōden · · · · · · · · · · · · · · 7:18a
Kita Sadakichi · · 喜田貞吉 · 1:77b; 4:228b
Kita school · · · · · 喜多流 · · 4:228b-229a
Kitaura · · · · · · · · · 北浦 · · · · · · 4:229a
Kita Ward · · · · · · · 北区 · · · · · · 4:229a
Kitayama culture 北山文化 · · · 4:229a
Kitazato Institute · · · · · · · · · · · · · 4:229a
Kitazato Shibasaburō
  · · · · · · · · · 北里柴三郎 · 4:229a; 7:89b
Kitazono Katsue · 北園克衛 · · · 4:229a

Kite, black [(tobi) *Milvus migrans*] 4:229b
Kite battles · · · · · · · · · · · · · · 4:230a, 231a
Kite makers · · · · · · · · · · · · · · 4:229b-232a
Kites · 2:296a; 4:229b-230a, *230b*, 231a-231b
  for Children's Day · · · · · · · · · · · 1:279b
  decoration · · · · · · · · · · · · · 4:230a-231a
  as folk craft · · · · · · · · · · · · 4:231a-231b
  military history · · · · · · · · · · · · · 4:230a
  modern · · · · · · · · · · · · · · · 4:230b-231a
  premodern · · · · · · · · · · · · · 4:229b-230b
Kitō · · · · · · · · · 几董 · · · · · 6:297b, 298b
Kitō Bōkyō Jichi Seifu
  · · · · · · · 冀東防共自治政府 · · · · 2:142b
Kitsuki · · · · · · · · · 杵築 · · · · · · 4:231b
Kitsune · 2:330a
Kitsuneken · · · · · · · · · · · · · · · · · 4:193a
Kitsutsuki · · · · · · · · · · · · · · · · · · 8:269b
Kiuchi Sekitei · · 木内石亭 · 1:75b; 4:231b
Kiuchi Shinzō · · 木内信蔵 · · · 4:231b
  Geography in Japan · · · · · · · · · 3:26a
Kiuchi Sōgorō. 木内惣五郎 *See* **Sakura
  Sōgorō**
Kiwanis Club · · · · · · · · · · · · · · 4:231b
Kiwanis Japan · · · · · · · · · · · · · · 4:231b
"**Kiyō bimbō**" (Clever
  Poverty) · · · · · · · 器用貧乏 · · · · 8:173b
Kiyokawa Shōji · · 清川正二 · · · 4:231b
Kiyomizudera · · · · 清水寺 · · · · 3:9a;
      4:231b-232a, *334b*, 336a; 7:256b
Kiyomizudera engi
(Legends of
Kiyomizudera)
  · · · · · · · · · 清水寺縁起 · · · · · 6:153b
Kiyomizu monogatari
  · · · · · · · · · · 清水物語 · · · · · · 4:136a
Kiyomizu ware. 清水焼　　*See* **Kyōto
ceramics**
Kiyomizuyaki · · · · · 清水焼 · · · · · 4:337a
Kiyomoto-bushi · · 清元節 · · · 4:91b, 99a,
                        232a-232b
  tokiwazu-bushi · · · · · · · · · · · · · 8:43b
Kiyonaga. 清長　　　*See* **Torii Kiyonaga**
Kiyono Kenji · · · · 清野謙次 · · · 4:232b
Kiyooka Takayuki
  · · · · · · · · · · 清岡卓行 · · · · · 4:232b
Kiyosato · · · · · · · · 清里 · · · · · · 4:232b
Kiyosawa Kiyoshi · 清沢洌 · · · 4:232b
Kiyose · · · · · · · · · 清瀬 · · · · · · 4:232b
Kiyosumiyama · · · · 清澄山 · 4:232b-233a
Kiyoura Keigo · · 清浦奎吾 3:198a; 4:233a;
                          7:55a
  cabinet · · · · · · · · · · · · · · 4:120a, 198a
Kiyozawa Manshi 清沢満之 · · · 4:233a
  Jōdo Shin sect · · · · · · · · · · · · · 4:68b
Kiyū shōran (Diversions
for One's Amusement)
  · · · · · · · · · · 嬉遊笑覧 · · · · · · 4:233b
Kizetsukyō gorge 奇絶峡
  Tanabe · · · · · · · · · · · · · · · · · · 7:335a
Kizewa-mono · · · · 生世話物 · · · · 4:91b-92a
Kizokuin. 貴族院 *See* **House of Peers**
Kizugawa · · · · · · · 木津川 · · · · 4:233b
Knitting · · · · · · · · · · · · · · · · · 7:106b
Knives (hōchō) · · · · · · · · · · · · · · 2:24b
Know-how · · · · · · · · · · · · · · · · 4:233b
Ko (household) · · · · · · · · · · 4:233b-234a
Kō (associations) · · · · · 講 · · · · 4:234a
Kōain · · · · · · · · · · 興亜院 · · · · 1:102b
Kōan · · · · · · · · · · 4:234a; 8:373b
  Hakuin · · · · · · · · · · · · · · · · · · 3:88a
  riddles · · · · · · · · · · · · · · · · · · 6:311b
Kōan Chōsa Chō　公安調査庁 · · · · 6:266b
Kōan jōrei · · · · · 公安条例 · 4:234a-234b
  Tōkyō ordinance decision (20 July 1960)
  · 8:68b
Kōa Oil Co, Ltd · · · · · · 4:234b; 6:181b
Kobachi (*chalcids*) · · · · · · · · · · · 1:149a
Koba Ichirō · · · · · · 木庭一郎 · 5:315a-315b

Koban (gold coins) · · 小判 · 4:234b; 7:67b
  ōban (coins) · · · · · · · · · · · · · · · 6:47b
Kōban (police box) · · · · · · 4:234b-235a
Kobanashi · · · · · · · · · · · · · 4:235a-235b
Kobayakawa Hideaki
  · · · · · · · 小早川秀秋 · 4:235b-236a;
                        7:56b, 99a
  Kamiya Sōtan · · · · · · · · · · · · · 4:127b
Kobayashi · · · · · · · 小林 · · · · · 4:236a
Kobayashi Ataru 小林中 · · · · · 4:236a
Kobayashi Hideo 小林秀雄 · · 1:209a;
                        4:236a-236b
  literary criticism · · · · · · · · · · · · 5:13a
Kobayashi Ichizō 小林一三 · · · 4:236b
  Furukawa Roppa · · · · · · · · · · · 2:373a
  Hankyū Corporation · · · · · · · · · 3:99a
  Itsuō Art Museum · · · · · · · · · · · 3:357b
Kobayashi Issa. 小林一茶　　*See* **Issa**
Kobayashi Kiyochika
  · · · · · · · · · 小林清親 · 4:236b-237a
  modern prints · · · · · · · · · · · · · · 5:232a
Kobayashi Kokei 小林古径 · · · 4:237a
Kobayashi Masaki
  · · · · · · · · · 小林正樹 · 2:272a-272b,
                      274a; 4:237a
  Seppuku · · · · · · · · · · · · · · · · 7:68b
Kobayashi Shigeru 小林茂 · · · 4:237a
Kobayashi Takiji
  · · · · · · · · · 小林多喜二 · 4:237a-238a;
                        7:25a, 66b
  proletarian literature movement
  · · · · · · · · · · · · · · · · · · 6:255b-256a
Kobayashi Yukio 小林行雄 · · · 1:77b
Kōbe · · · · · · · · · · 神戸 · 4:238a, *238b*
Kōbe Bank Ltd · · · · · · · · · · · · · · 8:96a
Kōbe Port Island · · · · · · · · · · · · · 4:364b
Kōbe Steel, Ltd · · · · · · · 4:139a, 238a
Kōbetsu · · · · · · · · · · · · · · · · · 7:124b
Kōbe University · · 神戸大学 · 4:238a-238b
Kōbō Daishi. 弘法大師　　*See* **Kūkai**
Kōbō Daishi gyōjō
  · · · · · · · · · 弘法大師行状 · · · · 4:295a
Kobori Enshū · · 小堀遠州 · · · 4:238b
  Furuta Oribe · · · · · · · · · · · · · · 2:373b
  Iga ware · · · · · · · · · · · · · · · · · 3:261b
  Kōrakuen · · · · · · · · · · · · · · · · 4:276a
Kobori Jinji · · · · 小堀甚二 · · · 3:141a
Kobotoke Pass · · 小仏峠 · · · · 4:238b
Kōbu Bijutsu Gakkō (Technical Fine
  Arts School) · · · · · · · · · · · · · · 7:43b
Kōbu currency · · · 洪武銭 · · · · 4:239a
Kōbu gattai · · · · · 公武合体 · 5:260a-260b
Kōbu Gattai Undō. 公武合体運動　　*See*
**Movement for Union of Court and
Shogunate**
Kōbun, Emperor · 弘文天皇 · 4:238b-239a
  Jinshin Disturbance · · · · · · · · · · 4:60b
Kobunjigaku · · · · 古文辞学 · · 4:239a
Kōbusen · · · · · · · 洪武銭 · · · · 4:239a
Kobushi (*Magnolia kobus*) · · · · · 4:239a
Kobushigadake
  · · · · · · · 甲武信ケ岳 1:272a; 4:239a
Kobushin · · · · · · · 小普請 · · · 4:239a-239b
Kobutori jijii ("The Old
Man Who Lost His
Wen") · · · · · · · · 瘤取爺 · · · · 4:239b
Kōbu tsūhō · · · · 洪武通宝 · · · 4:239b
Kobuuri · · · · · · · · 昆布売 · · · · 4:328a
Kōchi (city) · · · · · 高知 · · · · · · 4:239b
Kōchi kōmin system
  · · · · · · · · · · 公地公民制 · · · · 5:333b
Kōchi Plain · · · · · 高知平野 · · · 4:239b
Kōchi Prefecture · · 高知県 · · · 4:239b
Kochō · · · · · · · · · · 蝴蝶 · · · · · · 8:288b
Kōchō jūnisen · 皇朝十二銭 · 4:239b-240a;
                        7:277a
  Wadō kaihō · · · · · · · · · · · · · · · 8:198a
Kōda Aya · · · · · · · · 幸田文 · · · · 4:240a

Kodai · **4:258a**
Kōdaiji maki-e · 高台寺蒔絵 · **4:240a-240b;**
4:360b
Kodai kenkyū (The Study
of Ancient Times)
· · · · · · · · 古代研究 **4:240b; 6:119a**
Kodaira · · · · · · · · · · · 小平 · **4:241a**
Kodaira Kunihiko 小平邦彦 · **4:241a**
Kodakara ("child-treasure") · **1:277a**
Kodama (train) · · · · · · · · · · · **6:279a**
Kodama administration
Taiwan · · · · · · · · · · · · · · **7:307b**
Kodama Gentarō
· · · · · · · · · · 児玉源太郎 · **4:241a**
Kodama Yoshio
· · · · · · · · · · 児玉誉士夫 · **4:241a**
Kōdan · · · **4:241a-241b; 6:263a-264a; 7:65a**
film influence · · · · · · · · · · **2:267b**
Kōdansha, Ltd · **4:241b-242a; 6:246a, 268a**
Noma Seiji · · · · · · · · · · · · **4:212b**
Kōda Rohan
· · · · · · · · · · 幸田露伴 · **2:291b;**
4:242a-243a; 5:13a; 7:103a
fūryū concept · · · · · · · · · · **2:374b**
Ken'yūsha · · · · · · · · · · · · **4:199a**
life · · · · · · · · · · · **4:242a-243a**
Shinshōsetsu · · · · · · · · · · **7:125b**
works · · · · · · · · · · **4:242a-243a**
Kodemari
shimotsuke · · · · · · · · · · · · **7:107a**
Kōden · · · · · · · · · · · 公田 · **4:243a**
Kodera Kambyōe
· · · · · · · · · · 小寺宮兵衛 · **4:315a**
Kōdō · · · · · · · · · · · 講堂 · **1:182b**
Kōdō · · · · · · · · · · · 香道 · **3:284a-285a**
Kōdōha · · · · · · · · · · 皇道派 · **4:243a**
Nagata Tetsuzan · · · · · · · · **5:307a**
Tōseiha · · · · · · · · · · · · · · **8:82b**
Watanabe Jōtarō · · · · · · · · **8:235b**
Kōdōkan · · · · · · · · · 講道館 · **4:243a**
kangeiko · · · · · · · · · · · · · **4:140b**
Kōdōkan (school for Western Learning)
· · · · · · · · · · · · 弘道館 · **8:52a**
Kōdōkan Jūdō school · · · · · · **4:82b**
Kōdōkan ki jutsugi
· · · · · · · · 弘道館記述義 · **4:243b**
Kōdō Kyōkai · · · · 公道協会 · **3:262b**
Kodomo no Hi · · · 子供の日 · **1:279a-279b**
Kodomo no shiki
· · · · · · · · · · 子供の四季 · **8:110a**
Kōeki kokusan kō
· · · · · · · · · · 広益国産考 · **6:98a**
Kōen · · · · · · · · · · · 皇円 · **3:153a**
Kōenkai · · · · · · · · · · · · · · **7:272b**
Kōetsu. 光悦 · · · See Hon'ami Kōetsu
Kōfu (city) · · · · · · · 甲府 · **4:243b**
Kōfu Basin · · 甲府盆地 · **4:243b**
Kōfukuji · · 興福寺 · **1:152b, 182a;**
4:243b-244a; 5:270b-271a,
331a, 332a; 7:74a
edokoro
Kose-school painters in · · · · · **4:295a**
hiden'in · · · · · · · · · · · · · · **3:130b**
Taira-Minamoto War · · · · · · **7:299b**
Tamon'in nikki · · · · · · **7:334a-334b**
Kōfukuji Treasure House · · · · **4:244a**
Ashura · · · · · · · · · · · · · · **4:244b**
Kofun · · · · · · · · · · 古墳 · **4:244a-245b;**
7:30b, 256a
early-period · · · · · · · · **4:244a-245b**
Eta Funayama tomb · · · · · · · **2:231b**
first systematic investigation · · · · · · **1:76b**
Horse-rider theory · · · · · · · · **4:277a**
Ishibutai tomb · · · · · · · · · · **3:339a**
Iwase "thousand-mound" tomb cluster
· · · · · · · · · · · · · · · · · **3:363a**
Kakogawa · · · · · · · · · · · · **4:117b**
late-period · · · · · · · · **4:245b-246a**
middle-period · · · · · · · **4:245a-245b**

Nagoya · · · · · · · · · **5:308b-309a**
Nintoku Mausoleum · · · · · · · · **4:246b**
Ōzuka tomb · · · · · · · · · · · · **6:141a**
Shintō · · · · · · · · · · · · · · **7:126a**
Takamatsuzuka tomb · · · · **7:314b-315a**
Takehara tomb · · · · · · · · · · **4:247a**
Yame tomb cluster · · · · · **8:313a-313b**
Kofun period · · · · 古墳時代
· · · · · · · · · · **3:160b-161b; 4:246a**
archaeology of · · · · · · · · · · **4:246a**
economy · · · · · · · · · · · · · **2:147a**
periodization · · · · · · · · · · · **6:175b**
religion during · · · · · · · · · · **7:126a**
Kofun studies
new trends · · · · · · · · · · · · **1:79a**
protohistoric · · · · · · · · **1:77a, 78b**
Kofun to jōdai bunka
· · · · · · · · 古墳と上代文化 · **7:312a**
Koga · · · · · · · · · · · 古河 · **4:246a**
Koga bikō · · · · · 古画備考 · **4:156a**
Kōgai · · · · · · · · · 笄 · **4:246a, 295b**
Kōgaibyō · · · · · · · · · · · · **6:217a-220a**
Koga Issaku · · · · 古賀逸策 · **4:246a-246b**
Kogaku (Ancient
Learning) · · · · · 古学 · **4:246b-248a,**
258b; 7:71a, 190b-191a
Itō Jinsai · · · · · · · · **3:354a; 4:247b**
Ogyū Sorai · · · · **4:247b-248a; 6:72b-73a**
Yamaga Sokō · · · · **4:247a-247b; 8:290a**
Koga kubō · · · · · 古河公方 · **4:248a**
Koga Masao · · · · 古賀政男 · **4:248a**
Koganei · · · · · · · · 小金井 · **4:248a**
Koganei Yoshikiyo
· · · · · · · · 小金井良精 · **4:248a-248b**
Koganemaru (Golden Boy)
· · · · · · · · · · · こがね丸 · **4:199a**
Koganemushi · · · · · · · · · · · **3:43b**
Koganemushi · · · こがね蟲 · **4:139a**
Kōgei · · · · · · · **2:293b-294a; 4:179a**
Kōgei (Decorative Arts)
· · · · · · · · · · · · 工芸 · **8:314a**
Kogen eeben shōho
· · · · · · · · 古言衣延弁小補 · **6:138b**
Kogentei · · · · · 古言梯 · **4:134a, 169a**
Kōgi · · · · · · · · · · · 公儀 · **4:248b**
Kogidō · · · · · · · 古義堂 **3:354a; 4:248b;**
7:94b
Kogidō Bunko · 古義堂文庫 · **8:8b**
Kogigaku · · · · · · 古義学 **3:354a; 4:247b**
Kogin · · · · · · · · · **2:295a; 7:24b**
Kōgi seitai ron 公議政体論 · **4:248b-249a**
Taisei Hōkan · · · · · · · · · · **7:303a**
Kogito · · · · · · · · · コギト · **7:176a**
Kōgō · · · · · · · · 皇后 **2:356b; 4:249a**
Kōgoishi · · · · · · · · 神籠石 · **4:249a**
Kōgō Kaikaku · · · · 甲午改革 · **4:90a**
Kōgon, Emperor · 光厳天皇 · **4:249a**
Kōgonen-jaku · · · 庚午年籍 · **4:249a-249b**
Kogosho Kaigi 小御所会議 · **4:249b**
Kogo shūi · · · · · 古語拾遺 · **4:249b; 5:26a**
mythology · · · · · · · · · · · · **5:292a**
thought and culture · · · · · · · **8:25b**
Wani · · · · · · · · · · · · · · · **8:223a**
Koguryō · · · · · · · · · · · · **1:159b;**
2:287b, 303b; 4:249b; 6:146a; 7:16b
in Korean Three Kingdoms period · **4:292a**
language of · · · · · · · · · · · · **4:291a**
Kōgyō Gijutsu In
· · · · · · · · · · 工業技術院 · **1:21b**
Kōgyō iken · · · 興業意見 · **4:249b; 6:232a**
Kōgyō keiei sōron
· · · · · · · · 工業経営総論 · **6:93a**
Kōgyoku, Empress. 皇極天皇 See Saimei,
Empress
Kohan shuki · · · 湖畔手記 · **4:160b**
Kohitsugire · · · · · 古筆切 · **1:233b**
Kōhōdō · · · · · · · · · · · · · · **1:16b**
Koi · · · · · · · · · · · · · · · · **1:244a**

Koicha · · · · · · · · · · · · · · · **7:363a**
Koicha-demae · · · · · · · **7:363a-363b**
Koichijō In · · · · · · 小一条院 · **4:249b-250a**
Koide Narashige 小出楢重 · **4:250a**
Koihō school · · · · · 古医方
natural sciences · · · · · · · · · **5:356b**
Koikawa Harumachi
· · · · · · · · 恋川春町 · **4:250a; 7:95a,**
97a
Koikawa Sukimachi
· · · · · · · · 恋川好町 · **7:95a**
Kōiki shichōsonken · · · · · · · · **4:250a**
Koinuma Kuhachirō 鯉沼九八郎 · **4:89a**
Koishibara ware · 小石原焼 · **4:250b**
Koishikawa Botanic Garden · · · · · **1:165b;**
4:250a; 8:320a
Koishikawa Yōjōsho
· · · · · · · · 小石川養生所 · **4:250a-250b**
Koishiwara ware 小石原焼 **2:295b; 4:250b**
Onta ware · · · · · · · · · · · · **6:113a**
Koiso Kuniaki · 小磯国昭 **4:250b; 7:258b**
Koizumi Chikashi
· · · · · · · · 古泉千樫 · **4:250b**
Koizumi Shinzō 小泉信三 · **4:250b-251a**
Koizumi Yakumo. 小泉八雲 See Hearn,
Lafcadio
Kojidan (Stories About the
Past) · · · · · · · · · 古事談 · **4:251a**
Kōjien · · · · · · · · · 広辞苑 · **4:31b**
Kojiki (Record of Ancient
Matters) · · · · · · 古事記 · **1:20a, 151b,**
293a; 2:101a; 4:251a-251b; 5:25b, 27a;
6:290b; 7:48a, 128a, 143b, 310b, 324b, 376a,
382b
analysis · · · · · · · · · · **5:27a-28a**
Chinkon ritual · · · · · · · · · · **4:107a**
content · · · · · · · · · · · · · · **5:27b**
dance, traditional · · · · · · · · **2:73b**
early Japanese song · · · · **2:137a-138a**
English translation · · · · · · · **1:266b**
falconry · · · · · · · · · · · · · **2:241b**
fishing references · · · · · · · · **2:283b**
folktales · · · · · · · · · · · · · **2:302b**
frogs · · · · · · · · · · · · · · · **2:340a**
historiography · · · · · · · · · · **3:152b**
Hieda no Are · · · · · · · · · · **3:130b**
Japanese language, history · · · · **4:28b**
jellyfish · · · · · · · · · · · · · **4:50b**
Jimmu, Emperor · · · · · · **4:57a-57b**
Kada no Azumamaro lectures · · · · **4:100b**
Kakei Katsuhiko · · · · · · · · **4:115b**
literary analysis · · · · · · · · · **2:346b**
Motori Norinaga's study of · · · · **4:258b**
mythology · · · · · · · · · **5:292a-295a**
nature in · · · · · · · · · · · · · **5:357b**
Ōkuninushi no Mikoto · · · · · · **6:97b**
Ō no Yasumaro · · · · · · · · · · **6:112a**
pheasants · · · · · · · · · · · · **6:182b**
preface · · · · · · · · · · · · · · **5:27a**
rabbits · · · · · · · · · · · · · · **6:275a**
religious symbolism · · · · · · · **6:295b**
Shintō · · · · · · · · · · · · · · **7:126a**
Tokoyo · · · · · · · · · · · · · · **8:44a**
use of language · · · · · · · · · · **5:104a**
waka · · · · · · · · · · · · · · · **8:204a**
Wani · · · · · · · · · · · · · · · **8:223a**
Watarai Shintō · · · · · · · · · · **8:236b**
whales · · · · · · · · · · · · · · **8:249a**
women in Japan · · · · · · · · · · **8:258a**
women in Japanese religion · · · · **8:256b**
women's education · · · · · · · · **8:267a**
Yamatotakeru, Prince · · · · **8:311a-311b**
Kojiki den · · · 古事記伝 **2:102b; 4:188a,**
251b, 258
Kōjima · · · · · · · · · 幸島 · **4:251b**
Kojima Bay · · · · · · · 児島湾 · **4:251b**
reclamation · · · · · · · · · · · · **4:364a**

Kojima Gen'nosuke
················小島源之助 ···4:157a
Kojima Iken······児島惟謙·····4:251b–252a
Kōjima Island ·····幸島······4:251b
Kojima Korekata·児島惟謙·····4:251b–252a
Kojima Moriyoshi 小島守善·····4:308a
Kojima Nobuo·····小島信夫 1:209a; 4:252a
Kojima Takanori·児島高徳·····4:252a
Kōjin·············荒神·······4:252a
Kōjinsama·········荒神様·····4:120b
Koji ruien········古事類苑·····4:252a
  Ōtsuki Fumihiko ···········6:134b
Kōjō Hō··········工場法··2:241a–241b
Kojong, King ··4:140b, 252a–252b; 7:259b;
                                   8:293b
  Japanese gunboat diplomacy ·····4:279b
  Kabo Reform ···············4:90a
  pro-Russian, anti-Japanese activities
                                 ·····4:281b
  Samil Independence Movement ·····7:6b
  Taewŏn'gun ············7:293b–294a
  Tonghak Rebellion ············8:74b
"Kōjō no tsuki" (The
  Moon over the Ruined
  Castle) ········荒城の月 ··2:126a–126b
Kōjo ryōzoku···············4:252b
Kō Junken ·········黄遵憲·····3:247b
Kōjunsha·········交詢社··2:1b; 4:252b
Kōkaido Ō ryō hi. 広開土王陵碑   *See*
  Kwanggaet'o monument
Kōka no Miya ·······甲賀宮····7:91a
Kokan Shiren ··虎関師錬·4:252b–253a;
                          7:70b; 8:341b
  calligraphy ···············1:235b
  Genkō shakusho ············3:21a
Kōkatō Jōyaku 江華島条約 ·4:140b–141a
Kōkato Treaty. *See* **Kanghwa, Treaty of**
Kōke············高家 4:253a; 5:256b
Kōkechi (tie-dyeing)·纐纈·7:13b
Kōkei············康慶 1:199a; 4:253a
  Fukū Kensaku Kannon ·········4:253a
  Kaikei ·················4:111a
  Kōfukuji commission ·········4:244a
Kokei sanshō ("The Three Laughters of
  Tiger Ravine") 虎渓三笑 ·····4:253b
Kokemi ·········小検見·····4:191a
Koken (bill of sale) ·沽券····4:253b
Kōken, Empress 孝謙天皇·····4:253b
  Fujiwara no Nakamaro ·········2:353b
Kōkennin··········4:253b–254a
Kokeshi···········5:254a–254b
  Shiroishi ················7:148a
Kōki············皇紀·····1:232a
Kōkigyō·················6:263a–264a
Kokin chomonshū
··················古今著聞集 ·····4:256b
Kokin Denju ····古今伝授·4:254a–254b
Kokinshū········古今集·1:293b; 2:57a;
  4:*133a*, 254b–255a; 5:31b; 6:299a; 7:12b,
  42b, 61b, 95a, 161b–162a; 8:114b, 287b,
                                   328b
  commentaries ··········4:188a, 198b
  compilation ···············2:352b
  Fujiwara no Kanesuke ·········2:351b
  Gosen wakashū ············3:48b
  imperial anthologies ·········3:275b
  kagura uta ···············4:108a
  Ki no Tomonori ·········4:216a–216b
  Ki no Tsurayuki ·········4:216b–217a
  Mibu no Tadamine ·········5:166a–166b
  Ono no Takamura ···········6:111b
  Ōshikōchi no Mitsune ·········6:125a
  preface ············1:85b; 2:353a
  Rokkasen ················6:334b
  Senzai wakashū ············7:68a
  Tō no Tsuneyori ············8:75a
Kokinshū style ············5:31a

*Kokin waka rokujō (*Six Books of
  Japanese Poetry Ancient
  and Modern)
··········古今和歌六帖 ·5:35a; 8:204b
*Kokin wakashū.*古今和歌集
  See **Kokinshū**
Kokin wakashū seigi
········古今和歌集正義 ·····4:103a
Kokiroku ·········古記録·4:255a–255b
Kokka ············国華·····1:154b;
                          4:255b; 6:204b
*Kokka hachiron (*Eight
  Matters of Concern in
  the National Poetry)
··················国歌八論 4:100b; 8:215b
Kokkai. *See* **Diet**
Kokkai Kisei Dōmei. 国会期成同盟   *See*
  **League for Establishing a National
  Assembly**
Kokka Kōan Iinkai. *See* **National Public
  Safety Commission**
Kokkakuki ·······骨角器···1:160a–160b
Kokka Shintō. *See* **State Shintō**
Kokka shugi ············5:342a–343b
Kokka Sōdōin Hō. 国家総動員法
  See **National Mobilization Law**
Kokka taikan ·····国歌大観····5:140b
Kokkeibon ········滑稽本· 4:61b, 256a;
                                   7:18a
  Hiraga Gennai ···········3:142a
  late Edo ·················5:49a
  sharebon ·················7:80a
  Shikitei Samba ·········7:96b–97b
Kokkeibon fiction ···········5:49a
Kokkei wagōjin 滑稽和合人 ·····6:359a
Kokken hanron ·国憲汎論·····6:109a
Kokkuri·················4:256a
Kō Kō ············黄興····3:247b
Kōkō Emperor ····光孝天皇····1:45a
Kōkogaku Kenkyūkai
·····················1:77b
Kokon chomonjū
··········古今著聞集 4:256b; 7:328a
Kokoro·············心·····4:85a
Kokoromi no kishi
·················試みの岸·····6:69b
Kokoronashi ······心無し····5:282a
Kokorozuke·················4:256b
Kōkotsu no hito ·恍惚の人····6:99a
Koku·············石 2:340a; 4:256b
Kokubō ·················5:336b–338b
Kokubō Fujinkai. *See* **Dai Nippon
  Kokubō Fujinkai**
Kokubō Kaigi ·············5:338b
Kokubu············国分·····4:256b
Kokubungaku Kenkyū Shiryōkan
·················4:256b–257a
Kokubunji (city)····国分寺·····4:257a
Kokubunji (provincial
  temple) ··········国分寺····4:257a
  Kōmyō, Empress ·········4:268b
Kokubunniji 国分尼寺······4:268b
Kokudainō········石代納·····4:257a
Kokudaka·········石高·····3:188a;
                          4:257a–257b; 5:360b
  shimpan ·················7:108a
  shinden kaihatsu ············7:109b
  Tanuma Okitsugu ·········7:345a–346a
Kokudo Chiriin ············3:25a
Kokudochō. *See* **National Land Agency**
Kokufu············国府·····4:257b
  kokushi assigned to ·········4:262a
Kokugaku (National
  Learning) ··········国学 2:172b; 4:140a,
  257b–259b; 6:306b; 7:28b, 190b, 256b
  Edo period ···········4:257b–259b
  Ban Nobutomo ···········1:141b
  Hirata Atsutane ············4:259a

  Kada no Azumamaro ·····4:258a
  Kamo no Mabuchi ·····4:129a–129b
  Keichū ·············4:257b–258a
  Motoori Norinaga ·····4:258a–258b
  Ōkuni Takamasa ············6:97b
  Tayasu Munetake ············7:359a
  historiography ············3:155a
  Japanese language studies ·····4:31a
  Kojiki's status ············4:251b
  kokutai and ···············4:263a
  later developments ·····4:257b–259b
  nationalism ···············5:342b
  objectivism ···············4:188a
  Shintō and Buddhism, separation of
                          ·····7:132a
  Tanigawa Kotosuga ·········7:341b
  Tarui Tōkichi ············7:347a
  thought and culture ·········8:25a
Kokugakuin University·······4:259b
Kokugaku no hongi
··················国学の本義 ····4:259a
Kokugaku scholars ············5:17a
Kokugaryō (public lands)·国衙領····4:193a
Kokuga Sōsaku Kyōkai (National
  Creative Painting Association) ···8:111b
  modern painting ············6:156b
Kokugikan·················4:259b
Kokugo Chōsa Iinkai ·········4:31a
Kokugogaku shi (History
  of Japanese Language
  Studies) ·······国語学史····8:290a
Kokugo jiten ·······国語辞典··2:93b–94a
Kokugo Shingikai. *See* **Council on the
  National Language**
Kokugun system   国郡制 2:104a; 4:259b
  agatanushi in ·············1:21a
  ko (household) unit ·····4:233b–234a
  provinces ·········6:258b, 260a
  ritsuryō system ············6:329a
  Tōkyō ·················8:61b
Kokuhō *See* **National Treasures**
Kokuhonsha ·······国本社·4:259b–260a
  Hiranuma Kiichirō ·········3:144a
  Toranomon Incident ·········8:76b
Kokuikō ·········国意考····4:129b
Kokujin·············国人 2:265a; 4:260a;
                                   7:64b
  Akutō as ·················1:46a
  kuni ikki ·················4:309a
  shōen ·················7:158a
Kokumin Bungei Kai ·········5:19a
Kokumin Chōyō Rei. 国民徴用令
  See **National Service Draft Ordinance**
Kokumin Dōmei ·国民同盟·····4:260a
  Adachi Kenzō ···············1:11a
  Russo-Japanese War ·········6:346a
  Tairo Dōshikai ············7:303a
  Tōhōkai (Far East Society) ·····8:36b
Kokumin Dōshikai
··················国民同志会 ····4:64a
Kokumin gakkō · 4:260a–260b; 7:36a, 51a,
Kokumin Jissen Yōryō
  国民実践要領 ·············4:260b
Kokumin kenkō hoken. *See* **National
  health insurance**
Kokumin Kyōdōtō
  (National Cooperative
  Party) ·······国民協同党 4:260b; 6:212a
Kokumin Kyōkai ·国民協会·····1:40a;
                          4:260b–261a
  ritō ·················6:321b
  Shinagawa Yajirō ············7:109a
  Teikokutō ················7:376b
Kokumin no tomo (Friend
  of the People) ·国民之友 ·4:261a; 8:60a;
                                   296a
Kokumin seikatsu hakusho ·······8:251b

Kokumin Seikatsu Shingikai · 2:168a-168b
Kokumin Seishin Bunka Kenkyūjo 4:204b
Kokumin Seishin Sōdōin
  Remmei
    国民精神総動員連盟 ········ 4:284a
Kokumin Seishin Sōdōin Undō. See
  **National Spiritual Mobilization
  Movement**
Kokumin shimbun
    国民新聞 ········ 4:261a
Kokumin shukusha ········ 4:261a
Kokumin Taiiku Taikai ········ 5:348a
Kokumintō (National People's Party)
    国民党 ········ 5:311b-312a
Kōkuri. 高句麗 See **Koguryō**
Kokuritsu Daigaku Kyōkai ········ 4:10b
Kokuritsu ginkō. See **National banks**
Kokuritsu Kagaku Hakubutsukan
    ········ 5:346a
Kokuritsu Kōbunshokan. See **National
  Archives**
Kokuritsu Kokkai Toshokan
    国立国会図書館 ·· 5:338b-339a
Kokuritsu Kokugo Kenkyūjo ······ 5:343b
Kokuritsu Kyōiku Kenkyūjo ······· 2:181a
Kokuritsu Minzokugaku
  Hakubutsukan
    国立民族学博物館 ··· 5:344a
**Kokuritsu Rekishi Minzoku
  Hakubutsukan**
    国立歴史民俗博物館 ···· 4:261b
Kokuritsu Seiyō Bijutsukan ······ 5:344b
Kokurō (National Railway
  Workers' Union) · 国労 ·· 6:238a
Kokuryūkai ········ 黒龍会 ····· 1:53b
Kokusai Bunka Shinkōkai ··· 3:319b; 4:41a
Kokusai Denshin Denwa Co, Ltd (KDD)
    4:261b; 7:86b
  radio law ········ 6:276a
  telephones ········ 7:380a
Kokusai Kirisutokyō
  Daigaku · 国際基督教大学 ···· 3:318b
Kokusai Kōryū Kikin ········ 4:46a
Kokusai shihō (Private International
  Law) ········ 国際私法 ···· 8:289a
Kokusaku kaisha 国策会社 ·· 4:261b-262a
Kokusan kaisho · 国産会所 ·· 4:262a
Kokusei chōsaken ········ 4:262a
  Diet ········ 4:262a
Kokusen (Black Fan) · 黒扇 ·· 2:346b
Kokusen'ya Kassen
    国性爺合戦 ····· 1:275b
Kokushi ········ 国司 · 4:262a-262b
  kageyushi ········ 4:104b
  Taika Reform ········ 7:296a
  yōnin ········ 8:338a
Kokushigatake 国師ケ岳 ···· 4:153b
Kokushi musō (Peerless
  Patriot) ········ 国士無双 ···· 8:289a
Kokushi no kenkyū
    国史の研究 ········ 6:176a
Kokushi taikei · 国史大系 ··· 4:262b
  Kuroita Katsumi and ········ 4:316a
Kokusho kaidai 国書解題 ···· 1:154a-154b
Kokusho sōmokuroku
    国書総目録 ········ 1:154b
Kokushunrō ········ 国春楼 ···· 4:189b
Kokuso ········ 国訴 ········ 4:262b
Kokutai (national polity)
    国体 · 4:262b-263b;
        5:348a; 6:204b, 236b; 7:190b
  academic freedom ········ 1:6b
  Imperial Rescript on Education ·· 3:279a
  Kanamori Tokujirō ········ 4:135a
  Kokugaku as the elucidation of ··· 4:257b
  Kokutai no hongi ········ 4:264a
  nationalism ········ 5:343a
  Occupation ········ 6:51a

Kokutai debate ········ 4:263b-264a
Kokutai meichō mondai. 国体明徴問題
  See **Kokutai debate**
Kokutai no hongi
    国体の本義 ········ 4:264a
  kokutai ········ 4:263b
  nationalism ········ 5:342b
Kokutai shinron · 国体新論 · 4:168a, 263a
Kokutetsu. See **Japanese National
  Railways**
Kokutōkai ········ 6:159a
Kōkū Uchū Gijutsu Kenkyūjo ···· 5:336a
Kokuyaku ········ 国役 ····· 4:310a
Kokuyo Co, Ltd ········ 4:264b
Kokuzei. See **Taxes, national and local**
Kokyakujō (deed) ········ 4:253b
Kōkyō Kigyōtai Tō Rōdō Kumiai
  Kyōgikai ········ 4:294a
Kokyū ········ 4:264b
  jiuta ········ 4:64b
  ryūkōka ········ 6:354a
Kokyū wasureubeki
    故旧忘れ得べき · 7:176a, 315a
Kolchak, Aleksander Vasilievich · 7:192a
Koma. See **Tops**
Komachishū ········ 小町集 ···· 6:111a
Komadori [(Japanese robin) *Erithacus
  akahige*] ········ 4:264b
Komae ········ 狛江 ········ 4:264b
Komagaku ········ 高麗楽 ···· 3:1a
Komagane ········ 駒ケ根 ···· 4:264b
Komagatake (mountain,
  Akaishi) ········ 駒ケ岳 ··· 4:265a
Komagatake (mountain,
  Kiso) ········ 駒ケ岳 ···· 4:265a
Komagatake (mountain,
  northern Honshū) 駒ケ岳 ··· 4:265a
Komagatake (volcano,
  Hokkaidō) ········ 駒ケ岳 ··· 4:264b
Komagatake (volcano,
  Honshū) ········ 駒ケ岳 · 4:264b-265a
Komainu ········ 狛犬 ····· 4:265a
Komaki ········ 小牧 ····· 4:265a
Komaki Dam ········ 小牧ダム ·· 2:72b
Komaki Nagakute Campaign
    小牧・長久手の戦 ··· 4:265a
  Toyotomi Hideyoshi ········ 8:95a
Komatsu ········ 小松 ···· 4:265a
Komatsubara Eitarō
    小松原英太郎 ···· 4:265a
Komatsu, Ltd ········ 4:265b-266a
Komatsu Minoru ··· 小松実 ···· 4:266a
Komatsu Ryūnosuke
    小松竜之介 ···· 2:170b
Komatsu Sakyō · 小松左京 ···· 4:266a
  science fiction ········ 7:38b
Komatsu Seisakusho ········ 4:265b
Komatsushima · 小松島 ···· 4:266a
Komatsu Tatewaki
    小松帯刀 ···· 4:266a
Koma-yaki ········ 高麗焼 ···· 7:226a
Komayubachi (*braconids*) ···· 1:149a
Kombu (seaweed) ········ 7:47a
Kome ········ 6:308b-310a
Kōmei bijin rokkasen ········ 8:142b
Kōmei, Emperor · 孝明天皇 · 4:266a-266b
Kōmei Political Federation ···· 4:266b
Kōmeitō (Clean
  Government Party)
    公明党 · 4:266b-267a;
        6:205b, 212b, 213a
  future outlook ········ 4:266b-267a
  Ikeda Daisaku ········ 4:265a
  national defense ········ 5:336b-338b
  organization ········ 4:266b
  policies ········ 4:266b
  postwar status ········ 3:205a
  Takeiri Yoshikatsu ········ 7:324a

Kome kitte ········ 米切手 ······· 4:267a
Kome sōdō.   米騒動
  See **Rice riots of 1918**
Kome Yokose Mēdē. 米よこせメーデー
  See **Shokuryō Mēdē**
Kōmin ········ 公民 ···· 6:352b
  koshiro and nashiro relabeled ···· 4:296a
Kōminkan ········ 1:341a
Komiya Toyotaka 小宮豊隆 1:155b; 4:267a
Kommintō ········ 困民党 ···· 4:267a
Komon ········ 4:267a
Komonjo. 古文書   See **Diplomatics**
Komonjo gaku ··· 古文書学 · 2:97a-100b
Komononari ········ 小物成 ·· 4:267a-267b;
        5:360b
Kōmori ········ 1:146b
Kōmorigasa ("bat umbrellas") ·· 1:146b
Komoro ········ 小諸 ···· 4:267b
Komparu Nobutaka
    金春信高 ···· 4:267b
Komparuryū ········ 金春流 ···· 4:267b
Komparu school · 金春流 · 4:267b; 6:24a
Komparu Ujinobu 金春氏信 ···· 4:267b
Komparu Zempō · 金春禅鳳 · 4:267b
Komparu Zenchiku
    金春禅竹 · 4:267b; 5:15b
Kompira. 金毘羅   See **Kotohira Shrine**
Kompon Chūdō ·· 根本中堂 · 2:220b
Kompon Daitō ·· 根本大塔 · 4:269b
Komugi ········ 8:251a
Kōmundo Incident
    巨文島事件 ··· 4:267b-268a
Komura Jutarō 小村寿太郎 · 4:268a-268b
Komura-Vaeber Memorandum
    小村-ウェーバー覚書 · 4:268a, 281b;
        5:196b-197a; 8:293b
  Russo-Japanese War ········ 6:346a
Komusō. See **Shakuhachi**
Komusubi ········ 7:272a
Kōmyō, Empress 光明皇后 ···· 4:268b
  calligraphic collections ········ 1:234a
  Fujiwara no Nakamaro ········ 2:353b
  Hiden'in ········ 3:130b
Kōmyōshi ········ 光明子 ···· 4:268b
Kōnan ········ 江南 ···· 4:268b
Kondei ········ 健児 ···· 4:268b
Konden ········ 7:109b-110a
Konden Einen Shizai Hō. 墾田永年私財法
  See **Konden Eisei Shizai Hō**
Konden Eisei Shizai Hō
    墾田永世私財法 · 4:268b-269a;
        7:19b
Kondō (main hall) ··· 1:182b; 3:232b; 8:83a,
        285a, 376b
Kondō butsu ········ 4:269a
Kondō Heisaburō
    近藤平三郎 ········ 4:269a
Kondō Isami ··· 近藤勇 ···· 4:269a
  Shinsengumi ········ 7:124a
Kondō Jūzō ··· 近藤重蔵 ···· 1:154a;
        4:269a-269b
Kondō Keitarō 近藤啓太郎 · 4:269b
Kondō Kenzō ··· 近藤賢三 ···· 4:69a
Kondō Morishige. See **Kondō Jūzō**
Kondō Yoshirō · 近藤義郎 ···· 1:79a
Kondō Yūzō ··· 近藤悠三 ···· 1:261a
Kongōbuji ········ 金剛峰寺 ···· 4:269b
  Takuma Tametō ········ 7:328a
Kongōchō-gyō ··· 金剛頂経 ···· 4:270a
Kongōfukuji, temple of
    金剛福寺 ········ 1:102b
Kongō Iwao ········ 金剛巌 ···· 6:26b
Kongōkai ········ 金剛界 ··· 4:269b-270a
  Dainichi ········ 2:64b
  Shingon sect ········ 7:115a
Kongōkai mandara
    金剛界曼荼羅 4:270a; 6:347b,
        348b, 349a-351a

Kongōsan ········ 金剛山 ····· **4:270a**
Kongō school ······ 金剛流 ····· **4:270a**
Kongōsen ········ 金剛山 ····· **4:270a**
Kon Hidemi ······ 今日出海 ····· **4:270a**
Konica ····· **4:270b**
Kō Nihon bunten
  (Comprehensive
  Grammar of Japanese)
  ········ 広日本文典 ······ **6:134b**
Konishi Jin'ichi ·· 小西甚一 ···· **6:297a**
Konishi Raizan ·· 小西来山 ··· **4:270a**
Konishiroku Photo Industry Co, Ltd
  ····· **4:270b**
Konishiroku Shashin Kōgyō ·· **4:270b**
Konishi Yukinaga
  ········ 小西行長 · **1:83b; 4:270b;**
  7:56b, 83b, 98b-99a
  Christian daimyō ······· **1:306a**
  invasions of Korea in 1592 and 1597
  ····· **3:327a**
  Luis Frois ····· **2:340a**
Konjaku monogatari
  ········ 今昔物語 **1:180b; 2:296a;**
  4:132b, 270b-271a; 5:44a; 7:61b, 72a
  Chinese literature ····· **1:294a**
  folktales ····· **2:304a**
  fox legends ····· **2:330a**
  Fujiwara no Kintō ····· **2:352a**
  obasute ····· **6:48a**
  Obasuteyama ····· **6:48b**
  Warashibe chōja ("The Straw
  Millionaire") ····· **8:223b**
Konjiki yasha (The Golden
  Demon) ···· 金色夜叉 **4:199a; 6:221a;**
  7:107b
Konjin ········ 金神 ····· **4:271a**
Konketsuji ····· **4:271a-271b**
Konkō Daijin ···· 金光大神 ··· **4:271b**
Konkō Daijin Oboe
  ········ 金光大神覚え ···· **4:272a**
Konkō Daijin Rikai
  ········ 金光大神理解 ···· **4:272a**
Konkōkyō ······ 金光教 ···· **2:300b;**
  4:271b-272a; 7:48a
Konkōmyō Shitennō
  gokoku no tera
  ···· 金光明四天王護国寺 ·· **4:257a**
Konnyaku ····· **7:105a**
Kōno Bairei ···· 幸野楳嶺 ··· **4:272a**
Konoe Atsumaro 近衛篤麿 ·· **4:272a-272b**
Konoe family ····· 近衛家 · **4:272b; 7:29b**
  Gosekke ····· **3:48a**
Konoe Fumimaro 近衛文麿 ·· **2:3b;**
  4:272b-273b; 7:258b
  Gotō Ryūnosuke ····· **3:53b**
  Imperial Rule Assistance Association
  ····· **3:280a**
  New Order Movement ····· **5:365b**
  Sasaki Sōichi ····· **7:23a**
Konoe Fumimaro cabinet
  Araki Sadao ····· **1:74a**
  Arima Yoriyasu ····· **1:84a**
  Arita Hachirō ····· **1:85a**
  Nagai Ryūtarō ····· **5:301a**
  Yonai Mitsumasa ····· **8:337a**
Konoe Hidemaro 近衛秀麿 ·· **5:286b**
Konoe Iehiro ···· 近衛家熙 ··· **4:273b**
Konoe Nobutada 近衛信尹 ·· **4:273b**
Konohanasakuya Hime
  ········ 木花開耶姫 ····· **5:294b**
Kōno Hironaka · 河野広中 · **4:273b-274a**
  Freedom and People's Rights Movement
  ····· **2:335a**
  Fukushima Incident ····· **2:366a**
  Futsū Senkyo Kisei Dōmeikai ·· **2:376b**
  League for Establishing a National
  Assembly
  ····· **4:372b**
Kōno Hisashi ······ 河野寿 ···· **2:250a**

Kōno Ichirō ···· 河野一郎 ··· **4:274a**
Kōnoike family ··· 鴻池家 · **4:274a-274b**
Kōnoike shinden 鴻池新田 ·· **4:274b**
Kōnoike Zen'emon. *See* **Kōnoike family**
Kōno Kenzō ···· 河野謙三 ··· **4:274b**
Kōno Michiari ·· 河野通有 ··· **4:274b**
Kō no Moronao ·· 高師直 ··· **4:274b-275a**
  Kannō Disturbance ····· **4:144b**
Kōnosu ········ 鴻巣 ····· **4:275a**
Kōno Togama ··· 河野敏鎌 ··· **4:275a**
Kōno Yōhei ····· 河野洋平 ··· **4:275a**
Konrad, Nikolai Iosifovich ····· **4:275b**
Konsei ········ 金精 ····· **4:275b**
Konsei Pass ···· 金精峠 ···· **4:275b**
Konsei sama ····· 金精さま ·· **4:275b**
Konsen Highlands
  ········ 根釧台地 ····· **4:275b**
Kon Tōkō ······ 今東光 ···· **4:275b**
"Ko o kashiya" 子を貸し屋 ·· **8:173b**
Kōrai ········ 高麗 ····· **4:294a**
Kōraimon (castle gate)
  ········ 高麗門 ····· **1:248b**
Kōrakuen ······ 後楽園 ···· **4:198a, 276a,**
  276b
Kōrakuen Garden (Tōkyō)
  ········ 後楽園(東京) ····· **4:276a**
Korea
  annexation ····· **4:287a-287b**
  cultural sphere ····· **2:142a**
  historical works
    Samguk sagi (History of the Three
    Kingdoms) ····· **7:6a**
    Samguk yusa (Memorabilia of the Three
    Kingdoms) ····· **7:6a**
  language
    han'gŭl ····· **3:96b**
  religion ····· **6:290a-293b**
  Samil Independence Movement ··· **7:6a-6b**
  wakō ····· **8:220b**
  See also **Korea and Japan**
Korea, annexation of ····· **4:287a-287b**
  historical context ····· **4:282a**
  Korean-Japanese Convention of 1905
  ····· **4:289b**
Korea and Japan ····· **4:276a-287b**
  Democratic People's Republic of Korea
  (1953-) ····· **4:286a-287a**
  early modern relations
    Chemulp'o, Treaty of ····· **1:268b**
    Japanese control and annexation
    ····· **4:281b-282a**
    Kanghwa, Treaty of ···· **4:140b-141a**
    Kōmundo Incident ····· **4:268a**
    Korea, annexation of ····· **4:287a-287b**
    Korean-Japanese Convention of 1905
    ····· **4:289b**
    opening of Korea ····· **4:279b-280a**
    reaction to Japanese control **4:282a-282b**
    Russian influence ····· **4:281b**
    Sino-Japanese War of 1894-1895
    ····· **4:281a-281b; 7:197b-198a**
    Treaty of Shimonoseki ····· **7:106a**
  early postwar (1945-1952) ·· **4:284a-284b**
  independence ····· **7:106a**
  invasions of Korea in 1592 and
  1597 ····· **3:326b-327a**
  Japanese Colonial Control of Korea
  (1910-1945)
    Korea, annexation of ····· **4:287b**
  Japanese colonial control (1910-1945)
  ····· **4:283a-284a**
    administration ····· **4:283a**
    establishment ····· **4:283a-283b**
    Japanese militarization ····· **4:284a**
    reforms ····· **4:283b-284a**
  Koreans in Japan ····· **4:292a**
  patriotic groups of ····· **7:196a**
  premodern relations (to 1875) **4:276a-279b**

  foreign influences and consolidation of
  Yamato State ····· **4:277a-277b**
  Jingū, Empress ····· **4:59a**
  Kaya ····· **4:185a**
  Koryŏ Period (935-1391) ··· **4:278a-278b**
  prehistoric and protohistoric **4:276b-277a**
  Silla ····· **4:277b-278a; 7:196a**
  wakū ····· **8:220b**
  Yi Dynasty to 1875 ····· **4:278b-279a;**
  8:324b-325a
  Republic of Korea (1953-) ····· **3:324a;**
  4:284b-286a
    deterioration in 1950s ····· **4:284b-285a**
    normalization ····· **4:285a-285b**
    postnormalization ····· **4:285b-286a**
    tensions ····· **4:286a**
  Silla kingdom ····· **7:196a**
  Sino-Japanese War of 1894-1895 · **7:197b**
  YMCA ····· **7:196a**
Korea-Japan Treaty of 1965 · **4:287b-288a**
  historical context ····· **4:285b**
  supplementary agreements ··· **4:288a-288b**
Korea-Japan Treaty of 1965,
  supplementary agreements 4:288a-288b
  historical context ····· **4:285b**
Korean Armistice ····· **4:286b**
Korean campaigns of 1592 and 1597.
  See **Invasions of Korea in 1592 and**
  1597
Korean Central Intelligence Agency
  ····· **4:286a**
Korean Communist Party ····· **4:283b**
Korean Daily News ····· **4:282a**
Korean debate ····· **2:334a**
Korean Empire ····· **7:293b**
Korean "Independence Party." *See*
  Kaehwap'a
Korean-Japanese Convention of 1905
  ····· **4:289a-289b; 26a**
  historical context ····· **4:282a**
  Itō Hirobumi ····· **3:353b**
  Resident General ····· **6:306a**
  Russo-Japanese War ····· **6:347a**
  territory of Japan ····· **8:14a**
Korean language ····· **4:289b-291a**
  grammar ····· **4:290b**
  history ····· **4:291a**
  romanization ····· **4:289b-290a**
  sounds ····· **4:290a-290b**
  spelling ····· **4:289b**
  writing ····· **4:289b**
Korean National Art Museum ·· **2:293b**
Korean National Association ·· **4:208b**
Korean Patriotic League ····· **8:357b**
Korean People's Liberation Army · **4:208b**
Korean phonetic alphabet ······ **7:163a**
Korean Railway ····· **6:346b**
Koreans in Japan ····· **4:291a-292a**
  konketsuji ····· **4:271b**
  Korea-Japan Treaty of 1965,
  supplementary agreements ··· **4:288a**
  minorities ····· **5:195a-195b**
  resident foreigners ····· **2:313a-313b**
Korean Three Kingdoms period · **4:292a;**
  7:6a
  Koguryo ····· **4:249b**
  Tachan Empire ····· **7:293b**
  "Korean Tripitaka" ····· **4:278b**
Korean War ····· **4:292a-292b**
  Acheson statement ····· **1:10a-10b**
  foreign procurements (tokuju) ····· **8:57b**
  Japanese economy ····· **2:158a**
  Korean-Japanese relations ····· **4:284a**
  Occupation ····· **6:54b**
  Ōsu Incident ····· **6:128a**
  role in Self Defense Forces creation · **7:58b**
Korea Strait ····· 朝鮮海峡 ·· **4:292b**
Korematsu v *US* (323 US 214) ····· **4:18a**

Koretaka, Prince ·惟喬親王 ········ 4:205a
Koretō Hyūga no Kami. 惟任日向守
  See **Akechi Mitsuhide**
Koreyuki ············ 尹行 ···· 1:234b-235a
Kōrin ················ 光琳 ··· 1:166b, 262b;
  2:346a; 4:292b-293b; 6:153a, 154a-154b;
                                     7:43a
  Red and White Plum Trees (Kōhakubai zu)
  ···························· 4:293a-293b
  Rimpa ···························· 6:317b
Kōriyama ········· 郡山 2:367a; 4:293b
Kōriyama Basin ·郡山盆地 ···· 4:293b
Kōrogi ···························· 2:43b-44a
Kōrokan ············· 鴻臚館 4:293b-294a
Kōrōkyō ······················ 4:294a
Koryŏ ······················ 4:294a; 7:6a
  Japanese relations ············ 4:278a
  Mongol invasions of Korea and ·· 5:245a
Kōryūji ············· 広隆寺 4:294a-294b,
                                     334b
Kosai ················ 湖西 ···· 4:294b
Kosaka Zentarō
  ············ 小坂善太郎 ···· 4:285a
Kosaku sōgi. *See* **Tenant farmer**
  disputes
Kōsei shimpen ·· 厚生新編 ·· 4:294b
Kōseishō. 厚生省 *See* **Ministry of Health**
  and Welfare
Koseki. *See* **Household registers**
Kose no Kanaoka
  ············ 巨勢金岡 ···· 4:294b
  Kose school ···················· 4:295a
Kose school ······· 巨勢派 ·· 4:295a
  Kose no Kanaoka, founder ·· 4:294b
Kōsha ···················· 6:263a-264a
Kōshaku ························ 4:241a
Kōshakushi ···················· 4:241b
Koshi ························ 4:295a
Koshigaya ·········· 越谷 ···· 4:295b
Koshiki ························ 2:305a
Koshikijima Islands
  ············ 甑島列島 ···· 4:295b
Koshimino ···················· 7:249a
Kōshin ················ 庚申 ·· 4:295b
Kōshin Jihen ····· 甲申事変 4:156b-157a
Kōshin machi ····· 庚申待 ·· 4:295b
Koshirae ···················· 4:295b
Koshiro ············· 子代 1:147b; 7:296a
Koshiro and nashiro
  ············ 子代, 名代 ···· 4:296a
Kōshitsu ···················· 3:277b
Koshitsū (Survey of
  Ancient History) ·· 古史通 2:102b; 8:306a
Kōshitsu Tempan. 皇室典範
  See **Imperial Household Law**
Koshō ··········· 小姓 · 4:296a, 304b,
                                     322b
Kōshōgaku school
  ············ 考証学派 ···· 3:155b
Kōshoku ············· 更埴 ·· 4:296a
Kōshokubon ···· 好色本 4:296a; 8:144a
Kōshoku ichidai otoko
  ············ 好色一代男 4:136b; 8:144a
Kōshoku-mono (armorous
  pieces) ············ 好色物 ···· 8:144a
Kōshoku Tsuihō ··········· 6:57b-58b
Koshoku zensho 古織全書 ·· 4:159b
Koshu ············· 戸主 ···· 4:60b-61a
Kōshū Gakusei Jiken
  ············ 光州学生事件 ·· 4:323b
Kōshū Kaidō ····· 甲州街道 ···· 3:41a
Kōshūwan soshakuchi
  ············ 膠州湾租借地 ···· 4:53a
Kōsō ··········· 高宗 · 4:252a-252b
Kosode ················ 小袖 ·· 8:23a
  designs ························ 2:90b
Kōsō wasan ····· 高僧和讃 ·· 8:231a
Kosugi Isamu ··· 小杉勇 2:269a, 270b

Kosugi Tengai ··· 小杉天外 ·· 4:296a-296b
  fūzoku shōsetsu ············ 2:378b
"Kosui to karera" 湖水と彼等 ····· 8:92b
Kōtai Ō hi ············ 好太王碑 4:323a-323b
Kōtaishi Shōtoku hōsan
  ············ 皇太子聖徳奉讃 ·· 8:231a
Kotani Kimi ··· 小谷喜美 ·· 4:296b
Kotani Yasukichi ·小谷安吉 ··· 6:289a
Kotatsu ························ 1:267a
Kōten Kōkyūjo ·皇典講究所 ·· 4:259b
Koto ···················· 4:296a;
                       7:75b, 87b, 225b-226a
  gagaku ························ 3:2a
Kotobagaki ···················· 4:297a
Kotoba no tama no o
  ············ 詞玉緒 ···· 4:31b
Kotoba no yachimata
  ············ 詞八衢 ···· 4:31b
Koto hajime ···················· 4:298a
Kotohira ············· 琴平 ·· 4:297a
Kotohira Shrine 金刀比羅宮 · 4:103b, 297a
  main hall (honden) ············ 4:297a
Kōtō jogakkō ···················· 4:297a-297b
Kōtoku, Emperor 孝徳天皇 ·· 4:297b
  Taika Reform ················ 7:296a
Kōtoku Incident · 幸徳事件 ··· 3:135a
Kōtoku Shūsui ·· 幸徳秋水 · 4:297b-298a;
                       7:56a, 74a-74b; 8:296b
  Fukuda Hideko ··············· 2:362b
  Futsū Senkyo Kisei Dōmeikai ·· 2:376b
  Heiminsha ···················· 3:125b
  High Treason Incident of 1910 ·· 3:135a
  Kamitsukasa Shōken ··········· 4:127b
  Kanno Suga ···················· 4:145a
  pacifism ························ 6:144a
Koto osame ···················· 4:298a
Kōtō semmon gakkō. *See*
  Technical colleges
Kōtō Ward ············· 江東区 ·· 4:298a
Kotowaza ························ 6:258b
Kotoyōka ······· 事八日 3:208b; 4:298a
Kōtsu ···················· 4:131a
Kōtsū Hakubutsukan ············ 8:104a
Kotsutsubo ···················· 2:370a
Kottai-san 太夫さん
  shimpa ························ 7:108a
Kouta ············· 小唄 ··· 4:298a-298b
Kouta (small song) ············ 4:328a
Kōwaka (ballad-drama)
  ············ 幸若 · 4:298b; 5:45a
Kōwaka-mai ····· 幸若舞 ·· 4:298b
Kōwa Mondai Dōshi Rengōkai
  ······ 講和問題同志連合会 ·· 3:129a-129b
  Tairo Dōshikai ··············· 7:303a
Kōya ··········· 空也 ·· 4:322a-322b
Kōyagire ············ 高野切 ·· 4:133a
Koyairi ························ 4:195a
Koyama Shōtarō
  ············ 小山正太郎 ···· 8:341a
Koyama Yūshi ··· 小山祐士 ·· 4:298b-299a
Kōyasan (monastic
  complex) ········· 高野山 ·· 4:299a-299b,
                          304a; 6:248a
Kōyasan (mountain)
  ············ 高野山 ···· 4:299a
Kōyasan Treasure House ···· 4:299b
Kōyō gunkan ··· 甲陽軍鑑 ·· 4:299b
Koyori ···················· 4:299b
Kōyō Seikō Co, Ltd ············ 4:299b
Kōyō sekiyō sonsha shi
  ············ 黄葉夕陽村舎詩 ·· 4:152a
Kōyōsha ························ 8:88a
Kōyō wakaskū 黄葉和歌集 ·· 4:158a
Kō Yūi ············ 康有為 ·· 4:141a-141b
Kōyū Kurabu · 公友倶楽部 ·· 4:198a
Kōzaha ············· 講座派 · 4:299b-300a;
                          7:3a; 8:289a
  Rōnōha ························ 6:337b

Kozai Shikin ····· 古在紫琴 ·· 4:300a
Kozaki Hiromichi 小崎弘道 ·· 4:300a
Kōzanji ············· 高山寺 · 4:300a-300b
Kōzen gokoku ron
  ············ 興禅護国論 2:187a; 4:300b
Kōzo ············· 4:167b
Kozuka ························ 4:295b
Kōzuke monuments 上野三碑 ···· 4:300b
Kōzuki ············· 上月 ·· 8:301a
Kū. 空 *See* **Emptiness**
Kuan-yin ···················· 4:144b-145a
Kuan Yü. *See* **Kan U**
Kubō ············· 公方 · 4:121a, 300b
Kubo Kakutarō 久保角太郎 ·· 6:289a
Kubokawa Tsurujirō
  ············ 窪川鶴次郎 · 4:300b; 7:25a
Kubo Ryōgo ··· 久保亮五 · 4:300b-301a
Kubo Sakae ··· 久保栄 ·· 4:301a
  shingeki ························ 7:113a
Kubo Shumman ··· 窪俊満 · 4:301a
Kubota, Ltd ···················· 4:301a
Kubota Mantarō
  ············ 久保田万太郎 ··· 4:301a-301b
  shin kabuki ···················· 4:92a
Kubota Michiharu
  ············ 久保田通治 ···· 4:301b
Kubota Utsubo · 窪田空穂 ·· 4:301b
Kubunden ············· 口分田 ·· 4:301b
Kubushiro Ochimi
  ············ 久布白落実 ···· 4:301b
  fusen Kakutoku Dōmei ········· 2:374b
Kuchiei and kuchimai
  ············ 口永, 口米 4:301b; 5:360b
Kuchigin ············· 口銀 ·· 4:301b
Kuchimane muko 口真似聟 ·· 4:327a
Kuchinashi (gardenia) ············ 3:8a
Kuchizeni ············· 口銭 ·· 4:301b
Kūchō ···················· 6:357b
Kudamatsu ············· 下松 ·· 4:302a
Kudara ············· 百済 · 6:146a-146b
Kudara Daiji ··· 百済大寺 ·· 2:55a
Kudaradera remains
  ············ 百済寺址 ···· 4:302a
Kudashibumi ········· 下文 ·· 4:302a
  chōsen ························ 1:303b
  gejijō ························ 3:15a
Kuden. 公田 *See* **Kōden**
Kudo ···················· 4:120b
Kudō Heisuke ··· 工藤平助 ·1:39a; 4:302a
Kudō Suketsune · 工藤祐経 ·· 3:356a
Kudzu vine ···················· 4:323a
Kueiden (publicly
  managed fields) ·· 公営田 ·· 2:104b
Kuga Katsunan ··· 陸羯南 ·· 4:302a-302b
Kugatachi ············· 盟神探湯 ·· 4:302b
Kuge (Court nobles) · 公家 ·· 4:191a
Kuge (age of aristocratic houses) · 6:176b
Kuge bunko (private libraries) · 8:174a
Kūge nichiyō kufū ryakushū.
  空華日用工夫略集 *See* **Kūge nikkushū**
Kūge nikkushū 空華日工集 ·· 4:302b
Kugo ···················· 7:195a
Kugutsume ············· 傀儡女 ·· 8:259a
Kugyō ···················· 1:96b; 2:40a;
                                     4:302b
Kuhara Fusanosuke
  ············ 久原房之助 · 4:302b-303a;
                                     7:276b
Kuiawase ···················· 6:277b
Kuina ···················· 6:277b
Kuji ············· 旧辞 ·· 4:340b
Kuji (city) ············· 久慈 ·· 4:303a
Kuji ("public matters")
  ············ 公事 ···· 4:303a
Kujigawa ············· 久慈川 ·· 4:303a
Kujikata Osadamegaki
  ············ 公事方御定書 · 4:303a-303b
  Ofuregaki Shūsei ············ 6:68a

shioki · · · · · · · · · · · · · · · · 7:140b
Kujikata Osadamegaki
  code · · · · · · 公事方御定書 · · 8:53a, 113b
Kuji kongen · · · 公事根源 · · · · · 4:303b
Kujira · · · · · · · · · · · · · · 8:249a-249b
Kujō family · · · · · 九条家 · 4:303b; 7:58a
  Fujiwara no Nobuzane · · · · · · 2:353a
Kujō Kanezane · · 九条兼実 · · · · 4:303b
  Fukuharakyō · · · · · · · · · · · 2:363a
  Gyokuyō · · · · · · · · · · · · · 3:71b
  Jien · · · · · · · · · · · · · · · · · 4:53b
  Kujō family descended from · · 4:303b
  literature · · · · · · · · · · · · · · 5:40a
Kujū Kōgen · · · 久住高原 · · · · · 4:303b
Kujūkurihama · · 九十九里浜 · 1:92a; 4:303b
Kujūsan · · · · · · · 久住山 · · · · 4:303b
Kukadachi · · · · · 盟神探湯 · · · · 4:302b
Kūkai · · · · · · · · 空海 1:178b; 4:183a,
                      304a; 5:30a, 295a
  Buddhist sculpture · · · · 1:198a-198b
  charcoal making · · · · · · · · · 1:267a
  Chinese poetry · · · · · · · · · · 1:293b
  collection in Kōyasan Treasure House
   · · · · · · · · · · · · · · · · · · · 4:299b
  education · · · · · · · · · · · · · · 2:172b
  esoteric ritual implements · · · · 1:196a
  Fushimi Inari Shrine · · · · · · · 2:375a
  iroha poem · · · · · · · · · · · · · 3:332a
  Jingoji · · · · · · · · · · · · · · · · 4:58b
  Kakuban · · · · · · · · · · · · · · 4:118a
  Kammu, Emperor · · · · · · · · · 4:128a
  Kongōbuji · · · · · · · · · · · · · 4:269b
  Kōshō · · · · · · · · · · · · · · · · *4:304b*
  monasticism · · · · · · · · · 5:237b-238a
  Shingon sect · · · · · · · · · · · · 7:113b
  Shinshōji · · · · · · · · · · · · · · 7:125a
  Shintō · · · · · · · · · · · · · · · · 7:127a
Kukatachi · · · · · 盟神探湯 · · · · 4:302b
Kuki · · · · · · · · · 久喜 · · · · · 4:304a
Kuki Ryūichi · · · 九鬼隆一 · · · · 4:255b
Kuki Shūzō · · · · 九鬼周造 · · · · 4:304b
Kuma (bears) · · · · · · · · · · · · 1:148b
Kumade · · · · · · · · · · · · · · · · *8:80b*
Kumadori · · · · · · 隈取 · · · · · · 4:95b
Kumagai Gumi Co, Ltd · · · · · · · 4:304b
Kumagai Hisatora 熊谷久虎 · · · · 2:270b
Kumagai Naoyoshi
   · · · · · · · · · · 熊谷直好 · · · · 4:304b
Kumagai Naozane
   · · · · · · · · · · 熊谷直実 · · · · 4:305a
Kumagaisō (*Cypripedium japonicum*)
   · · · · · · · · · · · · · · · · · · · 4:305a
Kumagai Taizō · 熊谷岱蔵 · · · · 4:305a
Kumagawa · · · · 球磨川 · 4:305a-305b
Kumagaya · · · · · · · 熊谷 · · · · 4:305b
Kumai Kei · · · · · 熊井啓 · · · · 4:305b
Kumamoto · · · · · · 熊本 · · · · · 4:305b
"Kumamoto Band" · · 4:306b; 6:258a
Kumamoto Plain ·熊本平野 · · · 4:305b
Kumamoto Prefectural Art Museum
   · · · · · · · · · · · · · · · · · · · 4:305b
Kumamoto Prefecture
   · · · · · · · · · · · · · 熊本県 · · · · 4:306a
Kumamoto Yōgakkō
   · · · · · · · · · 熊本洋学校 · · 4:306a-306b
  Janes, Leroy Lansing · · · · · · · 4:2a
Kumano · · · · · · · · 熊野 · · · · 4:306b
Kumanogawa · · · · 熊野川 · · · · 4:306b
Kumano Sanzan Shrines
   · · · · · · · · · 熊野三社 · 4:306b-307a;
                      5:300a
  Shingū · · · · · · · · · · · · · · · 7:115a
Kumano Sea · · · · · 熊野灘 · · · · 4:307a
Kumano Shingū 熊野新宮 · · · · 6:124b
Kumano shrines 熊野神社 · · · · 7:160a
Kumārajīva · · · · · · · · · · · · · 4:71a

Kumashiro Hi · · · · · 熊代斐 · · · · 4:307a
Kumashiro Tatsumi
   · · · · · · · · · · 神代辰巳 2:275b; 4:307a
Kumashiro Yūhi ·熊代熊斐 4:307a; 5:306a;
                      7:83b
Kumaso · · · · · · · · 熊襲 · · · · · 4:307a
  Kagoshima Prefecture · · · · · · 4:105a
  suppression · · · · · · · · · · · · 4:189a
  Yamatotakeru, Prince · · · · · · 8:311a
Kumaya Art Museum · · · · · · · · 3:77a
Kumazasa (*Sasa albo-marginata*) · 1:136a
Kumazawa Banzan
   · · · · · · · · · · 熊沢蕃山 · 4:307a-307b;
                      5:16b; 8:335a
Kumejima · · · · · 久米島 · · · · 4:307b
Kume Kunitake · 久米邦武 3:359b; 4:307b;
                      7:92b
  historiography · · · · · · · · · · · 3:156a
Kume Masao · · · 久米正雄 · · 4:307b-308a
  fūzoku shōsetsu · · · · · · · · · · 2:378b
  Shinshichō · · · · · · · · · · · · · 7:125a
Kume no Sennin 久米仙人 · 5:295b-296a
Kumi · · · · · · · · · 組 · · · · · · 4:308a
Kumiai batsu (labor-union
  clique) · · · · · · 組合閥 · · · · 6:205b
Kumiai Chemical Industry Co, Ltd 4:308a
Kumigashira · · · · 組頭 · 4:55a; 5:270a
Kumihimo · · · · · · · · · · · · · · 4:308a
Kumo · · · · · · · · · · · · · · · · · 7:242b
  shingeki · · · · · · · · · · · · · · · 7:113b
Kumoi Tatsuo · 雲井龍雄 · · 4:308a-308b
Kumon · · · · · · · · 公文 · · · · · 4:308b
Kumonjo · · · · · · 公文所 · 4:308b; 7:8b
  Taira-Minamoto War · · · · · · · 7:300b
Kumo no hate · 雲の涯 · · · · · · 7:335b
Kumonosujō · · · 蜘蛛巣城 · · · · 7:108b
Kumootoko · · · · · 蜘蛛男 · · · · 2:170b
Kumosuke · · · · · · 雲助 4:308b; 7:265b
Kunaichō. 宮内庁
   See Imperial Household Agency
Kunaichō Shoryōbu. *See* Archives and
  Mausolea Department,
  Imperial Household Agency
Kunaichō Zushoryō
   · · · · · · · · 宮内庁図書寮 · · · · 1:82b
Kunashiri · · · · · · 国後 · · · 4:308b-309a
Kundoku kambun · · · · · · · · · · 4:124a
Kung-an · · · · · · · · · · · · · · · · 4:234a
Kuni · · · · · · · · · · · · · 6:258b-260a
Kuni ikki · · · · · · 国一揆 3:268b; 4:309a
  kokujin leadership · · · · · · · · · 4:260a
Kunikida Doppo
   · · · · · · · · · 国木田独歩 · · 4:309a-309b
  naturalism · · · · · · · · · · · · · 5:351a
Kunimidake · · · · · 国見岳 · · · · 4:309b
Kuninaka no Muraji
  Kimimaro · 国中連公麻呂 1:199b; 4:309b
Kuni no mikotomochi 国司 · · · · 4:310a
Kuni no Miya · · · 恭仁京 · · 4:309b-310a
Kuni no miyatsuko · · 国造 · · 1:21a, 147b;
                      4:310a
  uji-kabane system · · · · · · · · · 8:134a
Kunisada. 国貞　*See* Utagawa Kunisada
Kunisada Chūji 国定忠治
  Shimozawa Kan · · · · · · · · · · 7:107b
  Shinkokugeki · · · · · · · · · · · · 7:121a
Kunisaki Peninsula
   · · · · · · · · · · 国東半島 · · · · 4:310a
Kunishū (provincials) 国衆 · · · · 4:260a
Kunitachi · · · · · · · 国立 · · · · 4:310a
Kunitsukami · · · · 国津神 · · · · 4:125b
Kunitsu tsumi · · · 国津罪 · · · · 3:101a
Kuniyaku · · · · · · · 国役 · · · · 4:310a
Kuniyakukin · · · · 国役金 · · · · 4:310a
Kuniyoshi. 国芳　*See* Utagawa Kuniyoshi
Kuniyoshi, Yasuo 国吉康雄 · · · · 4:310b
Kunji · · · · · · · · · · · · · · · · · · 4:143b
Kunōji kyō · · · · · · 久能寺経 · · · · 8:183a

Ku no sekai (World of
  Woe) · · · · · · · 苦の世界 · · · · 8:173b
Kuno Yasu · · · · · 久野寧 · · · · 4:310b
Kuno Yasushi · · · 久野寧 · · · · 4:310b
Kunōzan · · · · · · · 久能山 · · · · 4:310b
Kunōzan-Tōshōgū
   · · · · · · · 久能山東照宮 · · · · 7:153b
Kun readings · · · 4:310b; 5:324b
  ideographs · · · · · · · · · · 4:143a-143b
  Shinsen jikyō · · · · · · · · · · · 7:124b
Kunshō · · · · · · · · · · · · · · · · 2:81b
Kunugi · · · · · · · · · · · · · · · · · 4:22b
Kunuhi · · · · · · · · 公奴婢 · · · · 7:62a
Kuo Mo-jo. *See* Guo Moruo (Kuo Mo-jo)
Kuonji. 久遠寺 *See* Minobusan
Kuo Sung-ling. *See* Guo Songling (Kuo
  Sung-ling)
Kura · · · · · · · · · · · · · 4:106b; 7:248b
Kurabō Industries, Ltd · · · · · · · 4:311a
Kurage · · · · · · · · · · · · 2:305b; 4:50b
Kurahara Korehito
   · · · · · · · · · · 蔵原惟人 · 4:311a; 7:66b,
                      122a
  proletarian literature movement
   · · · · · · · · · · · · · · · · · 6:255-255b
Kurahashijima · · · 倉橋島 · · · · 4:311a
Kurahashi Juhei 倉橋寿平 · · · · 4:201a
Kurahashi Kaku · 倉橋格 · · · · 4:250a
Kurahashi Yumiko
   · · · · · · · · · 倉橋由美子 · · · · 1:209a;
                      4:311a-311b
  Shinchō · · · · · · · · · · · · · · · 7:109a
Kurai · · · · · · · · · · 位 · · · · · 7:248b
Kurai e (Dark Pictures)
   · · · · · · · · · · · · 暗い絵 · · · · 6:230b
Kurakata no Okite
   · · · · · · · · · · 倉方の掟 · · · · 4:59a
Kuramai · · · · · · · · 蔵米 · · · · 4:311b
  kokudainō and · · · · · · · · · · · 4:257a
Kuramayama · · · · 鞍馬山 · · · · 4:311b
Kuramoto · · · · · · 蔵元 · · · · · 4:312a
"Kura no naka" · · 蔵の中 · · · · 8:173b
Kuraray Co, Ltd · · · · · · · · · · · 4:311b
Kurashiki · · · · · · · 倉敷 · · · · 4:311b
  Kurashiki Folkcraft Museum · · · *4:311a*
Kurata Chikara · 倉田主税 · 4:311b-312a
Kurata Hyakuzō 倉田百三 · 4:312a; 7:81a
Kuratsukuribe · · · 鞍作部 · · · · 1:147b
Kuratsukuri no Tori
   · · · · · · · · · · 鞍作鳥 · 1:197a; 2:55b;
                      4:312a; 7:85a
  sanzonzō · · · · · · · · · · · · · · · 7:20a
Kurayashiki · · · · · 蔵屋敷 · · · · 4:312a
  kome kitte · · · · · · · · · · · · · · 4:267a
Kurayoshi · · · · · · · 倉吉 · · · · 4:312a
Kurayoshi Plain 倉吉平野 · · 4:312a-312b
Kure · · · · · · · · · · · 呉 · · · · 4:312b
Kureha Chemical Industry Co, Ltd 4:312b
Kure Ken · · · · · · · · 呉健 · · · · 4:312b
Kuri · · · · · · · · · · · · · · · · · · · 1:270a
Kurihama · · · · · · 久里浜 · · · · 4:312b
Kurihara, Thomas
   · · · · · · · · · 栗原トーマス · · · · 2:268a
Kurikaradani, Battle of
   · · · · · · · · · 倶利伽羅谷の戦 · · · · 4:312b
Kurikara Pass 倶利伽羅峠 · · 4:312b-313a
Kurikomayama · · 栗駒山 · · · · 4:313a
Kuril Current. 千島海流　*See* Oyashio
Kuril Islands · · · · 千島列島 · · · · 4:313a
  Russia and Japan · · · · · 6:340b, 344a
Kurimoto Hōan · 栗本鋤庵 · · · · 4:313a
Kurimoto Iron Works, Ltd · · · · · 4:313a
Kurimoto Joun · 栗本鋤雲 · 4:313a-313b
  French-Japanese relations · · · · 2:331b
Kurimoto Kon · · · 栗本鯤 · · · · 4:313a
Kurishima Sumiko
   · · · · · · · · · 栗島すみ子 · · · · 4:313b

Kuriyagawa Hakuson
·········· 厨川白村 ····· 4:313b
Kuriyama Sempō 栗山潜鋒 ····· 4:313b
Kurobe ············ 黒部 ····· 4:313b
Kurobe Dam · 2:73a; 4:151b; 313a, 313b
Kurobegawa ········ 黒部川 ····· 4:314a
Kurobe Kyōkoku 黒部峡谷 ····· 4:314a
Kurobon ············ 黒本 ····· 4:201b
Kurochiku (Phyllostachys nigra) · 1:136a
Kuroda family ········ 黒田氏 ····· 7:320a
Kuroda Hisao ···· 黒田寿男 ····· 4:314a
Kuroda Josui ···· 黒田如水 ····· 4:315a
Kuroda Kiyotaka 黒田清隆 · 3:213a-213b;
4:314a-314b
Kaitakushi ········· 4:113a
Kanghwa, Treaty of ········· 4:140b
Sakhalin ········· 7:1b
Kuroda Kiyoteru. See **Kuroda Seiki**
Kuroda Nagamasa
········· 黒田長政 · 4:314b; 7:56b,
99a
Fukuoka ········· 4:127b
Kurodani shōnin gotō
roku ····· 黒谷上人語燈録 ····· 6:248a
Kuroda Seiki ···· 黒田清輝 · 4:314b-315a;
6:156b; 8:328a
Maiko ········· 4:315a
modern painting ········· 6:155b
Kuroda Yoshitaka
········· 黒田孝高 · 4:315a-315b
Kurōdo-dokoro ···· 蔵人所 ···· 2:350b;
4:315b; 7:65b
rinji ········· 6:318a
takiguchi no bushi ········· 7:326b
Kurofune ············ 黒船 ····· 4:315b
technology transfer ········· 7:374a
Kurohimeyama ···· 黒姫山 ····· 4:315b
Kurohon ············ 黒本 ····· 4:319b
Kuroi ame ········· 黒い雨 ····· 3:255a
Kuroi kiri ······ 黒い霧 · 4:315b-316a
Kuroi Senji ······ 黒井千次 ····· 4:316a
Kuroishi ············ 黒石 ····· 4:316a
Kuroiso ············ 黒磯 ····· 4:316a
Kuroita Katsumi · 黒板勝美 1:154a; 4:316a
historiography ········· 3:156b
Shintei zōho kokushi taikei editor ···· 4:262b
Kuroiwa Jūgo ···· 黒岩重吾 ····· 4:316b
Kuroiwa Ruikō ··· 黒岩涙香 · 4:316b; 8:339a
Futsū Senkyo Kisei Dōmeikai ··· 2:376a
Kuroiwa Shūroku 黒岩周六 ····· 4:316b
Kurokamiyama. 黒髪山 See **Nantaisan**
Kurokawa Kishō · 黒川紀章 ····· 4:316b
Kurokawa Toshio 黒川利雄 ····· 4:316b
Kurokawa v Chiba Prefectural Election
Administration Commission · 4:80a
Kuromaru odori (dance)
········· 黒丸踊 ···· 2:299a
Kuromoji [(Japanese spicebush)
Lindera umbellatum; Benzoin
umbellatum] ········· 4:316b
Kuro no shisōsha
········· 黒の試走車 ····· 4:115a
Kuropatkin, Aleksei Nikolaevich · 4:317a
Kurosawa Akira ···· 黒沢明 · 2:56b, 272a,
273a, 274a; 4:317a, 317b-318a
Hashimoto Shinobu ········· 3:110b
Ikiru ········· 3:268b
Rashōmon ········· 6:283b
Seven Samurai ········· 7:73a
Shimura Takashi ········· 7:108b
Kuroshima Denji 黒島伝治 · 4:318a-318b
Kuroshio ···· 黒潮 · 2:284a; 4:318b
Kuroshio current ········· 8:118a
Kuroshoin ············ 黒書院 ····· 7:162b
Kurotokage 黒蜥蜴 3:151a; 4:199a
Kurozumikyō ······ 黒住教 · 4:318b; 7:48a

Kuruidako ········· 狂ひ凧 ····· 8:147b
Kurume ········· 久留米 · 1:276b;
2:365b; 4:318b
Kurume Civic Center ········· 4:207b
Kurume-gasuri ···· 久留米絣 ····· 1:276b
Kurusu Saburō 来栖三郎 ····· 4:318b
Kurutta ippeiji (A Page Out of Place)
········· 狂った一頁 · 2:268b; 4:176a
Kuruwa kotoba ········· 2:92b
Kuruwa zōdan (Tales of
the Pleasure District)
········· 廓雑談 ····· 3:95a
Kusaboke ········· 6:274b
Kusaka Genzui 久坂玄瑞 · 3:90a; 4:319a
Kusakezuri kuwa ········· 4:322a
Kusama Isuke ···· 草間伊助 ····· 4:319a
Kusamakura ········· 草枕 ····· 5:350a
Kusama Naokata 草間直方 ····· 4:319a
Kusanagi ········· 草薙 ····· 5:293b
Kusanagi no Tsurugi
("grass-cutting"
sword) ········· 草薙剣 · 1:115b-116a
Kusano Shimpei 草野心平 ····· 4:319a
Kusarigama ········· 4:319a
Kusarigamajutsu ········· 4:319a
Kusatsu (city) ······ 草津 · 4:319a-319b
Kusatsu (town) ······ 草津 ····· 4:319b
Kusatsu Shirane. See **Shiranesan**
Kusawakaba ····· 草わかば ····· 4:123a
Kusazōshi ········· 草双紙 · 1:163b;
4:201b, 319b-320a; 5:49a; 7:103a
akahon ········· 4:319b
Bakin ········· 1:130b
Izumi Kyōka ········· 3:365b
kibyōshi ···· 4:201b-202a, 319b
kurohon ········· 4:319b
Kusemai ········· 曲舞 ····· 4:135b
Kusharon ··· 倶舎論 1:178b; 4:320a;
5:332b
Kusha school ···· 倶舎派 1:178b; 4:320a
Kushida Tamizō · 櫛田民蔵 ····· 4:320a
Kushida Tamizō zenshū
········· 櫛田民蔵全集 ····· 4:320a
Kushikino ········· 串木野 ····· 4:320a
Kushima ········· 串間 ····· 4:320a
Kushimoto ········· 串本 · 4:320a-320b
Kushiro ········· 釧路 ····· 4:320b
Kushirogawa ···· 釧路川 ····· 4:320b
Kussharo, Lake · 屈斜路湖 ····· 4:321a
Kusu (camphor tree) ········· 1:237a
Kusuko Incident · 薬子の変 ····· 4:320b
Fujiwara no Fuyutsugu ··· 2:350a
Kurōdo-dokoro ········· 4:315a
Kusumi Morikage
········· 久隅守景 · 4:320b-321a
Kusunoki. See **Camphor tree**
Kusunoki Masashige
········· 楠木正成 ····· 4:321a
Chihaya Castle ········· 4:270a
Kusunoki Masatsura
········· 楠木正行 ····· 4:275a
Kusunokiryū hanami no
makubari 樟紀流花見幕張 · 4:187a
Kutaiji ········· 九体寺 ····· 4:77b
Kutani ware ········· 九谷焼 · 4:136a, 321b,
337a
Kaga ········· 4:102b
Komatsu ········· 4:265b
medieval ········· 1:263b
museums ········· 5:279b
plate ········· 1:261a
Kutcharo, Lake · 屈斜路湖 ····· 4:321a
Kutōten. See **Punctuation marks**
Kutsukake Tokijirō
········· 沓掛時次郎 ····· 3:107a
Kutsuki Masatsuna
········· 朽木昌綱 ····· 4:321b
Kuttara, Lake ···· 倶多楽湖 · 4:321b; 7:98a

Kuwa ········· 4:322a; 7:265b
Kuwabara Takeo 桑原武夫 ····· 4:322a
haiku ········· 3:80b
Kuwada Yoshinari
········· 桑田義備 ····· 4:322a
Kuwaki Gen'yoku 桑木厳翼 ····· 4:322a
modern philosophy ········· 5:230b
Kuwana ········· 桑名 ····· 4:322a
Kuwayama kofun shikō
········· 桑山古墳私考 ····· 1:76b
Kuwayoboro ········· 鐷丁 ····· 8:327a
Kūya ········· 空也 · 4:322a-322b;
6:335a
Kōshō ········· 4:322b
nembutsu ········· 4:67a
Kuze Hirochika · 久世広周 ····· 1:55a;
4:322b-323a
Kuzu [(kudzu vine) Pueraria
thunbergiana] ········· 4:323a
Kuzu no matsubara
········· 葛の松原 ····· 4:102b
Kuzuryūgawa ···· 九頭竜川 2:364a; 4:323a
Kwanggaet'o monument ········· 4:323a,
323a-323b; 8:220a
Japanese battles in Korea ··· 4:277a
Kwangju Student Resistance Movement
········· 7:6b
historical context ··· 4:284a, 323b
Kwantung Army. See **Guandong
(Kwantung) Army**
Kwantung Territory. See **Guandong
(Kwantung) Territory**
Kyahan ········· 4:323b
Kyaku and shiki. 格,式 See **Engi Shiki**
Kyakushiki compilations
········· 格式編纂 ····· 4:376a
Kyan taiheiki mukō
hachimaki
········· 俠太平記向鉢巻 ········· 7:97a
Kyaramakura (Aloewood
Pillow) ········· 伽羅枕 ····· 4:199a
Kyobuntō jiken 巨文島事件 · 4:267b-268a
Kyōbushō ········· 教部省 ····· 4:323b
Taikyō Sempu ········· 7:297b
Kyōdai Jiken. 京大事件
See **Kyōto University Incident**
Kyōdō Bokin ········· 1:341a-341b
Kyōdo geinō ········· 2:296b
Kyōdō Insatsu sōgi. 共同印刷争議
See **Kyōdō Printing Company strike**
Kyōdo kenkyū ···· 郷土研究 · 4:323b-324a
Kyōdō News Service · 4:324a; 5:369a
international communications · 3:318b
Kyōdō Oil Co, Ltd ········· 4:324a
Kyōdō Printing Company strike · 4:324a
Kyōdō Shimbun Kisha Kurabu
(Associated Newspapers Journalist
Club) ········· 6:236a
Kyōdo shinsho ···· 郷土新書 ····· 6:288a
Kyōdō Shiryō Co, Ltd ········· 4:324a
Kyōdō Tsūshinsha ········· 4:324a
Kyōdō Un'yu Kaisha ········· 7:109a
Kyōfūkai ········· 矯風会 · 4:324b; 7:23b,
54a; 8:257b
Kanno Suga ········· 4:145a
prostitution ········· 6:257a
Yajima Kajiko ········· 8:284b
Kyōga ········· 4:201a
Kyōgaku Taishi · 教学大旨 · 2:175b-176a
Kyōganoko musume
Dōjōji ···· 京鹿子娘道成寺 ····· 4:93a
Kyōgen ········· 狂言 · 2:74b-75a;
4:324b-329a, 336b; 5:15b; 7:80b; 8:21b-22a
Bōshibari ········· 4:326b
classification and content · 4:326b-328a
daimyō (feudal lord) ········· 4:327a
first-group plays ········· 4:327a
Mai (dance) ········· 4:327b

Muko (bridegroom, son-in-law) ·········· **4**:327a–327b
Oni (Devil) ·········· **4**:327b
Shukke (Buddhist priest) ·········· **4**:327b
Tarō Kaja or Shōmyō ·········· **4**:327a
Yamabushi (mountain ascetic) ·········· **4**:327b
Zatō (blind men) ·········· **4**:327b
costume ·········· **4**:328b; **8**:23b
Fuku no kami ·········· **4**:325a
Fuse nai kyō ·········· **4**:328b
general characteristics ·········· **4**:388b–329a
history ·········· **4**:324b–325b
Iizawa Tadasu ·········· **3**:264a
independent plays ·········· **4**:326b
Izumi Motohide ·········· **4**:327a
Jippensha Ikku ·········· **4**:61b
kabuki ·········· **4**:90b–91a
kabuki adaptations ·········· **4**:92a
masks ·········· **4**:328b
Nakajima Noboru ·········· **4**:325a
name and variants ·········· **4**:324b
Nomura Mansaku ·········· **4**:326b
Nomura Matasaburō ·········· **4**:327a
Nō plays ·········· **4**:326a–326b
sarugaku and ·········· **7**:22a
schools
  Izumi ·········· **3**:366a
  Ōkura ·········· **6**:98a
schools and players ·········· **4**:325b–326a
Setsubun ·········· **4**:327a
Shigeyama Sengorō ·········· **4**:328b
Shigeyama Sensaku ·········· **4**:329a
song, music and dance ·········· **4**:328a
stage properties ·········· **4**:328a–328b
Takai Noriyasu ·········· **4**:325a
Tsukimi zatō ·········· **4**:329a
Yamamoto Tōjirō ·········· **4**:325a
Kyōgen ki ·········· 狂言記 ·········· **4**:328a
Kyōgen mask ·········· **5**:127b
Kyōgen nō ·········· 狂言能 ·········· **4**:324b
Kyōgen plays, masks for ·········· **5**:127a–127b
Kyōgoku ·········· 京極 ·········· **2**:186a
Kyōgoku family ·········· 京極氏 ·········· **4**:329a–329b;
  7:8b
  Fujiwara no Sadaie ·········· **2**:355a
Kyōgoku Tamekane
  ·········· 京極為兼 ·· **4**:329a–330a;
  5:14b
Kyōgyōshinshō ·· 教行信証 ·········· **4**:68a,
  330a–330b; **8**:28a
  Shinran ·········· **7**:123a
Kyōha Shintō. 教派神道 *See* **Sect
Shintō**
Kyōha Shintō Rengōkai
  ·········· 教派神道連合会 ·········· **7**:48a–48b
Kyōhō Famine · 享保の飢饉 ·········· **4**:330b
  rice storage ·········· **4**:117b
Kyōhō Reforms 享保の改革 ·········· **3**:189a;
  4:330b–331b
  meyasubako ·········· **5**:165b
  tashidaka ·········· **7**:347b
  Tokugawa shogunate ·········· **8**:55b
  Tokugawa Yoshimune ·········· **8**:56b
Kyōiku ·········· 教育 ·········· **7**:335b
Kyōiku Chokugo. 教育勅語 *See*
Imperial Rescript on Education
*Kyōiku chokugo
seiritsushi no kenkyū*
  ···· 教育勅語成立史の研究 ·········· **4**:109b
Kyōiku kaikaku ron
  ·········· 教育改革論 ·········· **1**:4b
Kyōiku kanji ·········· **4**:331b; **7**:34b
Kyōiku Kihon Hō
  ·········· 教育基本法 ·· **2**:182a–182b
Kyōiku kihonhō no riron
  ·········· 教育基本法の理論 ·········· **7**:337b
Kyōiku mama ·········· **2**:181b
Kyōikurei ·········· 教育令 ·········· **2**:183a

Kyōiku Sasshin Iinkai ·········· **2**:183a
Kyōiku shinron ·········· 教育新論 ·········· **7**:315b
*Kyōja no kenri no kyōsō/
  Der kampf ums Recht
  des Stärkeren
  und seine Entwicklung*
  ·········· 強者の権利の競争 ·········· **4**:168a
Kyo-jitsu (emptiness-fullness) ·········· **5**:151a
Kyōka ·········· 狂歌 ·········· **4**:331b–332a;
  7:18a
  Karagoromo Kisshū ·········· **4**:157a
  later Edo period ·········· **5**:48a
  Ōta Nampo ·········· **6**:129a
  Shikatsube Magao ·········· **7**:95a
  travel diaries ·········· **8**:105b
Kyōka iezuto ··· 狂歌家づと ·········· **4**:332a
Kyōkai jigen ······ 教界時言 ·········· **4**:233a
Kyōkaku ·········· **4**:332b
Kyōka poets
  Ishida Mitoku ·········· **3**:340a
  Ishikawa Masamochi ·········· **3**:343b
  Karagoromo Kisshū ·········· **4**:157a
  Kubo Shumman ·········· **4**:301a
  Nagata Teiryū ·········· **5**:307a
  Nakarai Bokuyō ·········· **5**:317b
  Ōta Nampo ·········· **6**:129a
  Shikatsube Magao ·········· **7**:95a
Kyōka sakehyakushu
  ·········· 狂歌酒百首 ·········· **4**:331b
Kyōkasho Gigoku 教科書疑獄 ·········· **8**:16a
Kyōka wakabashū
  ·········· 狂歌若葉集 ·········· **4**:157a
Kyōkechi (block-resist
  technique) ·········· 夾纈 ·········· **7**:13b
Kyokutei Bakin. 曲亭馬琴 *See* **Bakin**
Kyokutō Hōsō (JOTF) ·········· **4**:332b
Kyokutō Iinkai ·········· **2**:248a
Kyokutō Kyōwakoku ·········· **2**:248b
Kyokuyō Co, Ltd ·········· **2**:284a; **4**:332b
Kyō Machiko ·········· 京マチ子 ·········· **4**:332b
Kyōnyo Kōju ·········· 教如光寿 ·········· **3**:346b
Kyōō Gokokuji 教王護国寺 ·········· **8**:38a
Kyorai ·········· 去来 ·········· **6**:299b
Kyoraishō ·········· 去来抄 ·········· **4**:169a
Kyorin ·········· **4**:140b
Kyoryūchi ·········· **4**:333a
Kyōsai. 狂斎 *See* **Kawanabe Gyōsai**
Kyōsai gafu ······ 狂斎画譜 ·········· **4**:182a
Kyōsei shikkō ·········· **4**:333a
Kyōshi and kyōbun ·········· **4**:333a–334a
  poets ·········· **4**:333b
  themes and techniques ·········· **4**:334b–335a
Kyōtai kushū ···· 暁台句集 ·········· **4**:169a
Kyōtaku ·········· **4**:334a
Kyōto ·········· 京都 · **4**:334a–335b
  Arashiyama ·········· **1**:74b
  chōnin class ·········· **1**:301a–301b
  gardens ·········· **3**:8b–9a
  Gion Festival ·········· **4**:336b
  growth ·········· **2**:149a–150b
  Heiankyō ·········· **3**:121b–122b
  Kiyomizudera ·········· **4**:334b
  Kyōto Imperial Palace ·········· **4**:336b
  language ·········· **4**:24a
  map ·········· **4**:335a–335b
  Nijō Castle ·········· **4**:334b
Kyōto Art Association ·········· **4**:272a
Kyōto Basin ·········· 京都盆地 · **4**:336b–337b
Kyōto ceramics ·········· 京焼 · **1**:262b, 263b;
  2:295b; **4**:336a, 337a–338a; **6**:35a
Kyōto Ceramics Testing Institute ·· **4**:178b
Kyōto Daigaku Jimbun Kagaku
  Kenkyūjo. *See* **Kyōto University
  Research Institute
  for Humanistic Studies**
Kyōto Fu Tojaku Shihō of 1868 ···· **4**:60b
Kyōto Gozan. 京都五山 *See* **Gozan**
Kyōto Imperial Palace 京都御所 ···· **4**:336b

Kyōto Institute for the Blind and Deaf
  ·········· **7**:241b
Kyōto National Museum ·········· **4**:336a, 337b
Kyōto Prefectural Painting School **4**:272a
  Tanomura Chokunyū ·········· **7**:344b
Kyōto Prefecture ·········· 京都府 · **4**:337b–338b
  geography and climate ·········· **4**:337b–338a
  history ·········· **4**:338a
  industries ·········· **4**:338a
  tourism and culture ·········· **4**:338a–338b
Kyōto printing ·········· **6**:248a
Kyōtō shoshidai
  ·········· 京都所司代 ·········· **4**:338b
  Itakura Katsushige ·········· **3**:350a
Kyōtō shugoshoku
  ·········· 京都守護職 ·········· **4**:338b–339a
  Shinsengumi ·········· **7**:124b
Kyōto University ·········· **4**:339a
  Tanimoto Tomeri ·········· **7**:342a
Kyōto University Incident
  ·········· 京大事件 · **4**:339a–339b;
  7:251b, 255b; **8**:116a
  Gakuren Incident ·········· **4**:339a
  Takikawa Incident ··· **4**:339b; **7**:326b–327a
**Kyōto University Research Institute for
  Humanistic Studies** ·········· **4**:339b
Kyōto ware ·········· 京焼 ·········· **6**:35a
  plate ·········· **1**:262b
Kyōwa Bank, Ltd ·········· **4**:339b–340a
Kyōwa Hakkō Kōgyō Co, Ltd ·········· **4**:340a
Kyōwakai. 協和会 *See* **Concordia
  Society**
Kyō-yaki. 京焼 *See* **Kyōto ceramics**
Kyōyujo ·········· 教諭所 ·········· **4**:340a
Kyōzon Dōshū ·········· **6**:109a
Kyōzuka ·········· 経塚 ·········· **7**:280a
Kyū. *See* **Moxa treatment**
Kyūchū Bō Jūdai Jiken
  ·········· 宮中某重大事件 ·········· **4**:340a
Kyūdō ·········· 弓道 · **4**:340a–340b
Kyūha ·········· **2**:267b
Kyūji ·········· 旧辞 **1**:151a; **4**:340b
  historiography ·········· **3**:152a
  Kojiki based on · ·········· **4**:251a
Kyūjutsu ·········· **4**:340a
Kyūkakoku Jōyaku
  ·········· 九か国条約 ·········· **6**:4b
Kyūketsu hime ·········· 吸血姫 ·········· **4**:157b
Kyūkokukai ·········· **5**:346a
Kyū nihonhei mondai ·········· **8**:278b–279a
Kyūritsū (Physics) ·········· 窮理通 ·········· **6**:187a
Kyūrō gafu ·········· 九老画譜 ·········· **4**:201a
Kyūsei Atami Art Museum. *See* **MOA
  Museum of Art**
Kyūseigun ·········· 救世軍 ·········· **7**:5b–6a
Kyūsei Hakone Art Museum. *See*
  Hakone Museum of Art
Kyūsei kōtō gakkō ·········· **3**:135a
Kyūsekki bunka
  ·········· 旧石器文化 ·········· **6**:159b–160a
Kyūsekki jidai · 旧石器時代 ·········· **6**:160a
Kyūshū ·········· 九州 ·········· **4**:2b
  area ·········· **4**:2b
  dialects ·········· **2**:91b
  population density ·········· **4**:2b, 7a
Kyūshū Electric Power Co, Inc ··· **4**:340b
Kyūshū Matsushita Electric Co, Ltd
  ·········· **4**:340b–341a
Kyūshū Mountains
  ·········· 九州山地 ·········· **4**:341a
  Kunimidake ·········· **4**:309b
Kyūshū region ·········· 九州地方 ·········· **4**:341a
Kyūshū theory ·········· 九州説 ·········· **8**:306a
Kyūshū University ·········· **4**:341b
Kyūtei Edokoro (Imperial Court Office of
  Painting) ·········· 宮廷絵所 ·········· **2**:171a

L

LaBarre, Weston · · · · · · · · · · · · · · 4:38b
Labor · · · · · · · · · · · · · · · · · 4:343a-349b
  Allied Occupation labor reforms
  · · · · · · · · · · · · · · · · · · 4:345b-346a
  arubaito (part-time student) · · · · 2:209b
  "closed" employment systems
  · · · · · · · · · · · · · · · · · 4:344a-344b
  collective bargaining · · · · · · · · 4:348a-348b
  company welfare system · · · · · · · · 2:209b
  compensation · · · · · · · · · · · · · · 4:346a
    bonus · · · · · · · · · · · · · · · 4:348a
    nenkō and benefits · · · · · · · · 4:348a
    shuntō wage pattern · · · · · · · 4:348a
  corvée · · · · · · · · · · · · · · · 1:226a-226b
  corvée (yōeki) · · · · · · · · · · · · · 8:327a
  distribution · · · · · · · · · · · · 2:162a-162b
  dualistic labor markets · · · · · · · · 4:343b
  early patron-client system · · · · 4:343b-344a
  economic growth · · · · · · · · · · 2:160a-161b
  General Strike of 1947 · · · · · · · · · 3:18b
  government role · · · · · · · · · · · · 4:348b
  growth of unionism (1945-1950)
  · · · · · · · · · · · · · · · · · 4:346a-346b
  indentured servants · · · · · · · · · · 2:211b
  industrial labor force, emergence of
  · · · · · · · · · · · · · · · · · 4:343a-343b
  industrial structure · · · · · · · · · · 3:301a
  inflation and price stability · · · · · · · 3:303a
  Japanese emigrants · · · · · · · · 2:200b, 201b
  labor-management relations outlook
  · · · · · · · · · · · · · · · · · 4:348b-349b
  managerial ideology · · · · · · · · · · 5:91b-92b
  Meiji period · · · · · · · · · · · · 2:152a-152b
  minors · · · · · · · · · · · · · · · · · 2:209b
  modern employment system · 2:210a-211a
  nenkō wages and benefits · · · · 4:344b-345a
  premodern system · · · · · · · · · 2:211b-212b
  pressure groups · · · · · · · · · · · · 6:237a
  pre-World War II labor movement 4:345a
  Proletarian literature movement · · · 6:254b
  reemergence of rival labor federations
  · · · · · · · · · · · · · · · · · · · 4:346b
  restraints on unionism after 1947
  · · · · · · · · · · · · · · · · · 4:346b-347a
  salaried · · · · · · · · · · · · · · · · 8:251b
  Sampō: wartime labor front · · · · · · 4:345b
  shagaikō (noncompany workers) · · · 2:209b
  shortage · · · · · · · · · · · · · · · · 2:211a
    industrial robots · · · · · · · · · 3:298b-299a
  shuntō wage pattern · · · · · · · · · · 4:348a
  Sōhyō and Dōmei · · · · · · · · · 4:347a-347b
  structure and function of Japanese
  unionism · · · · · · · · · · · · · 4:347b-348a
  white-collar workers · · · · · · · · 8:251a-251b
  women's rights
    Tanino Setsu · · · · · · · · · · · 7:342a
  worker's compensation · · · · · · · · 8:270a
  work hours · · · · · · · · · · · · 8:270a-270b
  work regulations · · · · · · · · · · · · 8:270b
  Yūaikai and Sōdōmei · · · · · · · 4:345a-345b
  yui · · · · · · · · · · · · · · · · · · · 8:356a
Labor boss system · · · · · · · · · · · · 3:91b
Labor centers · · · · · · · · · · · · · · 4:359b
Labor Dispute Mediation Law (Rōdō
  Sōgi Chōtei Hō) · · · · · · · · · · · 4:351a
Labor disputes · · · · · · · · · · · 4:349b-351a
  Ashio Copper Mine · · · · · · · · · · 1:102a
  at Besshi Copper mine · · · · · · · · 1:150a
  in Hawaii
    Gotō Katsu · · · · · · · · · · · · 3:53a
  pre-World War II · · · · · · · · · · · · 4:345a
  resolution procedures · · · · · 4:349b-350a
  strikes · · · · · · · · · · · · · · 7:250b-251a
  Takita Minoru · · · · · · · · · · · · 7:327a
  work slowdowns · · · · · · · · · 7:250b-251a
Laborers
  dekasegi (work away from home)
  · · · · · · · · · · · · · · · · · 2:83b-84a
  hereditary occupations · · · · · · · · 1:147b
Labor-Farmer Party. *See* **Rōdō Nōmintō**
Labor federations · · · · · · · · · · · · 4:360a
  IMF-JC · · · · · · · · · 3:274b-275a
Labor force
  contemporary · · · · · · · · · · · · 2:161a
  employee dismissal · · · · · · · · · 2:117a
  industrial · · · · · · · · · · · · · · 4:343a
  participation · · · · · · · · · · 4:354b-355b
  women · · · · · · · · · · · · · 8:264a-266a
    protective legislation · · · · · · · 8:269a
Labor laws · · · · · · · · · · · · 4:351a-353b
  Allied Occupation reforms · · · 4:351a-351b
    Labor Relations Adjustment Law
    of 1946 · · · · · · · · · · · · · 4:351b
    Labor Standards Law of 1947 · · 4:351b
    Labor Union Law of 1945 · · · · · 4:351b
  company welfare system · · · · · · · · 1:342b
  labor protection · · · · · · · · · · · · 4:352b
    Labor Standards Law of 1947 · · · 4:352b
    Minimum Wage Law of 1959 · · · 4:352b
    Vocational Training Law of 1958 · 4:352b
  prewar legislation · · · · · · · · · · · 4:351a
    Factory Law of 1911 · · · · · · · · 4:351a
    Labor Dispute Mediation Law of 1926
    · · · · · · · · · · · · · · · · · 4:351a
    Public Order and Police Law of 1900
    · · · · · · · · · · · · · · · · · 4:351a
  revisions · · · · · · · · · · · · · 4:351b-352a
    Public Corporations and Government
    Enterprises Labor Relations Law
    of 1948 · · · · · · · · · · · · · 4:352a
  rights under collective
  bargaining · · · · · · · · · · · · · · 1:334b
  social security · · · · · · · · · · 4:352b-354a
    Employment Security Law of 1947
    · · · · · · · · · · · · · · · · · 4:352b
    Unemployment Insurance Law
    of 1947 · · · · · · · · · · · · 4:352a-353b
  unfair labor practices · · · · · · · · · 8:149b
Labor management relations
  government role · · · · · · · · · · · · 4:348b
  outlook · · · · · · · · · · · · · · · · 4:348b
Labor market · · · · · · · · · · · 4:353b-357b
  changing nature · · · · · · · · · · · · 4:353b
  dualistic · · · · · · · · · · · · · · · · 4:343b
  industrial · · · · · · · · · · · · · 4:343a-343b
  job tenure · · · · · · · · · · · · 4:356b-357b
  labor force participation · · · · · 4:354b-355b
  retired workers · · · · · · · · · · 4:355b-356a
  unemployment workers · · · · · 4:356a-356b
  women · · · · · · · · · · · · · · · · · 4:355b
Labor organizations · · · · · · · · · · · 7:164a
Labor protection laws · · · · · · · · · · 4:352b
Labor reforms of 1945-1947 · 4:357b-358b
  Employment Security Law (1947) · 4:358a
  Labor Relations Adjustment Law (1946)
  · · · · · · · · · · · · · · · · · · · 4:357b
  Labor Standards Law (1947) · · 4:357b-358a
  Labor Union Law (1945) · · · · · · · 4:357b
  National Personnel Law (1948) · · · 4:358b
  Public Corporation Labor Relations
  Law (1948) · · · · · · · · · · · · · 4:358b
  Unemployment Compensation
  Law (1947) · · · · · · · · · · · · · 4:358a
  Workers' Accident Compensation
  Law (1947) · · · · · · · · · · · · · 4:358a
Labor relations
  collective labor agreements · · · · · · 1:334b
  conditions of factory workers, study of
  · · · · · · · · · · · · · · · · · · · 7:164a
  iron and steel industry · · · · · · · · 3:335a
Labor Relations Adjustment Law of 1946
  (Rōdō Kankei Chōsei Hō) · 4:351b, 358a
  amendments · · · · · · · · · · · · · 4:346b
  labor dispute resolution · · · · · · · · 4:349b
  1952 amendment · · · · · · · · · · · 4:352a
Labor relations commissions · · · · 4:346a,
                              358b
  collective bargaining · · · · · · · · · · 1:334b
  conciliation · · · · · · · · · · · · · · · 4:349b
  labor reform · · · · · · · · · · · · · · 4:358a
  unfair labor practices · · · · · · · · · 8:149b
Labor relations laws · · · · · · · 4:351a-352b
Labor rights
  establishment · · · · · · · · · · · · · 4:359a
  fundamental · · · · · · · · · · · · · · 4:345a
Labor Safety and Sanitation Law · · 3:292a
Labor Safety Law · · · · · · · · · · · · 4:358b
Labor Standards Act of 1947
  women · · · · · · · · · · · · · · · · · 8:265b
  workers' compensation · · · · · · · · 8:270a
Labor standards inspection offices
  · · · · · · · · · · · · · · · 2:117a; 4:358b
  work regulations · · · · · · · · · · · · 8:270b
Labor Standards Law (1947)
  · · · · · · · · · · 2:6b; 2:209b, 241b; 4:87a,
             346a, 351b, 352b, 358a
  enforcement · · · · · · · · · · · · · · 4:358b
  industrial injuries · · · · · · · · · · · 3:292a
  women in · · · · · · · · · · 8:261b, 8:269a
  work regulations · · · · · · · · · · · · 8:270b
  See also **Labor laws**
Labor Standards Law (1949)
  work hours · · · · · · · · · · · · · · 8:270a
Labor Thanksgiving Day · · · · · · · · 2:262a
Labor Union Law. *See* **Labor laws**
Labor Union Law (1946) · · · · 4:345b-346a,
             351b, 357b; 6:313a
  since 1948 · · · · · · · · · · · · · · · 4:352a
  1948 revision · · · · · · · · · · · · · · 4:358a
  1949 revisions · · · · · · · · · · · · · 4:352a
  unfair labor practices · · · · · · · · · 8:149b
  See also **Labor laws**
Labor Union Law (1949) · · · · · · · · 6:264b
Labor unions 2:32b, 36b-37a; 4:358b-360a;
           6:206b; 7:219a; 8:376b
  chartering · · · · · · · · · · · · · · · 4:360a
  collective bargaining · · · · · · · · · · 4:360a
  Dōmei · · · · · · · · · · · · · · · · · 2:130a
  enterprise · · · · · · · · · · · · · · · 2:211a
  internal involvement · · · · · · · · · · 4:360a
  national labor federations · · · · · · · 4:359b
  organization · · · · · · · · · · · · · · 4:358b
  post-World War II · · · · · · · · · 2:156a-156b
  public corporations · · · · · · · · · · 6:263b
  rights · · · · · · · · · · · · · · · · · 4:360a
  right to organize · · · · · · · · · · 6:312a-312b
  secondary · · · · · · · · · · · · · · · 4:359a
  Shinsambetsu · · · · · · · · · · · · · 7:124a
  Takano Minoru · · · · · · · · · · · · 7:317a
  wage level · · · · · · · · · · · · · · · 8:198b
Lacquer
  making · · · · · · · · · · · · · · · · · 4:361a
  production · · · · · · · · · · · · · · · 4:361a
  uses · · · · · · · · · · · · · · · · · · 4:361a
  See also **Lacquer ware**
Lacquer pictures · · · · · · · · · · · · 8:181a
Lacquer sap · · · · · · · · · · · · · · · 4:360a
Lacquer tree [(urushi) *Rhus verniciflua*]
  · 4:360a
Lacquer ware · · · · · · · · · · · 4:360b-362a
  boxes · · · · · · · · · · · · · · · 1:166b-167a

decorative techniques ········· 5:85a-85b
general ············· 4:360b-361a
gold- or silver-leaf ············· 4:220b
hira maki-e ················· 4:360b
history ················· 4:361a-362a
  Azuchi-Momoyama period
  (1568-1600) ··············· 4:361a
  early ····················· 4:361a
  Edo period (1600-1868) ········· 4:361b
  Heian period (794-1185) ···· 4:361a-361b
  Kamakura and Muromachi
  (1133-1568) ················ 4:361b
  Kamakura period (1185-1333) ···· 4:361b
  Meiji period ················ 4:361b
  Nara period (710-794) ········· 4:361a
kamakura-bori ·············· 4:121a
kijiya ····················· 4:205a
maki-e ················· 5:85a-85b
museums ················· 5:280a
negoro-nuri ··········· 5:359a-359b
Ladybird Incident ··········· 4:362a
Lady Chatterley's Lover case ··· 4:362a
  Itō Sei ·············· 3:355b-356a
  obscenity ················· 6:50b
Lady Ōtomo of Sakanoue
  大伴坂上郎女 ········ 6:131a
Lafcadio Hearn Bunko ·········· 8:9a
Lagoons
  Hachirōgata ··············· 3:74b
  Hinuma ················· 3:141a
  Jūsan ···················· 4:86a
  Kahokugata ··············· 4:108a
  Saroma ·················· 7:22a
Laity ···················· 4:362a
  lay Buddhist movement ········ 4:372a
  ubasoku ················· 8:123a
  zaike ··················· 8:367b
Lakes
  Hokkaidō
    Abashiri ··············· 1:1b-2a
    Akan ··················· 1:40b
    Fūren ·················· 2:370b
    Kutcharo ··············· 4:321b
    Kuttara ················ 4:321b
    Mashū ················· 5:125b
    Notoro ················· 6:41b
    Ōnuma ················· 6:113a
    Saroma ················· 7:22a
    Shikotsu ················ 7:98a
    Tōfutsu ················ 8:35b
    Tōya ··················· 8:87b
    Uryū ·················· 8:181a
  Honshū
    Biwa ·············· 1:157b-158a
    Chūzenji ··············· 1:315a
    Fuji Five ··············· 2:342b
    Hachirōgata ············· 3:74b
    Hamana ················ 3:91a
    Haruna ················ 3:105b
    Hibara ················· 3:129a
    Hyō ··················· 3:252a
    Imbanuma ·············· 3:274b
    Inawashiro ·············· 3:283b
    Kasumigaura ············· 4:164a
    Kawaguchi ·············· 4:177b
    Kitagata ················ 1:125a
    Kitaura ················ 4:229a
    Mikata Five ············· 5:170b
    Nojiri ·················· 6:32b
    Shinji ················· 7:115a
    Shirakaba ··············· 7:145b
    Tama ·················· 7:332b
    Tazawa ················ 7:359a
    Towada ················ 8:87a
    Yamanaka ·············· 8:300b
  Kyūshū
    Ikeda ·················· 3:265b

"Lamenting the Deviations." *See*
  Tannishō
"Lampoons." *See* **"Nijōgawara no
  rakusho"**
Lamps ····················· 5:9a
Land
  distribution systems
    handen shūju system · 2:104b; 3:95a-96a
  private estates
    shitaji chūban ············· 7:149b
Land allotment system ······ 3:95a-96a
Land conservation ············ 2:326b
Landed estates ··········· 7:155a-158a
  managers ················· 7:163a
Landholders, local (myōshu) ····· 5:291b
Land laws
  Sanze Isshin no Hō (Law of Three
  Generations or a Lifetime) ····· 7:19a
Landlordism ········ 4:362b-363a; 6:353a
  cooperatives ··············· 1:22a
  decline ·················· 4:363b
  development ·········· 4:362b-363a
  land reforms of 1946 ········· 4:365a
  Land Tax Reform of 1873-1881 ··· 4:365b
  origins ·················· 4:362b
Landlord-tenant relationships ···· 2:107b
Land of the Wa ·············· 8:305a
Landowners ················ 6:137b
  collective
    iriai ·············· 3:329b-331a
  ichien chigyō ·············· 3:255a
  rights and obligations ········ 3:255b
  shiryō ··················· 7:148a
Land problem ·········· 4:363b-364a
  housing developers ·········· 3:242b
Land Purchase and Mortgage
  Regulation of 1873 ··········· 2:151a
Land reclamation ··········· 4:364a
  Edo period ················ 4:364a
  Kōbe Port Island ············ 4:364b
  Meiji period ··············· 4:364a
  post-World War II ··········· 4:364a
Land reform
  Kansei Reforms ············· 4:152b
  religion and ··············· 6:292b
Land reforms of 1946 · 1:31a; 4:364a-365b;
                 6:52b, 212a
  agriculture ················ 1:24b
  income distribution ·········· 3:285b
  Okinawa ·················· 6:87b
  women, rural ·············· 8:266b
Land registers ············· 6:128a-128b
Land rent ·················· 4:62b
Land Requisition Orders ········· 1:21a
Land rights ················· 1:274a
Landscape ················· 4:110b
Landscape of the Four Seasons ··· 3:306b
Landscape painting, traditional. *See*
  Sansuiga
Landscapes in miniature ········· 1:161a
Land System History Association · 8:289a
Land Tax Reform Agency ········ 4:366a
Land Tax Reform of 1873-1881 ·· 2:151b,
          361a; 4:365b-366b
  bureaucratic development ····· 1:217a
  chitsuroku shobun ··········· 1:297a
  general description ········ 4:365b-366a
  Ise Rebellion ·············· 3:337b
  Kanda Takahira ············ 4:137b
  kemi discontinuation ········· 4:191b
  kenchi ·················· 4:195a
  ketsuzei ikki ·············· 4:200a
  komononari abolished ········ 4:267b
  Mutsu Munemitsu ··········· 5:288b
  nengu ·················· 5:360b
  reforms ·················· 4:366a
  results ·················· 4:366b
  shizoku ·················· 7:151a

women, rural ··············· 8:266b
Land tenancy ··············· 2:186b
Land tenure system ··········· 4:362b
Language. *See* **Japanese language**
Language of the court ladies ··· 6:45a-45b
Lan-chi tao-lung ············· 6:283b
Lansing-Ishii Agreement ······· 3:341b;
      4:366b-367b; 8:271a
  Terauchi Masatake ··········· 8:12b
  Washington Conference ····· 8:234a-235a
Lansing, Robert ············ 4:367b
  Ishii Kikujirō ·············· 3:341b
Lantern plants, Chinese ···· 3:246a-247a
Lanterns ···· 2:371b; 4:367b-368a; 5:9a
  andon ··················· 4:368a
  bombori ·················· 4:368a
  chōchin ·················· 4:368a
  ishi-dōrō ················· 4:368a
  tōrō ···················· 4:368a
Langi Daolong ·············· 6:283b
Laos refugees ·············· 6:286a
LARA (Licensed Agencies for Relief in
  Asia) ··················· 4:368a
Larch, Japanese [(karamatsu) *Larix
  leptolepis*] ··············· 4:368b
Large Japanese-Russian Dictionary
  ····················· 4:275b
Larks [(hibari) family Alaudidae] · 4:368b
Later Collection of Japanese Poetry
  ····················· 3:48b
Later Three Years' War · 1:4a; 4:368b-369a
  samurai in ················ 7:7b
Lathes ··················· 6:335b
Latin America and Japan ···· 4:369a-370a
  diplomatic relations ······· 3:323a-323b
  economic relations ········ 4:369b-370a
  premodern relations ······· 4:369a-369b
  since 1868 ················ 4:369b
  trade ················· 3:323a-323b
Latitude Observatory of Mizusawa 7:336a
Latter Age of the Law (mappō) ····· 5:43b
Lattimore, Owen ············· 3:316a
Laurel, José Paciano ········· 4:370a
Laures, Johannes ··········· 4:370a
Laurilignosa culture. *See* **Shōyō jurin
  bunka**
Laver ·················· 6:37a-37b
Law ·················· 4:375b-380b
  Absolute Government under Military
  Law (ca 1500-1868) ········· 4:377b-378a
  Chinese
    ritsuryō system ············ 6:324b
  consumer protection ······· 2:15b-16b
    Installment Sales Law ········ 3:315b
  contemporary ··········· 4:379a-381b
    criminal justice ············ 4:380a
    custom ·············· 4:379a-379b
    disputes and their settlement ··· 4:379b
    legal profession and public ···· 4:380a
    legal tensions ·········· 4:380a-380b
    perceptions and uses ······ 4:379b-380a
    sources ················· 4:379a
  copyright ··············· 2:25b-26a
  Corporate Reorganization Law of 1952
    ···················· 2:33b-34a
  criminal ··············· 2:47b-49b
    Keihō ··············· 7:123b-124a
  Criminal Compensation Law of 1950 2:47a
  Cultural Properties Law of 1950 2:52b-53a
  customary (kanshūhō) ········ 2:53b
  early state (600-800) ······ 4:376a-376b
  equality ··············· 2:230a-230b
  equality of sexes ········· 2:229b-230a
  Institutionalization of Absolutist
  Monarchy (1868-1945) ········· 4:378a
  land
    bunchi seigen rei ··········· 1:208a

legal liability of a third party
(suretyship) ················· 7:278a
military houses ········· 1:206b–207a
morality ···················· 5:248b
to preserve Buddhist temples · 1:203b
rule of law (1945 to present) · 4:378a–379a
Shōen period: decentralized jurisdiction
(800–1500) ············· 4:376b–377b
warrior class ················ 1:206b
See also **Legal system**
Law, attitudes toward ······· 4:370a–370b
Law, constitutional litigation under · 2:13a
Law concerning Compensation for
Nuclear Energy Damages of 1961
··························· 1:114b
Law concerning Prevention of Radiation
Sickness Due to Radioactive Isotopes
of 1957 ···················· 1:114b
Law concerning Regulation of Nuclear
Raw Materials, Nuclear Fuel Materials,
and Nuclear Reactors of 1957 ··· 1:114b
Law concerning Technical Standards
for the Prevention of Radiation
of 1957 ···················· 1:114b
**Law concerning the Control of Important
Industries** ················ 4:370b
Law Concerning the Counting of Age
(1902) ····················· 1:21a
Law concerning the Settlement of
Environmental Pollution Disputes 2:225a
Law concerning the Special Measures
for Atomic Bomb Sufferers of 1968
··························· 1:110b
Law concerning the Treatment and
Clearing of Discharge ········· 3:302b
Law examination ········· 4:370b–371a
Law Examination Control Committee
··························· 4:370b
Law for Examination and Control of
Chemical Materials ··········· 6:220a
Law for Health Protection and Medical
Care for the Atomic Bomb Explosion
Sufferers ··················· 1:110b
Law for the Acceleration of Electric
Power Development ··········· 2:191b
Law for the Payment of Compensation to
Crime Victims (Hanzai Higaisha Tō
Kyūfukin Shikyū Hō) ·········· 2:46b
Law for the Prevention of Capital Flight
··························· 2:320a
Law for the Punishment of Crimes
Relating to the Environmental Pollution
that Adversely Affects the Health of
Persons ···················· 2:224b
Law Governing Monks and Nuns ·· 4:372a
Law of evidence ··· 2:50b; 4:371a–371b
Law of Fire Defense Organization · 2:279b
Law of Summary Procedures for Police
Offenses ··················· 5:196a
Law on Provisional Measures relating to
the Fisheries Zone ············ 2:283a
Law on Territorial Waters (No. 30 of 2
May 1977) ·················· 8:13b
Laws for the Military Houses · 1:206a–207a
Laws Governing the Imperial Court
and Nobility ················ 4:212a
Laws restricting the partitioning of
farm lands ·················· 1:208a
Law to Prevent Excessive Premiums and
Unreasonable Representations ··· 1:67b
Lawyers ················· 4:371b–372a
court-appointed ············· 2:39b
law examination ········· 4:370b–371a
limited role ················ 4:371b
Laxman, Adam Erikovich · 2:60b; 4:372a
Golovnin, Vasilii Mikhailovich ····· 3:44a
Russia ····················· 6:341a
Laxman, Kiril ················ 2:60b

Lay, Horatio Nelson ··········· 4:372b
Lay Buddhist movement ········· 4:372a
LDP (Liberal Democratic Party)
··························· 4:384b–386b
Le ························· 3:304a
Leach, Bernard Howell ·· 2:294a; 4:372b
Leach Pottery, The ············· 4:372b
Lead-glazed wares. *See* **Ceramics**
**League for Establishing a National
Assembly** (Kokkai Kisei Dōmei) · 1:34b;
2:334b; 4:372b–373a; 6:207a
League for the Establishment of
Universal Suffrage ··········· 8:169a
League of Blood Incident (1932) ·· 4:373a
Dan Takuma ················· 2:77b
League of Nations ············· 3:199a
Thailand and Japan ··········· 8:20b
Tripartite Pact ·············· 8:107a
Washington Naval Treaty of 1922 · 8:235a
League of Nations and Japan
··························· 4:373a–373b
League of the Divine Wind. *See*
Jimpūren Rebellion
League to Petition for Universal
Suffrage ··················· 2:376a–376b
Lealand, George A. ············· 7:242b
Learned societies ·········· 4:373b–374a
legal ····················· 4:375b
Learning of the Southern Barbarians
··························· 8:241a
Leased House Law ············· 4:374a
freedom of contract ··········· 2:337b
Leased house rights ·········· 4:374a
Leased Land Law
freedom of contract ··········· 2:337b
land lease rights ············· 4:374a
Leased land rights ·········· 4:374a–374b
Leasing
deposit money ·············· 2:87b
Orient Leasing Co, Ltd ······ 6:116a–116b
Leaves of Jade ·············· 3:71b
"Lectures" faction ············· 4:299b
Lectures on the Development of
Japanese Capitalism ·········· 8:289a
Leeches [(hiru) class Hirudinea] · 4:374a
Lee Hwe-song ··············· 4:374b
Left-wing Socialist Party ········ 8:296b
Legal Affairs Bureaus ··········· 4:80b
Legal cases
After the Banquet case ······· 1:20a–20b
Naganuma case ·············· 5:303a
Legal education ··········· 4:374b–375a
*Legal Reform in Occupied Japan: A
Participant Looks Back* ········ 6:115b
Legal rights ················· 3:252b
Legal scholarship ········· 4:375a–375b
associations ················ 4:375a
civil law ··················· 4:375a
constitutional law ············ 4:375a
criminal law ················ 4:375a
"Japanese philosophy of law" ····· 4:375a
Legal specialists ············· 6:323a
Legal system ············ 4:375a–380b
administrative law ········· 1:13a–13b
administrative litigation ····· 1:13b–14a
administrative procedures ······· 1:14a
administrative scrivener ····· 1:14a–14b
attitudes toward ········· 4:370a–370b
cabinet orders (seirei) ········· 1:229a
confessions ················· 1:350a
contracts ················ 2:20a–20b
criminal procedures ······· 2:49b–51a
domainal ·················· 1:212a
education ·················· 2:182b
history ················· 4:375b–376a
absolutist government under military
law (CA 1500–1868) ······· 4:377b–378a
absolutist monarchy (1868–1945) · 4:378a

contemporary ··········· 4:379a–380b
early state (600–800) ······· 4:376a–376b
rule of law (1945 to the present)
··························· 4:378a–379a
Shōen period: decentralized jurisdictions
(800–1500) ············· 4:376b–377b
Legal Training and Research Institute
··················· 2:246a; 4:380a–381a
Chūō University ············· 1:313b
law examinations ············ 4:371a
structure ·················· 4:380b
Le Gendre, Charles William ····· 4:381a
Legends
fireflies ················ 2:280a–280b
ochiudo ···················· 6:60a
Legends of Mt. Shigi, The ··· 7:92b–93a
Legends of Tōno, The ·········· 8:75a
Legislation
delegation of power ··········· 2:84a
modernization of business ······· 2:30a
small- and medium-sized businesses
··························· 7:205b
Legislative reapportionment ······ 4:80a
Legislative supremacy ··········· 4:81a
Legislature. *See* **Diet**
Leisure dress ·············· 5:7b–8a
Leisure-time activities ······· 4:381a–382b;
5:7a–7b
early historical period: courtly pastimes
··························· 4:381a
early modern period: leisurely pursuits of
the townspeople ············· 4:381b
industry growth ············· 4:382a
introduction of Western ····· 4:381b–382a
mass ··················· 4:382a–382b
participation sports ·········· 4:382a
television ·················· 4:382a
medieval period: warrior pastimes · 4:381a
post–World War II ············ 4:382a
western influence ·········· 5:7b–8a
Lelang (Lolang) ·············· 4:382b
commerce of, in prehistory ······ 4:276b
Japanese and Korean ties ········ 4:276a
Lenin, Vladmir Il'ich. *See* **Lenin and
Japan**
Lenin and Japan ········· 4:382b–383a
conversations with Japanese journalists
··························· 4:383a
publication of works in Japan ······ 4:383a
Russia and Japan ············· 6:342b
view of Japan ··············· 4:383a
Lennon, John ················ 6:112a
Léonard, Foujita ·············· 2:347a
Leontief, Wassily ············· 2:144b
Lerch, Theodore von ····· 1:120a; 4:383a;
7:242b
Les Aïnou des Iles Kouriles ······ 1:36a
Lese majesty ············ 4:383a–383b
food demonstrations ·········· 7:165a
Les Grimmaces ·············· 4:178a
Letters, Japanese ············· 7:231b
Leyte Gulf, Battle of
レイテ沖海戦 ········· 4:383b;
5:307b; 8:276a
Li ························· 6:288b
Liability ················ 4:383b–384a
Automobile Liability Security Law of
1955 ····················· 1:120b
compensation for damages ······ 7:226a
employers' ················· 2:209a
government ················· 3:55a
for negligence ············ 4:383b
without fault ·········· 4:383b–384a
Liancourt Rocks ·········· 7:325a–325b
Liang Kai ··················· 4:78a
Liang Qichao (Liang Ch'i-ch'ao) · 1:229b;
4:384a–384b
influence of seiji shōsetsu ········ 7:50a

Liao Chengzhi (Liao Ch'eng-chih) 4:384b
Libel Law of 1875 ·· 1:252a; 4:384b; 6:262b
  Press Ordinance of 1875 ·············· 6:236a
Liberal Democratic Party (LDP) ··· 1:220a;
  2:85a; 4:384b-386b; 6:212b, 215a, 216b;
  7:26a, 28b, 215b
  committees ·························· 4:384b
  Diet ···································· 2:95a
  as government ················ 4:386a-386b
  factions ···························· 4:385b
  funding ···························· 4:384b
  Hatoyama Ichirō ···················· 3:113a
  ideology and policies ·············· 4:385a
  Ishii Mitsujirō ···················· 3:341b
  Japan Socialist Party ················ 4:48a
  Kishi Nobusuke ············ 4:223a-223b
  Kōno Kenzō ······················ 4:274b
  "money politics" ·················· 4:385b
  national defense ············ 5:336b-338b
  New Liberal Club ·················· 5:365a
  Ōno Bamboku ···················· 6:109a
  organization of leadership ···· 4:385a-385b
  pacifism ·························· 6:145a
  peace movement ·················· 6:166b
  postwar dominance ················ 3:204b
  pressure groups ·················· 6:236b
  prime minister and cabinet ········ 6:242b
  reform ···················· 4:385b-386a
  support ···························· 4:384b
  Tanaka Kakuei ···················· 7:337a
Liberalism ···················· 4:386b-387a
Liberal Party (post-World War II) · 4:66a,
  223a-223b, 387b; 6:211b; 7:26a
Liberal Party (prewar). *See* **Jiyūtō**
Librarians (shisho) ········ 5:1b; 7:36a-36b
  assistant (*shishoho*) ················ 5:2b
Libraries ······················ 5:1a-3a
  Asakusa Bunko ·············· 1:95a-95b
  Ashikaga Gakkō Iseki Toshokan ··· 1:100a
  Cabinet Library ·················· 1:229a
  cataloging ························ 5:2b
  classification system ·············· 5:2b
  film ····························· 2:276a
  history ···························· 5:1a
  Hōsa Bunko ······················ 3:234b
  Japan Foundation Library ·········· 4:46a
  Jingū Bunko ·················· 4:58b-59a
  Kanazawa Bunko ·················· 4:136a
  Matsugaoka Bunko ················ 5:133a
  Mitsui Research Institute for Social and
   Economic History ·············· 5:212b
  Nanki Bunko ······················ 5:329a
  National Diet Library ········ 5:338b-339a
  problems ·························· 5:3a
  profession ························ 5:2a
  professional journals for ············ 5:2b
  roles and functions of modern ······ 5:1b
  school ···················· 7:36a-36b
  Seikadō Bunko ···················· 7:50b
  Sonkeikaku Library ······ 1:151b; 7:228a
  subject heading assignments ········ 5:2b
  technical processing ·············· 5:2b
  Tenri Central Library ·········· 8:8b-9a
  Tōkyō Metropolitan Archives and
   Records Institute ················ 8:67b
  Tōkyō Metropolitan Hibiya Library · 8:67b
  Tōyō Bunko ·················· 8:89b-90a
  types ······················ 5:1b, 5:3a
   academic ···················· 5:2a, 5:3a
   children's ························ 5:2a
   national ·························· 5:1b
   prefectural ······················ 5:2a
   public ······················ 5:2a, 5:3a
   school ···················· 5:3a; 7:36a
   special ·························· 5:2a
  Untei ···························· 8:174a
  Yōmei ···························· 8:335a
  Zushoryō ···················· 8:381a-381b

Library Law of 1950 ················ 5:1b
Licensed Agencies for Relief in Asia
  (LARA) ························ 4:368a
Licensing System ·················· 6:276a
Liefde ·············· 1:11a; 2:135b; 5:3a
Life Composition Movement (Seikatsu
  Tsuzurikata Undō) ·············· 6:233a
Life cycle ······················ 5:3b-5b
  age reckoning and ················ 5:3b
  change and conflict ················ 5:5a
  childhood ························ 5:4a
  infancy ·························· 5:4a
  maturity ······················ 5:4b-5a
  old age ·························· 5:5a
  postmortem ······················ 5:5a
  religious rituals ·················· 6:292a
  youth ················ 5:4a; 8:352a-353a
Life expectancy ·················· 6:222a
  economic implications ············ 6:232a
Life insurance ·················· 5:5b
Lifelong learning ················ 5:5b
Life of Jesus, A ·················· 2:214a
Life stages ························ 5:3b
Lifestyles ······················ 5:5b-8b
  education ························ 5:6b
  elderly ·························· 5:7a
  home life ························ 5:7b
  housing ·························· 5:6a
  modern and traditional elements · 5:7b-8b
   education ························ 5:8b
   food and diet ···················· 5:8a
   household furnishings ············ 5:8a
   leisure time activities ············ 5:8a
   occupations ···················· 5:8a
   social status ···················· 5:8b
   women ·························· 5:8b
  schoolchildren ···················· 5:6b
  standard of living and leisure time · 5:7a
  time and space ·················· 5:6a
  women ·························· 5:6b-7a
Lighting equipment ······ 2:370b; 5:8b-9b
Li Hongzhang (Li Hung-chang) ······ 5:9b
  Treaty of Shimonoseki ············ 7:106a
Li ji ···························· 4:165b
Lilies [(yuri) *Lilium* spp.] ······ 5:9b-10a
Limestone ························ 7:278b
Limited liability company ···· 2:31b, 37b;
  5:10a
Limited Liability Company Law (Yūgen
  Kaisha Hō) of 1938 ·············· 5:10a
Limited partnership company · 2:31b, 37b;
  5:10b; 6:164a
Lin Biao ·························· 7:200a
Lindera ·························· 4:316b
Linguistics ···················· 4:30b-32a
Linji Yixuan (Lin-chi I-hsüan; Rinzai
  Gigen) ···················· 6:318b-319a
Lion Corporation ················ 5:10b
Lion dance ························ 2:74a
Lions Club ···················· 5:10b
Li-po y otros Poemas ·············· 7:291a
Li-qi dualism ···················· 7:191a
Li-qi monism ···················· 7:191a
Liquefied natural gas (LNG) · 2:216a, 217a
  Tōkyō Electric Power Co, Inc ······ 8:67a
  Tōkyō Gas Co, Ltd ················ 8:67a
Liquor Tax Law ·················· 2:276b
Literacy ······················ 2:174b-175a
Literacy rate ·················· 5:10b-11a
Literary Age ·················· 1:209a-209b
Literary Arts ···················· 1:209a
Literary Club ···················· 1:209b
Literary criticism ············ 5:11a-17b
  modern ···················· 5:11a-13b
   first modernists ················ 5:11a
   practical critics ················ 5:13a
   professional critics ·············· 5:13a
   traditionalists ················ 5:11b-12a

   Western influence ················ 5:11a
   Westernization, second wave ······ 5:12a
  premodern ···················· 5:13b-17b
   conclusions ···················· 5:17b
   didactic theories ············ 5:16b-17a
   early thoughts ·············· 5:13b-14a
   fiction ·························· 5:14a
   haikai and haiku ················ 5:16a
   Heian Court poetry ·············· 5:14a
   jōruri and kabuki ················ 5:16a
   Kokugaku scholars ············ 5:17a-17b
   medieval waka aesthetics ·········· 5:14b
   Nō drama ···················· 5:15b-16a
   renga and structural principles ···· 5:15a
   valuational criticism in poetry contests
   ·························· 5:14b-15a
Literary critics
  Ara Masahito ···················· 1:74a
  Etō Jun ·························· 2:234a
  Fukuda Tsuneari ·················· 2:362b
  Hanada Kiyoteru ·················· 3:93a
  Haniya Yutaka ·················· 3:98a-98b
  Hirabayashi Hatsunosuke ·········· 3:141a
  Hirano Ken ······················ 3:143b
  Hirotsu Kazuo ···················· 3:151a
  Honda Shūgo ···················· 3:219b
  Ikuta Chōkō ······················ 3:271a
  Ishibashi Ningetsu ················ 3:339a
  Ishikawa Jun ·············· 3:342b-343b
  Itō Sei ···················· 3:355b-356a
  Iwano Hōmei ···················· 3:361a
  Kamei Katsuichirō ········ 1:209a; 4:125a
  Katō Shūichi ···················· 4:169b
  Katsumoto Seiichirō ·············· 4:172a
  Kawakami Tetsutarō ·············· 4:181b
  Kimura Ki ························ 4:211a
  Kitamura Tōkoku ················ 4:227b
  Kobayashi Hideo ············ 4:236a-236b
  Komiya Toyotaka ················ 4:267b
  Kubokawa Tsurujirō ······ 1:209a; 4:300b
  Kurahara Korehito ················ 4:311a
  Kuriyagawa Hakuson ·············· 4:313b
  Masaoka Shiki ·············· 5:123b-124a
  Nakamura Mitsuo ············ 5:315a-315b
  Nakamura Shin'ichirō ············ 5:315b
  Nakano Shigeharu ············ 5:316b-317a
  Nakano Yoshio ·············· 5:317a-317b
  Narushima Ryūhoku ·············· 5:335b
  Odagiri Hideo ···················· 6:61a
  Oda Makoto ······················ 6:61b
  Ozaki Hotsuki ···················· 6:139a
  Shimamura Hōgetsu ·········· 7:99b-100a
  Takayama Chogyū ················ 7:320a
  Taoka Reiun ···················· 7:346a
  Terada Tōru ······················ 8:11a
  Uno Kōji ························ 1:209a
  Usui Yoshimi ···················· 8:182a
  Yamamoto Kenkichi ·············· 8:298b
  Yamazaki Masakazu ·········· 8:312b-313a
  Yasuda Yojūrō ···················· 8:318a
  Yoshimoto Takaaki ················ 8:348a
Literary Front ···················· 1:209b
Literary groups ················ 5:17b-21b
  bundan ···················· 1:208a-208b
  modern ···················· 5:18b-21b
   fiction ······················ 5:18b-19b
   haiku ·························· 5:20a
   other special-purpose ············ 5:21a
   poetry ·························· 5:20a
   politically oriented ············ 5:20b-21a
   tanka ························ 5:19b-20a
   women's ························ 5:20b
  premodern ···················· 5:17b-18b
   Chinese learning ················ 5:18b
   haikai ·························· 5:17b
   publishers and printers ·········· 5:18a
   renga ·························· 5:17b
   writers and artists ·············· 5:18a

Literary magazines ············ 5:21b-24b
　early development (1868-1885) ····· 5:22a
　large literary and comprehensive
　　magazines (1895-1900) ············ 5:22a
　Leftist literary movement (1925-1935)
　　···································· 5:23a
　mid- and late Taishō period (1915-1925)
　　···································· 5:23a
　modern developments (1955-1975) ·· 5:24a
　modern literature (1885-1895) ····· 5:22a
　naturalist literature (1905-1910) ····· 5:22b
　　journals opposing (1910-1915) 5:22b-23a
　non-leftist ······················· 5:23b
　postwar (1945-1955) ··············· 5:24a
　types ·························· 5:21b-22b
　　dōjin zasshi ···················· 5:22a
　　kikanshi ······················· 5:22a
　War (1935-1945) ··············· 5:23b-24a
Literary names ············· 5:325a-326a
Literary prizes ··············· 5:24b-25a
　Akutagawa Ryūnosuke ············· 1:46a
　Akutagawa Ryūnoske Shō (Akutagawa
　　Prize) ·························· 5:24b
　Dazai Osamu Shō (Dazai Prize) ····· 5:24b
　Edogawa Rampo Prize ············· 2:171a
　H-Shi Prize ······················· 5:25a
　Mainichi Geijutsu Shō (Mainichi Art
　　Award) ························· 5:24b
　Naoki Sanjūgo Shō (Naoki Prize) ··· 5:24b
　Nihon Geijutsuin Shō (Japan Art
　　Academy Award) ················· 5:24b
　Noma Bungei Shō (Noma Literary Prize)
　　···································· 6:344b
　Shinchō Bungaku Shō (Shinchō Literary
　　Prize) ·························· 5:24b
　Tanizaki Jun'ichiro Shō (Tanizaki Prize)
　　···································· 5:24b
　Yomiuri Bungaku Shō (Yomiuri Literary
　　Prize) ·························· 5:25a
Literary societies ················· 1:208a
Literary vocational organizations
　···························· 5:21a-21b
Literary World, The ·········· 1:208a-208b
Literati painters ················· 6:154a
Literati painting. *See* **Bunjinga**
Literature ····················· 5:25a-60a
　authors (premodern). *See* Authors,
　　premodern
　criticism
　　modern ················ 5:11a-13b
　　premodern ·············· 5:13b-17b
　critics. *See* Literary critics
　essayists. *See* Essayists
　foreign influence
　　Chinese ·················· 1:292b-296a
　　Western ·················· 8:243a-247b
　genre (modern)
　　biography and biographical · 1:155a-155b
　　book illustration ·········· 1:163b-164a
　　children's ················ 1:279b-280a
　　chūkan shōsetsu ·········· 1:312b-313a
　　drama ···················· 5:57b-60a
　　fūzoku shōsetsu ·········· 2:378a-378b
　　I-novel ····················· 3:312a
　　mystery stories ·········· 5:291b-292a
　　naturalism ·············· 5:351a-351b
　　poetry ···················· 5:56a-57b
　　popular fiction ·········· 6:220b-221a
　　proletarian literature ······ 6:254b-256a
　　science fiction ············ 7:38a-39a
　　seiji shōsetsu ············ 7:50a-50b
　　shimbun shōsetsu ········· 7:103a-104a
　　tanka ······················· 7:343a
　　war literature ············ 8:225b-228a
　genre (premodern)
　　chōka ·················· 1:299a-299b
　　enkyoku ····················· 2:218b
　　fūryū ···················· 2:374a-374b

gesaku ···················· 3:28a-29a
giko monogatari ················· 3:32b
gōkan ························· 3:42a
Gozan literature ············· 3:58a-59b
gundan ························· 3:68b
gunki monogatari ··········· 3:69a-69b
hachimonjiya-bon ··············· 3:74b
haibun ···················· 3:77a-78a
haiku ···················· 3:78b-82a
honkadori ····················· 3:223b
imperial anthologies ············ 3:275b
jitsurokumono ··················· 4:64a
jokotoba ···················· 4:71a-72a
kakekotoba ····················· 4:115b
kana-zōshi ····················· 4:136b
kawaraban ····················· 4:182b
kibyōshi ·················· 4:201b-202a
kobanashi ·············· 4:235a-235b
Kokin denju ····················· 4:254a
kokkeibon ····················· 4:256a
kotobagaki ····················· 4:297a
kusazōshi ·················· 4:319b-320a
kyōka ···················· 4:331b-332a
kyōshi and kyōbun ········· 4:333a-334a
makura kotoba ············· 5:87b-88a
monogatari bungaku ········· 5:245b-246a
nikki bungaku ················· 6:2a-2b
ninjōbon ····················· 6:5b-6b
otogi-zōshi ·············· 6:129b-130b
poetry and prose in Chinese
　···················· 6:193b-197b
renga and haikai ··········· 6:296b-300a
Rokkasen ····················· 6:344b
saijiki ························· 6:369a
sakimori uta ···················· 7:2a-2b
senryū ···················· 8:368a-368b
setsuwa bungaku ············· 7:72a-72b
sharebon ···················· 7:79b-80a
shikashū ···················· 7:94b-95a
travel diaries ·············· 8:104b-106a
ukiyo-zōshi ·············· 8:144a-144b
uta-awase ·················· 8:182a-182b
utagaki ························· 8:183a
uta makura ····················· 8:185b
uta monogatari ··········· 5:245b-246a
waka ···················· 8:201b-217a
yomihon ···················· 8:336a-336b
zappai and senryū ··········· 8:368a-368b
zuihitsu ···················· 8:380a-380b
groups (modern) ············· 5:17b-21b
　bundan ·················· 1:208a-208b
　Ken' yūsha ·············· 4:198b-199b
　Nihon Bungaku Hōkokukai ······ 5:379a
　Nihon Rōman Ha ··············· 5:381b
　Pan no Kai ··················· 6:161b
　Shinkankaku school ········· 7:116a-116b
　Shinkō Geijutsu Ha ··············· 7:119b
　Shirakaba school ········· 7:145b-146b
　Zen Nihon Musansha Geijutsu Remmei
　　(NAPF) ···················· 6:255b
history
　early
　　early ·················· 5:25b-28b
　　Edo ···················· 5:46a-50b
　　Heian ·················· 5:28b-41b
　　medieval ················ 5:41b-46a
　　modern ················· 5:50b-60a
　　postwar ················ 6:230a-231b
　　Shōwa ················ 7:174b-176b
institutions
　Kokubungaku Kenkyū Shiryōkan
　　···················· 4:256b-257a
　Museum of Modern Japanese Literature
　　····························· 5:275b
novelists. *See* Novelists (modern)
playwrights. *See* Playwrights

poets
　free verse. *See* Poets
　haiku. *See* Haiku poets
　renga. *See* Renga poets
　tanka. *See* Tanka poets
　waka. *See* Waka poets
religion and literature
　Buddhism ················ 1:180a-182a
　Christianity ··················· 4:32a
works (modern)
　"Abe ichizoku" ················· 5:252b
　An'ya kōro ····················· 7:90a
　Bokutō kidan ················· 5:300b
　Gan ························· 5:252b
　"Haguruma" ····················· 1:45b
　Hakai ························· 7:101a
　Hototogisu ···················· 8:59b
　"Jigokuhen" ····················· 1:45b
　Kamen no kokuhaku ············· 5:200b
　"Kani kōsen" ················· 4:237b
　Kuroi ame ·················· 3:255b
　"Maihime" ····················· 5:252a
　Miyamoto Musashi ············· 8:347a
　Mon ························· 5:350b
　Sanshirō ····················· 5:350a
　Sasameyuki ··················· 7:343a
　Sembazuru ··················· 4:176b
　Shōsetsu shinzui ··············· 8:110b
　Sorekara ····················· 5:350a
　Suna no onna ··················· 1:3a
　"Takekurabe" ················· 3:136b
　Tsuchi ····················· 5:307b
　Ukigumo ····················· 2:375b
　Yama no oto ··················· 4:176b
　Yoakemae ··················· 7:101b
　Yukiguni ····················· 4:176a
works (premodern)
　Azuma kagami ············ 1:127a-127b
　fudoki ·················· 1:341a-341b
　Hamamatsu Chūnagon monogatari
　　···················· 3:90b-91a
　Heichū monogatari ·········· 3:122b-123a
　Heiji monogatari ·········· 3:123a-123b
　Heike monogatari ·········· 3:124a-125a
　Hōgen monogatari ············· 3:209b
　Hōjōki ····················· 3:129a
　Ise monogatari ············· 3:337a-337b
　Izumi Shikibu nikki ············· 3:366b
　Kagerō nikki ············ 4:104a-104b
　Kaifūsō ····················· 4:109a
　Kinkai wakashū ··············· 4:212b
　Kojiki ·················· 4:251a-251b
　Kokinshū ·············· 4:254b-255a
　Konjaku monogatari ·········· 4:270b-271a
　Makura no sōshi ············· 7:52a-53a
　Man'yōshū ·············· 5:102b-110b
　Nansō Satomi hakkenden ····· 5:329a-329b
　Ochikubo monogatari ·········· 6:59b-60a
　Ōkagami ····················· 6:79a
　Sarashina nikki ············· 7:21a-21b
　Shasekishū ··············· 7:80b-81a
　Shin kokinshū ·········· 7:119b-120b
　Taiheiki ····················· 7:295a
　Taketori monogatari ·········· 7:325a-326b
　Tale of Genji ············· 7:328b-331b
　Tōkaidōchū hizakurige ············· 4:61a
　Tosa nikki ·············· 4:216b-217a
　Towazugatari ··············· 8:87a-87b
　Tsurezuregusa ············· 8:341b-342b
　Tsutsumi Chūnagon monogatari
　　···················· 8:118b-119a
　Uji shūi monogatari ············· 8:137b
　Utsubo monogatari ·········· 8:187a-188a
Lithography ·············· 5:233a-233b
Litigation ···················· 4:81b
Liutiaogou (Liu-t'iao-kou) Incident 5:60a
　Vaughn, Miles W. ··············· 8:189a

Liu Yongfu (Liu Yung-fu) ·········· 5:60a
Livelihood Protection Law (Seikatsu
Hogo Hō) · 4:353a; 5:60a-60b; 7:55b, 209b
Livestock. *See* **Agriculture**
Livestock Communicable Disease
Control Law ···················· 6:274a
Livestock production ········· 1:27b-28a
climate ·························· 1:28a
historical perspective ········· 1:28a
native breeds ················· 1:28b
Living National Treasures ······ 5:60b-61a
Arakawa Toyozō (1955) ········ 1:73b
Cultural Properties Law of 1950 ··· 2:52b
Hamada Shōji ················· 3:89b
Hanayagi Shōtarō ············· 3:95a
Hirata Gōyō ·················· 3:145b
Hori Ryūjo ··················· 3:228a
Ishiguro Munemaro ····· 3:340a-341a
kabuki actors ················· 4:95b
Kaneshige Tōyō ··············· 4:140a
Katō Hajime ·················· 4:168a
Kiritake Monjūrō II ··········· 4:222a
Miwa Kyūwa ·················· 5:216a
Nakamura Utaemon VI ········ 5:315a
Nakazato Tarōemon XII ······· 4:159b
potters ······················· 1:260b
puppeteers ·················· 1:215b
Serizawa Keisuke ·············· 7:69a
Shōno Shōunsai (1967) ········ 1:136a
Tomimoto Kenkichi ······· 8:71a-71b
Toyotake Yamashiro no Shōjō ·· 8:93b
Lizards ·························· 8:40a
Loans ······················· 3:56b-57a
education ···················· 6:174a
goods (suiko) ················ 7:264a
interest rate structure ····· 3:317b-318a
priority system ··············· 3:291b
seed rice (suiko) ·············· 7:264a
small and medium-sized businesses
····················· 6:174a; 7:205b-206a
Loanwords ················ 5:61a-62a
Chinese ······················ 5:61b
differences in meaning ········· 5:62a
Dutch ························· 5:61b
English ······················ 5:61b
French ······················ 5:61b
general description ········· 5:61a-61b
introductory form ············· 5:61b
Japanese language ····· 4:23b-24a, 27a-27b
Portuguese ··················· 5:61b
Russian ······················ 5:61b
Spanish ······················ 5:61b
transformation into Japanese ···· 5:62a
Local autonomy ············ 5:62a-62b
Local Autonomy Law of 1947 3:56a; 4:84a
direct demand ················· 2:101a
Local Civil Service Law (Chihō Kōmuin
Hō), Law No. 261 (1950) · 4:351b; 6:264b
Local government ·········· 5:62b-71a
Allied Occupation ·········· 5:65b-67a
decentralization ·········· 5:65b-66a
new system ··············· 5:66a-66b
problems ···················· 5:66b
Assembly of Prefectural Governors 1:103b
early Meiji period (1868-1878) ··· 5:63a
grants-in-aid ················· 3:56a
Meiji local autonomy system ··· 5:63b-64b
administrative justice ········· 5:64b
district code ················· 5:64b
municipal code ··············· 5:64a
prefectural code ··········· 5:64a-64b
reform ··················· 5:64b-65b
town code ···················· 5:64a
village code ·················· 5:64a
politics ···················· 5:69a-71a
prewar ···················· 5:69a-69b
post-Occupation evolution ··· 5:67a-69a
administrative recentralization 5:67a-68a

finance ···················· 5:68b-69a
local control ··············· 5:68a-68b
stable growth adjustment ········ 5:68b
postwar ···················· 5:69b-71a
prewar ··············· 5:65b, 69a-69b
Three New Laws System (1878-1888)
····························· 5:63a-63b
districts ····················· 5:63b
local taxes ··················· 5:63b
prefectural assemblies ········· 5:63b
towns ························ 5:63b
villages ······················ 5:63b
wards ························ 5:63b
time of Restoration ········· 5:62b-63a
wartime ······················ 5:65b
Local history ················ 5:71a
birthplace history ············· 5:71b
forerunners ··················· 5:71a
"Study of the Lore of Rural Localities"
····························· 5:71b
Local ordinances ············· 5:71b
Lo Chen-yü. *See* **Luo Zhenyu (Lo
Chen-yü)**
Lockheed Scandal ··· 2:45a; 4:386a; 5:72a;
8:160b
Kodama Yoshio ················ 4:241a
Tanaka Kakuei ················ 7:337a
Locusts (inago) ················ 5:72a
Loew, Oscar ··················· 5:72a
London, Jack ················· 5:72a
London Naval Armaments Limitation
Treaty
Uchida Ryōhei ················ 8:124a
London Naval Conferences ···· 5:72b-73a;
7:88b
Hamaguchi Osachi ············· 3:90a
militarism ··········· 5:173a, 174b
Nagano Osami ················ 5:302b
United States ················· 8:158b
Wakatsuki Reijirō ············· 8:219a
London Naval Limitations Treaty
power of supreme command ····· 8:85a
London Naval Treaty ·········· 8:308a
Takarabe Takeshi ············· 7:317b
London Telegram ·············· 7:193b
Long-Term Credit Bank of Japan, Ltd
····················· 1:139b; 5:73a
Long-term credit banks ·········· 1:139b
establishment ················· 1:139b
floating debentures ············ 1:139b
Looms ···················· 5:73a-73b
Lord keeper of the privy seal. *See*
Naidaijin
"Lord of a sixth" ··············· 7:184a
"Lord Tamesuke's Thousand-Poem
Sequence" ···················· 6:290a
Loti, Pierre ···················· 5:73b
Lotte Co, Ltd ·················· 5:73b
Lotteries, public ·············· 5:73b
Dai-Ichi Kangyō Bank, Ltd ····· 2:58b
Lotus [(hasu) *Nelumbo nucifera*]
····························· 5:73b-74a
Lotus Confederation ············· 1:267b
Lotus Sutra 1:177b, 178b-179a, 180b, 186a,
187b, 193b, 282b, 292b; 5:74a, 74b; 7:172a
Eisai ························· 2:187a
exorcism ················· 2:236b-237a
Fuju Fuse sect ················ 2:359b
Genshin ······················ 3:23b
Kannon ······················ 4:144b
Lotus Sutra scroll ············· 5:74b
Namu Myōhō renge kyō ········· 5:327b
new religions ················· 5:366b
Nichiren ······················ 5:375b
Nichiren sect ················· 5:376b
Rinzai sect ··················· 6:319b
Sangyō gisho ················· 7:11b
Tendai sect ··················· 8:4b

thought and culture ··········· 8:26b
uta-e ······················· 8:183a
Love marriage (ren'ai kekkon) ···· 5:320b
Love Suicides at Sonezaki, The ···· 4:77a
Lowborn (semmin) ·············· 7:62a
Lowell, Percival ············· 5:74a
Low-income family slums ········ 7:202b
Low-pollution engines ····· 5:74a-75a
catalytic converter ············ 5:75a
CVCC (combined vortex controlled
combustion) ················· 5:75a
electric automobile ············ 5:75a
ERG (exhaust gas recirculation) ···· 5:75a
general description ········· 5:74a-74b
hydrogen ···················· 5:75a
TGP (turbulence-generating pot) ·· 5:75a
Loyalty ······· 5:75a; 6:163a; 7:213b
filial piety ··················· 2:267a
Seiken igen ·················· 7:51b
Loyalty to the emperor ········ 5:75b
Luck of the Mountains ····· 5:294b-295a
Luck of The Sea ·········· 5:294b-295a
Lucky Dragon Incident ··· 1:113b, 114b;
5:75b-76a; 6:166a
peace movement ··············· 1:111a
Luedorf, August ················ 3:26b
Lu Hsün. *See* **Lu Xun (Lu Hsün)**
Lunch box (warigo) ············· 8:225b
Luncheonettes ················· 7:164b
Luo Zhenyu (Lo Chen-yü) ······ 5:76a
Lüshun ··············· 6:226a-226b
Lute priest ···················· 1:157b
Lutheran Church ············· 5:76a
Lu Xun (Lu Hsün) ············ 5:76b
Luzon ························· 8:276a
Lyman, Benjamin Smith ········ 5:76b
Lytton Commission
·········· リットン調査団 · 1:253a; 5:76b;
7:246b

M

Ma ························ 間 · 1:82a-82b;
5:77a
Mabechigawa ······· 馬淵川 ···· 5:77a
Mabe Manabu ······· 間部学 ···· 5:77a
Mabuchi Kazuo · 馬淵和夫 ······ 4:31b
Mabuta no haha (Mother
in My Dreams) ··· 瞼の母 3:107b; 4:166a
Macaque ·················· 5:245a-245b
MacArthur, Douglas ····· 2:4b, 185b, 248a;
5:77a, 77b, 78a; 6:302b; 7:32b, 47a, 89a,
278a, 245b
Aguinaldo, Emilio ············· 1:32b
Akahata ····················· 1:39b
Diet ························· 2:94b
Dulles, John Foster ············ 2:135a
General Strike of 1947 ··· 3:18b; 4:11b
Korean War ·················· 4:292b
Nine Principles for Economic Stabilization
····························· 6:5a
Occupation ··················· 6:51b
Red Purge ··················· 6:285b
renunciation of war ············ 6:301b
role in constitutional revision ··· 2:3b
San Francisco Peace Treaty and 7:10a-10b
Self Defense Forces ············ 7:58b
United States-Japan security treaties
····························· 8:165b

World War II · · · · · · · · · · · **8:**273a
*MacArthur, His Rendezvous with
History* · · · · · · · · · · · · · · **8:**252b
MacArthur Line · · · · · · · · · · **6:**307b
MacArthur, 1941-1951 · · · · · · **8:**253b
McCarran-Walter Act · · · · · · · · **8:**164b
McCarthy, Joseph · · · · · · · · · **3:**316a
McDonald, Davidson · · · · · · · · **1:**237b
MacDonald, Ranald · · · · · · · · **5:**78a
Machi bugyō · · · · 町奉行 · **5:**78b; **8:**338b
Edo · · · · · · · · · · · · · · · · **2:**171a
Machibure · · · · · · · 町触 · · · · · **5:**78b
Machida · · · · · · · · · 町田 · · · · · **5:**78b
Machieshi (town painters) · · **4:**149b; **7:**43a
Machi hikyaku · · · · 町飛脚 · · · · · **3:**138a
Machine industries
Ebara Corporation · · · · · **2:**142b-143a
Katō Works Co, Ltd · · · · **4:**170b-171a
Komatsu, Ltd · · · · · · · **4:**265b-266a
Kubota, Ltd · · · · · · · · · · · **4:**301a
Nachi-Fujikoshi Corporation · · · · · · **5:**299b
NHK Spring Co, Ltd · · · · · · · **5:**374b
Niigata Engineering Co, Ltd · **5:**385a-385b
Nippon Seikō · · · · · · · · · · · **6:**12a
Sumitomo Heavy Industries, Ltd · · · **7:**268b
Tōshiba Machine Co, Ltd · · · · **8:**82b
Toyoda Automatic Loom Works, Ltd
· · · · · · · · · · · · · · · · · · **8:**90a
Yanmar Diesel Engine Co, Ltd · · · · **8:**316a
Machine Poetiku (*Matinée Poetique*)
· **5:**19a
Machine tool industry · · · · · · · · **5:**78b
"Machi no odoriba"
· · · · · · · · · · 町の踊り場 · · · **7:**176a
Machishū · · · · · · · · 町衆 · **5:**78b-79a;
7:64b
Machi yakko · · · · · · 町奴 · **4:**332b; **5:**79a;
6:221a
Machi yakunin · · · · 町役人 · · · · · **5:**79a
Mackerel [(saba) *Scomber japonicus*]
· · · · · · · · · · · · · **2:**284b; **5:**79a
Macroeconomics · · · · · · · · · **2:**144a-144b
Madai (sea bream) · · · · · · · · · · **7:**45a
Madake · · · · · · · · · · · · · · · **1:**135b
Madenokōji Tokifusa
· · · · · · · · · · 万里小路時房 · · · **4:**196b
Madre de Deus Incident · **1:**83b; **5:**79a-79b,
323a-323b
Mad verse · · · · · · · · · · · · **4:**331b-332a
Maebara Issei · · · 前原一誠 · **5:**79b
Maebashi · · · · · · · · 前橋 · · · · · **5:**79b
Maeda Construction Co, Ltd · · · · · · **5:**79b
Maeda family · · · · · · · 前田氏 · · · **5:**79b-80a
Ishikawa Prefecture · · · · · · · **3:**344a
Kaisakuhō · · · · · · · · · · · · **4:**112a
Kanazawa · · · · · · · · · · · · **4:**136a
Maeda Ikutoku Kai Sonkeikaku Bunko
· · · · · · · · · · · · · · · · · · **7:**228a
Maedakō Hiroichirō
· · · · · · · · · · 前田河広一郎 · · · **5:**80a
Maeda Magoemon
· · · · · · · · · · 前田孫右衛門 · · · **5:**80a-80b
Maeda Seison · · · 前田青邨 · · · **5:**80b
Maeda Tamon · · · 前田多門 · · · **5:**80b
Maeda Toshiie · · · 前田利家 · · · · **5:**80b-81a
Maeda Tsunanori 前田綱紀 · · · **5:**81a-81b
Kaisakuhō · · · · · · · · · · · · **4:**112a
Kanazawa Bunko · · · · · · · · · **4:**136a
Sonkeikaku Library · · · · · · · · **7:**228a
Maeda Yoshinori 前田吉徳 · · · **5:**81b
Maeda Yūgure · · 前田夕暮 · · · **5:**81b
Maegashira · · · · · · · · · · · · · **7:**272a
Maehata Hideko · · 前畑秀子 · · · **5:**81b
Maejima Hisoka · · 前島密 · · · **5:**81b-82a
Maekawa Kunio · 前川国男 · **1:**81a; **5:**82a
Kumamoto Prefectural Art Museum
· · · · · · · · · · · · · · · · · · **4:**305b
Tange Kenzō · · · · · · · · · · · **7:**340b

Maeku zuke · · · · · · · · · · · · **4:**157a
Maeno Ryōtaku · · · 前野良沢 · · **5:**82a-82b,
313a; **7:**258b
Maezumō · · · · · · · · · · · · · · **7:**273a
Mafune Yutaka · · · 真船豊 · · · · · **5:**82b
Mafutsusan · · · · · 麻沸散 · · · · · **3:**94b
Magariya · · · · · · · · · · · · · · · **5:**193a
Magatama. *See* Beads, ancient
Magazine of Women's Learning · · · · **4:**69a
Magazines · · · · · · · · · · · · · **5:**82b-83a
advertising · · · · · · · · · · · · · **1:**17a
censorship · · · · · · · · · **1:**253a, 254b
current trends · · · · · · · · · · · **5:**83a
literary · · · · · · · · · · · · **5:**21b-24b
Meiji period · · · · · · · · · · · · · **5:**82b
personal advice columns (minoue
sōdan) · · · · · · · · · · · · · · **5:**196a
post-World War II · · · · · · · · · · **5:**83a
publishing · · · · · · · · · · · · · **6:**267b
Taishō and Early Shōwa periods **5:**82b-83a
weekly · · · · · · · · · · · · **8:**239a-239b
women's · · · · · · **6:**221a; **8:**268a-268b
Magemono · · · · · · **2:**294b, 295a; **5:**83a
Magic · · · · · · · · · · · · · · · · **8:**273b
dog, Japanese · · · · · · · · **2:**125b-126a
dolls · · · · · · · · · · · · · **2:**128a, 129b
Magnolia Kobus · · · · · · · · · · · **4:**239a
Magnolias · · · · · · **3:**224a-224b; **4:**239a
Mago · · · · · · · · · · · · · · · · **5:**83a-83b
Magome Pass · · · · · 馬籠峠 · · · · · **5:**83b
Magoshi Kyōhei · · 馬越恭平 · · · · · **5:**83b
Maguro · · · · · · · · · · · · · · · · **8:**120a
Magusaba · · · · · · · 粔場 · · · · · · · **5:**83b
Mahāvairocana · · · · · · · · · · · · **2:**64b
Mahāvairocana-sūtra · · · · · · · · · **7:**113b
Mahāyāna Buddhism
· · · · · · · · · · マハーヤーナ教 · **1:**177b-179b;
4:67a, 68b; **6:**270a
architecture · · · · · · · · · **1:**184b-187b
art · · · · · · · · · · · · · · · **1:**184b-187b
calligraphy · · · · · · · · · · **1:**187a-187b
early texts · · · · · · · · · · · · · **1:**177b
Lotus Sutra · · · · · · · · · · · · · **5:**74a
Mādhyamika school · · · · · · · · · **1:**177b
printing · · · · · · · · · · · · **1:**187a-187b
Yogācāra school · · · · · · · · · · · **1:**177b
Mahiru no ankoku
(Darkness at Noon)
· · · · · · · · · · 真昼の暗黒 · **5:**83b-84a;
8:284b
Mahito · · · · · · · · · · 真人 · · · · · **1:**103a
Mah-Jongg · · · · · · **4:**382a; **5:**7b, 84a
"Maiden Sano no Chigami, The"
· · · · · · · · · · · · · · · · · · **7:**15b-16a
Maigoto · · · · · · · · · · 舞事 · · · · **2:**74b
Maihara · · · · · · · · 米原 · · · · **5:**84a-84b
Maiko (apprentice geisha) · · · · · · · · **3:**14a
Maiko · · · · · · · · · · 舞子 · · · · · **5:**84b
Maikov, Nikolai Apollonovich · · · · · **3:**44b
Mai-mai · · · · · · · · · · 舞舞 · · · · **4:**298b
Mainichi Book Award
Kita Morio (1964) · · · · · · · · · **4:**227a
Mainichi Broadcasting System, Inc
(MBS) · · · · · · · · · · · **1:**311a; **5:**84b
Mainichi shimbun
· · · · · · · · · · 毎日新聞 · **1:**4b; **5:**84b;
8:330b
Mai no hon · · · · · 舞の本 · · · **4:**298b
Mai (dance) plays · · · · · · · · · · **4:**327b
Maisaka · · · · · · · · 舞阪 · · · · **5:**84b-85a
Maison Franco-Japonaise · · · · · · · **2:**332b
Maitreya. *See* Miroku
Maitreya, age of · · · · · · · · · · · **8:**337b
Maizuru · · · · · · · 舞鶴 · **4:**337b; **5:**85a
Mājan · · · · · · · · · · · · · · · · · **5:**84a
Majima Toshiyuki
· · · · · · · · · · 真島利行 · **1:**268b; **5:**85a

Majime ningen (A Serious
Person) · · · · · · マジメ人間 · · · · **8:**294b
Major Industries Control Law · · · **3:**293a
Makekoshi · · · · · · · · · · · · · · **7:**273a
Maki · · · · · · · · · · · · 牧 · · · · · **5:**85a
Maki Asami Ballet Company · · · · · **2:**76a
Maki-e · · · · · · **4:**136a, 361a; **5:**85a-85b
inrō · · · · · · · · · · · · · · · · **3:**313b
mother-of-pearl inlay · · · · · · · **5:**256b
wooden ware · · · · · · · · · · · · **8:**269b
Maki Fumihiko · · · 牧文彦 · · · · · **5:**85b
Makiguchi Tsunesaburō
· · · · · · · · · · 牧口常三郎 · · · **5:**85b
Makihanashi · · · · · · · · · · · · · **4:**240b
Maki Itsuma · · · · · 牧逸馬 · · · **3:**116a
Maki Izumi · · · · · · 真木和泉 · · **5:**86a
Hamaguri Gomon Incident · · · · · **3:**90a
Makimono · · · · · · · · · · · · · · **4:**116a
Makino Eiichi · · · 牧野英一 · · · **5:**86a
Makinohara · · · · · 牧ノ原 · **4:**136a; **5:**86b
Makino Masahiro マキノ雅弘 **2:**268b; **5:**86b
Fuji Junko · · · · · · · · · · · · · **2:**343a
Makino Nobuaki · 牧野伸顕 · · · **5:**86b
February 26th Incident · · · · · · · **2:**249b
Makino Shin'ichi 牧野信一 · · · · · **5:**86b
Makino Shinken. *See* Makino Nobuaki
Makino Shōzō · · 牧野省三 · **2:**267b; **5:**87a
Makino Tomitarō
· · · · · · · · · · 牧野富太郎 · · **1:**156a; **5:**87a
Makioka Sisters, The · · · · · · · · **1:**102a
Maki Ryōko · · · · · 巻菱湖 · **5:**87a-87b
Makisu · · · · · · · · · · · · · · · · **2:**25a
Maki Yasuomi. 真木保臣 *See* Maki Izumi
Maki Yūkō · · · · · · 槇有恒 · · · · **5:**87b
"**Makkō Chō**" · · · · 抹香町 · · · · **4:**183a
Makoto · · · · · · · · · · · · · · · · **5:**87b
Kogaku concept · · · · · · · · · · · **4:**247a
in Konishi Raizan's verse · · · · · · **4:**270a
Maksimovich, Kark Ivanovich · · · · **5:**87b
Maku ga orite kara
· · · · · · · · · · 幕が下りてから · **8:**319b
Makura-e · · · · · · · · · · · · · · · **7:**187a
Makura kotoba · · · · **4:**115b; **5:**87b-88a
jokotoba · · · · · · · · · · · · · · **4:**72a
waka · · · · · · · · · · · · · · · · **8:**203a
Makura no sōshi · · · 枕草子 · **4:**166b; **7:**52a,
241a
cats · · · · · · · · · · · · · · · · **1:**251a
cattle · · · · · · · · · · · · **1:**251a-251b
Makurazaki · · · · · · 枕崎 · · · · · **5:**88a
Makushita · · · · · · · · · · **7:**272a, 273a
Makuuchi · · · · · · · · · · **7:**272a, 273a
Malayan Campaign · · · · · · · · · **5:**88a
Malayo-Polynesian languages, Japanese
and · · · · · · · · · · · · · · · **4:**20a-21b
Malay Peninsula · · · · · · · · · · · **5:**88a
Malaysia and Japan · · · · · · · · · **5:**88a-88b
Japanese occupation of · · · · · · · **5:**88a
Japanese settlement in · · · · · · · **5:**88a-88b
postwar Japanese relations · · · · · · **5:**88b
World War II campaign · · · · · · · **2:**348b
Mamako nagare · 継子流れ · · · **4:**166b
Mameita gin · · · · · · · · · **5:**242a-242b
Mamiya Rinzō · · · 間宮林蔵 · **5:**88b-89a
Sakhalin · · · · · · · · · · · · · · · **7:**1b
Mamizukurage · · · · · · · · · · · · **4:**50b
Mammals · · · · · · · **1:**59a-59b, 61b
bats · · · · · · · · · · · · · · · · · **1:**146b
bears · · · · · · · · · · · · · · · · **1:**148b
cats · · · · · · · · · · · · · · · · · **1:**251a
cattle · · · · · · · · · · · · **1:**251a-251b
deer, Japanese · · · · · · · · · · · · **2:**82a
dog, Japanese · · · · · · · · **2:**124b-126a
dormouse, Japanese · · · · · **2:**131a-131b
flying squirrels · · · · · · · · · · · **2:**293b
foxes · · · · · · · · · · · · · · · · **2:**330a
horses · · · · · · · · · · · · · · · · **3:**231a
Japanese spaniel · · · · · · · · **4:**40b-41a

Japanese terrier ··············· **4**:45a
Kamoshika ···················· **4**:129b
Kawauso ····················· **4**:184b
marine mammals ·············· **5**:114a
moles ························· **5**:235b
monkeys ·················· **5**:245a–245b
rabbits ······················ **6**:275a
rats and mice ················· **6**:284a
tanuki ······················· **7**:345a
Tosa dog ··················· **8**:81a–81b
weasels ······················ **8**:238a
whales ···················· **8**:249a–249b
wild boar ···················· **8**:253a
wildcats ····················· **8**:253a
wolf, Japanese ············ **8**:255b–256a
Mammō Dokuritsu Undō
·············· 満蒙独立運動 **5**:99a–99b
Mampukuji ·········· 万福寺 **5**:89a
Ingen ······················· **3**:303b
Manabe Akifusa · 間部詮房 · **5**:89a–89b
Manabe Akikatsu 間部詮勝 · **5**:89b
Management ··············· **5**:89b–91a
conflict resolution ············ **1**:351a
foreign executives ·········· **2**:318a–318b
multinational enterprises ····· **5**:263b
organizational structure and decision
making ···················· **5**:90a–91a
personnel practices ·········· **5**:89b–90a
seniority system ·············· **5**:92b
Management familism ········· **4**:356b
Management of affairs ······· **5**:91a
Managerial careers ········· **5**:91a–91b
Managerial ideology ········· **5**:91b–92b
antibusiness activities ········ **5**:92a
contracts ···················· **5**:92a
definition ··················· **5**:91b
postwar ···················· **5**:92a–92b
prewar ····················· **5**:91b–92a
vs government regulation ····· **5**:92a
Managers
career development ··········· **5**:91b
industrial
managerial ideology ········ **5**:91b–92b
promotion ·················· **5**:91b
recruitment ················· **5**:91a–91b
retirement ·················· **5**:91b
Ma namako (sea cucumber) ······· **7**:45a
Man and vegetation in prehistoric Japan
······························ **5**:92b–96a
anthropogenic period ········· **5**:95b–96a
late-glacial period ············ **5**:93b
paleolithic period ············ **5**:92b–94a
postglacial period ············ **5**:93b–95b
Manase Dōsan 曲直瀬道三 ··· **5**:96a
Manazuru ·········· 真鶴 ··· **5**:96a
Manchukuo ········· 満州国 · **5**:96a–97b;
6:302a; **7**:78a, 264b
Anti-Comintern Pact ·········· **1**:65b
"bandits" and border skirmishes · **5**:97a
formation ·················· **5**:96b–97a
immigration ················· **5**:97a
industries ··················· **5**:97a
land and people ·············· **5**:96b
Provisional Government of the Republic
of China ··················· **6**:260a
Russia and Japan ············· **6**:343a
South Manchuria Railway ····· **7**:237b
war in the Pacific ············ **5**:97a–97b
World War II role ············ **5**:97a–97b
Manchuria
Bohai (Po-hai) ··············· **1**:159b
Concordia Society ············ **1**:349a
Guandong Army ·············· **3**:64a–64b
Japanese conquest
Manchukuo ················· **5**:96a–97b
U.S. reaction ··············· **5**:96b
Japanese immigration ········· **2**:200b
Japanese takeover ············ **5**:98a–98b

Manchurian Incident ··········· **5**:97b–99a
Toi ························· **8**:38a
U.S.-Japanese confrontation ······ **3**:321a
Manchurian Incident 満州事変 **1**:11a,
88a, 237b; **5**:97b–99a; **7**:74b, 92a, 199a,
228a, 251b; **8**:271b
background ·················· **5**:97b–98a
colonial rule in Korea ·········· **4**:283b
Dai Jitao (Tai Chi-t'ao) ········· **2**:59a
foreign trade ················ **2**:320a
freedom of speech restrictions ··· **2**:339a
Grew, Joseph Clark ··········· **3**:62a
Inukai Tsuyoshi ·············· **3**:326a
Itagaki Seishirō ·············· **3**:349a
Kellogg-Briand Pact ··········· **4**:191a
League of Nations ············ **4**:373b
Lytton Commission ··········· **5**:76b
military operations ··········· **5**:98a–98b
Puyi (P'u-i) ················· **6**:271a
Russia and Japan ············· **6**:343a
Shanghai Incident ············ **7**:77b–78a
Shidehara Kijūrō ············· **7**:89a
significance ················· **5**:99a
socio-political context ········· **2**:250a
takeover ···················· **5**:98a–98b
Tatekawa Yoshitsugu ·········· **7**:349a
Tripartite Pact ··············· **8**:107a
Uchida Kōsai ················ **8**:123b
United Kingdom ·············· **8**:152a
Wakatsuki Reijirō ············· **8**:219a
women's suffrage ············· **8**:268b
Manchurian Industrial Development
Company ··················· **7**:237b
**Manchurian-Mongolian Independence
Movement** ················· **5**:99a–99b
Koiso Kuniaki ················ **4**:250b
Mandala ··········· 曼荼羅 **1**:188a, 196a;
5:99b–100b
Dainichi ("Great Sun") ········· **2**:64b
Japanese ···················· **5**:100a–100b
meanings ··················· **5**:99b
Ryōbu mandara ·············· **6**:347b–351b
Shingon sect ················· **7**:113b–115a
types ······················ **5**:99b–100a
general ···················· **5**:99a
Kongōkai mandara · **5**:100a; **6**:349a–351a
Taizō mandara ···· **5**:100a; **6**:348a–349a
Mandara. See **Mandala**
Mandarin duck [(oshidori) *Aix
galericulata*] ··············· **5**:100b–101b
Mandokoro ········ 政所 · **5**:101b; **7**:97b
keishi ······················ **4**:190a
Minamoto no Yoritomo ········ **4**:122a
Ōe no Hiromoto ·············· **6**:67a
proclamations ··············· **4**:90a
Manekineko ········· **5**:*101a*, 101b
Manekogane ·················· **4**:22b
Man'en Kembei Shisetsu
·············· 万延遣米使節 **8**:168b
Manga ···················· **5**:101b–102a
Ancient period ··············· **5**:101b–102a
Edo period ·················· **5**:102a
Hokusai ···················· **5**:*101a*
Middle Ages ················· **5**:102a
modern times ················ **5**:102a
Mange jigoku ···· 万花地獄 **4**:166a
Manginshū ······ 漫吟集 **4**:188a
Manila Declaration ············· **7**:236a
Manji ·············· 卍 **7**:342b
Manjirō, John ················· **5**:313a
Manjushage ·················· **3**:131a
Mannensha ··················· **1**:17a
Manners. See **Etiquette**
Mannō Pond ······ 満濃池 **5**:102a
Manor Regulation Edit of 902 ····· **4**:364a
Mansai ············ 満済 **2**:57b;
5:102a–102b
Mansaku ···················· **8**:255a

Manshū Jihen. 満州事変
See **Manchurian Incident**
Manshūkoku. 満州国 *See* **Manchukuo**
Mantetsu. *See* **South Manchuria Railway**
Mantra ···················· **5**:102b
Shingon sect ················· **7**:113b
Manufacturing ················ **7**:47b
distribution system ··········· **2**:119b
industrial robots ············· **3**:298b–299a
industrial structure ··········· **3**:300b–301b
iron
Tetsuzan hitsuyō kiji ········ **7**:348a
light vs heavy ··············· **3**:300b–301b
Manuscripts ················· **1**:152a
binding ···················· **1**:153a–153b
paper ······················ **1**:153b
script styles ················· **1**:153b
Man'yō Botanical Gardens ········ **4**:257a
Man'yō daishō ki 万葉代匠記 **4**:188a, 258a
Man'yōgana ······· 万葉仮名 · **4**:131b, *133a*;
5:109a–109b
Man'yōkō ········· 万葉考 **4**:129b
Man'yōshū ········ 万葉集 **1**:151b, 165b,
180b; **5**:26a, 28a–28b, 102b–111a;
7:96a–96b, 131a; **8**:286b
anonymous poems and problem of social
range ······················ **5**:108b–109a
chōka ······················ **1**:299b
commentaries ················ **4**:188a, 198b
compilation ················· **2**:352b
content and structure ········· **5**:105a–107a
Book 1 ····················· **5**:105a
Book 2 ····················· **5**:105a–105b
Book 3 ····················· **5**:105b
Book 4 ····················· **5**:105b
Book 5 ····················· **5**:105b
Book 6 ····················· **5**:105b
Book 7 ····················· **5**:105b–106a
Book 8 ····················· **5**:106a
Book 9 ····················· **5**:106a
Book 10 ···················· **5**:106a
Books 11 and 12 ············· **5**:106a
Book 13 ···················· **5**:106a–106b
Book 14 ···················· **5**:106b
Book 15 ···················· **5**:106b
Book 16 ···················· **5**:106b–107a
Book 17 ···················· **5**:107a
Book 18 ···················· **5**:107a
Book 19 ···················· **5**:107a
Book 20 ···················· **5**:107a
decipherment and exegesis · **5**:109b–111a
early Japanese song ···· **2**:137a, 138a–138b
firefly viewing ··············· **2**:280b
folk songs ··················· **2**:301b
Fujiwarakyō references ········· **2**:350a
Fujiwara no Toshinari ········· **2**:357b
historical context ············ **5**:103a–105a
Japanese language, history ······ **4**:28b
Japanese language studies ······ **4**:31a
Kada no Azumamaro lectures ···· **4**:100b
kakekotoba ·················· **4**:115b
Kakinomoto no Hitomaro ······ **4**:117a
Kamo no Mabuchi ············ **4**:129a
Keichū's study ··············· **4**:258a
Kodai kenyū ················· **4**:240b
Kojiki quotations ············ **4**:251b
literary analysis ············· **2**:346b
literary criticism ············· **5**:13b
major poets ·················· **5**:107a–108b
Kakinomoto no Hitomaro **4**:117a; **5**:107b
Kasa no Kanamura ····· **4**:161a; **5**:107b
Nukata no Ōkimi ····· **5**:107a–107b; **6**:44a
Ōtomo no Sakanoue no Iratsume
····················· **5**:108a–108b; **6**:131a
Ōtomo no Tabito ····· **5**:108a; **6**:131b
Ōtomo no Yakamochi ·· **5**:108b; **6**:131b
Takahashi no Mushimaro · **5**:107b–108a;
7:313a

Tanabe no Fubito Sakimaro · · · · · 5:108a
Yamabe no Akahito · · · 5:107b; 8:287b
Yamanoue no Okura · · · · · · · 5:108a;
8:302a-303a
Man'yō writing system · · · · · · 5:109a-109b
Motoori Norinaga · · · · · · · 5:257b
matsuri · · · · · · · · · · · 2:253b
mythology · · · · · · · · 5:292a-292b
nature in · · · · · · · · · 5:357b
Ōnakatomi no Yoshinobu · · · · · 6:105b
orthography · · · · · · · · · 4:134b
pheasants · · · · · · · · · 6:182b
poetry of sakimori · · · · · · · 7:2a
poets · · · · · · · · · · · 5:28a
prosodic features · · · · · 5:104a-104b
sakimori uta · · · · · · · · 7:2a-2b
Sano no Chigami no Otome · · · · 7:15a
Sasaki Nobutsuna · · · · · · 7:23a
scholarship · · · · · · · · 5:109a
Senkaku's study of · · · · · · 7:66a
Shimokōbe Chōryū's research · · 7:105a
Tachibana Akemi · · · · · 7:291b-292a
Tayasu Munetake · · · · · · 7:359a
thought and culture · · · · · · 8:25b
title and compilation · · · · · 5:103a
Tokoyo · · · · · · · · · · 8:44b
travel diaries · · · · · · · 8:104b
waka · · · · · · · · · · · 8:204a
women in Japan · · · · · · · 8:258a
writing system · · · · · · · 4:131b
Man'yōshū kogi
· · · · · · · · · · 万葉集古義 · · 4:128a
Man'yōshū ryakuge
· · · · · · · · 万葉集略解 · · 4:167b
Manza Hot Spring
· · · · · · · · · · 万座温泉 · · 5:111a
Manzai · · · · · · · 5:111a; 7:250a
Manzai kyōkashū
· · · · · · · · 万載狂歌集 · · 4:157a
Manzanar Relocation Center 5:111a-111b
Mao Zedong (Mao Tse-tung) · · · · 1:289a;
5:111b
Maples [(kaede; momiji) *Acer* spp.]
· · · · · · · · · · · · 5:111b-112a
Maple Viewing at Takao · · · · 4:150a
Mappō. *See* **Eschatology**
Maps · · · · · · · 2:65a; 5:112a-112b
cartographers
Inō Tadataka · · · · · · · 3:309a
Nagakubo Sekisui · · · · 5:301b-302a
Dai Nihon enkai jissoku zenzu · · 5:112b
Marathons · · · · · · · · 5:112b
March 15th Incident · · 5:112a-113b; 7:99b,
251b
Shinjinkai · · · · · · · · 7:115b
Tanaka Giichi · · · · · · 7:336a-336b
Tanno Setsu · · · · · · · 7:344a
"Thought Criminal" Probation Law · 8:29a
Watanabe Masanosuke · · · · · 8:236a
March Incident · · 三月事件 · 5:112b-113a
Koiso Kuniaki's role · · · · · 4:250a
Tatekawa Yoshitsugu · · · · · 7:349a
Ugaki Kazushige · · · · · · 8:130b
Marco Polo Bridge
Incident · · · · · · 蘆溝橋事件 · · · 3:201b;
5:113b; 7:199a, 228a; 8:272a, 344a
Tanggu (Tangku) Truce · · · 7:340b-341a
Marebito · · · · · · 客人 · 5:113b; 8:44b
Marē Oki Kaisen
· · · · · マレー沖海戦 · · · · 7:234b
Marē Ran'in kikō
· · · · · マレー蘭印紀行 · · · 4:139a
Mari · · · · · · · · · 毬(鞠) · 4:191a
Maria Luz Incident · 5:113b-114a; 6:178b
DeLong, Charles E. · · · · · 2:84a
Terashima Munenori · · · · · 8:12a
Maria no kubi · マリアの首 · · 7:335b
shingeki · · · · · · · · · 7:113a

Marijuana · · · · · · · · 2:134a-134b
Marine accidents inquiry · · · · 5:114a
Marine insurance · · · · · · 3:316b
Marine mammals · · · · · · 5:114a
Marine parks · · · · · · · 5:114a
Ocean resource development · · · 6:59a
Marine products, processing of · · 7:105a
Marine resources
Ocean resource development · · 6:58b-59a
Marine Science and Technology Center
Ocean resource development · · · 6:59a
Marine transportation · · · · · 8:102a
Maritime Guard · · · · · · · 7:59a
Maritime policies · · · · · · · 3:3b
Maritime Self Defense Forces · · 7:60a-60b
Marketing interdependency · · · · 2:318a
Markets · · · · · · · · 5:114b-115a
consumer · · · · · · · · · 2:17b
Market towns · · 2:148a-148b; 5:115a-115b
premodern · · · · · · · · 2:148a
urban planning · · · · · · · 8:179b
Marquat, William Frederic · · · · 5:115b
Marriage · · · · · · · · 5:115b-118a
adoptive · · · · · · · · 2:242a-242b
age for · · · · · · · · · · 5:4b
"arranged" (miai) · · · · · · 5:320b
changes · · · · · · · · 5:116a-116b
common-law · · · · · · 1:340a-340b
consanguineous · · · · · · · 4:38a
dissolving · · · · · · · · 5:118b
Edo period · · · · · · · · 5:117a
family decisions · · · · · 2:243b-244a
go-betweens, role of · 5:116a, 117a-118a
housewives · · · · · · · 3:241a-242a
husbands · · · · · · · · 3:242a
ie · · · · · · · · · · · 5:116a
industrialization · · · · · 5:117a-118a
investigations · · · · · · · 1:217a
legal requirements · · · · 5:118a-118b
love · · · · · · · · · · 2:244a
"love" (ren'ai kekkon) · · · · 5:320b
matrilocal · · · · · · · · 5:262b
matrilocal (mukoirikon) · · · · 5:262b
miai · · · · · · · · · · 5:166a
minors · · · · · · · · · · 1:16a
modern trends · · · · · · 5:117a-118a
permanent · · · · · · · 5:116b-117a
polygamous · · · · · · · 5:116a-116b
regulation · · · · · · · · 5:117a
social factors · · · · · · 5:115a-116b
traditionally arranged · · · · · 2:244a
Marriage alliances · · · · · 5:116b-117a
Marriage customs
abalones · · · · · · · · · · 1:1b
yomeirikon · · · · · · · · 8:336a
Marriage interview · · · · · · · 5:4b
Marriage law · · · · · · · 5:118a-118b
Marriage negotiations · · · · 5:320b-321a
Marshal · · · · · · · · · 5:118b
Martha Graham Dance Company · 2:76a
Martial arts · · · · · · · 5:118b-120a
aikidō · · · · · · · · · · 1:34a
bugei jūhappan · · · · · · · 1:206a
characteristics · · · · · · · 5:119a
essence · · · · · · · · · 5:119b
iai · · · · · · · · · · · 3:253a
implements for training of samurai 1:206a
jūdō · · · · · · · · · 4:82a-83a
karate · · · · · · · · 4:158a-159a
kendō · · · · · · · · 4:195b-196b
kusarigamajutsu · · · · · · · 4:319a
kyūdō · · · · · · · · 4:340a-340b
methods of practice · · · · 5:119b-120a
philosophy · · · · · · · 5:119a-119b
skills · · · · · · · · · · 5:119b
sōjutsu · · · · · · · · · 7:224a
spiritual training · · · · · 5:119a-119b
Martial law · · · · · · · · 5:120a

Marubashi Chūya
· · · · · · · · 丸橋忠弥 · 5:120a-120b
Maruba shimotsuke · · · · · · 7:107a
Marubeni Corporation · · · · · 5:120b
Marudai · · · · · · · · · · 4:308a
Marudai Food Co, Ltd · · · · · 5:120b
Marugame · · · · · · 丸亀 4:103b; 5:120b
Maruhon-mono · · · 丸本物 · 4:91b, 93b
dialogue · · · · · · · · · 4:94a
Maruichi Steel Tube, Ltd · · · 5:120b-121a
Marui Co, Ltd · · · · · · · 5:121a
Marumino · · · · · · · · · 7:249b
Maruoka Hideko · 丸岡秀子 · 5:121a-121b
Maruoka Kyūka · 丸岡九華 · · 4:198b
Maruyama Hiroshi · 丸山博 · · 5:251a
Maruyama Kaoru · 丸山薫 · · 5:121b
Maruyama Kenji · 丸山健二 1:209a; 5:121b
Maruyama Masao
· · · · · · · · 丸山真男 · 5:121b; 6:73b
gekokujō · · · · · · · · · 3:16a
Maruyama Ōkyo · 円山応挙 1:156b; 5:121a,
121b-122a; 7:17b
Maruyama-Shijō school
· · · · · · · 円山四条派 · 5:122a-122b
Atomi Kakei · · · · · · · · 1:115a
Hiroshige · · · · · · · · · 3:148a
Kanō Tan'yū · · · · · · · · 4:150a
Kōno Bairei · · · · · · 4:178b, 272a
Maruyama Ōkyo · · · · · 5:121b-122a
Matsumura Goshun · · · · · 5:138a
modern painting · · · · · · 6:155b
painting · · · · · · · · · 6:153b
Takeuchi Seihō · · · · · · · 7:326a
Tani Bunchō · · · · · · · · 7:341a
Terazaki Kōgyō · · · · · · · 8:13a
Uemura Shōen · · · · · · · 8:128a
ukiyo-e · · · · · · · · · 8:144a
Maruzen Co, Ltd · · · · · · 5:122b
Maruzen Oil Co, Ltd · · · · 5:122b; 6:182a
Daikyō Oil Co, Ltd · · · · · 2:60b-61a
Marxism · · 2:102b-103a, 142b; 4:11b, 85b
historiography · · · · · · 3:157b-158a
philosophical aspects · · · · 5:231a-232a
postwar adoption · · · · · · 3:203b
pragmatism · · · · · · · · 6:232b
Masakadoki. 将門記 *See Shōmonki*
Masamune Hakuchō
· · · · · · · · 正宗白鳥 · · · · 5:13a,
122b-123a
middle years and turn to drama · 5:123a
move to Tōkyō · · · · · · · 5:123a
Shinshichō · · · · · · · · 7:124b
Masanobu. 正信 *See* **Kanō Masanobu**
Masaoka Shiki · · · 正岡子規 · 4:103a; 5:11b,
123b-124a, 315a; 7:27b, 99b, 311b; 8:216b
Araragi · · · · · · · · · 1:74b; 5:19b
haiku · · · · · · · · · · 3:78b-79a
haiku reform · · · · · · · · 3:79b
Hototogisu · · · · · · · 3:237b; 5:20a
Itō Sachio · · · · · · · · 3:355b
Nagatsuka Takashi · · · · · · 5:307b
Shin kokinshū · · · · · · · 7:120b
Masculine language · · · · 5:124a-125a
Mashi · · · · · · · · · · 1:153b
Mashiko (town) · · · · 益子 · 5:125a
Mashiko ware · · · 益子焼 · 5:125a
teapot · · · · · · · · · · 2:294b
Mashū, Lake · · · 摩周湖 · 5:124b, 125b
Masks · · · · · 1:197a; 5:125b-127b
festivals · · · · · · · · 5:126b-127a
Karura, gigaku mask · · · · · 5:125a
Katen, gyōdō mask · · · · · 5:126a
Kobuaku, kyōgen mask · · · · 5:127b
Koomote, Nō mask · · · · · 5:126b
museums · · · · · · · · · 5:280a
Okame and Hyottoko · · · · · 6:80a
Okina, Nō mask · · · · · · 5:127a
ryōō bugaku mask · · · · · · 5:125b

Mason, Luther Whiting · 5:127b-128a, 286a
Massage
  amma method ················· 1:53a
  shiatsu vs ················· 7:83b
Mass Communication Ethics Group
  ····················· 1:255a
Mass communications ····· 5:128a-129b
  broadcasting ··········· 1:171b-173a
  education, culture and society 5:129a-129b
  historical development ········· 5:128a
  international communications 3:318b-319a
  journalists and their audience · 5:128-129a
  news, opinion and politics ······· 5:129a
  newspapers ············ 5:369a-370a
  structures and functions ····· 5:128a-128b
  treatment of law ············ 4:380a
Massey, Elizabeth and Joseph ···· 4:41b
Master of Go, The ············· 4:176a
Masu ····················· 7:5b
Masuchi Yōjirō 増地庸治郎 ····· 5:129b
Masuda ········· 益田 5:129b; 7:101a
Masuda Takashi · 益田孝 · 5:129b-130a
Masugata (castle
  entrance) ······· 枡形 · 1:248b
Masugatamon ············· 3:13a
Masukagami ········· 増鏡 5:130a
Masumoto Hakaru 増本量 5:130a
Masumura Yasuzō
  增村保造 · 2:272b, 273b
Masutomi Hot Spring
  增富温泉 5:130a
Masuzawa Dam · 桝沢ダム · 7:116a
Matabei. 又兵衛 *See* **Iwasa Matabei**
Matagi ····················· 5:130a
Matamono ········· 又者 · 1:130a
Matatabi-mono ····· 股旅物 · 3:108a
Matchlocks. *See* **Hinawajū**
Materialism Study Society ········ 5:231b
*Material on the History of Northern
  Japan and Her Relations with the
  Asiatic Continent and Russia* ···· 6:232b
Mathematicians
  Hironaka Heisuke ········· 3:147b
  Kakeya Sōichi ············· 4:116b
  Kikuchi Dairoku ··········· 4:206a
  Kodaira Kunihiko ··········· 4:241a
  Ogura Kinnosuke ··········· 6:71a
  Oka Kiyoshi ··············· 6:79b
  Seki Takakazu ············· 7:57b
  Shōda Kenjirō ············· 7:154b
  Takagi Teiji ··············· 7:311a
  Takebe Katahiro ··········· 7:321b
  Yoshida Mitsuyoshi ········· 8:342b
Mathematics
  abacus ··················· 1:1a
  modern ··········· 5:130a-131a
  premodern. *See* **Wasan**
  school curriculum ········· 7:35a
  Taisei sankyō ············· 7:321b
  Takagi class-field theory ······· 7:311a
  yōsan ··················· 8:231a
Matrix Realm ················· 7:310a
Matsu. *See* **Pines**
Matsubame-mono
  (adaptations of Nō
  drama) ········· 松羽目物 5:235a
Matsubara ········· 松原 · 5:131a
Matsuda Eiko · 松田英子 · 2:275a
Matsudaira family. *See* **Tokugawa family**
Matsudaira Hirotada
  松平広忠 · 8:49a
Matsudaira Ietada
  ········· 松平家忠 ····· 5:131a
Matsudaira Katamori
  ········· 松平容保 · 5:131a-131b
Matsudaira Keiei. *See* **Matsudaira
  Yoshinaga**

Matsudaira Nobutsuna
  松平信綱 ····· 5:131b
Matsudaira Sadanobu
  松平定信 · 5:49a,
  131b-132a; 7:84a, 87a
  bakuhan state ············ 3:189b
  Bunka and Bunsei eras ······· 1:211b
  education ················· 2:174a
  Hayashi Jussai ········· 3:116b-117a
  hitogaeshi ················· 3:208a
  Kansei Reforms ············ 4:152a
Matsudaira Tadanao
  松平忠直 ····· 5:132a
Matsudaira Tadayoshi
  松平忠吉 · 5:132b; 7:56b
Matsudaira Yoshinaga
  松平慶永 5:132b; 8:302b
Matsuda Masaki
  松田正恭 ····· 5:135a
"Matsuda reorganization" ······· 6:158a
Matsudo ········· 松戸 ····· 5:132b
Matsue ········· 松江 · 5:132b; 7:100b
Matsue Hot Spring 松江温泉 · 7:115a
Matsue Plain 松江平野 ····· 5:133a
Matsue Shigeyori 松江重頼 ····· 5:133a
Matsugaoka Bunko
  松ヶ岡文庫 ····· 5:133a
Matsui Sumako
  松井須磨子 4:181b; 5:133a;
  7:31a
Matsukata fiscal policy ·········· 2:361a;
  5:133a-134b
  financial crisis of 1878-1880 ····· 5:133b
  impact ············· 5:134a-134b
  industrial revolution in Japan · 3:298a
  kan'ei jigyō haraisage ········· 4:138a
  Matsukata Reform ····· 5:133b-134a
  national banks ············ 5:336b
Matsukata Masayoshi
  松方正義 1:140b; 3:194a;
  5:134a-136a; 7:66b, 263b
  Aoki Shūzō ··············· 1:69a
  Chichibu Incident ········· 1:271b
  Kabasan Incident ··········· 4:89a
  Kabayama Sukenori ········· 4:89b
  Kiyoura Keigo ············· 4:233a
  military career ············· 5:135a
  political career ········· 5:135b-136a
  Shimpotō ················· 7:108b
  Shinagawa Yajirō ··········· 7:109a
Matsukawa Incident
  松川事件 · 5:136a-136b;
  7:25a, 147b
  Hirotsu Kazuo ············· 3:151a
  Shimoyama Incident ········· 7:107b
  Tanaka Kōtarō ············· 7:337b
  Matsukaze ··············· 4:135a
Matsukura Shigemasa
  松倉重政 · 5:136b-137a
Matsumae (town) · 松前 ····· 5:137a
Matsumae family · 松前氏 ····· 5:137a
  Russia ··················· 6:340b
Matsumoto (city) · 松本 ····· 5:137b
Matsumoto Basin 松本盆地 ····· 5:137b
Matsumoto Castle · 松本城 ····· 5:137b
Matsumoto Folk Arts Museum ···· 5:137b
Matsumoto Hikoshichirō
  松本彦七郎 ····· 1:76a
Matsumoto Jōji · 松本烝治 · 2:3b, 319a;
  5:137b
Matsumoto Kōshirō VIII 松本幸四郎(八代)
  ····················· 4:94b
Matsumoto Nobuhiro
  松本信広 ····· 4:20a
Matsumoto Seichō
  松本清張 5:138a; 6:268b;
  7:103b

  Shimoyama Incident ········· 7:107a-107b
Matsumura Akira ··· 松村瞭 ····· 4:35a
Matsumura Goshun
  松村呉春 · 1:211a, 224b;
  5:138a
  Kōno Bairei influenced by ··· 4:272a
Matsumura Jinzō 松村任三 ····· 5:138a
Matsumura Keibun
  松村景文 · 5:138a-138b
Matsumura Kenzō
  松村謙三 ····· 5:138b
Matsumushisō [(Japanese scabiosa)
  Scabiosa japonica] ····· 5:138b
Matsunaga Memorial Gallery ····· 5:138b
Matsunaga Sekigo
  松永尺五 · 5:138b; 7:94b
  Fujiwara Seika ············· 2:358b
  Kaibara Ekiken ············· 4:108b
Matsunaga Teitoku
  松永貞徳 · 2:77a-77b;
  5:18a, 138b-139a, 317b; 6:298b; 7:96a
  haikai ··················· 3:79a
Matsunaga Yasuzaemon 4:205b; 5:139a
  Matsu no koe ··· 松の声 · 4:102a
  Matsu no uchi ··· 松の内 · 8:110b
Matsuo Bashō. 松尾芭蕉 *See* **Bashō**
Matsuoka Eikyū
  松岡映丘 ····· 5:139a
  Kaburagi Kiyokata ········· 4:100b
Matsuoka Gentatsu
  松岡玄達 ····· 1:75b
Matsuoka Joan · 松岡恕庵 ····· 5:139a
Matsuoka Komakichi
  松岡駒吉 ····· 5:139a
Matsuoka Yōsuke
  松岡洋右 · 5:139a-139b
  League of Nations ········· 4:373b
Matsuo Munefusa
  松尾宗房 ····· 1:144a
Matsuratō ········· 松浦党 · 5:139b-140a
Matsuri ········· 1:22b-23a; 2:252b-258a;
  7:139a-139b
  dancing ················· 2:255b
  essentials ··········· 2:254a-255b
    communion ········· 5:331a-331b
    offerings ··············· 2:254b
    purificatory asceticism ······· 7:139a
  hare and ke ··············· 7:362a
  modern society ··········· 2:258a
  seasons ················· 2:254a
  ujigami ············· 8:131a-131b
  ujiko ··················· 2:255b
  village and city festivals ······· 2:255b
  See also **Festivals**
Matsusaka ········· 松阪 ····· 5:140a
Matsushima ····· 松島 · 5:140a, *140b*
Matsushima Bay 松島湾 ····· 5:140a
Matsushiro ········· 松代 ····· 5:140a
**Matsushita Communication Industrial
  Co, Ltd** ················· 5:140a
Matsushita Daizaburō
  松下大三郎 · 5:140a-140b
**Matsushita Electric Industrial Co,
  Ltd** ········· 4:340b-341a; 5:140b; 7:19a
Matsushita Electric Trading Co, Ltd
  ····················· 5:140b
Matsushita Electric Works, Ltd
  ················· 5:140b-141a
Matsushita Kenrin
  松下見林 ····· 3:347b
Matsushita Kōnosuke
  松下幸之助 ····· 5:141a
**Matsushita-Kotobuki Electronics
  Industries, Ltd** ········· 5:141a-141b
Matsushita Reiki Co, Ltd ····· 5:141b
Matsuura ········· 松浦 ····· 5:141b
Matsuura Historical Museum ······ 5:276b

Matsuura Takeshirō
　　　松浦武四郎 ······· **5:**141b
Matsuyama ········· 松山 ······· **5:**141b
　　Dōgo Hot Spring ············· **5:**141a
Matsuyama Plain 松山平野 ··· **5:**141b
Matsuyama Zenzō
　　　松山善三 ··· **5:**141b–142a
Matsuzaka. 松阪 *See* **Matsusaka**
Matsuzakaya Co, Ltd ··········· **5:**142a
Matsuzaki tenjin engi
　　　松崎天神縁起 ······· **7:**42b
"Matters to be announced" ······· **6:**67b
Mattō ············· 松任 ······· **5:**142a
Mawaributai ············· **4:**91b, 95b
Mawari-dōro ··················· **5:**142a
Mawashi ····················· **7:**271b
Mayama Seika 真山青果 ···· **5:**142a
　　shin kabuki ················· **4:**92a
　　Shinseisakuza ··············· **7:**124a
May Day Incident ···· **5:**142a–142b; **7:**252a
Mayet, Paul ··············· **3:**27a; **5:**142b
May 15th Incident
　　　五・一五事件··· **5:**142b–143a
　　Aikyōjuku ··················· **1:**34b
　　Inukai Tsuyoshi ············· **3:**326b
　　Shimpeitai Incident ·········· **7:**108b
　　Tachibana Kōzaburō ·········· **7:**292a
May Fourth Movement 五・四運動
　　　············· **1:**288a; **5:**143a–143b
　　Kita Ikki ··················· **4:**226a
　　Nishihara loans ·············· **6:**16a
　　Shandong (Shantung) Question ···· **7:**77b
Mayoke ······················ **5:**143b
Mayors ······················ **3:**56b
May 30th Incident
　　　五・三〇事件 · **5:**143b; **7:**78a
Mayuzumi Toshirō 黛敏郎 · **5:**144a
Mazaki Jinzaburō
　　　真崎甚三郎 ··········· **5:**144a
　　February 26th Incident ······· **2:**250a
　　Hayashi Senjūrō ············· **3:**117b
　　Kōdōha leader ··············· **4:**243a
Mazda ······················ **6:**339b
Mazushiki shinto
　　　貧しき信徒 ·········· **8:**284a
Mead, George H. ············· **2:**184b
Meakandake ····· 雌阿寒岳 ·· **5:**144a
Meakashi ············· 目明 **5:**144a; **8:**338b
Meanings of Sound, Word, and Reality,
　The ······················ **7:**114b
Measure
　　architectural units ·········· **1:**82b
　　weights and measures ······· **8:**239b–240a
Meat packing industries
　　Itō Ham Provisions Co, Ltd ·· **3:**352a
　　Marudai Food Co, Ltd ······· **5:**120b
　　Nippon Meat Packers, Inc ··· **6:**11a
　　Prima Meat Packers, Ltd ···· **6:**239b
Meckel, Klemens Wilhelm Jakob · **1:**86b;
　　　　　　4:241a; **5:**144a
Medake (*Arundinaria simonii*) ···· **1:**136a
Medals of honor ········· **5:**144a–144b
Mēdē Jiken ··· メーデー事件 · **5:**142a–142b
Median Tectonic line ········· **4:**8b
Mediation
　　contemporary law ··········· **4:**379b
　　labor
　　　Tripartite commissions ··· **4:**351b
　　litigation vs ················ **4:**370b
Medical and health insurance ···· **4:**353a;
　　　　　　　　5:144b–145b
　　financing ··················· **5:**145a
　　health insurance society ······· **5:**145a
　　national ··············· **5:**339a–339b
　　structure ··················· **5:**144b
Medical care
　　health care system ··· **3:**119b–120b

Medical research. *See* **Medicine**
Medicine ··············· **5:**145b–152a
　　acupuncture ················· **1:**10b
　　diseases ··············· **5:**147b–149a
　　　characteristics ········ **5:**147b–149a
　　　common ··············· **5:**147b
　　drugs ················· **5:**150a–150b
　　　approval and reevaluation ···· **5:**150a
　　　consumption and related problems
　　　　　　　　5:150a–150b
　　　manufacture and supply ···· **5:**150a
　　euthanasia ············· **2:**235b–236a
　　general ···················· **5:**145b
　　history ················ **5:**145b–147a
　　　Chinese medicine and Western medicine
　　　　(16th–19th centuries) ··· **5:**146b–147a
　　　classicist school (17th–19th
　　　　centuries) ·········· **5:**146a–146b
　　　from 8th century ········ **7:**170a
　　　introduction of Chinese ··· **5:**146a
　　　latter-day school (16th–19th centuries)
　　　　　　　　5:146a
　　　modernization ········· **5:**147a–147b
　　industrial
　　　occupational diseases ······· **6:**55b
　　Kampō ················· **5:**150b–151b
　　Old-Age Welfare Law ······· **6:**100a
　　physicians
　　　Adachi Buntarō ··········· **1:**11a
　　　Aoyama Tanemichi ········· **1:**71a
　　　Asada Gōryū ··············· **8:**292a
　　　Asada Sōhaku ··············· **1:**92a
　　　Bälz, Erwin von ············· **1:**135b
　　　Dohi Keizō ················ **2:**126a
　　　Furuhata Tanemoto ······· **2:**371b–372a
　　　Gotō Konzan ··············· **3:**53a
　　　Hanaoka Seishū ············· **3:**94b
　　　Iinuma Yokusai ············· **3:**263b
　　　Imamura Arao ··············· **3:**273b
　　　Inada Ryōkichi ············· **3:**282a
　　　Itō Gemboku ··············· **3:**352a
　　　Kaempfer, Engelbert ······· **4:**101b–102a
　　　Kagawa Gen'etsu ··········· **4:**102b
　　　Kagawa Shūtoku ············· **4:**103b
　　　Katsunuma Seizō ··········· **4:**172a
　　　Katsuragawa Hoshū ········· **4:**173a
　　　Kumagai Taizō ············· **4:**305a
　　　Kure Ken ·················· **4:**312b
　　　Kurokawa Toshio ··········· **4:**316b
　　　Maeno Ryōtaku ············· **5:**82a–82b
　　　Manase Dōsan ············· **5:**96a
　　　Mitsuda Kensuke ··········· **5:**209b
　　　Mitsukuri Gempo ··········· **5:**213b
　　　Miura Kinnosuke ··········· **5:**215b
　　　Nagoya Gen'i ·············· **5:**309b
　　　Nakagawa Jun'an ··········· **5:**313a
　　　Ogata Kōan ················ **6:**69a
　　　Ogata Koreyoshi ··········· **6:**69a
　　　Ogino Ginko ·········· **6:**70a–70b
　　　Ogino Kyūsaku ············· **6:**70b
　　　Okinaka Shigeo ············· **6:**84b
　　　Shimazono Junjirō ········· **7:**101b
　　　Shioda Hiroshige ··········· **7:**140a
　　　Sugita Gempaku ············· **7:**258b
　　　Taki Mototaka ·············· **7:**327a
　　　Tamba Yasuyori ············· **7:**333b
　　　Tashiro Sanki ·············· **7:**347b
　　　Udagawa Yōan ·············· **8:**125b
　　　Yamawaki Tōyō ·········· **8:**311b–312a
　　　Yoshimasu Tōdō ············· **8:**347b
　　　Yoshioka Yayoi ············· **8:**349b
　　public health ··········· **5:**149a–150a
　　　aging ·················· **5:**149a
　　　death trends ·········· **5:**149a–149b
　　　future problems ········ **5:**149b–150a
　　　Health Service System ····· **5:**149a
　　　prevention of infectious diseases · **5:**149b
　　　Public Health Service ····· **5:**149b

　　research ················ **5:**151b–152a
　　smallpox vaccine ············· **3:**352a
　　traditional ············· **5:**150b–151b
　　　characteristics ··········· **5:**151a
　　　examination methods ······· **5:**151b
　　　febrile disease ············· **5:**151b
　　　shiatsu ··················· **7:**83b
　　　Shō ················· **5:**151a–151b
　　　two major schools ······· **5:**150b–151a
　　venereal disease ············· **8:**189b
Medieval ceramics. *See* **Ceramics**
Medieval literature. *See* **Literature**
Meditation (zazen) ············· **8:**372b
　　music ····················· **7:**75b
Medium (shamanism) ············ **7:**76b
Megijima ············· 女木島 ·· **5:**152a
Meguro Ward ········· 目黒区 ·· **5:**152a
Meian ····················· 明暗 ·· **5:**350b
Meiboku sendai hagi
　　　伽羅先代萩 ··· **4:**94a, 94b
Meibutsugire ·················· **5:**152b
Meidensha Electric Mfg Co, Ltd ·· **5:**152b
Meigen ················ 鳴弦 ·· **5:**152b
Meigetsuki 明月記 **2:**354b; **5:**152b
Meigō ōrai ··· 明衡往来 ·· **2:**350a;
　　　　　　5:152b–153a
　　ōraimono ·············· **6:**115b
Meigō shōsoku. *See* **Meigō ōrai**
Meiji, Emperor ··· 明治天皇 ·· **5:**153a,
　　　　153b–154a; **7:**27a
　　Iwakura mission ········ **3:**358b–360a
　　plot to assassinate ········· **3:**135a
Meiji Bijutsukai (Meiji Fine Arts Society)
　　　　　　　　6:155b
Meiji Bunka Kenkyūkai ······· **4:**211a
Meiji bunka zenshū
　　　明治文化全集 ········ **8:**349a
Meiji Canal ······ 明治用水 ·· **5:**153a
Meiji Colonization Company ····· **6:**178b
Meiji Constitution. *See* **Constitution;**
　Constitution of the Empire of Japan
Meiji Enlightenment ····· **5:**154a; **7:**54b
　　Mori Arinori ··············· **5:**249a
　　shogunate missions to the West ·· **7:**161b
　　technological innovation ····· **7:**371b
Meiji era ················ 明治時代 · **6:**176a
Meiji Fine Arts Society (Meiji Bijutsukai)
　　　　　　　　8:328a
Meiji Gakuin University ···· **5:**154a; **6:**258a
　　Hepburn, James Curtis ···· **3:**127a–127b
Meiji government. *See* **Government,**
　modern
Meiji history. *See* **History of Japan**
Meiji ichidai onna 明治一代女 ···· **7:**108a
Meiji Ishin. *See* **Meiji Restoration**
Meiji Jogakkō ················· **3:**360b
Meiji Jūyonen no Seihen. *See* **Political**
　Crisis of 1881
Meiji Kempō ······ 明治憲法 ······· **2:**1a–3b
Meiji Milk Products Co, Ltd ······· **5:**154b
Meiji-mono ···················· **2:**271a
Meiji Mura ············ 明治村 ·· **5:**154b
Meiji Mutual Life Insurance Co ·· **5:**154b
Meijin ················· 名人 ·· **4:**176a
Meiji no Mori Takao Quasi-National
　Park 明治の森高尾国定公園 ··· **7:**317b
Meiji period ········· 明治時代 ·· **5:**155a
Meiji Restoration (1868)
　　　明治維新 · **1:**159b, 223a;
　　　2:1a; **5:**155a–160b; **7:**30a, 7:31b, 102a
　　background ·········· **5:**155a–155b
　　chōnin ··················· **1:**301a
　　educational policies ········· **3:**279a
　　emperor ·············· **2:**205a–206b
　　fudasashi ················· **2:**340b
　　fukoku kyōhei ·············· **2:**360b
　　genrō ···················· **3:**21b
　　gesaku ···················· **3:**29a

Gobō no Keiji ··············· 3:38b
hambatsu ·················· 3:91b
impact of Ii Naosuke ········ 5:156a-157a
industrialization ············ 4:14a
interpretations ············ 5:160a-160b
Iwakura Tomomi ············ 3:360a
Japanese emigration ········ 4:14a
Japanese language ········· 4:24a
kōgi seitai ron used on the eve of · 4:248b
Meiji, Emperor ············ 5:153a
nationalism ··············· 5:342b
natural science ············ 5:356b
Occupation ··············· 6:51a
Okinawa ·················· 6:87a
Ōkubo Toshimichi ·········· 6:93b
Opening of Japan ·········· 6:115a
painting ·················· 6:154a
peerage ·················· 6:170b
periodization ·············· 6:177a
provinces ················· 6:260a
regional reform ··········· 5:158a-159a
religion ·················· 6:290b
restoration ··············· 5:159a-160a
rōnin ···················· 6:337a
Russo-Japanese War ········ 6:347a
samurai ·················· 7:8b
Shinritsu Kōryō ············ 7:124a
tattoos ·················· 7:350a-350b
technological development ··· 7:368a
textiles ·················· 8:16a
Tōkyō ···················· 8:61b
"Union of Court and Shogunate"
························· 5:157a-158a
World War II ·············· 8:271b
United Kingdom ············ 8:151a
Meiji Seika Kaisha, Ltd ······ 5:160b
Meiji Shrine ····· 明治神宮 · 5:160b
Meiji Shrine games ········· 7:243a
Meiji 6 Society ············ 5:161a-161b
Meiji Sugar Mfg Co, Ltd ····· 5:160b
Meiji University ·········· 5:160b-161a
Meiji Village Museum ······· 5:278b
Meireki Fire ··· 明暦の大火 4:182a; 5:161a;
························· 8:350a
Meirokusha ········ 明六社 · 5:161a-161b
Meiroku zasshi (Journal of
Meiji) ········· 明六雑誌 · 6:246a
Meiryō kōhan ···· 明良洪範 · 4:85a; 5:161b
Meisaku gekijō
(Masterpiece Theater)
··············· 名作劇場 · 6:275b
Meishi. *See* Name cards
Meishin Expressway ········· 4:46b
Meisho-e (famous places) paintings
··············· 名所絵 · 8:309b
Meisho zue ······ 名所図絵 · 5:161b-162a
Meitokuki ··········· 明徳記 · 4:84b
Meitoku Rebellion
··············· 明徳の乱 · 5:162a
Meitō Tax Evasion Case ······ 6:201b
Meiwa Incident · 明和事件 5:162a; 8:292b
Mekiki ··················· 4:177b
Membranophones ··········· 5:282b
Memorial services ·········· 8:319b
Memorial tablet (ihai) ······· 5:5a
Memushiri kouchi 芽むしり仔撃ち · 6:66a
Men ················· 面 · 8:73a
Mencius ················· 4:58a
Itō Jinsai's study ········· 4:247b
Mendenhall, Thomas Corwin · 5:162a
Mengjiang ················ 7:201a
Menko ················ 5:162b
Men's names ·············· 5:325a-326a
artistic and literary ······· 5:325a-326a
Buddhist ··············· 5:325a-326a
until 8th century ········· 5:325a-326a
premodern ·············· 5:325a-326a
scholars ················ 5:325a-326a

Mental illness ······· 5:162b-163b; 6:261a
attitudes toward ········· 5:163b
changes in symptoms over time
························· 5:163a-163b
introduction ············ 5:162b
social causes ··········· 5:162b-163a
Mental impairment ········· 2:48a
Mentally Disabled Welfare Law · 7:209b
Menuki ··················· 4:295b
Meoto-jawan ············ 5:163b
Meoto zenzai (Marital
Relations) ······· 夫婦善哉 · 8:319b
Meranoshō ········ 米良荘 · 5:164a
Merchant class ············ 1:300b
Merchant guilds. *See* Kabunakama
Merchant houses ······ 2:29b-30a; 6:110a
Merciful Mother Kannon (Hibo kannon)
··············· 4:147a; 5:378b
Mercury pollution ········· 6:218a-218b
Merger, corporate ········ 5:164a
regulation of ··········· 1:66a-66b
Meriyasu ················· 4:99b
Merodorama ··············· 2:269b
Merrimac ················ 1:175b
*Merrymaking under the Cherry
Blossoms* ········· 4:150a; 6:155a
Meshi ·············· めし 5:164a; 5:335a
Metabolist group ··········· 4:207b
Metal industries
Mitsubishi Metal Corporation · 5:208a
Mitsui Mining & Smelting Co, Ltd · 5:211b
Nippon Mining Co, Ltd ······ 6:11a
Sumitomo Metal Mining Co, Ltd · 7:269b
Tōhō Zinc Co, Ltd ········· 8:37b-38a
Metallurgists
Masumoto Hakaru ········· 5:130a
Mishima Tokushichi ······· 5:199a
Murakami Takejirō ········ 5:266b
Noro Kageyoshi ·········· 6:39a
Ōshima Takatō ··········· 6:126a
Metallurgy ················ 7:266b
Metals and minerals ········ 5:353b-354a
iron and steel ··········· 3:333a-333b
nonferrous ·············· 6:34b
manufacturers ·········· 7:268b-269a
Metalwork ········· 5:164a, 164b, 165a
folk craft ··············· 2:295b
"Metamorphosis" ··········· 7:109a
Metempsychosis ············ 1:20a
Meteorological Agency ······ 5:165a
typhoons ··············· 8:122b
Metric system ············· 8:239b
**Metropolitan Expressway Public
Corporation** ··········· 5:165a
expressways ············ 2:238a
Metropolitan Police Department (MPD)
························· 8:68a
Metsuke ·········· 目付 · 5:165a
Mexico and Japan ········ 5:165b
diplomatic ties ·········· 4:369b
Meyasubako ······· 目安箱 · 5:165b
Mi ··················· 5:165b
Miai ········· 見合 2:244a; 5:166a
Mibuchi Tadahiko
··············· 三淵忠彦 · 5:166a
Mibudera ········· 壬生寺 · 5:166a
Mibunkei ·········· 身分刑 · 7:140b
Mibu no Tadamine
··············· 壬生忠岑 · 5:166a-166b;
························· 7:13a
Kokinshū ·············· 4:254b
Mice. *See* Rats and mice
Michi ················· 5:166b
ancient Japanese literature ·· 4:258b
kogaku ················· 4:247b
Michiko, Princess
··············· 美智子妃 3:277a; 5:166b
Michikusa ·········· 道草 4:183a; 5:350b

Michinoku no Kuni 陸奥国 · 5:289a-289b
Michiyukiburi ·· 道ゆきぶり · 3:272b
Microeconomics ············ 2:144b
Midagahara ······· 弥陀ケ原 · 5:166b
Midaregami ······· みだれ髪 · 8:340a
Middle East and Japan ····· 5:167a-167b
diplomatic relations ······· 3:322a-322b
trade ················· 3:322a-322b
Middle Kingdom, The ······· 8:253b
Middle schools. *See* Elementary and
secondary education
Midō Kampaku. 御堂関白 *See*
Fujiwara no Michinaga
Midō Kampaku ki
··············· 御堂関白記 2:353a; 4:255b;
························· 5:167b
Midorikawa ········ 緑川 · 5:167b
Midway, Battle of
··············· ミッドウェー海戦 · 5:167b, 307b
Mie ···················· 4:94a
Mieidō ·················· 1:182b
Mie Prefecture ····· 三重県 · 5:167b-168a
Mifune Kyūzō ····· 三船久蔵 · 5:168a
Mifune Toshirō 三船敏郎 · 2:270b,
························· 271a; 5:168a-168b
Migration ················ 4:15a
Migration routes ·········· 4:33b
Migyōsho ················· 2:98a-98b
Mihara ·········· 三原 · 5:168b-169a
Miharayama ······· 三原山 2:347b; 5:169a
Mihashi Michiya 三橋美智也 · 6:355a
Miho no Matsubara
··············· 三保ノ松原 5:169a; 7:103a,
························· 104a
Mihonoseki ······· 美保関 · 5:169a
Mihoro Dam ······ 御母衣ダム · 2:73b; 5:169a
Miidera ········· 三井寺 · 5:169a; 7:91a
ōtsu-e ················· 6:133b
Miike Coal Mines 三池炭鉱 · 1:74b; 2:31b;
························· 5:169b
Dan Takuma ············ 2:77b
Miike strike 三池争議 · 4:349b; 5:169b-170a
Sakisaka Itsurō ·········· 7:3a
Miira no kuchibeni
··············· 木乃伊の口紅 · 7:334b
Mikage ·········· 御影 · 5:170a
Mikagura ·········· 御神楽 · 4:107a
Mikami Akira ······ 三上章 · 5:170a
Mikami Sanji ···· 三上参次 · 5:170a
Mikan [(citrus) family Rutaceae]
························· 5:170a-170b
Mikasa, Prince ····· 三笠宮 · 5:170b
Mikasa (city) ······ 三笠 · 5:170b
Mikata Five Lakes
··············· 三方五湖 · 5:170b
Mikatagahara ······· 三方ケ原 · 6:63a
Mikatahara ······· 三方原 · 5:170b
Mikawa Bay ······· 三河湾 · 5:170b
Mikawa monogatari
··············· 三河物語 · 5:170b-171a
Ōkubo Hikozaemon ········ 6:93b
Mikazuki (Crescent Moon)
··············· 三日月 · 6:221a
Miki ················· 5:171a
Miki Bukichi ····· 三木武吉 · 5:171a
Miki Kiyoshi ······ 三木清 · 5:171a
Miki Kiyoshi ni okeru ningen no kenkyū
三木清に於ける人間の研究 ···4:270a
Mikimoto Kōkichi
··············· 御木本幸吉 · 1:21b;
························· 5:171a-171b
Miki Rofū ······· 三木露風 · 5:171b
Miki Takeo ····· 三木武夫 2:333a; 5:171b
Miki Tokuchika · 御木徳近 · 5:171b
Mikkabi ········· 三ケ日 · 5:171b-172a
Mikkyō. *See* Esoteric Buddhism
Miko ················· 5:172a
shamanism ············· 7:76b

Miko kagura ·················· **4**:106b, 107b
Miko mai ······················· **4**:107b
Mikoshi 御輿··· **4**:137a; **5**:172a-172b; **7**:74a
  festivals ························ **2**:253b
  Sanja Festival ·················· **5**:*172b*
Mikoto ··························· **1**:62a
Mikotonori. 詔 *See* **Imperial edict**
Mikudarihan 　　 三行半 **5**:172b
Mikuni Mountains
  ···················· 三国山脈 ······· **5**:172b
Mikuni Pass 　　 三国峠 ······· **5**:172b
Mikuni Rentarō 三国連太郎 ·· **5**:172b-173a;
  　　　　　　　　　　　　　　　　　7:68b
Milestones ······················ **3**:258b
Militarism ···················· **5**:173a-175a
  growth ························ **5**:173a
  international relations ·········· **3**:321a
Military Armory Bribery case ····· **6**:201b
Military brigade ················· **6**:317a
Military chronicles. *See* **Gunki**
  monogatari
Military cliques. *See* **Gumbatsu**
Military commissioner for Kyōto
  ·······················**4**:338b-339a
Military education in the schools · **5**:175a
Military factions. *See* **Gumbatsu**
Military forces. *See* **Armed forces,**
  imperial Japanese; National defense;
  Self Defense Forces
  Combined Fleet, Imperial Japanese Navy
  ···························· **1**:336b
  Imperial Japanese Army ·········· **3**:278a
  Imperial Japanese Navy ·········· **3**:278a
  Indian National Army ······· **3**:289b-290a
  self-defense ···················· **3**:266a
  training ·················· **3**:279b-280a
Military governors ············· **7**:183a-184a
Military kites ··················· **4**:230a
Military leaders, modern
  Army
    Abe Nobuyuki ··············· **1**:3b-4a
    Anami Korechika ·············· **1**:53b
    Araki Sadao ··················· **1**:74a
    Doihara Kenji ················ **2**:126b
    Fukushima Yasumasa ··········· **2**:367a
    Hashimoto Kingorō ············ **3**:110a
    Hayashi Senjūrō ··············· **3**:117b
    Higashikuni Naruhiko ·········· **3**:132a
    Ishiwara Kanji ··········· **3**:345b-346a
    Itagaki Seishirō ··············· **3**:349a
    Katsura Tarō ············· **4**:173b-174a
    Kawakami Sōroku ·············· **4**:181b
    Kodama Gentarō ··············· **4**:241a
    Koiso Kuniaki ·················· **4**:250b
    Mazaki Jinzaburō ·············· **5**:144a
    Minami Jirō ·················· **5**:176b
    Miura Gorō ··············· **5**:215a-215b
    Mutō Akira ···················· **5**:288a
    Nagata Tetsuzan ·············· **5**:307a
    Nogi Maresuke ············· **6**:31a-31b
    Ōmura Masujirō ················ **6**:104b
    Ōyama Iwao ·············· **6**:138a-138b
    Saigō Takamori ··········· **6**:366a-367a
    Sugiyama Hajime ··············· **7**:258a
    Tachibana Shūta ··············· **7**:293a
    Tanaka Giichi ············ **7**:336a-336b
    Tani Kanjō ··············· **7**:341b-342a
    Tatekawa Yoshitsugu ············ **7**:349a
    Terauchi Hisaichi ·············· **8**:12a
    Terauchi Masatake ·············· **8**:12b
    Tōjō Hideki ················ **8**:39b-40a
    Tsuji Masanobu ··········· **8**:113b-114a
    Uehara Yūsaku ················· **8**:127a
    Ugaki Kazushige ·········· **8**:130b-131a
    Umezu Yoshijirō ················ **8**:147b
    Watanabe Jōtarō ················ **8**:235b
    Yamagata Aritomo ········· **8**:290a-292a
    Yamashita Tomoyuki ············ **8**:305a

  Navy
    Genda Minoru ·············· **3**:17a-17b
    Hiraga Yuzuru ················· **3**:142b
    Hirose Takeo ·················· **3**:148a
    Kabayama Sukenori ·············· **4**:89b
    Katō Hiroharu ················· **4**:168a
    Katō Tomosaburō ··············· **4**:170b
    Nagano Osami ················· **5**:302b
    Nomura Kichisaburō ············· **6**:34a
    Okada Keisuke ·············· **6**:78a-78b
    Saigō Tsugumichi ··············· **6**:367a
    Saitō Makoto ·················· **6**:374a
    Suzuki Kantarō ················· **7**:282a
    Takarabe Takeshi ·········· **7**:317b-318a
    Tōgō Heihachirō ··········· **8**:36a-36b
    Yamamoto Gonnohyōe ············ **8**:297b
    Yamamoto Isoroku ·············· **8**:298a
    Yonai Mitsumasa ··············· **8**:337a
Military police (pre-World War II) · **6**:198b
  Tōkyō Earthquake of 1923 ········· **8**:66b
Military Procurement Ministry (Gunjushō)
  ···························· **8**:40a
Military tales (gunki monogatari) · **5**:246a
Military uniforms ················ **1**:332b
Military Vehicle Subsidy Law (1918)
  ···························· **1**:121a
Milne, John ··················· **5**:175a
  seismology ···················· **2**:140b
Mimai ······················ **5**:175a-175b
Mimana 　　　 任那 · **4**:185a, 276a
Mimasaka 　　 美作 ········· **5**:175b
Mimashi ············· 味摩之 ······· **3**:32a
Mimikawa 　　　 耳川 ········· **5**:175b
Miminashiyama ····· 耳成山 ········· **8**:310b
Mimizu ··············· **2**:141a-141b
Mimpō no hone · 民法の骨 ····· **6**:109a
Mimpon shugi · 民本主義 ····· **5**:175b
Mimpōten. 民法典 　　 *See* **Civil Code**
Mimpōten ronsō
  ··············· 民法典論争 ···· **1**:316b-317b
Mimpō yōgi ····· 民法要義 ····· **8**:147a
Min, Queen ················ **5**:196b-197a
Min. *See* **Min, Queen; Sōmin** (Buddhist
  priest)
Minabuchi no Shōan
  ··············· 南淵請安 **5**:175b; **7**:260a
Minakami ············· 水上 ····· **5**:176a
Minakami Takitarō
  ·············· 水上滝太郎 ····· **5**:176a
Minakami Tsutomu 水上勉 **5**:176a; **7**:103b
Minakata Kumakusu
  ··············· 南方熊楠 ····· **5**:176a
Minakuchi ············ 水口 ····· **5**:176a
Minamata (city) ······ 水俣 ····· **5**:176a
Minamata disease ··· 水俣病 ····· **2**:224a,
  　　　　　 226a-226b, 304a; **6**:218b
Minami Arupusu Kokuritsu
  Kōen 南アルプス国立公園 ····· **7**:236a
Minami Ashigara ··· 南足柄 ····· **5**:176b
Minami Bōsō
  Quasi-National Park
  ··············· 南房総国定公園 ····· **1**:277a
Minami Chita ······· 南知多 ····· **5**:176b
Minami Daitōjima 南大東島 ····· **5**:176b
Minami Jirō ········· 南次郎 ····· **5**:176b
Minami Kikan ······ 南機関 **1**:221a; **5**:176b
Minami Manshū Tetsudō
  ··············· 南満州鉄道 ····· **7**:237a-238a
Minami Torishima 南鳥島 · **4**:2b; **5**:176b
Minamoto family ······ 源氏 ·· **5**:176b-178b,
  　　　　　　　　　　　　　　　　177a-177b
  alliances ······················ **2**:264a
  flags and banners ··············· **2**:288a
  Fujiwara no Michinaga ··········· **2**:353a
  Heike monogatari ··········· **3**:124a-124b
  Kitabatake Chikafusa ········· **4**:224a-224b
  Murakami Genji ··············· **5**:177b-178a
  Musashi Shichitō ··············· **5**:275b

  Ogasawara family ················ **6**:68b
  origins ···················· **5**:176b-177a
  samurai ························ **7**:7b
  Seiwa Genji ·················· **5**:178a-178b
  structure ···················· **5**:177a-177b
  Taira-Minamoto War ············· **7**:299b
  Wada Yoshimori ················ **8**:197b
  warrior government ·············· **8**:229a
Minamoto no Akikane
  ·················· 源顕兼 ······· **4**:251a
Minamoto no Michichika
  ·················· 源通親 ······· **3**:52a
Minamoto no Raikō. 源頼光
  See **Minamoto no Yorimitsu**
Minamoto no Sanetomo
  ·················· 源実朝 ······· **1**:11a;
  　　　　　　　5:178b-179a; **7**:58a, 97b
  character and cultural interests ···· **5**:178b
  Fujiwara no Sadaie ·············· **2**:354a
  Kamo no Chōmei ················ **4**:128b
  Kinkai wakashū ··············· **4**:212b
  Minamoto no Yoritomo ··········· **4**:122a
  poetry ···················· **5**:178b-179a
Minamoto no Shitagau
  ·················· 源順 **5**:179a; **7**:13a
Minamoto no Takakuni
  ·················· 源隆国 ······· **4**:270b
Minamoto no Tametomo
  ·················· 源為朝··· **5**:179a-179b
  harakiri ······················· **3**:101b
Minamoto no Tameyoshi. 源為義
  See **Hōgen Disturbance**
Minamoto no Toshiyori
  ·················· 源俊頼 ······· **5**:14a, 38a,
  　　　　　　　179b-180a; **7**:68a, 95a
  Fujiwara no Akisuke ············· **2**:350a
  Fujiwara no Mototoshi ············ **2**:353b
  Fujiwara no Toshinari ············ **2**:357b
  Kamo no Chōmei ················ **4**:128b
  poetic style ················· **5**:179b-180a
  works ························· **5**:180a
Minamoto no Tsunenobu
  ·················· 源経信 ······· **5**:38a,
  　　　　　　　180a-180b; **8**:210a
  Shin kokinshū ················· **7**:120a
Minamoto no Yoriie 源頼家 · **5**:180b; **7**:58a
  Kajiwara Kagetoki ··············· **4**:114b
  Minamoto no Yoritomo ··········· **4**:122a
Minamoto no Yorimasa
  ·················· 源頼政 **2**:280b; **5**:180b
  rebellion ······················ **2**:363a
Minamoto no Yorimitsu
  ·················· 源頼光··· **5**:180b-181a
Minamoto no Yoritomo
  ·················· 源頼朝 ······· **5**:181a-182b;
  　　　7:7b-8a, 25b, 57b, 85b, 97b, 101b
  assessment ················· **5**:182a-182b
  Battle of Fujigawa ··············· **2**:342b
  bugyō ························· **1**:206a
  collection in Kōyasan Treasure House
  ···························· **4**:299b
  consolidation of power ··········· **5**:182a
  feudalistic government ············ **2**:264a
  Fujiwara no Takanobu ······· **2**:355b; **5**:*181a*
  Gikeiki ······················ **3**:32b
  gokenin ······················· **3**:42b
  Ike no Zenni ··················· **3**:267a
  Itō Sukechika ·················· **3**:356a
  jitō ·························· **4**:63a
  Kajiwara Kagetoki ··············· **4**:114b
  Kamakura ····················· **4**:120b
  Kamakura shogunate ········· **4**:121b-122b
  Kōfukuji rebuilt ················· **4**:244a
  portrait painting ················ **6**:227a
  post-station system ·············· **2**:188b
  revolt against Taira family ········· **2**:363a
  rule ······················ **2**:204a-204b
  Samurai-dokoro ················· **7**:8b

Sasaki Takatsuna ············· 7:23a
shugo ····················· 7:183a
Taira-Minamoto War ········ 5:181a–182a
warrior ethic ··············· 1:221b
warrior government ·········· 8:229a
Minamoto no Yoshiie
················ 源義家 ·· 5:182b; 7:7b
Earlier Nine Years' War ······ 2:137a
Later Three Years' War ········· 4:369a
Minamoto no Yoshinaka
················· 源義仲 ········ 5:182b
Minamoto no Yoshitomo
················· 源義朝 ······· 5:182b
Fujiwara no Michinori ········ 2:353a
Heiji Disturbance ··········· 3:123a
Minamoto no Yoshitsune
················· 源義経 ······· 5:44b,
                              182b–183a;
Benkei ··················· 4:98a
biography ················· 3:32b
collection in Kōyasan Treasure House
······················· 4:299b
Dannoura, Battle of ········· 2:77a
Kajiwara Kagetoki ·········· 4:114b
Sasaki Takatsuna ··········· 7:23a
Minamoto-Taira War. 源平の争乱
See **Taira-Minamoto War**
Minase sangin hyakuin
············· 水無瀬三吟百韻 ······· 6:297a
Minashiguri ········· 虚栗 ···· 8:295b
Minasu ················ 5:183a–183b
Minatogawa, Battle of
················ 湊川の戦 ······ 5:183b
Minato machi. *See* **Port towns**
Minato Ward ····· 港区 ···· 5:183b
Minatsuki-barae ············· 5:308b
Minazuki no tsugomori no
    ōharae 水無月の晦の大祓 ······ 2:232a
Minchō ······· 明兆 · 1:192a, *192b*;
                              5:183b–184a
Nanzenji ·················· 5:330a
works ··················· 5:183b–184a
Mine ················ 美祢 ···· 5:184a
Mineral rights ············· 5:184a
Minerals ················· 5:353a–354b
Mines Law (Kōgyō Hō) ······· 6:181b
Ming dynasty
    invasions of Korea in 1592 and 1597
    ······················· 3:327a
    Ryūkyū trade ············· 6:358a
    script style ··············· 7:170a
Mingei. *See* **Folk crafts**
Mingu ········· 2:295b; 5:184a
Miniature gardens. *See* **Hakoniwa**
Minidoka Relocation Center ····· 5:184b
Minimum Wage Law (1959) ······· 4:352b;
                              5:184b
enforcement ·············· 4:358b
Mining ················ 5:184b–185a
coal ····················· 1:333a–333b
history ··················· 5:184b
Meiji period ·············· 2:151b
modernization ············· 2:31a–31b
Mining industry ·············· 5:185a
Mining industry companies ········ 5:185a
Dōwa Mining Co, Ltd ······· 2:132b–133a
Mitsubishi Mining & Cement Co, Ltd
······················· 5:208a–208b
Mitsui Mining & Smelting Co, Ltd · 5:211b
Mitsui Mining Co, Ltd ······· 5:211b–212a
Nittetsu Mining Co, Ltd ······· 6:22b
Takashima Coal Mine ········ 7:318b–319a
Mining Law (Kōgyō Hō) ········· 5:184a
Mining Memorandum of 1872 ······· 2:151b
Mining pollution ············· 5:185a–186a
Ashio Copper Mine Incident · 1:101b–102a
classification ·············· 5:185a

countermeasures and problems in future
······················· 5:186a
history ··················· 5:185b
recent problems ············ 5:185b
Tanaka Shōzō ············· 7:338b–339b
Ministerial deliberative council ···· 1:12b;
                              5:186a
Ministers of State ············· 2:7b
Ministries, governmental ····· 1:218b–219a
Ministry of Agriculture and Commerce
······················· 6:41a–41b
Ministry of Agriculture and Commerce
    Ordinance ·············· 8:250a
**Ministry of Agriculture, Forestry, and
    Fisheries** ······· 2:284a; 5:186a; 6:238a
Ministry of Central Imperial Affairs · 7:62b
Ministry of Construction ··········· 4:190b;
                              5:186a–186b
roads ···················· 6:332b
transportaton ·············· 8:99a
urban planning ············· 8:180b
Ministry of Education ········· 5:186b; 7:34a
educational research ········· 2:180b
educational technology ······· 2:181b
education law ·············· 2:182b
function ·················· 2:177b–178a
higher education system ········· 3:133a
Historical Documents Division
    in Kokubungaku Kenkyū Shiryōkan
    ······················· 4:257a
Imperial Rescript on Education ····· 3:279a
influence ················· 2:175b
teachers ·················· 7:365a–367a
universities and colleges ········· 8:170b
university autonomy ········· 8:171a
Ministry of Education Fine Arts
    Exhibition ·············· 1:215b
Ministry of Finance ··· 4:190b; 5:186b–188a;
                              7:48b
advisory council ············ 2:316b
auditing practices ··········· 1:9a
budgeting ················ 5:187b–188a
Business Accounting Council ······· 2:278a
foreign exchange control ········· 2:315b
foreign trade policy ·········· 2:325b
history ··················· 5:187a
monetary policy ············ 5:239b
monopolies ··············· 4:50a
other functions ············· 5:188a
regulatory agent
    insurance ·············· 3:316b–317a
role in economic growth ····· 5:187a–187b
Securities Bureau ········· 1:8b; 2:278a
status ···················· 5:187b
technological development ········· 7:369a
transportation ············· 8:99a
Ministry of Foreign Affairs ····· 5:188a–189b;
                              6:244b
functions ················· 5:189a
future prospects ············ 5:189b
organization and personnel ··· 5:189a–189b
origin and development ······· 5:188a–189a
Ministry of Health and Welfare · 3:119b;
                              5:189b; 7:211a
establishment ············· 4:351b
Maternal and Child Health Division of the
    Children and Families Bureau · 2:247b
public health ·············· 5:149a
Ministry of Home Affairs ········· 5:189b
kōiki shichōsonken ········· 4:250a
**Ministry of International Trade and
    Industry** (MITI) · 1:12a; 2:315b; 4:190b;
    4:62a; 5:189b–191b; 6:304a; 7:253a
automotive industry ········· 1:122a
computer technology ········· 1:346b
electronics industry ········· 2:193b–194a
foreign trade ·············· 2:320b
foreign trade regulation ········· 2:325a

function ·················· 2:165b–168a
industrial policy ············ 3:296b
Industrial Structure Council ······· 3:302a
legal cartels ·············· 3:295b–296b
Ministry of Foreign Affairs ······· 5:189a
origins and development ····· 5:190a–191a
pollution standards ··········· 2:226a
powers and influence ······· 5:191a–191b
public utilities ············· 6:266b
technological development ········· 7:370a
technology, modern ········· 7:373a
transportation ············· 8:99a
United States economic relations
    (1945–1973) ············· 8:162a
Ministry of Justice ··· 4:80b; 5:191b; 6:198a;
                              7:93b
civil liberties ············· 1:317b
Public Security Investigation Agency
    ······················· 6:266b
Ministry of Labor ········· 4:190b; 5:191b
Central Labor Relations Commission
    (Chūō Rōdō Iinkai) ········· 1:256a
establishment ············· 4:351b
group hiring ·············· 3:62b
Labor Relations Commission ······ 4:358b
retirement ················ 6:306b
shuntō negotiations ··········· 7:189b
**Ministry of Posts and
    Telecommunications** ····· 5:191b; 6:276a
Ministry of Public Works ········ 7:165b
Ministry of Punishments ········· 4:185b
Ministry of Religion ········· 4:323b
Ministry of Transport 4:190b; 5:191b–192a;
                              8:99a–103b
marine accidents inquiry ········· 5:114a
Minjihō Hanrei Kenkyūkai (Civil Case
    Study Group) ············ 4:375a
Minjuūiwōn ··············· 4:208a
Minka ················· 5:192a–194a
design characteristics ······· 5:192a–192b
differences in ············· 5:193b–194a
farmhouses ··············· 5:192b–193b
gasshō-zukuri ············· 7:158b
preservation ··············· 5:194a
roof forms ················ 5:192b
townhouses ··············· 5:193b
types and construction materials ··· 5:192a
Minkan denshō · 民間伝承 2:302a; 5:194a
Minkan geinō ············· 2:296b
Minkan Jōhō Kyōiku Kyoku ······· 1:317b
Minkan kagura ············· 4:107b
Minkan shinkō ············· 2:298a
Minkan Shintō ····· 民間神道 ···· 2:300b
Minken jiyūron 民権自由論 ······ 8:127b
Mino (city) ········· 美濃 ···· 5:194a
Mino. *See* **Straw raincoats**
Minobe Ryōkichi
················ 美濃部亮吉 ···· 5:194a
Minobe Tatsukichi
················ 美濃部達吉 ···· 5:194b
emperor-as-organ of state theory ·· 4:375a;
                              8:8a
Kanamori Tokujirō ········· 4:135b
kokutai debate ············· 4:263b
kokutai interpretation ········· 4:263b
Minobōshi ················ 7:249b
Minobu ········· 身延 ···· 5:194b
Minobusan ······· 身延山 ···· 5:194b
Mino Kamo ····· 美濃加茂 ···· 5:194b
Minolta Camera Co, Ltd ······· 5:194b–195a
Minomura Rizaemon
················ 三野村利左衛門 ···· 5:195a
Minoo ············ 箕面 ···· 5:195a
Mino Province ····· 美濃国 ···· 5:195a
Minorities ·········· 5:195a–195b; 7:217a
Minority rights ············· 5:195b–196a
among konketsuji ·········· 4:271b

Minority shareholders · · · · · · · · · · 4:71a
Minor Offenses Law · · · · · · · · · · 5:196a
Minors · 1:16a
Minoue sōdan · · · · · · · · · · · · · · · 5:196a
Mino ware · · · · · · · 美濃焼 1:259a; 2:295b;
                       5:196a-196b
  Arakawa Toyozō · · · · · · · · · · · 1:73b
  museums · · · · · · · · · · · · · · · · 5:279b
  Tajimi · · · · · · · · · · · · · · · · · · 7:310a
  tea ceremony · · · · · · · · · · · · · 7:364b
Minsei · · · · · · · · · · 民青 5:197a; 7:252b
Minsei Dōmei · · · · · · · · · · · · · · · 4:12a
Minshatō. 民社党 *See* **Democratic**
  Socialist Party
Minshingaku · · · · · · · 明清楽 5:197a-197b
Minshu Chōsen · · · · 民主朝鮮 · · · · 4:211a
Minshu Jiyūtō (Democratic
  Liberal Party) 民主自由党 · · · · · · 6:212a
Minshuka Dōmei
  (Democratization
  League) · · · · · · · 民主化同盟 · · · 6:212b
Minshuku · · · · · · · · · · · · · · · · · 5:197b
Minshū no teki (Enemy of
  the People) · · · · 民衆の敵 · · · · · · 8:319b
Minshu Shakaitō
  · · · · · · · · · · · · 民主社会党 · · 2:85a-85b
Minshutō (Democratic
  Party) · · · · · · · 民主党 5:197b; 6:212a
  Japan Socialist Party · · · · · · · · 4:48b
Mintō · · · · · · · · · · · · 民党 · · · · · · 2:335a;
                    5:197b-198a
  ritō · 6:321b
Minumadai Canal
  · · · · · · · · · · · 見沼代用水 · · 5:198a
Min'yō · · · · · · · · · · · · · · · · 2:300b-301b
Min'yūsha (Society of the
  People's Friends) 民友社 · · · · · · 4:261a
Minzokugaku · · · · · · · · · · · · 2:296a-296b
Minzoku geinō · · · · · · · · · · · 2:296a-298a
Minzoku shugi · · · · · · · · · · · 5:342a-343b
Minzoku to rekishi (Race
  and History) · 民族と歴史 · · · · 4:228b
Mio. 三尾   *See* **Amerika Mura**
"Miraculous Teakettle, The" · 1:207a-207b
Miroku · · · 1:159b; 2:83a; 5:198a; 8:337b
  image in Kōryūji · · · · · · · · · · · 4:294a
  Shinran · · · · · · · · · · · · · · · · · 7:123b
  statues · · · · · · · · · · · · 1:197b; 4:111a
Mirror of Eastern Japan · · · · · 1:127a-127b
Mirror of Gesture, The · · · · · · · · · · 8:21b
Miruna no zashiki
  · · · · · · · · · · · 見るなの座敷 · · 5:198a
Misasa · · · · · · · · · · · 三朝 · · · · · · 5:198a
Misato · · · · · · · · · · · 三郷 · · · · · · 5:198a
Misawa · · · · · · · · · · · 三沢 · · · · · · 5:198a
Misawa Homes Co, Ltd · · · · · · · 5:198a
Miscellaneous schools · · · · · · · · 5:198a
  gaikokujin gakkō · · · · · · · · · · · 3:3a
Miserables, Les · · · · · · · · · · · · · 4:316b
Mishihase · · · · · · · 粛慎 · · · · · · · 5:198b
Mishima (city) · · · · · · 三島 · · · · · 5:199a
Mishima (island) · · · · · 見島 · · · · · 5:199a
Mishima Michitsune
  · · · · · · · · · · · 三島通庸 · · · · 5:199a
  Fukushima Incident · · · · · · · · · 2:366a
  Kabasan Incident · · · · · · · · · · · 4:89a
Mishima Tokushichi
  · · · · · · · · · · · 三島徳七 · · · · 5:199a
Mishima Tsūyō. 三島通庸
  See **Mishima Michitsune**
Mishima Yukio 三島由紀夫 1:3a, 20b, 85a,
  223b; 2:274a; 5:199a-202a, 315b; 7:261a
  February 26th Incident · · · · · · · 2:250b
  first writings · · · · · · · · · · · 5:199b-200b
  harakiri · · · · · · · · · · · · · · · · · 3:102a
  1950s · · · · · · · · · · · · · · · 5:200b-201a
  1960s · · · · · · · · · · · · · · · 5:201a-202a
  obscenity case · · · · · · · · · · · · 1:255a

Shinchō · · · · · · · · · · · · · · · · · · 7:109a
Shingeki · · · · · · · · · · · · · · 7:112a, 113b
Mishina Shōei · · · 三品彰英 · · · · 8:307a
Mishōtai · · · · · · · · · · · · · · · · · · 5:202a
  Shintō art · · · · · · · · · · · · · · · 7:135a
Miso · · 2:305a, 306b; 5:202a; 6:283a; 7:239a,
                        265b
  brewing · · · · · · · · · · · · · · · · 1:170a
  Shimo Suwa · · · · · · · · · · · · · 7:106b
Misogi · · · · · · · · · 3:100b; 5:202a-202b
Misogikyō · · · · · · · · 禊教 · · · · · 5:202b
Misora Hibari · · · 美空ひばり · · · 5:202b
  ryūkōka · · · · · · · · · · · · · · · · 6:355a
Missan roku · · · · · · · 密参録 · · · · 7:234a
Missionaries, Christian · · · · · · · · · 1:306a
  Catholic · · · · · · · · · · · · · 1:249b-251a
  English · · · · · · · · · · · · · · · · · 8:249a
  friars · · · · · · · · · · · · · · · · · · 1:307a
  Jesuit · · · · · · · · · · · · · · · · · 1:306b
Mission schools · · · · · 5:202b-203a; 8:257b
Mission to Europe of 1582 · · 5:203a-203b
  achievements · · · · · · · · · · 5:203a-203b
  aims · · · · · · · · · · · · · · · · · · 5:203a
  Arima Harunobu · · · · · · · · · · · 1:83a
  Chijiwa Miguel · · · · · · · · · · · 1:274b
  Hara Martinho · · · · · · · · · · · · 3:102a
  Itō, Mancio · · · · · · · · · · · · · · 3:355a
  journey · · · · · · · · · · · · · · · · 5:203a
  members · · · · · · · · · · · · · · · 5:203a
  Nakaura Julião · · · · · · · · · · · 5:318b
  Ōmura Sumitada · · · · · · · · · · 6:104a
  Ōtomo Sōrin · · · · · · · · · · · · · 6:132b
Misumi · · · · · · · · · · 三角 · · · · · 5:203b
Mita bungaku · · · · · 三田文学 2:214a; 4:301a;
                    5:203b, 300b
Mitaka · · · · · · · · · · 三鷹 · · · 5:203b-204a
Mitaka Incident · · · 三鷹事件 5:204a; 7:147b
  Shimoyama Incident · · · · · · · · 7:107b
Mitake Shrine · · · · · 御岳神社 · · · 1:272a
  Ontake · · · · · · · · · · · · · · · · 6:112b
Mitama. *See* **Tama**
Mitamura Engyo
  · · · · · · · · · · · 三田村鳶魚 · · 5:204a
Mitasareta seikatsu
  · · · · · · · · · · · 充たされた生活 · 1:83a
Mitate-e (parodies of
  classics) · · · · · · · · 見立絵 · · 8:140b
Mitaue Matsuri · · · · · 御田植祭 · · · 1:103b
Mitegura. *See* **Gohei**
Mitford, Algernon · · · · · · · · · 5:204a-204b
MITI. *See* **Ministry of International Trade
and Industry**
Mito · · · · · · · · · · · · 水戸 · · · · · 5:204b
Mito Civil War · 天狗党の乱 · · 5:204b-205a
  Takeda Kōunsai · · · · · · · · · · · 7:322b
Mito Kōmon. *See* **Tokugawa Mitsukuni**
"Mito Kōmon" (television
  series) · · · · · · · · 水戸黄門 · · 2:219b
Mito school · · · · · · · 水戸学 · · 5:205a-205b
  Gamō Kumpei · · · · · · · · · · · · 3:6a-6b
  kokutai · · · · · · · · · · · · · · · · 4:263a
  National Seclusion · · · · · · · · · 5:347b
  scholars
    Aizawa Seishisai · · · · · · · · · 1:38a
    Asaka Tampaku · · · · · · · · · 1:94b
    Kuriyama Sempō · · · · · · · · · 4:313b
  Shinron · · · · · · · · · · · · · · · · 7:124a
  sonnō jōi · · · · · · · · · · · · · · · 7:228b
Mitoshiro · · · · · · · · · · · · · · · · · 7:109a
Mitoshiroda · · · · · · · · · · · · · · · · 7:109b
Mitsuba · · · · · · · · · · · · · · · · · · 3:127b
Mitsubachi (honey bees) · · · · · · · · 1:149a
Mitsubishi · · · · · · · · · 三菱 · 5:205b-206b;
              7:30b, 50b, 88a, 266b
  government enterprise sales · · · · 4:138a
  Ikuno Silver Mine · · · · · · · · · · 3:271a
  interaffiliate stockholding · · · · · · 3:295a
  Iwasaki Koyata · · · · · · · · · · 3:361b-362a

  Iwasaki Yatarō · · · · · · · · · · · 3:362b
  seishō · · · · · · · · · · · · · · · · · 7:52a
  Takashima Coal Mine · · · · · · · · 7:319a
  Tōyama Mitsuru · · · · · · · · · · · 8:88b
Mitsubishi Bank, Ltd · · · · · 5:206b-207a
Mitsubishi Chemical Industries, Ltd
                        5:207a
Mitsubishi Corporation 3:18b-20a; 5:207a;
                        7:258a
Mitsubishi Electric Corporation · · 2:82b;
                     5:207a-207b
Mitsubishi Estate Co, Ltd · · · · · 5:207b
Mitsubishi Gas Chemical Co, Inc
                     5:207b-308a
Mitsubishi Gōshi · · · · · · · · · 3:361b-362a
Mitsubishi group · · · · · · · · · · · · · 1:92b
Mitsubishi Heavy Industries, Ltd · 4:183b;
                        5:208a
  automotive · · · · · · · · · · · · · · 1:121b
  defense industry · · · · · · · · · · · 2:82b
  Nagasaki Shipyards · · · · · · · · · 5:306a
Mitsubishi Metal Corporation · · · 5:208a
Mitsubishi Mining & Cement Co, Ltd
                  5:208a-208b; 7:267b
Mitsubishi Motors Corporation · · 5:208b
Mitsubishi Oil Co, Ltd · · · · 5:208b; 6:181b
Mitsubishi Paper Mills, Ltd · · · · 5:208b
Mitsubishi Petrochemical Co, Ltd
                   5:208b-209a; 6:180a
Mitsubishi Rayon Co, Ltd · · · · · 5:209a
Mitsubishi Steel Mfg Co, Ltd · · · 5:209a
Mitsubishi Trust & Banking Corporation
                        5:209a
  Kagami Kenkichi · · · · · · · · · · 4:102b
**Mitsubishi Warehouse & Transportation
Co, Ltd** · · · · · · · · · · · · · · · · · 5:209b
Mitsuchi Chūzō · · · 三土忠造 · · · 5:209b
Mitsuda-e · · · · · · · · · · · · · · · · 5:209b
Mitsuda Kensuke 光田健輔 · · · · · 5:209b
Mitsui · · 三井 · · 1:138a, 165a;
  2:30a, 359a; 5:209b-210b; 7:86a, 266b
  Chōnin kōkenroku · · · · · · · · · 1:303a
  government enterprise sales · · · · 4:138a
  Ikeda Shigeaki · · · · · · · · · · · · 3:266a
  Inoue Kaoru · · · · · · · · · · · · · 3:310a
  interaffiliate stockholding · · · · · · 3:295a
  seishō · · · · · · · · · · · · · · · · · 7:52a
Mitsui & Co, Ltd · · 3:18b-20a; 5:210b-211a
  international communications · · · 3:319a
  Mukai Tadaharu · · · · · · · · · · · 5:262a
  Tashiro Shigeki · · · · · · · · · · · 7:347b
Mitsui Bank, Ltd · · · · · · · · · · · 5:211a
  Dai-Ichi Kangyō Bank, Ltd · · · · · 2:58b
  Mitsui Bunko · · · · · 三井文庫 · · 5:212b
Mitsui Bussan Company · · · · · · · · 7:193b
Mitsui Construction Co, Ltd · 5:211a-211b
**Mitsui Engineering & Shipbuilding Co,
Ltd** · 5:211b
Mitsui group · · · · · · · · · · · · · · · 7:305b
Mitsui Mining & Smelting Co, Ltd · 4:61a;
                  5:211b; 6:219a
Mitsui Mining Co, Ltd · · · · · 5:211b-212a
  Miike Coal Mines · · · · · · · · · · 5:169b
Mitsui O.S.K. Lines, Ltd · · · · · · · 5:212a
  Daiichi Chūō Kisen Kaisha · · · · · 2:58b
Mitsui Petrochemical Industries, Ltd
                    5:212a; 6:180a
**Mitsui Real Estate Development Co,
Ltd** · · · · · · · · · · · · 4:190a; 5:212a-212b
**Mitsui Research Institute for Social and
Economic History** · · · · · · · · · · · 5:212b
Mitsui Sugar Co, Ltd · · · · · · · · 5:212b
Mitsui Takatoshi 三井高利 · · · · · 5:212b
Mitsui Tōatsu Chemicals, Inc · · · 5:212b
Mitsui Trust & Banking Co, Ltd
                   5:212b-213a
Mitsui Warehouse Co, Ltd · · · · · 5:213a
Mitsukaidō · · · · · · · · 水海道 · · · 5:213a

Mitsuke ············ 見附 ······ 5:213a
Mitsukoshi, Ltd ········· 5:213a-213b
Mitsukuri Gempachi
　　　　箕作元八 ········ 5:213b
Mitsukuri Gempo 箕作阮甫 ····· 5:213b
Mitsukuri Kakichi 箕作佳吉 ···· 5:213b
Mitsukuri Rinshō 箕作麟祥 ···· 5:213b
　Civil Code ·················· 2:319a
Mitsukuri Shūhei ·箕作秋坪 ·· 5:213b
Mitsuminesan ····三峰山 ····· 5:214a
Mitsumine Shrine三峰神社 1:272a; 5:214a
Mitsunaga Hoshio
　　　　　光永星郎 ······· 5:214a
Mitsu no hamamatsu (The
　Pine on the Beach at the
　Royal Port) ·· 御津の浜松 ···· 5:36a
Mitsutani Kunishirō
　　　　満谷国四郎 ······· 5:214a
Mitsuya plan ················· 5:214a
Mitsuzōin ······ 密蔵院 ····· 4:163b
Miura ············ 三浦 · 5:214a-214b
Miura Anjin.　　　三浦按針
　　See Adams, William
Miura Baien ······ 三浦梅園 · 5:214b-215a
　jōri ·············· 4:247a; 5:214b
　main works ············· 5:214b-215a
　　Gengo ················ 5:214b
　　Kango ················· 5:215a
　　Zeigo ············ 5:214b-215a
　social and educational activity ···· 5:215a
Miura Chora ···三浦樗良 ····· 5:215a
Miura family ···三浦氏 ······· 5:215a
Miura Gorō ·····三浦梧楼 ····· 4:281b;
　　　　　　　　5:215a-215b
Miura Hiroyuki ··三浦周行 ····· 5:215b
　historiography ·············· 3:156b
Miura Jōshin ···三浦浄心 ····· 4:187b
Miura Ken'ya ···三浦乾也 ····· 5:215b
Miura Kinnosuke
　　　　　　三浦謹之助 ····· 5:215b
Miura Peninsula ·三浦半島 · 5:215b-216a
Miura Saku ·····三浦繋 ······ 5:216a
Miura Shumon ··三浦朱門 ····· 5:216a
Miura Tetsuo ···三浦哲郎 ····· 5:216a
Miwa Kyūwa ···三輪休和 ····· 5:216a
Miwa Shissai ···三輪執斎 5:216a; 8:335b
Miwata Masako
　　　三輪田真佐子 · 5:216a-216b
Miwayama ······三輪山 ······ 5:216b
Mixed-blood children ··· 4:271a-271b
Miyabe Kingo ··宮部金吾 ····· 5:216b
Miyagawa ······宮川 ········· 5:216b
Miyagawa Chōshun
　　　　　宮川長春 ······· 5:216b
Miyagawa Kazuo 宮川一夫 · 5:216b-217a
Miyage ···················· 5:217a
Miyagi Michio ··宮城道雄 · 5:217a-217b
Miyagi Prefecture ·宮城県 · 5:217b-218a
　attractions ················· 5:218a
　history ···················· 5:217b
　Tagajō ···················· 7:294a
Miyagi Tamayo 宮城タマヨ ···· 5:218a
Miyagi Yotoku ·宮城与徳 5:218a; 7:229b
Miyajima. 宮島　　　See Itsukushima
Miyajima Seijirō
　　　　宮嶋清次郎 ······· 5:218a
Miyake Issei ···三宅一生 ····· 5:218a
Miyakejima ····三宅島 ······· 5:218a
Miyake Kaho ···三宅花圃 ····· 5:218b
Miyake Kanran ·三宅観瀾 ····· 5:218b
Miyake Sekian ·三宅石庵 ····· 5:218b
　Kaitokudō ················· 4:113b
Miyake Setsurei 三宅雪嶺 · 5:218b-219a,
　　　311a; 7:51b, 91b, 258b
　Ernest Francisco Fenollosa ····· 2:251b
Miyake Shōsai ·三宅尚斎 ····· 5:219a
Miyake Yonekichi
　　　　　三宅米吉 ·· 1:77a; 5:219a

Miyake Yoshinobu
　　　　三宅義信 ······· 5:219a
Miyako ·········宮古 ········ 5:219a
　Ryūkyū Islands ·············· 6:357a
Miyakogusa (Lotus corniculatus var.
　Japonicus) ················· 5:219a
Miyako Islands ·宮古諸島 · 5:219b; 7:3a
Miyakoji Bungonojō 宮古路豊後掾 8:43b
Miyakojima ····宮古島 ······ 5:219b
Miyako no hana ·都の花 ····· 4:199a
Miyakonojō ·····都城 ······· 5:219b
Miyakonojō Basin
　　　　都城盆地 ········ 5:219b
Miyako no Nishiki 都の錦 ···· 5:219b
Miyako no Yoshika 都良香 ···· 5:219b
Miyako shimbun ·都新聞 · 5:219b-220a
　Kokumin shimbun merged with ···· 4:261a
Miyamairi ·······宮参り ····· 5:220a
Miyamoto Kenji ·宮本顕治 · 5:220a; 7:25a
Miyamoto Musashi
　　　　宮本武蔵 ·1:193b, 222a;
　　　　　5:220a; 8:295a-295b
Miyamoto Musashi series ········ 6:221b
Miyamoto Yuriko
　　　　宮本百合子 ·····1:155b;
　　　　　5:220a-221a; 7:25a
　Shin Nihon bungaku ············ 7:122a
　works ················· 5:220b-221a
Miyanouradake · 宮之浦岳 4:105b; 5:221a
Miyashita Takichi 宮下太吉 · 3:135a-136a
Miyatake Gaikotsu
　　　　宮武外骨 ········ 5:221a
Miyatsuko ······　　造 ····· 4:89a
Miyaza ·········宮座 4:145b; 5:221a
Miyazaki ·······宮崎 · 5:221a-221b
Miyazaki Ichisada
　　　　宮崎市定 · 5:221b, 311b
Miyazaki Plain ·宮崎平野 ···· 5:221b
Miyazaki Prefecture宮崎県 ··· 5:221b
Miyazaki Shrine ·宮崎神宮 ···· 5:222a
Miyazaki Tōten ·宮崎滔天 · 5:222a-222b;
　　　　　　　　　　7:276b
　tairiku rōnin ················ 7:302b
Miyazaki Yasuji ·宮崎康二 ···· 5:222b
Miyazaki Yasusada
　　　　宮崎安貞 · 1:24a; 5:222b
Miyazawa Kenji ·宮沢賢治 · 5:222b-223b
　works ····················· 5:223a
Miyazawa Toshiyoshi
　　　　宮沢俊義 · 2:13b; 5:223b
Miyazu ·········宮津 ········ 5:223b
Miyoshi ········三次 ········ 5:223b
Miyoshi Basin ·三次盆地 ····· 5:223b
Miyoshi Jūrō ···三好十郎 · 5:223b-224a
Miyoshi Kiyoyuki 三善清行 ··· 5:224a
Miyoshi Manabu ·三好学 ····· 5:224a
Miyoshi Masayasu
　　　　三好政康 ········ 5:224a
Miyoshi Nagayoshi
　　　　三好長慶 ········ 5:224a
Miyoshi Nagayuki 三好長逸 ··· 5:224a
Miyoshi Sanninshū
　　　　三好三人衆 ······ 5:224a
Miyoshi Tatsuji ·三好達治 · 5:224a-224b
　Kajii Motojirō ··············· 4:114b
Miyoshi Yasunobu
　　　　三善康信 ······· 5:57b,
　　　　　　　224b-225a
　works ····················· 5:224b
Mizoguchi Kenji · 2:268b-269a, 270b-271a,
　　　　溝口健二　272a; 5:225a-225b
　Shindō Kaneto ··············· 7:111a
　Shinoda Masahiro ············· 7:122a
Mizuhara Shūōshi
　　　　水原秋桜子 · 5:20a, 225b;
　　　　　　　　　8:295a
　haiku ····················· 3:80b
Mizuhiki ···················· 5:225b-226a

kokorozuke placed in ········· 4:256b
Mizuho Station ·瑞穂基地 ···· 1:64b
Mizukata ·······水方 ········ 4:119b
Mizuki ··········水城 ········ 5:226a
Mizuki Yōko ····水木洋子 ···· 5:226a
Mizukurage ················· 4:50b
Mizunami ······瑞浪 ········ 5:226a
Mizuno Corporation ·········· 5:226a
Mizunomi-byakushō
　　　　水呑百姓 · 5:226a-226b
Mizuno Rentarō
　　　　　水野錬太郎 ····· 5:226b
Mizuno Seiichi ··水野清一 ···· 1:78b
Mizuno Shigeo ··水野成夫 ···· 5:226b
　Sankei shimbun ············ 7:13b-14a
Mizuno Tadakuni 水野忠邦 ···· 1:21a;
　　　　5:226b-227b; 7:28b
　as rōjū ················· 5:227a-227b
　hitogaeshi ················· 3:208a
　Tempō Reforms ···· 3:189b; 5:226b, 227b;
　　　　　　　　　　8:2a
Mizusawa ······水沢 ········ 5:227b
Mizusawa Ken'ichi
　　　　水沢謙一 ········ 2:302b
Mizusawa, Latitude Observatory of
　　　　　　　　　　5:227b
　discoveries ················ 1:104b
Mizushima ·····水島 · 5:227a, 227b
Mizushima Coastal Industrial Region
　　　　水島臨海工業地域 ··· 6:83a;
　　　　　　　　　　7:312a
Mizushima San'ichirō
　　　　水島三一郎 ·····1:268b;
　　　　　　　　5:227b-228a
Mizutani Yaeko水谷八重子 ···· 5:228a
　shimpa ···················· 7:108a
MOA Museum of Art ···· 5:228a; 7:56a
Mobara ········茂原 ········ 5:228a
Mobil Sekiyu ················ 5:228a
　Tōa Nenryō Kōgyō ··········· 8:30b
Mochi ················· 2:253b, 262a
Mochizuki Yūko ·望月優子 ···· 5:228b
Modern age ·················· 6:176b
Modern Art Association ········· 8:294b
Modern art museums ··········· 5:279a
Modernization ·········· 5:228b-229b
Modern philosophy ······· 5:229a-232a
　formation of academic philosophy 3:112b;
　　　　　　　　　　4:322a
　Hiratsuka Un'ichi ············ 5:232b
　introduction of Western philosophy
　　· 5:161a-161b, 311b-312a; 6:14a-14b
　Marxist philosophy ···· 4:180b; 5:171a;
　　　　　　　　6:367a-367b
　Nishida and Tanabe ········ 6:14b-15b;
　　　　　　　　7:335a-335b
　post-World War II ············ 5:232a
　Taishō democracy and philosophy
　　　　· 1:2b; 4:304b; 8:237b
　traditional thought ······· 5:229b-230a
Modern poetry literary groups · 5:20a-20b
Modern prints ·········· 5:232a-233b
　Munakata Shikō ············· 5:233a
　1960s and 1970s ········· 5:233a-233b
　Nyonin Kanzeon ············· 5:233a
　Onchi Kōshirō ·············· 5:232b
　sōsaku hanga ··········· 5:232b-233a
Mo Di ···················· 4:58b
Modorikago ·····戻駕 ······· 8:43b
Modoshi ···················· 4:119b
Moetsukita chizu (1968,
　The Burned-up Map)
　　　　燃えつきた地図 ·· 1:3a; 8:15a
Mogamigawa ·····最上川 ···· 5:233b
Mogami Tokunai 最上徳内 ···· 5:233b
Mogi Keizaburō
　　　　茂木啓三郎 ······ 5:233b
Mogura ···················· 5:235b

Mohan Singh ·················· 7:197a
Mō hitori no Keitarō
　もう一人の啓太郎 ······· 6:275b
Mōka ·············· 真岡 ·········· 5:234a
Mokkan ·········· 木簡 · 1:80a; 5:234a
　inscriptions ···················· 3:314a
Mokkei ········· 牧谿 · 1:192a-192b;
　　　　　　　　　　　　　　5:234a
Mōko Shūrai ····· 蒙古襲来 ··· 5:243b-245a
Mōko shūrai ekotoba
　·········· 蒙古襲来絵詞 · 1:89b; 4:274b;
　　　　　　　　　　　5:243a-243b
Mokuami ········· 黙阿弥 ········· 5:50a,
　　　　　　　　　　　234b-235a
　kabuki plays ··················· 4:91b
　Sakura Sōgorō tale ············· 7:5a
Mokuami, Kawatake
　········· 河竹黙阿弥 ············· 7:4a
Mokuan Reien ··· 黙庵霊淵 ··· 5:235a-235b
　ink painting ··················· 3:306b
　works ···················· 5:235b
Mokubei. 木米 *See* **Aoki Mokubei**
Mokugyo. 木魚 *See* **Asai Chū**
Mokujiki ············· 木食 1:199b; 5:235b
Mokujiki Gogyō · 木食五行 1:194a; 5:235b
Mokujiki Ōgo ··· 木食応其 ······· 5:235b
Mokuyōkai (Thursday
　Club) ················ 木曜会 ··· 5:18b
Moles [(mogura) family Talpidae] · 5:235b
Mollusks. *See* **Shellfish**
Molony, James Clark ··········· 4:38b
Mombatsu ···················· 1:147a
Mombetsu ········· 紋別 ········· 5:236a
Mombi ·························· 7:58a
Mombushō. *See* **Ministry of Education**
Momiji ················· 5:111b-112a
Momijigari ········· 紅葉狩 4:154b; 5:236a
Momijioroshi ·················· 2:25b
Momi no ki wa nokotta
　(The Fir Tree Still
　Stands) · 樅の木は残った ··· 6:221b
Mommu, Emperor
　········· 文武天皇 · 5:236a; 7:62b
　court ···················· 2:350a
　Fujiwara family ······· 2:348a, 350b
　Kakinomoto no Hitomaro ······· 4:117a
Momo ·························· 6:169b
"**Mōmoku**" ············ 盲目 ······· 7:176a
Mōmoku monogatari
　·············· 盲目物語 ······· 7:342b
Momonga ···················· 2:293b
Momo sumomo ····· 桃李 ······· 6:298b
Momotarō ······· 桃太郎 2:302a; 5:236a;
　　　　　　　　　　　　　7:149b
Momoyama period. 桃山時代 *See*
　Azuchi-Momoyama period
Mon ·················· 門 ······· 5:350a
Monasticism ················ 5:236a-239a
　administrative framework ··· 5:236b-237a
　discipline problems ········ 5:236b-237a
　Ganjin ···················· 3:7a-7b
　reform movement ··········· 5:238a-238b
　secular control ················ 5:237a
　Tokugawa Reform ········· 5:238b-239a
　warrior control ················ 5:238b
　wealth and power ·············· 5:237b
Monchūjo ········· 問注所 · 5:239a; 7:8b
　keishi ···················· 4:190a
　Minamoto no Yoritomo ········· 4:122a
　Taira-Minamoto War ·············· 7:300b
Monetary expansion ············· 2:148a
Monetary policy ············ 5:239b-242a
　banking system ················ 5:240a
　before the late 1960s ······· 5:240b-241a
　industrial policy ················ 3:296b
　mechanics ··············· 5:239b-240b
　1970s and beyond ········· 5:241a-242a
　reserve money ············· 5:239b-240a

Monetary system
　Meiji period ················· 2:151b
　Muromachi history ········· 3:175a-176b
　premodern ··············· 2:147b-148a
　Wadō kaihō ················· 8:198a
Money. *See* **Money, premodern; Yen**
Money changers (ryōgaeshō) ····· 6:351b
Money offerings ················ 5:242a
Money, premodern ········· 5:242a-243a
　eirakusen ···················· 2:186b
　hansatsu ················ 5:242a-242b
　ichibukin ················ 5:242a-242b
　Kan'ei tsūhō ·············· 5:242a-242b
　Keichō koban ·············· 5:242a-242b
　kōchō jūnisen ················· 4:239b
　mameita gin ·············· 5:242a-242b
　Tenshō naga ōban ·········· 5:242a-242b
　Wadō kaihō ·············· 5:242a-242b
　See also Coins
Mongaku ············ 文覚 · 5:243a-243b;
　　　　　　　　　　　　　7:85b
　Jingoji ···················· 4:58b
Mongolia ···················· 4:18b
　Manchurian-Mongolian Independence
　Movement ················· 5:99a-99b
Mongol invasions of Japan · 5:243a-245a;
　　7:70b, 94b, 97b, 183b, 263a
　Akutō ···················· 1:46a
　challenge and response ····· 5:243b-244a
　effects ···················· 5:244a
　Eizon ···················· 2:188a
　fortifications ·················· 2:364b
　Hōjō Tokimune ················· 3:212a
　Japanese defense ··············· 5:244a
　kamikaze ···················· 4:126b
　Kikuchi Takefusa ··············· 4:206b
　Kōno Michiari ··················· 4:274b
　Koryŏ-Japan relations ·········· 4:278a
　location ···················· 2:365a
　Mōko shūrai ekotoba ········ 5:243a-243b
　national flag ·················· 5:339a
　regency politics ················ 4:122a
　Takezaki Suenaga ·············· 7:326b
　warrior government ············· 8:229b
Mongol invasions of Korea ······· 5:245a
Mongoloid features ··········· 4:35a-35b
Monkeys [(saru) *Macaca fuscata*]
　························ 5:245a-245b
　Mori Sosen ··················· 5:253a
Monnō ················ 文雄 ··· 5:245b
　phonological works ·············· 4:134a
Mono-awase ···················· 4:381a
Monobi ························ 7:58a
Monochrome ink painting ········· 6:150b
Monogatari bungaku ········· 5:245b-246b
　Chinese literature ··············· 1:293b
　gunki monogatari (military tales)
　　················· 3:69a-69b; 5:246a
　rekishi monogatari (historical tales) 5:246a
　rise ······················ 5:14a
　setsuwa bungaku ·········· 5:246b; 7:72a-72b
　Tale of Genji ················· 7:330a
　tsukuri monogatari (courtly romances
　or prose fiction) ··············· 5:246a
　uta monogatari (stories about poems or
　poem tales) ··············· 5:245b-246a
Monograms ··············· 4:155a-156a
Monographs ···················· 4:23b
Mono no aware
　········· 物のあはれ · 2:273b; 5:17a,
　　　　　　　　　　　246b-247a
　Motoori Norinaga ··············· 4:258b
Mononobe family · 物部氏 5:247a; 7:264a
　Buddhism ···················· 4:277a
　Keitai, Emperor ················· 4:190a
　Nakatomi family alliance ········· 2:351a
　Yamato court ·················· 8:308b

Mononobe no Moriya
　············ 物部守屋 ··· 5:247a
Mononoke ···················· 5:247a
Monopolization, private ······· 1:65b-66b
Monopoly and oligopoly ···· 5:247a-247b
　coin mints ···················· 4:219b
　domainal ················· 3:96a-96b
　industrial organization ······· 3:292b-293b
　private
　　control ···················· 1:66a
　　definition ···················· 1:65b
　　exclusion ···················· 1:65b
　　public interest and particular field of
　　trade ···················· 1:66a
　　regulation of stock acquisitions and
　　mergers ··············· 1:66a-66b
　　silk trade ···················· 3:356b
Monopoly Bureau ················ 4:50a
Monosodium glutamate (MSG) ··· 3:265b
Monshō ··············· 2:42a-43b
Monshō (Family Crest)
　············ 紋章 ······· 8:333a
Montages ···················· 2:378a
Montblanc, Charles, Comte des
　Cantons de ················ 5:247b
Months ················· 1:232a-232b
Monumenta Nipponica ············ 1:250a
Monuments, natural ········· 5:352a-352b
Monzen machi ······· 門前町 · 5:247b-248a
Moon and agricultural rites ········· 1:23a
Moon viewing ················ 5:248a
　cooking ···················· 2:22a
Moraes, Wenceslau de ············ 5:248a
Moral Adoption program ··········· 1:111a
Moral education ······ 2:181a; 5:248a-248b;
　　　　　　　　　　　7:34a-34b
Moral excellence (toku) ··········· 4:141b
Morality ···················· 5:248b
　vs etiquette ···················· 2:232b
"Moral" training ················· 7:191b
Morgan, George Dennison ········· 5:248b
Morgan, Yuki ···· モルガン雪 ··· 5:248b
Mori Arimasa ········ 森有正 ··· 5:248b
Mori Arinori ········· 森有礼 · 5:248b-249b
　education ···················· 2:176a
　educational policies ············· 3:279a
　Japanese language reform ······· 4:29b
　Meirokusha ··················· 5:161a
　school orders ·················· 7:36b
Moribana ··············· 2:290b-291a
Moribana-style ················· 2:291a
Mōri family ··········· 毛利氏 5:249b; 7:104a
Moriguchi ··········· 守口 ··· 5:249b
Mori Hanae ········· 森英恵 ··· 5:249b
Mori Kaku ········· 森恪 · 5:249b; 7:276b
Mori Kansai ········· 森寛斎 · 5:249b-250a
　style ···················· 5:250a
Morikawa Kyoroku
　········· 森川許六 · 1:295b; 5:16a,
　　　　　　　　　　　250a
Morikawa Yoshinobu
　········· 森川義信 ··· 1:82b
Mori Masayuki ····· 森雅之 2:272b; 5:250a
Morimoto Kaoru ··· 森本薫 · 5:250a-250b
　shingeki ···················· 7:113a
Mōri Motonari ··· 毛利元就 5:250b; 7:277a
　kakun ···················· 4:118b
Morimoto Rokuji · 森本六爾 · 1:77b; 5:250b
Mōri Museum ·················· 5:276b
Morinaga, Prince 護良親王 ··· 5:251b
Morinaga & Co, Ltd ············· 5:250b
Morinaga Milk Industry Co, Ltd ··· 5:251a;
　　　　　　　　　　　6:220a
Morinaga Powdered Milk Incident 2:304b;
　　　　5:251a-251b; 6:253b
Mori Nobuteru ······· 森矗昶 ··· 5:251b
Mori Ōgai ········· 森鷗外 · 1:155b; 5:11b,
　52b-54a, *251a*, 251b-252b; 7:103b, 253b

education · · · · · · · · · · · · · · · · **5:**251b
Nakamura Fusetsu · · · · · · · · · · · **5:**314b
works · · · · · · · · · · · · · · · **5:**252a–252b
Morioka · · · · · · · · · · · · · 盛岡 · · · **5:**252b
Morioka Emigration Company · · · · · **6:**178b
Mori Rammaru · · · · · 森蘭丸 · · · · **5:**252b
Mori Rintarō · · · 森林太郎 · · **5:**251b–252b
Morisada mankō 守貞漫稿 · · · · · **2:**296a;
　　　　　　　　　　　　　　　 5:252b–253a
Morishige Hisaya 森繁久弥 · · · · **5:**253a
Morishima Michio
　　　　　　　　 森嶋通夫 · · · · · · **5:**253a
Morishita Yōko · 森下洋子 · · · · · · · **2:**76a
Mori Shushō · · · · · · 森守象 · · · · **5:**253a
Mori Sosen · · · · · 森狙仙 · · · · **5:**253a
Morita Akio · · · 盛田昭夫 · · · · **5:**253a
Morita Kan'ya · 守田勘弥 · · · · **5:**253b
　kabuki leadership · · · · · · · · · · · **4:**92b
Moritake senku · 守武千句 · · · · · · **1:**73b
Morita Masatake 森田正馬 · · · **5:**253b–254a
Morita Sōhei 森田草平 · · · · · · **5:**253b
Morita therapy · · **5:**253b–254a; **6:**261b
　central tenet · · · · · · · · · · · · · · **5:**254a
Moritaza · · · · · · · · · · 守田座 · · · **5:**253b
Morito Incident · · 森戸事件 · · **5:**254a–254b
Morito Tatsuo · · 森戸辰男 · · · · **5:**254b
　dispute · · · · · · · · · · · · · · · · · **4:**48b
Mori Tsutomu · · · · · 森格 · · · · **5:**249b
Moriyama · · · · · · · · 守山 · · · · **5:**254b
Moriyama Shigeru 森山茂 · · · · · · · **4:**279a
Moriyama Takichirō
　· · · · · · · · · · · 森山多吉郎 · · **5:**254b–255a
Moriyoshi, Prince 護良親王 　　*See*
　Morinaga, Prince
Morning glories [(asagao) *Pharbitis nil;*
　Ipomoea nil] · · · · · · · · · · · · · **5:**255a
Morning glory fair · · · · · · · · · · **5:**255a
Morning Toilette · · · · · · · · · · · · **8:**328a
Morohashi Tetsuji
　· · · · · · · · · · · · 諸橋轍次 · · · **2:**60a;
　　　　　　　　　　　　　　　 5:255a–255b
Moromoriki · · · · · · 師守記 · · · · **5:**255b
Moronobu · · · · · · · 師宣 · · · **1:**163b;
　2:373b; **5:**255b–256a; **6:**155b; **7:***258a;* **8:***138b*
　Kaigetsudō school · · · · · · · · · · **4:**109b
　Kambun Master · · · · · · · · · · · · **4:**124b
　style · · · · · · · · · · · · · · · · · · **5:**255b
Morrison Bunko · · · · · · · · · · · · · **8:**90a
Morrison expedition · · · · · · · · · · **6:**258a
Morrison Incident
　· · · · · · · · · · · · モリソン号事件 · · **5:**256a
　Gaikokusen Uchiharai Rei · · · · · · **3:**3b
　Shinkiron · · · · · · · · · · · · · · · **7:**119a
Morse, Edward Sylvester · · · **1:**75b, 155b;
　　　　　　　　　　　2:311a; **5:**256a
　Faulds, Henry · · · · · · · · · · · · · **2:**249b
　Fenollosa, Ernest Francisco · · · · · · **2:**251b
　Ōmori shell mounds · · · · · · · · · · **6:**103a
　shell mounds · · · · · · · · · · · · · · **7:**81b
Mortality rates · · · · · · · · · · **5:**149a–149b
Mortars. *See* **Usu**
Moscow · · · · · · · · · · · · · · · · · **4:**44a
Mōsōchiku (Phyllostachys pubescens)
　· **1:**135b
Mosse, Albert · · · · · · · **2:**2b; **5:**256a–256b
　Meiji Constitution · · · · · · · · · · · **3:**195a
Mosses [(koke) division *Bryophyta*]
　· **5:**256b
Mō Takutō · · · · · · 毛沢東 · · · · **5:**111b
Moteru kuni Nihon
　· · · · · · · · · · · 持てる国日本 · · · · **6:**93a
Motherhood Protection League [Boshi
　Hogo Remmei (Bosei Hogo Dōmei)]
　· · · · · · · · · · · · · · · · · **8:**289b, 307b
Mother-of-pearl inlay · · · **2:**371b; **5:**256b
Motion Picture Code Committee · **2:**273a;
　　　　　　　　　　　　　　　　 5:256b
Motion Picture Code of Ethics · · · · **1:**254b

Motion Picture Film Censorship
　Regulations · · · · · · · · · · · · · · **2:**339a
Motion Picture Law · · · · · · · · · · **2:**339a
Motion pictures. *See* **Film, Japanese**
Motivation
　employment
　　internal organization of Japanese
　　companies · · · · · · · · · · · **3:**318a–318b
　group · · · · · · · · · · · · · · · · · **3:**63a
Moto · · · · · · · · · · · · · · · · · · **4:**108a
Motobu · · · · · · · · · · 本部 · · · · **5:**256b
Motoda Nagazane
　· · · · · · · · · · · · · 元田永孚 · · · **5:**257a
　Imperial Rescript on Education · · · · **3:**279a
　nationalism · · · · · · · · · · · · · · **5:**342b
Moto Gangōji. *See* **Asukadera**
Motoki Shōzō · · · · · 元木昌造 · · · **6:**245b
Motomezuka · · · · · · 求塚 · · · · **4:**135b
Motonobu. *See* **Kanō Motonobu**
Motoori Haruniwa
　· · · · · · · · · · · · 本居春庭 **5:**257a; **7:**281a
　Fujitani Nariakira · · · · · · · · · · · **2:**346b
Motoori Norinaga本居宣長 · · **1:**20a, 154a;
　2:346b; **3:**155a; **5:**13a, 17a, 257a–258b;
　　　　7:94b, 263b–264a, 281a; **8:**216a
　childhood and youth · · · · · · · · · · **5:**257b
　early works in literary criticism
　· · · · · · · · · · · · · · · · · **5:**257b–258a
　Genji monogatari tama no ogushi · · · **5:**258a;
　　　　　　　　　　　　　　　　 7:331a
　Hirata Atsutane · · · · · · · · · · · · **3:**145a
　impact · · · · · · · · · · · · · · · · · **5:**258b
　influenced by Ogyū Sorai · · · · · · · **4:**248a
　Japanese language studies · · · · · · · **4:**31a
　Kamo no Mabuchi · · · · · · · · · · · **4:**129b
　Kojikiden · · · · · · · · · · · · · · · **4:**251b
　Kokugaku · · · · · · · · · · · **4:**257b, 258a
　later years · · · · · · · · · · · · **5:**258a–258b
　literary scholar to classicist · · · · · · **5:**258a
　mono no aware · · · · · · · · · **5:**246b–247a
　orthographic studies · · · · · · · · · · **4:**134a
　self-portrait · · · · · · · · · · · · · · **5:**257a
　writings · · · · · · · · · · · · · **5:**258a–258b
Motoori Ōhira · · · · 本居大平 · · · **5:**259a
Motorcycle gangs · · · · · · · · · · · · **4:**86b
Motorcycle theft · · · · · · · · · · · · · **4:**86b
Motor vehicles · · · · · · · · · · · · · **8:**102a
Motoyakushiji remains
　· · · · · · · · · · · · 本薬師寺跡 · · · **5:**259a
Motoyama Hikoichi
　· · · · · · · · · · · · 本山彦一 · · · · **5:**259a
Mōtsuji · · · · · · · · 毛越寺 · · **3:***8b;* **5:**259a
Mōtsuji remains 毛越寺跡 · · **5:**259a–259b
Mt. Asama · · · · · · · · 浅間山 · · · **8:**194b
Mt. Bandai · · · · · · · · 磐梯山 · · · **8:**194a
Mt. Fuji · · · · · · · · · · 富士山 · · **2:**344b–345b;
　　　　　　　　　　　　　　　　 8:194a
Mt. Fuji Pilgrimage Mandala · · · · · · **7:**136a
Mountain ash · · · · · · · · · · · · · · **5:**327b
Mountain climbing · · · · · · · · · · · **8:**287b
Mountaineering · · · · · · · · · · · · **5:**259b
*Mountaineering and Exploration in the
　Japanese Alps* · · · · · · · **4:**12b; **8:**249a
Mountain fort · · · · · · · · · · · · · · **1:**246b
Mountain fortress (yamajiro) · · · · · · **1:**246a
Mountain passes
　Abō · · · · · · · · · · · · · · · · · · · **1:**5a
　Amagi · · · · · · · · · · · · · · · · · **1:**49a
　Daibosatsu · · · · · · · · · · · · · · · **2:**55b
　Hakone · · · · · · · · · · · · · · · · · **3:**87a
　Harinoki · · · · · · · · · · · · · · · · **3:**104a
　Jikkoku · · · · · · · · · · · · · · · · · **4:**57a
　Karikachi · · · · · · · · · · · · · · · **4:**160a
　Kimi · · · · · · · · · · · · · · · · · · **4:**208b
　Kobotoke · · · · · · · · · · · · · · · · **4:**238b
　Konsei · · · · · · · · · · · · · · · · · **4:**275b
　Kurikara · · · · · · · · · · · · · · **4:**312b–313a
　Magome · · · · · · · · · · · · · · · · · **5:**83b

Mikuni · · · · · · · · · · · · · · · · · · **5:**172b
Ningyō · · · · · · · · · · · · · · · · · · **6:**5b
Nomugi · · · · · · · · · · · · · · · · · · **6:**34a
Sayo no Nakayama · · · · · · · · · · · · **7:**31b
Torii · · · · · · · · · · · · · · · · · · · **8:**79a
Usui · · · · · · · · · · · · · · · · · · · **8:**182a
Wada · · · · · · · · · · · · · · · · · · · **8:**197b
"Mountain people" · · · · · · · · · · · · **7:**13b
"Mountain preserves" regulations
　(tomeyama) · · · · · · · · · · · · **8:**70b–71a
Mountain ranges
　Akaishi · · · · · · · · · · · · · · · · · **1:**39b
　Abukuma · · · · · · · · · · · · · · · · · **1:**5b
　Asahi · · · · · · · · · · · · · · · · **1:**92b–93a
　Chūgoku · · · · · · · · · · · · · · · · **1:**312a
　Dewa · · · · · · · · · · · · · · · · · · **2:**91a
　Echigo · · · · · · · · · · · · · · · · · **2:**143b
　Ezo · · · · · · · · · · · · · · · · **2:**239a–239b
　Hidaka · · · · · · · · · · · · · · · · · **3:**130a
　Hida · · · · · · · · · · · · · · · · · · **3:**130a
　Hira · · · · · · · · · · · · · · · · · · **3:**143a
　Ishikari · · · · · · · · · · · · · · · · · **3:**342a
　Izumi · · · · · · · · · · · · · · · · · · **3:**366a
　Japanese Alps · · · · · · · · · · · · · · **4:**12b
　Kantō · · · · · · · · · · · · · · · · · · **4:**153a
　Kii · · · · · · · · · · · · · · · · · · · **4:**204b
　Kiso · · · · · · · · · · · · · · · · · · **4:**224a
　Kitakami · · · · · · · · · · · · · · · · **4:**226a
　Kitami · · · · · · · · · · · · · · · · · **4:**226b
　Kyūshū · · · · · · · · · · · · · · · · · **4:**341a
　Mikuni · · · · · · · · · · · · · · · · · **5:**172b
　Oku Chichibu · · · · · · · · · · · · · · **6:**95a
　Oku Tama · · · · · · · · · · · · · · · · **6:**98b
　Ōu · · · · · · · · · · · · · · · · **6:**135b–136a
　Sanuki · · · · · · · · · · · · · · · · · **7:**18b
　Sefuri · · · · · · · · · · · · · · · · · · **7:**48b
　Shikoku · · · · · · · · · · · · · · · · · **7:**97b
　Suzuka · · · · · · · · · · · · · · · · · **7:**280b
　Tamba · · · · · · · · · · · · · · · · · **7:**333a
　Tango · · · · · · · · · · · · · · · · · · **7:**341a
　Teshio · · · · · · · · · · · · · · · · · · **8:**15b
　Tsukushi · · · · · · · · · · · · · · · · **8:**115a
　Yamizo · · · · · · · · · · · · · · · · · **8:**313b
　Yūbari · · · · · · · · · · · · · · · · · **8:**354b
Mountains
　Hokkaidō
　　Ashibetsudake · · · · · · · · · · · · · **1:**97a
　　Daisetsuzan · · · · · · · · · · · · · · **2:**67b
　　Ishikaridake · · · · · · · · · · · · · · **3:**341b
　　Yūbaridake · · · · · · · · · · · · · · · **8:**354b
　Honshū
　　Adatarasan · · · · · · · · · · · · · · · **1:**11b
　　Akaishidake · · · · · · · · · · · · · · **1:**39b
　　Amagisan · · · · · · · · · · · · · · · · **1:**49b
　　Bukōsan · · · · · · · · · · · · · · · · **1:**207a
　　Daisen · · · · · · · · · · · · · · · · · **2:**67a
　　Dōgoyama · · · · · · · · · · · · · · · **2:**126a
　　Enasan · · · · · · · · · · · · · · · · · **2:**213a
　　Fujisan · · · · · · · · · · · · · **2:**344b–345b
　　Hagurosan · · · · · · · · · · · · · · · **3:**77a
　　Hakusan · · · · · · · · · · · · · · · · **3:**88b
　　Hayachinesan · · · · · · · · · · · · · **3:**114b
　　Hieizan · · · · · · · · · · · · · · · · · **3:**130b
　　Hodosan · · · · · · · · · · · · · · · · **3:**209a
　　Hōōzan · · · · · · · · · · · · · · · · · **3:**227a
　　Hōraijisan · · · · · · · · · · · · · · · **3:**227a
　　Hotakadake · · · · · · · · · · · · · · · **3:**237b
　　Ikomayama · · · · · · · · · · · · · · · **3:**270b
　　Kammuriyama · · · · · · · · · · · · · **4:**128a
　　Kashima Yarigatake · · · · · · · · · · **4:**162b
　　Kimpokusan · · · · · · · · · · · · · · **4:**210b
　　Kimpusan · · · · · · · · · · · · · · · **4:**211a
　　Kitadake · · · · · · · · · · · · · · · · **4:**224b
　　Kobushigadake · · · · · · · · · · · · · **4:**239a
　　Komagatake (central Honshū/Akaishi)
　　· **4:**265a
　　Komagatake (central Honshū/Kiso)
　　· **4:**265a

Komagatake (northern Honshū) ·· **4:**265a
Kongōsan ················· **4:**270a
Kōyasan ················· **4:**299a
Mitsuminesan ·············· **5:**214a
Myōgisan ················· **5:**290b
Nachisan ················· **5:**300a
Obasuteyama ·········· **6:**48a–48b
Ōdaigaharasan ·············· **6:**61a
Ōeyama ·················· **6:**67b
Ōminesan ················· **6:**102a
Ōtakineyama ··············· **6:**129a
Ōyama ··················· **6:**137b
Rokkōsan ············· **6:**334b–335a
Rokkōzan ················· **1:**83b
Ryōzen ··················· **6:**353a
Senjōgatake ················ **7:**66a
Sentsūzan ················· **7:**67b
Shiomidake ················ **7:**141a
Shirane Sanzan ············· **7:**147a
Shiroumadake ·············· **7:**148a
Taishakusan ················ **7:**303b
Takaosan ·················· **7:**317b
Tanigawadake ·········· **7:**341a–341b
Tanzawasan ················ **7:**346a
Tateyama ················· **7:**349b
Togakushiyama ············· **8:**35b
Tsubakurodake ·············· **8:**109b
Tsukubasan ················ **8:**114b
Tsurugidake ················ **8:**116b
Yahikoyama ················ **8:**284b
Yakushidake ··············· **8:**285b
Yarigatake ················· **8:**316b
Kyūshū
  Hikosan ················· **3:**138b
  Kujūsan ················· **4:**303b
  Kunimidake ·············· **4:**309b
  Miyanouradake ············ **5:**221a
  Sobosan ················· **7:**207b
Shikoku
  Ishizuchisan ············· **3:**347a
  Tsurugisan ··············· **8:**116b
  worship ············· **5:**259b–260a
Mountains, worship of ····· **5:**259b–260a
Mourning ············ **2:**370a; **5:**260a
**Movement for Union of Court and
  Shogunate** ·········· **1:**55a–55b; **4:**308b;
            5:260a–260b, 317b; **7:**102a
  Iwakura Tomomi ··········· **3:**360a
  Kōmei, Emperor ··········· **4:**266a
  Nabeshima Kansō ·········· **5:**299a
  Sakuma Shōzan ············ **7:**4a
  Tokugawa Iemochi ·········· **8:**48a
**Movement to Memorialize Three
  Important Items** ·········· **7:**9b
**Movement to Protect Constitutional
  Government** · **3:**198a; **5:**260b–261a; **6:**211a
  Imperial Diet ············· **3:**276b
  Kakushin Kuarabu ·········· **4:**120a
  Kenseikai ················ **4:**198a
  Kiyoura Keigo ············· **4:**233a
  Kōjunsha ················· **4:**252b
  Rikken Seiyūkai ··········· **6:**315a
  Taishō political crisis ········ **7:**305b
  Takahashi Korekiyo ········· **7:**312b
Moxa treatment ······ **1:**10b; **5:**261a–261b
Moxibustion ········ **5:**146a, 261a–261b
Moyoro shell mound
  ············ モヨロ貝塚 · **1:**1b; **5:**261b
  Okhotsk culture ··········· **6:**84a
Mozaemon IV
  ············· 茂左衛門(四代)··**5:**334b
Mozu ···················· **7:**179b
Mozume Takami · 物集高見 ·· **5:**261b
M. R. Seni Pramot ··········· **7:**65b
Mu ······················ **6:**41b
Mube (Stautonia hexaphylla) ····· **5:**261b
Muchaku ········· 無著 ···· **1:***186b*

Mu-ch'i. See **Mokkei**
Muchigoma ("whip top") ········ **1:**149b
Muchō (pen name). See **Ueda Akinari**
Muchū mondōshū
  (Collections of
  Questions and Answers
  [Exchanged] in a Dream)
  ············· 夢中問答集 ···· **8:**28a
Mudaiki ········ 無益委記 ···· **4:**250a
Mudrā ·················· **3:**328a
Mugaen ········· 無我苑 ···· **4:**180b
Mugenkyū ········ 無弦弓 ···· **4:**179b
Mugen no michi · 無限の道 ···· **4:**165a
Mugi ··················· **8:**251a
Mugi to heitai ·· 麦と兵隊 ···· **7:**176b
Mugiwara-bōshi ············· **3:**119a
Muharras Oil Co, Ltd ········· **2:**61a
Muika ············ 六日 · **5:**261b
Mujin ············ 無尽 · **5:**261b–262a
  insurance system ········· **3:**316b–317a
Mujina. See **Tanuki**
Mujō ············· 無常 · **1:**180b, 181b;
            4:129a; **5:**262a; **6:**299a
  kabuki interpretations ······ **4:**93b
Mujū Ichien. 無住一円 See **Shasekishū**
Mukai Kyorai ···· 向井去来 · **5:**16a, 262a;
                        6:299b
Mukai Tadaharu · 向井忠晴 ···· **5:**262a
Mukashi-banashi kenkyū
  ············· 昔話研究 ···· **2:**302a
*Mukashi-banashi saishu
  techō* ······ 昔話採取手帖 ···· **2:**302a
Mukawa ········· 鵡川 · **5:**262a–262b
Mukden, Battle of
  ········· 奉天会戦 **3:**197a; **5:**262b
  Russo-Japanese War ········ **6:**347a
Mukō (city) ······· 向日 · **5:**262b
Mukōgaoka shell mound
  ············ 向ケ岡貝塚 · **1:**76b; **5:**262b
Mukogawa ······· 武庫川 · **5:**262b
Mukoirikon ·············· **5:**262b
Muko (bridegroom, son-in-law) plays
  ····················· **4:**327a
Muko yōshi ··········· **2:**242a–242b
Mukyōkai (non-church
  movement) ········ 無教会 · **5:**262b–263a,
                        323b
  Uchimura Kanzō ··········· **8:**124b–125a
Multinational enterprises ···· **5:**263a–264a
  investment character ······· **5:**263b
  Japanese ··············· **5:**263a–263b
  problems in 1980s ········· **5:**263b–264a
Mumeiō ·········· 無名翁 ···· **4:**189b
Mumyōshō ········ 無名抄 ···· **4:**128b
Mumyō-zōshi ··· 無名草子 · **5:**39b, 264a
Munabetsusen ··· 棟別銭 ···· **5:**264a
Munakata Shikō · 棟方志功 **2:**294a; **5:***233a*,
                        264a–264b
  Aomori Prefectural Museum ··· **1:**69b
  modern prints ············ **5:**232b
  style ·················· **5:**264b
Munakata Shrines
  ··········· 宗像神社 · **5:**264b–265a
  Okinoshima ·············· **6:**92b
Munakata Taisha Treasure House **5:**277b
Muneage ·················· **4:**195a
Munebetsusen. See **Munabetsusen**
Munenaga, Prince
  ··········· 宗良親王 ···· **5:**265a
Munetaka, Prince 宗尊親王 ···· **5:**265a
Mung, John ··········· **5:**313a–313b
Municipal museums ·········· **5:**279a
Muqi (Mu-ch'i). See **Mokkei**
Mura ··············· **5:**265a–265b
Muragaki Norimasa
  ··········· 村垣範正 ···· **5:**265b
Murahachibu ····· 村八分 · **5:**265b–266a

Muraji.   連
  See **Kabane**
Murakami ········· 村上 · **5:**266a
Murakami Genzō 村上元三 **2:**274a; **5:**266a;
                        7:103b
Murakami Kagaku
  ··········· 村上華岳 ···· **5:**266a
Murakami Kijō 村上鬼城 · **5:**266a–266b
Murakami Makoto ·· 村上信 ···· **5:**266b
Murakami Namiroku
  ··········· 村上浪六 ···· **5:**266b
Murakami Naojirō
  ········· 村上直次郎 ···· **5:**266b
Murakami Shōtarō
  ········· 村上荘太郎 · **5:**266a–266b
Murakami Takejirō
  ········· 村上武次郎 ···· **5:**266b
Murakami Yoshiteru
  ········· 村上義光 ···· **3:**101b–102a
Mural painting. See **Screen and wall
  painting**
Muramatsu Aizō · 村松愛蔵 ···· **3:**262b
Muramatsu Giichi 村松義一 ···· **5:**266b
Muramatsu Shōfū
  ··········· 村松梢風 ···· **5:**266b
"Mura no ie" ····· 村の家 ···· **7:**176a
Murano Shirō ··· 村野四郎 · **5:**266b–267a
  style ·················· **5:**267a
Murano Tōgo ···· 村野藤吾 ···· **5:**267a
Muraoka Hanako 村岡花子 ···· **5:**267a
Muraoka Iheiji · 村岡伊平治 · **5:**267a–267b
Muraoka Tsunetsugu
  ··········· 村岡典嗣 ···· **4:**259a
Murasaki (Lithospermum erythrorhizon) ·
                        5:267b
Murasaki no hitomoto
  ··········· 紫の一本 ···· **8:**34b
Murasaki Shikibu ·· 紫式部 · **1:**18a, 266a;
  2:280a; **5:**14a–14b, 267b–269a, 325a; **7:**52b
  Chinese literature ·········· **1:**293b
  at court ·············· **5:**268a–269a
  Fujiwara no Kintō ········· **2:**352a
  Fujiwara no Teishi ········· **2:**356b
  Kagerō nikki ············· **4:**104a
  late years and achievement ··· **5:**268b–269a
  middle years ·········· **5:**268a–268b
  name, family and early life ·· **5:**267b–269a
  Sei Shōnagon ············· **7:**52b
  Tale of Genji ············· **7:**328b–331a
Murasaki shikibu [[Japanese beauty-
  berry) Callicarpa japonica] ··· **5:**269b
Murasaki Shikibu nikki
  ·········· 紫式部日記 ········ **2:**186a;
                        5:267b–268a
Murasaki Shikibu shū
  ··········· 紫式部集 ···· **5:**269a
Murasaki susuki ··········· **7:**279a
Murasakizome (purple dye) ···· **1:**237a
Murata Harumi ·· 村田春海 ···· **5:**269b
  Kamo no Mabuchi ········· **4:**129b
Murata Kiyokaze · 村田清風 · **5:**269b–270a
Murata Minoru ·· 村田実 **2:**268a; **5:**269b;
                        7:102b
Murata Seifū ···· 村田清風 · **5:**269b–270a
Murata Shōzō ··· 村田省蔵 ···· **5:**270a
Mura (village) ············· **5:**265b
Mura yakunin ···· 村役人 ···· **5:**270a
Murayama ········ 村山 ···· **5:**270a
Murayama Reservoir. See **Tama, Lake**
Murayama Ryōhei
  ··········· 村山龍平 · **5:**270a–270b
Murayama Shichirō
  ·········· 村山七郎 · **1:**36b; **4:**18b,
                        20b
Murayama Tomoyoshi
  ··········· 村山知義 ···· **5:**270b
Murdoch, James ··········· **5:**270b
Muri shinjū ················ **7:**262a

Murō-Akame-Aoyama
  Quasi-National Park
  ····室生赤目青山国定公園 ····· 5:299a
Murōji   室生寺 ··· 5:270b-271a
Muro Kyūsō ····· 室鳩巣 ··· 5:271a-271b
  Forty-Seven Rōnin Incident ····· 2:327b
Muromachi bakufu. 室町幕府
  See **Muromachi shogunate**
Muromachi history. *See* **History of**
  Japan
Muromachi ki ····· 室町記 ····· 4:101b
Muromachi period
  ····· 室町時代 ····· 5:271b
Muromachi shogunate
  ····· 室町幕府 ····· 1:212a;
        5:271b-274a;
        7:8a, 12a, 64b, 161a
  Council of State ····· 3:252a
  decline and demise ····· 5:274a
  distribution of power ····· 5:272b-273a
  feudalism ····· 2:265a
  founding ····· 1:99a
  Kamakura shogunate military governors
    under ····· 7:184a
  machinery of government ··· 5:273a-274a
  patronage of arts ····· 5:273a
  powers of the shogunate ····· 5:273a
  shōgun and shugo ····· 5:272a-272b
  warrior government ····· 8:229b
Muroo Saisei 室生犀星 ··· 5:274a-274b
  Hagiwara Sakutarō ····· 3:76a
Muroran ····· 室蘭 ····· 5:274b
Muroto ····· 室戸 ····· 5:274b
Muroto-Anan Coast
  Quasi-National Park
  ···室戸阿南海岸国定公園 ····· 1:53b
Murotozaki ···· 室戸岬 ····· 5:274b
Murray, David ····· 2:311a; 5:275a; 7:35b
Musan Fujin Geijutsu Remmei ··· 7:316b
Musansha undō to fujin
  no mondai (The
  Proletarian Movement
  and Problems of
  Women)
  ·無産者運動と婦人の問題 ··· 8:297a
Musasabi····· 2:293b
Musashi ····· 武蔵 ··· 5:275a
  loss ····· 4:383b
Musashi Murayama
  ····· 武蔵村山 ··· 5:275a
Musashino ····· 武蔵野 ··· 5:275a
Musashino Department Store ··· 7:49a
Musashino Plateau
  ····· 武蔵野台地 ··· 5:275a
Musashino Tetsudō ····· 7:49b
Musashi Province 武蔵国 · 5:275a-275b
Musashi Shichitō 武蔵七党 ··· 5:275b
Muscular dystrophy ····· 2:143a
Museki isshi ····· 夢跡一紙 ··· 4:154a
Museum of Modern Japanese Literature
  ····· 5:275b
  Takami Jun ····· 7:315a
Museums ····· 5:275b-280b
  archaeological ····· 5:277b-278a
  ceramics ····· 5:279b
  educational activities ····· 5:280a-280b
  ethnographical ····· 5:278a-278b
  exhibition principles ····· 5:280b
  foreign ····· 5:280b
  funding ····· 5:280a-280b
  individual artists ····· 5:279b-280a
  modern art ····· 5:279a
  municipal ····· 5:279a
  national ····· 5:276a-276b
  prefectural ····· 5:278b
  private ····· 5:276b-277b
  religious foundation ····· 5:280a
  special ····· 5:280a

treasure houses ····· 5:277b
Western-art ····· 5:279a-279b
Musha Incident 霧社事件 ····· 5:280b
Mushanokōji Saneatsu
  ····· 武者小路実篤 2:344a; 4:114a;
        5:281a-281b
  Christianity ····· 4:32a
  Shirakaba school ····· 7:145b-146b
Mushi ····· 5:281b-282a
Mushifūji ····· 5:282a
Mushi mo ki mo 虫も樹も ····· 6:139b
Mushin ····· 無心 5:282a; 6:297a
Mushi no iroiro
  ····· 虫のいろいろ ····· 6:139b
Mushin (poetry term) 無心 ····· 8:181b
Mushi okuri ····· 虫送り ····· 6:309b
Mushiro ····· 7:249b
Mushrooms (kinoko) ····· 5:282a-282b
  production ····· 1:27b
Music
  accompaniment ····· 3:115b
  Ainu ····· 1:36a
  from Bohai ····· 1:159b
  children's songs ····· 1:280a
  composers
    Akiyoshi Toshiko ····· 1:44b
    Dan Ikuma ····· 2:76b
    Fukushima Kazuo ····· 2:366b
    Koga Masao ····· 4:248a
    Mayuzumi Toshirō ····· 5:144a
    Miyagi Michio ····· 5:217a-217b
    Nakanoshima Kin'ichi ····· 5:317a
    Nakayama Shimpei ····· 5:319a
    Takemitsu Tōru ····· 7:324b
    Taki Rentarō ····· 7:327a
    Yamada Kōsaku ····· 8:289a
  conductors
    Ozawa Seiji ····· 6:140b
  dengaku ····· 2:86a-86b
  folk song ····· 2:300b-301a
  gagaku ····· 3:1a-2a
  gidayū-bushi ····· 3:30a-30b
  gigaku ····· 3:31b-32a
  hayashi ····· 3:115b
  heikyoku ····· 1:157a
  Italian influence ····· 3:351a
  of Japanese imperial court ····· 3:1a-2a
  jiuta ····· 4:64b-65a
  jōruri ····· 4:76a-77b
  kabuki music ····· 4:99a-100a
  kiyomoto-bushi ····· 4:232a-232b
  kouta ····· 4:298a-298b
  meter in Ryūkyū ····· 6:357b-358a
  military songs (gunka) ····· 3:69a
  minshingaku ····· 5:197a-197b
  modal systems ····· 3:2a-2b
  nagauta ····· 5:307b
  naniwa-bushi ····· 5:328a
  national anthem ····· 5:336a
  notation ····· 6:86b
  puppet theater ····· 1:214a
  religious ····· 5:283a-284a
    Buddhist ····· 5:283a-283b
    Christian ····· 5:283b-284a
    Shintō ····· 5:283a
  ryūkōka ····· 6:353b-355a
  Ryūkyū music ····· 6:357a-358a
  saibara ····· 6:365a
  sōkyoku ····· 7:225b-226a
  song, early ····· 2:137a-138a
    Heian sources ····· 2:137b
    singers and song use ····· 2:138a
    sources ····· 2:137a
  tokiwazu-bushi ····· 8:43b
  traditional ····· 5:284a-285a
    early history (400-1200) ···· 5:284a-284b
    modern period ····· 5:285a-285b
    1200-1500 ····· 5:284b

      1500-1868 ····· 5:284b-285a
  Western ····· 5:285b-287b
    Meiji period (1868-1912) ··· 5:285b-286a
    ryūkōka ····· 6:354a
    Taishō and prewar Shōwa periods
      (1912-1940) ····· 5:286a-287a
    World War II and after (1940-   )
      ····· 5:287a-287b
Musical instruments ····· 5:282b
  aerophones ····· 5:282b
  Ainu ····· 1:37b
  biwa ····· 1:157a-157b
  chordophones ····· 5:282b
  companies
    Kawai Musical Instruments Mfg Co, Ltd
      ····· 4:179a
    Nippon Gakki Co, Ltd ····· 6:9b-10a
  denden taiko ····· 2:85b-86a
  Esoteric Buddhist rites ····· 1:195b-196a
  gagaku ····· 3:1b-2a
  hichiriki ····· 3:129b
  hitoyogiri ····· 3:208b
  idiophones ····· 5:282b
  kokyū ····· 4:264b
  koto ····· 4:296b-297a
  lute ····· 1:157a-157b
  membranophones ····· 5:282b
  percussion ····· 3:2a
  Pure Land Buddhist rites ····· 1:196a-196b
  sasara ····· 7:24a
  shakuhachi ····· 7:75a-76a
  shamisen ····· 1:157a, 212b-214a
  shichigenkin ····· 7:87b
  shō ····· 7:154a
  stringed ····· 3:2a
  taiko ····· 7:297b
  tsuzumi ····· 8:119b-120a
  Western ····· 5:285b-287b
  wind ····· 3:1b-2a
  Zen rites ····· 1:196b
Musket, matchblock ····· 3:140a
Musō Soseki 夢窓疎石 · 3:33a; 5:287b;
        6:*152b*
  gardens ····· 3:9a-9b
  Josetsu ····· 4:77b
  kakun ····· 4:118b
  portrait painting ····· 6:227b
Musubinokami (god)
  ····· 産霊神 ····· 4:259a
Musume Dōjōji · 娘道成寺 ····· 6:108a
Musume-gumi ····· 娘組 ····· 8:353b
Musume to watashi 娘と私 ····· 7:148b
Mutai Risaku ····· 務台理作 · 5:287b-288a
Mutō Akira ····· 武藤章 ··· 5:288a
Mutobe Yoshika
  ····· 六人部是香 ····· 4:259a
Mutō Nobuko · 武藤能婦子 ····· 2:66a
Mutō Sanji ····· 武藤山治 · 2:32b; 5:288a
Mutō Shūji ····· 6:*152b*
Mutsu (city) ····· むつ ··· 5:288a
Mutsu (battleship) ··· 陸奥 · 5:288a, 307b
Mutsu (nuclear-powered
  ship) ····· むつ · 5:288a-288b
Mutsu Bay ····· 陸奥湾 ··· 5:288b
  ····· 5:288a
Mutsu family ····· 陸奥氏 · 6:126b-127a
Mutsu Munemitsu
  ····· 陸奥宗光 · 5:288b-289a;
        7:99a
  Hara Takashi ····· 3:102b
Mutsu Province ····· 陸奥国 ····· 3:363b;
        5:289a-289b
Mutsu waki 陸奥話記
  Earlier Nine Years' War ····· 2:137a
Mutual company ····· 5:289b
Mutual Cooperation and Security,
  Treaty of ····· 6:167a

United States-Japan Administrative Agreement. *See* **United States-Japan security treaties**
Mutual Security Agreement 5:289b; 8:345a
  Occupation ················ 6:55a
Mutual Security Agreement of 1952
  ···························· 7:252a
My Fair Lady (Japanese) ···· 4:207b
"My heart is Buddha" ········ 8:27a-27b
My Lantern ················ 4:179a
Myōe ········· 明恵 · 5:289b-290a;
  7:85b
  Hōnen ················· 4:67b
  portrait ··············· 5:289a
  writings ··············· 5:290a
Myōen ········· 明円 ··· 5:290a
Myōga ····················· 3:127b
Myōgakin ········ 冥加金 4:100a; 5:290a,
  360b
  unjō ·················· 8:172a
Myōgisan ········ 妙義山 · 5:290b
Myōjinshō ······· 明神礁 · 5:290b
Myōji taitō ······ 苗字帯刀 · 5:290b
Myōjō ·········· 明星 2:346a; 5:290b;
  8:340b
  founding ··············· 5:19b
Myōkensan ······· 妙見山 · 5:290b
Myōkō, Naganuma 妙佼長沼 · 6:321a
Myōkōnin ········ 妙好人 · 5:290b-291a
Myōkōsan ········ 妙高山 2:347b; 5:291a
Myōō ···················· 5:291a
  Tankai ················· 7:343a
Myōren ············ 妙蓮 · 2:199b; 7:92b,
  93a
Myōshinji ········ 妙心寺 · 5:291a; 7:76a
  paintings ··············· 4:148a
Myōshu ········· 名主 ··· 5:291b
  bushidan ··············· 1:221a
  gōson system ··········· 3:50a-51a
  nago ·················· 5:308b
  shōen ················· 7:157a
Myōtei mondō ··· 妙貞問答 · 2:241a
Mystery stories · 2:170a-171a; 5:291b-292a;
  6:221b
  orthodox vs innovative authors · 5:292a
Mythology ················ 5:292a-297b
  Amaterasu and Susanoo ····· 5:293a-294b
    birth ················· 5:293a
    disappearance of Sun ······ 5:293b
    feuding ··············· 5:293a-293b
  badgers ················ 5:296b
  cats ·················· 5:296b
  cycles
    Izumo ················ 5:293b-295a
    Yamato ··············· 5:292b-293b
  Dragon Palace ·········· 5:295b
  fairies and celestial beings ··· 5:295a-295b
  fountains ·············· 5:295a
  foxes ················· 5:296b
  heaven ················ 3:121a-121b
  heroic tales ··········· 5:296a-296b
  Hoderi no Mikoto ······· 5:294b
  Hoori no Mikoto ········ 5:294b
  Izanagi and Izanami ····· 3:364b-365a;
    5:292b-293a
    land of Yomi ·········· 5:293a
  nefarious spirits ········· 5:296a
  Ninigi no Mikoto ······· 5:294b; 6:5b
  Ōkuninushi no Mikoto ··· 5:293b-294a
    Amaterasu's messengers ··· 5:294a-294b
    hare of Inaba ·········· 5:293b
    Sukunahikona no Mikoto ·· 5:294a
    trials ················ 5:293b-294a
    sennin ··············· 5:295b-296a
  Seven Gods of Good Fortune ····· 5:296a

Shintō ···················· 7:130b
  sources
    Kogo shūi (Gleanings from Ancient
    Stories) ··············· 5:292a
    Kojiki ("Records of Ancient
    Matters") ·············· 5:292a-295a
    Izumo fudoki ·········· 2:341a
    Nihon shoki ("Chronicles of Japan")
    ····················· 5:383b-384a
    Shoku nihongi (Chronicles of Japan,
    Continued) ············· 5:292
  sparrow ················ 5:296b
  Takamagahara ·········· 7:314a
  Tanabata ··············· 5:105a
Myths
  Chinese ················ 7:163b
  discipline of Japanese history · 2:101a-101b
  monkeys ··············· 5:245a-245b
Myths, agricultural ········ 7:177b

N

Nabari ··············· 名張 ··· 5:299a
Nabe (saucepans or pots) ········· 2:24b
Nabeshima family · 鍋島氏 ····· 5:299a
Nabeshima Kansō
  ············· 鍋島閑叟 ··· 5:299a
Nabeshima Naomasa. 鍋島直正
  See **Nabeshima Kansō**
Nabeshima Naoshige
  ············· 鍋島直茂 ··· 5:299a
Nabeshima ware · 鍋島焼 ······ 1:85b;
    5:299a-299b
  Edo period ············· 1:263b
  museums ·············· 5:279b
Nachi Falls ····· 那智滝 · 5:299b, 300a;
    8:348b
Nachi-Fujikoshi Corporation ······ 5:299b
Nachi-Katsuura · 那智勝浦 ······ 5:300a
Nachisan ········ 那智山 ····· 5:300a
Nada ············· 灘 ······· 5:300a
Nademono ·················· 4:166a
Naeba International Skiing Ground 5:300a
Naebasan ········ 苗場山 ···· 5:300a
Nagahama ······· 長浜 ····· 5:300a
Nagai ············ 長井 ····· 5:300a
Nagai Kafū ······ 永井荷風 1:164a; 2:274a;
    5:55b, 300a-301a; 7:26b, 103b, 125b, 253b;
    8:328b
  education and early career ······ 5:300a
  Ken'yūsha ··············· 4:199a
  western influence ········ 5:300b
  works ················· 5:300b-301a
Nagai Nagayoshi 長井長義 1:268a; 5:301a
Nagai Ryūtarō · 永井柳太郎··· 5:301a-301b
  education ··············· 5:301a
  political career ·········· 5:301a
Nagai Tatsuo ··· 永井龍男 ···· 5:301b
Nagai Uta ······ 長井雅楽 ···· 5:301b
Nagajuban ················· 4:210b
Nagako, Empress
  ············· 皇后, 良子 3:277a; 5:301b
Nagakubo Sekisui
  ············· 長久保赤水 · 5:301b-302a
Nagamaki ·················· 1:89a
Nagamochi ············· 5:302a
Nagano ············ 長野 ···· 5:302a
Nagano Basin ···· 長野盆地 ··· 5:302b
Nagano Osami · 永野修身 ······ 5:302b

Nagano Prefecture · 長野県 · 5:302b-303a;
    8:355a
Nagano Shigeo ··· 永野重雄 ··· 5:303a
Naganuma case ········· 5:303a; 7:275b
Nagaoka ·········· 長岡 ··· 5:303b
Nagaoka Hantarō
  ············· 長岡半太郎 ··· 5:303b
Nagaokakyō (city) · 長岡京 ··· 5:303b
Nagaokakyō (Imperial
  capital) ········· 長岡京 4:128a; 5:303b
Nagaragawa ······ 長良川 ··· 5:303b
Nagareru ········· 流れる ···· 4:240a
Nagareyama ······ 流山 ···· 5:303b
Nagasaki ········· 長崎 ·· 5:303b-304a;
    8:276a
  atomic bomb related diseases 1:111a-112b
  food riot ··············· 8:124a
Nagasakibana ····· 長崎鼻 ··· 5:304a
Nagasaki boat races ········ 6:171b
Nagasaki Flag Incident ········ 5:304a
  Korean (Democratic People's
  Republic)-Japanese trade suspended
  ····················· 4:286b
Nagasaki Haruma
  ············· 長崎波留麻 ······· 2:123a
Nagasaki Kaisho 長崎会所 · 5:304a-304b,
    306a
Nagasaki miyage ··········· 5:305a
Nagasaki Naval Training Academy. *See*
  Kaigun Denshūjo
Nagasaki Prefecture
  ············· 長崎県 · 5:304b-305a
  capital ················ 5:303b
  port ·················· 5:304b
  principal products ········ 5:304b
  tourist attractions ········ 5:304b
Nagasaki school · 長崎派 · 5:305a-306a;
    7:83b
  individualists ··········· 5:306a
  official painters ········· 5:305b
  screen and wall painting ···· 7:43a
  Shen Nanpin school ······· 5:305b-306a
  woodblock prints ········ 5:305a-305b
Nagasaki Shipyards
  ···················· 2:31a; 5:306a,
    306b
Nagasaki trade · 長崎貿易 1:211b; 5:306a;
  Dutch trade ············· 2:135b
  strict regulation ········· 7:171a
Nagasawa, Kanaye ········ 5:306a-306b
Nagasawa Rosetsu. 長沢蘆雪
  See **Rosetsu**
Nagase & Co, Ltd ·············· 5:306b
Nagashikan ················ 2:25a
Nagashino ·········· 長篠 ···· 6:63b
Nagashino, Battle of
  ············· 長篠の戦 ··· 5:306b
  ashigaru ··············· 1:98a
  firearms usage ·········· 2:279a
  Takeda Katsuyori ········ 7:322b
Nagashizuki (method of molding paper)
  ····················· 8:234a
Nagata Masaichi 永田雅一··· 5:306b-307a
Nagata Teiryū ··· 永田貞柳 ··· 5:307a
Nagata Tetsuzan 永田鉄山 ···· 5:307a
  February 26th Incident ····· 2:250a
Nagata Tokuhon 永田徳本 ····· 5:307a
Nagata Zenkichi. *See* **Aōdō Denzen**
Nagato (battleship) ··· 長門 · 5:307a-307b
Nagato (city) ····· 長門 ···· 5:307b
Nagatoro ········ 長瀞 · 1:73b; 5:307b
Nagatsuka Takashi 長塚節 5:307b; 7:103b
Nagauta ········· 長唄 · 2:301a; 4:77a,
    99a; 5:307b; 7:149a
  Tōkyō ················· 8:63b
Nagauta school ·········· 4:91b
Nagaya ·················· 3:245a
Nagayamon (gate) ········· 3:13a

Nagaya no Ō, Rebellion of
　　　　　長屋王の変 ···· 5:307b-308a
Nagayo Sensai ·長与専斎 ······ 5:308a
Nagayo Yoshirō 長与善郎 1:155b; 5:308a
Nagegane ···· 投銀 ············ 5:308a
Nageire (modern, free-style) ·2:289b, 291a
Nageshi ···························· 7:265b
Nagewaza ·························· 4:82b
Nagai michi ······ 長い道 ···· 4:162b
Naginata ····· 1:89a-89b; 5:308a-308b
Nago (city) ········ 名護 ······ 5:308b
Nago (peasant status)
　　　　　　　　名子 ········ 5:308b
Nago Bay ····· 名護湾 ·········· 5:308b
Nagoshi ······ 夏越 ············ 5:308b
Nagoya ····· 名古屋 · 5:308b, 309a
　Chūbu region ···················· 1:311a
　history ···················· 5:308b-309a
　products ·················· 5:309a-309b
　tourist attractions ········ 5:309a-309b
Nagoya Castle ·名古屋城 · 5:309a-309b
　paintings ························ 4:151a
Nagoya Gen'i ·名古屋玄医 ···· 5:309b
Nagoya Railroad Co, Ltd ······ 5:309b
Nagoya Tansuishi
　　　　　名古屋丹水子 ········ 5:309b
Nagoya University ············ 5:309b
Nagusazan Gokokuin
　　　　名草山護国院 ········ 4:208a
Naha ······ 那覇 ·············· 5:309b
Nahiko kashū ···魚彦歌集 ···· 4:169a
Naichi zakkyo ·内地雑居 ···· 4:333a;
　　　　　　　　　　5:309b-310a
Naidaijin ······ 内大臣 ···· 5:310a-310b
　inner minister ············ 5:310a-310b
　lord keeper of the privy seal · 5:310a-310b;
　　　　　　　　　　　　6:242a
Naikaku Bunko. 内閣文庫 *See* **Cabinet
　Library**
Naikan therapy ······· 5:310b-311a; 6:261b
Naikasho ····· 内科書 ········ 4:312b
Naiken ······ 内検 ············ 4:191a
Naikoku Kangyō Hakurankai
　　　　内国勧業博覧会 ········ 5:341b
Naimushō. 内務省 *See* **Home Ministry**
Naitō Jōsō ····· 内藤丈草 ···· 5:311a
Naitō Konan ·内藤湖南 ·5:311a; 7:51b
Naitō Torajirō. 内藤虎次郎 *See* **Naitō
　Konan**
Naizai hihyō ijō no mono
　···· 内在批評以上のもの ······ 4:165a
Nakabashira ······················ 7:266a
Nakabayashi Chikutō
　　　　　中林竹洞 ······ 1:211a;
　　　　　　　　　　5:311a-311b
Nakadai Motohisa
　　　　　仲代元久 ········ 5:311b
Nakadai Tatsuya 仲代達矢 2:273a; 5:311b;
　　　　　　　　　　　　7:68b
Nakada Kaoru ···· 中田薫 ···· 5:311b
Nakae Chōmin ··中江兆民 · 1:19a; 2:2a,
　　　　　　332a; 5:311b-312a
　education ················· 5:311b-312a
　Freedom and People's Rights Movement
　　　　　　　　　　　···· 2:335b
　fukoku kyōhei ················ 2:361a
　Genrōin ·················· 5:311b-312a
　political activities ········· 5:311b-312a
　Tōyō jiyū shimbun (Oriental Free Press)
　　　　　　　　　　5:311b-312a
　works ···················· 5:311b-312a
Nakae Tōju ···· 中江藤樹 · 5:312a-312b;
　　　　　　　　7:94b; 8:335a
　Shingaku ························ 7:111b
Nakagawa (Honshū) 那珂川···· 5:312b
Nakagawa (Shikoku) 那賀川···· 5:312b
Nakagawa Gorōji
　　　　　中川五郎治 ···· 5:312b-313a

Nakagawa Jun'an
　　　　　中川淳庵 5:313a; 7:258b
Nakagawa Yoichi 中河与一 ······ 5:313a
Nakagawa Zennosuke
　　　　　中川善之助 ········ 5:313a
Nakahama Manjirō
　　　　　中浜万次郎 ···· 5:313a-313b
Nakahara Chūya ·中原中也 ···· 5:313a
Nakahara Moromori
　　　　　中原師守 ········ 5:255a
Nakai Riken ··· 中井履軒 ···· 5:313b
Nakajima Atsushi 中島敦 ···· 5:313b
Nakajima Chikuhei
　　　　中島知久平 2:343a; 5:313b
Nakajima Mitsuzō. *See* **Takamura Kōun**
Nakajima Nobuyuki
　　　　　中島信行 ···· 5:313b-314a
Nakajima Shōen. *See* **Kishida Toshiko**
Nakajima Toshiko. *See* **Kishida Toshiko**
Nakajō ······ 中条 ············ 5:314a
Naka Kansuke ··· 中勘助 ···· 5:314a
Nakama ······ 仲間 4:100a; 5:314a
Naka Michiyo ···那珂通世 ···· 5:314a
Nakamigawa Hikojirō
　　　　中上川彦次郎 ··· 5:314a-314b
　Fujiyama Raita ················ 2:359a
Nakaminato ···· 那珂湊 ···· 5:314b
Nakamura ····· 中村 ·········· 5:314b
Nakamura Chōhachi
　　　　　中村長八 ········ 5:314b
Nakamura Fusetsu
　　　　　中村不折 ········ 5:314b
Nakamura Gakuryō
　　　　　中村岳陵 ········ 5:314b
Nakamura Hajime 中村元 ···· 5:314b-315a
Nakamura Kanzaburō XVII
中村勘三郎（十七代）
　　　　　　　　　　·········· 4:94b
Nakamura Keiu ··中村敬宇 ···· 5:315a
Nakamura Kenkichi 中村憲吉 ···· 5:315a
Nakamura Kichiemon
　　　　中村吉右衛門 ······ 2:274b
Nakamura kiln ···· 中村窯 ···· 7:226b
Nakamura Kinnosuke 中村錦之助 8:339a
Nakamura Kusatao
　　　　　中村草田男 ······ 5:315a
　haiku ···························· 3:80a
Nakamura Masanao
　　　　　中村正直 1:237b; 5:315a
　liberalism ························ 4:387a
Nakamura Mitsuo
　　　　　中村光夫 ········ 5:13a,
　　　　　　　　　　315a-315b
Nakamura Sakutarō
　　　　　中村鋸太郎 ······ 5:314b
Nakamura Seiichirō
　　　　　中村清一郎 ······ 5:315a
Nakamura Shin'ichirō
　　　　　中村真一郎 ······ 5:315b
Nakamura Tekisai
　　　　　中村惕斎 ········ 5:315b
Nakamura Tsuruzō
　　　　　中村鶴蔵 ······ 6:109b
Nakamura Utaemon
　　　　　中村歌右衛門 ······ 5:315b
　kabuki leadership ·············· 4:92b
Nakamura Utaemon VI ···· 4:93a, 94b
Nakamura v Japan (1962) ······ 2:13a
Nakane Chie ··中根千枝 ···· 7:218a
　vertical society ················ 8:191a
Nakanishi Seiko. *See* **Arima Ineko**
Nakano ······· 中野 ···· 5:315b-316a
Nakano kennel ················ 7:167a
Nakanomikado, Lord 中御門殿 ··· 2:358a
Naka no Ōe, Prince. 中大兄皇子
　See **Tenji, Emperor**
Nakano School ················ 5:316a
Nakano Seigō ···中野正剛 ··· 5:316a-316b
　ideas ······················· 5:316a-316b

　Kokumin Dōmei ············ 4:260a
　political activities ········· 5:316a-316b
Nakano Shigeharu
　　　　　中野重治 ········ 5:13a,
　　　　　　316b-317a; 7:66b
　Kurahara Korehito ········· 5:316b-317a
　novels ···················· 5:316b-317a
　proletarian literature movement ·· 6:255a
　Sata Ineko ···················· 7:25a
　Shinjinkai ······················ 7:115b
　Shin Nihon bungaku ············ 7:122a
Naka no Shima ···中之島 ···· 6:119a
Nakanoshima Kin'ichi
　　　　　中能島欣一 ········ 5:317a
Nakano Tomonori
　　　　　中野友礼 ········ 5:317a
Nakanoumi ···· 中海 ·········· 5:318b
Nakano Ward ···中野区 ···· 5:317a
Nakano Yoshio ·中野好夫 ···· 1:155b;
　　　　　　　　　　5:317a-317b
Nakaoka Shintarō
　　　　中岡慎太郎 · 5:317b; 7:3b
Nakaoku koshō ·中奥小姓 ·· 4:296a
Nakao Kumaki ·中尾熊喜 ···· 5:317b
Nakarai Bokuyō 半井卜養 ···· 5:317b
Nakarai Tōsui 半井桃水 ···· 3:136a
Nakasendai Rebellion
　　　　　中先代の乱 ········ 5:317b
Nakasendō ······ 中山道 · 3:40b-41a;
　　　　5:303a, 318a; 6:229b; 8:41a
　railways ························ 6:278a
Nakasone Yasuhiro
　　　　中曽根康弘 · 2:82b; 5:318a
Nakatsu ······ 中津 ·········· 5:318a
**Nakatsukasa Naishi no
　nikki** ····· 中務内侍日記 ·· 5:318a-318b
Nakatsu Keikoku 中津渓谷 ···· 5:318b
Nakatsukyō ······ 中津峡 ···· 5:318b
Nakatsumiya Shrine
　　　　　中津宮 ·········· 5:265a
Nakauchi Isao ·· 中内功 ···· 2:56b
Nakaumi ······ 中海 ·········· 5:318b
Nakaura Julião 中浦ジュリアン · 5:318b
Nakayama Gishū 中山義秀 ···· 5:318b
Nakayama Heijirō
　　　　中山平次郎 ········ 1:77a
Nakayama Ichirō
　　　　　中山伊知郎 ······ 5:318b
Nakayama Miki ·中山みき · 5:319a; 7:76b
　Tenrikyō ························ 8:9a
Nakayama Shichiri
　　　　　中山七里 ········ 5:319a
Nakayama Shimpei
　　　　　中山晋平 ········ 5:319a
Nakayama Sohei 中山素平 ···· 5:319a-319b
Nakayama Steel Works, Ltd ···· 5:319b
Nakayama Tadamitsu
　　　　　中山忠光 ········ 5:319b
Nakayama Yoshihide
　　　　　中山義秀 ········ 5:318b
Nakaya Ukichirō
　　　　　中谷宇吉郎 ······ 5:319b
Nakazato Kaizan 中里介山 1:164a; 2:268a;
　　　　　　　　5:319b-320a
　Daibosatsu Tōge ···· 5:320a; 6:221a; 7:121a
　early career ···················· 5:319b
　later period ···················· 5:320a
Nakazawa Dōni ·中沢道二 ···· 5:320a
　Shingaku ························ 7:112a
Nakijin castle remains
　　　　　今帰仁城跡 ········ 5:320b
Nakōdo ················· 5:320b-321a
　love marriage and arranged marriage
　　　　　　　　　　　···· 5:320b
　marriage negotiations ······ 5:320b-321a
　social context ·················· 5:320b
Nakoku ··········· 奴国 · 5:321a-321b;
　　　　　　　　　　　7:266a

Nakoso no Seki ········ 勿来関 ······· 5:321b
Namahage ····························· 5:321a, 321b
Namako. See Sea cucumbers
Namamugi Jiken. 生麦事件 See
 Richardson Affair
Namazu ····················· 1:249b; 6:44b
Namba Daisuke. 難波大助
 See Toranomon Incident
Namban ············· 5:321b-322a; 7:104b
Namban art 5:322a-323a, 322a-322b, 6:153a
 Kanō school ························· 4:150a
 museums ··························· 5:280a
Nambanji ················ 南蛮寺 ······ 5:323a
Namban maki-e (lacquer
 ware) ············· 南蛮蒔絵 ·· 4:240b, 361b
Namban screens ··············· 5:322a-323a
Nambantetsu ······················· 3:333a
Namban trade ················· 5:323a-323b
 ships ····························· 7:144a
Nambara Shigeru ·· 南原繁 ········· 5:323b
 Shimoyama Incident ················ 7:107b
Nambokuchō period. See Northern and
 Southern Courts
Nambokuchō seijun ron
        南北朝正閏論 ·· 5:323b-324a
Namboku sōhō · 南北相法 ········· 6:160b
Nambu Chūhei · 南部忠平 ········· 5:324a
Nambu Yoshikazu
        南部義籌 ········· 4:30a
Nambyō ················ 難病 ······ 2:116b
Name cards ························· 5:324a
Namerikawa ············ 滑川 ······ 5:324a
Names ························· 5:324a-326b
 group (clan and family) ····· 5:324b-325a
 men's ······················· 5:325a-326a
 people's ··························· 5:324b
 personal ·························· 5:325a
 place ······················· 5:326a-326b
 women's ·························· 5:326a
Nametoko ············· 滑床 ······ 5:326b
Nami ················ 波 ······ 4:179b
Namida o shishi no tategami ni
 Shinoda Masahiro ·················· 7:122a
Namiki Gohei ····· 並木五瓶 · 4:91b; 5:50a,
                        326b-327a
Namiki Shōzō ··· 並木正三 · 4:91b; 5:50a,
                        327a
Namiki Shōzō II ····················· 5:16b
Namiki Sōsuke ·· 並木宗輔 ········· 5:327a
Namiko ················ 浪子 ······ 8:59b
Nam Il ···························· 4:286b
Nampo Jōmyō ·· 南浦紹明 ········· 5:327a
Namu Amida Butsu
        南無阿弥陀仏 ·· 5:327a-327b
Namu Myōhō renge kyō
        南無妙法蓮華経 ··· 5:327b
Namura Shipbuilding Co, Ltd ······· 5:327b
Nanakamado [(mountain ash) Sorbus
 commixta] ························· 5:327b
Nanao ················ 七尾 ······ 5:327b
Nanatsugama ········ 七ツ釜 ······ 5:327b
Nanatsumen ········ 七つ面 ······ 4:98b
Nandin ························· 5:329b-330a
Nando ···························· 7:248b
Nanga ················ 南画 ·· 5:327b-328a
 See also Bunjinga
Nangakuha ············ 南学派 ······ 5:328a
 Tani Jichū ························· 7:341b
Nangawara kiln 南川原窯 ······· 5:299a
Nangnang ·························· 4:382b
Nangoku ················ 南国 ······ 5:329a
Naniwa (now Ōsaka) ·· 難波 ······ 8:176a
Naniwa-bushi ······ 浪花節 ······ 5:328a
 kōdan ························· 4:241a-241b
Naniwa erejii (Ōsaka
 Elegy) ············· 浪花エレジー · 8:289a
Naniwakyō ······ 難波京 · 5:328b; 7:91a
Naniwa miyage · 難波土産 ······ 5:328a

Naniwa Palace ····· 難波京 ········ 2:58a
Nanjing (Nanking) Incident ·· 5:328b-329a
 1927 ····················· 1:288b; 5:328b
 1937-1938 ························· 5:329a
 Shidehara Kijūrō ··················· 7:88b
Nanjō Bun'yū ···· 南条文雄 ········ 5:329a
Nanki Bunko ···· 南葵文庫 ········ 5:329a
Nankoku ················ 南国 ······ 5:329a
Nankyō shinshō · 南京新唱 ········· 1:38b
Nansei Islands. 南西諸島 See Ryūkyū
 Islands
Nansenshō Somabito. 南仙笑楚満人
 See Tamenaga Shunsui
Nanshinron. 南進論 See Southern
 expansion doctrine
Nansō Satomi hakkenden
        南総里見八犬伝 · 1:130b, 295b;
                5:16b, 329a-329b; 8:336b
Nan taiheiki.   難太平記 See Imagawa
 Sadayo
Nantaisan ·········· 男体山 · 5:329b; 6:3a
Nanten [(nandin) Nandina domestica]
        ······················· 5:329b-330a
Nanushi.   名主 See Shōya
Nan'yō ················ 南陽 ······ 5:330a
Nan'yō Eiga Kyōkai ················ 4:202a
Nan'yō no daiharan
        南洋の大波瀾 ······ 6:332b
Nanzan University ················· 5:330a
Nanzenji ········· 南禅寺 · 4:125b, 336a;
                5:330a-330b; 7:255a
 paintings ·························· 4:151a
 tea gardens
  Kobori Enshū ···················· 4:238b
Nanzonghua ························ 5:328a
Naobi no Kami · 直毘の神 ········· 5:330b
Naohi no Kami. See Naobi no Kami
Naoki Prize ························· 7:293a
 Dan Kazuo ·························· 2:76b
 Genji Keita ························· 3:20a
 Hisao Jūran ······················· 3:151b
 Ibuse Masuji ·················· 3:254a-255b
 Kaionji Chōgorō ···················· 4:112a
 Kikuchi Kan ······················· 4:206b
 Kon Hidemi ························ 4:270a
 Kon Tōkō ·························· 4:275b
 Kuroiwa Jūgo ······················ 4:316b
 Minakami Tsutomu ·················· 5:176a
 Nosaka Akiyuki ····················· 6:40b
 Shiba Ryōtarō ······················ 7:84b
 Shiroyama Saburō ·················· 7:148a
 Tachihara Masaaki ·················· 7:293a
 Umezaki Haruo ····················· 8:147b
 Yamaguchi Hitomi ·················· 8:294b
Naoki Sanjūgo ···· 直木三十五 ··· 5:330b-331a
 Bungei Shunjū, Ltd ················· 1:210a
Naorai ················ 直会 · 2:254b-255b;
                5:331a-331b; 7:139b
 Daijōsai ······················· 2:59a-59b
Naoshima Islands
        直島諸島 ······ 5:331b
NAPF (All Japan Proletarian Arts
 League) ·························· 7:175b
Nara. See Oaks
Nara (city)   奈良 · 5:331b-332a;
                        6:47a
 contemporary ····················· 5:331b
 excavations ························ 5:331b
 Heijōkyō ·························· 3:124a
 history ···························· 5:331b
 Kasuga Shrine ····················· 5:331a
 natural features ··················· 5:331b
 pagoda ···························· 5:331a
 Sarusawa Pond ···················· 5:331a
 tourism and culture ················ 5:332a
Nara Basin ······ 奈良盆地 · 5:332a-332b
Nara Buddhism ······ 2:178a-178b; 5:332b

Narachō bumpō shi
 (History of Nara Period
 Grammar) ·奈良朝文法史 ······· 8:290a
Narahara Shigeru 奈良原繁 ········ 4:1a
Nara history. See History of Japan
Narai ················ 奈良井 · 5:332b-333a
Nara Kashiwara Archeology Research
 Institute
 Takamatsuzuka tomb ·········· 7:314b-315a
Nara Kokuritsu Bunkazai Kenkyūjo. See
 Nara National Research Institute of
 Cultural Properties
Nara Kokuritsu Hakubutsukan. See Nara
 National Museum
Nara National Museum ···· 5:276b, 333a;
                        7:170a
Nara National Research Institute of
 Cultural Properties ········· 5:333a-333b
Nara Park ························· 5:332a
Nara period ········ 奈良時代 ······ 5:333b
Nara Prefecture ···· 奈良県 · 5:333b-334a
 geography and climate ·············· 5:334a
 history ···························· 5:334a
 industries ························· 5:334a
 tourism and culture ················ 5:334a
Narashino ············ 習志野 ······ 5:334a
Nara Women's University ············ 5:334a
Narayama-bushi kō ················· 6:99a
Naraya Mozaemon
        奈良屋茂左衛門 · 5:334a-334b
Narcotics. See Drug abuse
Narcotics Control Law ···· 2:134a-134b;
                        5:334b
Narihiradake (Semiarundinaria
 fastuosa) ························· 1:136a
Narikane-bon ······ 業兼本 ······ 4:161b
Narikin ················ 成金 ······ 5:334b
Narita ················ 成田 ······ 5:334b
Narita Airport. See New Tōkyō
 International Airport
Narita Shinkansen ·················· 6:279b
Narita Tomomi ··· 成田知巳 ········ 5:334b
 Japan Socialist Party ················ 4:49a
Narōdo ···························· 7:115b
Narrative literature ············ 5:245b-246b
Narrative of the Expedition of an
 American Squadron to the China Seas
 and Japan ················· 6:177b, 185b
Narrow Road through the Provinces
        ························· 6:297b
Narrow Road to The Deep North, The
        ························· 8:185b
Narukami ············ 鳴神 ··· 4:97b, 98b
Narukami Fudō kitayama-zakura
        鳴神不動北山桜 ······ 4:98a
Naruko (town) ········ 鳴子 ······ 5:334b
Naruko ("bird rattles")
        鳴子 ······ 5:334b
Naruse Jinzō ···· 成瀬仁蔵 ········ 5:335a
Naruse Mikio · 成瀬巳喜男 · 2:270a, 271a,
                272a; 5:335a-335b
Narushima Ryūhoku
        成島柳北 ······ 5:335b
Narutaki Gumi · 鳴滝組 ········· 2:270a
Naruto ················ 鳴門 ······ 5:335b
Naruto Strait ···· 鳴門海峡 · 5:335a, 335b
Nashi ···························· 6:170a
Nashiji ···························· 4:240b
Nashimotoshū · 梨本集 ········· 8:34b
Nashiro ················ 名代 ······ 1:147b
Nasu ················ 那須 2:184b; 5:335b
Nasudake ············ 那須岳 ······ 5:335b
Nasu Kōgen ···· 那須高原 · 5:335b-336a
Nasu no Yoichi · 那須与一 · 4:326b; 5:336a
Nasu Volcanic Zone
        那須火山帯 ··· 1:11b;
                5:335b-336a; 8:352a, 368a
Nation, The ························· 4:261a

National Administrative Organization
Law ·················
                               1:13a
National Aerospace Laboratory ··· **5**:336a;
                               7:38a
National Alliance. *See* **Kokumin Dōmei**
National anthem ·················· **5**:336a
National Archives ···· **1**:218b; **5**:336a–336b
Cabinet Library ···················· **1**:229a
National assemblies ················· **3**:275b
National Association of Chairmen of
Town and Village Assemblies ···· **6**:238a
**National Association of Commercial
Broadcasting in Japan** ·········· **5**:366b
National Association of Progressive
Mayors ·························· **1**:107b
National Association of Towns and
Villages ·························· **6**:238a
National Atlas of Japan ········ **5**:336b
National Bank Act ··············· **4**:184b
National Bank Ordinance of 1872 · **1**:138a
national banks ··················· **5**:336b
shizoku ·························· **7**:151b
National Banks ················· **5**:336b
founding ························· **2**:30b
National Capital Region Development
Law (Shutoken Seibi Hō) ······· **8**:67b
National Center for University Entrance
Examinations ··················· **2**:222b
National character ········ **4**:38a–39b
opinion surveys ·················· **4**:40a
National Chemical Laboratory for
Industry ························ **1**:21b
National Civil Service Law (1948) · **4**:351b;
                               6:264b
National Personnel Authority ······ **5**:344b
National Council for Peace and against
Nuclear Weapons ··············· **6**:166b
National Council of State Garden Clubs
································· **2**:292a
National Council of Women's
Organizations
of Agricultural Cooperatives ····· **8**:263b
National defense ········· **5**:336b–338b
evolving attitudes ··············· **5**:337b
Japanese-American relations ····· **5**:338a
policy of major political parties
······························· **5**:337b–338a
public attitudes ················· **5**:338a–338b
Self Defense Forces ·········· **7**:58b–60b
National Defense Academy · **5**:338b; **7**:60a
National Defense College ······ **5**:338b
National Defense Council ·· **1**:218b; **2**:82a;
                       5:338b; **6**:244a; **7**:60a
National Defense Program ·········· **7**:60a
National Defense Women's Association.
See **Dai Nippon Kokubō Fujinkai**
National Diet Library · **2**:95a; **5**:338b–339a;
                       7:50b; **8**:90a
Cabinet Library ···················· **1**:229a
Kanamori Tokujirō ················ **4**:135b
National Education Association ··· **2**:180b
National Enterprise and Public
Corporation Labor Relations
Commission (Kōkyō
Kigyōtai Tō Rōdō Iinkai) ········ **6**:265a
National Environmental Policy
Act ······················ **2**:224a, 225a
"National era" ·················· **1**:232a
periodization ···················· **6**:175a
National Eugenic Law ····· **2**:234b; **6**:224a
National Federation of Industrial Labor
Organizations ·················· **7**:124a
National Federation of Regional
Women's Organization ·········· **1**:273b
National Federation of Research
Institutes for School Curricula ··· **2**:180b
National flag ·················· **5**:339a

National Foundations Society **4**:259b–260a
National health insurance ··· **5**:339a–339b
National Health Resort Hot Spring **7**:351b
National Herbarium (Leyden) ····· **7**:193a
National holidays ················· **2**:262a
National income ········· **5**:339b–341b
complementary structure and economic
growth ························· **5**:340a–340b
flow of funds ···················· **2**:292a
public sector ···················· **5**:340b–341a
size and structure ··············· **5**:339b–340a
transfer payments ··············· **5**:341a–341b
National Income Taxation ···· **7**:355a–358b
National Industrial Exhibition ····· **5**:341b
**National Institute for Research
Advancement** (NIRA) ··········· **3**:127b;
                               5:341b–342a
National Institute of Genetics ··· **4**:204b
National Institute of Japanese
Literature ···················· **4**:256b–257a
Nationalism ··· **5**:342a–343b; **6**:214a; **7**:214a
education ················ **2**:172a, 183b
historiography ··················· **3**:157b
managerial ideology ·········· **5**:91b–92a
patriots and nationalists 1850–1890 **5**:342b
popular ·························· **5**:342b–343a
popular 1890–1945 ·············· **5**:342b–343a
postwar ························· **5**:343a–343b
premodern patriotism ·········· **5**:342a–342b
statist 1890–1945 ··············· **5**:342b
ultranationalism ················· **8**:145a
Nationalist Association ········· **4**:260b–261a
Nationalist Labor Party ·········· **1**:2b
Nationality, legal
loss of ······················· **4**:32b–33a
Nationality Law. *See* **Japanese
nationality**
**National Japanese Language Research
Institute** ······················ **5**:343b
National Laboratory for High Energy
Physics ························ **6**:306a
National Land Agency ····· **1**:219a; **5**:343b
National Learning School (Kokugaku)
································· **1**:75b
National Mobilization Law ········ **1**:229a;
                               5:343b–344a
China War ····················· **3**:201b
Konoe Fumimaro ················ **4**:273b
National Service Draft Ordinance · **5**:347b
National Museum of Ethnology ··· **5**:344a;
                       6:306a; **7**:193a
National Museum of Japanese History
································· **4**:261b
National Museum of Modern Art, Tōkyō
································· **5**:344a–344b
National Museum of Natural History
(Leyden) ······················· **7**:193a
National Museum of Western Art · **5**:344b
National museums ········· **5**:276a–276b
National parks and quasi-national parks
································· **5**:344b
Abashiri ·························· **1**:1b
Akan ···························· **1**:40b
Akiyoshidai ····················· **8**:295a
Ashizuri-Uwakai ················· **1**:102b
Aso ······················ **1**:103a; **6**:76a
Bandai-Asahi ····· **1**:11b, 127b, 136b–137a
Chichibu-Tama ········ **1**:272a; **6**:239a
Chōkai ·························· **8**:293b
Chūbu Sangaku ··········· **1**:5a, 127b
Daisen-Oki ············ **2**:67a–67b; **6**:84b
Daisetsuzan ············· **1**:92b; **2**:67b
Fuji-Hakone-Izu **1**:49b, 107b; **2**:342b–343a;
                               6:125a
Hakusan ············· **3**:88b–89a; **7**:375a

Inland Sea ·········· **1**:124b; **6**:76a, 335a
Iriomote ··············· **3**:331a; **6**:92a
Ise-Shima ·············· **1**:21b; **3**:338a
Jōshin'etsu Kōgen ·········· **1**:95b; **4**:78a
Kirishima-Yaku ·················· **7**:310b
Kita Nagato Coast ··············· **6**:102a
Kongō-Ikoma ···················· **6**:122a
Kurikoma ······················· **8**:293b
Meiji no Mori Minoo ············· **6**:122b
Myōgi-Arafune-Saku Kōgen ····· **7**:105b
Nikkō ···························· **6**:3a
Oga ····························· **6**:68a
Ogasawara ·················· **6**:68b–69a
Okinawa Coast ·················· **5**:308b
Rikuchū Coast ··················· **6**:67b
Rishiri-Rebun-Sarobetsu ········· **6**:320b
Saikai ·························· **6**:369b
San'in Coast ···················· **4**:338a
Shikotsu-Tōya ··················· **7**:347a
Shiretoko ························ **7**:147b
Sobo-Katamuki ·················· **7**:310b
Southern Alps ············· **1**:39b; **7**:236a
Southern Bōsō ··················· **7**:349a
Suigō-Tsukuba ··················· **8**:313b
Tanzawa-Ōyama ················· **7**:346a
Towada-Hachimantai ············· **1**:43a
Unzen-Amakusa ·················· **1**:50a
Yōrō-Sekigahara-Ibi ············· **6**:68a
Yoshino-Kumano ·········· **6**:125a; **7**:115a
Zaō ····························· **8**:293b
National Pearl Research Institute ··· **1**:21b
National Pension Insurance ······· **7**:211b
National Pension Law (Kokumin
Nenkin Hō) ············ **6**:173a; **7**:55b
pensions ························ **4**:353a
National People's School Order ··· **4**:260b
National Personnel Authority ··· **1**:218b;
                       4:351b; **5**:344b; **6**:264b
impeachment ···················· **3**:275b
Occupation ······················ **6**:53b
public employees ················· **6**:264b
recommendations ········· **5**:344b–345a
Satō Tatsuo ····················· **7**:29a
shuntō ·························· **4**:352a
National Personnel Law (Kokka Kōmuin
Hō) of 1948 ···················· **4**:358a
National Police Agency ····· **6**:198a–198b
National Police Reserve ·· **5**:345b; **6**:198b;
                       7:58b–59a; **8**:344b
defense industry ················· **2**:82b
national defense ················· **5**:336b–338b
National Safety Forces ············ **5**:346a
Occupation ······················ **6**:54b
United States-Japan security treaties
································· **8**:166a
United States military bases, disputes
································· **8**:168a
"National polity." *See* **Kokutai**
National Public Safety Commission
································· **1**:219a; **5**:345b–346a
Tōkyō Metropolitan Police Department
································· **8**:67b
National Railway Workers' Union · **7**:107a
National Research Institute of Police
Science ························ **2**:47a
National Research Laboratory of
Metrology ······················ **1**:21b
National Rural Police (Kokka Chihō
Keisatsu) ······················· **6**:198b
National Safety Forces ····· **5**:346a; **7**:59a;
                               8:344b
national defense ················· **5**:336b–338b
National Police Reserve ··········· **5**:345b
United States military bases, disputes
································· **8**:168a
National Salvation Association ··· **5**:346a;
                       7:78b; **8**:380a
December Ninth Movement ······ **2**:81b

National Science Museum · · · · · · · ·**5:**346a
National Seclusion · · **1:**161b; **5:**346a-347b;
 7:8a, 256b, 263a, 266b
 abandonment · · · · · · · · · · · · · · · · **3:**192a
 Austro-Hungarian relations · · · · · · · **1:**119b
 China · **1:**284b
 Chōsen tsūshinshi · · · · · · · · · · · · · · **1:**304a
 criticism · · · · · · · · · · · · · · · · **1:**39a, 141b
 Daikokuya Kōdayū · · · · · · · · · · · · · **2:**60b
 Dutch Factory · · · · · · · · · · · · · · · · **2:**135b
 eating habits · · · · · · · · · · · · · · · · · **2:**305a
 Edo period · · · · · · · · · · · · · · · · · · · **3:**185b
 foreign trade policy · · · · · · · · · · · · **2:**324b
 Gaikokusen Uchiharai Rei · · · · · · · · · **3:**3b
 Indonesia and Japan · · · · · · · · · · · · **3:**290b
 Kaempfer, Engelbert · · · · · · · · · · · · **4:**102a
 Kaigai Tokō Kinshi Rei · · · · · · · · · · **4:**109b
 Kakure Kirishitan · · · · · · · · · · · · · · **4:**119a
 Kanagawa Treaty · · · · · · · · · · · · · · **4:**135b
 Kawai Tsugunosuke · · · · · · · · · · · · · **4:**179b
 Kawaji Toshiakira · · · · · · · · · · · · · · **4:**179b
 missionary work · · · · · · · · · · · · · · · **2:**330b
 Morrison Incident · · · · · · · · · · · · · · **5:**256a
 Nagasaki trade · · · · · · · · · · · · · · · · **5:**306a
 naichi zakkyo · · · · · · · · · · · · **5:**309b-310a
 Nakahama Manjirō · · · · · · · · · **5:**313a-313b
 Opening of Japan · · · · · · · · · · · · · · **6:**114b
 Perry, Matthew Calbraith · · · · · · · · · **6:**177b
 Phaeton Incident · · · · · · · · · · · · · · **6:**182a
 plants · **6:**191a
 port towns · · · · · · · · · · · · · · · · · · · **6:**228b
 Russia · **6:**340b
 Sakuma Shōzan's violation · · · · · · · · · **7:**3b
 Shinkiron · · · · · · · · · · · · · · · · · · · **7:**119a
 Shinron · **7:**124a
 Shinsui Kyōyo Rei · · · · · · · · · · · · · · **7:**125b
 Spanish relations · · · · · · · · · · · · · · **4:**369b
 technological development · · · · · · · · **7:**368b
 temples · **8:**1b
 Thailand and Japan · · · · · · · · · · · · · **8:**20b
 Tokugawa Iemitsu · · · · · · · · · · · · · · **8:**48a
 Tokugawa shogunate · · · · · · · · · · · · **8:**56a
 trade regulations · · · · · · · · · · · · · · **7:**171a
 transportation · · · · · · · · · · · · · · · · · **8:**98a
 United Kingdom · · · · · · · · · · · · · · · **8:**150b
 United States · · · · · · · · · · · · · · · · · **8:**154b
 Vietnam · **8:**191b
 warriors · **1:**222b
 Watanabe Kazan · · · · · · · · · · · · · · · **8:**235b
 Western learning · · · · · · · · · · · · · · · **8:**241b
 whaling · **8:**249b
National Service Draft Ordinance **5:**347b;
 8:277b
 Koreans in Japan · · · · · · · · · · · · · · **4:**291a
National Socialist Party · · · · · · · · · · **8:**296a
**National Space Development Agency of
 Japan** · · **1:**172b; **5:**347b; **7:**38a, 240a
**National Spiritual Mobilization
 Movement** · · · · · · · · · · · **5:**348a; **8:**277a
National Sports Festival · · **5:**348a; **7:**243a
National Sports Stadium · · · · · · · · · **7:**116a
National Tax Administration Agency
 · **5:**188a
 tax office · **7:**358b
National Tax Agency · · · · · · · · **7:**355a-358b
National Tax Tribunal · · · · · · · **5:**348a-348b
National Trade Union of Metal and
 Engineering Workers · · · · · · · · · · · · **1:**72a
National Union of Agricultural
 Cooperative Women's Guild · · · · · **8:**267a
National University of Singapore · · **7:**196b
National Vacation Village · · · · · · · · · **7:**303b
National Veterans' Association
 (Gōyūren) · · · · · · · · · · · · · · · · · · **6:**238b
National wealth · · · · · · · · · · · **5:**349a-349b
Natori · · · · · · · · · · · 名取 · · · · · · · **5:**349a
Natorigawa · · · · · · · · 名取川 · · · · · · **4:**328a
Natsuigawa · · · · · · · 夏井川 · · · · · **5:**349b

Natsukodachi · · · · · 夏木立 · · · · · · · **8:**288b
Natsume Sōseki · 夏目漱石 · · · · **1:**5a, 74a,
 155b; **2:**274a, 291b; **5:**12b, 314a, 349b-350a,
 350b, 351a; **7:**103b, 125b
 biography · · · · · · · · · · · · · · · · **5:**349b-350a
 fūryū concept · · · · · · · · · · · · · · · · · **2:**374b
 Komiya Toyotaka's teacher · · · · · · · **4:**267a
 works · · · · · · · · · · · · · · · · · · **5:**350a-351a
Natsu no heitai (Summer
 Soldiers) · · · · · · · · · 夏の兵隊 · · · · · **8:**15a
Natsu no yami · · · · · 夏の闇 · · · · · · **4:**111b
Nattō · · · · · · · · · · · · · · · · · **2:**306a; **5:**351a
Natural disasters · · · · · · · · · · · · · · **5:**351a
Natural features. *See* **Japan**
Natural gas · · · · · · **2:**216a; **3:**344b; **5:**353a
Naturalism · · · · · · · · · · · · · · · **5:**351a-351b
 Iwano Hōmei · · · · · · · · · · · · · · · · · **3:**361b
 literary criticism · · · · · · · · · · · · · · · **5:**12a
 literary expression · · · · · · · · · · · · · · **2:**378b
 modern · · · · · · · · · · · · · · · · · · **5:**54a-54b
 Shimazaki Tōson · · · · · · · · · · · · · · · **7:**101a
 Tayama Katai · · · · · · · · · · · · **7:**358b-359a
 Tokuda Shūsei · · · · · · · · · · · · · · · · **8:**44b
 Uno Kōji · **8:**173b
Naturalist literary movement
 Iida Dakotsu · · · · · · · · · · · · · · · · · **3:**262b
 I-novel · **3:**312a
Naturalization · · · · · · · · **4:**32b-33a; **5:**351a
 grand · **4:**33a
 of Koreans in Japan · · · · · · · · · · · · **4:**291b
 ordinary · · · · · · · · · · · · · · · · **4:**32b-33a
 special · **4:**33a
**Natural monuments and protected
 species** · · · · · · · · · · · · · · · **5:**352a-352a
 animals · **5:**352a
 plants · · · · · · · · · · · · · · · · · · **5:**352a-352a
 protected areas · · · · · · · · · · · · · · · · **5:**352a
Natural resources · · · · · · · · · · **5:**352b-355a
 coal · **5:**352b-353a
 economic efficiency · · · · · · · · · · · · · **2:**146a
 hydroelectric power · · · · · · · · **5:**353a-353b
 metals and minerals · · · · · · · · **5:**353b-354a
 natural gas · · · · · · · · · · · · · · · · · · **5:**353a
 nuclear power and alternative sources
 · **5:**353b
 petroleum · · · · · · · · · · · · · · · · · · · **5:**353a
 prospects · · · · · · · · · · · · · · · · **5:**354b-355a
 wood and pulp · · · · · · · · · · · · **5:**354a-354b
Natural sciences · · · · · · · · · · · **5:**355a-357a
 Chinese influences · · · · · · · · · · · · · **5:**355a
 early Edo period · · · · · · · · · · · **5:**355a-355b
 after Meiji period · · · · · · · · · · **5:**356b-357a
 modern science and Western
 Learning · · · · · · · · · · · · · · · **5:**355b-356b
 postwar era · · · · · · · · · · · · · · · · · · **5:**357a
 western (Namban) culture · · · · · · · · **5:**355a
Nature, concept of · · · · · · · · · **5:**357a-357b
 religious symbolism · · · · · · · · · · · · **6:**295b
Nature Conservation Law · · · · · · · · · **2:**228a
Nature in Japanese religion **5:**357b-358a
Nature Protection District · · · · · · **5:**352a-352b
Nature religion · · · · · · · · · · · · · · · · **6:**291a
Naumann, Edmund · · · · · · · · · **5:**358a-358b
 geology · **2:**141a
Naval Academy · · · · · · · · · · · · **5:**358a-358b
 National Defense Academy · · · · · · · · **5:**338b
Naval bases · · · · · · · · · · · · · · · · · · **1:**296a
Naval General Staff Office · · · · · · · · **5:**358b
 independence · · · · · · · · · · · · · · · · · · **1:**87a
 power · **8:**85a
Naval Institute. *See* **Kaigun Denshūjo**
Navy, Imperial Japanese · · · · · · · · · · **3:**278a
 militarism · · · · · · · · · · · · · · **5:**173b-174b
 shipbuilding industry · · · · · · · · **7:**141b-142a
 World War II · · · · · · · · · · · · · · · · · **8:**271b
Navy Day · **6:**347a
Navy Ministry · · · · · · · · · · · · · · · · **5:**358b
Nawabari · **5:**358b

Nawa Nagatoshi · 名和長年 · · · · · · · · **5:**358b
Naya Sukezaemon
 · · · · · · · · · · · · 納屋助左衛門 · · · · · · · **6:**340b
Nayoro · · · · · · · · · · 名寄 · · · · · · · · · **5:**358b
Nayosechō · · · · · · · · 名寄帳 · · · · · · · **5:**359a
Nayotake · · · · · · · · · · なよたけ · · · · · · **4:**169a
Naze · · · · · · · · · · 名瀬 **4:**106a; **5:**359a
Nazo nazo · · · · · · · · · · · · · · · · · · · **6:**311b
NCR Japan, Ltd (Nippon NCR) · · · · **5:**359a
NDL (National Diet Library) · · **5:**338b-339a
Nebuta Festival ねぶた祭 · **1:**69b, 160b;
 2:*255a;* **5:**359a
Neesima, Joseph Hardy. *See* **Niijima Jō**
Negi. *See* **Welsh onion**
Negishi Tanka Kai
 (Negishi Tanka Society)
 · · · · · · · · · · · · 根岸短歌会 · **5:**19b; **8:**216b
Negoro-nuri · · · · · · · 根来塗 · · · · · **2:**295a;
 5:359a-359b
Nehru, Jawaharlal · · · · · · · · · · · · · · **3:**289a
Neighborhood associations · · · **1:**300a;
 5:359b; **8:**277b
 Imperial Rule Assistance Association
 · **3:**281a
Neighborhood groups · · · · · · · · · · · **5:**359b
Nekki · **5:**359b
Nekkoku no maki (The Tropics) · · · **6:***158b*
Neko · **1:**251a
*Neko to Shōzō to futari no
 onna* (A Cat, Shōzō, and
 Two Women)
 · 猫と庄造と二人のをんな · · · · · · **8:**319b
Nema · **7:**248b
Nembutsu · · · · · · · 念仏 · **1:**194b; **4:**67a;
 5:359b; **6:**270a; **7:**63a; 347a
 Ippen · · · · · · · · · · · · · · **3:**328b-329b; **4:**62a
 kakun · **4:**118b
 religious symbolism · · · · · · · · · · · · **6:**295b
 Shinran · **7:**123a
 Yūzū Nembutsu sect · · · · · · · · · · · · **8:**359b
Nembutsu odori · 念仏踊 · **2:**374a; **4:**62a;
 5:360a; **7:**149a
Nemure Pari · · · · · 眠れパリ · · · · · · **4:**139a
Nemureru bijo · 眠れる美女 · · · · · · **4:**176b
Nemuro · · · · · · · · · · 根室 · · · · · · · · · **5:**360a
Nemuro harbor · · · · · · · · · · · · · · · · **5:***360b*
Nemuro Peninsula
 · · · · · · · · · · · · 根室半島 · · · · · · · · · **5:**360a
Nemuro Strait · · · 根室海峡 · · · · · · · **5:**360a
Nenashigusa · · · · · 根なし草 · · · · · · · **4:**256a
Nenchū gyōji · · · · · 年中行事 · **2:**252b-253a,
 258a-262a, 299a
 Heian period · · · · · · · · · · · · · **2:**259b-261b
 post-Heian period · · · · · · · · · · **2:**260b-262a
 pre-Heian antecedents · · · · · · **2:**258b-259b
 sources · · · · · · · · · · · · · · · · · **2:**258a-258b
 See also **Festivals**
Nenchū gyōji emaki
 · · · · · · · · · · · · 年中行事絵巻 · · · · · · · **7:**42b
 shinden-zukuri · · · · · · · · · · · · · · · · **7:**110b
 Sumiyoshi school · · · · · · · · · · · · · · **7:**270a
Nengajō · **5:**372b
Nengō · · · · · · · · · · 年号 · · **1:**231b-232a;
 5:360a
Nengu · · · · · · · · · · · 年貢 · · · **5:**360a-361b
 kokudainō · · · · · · · · · · · · · · · · · · · **4:**257a
 tansen and tammai · · · · · · · · · · · · · **7:**344b
Nenjū gyōji emaki. 年中行事絵巻 *See*
 Nenchū gyōji emaki
Nenki · · · · · · · · · · · 年紀 · · · · · · · · · **5:**361b
Nenkō joretsu · · · · · · · · · · · · · · · · · **7:**189a
Nenkō system. *See* **Seniority system**
Nenkō wages and benefits · · · · · · · · **4:**344b
''Nennen saisai'' · 年年歳歳 · · · · · · · · **1:**21a
Neo-Confucianism. *See* **Confucianism;**
 Shushigaku; Yōmeigaku
Neo-Kantian school · · · · · · · · · · **7:**335a-335b
Neolithic period · · · · · · · · · · · · · · · **5:**361b

Neo-Thomism · · · · · · · · · · · · · · · 4:85b
Nerima Ward · · · · · · 練馬区 · · · 5:361b
Nerimiso (miso paste) · · · · · · · · · 2:25b
Netherlands and Japan · · · · · 5:361b-363a
  influence on medicine · · · · · · · 5:146b-147a
  Japanese studies · · · · · · · · · · · · 4:43a-43b
  modern period · · · · · · · · · · · · 5:362b-363a
  premodern period · · · · · · · · · · · · 5:362a
Netherlands Trading Company · · · 5:362b;
                      7:193a
Netsuke · · · · · · · · 3:313a; 5:363a, 363b-365a
  inrō · 3:313b
Neuer Tanz (new dance) · · · · · · · · · 2:76a
Nevskii, Nikolai Aleksandrovich · · · 5:365a
New Asian order · · · · · · · · · · · · · · 8:159a
New Collection of Ancient and
  Modern Times · · · · · · · · · · · 7:119b-121a
New Drama · · · · · · · · · · · · · · · · · · 7:112a
New Education Movement · · · 7:367a-367b
New Fourth Army Incident · · · · · · · 7:48a
New industrial cities · · · · · · · · · · 5:365a
New Japan Philharmonic Orchestra
                      6:140b
New Left Movement · · · · · 6:284b; 7:252a
New Liberal Club · · · · · · 5:365a; 6:213a
  Kōno Yōhei, founder and chairman 4:275a
"New Order in East Asia." See **Tōa
Shinchitsujo**
New Order in Europe and Greater East
  Asia · 8:107b
New Order Movement 5:365a-366a; 8:277b
  Asō Hisashi · · · · · · · · · · · · · · · · 1:103a
  Imperial Rule Assistance Association
                      3:280a
  Konoe Fumimaro · · · · · · · · · · · · 4:273a
  National Mobilization Law · · · 5:343b-344a
New People's Society · · · · · · · · · · 8:281b
New Photography Movement · · · · · 6:186a
New religions · 2:300a; 5:366a-368b; 6:292a
  early development · · · · · · · · · 5:367a-367b
  lay Buddhist movement · · · · · · · · 4:372a
  priesthood · · · · · · · · · · · · · · · · · 6:238b
  Shintō · 7:129b
  significance · · · · · · · · · · · · · · · · 5:368b
  social and religious background
                  5:366b-367a
  twentieth century · · · · · · · · · 5:367b-368b
  Union of New Religious Organizations of
    Japan · · · · · · · · · · · · · · · · · · · 8:150a
  women in · · · · · · · · · · · · · · · · · · 8:257b
News agencies · · · · · · · · · · · · 5:368b-369a
  mass communications · · · · · · · · · 5:128b
Newspaper Law · · · · · · · · · · · · · · 2:339a
Newspapers · · · · · · · · · · · · · · 5:369a-370a
  advertising · · · · · · · · · · · · · · · · · · 1:16b
  censorship · · · · · · · 1:252a-252b, 253b
  history · · · · · · · · · · · · · · · · · 5:369a-369b
  journalists · · · · · · · · · · · · · · · · · 5:370a
  local · · · · · · · · · · · · · · · · · 5:370a-370b
  mass communications · · · · · · 5:128a-128b
  mass media · · · · · · · · · · · · · 5:369b-370a
  Meiji period (1868-1912) · · · · · · · · 4:46a
  monopoly dealerships · · · · · · · · · 5:370a
  nationwide · · · · · · · · · · · · · · · · 5:370b
  publishing · · · · · · · · · · · · · · · · · 6:267b
  sociocultural contributions · · · · · · · 5:129a
News services · · · · · · · · · · · · · · · · 3:318b
New Theater movement · · · · · · · · · 8:300a
New Tōkyō International Airport · · · 1:37b;
                5:370b, 371a-371b
Newtonianism · · · · · · · · · · · · · · · · 5:356a
New Trunk Line. See **Shinkansen**
Newt. See **Imori**
New Tsukiji Theater Company (Shin
  Tsukiji Gekidan) · · · · · · · · · · · · · 8:299b

New Woman's Association. See **Shin
Fujin Kyōkai**
New Year · · · 1:160b; 2:258a-260a, 262a;
                 5:371b-372a
  cooking · 2:22a
  enkai (banquet) · · · · · · · · · · · · · · 2:218a
  folk religion · · · · · · · · · · · · · · · · 2:299a
  games · 2:367a
  joya no kane · · · · · · · · · · · · · · · · 5:371a
  kadomatsu · · · · · · · · · · · · · · · · · 5:371a
  New Year's Day · · · · · · · · · · · · · · 5:371b
  New Year's Eve · · · · · · · · · · · · · · 5:371b
  Ōshōgatsu and Koshōgatsu · · · · · 5:372a
  religion · · · · · · · · · · · · · · · · · · · 6:291b
  rice growing rites · · · · · · · · · · · · · 1:23a
New Year's cards · · · · · · · · · · · · · 5:372b
New Year's Scene at Nihombashi · · 8:78b
New York City Ballet · · · · · · · · · · · 2:76a
New York Herald Tribune · · · · · · · · 3:151a
New Zealand and Japan · · · · · 5:372b-373a
  Japanese studies · · · · · · · · · · · · · 4:44b
Neyagawa · · · · · · · · 寝屋川 · · · 5:373a
Nezame monogatari
  emaki · · · · · · 寝覚物語絵巻 · · 5:373a-373b
Nezamenotoko · 寝覚ノ床 · · · 5:373b
Nezu Art Museum · · · · · · 5:276b, 373b
Nezu Bijutsukan · · · · · · · · · · · · · · 5:373b
Nezu Kaichirō ·根津嘉一郎 · · · 5:373b-374a
Nezumi · 6:284a
Nezumimochi [(Japanese privet)
  Ligustrum japonicum] · · · · · · · · · 5:374a
Nezu no seki · · · · · 念珠関 · · · 7:146b
NGK Insulators, Ltd · · · · · · · · · · 5:374a
NHK (Japan Broadcasting Corporation)
  1:4b, 93a, 171b-173b; 5:374a-374b; 6:275a
  folk song collection · · · · · · · · · · · 2:301a
  international communications · · · · · 3:318a
  wire-relayed broadcasting · · · · · · · 8:254b
NHK Spring Co, Ltd · · · · · · · · · · 5:374b
Nichibei Gakusei Kaigi · · · · · · · 4:10a-10b
Nichibei Gyōsei Kyōtei · · · · · · · 8:165a-165b
Nichibei Kyōiku Iinkai · · · · · · · · 4:50a-50b
Nichibei Shinshi Kyōyaku
        日米紳士協約 · · · 3:24a-24b
Nichibei Shūkō Tsūshō Jōyaku. See
  Harris Treaty
Nichibei Sōgo Bōei Enjo Kyōtei · · 8:165a
Nichibei Washin Jōyaku. 日米和親条約
  See **Kanagawa Treaty**
Nichidokui Sangoku
  Dōmei · 日独伊三国同盟 · · · 8:107a-107b
Nichiei Dōmei. 日英同盟 See
  Anglo-Japanese Alliance
Nichietsu Bōeki Kai (Japan-Vietnam
  Trade) · · · · · · · · · · · · · · · · · · · 8:192a
Nichiei Tsūshō Kōkai Jōyaku.
  日英通商航海条約 See **Anglo-Japanese
Commercial Treaty of 1894**
Nichifutsu Kyōyaku
        日仏協約 · · · 2:333b
Nichifutsu tsūshin
        日仏通信 · · · 7:310b
Nichii Co, Ltd · · · · · · · · · · · · · · 5:374a
Nichimen Co Ltd · · · · · · · · · · · · 5:374b
Nichinan · · · · · · · · 日南 · · · 5:375a
Nichinan Coast, Quasi-National Park
     日南海岸国定公園 · · · 1:70b
Nichinichi shimbun
     日日新聞 · · · 4:100a
Nichiō · · · · · · · · · 日奥 · · · 5:375a
  Fuju Fuse sect · · · · · · · · · · · · · · 2:359b
Nichiren · · · · · · · · 日蓮 · · 5:375a-376b
  daimoku · · · · · · · · · · · · · · · · · · 5:327b
  Fuju Fuse sect · · · · · · · · · · · · · · 2:359b
  Hōnen · 4:67b
  Lotus Sutra · · · · · · · · · · · · · · · · · 5:74a
  portrait · · · · · · · · · · · · · · · · · · · 5:375a
  Risshō ankoku ron · · · · · · · · · · · · 6:321a

Tainoura · · · · · · · · · · · · · · · · · · · 7:298b
Nichiren sect · · · · · 日蓮宗 · · 1:178b-179a;
                5:376b-377b
  Azuchi Disputation · · · · · · · 1:126b-127a
  basic doctrines and controversies
                5:376b-377a
  climax and decline · · · · · · · · 5:377a-377b
  Fuju Fuse branch · · · · · · · · · · · · 2:359b
  mandalas · · · · · · · · · · · · · 5:100b, 376a
  modern period (1868-   );
    "Nichirenism" · · · · · · · · · · · · · · 5:377b
  Nichiren · · · · · · · · · · · · · · · 5:375a-376b
  Namu Myōhō renge kyō · · · · · · · · 5:327b
  Nichiō · 5:375a
  Temmon Hokke Rebellion · · · · · · 7:381b
  Nichiren Shōshū · · · · · · · · · · · · · 7:303b
  Nichirenshū Fujiha · · · · · · · · · · · 7:303b
Nichiren: the Buddhist Prophet · · · · 1:56b
Nichirin (The Sun) · · · 日輪 · · · 8:332a
Nichiro Gyogyō Kaisha, Ltd · · · · 2:284a;
                   5:378a
  Hiratsuka Tsunejirō · · · · · · · · · · · 3:146a
Nichiro kyōyaku. See **Russo-Japanese
agreements of 1907-1916**
Nichiro Sensō. 日露戦争   See
  Russo-Japanese War
Nichirōto. 日労党   See **Nihon Rōnōtō**
Nichiyō gorakuban
     日曜娯楽版 · · · 6:275b
Nicknames · · · · · · · · · · · · · · · 5:325a-326a
Nifon no cotoba to historia uo narai
  xiran to fossvrv fito no tameni xeva
  ni yava ragvetarv Feige no monogatari
                     2:241a
Night Drum · · · · · · · · · · · · · · · · · 8:339b
Night schools · · · · · · · · · · · · · · · 5:378a
"Nights of Fitful Waking" · · · · 8:339a-339b
Night View of Kanazawa in Musashi
  Province · · · · · · · · · 8:143b-144a, 144b
Nigite. See **Gohei**
Nihommachi · · · · · · 日本町 · · 5:378a-378b
Nihommatsu · · · · · · 二本松 · · · 5:378b
Nihon · · · · · · · · · · · 日本 · · · 5:378b
Nihon Aeroplane Manufacturing Co,
  Ltd · 8:353b
Nihon Apatchi zoku
     日本アパッチ族 · · · 4:266a
Nihon Arupusu · · · · · · · · · · · · · · · 4:12b
Nihon Baputesuto Dōmei · · · · · · · 1:142a
Nihon Baputesuto Remmei · · · · · · 1:142a
Nihon Beikoku Kabushiki
  Kaisha (Japan Rice
  Company, Ltd)
     日本米穀株式会社 · · · · · · 2:127a
Nihon-Betonamu Yūkō Kyōkai
  (Japan-Vietnam Friendship
  Association) · · · · · · · · · · · · · · · 8:192a
Nihon Bijutsuin.日本美術院   See **Japan
Fine Arts Academy**
Nihon bukkyō shi:
  Jōseihen (History of
  Buddhism in Japan,
  Ancient Period)
     日本仏教史:上世編 · · · · 2:105a
Nihon bukkyō shi no
  kenkyū (Studies on the
  History of Buddhism in
  Japan) 日本仏教史の研究 · · · · · 8:114a
Nihon bumpōgaku gairon
  (Outline of Japanese
  Grammar)
     日本文法学概論 · · · · 8:290a
Nihon bumpōron
  (Japanese Grammar)
     日本文法論 · · · 8:290a
Nihon bumpō yōron
  (Essentials of Japanese
  Grammar) ·日本文法要論 · · · · 8:290a

Nihon Bungaku Hōkokukai · · · · · · 5:379a
Nihon Bunka Kenkyūjo
　　　　日本文化研究所 · · · · · 1:2b
Nihon buppō chūkō gammon
　　　日本仏法中興願文 · · · · · · 2:187a
Nihon Cement Co., Ltd. · · · 1:96a; 5:379a
Nihon chimbotsu 日本沈没 · · · · 4:266a
Nihon Chiri Gakkai · · · · · · · · · 1:103b
Nihon chishi · · · · 日本地誌 · · · 6:288a
Nihon Chōkoku Kai · · · · · · · · · 3:143a
Nihon dai bunten
　　　　　日本大文典 · · · · · · 6:59b
Nihon daijisho 日本大辞書 · · · · 5:379a
Nihondaira 　　日本平 5:379a; 7:104a
Nihon Dempō Tsūshinsha (Dentsū) 1:16b
Nihon eitaigura 日本永代蔵 · · · · 8:144a
Nihonga · · · · · · · · · · · 5:379a-380a
　Japan Fine Arts Academy · · · · 4:45b
Nihon gaikō shi
　　　　日本外交史 · · · 4:232b
Nihon Gakujutsu Kaigi. **See Science
　Council of Japan**
Nihon Gakujutsu Shinkōkai. **See Japan
　Society for the Promotion of Science**
Nihon Gakushiin. **See Japan Academy**
Nihon Geijutsuin. **See Japan Art
　Academy**
Nihon Genshiryoku Kenkyūjo · · · · 1:114b
Nihongi. 日本紀　**See Nihon shoki**
Nihon Ginkō. **See Bank of Japan**
Nihon Harisuto Seikyōkai
　· · · · 日本ハリスト聖教会 · · · 3:216b
Nihon Heimintō (Japan
　Commoners' Party)
　　　日本平民党 · · · · · · 6:210b
Nihon Heiwa Gakkai (Peace Studies
　Association of Japan) · · · · · · · 6:145b
Nihon Heiwa Kenkyū Kondan Kai (Japan
　Peace Research Group) · · · · · 6:145b
Nihon hyōron (Japan
　Review) · · · 日本評論 5:380a; 8:127b
Nihon infureishon no kenkyū (Study of
　Japanese Inflation) · · · · · · · 6:135b
Nihon Ishikai · · · · · · · · · · 4:47a-47b
Nihon Jidō Bungakusha Kyōkai · · · · 5:19a
Nihon Jidō Bungeika Kyōkai · · · · · 5:19a
Nihonjin · · · · · 日本人 · 5:11b, 380b;
　　　　　　　　　7:51b, 258b
Nihonjin no hōishiki
　· · · · 日本人の法意識 · · · 4:184b
*Nihonjin no seishin shi
　kenkyū*
　· · · · 日本人の精神史研究 · · · · · · 4:125b
Nihonjin reika · 日本人霊歌 · · · 8:114a
Nihon Jiyūtō · 日本自由党 4:274a; 6:211b
　Ashida Hitoshi · · · · · · · · · 1:97b
Nihon Joshi Daigaku
　· · · · · · · · · · · · · · · · · 4:50b
Nihonkai · · · · · · · · · 日本海 · · · 7:46a
Nihon Kaigai Kyōkai Rengōkai · · · 2:201a
Nihonkai Kaisen
　　　　日本海海戦 · · · · · · 8:118a
Nihon kaika shōshi
　　　　日本開化小史 · · · · · 7:294b
Nihon kaizō hōan taikō
　　　日本改造法案大綱 4:225b; 8:359a
Nihon Kajin Kyōkai
　· · · · · · · · · · · · · · · · · 5:19b
Nihon Kakushintō (Japan
　Reform Party) 日本革新党 · 1:40a; 4:261a
Nihon keizai shimbun
　　　　日本経済新聞 · · · · · 5:380b
　Television Tōkyō Channel 12, Ltd · 7:380b
Nihon keizai shinshi
　　　　日本経済新誌 · · · · · 4:180b
Nihon Kiin 日本棋院 · · · · · · 5:380b
Nihon Kindai Bungakukan
　· · · · · 日本近代文学館 · · · 5:275b

Nihon Kirisuto Kyōdan · · · · · · · · 8:150a
Nihon Kirisutokyō Fujin
　Kyōfūkai
　　　日本基督教婦人矯風会 · · · 4:324b
Nihon Kirisutokyō Rengōkai · · · 1:305a
Nihon kirui. 日本紀類　**See Nihon kiryaku**
Nihon kiryaku 　日本紀略 · · · 5:381a
Nihon Kōfuku Bunsho · · · 7:278a-278b
Nihon kōki 　日本後紀 · · · · 6:315b
Nihon Kokka Shakaitō
　　　　日本国家社会党 · · · 1:40a
Nihon Kōkokunushi Kyōdan · · · · 4:9b
Nihon Kōkoku Shinsa Kikō · · · · 4:9b-10a
Nihon Koku 　　　日本国 · · · 4:7a
*Nihonkoku genzaisho
　mokuroku*
　　　日本国見在書目録 · · · 1:154a
Nihon kokugo daijiten
　　　日本国語大辞典 · · · 2:93b
Nihonkoku kokken an
　　　　日本国国憲按 · · · 8:127b
Nihon kokusei chizu 日本国勢地図 · 5:336b
*Nihon koten bungaku
　taikei* (Compendium of
　Japanese Classical
　Literature)
　　　日本古典文学大系 · · 2:104b
Nihon Kyōdōtō (Japan
　Cooperative Party)
　　　　日本協同党 · · · 6:211b
Nihon kyōiku shōshi
　　　　日本教育小史 · · 4:109b
Nihon Kyōsantō. 日本共産党 **See Japan
　Communist Party**
Nihon Kyōshokuin Kumiai
　Rengō
　　　日本教職員組合連合 · · · 7:366b
Nihon Kyōshokuin
　Remmei · 日本教職員連盟 · · 7:366b
Nihon meizan zue
　　　　日本名山図絵 · · · 7:341a
Nihon Mingeikan · · · · · · · · · 4:46a
Nihon Mingei Kyōkai · · · · · · · · 4:179a
Nihon Minkan Hōsō Remmei · · · 5:336b
Nihon Minshutō (Japan
　Democratic Party)
　　　　日本民主党 · · · 5:381a
　Hatoyama Ichirō · · · · · · · · 3:113a
　Rikken Minseitō · · · · · · · · 6:315a
　Tanaka Kakuei · · · · · · · · · 7:337a
Nihon Montoku Tennō jitsuroku.
　日本文徳天皇実録　**See Rikkokushi**
Nihon Musantō (Japan
　Proletarian Party)
　　　日本無産党 5:381a; 6:211b
Nihon no autosaidā
　· · · 日本のアウトサイダー · · · 4:181b
*Nihon no fujin: Fujin undō no hatten o
　megutte* · · · · · · · · · · · 7:349b
*Nihon nōgyō no tenkai
　katei* (The Development
　of Japanese Agriculture)
　· · · · · 日本農業の展開過程 · · · 8:36b
*Nihon nōgyō seisanryoku
　kōzō* 日本農業生産力構造 · · · 8:289a
Nihon no kasō shakai
　(Japan's Lower Classes)
　　　日本の下層社会 7:164a; 8:264a,
　　　　　　　　　　334b
Nihon no kōkogaku
　　　　日本の考古学 · · · 1:76a
Nihon no kuroi kiri
　　　　日本の黒い霧 · · · 4:315a
Nihon Nōmin Kumiai
　　　　日本農民組合 · · · 1:84a
Nihon no rōdō mondai
　　　　日本の労働問題 · · · 7:281a
Nihon Nōsan Kōgyō · · · · · 5:381a

Nihon nōson fujin mondai
　(The Problems of Rural
　Women in Japan)
　　　　日本農村婦人問題 · · · 8:266b
Nihon oyobi nihonjin
　(Japan and the
　Japanese) · 日本及日本人 · · · 5:316a
*Nihon oyobi nihonjin no
　michi* 日本及び日本人の道 · · · 6:82a
Nihon Pen Kurabu · · · · · · · · 4:47b-48a
Nihon Radiator Co, Ltd · · · · · 5:381b
Nihon reiiki. **See Nihon ryōiki**
Nihon Rekishi Chiri Gakkai · · · · 3:156b
Nihon rekishi dai jitten
　　　日本歴史大辞典 · · · 8:240a
Nihon rettō kaizō ron
　　　日本列島改造論 · · · 5:381b
Nihon Rōdō Kumiai
　Zenkoku Hyōgikai
　(All-Japan Council of
　Labor Unions)
　· 日本労働組合全国評議会 · · · 6:222a
Nihon Rōmanha
　　　日本浪曼派 · · 5:19a, 381b;
　　　　　　　　　　7:176a
　Kamei Katsuichirō · · · · · · · · 4:125a
Nihon Rōnōtō (Japan
　Labor-Farmer Party)
　　　　日本労農党 · · · 5:382a
　Asō Hisashi · · · · · · · · · · 1:102b
Nihon ryōiki · 日本霊異記 · 1:180b; 5:26a,
　　　　　　　29b, 382a; 7:67a, 72a
　folktales · · · · · · · · · · · · 2:304a
　Shintō · · · · · · · · · · · · · 7:126b
Nihon sammon opera
　　　日本三文オペラ · · · 4:111b
Nihon sandai jitsuroku.
　日本三代実録　**See Rikkokushi**
Nihon Sankei · 日本三景 · · · 5:382a
Nihon seiji shisōshi kenkyū
　· 日本政治思想史研究 4:259a; 5:121b
Nihon seiki 日本政記 · · · 6:281a
Nihon Seikōkai 日本聖公会 · · · 7:51b
Nihon Seinen Kaigai Kyōryoku Tai · 4:47b
Nihon seishin (The Spirit
　of Japan) · · · · 日本精神 · · · 4:204b
Nihon Sekijūjisha · · · · · · · · · 4:40b
*Nihon shakai no
　kazokuteki kōsei*
　· 日本社会の家族的構成 · · · 4:184b
**Nihon Shakai Shugi
　Dōmei** (Japan Socialist
　League)
　· · · · · · 日本社会主義同盟 · · 5:382a-382b;
　　　　　　　　　　6:210b
　Sekirankai auxiliary · · · · · · · 7:57a
Nihon Shakaitō. 日本社会党 **See Japan
　Socialist Party**
**Nihon shihon shugi
　hattatsu shi kōza**
　· 日本資本主義発達史講座 3:361a; 5:382b
Nihon shihon shugi ronsō
　　　日本資本主義論争 · 4:362b; 5:382
　central issues · · · · · · · · · 5:382b-383a
　historical context · · · · · · · 5:383a-383b
　postwar significance · · · · · · 5:383b
Nihonshi jiten · 日本史辞典 · · · 8:240a
Nihon Shimbun Kyōkai · · · · · · 4:47b
Nihon Shimpotō (Japan
　Progressive Party)
　　　　日本進歩党 · · · 6:211b
Nihon shoki · · · · 日本書紀 · 1:106a, 141b,
　151b, 353b; 2:259b; 4:259b; 5:25b,
　383b-384a; 6:290b; 7:69a, 85a, 143b,
　296a-297a, 310b, 324b, 376a, 382b; 8:285b
　analysis · · · · · · · · · · · · 5:27a
　Chinese literature · · · · · · · 1:293a
　commentaries · · · · · · · · · 5:384a

compilation · · · · · · · · · 5:383b–384a
early Japanese song · · · · · 2:137a, 138b
Five Kings of Wa · · · · · · · · · · 2:287b
folktales · · · · · · · · · · · · · · · 2:303b
fudoki · · · · · · · · · · · · · · · · · 2:341a
Fujiwarakyō references · · · · · · 2:350a
historiography · · · · · · · · 3:152b–153a
horse-rider theory · · · · · · · · · 3:230a
Japanese language, history · · · · 4:28b
Jimmu, Emperor · · · · · · · · · 4:57a–57b
Kada no Azumamaro lectures · · · 4:100b
Keitai, Emperor · · · · · · · · · · · 4:190a
kikajin · · · · · · · · · · · · · · · · · 4:205a
Kojiki compared · · · · · · · · · · 4:251a
mythology · · · · · · · · · · 5:292a–295a
nature, concept of · · · · · · 5:357a–357b
nature in · · · · · · · · · · · · · · · 5:357a
Ōjin, Emperor · · · · · · · · · · · · 6:76b
orthography · · · · · · · · · · · · · 4:134b
periodization · · · · · · · · · · · · · 6:176a
pheasants · · · · · · · · · · · · · · · 6:182b
religious symbolism · · · · · · · · · 6:295b
Rikkokushi · · · · · · · · · · · · · · 6:315b
roof tiles · · · · · · · · · · · · · · · 6:337b
Shaku nihongi · · · · · · · · · · · · 7:76a
Shintō · · · · · · · · · · · · · · · · · 7:126a
tattoos · · · · · · · · · · · · · · · · · 7:350a
tokoyo · · · · · · · · · · · · · · · · · 8:44a
use of language · · · · · · · · · · · 5:104a
wagtails · · · · · · · · · · · · · · · · 8:201a
waka · · · · · · · · · · · · · · · · · · 8:204a
Wani · · · · · · · · · · · · · · · · · · 8:223a
wild ducks · · · · · · · · · · · · · · · 8:253a
women in Japan · · · · · · · · · · · 8:258a
Yamato court · · · · · · · · · · · · · 8:308b
Yamatotakeru, Prince · · · · 8:311a–311b
Nihon shoki tsūshō
· · · · · · · · · · 日本書紀通証 · · · · · · 7:341b
Nihon Shōkō Kaigisho
· · · · · · · · · · 日本商工会議所 · · · · · · 4:11a
Nihon shomin kyōikushi
· · · · · · · · · · 日本庶民教育史 · · · · · · 6:133a
Nihon Shoseki Shuppan Kyōkai · · · · 4:10b
Nihonshu (Japanese sake) · · · · · · 7:1a
Nihon shugi · · · · · 日本主義 · · 5:384a–384b
Daitōjuku · · · · · · · · · · · · · · · 2:68a
ultranationalism · · · · · · · · · · · 8:144b
Nihon Shūkyō Remmei. *See* **Japan**
Federation of Religions
Nihon suidokō · 日本水土考 · · · · · · 3:25b
Nihon Tenji Toshokan · · · · · · 4:10b–11a
Nihon Tetsudō Kaisha · · · · · · · · 5:384b
· 6:278b–279a
Nihon Tokushukō, Ltd · · · · · · · · 2:56b
Nihon University · · · · · · · · · · · 5:384b
university upheavals of 1968–1969 · 8:171a
Nihon yakkyokuhō · · · · · · · · · · 6:182b
Nihon yūyō shokubutsu
zusetsu
· · · · · · · · · · 日本有用植物図説 · · · · 7:339b
Nihon Zasshi Kyōkai · · · · · · · · · 4:47a
Niichi Suto. *See* **General Strike of 1947**
Niigata · · · · · · · · · · 新潟 · · · · · · 5:385a
Niigata Engineering Co, Ltd · 5:385a–385b
Niigata hanjō ki 新潟繁昌記 · · · · · · 8:11b
Niigata Plain · · · · · · 新潟平野 · · · 5:385b
Niigata Prefecture · · · 新潟県 · · 5:385b–386a
Niihama · · · · · · · · · · 新居浜 · · · · 5:386a
Niijima Jō · · · · · · · · · 新島襄 · · 5:386a–386b
Niimanabi にひまなび（新学） · · 4:129b
Niimanabi iken · 新学異見 · · · · · · 4:103a
Niimi · · · · · · · · · · · 新見 · · · · · 5:386b
Niinamesai (harvest rites)
· · · · · · · · · · 新嘗祭 5:386b; 8:311a
Niitsu · · · · · · · · · · · 新津 · · · · · 5:386b
Niiza · · · · · · · · · · · 新座 · · · · · 5:386b
Niji · · · · · · · · · · · · · 虹 · · · · · 7:311b
Niji no Matsubara · · · · 4:159a; 5:386b–387a

Nijō, Lady · · · · · · · · · 二条后 · · · · 8:87a
Nijō Castle · · · · · · · · 二条城 2:375a; 4:334b;
· · · · · · · · · · · · · · · · 5:387a; 7:162b
Kobori Enshū · · · · · · · · · · · · · 4:238b
paintings · · · · · · · · · · · · · · · 4:151a
Nijōgawara no rakusho
· · · · · · · · · · 二条河原落書 · · · · · · 5:387a
transcriptions · · · · · · · · · · · · 4:191b
Nijō poetic school · 二条流 · · · · · · 7:170b
Nijō school · · · · · · · · · 二条派 · · · · 8:213b
Nijō Tameyo · · · · · · · · 二条為世 · · 5:387a–387b
Kokin denju · · · · · · · · · · · · · 4:254a
Nijō Yoshimoto · · · · 二条良基 · 1:181b; 5:15a,
· · · · · · · · · · · 43a, 387b; 6:297a, 298b
Nijūhasshuku · · · · · 二十八宿 · · · · 8:334a
Nijūichinichi Kai
· · · · · · · · · · 二十一日会 · · · · · · 6:221a
Nijūsannen miraiki
· · · · · · · · · · 二十三年未来記 · · · · 7:255b
Nijūshikumi-doiya
· · · · · · · · · · 二十四組問屋 · · · · · · 6:1a
kaisen management · · · · · · · · · 4:113a
monopolistic trade rights · · · · · · 4:100a
Nijūshi no hitomi
· · · · · · · · · · 二十四の瞳 · · 2:272b, 272b;
· · · · · · · · · · · · · · · · 6:1a; 8:110a
Nikaidō family · · · · · · 二階堂氏 · · · · 6:1a
Nikakai · · · · · · · · · · · 二科会 · · 6:156a, 157b
Nika Society . *See* **Nikakai**
Nikkan gendai · · · · · 日刊現代 · · · 6:268a
Nikkan Kihon Jōyaku
· · · · · · · · · · 日韓基本条約 · · 4:287b–288a
Nikkan Kyōyaku, Dai
Niji · · · · 日韓協約（第二次）· · 4:289a–289b
Nikkatsu · · · · · · · · · · · · · · · · 2:275a
Imamura Shōhei · · · · · · · · · · · 3:274a
Nikkatsu Corporation
· · · · · · · 2:267b–268a, 270b; 3:102a; 6:1a–1b
Daiei Co, Ltd · · · · · · · · · · · · · 2:56b
Tasaka Tomotaka · · · · · · · · · · · 7:347b
Uchida Tomu · · · · · · · · · · · · · 8:124a
Nikka Whisky Distilling Co, Ltd · · · · 6:1b
Nikkeiren (Japan
Federation of Employers'
Associations) · · · · · 日経連 · 4:188a, 348a;
· · · · · · · · · · · · 6:1b, 237b; 8:199a, 367a
Sakurada Takeshi · · · · · · · · · · · 7:4b
Nikki bungaku · · · · · 日記文学 · · 6:2a–2b
Nikkō · · · · · · · · · · · 日光 · · · 1:187a;
· · · · · · · · · · · · · · · · 6:2b–3a; 7:15b
Nikkō Kaidō · · · · · · · · 日光街道 · · · 3:41a
Nikkō National Park
· · · · · · · · · · 日光国立公園 · · · · · · 6:3a
Irohazaka · · · · · · · · · · · · · · · 3:332b
Lake Chūzenji · · · · · · · · · · · · · 6:3a
Nantaisan · · · · · · · · · · · · · · · 6:3a
Tōshōgū · · · · · · · · · · · · · · · · 8:84b
Nikkō Onari Kaidō
· · · · · · · · · · 日光御成街道 · · · · · · 8:220a
Nikkō Securities Co, Ltd · · · · · · · 6:3a
Nikkō Shirane. *See* **Shiranesan**
Nikkyōso (Japan
Teachers' Union) · 日教組 · 6:3a–3b, 237a,
· · · · · · · · · · · · · · · · · · · 238a
atom bomb film · · · · · · · · · · · 7:111a
teachers · · · · · · · · · · · · · · · 7:366a
Nikō Jiken. *See* **Nikolaevsk Incident**
Nikolaevsk Incident · · · · · · · 6:3b; 7:238a
Nikolai, Archbishop · · · · · · · · 6:3b–4a
Holy Orthodox Church · · · · · · · · 3:216a
spread of Christianity · · · · · · · · 1:308a
Nikutai no mon (The Gate
of Flesh) · · · · · · · 肉体の門 6:221b; 7:334b
Nimbetsu aratame · 人別改 · · · · · · 6:4a
Nimbetsuchō · · · · · · · 人別帳 · · · · 6:4a
Nimono · · · · · · · · · · · · · · · · · 2:306a

Ninagawa Torazō 蜷川虎三 · · · · · · 6:4a–4b
Nin'ami Dōhachi
· · · · · · · · · · 仁阿弥道八 · · · · · · 6:4b
Nindō · · · · · · · · · · · · · · · · · · 3:221a
Nine-Power Treaty (1922) · · · 6:4b; 8:272b
China · · · · · · · · · · · · · · · · · 1:288a
Lansing-Ishii Agreement · · · · · · · 4:367a
United States · · · · · · · · · · · · · 8:157a
Nine Principles for Economic
Stabilization · · · · · · · · · · 6:4b–5b
evaluation · · · · · · · · · · · · · · · 6:5a
implementation · · · · · · · · · · · · 6:5a
inflation · · · · · · · · · · · · · · · · 6:5a
prior attempts · · · · · · · · · · · · · 6:5a
provisions · · · · · · · · · · · · · · 6:4b–5b
Ningen Kokuhō · · · · · · · · · · 5:60b–61a
Ningen no higeki · · · 人間の悲劇 · · 4:139a
Ningen no jōken (The Human
Condition) · · · 人間の条件 · · 2:273a
''Ningen ōrai'' (Human
Comings and Goings)
· · · · · · · · · · 人間往来 · · · · · · 8:173b
Ningen shikkaku 人間失格 · · · · · · 2:80a
Ningyō jōruri · · · · · 人形浄瑠璃 · · · 1:275a
Ningyō mawashi · · · · · · · · · · · · 7:250a
Ningyō Pass · · · · · · · 人形峠 · · · · 6:5b
Ningyō Sashichi torimonochō
· · · · · · · · · · 人形佐七捕物帳 · · · · 8:333a
Ningyō shibai · · · · · · · · · · · · · 2:267b
Ninigi no Mikoto · 瓊瓊杵尊 · 5:294b; 6:5b
imperial regalia · · · · · · · · · · · 3:278b
story in *Kojiki* · · · · · · · · · · · · 4:251a
Niniroku Jiken. 二・二六事件
See **February 26th Incident**
Ninja. *See* **Ninjutsu**
Ninjin kōsakuki 人参耕作記 · · · · · · 7:334b
Ninjō · · · · · · · · · · · · · · · · · 2:269b
Ninjōbon · · · · · · · · · 人情本 5:49b; 6:5b–6b;
· · · · · · · · · · · · · · · · · · · 7:97a
Hanasanjin · · · · · · · · · · · · · · 3:94b
Santō Kyōden · · · · · · · · · · · · · 7:18a
sharebon · · · · · · · · · · · · · · · 7:80a
Tamenaga Shunsui · · · · · · · 7:333b–334a
Ninjō kamifūsen
(Humanity and Paper
Balloons) · · · · · 人情紙風船 · · 8:300b
Ninjutsu · · · · · · · · · 忍術 · · · · 6:6b–7a
Ninkyō gaiden: Genkainada
· · · · · · · · · · 任侠外伝:玄海灘 · · · · 4:157a
Ninkyō Tōkaidō 任侠東海道 · · · · · · 4:166a
Ninnaji · · · · · · · · · · 仁和寺 · · 4:336b; 6:7a
Kakuban · · · · · · · · · · · · · · · · 4:117b
Shingon sect · · · · · · · · · · · · · 7:115a
Ninnaji shojaku mokuroku
· · · · · · · · · · 仁和寺書籍目録 · · · · 3:219a
Ninohe · · · · · · · · · · 二戸 · · · · · 6:7a
Ninomiya Sontoku
· · · · · · · · · · 二宮尊徳 · · · · 6:7a–8a;
· · · · · · · · · · · · · · · · · · · 7:338b
Ninsei. 仁清 *See* **Nonomura Ninsei**
Ninshikiron · · · · · · · 認識論 · · · · 4:204b
Ninshō · · · · · · · · · · · 忍性 · · 2:187b–188a;
· · · · · · · · · · · · · · · · · · · 5:238b
Ninsoku yoseba · 人足寄場 · · · · · 6:8a
Nintoku, Emperor
· · · · · · · · · · 仁徳天皇 · · · 2:287b; 6:8a
tomb · · · · · · · · · · · · · · · · · 2:303b
Nintoku Mausoleum
· · · · · · · · · · 仁徳陵 4:246b; 6:8a–8b
Niō · · · · · · · · · · · · · · · · · · · 1:186b
Nippara Shōnyūdō
· · · · · · · · · · 日原鍾乳洞 · · · · · · 6:8b
Nippo jisho · · · · · · · 日葡辞書 · · 6:8b, 228b
Nippon · · · · · · · · · · · 日本 · · 1:76b, 123a
Nippon, Archiv zur Beschreibung von
Japan · · · · · · · · · · · · · · · · 7:192b
Nippon Beet Sugar Mfg Co, Ltd · · · · 6:8b

Nippon Broadcasting System, Inc 1:173b; 2:347a; 6:8b; 7:14a
Nippon Chisso Fertilizer Co ······· 7:57b
Nippon Columbia Co, Ltd ·········· 6:8b
Nippon Credit Bank, Ltd ·· 1:139b; 6:9a
Nippon Cultural Broadcasting, Inc
········· 1:173b; 2:347b; 6:9a; 7:14a, 86b
Nippon Dempō Tsūshinsha (Japan Telegraphic News Agency) ····· 5:369a
Nippondensō Co, Ltd ··············· 6:9a
Toyota Motor Co, Ltd ············ 8:93b
Nippon Educational Television (NET) ····················· 1:93a
Nippon Electric Co, Ltd (NEC) 6:9a-9b
Nippon Electric Industries ········· 7:173a
Nippon Express Co, Ltd ············· 6:9b
Nippon Flour Mills Co, Ltd ······· 6:9b
Nippon Formula Feed Mfg Co, Ltd · 6:9b
Nippon Gakki Co, Ltd ····· 3:90b; 4:179a; 6:9b-10a
Kawakami Gen'ichi ·············· 4:180b
Nippon Hodō Co, Ltd ·············· 6:10a
Nippon Hōsō Kyōkai
··········· 日本放送協会 ·· 2:179a, 182a; 5:374a-374b
establishment ················· 2:192a
Nippon Iodine Co ·················· 7:173a
Nipponjin no higeki
········· 日本人の悲劇 ····· 4:139a
Nippon Kangyō Bank ·············· 1:139a
Nippon Kangyō Bank, Ltd ········· 2:58b
Nippon Kayaku Co, Ltd. ············ 6:10a
Hara Yasusaburō ·············· 3:103b
Nippon Kōgaku ··················· 6:10a
Nippon Kōkan ··········· 6:10a-10b; 7:269a
Tōshin Steel Co, Ltd ············· 8:83b
Nippon Koku ····· 日本国 ···· 4:7a
Nippon konchūki (The Insect Woman) ········· にっぽん昆虫記 ·· 2:274b
Nippon Life Insurance Co ········· 6:10b
Nippon Light Metal Co, Ltd ······· 2:372b; 6:10b-11a
Nippon Meat Packers, Inc ········· 6:11a
Nippon Menka Kaisha (Japan Cotton Trading Company) ············ 5:374b
Nippon Metal Industry Co, Ltd ··· 6:11a
Nippon Mining Co, Ltd ············· 6:11b
Nippon mukashi-banashi meii ······· 日本昔話名彙 ·· 2:302b
Nippon mukashi-banashi shūsei ······· 日本昔話集成 ·· 2:302b
Nippon News Network (NNN) ····· 8:337a
Nippon no mukashi-banashi ·········· 日本の昔話 ···· 2:302a
Nippon Oil & Fats Co, Ltd ········· 6:11b
Nippon Oil Co, Ltd ········ 6:11b, 182a
Nippon Paint Co, Ltd ·············· 6:11b
Nippon Petrochemical ············· 6:180a
Nippon Reizō ··············· 6:11b-12a
Nippon Sanso ···················· 6:12a
Nippon Seikō ···················· 6:12a
Nippon Sharyō Seizō Kaisha, Ltd · 6:12a
Nippon Sheet Glass Co, Ltd ······ 6:12a
Nippon shimbun · 日本新聞 ······· 7:258b
Nippon Shimbun Rengōsha (Japan Associated Press) ······· 3:360b; 5:369a
Nippon Shinpan Co, Ltd ··········· 6:12a
Nippon Shokubai Kagaku Kōgyō Co, Ltd ···················· 6:12a-12b
Nippon Soda Co, Ltd ······· 5:317a; 6:12b
Nippon Stainless Steel Co, Ltd ··· 6:12b
Nippon Steel Corporation · 2:343a; 3:333a, 333b; 6:12b-13a; 7:269a
Inayama Yoshihiro ············· 3:284a
Nagano Shigeo ················· 5:303a
Pacific Metals Co, Ltd ·········· 6:143b
Sankyū, Inc ···················· 7:15a

Shinwa Kaiun Kaisha, Ltd ········ 7:139b
Topy Industries, Ltd ············· 8:76a
Nippon Suisan Kaisha, Ltd · 2:284a; 6:13a
Nippon Telegraph and Telephone Public Corporation ···· 6:13a, 263b; 7:14b
administrative committee ········ 2:373a
fiscal system ·················· 2:281b
Kokusai Denshin Denwa Co, Ltd separated from ·············· 4:261b
Kōrōkyō membership ··········· 4:294a
radio law ···················· 6:276a
telecommunications systems ···· 7:377a
telephones ···················· 7:380a
Nippon Television Network Corporation (NTV) ············ 1:172a; 6:13a-13b
Nippon teriya ·················· 4:45a
Nippon Times ·················· 4:50a
Nippon Univac Kaisha, Ltd ······· 6:13b
Nippon Yakin Kōgyō Co, Ltd ····· 6:13b
Nippon Yūsen ············ 2:31a; 6:13b
history ················ 2:151b, 153a
Kagami Kenkichi ·············· 4:102b
Nippon Zeon Co, Ltd ·············· 6:13b
NIRA. *See* National Institute for Research Advancement
Nirasaki ·········· 韮崎 ···· 6:13b-14a
Nireke no hitobito ········· 楡家の人びと ········ 4:227a
Niroku shimpō ·· 二六新報 ···· 1:44a
Nirvāna ····················· 1:177a
Nisai tōki ········ 二彩陶器 ··· 1:262a
Nisei ······· 4:12b-13a, 13a-15a; 6:179a
dual citizenship ··············· 4:16b
Hawaiian politics ·············· 4:16b
Japan ······················· 4:15a
United States Immigration Acts of 1924, 1952, and 1965 ············ 8:165a
wartime relocation ············· 4:18a
Nisei hibakusha ················· 4:15a
Niseko ·········· ニセコ ···· 6:14a
Nise monogatari · 仁勢物語 ···· 4:136b
Nise Murasaki inaka Genji (Rustic Genji, Imitation Murasaki) ·· 偐紫田舎源氏 ·· 3:42a; 5:49a; 6:359a
"Nisen dōka" ···· 二銭銅貨 ····· 2:170b
Nisengohyakunen shi ············ 二千五百年史 ···· 7:324a
Nishi Amane ········ 西周 ·· 6:14a-14b, 260b
Freedom and People's Rights Movement ················· 2:335b
Imperial Rescript to Soldiers and Sailors ···················· 3:280a
shigi kempō ·················· 7:92b
Nishida Kitarō · 西田幾多郎 6:14b, 15a-15b
philosophies ············· 5:230a-230b
Nishida Mitsugi ···· 西田税 ··· 6:15b-16a
February 26th Incident ·········· 2:250a
Nishigoribe ········ 錦織部 ··· 1:147b
Nishihara loans ·· 西原借款 · 3:199a; 6:16a
Duan Qirui (Tuan Ch'i-jui) ····· 2:134b
Terauchi Masatake ············· 8:12b
Nishi higashi ········ 西東 ··· 4:139a
Nishi Honganji ··· 西本願寺 ··· 6:16a-17a
Nishijin-ori ········ 西陣織 · 4:338a; 6:17a
Nishikawa Joken 西川如見 ··· 4:1a; 6:17a
geography studies ·············· 3:25b
Nishikawa Kōjirō. *See* Nishikawa Mitsujirō
Nishikawa Mitsujirō ········· 西川光二郎 ·· 6:17a
Nishikawa Shōji · 西川正治 ··· 6:17a
Nishikawa Sukenobu ········· 西川祐信 ··· 6:17a-17b; 7:187b
Nishiki ············ 4:158a; 6:17b
Atsuita ····················· 1:115b

Nishiki-e origami ··············· 6:118a
Nishikigoi (carp) ··············· 1:244a
Nishimatsu Construction Co, Ltd ·· 6:17b
Nishimura Isaburō ········ 西村伊三郎 ········· 2:66a
Nishimura Shigeki ········ 西村茂樹 ··· 6:17b-18b; 7:3b
Koji ruien ·················· 4:252a
Nishimura Shigenaga 西村重長 ·· 8:141a
Nishin ····················· 3:128a
Nishina Yoshio ·· 仁科芳雄 ··· 6:18b
Nishi-Nippon Railroad Co, Ltd ···· 6:18b
Nishi Nippon shimbun ········ 西日本新聞 ··· 6:18b
Nishinomiya ········ 西宮 ··· 6:19a
Nishinoomote ······ 西之表 ··· 6:19a
Nishio ·········· 西尾 ··· 6:19a
Nishio Suehiro ···· 西尾末広 ··· 6:19a
Democratic Socialist Party ·········· 2:85b
Japan Socialist Party ··········· 4:48b
Nishi-Rosen Agreement · 6:19a; 8:293b
Korea ······················· 4:281b
Russo-Japanese War ············ 6:346a
Nishi Sonogi Peninsula ········ 西彼杵半島 · 6:19a-19b
Nishi Takeichi ··· 西竹一 ··· 6:19b
Nishiwaki ········ 西脇 ··· 6:19b
Nishiwaki Junzaburō ········ 西脇順三郎 ··· 6:19b-20a
Nishiyama Sōin · 西山宗因 ··· 2:77a-77b; 6:20a, 297a
haikai ······················ 3:79a
Nishiyama Suishō ········· 西山翠嶂 ··· 6:20a
Nishiyama Usaburō. 西山卯三郎 *See* **Nishiyama Suishō**
Nishizawa Ippū · 西沢一風 · 5:48b; 6:20a
Nissan Chemical Industries, Ltd · 6:20a
Ishikawa Ichirō ················ 3:342a
Nissan Diesel Motor Co, Ltd ····· 6:20b
Nissan Motor Co, Ltd 1:33b; 2:343a; 6:20b
Atsugi Motor Parts Co, Ltd and · 1:115b
Daidō Steel Co, Ltd ············· 2:56b
early automotive industry ······· 1:121b
unions ······················ 4:53b
Nissan Shatai Co, Ltd ············· 6:20b
Nisshin Flour Milling Co, Ltd · 6:20b-21a
Nisshin Oil Mills, Ltd ············· 6:21a
Nisshin Sensō. *See* Sino-Japanese War of 1894-1895
Nisshin Shūkō Jōki ········· 日清修好条規 ···· 7:197b
Nisshin Spinning Co, Ltd ········· 6:21a
Sakurada Takeshi ·············· 7:4b
Takita Minoru ················ 7:327a
Nisshin Steel Co, Ltd ············· 6:21a
Nisshō ······················ 4:11a
Nisshō-Iwai Co, Ltd ·········· 6:21a-21b
Takahata Seiichi ·············· 7:313b
Nissin Food Products Co, Ltd ····· 6:21b
Nissin Sugar Mfg Co, Ltd ········· 6:21b
Nisso Kihon Jōyaku ········· 日ソ基本条約 ···· 7:238a
Nisso Kyōdō Sengen ········· 7:238b-239a
Nitaika fūga ··· 二大家風雅 ··· 4:333b
Nitchū Heiwa Yūkō Jōyaku 日中平和友好条約 ···1:291b-292a
Nitchū Sensō. *See* Sino-Japanese War of 1937-1945
Nitobe Inazō · 新渡戸稲造 ········ 1:223a; 6:21b-22a
League of Nations ·············· 4:373a
Nito monogatari ··· 二都物語 ··· 4:157b
Nitta family ············ 新田氏 ··· 6:22a
Nittai Dōmei ··· 日・タイ同盟 ··· 8:20a
Nitta Isamu ·· 仁田勇 · 1:268b; 6:22a
Nitta Yoshisada · 新田義貞 ··· 6:22a-22b

betrayal · **4:**192a
defeat · **1:**94b
Nitten (Nihon Bijutsu Tenrankai; Japan Art Exhibition) · · · · **1:**215b; **6:**158a
Nittetsu Mining Co, Ltd · · · · · · · · **6:**22b
Nittō Bōseki Co, Ltd · · · · · · · · · · **6:**22b
Nittō Chemical Industry Co, Ltd · · · **6:**22b
Nittō guhō junrei kōki
　　入唐求法巡礼行記 · · · · · **8:**105b
Nittsū. *See* **Nippon Express Co, Ltd**
Niwaban · · · · · · · · · 庭番 · · · · · · **6:**22b
Niwabi · **4:**108a
Niwa Fumio · · · · · · 丹羽文雄 · · · · · · **2:**274a;
　　　　　　　　　　　　　　　6:22b-23a
　fūzoku shōsetsu · · · · · · · · · · · · **2:**378b
Niwaka · · · · · · · · · · · 俄 · · · · · · · **7:**221b
Niwano Nikkyō · · · · 庭野日敬 · **6:**23a; **6:**321a
Niwatori · · · · · · · · · · · · · · · **1:**272b-273a
Niwa Yasujirō · 丹羽保次郎 · · · · · · **6:**23a
Nixon shocks · · · · · · · · · · · · · · **6:**23a-23b
　foreign trade policy · · · · · · · · · **2:**326a
　Satō Eisaku · · · · · · · · · · · · · · · · **7:**26b
Niyodogawa · · · · · · · · 仁淀川 · · · · · · **6:**23b
NLC · **5:**365a
Nō · · · · · · · · · · · · · · 能 · **2:**73a; **4:**336b;
　　6:23b-29b, 298b; **7:**64b, 79a; **8:**21b-22a
　audience · · · · · · · · · · · · · · · · **6:**27b-28a
　costume · · · · · · · · · **4:**158a; **6:**26a; **8:**23b
　criticism · **5:**15b
　dance, traditional · · · · · · · · · · · · **2:**75b
　evolution · · · · · · · · · · · · · · · · **6:**24a-24b
　fans · **2:**248a
　folk versions · · · · · · · · · · · · · · · · **2:**296b
　Hōshō school · · · · · · · · · · · · · · · · **3:**235b
　kabuki adaptations · · · · · · · · · · · **4:**92b
　Kanze school · · · · · · · · · · · · · · · · **4:**155a
　Kita school · · · · · · · · · · · · **4:**228b-229a
　Komparu school · · · · · · · · · · · · · **4:**267b
　kyōgen · **5:**43a
　ma, use of · · · · · · · · · · · · · · · · · · · **5:**77a
　masks · · · · · · · **5:***127a-127b;* **6:**26a
　musical influence · · · · · · · · · · · · **2:**366b
　Ōkura school · · · · · · · · · · · · · · · · **6:**98a
　origins · · · · · · · · · · · · · · · · · · · **6:**23b-24a
　performance · · · · · · · · · · · · · · **6:**26a-27b
　performers · · · · · · · · · · · · · · · **6:**25b-26a
　plays · · · · · · · · · · **6:**26a-27a; **7:**61b
　properties · · · · · · · · · · · · · · · · · · · **6:**26a
　sarugaku · · · · · · · · · · · **5:**43a; **7:**22b
　shingeki · **7:**112a
　stage · · · · · · · · · · · · · · · · · · · **6:**24b-25b
　tsuzumi · **8:**119b
　Zen influence · · · · · · · · · · · · · · · · **5:**43a
Nōami · · · · · · · · · · 能阿弥 · · · · · · **1:**52b;
　　　　　　　　　　　　　　6:29b-30a
Nobel Prize
　Esaki Reona · · · · · · · · · · · · · · · · **2:**231b
　Fukui Ken'ichi · · · · · · · · · · · · · · · **2:**363b
　Kawabata Yasunari · · · · · · · · · · · **4:**176b
　Satō Eisaku · · · · · · · · · · · · · · · · · **7:**26a
　Tomonaga Shin'ichirō · · · · · · · · · **8:**73a
　Yukawa Hideki · · · · · · · · · · · · · · **8:**356b
Nobeoka · · · · · · · · · · 延岡 · · · · · · **6:**30a
Nobeyama · · · · · · · · 野辺山 · · · · · · **6:**30a
Nobi (Fires on the Plain)
　　　　　　　　 野火 **2:***273a;* **6:**113b
Nōbi Earthquake of 1891 · · · · · · **8:**194b
Nōbi Plain · · · · · 濃尾平野 · · · · · · **6:**30a
　Nagoya · · · · · · · · · · · · · · · **5:**308b-309a
Nobori · **2:**288a
Noboribetsu · · · · · · · · 登別 · · · · · · **6:**30a
Noborigama (climbing kiln) · · · · **1:**263b,
　　　　　　　　　　　　264b; **4:**159b
Nobunaga Kō ki 信長公記 · **7:**109a-109b
Nobushi (armed peasants) · **1:**97b; **6:**30a
Nobuzumi · · · · · · · · · · 信澄 · · · · · · **3:**117a
Noda · · · · · · · · · · · · · 野田 · **6:**30a-30b
Noda Kōgo · · · · · 野田高梧 · **2:**272a; **6:**30b

Noda Shōyu Co · · · · · · · · · · · · · · **4:**206a
Noda Soy Sauce Co, case of 1957 · **1:**66a
Nogami Yaeko 野上弥生子 · · · · · **6:**30b-31a
Nōgata · · · · · · · · · · · · 直方 · **2:**365a; **6:**31a
Nogawa site · · · · · 野川遺跡 · · · · · · **6:**31a
Nogi Maresuke · · · · 乃木希典 · **1:**87b, 223a;
　　　　　　　　3:102a; **6:**31a-31b
Noguchi, Isamu · · · · · · · · · · · · · · **6:**31b
Noguchi Hideyo 野口英世 · · · · · · **6:**31b
Noguchi Shitagau 野口遵 · · · · · · **6:**32a
Noguchi Yonejirō
　　　　　　　野口米次郎 · · · · · · **6:**32a
Nōgyōkai (Agricultural Association) **1:**22a
Nōgyō kyōdō kumiai · · · · · · · **1:**21b-22b
Nōgyō zensho · · · 農業全書 · **1:**24a; **6:**32a
Nōhon shugi · · · · · 農本主義 · **6:**32a-32b;
　　　　　　　　　　　　　　8:144b
Noibara. *See* **Roses**
Nōin · · · · · · · · · · · · · · 能因 · **6:**32b; **8:**210b
Nōin uta makura · 能因歌枕 · · · · · · **8:**185b
Noise pollution · · · · · · · · · · · · · · **2:**228a
Noise Regulation Law · · · · · · · · · **2:**228a
Nojima Kōzō · · · · 野島康三 · · · · · · **6:***185a*
Nojiri, Lake · · · · · 野尻湖 · · · · · · **6:**32b
Nojiri Kiyohiko · 野尻清彦 · · · · · · **6:**123b
Nōkō girei · · · · · · · · · · · · · · · **1:**22b-23a
Nokogiriyama · · · · · · 鋸山 · · · · · · **6:**32b
Nōkyō · · · · · · · · · · · · · · · · · · · **1:**21b-22b
Noli me Tangere · · · · · · · · · · · · · · **6:**332b
Noma Hiroshi · · · · 野間宏 · · · · · · **6:**32b-33a
　Shin Nihon bungaku · · · · · · · · · **7:**122a
**Noma Institute of Educational
　Research** · · · · · · · · · · · · · · · · · **6:**33a-33b
Noma Kyōiku Kenkyūjo. *See* **Noma
　Institute of Educational Research**
Nomaoi Matsuri 野馬追祭 · · · · · · **2:***254b*
Noma Prize
　Endō Shūsaku · · · · · · · · · · · · · · · **2:**214a
　Nagai Tatsuo · · · · · · · · · · · · · · · · **5:**301b
　Nakayama Gishū · · · · · · · · · · · · · **5:**318b
　Shōno Junzō · · · · · · · · · · · · · · · · **7:**167a
　Takami Jun · · · · · · · · · · · · · · · · · **7:**315a
　Yasuoka Shōtarō · · · · · · · · · · · · · **8:**319b
Noma Seiji · · · · · · · 野間清治 · · · · · · **6:**33b
　Dai Nippon Yūben Kai Kōdansha · **4:**241b
Noma Shōichi · · · · · 野間省一 · · · · · · **6:**33b
　Kōdansha's president · · · · · · · · · · **4:**242a
Nō mask · · · · · · · · · · · · · · **5:***126b-127a*
Nōmijima · · · · · · · · 能美島 · **6:**33b-34a
**Nōmin Bungaku Konwa
　Kai** · 農民文学懇話会 · · · · · · **5:**19a
Nōmin Bungei Kondankai · · · · · · **7:**176b
Nomonhan Incident
　(1939) · · · ノモンハン事件 · **1:**88b; **6:**34a,
　　　　　　　　　　　　343b
　Tsuji Masanobu · · · · · · · · · · · · · · **8:**113b
Nomori no kagami
　　　　　　　野守の鏡 · · · · · · **4:**329b
Nomugi Pass · · · · · 野麦峠 · · · · · · **6:**34a
Nomura Hōtei · · · 野村芳亭 · · · · · · **2:**268a
Nomura Kichisaburō
　　　　　　　野村吉三郎 · · · · · · **6:**34a
Nomura Kodō · · · 野村胡堂 · · · · · · **6:**34a
Nomura Mansaku 野村万作 · · · · · · **4:***326b*
Nomura Matasaburō 野村又三郎 · **4:***327a*
Nomura Motoni
　　　　　　　野村望東尼 · · · · · · **6:**34a-34b
Nomura Securities Co, Ltd · · · · · · **6:**34b
　Tōyō Trust & Banking Co, Ltd · · · · · **8:**96a
Nonaka Kenzan 野中兼山 · · · · · · **6:**34b
Nonaka Shirō · · · 野中四郎 · · · · · · **2:**250a
Nonchurch Christianity. *See* **Mukyōkai**
Nonchurch Movement. *See* **Mukyōkai**
Nonferrous metals industry · · · · · · **6:**34b
Nonki-megane · · 暢気眼鏡 **6:**139b; **7:**176a
Nonki na kanja
　　　　　　のんきな患者 · · · · · · **4:**114a
Non-nuclear principles · · · · · · · · · **8:**168b

Nonoguchi Ryūho
　　　　　　野々口立圃 · · · · **6:**34b-35a
Nonomura Ninsei
　　　　　　野々村仁清 · **2:**346a; **6:**35a
　Kyōto ware · · · · · · · · · · · · · · · · · **6:***35a*
Nonpenal fines · · · · · · · · · · · · · **6:**35a-35b
Nonprint media · · · · · · · · · · · · · · **6:**268a
Nonrecognition policy · · · **6:**35b; **7:**246b
　Shandong (Shantung) Question · · · **7:**77b
Nonverbal communication · · · · **6:**36a-37a
　historical factors · · · · · · · · · · · · · **6:**36a
　social factors
　　artifacts · · · · · · · · · · · · · · · · **6:**36b-37a
　　body motion (kinesics) · · · · · · · · **6:**36b
　　group importance · · · · · · · · · · · **6:**36a
　　long-range goal perseverance · **6:**36a-36b
　　mother-child closeness · · · · · · · · **6:**36a
　　paralanguage · · · · · · · · · · · · · · **6:**36b
　　social obligations · · · · · · · · · · · **6:**36a
　　space (proxemics) · · · · · · · · · · · **6:**36b
Noodles (menrui) · · · · · · · · · · · · · **6:**283a
　Japanese cooking methods · · · · · **2:**24a-24b
Norainu · · · · · · · · · · 野良犬 · · · · · · **7:**108b
Noren · · · · · · · · · · · · · · · · · **2:**295b; **6:***37a*
Nori, Princess · · · · · · · · · · · · · · · **3:***277a*
Nori (laver) · · · · **2:**281b-282a; **6:**37a-37b
Norikuradake · · · · · 乗鞍岳 · · · · · · **6:**37b
Norikura Volcanic Zone
　　　　　　　乗鞍火山帯 · · · · · · **6:**37b
Norimono · · · · · · · · · · · · · · · · · · · **4:**104b
Nōrin Chūkin Bank · · · · · · **1:**22a; **6:**37b
Nōrin Suisan Shō. 農林水産省
　See **Ministry of Agriculture,
　Forestry, and Fisheries**
Noritake Co, Ltd · · · · · · · · · · · **6:**37b-38a
　Tōtō, Ltd · · · · · · · · · · · · · · · · · · · **8:**85b
Norito · · · · · · · · · · · · 祝詞 · · · · · · **6:**38a
　Shintō rites · · · · · · · · · · · · · · · · · **7:**138b
Normal schools · · · · · · · · · · · · · · **6:**38a
　teachers · · · · · · · · · · · · · · · · · · · **7:**365b
Norman, Egerton Herbert · **1:**238a; **6:**38b
Normanton Incident
　　　　　ノルマントン号事件 · **6:**38b; **8:**151b
Noro Eitarō · · · 野呂栄太郎 · · · · · · **6:**38b
Noro Genjō · · · · · 野呂元丈 · · · · · · **6:**39a
Noro Kageyoshi 野呂景義 · · · · · · **6:**39a
North China Area Army · · · · · · · · **6:**260a
North China Incident · · · · · · · · · · **7:**199a
North China Political Council · · · · · **6:**260b
Northern and Southern Courts · **6:**39a-40a
　estate stewards · · · · · · · · · · · · · · **4:**63b
　feudalism · · · · · · · · · · · · · · · · · · · **2:**265a
　Go-Kameyama, Emperor · · · · · · **3:**41b-42a
　Jinnō shōtōki · · · · · · · · · · · · · **4:**59b-60a
　Kaei sandai ki · · · · · · · · · · · · · · **4:**101b
　Kōgon, Emperor · · · · · · · · · · · · · **4:**249a
　periodization · · · · · · · · · · · · · · · · **6:**175b
　reunification · · · · · · · · · · · · · · **3:**41b-42a
　Taiheiki · · · · · · · · · · · · · · · · · · · **7:**295a
Northern sea operations · · · · · · · · **2:**285b
Northern Territory issue. *See* **Territory
　of Japan**
North Korea, Japanese relations with.
　See **Korea and Japan**
North Kyūshū Industrial Zone · · · · · **6:**40b
North Pacific Paper Corporation · · · **4:**83b
Norway · **4:**43b
Noryang, Battle of · · · · · · · · · · · · · **3:**327b
Nosaka Akiyuki · 野坂昭如 · **6:**40b; **8:**328b
Nosaka Sanzō · · · 野坂参三 · · · · · · **6:**40b
　Japan Communist Party · · · · · · · **4:**11a-11b
　Shinjinkai · · · · · · · · · · · · · · · · · · **7:**115b
Nosappumisaki · 野寒布岬 · · · · · · **6:**40b
"Nose, The" · · · · · · · · · · · · · · · · · · **1:**45a
Noshappumisaki 納沙布岬 · · · · · · **6:**41a
Noshi · · · · · · · · · · · · · · · · · · · **1:**1b; **6:**41a
　kokorozuke placed in · · · · · · · · · · **4:**256b
Noshi awabi · · · · · · · · · · · · · · · · · **6:**118a

Noshiro ············ 能代 ······· **6**:41a
Noshiro Plain ···· 能代平野 ······· **6**:41a
Nōshōmushō ···· 農商務省 · **6**:41a–41b
Nōshū ············· 能衆 ······· **2**:297b
"Nosongdang Ilbon haengnok" ·· **4**:278b;
 7:227b
Notary public ············· **1**:16a; **6**:41b
Notes on the Rectification of the
 Japanese Writing ······· **8**:201a
Nothingness ···· **2**:212b–213a; **6**:41b
Notkome ··············· **6**:340b
Noto Peninsula · 能登半島 ······· **6**:41b
Notoro, Lake ···· 能取湖 ······· **6**:41b
Notsukezaki ········· 野付崎 ······· **6**:41b
Novelists
 Abe Kōbō ············· **1**:2b–3b
 Abe Tomoji ············· **1**:4b
 Aeba Kōson ············· **1**:18a
 Agawa Hiroyuki ············· **1**:21a
 Akutagawa Ryūnosuke ········· **1**:45a–46a
 Amino Kiku ············· **1**:52a–52b
 Aono Suekichi ············· **1**:70a–70b
 Arishima Takeo ············· **1**:84b
 Ariyoshi Sawako ············· **1**:86a
 Chikamatsu Shūkō ······· **1**:276a–276b
 Dan Kazuo ············· **2**:76b
 Dazai Osamu ············· **2**:79b–80a
 Edogawa Rampo ········· **2**:170b–171a
 Enchi Fumiko ············· **2**:213b
 Endō Shūsaku ············· **2**:214a
 Fujieda Shizuo ············· **2**:342a
 Fujimori Seikichi ············· **2**:343b
 Fujioka Sakutarō ········· **2**:344a–344b
 Fujisawa Takeo ············· **2**:345b
 Fukazawa Shichirō ············· **2**:360a
 Fukunaga Takehiko ············· **2**:364a
 Funahashi Seiichi ············· **2**:368b
 Furui Yoshikichi ············· **2**:372a
 Furuyama Komao ············· **2**:373b
 Futabatei Shimei ········· **2**:375a–376a
 Genji Keita ············· **3**:20a
 Gomi Yasusuke ············· **3**:44b
 Haji Seiji ············· **3**:84b
 Haniya Yutaka ············· **3**:98a–98b
 Hara Tamiki ············· **3**:103b
 Hasegawa Shirō ············· **3**:108a
 Hayama Yoshiki ············· **3**:115a–115b
 Hayashi Fubō ············· **3**:116a
 Hayashi Fumiko ············· **3**:116a–116b
 Hayashi Fusao ············· **3**:116b
 Hino Ashihei ············· **3**:140b
 Hirabayashi Taiko ············· **3**:141b
 Hirotsu Kazuo ············· **3**:151a
 Hirotsu Ryūrō ············· **3**:151a
 Hisao Jūran ············· **3**:151b
 Hōjō Tamio ············· **3**:211b–212a
 Honjō Mutsuo ············· **3**:223b
 Hori Tatsuo ············· **3**:228a
 Hoshi Shin'ichi ············· **3**:235a
 Hotta Yoshie ············· **3**:239b–240a
 Ibuse Masuji ············· **3**:255a
 Inagaki Taruho ············· **3**:282a–282b
 Inoue Hisashi ············· **3**:309b
 Inoue Mitsuharu ············· **3**:311a
 Inoue Yasushi ············· **3**:311b
 Ishihara Shintarō ············· **3**:341a
 Ishikawa Jun ············· **3**:342b–343b
 Ishikawa Tatsuzō ············· **3**:345a
 Ishizaka Yōjirō ············· **3**:347a
 Itō Einosuke ············· **3**:352a
 Itō Sei ············· **3**:355b–356a
 Itsuki Hiroyuki ············· **3**:356b–357a
 Iwano Hōmei ············· **3**:361a–361b
 Izumi Kyōka ············· **3**:365b
 Kaga Otohiko ············· **4**:102b
 Kaikō Ken ············· **4**:111a–111b
 Kaionji Chōgorō ············· **4**:112a
 Kajii Motojirō ············· **4**:114a–114b

 Kajiyama Toshiyuki ············· **4**:115a
 Kambayashi Akatsuki ············· **4**:123a
 Kamitsukasa Shōken ············· **4**:127b
 Kamura Isota ············· **4**:120b
 Kanō Sakujirō ············· **4**:148b
 Kasai Zenzō ············· **4**:160b
 Kashiwabara Hyōzō ············· **4**:162b
 Kataoka Teppei ············· **4**:166a
 Kawabata Yasunari ············· **4**:175b–177a
 Kawaguchi Matsutarō ············· **4**:177b
 Kawakami Bizan ············· **4**:179b–180a
 Kawasaki Chōtarō ············· **4**:183a
 Kida Minoru ············· **4**:202a
 Kikuchi Kan ············· **4**:206a–207a
 Kikumura Itaru ············· **4**:207a
 Kikuta Kazuo ············· **4**:207a
 Kim Tal-su ············· **4**:211a
 Kinoshita Naoe ············· **4**:215b–216a
 Kitahara Takeo ············· **4**:255a–255b
 Kita Morio ············· **4**:227a
 Kobayashi Takiji ············· **4**:237a–237b
 Kōda Rohan ············· **4**:242a–243a
 Kojima Nobuo ············· **4**:252a
 Komatsu Sakyō ············· **4**:266a
 Kondō Keitarō ············· **4**:269b
 Kon Tōkō ············· **4**:275b
 Kosugi Tengai ············· **4**:296a
 Kubota Mantarō ············· **4**:301a
 Kunikida Doppo ············· **4**:309a–309b
 Kurahashi Yumiko ············· **4**:311a–311b
 Kuroi Senji ············· **4**:316a
 Kuroiwa Jūgo ············· **4**:316b
 Kuroshima Denji ············· **4**:318a–318b
 Lee Hwe-song ············· **4**:374b
 Maedakō Hiroichirō ············· **5**:80a
 Makino Shin'ichi ············· **5**:86b
 Maruyama Kenji ············· **5**:121b
 Masamune Hakuchō ············· **5**:122b–123a
 Matsumoto Seichō ············· **5**:138a
 Minakami Takitarō ············· **5**:176a
 Minakami Tsutomu ············· **5**:176a
 Mishima Yukio ············· **5**:199a–202a
 Miura Shumon ············· **5**:216a
 Miura Tetsuo ············· **5**:216a
 Miyamoto Yuriko ············· **5**:220a–221a
 Mori Ōgai ············· **5**:251b–252b
 Morita Sōhei ············· **5**:253b
 Murakami Genzō ············· **5**:266a
 Muramatsu Shōfū ············· **5**:266b
 Muroo Saisei ············· **5**:274a–274b
 Mushanokōji Saneatsu ············· **5**:281a–281b
 Nagai Kafū ············· **5**:300a–300b
 Nagai Tatsuo ············· **5**:301b
 Nagatsuka Takashi ············· **5**:307b
 Nagayo Yoshirō ············· **5**:308a
 Nakagawa Yoichi ············· **5**:313a
 Nakajima Atsushi ············· **5**:313b
 Naka Kansuke ············· **5**:314a
 Nakamura Shin'ichirō ············· **5**:315b
 Nakano Shigeharu ············· **5**:316b–317a
 Nakayama Gishū ············· **5**:318b
 Nakazato Kaizan ············· **5**:319b–320a
 Naoki Sanjūgo ············· **5**:330b–331a
 Narushima Ryūhoku ············· **5**:335b
 Natsume Sōseki ············· **5**:349b–351a
 Niwa Fumio ············· **6**:22b–23a
 Nogami Yaeko ············· **6**:30b–31a
 Noma Hiroshi ············· **6**:32b–33a
 Nomura Kodō ············· **6**:34a
 Nosaka Akiyuki ············· **6**:40b
 Oda Makoto ············· **6**:61b
 Oda Sakunosuke ············· **6**:65a
 Ōe Kenzaburō ············· **6**:66a–66b
 Ogawa Kunio ············· **6**:69b
 Ogawa Mimei ············· **6**:70a
 Oguri Fūyō ············· **6**:71b
 Okamoto Kanoko ············· **6**:80a
 Okamoto Kidō ············· **6**:80b

 Ōoka Shōhei ············· **6**:113b
 Osaragi Jirō ············· **6**:123b–124a
 Ozaki Kōyō ············· **6**:139b–140a
 Ozaki Shirō ············· **6**:140a
 Saitō Ryokuu ············· **6**:374b
 Sakagami Hiroshi ············· **6**:375a
 Sakaguchi Ango ············· **6**:375a–375b
 Sata Ineko ············· **7**:25a–25b
 Satō Haruo ············· **7**:26b–27a
 Satomi Ton ············· **7**:27b
 Serizawa Kōjirō ············· **7**:69a
 Setouchi Harumi ············· **7**:71a
 Shiba Ryōtarō ············· **7**:84b
 Shibata Renzaburō ············· **7**:85a
 Shibata Shō ············· **7**:85a
 Shiga Naoya ············· **7**:89b–90a
 Shiina Rinzō ············· **7**:93b–94a
 Shimaki Kensaku ············· **7**:99b
 Shimao Toshio ············· **7**:101a
 Shimazaki Tōson ············· **7**:101a–101b
 Shimozawa Kan ············· **7**:107b
 Shiroyama Saburō ············· **7**:148a
 Shishi Bunroku ············· **7**:148b
 Shōji Kaoru ············· **7**:163a
 Shōno Junzō ············· **7**:167a
 Sono Ayako ············· **7**:228b
 Suzuki Miekichi ············· **7**:282b
 Tachihara Masaaki ············· **7**:293a
 Takahashi Kazumi ············· **7**:312a
 Takami Jun ············· **7**:315a
 Takayama Chogyū ············· **7**:320a
 Takeda Rintarō ············· **7**:322b–323a
 Takeda Taijun ············· **7**:323b
 Takii Kōsaku ············· **7**:326b
 Tamura Taijirō ············· **7**:334a
 Tamura Toshiko ············· **7**:334b
 Tanabe Seiko ············· **7**:335b
 Tanaka Hidemitsu ············· **7**:336b
 Tanizaki Jun'ichirō ············· **7**:342a–343b
 Tayama Katai ············· **7**:358b–359a
 Tōkai Sanshi ············· **8**:42a
 Tokuda Shūsei ············· **8**:44b–45a
 Tokunaga Sunao ············· **8**:58a
 Tokutomi Roka ············· **8**:59b–60a
 Tomita Tsuneo ············· **8**:73a
 Tonomura Shigeru ············· **8**:75a
 Tsuboi Sakae ············· **8**:110a
 Tsubota Jōji ············· **8**:110a
 Tsubouchi Shōyō ············· **8**:110a–111a
 Tsuji Kunio ············· **8**:113b
 Uchida Hyakken ············· **8**:123b
 Umezaki Haruo ············· **8**:147a–147b
 Uno Chiyo ············· **8**:173a
 Yamada Bimyō ············· **8**:288b
 Yamada Tomohiko ············· **8**:289b
 Yamamoto Shūgorō ············· **8**:299a–299b
 Yamamoto Yūzō ············· **8**:300a
 Yamate Kiichirō ············· **8**:307b
 Yoshikawa Eiji ············· **8**:347a
 Yasuoka Shōtarō ············· **8**:312b
 Yokomitsu Riichi ············· **8**:331b–333b
 Yoshiya Nobuko ············· **8**:351a–351b
 Yoshiyuki Junnosuke ············· **8**:351a–352a
Novelists (premodern). *See* Authors
 (premodern)
Novels
 home (katei shōsetsu) ············· **4**:199b
 opinion (kannen shōsetsu) ············· **4**:199a
November Incident
 ············· 十一月事件 ···· **6**:41b–42a
Nozarashi kikō
 ············· 野ざらし紀行 ···· **1**:144a
Nozawa Bonchō · 野沢凡兆 ······· **6**:42a
Nozoe Tetsuo ···· 野副鉄男 · **1**:268b; **6**:42a
Nozomi naki ni arazu (Not
 without Hope)
 ············· 望みなきに非ず ···· **6**:221b

NSK (Japanese Newspaper Publishers and Editors Association) ········ 4:47b
NTN Tōyō Bearing Co, Ltd ········ 6:42a
Nuchi ·································· 6:324b
Nuclear energy ····· 1:114a–114b; 2:216b; 5:353a
　laws ······················· 1:114a–114b
　peaceful use ··············· 1:114a–114b
Nuclear energy policy ·········· 6:42a–43b
　history ·························· 6:42b
　need ··························· 2:191b
　unresolved problems ·············· 6:43a
Nuclear family ··················· 7:208b
Nuclear Non-Proliferation Treaty · 4:386b; 8:154a
Nuclear policy ······· 3:137b; 6:43b–44a
　military ····················· 6:43b–44a
　peaceful ························ 6:44a
Nuclear reactors ················· 2:216b
Nuclear Test Ban Treaty (1963) ········ 6:166b; 8:154a
Nuclear weapons ············· 1:114–115a
Nue ······························ 6:44a
Nuhi ··············· 奴婢 · 1:147b; 6:44a; 7:62a
Nukata no Ōkimi ··· 額田王 ····· 6:44a
　poems in Man'yōshū ········· 5:107a–107b
Nukina Kaioku · 貫名海屋 ········ 6:44b
Numa Morikazu ·沼間守一········ 6:44b
Numata ·········· 沼田 ·········· 6:44b
Numazu ········· 沼津 ·········· 6:44b
Numeral classifiers ············· 2:39a
Nunobiki maru ····· 布引丸 ······ 1:32a
Nunohiki Dam · 布引ダム ········· 2:72b
Nurigome ······················· 7:111a
Nursery songs. See Children's songs
Nurses ····················· 3:119b–120a
Nusa. See Gohei
Nutari no ki ····· 淳足柵 ····· 6:44b–45a
Nu, U ··························· 6:45a
Nyōbō hōsho ··· 女房奉書 ······· 6:45a
Nyōbō kotoba ····· 女房詞 ···· 6:45a–45b
Nyohōzan ········ 女峰山 ········ 6:45b
Nyoirin Kannon ················· 1:188b
Nyokōba ························· 6:45b
Nyonin Kanzeon ················· 5:233a
Nyonin kinzei ··················· 6:45b
Nyorai ·················· 2:64b; 6:45b
　Shinran ······················· 7:123b
Nyoraidō ······ 如来堂 ·········· 1:182b
Nyūan zakki (Miscellaneous Record of a Sexton) ······· 入庵雑記 · 6:139a
Nyūtōzan ········ 乳頭山 ········ 6:45b

O

Oakandake ····· 雄阿寒岳 ····· 6:47a
Oaks [(kashi; nara) Quercus spp.] · 6:47a
Ōama, Prince · 大海人皇子 ····· 4:60a
Ōarai ············ 大洗 ········· 6:47a
Ōashi. See Tageta
Ōatari kyōgen (Successful Plays) · 8:183a
Oats ···························· 8:251a
Ōaza ··························· 5:265b
Ōba Hideo ······ 大庭秀雄 ····· 2:272b
Ōbaiin ·························· 8:172b
Obake ··························· 1:130b

Ōbaku Sampitsu · 黄檗三筆 ······· 1:236a
Ōbaku sect ······ 黄檗宗 ······ 1:179b; 6:47a–47b; 8:371b
　Ingen ························· 3:303b
　Itsunen ······················ 3:357a
　Tetsugen ····················· 8:16a
Ōbakushū ······ 黄檗宗 ····· 6:47a–47b
Obama (city) ····· 小浜 ········ 6:47b
Obama (town) ···· 小浜 ········ 6:47b
Ōban ··········· 大判 ······ 6:47b–48a
Obanazawa ····· 尾花沢 ········ 6:48a
Obara Kuniyoshi 小原国芳 ······ 6:48a
　Shin Kyōiku Undō ············· 7:121b
Obasute ········ 姨捨 ·········· 6:48a
　Fukazawa Shichirō ············ 2:360a
　old age and retirement ·········· 6:99a
Obasuteyama ··· 姨捨山 ····· 6:48a–48b
　obasute ······················ 6:48a
Ōbe Masuo ····· 大邊男 ········ 6:93a
Obi ·············· 帯 ······ 4:308a; 6:48b–49a; 7:87b
Obidome ······················· 4:308a
Obihiro ········· 帯広 ········· 6:49a
Obi iwai ········ 帯祝 ········· 6:49a
Obito ··········· 首 ·········· 4:89a
Obligation, default of ········ 6:49a–49b
Obligations ····················· 6:301a
　human feelings (ninjō) ·········· 3:34b
　social (giri) ··················· 3:34b
Oblomov ······················· 3:44b
Oboe ·························· 3:129b
Ōboke ········· 大歩危 · 6:49a; 7:97b
Ōbora shell mounds 大洞貝塚 ···· 4:75b
Obscenity ··················· 6:49b–50b
　censorship ···················· 1:254a
　freedom of speech ······· 2:338a, 339a
　Japanese Supreme Court ·········· 6:50b
　law today ················· 6:49b–50a
　pictures ······················ 6:50a
　writings ·················· 6:50a–50b
Ōbu ··········· 大府 ·········· 6:50b
Ōbunsha Publishing Co, Ltd ·· 6:50b–51a
Occupation · 2:13b; 6:51a–55b; 7:29a, 58b, 93b; 8:278a
　bureaucracy ··············· 1:218a–218b
　business reforms ··············· 2:34b
　censorship ················ 1:254a–255b
　censorship repeal ·············· 2:339a
　Commercial Code ··············· 1:338a
　conclusion ················ 6:55a–55b
　Constitution, enactment of ········ 2:3b
　Crisis of 1947 ·············· 6:53a–54a
　Crisis of 1950 ·············· 6:54b–55a
　Daitōjuku ····················· 2:68a
　Diet ························· 2:94b
　economic reforms ··········· 6:52b–53a
　economy ················· 2:154a–158a
　educational reforms · 2:180a–180b; 6:53a
　Eichelberger, Robert Lawrence ····· 2:185b
　Far Eastern Commission (FEC) ····· 2:248a
　film censorship policy ··········· 2:271b
　foreign trade regulation ········· 2:314b
　foreign trade restoration ········· 2:320a
　General Strike of 1947 ··········· 3:18b
　general trading companies ········ 3:19a
　imperial ordinance ············· 3:278b
　international relations ··········· 3:324a
　iron and steel industry ·········· 3:334a
　Japanese language reform ········· 4:30a
　labor rights, fundamental ········ 4:359a
　land reforms ············ 4:345b, 364a
　life under ···················· 6:55a
　local government ··········· 5:65b–71a
　MacArthur, Douglas. See MacArthur, Douglas
　Ministry of Finance ············· 5:187a
　Occupation Purge ··············· 6:57b
　Okinawa ······················ 6:88b

Oppler, Alfred C. ··············· 6:115a
Ōsu Incident ··················· 6:128a
　policy and structure ············ 6:51b
　political parties ·········· 6:207a, 211b
　political reforms ············ 6:51b–52b
　political trends ············ 6:54a–54b
　prostitution ··················· 6:257a
　public assistance during ········· 7:210a
　Red Purge ···················· 6:285b
　renunciation of war ············ 6:301b
　Russia and Japan ·············· 6:343b
　San Francisco Peace Treaty · 7:10a–11a
　SCAP during ·················· 7:32b
　science ······················ 5:357a
　Shimoyama Incident ········ 7:107a–107b
　social prejudice ··············· 4:271a
　social reforms ················ 7:211a
　student movements ········ 7:251b–252a
　surrender terms ··············· 6:51a
　technological development ··· 7:369b–370a
　technology transfer ············· 7:374b
　United States economic relations ··· 8:161a
　war criminals ················· 4:273a
　Warner, Langdon ··············· 8:228a
　Willoughby, Charles Augustus ····· 8:253b
　women in ····················· 8:261b
　women's suffrage ·············· 8:268b
　World War II, Japanese society during ···················· 8:278b
Occupational diseases ············ 6:55b
Occupational structure ········ 6:55b–57b
　individual behavior ············· 6:57b
　1920–1940 ···················· 6:56b
　postwar recovery ········· 6:56b–57b
　pre-1920 ················· 6:56a–56b
Occupation-period economy. See Economic history
Occupation Press Code ··········· 1:254a
Occupation Purge ····· 6:57b–58b; 7:86b; 8:344b
Occupations
　lifestyle ······················ 5:8a
　self-employment ··············· 7:60b
Ocean resource development ··· 6:58b–59a
Ochanomizu University ··········· 6:59a
Ochanomizu Women's University · 6:59a
Ochiai Eiji ······ 落合英二 ····· 6:59a
Ochiai Naobumi · 落合直文 ··· 6:59a–59b
Ochi Etsujin ···· 越智越人 ····· 6:59b
Ochikubo monogatari ··· 落窪物語 · 5:34a, 246a; 6:59b–60a
Ochitaru tennyo ··· 堕ちたる天女 ········ 8:289a
Ochiudo legends ················ 6:60a
Ō Chōmei ······· 汪兆銘 ······· 8:222a
Ochūdō ······················· 2:345b
October Incident ················ 6:60a
Octopuses [(tako) order Octopoda] ··· 2:287a; 6:60a–60b; 7:81b
Ōda ············ 大田 ·········· 6:60b
Oda family ······ 織田氏 ····· 6:60b–61a
Odagiri Hideo · 小田切秀雄 ····· 6:61a
　Shin Nihon bungaku ············· 7:122a
Oda Gōichi. 小田剛一 See Takakura Ken
Ōdaigaharasan 大台ケ原山 ······ 6:61a
Odaira Namihei · 小平浪平 ····· 6:61a
Odaishi Sama ··· 御大師様 ····· 4:269b
Odaka Tomoo · 尾高朝雄 ···· 6:61a–61b
Oda Makoto ···· 小田実 · 6:61b; 7:85a
Oda Mikio ····· 織田幹雄 ····· 6:61b
Odani no Kata · 小谷の方 ····· 6:61b
Oda Nobukatsu · 織田信雄 ····· 4:265b
Oda Nobunaga · 織田信長 ····· 1:193a; 6:61b–65a; 7:8a, 14a, 64a, 67a, 84a, 90b–91a, 104a
　abolition of barrier stations ······ 7:57a
　Anegawa, Battle of ············· 1:56a

assassination · · · · · · · · · · · 1:41a; 3:224a
Azuchi Castle · · · · · · · · · 1:126b; 4:146a
Azuchi Disputation · · · · · · 1:126b-127a
campaigns · · · · · · · · · · · · · · · · · 3:178b
chōnin · 1:301a
Christianity · · · · · · · · · · · · · · · · · 5:323a
climax and end of career · · · · · 6:63b-65a
corvée labor · · · · · · · · · · · · · · · · · 1:226b
Enryakuji temple · · · · · · · · 2:220b-221a
feudalism · 2:266a
free markets · · · · · · · · · · · · · · · · · 6:283a
Furuta Oribe · · · · · · · · · · · · · · · · 2:373b
Gamō Ujisato · · · · · · · · · · · · · · · · · · 3:6b
government · · · · · · · · · · · · · · · · · · 3:178b
Honganji vs. · · · · · · · · · · · · 3:221a-222b
Honnōji Incident · · · · · · · · · · · · · 3:224a
Imai Sōkyū · · · · · · · · · · · · · · · · · · 3:273a
Kaihō Yūshō · · · · · · · · · · · · · · · · · 4:110b
Kanemi kyō ki · · · · · · · · · · · · · · · · 4:139b
Kanō Motohide · · · · · · · · · · · · · · · · 6:62b
Komaki developed · · · · · · · · · · · · · 4:265a
Luis Frois · · · · · · · · · · · · · · · · · · · 2:340a
military practices · · · · · · · · · · · · · 2:279a
monasticism · · · · · · · · · · · · · · · · · 5:238b
Nagashino, Battle of · · · · · · · · · · · 5:306a
Nagoya Castle · · · · · · · · · · · 5:309a-309b
provenance and early career · · · · 6:62a-62b
rise to hegemony · · · · · · · · · · · 6:62b-63b
seal of · 7:45b
Shibata Katsuie · · · · · · · · · · · · · · · 7:84b
Shinchō kō ki · · · · · · · · · · · · 7:109a-109b
Shokuhō seiken · · · · · · · · · · · · · · · 7:164b
Odano Naotake
· · · · · · · · · · · 小田野直武 · 6:65a; 7:25b
Oda Sakunosuke
· · · · · · · · · · · · · · · · · 織田作之助 · 6:65a
fūzoku shōsetsu · · · · · · · · · · · · · · 2:378b
Ōdate · · · · · · · · · · · · · · · 大館 · 6:65a
Ōdate Basin · · · · · · 大館盆地 · 6:65a
Oda-Toyotomi regime
· · · · · · · · · · · 織田豊臣政権 · 3:178b
accomplishments · · · · · · · · · · · · · 3:180b
Oda Uraku · · · · · · 織田有楽 · 6:65a-65b
Odawara · · · · · · · · · · · 小田原 · 6:65b
Odawara Campaign
· · · · · · · · · · · 小田原征伐 · 6:65b
firearms usage · · · · · · · · · · · · · · · 2:279a
Fukushima Masanori's role · · · · · · · 2:366b
Keichō kemmon shū · · · · · · · · · · · 4:187b
Sanada Yukimura · · · · · · · · · · · · · · · 7:9a
Toyotomi Hideyoshi · · · · · · · · · · · · 8:95b
Uesugi Kagekatsu · · · · · · · · · · · · · 8:129b
Ukita Hideie · · · · · · · · · · · · · · · · · 8:137b
**OECD (Organization for Economic
Cooperation and
Development)** · · · · · 1:238a; 6:65b
Ōei Invasion · · 応永の外寇 · 6:65b-66a
Ōei Rebellion · · 応永の乱 · 6:66a
Ōe Kenzaburō · 大江健三郎 1:209a; 2:274a;
6:66a-66b; 7:109a
Ōendan · 6:66b
Ōe no Hiromoto · 大江広元 · 6:66b-67a
Ōe no Masafusa · 大江匡房 · 1:151b; 6:67a;
7:72a, 95a
Fujiwara no Michitoshi · · · · · · · · · 2:353a
Gōke shidai · · · · · · · · · · · · · · · · · · 3:43a
Ōe Taku · · · · · · · 大江卓 · 6:67a-67b
Ōeyama · · · · · · · · · 大江山 · 6:67b
Tango Mountains · · · · · · · · · · · · · · 7:341a
Ōeyama emaki 大江山絵巻 · 6:106b
Offenders Rehabilitation Law · · · · · 2:49a
Offerings, Shintō rites · · · · · · · · · 7:138b
Office of Municipal Affairs · · · · · · · 4:185b
Officers, imperial court · · · · · · 1:206a-206b
**Official Development Assistance
(ODA)** · · · · · · · · · · · · · · · 2:308b
Africa · 1:19b
Official documents · · · · · · · · · · · · 4:308b

Official Gazette (Kampō) · · · 6:67b; 8:106a
Offset printing · · · · · · · · · · · · · · · 6:246a
Ofuda · 3:39b
Ofudesaki · 2:82b
Ofukuro · · · · · · · · おふくろ · 7:335b
Ōfunato · · · · · · · · 大船渡 · 6:67b
Ofuregaki · · · · · · · · 御触書 · 6:67b-68a
Ofuregaki Shūsei
· · · · · · · · · · · 御触書集成 · 6:68a
Oga · · · · · · · · · · · 男鹿 · 6:68a
Ōgaki · · · · · · · · · · · 大垣 · 6:68a
Oga Peninsula · 男鹿半島 · 6:68a-68b
Ogasawara family
· · · · · · · · · · · 小笠原氏 · 6:68b
Ogasawara Islands
· · · · · · · · · 小笠原諸島 4:2b, 7a; 6:68b
Ogasawara National Park
· · · · · · · 小笠原国立公園 · 1:272b;
6:68b-69a
Ogasawara school of etiquette · · · 2:258b;
6:69a
Ogasawara family · · · · · · · · · · · · · 6:68b
Ogata Kenzan · 尾形乾山 1:262b; 4:199b,
337a
Ogata Kōan · · · · · 緒方洪庵 · 6:69a
Nagayo Sensai · · · · · · · · · · · · · · · 5:308a
school for Dutch studies · · · · · · · · 2:367b
Ogata Koretomi · 尾形惟富 · 4:292b-293b
Ogata Koreyoshi · 緒方惟準 · 6:69a
Ogata Kōrin · · · 尾形光琳 · 4:292b-293b;
6:153a
Ogata Shinsei · · · · 尾形深省 · 4:199b
Ogata Taketora · 緒方竹虎 · 6:69a-69b
Ogata Tomosaburō
· · · · · · · · · · · 緒方知三郎 · 6:69a; 7:101b
Ogawa Heikichi · 小川平吉 · 6:69b
Ogawa Isshin · · · 小川一真 · 6:184b
Ogawa Kunio · · · 小川国夫 · 6:69b
Ogawa Mimei · · · 小川未明 · 1:279b; 6:70a
Ogawa Mokichi · · 小川茂吉 · 6:70a
Ogawa Shinsuke 小川紳介 · 2:275b
Ogawa Takuji · · · 小川琢治 · 6:70a
Ogawa Usen · · · 小川芋銭 · 4:156b; 6:70a
Ōgi. See Fans
Ogidō · · · · · · · · · · · 荻堂 · 6:85a
Ogidō shell mound
· · · · · · · · · · · 荻堂貝塚 · 6:70a
Ogino Ginko · · · · 荻野吟子 · 6:70a-70b
Ogino Kyūsaku · 荻野久作 · 2:247a; 6:70b
Ogin sama · · · · · · お吟さま · 4:275a
Ogiwara Morie · · · 荻原守衛 · 6:70b; 7:44b
Ogiwara Seisensui
· · · · · · · · · · · 荻原井泉水 · 6:70b
haiku · 3:79b
Ogiwara Shigehide
· · · · · · · · · · · 荻原重秀 · 6:70b
Ogōchi Dam · · · 小河内ダム · 6:71a
Ōgon kamen · · · 黄金仮面 · 2:170b
Ogōri (city) · · · · · · 小郡 · 6:71a
Ogōri (town) · · · · · · 小郡 · 6:71a
Ōgosho · · · · · · · · 大御所 · 6:71a
Oguma Hideo · · · 小熊秀雄 · 6:71a
Ogura hyakunin isshu
· · · · · · · · · · · 小倉百人一首 · 3:248b
Ogura Kinnosuke
· · · · · · · · · · · 小倉金之助 · 6:71a
Ogura Masatsune
· · · · · · · · · · · 小倉正恒 · 6:71a
Ogura Shimpei · 小倉進平 · 6:71b
Ogurayama · · · · 小倉山 · 6:71b
Oguri Eijirō · · · 小栗栄次郎 · 6:71b
Oguri Fūyō · · · · 小栗風葉 · 6:71b; 7:124b
fūzoku shōsetsu · · · · · · · · · · · · · · 2:378b
Oguri Mushitarō
· · · · · · · · · · · 小栗虫太郎 · 6:71b; 7:38b
Oguri Ryōun · · · 小栗了雲 · 3:339b
Oguri Sōtan · · · · 小栗宗湛 · 6:72a
Oguri Tadamasa · 小栗忠順 · 6:72a-72b

Ogyū Sorai · · · · · 荻生徂徠 · 4:247b-248a;
6:72b-73a; 7:281a
education · · · · · · · · · · · · · · · · · · · 2:173b
Forty-Seven Rōnin Incident · · · · · · · 2:327b
Kobunjigaku exponent · · · · · · · · · · 4:239a
Kogaku proponent · · · · · · · · · · · · · 4:246b
Motoori Norinaga's study of · · · · · · · 4:258a
Seidan · 7:49a
Ohachimeguri · · · · · · · · · · · · · · · · 2:345b
Ohajiki · 6:73a
Ōhara · · · · · · · · · · · 大原 · 6:73a
Ōhara Art Museum · · · · · · · · · · · · 5:279a
Ōharae · · · · · · · · · · 大祓 · 3:101a
Ohara Hōun · · · 小原豊雲 · 2:291b
Ōhara Institute for Social Research
· · · · · · · · · · · 5:254b; 6:73b, 305b
Miyagi Tamayo · · · · · · · · · · · · · · · 5:218a
Ōhara Magosaburō · · · · · · · · · · · · · 6:73b
Takano Iwasaburō · · · · · · · · · · · · · 7:317a
Ōhara Magosaburō
· · · · · · · · · · · 大原孫三郎 · 2:294a; 6:73b
Western-art museums · · · · · · · · · · 5:279a
Oharame · · · · · · · · 大原女 · 6:73a
Ōhara Shakai Mondai Kenkyūjo. See
Ōhara Institute for Social Research
Ōhara shakai mondai kenkyūjo
zasshi 大原社会問題研究所雑誌 6:337b
Ōhara Sōichirō 大原総一郎 · 6:73b
Ohara Unshin · · · 小原雲心 · 2:290a
Ōhara Yūgaku · · · 大原幽学 · 6:73b
Ōhashi Sahei · · · 大橋佐平 · 6:73b-74a
Hakubunkan · · · · · · · · · · · · · · · · · 3:87b
Ohayō · · · · · · · · · · · おはよう · 8:146b
Ohbayashi-Gumi, Ltd · · · · · · · · · · 6:74a
Ōhira Masayoshi · 大平正芳 · 2:309b; 6:74a
election · 4:386a
Ōhiroma · · · · · · · · 大広間 · 6:74a
Oichi no Kata · · · お市の方 · 6:61b
Ōichōmage · · · · · · · · · · · · · 7:272a-272b
Ōi Dam · · · · · · · · · 大井ダム · 2:72b
Oie sōdō · · · · · · · 御家騒動 · 6:74a-74b
Ōigawa · · · · · · · · 大井川 · 6:74b
Oikawa Heiji · · · 及川平治 · 6:74b-75a
Shin Kyōiku Undō · · · · · · · · · · · · · 7:121b
Ōi Kentarō · · · · 大井憲太郎 · 6:75a
Freedom and People's Rights Movement
· 2:335a
Fukuda Hideko · · · · · · · · · · · · · · · 2:362a
Ōsaki Incident · · · · · · · · · · · · · · · · 6:121b
Oil, dependence on Middle East
· 5:167a-168a
Oil crisis of 1973 · 2:214b-215b; 6:75a-75b;
7:24a, 204a-204b, 253b
balance-of-trade effects · · · · · · · · · 2:326a
coal · 1:333b
consumer movements · · · · · · · · · · · 2:15a
declining industries · · · · · · · · · · · · · 2:81b
economic effects · · · · · 2:164a-164b, 292b
employment system, effect on · · · · · · 2:34b
IMF and · 3:274b
iron and steel industry · · · · · · · · · · 3:336a
Japanese economy · · · · · · · · · · · · · 1:133b
nuclear energy policy · · · · · · · · 6:42a-44a
personal consumption · · · · · · · · · · · 7:244a
quality control · · · · · · · · · · · · · · · · 6:273b
Sankō Steamship Co, Ltd (Sankō Kisen)
· 7:14b
transportation · · · · · · · · · · · · · · · · 8:99a
wage level · · · · · · · · · · · · · · · · · · · 8:199a
Oil refiners · · · · · · · · · · · · · · · · · · 7:176b
"Oil shock" · · · · · · · · · · · · · · · · · · 6:75a
Oirasegawa · · · 奥入瀬川 · 6:75b; 8:87a
Ōishi Hisatake · · · 大石久敬 · 4:55a
Ōishi Kuranosuke. 大石内蔵助
See **Ōishi Yoshio**
Ōishi Yoshio · · · 大石良雄 · 2:327b; 6:75b
Ōiso · · · · · · · · · · · 大磯 · 6:75b
Ōita · · · · · · · · · · · 大分 · 6:75b

Ōita Plain ········ 大分平野 ···· 6:75b
Ōita Prefecture ···· 大分県 ·· 6:75b-76a;
　　　8:355a
Oiwake ·············· 追分 ···· 2:301b
Ojigi ································ 6:76a
Ōjin, Emperor ···· 応神天皇 ·· 2:287b;
　　　6:76a-76b
　horse-rider theory ········ 3:230a
　Iwashimizu Hachiman Shrine ·· 3:363a
　Keitai, Emperor ············ 4:190a
Ōjin Mausoleum
　　　応神天皇陵 ·········· 6:76b
　Ōsaka Prefecture ·········· 6:122a
Ōji Paper Co, Ltd ···· 2:348b, 359a; 4:83a;
　　　6:77a; 7:86a
Ojiya ·············· 小千谷 ···· 6:77a
Ōjōya ·············· 大庄屋 ···· 5:270a
Ōjōyōshū ········ 往生要集 ·· 1:20a; 3:23b;
　　　6:77a
　nembutsu ················ 5:359b
Oka Asajirō ······ 丘浅次郎 ···· 6:77b
　Esperanto promotion ········ 2:231b
Okabe Kinjirō ···· 岡部金次郎 ···· 6:77b
　electronics ················ 2:192a
Okada Beisanjin
　　　岡田米山人 ·· 1:211a; 6:77b
Okada Eiji ······ 岡田英次 ···· 6:78a
Okada Hankō ···· 岡田半江 ·· 1:211a; 6:78a
Okada Keisuke ···· 岡田啓介 ·· 3:202a;
　　　6:78a-78b; 7:92a
　February 26th Incident ···· 2:249b
Okada Mokichi ···· 岡田茂吉 ···· 6:78b
　Sekai Kyūsei Kyō ·········· 7:56a
Okada Saburōsuke
　　　岡田三郎助 ·········· 6:78b
Okada Takematsu
　　　岡田武松 ·········· 6:78b
Okada Yasui ···· 岡田野水 ···· 6:299b
Okadera ·········· 岡寺 ···· 6:78b
Ōkagami ········ 大鏡 ·· 2:102b; 5:37a,
　　　246a; 6:79a
　Fujiwara no Kintō ·········· 2:352a
　narrative histories ········ 3:153a
Okage mairi ······ 御蔭参り ·· 6:79a-79b
Oka Kiyoshi ······ 岡潔 ···· 6:79b
Okakura Kakuzō ·· 岡倉覚三 ·· 1:154b; 5:12a;
　　　6:79b; 7:270b
　Fenollosa, Ernest Francisco ·· 2:251b
　Hishida Shunsō ·········· 3:151b
　Japan Fine Arts Academy ···· 4:45b
　Kokka founder ············ 4:255b
　Rimpa ···················· 6:318a
　Shimomura Kanzan ········ 7:105b
　Tagore, Rabindranath ······ 7:294b
Oka Masao ········ 岡正雄 ···· 1:120a
　horse-rider theory ········ 3:229b
Okame and Hyottoko ···· 6:80a, 80b
Okamezasa (Shibataea kamasaca) 1:136a
Okami ···················· 7:108a
Ōkami [(wolf) Canis lupus hodophilax]
　　　8:255b-256a
Okamisan ················ 7:273a
Okamoto Kanoko
　　　岡本かの子 ·· 6:80a; 7:71a
Okamoto Kansuke
　　　岡本監輔 ···· 6:80a
Okamoto Keiji ···· 岡本敬二 ···· 6:80b
Okamoto Kidō ···· 岡本綺堂 ···· 6:80b
　kabuki ···················· 4:92a
　radio drama ················ 6:275a
　Tamura Toshiko ·········· 7:334b
Okamoto Kihachi 岡本喜八 ···· 2:274a
Okamoto Toyohiko
　　　岡本豊彦 ···· 6:80b
Okanishi Ichū ···· 岡西惟中 ···· 6:80b
Okano Keijirō ···· 岡野敬次郎 ·· 2:319a;
　　　6:80b-81a
Okashi ·········· をかし ···· 6:81a

Oka Shigeki ········ 岡繁樹 ···· 6:81a-81b
Okauchi Hideo ···· 岡内英夫 ···· 6:81a-81b
Ōkawa ············ 大川 ···· 6:81b
Ōkawabata ········ 大川端 ···· 6:123b
Ōkawa Heizaburō
　　　大川平三郎 ···· 6:81b
Ōkawa Shūmei ···· 大川周明 ···· 6:81b-82b
Okaya ············ 岡谷 ···· 6:82b
Okayama ·········· 岡山 ···· 6:82b
Okayama Astrophysical
　Observatory ·············· 1:104b
Okayama Plain ···· 岡山平野 ·· 6:82b-83a
Okayama Prefecture
　　　岡山県 ···· 6:83b
Okazaki ·········· 岡崎 ···· 6:83b
Okazaki Katsuo 岡崎勝男 ···· 6:83b
Okazaki Kunisuke
　　　岡崎邦輔 ···· 6:83b
Oke ···················· 6:83b
Okegawa ·········· 桶川 ···· 6:83b
Okehazama, Battle of
　　　桶狭間の戦 ···· 6:83b
　Imagawa Yoshimoto ······ 3:272b
　Oda Nobunaga ············ 6:62a
　Takeda Shingen ············ 7:323a
Ōkemi ············ 大検見 ···· 4:191a
Okera (Atractylis ovata) ···· 6:83b
Okhotsk culture ·· 1:160a; 6:83b-84a; 7:30b
Okhotsk Current ················ 6:138b
Okhotsk Sea オホーツク海 ···· 6:84a
Okibumi ·········· 置文 ···· 6:84a
　kakun ···················· 4:118b
Okibutai ···················· 4:93b
Oki Electric Industry Co, Ltd ···· 6:84a
Okigome ···················· 4:117b
Oki Islands ······ 隠岐諸島 ·· 6:84a-84b
Okina ············ 翁 ···· 4:326a
Okina ebisugai ················ 7:81b
Okinaka Shigeo 沖中重雄 ···· 6:84b
Okina mondō (Dialogues
　with an Old Man) · 翁問答 ·· 5:312a-312b
Okina no fumi (Writings of
　an Old Man) ···· 翁の文 ···· 8:71b
Okinawa (Ryūkyū) ·· 沖縄 ·· 6:84a-91a
　agricultural rites ·········· 1:23a
　agricultural productivity ···· 6:86b-87a
　cultural characteristics ······ 6:85a
　dialects ···················· 6:385a
　earliest times to 1945 ···· 6:84b-85a
　early dynasties ············ 6:85b-86a
　economic grievances and protests
　　　6:87b-88a
　financial problems ·········· 6:87a
　Japanese militarism and Pacific War 6:88b
　liberalizing American control ·· 6:90a
　military bases and land issue ·· 6:89a-89b
　military government ········ 6:88b-89a
　postwar ···················· 6:88b
　prehistory ················ 6:85a-85b
　reversion issue ············ 6:90a-91a
　San Francisco Peace Treaty ·· 7:10b
　Satō-Nixon Communiqué ···· 7:28b
　Second Golden Age ········ 6:86a-86b
　sovereignty issue ·········· 6:87a-87b
　taxation ···················· 6:87a
　under dual sovereignty ······ 6:86a
　Western pressures ·········· 6:87a
　World War II ················ 8:276a
Okinawa (city) ···· 沖縄 ···· 6:84b
Okinawa Coast Quasi-National Park
　　　沖縄海岸国定公園 ···· 5:308b
Okinawa culture ················ 3:262a
Okinawa Day ···················· 6:284b
Okinawa Day demonstration of April 28
　university upheavals of 1968-1969 · 8:171b
Okinawa Development Agency
　　　沖縄開発庁 ·· 1:219a; 6:91a
Okinawa Islands · 沖縄諸島 ···· 4:2b; 6:91a

population density ·············· 4:2b
Okinawa issennen shi
　　　沖縄一千年史 ···· 6:88a
Okinawans ···················· 4:35a
Okinawan textiles ·· 2:294a; 6:91a-91b
Okinawa People's Party
　　　沖縄人民党 ···· 7:63a
Okinawa Prefecture 沖縄県 ·· 6:91b-92a
　capital ···················· 5:309b
　Ryūkyū Islands ············ 6:357a
Okinoerabujima
　　　沖永良部島 ···· 6:92a
Okinoshima ······ 沖ノ島 ···· 6:92b
Okinoshima site
　　　沖ノ島遺跡 ···· 6:92b
Okinotorishima ·· 沖ノ鳥島 ·· 4:2b; 6:93a
Ōki Takatō ······ 大木喬任 ···· 6:93a
Ōkita Saburō ···· 大来佐武郎 ·· 2:154b
　economic planning ········ 2:168a
Okitsumiya Shrine
　　　沖津宮 ···· 5:265a
Okitsu Yagoemon no isho
　···· 興津弥五右衛門の遺書 ·· 4:85a
Okiya ···················· 3:14b
Ōkōchi Denjirō
　　　大河内伝次郎 ·· 2:268b; 6:93a
Ōkōchi Masatoshi
　　　大河内正敏 ···· 6:93a-93b
Ō Kokubin ········ 王克敏 ···· 8:222b
Ōkōmori [(flying fox) Pteropus spp.]
　　　1:146b
Ōkubi-e, (close-up bust
　portrait) ········ 大首絵 ···· 8:142b
Ōkubo Hikozaemon
　　　大久保彦左衛門 ···· 6:93b
　Mikawa monogatari ·· 5:170b-171a
Ōkubo Nagayasu
　　　大久保長安 ···· 6:93b
Ōkubo Toshimichi
　　　大久保利通 ·· 1:86b, 150a;
　　　2:30a, 332a; 6:93b-94b; 7:29b, 102a
　Freedom and People's Rights
　Movement ············ 2:334a-334b
　Political Crisis of 1881 ······ 6:202b
　sangi (councillor) ·········· 7:11b
　Seikanron issue ············ 7:50b
Ōkuchi ············ 大口 ···· 6:95a
Oku Chichibu ···· 奥秩父 ·· 1:272a; 6:95a
Okuda Eisen ······ 奥田穎川 ···· 6:95a
Okueshi ···················· 4:149b
Oku Koshō ········ 奥小姓 ···· 4:296a
Ōkuma cabinet ················ 6:95a
Ōkuma Kotomichi
　　　大隈言道 ·· 6:95a-95b
Ōkuma Shigenobu
　　　大隈重信 ···· 2:30a;
　　　5:314a-314b; 6:95b-96b; 7:29a, 66b, 86a,
　　　88a, 99a, 276b
　Freedom and People's Rights
　Movement ················ 2:334a
　Gen'yōsha ················ 3:24b
　Itagaki Taisuke ············ 3:349b
　Itō Hirobumi ·············· 3:353a
　Kenseitō ·················· 4:198b
　naichi zakkyo ············ 5:309b-310a
　Political Crisis of 1881 ······ 6:202a
　Rikken Kaishintō ·········· 6:314b
　Shimpotō ················ 7:108b
　Waseda University ·········· 8:232a
Okumiya Kenshi. See Okumiya Takeyuki
Okumiya Takeyuki
　　　奥宮健之 ···· 6:96b
Oku Mumeo ······ 奥むめお ···· 6:96b
　Shin Fujin Kyōkai ·········· 7:111b
Okumura Corporation ·········· 6:96b
Okumura Ioko ·· 奥村五百子 ·· 6:96b-97a
Okumura Masanobu
　　　奥村政信 ···· 6:97a

Okunchi ········ おくんち ······· 2:258b
Okuni ········ 阿国 · 3:184a; 4:90b; 6:97a
Ōkunimi ········ 大国見 ···· 4:309a
Ōkuninushi no Kami. See Ōkuninushi no Mikoto
Ōkuninushi no Mikoto
········ 大国主命 · 6:97a; 1:149a; 4:125b; 5:293b-294a; 6:97b; 7:73a, 280a
　Izumo Shrine ········ 3:367b
　Kanda Shrine ········ 4:137a
Ōkuni Takamasa 大国隆正 ····· 6:97b
　Fukuba Bisei ········ 2:361b
　Hirata Atsutane's influence ···· 4:259a
Oku no hosomichi (The Narrow Road to the Deep North) ···· 奥の細道 1:145a; 4:179a; 6:297b; 8:104a-104b; 185b
Ōkunojima ········ 大久野島 ··· 6:97b-98a
Ōkura & Co, Ltd ········ 6:98a
Ōkura Commercial School ····· 6:98a
Ōkura Kihachirō
········ 大倉喜八郎 ········ 6:98a
　collections ········ 5:277a
　Hakodate Dock Co, Ltd ···· 3:86a
　Ōkura Museum ········ 5:277a
Ōkura Nagatsune 大蔵永常 ···· 6:98a
Ōkura school ···· 大蔵流 4:325b; 6:98a
Ōkurashō ····· 大蔵省 · 5:186b-188a
Ōkura Toraakira · 大蔵虎明 · 5:15b-16a
Okushiri ········ 奥尻 ····· 6:98b
Oku Tadami Dam
········ 奥只見ダム · 2:73a; 6:98b
Oku Tama ····· 奥多摩 · 1:272a; 6:98b
Oku Tama, Lake · 奥多摩湖 · 1:272a; 8:62b
Ōkyo. 応挙 　See Maruyama Ōkyo
Old age ········ 5:5a
Old age and retirement 4:356a; 6:98b-100a
　family solidarity ········ 6:99b
　obasute ········ 6:48a
　population change ········ 6:98b
　prospects ········ 6:99b-100a
　social services ········ 6:99a-99b
　traditional themes ········ 6:98b
　work ········ 6:99a
Old-Age Welfare Law ···· 6:100a; 7:209b
Old Ash Spreader, The ···· 3:94b
Old Goose Hunter, The ···· 3:94b
"Old Man Who Lost His Wen, The" ········ 4:239b
Old Pine Tree in Snow (Setchū rōshō zu or Sesshōzu) ····· 5:121a
Oligopoly ········ 2:162b-163a
Oliphant, Laurence ······· 5:306b; 6:100a
　Harris, Thomas Lake ········ 3:104b
Olivetti ········ 7:196a
Olympic games ········ 7:243a
　Sapporo Winter Olympic Games · 7:20b
　Tōkyō ········ 8:61b, 353b
Olympus Optical Co, Ltd ········ 6:100a
Ōmachi ········ 大町 · 6:100a-100b
Omaezaki ········ 御前崎 · 6:100b
Ōmagari ········ 大曲 · 6:100b
Omamori ········ 3:39b
Ōmazaki ········ 大間崎 6:100b; 7:105a
Ombashira ········ 御柱 · 7:280b
Ombin ········ 6:100b-101a
Ombu ········ 6:101a
Ōme ········ 青梅 · 6:101a
Ōme Marathon
········ 青梅マラソン · 7:243a
Ōmetsuke ········ 大目付 · 6:101a
Omi ········ 臣 · 4:89a, 310a
　uji-kabane system ········ 8:131b
Ōmi Basin ······· 近江盆地 · 6:101a
Ōmi Code ········ 近江令 ··· 1:151a; 6:101a-101b

Kōgonen-Jaku
　Taika Reform ········ 7:296b
　ritsuryō system ········ 6:331a
Ōmi Hachiman ······· 近江八幡 ······· 6:101b
Ōmi Hakkei (Eight Views of Ōmi) ····· 近江八景 6:101b; 8:184b
Ōmikenshi Co, Ltd ········ 6:101b
Omikuji ········ 6:101b
Ōmi Mission ········ 8:195b
Ominaeshi (Patrinia scabiosaefolia)
········ 6:101b
Ōminesan ········ 大峰山 6:102a; 8:349b
Ōmi no Mifune ···· 淡海三船 · 6:102a
　Kaifūsō ········ 4:109a
Ōmiryō. 近江令 　See Ōmi Code
Ōmi sales ········ 8:195b
Ōmishima (Island, central Inland Sea) ···· 大三島 · 6:102a
Ōmishima (Island, Sea of Japan) ···· 青海島 · 6:102a
Ōmi Shrine ········ 近江神宮 · 6:102a
Ōmiwa Shrine ···· 大三輪神社 · 6:102a-102b, 259b-260a
　tama ········ 7:332a
Ōmiya ········ 大宮 · 6:102b
Omizutori ········ 御水取 · 6:102b
　Tōdaiji ········ 6:102b
Ommitsu ········ 隠密 · 6:102b-103a
Ommyōdō ···· 2:259a; 6:103a, 187a; 8:285a
　kaō ········ 4:156a
　Konjin's origins ········ 4:271b
Ommyōji ········ 陰陽師 · 4:166b
Omogashi, tea ceremony ···· 7:362b-363a
Omogokei ········ 面河渓 · 6:103a
Omoide no ki ···· 思出の記 · 1:155a; 8:59b
Omoide o uru otoko
········ 思ひ出を売る男 ··· 4:169a
Omoigawa (Love Stream)
········ 思ひ川 · 8:173b
Omonogawa ········ 雄物川 · 6:103a
Ōmori Fusakichi ···· 大森房吉 · 6:103a
　earth sciences ········ 2:141a
Ōmori shell mounds
········ 大森貝塚 · 1:75b; 6:103a-103b
Omoro sōshi おもろさうし
　Ryūkyū dialects ········ 6:355b
　Ryūkyū music ········ 6:357b
Omoshiro hambun
········ 面白半分 · 8:328b
Omotedaka ········ 表高 · 6:103a
Omoteeshi ········ 4:149b
Omote Nihon ········ 表日本 · 6:103b
Omoto (Rohdea japonica) · 4:195a; 6:103b
Ōmoto (new religion) 大本教 6:103b-104a; 7:48b, 56a, 76b
　Deguchi Nao ········ 2:82b-83a
　Deguchi Onisaburō ········ 2:83a
　Taniguchi Masaharu ········ 7:341b
Omron Tateisi Electronics Co, Ltd 6:104a
Ōmugaeshi bumbu no futamichi · 4:250a
Ōmugi ········ 8:251a
Ōmura ········ 大村 · 6:104a
Ōmura Bay ········ 大村湾 · 6:104b
Ōmura Masujirō
········ 大村益次郎 · 1:86a, 165a; 6:104b
Ōmura Sumitada 大村純忠 3:184b; 5:306a; 6:104b
　Christian daimyō ········ 1:305b, 306b
Omuro shojaku mokuroku
········ 御室書籍目録 · 3:219a
Ōmuta ········ 大牟田 · 2:365b; 6:104b-105a
On ········ 1:149b; 6:105a
Onagawa ········ 女川 · 6:105a-105b

Ōnakatomi no Yoshinobu
········ 大中臣能宣 · 6:105a-105b; 7:13a
Ōnanjiyama ········ 大汝山 · 7:349b
Onarimon ········ 1:183a
"On a Winter Garden" ········ 8:214a
Onchi Kōshirō · 恩地孝四郎 5:232b; 6:105b
　modern prints ········ 5:232b
Onda Moku ····· 恩田木工 · 6:105b-106a
Onda Takumi ···· 恩田木工 · 6:105b
Onda ware ···· 小鹿田焼 · 6:113a
Ondo Strait ···· 音戸瀬戸 · 6:106a
"One Arm" ········ 4:176b
One-set principle ········ 6:106a
Ongagawa ········ 遠賀川 · 6:106a
Oni ········ 6:106a, 133a
　Ōeyama emaki ········ 6:106b
On'i ········ 2:40b
Onibaba ········ 鬼婆 · 7:111b
Onibi ········ 鬼火 · 8:333a
Oni (devil) plays ········ 4:327b
Ōnie ceremony ···· 大嘗祭 · 2:128b
Oni no ko no uta
········ 鬼の児の唄 ···· 4:138b
Ōnin War ········ 応仁の乱 · 6:106a-107b; 7:19b, 45b, 64a, 84a
　Ashikaga hegemony ········ 6:106b-107a
　economic effects ········ 2:260b
　events ········ 6:107a-107b
　Gozan monasteries ········ 3:58a
　Hatakeyama family ········ 3:111a
　historiography ········ 3:154b
　role of Hino Tomiko ········ 3:141a
　samurai ········ 7:8a
　Shiba family ········ 7:84a
　Shinkei ········ 7:119a
　shōen ········ 7:158a
　shōgun ········ 7:160b
　sociopolitical consequences ········ 2:265a
　succession disputes ········ 6:107a
　textiles ········ 8:18b
　Toki family ········ 8:43a
　Uragami family ········ 8:174b
　warrior government ········ 8:229b
　Yamana family ········ 8:300b
Onioshidashi ········ 鬼押出 · 1:95b; 4:160b; 6:107b
Ōnishi Hajime ········ 大西祝 · 6:107b
Ōnishi hakase zenshū
········ 大西博士全集 ··· 6:107b
Onjōji. 　園城寺 　See Miidera
Onjō shugi ········ 6:165a-165b
Onjuku ········ 御宿 · 6:107b
Onkō, Jiun Sonja
········ 飲光慈雲尊者 ··· 1:179b
Onna (Woman) ········ 女 · 7:44b
Onna daigaku ···· 女大学 · 6:108a; 7:81a; 8:259a, 267a
Onnade ········ 4:133a
Onna-e painting ········ 6:150a
Onnagata (female impersonator) · 2:268a; 4:218b; 6:108a-109b; 7:48b
　development ········ 4:91a
　Hanayagi Shōtarō ········ 3:95a
　makeup ········ 4:95a
　Nakamura Utaemon ········ 5:315b
　Onoe Kikugorō ········ 6:109a-109b
　roles ········ 4:94a
　Sawamura Sōjūrō ········ 7:31a
　shimpa ········ 7:108a
Onnagoroshi abura no jigoku
········ 女殺油地獄 ··· 4:91a
Onnakeizu (Lineage of Women) ········ 婦系図 · 8:289a
Onnakotoba ········ 2:250b
Onna nidai no ki (A Story of Mother and Daughter)
········ 女二代の記 ········ 8:297a

Onna sakusha ···· 女作者 ······· 7:334b
*Onnazaka (The Waiting
  Years)* ············· 女坂 ······· 6:231a
Ono (city, Hyōgo
  Prefecture) ·········· 小野 ······ 6:108b
Ōno (city, Fukui
  Prefecture) ········ 大野 ······ 6:108b
Ono Azusa ······· 小野梓 ····· 6:108b-109a
  Fuzambō ····························· 2:377a
Ōno Bamboku ··· 大野伴睦 ····· 6:109a
Onoda ················ 小野田 ······ 6:109a
Onoda Cement Co, Ltd ·········· 6:109a
  Onoda Hiroo ·· 小野田寛郎 ····· 8:279a
Ōno Dam ········· 大野ダム ····· 6:358a
Onoe Hachirō ··· 尾上八郎 ····· 6:110a
Onoe Kikugorō 尾上菊五郎 ······· 4:92a;
  6:109a-109b
Onoe Matsunosuke
  ·············· 尾上松之助 ····· 2:267b;
  6:109a-109b
Onoe Saishū ··· 尾上柴舟 ····· 6:110a
  Onoe Shōroku ·· 尾上松緑 ····· *4:92b*
Ono ga tsumi ······· 己が罪 ····· 7:107b
Ōnogawa ········· 大野川 ····· 6:110a
Ono-Gumi ········ 小野組 ····· 6:110a
Ōno Harunaga ·· 大野治長 ····· 6:110a
Ōnojō ··············· 大野城 ····· 6:110a
  Ōnojō Castle ······ 大野城 ····· 6:110a
Onomatopoeia ···················· 6:110b
Onomichi ············· 尾道 ····· 6:110b
Ono no Imoko ··· 小野妹子 2:288a; 6:110b;
  7:253a, 260a
Ono no Komachi 小野小町 ·· 6:110b-111a;
  7:13a, 53b, 96b; 8:208b
  Ise ·························· 3:336a
  Kenuki ····················· 4:98a
  Kokinshū ·················· 4:254b
  Rokkasen ·················· 6:334b
Ono no Michikaze. *See* **Ono no Tōfū**
Ononomiya Sanesuke
  ·············· 小野宮実資 ····· 7:179a
Ono no Takamura 小野篁 ··· 6:111a-111b
Ono no Tōfū ··· 小野道風 1:234a; 6:111b
  Fujiwara no Sukemasa ······ 2:355a
Ono Ranzan ··· 小野蘭山 1:155b; 6:111b
Ono Seiichirō ··· 小野清一郎 ··· 6:111b-112a
Ōno Susumu ····· 大野晋 ····· 4:31b
Ono Tōzaburō ··· 小野十三郎 ··· 6:112a
Ō no Yasumaro ·· 太安万侶 ····· 6:112a
  Chinese literature ············ 1:293a
  Kojiki ····················· 4:251a
Ono Yōko ········· 小野洋子 ····· 6:112a
"On Parting from His Wife as He Set Out
  from Iwami for the Capital" ··· 8:206a
On readings ···· 4:57a; 5:324b; 6:112a-112b
  go on ····················· 3:46a
  ideographs ············· 4:143a-143b
  kan on ······················ 4:148a
  nengo ······················ 1:231b
  Shinsen jikyō ············· 7:124b
  tō on ······················ 8:75b
Onryō. See **Goryō**
Onryōken nichiroku
  ·············· 蔭凉軒日録 ····· 1:52b
Onsen. *See* **Hot springs**
Ontake ··············· 御岳 ····· 6:112b;
  259b-260a; 7:48a
Ontakesan ········· 御岳山 ··· 6:112b-113a
Ontake Shrine ··· 御岳神社 ····· 6:112b
Onta ware ········ 小鹿田焼 2:295b; 6:113a
On the Unity of Learning and Culture
  ····························· 1:207b
Ontleedkundige Tafelen ········· 7:258b
Ōnuma ················ 大沼 ····· 6:113a
Ōnuma Chinzan 大沼枕山 ····· 6:113a
On'yōryō ············ 陰陽寮 ··· 6:113a-113b

*Ōoka Echizen no Kami
  Tadasuke nikki*
  ······· 大岡越前守忠相日記 ····· 6:113b
Ōoka Makoto ··· 大岡信 ····· 6:113b
Ōoka seidan ······· 大岡政談 ····· 6:113b
Ōoka Shōhei ··· 大岡昇平 2:274a; 6:113b
Ōoka Tadamitsu 大岡忠光 3:189a; 8:292b
Ōoka Tadasuke · 大岡忠相 ····· 6:113b
Ōoku ·················· 大奥 ··· 6:113b-114a
OPEC, nuclear energy policy ··· 6:42a-44a
Open Door policy ····· 4:366b; 6:114a
  Franco-Japanese Agreement of 1907
  ························· 2:233b
  Roosevelt, Theodore ········· 6:339a
  Russo-Japanese agreements of 1907-
  1916 ··················· 6:344b
  Shandong (Shantung) Question ···· 7:77b
Open guilds ······················· 6:282b
Opening of Japan ········· 6:114a-115a
  consequences ············· 5:155b-156a
  Dutch trade ··············· 2:135b
  international relations ········ 3:320a
  Netherlands ··············· 5:362a
  periodization ·············· 6:176b
  Perry, Matthew Calbraith ····· 6:177b
  technological development ····· 7:368b
Opera. *See* **Music**
Operation Number One ········· 6:115a
Operation Victory ············ 6:115a
Opium ······················ 2:134a
Opium War ················· 6:114b
Oppekepei bushi
  ·············· オッペケペー節 ····· 4:181a
Oppler, Alfred C. ········ 6:115a-115b
Oraga haru ······· おらが春 ····· 6:298a
Ōraimono ············ 往来物 ····· 6:115b
  school textbooks ··········· 7:37b
Oral Folklore ··················· 5:194a
Oranda bōeki. See **Dutch trade**
Oranda chikyū zusetsu
  ·········· オランダ地球図説 ····· 5:355b
Oranda fūsetsugaki
  ·········· オランダ風説書 ··· 6:115b-116a
Oranda honzō wage
  (Dutch Botanicon
  Translated) 和蘭本草和解 ····· 8:242b
Oranda kotohajime 和蘭事始 ····· 6:283b
Oranda Shōgatsu
  ·············· オランダ正月 ····· 6:116a
  Ichikawa Gakusan ········ *6:116b*
Oranda Shōkan
  ·············· オランダ商館 ····· 2:135b
Oranda tsūji オランダ通辞 ····· 6:116a
Orange War ···················· 6:116a
  Rainbow plan ·············· 6:280a
Orashio ·············· オラショ ····· 4:119b
Orashū ··························· 4:119b
Order for the Repelling of Foreign
  Ships ···················· 3:3a-3b
Order of Culture ················· 2:81b
  Andō Hirotarō (1956) ········ 1:55a
  Asakura Fumio (1948) ········ 1:94b
  Nagai Tatsuo (1981) ········· 5:301b
  Nagaoka Hantarō (1937) ········ 5:303b
  Nitta Isamu (1966) ·········· 6:22a
  Nozoe Tetsuo (1958) ········· 6:42a
  Okada Saburōsuke (1937) ····· 6:78b
  Okada Takematsu (1949) ······ 6:78b
  Takagi Teiji (1940) ········· 7:311a
  Takahama Kyoshi (1954) ······ 7:311b
  Tamiya Hiroshi (1977) ········ 7:334a
  Tanakadate Aikitsu (1944) ····· 7:336a
  Tawara Kuniichi (1946) ······· 7:351b
  Yabe Hisakatsu (1953) ········ 8:283a
  Yabuta Teijirō (1964) ········ 8:283b
  Yagi Hidetsugu (1956) ········ 8:283b
  Yamagata Masao (1967) ······· 8:293b
  Yamamoto Yūzō (1965) ······· 8:300a

  Yasuda Yukihiko (1948) ······· 8:318a
  Yasui Sōtarō (1952) ········· 8:318a
  Yasui Takuma (1971) ········· 8:318b
  Yokoyama Taikan (1937) ······· 8:334a
Order of the Golden Kite ···· 2:81b; 4:217a
Order of the Precious Crown ······ 2:81b
Order of the Rising Sun ··· 2:81b; 4:381a
Order of the Sacred Treasure ······ 2:81b
Ordnance Manufacturing Law (1953)
  ························· 1:90b
"Organic Act" ··················· 7:54a
Organization for Economic Cooperation
  and Development (OECD) 2:159b, 175b;
  3:13b, 265a; 4:386b; 6:65b
  Development Assistance Committee
  ························· 2:308b
  Foreign Investment Council ······ 2:316b
  foreign trade ·············· 2:322b
  income distribution ········· 3:285b-286a
  technological assistance codes ···· 2:316a
  United States ·············· 8:162a
Organization for Pacific Trade and
  Development ············ 1:117b-118b
Organized crime ·················· 2:45a
Oribe ware 織部焼 ···· *1:258b*
  See also **Mino ware**
Oriental Development Company ···· 8:93b
Oriental Economic Review, The ··· 1:129a
Oriental Liberal Party ············ 8:91a
Oriental Socialist Party ····· 1:53b; 8:92b
Orient Emigration Company ······ 6:178a
Orient Leasing Co, Ltd ··· 6:116a-116b
Orient Steamship Company ······ 6:179a
Origami ···················· 6:116b-118b
  background ············· 6:116b-118a
  education and art ··········· 6:118b
  making ·················· 6:118a-118b
  outside Japan ·············· 6:118b
  types ···················· 6:118a
  Yoshizawa Akira ··········· *6:116b*
Origami Center of America ······ 6:118b
Orihon ·················· 折本 ····· 1:153a
Orikuchi Shinobu 折口信夫 · 2:296b, 297b;
  5:13b; 6:118b-119a
  Kodai kenkyū ············· 4:240b
Orimposu no kajitsu
  ·········· オリンポスの果実 ····· 7:336b
Oritaku shiba no ki
  ··········· 折たく柴の記 · 1:73a; 3:155a
Ornamental and ritual objects
  beads, ancient ············· 1:147b
Ornamented tombs ···· 4:247a; 6:119a-119b
  chokkomon ················ 1:299b
  fern frond design ··········· 2:252a
Oroshigane (grater) ·············· 2:25a
Orthodox Church. *See* **Holy Orthodox
  Church**
Ōryōshi ·············· 押領使 ····· 6:119b
Osabyakushō ······· 長百姓 ····· 6:119b
Ō Sadaharu ········· 王貞治 ····· 6:119b
Osadamegaki ······· 御定書 ····· 4:318a
Ōsaka ················ 大阪 4:58a; 6:120a
  chōnin class ·············· 1:301b
  Dōtombori ················ *6:119a*
  growth ················· 2:149a-150b
  language ················· 4:24a
  Nakanoshima ············· *6:119a*
**Ōsaka Asahi Hikka
  Incident**
  ······· 大阪朝日筆禍事件 2:338b; 6:120a
  Hasegawa Nyozekan ········· 3:107a
Ōsaka asahi shimbun
  ·········· 大阪朝日新聞 ····· 4:180b, 320a
Ōsaka Bay ········· 大阪湾 ····· 6:120a
Ōsaka Castle ······· 大阪城 ····· 2:375a;
  6:120a-120b; 7:274b
  jōdai ···················· 4:66b
  Kanō Mitsunobu ··········· 4:147b

Kimura Shigenari ············· 4:211b
Ōsaka Prefecture ············· 6:122b
  paintings ·················· 4:151a
  sieges of ·················· 6:120b
  Toyotomi Hideyoshi ········· 4:146a
Ōsaka Cement Co, Ltd ··· 6:120b-121a
Ōsaka Conference of 1875 1:34b; 2:334b;
                                   6:121a
  Assembly of Prefectural Governors 1:103b
  Itagaki Taisuke ·············· 3:349a
  Kido Takayoshi ·············· 4:203a
Ōsaka Dōjima Beikoku
  Torihikisho
    ····· 大阪堂島米穀取引所 ······· 2:127a
Ōsaka Dōjima Komeshō Kaisho
  Dōjima Rice Market ········· 2:127a
Ōsaka Expo '70. *See* **Expo '70**
Ōsaka Gas Co, Ltd ·········· 6:121a
Ōsaka Incident ·· 大阪事件······· 2:336a;
                                   6:121a-121b
Ōsaka International Airport ······ 1:37b
Ōsaka mainichi shimbun
    ········ 大阪毎日新聞 4:265b; 7:279b
Ōsaka Municipal Museum of Fine Arts
    ······························ 6:121b
Ōsaka no Jin. 大坂の陣
  See **Ōsaka Castle, Sieges of**
Ōsaka Plain ····· 大阪平野 ··· 6:121b
Ōsaka Prefecture 大阪府 ·· 6:122a-122b
Ōsaka school ····· 大坂派 ···· 6:123a
Ōsaka School of Foreign
  Languages ·················· 6:123a
Ōsaka Shōsen Kaisha Co ····· 5:270a
Ōsaka Spinning Mill ········ 6:123a
  industrial revolution in Japan ··· 3:298a
Ōsaka tube··················· 2:192a
Ōsaka University ··········· 6:123a
Ōsaka University of Foreign
  Studies ·················· 6:123a
Ōsakayama ····· 逢坂山 ·· 6:123a-123b
Ōsakazuki ·················· 4:180a
Osanai Kaoru ··· 小山内薫 2:268a; 6:123b
  shingeki ··················· 7:112b-113a
  Shinshichō ················ 7:124b
Osaragi Jirō ···· 大仏次郎 ··· 1:164a;
                          6:123b-124a; 7:103b
  contemporary novels ········ 6:123b-124a
  historical novels ············ 6:123b
  other works ················ 6:124a
Ōseidasaresho ··· 被仰出書 ···· 6:124a
  education theory ············ 2:182b-183a
Ō Seiei ········ 汪精衛 ······· 8:222a
Ōsei Fukko ···· 王政復古 ····· 6:124a
  Kogosho Kaigi ·············· 4:249b
Ō Seitei ······ 王正廷 ···· 8:222b-223a
Ōse Jintarō ··· 大瀬甚太郎 ·· 6:124a-124b
Osenkorogashi
    ······ おせんころがし 4:174b; 6:124b
Ōsetsuma ···················· 2:253b; 6:124b
Oshi ·············· 御師 ······ 6:124b
Oshidashibutsu ············· 6:125a
  Amida triad ················ 6:124b
Oshidori ··················· 5:100b-101a
Oshiekata ··········· 教方 ····· 4:119b
Oshika Peninsula 牡鹿半島 ·· 6:125a
Ōshikōchi no Mitsune
    ······· 凡河内躬恒 · 6:125a; 7:13a
  Kokinshū ················· 4:254b
Oshikōji ware ····· 押小路焼 ··· 4:337a
Oshima Fuji ······· 渡島富士 ·· 4:264b
Ōshima Hiroshi ···· 大島浩 ·· 6:125b
Ōshima (island,
  Wakayama Prefecture)
    ···························· 大島 ····· 6:125a
Ōshima (island, western
  Inland Sea) ····· 大島 ··· 6:125b
Ōshima (volcanic island)
    ···························· 大島 ····· 6:125a

Ōshima Nagisa ···· 大島渚 · 2:273b, 275b;
                          6:125b-126a; 7:122a
  obscenity case ·············· 1:255a
Oshima Peninsula
    ············ 渡島半島 ··· 6:126a
Ōshima Ryōta ···· 大島蓼太 ·· 6:126a
Ōshima Sadamasu
    ························ 6:126a
Ōshima Takatō ··· 大島高任 ·· 6:126a
  blast furnace construction ···· 4:120b
  iron and steel industry ······ 3:333b
Oshimodoshi ······· 押戻 ····· 4:98b
Ōshio Chūsai ······ 大塩中斎 ·· 6:126a
Ōshio Heihachirō
    ········· 大塩平八郎 ·······1:141b;
                          6:126a-126b; 8:335a
Ōshū Fujiwara family
    ······· 奥州藤原氏 · 1:189b-190a;
                          6:126b-127a
  Fujiwara no Hidesato ········ 2:350b
  seat
    Hiraizumi ················ 3:143a
  Taira-Minamoto War ········· 7:300b
Ōshū kikō (European
  Travel Diary) · 欧州紀行 ·· 8:333a
Osoreyama ········· 恐山 ····· 6:127a
Osorezan ······· 恐山 · 6:127a; 7:76b,
                                   105a
Osso ··············· 越訴 ····· 4:55b;
                          6:127a-127b
Osso bugyō (commissioner
  of appeals) ····· 越訴奉行 ·· 6:127a
Ostasien 1860–62 ············ 2:235a
Osteoporosis ················ 6:219a
Ostracism. *See* **Murahachibu**
Ōsuga Isao ····· 大須賀績 ··· 6:127b
Ōsuga Otsuji ··· 大須賀乙字 ·· 6:127b
Ōsugi Sakae ···· 大杉栄 · 1:54a, 155a;
                          6:127b-128a; 7:54b, 93b
  Itō Noe ··················· 3:355a
  Kaizō ···················· 4:113b
  Kamichika Ichiko ··········· 4:126a
  murder ···················· 4:125a
  Red Flag Incident ·········· 6:285a
Ōsu Incident ···· 大須事件 ·· 6:128a
Ōsumi Peninsula 大隅半島 ·· 6:128a
Ōsuzumebachi (*Vespa mandarinia
  latilineata*) ················ 1:149a
Ōta ··············· 太田 ····· 6:128a
Ōtabumi ········· 太田文 ···· 4:193a;
                          6:128a-128b
Ōta Dōkan ····· 太田道灌 ···· 6:128b
Ōtagaki Rengetsu
    ········· 太田垣蓮月 ··· 6:128b
Ōtagawa ········ 太田川 ···· 6:128b
Ōtaguro Tomoo
    ········· 大田黒伴雄 ···· 4:58a
Ōtaka Hiroshi ···· 大鷹弘 ·· 8:295b
Ōta Kaoru ······ 太田薫 ···· 6:129a
Ōtake ············ 大竹 ····· 6:129a
Otake Kōkichi ····· 尾竹紅吉 ·· 7:54b
Ōtakineyama ···· 大滝根山 ·· 6:129a
Ōta Nampo ···· 大田南畝 6:129a; 7:79a-79b
  kyōka ···················· 4:332a
  kyōshi ···················· 4:333b
Ōtani University ··········· 6:129a
Otaru ············ 小樽 · 6:129a-129b
Ōta Shokusanjin. 大田蜀山人
  See **Ōta Nampo**
Ōta Sukenaga ····· 太田資長 ·· 6:128b
Ōtaue (rice transplanting festival) 2:254b
Ōtawara ········· 大田原 ···· 6:129b
Ōta Ward ······· 大田区 ···· 6:129b
Ōta Zensai ········ 太田全斎 ·· 4:31b
Ōte ·············· 大手 ···· 1:248a
Otedama ·················· 1:148a
Ōtemmon Conspiracy
    ········· 応天門の変 ··· 6:129b

Fujiwara no Yoshifusa ········ 2:358a
Ōte Takuji ····· 大手拓次 ·· 6:129b
Ō Tō ············ 王韜 ····· 8:222a
Otogi bunko (The Companion
  Library) ····· 御伽文庫 ··· 6:130a
Otogishū ····· 御伽衆 · 6:129b, 282a
Otogi-zōshi ····· 御伽草子 · 2:303a; 5:45a;
                          6:129b-130b; 7:64b
  Ochikubo monogatari ······· 6:59b
  painting ·················· 6:150b
Otoko-e painting ············· 6:150a
*Otoko wa tsurai yo;
  Torajirō wasurenagusa*
  (Hard to Be a Man;
  Tora's Forget-me-not)
    ······· 男はつらいよ 1:115b; 2:275a
Otometsubaki ················ 1:237a
Ōtomo ············ 大友氏 ··· 7:102b
Ōtomo family (fl 8th
  century) ········ 大伴氏 ··· 6:130b
Ōtomo family (fl 12th-16th
  centuries) ······· 大友氏 ·· 6:130b
Ōtomo no Kanamura
    ········· 大伴金村··· 6:130b-131a
  Keitai, Emperor ············ 4:190a
Ōtomo no Kuronushi 大伴黒主 ·· 4:254b
Ōtomo no Miyuki 大伴御行 ···· 1:107a
**Ōtomo no Sakanoue no
  Iratsume** · 大伴坂上郎女 ·· 6:131a
  poems in *Man'yōshū* ···· 5:108a-108b
Ōtomo no Tabito 大伴旅人 · 5:104b-105a;
                          6:131a-131b; 8:206b, 303a
  poems in *Man'yōshū* ······· 5:108a
Ōtomo no Yakamochi
    ········· 大伴家持 ·· 6:131b-132a;
                          7:13a; 8:207a
  Man'yōshū compilation ····· 5:103a
  poems in *Man'yōshū* ······· 5:108b
  sakimori uta ··············· 7:2b
Ōtomo, Prince ··· 大友皇子 ·· 4:60a
Ōtomo Sōrin ···· 大友宗麟 · 6:132a-132b;
                          7:99a-99b
  Christian daimyō ··········· 1:305a
  Luis Frois ················· 2:340a
Ōtomo Yoriyasu · 大友頼泰 ·· 3:329a
Ōtomo Yoshishige
    ········· 大友義鎮 ··· 6:132a
Otona ··········· 乙名 ···· 6:132b
Ōtori Keisuke ··· 大鳥圭介 ·· 6:133a
  Kabo Reforms ·············· 4:281a
Otoshiana (Pitfall)
    ········· おとし穴 ···· 8:15a
Otoshidama ················· 6:133a
Otoshi no kyaku 大歳の客 ·· 6:133b
Ototake Iwazō ···· 乙竹岩造 ·· 6:133b
Otowa Nobuko ···· 乙羽信子 ·· 6:133b
Ōtsu ············ 大津 · 6:133b; 7:90b
  urbanization ··············· 8:176a
Ōtsubo Noboru ····· 7:93b-94a
Ōtsu-e ········· 大津絵 ··· 2:296a;
                          6:133b-134a
  Ki Baitei ·················· 4:201a
  oni ······················ *6:133a*
Ōtsu Incident ··· 大津事件 ·· 6:134a
  Kojima Iken's sentencing ····· 4:251b
Otsuji haironshū
    ········· 乙字俳論集 ··· 6:127b
Otsuji kushū ···· 乙字句集 ·· 6:127b
Otsuji shokanshū
    ········· 乙字書簡集 ··· 6:127b
Ōtsuka Hisao ··· 大塚久雄 ·· 6:134a
Ōtsuki ·········· 大月 ···· 6:134a
Ōtsuki Fumihiko 大槻文彦 · 2:57a, 377a;
                          6:134a-134b
Ōtsuki Gentaku · 大槻玄沢 6:134b; 7:258b
  Kōsei shimpen translator ···· 4:294b
  Rangaku kaitei ············ 6:283b
Ōtsuki Joden ···· 大槻如電 ··· 6:134b

Ōtsuki Nyoden ··········· 大槻如電 ·········· **6**:134b
Ōtsukyahan ··· **4**:323b
Otsuni, Iwama ········· 岩間乙二 ············· **3**:79b
Ōtsu no Miya ········ 大津宮 · **6**:134b-135a
Ōtsu pictures ·································· **6**:133b-134a
Ottama, U ··· **6**:135a
Ottawa Conference (1932) ·········· **8**:152b
Ott, Eugen ··· **6**:135a
Otter ··· **4**:184b
Ottō to yobareru nihonjin ··········· **7**:113a
Ōuchi family ·········· 大内氏 ············· **6**:135a
  Ōuchike Kabegaki ····················· **6**:135b
  Sesshū Tōyō ······························· **7**:69b
  tally trade ································· **7**:332a
Ōuchi Hyōe ········· 大内兵衛 ············· **2**:13b;
                                      6:135a-135b
  Sakisaka Itsurō ························· **7**:3a
Ōuchike Kabegaki
                    大内家壁書 ············· **6**:135b
  Ōuchi family ····························· **6**:135a
Ōuchi Yoshitaka 大内義隆 **6**:135b; **7**:277a
Ōuetsu Reppan Dōmei
                奥羽越列藩同盟 ············· **6**:135b
Ōu Mountains ··· 奥羽山脈 ············· **2**:366b;
                                      6:135b-136a
Ōura Kanetake ···· 大浦兼武 ··········· **6**:136a
  senkyo kanshō ··························· **7**:66b
Our Jungle Road to Tokyo ········· **2**:185b
Outcasts (semmin) ··························· **7**:62a
Outer Gardens of the Meiji Shrine
  Shinjuku Ward ························· **7**:116a
*Outline of a Theory of
  Civilization, An* ····················· **1**:207b
Overseas colonization theory ······· **7**:236b
Overseas Development Company · **6**:178b
**Overseas Economic Cooperation
  Fund** ···················· **6**:136a; **8**:324a
  foreign aid policy ····················· **2**:310a
  international friendship
  organizations ··························· **3**:319b
Overseer ······················ **6**:136a; **7**:254a
Ōwakudani ··········· 大涌谷 ············· **6**:136b
Ōwani ··················· 大鰐 ·············· **6**:136b
Owari Asahi ········ 尾張旭 ·············· **6**:136b
Owari no Kuni ········ 尾張国 ·············· **6**:136b
Owari Province ···· 尾張国 ··········· **6**:136b
*Owarishi michi no shirube
  ni* (Marking the Road I
  Have Come)
            終りし道の標べに ··········· **6**:230b
Owase ··················· 尾鷲 ·············· **6**:136b
Ownership rights ··· **6**:136b-137a, 288a
  abuse ··································· **1**:5b
Ōya ····················· 大家 ·············· **6**:137a
Oyabe ·················· 小矢部 ············· **6**:137a
Oyabun-kobun **2**:243a; **4**:344a; **6**:137a-137b
  "parent-child" relationship ····· **1**:207b
Oyakata ················ **1**:71a-71b; **7**:273a
Oyakata and hikan
              親方, 被官 ············· **6**:137b
Oyakata-kokata. *See* **Oyabun-kobun**
Oya-ko ··· **6**:204b
Oyakodaka ············ 父子鷹 ············· **7**:107b
Ōyama (city) ········· 小山 ·············· **6**:137b
Ōyama (mountain) ··· 大山 ·············· **6**:137b
Ōyama Ikuo ········· 大山郁夫 ········· **1**:313b;
                                      6:137b-138a
Ōyama Iwao ········· 大山巌 ··········· **1**:86b, 87b;
                                      6:138a-138b
Oyama Shrine ··· 雄山神社 ············· **7**:349b
Oyashio ·········· 親潮 **2**:284b; **6**:138b
Oyashirazu ··········· 親不知 ············· **6**:138b
Oyashirokyō ··········· 大社教 ············· **3**:367a
Ōya Sōichi ········· 大宅壮一 ········· **6**:138b
  literary prize ··························· **1**:209b-210a
Oyatoi gaikokujin ·························· **2**:310b-311a
Ōya Tōru ············· 大矢透 ·············· **6**:138b
Ōyodogawa ········· 大淀川 ············· **6**:138b

Ō Yōmei ··············· 王陽明 ············· **8**:335a
Oysters [(magaki) *Crassostrea
  gigas*] ································· **2**:282a
  cultivation ··············· **2**:231b; **7**:266a
Oyudono no Ue no nikki
              御湯殿上日記 ············· **4**:255b
Ōyu stone circles
        大湯環状列石 · **6**:139a, *139a,*
                                      235a
Ozaki Hōsai ········ 尾崎放哉 ·········· **6**:139a
Ozaki Hotsuki ······ 尾崎秀樹 ·········· **6**:139a
Ozaki Hotsumi **6**:139b; **7**:229b
Ozaki Kazuo ········ 尾崎一雄 ·········· **6**:139b
Ozaki Kōyō ········ 尾崎紅葉 · **1**:164a; **5**:11b;
                                      6:139b-140a
  fūzoku shōsetsu ····················· **2**:378b
  "Golden Demon, The" ············· **7**:121a
  Izumi Kyōka ··························· **3**:365b
  Ken'yūsha ······························· **4**:198b
Ozaki Memorial Hall ····················· **6**:140b
Ozaki Shirō ········ 尾崎士郎 ·········· **6**:140a
Ozaki Yukio ········ 尾崎行雄 · **6**:140a-140b
  Kakushin Kurabu ····················· **4**:120a
  Kenseitō ································· **4**:198b
Ozawa Roan ········ 小沢蘆庵 ··· **5**:17a-17b;
                                      6:140b
  Kagawa Kageki ························· **4**:103a
Ozawa Seiji ········ 小沢征爾 ·········· **6**:140b
Ozawa Shigeo ········ 小沢重男 ········· **4**:18b
Oze ····················· 尾瀬 ·············· **6**:*140b*
Ōzeki ··· **7**:272a
Ozeki San'ei ········ 小関三英 ···· **6**:140b-141a
Ōzu ····················· 大洲 ·············· **6**:141a
Ōzu Castle ·········· 大洲城 ············· **6**:141a
Ōzuka tomb ········· 王塚古墳 ·········· **6**:141a
Ozu Yasujirō · 小津安二郎 · **2**:269b-270a;
                    3:102a; **6**:*141a,* 141b-142b
  Shinoda Masahiro ····················· **7**:122a
Umarete wa mita keredo, (I Was Born,
  But . . .) ····························· **8**:146a

P

Pabst, Jean Charles ····················· **6**:143a
Pachinko ··············· **4**:382a; **5**:7b; **6**:*143a*
Pacific Affairs ······························· **3**:316a
**Pacific Basin Economic
  Council** ····························· **6**:143a-143b
  founding ································· **1**:118b-119a
Pacific Economic Committee ······· **4**:188a
Pacific Islands
  Japanese occupation ··········· **7**:235a
  relations with Japan ············· **7**:234b-236a
    diplomatic relations ··········· **3**:322a-322b
    trade ································· **3**:322a-322b
  Southern expansion doctrine · **7**:236a-237a
Pacific Islands Agency ····················· **7**:235b
Pacific Metals Co, Ltd ············· **6**:143b
Pacific Ocean
  earthquakes ······························· **2**:139b
  natural features of Japan ········· **4**:7b
Pacific Painting Society (Taiheiyō
  Gakai) ······················· **4**:175b; **8**:328a, 341a
Pacific plate
  volcanoes ······························· **8**:193b
Pacific War ········· 太平洋戦争 · **3**:202a-202b
  See also **World War II**
Pacifism ····························· **6**:143b-146a
  partisan politics ····················· **6**:145a-145b

  peace research ··················· **6**:145b-146a
  postwar era ······················· **6**:144b-145a
  post-World War I ················· **1**:88a
  prewar development ············· **6**:143b-144b
  United States-Japan security treaties
                                      8:165b
Packhorsemen ··························· **5**:83a-83b
Packhorse service (chūma) ········· **1**:313a
Pact of Paris ·································· **4**:191a
Paddy field remains
  historical ······························· **1**:80a
Paekche ··················· **2**:287b; **6**:146a-146b
  Chinese relations ····················· **6**:146b
  Hakusukinoe, Battle of ············· **3**:89a
  in Korean Three Kingdoms period · **4**:292a
  Japanese relations ····················· **6**:146b
  Kanroku ································· **4**:151b
  language of ······························· **4**:291a
  origins and society ················· **6**:146a
  relations among Korean Kingdoms
                                      6:146a-146b
  religion and culture ················· **6**:146b
Page ··· **4**:296a
Page of Madness, A ····················· **4**:176a
Pagès, Léon ····························· **6**:146b-147a
  works ··································· **6**:146a
Pagoda ······· **3**:*232b*; **5**:*331a*; **6**:147a-147b;
                    8:*285a,* 285b
  architecture ························· **1**:182a-182b
Painters
  Akita
    Odano Naotake ····················· **6**:65a
    Satake Shozan ····················· **7**:25b
  bunjinga
    Aoki Mokubei ····················· **1**:68b
    Buson ································· **1**:224b-225a
    Gion Nankai ······················· **3**:34a
    Ike no Gyokuran ················· **3**:266b
    Ike no Taiga ······················· **3**:267a
    Ki Baitei ····························· **4**:201a
    Nakabayashi Chikutō ··········· **5**:311a-311b;
                                      8:297a
    Okada Beisanjin ················· **6**:77b
    Okada Hankō ····················· **6**:78a
    Rai San'yō ························· **6**:28b
    Tani Bunchō ······················· **7**:341a
    Tanomura Chikuden ············· **7**:344b
    Tazaki Sōun ······················· **7**:359a
    Tomioka Tessai ················· **8**:72a-73a
    Totoki Baigai ····················· **8**:85b
    Tsubaki Chinzan ················· **8**:109b
    Uragami Gyokudō ··············· **8**:175a
    Uragami Shunkin ··············· **8**:175b
    Watanabe Kazan ················· **8**:235b
    Yamamoto Baiitsu ··············· **8**:297a-297b
    Yokoi Kinkoku ··················· **8**:330b-331a
  Chinese
    Itsunen ······························· **3**:357a
    Mokkei ······························· **5**:234a
    Shen Nanpin (Shen Nan-p'in) ····· **7**:83b
  emakimono
    Toba Sōjō ··························· **8**:31b-32a
  English
    Wirgman, Charles ··············· **8**:254b-255a
  French
    Bigot, Georges ··················· **1**:154b-155a
  Hasegawa
    Hasegawa Tōhaku ··············· **3**:108b
  illustrators
    Andō Hiroshige ················· **1**:163b
    Hanabusa Itchō ··················· **3**:92b-93a
    Ishikawa Tairō ··················· **3**:344a
    Kaburagi Kiyokata ··············· **1**:164a
    Katsushika Hokusai ··············· **1**:163b
    Kitagawa Utamaro ··············· **1**:163b
    Suzuki Harunobu ················· **1**:163b
    Takehisa Yumeji ················· **1**:164a; **7**:324a
    Torii Kiyonaga ··················· **1**:163b

ink
Gakuō Zōkyū ············· **3**:4b
Geiami ················· **3**:14a
Gyokuen Bompō ··········· **3**:71a-71b
Hasegawa Tōhaku ··· **3**:108b-109a, *307a*
Josetsu ················ **4**:77b-78a
Kaihō Yūshō ············· **4**:110b
Kameda Bōsai ·········· **4**:124b-125a
Kanō Masanobu ·········· **4**:147b
Kaō Ninga ··············· **4**:156a
Mokkei ················· **5**:234a
Minchō ················· **5**:183b
Mokuan Reien ·········· **5**:235a-235b
Nōami ················· **6**:29b-30a
Oguri Sōtan ············· **6**:72a
Sesshū Tōyō ············· **7**:69b
Sesson Shūkei ············ **7**:70a
Shōkei ················· **7**:163b
Shūbun ··············· **7**:180b-181a
Shūgetsu Tōkan ········· **7**:182b-183a
Sōami ················· **7**:207b
Sōen ················· **7**:219b-220a
Tesshū Tokusai ·········· **8**:15b-16a
Italian
Chiossone, Edoardo ······· **1**:296b
Fontanesi, Antonio ········ **2**:304a
Japanese-style, modern
Dōmoto Inshō ············ **2**:130b
Fukuda Heihachirō ········ **2**:362a
Hashiguchi Goyō ·········· **3**:109b
Hashimoto Kansetsu ······· **3**:110a
Hayami Gyoshū ··········· **3**:115b
Hirafuku Hyakusui ········ **3**:141b-142a
Hishida Shunsō ··········· **3**:151b-152a
Imamura Shikō ··········· **3**:273b
Itō Shinsui ·············· **3**:356a
Kaburagi Kiyokata ········ **4**:100a
Kawabata Ryūshi ·········· **4**:175b
Kawai Gyokudō ·········· **4**:178b
Kobayashi Kokei ·········· **4**:237a
Maeda Seison ············ **5**:80b
Murakami Kagaku ········· **5**:266a
Nakamura Gakuryō ········ **5**:314b
Nishiyama Suishō ········· **6**:20a
Ogawa Usen ············· **6**:70a
Shimomura Kanzan ······· **7**:105a-105b
Takeuchi Seihō ··········· **7**:326a
Terazaki Kōgyō ··········· **8**:13a
Tomita Keisen ··········· **8**:73a
Tsuchida Bakusen ········· **8**:111b
Uemura Shōen ··········· **8**:128a
Yasuda Yukihiko ·········· **8**:318a
Kaihō
Kaihō Yūshō ··········· **4**:110b-111b
Kanō
Hashimoto Gahō ·········· **3**:109b
Kanō Eitoku ············· **4**:146a
Kanō Hōgai ············· **4**:146b-147a
Kanō Masanobu ·········· **4**:147a
Kanō Mitsunobu ·········· **4**:147b
Kanō Motonobu ········· **4**:147b-148a
Kanō Sanraku ············ **4**:148b
Kanō Sansetsu ·········· **4**:148b-149a
Kanō Tan'yū ············· **4**:150b
Kusumi Morikage ········· **4**:320b
Mori Sosen ············· **5**:253a
Kishi
Ganku ················· **3**:7b-8a
Kose
Kose no Kanaoka ·········· **4**:294b
Maruyama-Shijō
Kawabata Gyokushō ······· **4**:175a
Kōno Bairei ············· **4**:272a
Maruyama Ōkyo ········· **5**:121b-122a
Matsumura Goshun ········ **5**:318a
Matsumura Keibun ······· **5**:138a-138b
Mori Kansai ············· **5**:249b-250a
Mori Sosen ············· **5**:253a

Okamoto Toyohiko ········ **6**:80b
Rosetsu ················ **6**:339a
Watanabe Nangaku ······· **8**:236a
nanga
See Painters, bunjinga
nihonga
See Painters, Japanese-style, modern
portraiture
Fujiwara no Nobuzane ····· **2**:353b-354a
Fujiwara no Takanobu ······ **2**:355b
Rimpa
Kenzan ················ **4**:199b
Kōrin ··············· **4**:292b-293b
Sakai Hōitsu ············· **6**:376b
Sōtatsu ················ **7**:232b
Watanabe Shikō ·········· **8**:236a
Soga
Soga Shōhaku ············ **7**:222a
Takuma
Takuma Eiga ············· **7**:327b
Takuma Shōga ··········· **7**:328a
Takuma Tamenari ····· **1**:190a; **7**:328a
Takuma Tametō ·········· **7**:328a
ukiyo-e
Chōkyōsai Eiri ··········· **1**:300a
Furuyama Moromasa ······· **2**:373b
Harunobu ············· **3**:106a-106b
Hiroshige ··············· **3**:148a
Hokusai ··············· **3**:215a-216a
Hosoda Eishi ············· **3**:235b
Ishikawa Toyonobu ········ **3**:345a
Isoda Koryūsai ··········· **3**:347b
Katsukawa Shunchō ······· **4**:171b-172a
Kawanabe Gyōsai ········· **4**:182a
Kobayashi Kiyochika ······ **4**:236b-237a
Miyagawa Chōshun ········ **5**:216b
Nishikawa Sukenobu ······· **6**:17a-17b
Sharaku ··············· **7**:78b-79a
Taiso Yoshitoshi ·········· **7**:306a
Torii Kiyonobu I ·········· **8**:78b-79a
Totoya Hokkei ············ **8**:85b
Utagawa Kunimasa ········ **8**:183a
Utagawa Kunisada ········· **8**:183a
Utagawa Kuniyoshi ········ **8**:183b-184a
Utagawa Toyoharu ········ **8**:184b
Utagawa Toyohiro ········· **8**:184b
Utagawa Toyokuni ········· **8**:184b
Utamaro ··············· **8**:185b-187a
Unkoku
Unkoku Tōgan ··········· **8**:172b-173a
Western-style
Aōdō Denzen ············· **1**:68a
Aoki Shigeru ············· **1**:69a
Asai Chū ··············· **1**:93b
Fujishima Takeji ·········· **2**:345b-346a
Fujita Tsuguharu ·········· **2**:347a
Harada Naojirō ··········· **3**:100b
Hasegawa Roka ··········· **3**:107a-107b
Kawahara Keiga ·········· **4**:177b-178a
Kawakami Tōgai ········· **4**:181b; **8**:327a
Kishida Ryūsei ··········· **4**:223a
Koide Narashige ·········· **4**:250a
Kuniyoshi, Yasuo ········· **4**:310a
Kuroda Seiki ············· **4**:314b
Mitsutani Kunishirō ······· **5**:214a
Nakamura Fusetsu ········· **5**:314b
Okada Saburōsuke ········· **6**:78b
Sakamoto Hanjirō ········· **6**:378a
Takahashi Yuichi ·········· **7**:313b
Umehara Ryūzaburō ······· **8**:146b
Wada Eisaku ············· **8**:197b
Yamaguchi Kaoru ········· **8**:294b
Yamamoto Hōsui ········· **8**:298a
Yasui Sōtarō ············· **8**:318b
yamato-e
Iwasa Matabei ··········· **3**:362b-363a
Matsuoka Eikyū ·········· **5**:139a

Reizei Tamechika ········· **6**:289b
Zen
Fūgai Ekun ············· **2**:341b
Hakuin ················· **3**:88a
Sengai Gibon ············ **7**:63b
Takuan Sōhō ············· **7**:327b
Painting ············· **6**:147b-158b
Amanohashidate ·········· **6**:152b
Ban Dainagon ekotoba (Picture Story of
the Courtier Ban Dainagon) ······· **6**:152a
Beauties beneath Trees (juka bijin) ··· **6**:149a
bird-and-flower ··········· **1**:156a-156b
Black Cat ··············· **6**:157a
bunjinga school ··········· **1**:210a-211a
Chinese influence ·········· **7**:167b
Diamond realm mandala ······· **6**:150b
dōshakuga ··············· **1**:192a
Engeki zukan ············· **6**:155b
esoteric Buddhist ·········· **1**:188b-189a
Fudō Myōō ············· **6**:151a
haboku ················· **1**:193a
handscrolls (emakimono) ····· **2**:198a-200a
Heiji monogatari ekotoba (Tale of Heiji
scrolls) ··············· **6**:152a
Hishida Shunsō ············ **6**:157a
Hishikawa Moronobu ········ **6**:155b
Illustrated Sutra of Cause and Effect
(E inga kyō) ············· **6**:149a
Imamura Shikō ··········· **6**:158b
ink painting ······ **1**:192a; **3**:305b-307b
Iris Screens (Kakitsubatazu) ···· **6**:154a-154b
Italian influence ··········· **3**:350b
Kanō Naganobu ··········· **6**:155a
Kanō Sanraku ············· **6**:153a
Kiyomizudera engi (Legends of
Kiyomizudera) ··········· **6**:153b
Kōrin ················· **6**:154a-154b
Kuroda Seiki ············· **6**:156b
latter-day Buddhist ········· **1**:193a-194b
Mahāyāna Buddhist ········· **1**:185a-187a
emakimono ············· **1**:186b-187a
Merrymaking under the Cherry Blossoms
··············· **6**:155a
modern ················ **6**:155a-158b
Shōwa period ··········· **6**:157b-158b
Taishō period ··········· **6**:156a-157b
Musō Soseki ············· **6**:152b
Mutō Shūi ··············· **6**:152b
nanga. See **Bunjinga**
Nekkoku no maki (The Tropics) ······ **6**:158b
premodern ·············· **6**:147b-148a
Azuchi-Momoyama and
Edo period ············· **6**:151b-155a
Buddhist ··············· **6**:148a-149b
ink ················· **6**:150b-151b
scroll ················· **6**:149b-150b
Pure Land Buddhist ········· **1**:189b-191a
raigōzu ·············· **1**:190a; **6**:151b
schools
Ami school ············· **1**:52b-53a
Kanō school ············ **4**:149a-151a
Maruyama-Shijō school ···· **5**:122a-122b
Rimpa ················ **6**:317a-318a
Takuma school ·········· **7**:328a
Sesshū Tōyō ············· **6**:152b
screen and wall ··········· **7**:41a-43b
subjects ················ **6**:158b-159a
suibokuga ··············· **1**:192a
Tamamushi Shrine ········· **6**:148b
Tanomura Chikuden ········ **6**:155a
Tosa Mitsunobu ··········· **6**:153b
Umehara Ryūzaburō ········ **6**:156b
wall painting ············· **6**:148b
Western-style (yōga) ······ **8**:327a-328b
yamato-e ··············· **6**:309b
early ················· **8**:248b-249a
Yokoyama Taikan ·········· **6**:157a
Yoshiwara ·············· **6**:155b

Yunazu · **6:**155a
Zen · · · · · · · · · · · **1:**192a–194a; **8:**374b–375b
Painting Appreciation Society · **4:**150b
Painting subjects · · · · · · · · **6:**158b–159a
  bird-and-flower painting (kachōga)
    · **6:**158b–159a
  figure painting (jimbutsuga) · · · · · · · **6:**158b
  landscape painting (sansuiga) · · · · · **6:**158b
Pak Chŏng-hŭi · · · · · · · · · · · · · · · · **6:**159a
Pak Chong-sŏk v. Hitachi, Ltd · · · · **4:**291b
Pakutari no saiban
  朴達の裁判 · · · · · · · · **4:**211a
Pak Yŏl · · · · · · · · · · · · · · · · · **6:**159a–159b
  plot · **6:**159a
Pak Yŏng-hyo · · · · · · · · · · · · · · · · **6:**159b
  Japanese visit · · · · · · · · · · · · · · · · · **4:**280b
  Kaehwap'a · **4:**101b
  Kapsin Political Coup · · · · · · · · · · · · **4:**156b
Palace Guards. *See* **Efu**
Paleolithic culture · · · · · · · **6:**159b–160a
  artifacts · **4:**153b
  Iwajuku site · · · · · · · · · · · · · · · · · · **3:**358a
Paleolithic period · · · · · · · · · · · · **6:**160a
Paleontological Society of Japan · **2:**329a
Paleontology · · · · · · · · · · · · · · · · · **2:**328a
  cenozoic · **2:**329a
  development · · · · · · · · · · · · · · · · · · **2:**328a
  mesozoic · **2:**328b
  paleozoic · **2:**328b
Palisades (ki) · · · · · · · · · · · · · · · · · · **1:**246b
Pallada · **6:**270b
Palmistry · **6:**160b
Palms
  Cycas revoluta · · · · · · · · · · · · · · · · **7:**233a
Pan American Treaty on Tropical
  Tuna · · · · · · · · · · · · · · · · · · · **2:**282b–283a
Pan-Asianism · · · · · · · **1:**164b; **6:**160b–161a;
    7:51b; **8:**144b
  Amur River Society · · · · · · · · · · · · · · **1:**53b
  nationalism · · · · · · · · · · · · · · · · · · · **5:**343b
  United States · · · · · · · · · · · · · · · · · · **8:**156a
  World War II · · · · · · · · · · · · · · · · · · **8:**272a
Panay Incident
  · · · · · · · · · · · パネー号事件 · **6:**161a–161b
Panē gō Jiken. *See* **Panay Incident**
Pan no Kai (Pan Society)
  · · · · · · · · · · · · · · · パンの会 · **5:**18b; **6:**161b;
    8:346b
Paper · · · · · · · · · · · · · · · · · · · **8:**232b–234a
  book · **1:**153b
  marbled design techniques · · · · · · · **7:**266b
  pattern technique · · · · · · · · · · · · · · **7:**280b
  traditional furniture material · · · · · **2:**371b
Paper, hand-made. *See* **Washi**
Paper and pulp industry
  Daishōwa Paper Mfg Co, Ltd · · · **2:**67b
  Honshū Paper Co, Ltd · · · · · · · · · · **3:**240a
  Jūjō Paper Co, Ltd · · · · · · · · · · **4:**83a–83b
  Ōji Paper Co, Ltd · · · · · · · · · · · · · · **6:**77a
Paperback books · · · · · · · · · · · · · · **6:**162a
  major series · · · · · · · · · · · · · · · · · · · **6:**162a
Paper balloons · · · · · · · · · · · · · · · **6:**162a
Paper-folding
  origami · · · · · · · · · · · · · · · · · **6:**116b–118b
"Paper Lining of the Sliding Doors of
  a Four-and-a-Half-Mat Room" · · · **8:**328b
Paper mill · **8:**233a
Paper Museum · · · · · · · · · · · · · · · · **6:**162a
Papier-mâché · · · · · · · · · · · · · · · · · · **2:**371b
Pardon · · · · · · · · · · · · · · · **2:**49a; **6:**162a–162b
Pardon Law of 1947 · · · · · · · · · · · · · **6:**162b
Parental power · · · · · · · · · · · · · · · · **6:**162b
Parent and child, legal
  definition of · · · · · · · · · · · · **6:**162b–163a
  adoptive · **6:**163a
  illegitimacy · · · · · · · · · · · · · · · · · · · **6:**163a
  legitimate · · · · · · · · · · · · · · · · **6:**162b–163a
  recorded and nonexistent · · · · · · · · **6:**163a

rights and obligations · · · · · · · · · · · · **6:**163a
Parenticide · · · · · · · · · · · · · · · **6:**163a–163b
Parhae · · · · · · · · · · · · · · · · · · · **1:**159b–160a
Paris Exposition of 1878 · · · · · · · · · **4:**182a
Paris Peace Conference · · · · · · · · · · **4:**367b
  United States · · · · · · · · · · · · · · · · · · **8:**157a
  Versailles, Treaty of · · · · · · · · · · · · **8:**190b
Parkes, Sir Harry Smith · · **1:**175b; **4:**372b;
    6:163b–164a
  French-Japanese relations · · · · · · · · **2:**331b
  Satow, Ernest Mason · · · · · · · · · · · · **7:**29a
  Shimonoseki Bombardment · · · · · · **7:**106a
Parlor · **6:**124b
Parole · **6:**172a
Parties himachi and tsukimachi · · · **3:**139a
Partnership · · · · · · · · · · · · · · · **6:**164a–164b
Pasture lands, regulation · · · · · · · · · **5:**85a
Patent agent · · · · · · · · · · · · · · · · · · · **1:**16a
Patent Law of 1959 · · · · · · · · **6:**164b–165a
Patent Office · · · · · · · · · · · · · · · · · · · **3:**297a
Patents, Design Law · · · · · · · · · · · · · **2:**91a
Paternalism · · · · · · · · · **6:**165a–165b; **7:**213b
  "closed" employment systems · · · · · **4:**344b
  job tenure · **4:**357a
  managerial ideology · · · · · · · · · **5:**91b–92a
Paternity suit · · · · · · · · · · · · · · · · · · **6:**163a
Pathologists
  Katsurada Fujio · · · · · · · · · · · · · · · · **4:**172a
  Kiyono Kenji · · · · · · · · · · · · · · · · · · **4:**232b
  Ogata Tomosaburō · · · · · · · · · · · · · · **6:**69b
  Tawara Sunao · · · · · · · · · · · · · · · · · **7:**351b
  Yamagiwa Katsusaburō · · · · · · · · · · **8:**294a
  Yoshida Tomizō · · · · · · · · · **8:**346a–346b
Patrimonial rule
  ritsuryō system · · · · · · · · · · · · · · · · **6:**322a
Patriotic Association for Japanese
  Literature · **5:**379a
Patriotic Labor Party · · · · · · · · · · · · **7:**108a
Patriotic Women's Association · · · · · **1:**34a;
    6:165b
Patriotism · **6:**165b
Patron-client system · · · · · · · · · **4:**343b–344a
Patterns of Culture · · · · · · · · · · · · · **4:**39a
Pauley, Edwin Wendell **6:**165b–166a, 302b;
    7:250b
Paulownia [(kiri) *Paulownia tomentosa*]
    2:371b; **6:**166a
Pavlova, Anna · · · · · · · · · · · · · · · · · · **2:**75b
Pawnbrokers · · · · · · · · · · · · · · · · **2:**148a–148b
Pawning · **7:**87a
Peabody Museum · · · · · · · · · · · · · · · **5:**256a
Peace for Vietnam Committee · · · · **6:**166a
  Oda Makoto · · · · · · · · · · · · · · · · · · · **6:**61b
  peace movement · · · · · · · · · · · · · · · · **6:**167a
Peace Memorial Park · · · · · · · **3:**149a, 149b
Peace movement · · · · · **1:**111a; **6:**166a–167b
  Anti-Nuclear-Bomb Movement
    · · · · · · · · · · · · · · · · · · · **6:**166a–166b
  Anti-Security-Treaty Movement
    · · · · · · · · · · · · · · · · · · · **6:**166b–167a
  Vietnam and Okinawa Movement
    · · · · · · · · · · · · · · · · · · · **6:**167a–167b
  women in · **8:**263b
"Peace police" · · · · · · · · · · · · · · · · · **7:**241a
Peace Preservation Law of 1887 · **1:**252b;
    6:167b
  Daidō Danketsu Movement · · · · · · · **2:**56a
  Freedom and People's Rights
    Movement · · · · · · · · · · · · · · · · · · **2:**336a
  Kishida Toshiko · · · · · · · · · · · · · · · · **4:**223a
  Kiyoura Keigo · · · · · · · · · · · · · · · · · **4:**233a
  Nakae Chōmin · · · · · · · · · · · · **5:**311b–312a
  Nakajima Nobuyuki · · · · · · · · · **5:**313b–314a
  Sandai Jiken Kempaku Movement
    (Movement to Memorialize Three
    Important Items) · · · · · · · · · · · · · · · · **7:**9b
Peace Preservation Law of 1925 · **1:**253a;
    2:337b–338a; **3:**198b; **4:**339a, 345b, 378a;

    6:168a–169b; **6:**266a; **7:**229a, 242a, 251b,
      254a
  democracy · **2:**84b
  fundamental liberties limitation · · · · **2:**369b
  Kakushin Kurabu · · · · · · · · · · · · · · · **4:**120a
  Kawakami Hajime · · · · · · · · · · · · · · **4:**181a
  Kenseikai · **4:**198a
  kokutai discussed · · · · · · · · · · · · · · · **4:**263b
  March 15th Incident · · · · · · · · · · · · · **5:**113a
  Planning Board Incident · · · · · · · · · · **6:**189b
  Taishō democracy · · · · · · · · · · · · · · · **7:**305a
  Tanaka Giichi · · · · · · · · · · · · **7:**336a–336b
  "Thought Criminal" Probation Law · **8:**29a
  Tosaka Jun · **8:**81b
  United States · · · · · · · · · · · · · · · · · · **8:**157b
  Wakatsuki Reijirō · · · · · · · · · · · · · · · **8:**218b
  Yokohama Incident · · · · · · · · · · · · · · **8:**330a
"Peach Boy" · · · · · · · · · · · · · · · **5:**296a–296b
Peaches (*Prunus persica*) · · · · · · · · **6:**169b
Pearl Harbor, attack on · · · **6:**169b; **8:**273a
  Genda Minoru · · · · · · · · · · · · · · **3:**17a–17b
  Grew, Joseph Clark · · · · · · · · · · · · · · **3:**62a
  Roosevelt, Franklin Delano · · · · · · · **6:**339a
  United States · · · · · · · · · · · · · · · · · · **8:**159a
Pearl industry · · · · · · · · · · · · · · · · · · **1:**21b
Pearls · · · · · · · · · · · · **2:**287a; **6:**169a, 169b–170a
  classification · · · · · · · · · · · · · · · · · · **6:**170a
  commercial production · · · · · · · · · · · **6:**170a
  composition · · · · · · · · · · · · · · · · · · · **6:**170a
  cultivation · **7:**266a
  cultured · **6:**169b
  formation · · · · · · · · · · · · · · · · **6:**169b–170a
  freshwater · **6:**170a
  shellfish · **6:**169b
Pears [(nashi) *Pyrus serotina*] · · **6:**170a
Peasant Family beneath a Hanging
  Gourd Trellis · · · · · · · · · · · · · · · · **4:**320b
Peasant landholders (hombyakushō)
    · **4:**362b
Peasant leagues. *See* **Tsuchi ikki**
Peasant protest · · · · · · · · · · · · · · · · · **8:**337b
Peasants · **3:**217a
  hyakushō · · · · · · · · · · · · · · · · **3:**249a–249b
  rebellions
    ikki · **3:**268b
    rōnin · **6:**336b
Peasant uprisings · · · · · · · · · · · **2:**107b–108a
Pecuniary sanctions · · · · · · · · · · · · · · **2:**49a
Peel Island · · · · · · · · · · · · · · · · **1:**272a–272b
Peerage · · · · · · · · · · · · · · **6:**170a–172b; **7:**151a
  abolition · **6:**171b
  adoption · · · · · · · · · · · · · · · · · **6:**170a–170b
  court ranks · · · · · · · · · · · · · · · · **2:**39b–41a
  historical evolution · · · · · · · · · · · · · **6:**170b
  House of Peers · · · · · · · · · · · · **6:**171a–171b
  Meiji Restoration · · · · · · · · · · · **6:**170b–171a
  Occupation · **6:**52a
  Peerage Act of 1884 · · · · · · · · · · · · · **6:**171a
  shi-nō-kō-shō · · · · · · · · · · · · · · · · · · **7:**122b
Peerage Act · **6:**171a
Peerage rights · · · · · · · · · · · · · · · · · · **4:**362b
Peers' School (Gakushūin) · · **1:**5a; **4:**82b;
    6:171a
Peiron boat race · · · · · · · · · **5:**304a; **6:**171b
Peiron Festival · · · · · · · · · · · · · · · · · · **1:**37b
Penal Code · **2:**339a
Penal sentences
  death · **2:**48b
  incarceration · · · · · · · · · · · · · · · **2:**48b–49a
  pecuniary sanctions · · · · · · · · · · **2:**48b–49a
Penal system · · · · · · · · · · **2:**45b; **6:**171b–172b
  contemporary · · · · · · · · · · · · · **6:**172a–172b
  capital punishment · · · · · · · · · · · · · · **6:**172b
  juvenile offenders · · · · · · · · · · · · · · · **6:**172a
  number of offenses · · · · · · · · · · · · · · **6:**172a
  parole · **6:**172a
  prison terms · · · · · · · · · · · · · · · · · · · **6:**172b
  prosecution · · · · · · · · · · · · · · · · · · · **6:**172b

exile (entō) ···················· **2:**222a
history ···················· **6:**171b–172a
premodern
banishment ·············· **1:**137b
Peninsulas
Atsumi ···················· **1:**115b
Bōsō ······················ **1:**165b
Chita ······················ **1:**297b
Higashi Matsuura ·········· **3:**132a
Izu ························ **3:**367b
Kii ························ **4:**205a
Kunisaki ·················· **4:**310a
Miura ···················· **5:**215b–216a
Nemuro ···················· **5:**360a
Nishi Sonogi ·············· **6:**19a–19b
Noto ······················ **6:**41b
Oga ···················· **6:**68a–68b
Oshika ···················· **6:**125a
Oshima ···················· **6:**126a
Ōsumi ···················· **6:**128a
Satsuma ·················· **7:**29b
Shakotan ·················· **7:**75a
Shima ···················· **7:**101a
Shimabara ················ **7:**98b
Shimane ·················· **7:**100b
Shimokita ················ **7:**105a
Shiretoko ················· **7:**147b
Tsugaru ·················· **8:**113a
Pensions ············ **6:**172b–173a
development ·············· **7:**210b
national ·················· **6:**173a
Onkyū system ············ **6:**172b
private ···················· **6:**172b
public ···················· **6:**172b
railroad workers ·········· **6:**172b
retirement plans ········ **6:**99a, 307a
social security ············ **6:**173a
Penta-Ocean Construction Co, Ltd
···················· **6:**173b
Peonies [(botan; shakuyaku)
family Ranunculaceae] ····· **6:**173b–174a
People's Cooperative Party ······· **4:**260b
**People's Council to Prevent the Security
Treaty Revision** ··········· **6:**167a
People's Finance Corporation ···· **6:**174a;
7:204b
People's Party (Kokumintō) ······ **4:**260b
People's Republic of China
postwar relations ·········· **1:**290a
Pēpābakku ················ **6:**162a
Perfect Liberty, The Church of. *See* **PL
Kyōdan**
Periodicals, censorship of ········ **1:**253a
Periodization ············ **6:**174a–177b
dating system ············ **6:**174b–175a
"national era" ············ **6:**175a
nengō (imperial name era) ······ **6:**174b
60-year cycles ············ **6:**174b–175a
sovereign reign ············ **6:**175a
historiographical ········· **6:**175a–177a
conceptual systems ······· **6:**176a–176b
era systems ············ **6:**175a–176b
European models ········ **6:**176b
jidai (epoch, age, period) ··· **6:**175b–176a
scholarly debates over ····· **6:**176b–177a
Permanent Court of International
Justice ·················· **4:**373a
Perry, Matthew Calbraith ··· **2:**64a; **6:**177a,
177b–178a; **7:**3b, 8b, 86a
bureaucratic development ···· **1:**217b
end of Tokugawa regime ···· **3:**192a–192b
imperial rule ·············· **2:**205b
Kanagawa Treaty ···· **2:**331a; **4:**135a, 140b
Nakahama Manjirō ·········· **5:**313a–313b
National Seclusion ········ **5:**346b–347b
Opening of Japan
daimyō response ········ **5:**155b–156a
Persecution, religious ·········· **6:**294b

Persecutions at Urakami (Urakami
kuzure) ···················· **6:**178a
Persimmons (*Diospyros kaki*) ····· **6:**178a
"Personal collections" (shikashū) · **8:**204a
Personal field allotment ··········· **4:**301a
Personal names ··········· **5:**324b–325a
kana ···················· **5:**325a
Personal suretyship ······· **6:**178a–178b
Personification, waka ············· **8:**203b
Personnel
foreign firms ·············· **2:**318a
training ·················· **2:**318a
Person without capacity ·········· **6:**178b
Peru, diplomatic ties ············· **4:**369b
Peru and Japan ··········· **6:**178b–179b
Japanese immigrants ········· **6:**178b–179a
Maria Luz Incident ·········· **6:**178b
World War II ·············· **6:**178b
PETA Army ················ **6:**179b
Petrochemical industry ········· **1:**267b;
6:180a–180b
companies
Kanegafuchi Chemical Industry Co, Ltd
···················· **4:**137b
Mitsubishi Petrochemical Co,
Ltd ················ **5:**208b–209a
Mitsui Petrochemical Industries,
Ltd ·················· **5:**212a
Sekisui Chemical Co, Ltd ········ **7:**57b
energy revolution ·············· **2:**214b
Petrochemicals, manufacturers ···· **7:**173a
Petroleum ········ **5:**353a; **6:**180a–182a
alternatives ················ **6:**181a
conservation ·············· **6:**181a
consumption ·············· **6:**181a
imports ················ **6:**180b–181a
production ··············· **6:**181b–182a
products ················· **6:**181a
Petroleum industries
Arabian Oil Co, Ltd ········· **1:**71b–72a
Daikyō Oil Co, Ltd ·········· **2:**60b–61a
Esso Standard Oil Co, Ltd ········· **2:**231b
Fuji Kōsan Co, Ltd ·········· **2:**343b
General Sekiyu ············ **3:**18a–18b
Idemitsu Kōsan Co, Ltd ······ **3:**258b–259a
Kōa Oil Co, Ltd ············ **4:**234b
Kyōdō Oil Co, Ltd ·········· **4:**324a
Maruzen Oil Co, Ltd ········· **5:**122b
Mitsubishi Oil Co, Ltd ········· **5:**208b
Mobil Sekiyu ·············· **5:**228a
Nippon Mining Co, Ltd ········ **6:**11a
Nippon Oil Co, Ltd ·········· **6:**11b
Shell Oil Co, Ltd ··········· **7:**83a–83b
Shōwa Oil Co, Ltd ·········· **7:**176b
Teikoku Oil Co, Ltd ········· **7:**376a–376b
Tōa Nenryō Kōgyō ·········· **8:**30b
Phaeton Incident
フェートン号事件 **1:**211b; **6:**182a
Doeff, Hendrik ············ **2:**123a
National Seclusion ·········· **5:**347b
Phan Boi Chau ········ **2:**53a; **6:**182a
Pharmaceutical industry ········· **5:**150a;
6:182a–182b
companies
Eisai Co, Ltd ············ **2:**187b
Fujisawa Pharmaceutical Co, Ltd · **2:**345b
Kanebō, Ltd ·············· **4:**137b
Sankyō Co, Ltd ············ **7:**15a
Shionogi & Co, Ltd ·········· **7:**141a
Takeda Chemical Industries, Ltd
···················· **7:**321b–322a
Tanabe Seiyaku Co, Ltd ········ **7:**335b
Pharmacists in health care system **3:**120a
Pharmacognosists. *See* Honzōgaku
Pharmacognosy ················ **1:**155b
Pharmacologists
Asahina Yasuhiko
···················· **1:**93a

Nagai Nagayoshi ············ **5:**301a
Tawara Yoshizumi ·········· **7:**351b
Pharmacopoeia of Japan ········ **6:**182b
Pheasants [(kiji; yamadori) family
Phasianidae] ·············· **6:**182b
Phenylthiocarbamide ·········· **4:**36b–37a
Phibul Songkhram ·········· **6:**183a; **7:**65b
Philip Jaisohn
Independence Club ········· **4:**281b
Philippine Executive Commission · **6:**184a
Philippines and Japan ········ **6:**183a–184b
before 1898 ············ **6:**183a–183b
Japanese-Philippine Trade
(1899–1941) ············ **6:**183b–184a
postwar relations ·········· **6:**184b
wartime relations ·········· **6:**184a–184b
Philippine Sea, Battle of ········ **5:**307b;
6:184b–185a
Philosophers
Aizawa Seishisai ············ **1:**38a
Andō Shōeki ············ **1:**55b–56a
Ban Nobutomo ············ **1:**141b
Dazai Shundai ············ **2:**80b
Fujita Tōko ··············· **2:**347a
Fujiwara Seika ············ **2:**358b–359a
Hasegawa Nyozekan ········· **3:**107a
Hashimoto Sanai ·········· **3:**110a–110b
Hatano Seiichi ············ **3:**112b
Hayashi Razan ············ **3:**117a–117b
Hisamatsu Shin'ichi ········· **3:**151b
Inoue Tetsujirō ············ **3:**311a
Ishida Baigan ············ **3:**339a–340a
Itō Jinsai ················ **3:**354a
Itō Tōgai ················ **3:**356a
Iwashita Sōichi ············ **3:**363a–363b
Jien ···················· **4:**53b–54a
Kaibara Ekiken ············ **4:**108a–108b
Kameda Bōsai ············ **4:**124b–125a
Kanō Kōkichi ·············· **4:**147a
Kawakami Hajime ·········· **4:**107b–181a
Kihira Tadayoshi ··········· **4:**204b
Kuki Shūzō ··············· **4:**304b
Kumazawa Banzan ·········· **8:**335b
Kuwaki Gen'yoku ·········· **4:**322a
Maruyama Masao ··········· **5:**121b
Miki Kiyoshi ·············· **5:**171a
Miura Baien ············ **5:**214b–215a
Mori Arimasa ············· **5:**248b
Muro Kyūsō ············ **5:**271a–271b
Mutai Risaku ············ **5:**287b–288a
Nakae Tōju ··············· **8:**335b
Nakamura Hajime ·········· **5:**314b–315a
Ninomiya Sontoku ·········· **6:**7a–8a
Nishi Amane ············ **6:**14a–14b
Nishida Kitarō ············ **6:**14b–15b
Nishimura Shigeki ········· **6:**17b–18b
Ogyū Sorai ··············· **6:**72b–73a
Oka Asajirō ··············· **6:**77b
Okakura Kakuzō ············ **6:**79b
Ōkuni Takamasa ············ **6:**97b
Ōnishi Hajime ············· **6:**107b
Ōshio Heihachirō ·········· **6:**126a–126b
Rai San'yō ··············· **6:**280b–281a
Saigusa Hiroto ············ **6:**366a–366b
Sakuma Shōzan ············ **7:**3b–4a
Shibukawa Shunkai ········· **7:**86a
Sugiura Shigetake ·········· **7:**258b
Suzuki Shōsan ············ **7:**283a–283b
Tachibana Shiraki ·········· **7:**293a
Takahashi Satomi ·········· **7:**313a
Tanabe Hajime ············ **7:**335a–335b
Tanaka Ōdō ··············· **7:**338a–338b
Teshima Toan ············· **8:**15a–15b
Tosaka Jun ··············· **8:**81b
Tsuda Sōkichi ············· **8:**112b
Watsuji Tetsurō ············ **8:**237b
Yamaga Sokō ············ **8:**290a–290b
Yamagata Bantō ··········· **8:**292a–292b

Yamakawa Hitoshi · · · · · · · · · · 8:296a-297b
Yamazaki Ansai · · · · · · · · · · · · 8:312a-312b
Yanagi Muneyoshi · · · · · · · · · · · · · · 8:314a
Yokoi Shōnan · · · · · · · · · · · · · · 8:331a-331b
Yoshida Shōin · · · · · · · · · · · · · 8:345b-346a
Yoshino Sakuzō · · · · · · · · · · · · 8:348b-349a
Philosophy
  comprehensive dialectical whole · · · 7:313a
  Confucianism · · · · · · · · · · · · · 1:352b-358b
  emptiness · · · · · · · · · · · · · · · · 2:212b-213a
  ethics · · · · · · · · · · · · · · · · · · · 2:232a-232b
  existentialism · · · · · · · · · · · · · · · · · 2:236b
  Marxist · · · · · · · · · · · · · · · · · · 5:231a-232a
  modern · · · · · · · · · · · · · · · · · · 5:229b-232a
  wakon yōsai (Japanese spirit, Western
    knowledge) · · · · · · · · · · · · · · · · · · 8:221a
Philosophy of law · · · · · · · · · · · · · · · · 4:85b
Phoenix Hall (Hōōdō) · · · · · · · · · · · · 1:226b
Phonetics. See Japanese language
Phonics, Ryūkyū dialects · · · · · · · 6:355a-357a
Phonorecord · · · · · · · · · · · · · · · · · · 6:354b
Photographers
  Ishimoto Yashuiro · · · · · · · · · · · · · 6:186b
  Kimura Ihei · · · · · · · · · · · · · · · · · · 6:185a
  Nojima Kōzō · · · · · · · · · · · · · · · · · 6:185a
  Ogawa Isshin · · · · · · · · · · · · · · · · · 6:184b
Photography · · · · · · · · · · · · · · · 6:185a-186a
  industry companies
    Asahi Optical Co, Ltd. · · · · · · · · · 1:93a
    Canon, Inc. · · · · · · · · · · · · · · · · · 1:239b
    Nippon Kōgaku · · · · · · · · · · · · · · 6:10a
    Olympus Optical Co, Ltd · · · · · · · 6:100a
    Ricoh Co, Ltd · · · · · · · · · · · · · · · 6:311b
  19th century · · · · · · · · · · · · · · 6:185a-185b
    professional photographers · · · · · 6:185b
    Shimazu Nariakira · · · · · · · · · · · 6:185a
    studios · · · · · · · · · · · · · · · · · · · 6:185b
    techniques · · · · · · · · · · · · · · · · 6:185b
  20th century · · · · · · · · · · · · · · 6:185b-186a
    artistic or salon photography
      · 6:185b-186a
    eizō or personal vision · · · · · · · · 6:186a
  wartime · · · · · · · · · · · · · · · · · · · 6:186a
Physical education · · · · · · · · · · 4:10a; 7:35b
Physically Handicapped Welfare Law of
  1949 · · · · · · · · · · · · 6:186a-186b; 7:209b
  investigation · · · · · · · · · · · · · 6:186a-186b
  rehabilitation · · · · · · · · · · · · · · · · 6:186a
  technical guidance · · · · · · · · · · · · 6:296a
Physicists
  Esaki Reona · · · · · · · · · · · · · · · · · 2:231a
  Honda Kōtarō · · · · · · · · · · · · · · · · 3:219a
  Ishiwara Jun · · · · · · · · · · · · · · · · · 3:345a
  Kaya Seiji · · · · · · · · · · · · · · · · · · 4:185a
  Kikuchi Seishi · · · · · · · · · · · · · · · 4:207a
  Kubo Ryōgo · · · · · · · · · · · · · · · · · 4:300b
  Nagaoka Hantarō · · · · · · · · · · · · · 5:303a
  Nakaya Ukichirō · · · · · · · · · · · · · · 5:319b
  Nishikawa Shōji · · · · · · · · · · · · · · · 6:17a
  Nishina Yoshio · · · · · · · · · · · · · · · · 6:18b
  Sakata Shōichi · · · · · · · · · · · · · · · 6:379b
  Terada Torahiko · · · · · · · · · · · · · · · 8:11a
  Tomonaga Shin'ichirō · · · · · · · · · · · 8:73a
  Yukawa Hideki · · · · · · · · · · · · · · · 8:356b
Physics · · · · · · · · · · · · · 3:133a; 6:186b-187a
Physiognomy · · · · · · · · · · · · · · 6:187a-187b
Physiologists
  Katō Gen'ichi · · · · · · · · · · · · · · · · 4:167b
  Katsuki Yasuji · · · · · · · · · · · · · · · 4:172a
  Kuno Yasu · · · · · · · · · · · · · · · · · · 4:310b
  Shibata Keita · · · · · · · · · · · · · · · · · 7:84b
  Tamiya Hiroshi · · · · · · · · · · · · · · · 7:334a
Physiology · · · · · · · · · · · · · · · · · · · 1:156a
Physiology of Human Perspiration, The
  · 4:310b
Physique · 4:37a
Piccadilly · · · · · · · · · · · · · · · · · · · 6:100a
Pickles · · · · · · · · · · · · · · 2:52b; 6:187b

Picture brides · · · · · · · · · · · · 6:187b-188a
  Hawaii · 4:16a
  Japanese American · · · · · · · · · · · · · 4:14a
  Japanese Associations of America · · · 4:22a
Picture scrolls. See Emakimono
Piggott, Francis Stewart · · · · · · · · · 6:188a
Pilgrimages · · · · · 1:194b; 6:188a-188b, 291a
  gankake · 3:7b
  Ise Shrine · · · · · · · · · · · · · · · 3:338a-339a
  prayer · 6:233a
Pillow Book. See Sei Shōnagon
Pillow words · · · · · · · · · · · · · · · 5:87b-88a
Pimiko · 3:139b
Pine and Hawk · · · · · · · · · · · · · · · · 4:150a
Pines [(matsu) Pinus spp.] · · · · · · 2:326b;
                                         6:188b-189a
Pines on a Beach · · · · · · · · · · · · · · 4:111a
Pine Trees · · · · · · · · · · · · · · · · · · · 3:108b
Ping-Pong. See Table tennis
Pinku · 2:275a
Pioneer Electronic Corporation · · · 6:189a
Pipe organs · · · · · · · · · · · · · · · · · 6:9b-10a
Pirates · · · · · · · · · · · · · · · · · · 8:220a-221a
Pit houses 1:78a; 4:72b; 6:189a-189b; 7:30b
  Hiraide site · · · · · · · · · · · · · · · · · · 3:143a
  Iba site · 3:253b
  Karako site · · · · · · · · · · · · · · · · · · 4:157b
  shell mounds · · · · · · · · · · · · · · 7:82b-83a
  Toro site · · · · · · · · · · · · · · · · · · · 6:189a
Pittosporum. See Tobera
Place names · · · · · · · · · · · · · · 5:326a-326b
  administrative · · · · · · · · · · · · 5:326a-326b
  Chinese · · · · · · · · · · · · · · · · · 5:326a-326b
  geographical · · · · · · · · · · · · · 5:326a-326b
  historical · · · · · · · · · · · · · · · · 5:326a-326b
Plain castle (hirajiro) · · · · · · · · · · · 1:247b
Plains
  Hokkaidō
    Ishikari · · · · · · · · · · · · · · · · · · · 3:342a
    Sarobetsu · · · · · · · · · · · · · · · · · · 7:22a
    Teshio · 8:15b
    Tokachi · · · · · · · · · · · · · · · · · · · 8:40a
  Honshū
    Akita · 1:42b
    Fukui · 2:363b
    Himeji · · · · · · · · · · · · · · · · · · · 3:139a
    Hiroshima · · · · · · · · · · · · · · · · · 3:149a
    Ise · 3:337b
    Izumo · 3:367a
    Kanazawa · · · · · · · · · · · · · · · · · 4:136a
    Kantō · 4:153b
    Kurayoshi · · · · · · · · · · · · · · 4:312a-312b
    Matsue · · · · · · · · · · · · · · · · · · · 5:133a
    Niigata · · · · · · · · · · · · · · · · · · · 5:385b
    Nōbi · 6:30a
    Noshiro · · · · · · · · · · · · · · · · · · · 6:41a
    Okayama · · · · · · · · · · · · · · · · 6:82b-83a
    Ōsaka · 6:121b
    Sendai · 7:63b
    Shizuoka · · · · · · · · · · · · · · · · · · 7:153b
    Shōnai · · · · · · · · · · · · · · · · · · · 7:166a
    Tonami · 8:73b
    Tottori · 8:86a
    Toyama · 8:88b
    Tsugaru · · · · · · · · · · · · · · · · · · · 8:113a
    Wakayama · · · · · · · · · · · · · · · · · 8:219b
  Kyūshū
    Fukuoka · · · · · · · · · · · · · · · · · · 2:364b
    Kumamoto · · · · · · · · · · · · · · · · · 4:305b
    Miyazaki · · · · · · · · · · · · · · · · · · 5:221b
    Ōita · 6:75b
    Tsukushi · · · · · · · · · · · · · · · · · · 8:115a
  Shikoku
    Kōchi · 4:239b
    Matsuyama · · · · · · · · · · · · · · · · · 5:141b
    Sanuki · 7:18b
    Tokushima · · · · · · · · · · · · · · · · 8:58b-59a
Planning Board Incident · · · · · · · · · 6:189b

Planning Board (Kikakuin) · · · · · · · 1:8a-8b
Plant breeding · · · · · · · · · · · · · · · · · 1:30a
Plant Communicable Disease
  Control Law · · · · · · · · · · · · · · · · · 6:274a
Plant conservation · · · · · · · · · · · · · 6:192a
Plant crops. See Agriculture
Plant diseases · · · · · · · · · · · · · · · · · 1:30b
  rice · 6:310a
Plant export · · · · · · · · · · · · · · · · · 6:190a
Plant hopper (unka) · · · · · · · · · · · · 6:190a
Plants · · · · · · · · · · · · · · · · · · 6:190a-192a
  folklore · · · · · · · · · · · · · · · · · · · 6:191b
  garden flowers · · · · · · · · · · · · · · · 6:192a
  in literature · · · · · · · · · · · · · · · · · 6:191a
  in visual arts · · · · · · · · · · · · · 6:191a-191b
  modern Japan · · · · · · · · · · · · · · · 6:192a
  protected · · · · · · · · · · · · · · · 5:352a-352b
  religion · · · · · · · · · · · · · · · · 6:191b-192a
  trees and shrubs · · · · · · · · · · · · · 6:192a
  types · · · · · · · · · · · · · · · · · · 6:190a-191a
    endemic species · · · · · · · · · · 6:190a-191a
    floricultural · · · · · · · · · · · · · · · · 6:191a
    naturalized · · · · · · · · · · · · · · · · 6:191a
    plant distribution zones · · · · · · · 6:190a
  uses · 6:191a
  wild flowers · · · · · · · · · · · · · · · · 6:192a
Playing cards · · · · · · · · · · · · · 6:192a-192b
Play therapy · · · · · · · · · · · · · · · · · 6:261b
Playwrights
  Abe Kōbō · 1:3b
  Akimoto Matsuyo · · · · · · · · · · · · · · 1:42a
  comic
    Shibuya Tengai · · · · · · · · · · · · · · 7:86b
    Soganoya Gorō · · · · · · · · · · · · · · 7:221b
  French
    Claudel, Paul Louis Charles · · · · · 1:325a
    Fujimori Seikichi · · · · · · · · · · · · · 2:343b
    Inoue Hisashi · · · · · · · · · · · · · · · 3:309b
  kabuki
    Chikamatsu Monzaemon · · · · · · · 1:276a
    Mokuami · · · · · · · · · · · · · · 5:234b-235a
    Okamoto Kidō · · · · · · · · · · · · · · · 6:80b
    Sakurada Jisuke · · · · · · · · · · · · · · · 7:4a
    Segawa Jokō · · · · · · · · · · · · · · · · 7:48b
    Tsuruya Namboku · · · · · · · · · · · · 8:117b
  Kawaguchi Matsutarō · · · · · · · · · · · 4:177b
  Kikuchi Kan · · · · · · · · · · · · · · · · · 4:206b
  Kinoshita Mokutarō · · · · · · · · · · · · 4:215b
  Kishida Kunio · · · · · · · · · · · · · · · · 4:222b
  Koyama Yūshi · · · · · · · · · · · · · · · · 4:298b
  Kume Masao · · · · · · · · · · · · · · · · · 4:307b
  Mafune Yutaka · · · · · · · · · · · · · · · · 5:82b
  Mayama Seika · · · · · · · · · · · · · · · · 5:142a
  Morimoto Kaoru · · · · · · · · · · · 5:250a-250b
  Murayama Tomoyoshi · · · · · · · · · · · 5:270b
  Nō
    Kan'ami · · · · · · · · · · · · · · · · · · · 4:135b
    Kanze Motomasa · · · · · · · · · · · · · 4:154b
    Kanze Nobumitsu · · · · · · · · · · · · · 4:154b
    Komparu Zenchiku · · · · · · · · · · · 4:267b
    Zeami · · · · · · · · · · · · · · · · · 8:369a-369b
  puppet theater (bunraku) · · · · · · · · 1:214a
    Chikamatsu Hanji · · · · · · · · · · · · 1:274b
    Chikamatsu Monzaemon · · · · · · · 1:214a,
                                         275a-276a
    Namiki Sōsuke · · · · · · · · · · · · · · 5:327a
  radio
    Kikuta Kazuo · · · · · · · · · · · · · · · 4:207a
    Kinoshita Junji · · · · · · · · · · · 4:214b-215b
    Kubota Mantarō · · · · · · · · · · 4:301a-301b
    Tanaka Sumie · · · · · · · · · · · · · · · 7:339a
    Uchimura Naoya · · · · · · · · · · · · · 8:125a
  Tanaka Chikao · · · · · · · · · · · · · · · 7:335b
  theater
    Hōjō Hideji · · · · · · · · · · · · · 3:211a-211b
    Iizawa Tadasu · · · · · · · · · · · · · · · 3:264a
    Kara Jūrō · · · · · · · · · · · · · · · · · · 4:157b
    Katō Michio · · · · · · · · · · · · · · · · 4:169a

Kikuta Kazuo ·············· 4:207a
Kinoshita Junji ·········· 4:214b-215b
Kubo Sakae ················ 4:301a
Kubota Mantarō ·········· 4:301a-301b
Osanai Kaoru ·············· 6:123b
Shimamura Hōgetsu ···· 7:99b-100a
Terayama Shūji ·········· 8:12b-13a
Tsubouchi Shōyō ········ 8:110a-111a
Yamamoto Yūzō ·········· 8:300a
Yamazaki Masakazu ········ 8:312b-313a
Yashiro Seiichi ············ 8:317a
Plea bargaining ·············· 6:172b
Pleasure quarters, popular
  fiction ················ 7:79b-80a
PL Kyōdan ·········· 5:171b; 6:192b
Plovers [(chidori) family Charadriidae]
  ···························· 6:192b
Plum, Japanese [(ume) Prunus mume]
  ···················· 6:192b-193b
Plum and Pine Discourse, The
  ···················· 1:130a-130b
Plural suicide ·············· 7:262a
Poetic Memoirs of Lady
  Daibu, The ·········· 4:197b-198a
Poetry ···················· 5:13b-14a
  chōka ················ 1:299a-299b
  early Japanese song ········ 2:137a-138b
  haiku ················ 3:78a-82a
  imperial anthologies ········ 3:275b
  kanshi ················ 6:193b-197b
  kyōka ················ 4:331b-332a
  kyōshi ················ 4:333a-333b
  modern ················ 5:56a-57b
  renga ················ 6:296b-300a
  senryū ················ 8:368b
  tanka ················ 7:343b
  waka ················ 8:201b-217a
  zappai ················ 8:368a
Poetry, Bureau of ············ 3:52a
  Ōnakatomi no Yoshinobu ···· 6:105a
Poetry and prose in Chinese ····· 4:109a;
                              6:193b-197b
  general ················ 6:193b
  history ················ 6:193b-195b
  Ishikawa Jōzan ············ 3:342b
  method and forms ········ 6:195b-197b
"Poetry Contest at the Residence of the
  Minister of Public Affairs" ······· 8:209b
Poetry Contest in Six
  Hundred Rounds ······ 4:1b, 198b; 5:40b
Poetry contests ············ 8:209b
Poetry match ·············· 8:182a-182b
Poetry, modern. See Literature
Poets
  haiku. See Haiku poets
  modern
    Anzai Fuyue ·············· 1:68a
    Doi Bansui ·············· 2:126a-126b
    Hagiwara Sakutarō ·········· 3:76a-76b
    Horiguchi Daigaku ·········· 3:227b
    Hori Tatsuo ·············· 3:228a
    Itō Shizuo ·············· 3:356a
    Kambara Ariake ············ 4:123a
    Kaneko Mitsuharu ·········· 4:138b-139a
    Kawaji Ryūkō ·············· 4:179b
    Kinoshita Mokutarō ·········· 4:215b
    Kitagawa Fuyuhiko ·········· 4:224b
    Kitahara Hakushū ············ 4:225a
    Kusano Shimpei ············ 4:319a
    Miki Rofū ·············· 5:171b
    Miyazawa Kenji ·········· 5:222b-223b
    Miyoshi Tatsuji ·········· 5:224a-224b
    Murano Shirō ·········· 5:266b-267a
    Nishiwaki Junzaburō ·········· 6:19b-20a
    Ōoka Makoto ·············· 6:113b
    Saijō Yaso ·············· 6:369b
    Satō Hachirō ·············· 7:26b
    Senke Motomaro ············ 7:66b

Susukida Kyūkin ············ 7:279b
Tachihara Michizō ············ 7:293a
Takahashi Mutsuo ············ 7:312b
Takahashi Shinkichi ············ 7:313a
Takamura Kōtarō ·········· 7:315b-316b
Ueda Bin ················ 8:126b-127a
Yagi Jūkichi ·············· 8:284a
Yamamura Bochō ············ 8:300a
Yosano Akiko ·············· 8:340a
renga. See Renga poets
tanka. See Tanka poets
waka. See Waka poets
Po-hai. See Bohai (Po-hai)
Poisoning ················ 5:148b-149a
Poland, Japanese studies ·········· 4:43b
Police, criminal investigation ······ 2:49b
Police box (kōban) ············ 6:200b
Police Duties Law of 1938 ········ 2:49b
Police Offenses Penal Regulations 5:196a
Police system ·············· 6:198a-201a
  administration (keimu) ·········· 6:200a
  brutality ················ 6:200b
  community relations ·········· 6:200a-201a
  counselors ················ 6:200b
  crime prevention (bōhan) ········ 6:200a
  criminal investigation (keiji) ······ 6:200a
  historical development ······ 6:198a-198b
  neighborhood association (chōnaikai)
                              6:200b
  police officers ·············· 6:200a
  present structure ·········· 6:198b-199b
  riot police (kidōtai) ·········· 6:200a
  security (kōan) ·············· 6:200a
  specializations ·········· 6:199b-200a
  traffic (kōtsū) ·············· 6:200a
  traffic safety ·············· 6:200b
Political asylum ·············· 6:201a
Political cliques ·············· 6:165a
Political commentary ············ 7:119a
Political concepts ············ 3:15b-16a
Political corruption ············ 6:201a-202a
  history ················ 6:201b
  postwar ················ 6:201b-202a
  prospects for reducing ·········· 6:202a
Political Crisis of 1881 ········ 4:113a;
                      6:202a-203a; 7:92b, 99a
Political culture ············ 6:203a-207a
  continuities and changes ····· 6:206a-207a
  emperor ················ 6:203b-204a
  hara, kan, newaza ·········· 6:205b-206a
  kenryoku (political power) ········ 6:206a
  political parties, cliques, and
    factions ················ 6:205b
  power ················ 6:203a-203b
  pragmatism ·············· 6:206a
  public ················ 6:205a-205b
  state ················ 6:204b-205a
  yokubō shizen shugi (Doctrine
    of Natural Desire) ·········· 6:204a-204b
Political Ethicization Movement (Seiji
  Rinrika Undō) ·············· 8:117a
Political Fund Control Law ········ 4:386a
Political Fund Regulations Law ···2:337b
Political groups, right-wing
  extremists ·············· 7:176b-177a
Political memorandum ············ 7:337b
Political movements, Marxist
  student ················ 7:251a-253a
"Political novel" ············ 7:50a-50b
Political parties ············ 6:207a-213a
  Diet (1890–1898) ············ 6:207b-210a
    Jiyūtō ················ 6:207b, 210a
    Shimpotō ·············· 6:207b, 210a
  Meiji constitutional government
                              3:195a-195b
  Military Takeover (1932-1945) ····· 6:211a
  Occupation (1945-1952) ····· 6:211b-212b
    communists ············ 6:212b

conservative parties ········ 6:211b-212a
  multiparty competition ·········· 6:212a
  reorganization ············ 6:211b
  Socialists ·············· 6:211a-211b
"One-and-a-Half-Party System"
  (1952-1977) ············ 6:212b-213a
origins (1874-1889) ·········· 6:207a-207b
  Itagaki Taisuke ·········· 6:207a-207b
  Ōkuma Shigenobu ·············· 6:207a
politics of compromise (1898-1924)
                          6:210a-211a
  civil bureaucracy ·········· 6:210b-211a
  Kenseikai vs. Seiyūkai ····· 6:210a-210b
  party cabinet of 1898 ·········· 6:210a
  proletarian groups ·········· 6:210b
  Yamagata cabinet of 1900 ····· 6:210a
"reformist" ·············· 3:280a-281a
rise of ················ 3:276b
temporary command (1924-1932)
                          6:211a-211b
  noncommunist proletarian groups 6:211a
  repression of proletarian groups ·· 6:211a
  Taishō democracy ············ 6:211a
Political scandals ··· 5:72a; 6:202a; 7:143a,
                          173a, 375b
Political Study Association ············ 1:2a
Political suppression of writers
  in Shōwa period ·········· 7:175b-176a
Political system ·············· 6:213b-217a
  conclusion ·············· 6:216b-217a
  democracy ·············· 2:84a-85a
  origins ················ 6:213b
  postwar ················ 6:214b-216b
    centralization ············ 6:215a-215b
    participation ············ 6:215b-216b
    structure ·············· 6:214b-215a
  postwar changes ·········· 3:204a-205a
  power structure under the Meiji
    Constitution ············ 6:213b-214b
Political thought, Confucianism
                          1:352b-358b
Politics, student movements ······· 7:115b
Polivanov, Evgenij Dmitrievich ···· 4:20b;
                                6:217a
  writings ················ 6:217a
Polluter Pays Principle (PPP) ···· 2:225a,
                          226a, 229a
Pollution
  automobile emissions ····· 2:236a-236b
  control ················ 2:224a, 225b
  industrial complexes ·········· 3:291b
  industrial waste ·············· 3:302b
  laws against ·············· 2:224a-225b
  mining ················ 5:185a-186a
  modern economy ············ 2:165a
  plants ················ 6:192a
  victim compensation ·········· 2:225a
See also Environmental quality
Pollution Control Public Works Cost
  Allocation Law ·············· 2:224b
Pollution Countermeasures
  Basic Law ·············· 6:217b
Pollution litigation ············ 6:217b
  Ashio Copper Mine Incident ······· 1:102a
Pollution-related diseases ·········· 2:224a,
                      226a-226b, 304a; 6:217b-220a
  air pollution ·············· 6:217b-218a
    photochemical smog ············ 6:218a
    respiratory disorders ·········· 6:217b-218a
  food poisoning ·············· 6:219b-220a
    dried milk poisoning (arsenic) ···· 6:220a
    milk contamination (BHC) ········ 6:220a
    rice oil poisoning (PCB) ········ 6:219b-220a
  land pollution ·············· 6:218b-219a
    arsenic poisoning, chronic ········ 6:219a
    itai itai disease ············ 6:218b-219a
Pollution-Related Health Damage
  Compensation Law ············ 6:219a-219b

pressure groups ··············· 6:237b
water pollution ·········· 6:218a-218b
  Minamata disease ········ 6:218a-218b
  Niigata mercury poisoning ······ 6:218b
Pollution-Related Health Damage
  Compensation Law ·············· 2:225a
Polyandry. *See* Polygamy
Polychlorinated biphenyl poisoning
  ··································· 2:304b
Polychrome Corporation ············ 4:23a
Polychrome screen and wall painting
  ··································· 6:151b
Polygamy ·················· 5:116a-117a
Polygyny. *See* Polygamy
Polytheism ····················· 6:290a
Po mo ······················ 3:73a-73b
Pompe van Meerdervoort, Johannes
  Lydius Catherinus ······· 6:220a-220b
Poporo Players case (1963) ······· 6:220b
  university autonomy ··········· 8:171a
Poppe, N. N. ··················· 4:18b
Popper, Karl ····················· 4:85b
Popular fiction ············· 6:220b-221b
  Daibosatsu Tōge ·············· 5:320a
Popular Front Incident ····· 6:221b-222a;
  7:74b; 8:296b
  Sakisaka Itsurō ················· 7:3a
Popular parties ············ 5:197b-198a
Popular Rights Movement. *See* **Freedom**
  and People's Rights Movement
Popular sovereignty ············ 6:222a
Population ·········· 4:7a; 6:222a-225b
  historical patterns ········ 6:222b-224b
    Edo-period (1600-1868) ·· 6:222b-223b
    1868 to 1940 ·········· 6:223b-224a
  postwar ················ 6:224a-225b
    changing patterns ········· 6:224b-225a
    decline of growth rate ······ 6:224a-224b
    increase ···················· 6:224a
    regional differences and redistribution
      ··························· 6:225a
  special features ·········· 6:225a-225b
  urban densities ·············· 7:214a
Population censuses ··············· 6:4a
Population density, land rents ····· 4:363b
Population Problems Council ······ 6:224a
Population Problems Research Council
  ··································· 2:247b
Population redistribution ···· 6:225b-226a
Porcelain ······················ 1:260a
Porcelain industry ················ 1:85a
Pork production ·················· 1:28b
Pornography ················ 6:49b-50b
Poroshiridake ····· 幌尻岳 ······· 6:226a
Port Arthur ······· 6:226a-226b; 7:277b
  Hirose Takeo ··················· 3:148a
Port Hamilton Incident ······· 4:267b-268a
Portman, Anton L. C. ··········· 6:226b
"Portrait of Tenshin" ············ 7:105b
Portrait painting ··········· 6:226b-228a
  Ashikaga Takauji ·············· 1:*100b*
  China ························ 1:283a
  early ························ 6:226b
  Edo ····················· 6:227b-228a
  Fujiwara no Takanobu ····· 5:*181a*; 6:227a
  Ikkyū ······················· 3:*270b*
  Kamakura ················ 6:227a-227b
  Muromachi and Momoyama ····· 6:227b
  Myōe ························ 5:*289a*
  Nichiren ····················· 5:*375a*
  Shōtoku, Prince ·············· 7:*172b*
  subjects ····················· 6:158b
  Taira no Shigemori ············ 6:*227a*
  Tokugawa Ieyasu ··············· 8:*49a*
  Toyotomi Hideyoshi ············· 8:*94b*
  Watanabe Kazan ··············· 8:236a
Portraits of Eminent Tendai Monks 6:227a

Portraiture
  kabuki actors ·················· 7:79a
  Sharaku ······················ 7:79a
Portsmouth, Treaty of
  ········· ポーツマス条約 ······· 3:197a;
  6:228a-228b; 7:88a, 237a, 238a
  China ······················· 1:288b
  Guandong Territory ·········· 3:64b-65a
  Hibiya Incendiary Incident ··· 3:129a-129b
  Japan's interest in Korea ········ 4:282a
  Komura Jutarō ················· 4:268a
  Korea's annexation ············· 4:287b
  mandates ····················· 6:228a
  Russo-Japanese fisheries ········· 6:345a
  Russo-Japanese War ············· 6:347a
  Tairo Dōshikai ················· 7:303a
  Takahira Kogorō ··············· 7:313b
Port towns ··················· 6:228b
  urban life ···················· 8:177b
  urban planning ················ 8:179b
Portugal and Japan ············ 6:228b
  Namban trade ············· 5:323a-323b
Possession ·················· 7:67b-68a
Postal savings system ············ 1:139b
Postal service ·············· 6:229a-229b
  founder of ·············· 5:81b-82a
  history ····················· 6:229a
  present state ·············· 6:229a-229b
Postal system, early ·············· 3:138a
Postindustrialism ··············· 3:302a
Poston Relocation Center ······· 6:229b
Post-station system ·············· 2:188b
Post-station towns ····· 6:229b-230a; 7:4b
  bashaku ····················· 1:144a
  urban planning ················ 8:179b
Postwar history. *See* **History of Japan**
Postwar literature ·········· 6:230a-231b
  chūkan shōsetsu ·········· 1:312b-313a
  decadence (buraiha) phenomenon · 6:230a
  democratic literature ············ 6:230a
  mass communications ·········· 6:231a
  renewed activity of major writers
    ······················· 6:230a-230b
  sengo bungaku school ··········· 6:230b
    "first wave" ················· 6:230b
    "second wave" ············ 6:230b-231a
    "third new generation" ········· 6:231a
  United States-Japan Security Treaty 6:231a
Postwar reforms. *See* **Occupation**
Post-World War II reparations ····· 7:235b
Potatoes and yams ············ 6:231b
Potsdam Declaration ····· 1:108a, 290a;
  6:231b-232a; 7:28a, 246b, 278a; 8:276b
  Anami Korechika ················ 1:53b
  Far Eastern Commission ········· 2:248a
  Government-General of Korea ···· 4:283a
  Hirohito, Emperor ·············· 3:147a
  Kido Kōichi ··················· 4:202a
  Occupation ···················· 6:51b
  Occupation Purge ··············· 6:57b
  religious freedom ·············· 6:294b
  Taiwan ······················ 7:309a
  women's suffrage ·············· 8:268b
Potter's Book, A ··············· 4:372b
Potter's wheels. *See* **Rokuro**
Pottery
  Agano ware ··················· 1:20b
  Arakawa Toyozō ················ 1:73b
  Asahi ware ···················· 1:93b
  Banko ware ··················· 1:141a
  Haji ························· 1:79b
  high-fired ···················· 1:258a
  Jōmon ······················· 1:76a
  Ōmori shell mounds ············ 6:103a
  Onta ware ···················· 6:113a
  paleolithic culture ············· 6:159b
  Sue ························· 1:79b
  Tamba ware ··················· 7:333a

yayoi ····················· 1:76b-77a
Poverty ·················· 6:232a-232b
Power of supreme command ······· 8:85a
Pozdneev, Dmitrii Matveevich ··· 6:232b
Pragmatism ····· 6:232b-233a; 7:149a-149b
Prajñapāramitā sutras ············ 2:213a
Pratītya-samutpāda ········· 2:217a-217b
Prawns. *See* **Shrimps, prawns, and**
  lobsters
Prayer ····················· 6:233a
Precepts for Health ············· 8:328b
Preceramic period ········· 6:233a-233b
Precision machinery industry ···· 6:233b
  companies ···· 1:239b, 316a; 4:200b; 6:10a;
  7:99a
Prefectural governor ·············· 4:197b
Prefectural museums ············ 5:278b
Prefectural public safety ordinance
  ·························· 4:234a-234b
Prefectural system, establishment of
  2:1a; 6:233a-235a; 7:30a
  abolition of domains ········ 6:234a-235a
  bureaucratic development ········ 1:217b
  compromise settlement ·········· 6:234a
  establishment ·················· 4:7a
  hambatsu ····················· 3:91b
  hanseki hōkan ············ 6:233b-234a
  provinces ····················· 6:260a
  Verbeck, Guido Herman Fridolin · 8:190a
Prefectures
  Hokkaidō ················· 3:212b-213a
  Honshū
    Aichi ······················ 1:33a
    Akita ····················· 1:42b-43a
    Aomori ··················· 1:69b-70a
    Chiba ····················· 1:271a
    Fukui ····················· 2:364a
    Fukushima ·············· 2:366b-367a
    Gifu ···················· 3:31a-31b
    Gumma ····················· 3:68a
    Hiroshima ·············· 3:149b-150a
    Hyōgo ····················· 3:251b
    Ibaraki ················· 3:253a-253b
    Ishikawa ···················· 3:344a
    Iwate ····················· 3:363b
    Kanagawa ··················· 4:135a
    Kyōto ·················· 4:337b-338b
    Mie ···················· 5:167b-168a
    Miyagi ················· 5:217b-218a
    Nagano ················· 5:302b-303a
    Nara ··················· 5:333b-334a
    Niigata ················· 5:385b-386a
    Okayama ····················· 6:83a
    Ōsaka ·················· 6:122a-122b
    Saitama ················· 6:372b-373a
    Shiga ·················· 7:90b-91a
    Shimane ····················· 7:100b
    Shizuoka ··············· 7:153b-154a
    Tōkyō ··················· 8:60b-66a
    Tochigi ······················ 8:33a
    Tottori ················· 8:86a-86b
    Toyama ················· 8:88b-89a
    Wakayama ···················· 8:219b
    Yamagata ···················· 8:293b
    Yamaguchi ··················· 8:295b
    Yamanashi ·············· 8:301a-301b
  Kyūshū
    Fukuoka ················ 2:364b-365b
    Kagoshima ·············· 4:105b-106a
    Kumamoto ··················· 4:306a
    Miyazaki ···················· 5:221b
    Nagasaki ··············· 5:304b-305a
    Ōita ··················· 6:75b-76a
    Saga ··················· 6:363b-364a
  Okinawa ·················· 6:91b-92a
  Shikoku
    Ehime ················· 2:185a-185b
    Kagawa ····················· 4:103a

Kōchi ·············· **4**:239b
Tokushima ············· **8**:59a
See also maps ············ **4**:4a–4b
Pregnancy ················ **6**:49a
Prehistoric burials ········· **6**:235a–235b
hōkei shūkōbo ··········· **4**:244a
Prehistoric relics ·········· **7**:82b–83a
Prehistory. *See* **History of Japan**
Preparatory Commission for Establishing a New Political Order ·········· **3**:280b
Preparatory school (Juku) ········ **5**:6b
Preschool education ····· **2**:195b; **6**:235b
Prescriptive period ······· **6**:235b–236a
Press
influence ··············· **5**:129a
regulation ·············· **5**:129a
Press clubs ········ **5**:128b–129a; **6**:236a
Press Code and Radio Code for Japan ············· **2**:339a
Press Law of 1909 ········ **1**:72a; **1**:252b; **2**:338a–338b; **6**:236a
Morito Incident ··········· **5**:254b
Torii Sosen ·············· **8**:80a
Press Ordinance of 1875 ·· **1**:252a; **6**:236a, 262b
Pressure groups ········· **6**:236a–238b
agriculture ············· **6**:238a
business ··············· **6**:237b–238a
Federation of Economic Organizations (Keidanren) ············· **6**:237b
Japan Chamber of Commerce and Industry (Nisshō) ········ **6**:237b–238a
Japan Committee for Economic Development (Keizai Dōyū Kai) · **6**:238a
Japan Federation of Employers' Associations (Nikkeiren) ········ **6**:237b
history ················ **6**:236b
interaction with government · **6**:236b–237a
labor ················· **6**:238a
General Council of Trade Unions of Japan (Sōhyō) ········· **6**:238a
Japanese Confederation of Labor (Dōmei) ············· **6**:238a
major ················ **6**:237b–238b
medical ··············· **6**:238a–238b
methods ··············· **6**:237a–237b
courts ··············· **6**:237b
election to Diet ········· **6**:237a–237b
information ············ **6**:237a
meetings ·············· **6**:237a
money ··············· **6**:237a
retired bureaucrats ······ **6**:237b
Preternatural beings ········· **1**:130b
Price changes ············· **3**:312b–313a
Price Control Order of 1946 ······ **6**:238b
Price controls ············· **6**:310a
Price stability ············· **3**:303a
Pridi Phanomyong ········ **2**:339b; **6**:238b
Priest and His Disciples, The ······ **4**:312a
Priesthood ············· **6**:238b–239b
Buddhism ············· **6**:239a–239b
new religions ··········· **6**:239b
Shintō ················ **4**:145b–146a
Priest of Hitachi, The ·········· **1**:42a
Primal Vow ··············· **4**:68b–69a
Prima Meat Packers, Ltd ······· **6**:239b
Primary industries ········· **6**:239b–240a
secondary industries ········· **7**:47b
"Primary union" ············· **4**:359b
Primate Research Institute ······· **6**:240a
Primate studies ············· **6**:240a–240b
infrahuman culture ········· **6**:240a
Macaca Fuscata society ······· **6**:240b
Prime minister and cabinet · **6**:240a–244a
cabinet system
origins ············· **6**:241a–241b
party to military ········· **6**:242a–242b
postwar changes ········· **6**:242b
powers and organizations ·· **6**:244a–244b

decentralization ·········· **6**:241b–242a
government, executive branch ·· **3**:55b–56a
prime minister
powers and functions ·········· **6**:242a
selection process ·········· **6**:242b–244a
"transcendental" cabinets ········· **8**:97b
Prime ministers
Abe Nobuyuki ············· **1**:3b–4a
Ashida Hitoshi ············· **1**:97b
Fukuda Takeo ············· **2**:362b
Hamaguchi Osachi ··········· **3**:90a
Hara Takashi ············· **3**:102b–103b
Hatoyama Ichirō ··········· **3**:113a
Hayashi Senjūrō ··········· **3**:117b
Higashikuni Naruhiko ········· **3**:132a
Hiranuma Kiichirō ········· **3**:143b–144a
Hirota Kōki ·············· **3**:150a
Ikeda Hayato ············· **3**:265a
Inukai Tsuyoshi ········· **3**:326a; **4**:373a
Ishibashi Tanzan ··········· **3**:339b
Itō Hirobumi ············· **3**:353a
Katayama Tetsu ············ **4**:167a
Katō Takaaki ············ **4**:169b–170b
Katō Tomosaburō ·········· **4**:170b
Katsura Tarō ············· **8**:291b
Kishi Nobusuke ········· **4**:223a–223b
Kiyoura Keigo ············· **4**:233a
Koiso Kuniaki ············· **4**:250b
Konoe Fumimaro ········ **4**:272b; **6**:189b
Kuroda Kiyotaka ·········· **4**:314a–314b
Matsukata Masayoshi ······· **5**:134b–136a
Miki Takeo ·············· **5**:171b
Nakasone Yasuhiro ·········· **5**:318a
Ōhira Masayoshi ··········· **6**:74a
Okada Keisuke ············ **6**:78a–78b
Ōkuma Shigenobu ·········· **6**:95b–96a
Saionji Kimmochi ········· **6**:371b–372b
Saitō Makoto ············· **6**:374a
Satō Eisaku ·············· **7**:26a–26b
Shidehara Kijūrō ·········· **7**:88a–89a
Suzuki Kantarō ············ **7**:282a
Suzuki Zenkō ············· **7**:284a
Takahashi Korekiyo ········ **7**:312a–312b
Tanaka Giichi ············ **7**:336a–336b
Tanaka Kakuei ············· **7**:337a
Terauchi Masatake ·········· **8**:12b
Tōjō Hideki ·············· **1**:32a
Wakatsuki Reijirō ········· **8**:218b–219a
Yamagata Aritomo ········· **8**:290b–292a
Yamamoto Gonnohyōe ········ **8**:297b
Yonai Mitsumasa ··········· **8**:337a
Yoshida Shigeru ·········· **8**:343a–345a
Prime Minister's Office ·········· **1**:218b; **6**:244b
Council for Science and Technology (Kagaku Gijutsu Kaigi) ·········· **7**:38a
external organs ············ **6**:244b
National Land Agency ········· **5**:343b
Primeval forest ············· **5**:352a–352b
Primogeniture ········· **2**:242a; **6**:244b
Primroses [(sakurasō) *Primula* spp.] ······························· **6**:245a
Principle of changed circumstances ······························· **6**:245a–245b
Principle of fidelity and good faith **6**:245b
Principles of Newspaper Ethics, The ······························· **1**:254b
Principles of Publishing Ethics, The ······························· **1**:254b
Printing ····· **1**:152a–153a, 187a–187b, 233b; **6**:245b–249a
modern ··············· **6**:245b–246b
history ··············· **6**:245b–246a
industry today ············ **6**:246a–246b
movable-type ············ **8**:325a
premodern ············· **6**:246b–249a
book illustration ·········· **6**:247a
Kyōto ················ **6**:247b–248a
legacy from China ········· **6**:246b–247a

luxury printing ··········· **6**:248b
movable type ··········· **6**:248a–248b
Nara ················ **6**:247b
origins ··············· **6**:247a–247b
woodblock printing ········· **6**:247a
17th to 19th centuries ······ **6**:248b–249a
Printing Bureau ············ **6**:246a
Print media ··············· **6**:268a
Prints. *See* **Ukiyo-e; Modern prints**
Priority production program ······· **6**:249a
business cycles ············ **1**:224a
Reconstruction Finance Bank ··· **6**:284b
Priority Production System ······· **1**:84b
Prisoners' rights ············· **6**:249b
Prison Law (Kangoku Hō) of 1908 **6**:249b
Prisons ········· **2**:51b; **6**:172a, 249a–249b
Kirishitan yashiki ·········· **4**:221b–222a
premodern ············· **6**:8a
Privacy, invasion of ··········· **1**:255a
Privacy, right of ············· **6**:249b–250a
After the Banquet case (1964) ······· **1**:20b
judicial decisions ·········· **6**:250a
privacy law ············· **6**:249b–2450a
society ··············· **6**:249b
Private international law ········ **1**:316b, 337b–339a; **6**:250a–252a
Private Investment Company for Asia (PICA) ··············· **6**:143b
Private museums ············· **5**:276b–277b
Private schools ········· **2**:179a; **6**:252a–252b; **7**:94a–94b
Private universities ············· **6**:252b
Privy Council ······· **2**:2b, 4a; **6**:214a, 242a, 252b–253b; **7**:304a
Hiranuma Kiichirō ·········· **3**:143b–144a
Imperial Diet ············ **3**:276a
Itō Hirobumi ············· **3**:353a
Konoe Fumimaro ·········· **4**:273a
Kōno Togama ············· **4**:275a
Meiji Constitution ········· **3**:195a
power of supreme command ····· **8**:85a
Probation ··············· **4**:87a–87b
Probation officers ············ **2**:246a
Proceedings of the Japan Academy or *Gakushiin kiyō* ··························· **4**:9b
Proclamation concerning the Encouragement of Education ··· **6**:124a
Proclamation of Neutrality (Proclamation No. 546 of 1870) ················ **8**:13b
Proclamation of the Great Doctrine. *See* **Taikyō Sempu**
Product distribution ··········· **2**:162a
Production Research Council ····· **7**:372b
Product liability ············· **6**:253b–254b
burden of proof ············ **6**:254a
government liability for negligence ······························· **6**:253b–254a
legal theories ············· **6**:253b
proximate causation ········· **6**:254a
scope ··············· **6**:254a–254b
standard of care ··········· **6**:254a
strict ··············· **6**:254a
Professional School Order (Semmon Gakkō Rei) ············ **7**:62a; **8**:170a
Professional Writers' Guild of Japan ················· **4**:207a
Profitability, Japanese corporate view ··················· **2**:35b
Progovernment parties ·········· **6**:321b
Progressive Education Movement ······························· **7**:367a–367b
Progressive Party ············· **7**:108b
The Progressive Woman ········ **4**:138b
Prohibitions of Foreign Voyages · **4**:109b
Proletarian literary groups ········· **5**:20b
Proletarian literature movement · **1**:209a–209b; **6**:254b–256a; **7**:25a, 66b, 69a

Aono Suekichi · · · · · · · · · · · · · · · · · 1:70a
areas of dispute · · · · · · · · · · · · · · 6:255b
Bungei sensen period (1924-1932)
· 6:254b-255b
children's literature · · · · · · · · · · · · · 1:279b
film · 2:269b
fūzoku shōsetsu · · · · · · · · · · · · · · · 2:378a
Hayama Yoshiki · · · · · · · · · · · · · · 3:115a
Hayashi Fusao · · · · · · · · · · · · · · · · 3:116b
Hirabayashi Hatsunosuke · · · · · · 3:141a
Hirabayashi Taiko · · · · · · · · · · · · · 3:141b
Hirotsu Kazuo · · · · · · · · · · · · · · · · 3:151a
Hisaita Eijirō · · · · · · · · · · · · · · · · · 3:151b
Itō Einosuke · · · · · · · · · · · · · · · · · · 3:352a
Kamei Katsuichirō · · · · · · · · · · · · · 4:125a
Kataoka Teppei · · · · · · · · · · · · · · · 4:166b
Kikuchi Kan · · · · · · · · · · · · · · · · · · 4:206a
Kindai bungaku · · · · · · · · · · · · · · · 4:212a
Kobayashi Takiji · · · · · · · · · · · · · · 4:237a
Kurahara Korehito · · · · · · · · · · · · · 4:311a
Maedakō Hiroichirō · · · · · · · · · · · · · 5:80a
Miyoshi Jūrō · · · · · · · · · · · · · · · · · 5:223b
Nakano Shigeharu · · · · · · · · · · 5:316b-317a
NAPF-KOPF period (1928-1934)
· 6:255b-256a
postwar literature · · · · · · · · · · · · · · 6:230a
schisms · 6:255a
Senki · 7:66b
Shinkō Geijutsu Ha · · · · · · · · · · · · 7:119a
Shin Nihon bungaku · · · · · · · · · · · 7:122a
Takeda Rintarō · · · · · · · · · · · · · · · 7:323a
Tane maku hito · · · · · · · · · · · · 7:340a-340b
Tane maku hito period (1920-1922) · · 6:254b
Tokunaga Sunao · · · · · · · · · · · · · · · · 8:58a
Tsuboi Sakae · · · · · · · · · · · · · · · · · 8:110a
Tsuboi Shigeji · · · · · · · · · · · · · · · · 8:110a
Tsubota Jōji · · · · · · · · · · · · · · · · · · 8:110a
Western literature in Japanese
translation · · · · · · · · · · · · · · · · · 8:248a
Proletarian theater movement
(puroretaria
engeki) · 6:255a
*Promotion of Zen in Defense of
the Country* · · · · · · · · · · · · · · · · 6:319a
Promotive establishment · · · · · · · · · 2:37b
*Propagation of Zen for the Protection
of the Country, The* · · · · · · · · · · · 8:370b
Property, ownership · · · · · · · · · 7:155a-158a
right to control · · · · · · · · · · · · · · · 6:312a
Property, registration of · · · · · 6:288a-288b
Property deed · · · · · · · · · · · · · · · · · 8:359b
Property law · · · · · · · · · · · · · · · · · · 8:238a
Property rights · · · · · · · · · · · · · · 6:256a-256b
abuse · 1:5b
ando · 1:55a
managerial ideology · · · · · · · · · · · · · 5:92b
ownership rights · · · · · · · · · · · · · · · 6:136b
principle rights · · · · · · · · · · · · · · · · 6:256a
shitaji chūbun · · · · · · · · · · · · · · · · · 1:101b
Proprietary lords · · · · · · · · · · · · · · · 6:353a
Proprietary province · · · · · · · · · 1:274a-274b
Proprietorship (chigyō) · · · · · 1:274a-274b;
3:255a
Prose, Buddhist · · · · · · · · · · · · 1:180b, 181b
Prosecution review commissions
(Kensatsu shinsakai) · · · · · · 6:256b, 266a
Prostitution · · · · · · · · · · · · · · · 6:256b-257b;
7:234b-235a
karayuki san · · · · · · · · · · · · · · · · · · 4:159b
Meiji to World War II · · · · · · · · · · · 6:257a
postwar · · · · · · · · · · · · · · · · · · 6:257a-257b
premodern · · · · · · · · · · · · · · · · 6:256b-257a
Shikidō ōkagami · · · · · · · · · · · · · 7:95b-96a
tsutome hōkō · · · · · · · · · · · · · · · 2:211b-212a
Prostitution Prevention Law · · · · · · 6:257b;
8:349b
Miyagi Tamayo · · · · 2:49a; 5:218a; 6:257b;
8:189b
Protected species · · · · · · · · · · · 5:352a-352b

Protectionism · · · · · · · · · · · · · · · · · 2:325a
Protectorate Treaty · · · · · · · · · · · · · 4:289a
Protestant missionaries · · · · · 6:257b-258b
Proto history. *See* History of Japan
Proverbs · 6:258b
Provinces · · · · · · · · · · · · · · · · · 6:258b-260a
Provincial capitals · · · · · · · · · · · · · 4:257b
Provincial governors · 3:174b; 4:262a-262b
"Provincial levies" · · · · · · · · · · · · · · 4:310a
Provisional disposition · · · · · · · · · 6:260a
**Provisional Government
of Free India** · · · · · · · · · · · · · · · 6:260a
Provisional Government of Korea 6:260a,
307b
**Provisional Government of the Republic
of China** · · · · · · · 6:260a-260b, 285b, 302a
Wang Kemin (Wang K'o-min) · · · 8:222b
Wu Peifu (Wu P'ei-fu) · · · · · · · · · 8:279b
Xinmin Hui (Hsin-min Hui), (New
People's Society) · · · · · · · · · · · · · · 8:281b
Provisional Joint Agreement · · · · · 4:281a
"Prussia of the Far East" · · · · · · · · · 1:86b
PS-1 seaplane · · · · · · · · · · · · · · · · · 6:260b
Psychodrama · · · · · · · · · · · · · · · · · · 6:261b
"Psychologism" · · · · · · · · · · · · · · · · 7:175b
Psychologists. *See* Psychology in Japan
Psychology, concepts in
akirame · 1:42a
amae · 1:48b
educational counseling · · · · · 2:179a-179b
ego · 2:184b
hara · 3:100a
Psychology in Japan · · · · · · · 6:260b-261a
Psychotherapy · · · · · · · · · · · · 6:261a-262a
Buddhist-based · · · · · · · · · · · · 6:261b-262a
morita · 6:261b
naikan · 6:261b
shadan · · · · · · · · · · · · · · · · · · 6:261b-262a
mental hospitals · · · · · · · · · · · · · · · 6:262a
mental process · · · · · · · · · · · · · · · · · 6:261b
naikan · 5:310a
physical process · · · · · · · · · · · 6:261a-261b
Ptarmigan [(raichō) *Lagopus mutus*]
· 6:262b
PTAs · 6:262b
Public Accounts law · · · · · · · · · · · · · 2:276b
Public assembly, restriction · · · · · · · 7:185a
Public Assembly Ordinance · · · · · · · 7:185a
Public assistance. *See* Social Welfare
Publication Law of 1893 · · · · · · · · 1:252b;
2:338a-338b; 4:339a; 6:236a, 262b
fundamental liberties limitation · · 2:369b
Kawai Eijirō · · · · · · · · · · · · · · · · · · 4:178b
Publication Ordinance of 1869 · · · · 1:252a;
6:262b
Publications, distributors · · · · · · · · · 1:163b
Publications Law · · · · · · · · · · · · · · · 2:339a
Public auction · · · · · · · · · · · · · 6:262b-263a
Public bathhouses. *See* Bath
Public Corporation Labor Relations Law
of 1948 · 4:358a
Public corporations · · · · · · · · · 6:263b-264a
bonds · 3:54b
finance · 1:139b
kokusaku kaisha · · · · · · · · · · · · · · · 4:262a
public investment · · · · · · · · · · · · · · 6:265a
role · 6:264a
types · 6:263a-264a
union members · · · · · · · · · · · · · · · · 4:348b
**Public Corporations and Government
Enterprises Labor Relations Law**
· · 4:352a, 358a, 360a; 6:264b; 7:189b, 279b
Kōrōkyō restricted · · · · · · · · · · · · · 4:294a
Public Corporations and National
Enterprise Labor Relations
Commission (Kōkyō
Kigyōtai Tō Rōdō Iinkai) · · · · · · · · · 4:358a

Public deposit · · · · · · · · · · · · · · · · · 4:334a
Public Employee Law · · · · · · · · · · · · 2:339a
Public employees · · · · · · · · · · · 6:264b-265a
legal restrictions · · · · · · · · · · · · · · · 4:360a
Public employment security offices
· 2:210a; 6:265a
Public fields (kōden) · · · · · · · · · · · · · 4:243a
Public Finance Law · · · · · · · · · · · · · · 3:54b
Public health · · · · · · · · · · · · · · 5:149a-150a
environmental law · · · · · · · · · · 2:224a-225b
Ministry of Health and Welfare · · · 5:189b
pollution · · · · · · · · · · · · · · · · · 2:226a-226b
Public Housing Law · · · · · · · · · · · · · 3:245b
Public Information and Cultural
Affairs Bureau · · · · · · · · · · · · · · · 3:319b
Public investment · · · · · · · · · · · 6:265a-265b
Public law · · · · · · · · · · · · · · · · · · · 6:265b
"Public matters" · · · · · · · · · · · · · · · · 4:303a
Public Office Election Law · · · · · · · · 2:189a
Public Opinion Survey Department 6:265b
Public opinion surveys · · · · · · 6:265b-266a
Public Order and Police Law of 1900
· · 2:337a-337b; 4:345a, 351a; 6:210b, 266a;
7:241b, 317a; 8:291b
sex discrimination · · · · · · · · · · · · · · 2:362a
women's suffrage · · · · · · · · · · · · · · · 8:268b
Public Order and Police Law (1922)
· 8:268b
Public Party of Patriots · · · · · · · · · · · 1:34b
Public Peace Police Law · · · · · · · · · · 2:337a
Public prosecutor · · · · · 2:45b; 6:256b, 266a
criminal investigation · · · · · · · · · 2:47a-47b
Public Safety · · · · · · · · · · · · · · 5:345b-346a
Public Safety Examination
Commission · · · · · · · · · · · · · · · · · 2:337a
Public schools, construction · · · · · · · · 7:33b
**Public Security Investigation
Agency** · 6:266b
Public Telecommunications Law · 6:276a
Public utilities · · · · · · · · · · · · · · · 6:266b
Public utility rates · · · · · · · · · 6:266b-267a
Public welfare · · · · · · · · · · · · · · · 6:267a
establishment of principal · · · · · · · · · 1:5b
Public works
national budget · · · · · · · · · · · · 1:205a-205b
Public Works Research Institute · 6:267a
Publishers' Weekly · · · · · · · · · · · · · 6:268a
Publishing · · · · · · · · · · · · · · · 6:267a-269a
freedom of the press · · · · · · · · · · · · 2:339a
industry structure · · · · · · · · · · · 6:268a-268b
buying and selling · · · · · · · · · · · · 6:268b
distribution system · · · · · · · · · · · · 6:268a
size · 6:268a
after Meiji Restoration · · · · · · · 6:267b-268a
contemporary book · · · · · · · · · · · 6:267b
magazine · · · · · · 5:82b-83a; 6:267b-268a
translations · · · · · · · · · · · · · · · · · · 6:267b
postwar reforms · · · · · · · · · · · · 6:268b-269a
printing · · · · · · · · · · · · · · · · · 6:267a-267b
reference · 7:105b
Publishing companies
Bungei Shunjū, Ltd · · · · · · · · · · · · 1:209a
Chikuma Shobō Publishing
Co, Ltd · · · · · · · · · · · · · · 1:276b; 7:309b
Chūō Kōron Sha, Inc · · · · · · · · · · · 1:313b
Fuzambō · · · · · · · · · · · · · · · · · 2:376b-377a
Gakken Co, Ltd · · · · · · · · · · · · · · · · · 3:3b
Hakubunkan · · · · · · · · · · · · · 1:209b; 7:309b
Heibonsha, Ltd, Publishers 3:122b; 7:309b
Iwanami Shoten Publishers · · 3:360b-361a;
7:149a
Kadokawa Publishing Co, Ltd · · · · 4:101a
Kaizōsha
Bungei · 1:209a
Kōdansha, Ltd · · · · · · · · · · · · · · · · 4:241b
Ōbunsha Publishing Co, Ltd · · · 6:506-51a
Shinchōsha Company · · · · · · · · · · · 7:109b
Shōgakukan Publishing Co, Ltd · · · 7:158a
Shūeisha Publishing Co, Ltd · · · · · 7:181a

Publishing Ordinance of 1869 · · · · · 2:338b
Pueraria thunbergiana · · · · · · · · · · · 4:323a
Pu Fa zhan ji (P'u-Fa chan chi; The
  Franco-Prussian War) · · · · · · · · · · 8:222b
P'u-i. *See* **Puyi (P'u-i)**
"Pulling boards." *See* **Naruko**
Pulp · · · · · · · · · · · · · · · · · · · 5:354a-354b
Punctuation marks · · · · · · · · · · 6:269a-269b
Punishments
  criminal · · · · · · · · · · · · · · · · · · · 3:138a
  heimin · 3:126a
  hell · 3:126a
  tojime · 3:126a
Puns · 8:269b
Puppeteers
  dress · · · · · · · · · · · · · · · · · · 1:213a-213b
  Kiritake Monjūrō II · · · · · · · · · · · 4:222a
Puppet heads · · · · · · · · · · · · · · · · 1:*214b*
Puppets · · · · · · · · · · · · · · · · · · 2:128a-129a
Puppet theater · · · · · · 1:212a-215b; 2:267b;
                          6:269b-270a
  Azuchi-Momoyama · · · · · · · · · · · 3:184a
  dolls · 2:128a
  kabuki adaptations · · · · · · · 4:91b, 93a, 99a
  music, traditional · · · · · · · · · · · · 5:284b
Pure Land Buddhism · 1:178b-179a, 185a;
                          6:270a-270b
  Amida · 1:189a
  architecture · · · · · · · · · · · · · · · · 1:189b
  art · 1:189a-191a
  Genshin · · · · · · · · · · · · · · · · · · · 3:23b
  Hōnen · 1:190b
  Ippen · · · · · · · · · · · · · · · · · 3:328b-329b
  Kakuban · · · · · · · · · · · · · · · · · · 1:191a
  Kannon · · · · · · · · · · · · · · · · · · · 4:144b
  modern philosophy · · · · · · · · · · · 5:230b
  monasticism · · · · · · · · · · · · · · · · 5:238a
  musical instruments · · · · · · 1:196a-196b
  Myōe · 5:289b
  Ōbaku sect · · · · · · · · · · · · · · · · 6:47a-47b
  painting · · · · · · · · · · · · · · · · 1:189b-191a
  poems and songs · · · · · · · · · · · · 8:231a
  Pure Land · · · · · · · · · · · · · · · · · 4:307b
  Rinzai sect · · · · · · · · · · · · · · · · · 6:319b
  Risshō ankoku ron · · · · · · · · · · · 6:321a
  ritual implements · · · · · · · · 1:196a-196b
  rosaries · · · · · · · · · · · · · · · · · · · 1:197a
  schools · · · · · · · · · · · · · · · · · · · 1:179a
  sculpture · · · · · · · · · · · · · · · 1:189b-191a
  *Senchakushū (Senchaku hongan
    nembutsu shū)* · · · · · · · · · · · · · · 7:63a
  Shinran · · · · · · · · · · · · · · · · · · · 1:190b
  Tannishō · · · · · · · · · · · · · · · · · · 7:344a
  thought and culture · · · · · · · · · 8:27a-28a
Purification. *See* **Misogi**
Puroretaria geijutsu
  (Proletarian Arts)
    プロレタリア芸術 · · · · · 6:255a
Putiatin, Evfimii Vasil'evich · 6:270b, 278a
  Goncharov, Ivan Aleksandrovich · · · 3:44b
Puyi (P'u-i) · · · · · · · · · · · · · · 6:270b-271b

Q

Qin (Ch'in) dynasty
  calligraphic styles · · · · · · · · · · · · 7:170a
Qincuxŭ (Kinkushū) · · · · · · · · · · · 2:241a

Qing (ch'ing) dynasty · · · · · · · · · · · 4:18b
Qingdao (Tsingtao) · · · · · · · · · · · 6:273a
  concession · · · · · · · · · · · · · · · · · · 4:53a
Qing period · · · · · · · · · · · · · · · 7:307a-307b
Qinqi shuhua · · · · · · · · · · · · · 4:213b-214a
Q. P. Corporation · · · · · · · · · · · · 6:273a
Quality control · · · · · · · · · · · 6:273a-274a
  automation · · · · · · · · · · · · · · 6:273b-274a
  Deming, Edward · · · · · · · · · · · · · 6:273b
  history · · · · · · · · · · · · · · · · · 6:273a-273b
  principles · · · · · · · · · · · · · · · · · · 6:273b
Quanfa · 4:158a
Quarantine · · · · · · · · · · · · · · · · · 6:274a
Quasi-legal professions · · · · · · · · · 4:371b
Quezon, Manuel Luis · · · · · · · 6:274a-274b
Quilting · · · · · · · · · · · · · · · · · · · 7:24a-24b
Quince, dwarf Japanese [(kusaboke)
  Chaenomeles japonica] · · · · · · · · 6:274b
Quinoform · · · · · · · · · · · · · · · · · · · 7:206a

R

Rabbits [(usagi) family Leporidae]
                          · · · · · · · · · · 6:275a
Rabies Prevention Law · · · · · · · · · · 6:274a
Raccoon dog. *See* **Tanuki**
Racial discrimination · · · · · · · · · · · 7:209a
Radar · 2:192a
Raden. *See* **Mother-of-pearl inlay**
Radiation Effects Research Foundation
  (RERF) · · · · · · · · · · · · · · · · · · · 1:112a
Radio
  broadcasting · · · · · · · · · 1:171b-172a, 173a
    educational · · · · · · · · · · · · · · · · 2:179a
    censorship · · · · · · · · · · · · · · · · 2:339a
    late-night · · · · · · · · · · · · · · · · · 1:173b
    mass communications · · · · · · · · · 5:128b
    technology · · · · · · · · · · · · 2:192a, 193b
Radioactive isotopes laws · · · · · · · 1:114b
Radio Code for Japan · · · · · · · · · · 2:339a
Radio drama · · · · · · · · · · · · · 6:275a-276a
Radio Law · · · · · · · · · 1:171b-172a; 6:276a
Radio Press (RP) · · · · · · · · · · · · · · 5:369a
Radio serials · · · · · · · · · · · · · · · · · 4:207a
Radishes [(daikon) *Raphanus
  sativus* var. *acanthiformis*] · 6:276a-276b
    production · · · · · · · · · · · · · · · · · 1:27a
Ragusa, Vincenzo · · · · · · · 2:304a; 6:276b
"Rai" · · · · · · · · · · · · · · · · 癩 · · 7:176a
Raichō · 6:262b
Raigō triptych · · · · · · · · · · · · · · · · 4:299b
Raigōzu · · · · · · · · 来迎図 · 1:190a-190b;
                    6:*151b*, 276b, 277a, 277b
Rails [(kuina) family Rallidae] · · · · · 6:277b
Railway industries
  Kinki Nippon Railway Co, Ltd · · · 4:213b
  Hankyū Corporation · · · · · · · · · · · 3:99a
  Nagoya Railroad Co, Ltd · · · · · · · 5:309b
  Nishi-Nippon Railroad Co, Ltd · · · · 6:18b
  Seibu Railway Co, Ltd · · · · · · · · · · 7:49b
  Tōbu Railway Co, Ltd · · · · · · · · 8:32b-33a
  Tōkyū Corporation · · · · · · · · · · · · 8:70a
Railway Nationalization Law · · · · · · 4:33b
Railways · · · · · · · · · 6:277b-280a; 8:99a-99b
  boxed meals (ekiben) · · · · · · · 2:188a-188b
  electric · · · · · · · · · · · · · · · · · · 7:116a-119a

  high-speed · · · · · · · · · · · · · · 7:116a-119a
  history · · · · · · · · · · · · · · · · · 6:278a-279a
  importance · · · · · · · · · · · · · · · · · 6:277b
  Meiji period · · · · · · · · · · · · · · · · · 2:153a
  nationalization · · · · · · · · · · 2:31a; 6:279a
  other service · · · · · · · · · · · · 6:279b-280a
  passenger · · · · · · · · · · · · · · · 7:116a-119a
  Shinkansen · · · · · · · · · · · · · 6:279a-279b
  size and complexity · · · · · · · · · · · 6:278a
  urban life · · · · · · · · · · · · · · · · · · 8:178b
Railway Technical Research Institute
                          · · · · · · · · · · 7:117b
Rain, rituals for · · · · · · · · · · · · · · 6:280b
Rainbow plan · · · · · · · · · · · · · · · 6:280a
Raingear, traditional · · · · · · · 6:280a-280b
Rain supplication (amagoi) rites · · · 1:23a
Rainy season · · · · · · · · · · · · · · · · · · 4:8a
Rai San'yō · · · · · · · · · 頼山陽 · 1:211a;
                    5:311a-311b; 6:280b-281a
  Kan Sazan · · · · · · · · · · · · · · · · · 4:152a
  Rai San'yō to sono jidai · · · · · · · · 5:315b
  Uragami Shunkin · · · · · · · · · · · · · 8:175b
Rajio monogatari (radio story) · · · · 6:275b
Rakan · · · · · · · · · · · · · · 羅漢 · 2:346a;
                          6:281a-281b
  Takuma Eiga · · · · · · · · · · · · · · · · 7:327b
Rakkan · · · · · · · · · · · · · · 落款 · 6:281b
Rakkasan · · · · · · · · · · · · · 落下傘 · 4:138b
Rakuchū rakugai 洛中洛外 · 7:270a
Rakuchū rakugai zu · · · · · · · · · · · 2:*377a*
Rakugaki (graffiti) · · · · · · · · · · · 3:59b-60a
Rakugo · · · · · · · · · · · · · 落語 · 2:267b;
                          6:281b-282b
  influence on Shikitei Samba · · · 7:97a
  Jippensha Ikku · · · · · · · · · · · · · · · 4:61b
  kōdan · 4:241a
  kokkeibon influenced · · · · · · · · · · 4:256a
  San'yūtei Enchō · · · · · · · · · · · · · · 7:19b
  Yanagiya Kosan V · · · · · · · · · · · · 6:*282b*
Rakuichi and rakuza
                    楽市楽座 · 6:282b-283a
Rakujitsu moyu · 落日燃ゆ · 7:148a
Rakujō · · · · · · · · · · · · · · · 落城 · 7:334a
Rakurō · · · · · · · · · · · · · · · · 楽浪 · 4:382b
Rakusho · 3:59b
Rakusho roken · · · · · · 落書露顕 · 3:272b
Raku ware · · · · · · · · · · 楽焼 · 1:20b; 4:337a;
                          6:283a; 7:67a
  originator · · · · · · · · · · · · · · · · · · 1:298b
  teabowl · · · · · · · · · · · · · · · · · · · 1:*258b*
  tea ceremony · · · · · · · · · · · · · · · 7:363b
Rakuzenkai Institute for the Blind · 7:241a
Rāmen · 6:283a
Ramies · 8:17b
Rangaku.   蘭学 *See* **Western
  Learning**
Rangaku kaitei 蘭学階梯 · 6:283b
  Ōtsuki Gentaku · · · · · · · · · · · · · · 6:134b
Rangaku kotohajime
            蘭学事始 6:283b; 7:258b
Rangakusha (Scholars of Dutch
  studies) · · · · · · · · · · · · · · · · · · · 8:235b
Ranke, Leopold von · · · · · · · · · · · 3:156a
Rankei Dōryū 蘭渓道隆 5:327a; 6:283b
Rantō kotohajime 蘭東事始 · 6:283b
Ranwa tsūben
  (Dutch-Japanese
  Conversations) ·蘭和通弁 · 6:245b
Ranzan · · · · · · · · · · · · · · · · 嵐山 · 1:74b
Rape of Nanjing · · · · · · · · · · 5:329a; 7:199b
Ra Shingyoku · · · · · · · · 羅振玉 · 5:76a
Rashōmon · · · · · · · · 羅生門 · 2:56b, 272a;
            4:154b, 317b; 5:217a, 307a; 6:283b-284a
  Daiei Co, Ltd · · · · · · · · · · · · · · · · 2:56b
  Hashimoto Shinobu · · · · · · · · · · · 3:110b
Rastvorov, Yuri · · · · · · · · · · · · · · · 6:284a
Rastvorov Incident · · · · · · · · · · · 6:284a
Ratification · · · · · · · · · · · · · · · · · 6:284a

Rationing, rice ·········· 6:310a
Rats and mice [(nezumi) suborder
  Myomorpha] ··············· 6:284a
Rausudake ········· 羅臼岳 ····· 6:284b
Raymond, Antonin ········· 6:284b
*Reading in the Bamboo Study (Chikusai
  dokusho zu)* ········ 7:181a, 181a
Real estate
  religious ownership ········· 7:109b
"Realizing Buddhahood" ········· 8:27a
Realm ············· 4:269b-270a
Real property registration ····· 6:288a
Realtors ··················· 6:137a
Rebirth ···················· 6:318a
Rebun ··········· 礼文 ····· 6:284b
  Rishiri-Rebun-Sarobetsu National Park
  ························ 6:320b
Recession ··· 2:146b, 157b-158a, 163b-164a
Reconstruction Finance Bank · 6:249a,
                                   284b
  Dodge line ··············· 2:122b
Reconstruction Finance Board
  economic reform ······ 2:155b-156a, 157a
*Record of three generations of flowery
  rule* ···················· 4:101a
Records, historiography ··· 3:152a-158a
Records of Ancient Matters ··· 4:251a-251b
Records of a Tibetan Journey ····· 4:177b
"Records of the Eastern Barbarians"
  ························ 7:264a
Red algae ················· 7:46b
*Red and White Plum Trees (Kōhakubai
  zu)* ················· 4:293a-293b
Red Army faction ····· 6:284b-285a; 7:252b
  pacifism ················· 6:145b
Red Bird ················· 1:39b
Red Cross ················· 4:40b
  Sano Tsunetami, founder ······· 7:16a
Red Cross Service Organization (Nisseki
  Hōshidan) ··············· 6:238b
Red Flag ················· 1:39b
Red Flag Incident of 1908 · 6:285a-285b;
                                8:296b
  High Treason Incident of 1910 ····· 3:135a
  Kanno Suga ··············· 4:145b
Red Purge · 6:285b; 7:91b, 252a; 8:344b
  Japan Communist Party ······· 4:11b
  Occupation ··············· 6:54b
  Sambetsu Kaigi (Congress of Industrial
  Labor Unions of Japan) ··········· 7:6a
Red Wave Society (Sekirankai) ····· 7:57a
"Reed script painting" ··········· 1:97b
Reed warblers [(yoshikiri) family
  Muscipapidae] ············· 6:285b
Reform Club ················ 4:120a
Reformed Government of the Republic
  of China
  Wu Peifu (Wu P'ei-fu) ········· 8:279b
**Reform Government of the Republic
  of China** · 6:285b-286a, 302a; 8:279b
  New Order in East Asia ········· 3:61a
Refractories
  Shinagawa Refractories Co, Ltd · 7:108b
Refugees ················· 6:286a
Refuge temples ·············· 4:115b
Regency government
  ········· 摂関政治 · 2:104b, 106b,
                  348b; 6:286a-288a
  culmination ··············· 6:286b
  decline ··············· 6:286b-287b
  establishment ············· 4:130a
  Fujiwara no Yoshifusa ········· 2:358a
  Fujiwara Regency ········· 6:286a-286b
  post of Regent ············· 6:286b
  ritsuryō state ······ 6:287b-288a, 322a
  Shirakawa, Emperor ········· 7:146b
  traditional and modern views ····· 6:287b
Regent (sesshō) ············· 7:69b

Regional development
  Comprehensive National Land
  Development Plan ··············· 1:343b
Regional geographies ·········· 6:288a
Register of Foreign Affairs ······ 3:270b
Register of the Kōgo Year ······ 4:249a
Registration ················ 6:306a
Registration of property · 6:288a-288b
Regulations for the Control of
  Factory-Ship Whaling ········· 8:250b
Rei ················· 4:141b; 6:288b
Reichōrui Kenkyūjo ·········· 6:240a
Reign years ··············· 1:232a
Reiheishi Kaidō
  ··············· 例幣使街道 ····· 8:220a
Reikai monogatari 霊界物語
  Deguchi Onisaburō ··········· 2:83a
Reimeikai ········ 黎明会 2:362b; 6:288b
Reincarnation ··············· 2:80b
Reischauer, August Karl ···· 6:288b-289a
Reischauer, Edwin Oldfather ····· 2:196b;
                                   6:289a
  modernization ············· 5:228b
Reisho (clerical script) ··· 1:233b, 1:170b
Reiss, Ludwig ··············· 3:156a
Reiyūkai ········ 霊友会 6:289a-289b
Reizei family ········ 冷泉家 ····· 4:329b
Reizei Tamechika
  ··················· 冷泉為恭 ····· 6:289b
  Fukko Yamato-e school ········· 2:360b
Reizei Tamehide 冷泉為秀 ····· 3:272a
Reizei Tamesuke 冷泉為相 ····· 1:5b;
                                6:289b-290a
Rekishi chiri ···· 歴史地理 ····· 4:228b
Rekishi kagaku · 歴史科学 ····· 4:300a
Rekishi monogatari
  ··············· 2:186a; 5:246a;
                  6:79a; 7:153a; 8:242a
Rekishiteki kanazukai ······ 4:133b, 134b
Rekishō shinsho (New
  Book of Astronomical
  Calculations) ·· 暦象新書 7:153a; 8:242a
Relic hall (shariden) ··········· 1:191a
Religion ················· 6:290a-293a
  afterlife ··················· 1:20a
  animism ··················· 1:62a
  asceticism ················· 1:96b
  cosmogony ················· 2:38b
  eschatology ················· 2:231a
  freedom of religious faith ···· 2:337a-338a
  historical formation ······ 6:290a-291b
  heaven and hell ······ 3:121a-121b, 126a
  monasticism ··········· 5:236a-239a
  nature ··············· 5:357b-358a
  prayer ··················· 6:233a
  priesthood ··········· 6:238b-239b
  sacred, the ··········· 6:361b-362b
  sacrifice ··················· 6:362b
  society and ··········· 6:293b-294b
  state and ··········· 6:294a-295a
  sin ················· 8:115a-115b
  syncretism ··········· 7:288b-290b
  this-worldliness ············· 8:24b
  tolerance ··················· 8:70b
  See also **Buddhism, Christianity, New
  religions, Shintō**
Religion and modernization · 6:293a-293b
Religion and society ······· 6:293b-294b
**Religion and the state in modern
  Japan** ··············· 6:294b-295a
Religious associations (kō) ······· 4:234a
Religious education ······· 6:295a-295b
Religious foundation museums · 5:280a
Religious freedom ·········· 6:292b
Religious inquiry census registers 7:186b
Religious inquisition ······· 7:185b-186b
Religious Organizations Law ····· 8:150a
Religious symbolism ······· 6:295b-296a

Reliquary (sharitō) ·········· 1:195a
*Reluctant Admiral, The: Yamamoto and
  the Imperial Navy* ··········· 1:21a
Remon ··············· 檸檬 ····· 4:114a
Ren ····················· 4:295a
"Ren'ai kassen" 恋愛合戦 ····· 8:173b
Ren'ai kekkon ············· 2:244a
Rendai ··················· 6:296a
  Utagawa Toyokuni ··········· 6:296b
Rendaku ········ 連濁 · 6:296a-296b
  constraints ··············· 6:296a
  origins ············· 6:296a-296b
Renga and haikai 連歌俳諧 · 1:181b;
          6:296b-300a; 7:64b, 222b-223a
  canons ············· 6:298a-298b
  criticism and examples 5:15a; 6:298b-300a
  general description ······ 6:296b-297a
  history ············· 6:297a-298a
  kakekotoba ··············· 4:115b
  Kanemi kyō ki ············· 4:139b
  Shinsen tsukubashū ········· 7:124b
  Tsukubashū ··············· 8:144b
Renga poets
  Arakida Moritake ············· 1:73b
  Asayama Bontō ··············· 1:96a
  Gusai ··················· 3:70b
  Imagawa Sadayo ············· 3:272a
  Inawashiro Kensai ··········· 3:283b
  Nishiyama Sōin ············· 6:20a
  Satomura Jōha ··············· 7:27b
  Shōhaku ············· 7:161b-162a
  Takayama Sōzei ········· 7:320b-321a
  Yamazaki Sōkan ············· 8:313a
Renge Kokūzō 蓮華虚空像 ····· 1:187a
Rengeōin ········· 蓮華王院 ····· 7:13a
Rengetsu. 蓮月
  See **Ōtagaki Rengetsu**
Rengō Co, Ltd ············· 6:300a
Rengō Sekigun (United Red Army) 6:285a
Renju ··················· 6:300a
Rennyo ·········· 蓮如 ····· 4:68a;
                            6:300a-300b
  Honganji ················· 3:221b
  Ikkō ikki ················· 3:296b
  Ishiyama Honganji ··········· 3:346b
Rennyo Kenju. 蓮如兼寿 See **Rennyo**
Renown, Inc ··············· 6:300b
Rensageki ················· 2:267b
Rensha ················· 6:301a
Rensho ·········· 連署 ····· 6:301a
Rentai saimu ············· 6:301a
Rents, land ··············· 4:363b
Renunciation of war 2:82a; 4:378a; 6:166a,
                      301a-301b; 7:274b
  Occupation ··············· 6:52a
Renza ·········· 連坐 ····· 6:301a
Reorganization Loan ····· 1:287b; 6:302a;
                            7:277b
**Reorganized National Government of the
  Republic of China** ······· 6:260b, 286a,
                            302a-302b
  Wu Peifu (Wu P'ei-fu) ········· 8:279b
Reparations for Southeast Asia · 6:302b
Report cards ··········· 6:302b-303a
Report on the Ezo Lands ······· 1:39a
*Repoussé. See **Oshidashibutsu**
Reprieve (kei no shikkō menjo) ···· 2:49a
Reptiles ··········· 1:60a-60b, 62a
Republic of Korea, Japanese relations
  with. See **Korea and Japan**
Republic of the Philippines ····· 6:184a
Research and development · 6:303a-305b
  current efforts ············· 6:304a
  economic growth ············· 2:161b
  electric power ············· 2:192a
  electronics ········· 2:195a, 325a
  government ··········· 6:304a-304b
  historical background ······ 6:303a-304a

private sector ·············· 6:305a–305b
summary ·················· 6:305b
universities ··············· 6:304b–305a
**Research Institute for Iron, Steel and
Other Metals** ············· 6:305b
Research institutes ········· 6:305b–306a
Educational Research, National Institute
for ···················· 2:181a
Electric Power Industry, Central Research
Institute of ·············· 2:192a
Institute of Pacific Relations ·· 3:315b–316a
Institute of Physical and Chemical
Research ················· 3:316a
Nara National Research Institute of
Cultural Properties ·········· 5:333b
National Institute of Japanese Literature
························· 4:256b
National Japanese Language Research
Institute ················· 5:343b
National Laboratory for High Energy
Physics ·················· 3:133a
Ōhara Institute for Social Research · 6:73b
Science Council of Japan ······· 7:38a
Tōkyō National Research Institute of
Cultural Properties ··········· 8:68a–68b
Reservoirs ················· 2:72b
Resident General in Korea, Office of
························· 6:306a
opening of ··············· 4:282a
Resident registration ········· 6:306a
Resignation ················ 1:42a
Resist-dyed textiles. *See* **Sankechi**
Respect for the Aged Day ·· 2:254a; 5:5a
Responsibility
ethical concept ············ 2:232a
Restorationism ·············· 8:144b
Restoration of Imperial Rule
Ōsei Fukko ··············· 6:124a
Restoration of rights (fukken) ··· 2:49a
Restoration Shintō ········· 6:306a–306b;
7:129a–129b
Restoration War of 1868. *See* **Boshin
Civil War**
Restraint of trade, unreasonable
cartels ·················· 1:66b
definition ················ 1:66b
exemptions ··············· 1:66b
international cartels ········· 1:66b–67a
trade associations ·········· 1:66b
"Restructuring Theory" ········ 2:168b
Retailers
distribution system ········· 2:119b
Itō Yōkadō Co, Ltd ········· 3:356b
Retired shōgun ·············· 6:71a
Retirement ····· 2:245b; 4:348b, 356a; 5:5a;
6:306b–307a; 7:65a, 216b
head of household
inkyo ················· 3:307b–308a
lifestyles ··············· 5:7a
payments and benefits ······· 8:200a
pensions ················ 4:353a–353b
Return of Political Rule to the Emperor.
See **Taisei Hōkan**
Reverberatory furnace ·········· 3:99b
"Revere the Emperor, Expel the
Barbarians." *See* **Sonnō jōi**
Revised Kansei Genealogies ······ 4:152a
Rezanov, Nikolai Petrovich ······· 4:372a;
6:307a–307b
Gaikokusen Uchiharai Rei ·········· 3:3b
Golovnin, Vasilii Mikhailovich ····· 3:44a
Russia ·················· 6:341a
Rhee, Syngman ··········· 6:307b–308a
Korean independence activist ··· 4:284a
Rhee line established ········· 4:288a
Rhee line ················ 6:307b
fishing restrictions ·········· 4:285a

Korea-Japan Treaty of 1965,
supplementary agreements ········ 4:288b
Rhodesia ·················· 1:19b
Rhododendrons [(shakunage)
Rhododendron spp.] ········· 6:308a
Ri (village) ············· 里 6:308a
Ri (law, principle) ··········· 6:308a
Riccar Art Museum ········· 6:308a–308b;
7:190a–190b
Rice ···················· 6:308b–310a
botanical characteristics ········ 6:308b
cooking methods ············ 2:305a
cultivation history ·········· 6:309a
religious aspects ··········· 2:254a
folk beliefs ·············· 6:309b–310a
food staple ·············· 2:306a
Japanese cooking methods ····· 2:24a
patterns in consumption ····· 6:309a–309b
plant damage ············· 6:309a
price stabilization ·········· 2:307b
production ·············· 2:149b 308a
seed rice loans ··········· 7:264a
storage ········· 4:117b; 7:248a–249a
straw sacks ·············· 7:351b
taxes ·················· 7:239b
ritsuryō system ··········· 6:326b
technique ··············· 6:309a
varieties and improvements ·· 6:308b–309a
See also **Agriculture**
Rice blight ··········· 6:309a, 310a
Rice Control Law ············ 6:310a
religious aspects ··········· 2:254a
Rice farming
development ·············· 7:178a
influence on village design ····· 7:179a
Iseki & Co, Ltd ··········· 3:337a
Rice growing rites
rain supplication ··········· 1:22b
seedling-transplanting ········ 1:22b
sowing ················· 1:22b
Rice Law ················· 6:310a
Rice planting techniques ······· 1:28b–29a
Rice price controls ········· 6:310a–310b
land reform programs ········ 1:24b
Rice riots of 1918 ····· 6:310b–311a; 7:242a;
8:124b
China ·················· 1:388a
cooperatives, role of ········ 1:22a
employment ·············· 4:344b
Korea ·················· 4:283b
Taishō democracy ·········· 7:304b
Terauchi Masatake ·········· 8:12b
World War I ·············· 8:271a
Rice stipend (kirimai) 切米 ······ 4:221a
Rice-transplanting dances ········ 2:86a
Rice wine. *See* **Sake**
Richardson, Charles ··········· 6:311a
Richardson Affair ··········· 6:311a
Kagoshima Bombardment ······ 4:105b
United Kingdom ············ 8:150b
Willis, William ············ 8:253b
"Rich Nation and a Strong Army" 2:311b
Richō 李朝 ··········· 8:324b–325b
Rickshaw ·········· 6:311a–311b; 8:350b
Ricoh Co, Ltd ············· 6:311b
Riddles ·················· 6:311b
Ridgway, Matthew Bunker ······· 2:248a;
6:311b–312a; 7:32b
Riess, Ludwig ·············· 6:312a
Rigaku kōgen (An
Exploration of the
Principles of Philosophy)
············· 理学鉤玄 5:311b–312a
Rigen shūran 俚言集覧 ········ 6:312a
Japanese dialects ··········· 4:31b
Righteous Army Movement ······· 4:282a
resistance of Japanese control through
························· 4:282b

Righteousness (gi) ············ 4:141b
Rights
abuse ·················· 1:5b
control property ··········· 6:312a
in things ················ 6:312a
of possession ············· 7:67b–68a
proprietary ·············· 1:55a
to organize labor unions ···· 6:312a–312b
collective bargaining ········ 1:334b
to remain silent ········· 6:312b
to strike ········· 6:312b–313a; 7:250b
to sunshine ············ 6:313a
Rights in things ··········· 6:312a
Right to organize labor unions
························· 6:312a–312b
collective bargaining ········· 1:334b
Right to remain silent ········ 6:312b
Right to strike ······· 6:312b–313a; 7:250b
collective bargaining ········ 1:334b
Right to sunshine ··········· 6:313a
Right wing ············· 6:313a–314b
Amur River Society ········· 1:53b
Gen'yōsha ··············· 3:24b–25a
Kita Ikki ················ 4:225a
Kodama Yoshio ············ 4:241a
Ōkawa Shūmei ············ 6:81b
Tōyama Mitsuru ··········· 8:88a
Uchida Ryōhei ············ 8:124a
ultranationalism ··········· 8:144b–146a
Rijichō ·················· 7:274a
Rikagaku Kenkyūjo. *See* **Institute of
Physical and Chemical Research**
Ri Kaisei. 李恢成   *See* **Lee Hwe-song**
Ri Kan'yō   李完用 ·········· 8:326a
Rikka ············· 2:288b–289b, 293a
Rikka-style ················ 2:288b
Rikken Dōshikai
(Constitutional
Association of Friends)
············· 立憲同志会 · 6:210a, 314b;
7:66b
Adachi Kenzō ············· 1:11a
Katsura Tarō ············· 4:173b
Kenseikai ··············· 4:198a
Taishō Political Crisis ········ 7:305b
Wakatsuki Reijirō ·········· 8:218b
Rikken Kaishintō
(Constitutional Reform
Party) ······· 立憲改進党 · 6:207b, 314b;
7:99a, 255b
democracy ··············· 2:84b
Freedom and People's Rights Movement
························· 2:335a
Imperial Diet ············· 3:276b
Inukai Tsuyoshi ············ 3:326a
Jiyūtō ·················· 4:65a–65b
Kōno Togama founded ········ 4:275a
Ōkuma Shigenobu ·········· 6:96a
Rikken Teiseitō ············ 6:315b
senkyo kanshō ············· 7:66b
Shimpotō ················ 7:108b
Takada Sanae ············· 7:310b
Rikken Kokumintō
(Constitutional
Nationalist Party)
··············· 立憲国民党 ······· 6:210a,
314b–315a
Inukai Tsuyoshi ············ 3:326a
Kakushin Kurabu ··········· 4:120a
Universal Manhood Suffrage Movement
························· 8:169b
Rikken Minseitō
(Constitutional
Democractic Party)
··············· 立憲民政党 · 5:316a–316b;
6:211a, 315b; 7:52a, 55a, 66b, 74b
Kenseikai ··············· 4:198a
Tokonami Takejirō ·········· 8:44a

Rikken seitai ryaku
········立憲政体略 ·······**4**:168a
Rikken Seiyūkai (Friends of Constitutional Government Party)
········立憲政友会 ·**1**:97b; **3**:198a;
········**6**:210a, 315a-315b; **7**:52a, 55a, 66b
Arima Yoriyasu ·············**1**:84a
Hara Takashi ···············**3**:103a
Imperial Diet ···············**3**:227b
Itō Hirobumi ···············**3**:353a
Jiyūtō ······················**4**:65b
Kakushin Kurabu ············**4**:120a
Kaneko Kentarō ·············**4**:138b
Kenseikai ··················**4**:198a
Kenseitō ···················**4**:198b
Kiyoura Keigo ··············**4**:233a
Kōno Ichirō ·················**4**:274a
Mori Kaku ··················**5**:249b
Nakajima Chikuhei ··········**5**:313b
Ozaki Yukio ················**6**:140a
Pak Yŏl ····················**6**:159a
power of supreme command ··**8**:85a
Rikken Minseitō ············**6**:315a
Taishō democracy ·········**7**:304a-304b
Takahashi Korekiyo ·······**7**:312a-312b
Takegoshi Yosaburō ········**7**:324a
Tanaka Giichi ···········**7**:336a-336b
Teikokutō ··················**7**:376b
Tokonami Takejirō ··········**8**:44a
Universal Manhood Suffrage Movement
·······················**8**:169b

Rikken Teiseitō 立憲帝政党 **2**:366a; **6**:315a
Rikkokushi (Six National Histories) ·······六国史 ···**1**:354a;
········**6**:315b-317a; **7**:62b, 257a
Dai Nihon shiryō ············**2**:65b
general description ········**6**:315b-316a
historiography ···········**3**:152b-153a
Miyako no Yoshika ··········**5**:219b
Nihon kōki (Later Chronicle of Japan)
·······················**6**:316b
Nihon Montoku Tennō jitsuroku (Veritable Record of Emperor Montoku of Japan)
·······················**6**:316b
Nihon sandai jitsuroku (Veritable Record of Three Generations [of Emperors] of Japan) ·······**6**:316b; **7**:257a
Nihon shoki (Chronicle of Japan) ··**6**:316a
Shinkokushi ················**7**:121b
Shoku nihongi (Chronicle of Japan, Continued) ············**6**:316a-316b
Shoku Nihon kōki (Later Chronicle of Japan, Continued) ·······**6**:316b
Rikkyō University ··········**6**:317a
Ri Kō ···············李滉 ·**8**:325b
Rikord, Petr Ivanovich ·······**3**:44a
Ri Kōshō ············李鴻章 ·**5**:9b
Rikuchū Coast National Park ·陸中海岸国立公園 ·**6**:*317a*; **7**:16a
Rikuentai ·········陸援隊 ·**5**:317b; **6**:317a-317b
Rikugien Garden ·六義園 ·**6**:317b
Rikugō zasshi ·六合雑誌 **4**:300a; **8**:127b, 138a
Ōnishi Hajime ·············**6**:107b
Rikugun Nakano Gakkō ·······**5**:316a
Rikugun Shikan Gakkō. *See* **Army Academy**
Rikugunshō. 陸軍省 *See* **Army Ministry**
Rikuzen Takata ·陸前高田 ·**6**:317b
Rikyū ·············利休 ·**6**:299b
Rimpa ·········琳派 **1**:210a; **4**:361b; **6**:317b-318a
Fukuda Heihachirō ··········**2**:362a
Kōrin ·····················**4**:292b

painting ·········**6**:153a, *154a-154b*
screen and wall painting ·······**7**:43a
seals ······················**6**:281b
Rimpohan ···················**4**:308a
Rin ·······················**8**:323b
Rindō. *See* **Gentians**
Ringi system. *See* **Management**
Ringo ·····················**1**:71a
Rinji ···········綸旨 ·**6**:318a
Rinji Kyōiku Kaigi ·······**2**:176a; **6**:318b
Rinne ···················**6**:318b
Rinrigaku ·······倫理学 ·**8**:237b
Rinzai sect ·······臨済宗 ·**1**:179b, 294a; **6**:318b-320a; **7**:80b
China ····················**1**:253a
Chinese émigré masters ·····**6**:319b
Daitokuji ··················**2**:68a
founder ········**2**:187a; **6**:319a-319b
Gozan network ···········**6**:319b-320a
monks
Bankei Yōtaku··············**1**:137b
Eisai ·················**6**:319a-319b
Hakuin ··················**6**:320a
Jakushitsu Genkō ·········**4**:1b-2a
Shidō Bunan ··············**7**:89b
Yinyuan Longji (Yin-yüan Lung-chi; Ingen Ryūki) ··········**6**:320a
Ryōanji temple ············**6**:347b
Tenryūji ··················**8**:10b
Riot Police ··········**6**:320a-320b
Riron keizaigaku no kihon mondai
····理論経済学の基本問題 ···**7**:258a
Riryō ·············李陵 ·**5**:313b
Ri Sampei ·李参平 ·**1**:85b; **6**:320a
Rise and Fall of the Genji and Heike, The
·······················**3**:16b
Ri Seikei ··········李成桂 ·**8**:326a
Rishi keizairon (Economics of Ricardo)
···········李氏経済論 ·**6**:126a
Rishiri ···········利尻 ·**6**:320b
Rishiri-Rebun-Sarobetsu National Park
利尻礼文サロベツ国立公園 ···**6**:320b
Ri Shōban ··········李承晩 ·**6**:307b
Ri Shōban rain
········李承晩ライン ·**6**:307b
Ri Shunshin ·······李舜臣 ·**8**:326a
Risshakuji ·······立石寺 ·**6**:320b-321a
Risshisha ·········立志社 **1**:34b; **2**:334a, 373b; **6**:207a, 321a
Hayashi Yūzō ··············**3**:118a
Itagaki Taisuke ············**3**:349b
Taoka Reiun ···············**7**:346a
Risshō ankoku ron
·········立正安国論 **5**:375b; **6**:321a; **8**:28a
Risshō Gokoku Dō
·········立正護国堂 ·**3**:311a
Risshō Kōseikai
·········立正佼成会 ·**6**:321a-321b
Niwano Nikkyō ·············**6**:23a
Reiyūkai ··················**6**:289b
Risshū ···················**6**:332a
Ri Taiō ··········李太王 ·**4**:252a-252b
Rites and ceremonies
agricultural ···············**1**:22b-23a
Buddhist ···············**1**:194b-195a
for laity ················**1**:194b
for monks ············**1**:194b-195a
Confucianism ·············**4**:247b
religion ··················**6**:290b
Shintō ···················**7**:139a
Rites of passage ···········**2**:299b
Ritō ···········吏党 ·**6**:321b
Ritsu ···········律 ·**6**:327b-328b

ritsuryō system ············**6**:322b
Ritsuko, sono shi
·······リツ子・その死 ···**2**:76b
Ritsumeikan University ·····**6**:321b
Ritsurin Park ···栗林公園 ···**4**:103b; **6**:321b-322a, *322b*
Sanuki Folk Arts Museum ···**7**:18b
Takamatsu ·············**7**:314a-314b
Ritsuryō system ·····律令制 ·**2**:106b; **6**:322a-332a; **7**:11a, 57a, 89a-89b, 274b
agatanushi in ··············**1**:21a
barter ····················**6**:326b
classes defined ·············**7**:62a
Confucian influence ·········**1**:353b
Confucianism ·············**6**:322b
corvée labor ·····**1**:226a-226b; **8**:327a
court hierarchy ············**4**:141b
court rank ················**2**:40a
criminal law ··············**6**:327a
currency minting ··········**6**:328a
Dajōkan ················**2**:69a-70a
decline ··················**8**:338a
diplomatics ··············**2**:97b
economy ·················**2**:147a
filial piety ················**6**:325b
general principles of Ritsuryō Law
·······················**6**:322a-323a
Goki Shichidō ············**3**:43a
gōri system ·············**3**:46a-46b
hakase ···················**3**:84b
history ················**6**:330b-332a
Asuka Kiyomihara Code ········**6**:331a
compendium of regulations ···**6**:331b
Ōmi Code ···············**6**:331a
"revised ritsuryō" and "revised ryōkyaku" ··········**6**:331b-332a
Ryō no gige ··············**6**:332a
Taihō Code ············**6**:331a-331b
Taika Reform ············**6**:331a
Yōrō Code ···············**6**:331b
impeachment and legal process
·······················**6**:327a-328b
imperial edict ·············**3**:277a
imperial rule ···········**2**:203b-204b
inheritance ···············**6**:326a
inheritance law ············**3**:304a
kinship rules ··············**6**:325a
kōden under ···············**4**:243a
kōgō status ···············**4**:249a
ko (household) unit ········**4**:233b-234a
Koken under ··············**4**:253b
kokufu under ··············**4**:257b
kokugun system under ·······**4**:259b
law
education in ··············**6**:323a
philosophies of ···········**6**:322b
legal specialists ·······**6**:323a-327a
mura (village) ············**5**:265a
nengu ···················**5**:360a
official salaries ···········**2**:360b
premodern employment ·····**2**:211b
real property ·············**6**:326a
renza ····················**6**:301b
ri ·······················**6**:308a
ritsu ··················**6**:327b-333b
"ritsuryō state" ········**6**:329a-332a
ru ······················**6**:339b
ryō ······················**6**:347a
ryōge no kan ··············**6**:351b
ryō, rules of ···········**6**:324a-324b
sakimori ··················**7**:2a
Sanze Isshin no Hō (Law of Three Generations or a Lifetime) ·········**7**:19b
shichi ····················**7**:87a
shinden ··················**7**:109b
Shintō ···················**7**:126b
shōen ····················**7**:155b
uniforms ·················**8**:149b

warrior government ·············· 8:228b
yakko (slaves) ················· 8:285a
Ritsu school ···················· 5:238b
Ritsu sect ·········· 律宗 ·1:178a–178b;
6:332a
headquarters ················· 5:332b
Rittō ··················· 栗東 ·6:332a
Ritual impurity ············ 4:186a–186b
Ritualism ······················ 4:38b
Rivers
Hokkaidō
Ishikarigawa ················ 3:342a
Kushirogawa ··············· 4:320b
Mukawa ················5:262a–262b
Sarugawa ··················· 7:22b
Shiribetsugawa ············· 7:147b
Teshiogawa ················· 8:15b
Tokachigawa ················ 8:40a
Tokorogawa ················· 8:44a
Honshū
Abekawa ···················· 1:2b
Abugawa ···················· 1:5a
Abukumagawa ··············· 1:5a
Adogawa ··················· 1:14b
Aganogawa ················· 1:20b
Agatsumagawa ··············· 1:21a
Ajikawa ···················· 1:38b
Arakawa ················1:73a–73b
Aridagawa ·················· 1:83a
Asahigawa ·················· 1:92b
Asukagawa ················· 1:106b
Azusagawa ················· 1:127b
Chikumagawa ··············· 1:276b
Edogawa ··················· 2:170b
Fuefukigawa ················ 2:341b
Fujikawa ··················· 2:343b
Gōnokawa ·················· 3:46a
Hiikawa ··················· 3:136b
Hozugawa ·················· 3:246b
Ibigawa ··················· 3:253b
Iwakigawa ················· 3:358a
Jinzūgawa ·················· 4:61a
Jōganjigawa ················ 4:69a
Kakogawa ·················· 4:117b
Kamanashigawa ·············· 4:122b
Kamogawa ············4:128a–128b
Kanogawa ·················· 4:146b
Kinokawa ·················· 4:214a
Kinugawa ·················· 4:219a
Kisegawa ·················· 4:222b
Kisogawa ·················· 4:224a
Kitakamigawa ··············· 4:226a
Kizugawa ·················· 4:233b
Kujigawa ·················· 4:303a
Kumanogawa ················ 4:306b
Kurobegawa ················ 4:314a
Kuzuryūgawa ··············· 4:323a
Mabechigawa ··············· 5:77a
Miyagawa ·················· 5:216b
Mogamigawa ··············· 5:233b
Mukogawa ·················· 5:262b
Nagaragawa ················ 5:303b
Nakagawa ·················· 5:312b
Natsuigawa ················· 5:349b
Ōigawa ···················· 6:74b
Oirasegawa ················· 6:75b
Omonogawa ················ 6:103a
Ōtagawa ··················· 6:128b
Setagawa ··················· 7:70b
Shinanogawa ··············· 7:109a
Shōgawa ··················· 7:158b
Sumidagawa ················ 7:266a
Tadamigawa ················ 7:293b
Takahashigawa ·············· 7:312a
Tamagawa ·················· 7:332b
Tatsutagawa ················ 7:349b
Tedorigawa ················· 7:375a
Tenryūgawa ················· 8:10b

Tonegawa ··················· 8:74a
Totsukawa ·················· 8:85b
Ujigawa ··················· 8:131b
Watarasegawa ··············· 8:236b
Yahagigawa ···········8:284a–284b
Yamatogawa ···········8:309a–310a
Yasugawa ·················· 8:318b
Yodogawa ·················· 8:326b
Yoneshirogawa ·········8:337b–338a
Yōrōgawa ·················· 8:339a
Yoshiigawa ················· 8:346b
Yuragawa ·················· 8:358a
Kyūshū
Chikugogawa ·········· 1:83a, 276b
Gokasegawa ················ 3:42b
Kumagawa ················· 4:305a
Midorikawa ················ 5:167b
Mimikawa ················· 5:175b
Ongagawa ·················· 6:106a
Ōnogawa ··················· 6:110a
Ōyodogawa ················ 6:138b
Sendaigawa ················ 7:63b
Shirakawa ················· 7:146b
Yabegawa ·················· 1:83a
Yamakunigawa ·············· 8:297a
Shikoku
Hijikawa ··················· 3:136b
Nakagawa ·················· 5:312b
Niyodogawa ················· 6:23b
Shimantogawa ··············· 7:101a
Rizal, José ················· 6:332a
Roads ····················· 6:332b
Road Traffic Law ···· 2:48a; 6:332b–333a
drivers' licenses ·········· 2:133b–134a
Ro and sha ·················· 6:333a
Rōben ·················· 良弁 ·6:333a
Ishiyamadera ················ 3:346a
Roberts Commission
Warner, Langdon ············ 8:228a
Robertson, Walter S. ·········· 3:266a
Robins ····················· 4:264b
Robinson no matsuei
ロビンソンの末裔 ···4:111b
Robō no hana ··· 路傍の花 ···4:179b
Robō no ishi   路傍の石
Shindō Kaneto ·············· 7:111a
Robots, industrial ········3:298b–299b
Rochdale Society of Equitable Pioneers
······················· 1:22a
Roches, Léon ·· 1:229b, 267a; 6:333a–333b
French-Japanese relations ········ 2:331a
Rockets ················7:239b–241a
Rock formations ·············· 3:109b
Rōdō Kumiai Kiseikai
(Society for Formation of
Labor Unions)
······· 労働組合期成会 ·4:345a
Takano Fusatarō ············· 7:317a
Rōdō Nōmintō
(Labor-Farmer Party)
········ 労働農民党 ·1:96a; 6:333b;
7:74b
Japan Communist Party ········· 4:11a
Yamamoto Senji ·············· 8:299a
Rōdō sekai ····· 労働世界 4:167a; 7:164a
Rōdōsha Nōmintō
······· 労働者農民党 ····6:333b
Rōdōshō. 労働省 See **Ministry of Labor**
Rōdō undō nijūnen
········ 労働運動二十年 ·7:281a
Rōdō wa shinsei nari
········ 労働は神聖なり ·7:281a
Rodrigues, João ······4:51a; 6:334a
Jesuit mission press ··········· 3:1a
Rōei ·················· 朗詠 ·3:1a
Rōen (The Aging Monkey) 老猿 ·7:43a
Roesler, Karl Friedrich Hermann ·· 1:8a;
2:2b, 311a; 6:334a

Commercial Code ············· 1:338a
legal reform activities ·········· 2:319a
Rohen ·················· 炉辺 ·4:301b
Rohen sōsho ········ 炉辺叢書 ·2:302a
Rohwer Relocation Center ····· 6:334a
Roji ······················· 7:361b
Rojin ··················· 魯迅 ·5:76b
Rojō no reikon 路上の霊魂 ·5:269b
Rōjū ············· 老中 ·4:109b, 160a;
6:334a–334b
Roka Tokutomi Kenjirō
·········· 蘆花徳富健次郎 ·1:155b; 8:60a
Rōkechi ············· 藤纈 ·7:13b;
8:237b–238a
Rōketsu ················8:237b–238a
Rokkaku family ···· 六角氏 ·6:334b
free markets ················ 6:283a
Rokkakushi Shikimoku
············ 六角氏式目 ·8:346b
Rokkasen ········· 六歌仙 ·6:334b
Ariwara no Narihira ··········· 1:85b
Fujiwara no Kintō ············ 2:352a
Fujiwara no Sadaie ············ 2:354b
Henjō ···················· 3:126b
Ono no Komachi ·········6:110b–111a
Rokkō ·················· 六甲 ·4:207b
Rokkōsan ··········· 六甲山 ·1:83b;
6:334b–335a
Rokōkyō Jiken 蘆溝橋事件 ·5:113b
"Rōko shiiki" 聾瞽指帰 ·4:269b
Rokudai shōjiki 六代勝事記 ·3:154a
Rokuhara deputies 六波羅探題 ·6:335a
Rokuharamitsuji
············ 六波羅蜜寺 ·6:335a
Rokuhara tandai
········· 六波羅探題 6:335a; 7:340a
Rokujō Madenokōji
bussho 六条万里小路仏所 ·····3:313b
Rokujō no Akisuke
··········· 六条顕輔 ·2:350a
Rokujō poets ········· 六条派 ·4:1b
Rokumeikan ········ 鹿鳴館 ·6:335a–335b
Yōshū Chikanobu ············· 6:335a
Rokuon'indono
Itsukushima mōde no ki
········ 鹿苑院殿厳島詣記 ·3:272b
Rokuonji ·············· 鹿苑寺 ·4:213a
Rokuon nichiroku
·········· 鹿苑日録 ·1:264a–264b;
6:335b; 6:335b
Rokuro ···················· 6:335b
Karako site ················· 5:157b
Rokuroshi ·················· 4:205a
Rōkyoku ··············2:267b; 5:328b
Romances ·················· 5:246a
Romanization of Japanese ···· 6:335b–336b
difficulties ················· 6:336a
early systems ··············· 6:336a
general description ········· 6:335b–336a
Hepburn system ·············· 6:336a
Hyōjun system ··············· 6:336a
International Organization for
Standardization (ISO) ········· 6:336a
Kokutei system ·············· 6:336a
Kunrei system ···········6:336a–336b
Rōmajikwai ················· 6:336
Roman poruno ··············· 2:275a
Rōnin ············ 浪人 ·6:336b–337a;
7:75b
Forty-Seven Rōnin Incident ······ 2:327a
movie theme ················ 2:268a
Shinsengumi ················ 7:124a
Rōninkai ··········· 浪人会 ·6:337a–337b
Rōnō ············ 労農 6:337b; 8:297a
Rōnōha ···················· 6:337b
Rōnōha ······· 労農派 ·1:72a; 6:337b;
8:289a, 296b
Sakisaka Itsurō ·············· 7:3a

Rōnōtō. 労農党
See Rōdō Nōmintō; Rōdōsha Nōmintō
Roofs ·· 5:192b
Roof tiles ·································· 6:337b-339a
  general description ····················· 6:337b
  hongawara-buki ················ 6:337b-338a
  karakusa-gawara ······················· 6:338b
  onigawara ······················· 6:338b-338b
  sangawara-buki ······················· 6:338b
Roosevelt, Franklin Delano 6:339a; 7:246b
  atomic bomb ····························· 1:108a
  wartime relocation of Japanese
    Americans ······························· 4:17b
  World War II ··························· 8:272b
  Yalta Conference ····················· 8:286b
Roosevelt, Theodore ········· 6:339a; 7:49a
  Gentlemen's Agreement ········ 3:24a-24b
  Korean appeal to ····················· 4:282b
Root, Elihu ····························· 3:24a-24b
Rosanjin. 魯山人 See Kitaōji Rosanjin
Rosaries, Buddhist ····················· 1:197a
Rosario kiroku
  ·················· ロザリオ記録 ······· 7:241a
Rosario no kyō
  ·················· ロザリオの経 ······· 7:241a
Roses (Rosa spp.) ······················· 6:339a
Rosetsu ···················· 蘆雪 6:339a-339b
Roshia Gunkan Tsushima
  Senryō Jiken
    ロシア軍艦対馬占領事件 ······· 8:118a
Roshia shi ·········· ロシア史 ······· 4:173a
Rōshigumi
  Shinsengumi ··························· 7:124a
Rosny, Léon Louis Lucien Prunol de
  ··· 6:339b
Rōsōkai (Society of the
  Old and the Young)
    ···················· 老壮会 ······· 8:359a
Rossi, Giovanni V. ······················· 2:75b
Rossi, Vittorio ··························· 3:351a
Rotary Club ····························· 6:339b
Rotary engine ··························· 6:339b
Rotary press ····························· 6:246a
Rotenshō ································· 7:250a
Rōtō ····················· 郎党 ······· 3:261a
Rouge (beni) ····························· 2:38a
Royal Co ································· 7:196a
Royalty rights ··························· 6:164b
Rōyama Masamichi 蠟山政道 ··· 7:115b
Ru ···················· 流 ··· 6:339b-340a
Rubber industry
  Bridgestone Tire Co, Ltd ········· 1:170b
  Yokohama Rubber Co, Ltd ······· 8:330b
Ruijū fusen shō
  ·················· 類聚符宣抄 ······· 4:90a
Ruijū jingi hongen
  ·················· 類聚神祇本源 ······· 7:128a
Ruiju karin (Classified
  Forest of Verse) 類聚歌林 ······· 8:303a
Ruijū kokushi ··· 類聚国史 1:151b; 6:340a
Ruiju myōgi shō
  ·················· 類聚名義抄 ··· 1:7b; 6:340a
Ruijū uta-awase
  (Classified Texts of
  Poetry Contests)
    ···················· 類聚歌合 ······· 8:204b
Ruined Map, The ························· 1:3a
Rules of court ··············· 6:340a-340b
Rumoi ···················· 留萌 ······· 6:340b
Rumpen-mono
  Shindō Kaneto ······················· 7:111a
Runners. See Couriers
Rural Samurai ··················· 3:48b-49a
Rural women ··················· 8:266a-267a
Rushana ·········· 盧遮那 ······· 1:199a
Rusk, Dean ····························· 4:285b
Ruson Sukezaemon
  ·················· 呂宋助左衛門 ······· 6:340b

Russia and Japan ··············· 6:340b-344b
  early relations ················· 6:340b-341b
  Entente ···················· 6:341b-342a
  espionage ················ 7:229a-230a
  Ezo ····································· 2:238b
  Ioffe (Joffe), Adolf Abramovich ···· 3:328a
  Japanese studies ······················· 4:44a
  Korean Question ····················· 6:341b
  Laxman, Adam Erikovich ········· 4:372a
  neutrality ···················· 6:343a-343b
  Nishi-Rosen Agreement ··········· 6:19a
  normalization of relations ··· 6:344a-344b
  Northern Territories Issue ········· 6:344a
  occupation ··················· 6:343b-344a
  Pacific War ··························· 6:343b
  postwar relations ····················· 3:205b
  recognition of the USSR ··········· 6:343a
  refugees ································· 6:286a
  Shichihakase Jiken ··········· 7:87b-88a
  Siberian Intervention ······· 6:342b-343a
  Tairo Dōshikai (anti-Russian group) 8:88b
  Treaty of Portsmouth ········ 6:342a-342b
  Tripartite Intervention ··········· 6:341b
Russia Japan Expedition of 1852-1855
  Putiatin, Evfimii Vasil'evich ····· 6:270a
Russian Orthodox Church ········· 6:258a
  Archbishop Nikolai ··················· 6:3b
Russian Soviet Federated Socialist
  Republic ····························· 2:248b
Russo-Japanese agreements
  of 1907-1916 ····················· 6:344b
Russo-Japanese Alliance ··········· 6:342b
Russo-Japanese fisheries ··· 6:344b-345b
  Cooperative Fishery Agreement of 1978
    ··· 6:345b
  Fishery Convention of 1907 ······· 6:345a
  Fishery Convention of 1928 ·· 6:345a-345b
  Fishery Convention of 1956 ······· 6:345b
  Fishery Agreement of 1975 ······· 6:345b
Russo-Japanese Treaty of Amity · 6:270b
Russo-Japanese War ······· 1:166a; 6:342a,
  345b-347a; 8:287a
  Akiyama Saneyuki's battle plan ·· 1:144a
  annexation of Korea and ········· 4:281b
  background ··················· 6:345b-346b
  Denison, Henry Willard ··········· 2:86b
  Eastern European nations and Japan
    ··· 2:142a
  events ···················· 6:346b-347a
  French-Japanese relations ········· 2:332b
  Fukushima Yasumasa ··············· 2:367a
  Gen'yōsha ····························· 3:25a
  growth of business ··················· 2:30b
  Hibiya Incendiary Incident ······· 3:129a
  Hirose Takeo ··························· 3:148a
  Kaneko Kentarō ····················· 4:138b
  Komura Jutarō ······················· 4:268a
  Korean-Japanese relations ········· 4:279b
  Korea's annexation ··················· 4:287b
  Mukden, Battle of ··················· 5:262b
  nationalism ··························· 5:343a
  periodization ························· 6:177a
  photography ··························· 6:185b
  Portsmouth, Treaty of ······· 6:228a, 347a
  Roosevelt, Theodore ················· 6:339a
  Russian influence in Korea ········· 4:90a
  Russo-Japanese agreements of 1907-
    1916 ································· 6:344b
  Sakhalin ································· 7:2a
  Shichihakase Jiken ··········· 7:87b-88a
  Shimose Masachika ··················· 7:106b
  Tachibana Shūta ····················· 7:293a
  Tairo Dōshikai ······················· 7:303a
  Takahira-Root Agreement ········· 7:313b
  Tatekawa Yoshitsugu ··············· 7:349a
  Tōgō Heihachirō ······················· 8:36a
  territory of Japan ····················· 8:14a
  Tripartite Intervention ············· 8:107a

United Kingdom and Japan ······· 8:152a
  victory ································· 1:87b
  war literature ························· 8:226a
  World War I ··························· 8:271a
  Wu Peifu (Wu P'ei-fu) ··········· 8:279b
Rusui ···················· 留守居 ······· 6:347a
Rye and oats ··························· 8:251a
Ryō ···················· 令 · 6:324a-327b,
  347a-347b
  ritsuryō system ······················· 6:322b
Ryōanji ············· 龍安寺 · 3:8b; 6:347b
Ryōben ···················· 良弁 ······· 6:333a
Ryōbu
  Shintō ···················· 7:127b-128a
Ryōbu Mandara
  ···················· 両部曼荼羅 · 6:347b-351a
  general description ··········· 6:347a-348a
  Kongōkai ······························· 4:270a
  Kongōkai mandara ··········· 6:349a-351a
    Gōzanze katsuma e ··············· 6:350b
    Gōzanze sammaya e ··············· 6:351a
    Ichiin e ····························· 6:350b
    Kompon jōshin e ·········· 6:349b-350b
    Kuyō e ····························· 6:350b
    Misai e ····························· 6:350b
    Rishu e ····························· 6:350b
    Sammaya e ························· 6:350b
    Shiin e ····························· 6:350b
  Kongōkai mandara (Diamond Realm
    Mandala) ··························· 6:348b
  Taizō mandara ··············· 6:348a-349a
    Chūtai hachiyō in ··············· 6:348b
    Henchi in ···················· 6:348b-349a
    Jimyō in ····························· 6:348b
    Jizō in ····························· 6:349a
    Jogaishō in ························· 6:349a
    Kannon in ························· 6:349a
    Kokūzō in ························· 6:349a
    Kongōshu in ······················· 6:349a
    Monju in ··························· 6:349a
    Saige in ····························· 6:349a
    Shaka in ····························· 6:349a
    Soshitsuji in ······················· 6:349a
  Taizō mandara (Womb Mandala) · 6:348a
Ryōbun ································· 3:92b
Ryōbu Shintō ··· 両部神道 1:187b-188a;
  6:351a-351b; 7:289b
  Sannō Ichijitsu Shintō ··············· 7:15a
  Shingon sect ··························· 7:115a
  Shintō and Buddhism, separation ·· 7:132a
Ryōgae nendaiki
  ···················· 両替年代記 ······· 6:351b
Ryōgaeshō ········· 両替商 · 1:137b;
  6:351b; 7:268a
  Kōnoike family ······················· 4:274a
  Ryōgae nendaiki ····················· 6:351b
Ryōgen ···················· 良源 ······· 6:351b
Ryōge no kan ········· 令外官 ······· 6:351b
  kageyushi ······························· 4:104b
  kebiishi ······························· 4:185b
  naidaijin ···················· 5:310a-310b
  Sangi ································· 7:11a
Ryōjin hishō ········· 梁塵秘抄 · 3:49b; 5:40a;
  6:351b-352a
Ryojun ···················· 旅順 ······· 6:226a-226b
Ryōkai Mandara. 両界曼荼羅
  See Ryōbu Mandara
Ryokan. See Inns
Ryōkan ···················· 良寛 · 5:48a; 6:352a
Ryō Keichō ········· 梁啓超 · 4:384a-384b
Ryōken ···················· 亮賢 ······· 3:43a
Ryōko ···················· 良戸 ······· 7:62a
Ryokufūkai ········· 緑風会 · 6:352a-352b
Ryokuyū tōki ········· 緑釉陶器 · 1:263a
Ryōmin ···················· 良民 ······· 6:352b
  ritsuryō system ······················· 6:324a
Ryōmō Railway Company
  Taguchi Ukichi ······················· 7:294b

Ryōnin ············· 良忍 **6:**352b; **8:**359b
  nembutsu ··················· **4:**67a
  Sanzen'in ··················· **7:**20a
Ryō no gige ········ 令義解 **6:**352b; **7:**54a;
                              8:339a
  commentary ·················· **6:**352b
  ritsuryō system ·············· **6:**332a
Ryō no shūge ····· 令集解 · **6:**352b-353a;
                       7:295b; **8:**339a
Ryōō bugaku mask ·············· **5:***125b*
Ryō Shōshi ······· 廖承志 ··· **4:**384b
Ryōshu ····················· **6:**353a
  shitaji chūbun ··············· **7:**149a
  shōen ······················· **7:**156a
  yorioya-yoriko relationship ····· **8:**338b
Ryoshū (A Traveler's
  Sadness) ··········· 旅愁 · **8:**333a-333b
Ryōshun. 了俊 *See* **Imagawa Sadayo**
Ryōshun isshi den
              了俊一子伝 ···· **3:**272b
Ryōtsu ············· 両津 ··· **6:**353a
Ryōunshū ("Cloud-borne
  Collection") ······ 凌雲集 · **4:**109a, 189a;
                              5:29b
Ryōzen ············· 霊山 ··· **6:**353a-353b
Ryūchikai (Dragon Pond
  Society) ············· 龍池会 **6:**155a; **8:**327b
Ryū Chishū ········ 笠智衆 **2:***271a;* **6:**353b
Ryū Eifuku ········ 劉永福 · **5:**60a
Ryūgadō ············ 竜河洞 · **6:**353b
Ryūgaiji ············ 龍蓋寺 · **6:**78b
Ryūgasaki ········· 竜ヶ崎 · **6:**353b
Ryūgū Soga monogatari
              竜宮曽我物語 ···· **4:**319b
Ryūjōkō Jiken · 柳条溝事件 · **5:**60a
Ryūkōgo ····················· **6:**353b
Ryūkōka ·················· **6:**353b-355a
  early history ·············· **6:**353b-354a
  Edo-period ··················· **6:**354a
  late 1920s and 1930s ········ **6:**354b-355a
  after 1941 ··················· **6:**355a
  Meiji-period ············ **6:**354a-354b
  Taishō-period ··············· **6:**354b
Ryūkyū dialects ··········· **6:**355a-357a
  external history ············ **6:**355a-355b
  Okinawan ··················· **6:**355b-356b
    morphology and syntax ········ **6:**356a
    phonology ················ **6:**355b-356a
    written language ············· **6:**355b
  Outer Islands ·············· **6:**356b-357a
    Hirara ·················· **6:**356b-357a
    Sakishima ··················· **6:**356b
Ryūkyū Islands · 琉球諸島 · **6:**84b-91a,
               356b, 357a; **7:**30b; **8:**13b
  San Francisco Peace Treaty ····· **7:**10b
  Taiwan Expedition of 1874 ····· **7:**309a
Ryūkyū Kingdom. *See* **Okinawa**
Ryūkyū kizoku mondai ········ **6:**357a
Ryūkyū music ··········· **6:**357a-358a
Ryūkyū Rettō ····· 琉球列島 · **6:**357b
Ryūkyū territorial question ········ **6:**357a
Ryūkyū trade ············ **6:**358a-358b
Ryūkyū University ········· **6:**358b-359a
Ryūnōgiku (Chrysanthemum makinoi)
                              6:359a
Ryū Seiryū ········ 柳成龍 ··· **8:**358b
Ryūsendō ············ 竜泉洞 · **6:**359a
Ryūshi shinron · 柳子新論 · **8:**292b-293a
Ryūtanji Yū ······· 竜胆寺雄
  Hōrō jidai ················ **7:**119a
  Machi no nansensu ··········· **7:**119b
Ryūtei Rijō ········ 滝亭鯉丈 · **6:**359a
Ryūtei Tanehiko · 柳亭種彦 **1:**119b, 211b;
             3:42a-42b; **5:**49a; **6:**359a-359b
  fūzoku shōsetsu ··············· **2:**378a
Ryūzōji ············ 龍造寺 ··· **7:**102b
Ryūzōji family ···· 龍造寺氏 · **6:**359b

S

Saba ·························· **5:**79a
Sabae ············· 鯖江 **2:**364a; **6:**361a
Sabi ················· 寂び **1:**145a; **5:**42a;
            6:146a, 297b, 361a-361b; **7:**85b
  ferns ······················· **2:**252a
  Jakuren ····················· **4:**1b
Saburō Masaaki · 三郎正明 · **4:**270a
Sacks, straw ··················· **7:**351b
Sacred, the ············· **6:**361b-362b
  hare ····················· **2:**253b-254a
  kami ····················· **4:**125b-126a
  kami-hotoke ·············· **6:**361b-362a
  ke ······················· **2:**253b-254a
  kegare ··················· **4:**186a-186b
Sacred fire ··················· **4:**220a
Sacred Nachi Waterfall, The ····· **7:**136a
Sacrifice ··················· **6:**362b
Sacrifice, human ··············· **3:**207a
Sadae Party. *See* **Sugup'a**
Sada Keiji ········ 佐田啓二 · **6:**362b
Sadamisaki Peninsula
              佐田岬半島 ···· **6:**362b
Sadanobu ············· 定信 ··· **1:**234b
Saddlery ····················· **1:**90a
Sadō. *See* **Tea ceremony**
Sado ··············· 佐渡 **6:**363a-363b;
                       7:360a-365a
Sado bugyō ······ 佐渡奉行 · **6:**363a
Sado mines ······· 佐渡金山 · **6:**363a
  Ōkubo Nagayasu ··············· **6:**93b
Saekibe ············· 佐伯部 · **1:**147b
Safety Agency ··················· **7:**59a
Safety ordinances ··········· **4:**234a-234b
Saga-bon ············· 嵯峨本 **3:**182a; **6:**248b
Saga, Emperor ··· 嵯峨天皇 · **6:**363b
  Fujiwana no Yoshifusa ········ **2:**358a
  Fujiwara family ··············· **2:**350b
  rule ························· **2:**204a
Saga (city) ········ 佐賀 ··· **6:**363a
Sagae (city) ······ 寒河江 ··· **6:**363a
Sagami Bay ······· 相模湾 ··· **6:**363b
Sagamigawa (river) 相模川 **4:**135a; **6:**363b
Sagamihara (city) · 相模原 · **6:**363b
Sagamihara (upland)
                 相模原 · **6:**363b
Sagami, Lake ····· 相模湖 · **6:**363b
Saga ningyō ················· **2:***129a*
Saga Prefecture ··· 佐賀県 · **6:**363b-364a
Sagara Sōzō ······ 相楽総三 · **6:**364a
Saga Rebellion ··· 佐賀の乱 · **1:**34b;
                  6:364b-365a; **7:**152a
Sagi ························· **3:**127b-128a
Sagi school ··········· 鷺流 · **4:**325b
**Sagisō (*Habenaria radiata; Pecteilis*
  radiata)** ················· **6:**365a
Sagoromo monogatari
              狭衣物語 · **5:**36b; **6:**365a
Sahara Makoto ···· 佐原真 ··· **1:**78b
Sahogawa ········· 佐保川 · **6:**365a
Saiban shiyō shō
              裁判至要抄 ···· **4:**376b
Saibara ············ 催馬楽 **4:**108a; **6:**365a
  folk song ··················· **2:**138b
  gagaku ····················· **3:**1a
Saichō ············· 最澄 **1:**178b; **2:**60b;
                  5:30a; **6:**365a-366a

  autonomous ordination system
                  6:365b-366a
  Buddhist sculpture ········· **1:**198a-198b
  early life ················· **6:**365b-365b
  education ··················· **2:**172a
  Eisai ······················· **2:**187a
  Enryakuji temple ············ **2:**220b
  esoteric ritual implements ····· **1:**196a
  founding of Tendai sect ········ **6:**365b
  Kammu, Emperor ·············· **4:**128a
  monasticism ············· **5:**237b-238a
  portrait painting ············ **6:**227a
  relationship with Kūkai ········ **6:**365b
  Sanzen'in temple ············ **7:**19b
  Shintō ······················ **7:**127a
  voyage to China ············· **6:**365b
Saidaiji ············ 西大寺 · **6:**366a
Saifu ·············· 割符 **4:**102a; **6:**366a
Saifuya ············ 割符屋 ··· **4:**102a
Sai Gaku ·········· 蔡鍔 ··· **1:**229b
Saiga no tsugunoi (What
  Cai Wo [Tsai Wo] Wrote
  instead of Napping)
              宰我の償 ···· **8:**292a
Saigawa ············ 犀川 ··· **6:**366a
Saigoku risshi hen
              西国立志編 ···· **6:**366a
Saigō Takamori · 西郷隆盛 ·· **1:**87a, 165a;
              6:366a-367a; **7:**29b, 102a
  Chiossone, Edoardo ·········· **6:***366b*
  Freedom and People's Rights Movement
                              2:334a
  Itagaki Taisuke ·············· **3:**349a
  Iwakura Tomomi ············· **3:**360a
  Satsuma Rebellion ············ **7:**30a
  Seikanron issue ·············· **7:**50b
Saigō Tsugumichi
              西郷従道 ···· **6:**367a
  Kokumin Kyōkai founder ······ **4:**260b
  Shinagawa Yajirō ············ **7:**109a
Saigusa Hiroto ··· 三枝博音 · **6:**366a-366b
Saigyō ············· 西行 **1:**181a-181b;
      2:303b; **5:**39a; **6:**299b, 367b-368b; **7:**72a
  Fujiwara no Ietaka ··········· **2:**351a
  Fujiwara no Toshinari ········· **2:**357b
  Ihon Sankashū (variant Sankashū) ··· **6:**368b
  Kamo no Chōmei ············· **4:**128b
  Kikigakishū and *Kikigaki zanshū* ···· **6:**368b
  life ······················ **6:**367a-368a
  poetry ······················ **6:**368b
  Sankashū ··················· **6:**368b
  Shin kokinshū ·············· **7:**120a
Saihōji ············ 西芳寺 · **6:**368b-369a
  gardens ···················· **3:**9a-9b
Saiiki monogatari 西域物語 · **6:**369a
Saijiki ············· 歳時記 **2:**258b; **6:**369a
Saijō ·············· 西条 ··· **6:**369b
Saijō Yaso ········ 西条八十 · **6:**369b
Saika ···················· **7:**129a, 139a
Saikai National Park
              西海国立公園 ···· **6:**369b
Saikaku ········· **2:**77b; **5:**11b,
              47a; **6:**369b-371a
  fiction
    Kōshoku gonin onna (Five Women Who
      Loved Love) ········· **5:**47a; **6:**370b
    Kōshoku ichidai onna (The Life of an
      Amorous Woman) ····· **5:**47a; **6:**370b
    Kōshoku ichidai otoko (The Life of an
      Amorous Man) ······ **5:**47a; **6:**370a
    Kōshoku nidai otoko ········ **6:**370a
    Koyomi ··················· **6:**370b
    Nanshoku ōkagami ·········· **6:**370b
    Nippon eitaigura (The Japanese Family
      Storehouse) ········· **5:**47a; **6:**370b
    Saikaku shokokubanashi ····· **6:**370b
    Seken munesan'yō (Worldly Mental
      Calculations) ············· **6:**370b

Shoen ōkagami ············· **6**:370a-370b
fūzoku shōsetsu ············· **2**:378a
haikai ·········· **3**:79a; **6**:369b-370a
 "arrow counting" (yakazu) ······· **6**:370a
 "Dutch style" ·················· **6**:370a
 influence of *Shikidō ōkagami* ···· **7**:95b
 life ························· **6**:369b
 posthumously published works ··· **6**:370b
Saikaku ichidai onna (The Life of Oharu)
 ··········· 西鶴一代女 ····· **2**:*270b*
Saikaku shokokubanashi
 ···· 西鶴諸国噺 **6**:370b; **8**:144a
Saiken ············· 再建 ····· **7**:176b
Saiki ············· 佐伯 ······ **6**:371a
Saikontan ······ 菜根譚 ······ **6**:371a
Saikun ········· 細君 ······ **8**:110b
Saimei, Empress 斉明天皇 **5**:328b; **6**:371a
Saimoppo Jōyaku
 ············· 済物浦条約 ···· **1**:268b
"Saint of Kasuya" ·············· **8**:60a
St. Petersburg, Treaty of ··· **4**:7a; **6**:371a
 Russia and Japan ·············· **6**:344a
 Terashima Munenori ············ **8**:12a
Saionji, Prince ·西園寺公 ····· **3**:200b
Saionji family ··· 西園寺家 ··· **6**:371b
Saionji Kimmochi
 ········· 西園寺公望 ····· **1**:165b;
 2:332b; **5**:310a-310b; **6**:371b-372b
 genrō ····················· **3**:21b
 Hiranuma Kiichirō ············· **3**:144a
 Hirohito, Emperor ············· **3**:147a
 Nakae Chōmin ············· **5**:311b-312a
 Ritsumeikan University ········· **6**:321b
Saionji Kintsune
 ··········· 西園寺公経 ····· **6**:372b
Sairan igen ····· 采覧異言 **4**:369b; **8**:241b
Saisei itchi ··· 祭政一致 ······ **7**:245b
Saisen ······················ **5**:242a
 Saishōkōin wall paintings ······· **6**:227a
Saitama Bank, Ltd ··········· **6**:372b
Saitama Prefecture 埼玉県 ··· **6**:372b-373a
Saito ·········· 西都 ······ **6**:373a
 Saitobaru Burial Mounds Museum **5**:277b
Saitobaru tomb cluster
 ········· 西都原古墳群 ····· **6**:373a
 excavation ················· **1**:77b
 ships ····················· **7**:144a
Saitō Dōsan ·· 斎藤道三 ··· **6**:373a-373b
Saitō Gesshin ·· 斎藤月岑 ····· **6**:373b
Saitō Hiroshi ··· 斎藤博 ··· **6**:373b-374a
Saitō Makoto ··· 斎藤実 **3**:117b; **6**:374a;
 7:92a
 February 26th Incident ·········· **2**:249b
 Samil Independence Movement ··· **7**:6b
Saitō Mokichi ·· 斎藤茂吉 ·· **1**:74b; **5**:13a;
 6:374a-374b
 Kaminoyama museum ··········· **4**:127a
Saitō Mokichi nōto
 ········· 斎藤茂吉ノオト ·· **5**:316b-317a
Saitō Rinjirō. 斎藤林次郎
 See **Takayama Chogyū**
Saitō Ryokuu ·· 斎藤緑雨 · **5**:13a; **6**:374b
Saitō Sanemori ·· 斎藤実盛 ····· **6**:374b
Saitō Setsudō ·· 斎藤拙堂 ····· **6**:374b
Saitō Tatsuo ···· 斎藤達雄 ····· **2**:*269a*
Saiyūki ········· 西遊記 ······ **8**:106a
Saji Keizō ···· 佐治敬三 **6**:375a; **7**:276a
Sakado ········· 坂戸 ······ **6**:375a
Sakadoza 坂戸座
 Kongō school ················ **4**:270a
Sakagami Hiroshi ·坂上博 ····· **6**:375a
Sakaguchi Ango ·坂口安吾 · **6**:375a-375b
Sakaguchi Kin'ichirō
 ········· 坂口謹一郎 ······ **6**:375b
Sakai ············· 堺 **2**:295a; **4**:112b;
 6:375a-376b; **7**:99a
 Oda Nobunaga ··············· **6**:63a
 machishū ·················· **5**:78b

Sakai, Frankie
 ········ フランキー堺 ··· **6**:376a-376b
Sakaida Kakiemon
 ····· 酒井田柿右衛門 **1**:*261a*; **4**:116b
Sakaide ········· 坂出 **4**:103b; **6**:376a
Sakai Hōitsu ··· 酒井抱一 ····· **6**:376b
 Kameda Bōsai ················ **4**:125a
Sakai merchants ············· **6**:376b
 gokasho shōnin ··············· **3**:42b
 shipping ··················· **4**:113a
 tally trade ················ **7**:331b-332a
Sakaiminato ······ 境港 ·· **6**:376b-377a
Sakai Spinning Mill 堺紡績所 ·· **6**:377a
Sakai Tadakiyo ·酒井忠清 ····· **6**:377a
Sakai Toshihiko ·· 堺利彦 · **6**:377a; **7**:56a
 Baibunsha ················ **1**:129b-130a
 Fukuda Hideko ··············· **2**:362b
 Heiminsha ·················· **3**:125b
 Kaizō ····················· **4**:113b
Sakaki (*Cleyera ochnacea*) · **6**:377a-377b
Sakakibara Yasumasa
 ·········· 榊原康政 ······· **6**:377b
Sakaki Hyakusen 彭城百川 ···· **1**:211a;
 6:377b-378a
Sakakura Junzō 坂倉準三 ····· **6**:378a
Sakamoto Hanjirō
 ·········· 坂本繁二郎 ····· **6**:378a
Sakamoto Ryōma 坂本龍馬 ···· **5**:317b;
 6:378a-378b; **7**:3b, 23b, 29b
 Kaientai ···················· **4**:109a
Sakana ······················ **2**:25b
Sakanishi Shiho 坂西志保 · **6**:378b-379a
Sakanoue family ·· 坂上氏 ··· **6**:379a
 Aya family ··················· **1**:125b
**Sakanoue no
Tamuramaro**
 ······· 坂上田村麻呂 ····· **6**:379a
 pardon of Fun'ya no Watamaro ··· **2**:370b
 shōgun ····················· **7**:160a
Sakasafuji ·········· 逆富士 ····· **4**:177b
Sakashitamon Incident
 ········ 坂下門外の変 ····· **6**:379a
Sakata ············· 酒田 ····· **6**:379b
Sakata Shōichi ·· 坂田昌一 ····· **6**:379b
Sakata Tōjūrō · 坂田藤十郎 ··· **5**:16b, 47a
 acting style ·················· **4**:91a
Sakata Tōjūrō I
 ······· 坂田藤十郎(初代) ··· **6**:379b
Sakawagawa ······· 酒匂川 ··· **6**:379b
Sakaya ··············· **6**:379a-380b
Sakaya Kaigi ··· 酒屋会議 · **6**:380a-380b
Sake (dog salmon) ·············· **7**:5b
Sake · **1**:46b; **2**:306a; **4**:336a, 338a; **7**:1a-1b,
 5b, 207a, 257b
 brewing ·············· **1**:170a; **7**:1a-1b
 ceremonial use ················ **1**:46b
 current drinking patterns ········ **7**:1b
 economy ··················· **2**:148b
 origin ····················· **1**:46b
 present day
 social ···················· **1**:47a
 wedding ceremony ··········· **1**:47a
 present day use ··············· **1**:47a
 production ··················· **1**:46b
 refined ····················· **7**:1a
 rice consumption ·············· **6**:309b
 shōchū ··················· **7**:1a-1b
 songs
 Taue-zōshi ················ **7**:351a
 Takara Shuzō Co, Ltd ·········· **7**:318a
 tōji (brewer) ················ **8**:38a
 transport ··················· **4**:113a
Sake brewers ··············· **6**:379b-380a
Sake brewing ·················· **4**:226b
Sake Production Bureau ········· **1**:46b
Sakhalin ··················· **7**:1b-2a
 acquisition ··················· **4**:7a
 international relations ··········· **3**:320b

 Mamiya Rinzō ·············· **5**:88b-89a
Sakhalin-Kuril Islands Exchange Treaty.
 See **St. Petersburg, Treaty of**
Sakimori ········· 防人 ······ **7**:2a
Sakimori uta ···· 防人歌 ····· **7**:2a-2b
 defined ···················· **5**:106b
Sakisaka Itsurō ·向坂逸郎 ····· **7**:2b-3a
Sakishima Islands
 ·········· 先島諸島 ······· **7**:3a
 Ryūkyū dialects ··············· **6**:355a
Sakka shiron ··· 作家私論 ······ **8**:11a
Sakoku ······ 鎖国 · **5**:346b-347b
Saku (city) ······ 佐久 ······ **7**:3a
Saku Basin ···· 佐久盆地 ····· **7**:3a
Saku (stockades) ·· 柵 ······ **7**:3a
Sakugami. *See* **Ta no kami**
Sakuma Dam · 佐久間ダム **2**:73a; **7**:3a-3b
Sakuma Kanae · 佐久間鼎 ····· **7**:3b
Sakuma Kōho · 佐久間琈甫 · **2**:*129a*
Sakuma Shōzan
 ········ 佐久間象山 · **7**:3b-4a, 27a;
 8:221a-221b, 313b
 fukoku kyōhei ················ **2**:360b
Sakunami Hot Spring
 ·········· 作並温泉 ······· **7**:4a
Sakura (city) ······ 佐倉 ······ **7**:4a
Sakura (flowering cherry tree) · **1**:269a-270a
Sakurada Ichirō · 桜田一郎 · **1**:268b; **7**:4a
Sakurada Jisuke · 桜田治助 **4**:91b; **7**:4a-4b
 kabuki plays ················· **4**:91b
Sakuradamongai Incident
 ········ 桜田門外の変 · **1**:55a, 84a,
 263b; **7**:4b
Sakuradamon Incident
 ·········· 桜田門事件 ····· **7**:4b
Sakurada Takeshi 桜田武 ····· **7**:4b
Sakurai ·········· 桜井 ······ **7**:4b
 Sakurai Prize ················· **1**:268a
Sakurajima ······ 桜島 · **4**:105a-105b;
 7:4b; **8**:147b, 194a
Sakurakai ·········· 桜会 ····· **7**:5a
Sakurama Michio 桜間道雄 ·**4**:267b; **6**:*26b*
Sakurama Sajin · 桜間左陣 ····· **4**:267b
Sakurasō. *See* **Primroses**
Sakura Sōgorō 佐倉惣五郎 ····· **7**:5a
Sakushiki ········· 作職 ······ **7**:5a
Salamanders [(sanshōuo) family
 Salamandridae] ············· **7**:5a-5b
Sales contract ·············· **2**:20a-20b
Salmon and trout ·············· **2**:284a
Salmons [(sake; masu) family
 Salmonidae] ················· **7**:5b
Salt fields ··················· **2**:213b
Salvation Army ············ **7**:5b-6a
 prostitution ·················· **6**:257a
 Yamamuro Gumpei ············ **8**:300a
 Yamamuro Kieko ·············· **8**:300a
Samādhi ····················· **4**:304a
Sambesan ····· 三瓶山 · **7**:6a, 101a
Sambetsu Kaigi · 産別会議 · **4**:346b, 358a;
 6:212b; **7**:6a
 Shinsambetsu ················ **7**:124a
Sambō Hombu · 参謀本部 · **1**:90b-91a
Sambōin ········ 三宝院 ······ **2**:57b
Sambugyō ······ 三奉行 ······ **7**:6a
Same ··············· 鮫 ···· **4**:138a
Samgha
 monasticism ················· **5**:236b
Samguk sagi ·············· **6**:146a; **7**:6a
 Korean Three Kingdoms period ·· **4**:292a
 Samguk sidae ················ **4**:292a
Samguk yusa ················· **7**:6a
 Korean Three Kingdoms period ·· **4**:292a
Samil Independence Movement · **6**:159a;
 7:6a-6b, 242
 historical context ············· **4**:283b
Sammaioroshi ················· **2**:25b
Samma [(saury) *Cololabis saira*] · **7**:6b-7a

Sammon ·············· 1:183a
Sampitsu ······ 三筆 ····· 1:234a
Sampō (Industrial Patriotic Association)
··················· 4:345b
Samp'o Incident ········ 7:7a
Sampō kōjin (god)
········· 三宝荒神 ······ 4:252a
Sampo no Ran. See Samp'o Incident
"Sampō" (Sangyō Hōkoku Kai) ··· 4:351b
Sampū kushū ··· 杉風句集 ···· 7:259a
Samsara ················· 1:181a
Samurai ········ 侍 7:7a–8b, 247a,
                    251a, 258b, 261a
  abolition of class ········· 3:192a
  administrative units (yakukata) · 1:137b
  arms bearing ············· 1:88b–89a
  bakuhan system ········· 1:131a–131b
  bushidō ··············· 1:221b–223b
  Christian conversion ······· 1:308a
  Dampatsurei ············· 2:72a
  declassment ·········· 4:108b–109a
  descendants ············· 1:324b
  dissolution ············· 7:8b
  Edo ················ 2:168b–169b
  Edo period ·············· 3:186a
  education ·········· 2:172b, 174b
  employees ··········· 2:212a–212b
  ethics ······· 1:221b–223b, 276b
  feudalism ··········· 2:263b–264a
  fighting units (bankata) ······· 1:137b
  geisha ················· 3:15b
  Genroku era ·············· 3:22b
  gōshi (rural) ·········· 3:48b–49a
  hatamoto yakko ·········· 3:112a
  ie system ·············· 3:260a
  Japanese immigration to U.S. ··· 4:13b
  kana-zōshi ·············· 4:136b
  kenka ryōseibai ·········· 4:196b
  kirisute gomen (privilege to kill) · 4:222a
  leaders ················· 7:7b
  martial arts ············· 1:206a
  Medieval Age ·········· 7:7b–8a
  Meiji Restoration ········· 5:156b
  myōji taitō ·············· 5:290b
  militarism ·············· 5:173a
  organization ·········· 7:7a–7b
  origins ················· 7:7a
  pension ················· 2:151b
  physical characteristics ······· 4:35a
  salaries ················· 2:340a
  Satsuma Rebellion ········· 4:105b
  shimpan ················· 7:108a
  shi-nō-kō-shō ············ 7:122b
  sword fights (chambara) ······· 1:266a
  Taira and Minamoto struggle ···· 7:7b
  technological development ··· 7:368b
  Tokugawa shogunate ···· 7:8a–8b
  urban life ······ 2:150b–151a; 8:177b
Samurai declassment
  Edo period ·············· 4:108b
  Muromachi period ········· 4:108b
Samurai descent ······· 7:151a–152a
Samurai-dokoro ··· 侍所 4:122a; 5:273b;
                        7:8b, 97b
  Kajiwara Kagetoki ·········· 4:114b
  Minamoto no Yoritomo ······· 4:122a
Samurai society
  lineage ················· 7:108a
  related houses ············ 7:108a
Sanada Nobushige
  ················ 真田信繁 ···· 7:9a
Sanada Yukimura
  ················ 真田幸村 ···· 7:9a
  Sekigahara, Battle of ········ 7:56b
Sanage ·········· 猿投 ····· 1:258a,
              261b–262a; 7:9a–9b, 71a
  green-glazed wares ········· 1:263a
  Tokoname ware ············ 8:44a

Sancho Kurabu ········· 5:19a
Sanchū hōrō ··· 山中放浪 ···· 4:270a
Sanda ········· 三田 ····· 7:9b
Sandai Jiken Kempaku Movement
  ······ 三大事件建白運動 ····· 7:9b
Sandaikō   三大考
  Hirata Atsutane influenced ···· 4:259a
Sandaishū ("The Collections of Three
  Eras")   三代集 ····· 8:204a
Sandakan hachiban shōkan
  ···· サンダカン八番娼館 ··· 4:159b–160a
Sandakan hachiban shōkan: Bōkyō
  サンダカン八番娼館:望郷 ···· 7:337a
Sandamme ·········· 7:272a, 273a
San'en ··············· 8:29a–29b
Sanetaka Kō ki ··· 実隆公記 · 7:9b, 12b
San Felipe Incident ······ 7:9b–10a
San Francisco Board of Education · 7:49a
San Francisco Peace Treaty 6:178b, 302b;
  7:10a–11a, 28a, 275a; 8:160a–160b, 165b,
                        344b
  Article 14 ·············· 7:235b
  atomic bomb ············· 1:110b
  Cambodia ··············· 1:236b
  Canada ················· 1:238a
  Communist purge termination ··· 2:339a
  Dulles, John Foster ········· 2:135a
  Far Eastern Commission ······· 2:248a
  French-Japanese relations ····· 2:333b
  Hiratsuka Raichō ··········· 3:146a
  Indonesia and Japan and ······ 3:291a
  Latin American emigration ····· 4:369b
  Netherlands ·············· 5:362b
  New Zealand ·············· 5:372b
  Occupation ·············· 6:51a
  Okinawa ················· 6:88b
  Ōsu Incident ············· 6:128a
  peace movement ··········· 6:166b
  Philippines ·············· 6:184b
  postwar relations with China ···· 1:290a
  Russia and Japan ·········· 6:344a
  territory of Japan ·········· 8:14b
  United Kingdom ··········· 8:153a
  United States military bases, disputes
  ····················· 8:168a
San Francisco Symphony Orchestra
  Ozawa Seiji ·············· 6:140b
San Francisco World's Fair of 1939
  ····················· 8:228a
Sangaku   散楽 ····· 7:22a
Sangaku shinkō · 山岳信仰 · 5:259b–260a
Sangatsu Jiken ··· 三月事件 · 5:112b–113a
Sangawara-buki ············ 6:338a
Sanger, Margaret ······· 2:246b; 7:11a
Sangha ················· 1:177a
Sangi   参議 · 2:70a–70b;
                    7:11a–11b
Sangoku jidai ··· 三国時代 · 4:292a; 7:6a
Sangoku Kanshō.
  三国干渉
  See Tripartite Intervention
Sangoku shiki ··· 三国史記 ···· 7:6a
Sangō shiki ····· 三教指帰 ···· 4:304a
Sanguo zhi ··············· 7:264a
Sangyō gisho ··· 三経義疏 · 7:11b, 172a
Sangyō kumiai (production unions) 1:21b
San'ichi Dokuritsu Undō
  ····· 三・一独立運動 · 7:6a–6b
San'ichigo Jiken. See March 15th
  Incident   三・一五事件
San'in Coast National
  Park ··· 山陰海岸国立公園 ··· 4:338b
Sanja Festival ···· 三社祭 2:253a; 5:172b;
                        7:11b
Sanjiin ················· 8:291a
Sanjo (people) ······ 散所 · 7:11b–12a
Sanjō, Emperor 三条天皇 ···· 7:12a

Sanjō (city) ········ 三条 ···· 7:12a
Sanjōgatake ····· 山上ケ岳 ···· 6:102a
Sanjōnishi Sanetaka
  ·········· 三条西実隆 ··· 7:12a–12b
  diary ·················· 7:9b
  incense ceremony ·········· 3:285a
  Kokin denju ············· 4:254a
Sanjō Sanetomi · 三条実美 · 7:12b, 88a
  lord keeper of the privy seal · 5:310a–310b
  Seikanron issue ··········· 7:50b
Sanjō wasan ···· 三帖和讃 ···· 8:231a
Sanjūrokkasen 三十六歌仙 2:354a; 4:161b;
                        7:12b–13a
  Ariwara no Narihira ········· 1:85b
  Ōnakatomi no Yoshinobu ··· 6:105a–105b
Sanjūrokunin sen
  ········· 三十六人撰 ···· 4:161b
Sanjūrokunin Kashū
  (Collection of Thirty-six Master
  Poets)   三十六人歌集 7:266b; 8:233a
Sanjūsangendō
  ········ 三十三間堂 1:189a; 4:145a;
                     7:13a, 13b, 67b
Sanjūyonka no kotogaki
  (The Thirty-Four
  Articles) · 三十四箇事書 ···· 8:27a
Sanka ················· 7:13b
Sankan. 三関 See Sekisho
Sanka zui ······ 三貨図彙 ···· 4:319a
Sankechi ··········· 7:13b; 8:17b
Sankeien ········ 三渓園 ···· 7:13b
Sankei shimbun
  ········ サンケイ新聞 ··· 2:347b;
                     7:13b–14a
Sanki Engineering Co, Ltd ···· 7:14a
Sankin kōtai   参勤交代 · 1:131b, 132a;
                     7:14a–14b, 265a;
                        8:98a
  Edo ················ 2:168b, 170a
  Edo-period ·············· 2:171b
  feudalism ··············· 2:266b
  Gokaidō ············· 3:41a–41b
  Hakone no Seki ··········· 3:86b
  urban life ··············· 8:177b
Sankōsha gogengyō ········· 7:14b
Sankō Steamship Co, Ltd ···· 7:14b
Sankyō Aluminium Industry Co, Ltd
  ····················· 7:14b
Sankyō Co, Ltd ··········· 7:15a
Sankyō Seikō Co, Ltd ······· 7:15a
Sankyū, Inc ············· 7:15a
Sanlüe ················· 4:82a
Sannō ········· 山王 ···· 7:136a
Sannō Festival ··· 山王祭 · 4:137a; 7:15a
Sannō Ichijitsu Shintō
  ········ 山王一実神道 ··· 7:15a–15b
  Ichijitsu shintō ki ·········· 3:255b
  Shintō ················· 7:127b
Sannō Nijūissha
  ········ 山王二十一社 ··· 3:130b
Sano ·········· 佐野 ···· 7:15b
Sano Manabu ···· 佐野学 ···· 7:15b
Sano no Chigami no
  Otome ··· 狭野茅上娘子 ··· 7:15b–16a
Sano Tsunetami · 佐野常民 · 1:119b–120a;
                        7:16a
  Kaigun Denshūjo ·········· 4:110a
Sanoyasu Dockyard Co, Ltd ··· 7:16a
Sanraku. 山楽   See Kanō Sanraku
Sanriku Coast ··· 三陸海岸 · 2:285b; 7:16a
Sanrizuka ········ 三里塚 ···· 7:16a
Sanron ········· 産論 ···· 4:102b
Sanron school ··· 三論宗 · 1:178b; 4:71b;
                     5:332b; 7:16a–16b
Sansai tōki ··· 三彩陶器 ···· 1:263a
Sansei ··········· 4:13a–13b, 14b–15a
  Hawaiian politics ·········· 4:16b
  Japan ················ 4:15a–15b

marriage · · · · · · · · · · · · · · · · · **4**:17a
Sanseki (Three [Brush]
Traces) · · · · · · · · · 三蹟 · **1**:234a-234b
**Sanshimpō (Three New
Laws)** · · · · · · · · 三新法 · **1**:103b; **7**:16a
Sanshin
Ryūkyū music · · · · · · · · · · **6**:357a
Sanshirō · · · · · · 三四郎 · · · · · **5**:350a
Sanshō · · · · · · · · · · **2**:305a; **3**:127b
Sanshoku · · · · · · · · 三職 · **7**:16b-17a
Sanshōuo · · · · · · · · · · · · **7**:5a-5b
Sanshu no jingi
· · · · · · · 三種の神器 · **3**:278b-279a
Sanskrit drama · · · · · · · · · · **8**:22a
Sanskrit language · · · · · · · · **7**:192b
Sanskrit treatises · · · · · · · · · **8**:21b
Sansom, George Bailey · · · · **7**:17a-17b
works · · · · · · · · · · · · · · **7**:17a-17b
Sansui Electric Co, Ltd · · · · · · · **7**:17b
Sansuiga · · · · · · · 山水画 · **6**:151a, 158b;
7:17b
Autumn and Winter Landscapes · · · · · · **7**:17a
Sesshū Tōyō · · · · · · · · · · **7**:17a
subjects · · · · · · · · · · · · · **6**:158b
Santai (Three Truths) 三諦 · · · · **8**:29a
Santō Kyōden · · · 山東京伝 · **1**:130b; **5**:48b;
7:18a-18b, 96b
fūzoku shōsetsu · · · · · · · · · · · **2**:378a
gesaku · · · · · · · · · · · · · · · **3**:28b
sharebon · · · · · · · · · · · · · · **7**:79b
Santō Mondai. 山東問題
See **Shandong (Shantung) Question**
"Santō senkyaku" (The
Steerage Passengers)
· · · · · · · · · 三等船客 · · · · · **5**:80a
Sanuki Folk Arts Museum · · · · · **7**:18b
Sanuki Mountains
· · · · · · · · · 讃岐山脈 · **4**:103a; **7**:18b
Sanuki no Suke no nikki
· · · · · · · 讃岐典侍日記 · **5**:38b; **6**:2b;
7:18b
Sanuki Plain · · · · 讃岐平野 · **7**:18b
Sanwa Bank, Ltd · · · · · · · · **7**:18b-19a
Tōyō Trust & Banking Co, Ltd · · · · **8**:96a
San'yaku · · · · · · · · · · · · · · **7**:272a
San'yō Electric Co, Ltd · · · · · · · **7**:19a
San'yo-Kokusaku Pulp Co, Ltd · · · · **7**:19a
San'yūtei Enchō
· · · · · · · · · 三遊亭円朝 · · · · **7**:19b
Sanze Isshin no Hō
· · · · · · · · · 三世一身の法 · · · · **7**:19b
Sanzen · · · · · · · · · · · · · · · **7**:234a
Sanzen'in · · · · · 三千院 · **7**:19b-20a
Sanzenri · · · · · · 三千里 · · · · **4**:178a
Sanzonzō · · · · · · · 三尊像 · · · · **7**:20a
Saotome · · · · · · · · · · · · · · · **7**:20a
Sapporo · · · · · · · · 札幌 **7**:20a, *20b*, 98a
Sapporo band · · · · · · · · · · · **6**:258a
Sapporo Breweries, Ltd **4**:221a; **7**:20a-20b
Sapporo Winter Olympic Games · · · **7**:20b
Sararīman · · · · · · **7**:20b-21a; **8**:251b
urban life · · · · · · · · · · · · · · **8**:178b
Sarasa · · · · · · · · · · · · · · · · **7**:21a
Sarashina nikki · 更級日記 · **1**:154a; **5**:35b;
6:2a; **7**:21a-21b, 257b; **8**:104b
Sarcoli, Adolfo · · · · · · · · · · **3**:351a
Sardines [(iwashi) family Clupeiformes]
· · · · · · · · · · · · · **2**:284b; **7**:21b
Saris, John · · · · · · · · · · · **7**:21b-22a
Sarobetsu Plain
· · · · · · · サロベツ原野 · **7**:22a; **8**:15b
Rishiri-Rebun-Sarobetsu National Park
· · · · · · · · · · · · · · · · · **6**:320b
Saroma, Lake · サロマ湖 · **7**:22a
Saru · · · · · · · · · · · · · · · **5**:245a-245b
Sarugaku · · · · · · 猿楽 **1**:216a; **2**:297b;
5:43a; **7**:22a-22b
dance, traditional · · · · · · · · · **2**:74a-74b

Sarugaku nō · · · · · 猿楽能 · · · · **4**:324b
Sarugawa · · · · · · 沙流川 · · · · **7**:22a
Sarukani kassen 猿蟹合戦 · · · · **7**:22b
Saru mawashi · · · · · · · · · · · **7**:250a
Sarumino · · · · · · 猿蓑 · · · · · **6**:298a
Sarusawa Pond · · · 猿沢池 · **5**:*331a*; **7**:22b
Sasa · · · · · · · · · · · · · · **1**:135b-136a
Sasagawanagare 笹川流れ · · · · **7**:22b
Sasago Pass · · · · 笹子峠 · · · · **7**:22b
Sasaki Dōyo · · · 佐々木道誉 · · · · **7**:23b
Sasaki Eigyōbu Co, Ltd · · · · · · **6**:300b
Sasaki Kojirō 佐々木小次郎 · · · · **6**:221b
Sasaki Kōzō · · 佐々木更三 · **7**:22b-23a
Sasaki Nobutsuna
· · · · · · · · 佐佐木信綱 · · · · **7**:23a
Sasaki Ryōsaku
· · · · · · · · 佐々木良作 · · · · **7**:23a
Sasaki Sōichi · 佐々木惣一 · **2**:3b; **7**:23a
Sasaki Takaoki 佐々木隆興 · · · · **7**:23a
Sasaki Takasada
· · · · · · · · 佐々木高貞 · · · · **4**:275a
Sasaki Takatsuna
· · · · · · · · 佐々木高綱 · **7**:23a-23b
Sasaki Takauji 佐々木高氏 · · · · **7**:23b
Sasaki Takayuki
· · · · · · · · 佐々木高行 · · · · **7**:23b
Sasaki Toyoju · 佐々城豊寿 · · · · **7**:23b
Sasamegoto · · ささめごと · **7**:23b-24a, 80b
*Sasameyuki (The Makioka
Sisters)* · · · · · · · · · 細雪 **1**:102a; **6**:230a;
7:176b, 343a
Sasanqua · · · · · · · · · · · · · **7**:31b-32b
Sasara · · · · · · · · · · · · · · · **7**:24a
Sasayama · · · · · 篠山 · · · · · **7**:24a
Sasebo · · · · · · · 佐世保 · · · · **7**:24a
Sasebo Heavy Industries Co, Ltd · **7**:24a
Sase Yojiemon
· · · · · · · 佐瀬与次右衛門 · · · **1**:38b
Sashidashi · · · · · · 指出 · · · · **4**:193a
Sashi-e · · · · · · · · · · · · · · **1**:163b-164a
Sashi hijiki · · · · · · · · · · · · · **1**:183b
Sashiko · · · · · · · · **2**:294a; **7**:24a-24b
techniques · · · · · · · · · · · **7**:24a-24b
Sashimi · · · · · · **2**:305b-306a; **7**:24b; **8**:323b
Sāstra · · · · · · · · · · · · · · · **1**:177a
Sata · · · · · · · · · · 沙汰 · · · · **7**:25a
Sata Ineko · · · · 佐多稲子 · · · **6**:255a;
7:25a-25b, 66b
works · · · · · · · · · · · · · · · · **7**:25a
Satake-bon · · · · · 佐竹本 · · · · **4**:161b
Satake family · · · 佐竹氏 · · · · **7**:25b
Satake Shozan · 佐竹曙山 · · · · **7**:25b
Sata mirensho · 沙汰未練書 · · · · **7**:25b
kabegaki definition · · · · · · · · · **4**:90a
Satamisaki · · · · · 佐多岬 · · · · **7**:25b
Satchō Dōmei. 薩長同盟
See **Satsuma-Chōshū Alliance**
Satellites, artificial. *See* **Space
technology**
Sato · · · · · · · · · · · · · · · · · **6**:308a
Satodairi · · · · · · · 里内裏 · · · · **7**:26a
Satō Eisaku · · · 佐藤栄作 · **1**:159a;
7:26a-26b, 28a, 252b
Fujiyama Aiichirō defeat · · · · · · · **2**:359a
hikaku sangensoku · · · · · · · · · **3**:137a
Satō Genchō · · 佐藤元萇 · **5**:251b, 252b
Satogo · · · · · · · · · · · · · · · **7**:26b
Satō Hachirō
· · · · · · · サトウハチロー · **7**:26b, 27b
Satō Haruo · · · 佐藤春夫 · · · **5**:13a;
7:26b-27a, 253b
fiction · · · · · · · · · · · · · · · · **7**:27a
poetry · · · · · · · · · · · · · · · · **7**:27a
samma (saury) in poetry · · · · · · · · **7**:7a
Satō Issai · · · · 佐藤一斎 · **5**:315a; **7**:3b,
27a; **8**:335b
*Satokagami (Mirror of
Flower Town)* · · · · · 里鏡 · · · · **3**:95a

Sato kagura · · · · · · 里神楽 **4**:107b; **5**:283a
Satō Kōgyō Co, Ltd · · · · · · · **7**:27a-27b
Satō Kōroku · · · · 佐藤紅緑 · · · **7**:27b, 121a
Satō Hachirō · · · · · · · · · · · · **7**:26b
Satomi and the Eight "Dogs" **5**:329a-329b
Satomi Ton · · · · · 里見弴 · · · · **7**:27b
radio drama · · · · · · · · · · · · · **6**:275a
Satomura Jōha · 里村紹巴 · **6**:297a; **7**:27b
Satō Naokata
(Neo-Confucian
scholar) · · · · · · · · 佐藤直方 · · · **7**:27b-28a
Satō Naotake (diplomat)
· · · · · · · · · 佐藤尚武 · · · · **7**:28a
Satō Nempuku · 佐藤念腹 · · · · **7**:28a
Satō-Nixon Communiqué · · **7**:28a-28b;
8:160a
Japanese-Korean cooperation · · · · **4**:286a
trade with China · · · · · · · · · · **1**:291a
United States-Japan Security Treaties
· · · · · · · · · · · · · · · · · **8**:167b
Satō Nobuhiro · 佐藤信淵 · · · · **7**:28b
Satori · · · · · · · · **7**:28b; **8**:373b-374a
Satō Satarō · 佐藤佐太郎 · · · · **7**:28b
Satō Takeo · · · 佐藤武夫 · · · · **7**:28b
Satō Tatsuo · · · 佐藤達夫 · · · **7**:28b-29a
Satō Toshi. *See* Tamura Toshiko
Satow, Ernest Mason · · · · · · **1**:77a; **7**:22a,
29a-29b, 270b
Satsuban · · · · · · · · · · · · · · **2**:*260b*
Satsuei Sensō · · · 薩英戦争 · · · · **4**:105a
Satsuki *(Rhododendron indicum)*
· · · · · · · · · · · · · · **1**:126a-126b
Satsuma and Chōshū oligarchs. *See*
Hambatsu
Satsuma-Chōshū Alliance
· · · · · · · · 薩長同盟 **4**:109a; **5**:317b;
7:29b
Inoue Kaoru · · · · · · · · · · · · **3**:310a
Komatsu Tatewaki · · · · · · · · · **4**:266a
Shinagawa Yajirō · · · · · · · · · · **7**:109a
Satsuma Peninsula
· · · · · · · · 薩摩半島 · · · · **7**:29b
Satsuma Province 薩摩国 · · · **7**:29b-30a;
8:323b
Satsuma Rebellion
· · · · · · · · 西南戦争 · **1**:85a; **7**:16a,
30a, 152a; **8**:291a
chitsuroku shobun · · · · · · · · · · **1**:298a
Fujita Denzaburō · · · · · · · · · · **2**:346a
Hayashi Yūzō · · · · · · · · · · · **3**:118a
Kabayama Sukenori · · · · · · · · · **4**:89b
Kawakami Sōroku · · · · · · · · · · **4**:181b
Kido Takayoshi · · · · · · · · · · · **4**:203b
Kōno Togama · · · · · · · · · · · · **4**:275a
location · · · · · · · · · · · · · · · **4**:105b
Red Cross Society · · · · · · · · · · **4**:40b
Saigō Takamori · · · · · · · · · · · **6**:367a
samurai · · · · · · · · · · · · · · · · **7**:8b
Sasaki Takayuki · · · · · · · · · · · **7**:23b
Seikanron issue · · · · · · · · · · · **7**:51a
Shiroyama · · · · · · · · · · · · · **7**:148a
Takehashi Insurrection · · · · · · · · **7**:324a
Takenouchi Tsuna · · · · · · · · · · **7**:325a
Tani Kanjō · · · · · · · · · · · · **7**:341b-342a
Terauchi Masatake · · · · · · · · · **8**:12b
Willis, William · · · · · · · · · · · · **8**:253b
Satsuma Tayū · · 薩摩太夫 · **4**:76b-77a
Satsuma ware · · · 薩摩焼 · · · **7**:30a-30b
Satsumon culture
· · · · · · · · 擦文文化 · · · · **7**:30b
Satsunan Islands 薩南諸島 · **6**:357a; **7**:30b
Saury · · · · · · · · · · · · · · · · **7**:6b-7a
Savings, consumer · · · · · · · · · **2**:17b
Savings and loan banks (sōgo ginkō)
· · · · · · · · · · · · · · · · · **1**:139b
Savings Bank Ordinance of 1890 · **1**:138b
Sawada Miki · · · 沢田美喜 · · · · **7**:30b
Elizabeth Saunders Home · · · · · · **2**:196b

Sawada Shōjirō
　　　　　沢田正二郎 ······ 2:268a;
　　　　　　　　　　　7:30b-31a
　　Shinkokugeki ··········· 7:121a
Sawamura Sōjūrō
　　　　　沢村宗十郎 ······· 7:31a
Sawa Nobuyoshi ··· 沢宣嘉 · 7:31a-31b
Sawara ··········· 佐原 ······ 7:31b
Sawayanagi Masatarō
　　　　　沢柳政太郎 ······· 7:31b
　　school curriculum ········· 7:36a
　　Shin Kyōiku Undō ······· 7:121a
Saya ····················· 4:295b
Sayama ············ 狭山 ····· 7:31b
Sayama Kengyō · 佐山検校 ···· 4:65a
Sayama, Lake ······ 狭山湖 ··· 7:31a
Sayo no Nakayama
　　　　　小夜ノ中山 ······· 7:31b
Sazae san ······ サザエさん ······· 6:275b
Sazanka [(sasanqua) Camellia
　　sasanqua] ············· 7:31b-32b
Scandinavia
　　Japanese studies ··········· 4:43b
SCAP ·············· 7:32b-33a, 47a
　　civil information and education
　　　section ··············· 1:317a
　　deputy chief ············· 4:101a
　　normalization negotiations ···· 4:284b
　　Sorge Affair ············· 7:229b
Scapegoats
　　dolls ·················· 2:128a
Scarecrows ················ 4:115a
Scenes in and around Kyōto ······ 4:146a
Schnell, John Henry ········· 4:13b
Scholars' names ········· 5:325a-326a
Scholastic Shintō ·········· 2:300b
School Administration ········ 7:33a
School administration and finance. See
　　Education
School architecture ········· 7:33a-33b
Schoolchildren, life of ········· 5:6b
School course guidelines ········ 7:34a
　　textbooks ··············· 7:37b
School curriculum ········· 7:34a-36a
　　history of ············· 7:35b-236a
　　revision ················ 2:180a
　　structure ············· 7:34b-35b
　　　extracurricular activities ········· 7:35b
　　　foreign language ········· 7:35b
　　　health and physical education ···· 7:35b
　　　home economics ········· 7:35b
　　　language ············· 7:34b
　　　mathematics ··········· 7:35a
　　　music and art ··········· 7:35b
　　　science ··············· 7:35a
　　　social studies ········· 7:34b-35a
School Education Law of 1947 ··· 2:179b;
　　　　6:235b; 7:34a, 36a-36b, 241b
　　higher education ··········· 3:133a
　　outline ················· 2:180a
　　private schools ··········· 6:252a
　　structure ··············· 2:182b
School entrance examinations
　　··················· 2:222a-224b
School libraries ············ 7:36a-36b
School lunch program ········ 7:36b
School orders ············· 7:36a-36b
　　teachers ··············· 7:365b
Schools for Japanese children
　　abroad ·············· 7:36a-37b
School system. See Education
School system administration and
　　finance ·············· 2:177a-178b
School textbooks ············ 7:37b
Science and International Affairs
　　Bureau ················ 3:319b
Science and Technology, Council for
　　···················· 7:38a

Science and Technology Agency · 1:219a;
　　　　6:304a; 7:37b-38a
　　1977 White Paper on Science and
　　Technology ·············· 7:372b
　　Ocean resource development ······· 6:59a
　　technology, modern ········· 7:373a
Science Council of Japan · 1:218b; 7:38a
　　natural science ············· 5:357a
Science fiction ········· 6:221b; 7:38a-39a
　　Edo-period ············· 7:38a-38b
　　Meiji period to World War II ······· 7:38b
　　mystery stories ··········· 5:292a
　　post-World War II ········· 7:38b-39a
Scientific research
　　natural science ········· 5:356b-357a
Scientific thought, premodern · 7:39a-41a
　　astronomy ··········· 7:39a, 40a
　　Confucianism ··········· 7:40a-40b
　　emperor's mandate ········ 7:39a-39b
　　mathematics ····· 7:39b-40a; 8:231a-232a
　　medicine ············· 5:145b-147a
　　Shibukawa Shunkai ········· 7:40a, 86a
　　Western influences ········ 7:39b-40a
Scott, Marion McCarrell ····· 7:35b, 41a
Screen ·················· 2:371a
Screen and wall painting ···· 3:181a-183a;
　　　　6:151b; 7:41a-43b
　　byōbu-e ············· 7:41b-42a
　　Chinese Lions ········· 4:146a-146b
　　Cherries and Maples panels ····· 7:41a-41b
　　early shōbyōga ·········· 7:42a-42b
　　Edo-period shōbyōga ········ 7:43a-43b
　　Hikone byōbu ············ 2:377a
　　Iris Screens ··········· 6:154a-154b
　　Kanō school ··········· 4:149a, 150a
　　medieval shōbyōga ········ 7:42b-43a
　　shōhekiga ··············· 7:41b
　　rakuchū rakugai zu ·········· 2:377a
Script style ··············· 7:170a
"Scriptures of the Konkōkyō" ···· 4:272a
Scroll of Hungry Ghosts ········ 1:191a
Scrolls of Frolicking Animals and
　　Humans. See Chōjū giga
Scrolls of Hells ··········· 4:54a-54b
Sculptors
　　Buddhist
　　　Chōsei ··············· 1:303b
　　　Enkū ············· 2:218a-218b
　　　Inson ··············· 3:315a
　　　Jōchō ············· 4:66a-66b
　　　Kaikei ··············· 4:111a
　　　Kōkei ··············· 4:253a
　　　Kuninaka no Muraji Kimimaro · 4:309b
　　　Kuratsukuri no Tori ········ 4:312a
　　　Myōen ··············· 5:290a
　　　Tankai ··············· 7:343b
　　　Unkei ··············· 8:172a
　　　Yamaguchi no Atai Ōguchi ····· 8:294b
　　modern
　　　Asakura Fumio ············ 1:94b
　　　Hiragushi Denchū ········ 3:142b-143a
　　　Horiuchi Masakazu ········· 3:228b
　　　Noguchi, Isamu ··········· 6:31b
　　　Ogiwara Morie ············ 6:70b
　　　Takada Hiroatsu ········· 7:310b
　　　Takamura Kōun ·········· 7:316b
　　　Takeuchi Kyūichi ········· 7:326a
　　modern
Sculpture. See Buddhist sculpture;
　　Masks; Sculpture, modern
Sculpture, modern ·········· 7:43b-44b
　　international participation ········· 7:44b
　　Meiji and Taishō (1912-1926) ··· 7:43b-44a
　　neoclassicism ············ 7:44a
　　object in space ··········· 7:44b
　　Ogiwara Morie ··········· 7:44b
　　Onna (Woman) ··········· 7:44b
　　outdoor ··············· 7:44b

Rōen (The Aging Monkey) ········ 7:43a
　　romanticism ··········· 7:44a-44b
　　Shōwa period ··········· 7:44a-44b
　　Takamura Kōun ··········· 7:43a
　　Western-style ·········· 7:43b-44a
　　See also Sculptors
Sculpture, premodern. See Buddhist
　　sculpture
Sculptures
　　haniwa ············· 3:97b-98a
SDF ················ 7:58b-60b
Sea bream [(tai) family Sparidae] · 2:284a;
　　　　5:352a-352b; 7:45a
Sea cucumbers [(namako)
　　class Holothuroidea] ···· 2:287a; 7:45a
Seafood ················· 7:179b
Seagulls. See Gulls
Seals ············· 4:145a; 7:45b-46a
　　artist's ················ 6:281b
　　diplomatic ··········· 2:99b-100a
　　tensho ················ 1:233b
Seamen's Insurance Law ········ 6:172a
Sea of Japan ··············· 7:46a
Sea of Japan, Battle of. 日本海海戦
　　See Tsushima, Battle of
Search and seizure (sōsaku,
　　sashiosae) ·············· 2:49b
Seas, marginal ·············· 4:8b
Seasonal festival ·········· 7:58a-58b
Seasonal workers
　　dekasegi ··············· 2:83b
Seasonings ············· 2:21a-21b
Seasons ·················· 4:8a
　　festivals ··············· 2:254a
　　folk beliefs ··········· 2:297a-297b
　　folk religion ············· 2:298b
　　haiku ··············· 3:81b-82a
Sea urchins [(uni) class Echinoidea]
　　··················· 7:46a-46b
Seaweed ················ 7:46b
Seaweed cultivation ····· 2:284a; 7:46b, 47a
Sebald, William Joseph ········ 7:47a
Sebiki Kemi ······ 畝引検見 ···· 4:191a
Seburi Mountains 背振山地 ····· 7:48b
Sechie-zumō ······ 節会相撲 ···· 4:82a
SECOM Co, Ltd ·········· 7:47a-47b
Secondary education. See Education,
　　secondary
Secondary industries ···· 6:239b; 7:47b
"Secondary unions" ·········· 4:359b
Second National Bank ········ 4:184b
Second United Front ········ 7:47b-48a
Secret agents
　　ommitsu ·········· 6:102b-103a
Secret History of the Mongols ···· 4:18b
Secret language ········· 5:303b-304a
"Secret Selection of Dust and Motes"
　　················· 6:351b-352a
Sect Shintō ····· 教派神道 · 2:300b; 7:48a,
　　　　137a
Sect Shintō, Association
　　of ······ 教派神道連合会 ····· 7:48a-48b
Secularism ··········· 6:204a, 292b
Securities
　　American Depository Receipts (ADR)
　　··················· 1:51b
　　bonds, government ········· 1:160a
　　fixed-interest ············ 1:160a
Securities Bureau of the Ministry of
　　Finance ················ 7:48b
Securities Exchange Law · 1:8b-9a; 7:48b,
　　　　247a-247b, 254a
　　auditing practices ··········· 1:9a
　　financial reporting requirements
　　················· 2:277b-278a
　　tax accounting ··········· 7:352a
Securities Investment Trust Law · 3:327b

Security Consultative Committee
United States-Japan security treaties
·· **8**:167a
Sedōka 旋頭歌
waka ······································ **8**:202b
Seedlings Law ······················· **1**:30a
Sefuri Mountains 背振山地 ···· **7**:48b
Segawa Jokō 瀬川如皐 ········· **7**:48b
**Segregation of Japanese schoolchildren
in the United States** ··· **4**:14a; **7**:48b-49a
Sei 生 ·············· **7**:359a
Seian Jiken 西安事件 · **8**:281a-281b
Seibo ···································· **7**:49a
kaeshi ·································· **4**:102a
Seibu Department Stores, Ltd · **7**:49a, 55a
Seibu Railway Co, Ltd ········· **7**:49b
Tsutsumi Yasujirō ················ **8**:119a
Seibutsu 静物 ········· **7**:167a
Seichōkai ······························ **5**:18b
Seichō no Ie ····· 生長の家 ···· **7**:49b
Taniguchi Masaharu ·············· **7**:341b
Seidan 政談 ··········· **7**:49b
Seidō 西堂 ··········· **7**:49b
Seidōki jidai ·· 青銅器時代 ··· **1**:173b-174a
Seidōkyō ································ **1**:174a
Seifukugumi ·········· 制服組 ···· **7**:58b
Seifū sagen 清風瑣言 ·· **8**:126b
Seiiki monogatari
(Account of the West)
················ 西域物語 ·· **8**:242a
Seii tai shōgun
············ 征夷大将軍 **3**:172b; **4**:122a,
192b
Seiji Kenkyūkai ···················· **1**:2a
Seiji Kōgaku Kenkyūjo ········· **4**:275a
Seiji Shōsetsu ··· **7**:50a-50b, 255b
new literature ······················ **7**:50a
rehabilitation of novel ·········· **7**:50a
significance ·························· **7**:50a
Seikadō Bunko 静嘉堂文庫 · **5**:277a; **7**:50b
Seikanron 征韓論 ····· **7**:50b-51a
Seikan Tunnel 青函トンネル
Tappizaki ···························· **7**:346a
**Seikatsu Tsuzurikata
Undō** ····生活綴り方運動 ··· **7**:51a
Seiken igen 靖献遺言 · **1**:95b; **7**:51b
Seiki 清輝 ·· **8**:334a
Seikōkai 聖公会 ···· **7**:51b
Seikōsha Co, Ltd ·················· **4**:200b
Seikyōsha (Society for
Political Education)
·················· 政教社 ···· **7**:51b
Miyake Setsurei ··················· **5**:218b
Shiga Shigetaka ··················· **7**:91b
Seikyō yōroku ·· 聖教要録 · **4**:247a; **7**:51b;
8:290a
Seimeikei ········ 生命刑 ··· **7**:140b
Seimi kaisō ···· 舎密開宗 ··· **8**:125b
Seimikyoku 舎密局 · **7**:51b-52a
Seimino ································ **7**:249b
Seinan no Eki ·· 西南の役 ··· **7**:30a
Seinan Sensō. See **Satsuma Rebellion**
Seinen Bungaku Kai ·············· **5**:18b
Seinen gakkō 青年学校 ········ **7**:52a
training ······························ **2**:183b
Seinen Geijutsu Ha ··············· **5**:19a
Sei no yōkyū to bungaku
················ 生の要求と文学 ··· **4**:165a
Seiōbo ············ 西王母 ··· **5**:295b
Seirigaku 生理学 ··· **4**:167b
Seiryōji engi emaki
·············· 清凉寺縁起絵巻 ··· **4**:149b
Seiryōki 清良記 ···· **7**:52a
Seiryūsha (Blue Dragon Society)
modern painting ·················· **6**:157b
Seiryūtō-gata sekki
················ 青竜刀型石器 ··· **7**:248a

Seisetsu igen sūyō
·············· 西説医原枢要 ······ **7**:316b
Seishin shugi (spiritualism) ······ **4**:233a
Seishin shūyō ······················ **3**:63a
Seishō 政商 ·········· **7**:52a
kan'ei jigyō haraisage ··········· **4**:138a
Sei Shōnagon ··· 清少納言 · **1**:18a; **2**:280a;
5:325a; **7**:52a-54a
butterflies ·························· **1**:226a
classical Japanese language ···· **1**:322a
feminine language ················ **2**:250b
Fujiwara no Kintō ················ **2**:352a
Fujiwara no Teishi ··············· **2**:356b
literary significance ············· **7**:53b-54a
Makura no sōshi ··· **5**:34a-34b; **7**:52b-53a
personality ························· **7**:53a-53b
private life and career ··········· **7**:53b
Seisho no kenkyū (Bible
studies) ······ 聖書の研究 ··· **6**:144a
Russo-Japanese War ············ **6**:346b
Uchimura Kanzō ·················· **8**:124b
Seishū 勢州 ··· **3**:337b
Seismologists
Milne, John ························ **5**:175a
Ōmori Fusakichi ·················· **6**:103a
Seismology ·························· **2**:140b
Seisonkaku 成巽閣 ··· **5**:276b
Seisuishō 醒睡笑 · **1**:62a-63a;
6:282a
Seitai ·································· **4**:263a
Seitai no Eki ····· 征台の役 ··· **7**:309a-309b
Seitaisho 政体書 **7**:16b, 54a, 55a
Fukuoka Takachika ·············· **2**:365a
Seitō 青鞜 · **7**:54b; **8**:297a
Seitōsha 青鞜社 **7**:54a-54b; **8**:289b
Hiratsuka Raichō ················· **3**:146a
Itō Noe ······························ **3**:355a
Kamichika Ichiko ················· **4**:126a
Seiwa Genji. 清和源氏
See **Minamoto family**
Seiyō dōchū hizakurige
·············· 西洋道中膝栗毛 ··· **4**:135a
Seiyō jijō ····· 西洋事情 **1**:207b; **2**:368a;
4:387a; **7**:54b-55a
Seiyō kibun ······ 西洋紀聞 · **1**:72b; **7**:192b;
8:241b
Seiyō zasshi (Journal of
Western Affairs) 西洋雑誌 ········ **6**:245b
Seiyū Hontō (True Seiyū
Party) ············ 政友本党 · **6**:211a; **7**:55a,
66b
Kenseikai ··························· **4**:198a
Rikken Minseitō ·················· **6**:315a
Tokonami Takejirō ··············· **8**:44a
Seiyūkai. 政友会 See **Rikken Seiyūkai**
Seiyū Stores, Ltd ·············· **7**:55a
Seiza ("quiet sitting") ············· **6**:261b
Seizonken ·························· **7**:55a-55b
Seizure ····························· **7**:55b
Seji kembunroku
·············· 世事見聞録 ········ **7**:55b
Sekai 世界 · **7**:55b-56a
Iwanami Shoten Publishers ···· **3**:361a
Sekai fujin 世界婦人 · **2**:362a; **7**:56a
Sekai Heiwa Apīru Shichinin Iinkai **1**:340a
Sekaihō no riron
·············· 世界法の理論 ········ **7**:337b
Sekai Keizai Hihan Kai ··· **1**:84a-84b
Sekai Kirisutokyō Tōitsu Shinrei Kyōkai
·································· **3**:216b-217a
Sekai Kyūsei Kyō
·············· 世界救世教 ········ **7**:56a
Okada Mokichi ···················· **6**:78b
Sekai Meshiya Kyō
·············· 世界メシア教 ········ **7**:56a
Sekai no meisaku (World
Masterpieces) 世界の名作 ········ **6**:275b

Seken musuko katagi
·············· 世間子息気質 ········ **8**:144b
Seken tekake katagi
·············· 世間妾形気 ········ **8**:126a
Sekibō ······························· **7**:247b
Seki (city) 関 ··· **7**:56a
Seki (town) 関 ··· **7**:56a-56b
Sekigahara ·········· 関ケ原 · **7**:56b, 274b
Gifu Prefecture ··················· **3**:31a-31b
Ōgaki ································· **6**:68a
Sekigahara, Battle of
·············· 関ケ原の戦 · **1**:83b; **5**:299a;
7:9a, 25b, 56b, 98b, 101b
Date Masamune ··················· **2**:78a
fudai ·································· **2**:340b
Fukushima Masanori's role ····· **2**:366b
Ishida Mitsunari ·················· **3**:340a
Konishi Yukinaga ················· **4**:270b
Tōdō Takatora ···················· **8**:34b-35a
Tokugawa Ieyasu ··········· **3**:186a; **8**:50b
tozama (outside vassals) ········ **8**:97a
Uesugi family ······················ **8**:129a
warrior government ··············· **8**:230a
Sekigunha. See **Red Army faction**
Seki Hironao 瀬木博尚 ····· **7**:56b
Hakuhōdō, Inc ···················· **3**:88a
Sekihōji 石峰寺 ··· **3**:353b
Sekimon Shingaku. See **Shingaku**
Sekine Shōroku · 関根祥六 ···· **6**:27a
Sekino Tadasu 関野貞 ··· **1**:79b
Seki no to 関の扉
tokiwazu-bushi ···················· **8**:43b
Sekirankai ·············· 赤瀾会 · **7**:57a; **8**:260b
Itō Noe ······························ **3**:355a
Tanno Setsu ······················· **7**:344a
Yamakawa Kikue ················· **8**:297a
Sekirei ···························· **8**:200b-201a
Sekisen 関銭 · **7**:57a
Sekisho 関所 · **4**:153b; **7**:57a
Sekisui Chemical Co, Ltd ···· **7**:57b
Sekisui House, Ltd ··········· **7**:57b
Seki Takakazu 関孝和 ···· **7**:57b
natural sciences ··················· **5**:355b
Takebe Katahiro ·················· **7**:321b
Sekitori ························· **7**:272a, 273a
Sekiwake ························· **7**:272a
Sekiya Kiyokage 関谷清景
earth sciences ····················· **2**:140a
Sekkan ······························· **7**:248a
Sekkan seiji 摂関政治 · **6**:286a-288a
Sekke shōgun · 摂家将軍 · **7**:57b-58a
Sekki 節気 · **1**:231a, 259b
Sekku 節句 **2**:260a; **7**:58a-58b
"Selections of Poetry in the New Style"
(Shintaishi shō) ················· **8**:216a
Self-defense, national right of ···· **7**:60b
Self Defense Forces (SDF) · **1**:219a; **2**:52a;
6:198b; **7**:58b-60b; **8**:344b
arms and equipment ·············· **7**:60a-60b
budget ······························· **7**:59b-60a
constitutionality ·················· **2**:218a
constitution and SDF ············ **7**:60b
defense buildup ··················· **7**:60a
duties and operations ············ **7**:59a-59b
education and training ············ **7**:60a
history ································ **7**:58b-59a
judicial review ···················· **4**:79b
maritime ···························· **2**:231b
Naganuma case ··················· **5**:303a
national defense ·················· **5**:336b-338b
National Defense Academy ······ **5**:338b
National Police Reserve ········· **5**:345b
national right of self-defense ··· **7**:60b
Occupation ························· **6**:54b
organization and command ····· **7**:59a
pacifism ····························· **6**:145a
personnel ··························· **7**:59b
United States ······················ **8**:160a

United States-Japan security treaties
·········· 8:166b
United States military bases disputes
·········· 8:168a
units ·········· 7:60a
Self Defense Forces Law ·········· 7:59a
Self-employment ·········· 2:210b; 4:353b; 7:60b
Self-governing bodies ·········· 7:207a
Self-help ·········· 7:60b-61a
Self Help (Saigoku risshi hen) ·········· 5:315a
Self Help Society ·········· 6:321a
Sembakoki ·········· 千歯扱 ·········· 7:61a
*Sembazuru (Thousand
Cranes)* ·········· 千羽鶴 4:176b; 6:230a
Sembetsu ·········· 2:249a
Sembon Matsubara
·········· 千本松原 ·········· 7:61a
Semburi (Swertia japonica) ·········· 7:61a-61b
Sembutsu ·········· 1:176a-176b
Semenov, Grigorii Mikhailovich ·········· 7:61b
Semi ·········· 1:315a
Semiconductor industry
Ibuka Masaru ·········· 3:254a
silicon production ·········· 7:111b
Semimaru ·········· 蟬丸 ·········· 7:61b-62a
Semmen koshakyō
·········· 扇面古写経 ·········· 7:266b
Semmin ·········· 賤民 2:104a; 7:62a
ritsuryō system ·········· 6:324a
Semmon gakkō ·········· 7:62a; 8:170a
development ·········· 2:175b-176a
training ·········· 2:183b
Semmyō ·········· 宣命 ·········· 7:62a-62b
Rikkokushi ·········· 6:316a
Sempai-kōhai ·········· 7:62b
gakubatsu ·········· 3:4b
Sempūyō ·········· 1:153a-153b
Sen ·········· 8:323b
Senaga Kamejirō
·········· 瀬長亀次郎 ·········· 7:63a
Senate ·········· 3:22a
Sencha ·········· 7:365a
*Senchaku hongan
nembutsushū*
·········· 選択本願念仏集 4:67b; 7:63a
Senchakushū ·········· 選択集 3:220a-220b;
5:359b; 7:63a
Senchimentaru jānī
·········· 感傷旅行 ·········· 7:335b
Sendai (Honshū) ·········· 仙台 7:63a, 63b
Sendai (Kyūshū) ·········· 川内 ·········· 7:63b
Sendai Bay ·········· 仙台湾 ·········· 7:63b
Sendaigawa ·········· 川内川 ·········· 7:63b
Sendai Plain ·········· 仙台平野 ·········· 7:63b
Sendan ·········· 1:291b
Sendoki jidai ·········· 先土器時代 6:233a-233b
Sengai Gibon ·········· 仙厓義梵 1:194a; 7:63b;
8:374b
Idemitsu Art Gallery ·········· 3:258b
"Sengen hitotsu" 宣言一つ ·········· 1:84b
Sengen Shrine ·········· 浅間神社 2:359b; 7:64a,
153b
Sengokubune ·········· 千石船 ·········· 4:112b
Sengoku daimyō 戦国大名 1:212a; 3:175a;
7:64a
Sengokuhara ·········· 仙石原 ·········· 7:64a
Sengoku period 戦国時代 ·········· 7:64a-64b
kabegaki ·········· 4:90a
Ōnin War ·········· 6:106b
samurai ·········· 7:8a
Sen Hime ·········· 千姫 ·········· 7:64b-65a
Senior councillors ·········· 6:334a-334b
Seniority system ·········· 2:34a, 36a, 211a;
7:65a-65b, 214a
managerial ideology ·········· 5:92a-92b
job tenure ·········· 4:356b-357b
occupational structure ·········· 6:56a
retirement ·········· 6:306b

women in ·········· 8:265b
Seni Pramot ·········· 2:339b; 7:65b
Senji ·········· 宣旨 ·········· 7:65b
rinji ·········· 6:318a
Senjinkun ·········· 戦陣訓 ·········· 7:65b
Senjōgahara ·········· 戦場ケ原 ·········· 7:65b
Senjōgatake ·········· 仙丈ケ岳 ·········· 7:66a
Senjōsan ·········· 船上山 ·········· 7:66a
Senjuji ·········· 専修寺 ·········· 7:66a
Senju Seijūsho 千住製絨所 ·········· 7:66a
Senju Woolen Mill ·········· 7:66a
Senkaku ·········· 仙覚 ·········· 7:66a
Man'yōshū exegesis ·········· 5:110a
Senkaku Islands ·········· 尖閣諸島 ·········· 7:66a
Senkaku Islands, disputes over. *See*
Territory of Japan
Senkan ·········· 8:231a
Senkan Yamato
(Battleship Yamato)
·········· 戦艦大和 ·········· 8:319b
Senkawa Aqueduct ·········· 7:332b
Senke Motomaro 千家元麿 ·········· 7:66b
Senki ·········· 戦旗 ·········· 7:66b
*Senkō sanzenri (Three Thousand Miles
Underground)*
·········· 潜行三千里 ·········· 8:114a
Senku
Rōnōha ·········· 6:337b
Shinjinkai ·········· 7:115b
Senkyo kanshō ·········· 選挙干渉 ·········· 7:66b
Shinagawa Yajirō ·········· 7:109a
"Senkyūhyaku nijūhachinen sangatsu
jūgonichi" ·········· 4:237b; 7:242a
Sennan ·········· 泉南 ·········· 7:66b
Sennimbari ·········· 千人針 ·········· 7:67a
Sennin ·········· 仙人 · 5:295b-296a;
7:67a
Sen no Rikyū ·········· 千利休 · 1:136a, 158a;
2:21b, 289b; 3:197a; 4:337a; 7:67a-67b
Furuta Oribe ·········· 2:373b
tea ceremony ·········· 7:361a
tea ceremony fans ·········· 2:248a
tea gardens ·········· 3:9b
Sen'oku Hakkokan
·········· 泉屋博古館 ·········· 7:67b
Senryōbako ·········· 7:67b
Senryū. 川柳 *See* **Zappai and senryū**
Senryūhyō mankuawase
·········· 川柳評万句合 ·········· 4:157a
Senshi bankō ··· 千紫万紅 ·········· 4:199b
Senshindō satsuki
Ōshio Heihachirō ·········· 6:126a
Sensō to heiwa (War and
Peace) ·········· 戦争と平和 ·········· 8:319b
Sensuijima ·········· 仙酔島 ·········· 7:67b
Sentai butsu ·········· 7:67b
Senten sōhō ·········· 先天相法 ·········· 6:187a
Sentō ·········· 1:146a
Sentsūzan ·········· 船通山 ·········· 7:67b
Sen'yū ·········· 7:67b-68a
Sen'yū to shoyū
·········· 専有と所有 ·········· 7:255b
Senzaishū ·········· 千載集 ·········· 7:68a-68b
Senzai wakashū
·········· 千載和歌集 4:198b; 5:39a;
7:68a-68b, 96b, 302a
compilation ·········· 7:68a
composition and structure ·········· 7:68a
Fujiwara no Ietaka ·········· 2:351a
Fujiwara no Toshinari ·········· 2:356b
Jakuren ·········· 4:1b
major poets ·········· 7:68a
poetic styles ·········· 7:68a-68b
Senzui byōbu ·········· 山水屛風 ·········· 7:42a-42b
Senzui Kawaramono
·········· 山水河原者 ·········· 3:9b
Seoul, Treaty of ·········· 4:280b; 7:68b
Kapsin Political Coup ·········· 4:156b

Seoul-Inch'ŏn Railroad ·········· 4:281b
Seoul-Pusan Railroad ·········· 4:281b
Seppuku ·········· 切腹 ·········· 2:274b;
7:68b
See also **Harakiri**
Sequential voicing ·········· 6:296a-296b
Sericulture ·········· 7:68b-69a
Serizawa Chōsuke ·········· 3:358a
Serizawa Keisuke
·········· 芹沢銈介 2:294a; 7:69a
Serizawa Kōjirō
·········· 芹沢光治良 ·········· 7:69a-69b
Serow. *See* **Kamoshika**
Servants, hereditary ·········· 2:340b
Service population ·········· 7:12a
Sessai. 折柴 *See* **Takii Kōsaku**
Sesshō ·········· 摂政 · 2:204a; 7:69b
Sesshū Tōyō ··· 雪舟等楊 · 1:156a, 192b,
193a; 3:306b; 6:152b; 7:17a, 42b, 69b-70a;
8:371a
Gakuō Zōkyū ·········· 3:4b
Haboku Landscape ·········· 7:69a
ink painting ·········· 3:306b
sansuiga (landscape painting) ·········· 7:17b
Sesson Shūkei ··· 雪村周継 7:42b, 70a, 70b
Sesson Yūbai ··· 雪村友梅 · 1:150b; 7:70b
Setagawa ·········· 瀬田川 ·········· 7:70b
Setagaya Ward ·········· 世田谷区 · 7:70b-71a
Seta no Karahashi
·········· 瀬田唐橋 ·········· 4:333b
Setchōshū ·········· 節用集 ·········· 7:72b
Setchūbai ·········· 雪中梅 ·········· 7:255b
Setchūgakuha ·········· 折衷学派 ·········· 7:71a
Seto ·········· 瀬戸 ·········· 7:71a
Seto Naikai. 瀬戸内海 *See* **Inland Sea**
Setō Shōji ·········· 瀬藤象二 ·········· 7:71a
Setouchi ·········· 瀬戸内 ·········· 7:71a
Setouchi Harumi
·········· 瀬戸内晴美 ·········· 7:71a
Seto ware ·········· 瀬戸焼 · 1:258b;
2:295b; 4:337a; 7:71a-71b
jar ·········· 1:257b
museums ·········· 5:279b
tea ceremony ·········· 7:360b, 364b
Setsu ·········· 節 ·········· 1:231a
Setsubun ·········· 節分 · 2:259a-259b;
4:327a, 327b; 7:71b
cooking ·········· 2:22a
religious symbolism ·········· 6:296a
Setsuhei
Tominaga Nakamoto ·········· 8:71b
Setsuwa ·········· 1:180b; 3:154a
Setsuwa bungaku (tale
literature) ·········· 説話文学 · 5:26a, 246b;
7:72a-72b, 131b
Kodai kenkyū ·········· 4:240b
Setsuwa-mono (tales of
the strange) ·········· 説話物 ·········· 8:144a
Setsuyōshū ·········· 節用集 7:64b, 72b-73a
Setting Sun, The ·········· 2:80a
Settlement regions (teijūken)
urban planning ·········· 8:180b
Settsu ·········· 摂津 ·········· 7:73a
Seven Deities of Good Fortune · 5:296a;
7:73a, 250a
Daikokuten ·········· 2:60b
dolls ·········· 2:129b
Ebisu ·········· 2:60b, 143b
Ōkuninushi no Mikoto ·········· 6:97b
Shintō family altars ·········· 7:137b
Seven Sages ·········· 8:173a
Seven Sages in a Bamboo Grove · 4:110b
"Seven Sages of Renga" ·········· 7:320a
Seven Samurai · 七人の侍 2:272a; 4:317b;
7:73a
Seven Shingon Patriarchs ·········· 6:227a
Seventeen-Article Constitution · 6:205a;
7:73a-73b, 190b, 264a

China · · · · · · · · · · · · · · · · · 1:281b
codes of conduct · · · · · · · · · · 1:207a
Shōtoku · · · · · · · · · · · · · · · · 7:171b
Taika Reform · · · · · · · · · 7:295b-296a
Seventh-Day Adventists · · · · · · · · · 6:144b
Seven-Volume Haikai Collection · · · · 3:78a
Sewa-mono (domestic
plays) · · · · · · · · · · 世話物 · · 4:91a, 92a,
93a-94a; 5:234b
acting style · · · · · · · · · · · · · · 4:94a
dialogue · · · · · · · · · · · · · · · 4:94a
costume, wig and makeup · · · · · 4:95b
Sewing box · · · · · · · · · · · · · · · 3:103b
Sewing ceremonies · · · · · · · · · · · 3:104a
Sexagenary cycle. See Jikkan jūnishi
Sex education · · · · · · · · · · · · · · 7:73b
Sex in Japanese folk culture · 7:73b-74a
folk song · · · · · · · · · · · · · 7:73b-74a
religious observances · · · · · · · · 7:74a
Sexual discrimination · · · · · · 2:229b-230a
Seyakuin · · · · · · · · · · 施薬院 · · · 7:74a
Kōfukuji building · · · · · · · · · · 4:243b
Kōmyō, Empress · · · · · · · · · · 4:268b
Shadan therapy · · · · · · · · · · · · 6:261b
Shaga · · · · · · · · · · · · · · · · · · 3:331b
Shain (permanent members of a
company) · · · · · · · · · · · · · · 4:344b
Shaka · · · · · · · · · · · · · · · · · · 1:176a
Shakaigaku gairon
· · · · · · · · · · · · 社会学概論 · · 7:319b
Shakai keizaigaku
· · · · · · · · · · · · 社会経済学 · · 4:135b
Shakai Minshu Rengō
· · · · · · · · · · · · 社会民主連合 · · 8:154b
Shakai Minshutō (Social
Democratic Party)
· · · · · · · · · · 社会民主党 · · 1:2b, 40b;
6:210b; 7:74a-74b; 8:349a
Shakai mondai · · · 社会問題 · · 4:135b
Shakai Minshūtō
· · · · · · · · · · · 社会民衆党 · · · 7:74b
Shakai mondai kenkyū
· · · · · · · · · · 社会問題研究 · · 4:180b
Shakai Shimin Rengō. See United
Social Democratic Party
Shakai shōsetsu · · · · · · · · · · · 4:180a
"Shakaishugi hyōron"
· · · · · · · · · · 社会主義評論 · · 4:180b
Shakai Shugi Kenkyūkai
(Socialist Study Party)
· · · · · · · · · 社会主義研究会 · · 1:2a, 72a;
6:210b; 7:74b
Shakai Shugi Kyōkai
(Socialist Association)
· · · · · · · · · · 社会主義協会 · · 6:210b
Tazoe Tetsuji · · · · · · · · · · 7:359a-359b
Shakai shugi shinzui
· · · · · · · · · · 社会主義神髄 · · 4:297a
Shakai Taishūtō (Socialist
Masses Party) 社会大衆党 · 1:96a; 3:198b;
6:211a; 7:74a
Asō Hisashi · · · · · · · · · · 1:102b-103a
founding · · · · · · · · · · · · · · · 1:2b
tenkō · · · · · · · · · · · · · · · · · · 8:7a
Shakaitō · · · · · · · · 社会党 · · 7:74b-75a
Shakai to kokka
· · · · · · · · · 社会と国家 · · · 7:319b
Shaka Triad · · · · · · · · · · · · · · 1:197a
Shaken · · · · · · · · · · · · · · · · · 7:251b
Shakkintō · · · · · · 借金党 · · · 4:267a
Shakotan Peninsula
· · · · · · · · · · · · 積丹半島 · · · 7:75a
Shakubyōshi · · · · · · · · · · · · · · 4:108a
Shaku Chōkū · · · · · 釈迢空 · · · 6:118b
Shakuhachi · · · · · · · · · · · · · 7:75a-76a
history · · · · · · · · · · · · · · · 7:75a-76b
jiuta · · · · · · · · · · · · · · · · · · 4:64b
music · · · · · · · · · · · · · · · · · · 7:75b

musical instruments · · · · · · · · · 5:282b
Shakunage · · · · · · · · · · · · · · · 6:308a
Shaku nihongi · · · 釈日本紀 · · · 7:76a
Shaku Sōen · · · · · · 釈宗演 · · 7:76a, 281b
Shaku Unshō · · · · 釈雲照 · · · 5:239a
Shakuyaku. See Leased house rights
Shakuyaku. See Peonies
Shamanism · · · · · · · · · · · · · 7:76a-76b
kagura · · · · · · · · · · · · · · · · · 4:107b
miko · · · · · · · · · · · · · · · · · · 5:172a
Takamagahara · · · · · · · · · · · · 7:314a
women in · · · · · · · · · · 8:256b, 258a
yamabushi · · · · · · · · · · · · · · · 8:288a
Shame · · · · · · · · · · · · · · · · 3:83b-84a
Shamisen · · · · · · 1:161b; 7:75b, 76b-77a
film accompaniment · · · · · · · · · 2:267b
folk music accompaniment · · · · · 2:301a
kabuki music · · · · · · · · · · · · · 4:99a
musical instruments · · · · · · · · · 5:282b
nagauta · · · · · · · · · · · · · · · · 5:307b
Okinawa · · · · · · · · · · · · · · · 6:86b
ryūkōka · · · · · · · · · · · · · · · · 6:354a
Shamoji (spatula) · · · · · · · · · · · 2:25a
Shand, Alexander Allan · · · · · · · · 1:8a
Shandao · · · · · · · · · · · · · · · 4:67a-67b
Shandong (Shantung) Question
· · · · · · · · · · · 4:367a-367b; 7:77a-77b
Washington Conference · · · · · · · 8:234b
Shanghai Conspiracy: The Sorge Spy
Ring · · · · · · · · · · · · · · · · · 8:253b
Shanghai Incident
· · · · · · · · · · · · · · · 7:77b-78a, 92a
League of Nations · · · · · · · · · · 4:373b
nationalist government · · · · · · · · 1:289a
Sino-Japanese War 1937–1945 · · · 7:199a
Shanghai International Settlement
· · · · · · · · · · · · 7:78a-78b; 8:252b
Shanhai (Shanghai) · 上海 · 7:116b, 175b;
8:332b
Shanhai Jiken · · · · 上海事件 · · 7:77b-78a
Shanhai jing (Shan-hai ching; Classic of
Mountains and Waterways) · · · · 8:197a
Shan-hou Chieh-k'uan · · · · · · · · · 6:302a
Shanhou Jiekuan · · · · · · · · · · · 6:302a
Sharaku · · · · · · · · · 写楽 · · 7:78b-79b;
8:143a
drawings · · · · · · · · · · · · · · · 7:79a
identity · · · · · · · · · · · · · · 7:79a-79b
influence · · · · · · · · · · · · · · · 7:79b
prints · · · · · · · · · · · · · · · 7:78b-79a
Sanogawa Ichimatsu III · · · · · · · 7:78b
Sharebon · · · · · · 洒落本 · · 5:49a; 7:18a,
79b-80a; 8:141b
gesaku · · · · · · · · · · · · · · · · · 3:28b
Santō Kyōden · · · · · · · · · · · · · 7:18a
Shikitei Samba · · · · · · · · · · · · 7:97a
Tamenaga Shunsui · · · · · · · 7:333b-334a
Shareholders, general meetings of 7:247a
Shares · · · · · · · · · · · · · · · 4:70a-70b
Sharp Corporation · · · · · · · · 7:80a-80b
Shasei · · · · · · · · · · · · · · · · · · 3:79b
Shaseiga (painting subjects) · · · · · 6:159a
Shasekishū · · · · · · · 沙石集 · · 7:80b-81a
author · · · · · · · · · · · · · · · 7:80b-81a
Shasō · · · · · · · · · · · · 社倉 · · · 7:81a
Shaw, Glenn William · · · · · · · · · 7:81a
Shayō (The Setting Sun)
· · · · · · · · · · · · · 斜陽 · · · 6:230b
Shazensōsha · · · · 車前草社 · · · 5:19b
Shellfish [(kai) phylum Mollusca]
· · · · · · · · · · · · · · · · · · 7:81a-82b
important species · · · · · · · · · 7:81b-82b
Shell mounds · · · · · · · 貝塚 · 1:75a, 160a;
4:163b; 6:235a; 7:82b-83a
Shell Sekiyu Co, Ltd · · · · · · · · 7:83a-83b
Shenghuo zhoukan · · · · · · · · · · 8:380a
Shen Nanpin (Shen Nan-p'in) · · 1:211a;
5:305a; 7:83b

Shen Nanpin school · · · · · · · 5:305b-306a
Shen Weijing (Shen Wei-ching) · · · · 7:83b
Shenxiang quanbian · · · · · · · · · 6:160b
Shiatsu · · · · · · · · · · · · · · · · · 7:83b
Shiawase no kiiroi hankachi (Yellow
Handkerchief of Happiness) · · · · · 8:290a
Shiba family · · · · · · 斯波氏 · · 7:83b-84a
kanrei · · · · · · · · · · · · · · · · · 4:151a
Shiba Kōkan · · · · · · 司馬江漢 · · · 7:84a
Shibano Ritsuzan 柴野栗山 · · 7:84a-84b
Shibaraku · · · · · · · · · 暫 · · 4:92b, 98a
Shiba Ryōtarō · 司馬遼太郎 · · 7:84b, 103b
Shibata · · · · · · · · 新発田 · · · 7:84b
Shibata Katsuie 柴田勝家 · · · 7:84b
castle town · · · · · · · · · · · · · 2:363b
free markets · · · · · · · · · · · · · 6:283a
Shibata Keita · · · · · 柴田桂太 · 1:156a, 268b;
7:84b
Shibata Kyūō · · · · 柴田鳩翁 · · 7:84b-85a
Shingaku · · · · · · · · · · · · · · · 7:112a
Shibata Renzaburō
· · · · · · · · · · · 柴田錬三郎 · · 7:85a
Shibata Shō · · · · · · 柴田翔 · · · 7:85a
Shiba Tatto · · · · · · 司馬達等 · · · 7:85a
Shibata Zeshin · · · · 柴田是真 · · 7:85a-85b
Shiba Teikichi · · · · 斯波貞吉 · · · 8:296a
Shiba Yoshimasa 斯波義将 · · · 3:173b
Shiberia Shuppei · · · · · · · · · 7:192a-192b
Shiberiya monogatari
· · · · · · · · · シベリヤ物語 · · 3:108a
Shibetsu · · · · · · · · · 士別 · · · 7:85b
Shibori · · · · · · · · · · · · · · · · 8:29b-30a
Shiborizome · · · · · · · · · · · · · 8:29b-30a
Shibue Chūsai · · · · 渋江抽斎 · 1:155b; 7:85b
Shibugaki · · · · · · · · 渋柿 · · · 7:85b
Shibui · · · · · · · · · 6:361a; 7:85b-86a; 8:197a
Shibukan · · · · · · · · 四部官 · · 7:150b-151a
Shibukawa · · · · · · · · 渋川 · · · 7:86a
Shibukawa Shunkai
· · · · · · · · · · · 渋川春海 · · · 7:86a
Shibusawa Eiichi 渋沢栄一 · 2:58b, 332b;
7:52a, 86a-86b, 87b
Furukawa Ichibei · · · · · · · · · · 2:372b
Hakodate Dock Co, Ltd · · · · · · · 3:86a
Ōji Paper Co, Ltd · · · · · · · · · · 6:77a
Shibusawa Keizō 渋沢敬三 · 2:295b; 7:86b
Shibushi Bay · · · · · · 志布志湾 · 1:83a; 7:86b
Shibuya Tengai · · · · 渋谷天外 · · · 7:86b
Shibuya Ward · · · · · 渋谷区 · · · 7:87a
Shichi · · · · · · · · · · · · 質 · · · 7:87a
Shichibukin tsumitate
· · · · · · · · · · · 七分金積立 · 7:87a-87b
Shichidaiji junrei shiki
· · · · · · · · · 七大寺巡礼私記 · · · 1:79a
Shichifukujin · · · · · · · · · · · · · 7:73a
Shichigenkin · · · · · · · · · · · · · · 7:87b
Shichigosan · · · · · · 2:261b, 262a; 7:87b
Shichihakase Jiken
· · · · · · · · · · · 七博士事件 · · 7:87b-88a
Kanai Noburu · · · · · · · · · · · · 4:135b
Shichiire · · · · · · · · · · · · · · · · 4:117a
Shichijō Ōmiya bussho
· · · · · · · · · · 七条大宮仏所 · · 3:313b
Shichikyō Ochi · · 七卿落ち · · · 7:88a
Shichimi tōgarashi · · · · · · · · · · 3:127b
Shichinin no samurai
(Seven Samurai)
· · · · · · · · · · 七人の侍 · 2:277a; 7:73a
Shichirigahama 七里ケ浜 · · · 7:88a
Shichiseisha (Seven Lives Society)
Uesugi Shinkichi · · · · · · · · · · 8:130a
Shichiya · · · · · · · · · · · · · · · · 7:88a
Shichō · · · · · · · · · · · · · · · · · 1:149a
Shida · · · · · · · · · · · · · · · · · · 2:252a
Shide. See Gohei
Shidehara Kijūrō
· · · · · · · · · · · 幣原喜重郎 · 7:86b, 88a-89a
emperor's renunciation of divinity · 2:209a

Shiden ·············· 私田 · 7:89a-89b
Shidō Bunan ···· 至道無難 · 7:89b
Shidō yōroku ·················· 2:53a
Shie Incident ···· 紫衣事件 · 7:89b, 255a
Shields ···················· 1:89b
Shien (old paper owl kite) ···· 4:229b
Shier zhi ···················· 4:57a
"Shifun no Kao" · 脂粉の顔 ····· 8:173a
Shigajiku ("painting and poetry scrolls") ········ 4:116a; 6:151a
Shiga Kiyoshi ····· 志賀潔 · 7:89b
Shiga Kōgen ····· 志賀高原 · 7:89b
Shigaku ··················· 2:172b
Shigakukai ················· 6:312a
Shigaku kenkyū hō (Methods of Historical Research) ···· 7:109b-110a
Shigaku zasshi ··············· 2:115a;
6:312a
Shiga Naoya ···· 志賀直哉 1:313b; 2:274a;
4:114a; 7:89b-90b, 103b
I-novel ···················· 3:312a
Shiga Prefecture ··· 滋賀県 · 7:90b-91a
Shigaraki ········· 信楽 · 7:91a
Shigaraki no Miya
·············· 紫香楽宮 · 7:91a
Shigaraki Palace · 紫香楽宮 · 7:91a
Shigaraki ware ····· 信楽焼 · 4:337a;
7:91a-91b, 256a
similarity to Iga ware ······ 3:261b
Shiga Shigetaka · 志賀重昂 · 5:11b; 7:51b,
91b
Shiga Yoshio ···· 志賀義雄 · 4:12a; 7:91b
Shinjinkai ················· 7:115b
Shigemasa ········· 重政 · 3:149a
Shigemitsu Mamoru
················ 重光葵 · 6:302a;
7:91b-92a, 278a
Shigenobu ········· 重宣 · 3:149a
Shigeno Yasutsugu
············· 重野安繹 · 7:50b, 92b
historiography ············· 3:156a
Shigeta Sadakazu
··········· 重田貞一 · 4:61a-61b
Shigeyama Sengorō 茂山千五郎 4:328b
Shigeyama Sensaku 茂山千作 4:328b-329a
Shigi kempō ··· 私擬憲法 ······· 7:92b
Shigisan ······ 信貴山 ······· 7:92b
Shigisan engi emaki
········· 信貴山縁起絵巻 1:137a; 2:199b;
7:92b-93a; 8:32a
The Flying Granary ········· 7:93a
Shigisanji ······· 信貴山寺 · 7:93a-93b
Shihō Kenshūjo. See Legal Training and Research Institute
Shihon keiretsu ·········· 3:295b; 4:189b
Shihōshō ········· 司法省 ······· 7:93b
Shiiba ··········· 椎葉 ······· 7:93b
Shiin ····················· 1:183a
Shiina Etsusaburō
········ 椎名悦三郎 · 4:285b-286a
Shiina Rinzō ···· 椎名麟三 · 7:93b-94a
Christianity ················ 4:32a
Shijin ··········· 詩人 ······· 4:139a
Shijing
Kokinshū ················· 4:255a
Shi jing (Shih ching or Book of Odes)
······················ 8:209a
Shi ji (Records of the Historian)
Tokugawa Mitsukuni ······· 8:51b
Shijōnawate ······ 四条畷 ····· 7:94a
Shijō school. See Maruyama-Shijō school
Shijūhattai Butsu ·········· 7:94a, 94b
Shijuku ················· 7:94a-94b
Shika ····················· 2:82a
Shikakudake (Chimonobambusa quadrangularis) ··········· 1:136a

Shikan Gakkō Jiken
········· 士官学校事件 · 6:41b-42a
Shikanki ········· 史官記 ······· 3:219a
Shikano Buzaemon
············ 鹿野武左衛門 · 6:282a
Shikanoshima ····· 志賀島 · 7:94b
Shikashū ········· 私家集 · 4:117a;
7:94b-95b
Shikatsube Magao
·········· 鹿都部真顔 · 7:95a
Shika wakashū 詞花和歌集 · 2:350a; 5:38a;
7:95a-95b
Fujiwara no Toshinari ······· 2:357a
Shiki ············· 志木 ······· 7:95b
Shiki ··· 職 1:274a; 2:263b
shogunal bestowal ·········· 4:122a
Shikibō, Ltd ················ 7:95b
Shikibuton ················· 1:148a
Shikidō ōkagami 色道大鏡 · 7:95b-96a
Shiki-e (four seasons) paintings · 8:309a
Shikikin. See Deposit money
Shikimi (Illicium religiosum; Illicium anisatum) ················ 7:96a
Shikimoku ········· 式目 ······· 7:96a
Shikinaisha ······· 式内社 ····· 7:96a
Shikinai shrines ··· 式内社 ····· 7:96a
Shiki no Miko ···· 志貴皇子 · 7:96a-96b
Shikirisen ················· 7:271a
Shikisha ··················· 7:96a
Shikishi
Shin kokinshū ············· 7:120a
Shikishiban ················ 7:278a
Shikishi, Princess
·········· 式子内親王 · 2:357b; 7:96b
Shiki sōka
subjects ·················· 6:159a
Shikitei Samba ··· 式亭三馬 · 1:146a; 5:16b;
7:79a, 96b-97b
fūzoku shōsetsu ············ 2:378a
kamiyui descriptions ········· 4:127b
kokkeibon ················· 4:256a
works ·················· 7:96a-97a
Shikken ············ 執権 · 4:122a; 7:97b
hereditary nature ··········· 4:151a
rensho ··················· 6:301a
Shikkongōshin, statue of ······ 1:198b
Shiko ····················· 7:272b
Shikoku
area ····················· 4:2b
population density ········· 4:2b, 7a
Shikoku Electric Power Co, Ltd · 7:97b
Shikoku Kantai Shimonoseki Hōgeki Jiken
····· 四国艦隊下関砲撃事件 · 7:105b-106a
Shikoku karst
··········· 四国カルスト · 7:97b
Shikoku Mountains
··········· 四国山脈 ······· 7:97b
Shikoku region · 四国地方 · 7:97b-98a
Shikotan ········· 色丹 ······· 7:98a
Shikotsu, Lake ···· 支笏湖 ····· 7:98a
Shikotsu-Tōya National Park · 支笏洞爺国立公園 · 4:79a; 7:98a
Shikunshi ········· 四君子 · 5:311a-311b;
7:98a-98b
Shikyō ruijū ····· 私教類聚 · 4:201b
Shima, George ············· 4:22a
Shima ················ 島 · 2:302a
Shimabara ········· 島原 ····· 7:98b
Shimabara Peninsula
·············· 島原半島 · 7:98b
Shimabara Uprising · 5:323a-323b; 7:98b
anti-Christian policy ········ 3:188b
Dejima ···················· 2:83b
Dutch trade ··············· 2:135b
National Seclusion ········· 5:347b
Tokugawa Iemitsu ··········· 8:48a
Shimada ··········· 島田 ····· 7:99a

Shimada Saburō · 島田三郎 ····· 7:99a
Kakushin Kurabu ··········· 4:120a
Shimadzu Corporation ········· 7:99a
Shima Hot Spring
··········· 四万温泉 ······· 7:99a
Shimai Sōshitsu · 島井宗室 · 4:127b;
7:99a-99b
Shimai toshi ················ 7:202a
Shimaji Mokurai · 島地黙雷 · 7:99b
Fukuda Gyōkai ············· 2:362a
Shimaki Akahiko 島木赤彦 · 1:74b; 7:99b
Shimaki Kensaku 島木健作 · 7:99b
Shimamura Hōgetsu
··········· 島村抱月 · 5:12b; 7:31a,
99b-100a
Shimanaka Incident
·········· 嶋中事件 · 2:360a; 7:100a
Shimanaka Yūsaku
·········· 嶋中雄作 · 7:100a-100b
Shimane Peninsula
·············· 島根半島 · 7:100b
Shimane Prefecture 島根県 · 7:100b-101a
Shimantogawa ···· 四万十川 · 5:326b; 7:101a
Shimanto geosyncline
··········· 四万十地向斜 ····· 4:9b
Shimao Toshio ·· 島尾敏雄 · 7:101a
Shima Peninsula · 志摩半島 · 2:234b; 7:101a
Shimazaki Shōji
Shimura Takashi ············ 7:108b
Shimazaki Tōson 島崎藤村 · 5:52a-52b;
7:101a-101b, 103b
Japan P.E.N. club ··········· 4:47b
naturalism ············· 5:351a-351b
Shinshōsetsu ··············· 7:125b
Shimazono Junjirō
·········· 島薗順次郎 · 7:101b
Shimazu ·········· 島津 ······· 7:56b
Shimazu family ···· 島津氏 · 7:101b-102b
Kagoshima ················· 4:105a
Satsuma Province ··········· 7:29b
Shimazu Genzō · 島津源蔵 · 7:102a
Shimazu Hisamitsu
·············· 島津久光 · 7:102a
Richardson Affair ·········· 6:311a
Shimazu Nariakira
·············· 島津斉彬 · 7:102a-102b
Shimazu Yasujirō
·········· 島津保次郎 2:269a; 7:102a
Kamiyama Sōjin ············· 4:127b
Shimazu Yoshihiro
·············· 島津義弘 · 7:101b, 102b
invasions of Korea in 1592 and 1597
······················ 3:327b
Shimbunshi Hō · 新聞紙法 ······· 6:236a
Shimbunshi Jōrei. See Press Ordinance of 1875
Shimbun shōsetsu ········· 7:103a-104a
golden age ················ 7:103b
growth and development ···· 7:103a-103b
popularization ············· 7:103b
postwar period ············· 7:103b
Shimbutsu bunri · 神仏分離 · 7:132a
Shimbutsu Shūgō. See Syncretism
Shimenawa ················· 7:249b
Shintō ···················· 7:128b
shrines ··················· 7:180a
Shīmensu Jiken
·········· シーメンス事件 · 7:193a-193b
Shimizu ··········· 清水 · 7:103a, 104a
Shimizu Construction Co, Ltd ··· 7:104a
Shimizu Hamaomi
·············· 清水浜臣 · 7:104a
Shimizu Hiroshi ··· 清水宏 · 2:270a
Shimizu Muneharu
·············· 清水宗治 · 7:104a
Shimmei Masamichi
·········· 新明正道 · 7:104b
Shimmei-zukuri ············· 7:271a

Shimmi Masaoki ·新見正興 ········ **7**:104a
Shimminato ·······新湊 ········· **7**:104a
Shimminkai ····························· **8**:281b
Shimmura Izuru ·新村出 ········ **7**:104b
Shimobe ···············下部 ······· **7**:104b
Shimoda ·······下田 **2**:342b; **7**:104b
Shimodate ···········下館 ········ **7**:104b
Shimoda Utako ·下田歌子 ······ **7**:105a
Shimofuri ··························· **2**:25b
Shimo-Gamo Shrine
　Takehara ························· **7**:324a
Shimokita Peninsula
　下北半島 ······················ **7**:105a
Shimokōbe Chōryū
　下河辺長流 ··················· **7**:105a
　Man'yōshū study ············· **5**:110a
Shimokōbe Nagaru
　下河辺長流 ··················· **7**:105a
Shimomoto Kenkichi
　下元建吉 ····················· **7**:105a
Shimomura Kanzan
　下村観山 ··············· **7**:105a-105b
Shimonaka Yasaburō
　下中弥三郎 ··················· **7**:105b
　Committee of Seven to Appeal for World
　Peace ·························· **1**:340a
　Heibonsha, Ltd, Publishers ··· **3**:122b
Shimonita ···········下仁田 ······ **7**:105b
Shimonoseki ·······下関 ········ **7**:105b
　Chōfu ·························· **1**:298b
Shimonoseki, Treaty of
　下関条約 · **3**:196a; **5**:9b;
　　7:106a-106b, 197b, 198b
　Komura Jutarō and ··········· **4**:268a
　Mutsu Munemitsu ············ **5**:289a
　rejection ······················ **4**:141a
　relations with China ········· **1**:286b
　Shanghai International Settlement ··· **7**:78a
　Sino-Japanese War of 1894-1895 · **7**:198b
　Tripartite Intervention ······· **8**:106b
Shimonoseki Aquarium ·········· **7**:105b
Shimonoseki
　Bombardment ·馬関戦争 · **1**:86a; **5**:319b;
　　7:105b-106a
　Itō Hirobumi ·················· **3**:352b
　Kiheitai ························ **4**:204b
　Takasugi Shinsaku ············ **7**:319b
Shimose gunpowder
　developer ····················· **7**:106b
Shimose Masachika
　下瀬雅允 ····················· **7**:106b
Shimo Suwa ·······下諏訪 ······ **7**:106b
Shimotsuke (*Spiraea*
　japonica) ················ **7**:106b-107a
Shimotsuke Incident
　Taira no Yoritsuna ··········· **7**:302b
Shimotsuki kagura
　霜月神楽 ····················· **4**:107b
Shimotsuma ·······下妻 ········· **7**:107a
Shimoyama Incident
　下山事件 ··· **7**:107a-107b,
　　147b
　Furuhata Tanemoto ··········· **2**:371b
　Shimoyama Sadanori 下山定則 · **7**:107a
Shimozawa Kan ·子母沢寛 **2**:274a; **7**:107b
Shimpa ·······新派 **2**:267b;
　　4:218b; **7**:31a, 107b-108a
　Hanayagi Shōtarō ············· **3**:95a
　Kawakami Otojirō ············· **4**:181a
　Shinkokugeki ·················· **7**:121a
　Shimpa higeki ················· **2**:268b
Shimpai ···········信牌 ········· **7**:171a
Shimpan ···········親藩 ······· **1**:131b;
　　2:340b; **3**:186a; **7**:108a
Shimpeitai Incident
　神兵隊事件 ··· **7**:108a-108b
　Daitōjuku ····················· **2**:67b
Shimpotō ·······進歩党 **4**:141a; **7**:108b

Tanaka Kakuei ················· **7**:337a
Shimpukuji-bon ·真福寺本 ····· **4**:251b
Shimura Takashi ··志村喬 ···· **7**:108b
Shin ····················· **4**:141b, 295b
Shinabe (workers) ···品部 ···· **1**:147b
Shinagawa Refractories Co, Ltd · **7**:108b
Shinagawa Ward ·······品川区 · **7**:108b
Shinagawa Yajirō
　品川弥二郎 ···· **1**:21b; **7**:109a
　Kokumin Kyōkai founder ····· **4**:260b
Shinanogawa ·······信濃川 ···· **7**:109a
Shinano mainichi shimbun
　信濃毎日新聞 ················· **8**:296a
Shinano Province ·信濃国 ······ **5**:303a
Shina shisō kenkyū
　支那思想研究 ················· **7**:293a
Shin Buddhism ············ **4**:68a-69a
Shinchiku iwai ················· **4**:195a
Shinchō ···········新潮 ········ **7**:109a
　Shinkō Geijutsu Ha ·········· **7**:119a
Shinchō hyakushu (A Hundred New
　Volumes) ····· 新著百種 ···· **4**:199a
Shinchō Kō ki ·信長公記 ·· **7**:109a-109b
Shin chokusenshū (New
　Imperial Collection)
　新勅撰集 ····················· **8**:212a
Shinchō Literary Prize ········· **6**:66b
Shinchōsha Company ········· **7**:109b
Shinden ···········神田 ········ **7**:109b
Shinden kaihatsu 新田開発 ·· **7**:109b-110a
Shinden-zukuri ·······寝殿造 · **3**:243b;
　　7:110a-111a
　design ·························· **7**:110b-111a
　Fujiwara culture ·············· **2**:348a
　gardens ························ **3**:9a
　history ························· **7**:110b
　main hall ······················ **7**:111a
Shindō Kaneto ·新藤兼人 ···· **2**:275b;
　　7:111a-111b
　Hadaka no shima ············ **3**:75a
Shin'ei. *See* **Shinyei Kaisha**
Shi nengō ·········私年号 ······ **1**:232a
Shin'en (The Imperial
　Mausoleum) ·········寝園 ···· **8**:332b
Shin-Etsu Chemical Co, Ltd ·· **7**:111b
Shin Fujin Kyōkai (New
　Woman's Association)
　新婦人協会 ···· **7**:111b;
　　8:260b, 268b
　Hiratsuka Raichō ·············· **3**:146a
　Oku Mumeo ·················· **6**:96b
Shingaku ···········心学 ······ **6**:260b;
　　7:111b-112a
　Ishida Baigan ················· **3**:339b-340a
　Nakazawa Dōni ················ **5**:320a
　Shibata Kyūō ················· **7**:84b-85a
　Teshima Toan ················· **8**:15a
Shingaku tokeigusa
　心学時計草 ··················· **4**:61a
Shingei. *See* **Geiami**
Shingeki (magazine) 新劇
　film influence ················· **2**:268a
　shimpa ························· **7**:107b
　Shinshichō ··················· **7**:124b
　　7:112a
Shingeki (theater) ····· **7**:112a-113b, 368a
Shingen Kahō ·信玄家法 ····· **7**:113b
Shin Gesaku Ha ·新戯作派 ···· **5**:19b
Shingon (mantra) ·真言 **5**:102b; **6**:233a
Shingon sect ··· **1**:178b-179a; **7**:113b-115a
　Akishinodera ·················· **1**:42a
　Amida ·························· **4**:67a
　doctrines ······················ **7**:225a
　Hasedera ······················ **3**:106b-107a
　Jingoji ························· **4**:58b
　Jiun Onkō ····················· **4**:64a-64b
　Kakuban ······················ **4**:117b
　Kōfukuji ······················ **4**:244a

Kongōbuji ··········· **4**:299a-299b
Kūkai ························· **4**:304a
mandalas ····················· **5**:100a
mantra ························· **6**:233a
Mokujiki Ōgo ················ **5**:235b
monasticism ················· **5**:237b-238a
Mongaku ····················· **5**:243a-243b
Okadera ······················ **6**:78b
Ryōbu Mandara ·············· **6**:347a
Ryōbu Shintō ················· **6**:351a
Shinshōji ······················ **7**:125a
Shigisanji ····················· **7**:93a-93b
Tōji ···························· **8**:38b
Shingū ···········新宮 ········ **7**:115a
Shin Heike monogatari
　(New Tales of Heike)
　新平家物語 ·········· **6**:221b
Shin Ikei ·········沈惟敬 ······ **7**:83b
Shinji, Lake ·······宍道湖 ···· **7**:115a
Shinjin ························· **4**:68b
Shinjin (The New Person)
　·········新人 ········· **2**:143a
"Shinjin Celluloid Workers Union"
　Shinjinkai · **1**:40a; **7**:91b, 115b-116a, 251b
　Kamei Katsuichirō ············ **4**:125a
　Sano Manabu ················· **7**:15b
Shinjinkai (New Man
　Society) ·····新人会 ····· **5**:316b-317a
Shinjitsushō-gyo
　Ryōbu Mandara ·············· **6**:348a
Shin Jiyū Kurabu
　·········新自由クラブ · **5**:365a
Shinjō ···········新庄 ········· **7**:116a
Shinjō Basin ·····新庄盆地 ···· **7**:116a
Shinjō Hot Spring新庄温泉 ····· **7**:116a
Shinjū ······ **4**:93b; **7**:95b, 262a
Shinju fujin (Lady Pearl)
　·········真珠夫人 ···· **6**:221a
Shinjuku Gyoen National Garden **7**:116a
Shinjuku Ward ·······新宿区 · **7**:116a
Shinjū Ten no Amijima (Love Suicide at
　Amijima; Double Suicide)
　·········心中天網島 ···· **2**:274b
Shinkai ···········神誡 ········· **4**:272a
shinden kaihatsu ··············· **7**:109b-110a
Shinka Jōrei ·····新貨条例 ···· **8**:323b
Shin kanazukai ················· **4**:134a
Shinkankai ·······新幹会 ····· **7**:196a
Shinkankaku school
　·········新感覚派 · **2**:378b;
　　7:116a-116b, 175a
　Literary Age ················· **1**:209a
　Shinchō ······················ **7**:109a
　Nakagawa Yoichi ············· **5**:313a
　Western literature in Japanese
　　translation ················· **8**:248a
　Yokomitsu Riichi ············· **8**:331b-333b
Shinkansen ········· **2**:345a; **4**:336a; **6**:278a;
　　7:116b-119a
　development ··················· **7**:117a-117b
　extension ······················ **4**:33b
　operation and maintenance ··· **7**:118a-119a
　power source ·················· **7**:118a
　Shinkansen central control room ··· **7**:117a
　technical aspects ·············· **7**:117b-118a
Shinkei ···········心敬 · **1**:181b; **5**:15a,
　　42b; **6**:298b-299a; **7**:80b, 119a
　Sasamegoto (Murmured Conversations)
　　·········· **7**:23b
　Shinsen tsukubashū ·········· **7**:124b
Shinkeishitsu ··················· **5**:253b-254a
Shin kigen ·······新紀元 ······ **1**:2a
Shinkiron ·······慎機論 ····· **7**:119a
Shinkō Geijutsu Ha
　·········新興芸術派 · **2**:378b; **5**:19a;
　　7:119b
　Shinchō ······················ **7**:109a

Shinkō Geijutsu Ha
  Kurabu 新興芸術派倶楽部 ······· 7:175b
Shin kokinshū (New Collection of
  Ancient and Modern
  Times) ······· 新古今集 · 3:52a–52b;
  5:15a, 41a, 42b; 7:96b, 119b–121a; 8:211a
  Buddhist influence ············· 5:43a
  compilation ················· 7:120a
  compilers ··········· 2:351a; 5:41a
  Fujiwara no Sadaie ··········· 2:354a
  Fujiwara no Toshinari ········· 2:357a
  Fujiwara no Toshinari no Musume 2:357b
  Fujiwara no Yoshitsune ······· 2:358a
  influence on later literature ······· 7:120b
  Jakuren ···················· 4:1b
  Jien ······················ 4:54a
  Kamo no Mabuchi ············ 4:129b
  Kinkai wakashū ············· 4:212b
  Kokinshū compared ·········· 4:255a
  Kujō Kanezane in ············· 4:303b
  literary status ··············· 7:120b
  poets ····················· 7:120a
  qualities ················ 5:42b–43a
  structure ·············· 7:120a–120b
  styles ···················· 7:120b
  techniques ················· 5:42b
Shin kokin wakashū. 新古今和歌集
  See **Shin kokinshū**
Shinkoku ·············· 神国 · 4:59b
Shinkokugeki ······· 新国劇 2:268a; 7:121a
  Sawada Shōjirō ··········· 7:30b–31a
Shinkokushi ········ 新国史 · 7:121a–121b
  historiography ·············· 3:153a
Shinkoku shōsetsu ············ 4:199a
Shin Kokuzō ·········· 新国造 · 4:310a
Shinkō shūkyō ············ 5:366a–368b
Shinku (closely related
  verses) ··········· 親句 · 8:214b
Shinkun ············· 神訓 · 4:272a
Shin Kyōiku Undō
  ·············· 新教育運動 · 7:121b
  Tanimoto Tomeri ············· 7:342a
Shinkyoku Urashima
  ············ 新曲浦島 · 2:75b; 8:111a
Shinkyō Kyōdōtai
  ············· 心境共同体 · 7:121b
Shinkyō Taamidabutsu
  ··········· 真教他阿弥陀仏 · 4:62a
Shin Nampin ·········· 沈南蘋 · 7:83b
Shin Nan'yō ········· 新南陽 · 7:121b
Shin Nihon bungaku
  ············· 新日本文学 · 7:122a
Shin Nihon Bungakukai
  (Society for a New
  Japanese Literature)
  ·········· 新日本文学会 · 5:316b–317a;
  6:230b
  Shin Nihon bungaku ·········· 7:122a
  Tsuboi Shigeji ··············· 8:110a
Shin Nihon Bungaku Kyōkai ······· 5:19a
Shin Nihon Kajin Shūdan
  ·········· 新日本歌人集団 · 5:20a
Shin Nihon Shūkyō Dantai Rengōkai
  ····················· 8:150a
Shin Nippon (New Japan)
  ··············· 新日本 · 5:301a
Shinobunoya. *See* **Tachibana Akemi**
Shinobunoya kashū
  ·········· 志濃夫廼舎歌集 · 7:292a
Shinoda Masahiro
  ········· 篠田正浩 ··· 2:273b;
  7:122a–122b
Shi no genri ······· 詩の原理 · 3:76b
Shi-nō-kō-shō ······ 士農工商 · 7:122a
Shin onna daigaku
  Onna daigaku ·············· 6:108a
Shino ware. 志野焼 *See* **Mino ware**
Shinran ··········· 親鸞 ··· 3:171b;
  4:67b–68b, 125a; 7:66a, 122b–123b

Jinen hōn'i shō ············· 7:123a
Jōdo Shin sect ············· 4:68a
Kagami no miei ············ 7:122b
Kyōgyōshinshō ········· 4:330a–330b
monasticism ················ 5:238a
raigōzu ··················· 6:277a
Sen Amidabutsu ············· 7:122b
Tannishō ·················· 7:344a
wasan ···················· 8:231a
Shinran's Kyōgyōshinshō
  Kiyozawa Manshi ············ 4:233a
Shinrigaku kenkyū
  (Psychological
  Research) ···· 心理学研究 · 6:260b
Shinri ippan ······· 真理一般 · 8:127b
Shinritsu Kōryō (New
  Legal Principles)
  ············· 新律綱領 · 6:172a
  Kaitei Ritsurei ·············· 4:113b
Shinroku Ujimasa 新六氏正 · 4:270a
Shinron ······· 新論 · 1:38a; 7:124a
Shinrui (shinseki) ······ 4:217b, 218a
Shinsai Yobō Chōsakai ········· 2:140b
Shinsambetsu (National
  Federation of Industrial
  Organizations) ··· 新産別 · 4:347b, 360a;
  6:238a; 7:124a
Shin sarugaku ki 新猿楽記 · 4:325a
Shinsei   新声
  Shinchō ················· 7:109a
  Shinchōsha Company ·········· 7:109b
Shinseisakuza ············· 7:124a
Shinsei taii ······· 真政大意 · 4:168a
Shinsekki jidai · 新石器時代 · 5:361b
Shinsengumi ····· 新撰組 · 7:124a–124b
  Ikedaya Incident ············· 3:266b
  Kondō Isami, leader ··········· 4:269a
  Serizawa Kamo ·············· 7:124a
Shinsengumi shimatsuki
  Shimozawa Kan ············· 7:107a
Shinsen jikyō ···· 新撰字鏡 · 2:93a; 7:124b
Shinsen jisho
  Ōtsuki Joden ··············· 6:134b
Shinsen rōeishū (Newly
  Selected Collection for
  Recitation) ···· 新撰朗詠集 · 5:38b; 8:208a
Shinsen shōjiroku
  ············· 新撰姓氏録 ··· 1:151b;
  7:124b; 8:137a
  Kōgonen-Jaku cited ··········· 4:249a
Shinsen tsukubashū
  ·········· 新撰菟玖波集 · 7:12b, 124b,
  162a
Shinsetsu Ishikawa Goemon
  ········· 真説石川五右衛門 · 2:76b
Shinsha ··················· 4:179a
Shin shakai ········ 新社会 · 7:310a
Shinshibari ················· 4:210b
Shinshichō ······ 新思潮 · 7:124b–125a;
  8:300a
  "neorealist" school ··········· 5:19a
  Osanai Kaoru ··············· 7:124b
Shinshiro ········· 新城 · 7:125a
Shinsho ··················· 6:162a
Shinshō hōshi nikki
  ··········· 信生法師日記 · 8:105a
Shinshōji ······· 新勝寺 5:334b; 7:125a
Shinshōji temple ············· 1:271a
Shinshō maru (ship)
  Daikokuya Kōdayū ··········· 2:60b
Shinshōsetsu ····· 新小説 · 7:125a
Shin shūishū (New
  Collection of Gleanings)
  ··············· 新拾遺集 · 8:73b
Shinshūren ················· 8:150a
Shinshū temma kyō
  ·········· 神州天馬侠 · 7:166b
Shinsō zempen 神相全編 · 6:187a

Shinsui Kyōyo Rei
  ········· 薪水供与令 · 7:125a–125b
Shintaikei ·········· 身体刑 · 7:140b
Shin Taisei Undō
  ··········· 新体制運動 · 5:365a–366a
Shintaishi (new form poetry) style · 4:225a
Shintaishi shō · 新体詩抄 · 8:88a
Shin Tanka Kyōkai (New
  Tanka Society)
  ··········· 新短歌協会 · 5:19b
*Shintei zōho kokushi
  taikei* (Newly Revised
  and Supplemented
  Compendium of National
  History)
  ········· 新訂増補国史大系 · 2:104b–105a;
  4:262b; 7:262b
Shintō ·········· 神道 1:162b; 6:290a;
  7:48a–48b, 64a, 99b, 125a–132a
  afterlife ·················· 1:20a
  dance, traditional ············ 2:73b
  doctrine
    changeableness ········· 8:25a–25b
    community-ism ········· 8:25b–26a
    functionalism ············· 8:25b
  family altars ··············· 7:137b
  festivals ··············· 2:252b–258a
  folk religion ··············· 2:298a
  Gobusho ·············· 3:38b–39a
  government promotion ·········· 3:78a
  historical developments
    origins and formative
    period ·············· 7:125b–127a
    medieval period ········· 7:127a–128b
    Edo period ··········· 7:128b–129b
    Meiji period and after ········ 7:129b
  Inari ···················· 3:283a
  kami ················ 4:125b–126a
  lay believers (ujiko) ······· 4:362a–362b
  miko ···················· 5:172a
  music ···················· 5:283a
  mythology ················· 5:295a
  nature in ·················· 5:357b
  new religions ··········· 5:368a–368b
  prayer ···················· 6:233a
  priesthood ············· 6:238a–239a
  restructuring ·········· 2:206a–206b
  ritual codification ············ 7:126b
  ritual dimensions and thought 7:129b–132a
  ritual music and dance ········ 3:1a, 2a
  Sect Shintō
    Confucian ················ 7:48a
    Faith-healing ············· 7:48a
    Mountain ················ 7:48a
    Pure ··················· 7:48a
    Purification ·············· 7:48a
    Restoration ······· 7:48a, 129a–129b
    Ryōbu ·················· 7:127b
    Sannō Ichijitsu ············· 7:127b
    Suika ··················· 7:129a
    Watarai ············· 7:127b–128a
    Yuiitsu ·············· 7:128a–128b
  shimenawa ················ 7:128b
  Shingaku ·················· 7:112a
  taboo expressions ············ 7:291b
  Taikyō Sempu ·············· 7:297b
  tama ···················· 7:332a
  thought and culture ········ 8:25a–29a
  tolerance in Japanese religion · 8:70b
  types ···················· 2:300b
    Folk ··················· 2:300b
    Imperial ················· 2:300b
    Scholastic ··············· 2:300b
    Sect ··················· 7:48a
    Shrine ·················· 7:180b
    shūgyō ················· 4:271b
  weddings ·················· 8:239a
  women in ·········· 8:256b, 258a

Shintō and Buddhism, separation of
·· **7**:132a

Shintō architecture ········· **7**:132a–134a
origin ··························· **7**:132a–132b
reconstruction ························ **7**:134a
shrine complex buildings ········· **7**:134a
shrine complexes ··········· **7**:132b–134a
Shintō art ····················· **7**:134b–137b
anthropomorphism ············· **7**:126a
applied arts ························ **7**:136b
architecture ········· **7**:132a–134a, 135b
definition ···················· **7**:134b–135a
Hachiman ························· *7:134b*
history ··················· **7**:136b–137a
imperial regalia · **3**:278b–279a; **7**:135a–135b
Kitano tenjin engi ·············· *7:136b*
painting ··················· **7**:136a–136b
sculpture ························· **7**:136a
shūgō bijutsu ····················· *7:134b*
Shintō-Buddhist relationships **1**:179b–180a
Honji Suijaku theory
religious literature concerning **7**:127a–128b
Shintō charms ····················· **3**:91a
Shintō denju ·········· 神道伝授 **7**:128b
Shintō family altars **2**:307a; **6**:291a; **7**:137b
harvest rites ······················ **1**:22b
Shintō gobusho
·············· 神道五部書 **3**:38b–39a;
7:128a; **8**:236b
Shin Tōhō Co, Ltd ··· **2**:271b, 273b; **7**:137b
Shintō Jūsampa
············· 神道十三派 ········ **7**:48a
Shin Tōkyō Kokusai Kūkō ···· **5**:370b–371a
Shintō rites ··············· **7**:137b–139b
accessories and offerings ········ **7**:138b
body of worshipers ········· **7**:138a–138b
buildings and facilities ·········· **7**:138a
divisions ················· **7**:137b–138a
Engi Shiki ························ **2**:217b
festivals ························· **7**:139a
Norito ··························· **7**:138b
religious banquets ··············· **7**:139b
saikai ··················· **7**:139a–139b
shrine ··························· **7**:138a
Shintō shrines ················ **7**:179b–180b
Akama ·························· **1**:40a
Akiba ··························· **1**:41b
Aso ····························· **1**:103b
Atago ··························· **1**:107b
Atsuta ··················· **1**:115b–116a
Awa ···························· **1**:125a
Dazaifu ·························· **2**:79b
Fushimi Inari ···················· **2**:375a
Futarayama ······················ **2**:376a
Hakozaki ························· **3**:87a
Heian ··························· **3**:122b
Hie ····························· **3**:130b
Hikawa ·························· **3**:137b
Hirose ··························· **3**:147b
Hirota ··························· **3**:150b
Ikukunitama ··············· **3**:270b–271a
Ise ····················· **3**:338a–339a
Isonokami ························ **3**:348a
Itsukushima ······················ **3**:357a
Iwashimizu Hachiman ·············· **3**:363a
Izumo ··························· **2**:67a
Kamo ··························· **4**:130a
Kashihara ························ **4**:162a
Kashii ··························· **4**:162a
Kashima ·························· **4**:162b
Kasuga ··················· **4**:163b–164a
Katori ··························· **4**:169a
Kehi ····························· **4**:186b
Kitano ··························· **4**:228a
Kotohira ························· **4**:297a
Kumano Sanzan ·················· **4**:306a
land owned by ··················· **7**:109b
Meiji ···························· **5**:160b

Mitsumine ····················· **5**:214a
Miyazaki ······················· **5**:222a
money offerings ················· **5**:242a
Munakata ················· **5**:264b–265a
Ōmi ···························· **6**:102a
Ōmiwa ··················· **6**:102a–102b
pictorial votive offerings ····· **2**:196b–198a
public ··························· **7**:180b
Sengen ·························· **7**:64a
Shiogama ························ **7**:140a
Shōkonsha ······················· **8**:319a
Sumiyoshi ······················· **7**:270b
Tatsuta ························· **7**:350a
Tōshōgū ·························· **8**:84b
Tsurugaoka Hachiman ············ **8**:116b
Udo ···························· **8**:125b
Usa Hachiman ···················· **8**:181b
Yasukuni ··················· **8**:319a–319b
Shintō Shrines, Association of ···· **7**:139b
Shintō symbols ··············· **3**:49a–49b
Shinuhi ············· 私奴婢 ···· **7**:62a
Shinwa Kaiun Kaisha, Ltd ········ **7**:139b
Shin Yakushiji ····· 新薬師寺 **7**:139a–140b
Shinyei Kaisha ·················· **7**:140a
Shin'yōkai ······················· **5**:19a
Shinza ············· 神座 **4**:107a
Shinzei ············· 信西 **2**:353a
Shinzei kogakuzu
············· 信西古楽図 **3**:32a
Shinzō inu tsukubashū
············· 新増犬筑波集 **7**:140a
Shinzoku Hō (family law)
Tomii Masaaki ················· **8**:71a
Shin zoku kokinshū (New
Collection of Ancient
and Modern Times,
Continued, 1439)
············· 新続古今集 **7**:170b; **8**:204b
Shiobara ············· 塩原 **7**:140a
Shioda Hiroshige 塩田広重 **7**:140a
Shiogama ············· 塩竈 **7**:140a
Shiogama Jinja. *See* **Shiogama Shrine**
Shiogama Shrine 塩竈神社 **7**:140a
Shiohigari ····················· **7**:140b
Shioiri Matsusaburō
············· 塩入松三郎 **7**:140b
Shiojiri ············· 塩尻 **7**:140b
Shiokara ························ **2**:305a
Shioki ························· **7**:140b
Shiomidake ········· 塩見岳 **7**:141a
Shionogi & Co, Ltd ············· **7**:141a
Shionomisaki 潮岬 **7**:141a; **8**:348b
Shiotsuki Yaeko
············· 塩月弥栄子 **2**:233b
Shiozawa ············· 塩沢 **7**:141a–141b
Shiozawa Masasada
············· 塩沢昌貞 **7**:141b
Shipbuilding companies
Hakodate Dock Co, Ltd ··········· **3**:86a
Hitachi Zōsen Corporation ······· **3**:207b
Ishikawajima-Harima Heavy Industries
Co, Ltd ····················· **3**:342b
Kawasaki Heavy Industries, Ltd ··· **4**:183b
Mitsubishi Heavy Industries, Ltd ··· **5**:208a
Mitsui Engineering &
Shipbuilding Co, Ltd ········· **5**:211b
Namura Shipbuilding Co, Ltd ····· **5**:327b
Sanoyasu Dockyard Co, Ltd ····· **7**:16a
Sasebo Heavy Industries Co, Ltd
(Sasebo Jūkōgyō) ············· **7**:24a
Shipbuilding industry **7**:141b–143b; **8**:102b
Edo ···························· **2**:149b
electronics ······················ **2**:192a
industrial organization and
technology ············· **7**:142a–143a
Meiji ···················· **2**:151b, 153a
postwar ························· **7**:142a
pre-1945 ················· **7**:141b–142a

Shimonoseki ··················· **7**:108b
Shipbuilding Scandal of 1954
············· **7**:143a–143b; **8**:345a
Shipping industry companies ···· **7**:142a
Daiichi Chūō Kisen Kaisha ········ **2**:58b
Japan Line, Ltd ················ **4**:47a
Kawasaki Kisen Kaisha, Ltd · **4**:183b–184a
Mitsui O.S.K. Lines, Ltd ········ **5**:212a
Nippon Yūsen ·················· **6**:13b
Sankō Steamship Co, Ltd ········ **7**:14b
Shinwa Kaiun Kaisha, Ltd ······· **7**:139b
Shōwa Line, Ltd ················ **7**:174b
Yamashita-Shinnihon Steamship
Co, Ltd ····················· **8**:304b
Shippō ··················· **1**:328b–329a
Ships ··················· **7**:143b–145a
haniwa ························· *7:143a*
higaki kaisen (lozenge-fenced cargo ship)
············· **7**:144b
types ··················· **7**:143b–144a
vermilion seal ship (shuinsen) ····· *7:144b*
votive picture (ema) ············· *7:144b*
Shirabe ························· **4**:103a
Shirabyōshi ······· 白拍子 **7**:145a; **8**:259a
geisha ·························· **3**:15a
Shiragi ············· 新羅 **7**:196a
Shiragikukai ········· 白菊会 ····· **5**:19b
Shirahama (Chiba
Prefecture) ············· 白浜 **7**:145a
Shirahama (Wakayama
Prefecture) ············· 白浜 **7**:145a
Shirahone Hot Spring
············· 白骨温泉 **7**:145a
Shirahone Onsen. *See* **Shirahone Hot
Spring**
Shirai Kyōji ······ 白井喬二 **7**:103b, 145b
Shirai Rittoku. *See* **Tatebayashi Kagei**
Shirai Seiichi ········· 白井晟一 **7**:145b
Shiraito Falls ····· 白糸の滝 **4**:160b; **7**:145b
Shiraitowappu ··· 白糸割符 ···· **3**:356b
Shirakaba, Lake ··· 白樺湖 **7**:145b–146b
Shirakaba ············· 白樺 **5**:19a, 281a,
308a
Shirakabaha, "White Birch school."
See **Shirakaba school**
Shirakaba school ··· 白樺派 **1**:84b; **4**:237b;
7:27b, 90b, 145b–146b
Christianity ······················ **4**:32a
founding ························· **5**:19a
Leach, Bernard Howell ············ **4**:372b
literary criticism ················· **5**:12a
Shirakawa, Emperor
············· 白河天皇 · **7**:26a, 146b,
279b
insei ···························· **3**:314b
Shirakawa (Fukushima
Prefecture) ············· 白河 ······· **7**:146b
Shirakawa (Gifu
Prefecture) ············· 白川 ······· **7**:146b
Shirakawa (river) ····· 白川 ······· **7**:146b
Shirakawa no Seki 白河関 · **7**:146b–147a
Shiran (*Bletilla striata*) ·········· **7**:147a
Shiranami-mono (plays
depicting activities of
thieves) ············· 白浪物 **5**:234b
Shiranesan. *See* **Shirane Sanzan**
Shiranesan (Kusatsu)
············· 白根山 **7**:147a
Shiranesan (Nikkō) 白根山 **7**:147a
Shirane Sanzan 白根三山 **7**:147a
"Shirano Benjūrō"
Shinkokugeki ··················· **7**:121a
Shirase Nobu ····· 白瀬矗 **7**:147a
Shirashi (ash-glazed wares) · **1**:261b–262a
Shirasu ············· 白州 **7**:147a
Shirataki ························ **7**:265b
Shiratori Incident 白鳥事件 ····· **7**:147b

Shiratori Kurakichi
　　　　　　白鳥庫吉 ‥‥‥‥ 7:147b
Shirauo ‥‥‥‥‥‥‥‥‥‥‥‥‥ 8:251a
Shiretoko Hantō. *See* **Shiretoko Peninsula**
Shiretoko National Park
　　　　　　知床国立公園 ‥‥‥ 7:147b
Shiretoko Peninsula
　　　　　　知床半島 ‥‥‥‥‥ 7:147b
Shiribetsugawa ・ 尻別川 ‥‥‥ 7:147b
Shiritori (capping) ‥‥‥‥‥‥ 8:269b
Shiroi keshi ‥ 白い罌粟 ‥‥‥ 7:293a
Shiroi kyotō (The Ivory Tower) ‥ 白い巨塔 ‥‥‥ 8:299a
Shiroishi ‥‥‥‥ 白石 ‥‥‥ 7:148a
Shirō Katsuyasu ・ 四郎勝康 ‥ 4:270a
Shiron (Essays on Poetry)
　　　　　　詩論 ‥‥‥‥‥‥‥ 6:112a
Shirone ‥‥‥‥‥‥ 白根 ‥‥ 7:148a
Shiroumadake ‥ 白馬岳 ‥‥‥ 7:148a
Shiroyama ‥‥‥ 城山 ‥‥‥ 7:148a
Shiroyama Saburō
　　　　　　城山三郎 ‥‥‥‥‥ 7:148a
Shiryō ‥‥‥‥‥‥ 私領 ‥‥‥ 7:148a
Shiryō Hensanjo. *See* **Historiographical Institute, Tōkyō University**
Shisakajima ‥‥ 四阪島 ‥‥ 7:148a
Shisei ‥‥‥‥‥‥ 刺青 ‥‥‥ 7:342b
Shiseidō Co, Ltd ‥‥‥‥‥‥‥ 7:148b
Shisei System. *See* **Uji-kabane system**
Shisendō ‥‥‥‥ 詩仙堂 ‥‥ 3:342b
Shisen o koete
　　　　　　死線を越えて ‥‥‥ 4:103b
Shisetsu jikenshū
　　　　　　師説自見集 ‥‥‥‥ 3:272b
Shishi Bunroku ・ 獅子文六 1:164a; 7:148b
　fūzoku shōsetsu ‥‥‥‥‥‥‥ 2:378b
Shishigatani Conspiracy
　　　　　　鹿ヶ谷の変 ‥‥‥‥ 7:188b
　Taira no Shigemori ‥‥‥‥‥ 7:302a
Shishi kagura ‥ 獅子神楽 ‥ 4:106b, 107b
Shishi-mai ‥‥‥ 獅子舞 ‥‥ 7:148b, 148b–149a, 250a
　kadozuke ‥‥‥‥‥‥‥‥‥‥ 4:101b
Shishi odori ‥‥‥ 鹿踊 ・ 7:149a, 149a
Shishi yuebao ‥‥‥‥‥‥‥‥‥ 7:337b
Shishōsetsu ‥‥‥‥‥‥‥‥‥ 3:312a–312b
Shisō ‥‥‥‥‥ 思想 3:127b; 7:149a
Shiso doll ‥‥‥‥‥‥‥‥‥‥‥ 4:105b
Shisōhan Hogo Kansatsu Hō. *See* "Thought Criminal" Probation Law
Shisōhan Hogo Kansatsu Hō ‥‥ 8:29a
Shisō kenji ("thought prosecutors")
　　　　　　　　　　　　 ‥‥‥ 6:168b
Shisō no kagaku
　　　　　　思想の科学 ‥‥‥ 6:233a; 7:149a–149b
　members ‥‥‥‥‥‥‥‥‥‥‥ 7:149a
　pragmatism ‥‥‥‥‥‥‥ 6:232b–233a
　publications ‥‥‥‥‥‥‥‥‥ 7:149b
Shitaji chigyō ‥ 下地知行 ‥‥ 1:274a
Shitaji chūbun ‥‥ 下地中分 ‥ 7:149a
　Ashikaga Yoshimitsu ‥‥‥‥‥ 1:101b
　jitō ‥‥‥‥‥‥‥‥‥‥‥‥‥‥ 4:63b
　shōen ‥‥‥‥‥‥‥‥‥‥‥‥ 7:157b
Shitakiri suzume ・ 舌切雀 2:302b; 7:149b
Shitamachi ‥‥‥‥ 7:149b–150a, 266a
　chōnaikai ‥‥‥‥‥‥‥‥‥‥ 1:300a
　urban life ‥‥‥‥‥‥‥‥‥‥ 8:178a
Shitaobi ‥‥‥‥‥‥‥‥‥‥‥‥ 2:369b
Shite kata ‥‥‥‥‥‥‥‥ 4:267b, 270a
Shitennōji ‥‥‥‥ 四天王寺 ・ 1:182a; 7:74a, 150b
Shitōkan ‥‥‥‥ 四等官 ‥ 7:150b–151a
Shitomido ‥‥‥‥‥‥‥‥‥‥‥ 7:111a
Shiwaku Islands ‥ 塩飽諸島 ‥‥ 1:125a
Shiwaza no kotoba
　　　　　　為業の言葉 ‥‥‥‥ 7:281a

Shizen kankyō no hembō
　　　　　　自然環境の変貌 ‥‥‥ 7:293b
Shizen shin'eidō
　　　　　　自然真営道 ・ 1:55b; 4:147a; 7:151a
Shizen shugi ‥‥‥‥‥ 5:351a–351b
Shizen shugi no shukanteki yōso
　　‥‥‥ 自然主義の主観的要素 ‥‥‥ 4:165a
Shizoku ‥‥‥‥‥ 士族 ・ 7:151a–152a
　dissidence ‥‥‥‥‥‥‥ 7:151b–152a
　government policy ‥‥‥‥ 7:151a–151b
　shi-nō-kō-shō ‥‥‥‥‥‥‥‥‥ 7:122a
Shizoku jusan ‥ 士族授産 ・ 7:152a–152b
　shizoku ‥‥‥‥‥‥‥‥‥‥‥ 7:151b
Shizugatake, Battle of
　　　　　　賤ケ岳の戦 ‥‥‥‥ 7:152b
　Fukushima Masanori's role ‥‥ 2:366b
　Shibata Katsuie ‥‥‥‥‥‥‥‥ 7:84b
Shizugatake no Tatakai. *See* **Shizugatake, Battle of**
Shizuka Gozen ‥‥‥ 静御前 ‥ 7:152b
Shizukawa Hydroelectric Dam ・ 2:72b
Shizuki Tadao ‥‥ 志筑忠雄 ・ 7:152b–153a
　Kaempfer, Engelbert ‥‥‥‥‥ 4:102a
　natural sciences ‥‥‥‥‥‥‥ 5:356a
Shizuoka ‥‥‥‥‥‥ 静岡 ‥ 7:153a, 153a–153b
　shrines ‥‥‥‥‥‥‥‥‥‥‥‥ 7:153b
Shizuoka Bunko ・ 静岡文庫 ‥‥‥ 1:68a
Shizuoka Heiya. *See* **Shizuoka Plain**
Shizuoka Ken. *See* **Shizuoka Prefecture**
Shizuoka Municipal Toro Site Museum
　　　　　　　　　　　　 ‥‥‥ 7:153b
Shizuoka Plain ・ 静岡平野 ‥ 7:153b
Shizuoka Prefecture
　　　　　　静岡県 ・ 7:153b–154a; 8:355a
　cities ‥‥‥‥‥‥‥‥‥‥‥‥ 7:154a
　parks ‥‥‥‥‥‥‥‥‥‥‥‥ 7:154a
　rivers ‥‥‥‥‥‥‥‥‥‥‥‥ 7:153b
Shizuoka Shiritsu Toro Hakubutsukan. *See* **Shizuoka Municipal Toro Site Museum**
Shō ‥‥‥‥‥‥ 5:151a–151b; 7:154a
　determination ‥‥‥‥‥‥ 5:151a–151b
　use in gagaku ‥‥‥‥‥‥‥‥ 3:1b–2a
Shōan ‥‥‥‥‥‥‥ 咲庵 ‥‥ 5:318a
Shōbara ‥‥‥‥‥‥ 庄原 ‥‥ 7:154a
Shōbō genzō ‥‥ 正法眼蔵 2:123b; 7:154a; 8:28a
Shōbu [(sweet flag) *Acorus calamus* var. *asiaticus*] ‥‥‥‥‥ 7:154a–154b
Shōbungaku ‥‥‥‥‥‥‥‥‥‥ 4:199a
Shōbyōga ‥‥‥‥ 障屛画 ‥ 7:41a–43b
Shōchi. 勝知　*See* **Takuma Tametō**
Shōchiku ‥‥‥‥‥‥‥ 2:268a, 269b
Shōchiku Co, Ltd ‥‥‥‥ 7:102b, 154b
Shōchiku Kinema ‥‥‥‥‥‥‥ 3:351b
Shōchiku Motion Picture Company
　Imamura Shōhei ‥‥‥‥‥‥‥ 3:274a
Shōchiku New Wave ‥‥‥‥‥‥ 7:122a
Shōchū (alcoholic beverages) ‥・ 4:161a; 7:1a–1b
Shōchū Conspiracy
　　　　　　正中の変 ‥‥‥‥‥ 7:154b
Shock therapy ‥‥‥‥‥‥‥‥‥ 6:261a
Shōda Heigorō 荘田平五郎 ‥‥ 7:154b
Shōda Hidesaburō
　　　　　　正田英三郎 ‥‥‥‥ 7:154b
Shōda Kenjirō 正田建次郎 ‥‥ 7:154b
Shōdan chiyo ‥ 樵談治要 ‥‥ 7:155a
Shōden Jiken. *See* **Shōwa Denkō Scandal**
Shodō ‥‥‥‥‥‥‥‥‥‥ 1:232b–236b
Shodō kikimimi sekenzaru
　　　　　　諸道聴耳世間猿 ‥‥ 8:126a
Shōdoshima ‥‥‥ 小豆島 ‥‥ 7:155a

Shoemaker, The ‥‥‥‥‥‥‥‥ 8:328a
Shōen ‥‥‥‥‥‥ 荘園 ・ 7:155a–158a, 277a
　corvée labor ‥‥‥‥‥‥‥‥‥ 1:226b
　early ‥‥‥‥‥‥‥‥‥‥ 7:155b–156a
　economy ‥‥‥‥‥‥‥‥ 2:147b–148a
　feudalism ‥‥‥‥‥‥‥‥‥‥ 2:263b
　honke and ryōke ‥‥‥‥‥‥‥ 3:224a
　hyakushō ‥‥‥‥‥‥‥‥‥‥ 3:249a
　iriai ‥‥‥‥‥‥‥‥‥‥‥‥‥ 3:330a
　kaezeni ‥‥‥‥‥‥‥‥‥‥‥ 4:102a
　Kamakura shogunate ‥‥‥ 7:157a–158a
　kenchi ‥‥‥‥‥‥‥‥‥‥‥‥ 4:193a
　kokugun system ‥‥‥‥‥‥‥ 4:259b
　mature ‥‥‥‥‥‥‥‥‥ 7:156a–157a
　rice tax ‥‥‥‥‥‥‥‥‥‥‥ 4:112b
　ryōshu ‥‥‥‥‥‥‥‥‥‥‥ 6:353a
　samurai ‥‥‥‥‥‥‥‥‥‥‥‥ 7:7a
　sanjo ‥‥‥‥‥‥‥‥‥‥‥‥‥ 7:12a
　shitaji chūbun ‥‥‥‥‥‥‥‥ 7:149b
　tax exemption rights ‥‥‥‥‥ 2:376b
　warriors ‥‥‥‥‥‥‥‥‥‥‥ 4:121b
Shōen-kōryō system (private estate-public land system) ・ 荘園公領制 ‥ 2:106b–107a
Shōen landholding system ‥‥‥‥ 1:80a
Shōen nikki ‥‥‥ 湘烟日記 ‥‥ 4:223a
Shōga ‥‥‥‥‥‥‥‥ 2:305a; 3:127b
Shōgakukan Publishing Co, Ltd
　　　　　　　　　　　　 ‥‥‥ 7:158a–158b
Shōgatsu ‥‥‥‥ 正月 1:20a; 5:371b–372a
Shōgawa ‥‥‥‥‥‥ 庄川 ‥‥ 7:158b
Shōgi ‥‥‥‥‥‥ 将棋 ・ 5:7b; 7:12b; 158b–159b
　game ‥‥‥‥‥‥‥‥‥‥ 7:159a–159b
　history ‥‥‥‥‥‥‥‥‥‥‥‥ 7:158b
　Japan Shōgi Federation ‥‥ 7:158b–159a
Shōgi Magajin
　　　　　　将棋マガジン ‥‥‥ 7:159a
Shōgi sekai ‥‥ 将棋世界 ‥‥ 7:158b
Shōgitai ‥‥‥‥ 彰義隊 ‥‥ 1:165a; 7:159b–160a
Shōgoin ‥‥‥‥‥ 聖護院 ‥‥ 7:160a, 182a–182b
Shōgun ‥‥‥‥‥ 将軍 ‥‥ 7:160a–160b
　Kamakura shogunate ‥‥‥ 4:121a–142b
　Kamakura shōguns ‥‥‥‥‥‥ 4:122b
　Muromachi shogunate ‥‥‥ 5:271b–274a
　Ashikaga shōguns ‥‥‥‥‥‥ 5:272b
　Tokugawa shogunate ‥‥‥‥ 8:52b–56a
　Tokugawa shogunal line ‥‥‥‥ 8:45a
　seii tai shōgun ‥‥‥‥‥ 2:204a–204b
Shogunal deputy ‥‥‥‥‥‥‥‥ 4:151a
Shogunal regent ‥‥‥‥‥‥‥‥ 7:97b
"Shōgun art"
　Taut, Bruno ‥‥‥‥‥‥‥ 7:351a–351b
Shogunate ‥‥‥‥‥‥‥‥ 7:160b–161a
Shogunate missions to the West
　　　　　　　　　　　　 ‥‥‥ 7:161a–161b
Shōhaku ‥‥‥‥‥‥ 肖柏 ・ 6:298b–299a; 7:161b–162a
　Kokin denju ‥‥‥‥‥‥‥‥‥ 4:254a
Shōheikō ‥‥‥‥ 昌平黌 1:157a; 4:140a; 7:84b, 162a
　Ban on Heterodoxy ‥‥‥‥‥‥ 4:152b
　Confucian academy ‥‥‥‥‥‥ 7:335b
　Nakamura Masanao and ‥‥‥‥ 5:315a
　religious education ‥‥‥‥ 6:295a–295b
　Satō Issai ‥‥‥‥‥‥‥‥‥‥‥ 7:27a
Shōhei no shiki
　Kojiki described ‥‥‥‥‥‥‥ 4:251b
Shōheizaka Gakumonjo. *See* **Shōheikō**
Shōhekiga ‥‥‥‥ 障壁画 ‥ 7:41a–43b
Shōhisha undō ‥‥‥‥‥‥‥ 2:14a–15b
Shōhō Kōshūjo 商法講習所 ‥‥‥ 5:249a
Shōhō Kōshū Jo (School for Commercial Law) ‥‥‥‥‥‥ 2:208a
Shōhon ‥‥‥‥‥‥ 正本 ‥‥‥ 4:76b

Shoikō ············· 書意考 **4:**129b
Shoin ··············· **7:**266a
Shoin-zukuri ···· 書院造り **2:**295a;
　　　　　　　　7:162a-163a, 265b
　Kuroshoin ··············· **7:**162b
　Nijō Castle ············· **7:**162a
　shinden-zukuri ·········· **7:**110a
　shoin style ············· **7:**162b
Shōji ················ **1:**82b
Shōji Kaoru 　庄司薫 **7:**163a
Shōji ninen nido hyakushu
　　　　正治二年二度百首 ······· **4:**128b
Shōjin ryōri ········ **2:**21a, 22a
Shōji Tarō ····· 東海林太郎 **6:**355a
Shōka ··········· **2:**289b-290a, 293a
Shōkadō Shōjō 松花堂昭乗 **7:**163a
Shō Kaiseki ···· 蔣介石 **1:**270a-270b
Shōkai shingo 捷解新語 **7:**163a
Shōkai shingo bunshaku
　　　　　捷解新語文釈 **7:**163a
Shōkaku ········ 勝覚 **2:**57b
Shōkan ······· 荘官 **7:**163a-163b
Shōka-style ············· **2:**290b
Shōkei ········ 祥啓 **7:**163b
　Geiami ················ **3:**14a
Shō Ki ········· 鍾馗 **7:**163b
Shokikan ······ 書記官 **4:**180a
Shokkiri ················ **7:**272b
Shokkō Giyūkai
　　　　職工義友会 ········· **7:**164a
　Takano Fusatarō ········ **7:**317a
Shokkō jijō ···· 職工事情 **7:**164a; **8:**264b
Shōko ················· **3:**2a
Shōkō Chūkin Bank ····· **7:**164a
Shōkōkan 彰考館 **1:**94b; **2:**347a;
　　　　　　　　　　7:164a
Shōkō keiei ···· 商工経営 **8:**127a
Shōkōki. 照光記 *See* **Meigetsuki**
Shokoku Fūzoku Toijō Kotae. *See*
Yashiro Hirokata
Shōkokuji ········· 相国寺 **3:**57a; **7:**69b,
　　　　　　　　　　164b
　Ginkakuji ··············· **3:**33a
　Itō Jakuchū ············· **3:**353b
　Josetsu ··············· **4:**77b-78a
　Rokuon nichiroku ······· **6:**335b
Shokudō ··············· **7:**165
Shokugaku keigen
　　　　植学啓原 ······· **8:**125b
Shokugenshō 職原抄 **4:**224b; **7:**164b
Shokugyō fujin
　Oku Mumeo ············· **6:**96b
Shokuhō seiken · 織豊政権 **3:**178b;
　　　　　　　　7:164b-165a
　warrior government ······· **8:**230a
Shoku nihongi 続日本紀 **4:**249a; **7:**248b
　Kojidan, resource ······· **4:**251a
　Rikkokushi ············· **6:**315b
Shoku Nihon kōki 続日本後紀 **6:**315b
Shokunin ·············· **7:**165a
Shokuryō Mēdē ·· **4:**358a; **7:**165a
Shoku sandai jitsuroku ······· **7:**121b
Shokusan Jūtaku Sōgo Co, Ltd
　　　　　　　　　7:164a-164b
Shokusan kōgyō 殖産工業 **7:**165a-165b
　National Industrial Exhibition **5:**341b
　technological development ···· **7:**369a
Shoku senzaishū (Collection of a
　Thousand Years
　Continued) ····· 続千載集 **8:**73b
Shokushi, Princess. 式子内親王
　See **Shikishi, Princess**
Shōman, Queen · 勝鬘王妃 **2:**55b
Shōmei Incident 鐘銘事件 **5:**32b; **7:**165b
Shōmonki ···· 将門記 **2:**101b; **7:**165b
　Taira no Masakado ······· **7:**301b
Shōmono ·············· **7:**165b-166a
Shōmu, Emperor 聖武天皇 **1:**184b; **5:**308a;
　　　　　　　　7:91a, 166a; **8:**287b

　education ··············· **2:**172a
　Fujiwara family ······· **2:**348a, 350b
　Fujiwara no Nakamaro ···· **2:**353b
　Ishiyamadera ······· **3:**346a-346b
　kokubunji decree ········· **4:**257a
　Kōmyō, Empress, consort of · **4:**268b
　monasticism ············· **5:**237b
　Naniwakyō ············· **5:**328b
　Shigaraki no Miya ······· **7:**91a
Shōmyō ·········· 声明 **4:**327a;
　　　　　　　　　　5:283a-283b
　tonal system ············· **5:**283b
Shōmyō Falls ····· 称名の滝 **4:**69a
Shōnai Plain ···· 庄内平野 **7:**166a, 166b
Shōnandō ········· 小楠堂 **8:**331a
Shōnen ·········· 少年 **7:**166a, 342b
Shōnen kurabu 少年倶楽部 **4:**241b; **7:**166b
Shōnen sekai ···· 少年世界 **7:**309b
Shōni family ······ 少弐氏 **7:**166b
Shōnin ··············· **7:**166b-167a
Shōnindō ··············· **7:**112a
Shōno Junzō ···· 庄野潤三 **7:**167a
Shōnō ni kansuru kenkyū
　　　　小農に関する研究 ···· **8:**331b
Shōno Shōunsai
　　　　生野祥雲斎 ········· **1:**136a
Shōnyo Kōkyō ···· 証如光教 **3:**346b
Sho o suteyo machi e deyō (Throw Away
　the Books, Take to the Streets)
　·· 書を捨てよ街へ出よう ···· **8:**13a
Shoplifting ··············· **4:**86b
Shōriki Matsutarō
　　　　正力松太郎 ········· **7:**167a
Short stories ············· **5:**42b
Shōrui Awaremi no Rei
　　　　生類憐みの令 ··· **7:**167a-167b
Shōryōe Festival
　dance, traditional ········· **2:**74a
Shosagoto ········· 所作事 **2:**75b; **4:**91a,
　　　　　　　　93a-93b, 95b
　onnagata ··············· **6:**108a
Shosai yori gaitō ni
　　　　書斎より街頭に ··· **7:**338b
Shosaizu ··············· **3:**306a
Shōseikon (matrilocal
　marriage) ······ 招婿婚 **5:**262b
Shōseikon no kenkyū
　　　　招婿婚の研究 ··· **7:**316a
Shōsendō ········· 象先堂 **3:**352a
Shōsenkyō ········· 昇仙峡 **7:**167b
Shōsetsu Nihon ginkō
　　　　小説日本銀行 ··· **7:**148a
Shōsetsu shinzui 小説神髄 **5:**11a
Shoshi Hatto (Regulations for the
　Vassals)
　Tokugawa shogunate ······· **8:**53a
Shōshikai ······· 尚歯会 **1:**141b; **7:**167b
　Takano Chōei ············· **7:**316a
Shōshimin geki ········· **2:**270a
Shōshin dokugo · 称心独語 **4:**169b
"Shōshitsu" ······ 消失 **7:**163b
Shōsho ············· 詔書 **3:**277a-277b;
　　　　　　　　　　7:62a
Shōshō Hakkei · 瀟湘八景 **7:**167b
Shōshō Shigemoto no
　haha ········ 少将滋幹の母 **7:**343a
Shōshū reijō ·· 召集令状 **7:**167b-168a
Shōsōin ······ 正倉院 **2:**295a; **5:**277b;
　　　　　　　　7:42a, 168a-170a
　biwa ················· **7:**168b
　bodhisattva (bosatsu) ······· **7:**169a
　categories ············· **7:**169a-170a
　ceramic bowl ············· **7:**168b
　folding-screen panel ······· **7:**169b
　furniture collection ······· **2:**371a
　Kōmyō and Shōmu collection · **4:**268b
　lead-glazed wares ········· **1:**262b
　musical instruments ······· **1:**157a

　preservation of treasures ···· **7:**170a
　sankechi examples ········· **7:**13b
　textiles ················ **8:**17a
　treasures ··············· **7:**169a
Shōsōin documents
　　　　正倉院文書 **1:**234a
Shōsōin textiles 正倉院染織 **8:**17b
Shotai ··············· **4:**203a; **7:**170a
　calligraphy ············· **1:**233b
　gyōsho ················ **7:**171a
　kaisho ················ **7:**171a
　kanji ················· **7:**170b
　reisho ················ **7:**170b
　sōsho ················· **7:**171a
　tensho ················ **7:**170b
Shōta no uma ··· 正太の馬 **8:**110a
Shōtatsu ········· 聖達 **3:**328b-329a
Shōtetsu ········· 正徹 **5:**14b; **7:**170b;
　　　　　　　　　　8:215a
Shōtetsu monogatari
　　　　正徹物語 **7:**170b
Shotō chigyō ···· 所当知行 **1:**274a
Shōtō Kokushi ··· 正燈国師 **4:**1b-2a
Shōtoku, Empress
　　　　称徳天皇 **4:**253b
Shōtoku Nagasaki Shinrei
　　　　正徳長崎新令 **7:**171a
　Dutch trade ············· **2:**136a
Shōtoku no Chi ·· 正徳の治 **7:**171a
Shōtoku, Prince · 聖徳太子 **1:**234b, 151a,
197b; **7:**11b, 69b, 74a, 93a, 171b-172a, 260a,
　　　　　　　　　　264a
　codes of conduct ········· **1:**207a
　founding of Buddhism ····· **1:**178a
　historiography ··········· **3:**152a
　Ikaruga no Miya ········· **3:**264b
　imperial era ············· **4:**203a
　Jōgū Shōtoku Hōōtei Setsu ··· **4:**69a
　portrait ················ **7:**172b
　Seventeen-Article Constitution · **7:**73a
　Shinran ··············· **7:**123a
　treasure houses ········· **5:**277b
Shōtoku Taishi. *See* **Shōtoku, Prince**
Shōtoku Taishi · 聖徳太子 **4:**125a
　················ **1:**197b
Shoup mission ······· **7:**172a-173a
　taxes, national and local · **7:**354a-354b
Shōwa ················ 昭和 **3:**147a
Shōwa Aluminum Corporation ··· **7:**173a
Shōwa bungaku shi
　　　　昭和文学史 **7:**175a
Shōwa Denkō
　　　　　　　　　　7:173a
　pollution ··············· **2:**226b
Shōwa Denkō Scandal
　　　　昭和電工事件 **1:**97b; **7:**173a;
　　　　　　　　　　8:344b
　Fukuda Takeo's involvement ··· **2:**362b
Shōwa Depression
　　　　昭和恐慌 **7:**173b-174a
　cooperatives ············· **1:**22a
　economy ··············· **2:**153b
　Financial Crisis of 1927 ··· **2:**277a
　landlordism ············· **4:**363a
Shōwa Electric Wire & Cable Co, Ltd
　　　　　　　　　　7:174a
Shōwa Fertilizer Co ······· **7:**173a
Shōwa Ishin. *See* "**Shōwa Restoration**"
Shōwa Kenkyūkai
　　　　昭和研究会 **7:**174a-174b
Shōwa Line, Ltd ········· **7:**174b
Shōwa literature ······· **7:**174b-176b
　postwar literature ······· **6:**230a-231b
Shōwa Oil Co, Ltd ··· **6:**181b; **7:**176b
Shōwa period ···· 昭和時代 **7:**176b
Shōwa Research Association ··· **3:**53b;
　　　　　　　　　　7:174a
Shōwa Research Society ······· **7:**229b

Shōwa Restoration
　　　　　昭和維新 ···· **7:**176b-177a
Shōwa Sangyō Co, Ltd ···· **7:**177a
Shōwa Shinzan 昭和新山 ·· **7:**98a, 177a
Shōwa Station ···· 庄屋 **1:**64a-64b
Shōya 　　　　　　庄屋 **7:**177a-177b
Shōyō jurin bunka
　　　　照葉樹林文化 ···· **7:**177a-179a
　Laurilignosa culture ···· **7:**177b-178a
　development of agriculture · **7:**178a-178b
　Jōmon cultures ············· **7:**178b-179a
　material elements ··········· **7:**177b
　nonmaterial elements ···· **7:**177b-178a
Shōyu ············· **2:**305a, 306a; **7:**239b
Shoyūken hō no riron
　　　　　所有権法の理論 ···· **4:**184b
Shōyūki 　　　　小右記 ···· **7:**179a
Shozan ·························· **3:**57a
Shōzei ··············· 正税 ···· **7:**179a
Shōzōmatsu wasan
　　　　　正像末和讃 ···· **8:**231a
Shrikes [(mozu) *Lanius* **spp.]** ··· **7:**179b
Shrimps, prawns, and lobsters [(ebi)
　suborders Natantia and Palinura]
　　　　　　　　　　　···· **7:**179b
Shrine Forest ············· **5:**352a-352b
Shrine Library ··············· **4:**58b-59a
Shrine of Lady Tachibana
　　　　　橘夫人厨子 ······ **1:**21a
Shrines ········ **7:**138a, 179b-180b
　kagura ················ **4:**106a-107b
　Shintō ················ **7:**129b-131a
　Shintō architecture ····· **7:**132a-134b
　Shintō art ············· **7:**135b-136b
　Shintō rites ············ **7:**137b-139b
　ujigami ················ **8:**131a-131b
Shrine Shintō ···· 神社神道 **2:**300b; **7:**138a,
　　　　　　　　　　　　180b
　goshintai ················ **3:**49a-49b
　See also **Shintō**
Shūbun ············ 周文 ·· **7:**42b, 69b,
　　　　　　　　　　180b-181a
　Gakuō Zōkyū ············ **3:**4b-5a
　ink painting ············· **3:**306b
　Reading in the Bamboo Study (Chikusai
　　dokusho zu) ············· **7:**181a
　sansuiga (landscape painting) · **7:**17b
Shuchiteki bungakuron
　　　　　主知的文学論 ···· **1:**4b
Shūdan shūshoku ········· **3:**62b-63a
Shūeisha Publishing Co, Ltd ·· **7:**181a
Shufu no tomo ·· 主婦の友 **7:**181b; **8:**289b
Shufuren ······· 主婦連 **6:**238b; **7:**181b
　Oku Mumeo ················· **6:**96b
Shufu Rengōkai. *See* **Shufuren**
Shūgaishō ········· 拾芥抄 ···· **7:**181b
Shugakuin Detached
　Palace ··· 修学院離宮 · **4:**336a, 337a;
　　　　　　　　　　7:181b-182a
Shugakuin Rikyū. *See* **Shugakuin**
　Detached Palace
Shugei Shuchiin
　　　　綜芸種智院 ···· **7:**182a
　founding ················· **2:**172b
　Kūkai founded ············· **4:**304a
Shugendō ········· 修験道 **2:**57b, 88b;
　　　　　　7:67a, 182a-182b; **8:**288b
　En no Gyōja ··············· **2:**219b
　Shingon sect ··············· **7:**115a
　Shōgoin ··················· **7:**160a
Shūgetsu Tōkan 秋月等観 ···· **7:**70a,
　　　　　　　　　　182b-183a
Shūgi ······················· **7:**183a
　kokorozuke as ············· **4:**256a
Shūgigaisho 　集義外書 ···· **4:**307a
Shūgiwasho 　集義和書 ···· **4:**307b
Shugo ············ 守護 ···· **7:**64b,
　　　　　　　　　　183a-184a

　appointment ············· **4:**121b
　corvée labor ············· **1:**226b
　governmental functions ····· **2:**264a-264b
　kokujin ················· **4:**260a
　mediation with shogunate ····· **4:**151a
　Muromachi history ········· **3:**173a
　provincial decrees ········· **4:**90a
　shōen ··················· **7:**157a
　shogunate, shugodai and, relationships
　　between ············· **7:**183b-184a
Shugo daimyō 　守護大名 **1:**274a; **7:**184a
　Ōnin War and ············· **6:**106b
Shugō Incident ·· 殊号事件 ···· **7:**184a
Shūgō Shintō ················· **4:**271b
Shūgyō ····················· **1:**96b
Shūgyokushū ······ 拾玉集 ···· **4:**54a
Shūhōdō. *See* **Akiyoshidō**
Shūhō Myōchō. *See* **Sōhō Myōchō**
Shuihuzhuan [Shui-hu-chan (All Men Are
　Brothers)] ··············· **8:**336b
Shuinjō ·········· 朱印状 · **7:**184a-184b,
　　　　　　　　　　256b, 266b
　vermilion seal ship trade ····· **8:**190a
Shuinsen ········· 朱印船 ···· **7:**255a
Shuinsen bōeki 朱印船貿易 ··· **8:**190a-190b
　Shuinsen voyages ··········· **8:**190a
　　　　　7:184b-185a; **8:**204a
Shūi wakashū 拾遺和歌集 · **1:**41a; **5:**35a;
　　　　　　7:42b, 184b-185a; **8:**204a
　Fujiwara no Kintō ··········· **2:**352a
　kagura uta ················· **4:**108a
Shūji. *See* **Calligraphy**
Shūkai Jōrei 　集会条例 ···· **7:**185a
Shūkai Oyobi Seisha Hō ···· **6:**266a
Shūkan shinchō 週刊新潮 ···· **6:**267b
　Shinchōsha Company ········· **7:**109a
Shūkan tōyō keizai (Weekly Eastern
　Economic Review) 週刊東洋経済 **8:**91b
Shūkiku ·········· 蹴鞠 ···· **4:**191a
Shukke (Buddhist priest) **plays** · **4:**327b
Shukke taikō ···· 出家大綱 ···· **2:**187a
Shukke to sono deshi
　　　　出家とその弟子 ···· **4:**312a
Shukkō ··················· **7:**185a
Shū Kōkei Jiken
　　　　周鴻慶事件 ···· **8:**379a
Shukuba machi. *See* **Post-station**
　towns
Shukushi (recycled paper)
　　　　　　　宿紙 ···· **8:**233a
Shukuzu ·········· 縮図 ···· **7:**176b
　Shindō Kaneto ············· **7:**111a
Shukuzu (Miniature)
　Tokuda Shūsei ············· **8:**45a
Shukyūha ·········· 守旧派 ···· **7:**259b
Shūmei ····················· **4:**95a
Shūmeigiku ··················· **1:**56a
Shummusō ········· 春夢草 ···· **7:**162a
Shūmon aratame · 宗門改 · **7:**185b-186b
　Jinshin Koseki ············· **4:**60b
Shumpuden ········· 春婦伝 ···· **7:**334b
Shun ····················· **7:**68a
Shunchōshū ········ 春鳥集 ···· **4:**123a
Shundō Junko 　俊藤純子 ···· **2:**343a
Shun'e ·········· 俊恵 ···· **7:**186b-187a
Shunga ····· **7:**187a-188a, 258a; **8:**138b
Shungiku ··················· **7:**265a
Shunkan (*Cymbidium virescens*) · **7:**188b
Shunran (*Cymbidium virescens*) · **7:**188b
Shunshoku tatsumi no
　sono 　　春色辰巳園 ···· **7:**334a
Shunshoku umegoyomi
　　　　春色梅児誉美 · **7:**333b-334a
Shuntō (spring labor offensive)
　　　　　7:188b-190a, 250b
　"Base-up" ················· **7:**189
　collective bargaining ········· **4:**360a
　enterprise-level unions ······· **7:**189a

　Iwai Akira ················· **3:**357b
　labor disputes ············· **4:**349b
　negotiations ············· **7:**189b
　origins ················· **7:**188b
　Ōta Kaoru ················· **6:**129a
　people's ················· **7:**189b-190a
　spread ················· **7:**189a-189b
　wage campaigns 1945-1955 · **7:**188b-189a
　wage level ················· **8:**198b
　Shuntō wage pattern ········· **4:**348a
Shun'yōdō ········· 春陽堂 ···· **4:**199a
Shun'yōshū ········ 春葉集 ···· **4:**101a
Shū Onrai ········ 周恩来 · **8:**378b-379a
Shuppan Hō ······ 出版法 ···· **6:**262b
Shuppan Jōrei ··· 出版条例 ···· **6:**262b
Shuppan nenkan
　(Publisher's Yearbook)
　　　　　　出版年鑑 ···· **8:**268a
Shuppan Rei ····· 出版令 ···· **1:**252a
Shurei no Mon · 守礼の門 ···· **6:**84b
Shuri castle ······ 首里城 ···· **6:**84b
Shuri castle remains
　　　　　首里城遺構 ···· **7:**190a
Shuriken ··················· **7:**190a
Shū Sakujin ····· 周作人 · **8:**379a-379b
Shushi ····················· **4:**325a
Shushigaku
　(Neo-Confucianism)
　　　　　　朱子学 **1:**354b-355a;
　　　　　　4:140a; **7:**71a, 190a-191b
　basic teachings ············· **7:**190a
　education ················· **2:**173b-174a
　new religions ············· **5:**366b
　Shingaku ················· **7:**112a
　shogunate patronage ········· **1:**355a
　Shōheikō ················· **7:**162a
　Tokugawa shogunate ········· **8:**53a
　view of history ············· **3:**154b
　view of literature ··········· **5:**16b
　warrior government ········· **8:**230b
　Zhu Xi School ············· **7:**190b-191b
Shūshin ······· 修身 · **7:**35b, 191b
Shūshin kōyō seido
　technological development ····· **7:**369b
Shu Shunsui ····· 朱舜水 ···· **7:**191b
Shūsō Dōjin. 秋艸道人 　*See* **Aizu Yaichi**
Shusse Kagekiyo 出世景清 · **1:**275b; **4:**77a
Shutaisei ("sense of self") **debates**
　　　　　　　　　6:232b-233a
Shūto ················· **8:**230b-231a
Shūtō fukko ······ 宗統復古 ···· **7:**234a
Shutoken ··················· **8:**67b
Shutsujin'ei
　portrait painting ··········· **6:**227a
Shutsujō kōgo (Buddha's
　Comments After His
　Meditation) ···· 出定後語 ···· **8:**71b
Shuzenji ········· 修善寺 ···· **7:**191b
Sian Incident. *See* **Xi'an (Sian) Incident**
Siberia
　expedition of Japanese troops ····· **7:**192a
　geological exploration ········· **7:**238b
　natural resources ··········· **7:**238b
　Soviet-Japanese development ····· **7:**238a
Siberia, Japanese prisoners of war in
　　　　　　　　　7:191b-192a
Siberian Intervention · **1:**74a; **7:**192a-192b
　China ················· **1:**288a
　failure ················· **1:**88a
　Kenseikai ················· **4:**198a
　Tanaka Giichi ············· **7:**336a-336b
　Terauchi Masatake ········· **8:**12b
　Ugaki Kazushige ············· **8:**130b
　United States ············· **8:**156b
Sickles. *See* **Kama**
Siddham ············· **1:**179a; **7:**192b
　Jakugon ················· **4:**1b
Sidotti, Giovanni Battista ···· **7:**192b

Siebold, Heinrich von · · · · · · · · · · · 1:120a
Siebold Philip Franz von · · · · · · · · 1:76b;
7:192b-193a
German-Japanese relations · · · · · · · · 3:26a
Inō Tadataka · · · · · · · · · · · · · · · 3:309b
Itō Gemboku · · · · · · · · · · · · · · · 3:352a
Sakhalin · · · · · · · · · · · · · · · · · · · 7:1b
Siemens Incident 7:99a, 193a-193b; 8:298b
Takarabe Takeshi · · · · · · · · · · · · · 7:317b
Signboards · · · · · · · · · · · · · · 7:193b-194a
Silence · · · · · · · · · · · · · · · · · · 2:214a
Silent Temple in Autumn Mountains
· 6:77b
Silk · · · · · · · · · · · 7:21a, 194a-194b
fibers and yarns · · · · · · · · · · : · · · 7:194a
history · · · · · · · · · · · · · · · 7:194a-194b
plain weave · · · · · · · · · · · · · · · · · 8:17a
production, sericulture · · · · · · · · · · · 7:68b
Silk crepe · · · · · · · · · · · · · · · · · 1:297a
Silk fabric · · · · · · · · · · · · · · · · · 7:194a
Silk industries
Shinyei Kaisha · · · · · · · · · · · · · · 7:140a
Tomioka Silk-Reeling Mill · · · · · · · · 8:72a
Silk Road · · · · · · · · 1:26b; 7:194b-196a
in Japan · · · · · · · · · · · · · · 7:195a-196a
motifs · · · · · · · · · · · · · · · · · · 7:195b
musical instruments and game
objects · · · · · · · · · · · · · 7:195a-195b
theater and acrobatics · · · · · · · · · 7:195a
West Asian design composition
· · · · · · · · · · · · · · · · · · 7:195b-196a
West Asian materials · · · · · · · · 7:195b
West Asian objects and shapes · 7:195b
Silkscreen · · · · · · · · · · · · · · · · · 5:233a
Silk trade · · · · · · · · · · · · · 5:323a-323b
itowappu system · · · · · · · · · · · · · 3:356b
Taiwan · · · · · · · · · · · · · · · 7:306b-307a
Silkworms [(kaiko) *Bombyx mori*] · 7:196a
raising · · · · · · · · · · · · · · · · · · · 7:68b
Silla · · · · · · · · · · · · · · 2:347b; 7:196a
in Korean Three Kingdoms period · 4:292a
language during · · · · · · · · · · · · · 4:291a
Silver mining · · · · · · · · · · · · 5:184b-185a
Iwami Silver Mine · · · · · · · · · · · · 3:360a
Silver Seikō, Ltd · · · · · · · · · · · · 7:196a
Silver World · · · · · · · · · · · · · · · 8:143a
Simeāo · · · · · · · · · · · · · · · · · · 4:315a
Sin. *See* **Tsumi**
Sin'ganhoe · · · · · · · · · · · · · · · 7:196a
formation · · · · · · · · · · · · · · · · · 4:283b
Singapore and Japan · · · · · · · · · 7:196b
Malayan Campaign · · · · · · · · · · · · 5:88a
postwar relations · · · · · · · · · · · · · 7:196b
Singapore-Malaya merger controversy
"Blood Debt" Incident · · · · · · · 1:158b-159a
Singer Sewing Machine Co · · · · · · · · 7:196a
Singh, Mohan · · · 1:164b; 2:348b; 7:197a
Indian National Army · · · · · · · · · · 3:289b
Single Poems by 100 Poets · · 3:248b-249a
Sino-French War · · · · · · · · · 7:197a-197b
Sino-Japanese Amity Treaty of 1871
· 7:197b
Taiwan · · · · · · · · · · · · · · · · · · 7:307a
Sino-Japanese Joint Defensive Military
Agreement · · · · · · · · · · · · · · 6:336a-336b
Sino-Japanese relations. *See* **China and**
Japan
Sino-Japanese War of 1894-1895 · 1:286a;
7:29a, 197b-198b; 8:287a
Denison, Henry Willard · · · · · · · · · 2:86b
Ding Ruchang · · · · · · · · · · · · 2:96b-97a
drama during · · · · · · · · · · · · · · · 7:107b
French-Japanese relations · · · · · · · · 2:332b
Fukushima Yasumasa · · · · · · · · · · 2:367a
Gen'yōsha · · · · · · · · · · · · · · · · · 3:25a
growth of business · · · · · · · · · · · · 2:30b
Imo Mutiny · · · · · · · · · · · · · · · · 3:275a
Imperial Japanese armed forces · · · · · 1:87a

Kabayama Sukenori · · · · · · · · · · · · 4:89b
Kanghwa, Treaty of · · · · · · · · · · · 4:140b
Kawakami Sōroku · · · · · · · · · · · · 4:181b
Kiguchi Kohei · · · · · · · · · · · · · · · 4:204a
Korean-Japanese relations · · · · · · · · 4:279b
Mutsu Munemitsu · · · · · · · · · · · · 5:288b
nationalism · · · · · · · · · · · · · · · · 5:343a
Okinawa · · · · · · · · · · · · · · · · · · 6:87b
Russo-Japanese War · · · · · · · · · · · 6:346a
Shimonoseki, Treaty of · · · · · · · · · 4:141a
Taewǒn'gun · · · · · · · · · · · · · · · · 7:294a
Taiwan · · · · · · · · · · · · · · · · · · · 7:306a
Tanaka Giichi · · · · · · · · · · · · 7:336a-336b
territory of Japan · · · · · · · · · · · · · 8:14a
Tianjin (Tientsin) Convention · · · · · · 8:29b
Tōgō Heihachirō · · · · · · · · · · · · · 8:36a
Tonghak Rebellion · · · · · · · · · · · · 8:74b
treaty concluding · · · · · · · · · 7:106a-106b
Tripartite Intervention · · · · · · · · · · 8:106b
war literature · · · · · · · · · · · · · · · 8:225b
Sino-Japanese War of 1937-1945
· 1:286b-287a, 289b; 7:48a, 65b, 199a-202a
anticommunism · · · · · · · · · · · 7:201b-202a
background · · · · · · · · · · · · · 7:199a-199b
China · 6:302a
critics · · · · · · · · · · · · · · · · 7:200a-200b
December Ninth Movement · · · · · · · · 2:81b
Eastern European nations and Japan
· 2:142a
French-Japanese relations · · · · · · · · 2:333b
Guomindang (Kuomintang) government
during · · · · · · · · · · · · · · · · · · · 1:300b
hostilities · · · · · · · · · · · · · · · · · 7:199a
Hundred Regiment Offensive · · · · · · 3:248a
Imperial Japanese armed forces · · · · · 1:88b
Ishiwara Kanji · · · · · · · · · · · · · · · 3:346a
Konoe Fumimaro policy · · · · · · · · · 4:272b
Ladybird Incident · · · · · · · · · · · · 4:362a
Marco Polo Bridge Incident · · · · · · · 5:113b
militarism as cause · · · · · · · · · · · · 2:250a
military operations · · · · · · · · · 7:200a-200b
Nanjing Incident · · · · · · · · · · 5:328b-329a
"New Policy for China" · · · · · · · · · 7:201b
peace initiatives and collaborationist
governments · · · · · · · · · · · · 7:200b-201b
photography · · · · · · · · · · · · · · · · 6:185b
Puyi (P'u-i) · · · · · · · · · · · · · · · · 6:271b
Reorganized National Government of the
Republic of China · · · · · · · · · · · · 1:289b
Russia and Japan · · · · · · · · · · · · · 6:344a
Shōwa Research Association · · · · · · · 7:174b
stalemate · · · · · · · · · · · · · · · · · · 7:200a
Tanggu (Tangku) Truce · · · · · · 7:340b-341a
Tripartite Pact · · · · · · · · · · · · · · · 8:107a
United Kingdom · · · · · · · · · · · · · · 8:152b
Wang Jingwei (Wang Ching-wei) · · · · 8:222a
war literature · · · · · · · · · · · · · · · 8:226b
Sister cities · · · · · · · · · · · · · · · 7:202a
Six National Histories · · · · · · · 6:315b-317a
"Six Poetic Geniuses" (Rokkasen) 8:207b
Six Poetic Sages, The · · · · · · · · · · 6:334b
Six Scripts · · · · · · · · · · · · · · 4:142a-142b
Sjahrir, Sutan. *See* Syahrir, Sutan
Skiing · 4:69a
introduction to Japan · 1:119b-120b; 4:383a
Sky House · · · · · · · · · · · · · · · · · 4:207b
Slang · · · · · · · · · · · · · · · · · 3:303b-304a
Slaves (yakko) · · · · · · · · · · · 6:44a; 8:285a
Slawik, Alexander · · · · · · · · · · · · · 4:43a
Slogans, political · · · · · · · · · · · · · 6:206a
Slums · · · · · · · · · · · · · · · · 7:202a-203a
Small and Medium Business Cooperative
Association · · · · · · · · · · · · · · · · 7:164a
Small and Medium Enterprise Credit
Insurance Finance Corporation Law
· 7:205b
Small and Medium Enterprise Credit
Insurance Law · · · · · · · · · · · · · · 7:205b

Small and Medium Enterprise Group
Organization Law · · · · · · · · · · · · 3:295b
Small and Medium Enterprise
Modernization Law · · · · · · · · · · · 7:205b
Small and medium enterprises
· · · · · · · · · · · · · 7:203a-205b, 253b
bank for · · · · · · · · · · · · · · · · · · 7:164a
developments · · · · · · · · · · · · · · · 7:204b
diversity of industries · · · · · · · · · · 7:203b
foreign trade · · · · · · · · · · · · · · · · 2:324a
government assistance · · · · · · · 7:204b-205a
growth · · · · · · · · · · · · · · · · 7:203b-204a
international comparisons · · · · 7:203a-203b
large companies · · · · · · · · · · · · · · 7:203b
medium firms · · · · · · · · · · · · · · · 7:205a
national economy · · · · · · · · · · 7:204a-204b
prospects · · · · · · · · · · · · · · · · · · 7:205b
Small and medium enterprises, laws
concerning · · · · · · · · · · · · · · · 7:205b
Small business. *See* **Small and medium**
enterprises
Small Business Finance Corporation
· · · · · · · · · · · · · · · · 7:204b, 205b-206a
Smallpox vaccination · · · · · · · · 5:312b-313a
Small-Scale Whaling Control
Regulations · · · · · · · · · · · · · · · · 8:250b
Smiths · · · · · · · · · · · · · · · · · · 7:206a
Smiths, Bureau of · · · · · · · · · · · · · 7:206a
Smithsonian Agreements
United States economic relations
(1945-1973) · · · · · · · · · · · · 1:135a; 8:164a
Smog · 2:227b
SMON disease · · · · · · 6:254a; 7:206a-206b
Tanabe Seiyaku Co, Ltd · · · · · · · · · 7:335b
Snails · 7:81b
Snakes [(hebi) suborder Serpentes]
· 7:206b
"Snow" · · · · · · · · · · · · · · · · · · 8:212b
Snowbell (tree), Japanese · · · · · · · · 2:184b
Snow Brand Food Co, Ltd · · · · · · · 7:206b
Snow Brand Milk Products Co, Ltd
· 7:206b
Snow Country · · · · · · · · · · · · · · · 4:176a
Snow Festival (Yuki Matsuri) · · · · · 2:252b;
7:206b-207a
Snow viewing · · · · · · · · · · · · · · · 7:207a
Snyder, Gary · · · · · · · · · · · · · · · · 7:207a
Sō · · · · · · · · · · · · · · · · 惣 7:207a-207b
Sōami · · · · · · · · · · · 相阿弥 · · 1:52b; 7:42b,
70a, 207b
works · 1:52b
Sobayōnin · · · · · · · · · · · 側用人 · · · 7:207b
Sōbin. 僧旻 *See* **Sōmin**
Sobosan · · · · · · · · · · · · 祖母山 · · · 7:207b
Sōbō Suisan Co · · · · · · · · · · · · · · 7:173a
Sō Chae-p'il · · · · · · · · · · · · · · · · 3:287b
Independence Club · · · · · · · · · · · · 4:281b
Sōchō · · · · · · · · · · · · · 宗長 6:298b; 7:208a
Sōchū · · · · · · · · · · · · · 惣中 · · · 7:207a
Social Affairs Bureau of the Home
Ministry · · · · · · · · · · · · · · · · · · 7:211a
Japanese conception of · · · · · · · · · 1:324a
Social Democratic Party · · · · · · · 7:74a-74b
modern philosophy · · · · · · · · · · · · 5:231a
Social hierarchy, class distinction · 7:122a
Social Insurance. *See* **Social security**
programs
Social insurance · · · · · · · · · · · · · · 3:317a
Social Insurance Payment Fund · · · 5:145a
Socialism
Arahata Kanson · · · · · · · · · · · 1:72a-72b
Asanuma Inejirō · · · · · · · · · · · · · 1:96a
censorship · · · · · · · · · · · · · · · · · 1:252a
High Treason Incident of 1910
· · · · · · · · · · · · · · · · · · 3:135b-136a
labor federations · · · · · · · · · · · · · 4:346a
leaders
Abe Isoo · · · · · · · · · · · · · · · · · 1:2a

Harris, Thomas Lake ········ **3**:104a-104b
Ishikawa Sanshirō ············ **3**:344a
Kagawa Toyohiko ················ **1**:2a
Kita Ikki ·············· **4**:225b-226a
Nishikawa Mitsujirō ············ **6**:17a
Ōyama Ikuo ···················· **1**:2a
modern philosophy ············ **5**:231a
national leadership ············ **3**:198b
organizations
  Baibunsha·············· **1**:129b-130a
  Heiminsha ················ **3**:125b
pacifism ···················· **6**:144a
Shakai Shugi Kenkyūkai ······ **7**:74b
Socialist Democratic Party ······ **1**:2a
Socialism Study Society ········ **5**:231a
Socialist Citizens League
  Eda Satsuki ·············· **2**:168b
Socialist Democratic Party ·········· **1**:2a
Socialist Masses Party ··· **1**:2b, 96a; **7**:74b
"Socialist" novel
  Proletarian literature movement ·· **6**:254a
Socialist Party of Japan ········ **4**:48a-48b
Socialist People's Party ··· **1**:2b; **7**:74b
Socialist Woman, The ············ **4**:138b
Socialization ···················· **4**:39a
Social organization ············ **2**:233a
  ie ···················· **3**:259a-260b
Social problems ······· **7**:208a-209a, 217b
Social relationships ········ **2**:232b-234a
Social security, national budget
···················· **1**:204b-205a
Social security legislation ··· **4**:352b-354a;
                           7:209a-209b
  Employment Security Law of 1947 · **4**:352b
  Livelihood Protection Law of 1950 · **4**:353a
  National Pension Law of 1959 ····· **4**:353a
  Unemployment Insurance Law of 1947
                          4:352b
Social security programs ···· **7**:209b-210b
  Ministry of Health and Welfare · **5**:189b
  Occupation reforms ··········· **4**:346a
Social Security System structure ·· **7**:210a
Social Service Law (Shakai Jigyō Hō)
························· **6**:235b
Social status, lifestyle ··········· **5**:8b
Social welfare ····· **7**:210b-213a, 217b
  aged ··················· **7**:211b-212a
  early development ·········· **3**:71a; **7**:210b
  income maintenance ····· **7**:211a-211b
  industrialization ············· **7**:211a
  Ministry of Health and Welfare · **5**:189b
  other services ········· **7**:212a-212b
  postwar period ·············· **7**:211a
  prospects ············· **7**:212b-213a
  social administration ········· **7**:212b
Social Welfare Activities Law · **7**:55b, 209b
Société Franco-Japonaise ········· **2**:332b
Society ··············· **7**:213a-218b
  class structure ············· **1**:322b-324b
  education ············· **7**:215a-215b
  employment ··········· **7**:216a-216b
  government and business ··· **7**:215b-216a
  history, 1868-1945 ······· **7**:213b-214a
  income distribution ··········· **7**:216b
  interpretations ········· **7**:217b-218a
  legacies ············· **7**:213a-213b
  marriage and family ······ **7**:214b-215a
  minorities ············· **7**:216b-217b
  occupation and postwar changes ··· **7**:214a
  problems ···················· **7**:217b
  religion ···················· **7**:217a
  stratification ··············· **7**:216a
  unions ················· **7**:216b-217a
  urbanization and rural ····· **7**:214a-214b
Society for Study of Meiji Civilization
  (Meiji Bunka Kenkyūkai) ········· **8**:313b
Society for the Preservation of the
  Japanese Dog ·············· **2**:125b

Society for the Study of Marxist Arts
(Marukusu Shugi Geijutsu Kenkyūkai)
························· **6**:255a
Society for the Study of Socialism ·· **1**:2a;
                             7:74b
Society of Commoners ··········· **3**:125b
Society of Masterless Samurai ···· **6**:337a
Society of Patriots ··············· **1**:34b
Society of the Chemical Industry ·· **1**:268a
Society to Protect Children ······· **1**:255a
Sociologists
  See **Sociology in Japan**
Sociology in Japan ········· **7**:218b-219a
  empirical ············· **7**:218b-219a
  formal ···················· **7**:218b
  historical ············· **7**:218b-219a
  Marxist ··············· **7**:218b-219a
  Meiji period ················ **7**:218b
  psychological ··············· **7**:218b
  today ······················ **7**:219a
Sōda Kiichirō
       左右田喜一郎 · **7**:219a, 258a
"Sodezukin"   袖頭巾 ········ **4**:180a
Sōdōmei (Federation of
  Labor) ·········· 総同盟 ··· **1**:2a, 150b;
    4:345a, 346b; **6**:212b; **7**:74b, 219a-219b
  democracy ···················· **2**:84b
  Takano Minoru ··············· **7**:317a
  Watanabe Masanosuke ········· **8**:236a
Soejima Taneomi 副島種臣 · **3**:349b; **7**:54a,
                           219b
  Seikanron issue ··············· **7**:50b
Sōen   宗淵 ··· **7**:219b-220a
Sō family   宗氏 ······· **7**:220a
  trade policy ················· **4**:278b
  waegwan ···················· **8**:198a
Soft drinks ············ **7**:220a-220b
Soga brothers. *See* **Soga monogatari**
Soga family ········ 蘇我氏 · **7**:220b-221a,
                           264a
  Aya family ·················· **1**:125b
  Buddhism as power ploy ········· **4**:277a
  Fujiwara family rivalry ········· **2**:348a
  monasticism ················· **5**:236b
  Nakatomi family rivalry ········· **2**:351a
Soga monogatari 曽我物語 · **1**:294a; **5**:44b,
                           47a;
                     7:221a-221b
  kabuki depiction ·············· **4**:98a
  otogi-zōshi ·················· **6**:130a
Sōgana ···················· **4**:131b
Soga no Emishi · 蘇我蝦夷 ······· **8**:303b
Soga no Iruka 蘇我入鹿 **2**:351b; **7**:221b
Soga no Umako · 蘇我馬子 · **7**:85a, 221b,
                           264a
  Gangōji ······················ **3**:6b
  monasticism ················· **5**:236b
Soganoya Gorō
       曽我廼家五郎 ··· **7**:221b-222a
Soga school   曽我派 ······· **7**:222a
Soga Shōhaku   曽我蕭白 · **7**:222a-222b
Sōgetsu Kaikan ··············· **8**:15a
Sōgi ·············· 宗祇 · **5**:15a; **6**:297a,
     298a, 299b; **7**:24a, 222b-223b
  Sanjōnishi Sanetaka ··········· **7**:12b
  Shinkei ····················· **7**:119a
  Shinsen tsukubashū ··········· **7**:124b
Sōgi dokugin nanibito
hyakuin
     宗祇独吟何人百韻 ··· **6**:298b
Sōgi shūenki · 宗祇終焉記 ······· **7**:208a
Sogō Co, Ltd ················· **7**:223b
Sōgō shōsha ············ **3**:18b-20a
Sōhei ············· 僧兵 · **8**:230b-231a
Sōhō Myōchō ···· 宗峰妙超 · **1**:235a; **2**:68a;
                         7:223b
  calligraphy ·················· **1**:235b

Sōhyō (General Council of
  Trade Unions of Japan)
                総評 ·· **2**:7a; **4**:347a,
     359b; **6**:212b; **7**:223b-224a, 366b
  Iwai Akira ·················· **3**:357b
  Japan Socialist Party ········· **4**:48b-49a
  Kōrōkyō affiliation ············ **4**:294a
  labor unions ················ **1**:313b
  national bureaucracy ·········· **1**:220b
  Ōta Kaoru ·················· **6**:129a
  Shinsambetsu ················ **7**:124a
  Takano Minoru ··············· **7**:317a
  Takita Minoru ··············· **7**:327a
Sōja ·············· 総社 ····· **7**:224a
Sōjiji ············· 総持寺 ····· **7**:224a
Sojinkan zenshū
          楚人冠全集 ······· **7**:258a
Sō Jorin ········ 曹汝霖 ······· **1**:239b
Sōjutsu ················ **7**:224a-224b
Sōka ·············· 草加 ······· **7**:224b
Sōka Gakkai ···· 創価学会 ······· **6**:212b;
                     7:224b-225a
  Ikeda Daisaku ················ **3**:265a
  Makiguchi Tsunesaburō ········· **5**:85b
  Toda Jōsei ·················· **8**:34b
Sōkaiya ···················· **7**:225a
  Sōkaiya kinjō · 総会屋錦城 ······· **7**:148a
Sō Kikei ········· 宋稀璟 ······· **7**:227b
Sōkonshū   草根集
                     7:170b
Soku (distantly related
  verses) ··········· 疎句 ····· **8**:214b
Sokushin jōbutsu 即身成仏 ······· **7**:114a,
                     225a-225b
Sokushin jōbutsu gi
        即身成仏義 ······· **4**:304a
Sō Kyōjin ········ 宋教仁 ······· **7**:227b
Sōkyoku ················ **7**:225b-226a
  Sōkyoku koto music ··········· **5**:317a
Solar energy ··········· **2**:216a-216b
Solatium ·············· **7**:226a-226b
Solf, Wilhelm ················· **3**:27a
Sōma ·············· 相馬 ······· **7**:226b
Sōma family ······· 相馬氏 ······· **7**:226b
Sōmagahara Incident
            相馬原事件 ··· **3**:34a-34b
Sōma Kokkō ····· 相馬黒光 **1**:164b; **7**:226b
Sōma Nomaoi Festival
            相馬野馬追い ··· **7**:226b
Sōma ware ······· 相馬焼 · **7**:226b-227a
Sōmin ············ 僧旻 · **7**:227a, 260a
  assassination ················· **4**:90a
Sōmoku chūgyo 艸木虫魚 ······· **7**:279b
Sōmon ···················· **1**:183a
Sōmon poetry, defined ··········· **5**:105a
Sompi bummyaku
        尊卑分脈 · **3**:17a; **7**:227a
Sōmura ········· 惣村 ······· **7**:207a
Sone no Yoshitada
       曽禰好忠 ··· **5**:34b; **7**:95a,
                     227a-227b
  Fujiwara no Akisuke ··········· **2**:350b
  Shin kokinshū ··············· **7**:120a
Sonezaki shinjū
       曽根崎心中 · **1**:212b; **4**:77a
Songai hoken ················· **3**:316a
Songbirds ··················· **7**:179b
Song contests, early ············ **2**:138a
Song Hŭi-gyŏng ··············· **7**:227b
  envoy to Japan ··············· **4**:278b
Song Jiaoren (Sung Chiao-jen) ··· **7**:227b
Sŏng, King ·················· **6**:146b
Songs. *See* **Music**
Song shu ···················· **7**:264a
"Song [Sung] coins" ········ **7**:232a-232b
Song Zheyuan (Sung Che-yüan) ·· **7**:228a
Sonkeikaku Library ······· **5**:1a; **7**:228a
Sonnō jōi ······· 尊王攘夷 · **1**:86a; **2**:102a,
      347a; **7**:228a-228b; **8**:291a

Inoue Kaoru · · · · · · · · · · · · · 3:310a
Meiji Restoration · · · · · · · · · 5:156a
Mito school · · · · · · · · · · · · · 5:205b
nationalism · · · · · · · · · · · · · 5:342b
Ōkubo Toshimichi · · · · · · · · 6:94a
Sakuradamongai Incident · · · · 7:4b
Sanjō Sanetomi · · · · · · · · · · 7:12b
Shimonoseki Bombardment · · · · · 7:106a
Shinagawa Yajirō · · · · · · · · · 7:109a
Shinron · · · · · · · · · · · · · · · 7:124a
Tachibana Akemi · · · · · · · · · 7:292b
Takechi Zuizan · · · · · · · · · · 7:321b
Takeda Kōunsai · · · · · · · · · · 7:322b
Tenchūgumi Rebellion · · · · · · · 8:4a
Tokugawa Nariaki · · · · · · · · · 8:52a
Umeda Umpin · · · · · · · · · · · 8:146b
Yoshida Shōin · · · · · · · · · · · 8:346a
Sonnō jōi movement · · · · 5:317b, 319b
Sono Ayako　曽野綾子 · · · · 7:228b
Sony Corporation · · · · · · · 7:228b-229a
Ibuka Masaru · · · · · · · · · · · 3:254a
Sōōji byōbu　相応寺屏風 · · 2:378a
Sophia University · · · · · · · · · 7:229a
Sora utsu nami　天うつ浪 · · 4:242b
Sorekara　それから · · · · · · 5:350a
Sorge Incident · · · · · · · · · 7:229a-230a
Sorge, Richard. See Sorge Incident
Sōrifu　総理府 · · · · · · · · · 6:244b
Soroban · · · · · · · · · · · · · · · · · 1:1a
Sōrōbun · · · · · · · · · · · · · 7:230a-231b
epistolary form · · · · · · · · · · 7:231b
grammar · · · · · · · · · · · 7:230b-231b
history · · · · · · · · · · · · · · · 7:230a
ōraimono · · · · · · · · · · · · · · 6:115b
writing system · · · · · · · · 7:230a-230b
Sōrui · · · · · · · · · · · · · · · · · · 7:46b
Sōryō system　惣領制 · · · · · 7:232a
warrior government · · · · · · · · 8:229b
Sōsaku hanga 3:146b; 4:236b; 5:232b-233a
Onchi Kōshirō · · · · · · · · · · · 6:105b
Sosei　素性 · · · · · · · 7:13a, 232a
Kokinshū · · · · · · · · · · · · · · · 4:254b
Sōseki no geijutsu
　　　漱石の芸術 · · · · · · · · 4:267a
Sōsen　宋銭 · · · · · · · 7:232a-232b
"Sōshin"　喪神 · · · · · · · · · · 3:44b
Sōsho ("grass writing")
　　　　　　　　　　1:233b; 7:171a,
　　　　　　　　　　　　　207a
Sōshoku gakku　装飾楽句 · · 8:114a
Sōshoku kofun · · 装飾古墳 · 6:119a-119b
Sōshū Masamune 相州正宗 · 7:285a-285b
Sosogi Coast · 曽々木海岸 · · 7:232b
Sōtan.　宗湛　　See Oguri Sōtan
Sōtatsu　宗達 · · · · · · · · · 7:43a,
　　　　　　　　　　232b-233a
Hon'ami Kōetsu · · · · · · · · 3:182a-182b
rimpa · · · · · · · · · · · · · · · · 6:317b
Wind and Thunder Gods · · · · · · 7:232a-232b
Sotetsu [(Japanese sago
palm) Cycas revoluta]
　　　　　　　　　　　　　　7:233a
Sō Tetsugen　宋哲元 · · · · · 7:228a
Sōtō, China · · · · · · · · · · · · · 1:283a
Sotomo　蘇洞門 · · · · · · · · 7:233a
Sōtō sect · · · · · · · · 曹洞宗 · 1:179b;
　　　　　　　　　　7:233a-234b
Dōgen · · · · · · · · · · · · · · · · 2:123b
Edo period and revitalization · 7:234a-234b
Eiheiji temple · · · · · · · · · 2:186a-186b
history · · · · · · · · · · · · · · · 7:233b
popularization · · · · · · 4:190b; 7:224a
teachings · · · · · · · · · · · · · · 7:233b
Sound of a Waterfall · · · · · · · · 6:77b
Sōunji Dono Nijūikkajō
　　　早雲寺殿廿一箇条 · · 7:234b
Sōunkyō　層雲峡 · · · · · · · · 7:234b
Soups · · · · · · · · · · · · · · · · · 2:22b

South Africa · · · · · · · · · · · · · 1:19b
South America, Japanese studies · · 4:45a
South China Sea, Battle of · · · · · 7:234b
Southeast Asia, Pacific Islands, and
　Japan · · · · · · · · · · · · · 7:234b-236a
anti-Japanese sentiment · · · · · · 7:236a
expansion · · · · · · · · · · · · · · 7:235a
Japanese influence · · · · · · · 7:235b-236a
Meiji period · · · · · · · · · · 7:234b-235a
post-World War II relations · · · · 7:235b
World War II · · · · · · · · · · · · 7:235a
Southern Alps. See
　Akaishi Mountains
Southern Alps National
　Park　南アルプス国立公園 · 1:39b; 7:236a
Southern Baptist Mission · · · · · 1:142a
"Southern barbarian" · · · · · · 5:321b-322a
Southern expansion doctrine · · 1:87b;
　　　　　　　　7:235a, 236a-237a
elements · · · · · · · · · · · · · · 7:236b
history · · · · · · · · · · · · · 7:236b-237a
United Kingdom · · · · · · · · · · 8:152b
"Southern Learning" school · · · · 5:328a
"Southern painting" · · · · · · 5:327b-328a
Southern Song · · · · · · · · · · · 7:167b
South Islands · · · · · · · · · · · · · 6:35a
South Korea, Japanese relations with.
　See Korea and Japan
South Manchuria Railway
　　　　　　　南満州鉄道 · · 6:278b;
　　　　　　　　　　7:237a-238a
administration, 1906-1937 · · · · · · 7:237a
conflict with China · · · · · · · · 7:237b
empire, 1906-1931 · · · · · · 7:237a-237b
founding · · · · · · · · · · · · · · 7:237a
Japanese interest · · · · · · · · · 1:288b
Komura Jutarō · · · · · · · · · · 4:268a
Manchukuo · · · · · · · · · · · 5:96b-97a
Matsuoka Yōsuke · · · · · · · · · 5:139b
after 1937 · · · · · · · · · · · 7:237b-238a
Shiratori Kurakichi · · · · · · · · 7:147b
Twenty-One Demands · · · · · · · 8:120b
Uchida Kōsai · · · · · · · · · · · 8:123a
South Manchuria Railway Research
　Institute · · · · · · · · · · · · · 7:293a
Souvenirs, commemorative · · · · 3:138a
Sovereign, priestly retired · · · · 3:227a
Sovereigns
Emperor Shōmu · · · · · · · · · 7:166a
residences · · · · · · · · · · · · · 1:105a
Soviet-Japanese Basic Convention
　　　　　　　　　　　　　　7:238a
Russia and Japan · · · · · · · · · 6:343a
Russo-Japanese fisheries · · · · · 6:345a
Soviet-Japanese development of
　Siberia · · · · · · · · · · · · 7:238a-238b
Soviet-Japanese Joint Declaration
　　　　　　　　　　7:238b-239a
Cold War · · · · · · · · · · · · · 3:324a
United Nations · · · · · · · · · · 8:153b
Soviet-Japanese Joint Economic
　Committee · · · · · · · · · · · · 7:238b
Soviet-Japanese Neutrality Pact · · 6:343b
Sōya Kaikyō · · · · 宗谷海峡 · 7:239a
Sōyamisaki · · · · · · 宗谷岬 · 7:239a
Sōya Strait · · · · · 宗谷海峡 · 7:239a
Soybeans [(daizu) Glycine max] · 7:239a
production · · · · · · · · · · · · · · 1:27a
So, yō, and chō　祖, 庸, 調 · 7:239a-239b,
　　　　　　　　　　　296a
Soy sauce · · · · · · 2:305a, 306b; 7:239b
brewing · · · · · · · · · · · · · · 1:170a
production · · · · · · · · · · · · · 5:233b
Sōzei　　　　　　宗砌 · · · · 6:297a
Sozō · · · · · · · · · · · · · · · · · 7:239b
Sōzoku Hō (inheritance law) · · · · 8:71a
Sozoro monogatari
　　　そぞろ物語 · · · · · · 4:187b

Space program. See Aerospace
Space technology · · · · · · · 7:239b-241a
applications satellites · · · · · · · 7:240b
plans · · · · · · · · · · · · · · 7:240b-241a
rockets · · · · · · · · · · · · · · · 7:240a
scientific satellites · · · · · · · 7:240a-240b
Spain and Japan · · · · · · · · · · 7:241a
San Felipe Incident · · · · · · · 7:9b-10a
Spaniel, Japanese · · · · · · · · 4:40b-41a
Sparrows [(suzume) Passer spp.]
　　　　　　　　　　7:241a-241b
mythology · · · · · · · · · · · · · 5:296a
Spearheads, bronze · · · · · · · · 1:175a
Spears · · · · · · · · · · · · · 1:89b; 7:224a
Special accounts · · · · · · 2:281a-281b, 307a
Special education · · · · · · · · · 7:241b
Special Higher Police (Tokubetsu Kōtō
　Keisatsu or Tokkō) · · · · · 1:253a; 6:198b;
　　　　　　　　　　7:241b-242a
Yokohama Incident · · · · · · · · 8:330a
Special Measures Law · · · · · · · 2:182b
Special procurements · · · · · · 8:57b-58a
Special tax measures · · · · · · 7:242a-242b
Spell master · · · · · · · · · · · · · 4:325a
Spencer, Herbert · · · · · · · · · · 7:218b
Spices · · · · · · · · · · · · 2:306a; 3:127b
Japanese cooking · · · · · · · · 2:21a-21b
Spiders [(kumo) order Araneae] · 7:242b
Spinning industries
Kanebo, Ltd · · · · · · · · · · · 4:137b
Nisshin Spinning Co, Ltd · · · · · 6:21a
Nittō Bōseki Co, Ltd · · · · · · · 6:22b
Tōyōbō Co, Ltd · · · · · · · · · · 8:89b
Unitika, Ltd · · · · · · · · · · · · 8:168b
Spinning mills · · · · · · · · · · · · 2:31a
Spirit of Jesus Church · · · · · · · 7:242b
Spirits
ancestral · · · · · · · · · · · · · · 5:260a
nefarious · · · · · · · · · · · 5:296a-296b
Spiritual exercises · · · · · · · · · · 1:96b
Spitzer, H. M. · · · · · · · · · · · · 4:38b
Sponge bath · · · · · · · · · · · · · 3:72b
Sporting goods manufacturers · · · 7:269b
Sports · · · · · · · · · · · · · · · 7:242b-243a
Sports and recreation regulation · · 4:10a
"Spring pictures" · · · · · · · · 7:187a-188a
Spring wage offensive · · · · · 7:188b-190a
Spy ring · · · · · · · · · · · · · · · 7:229a
Squid and cuttlefish [(ika) order
　Decapoda] · · · · · · · · 2:284b; 7:243a-243b
Squid fishing · · · · · · · · · · · · 2:286a
Stalactite grottos · · · · · · · · · · 7:312a
Stalin, Joseph · · · · · · · · · · · · 8:286b
Standard Classification of Occupations
occupational structure · · · · · · · 6:55b
Standard-form contract · · · · · · 7:243b
Standard of living · · · · · 2:165a; 6:225b;
　　　　　　　　　7:243b-245a
changes in consumption patterns
　　　　　　　　　　7:244a-245a
leisure time · · · · · · · · · · · · · 5:7a
living conditions · · · · · · · 7:243b-244a
personal consumption · · · · · · · 7:244a
Standing to sue doctrine · · · · · · 4:80a
State Ceremonials, Board of · · · · 7:180b
Statement on the Expulsion of the
　Bateren · · · · · · · · · · · · · · 1:65a
State policy company · · · · · 4:261b-262a
State Shintō · · · · · · 国家神道 · 2:300b;
　　　　　　　6:204b; 7:138a, 245b-246a
Deguchi Nao · · · · · · · · · · · · 2:82b
Fukko Shintō · · · · · · · · · · · 6:306b
ikigami · · · · · · · · · · · · · 3:268a-268b
Statistical Mathematics, Institute of
　　　　　　　　　　　　　　7:246a
Stature · · · · · · · · · · · · · · · · · 4:37b
Status, concept of · · · · · · · · · 1:207b

Status of Forces Agreement (SOFA)
United States-Japan Administrative
Agreement · · · · · · · · · 8:165a-165b
United States military bases, disputes
· · · · · · · · · · · · · · · · · · · 8:168a
United States-Japan security treaties
· · · · · · · · · · · · · · · · · · · 8:167a
Statutory Law · · · · · · · · · · · · · 1:13a
Steaming, Japanese cooking method
· 2:23b
Steel Industries
Aichi Steel Works, Ltd · · · · · · 1:33a-33b
Daidō Steel Co, Ltd · · · · · · · · · 2:56b
Hitachi Metals, Ltd · · · · · · · · · 3:207a
Japan Steel Works, Ltd · · · · · · · 4:49b
Kamaishi · · · · · · · · · · · · · · 4:120b
Kawasaki Steel Corporation · · · · · 4:184a
Kōbe Steel, Ltd · · · · · · · · · · · 4:238a
Maruichi Steel Tube, Ltd · · · · 5:120b-121a
Mitsubishi Steel Mfg Co, Ltd · · · · 5:209a
Nakayama Steel Works, Ltd · · · · · 5:319b
Nippon Kōkan · · · · · · · · · 6:10a-10b
Nippon Steel Corporation · · · · 6:12b-13a
Nippon Yakin Kōgyō Co, Ltd · · · · · 6:13b
Nisshin Steel Co, Ltd · · · · · · · · 6:21a
Pacific Metals Co, Ltd · · · · · · · 6:143b
Sankyū, Inc · · · · · · · · · · · · · 7:15a
Shin Nan'yō · · · · · · · · · · · · 7:121b
Sumitomo Metal Industries, Ltd · · · 7:269a
Tōkyō Steel Mfg Co, Ltd · · · · · · 8:69a
Tōshin Steel Co, Ltd · · · · · · · · 8:83b
Yawata Iron and Steel Works 8:320b-321a
Yodogawa Steel Works, Ltd · · · · · 8:326b
See also Iron and steel industry
Stein, Lorenz von · · · · · 1:120a; 2:2b; 7:246a
Stencil dyeing · · · · · · · · · · · · 4:167b
Stevens, Durham W. · · · · · · · · · 4:282a
Stews, Japanese cooking methods · 2:23a
Stick dance · · · · · · · · 棒踊り · 7:246a
Ryūkyū music · · · · · · · · · · · 6:357b
Stilts · · · · · · · · · · · · · · · · 7:246a
Stilwell, Joseph W. · · · · · · · · · 7:200b
Stimson, Henry Lewis · · · · · · · · 7:246b
Stimson Doctrine. See Nonrecognition
policy
Stipend · · · · · · · · · · · · · · · 7:347b
Stock acquisitions, regulation of
· · · · · · · · · · · · · · · · · 1:66a-66b
Stock exchanges · · · · · · 4:48a; 7:246b-247a
Stockholder, professional · · · · · · 7:225a
Stockholders' general meeting · 1:159a;
7:247a-247b
overseer · · · · · · · · · · · · · · 6:136a
Stockholm Appeal (1950) · · · · · · · 1:111a
Stock market · · · · · · · · · · · · · 2:35a
Stock ownership dividends · · 2:120b-121a
Stocks, corporate · · · · · · · · · · 2:34a
Stoddard, George D. · · · · · · · · · 2:180a
Stone tools · · · · 1:75b; 6:159b; 7:247b-248a
Fukui Cave · · · · · · · · · · · · · 2:363b
Iwajuku site · · · · · · · · · · · · 3:358a
Kamegaoka site · · · · · · · · · · · 4:125a
Karako site · · · · · · · · · · · · · 4:157b
Okhotsk culture · · · · · · · · · · · 6:84a
paleolithic culture · · · · · · · · · 6:159a
Stoneware · · · · · · · · · · · 1:259b-260a
Stop Venereal Disease Week · · · · · 8:189b
Storehouses, traditional 7:248a-249a, 248b
modernization · · · · · · · · · · · 7:249a
premodern · · · · · · · · · · · 7:248b-249a
Stories about the past · · · · · · · · 4:251a
Storyteller · · · · · · · · · · · · · · 6:281a
medieval · · · · · · · · · · · · 5:44b-45a
Storytelling · · · · · · · · · · · · · 2:172a
kōdan (oral) · · · · · · · · · · 4:241a-241b
Straight, Willard Dickerman · · · · · 7:249a
Straits
Kammon · · · · · · · · · · · · · · 4:128a

Korea · · · · · · · · · · · · · · · · 4:292b
Naruto · · · · · · · · · · · · · · · 5:335b
Nemuro · · · · · · · · · · · · · · · 5:360a
Ondo · · · · · · · · · · · · · · · · 6:106a
Sōya · · · · · · · · · · · · · · · · 7:239a
Tsugaru · · · · · · · · · · · · · · · 8:113a
Tsushima · · · · · · · · · · · · 8:118a-118b
Strange, Fredric W. · · · · · · · · · 7:242b
Stranger, The · · · · · · · · · · · · 7:109a
Strategic Bombing Survey, United
States · · · · · · · · · · · · · · · 7:249a
Stratification, social · · · · · · · · · 7:216a
Stratovolcanoes · · · · · · · · · · · 8:194a
Straw boots. See Waragutsu
Straw raincoats · · · · · 6:280a; 7:249a-249b
Straw sandals. See Waraji
Straw ware · · · · · · · · · · · · · · 7:249b
Stray Thoughts · · · · · · · · · · · · 4:138b
Street dances · · · · · · · · · · · · · 2:74a
Street entertainment · · · · · · 7:249b-250a
monkeys · · · · · · · · · · · · · · 5:245b
Street stalls · · · · · · · · · · · · · 7:250a
Street vendors · · · · · · · · · · · · 7:250b
Strike, Clifford Stewart · · · · · · · 7:250b
Strike, right to · · · · · · · · · · 6:312b-313a
Strike for the Right to Strike · · · · · 7:279b
Strikes and other forms of labor
dispute · 2:369a; 4:349b-350a; 7:250b-251a
Allied Occupation · · · · · · · · · · 7:189a
injunctions · · · · · · · · · · · · · 4:352a
political implications · · · · · · · 4:350b-351a
public employees · · · · · · · 4:351a; 6:265a
Takita Minoru · · · · · · · · · · · · 7:327a
Student associations. See Zengakuren
Student Federation of Social Science
(Gakuren) · · · · · · · · · · · · · 6:168a
Student movement · · · · · · · 7:251a-253a;
8:375a-375b
armed confrontation · · · · · · · · 7:252b
crisis of 1968-1969 · · · · · · · 7:252b-253a
Japan Communist Party (JCP) · · · · 4:12a;
7:252a-252b
origins · · · · · · · · · · · · · 7:251a-251b
postwar reconstruction · · · · · 7:251b-252a
prewar Gakuren · · · · · · · · · · · 7:251b
revenue for higher education · · · · 3:134a
Shinjinkai · · · · · · · · · · · · · · 7:115b
suppression and decline · · · · · · · 7:251b
university autonomy · · · · · · · · · 8:171a
Zengakuren · · · · · · · · · · · · · 7:252a
Student protests of 1968-1969. See
University upheavals of 1968-1969
Students, foreign · · · · · · · · 2:319a-319b
Studies in Japanese Buddhism · · · · 6:288b
Studies in the Intellectual History of
Tokugawa Japan · · · · · · · · · · 4:259a
Studio potter · · · · · · · · · · · · · 1:260a
Study abroad · · · · · · · · · · 7:36b, 253a
Study of Ancient Times, The · · · · · 4:240b
Study of Good, A · · · · · · · · · 8:376a-376b
"Study of Local Rural Localities" · · 5:71b
Su, Prince · · · · · · · 肅親王 · 7:277b
Subarjo, Raden Akhmad · · · · · · · 7:253b
Subaru · · · · スバル(昴) 2:343a; 7:253b
Subcontracting firms · · · · · · · · · 2:35a
Subcontractors · · · · · · · · · · · · 7:253b
Subscriptive establishment · · · · · · 2:37b
Subsidiaries, prevalence · · · · · · · 2:35b
Subsidiary companies · · · · · · 7:253b-254a
stock · · · · · · · · · · · · · · · · 4:189b
Subversive Activities Prevention Law of
1952 · · · · 1:254b; 2:337b, 339a; 6:266b;
7:254a-254b
Japan Communist Party · · · · · · · 4:11b
Subways · · · · · · · · 7:254b-255a; 8:103a
Succession
imperial household · · · · · · · · · 3:277b
principle of · · · · · · · · · · · 3:259b-260a

Sūden · · · · · · · · · 崇伝 · 7:255a
codes of conduct · · · · · · · · · · 1:206b
Ikoku nikki · · · · · · · · · · · · · 3:270b
Sudō Sadanori · · · · 角藤定憲 · 4:181a
Sue · · · · · · · · · · 須恵 · 7:255a
Embree, John Fee · · · · · · · · · · 2:200a
Sue Harukata · · · · · · 陶晴賢 · 5:250b
Suehiro Izutarō 末弘厳太郎 · 7:255a-255b
case study approach · · · · · · · · · 4:375a
Suehiro Tetchō 末弘鉄腸 · 7:255b
fūzoku shōsetsu · · · · · · · · · · · 2:378b
hambatsu · · · · · · · · · · · · · · 3:92a
seiji shōsetsu · · · · · · · · · · · · 7:50a
Suekawa Hiroshi · · · 末川博 · 7:255b
Sue kilns · · · · · · · · · · · · · · · 7:256a
Suematsu Kenchō
末松謙澄 1:159b; 7:255b
Suemitsu · · · · · · · · · 季光 · 5:249b
Suetsugu Heizō · 末次平蔵 · 7:255b-256a
Sue vessels · · · · · · · · · · · · · · 7:256a
Sue ware · · · · · · · 須恵器 · 1:78a, 158a,
258a; 2:305b; 7:256a
ash glazing · · · · · · · · · · · · · 1:261b
jar · · · · · · · · · · · · · · · · · 1:257a
of kofun · · · · · · · · · · · · · · · 4:245a
Okinawa · · · · · · · · · · · · · · · 6:85b
rokuro · · · · · · · · · · · · · · · 6:335b
Sanage · · · · · · · · · · · · · · 7:9a-9b
Sueyoshi Magozaemon
末吉孫左衛門 · 7:256a-256b
Suffrage. See Universal Manhood
Suffrage Movement; Women's suffrage
Suffrage movements · · · · · · · 8:169a-169b
Sugadaira · · · · · · · · · · · · · · 7:256b
Sugae Masumi · 菅江真澄 2:296a; 7:256b
Sugae Masumi yūranki
· · · · · · · 菅江真澄遊覧記 · 7:256b
Sūgaku kyōiku no kompon
mondai
· · · · · · 数学教育の根本問題 · 6:71a
Suganuma Teifū · 菅沼貞風 · 7:256b
Sugap'a · · · · · · · · · · · · · · · 7:259b
Sugar cane production · · · · · · · · 1:50a
Sugar industries
Dai-Nippon Sugar Manufacturing Co,
Ltd · · · · · · · · · · · · · · · · 2:66b
Ensuikō Sugar Refining Co, Ltd
· · · · · · · · · · · · · · · · 2:221a-221b
Meiji Sugar Mfg Co, Ltd · · · · · · · 5:160b
Mitsui Sugar Co, Ltd · · · · · · · · 5:212a
Nippon Beet Sugar Mfg Co, Ltd · · · 6:8b
Nissin Sugar Mfg Co, Ltd · · · · · · 6:21b
Taitō Co, Ltd · · · · · · · · · · · · 7:306a
Sugar industry · · · · · · · · · 2:152-153a
Sugata Sanshirō · 姿三四郎 · 8:36b, 73a
Sugawara Minoru. 菅原実
See Uchimura Naoya
Sugawara no Michizane 菅原道真 1:151b;
2:79a; 5:31a-31b; 7:21a, 256b-257b, 260a
China · · · · · · · · · · · · · · · · 1:283a
Chinese poem · · · · · · · · · · · · 1:293b
Fujiwara family · · · · · · · · · · · 2:348b
hero worship · · · · · · · · · · · · 3:128a
Ruijū kokushi · · · · · · · · · · · · 6:340a
Shin kokinshū · · · · · · · · · · · · 7:120a
Shintō · · · · · · · · · · · · · · · · 7:127a
vengeful spirit · · · · · · · · · · · 4:126a
works · · · · · · · · · · · · · · · · 5:31b
Sugawara no Takasue no
Musume · · · · 菅原孝標女 · 7:257b
diary · · · · · · · · · · · · · · · · 7:21a
Sarashina nikki · · · · · · · 5:35b; 7:21a-21b
Suggestion boxes · · · · · · · · · · · 5:165b
Sugi [(Japanese cedar) Cryptomeria
japonica] · · · · · · · · · · · · · · 7:257b
Sugihara Sōsuke 杉原荘介 · · · · · · 3:358a

Sugihara Yoshie
  Ai no aru mura: Shinkyō Kyōdōtai no Kiroku ··············· 7:121b
  Sensei and His People: The Building of a Japanese Commune ········· 7:121b
Sugi Michisuke ···· 杉道助 ·······7:257b
Sugimoto Eiichi · 杉本栄一 ·······7:258a
Sugimoto Ryōkichi
  ··············· 杉本良吉 ·······3:261a
Sugimura Jihei 杉村治兵衛 ····7:258a
  Kaigetsudō school ············ 4:109b
  Kambun Master ············· 4:124b
Sugimura Kōzō ·· 杉村広蔵 ·······7:258a
Sugimura Sojinkan
  ··············· 杉村楚人冠 ·······7:258a
Sugimura Yōtarō
  ··············· 杉村陽太郎 ·······4:373a
Suginami Ward ···· 杉並区 ·······7:153a
Sugita Gempaku · 杉田玄白 5:313a; 7:258b
  natural science ············· 5:356b
  Rangaku kotohajime ········· 6:283b
Sugiura Eiichi. 杉浦英一
  See **Shiroyama Saburō**
Sugiura Shigetake 杉浦重剛 4:340a; 7:51b, 258b
Sugiyama Gen. *See* **Sugiyama Hajime**
Sugiyama Hajime · 杉山元 ······· 7:258b
Sugiyama Naojirō
  ··············· 杉山直治郎 ······· 2:319a; 7:258a-259a
Sugiyama Sampū 杉山杉風 ······· 7:259a
Sugoroku ··············· 7:259a-259b
Sugup'a ··············· 7:259b
  Kaehwap'a clash ············· 4:101b
  Kaehwap'a thwarted ·········· 4:280b
  Kapsin Political Coup ········· 4:156b
Sui ··············· 粋 ··3:267b-268a
Sui and Tang (T'ang) China, embassies to ··············· 7:259b-261a
  abandonment ············· 7:260a-261a
  Sui ··············· 7:260a
  Tang ··············· 7:260a
Suibokuga. 水墨画 *See* **Ink painting**
Suichikushū ········ 酔竹集 ······· 4:157a
Suicide ···· 4:38b, 84b-85a; 7:261a-263a
  characteristics ············· 7:261b-262a
    age ··············· 7:261b
    marital status ··········· 7:261b-262a
    occupation ··············· 7:262a
    plural suicide ··············· 7:262a
    region ··············· 7:261b
    sex differential ············· 7:261b
  ethics ··············· 2:232a
  harakiri ··············· 3:101b-102a
  historical trends ··········· 7:261a-263a
  juvenile ··············· 4:87a
  psychological theories ······· 7:262a-263a
  sociological approach ······· 7:262a-263a
  statistics ··············· 7:261b
  theories ··············· 7:262a-263b
  types ··············· 7:261b-262a
Suiga Shintō ···· 垂加神道 ·······8:312a
Suigun ··············· 水軍 ·······7:263a
Suijakuga ··············· 垂迹画·7:263a-263b
Suijin ··············· 水神 ·······7:263b
Suijinroku ··············· 吹塵録 ·······7:263b
Suijin yoroku ··· 吹塵余録 ·······7:263b
Suika Shintō ···· 垂加神道 ·······2:300b; 7:263b-264a; 8:312a-312b
Suiko ··············· 出挙 ·······7:264a
  kōden ··············· 4:243a
Suiko, Empress · 推古天皇 · 7:69b, 264a
  Kanroku ··············· 4:151b
Suinin, Emperor · 垂仁天皇 · 4:84b
Suiren ··············· 8:237a
Suisei ··············· 水勢 ·······4:139a
Suisha ··············· 8:237a-237b
Suishō gensō ···· 水晶幻想 ·······4:176a

Sui shu ··············· 7:264a-264b; 8:308b
Suita ··············· 吹田 ·······7:264b
Suita Incident ··· 吹田事件 ·······7:264b
Suiteki ··············· 1:233a
  Suiteki (small water-dropper) ····· 1:233b
Suiyuan Incident ··············· 7:264b
Sujime ··············· 2:25b
Sujin, Emperor ·· 崇神天皇·2:376a; 4:576; 7:264b
Sukagawa ··············· 須賀川 2:367a; 7:265a
Sukarno ·········3:290b-291a; 7:265a
  Hatta, Mohammad ············· 3:113b
Sukayu Hot Spring
  ··············· 酸ケ湯温泉 ·······7:265b
Sukegō ··············· 助郷·· 7:265a-265b
Sukeroku ··············· 助六 ··4:98a-98b
Sukeroku yukari no edo-zakura
  ··············· 助六由縁江戸桜 4:90b, 93a, 94a
Sukhāvatī ··············· 6:270a
Sukhāvatī-vyūha ··············· 4:330a
Suki ··············· 7:265b
Sukiwatadono
  shinden-zukuri ··············· 7:111a
Sukiya ··············· 7:265b
Sukiyaki ··············· 7:265b
Sukiya-zukuri ··· 数寄屋造· 7:265b-266a
  Katsura Detached Palace ······· 7:265a
Sukumo ··············· 宿毛 ·······7:266a
Sukumo Bay ··············· 宿毛湾·7:266a
Sukunahikona no Mikoto
  ··············· 少彦名命 ·······5:294a
  Ōkuninushi no Mikoto ········· 6:97b
Suku site ··············· 須玖遺跡 4:163b; 7:266a
Suma ··············· 須磨 ·······7:266a
Sumi (Chinese ink) ···· 1:232b, 233a, 233b; 5:331b
Sumidagawa ··············· 隅田川 ·······4:154b; 7:266a-266b
  firefly viewing ··············· 2:280b
Sumida Ward ··············· 墨田区 ·······7:266b
Sumi-demae, tea ceremony ······· 7:362b
Sumi-e ··············· 墨絵 ·· 3:305b-307b
Suminagashi (marbled paper) ··············· 墨流し 7:266b; 8:233a
Suminokura Ryōi 角倉了以 ·······7:266b
Sumire ··············· 8:192a-192b
Sumitomo ··············· 住友 ·······2:30a; 7:266b-267a, 268a-268b
  Hirose Saihei ··············· 3:147b
  interaffiliate stockholding ······· 3:295a
Sumitomo Bakelite Co, Ltd ·· 7:267a-267b
Sumitomo Bank, Ltd ···· 7:267a-267b
Sumitomo Cement Co, Ltd ······· 7:267b
Sumitomo Chemical Co, Ltd ····· 6:180a; 7:267b-268a
Sumitomo Construction Co, Ltd ··· 7:268a
Sumitomo Corporation · 3:18b-20a; 7:268a
Sumitomo Electric Industries, Ltd ··············· 7:268a-268b
Sumitomo family ············· 7:52a, 268b
Sumitomo Forestry Co, Ltd ······· 7:268b
Sumitomo Heavy Industries, Ltd ···· 7:268b
  Sanoyasu Dockyard Co, Ltd ····· 7:16a
Sumitomo Kichizaemon
  ··············· 住友吉左衛門 ·······7:267b, 268b
  museums ··············· 5:277a
  Sen'oku Hakkokan ············· 7:67b
Sumitomo Light Metal Industries, Ltd
  ··············· 7:267b, 268b-269a
Sumitomo Metal Industries, Ltd · 7:269a
Sumitomo Metal Mining Co, Ltd · 7:269a
  pollution ··············· 2:226b
Sumitomo Mutual Life Insurance Co
  ··············· 7:267a, 269b
Sumitomo Rubber Industries, Ltd · 7:269b
Sumitomo Trust & Banking Co, Ltd
  ··············· 7:267a, 269b

Sumitomo Warehouse Co, Ltd ···· 7:269b
Sūmitsuin ··············· 枢密院 ·6:252b-253b
Sumiyaki chōja ···· 炭焼長者·7:269b-270a
Sumiyoshi
  Shintō ··············· 7:126b
Sumiyoshi monogatari
  ··············· 住吉物語 5:246a; 7:270a
Sumiyoshi school ·· 住吉派 ·······2:360b; 7:270a-270b
Sumiyoshi Shrine
  ··············· 住吉神社 ·······7:270b
Sumiyoshi-zukuri ··· 住吉造 ·······7:270b
Summary courts ············· 4:80b, 81b
Summers, James ··············· 7:270b
Sumō ··············· 7:270b, 271a, 271b-274a
  belt ··············· 7:271b
  ceremonies ··············· 7:272a-273a
  divisions and ranks ··········· 7:271b-272a
  dohyō ··············· 7:271a
  Japan Sumō Association ········· 7:274a
  kappa ··············· 4:156b
  Kokugikan ··············· 7:274a
  object of match ··········· 7:271a-271b
  practice ··············· 7:273b-274a
  stable system ··············· 7:273a-273b
  techniques ··············· 7:271b
  tournaments ··············· 7:273a
  wrestlers ··············· 7:271b
Sumoto ··············· 洲本 ·······7:274b
Sumō wrestlers
  fundoshi ··············· 2:369b
  physical adaptation ··········· 4:37a
Sumptuary edicts ··············· 4:198b
Sumpu ··············· 駿府 ·······7:274b
Sumpuki ··· 駿府記 ·······7:274b
Sunagawa ··············· 砂川 ·······7:274b
Sunagawa case · 砂川事件 ·7:274b-275b
  judicial review ··············· 4:80a
  Tanaka Kōtarō ··············· 7:337a
Suna no onna (Woman in the Dunes) ··············· 砂の女 ·· 1:3a; 8:15a
Sunao ··············· 7:275b-276a
Sundry goods industry ··············· 7:276a
Suneru ··············· 7:275b
Sung Che-yüan. *See* **Song Zheyuan (Sung Che-yüan)**
Sung Chiao-jen. *See* **Song Jiaoren (Sung Chiao-jen)**
Sun goddess. *See* **Amaterasu Ōmikami**
Sun I-hsien ··············· 7:276b
Sunlight, access to ··············· 6:313a
Sun, The. See **Taiyō**
Suntory, Ltd ··············· 7:276a
  Torii Shinjirō ··············· 8:79b
Sun Wen. *See* **Sun Yat-sen**
Sun worship ··············· 7:276a-276b
Sūnyatā ··· 1:177b-178a; 2:212b-213a
Sun Yat-sen ··· 6:302a; 7:48a, 199b, 276b, 277b
  Chiang Kai-shek ··············· 1:270b
  Dai Jitao (Tai Chi-t'ao) ··············· 2:59a
  Inukai Tsuyoshi ··············· 3:326a
  Ioffe (Joffe), Adolf Abramovich ··· 3:328a
  Kita Ikki ··············· 4:226a
  Provisional Government of the Republic of China ··············· 6:260b
Sun Yixian ··············· 7:276b
Suō no Kuni ··· 周防国 7:276b-277a
Suō Ōshima ····· 周防大島·6:125a-125b
Suō Province ··· 周防国 ·7:276a-276b
Supermarkets distribution system · 2:120b
Superstitions ··············· 5:245b
Support ··············· 7:277a
Supreme Commander for the Allied Powers (SCAP) ··············· 7:32b-33a
  Ball, William MacMahon ··· 1:135a-135b
  dissension ··············· 2:154b
  economic planning ··········· 2:167b-168a

economic reforms ············ **2:**155a-155b
educational reform ············ **2:**180a-180b
Japanese economy **2:**154b-155a, 156b-158a
labor unions ················ **2:**156b
LARA ····················· **4:**368a
trade ······················ **2:**157a
United States education missions to
Japan ····················· **8:**164b
United States-Japan security treaties
·························· **8:**166a
Supreme Court ··· **4:**79a-81a; **6:**214a; **7:**93b,
277a-277b
customs ···················· **4:**380a
delegation of power ··········· **2:**84a
obscenity rulings ············· **1:**254b-255a
prime minister and cabinet ······· **6:**244a
religion ···················· **6:**295a
rules of ···················· **6:**340a
Supreme Order of the Chrysanthemum
·························· **2:**81b
Suretyship ················ **7:**278a
Suretyship, personal ··········· **6:**178a-178b
Suribachi and surikogi (mortar and
pestle) ····················· **2:**24b-25a
Surimono ·········· **7:**278a; **8:**183b-184a
Ōsaka school ··············· **6:**123a
Surrender, Instrument of ······ **7:**278a-278b
Suruga Bay ········ 駿河湾 ··· **7:**278b
Susaki ··············· 須崎 ··· **7:**278b
Susanoo no Mikoto
············· 素戔嗚尊 **7:**278b; **8:**307a
birth ····················· **5:**293a
feuding with Amaterasu ··· **5:**293a-293b
Suseri Hime ··· 須勢理毘売 ····· **5:**294a
Sushi ······· **2:**24a, 306a; **7:**278b-279a
chirashizushi ·············· **7:**278b-279a
hakozushi ·················· **7:**278b
makizushi ·················· **7:**278b
nigirizushi ·················· **7:**278b
Susono ·············· 裾野 ··· **7:**279a
Sustenance allotments ·········· **4:**55b
Susuki [(eulalia) *Miscanthus sinensis*]
·························· **7:**279a
Susukida Kyūkin 薄田泣菫 ······· **7:**279b
Kambara Ariake ··············· **4:**123a
Susukita Rokuhei
········· 寿々喜多呂九平 ··· **2:**268a
Susumubeki haiku no
michi ·· 進むべき俳句の道 ··· **7:**311b
Sutego ··················· **7:**279b
Sū Tōfun ·········· 鄒韜奮 ··· **8:**380a
Suto Ken Suto ··············· **7:**279b
Sutoku, Emperor 崇徳天皇 ········ **7:**68a,
279b-280a
Fujiwara no Toshinari ··········· **2:**356b
Sūtra ····················· **1:**177a
Sutra mounds ·············· **7:**280a
gorintō ···················· **3:**46a
inscriptions ················· **3:**313b
shellfish ··················· **7:**82a
Suwa (city) ·········· 諏訪 ··· **7:**280a
Suwa, Lake ········ 諏訪湖 ··· **7:**280a
Suwa Basin ···· 諏訪盆地 ··· **7:**280a
Suwariwaza ················· **4:**82a
Suwa Seikōsha Co ············· **4:**200b
Suwa Shrine ····· 諏訪神社 ··· **7:**280a-280b
Suye Mura: A Japanese Village ··· **2:**200a;
7:255a
Suzaka ·············· 須坂 ··· **7:**280b
Suzaku, Shinkokushi ··········· **7:**121b
Suzu (city) ··········· 珠洲 ··· **7:**280b
·························· **7:**280b
Suzu (bell) ················· **7:**280b
Suzuka ·············· 鈴鹿 ··· **7:**280b
"Suzuka magouta"
················ 鈴鹿馬子唄 ··· **7:**281a
Suzuka Mountains
················ 鈴鹿山脈 ··· **7:**280b

Suzuka Pass ····· 鈴鹿峠 ··· **7:**280b-281a
Suzuka Quasi-National
Park ······· 鈴鹿国定公園 ··· **8:**357b
Suzuki Akira ········· 鈴鹿睃 ··· **7:**281a
Fujitani Nariakira ············· **2:**346b
Suzuki Bokushi ··· 鈴木牧之 ··· **3:**214b
Suzuki Bunji ····· 鈴木文治 ··· **7:**281a
Yūaikai ···················· **4:**345a
Suzuki Daisetsu ·· 鈴木大拙 ··· **7:**281b
Suzuki, Daisetz Teitarō
····· 鈴木大拙(貞太郎) ··· **7:**28b, 281b
Suzuki decision ······· **4:**79b; **7:**281b-282a
Suzuki Eitarō ···· 鈴木栄太郎 ··· **7:**282a
Suzuki Harunobu. 鈴木春信
See **Harunobu**
Suzuki Kantarō 鈴木貫太郎 ··· **7:**282a
February 26th Incident ··········· **2:**249b
World War II ················· **8:**276a
Suzuki Kiitsu ····· 鈴木基一 ··· **7:**282a
Suzuki Kisaburō
··············· 鈴木喜三郎 ··· **7:**282a-282b
senkyo kanshō ··············· **7:**66b
Suzuki Masatsugu 鈴木雅次 ··· **7:**282b
Suzuki Masaya 鈴木馬左也 ··· **7:**267a, 282b
Suzuki Masayuki · 鈴木雅之 ··· **4:**259a
Suzuki Miekichi
··············· 鈴木三重吉 · **1:**39b; **7:**282b
Seikatsu Tsuzurikata Undō development
·························· **7:**51a
Shinshōsetsu ··············· **7:**125b
Suzuki Mosaburō
··············· 鈴木茂三郎 ··· **7:**282b-283a
Japan Socialist Party ··········· **4:**48b
Suzuki Motor Co, Ltd ··········· **7:**283a
Suzuki Ryōichi ··· 鈴木良一 ··· **3:**16a
Suzuki Shigetane 鈴木重胤 ··· **7:**283a
Suzuki Shin'ichi · 鈴木鎮一 ··· **7:**283a
Suzuki Shōsan ··· 鈴木正三 ··· **1:**179b;
7:283a-283b
Suzuki Shōten ··· 鈴木商店 ·· **2:**31a, 277b;
4:139a; **7:**283b
Takahata Seiichi ··············· **7:**313b
Teijin Incident ··············· **7:**375b
Suzuki Umetarō
··············· 鈴木梅太郎 **1:**268b; **7:**283b
Suzuki violin method · **5:**287a; **7:**283b-284a
Suzuki Zenkō ··· 鈴木善幸 ··· **7:**284a
Suzume ··················· **7:**241a-241b
Suzumebachi (hornets) ·········· **1:**149a
Suzuri ··················· **1:**233a, 233b
Suzuribako (writing-equipment box)
·························· **1:**233b
Suzutake (*Sasa purpurascens*) ···· **1:**136a
Swallows [(tsubame) family
Hirundinidae] ··············· **7:**284a
Swami Vivekananda ········· **3:**288a-288b
Swearwords ················ **7:**284a
Sweden ···················· **4:**43b
Sweetfish (ayu) ··············· **1:**125b
Sweet flag ··················· **7:**154a-154b
Swimming ················· **7:**284a-284b
Swiss Civil code ··············· **4:**75b
Switzerland, Japanese studies ····· **4:**43a
Sword Ban Order of 1876 ········· **7:**151b
Sword-guards. *See* **Tsuba**
Sword hunt ······· **1:**89a; **7:**84b, 284b-285a
Edo social structure and class policy
·························· **3:**188a
Oda Nobunaga ··············· **6:**63b
Sword Hunt of 1588 ············ **7:**122b
Sword-making
process ···················· **3:**333a-333b
tatara furnace ··············· **3:**333a-333b
Swordsmanship
iai ······················· **3:**253a
kendō ····················· **4:**195b
training ···················· **5:**119b-120a
Sword mountings ·············· **4:**295b

Swordplay
jūjutsu vs. ·················· **5:**119a
training ···················· **5:**119b-120a
Swords ··················· **7:**285a-288a
bronze ···················· **1:**175a
early ······················ **1:**87a
forging ···················· **7:**285b-286a
Jōkotō (ancient sword) period ····· **7:**287a
Kotō (old sword) period ······· **7:**287a-287b
manufacture
Tawara Kuniichi ············· **7:**351b
modern period ··············· **7:**288a
museums ··················· **5:**280a
Shintō (new sword) period ··· **7:**287b-288a
Sōshū Masamune ······· **7:**285a-285b
swordsmiths ················· **7:**285b
tempering and polishing ····· **7:**286a-287a
Syahrir, Sutan ············· **7:**288b
Syllabic Dictionary of the Chinese
Language, A ··············· **8:**253b
"Symbol emperor system" (shōchō
tennō sei) ················· **2:**208a
Symbolist movement ··········· **6:**161b
Sympneumata ··············· **6:**100a
Syncretism ················ **7:**288b-290b
evolution ··················· **7:**288b-289a
examples ····· **6:**62a-62b; **8:**221a, 347b
religious ··········· **3:**223a; **6:**351a-351b;
7:182a-182b, 190a-190b
terms ····················· **7:**288b
Synthetic resins
manufacture ················· **7:**111b
Syphilis ··············· **6:**257a; **8:**189b

T

Taasobi ····················· **2:**86a
Tabaruzaka ········ 田原坂 ··· **7:**291a
Tabei Junko ···· 田部井淳子 ··· **7:**291a
Tabi ················ **4:**210a; **7:**291a
Tabi to densetsu · 旅と伝説 ··· **2:**302a
Tablada, José Juan ··········· **7:**291a
Table tennis ··············· **7:**291b
Tableware ··················· **2:**25a
bowls ····················· **2:**25a
chawan ···················· **2:**25a
hachi ····················· **2:**25a
chopsticks (hashi) ············· **2:**25a
plate (sara) ················· **2:**25a
sake bottle and cup ··········· **2:**25a
teapots (kyūsu and dobin) ······· **2:**25a
zen (table for one) ············ **2:**25a
Taboo ···················· **7:**291b
Taboo expressions ··········· **7:**291b
diplomatics ················· **2:**98a
Taboos ··················· **6:**204a
harae ····················· **3:**100b-101a
Tanabata Festival ··········· **7:**334b-335a
Tachiai ··················· **7:**271a
Tachibana Akemi ··· 橘曙覧 ··· **5:**48a;
7:291b-292a
Tachibana Chikage 橘千蔭 ··· **4:**167b
Tachibana family ····· 橘氏 ··· **7:**292a
Tachibana Kōsai 橘耕斎 ··· **3:**49b
Tachibana Kōzaburō
··············· 橘孝三郎 ··· **1:**34b;
7:292a-292b
Tachibana Moribe · 橘守部 ··· **7:**292b
travel diaries ················· **8:**106a

Tachibana no Hayanari
　　橘逸勢 ········ **7:292b**
　　Jōwa conspiracy ········ **4:78a**
　　Sampitsu ········ **1:234a**
Tachibana no Moroe
　　橘諸兄 ········ **7:292b**
　　Fujiwara no Hirotsugu, Rebellion of
　　········ **2:351a**
Tachibana no Narisue
　　橘成季 ········ **4:256b**
Tachibana no Norimitsu
　　橘則光 ········ **7:53a**
Tachibana no Tadakane
　　橘忠兼 ········ **3:332a**
Tachibana no Ujikimi
　　橘氏公 ········ **2:77a**
Tachibana Shiraki · 橘樸 ··· **7:293b**
Tachibana Shiraki
　chosakushū··橘樸著作集 ··· **7:293b**
Tachibana Shūta ··· 橘周太 ··· **7:293b**
Tachihara Masaaki
　　立原正秋 ········ **7:293b**
　　fūzoku shōsetsu ········ **2:378a**
Tachihara Michizō
　　立原道造 ········ **7:293b**
Tachikawa········ 立川 ········ **7:293b**
Tachikawa Bunko
　　立川文庫 ··· **7:293a-293b**
Tachimochi ········ **7:272b**
Tachimono ········ **7:293b**
Tachioyama ········ **4:95a**
Tachiyaku ········ **4:94a**
Tada Fumio ········ 多田文男 ··· **7:293b**
Tadagoto uta (poetry employing the
　diction of ordinary speech) ··· **6:140b**
Tadamigawa ····· 只見川 **2:366b; 7:293b**
Tadare (Festering) ····· 爛 ········ **8:45a**
Tadataka ········ 忠教 ········ **6:93b**
Tadayoshi ········ 直義 ········ **8:341b**
Tade ········ **2:305a**
Tade kuu mushi · 蓼喰ふ虫 ··· **7:342a**
Tadokoro ········ 田荘 ··· **7:293b, 296a**
Taehan Cheguk ········ **7:293b**
Taehan Empire ········ **7:293b**
　　Independence Club ········ **3:287b**
　　Korean-Japanese relations ··· **4:281b**
Taewŏn'gun ········ **7:259b, 293b-294a**
　　Japanese diplomacy ········ **4:279b**
　　Korean-Japanese relations ··· **4:140b**
Taft, William Howard ········ **4:173a**
Taga Castle ········ 多賀城
Tagajō (castle) ··· 多賀城 ···· **7:3a, 294a**
　　excavation ········ **1:79b**
Tagajō (city) ········ 多賀城 ···· **7:294a**
Taga no Ki. 多賀の柵 *See* **Tagajō**
Tagawa ········· 田川 ········ **7:294a**
Tageta ········ **4:143b; 7:294b**
Tagokura Dam 田子倉ダム ··· **7:294b**
Tagonoura ······· 田子ノ浦 **2:345a; 7:294b**
Tagore, Rabindranath **1:164a; 3:288a;**
　　7:294b
Taguchi Ukichi · 田口卯吉 ··· **7:294b**
　　historiography ········ **3:156a**
　　Kokushi taikei editor ········ **4:262b**
Tahata Eitai Baibai Kinshi
　Rei (of 1643)
　····· 田畑永代売買禁止令 ··· **1:131b;**
　　7:294b-295a
　　Prohibition Against Permanent
　　Alienation of Farm Lands ········ **1:208a**
　　Tokugawa Iemitsu ········ **8:48a**
Tai ········ **1:244a; 7:45a**
Taibei ········ **7:307a**
Tai Chi-t'ao. *See* **Dai Jitao (Tai Chi-t'ao)**
Taiga. 大雅 *See* **Ike no Taiga**
Taigyaku Jiken · 大逆事件 **3:135a-136a**
Taiheiki ········ 太平記 · **1:130b, 294a;**
　　4:121a, 252a, 275a;

5:44a, 246a; 7:23b, 295a; 8:105a
　　gunki monogatari ········ **3:69a**
　　historiography ········ **3:154a**
　　kōdan tradition ········ **4:241b**
Taihei kōki ····· 太平広記 ···· **4:121a**
Taiheiyō Coal Mining Co. ··· **7:295a-295b**
Taiheiyō Kouhatsu, Inc ···· **7:295a-295b**
Taiheiyō Kyōkai (Institute of the Pacific)
　　Tsurumi Yūsuke ········ **8:117a**
Taiheiyō Mondai Chōsakai ··· **3:315b-316a**
Taiheiyō no washi (Eagles
　of the Pacific) 太平洋の鷲 ···· **8:111b**
Taihō Code ····· 大宝律令 · **1:151a; 7:11a,**
　　62b, 295b
　　clothing styles ········ **1:329b**
　　compilation ········ **1:20b**
　　corvée labor ········ **8:327a**
　　court rank ········ **2:40a**
　　Daijōsai ········ **2:59a-59b**
　　Dazaifu ········ **2:79a**
　　education ········ **2:171b, 172b**
　　Fujiwara no Fuhito ········ **2:350b**
　　inheritance ········ **2:244b**
　　Kannamesai ········ **4:144a**
　　kokugun system ········ **4:259b**
　　ritsuryō system ········ **6:329b, 331a**
　　seals and ········ **7:45b**
　　Temmu, Emperor ········ **7:382b**
　　toneri ········ **8:74b**
　　uniforms ········ **8:149b**
Taihō Ritsuryō. 大宝律令 *See* **Taihō Code**
Taiinkun ········ 大院君 · **7:293b-294a**
Taika (Great Change) era ······· **6:174b**
Taika Nijūikkajō Yōkyū
　····· 対華二十一か条要求 ··· **8:120b-121a**
Taika no Kaishin. *See* **Taika Reform**
Taika Reform ···· 大化改新 **1:293a; 2:102b;**
　　7:2a, 90b, 100b, 172a, 260a, 295a-297a
　　China ········ **1:282a**
　　Chinese influence ········ **4:277a**
　　court rank ········ **2:39b**
　　corvée labor ········ **8:327a**
　　edict ········ **7:296a**
　　Fujiwara family ········ **2:348a, 351a**
　　immediate efforts ········ **7:296a**
　　iriai ········ **3:330a**
　　Jinshin Disturbance ········ **4:60b**
　　kokugun system ········ **4:259b**
　　Occupation ········ **6:51a**
　　opposition ········ **7:296b**
　　other reforms ········ **7:296b**
　　ritsuryō state ········ **7:296b-297a**
　　ritsuryō system ········ **6:331a**
　　sekisho establishment ········ **7:57a**
　　shōen ········ **7:155b**
　　645 Coup ········ **7:296a**
　　tadokoro ········ **7:293b**
　　technology transfer ········ **7:374a**
　　textiles ········ **8:17b**
　　uji-kabane system ········ **8:131b**
　　Uneme ········ **8:147b**
　　women in ········ **8:258b**
　　Yamato court ········ **7:295b-296a**
Taika Shakkandan
　········ 対華借款団 ·· **7:297a-297b**
Taiki ········ 台記 ········ **7:297b**
Tai Kitō ········ 戴季陶 ···· **2:59a**
Taiko (drum) ········ **2:301a; 4:193b;**
　　7:297b
　　gagaku ········ **3:2a**
　　Ryūkyū music ········ **6:357b**
Taikō (title) ········ 太閤 ···· **7:297b**
Taikō kenchi ····· 太閤検地 ·· **1:131b**
Taikū (Big Sky) ········ 大空 ···· **6:139a**
Taikyō Sempu 大教宣布 ···· **7:297b**
Taimadera ········ 当麻寺 ···· **7:298a**
Taima mandara engi
　········ 当麻曼荼羅縁起 ···· **7:42b**

Taimitsu ········ **2:231b**
Tainichi Rijikai ········ **1:47b-48a**
Tai no kotoba · 体の言葉 ···· **7:281a**
Tainoura ········ 鯛ノ浦 · **7:298a-298b**
Tainoya ········ **7:111a**
Taipei Asian Problems Study Group
　········ **4:385a**
Taiping Rebellion ········ **2:319b**
Taira ········ 平氏 ········ **7:7b**
Taira family ········ 平氏 ···· **1:187b;**
　　7:298a-298b, 298b-299a
　　alliances ········ **2:264a**
　　defeat ········ **4:121b-122a**
　　flags and banners ········ **2:288a**
　　Fujiwara family rivalry ········ **2:348b**
　　Hatakeyama family ········ **3:111a**
　　Heiji monogatari ········ **3:123a**
　　Heike monogatari ········ **3:124a-124b**
　　Ise Province ········ **3:337b**
　　ochiudo legends ········ **6:60a**
　　Sasaki Takatsuna ········ **7:23a**
　　warrior government ········ **8:229a**
Taira Incident ········ 平事件 ···· **7:299b**
Taira-Minamoto War
　········ 源平の争乱 · **1:51a, 67b;**
　　2:264a, 363a; 7:93b, 183a, 299a-300b
　　aftermath ········ **7:300b**
　　battlefield ········ **7:266a**
　　Battle of Fujigawa ········ **2:342b**
　　crests ········ **2:42b**
　　Dannoura, Battle of ········ **2:77a**
　　defeat of Taira ········ **7:300b**
　　Heike monogatari ········ **3:124b**
　　jitō ········ **4:63a**
　　Koryŏ-Japan relations ········ **4:278a**
　　Minamoto family ········ **5:178a**
　　Mochihito, Prince ········ **5:181a-181b**
　　outbreak ········ **7:299b**
　　shōgun ········ **7:160a**
　　Taira family ········ **7:299a**
　　Tōdaiji ········ **8:34a**
　　warrior government ········ **8:229a**
　　Yoritomo's revolt ········ **7:299b-300a**
　　Yoshinaka and fighting ···· **7:300a-300b**
Taira no Atsumori · 平敦盛 · **7:300b-301a**
Taira no Kiyomori ····· 平清盛 · **1:187b; 4:1a;**
　　5:39b, 43b; 7:301a-301b
　　China ········ **1:283a**
　　court politics involvement ······· **2:264a**
　　Heiji Disturbance ········ **3:123a**
　　Heiji monogatari ········ **3:123a**
　　jitō ········ **4:63a**
　　Kōfukuji razed ········ **4:244a**
　　Ondo Strait ········ **6:106a**
　　residential estate ········ **2:363a**
　　Sanjūsangendō ········ **7:13a**
　　Taira no Sukemori ········ **4:197b**
Taira no Masakado 平将門 **4:112a; 7:301b**
　　Fujiwara no Hidesato ········ **2:350b**
　　Fujiwara no Takanobu ········ **2:355b**
　　Kanda Festival ········ **4:137a**
　　Shinshōji ········ **7:125a**
　　vengeful spirit ········ **4:137a**
Taira no Munemori 平宗盛 ···· **7:301b**
Taira no Shigehira 平重衡 · **7:301b-302a**
Taira no Shigemori 平重盛 **6:227a; 7:302a**
　　Fujiwara no Takanobu ········ **2:355b**
　　portrait painting ········ **6:227a**
Taira no Tadamori · 平忠盛 ···· **7:302a**
Taira no Tadanori · 平忠度 · **5:39b; 7:302a**
Taira no Tadatsune,
　Rebellion of · 平忠常の乱 **7:302a-302b**
Taira no Tomomori 平知盛 ···· **7:302b**
Taira no Yoritsuna · 平頼綱 ···· **7:302b**
Tairiku nippō ········ 大陸日報 ···· **7:334b**
Tairiku rōnin ········ **7:302b**
　　rōnin ········ **6:337a**
Tairō ········ 大老 ···· **7:302b-303a**

Tairo Dōshikai 対露同志会 4:272b; 7:303a
　Tōyama Mitsuru ················ 8:88b
　Uchida Ryōhei ················· 8:124a
Taisei Corporation ············ 7:303a
　firms of ······················ 7:303a
Taisei Hōkan ·····大政奉還····· 7:303a–303b
Taisei Kensetsu. *See* **Taisei Corporation**
Taisei kokuhō ron (On
　Western Law) 泰西国法論 ······ 8:112a
Taisei santen kō (Study of
　Three Changes in the
　World) 大勢三転考 2:102a; 3:155b
Taisei yochi zusetsu
　············· 泰西輿地図説 ······ 4:321b
Taisei Yokusankai
　············· 大政翼賛会 ···· 3:280a–281a
Taisekiji ········ 大石寺 ······· 7:303b
Taisha ···························· 7:303b
Taishakukyō ······ 帝釈峡 ······ 7:303b
Taishakusan ······ 帝釈山 ······ 7:303b
Taishin'in. *See* **Great Court of Cassation**
Taishō, Emperor 大正天皇 ······ 7:69b,
　　　　　　　　　　　　　305a–305b
Taishō and early Shōwa history. *See*
　History of Japan
Taishō Democracy ··· 1:87a; 2:84b; 6:211a;
　　　　　　　　　　　7:303b–305a
　folk craft influence ············ 2:295a
　Gen'yōsha ···················· 3:25b
　Imperial Diet ················· 3:276b
　limits ························ 7:305a
　mimpon shugi ················· 5:175b
　modern philosophy ······ 5:230b–231a
　Nagai Ryūtarō ··········· 5:301a–301b
　popular involvement ··········· 7:304b
　private interests vs. state interests
　························· 7:304b–305a
　strengthening elected bodies · 7:304a–304b
　tennō kikan setsu ············· 8:7b
　theorists ···················· 2:362b
　Ukita Kazutami ··············· 8:138a
　Washington Conference ········· 8:235a
　women's suffrage ·············· 8:268b
Taishō Kaijō Kasai Hoken. *See* **Taishō**
　Marine & Fire Insurance Co, Ltd
Taishō Marine & Fire Insurance
　Co, Ltd ···················· 7:305a
Taishō period ····· 大正時代 ···· 7:305b
Taishō Political Crisis ····· 3:198a; 7:305b
　Imperial Diet ················· 3:276b
Taishō Seihen. 大正政変
　See **Taishō Political Crisis**
Taishū bungaku. *See* **Popular fiction**
Taishū bungaku ron
　(Theory of Popular
　Literature) ··· 大衆文学論 ······ 6:139a
Taishū tennōsei
　············· 大衆天皇制 ········ 6:204a
Taiso Hōnen. *See* **Taiso Yoshitoshi**
Taiso Yoshitoshi ·大蘇芳年 ····· 7:306a
　Kaburagi Kiyokata ············· 4:100a
Taitō Co, Ltd ················· 7:306a
Taitō Ku. *See* **Taitō Ward**
Taitō Ward ······ 台東区 ······ 7:306a
Taiwan ············台湾···· 1:286a;
　　　　　　　　　　　7:306a–309a
　acquisition of ·········· 4:7a; 7:198b
　Chiang Kai-shek ·············· 1:270b
　colonial politics ·············· 7:308b
　colonial rule ················· 7:307b
　colonial society ·········· 7:308a–308b
　Dutch and Zheng (Cheng)
　family periods ··········· 7:306b–307a
　early reforms ················· 7:307b
　economic policy and development
　························· 7:307b–308a
　Japanese contact ·············· 7:306b
　modernization ················ 7:308a

　Musha Incident ··············· 5:280b
　postwar era ·················· 7:309a
　Qing period ············· 7:307a–307b
　Ryūkyū dialects ··············· 6:355a
　Ryūkyū Islands ··············· 6:357a
　wartime period ··········· 7:308b–309a
Taiwan Expedition of 1874 ··· 1:87a, 160a;
　　　　　　　　　2:332a; 4:381a; 7:309a–309b
　Iwasaki Yatarō ··············· 3:362b
　Kido Takayoshi ··············· 4:203a
　Ryūkyū kizoku mondai ········· 6:357a
Taiwan Ginkō ····· 2:277a–277b; 7:309b
Taiwan Seitō Co. ··············· 7:306a
Taiwan Shuppei 台湾出兵 ··· 7:309a–309b
Taiya Teiryū ······ 鯛屋貞柳 ····· 5:307a
Taiyō ·················太陽···· 7:309b
Taiyō Fishery Co, Ltd 2:284a; 7:309b–310a
Taiyō Gyogyō. *See* **Taiyō Fishery Co,**
　Ltd
Taiyō Kōbe Bank, Ltd ···· 1:140a; 7:310a
Taiyō no kisetsu (Season
　of Violence) ··· 太陽の季節 ····· 6:231a
Taiyō no nai machi (Street
　without Sunshine)
　········· 太陽のない街 4:324a; 6:255b;
　　　　　　　　　　　　　7:175b
　Tokunaga Sunao ··············· 8:58a
Taiyōzoku ····················· 2:273b
Taizōkai ········ 胎蔵界 ······· 7:310a
　Kongōkai ················ 4:269b–270a
　Shingon sect ················· 7:115a
Taizōkai mandara 胎蔵界曼荼羅 ·· 7:310a
　Ryōbu Mandara ··········· 6:347b, 351a
Taizō mandara 胎蔵曼荼羅 ······ 7:310a
Taizō mandara (Womb
　Mandala) 胎蔵曼荼羅 ··· 6:348a
Tajima Naoto ···· 田島直人 ····· 7:310a
Tajimi ··········多治見··· 7:276a, 310a
Tajō takon (Much Love
　Much Regret) ··· 多情多恨 ····· 4:199a
Taka. *See* **Hawks and eagles**
Takabatake Motoyuki
　············· 高畠素之 ········· 7:310a
Takachiho ········ 高千穂 ······ 7:310b
Takachihokyō 高千穂峡 ····· 7:310b
Takachihonomine
　············· 高千穂峰 4:221a; 7:310b
Takadachi ········· 高館 ········ 4:76b
Takadai ······················· 4:308a
Takada Hiroatsu 高田博厚 ···· 7:310b
Takada Kenzō ··· 高田賢三 ····· 7:310b
Takada Sanae ··· 高田早苗 ····· 7:310b
　Fenollosa, Ernest Francisco ······ 2:251b
　Taka-Diastase ················ 7:315b
Takagari (falconry) ··· 鷹狩 2:241b; 4:381a
Takagi Kanehiro. *See* **Takagi Kenkan**
Takagi Kenkan ··· 高木兼寛 ···· 7:311a
Takagi Teiji ····· 高木貞治 ···· 7:311a
Takahagi ········ 高萩 ········ 7:311a
Takahama ······· 高浜 ········ 7:311a
Takahama Kyoshi
　············· 高浜虚子 ···· 5:123b;
　　　　　　　　7:311a–311b; 8:295a
　haiku ························ 3:80a
　Hototogisu ·················· 3:237b
Takahashi ········ 高梁 ······· 7:311b
Takahashi Deishū
　············· 高橋泥舟 ········ 8:303a
Takahashi Dōhachi. 高橋道八
　See **Nin'ami Dōhachi**
Takahashigawa ····高梁川··· 7:312a
Takahashi Kageyasu
　············· 高橋景保 ···· 7:1b, 312a
Takahashi Kazumi
　············· 高橋和巳 ··· 7:85a, 312a
Takahashi Kenji 高橋健自 · 1:77b; 7:312a
Takahashi Kenzō 高橋建三
　Kokka founder ··············· 4:255b

Takahashi Korekiyo
　············· 高橋是清 ·3:201a; 7:55a,
　　　　　　　　　　　312a–312b
　February 26th Incident ········· 2:249b
Takahashi Mitsutoki. 高橋光時
　See **Nin'ami Dōhachi**
Takahashi Mutsuo
　············· 高橋睦郎 ········ 7:312b
Takahashi no Mushimaro
　············· 高橋虫麻呂 7:313a; 8:207a
　poems in *Man'yōshū* ······· 5:107b–108a
　sakimori uta ·················· 7:2b
　"Takahashi no Mushimaro Collection"
　····························· 8:207a
Takahashi Oden · 高橋お伝 ···· 7:313a
Takahashi Satomi
　············· 高橋里美 5:230b; 7:313a
Takahashi Shinkichi
　············· 高橋新吉 ········ 7:313a
　Nakahara Chūya ··············· 5:313b
Takahashi Yoshitoki
　············· 高橋至時 ········ 7:313b
　Inō Tadataka ················· 3:309a
Takahashi Yuichi 高橋由一 ··· 7:313b
Takahata Seiichi · 高畑誠一 ··· 7:313b
Takahira Kogorō
　············· 高平小五郎 ······· 7:313b
Takahira-Root Agreement
　········· 高平－ルート協定 3:197a; 7:313b;
　　　　　　　　　　　　　8:136a
　Komura Jutarō ··············· 4:268b
Takaichi Kuroto. 高市黒人
　See **Takechi no Kurohito**
Takai Kitō ········ 高井几董 ···· 6:297b;
　　　　　　　　　　　7:313b–314a
Takai Noriyasu ··· 高井則安 ···· 4:325a
Takaishi ·········高石···· 7:314a
Takakura ····················· 1:50b
Takakura, Emperor 高倉天皇 ····· 1:67b
Takakura Ken ···· 高倉健 ····· 7:314
　Fuji Junko ··················· 2:343a
Takamagahara ··· 高天原 4:126a; 7:278b,
　　　　　　　　　　　　　314a
Takamanohara. *See* **Takamagahara**
Takamatsu ········ 高松 ····· 4:103a;
　　　　　　　　　　　7:314a–314b
Takamatsu, Prince· 高松宮 ···· 7:314a
Takamatsu Castle · 高松城 ·· 7:314a–314b
Takamatsu no Miya Nobuhito.
　高松宮宣仁 *See* **Takamatsu, Prince**
Takamatsuzuka tomb
　············· 高松塚古墳 ···· 7:314b, 314b–315a
　art objects ·············· 7:314b–315a
　wall murals ·················· 1:79a
Takama Yoshio. 高間芳雄
　See **Takami Jun**
Takami Jun ······ 高見順 ····· 7:315a
　February 26th Incident ········· 2:250b
Takamine Hideko 高峰秀子 2:272b; 7:315a
Takamine Hideo· 高嶺秀夫 ·· 7:315a–315b
Takamine Jōkichi
　············· 高峰譲吉 1:268a; 7:315b
　Institute of Physical and Chemical
　Research ···················· 3:316a
Takami Senseki · 鷹見泉石 ···· 7:315b
Takamuko no Kuromaro
　············· 高向玄理 7:260a, 315b
Takamura Kōtarō
　············· 高村光太郎 ······ 7:253b,
　　　　　　　　　　　315b–316b
Takamura Kōun 高村光雲 · 7:43a, 316b
Takamure Itsue · 高群逸枝 ···· 7:316b
　Fujin kōron publication ········· 2:344a
Takano Chōei · 高野長英 1:141b; 7:28b,
　　　　　　　　　　　316b–317a
Takano Fusatarō
　············· 高野房太郎 ······· 7:317a
　labor movement ··············· 4:345a

Workers' Fraternal Society · · · · · · 7:164a
Takano Iwasaburō
　　　　　高野岩三郎 · · · · · 7:317a
Takano Minoru · · · 高野実 · · · · 7:317a
Takano Sujū · · · · · 高野素十 · 7:317a–317b
haiku · 3:80a
Takaoka · · · · · · · · · · 高岡 · · · · · · 7:317b
Takaosan · · · · · · · · · 高尾山 · · · · · 7:317b
Takaosanji · · · · · · · · 高尾山寺 · · · · 4:58b
Takarabe Takeshi · · 財部彪 · · 7:317b–318a
Takarai Kikaku · · 宝井其角 1:225a; 7:318a
Ōshima Ryōta · · · · · · · · · · · · · · · · 6:126a
Takara kuji. See **Lotteries, public**
Takara Shuzō Co, Ltd · · · · · · · · 7:318a
Takarazuka · · · · · · · · 宝塚 · · · · · · 7:318a
Takarazuka Girls Opera Company. See
　Takarazuka Kagekidan
Takarazuka Kagekidan 1:83b; 7:318a–318b
Otowa Nobuko · · · · · · · · · · · · · · 6:133b
repertoire · · · · · · · · · · · · · · · · · · 7:318b
Shōchiku Co, Ltd · · · · · · · · · · · · 7:318b
Takarazuka · · · · · · · · · · · · · · · · · 7:318a
Takasago · · · · · · · · · 高砂 · · · · · · 7:318b
Takasago Netsugaku Kōgyō. See
　Takasago Thermal Engineering Co,
　Ltd
Takasago Thermal Engineering
　Co, Ltd · · · · · · · · · · · · · · · · · · · 7:318b
Takasaki · · · · · · · · · 高崎 · · · · · · 7:318b
Takasakiyama · · · · · 高崎山 · · · · · 7:318b
Takase Dam · · · 高瀬ダム · · · · 2:73b
Takasegawa · · · · · · · 高瀬川 · 7:318b–391a
Takashima Coal Mine
　· · · · · · · · · · · 高島炭坑 · · · · 2:31b;
　　　　　　　　　　　　　　7:318b–319a
Takenouchi Tsuna · · · · · · · · · · 7:325a
Takashimaryū teachings · · · · · · · · 7:319a
Takashima Shūhan 高島秋帆 · · · · 7:319a
Takashima Tankō. 高島炭坑
　See **Takashima Coal Mine**
Takashimaya Co, Ltd · · · · · · · · 7:319a
Takasugi Shinsaku
　· · · · · · · · · · · 高杉晋作 · · · · 1:86a;
　　　　　　　　　　　　　　7:319a–319b
Chōshū Expeditions · · · · · · · · · · 1:304a
Fujita Denzaburō · · · · · · · · · · · · 2:346a
Takataya Kahei 高田屋嘉兵衛 7:319b
Takata Yasuma · · 高田保馬 · · · 7:319b
Takatō · · · · · · · · · · · 高遠 · · · · · · 7:319b
Ejima Incident · · · · · · · · · · · · · · 2:188a
Takatō Castle · · · · · 高遠城 · · · · · 7:319b
Takatori ware · · · 高取焼 1:20b; 2:295b;
　　　　　　　　　　　　　　7:319b–320a
Kobori Enshū · · · · · · · · · · · · · · · 4:238b
Takatori-yaki. 高取焼 See **Takatori ware**
Takatsuki · · · · · · · · · 高槻 · · · · · · 7:320a
Takatsu Tamaki · · 高津環 · · · · 3:261a
Takaya Hikoshirō
　　　　　高屋彦四郎 · · · · 6:359a
Takayama · · · · · · · · · 高山 · · · · · · 7:320a
Takayama Basin · 高山盆地 · · · · 7:320a
Takayama Bonchi. See **Takayama Basin**
Takayama Chogyū
　　　　　高山樗牛 5:12a; 7:320a
Takayama Festival · 高山祭 · 7:320a, 320b
Takayama Hikokurō
　　　　　高山彦九郎 · · · · 7:320b
Takayama Sōzei · 高山宗砌 · 7:320b–321a
Takayama Ukon · 高山右近 · · · 7:321a
Takayanagi Kenjirō
　　　　　高柳建次郎 · · · · 7:321a
electronics · · · · · · · · · · · · · · · · · 2:192a
Takayanagi Kenzō
　　　　　高柳賢三 2:319a; 7:321a
Commission on the 1947 Constitution
　· 1:339b
Take · · · · · · · · · · · · · · · · 1:135b–136a
Takebe Ayatari · 建部綾足 · · · 7:321a–321b

Takebe Katahiro · 建部賢弘 · · 7:57b, 321b
Takebu. 武生 See **Takefu**
Takechi no Kurohito
　　　　　高市黒人 · · · · · · 7:321b
Takechi Tetsuji · 武智鉄二 · 2:274b–275a
Takechi Zuizan · 武市瑞山 5:317b; 7:321b
Kōno Togama · · · · · · · · · · · · · · · · 4:275a
Takeda Chemical Industries, Ltd
　· 7:321b–322a
Takeda family · · · · · · 武田氏 · · 7:322a–322b
Kōfu, based in · · · · · · · · · · · · · · 4:243b
Shingen Kahō · · · · · · · · · · · · · · · 7:113b
Uesugi Kenshin · · · · · · · · · · · · · · 8:130a
Takeda Izumo · · · 竹田出雲 · · · 5:49b;
　　　　　　　　　　　　　7:322a–322b
Forty-Seven Rōnin Incident · · · · · 2:328a
productions · · · · · · · · · · · · · · · · · 7:322b
Takeda Katsuyori 武田勝頼 · · · · 7:322b
Nagashino, Battle of · · · · · · · · · · 5:306b
Takeda Kōunsai
　· · · · · · · · · · · 武田耕雲斎 · · · · 7:322b
Takeda Rintarō 武田麟太郎 · 7:322b–323a
Takeda Shingen · 武田信玄 · · 7:274b,
　　　　　　　　　　　　　323a–323b
military practices · · · · · · · · · · · · 2:279a
Shingen Kahō · · · · · · · · · · · · · · · 7:113b
Takeda Shirō. 武田四郎
　See **Takeda Katsuyori**
Takeda Taijun · · · 武田泰淳 · · · 7:323b
February 26th Incident · · · · · · · · 2:250b
Takefu · · · · · · · · · · · 武生 2:364a; 7:323b
Takegoshi Yosaburō
　· · · · · · · · · · · 竹越与三郎 · · 7:323b–324a
Takehara · · · · · · · · · 竹原 · · · · · · 7:324a
Takehara tomb · · · 竹原古墳 · · · 4:247a
Takehashi Insurrection
　· · · · · · · · · · · 竹橋騒動 · · · · 7:324a
Takehashi Sōdō.
　See **Takehashi Insurrection**
Takehisa Shigejirō. 竹久茂次郎
　See **Takehisa Yumeji**
Takehisa Yumeji · 竹久夢二 · · · 7:324a
Takeiri Yoshikatsu
　· · · · · · · · · · · 竹入義勝 · · · 7:324a–324b
Takekoshi Yosaburō. 竹越与三郎
　See **Takegoshi Yosaburō**
Takemi Tarō · · · 武見太郎 · · · 4:47b
Takemitsu Tōru · · 武満徹 · · · · 7:324b
Shinoda Masahiro · · · · · · · · · · · · 7:122a
Takemoto Gidayū
　　　　　竹本義太夫 · · · · 4:77a
Takemoto Gidayū I
　· · · · · · · · · 竹本義太夫(初代) · 3:30a; 7:324b
Takemotoza
Takeda Izumo · · · · · · · · · · · · · · · 7:322a
Takemoto Gidayū I · · · · · · · 3:30a; 7:324b
Takenaka Kōmuten Co, Ltd · · · 7:324b
Takenouchi no Sukune
　· · · · · · · · · · · 武内宿禰 · · · 7:324b–325a
Takenouchi Shikibu
　· · · · · · · · · · · 竹内式部 · · · · 7:325a
Takenouchi Tsuna · 竹内綱 · · · 7:325a
Takenouchi Yasunori
　· · · · · · · · · · · 竹内保徳 · · · · 7:325a
Takeo · · · · · · · · · · · 武雄 · · · · · · 7:325a
Takeshima · · · · · · · · 竹島 · · · 7:325a–325b
Korea-Japan Treaty of 1965,
supplementary agreements · · · · · 4:288a
territorial claims · · · · · · · · · · · · · 4:285b
Taketa · · · · · · · · · · · 竹田 · · · · · · 7:325b
Taketombo · · · · · · · 竹蜻蛉 · · · · 7:325b
Taketomijima · · · · · 竹富島 · · · · 7:325b
Taketori monogatari
　· · · · · · · · · · · 竹取物語 · · · · 5:32b–33a,
　　　　　　　246a, 295a–295b; 7:325b–326a
Chinese literature · · · · · · · · · · · · 1:293b
monogatari bungaku · · · · · · · · · · 5:246a

Taketori no okina no monogatari. See
　Taketori monogatari
Takeuchi Kyūichi 竹内久一 · · · · 7:326a
Takeuchi Seihō · 竹内栖鳳 · 7:20a, 326a
Takeuchi Tsunekichi. 竹内恒吉
　See **Takeuchi Seihō**
Takeuma · · · · · · · · · · · · · · · · · · 7:246a
Takezaki Suenaga
　　　　　竹崎季長 · · · · 7:326b
Mōko shūrai ekotoba commissioned · 4:274b
Takiguchi no bushi 滝口の武士 · · · 7:326b
Takii Kōsaku · · · 滝井孝作 · · · 7:326b
Takikawa · · · · · · · · · 滝川 · · · · · · 7:326b
Takikawa Incident
　　　　　滝川事件 · · · · 4:339b
Takikawa Yukitoki
　　　　　滝川幸辰 · · · · 7:251b,
　　　　　　　　　　　　　326b–327a
Sasaki Sōichi · · · · · · · · · · · · · · · · 7:23a
Taki Mototaka · 多紀元孝 · · · 7:327a
Taki Rentarō · · · 滝廉太郎 · · · 7:327a
Takita Choin · · · 滝田樗陰 · 7:100a, 327a
Chūō kōron · · · · · · · · · · · · · · · · · 1:313a
Takita Minoru · · 滝田実 · · · · 7:327a
Takizawa Bakin · 滝沢馬琴 · · · 1:130b
Takizawa Eisuke · 滝沢英輔 · · · 2:271a
Takizawa Okikuni · 滝沢興邦 · · · 1:130b
Taki Zenzaburō · 滝善三郎 · 3:101b–102a
Tako. See **Kites**
Tako (kite) · · · · · · · · · · · · · · 4:229b–231b
Tako (octopus) · · · · · · · · · · · · · · 6:60a–60b
Taku · · · · · · · · · · · · 多久 · · · · · · 7:327b
Takuan Sōhō · · · 沢庵宗彭 1:193b; 7:89b,
　　　　　　　　　　　　　　　327b
Takuma Eiga · · 宅磨栄賀 2:346a; 7:327b
Takuma school · 宅磨派 1:190a; 7:328a
Takuma Shōga · 宅磨勝賀 · · · 7:328a
Takuma Tamenari
　　　　　宅磨為成 1:227b; 7:328a
Takuma Tametō 宅磨為遠 · · · 7:328a
Tale of Flowering Fortunes · · · · · · 1:41a
Tale of Genji · 1:293b; 4:188a; 5:35a–35b;
　　　6:299b; 7:12b, 52a, 87b, 328b–331b
Buddhism · · · · · · · · · · · · · · · 7:330b–331a
criticism · · · · · · · · · · · · · · · · · · · 7:331a
divisions · · · · · · · · · · · · · · · 7:328b–330b
early Japanese songs · · · · · · · · · · 2:138b
early stages · · · · · · · · · · · · · 7:328a–330a
eschatology · · · · · · · · · · · · · · · · · 7:331a
Fujiwara no Toshinari · · · · · · · · · 2:357a
gagaku · 3:1a
Genji monogatari emaki · 3:87b; 7:329a–329b
Ichikawa Danjūrō · · · · · · · · · · · · 3:257a
influence · · · · · · · · · · · · · · · 7:330b–331a
Kamo no Mabuchi commentary · · · 4:129b
later stages · · · · · · · · · · · · · · 7:330a–330b
model for hero · · · · · · · · · · · · · · 2:352b
Motoori Norinaga's study of · · · · 4:258b
Murasaki Shikibu · · · · · · · · · 5:267b–269a
Murasaki Shikibu nikki · · · · · · · · 7:328b
nature in Japanese religion · · · · · 5:357b
Ochikubo monogatari · · · · · · · · · · 6:59b
paintings · · · · · · · · · · · · · · · · · · · 4:148b
regency government · · · · · · · · · · · 6:286b
Sarashina nikki · · · · · · · · · 5:35b; 7:21b
Sengenshō · · · · · · · · · · · · · · · · · · 1:299b
studies of
　Kodai kenkyū · · · · · · · · · · · · · 4:240b
textual history · · · · · · · · · · · 7:330b–331b
themes · · · · · · · · · · · · · · · · · 7:330b–331a
translation · · · · · · · · · · · · · · · · · 7:343a
waka · 8:212b
women in Japan · · · · · · · · · · · · · 8:258a
Tale of Lady Ochikubo, The · · · · · · 6:59b
Tale of Sagoromo · · · · · · · · · · · · · 6:365a
Tale of the Bamboo Cutter, The
　(*Taketori monogatari*) · · · · · 7:325b–326a

Tale of the Hamamatsu Middle
    Counselor ·············· **3**:90b-91a
Tale of the Heike. See Heike monogatari
Tale of the Hollow Tree ······ **8**:187b-188a
Tale of the Soga Brothers ···· **7**:221a-221b
Tale of the Tsutsumi Middle Counselor
    ··························· **8**:118b-119a
Tales of Aesop ················· **2**:241a
Tales of Christians ·············· **4**:221b
Tales of Glory ··················· **2**:186a
Tales of Ise, The ··········· **3**:337a-337b
Tales of Moonlight and Rain ····· **8**:126a
Tales of the Major Counselor from Uji
    ··························· **8**:137b
Tales of the Spring Rain ········· **8**:126b
Tales of the West ··············· **6**:369a
Tales of Times Now Past ···· **4**:270b-271a
Tales of Yamato ················· **8**:310a
Talisman
    inu hariko ·············· **3**:325b
Talisman, protective ············· **8**:285a
Tally trade ···· **3**:174a; **7**:331b-332a; **8**:220b
    Ashikaga Yoshimitsu ········· **1**:101b
    kinds ······················ **7**:332a
    Kōbe prospered in ··········· **4**:238a
    Muromachi shogunate ········· **5**:273a
    National Seclusion ··········· **5**:347a
    Ōuchi family ··············· **6**:135a
Tama (city) ············· 多摩 **7**:332a
Tama **1**:62a, 147b-148a; **4**:126a; **7**:332a
    rites of pacification ········· **7**:332a
    types ······················ **7**:332a
Tama, Lake ········· 多摩湖 **7**:332b
Tamabachi (gall wasps) ·········· **1**:149a
Tamagawa ······· 多摩川 **1**:272a; **4**:135a;
    7:332b
Tamagawa Aqueduct ·········· **7**:332b
Tamagawa Daigaku. *See* **Tamagawa**
    University
Tamagawa Gakuen. *See* **Tamagawa**
    University
Tamagawa Jōsui. 玉川上水
    See **Tamagawa Aqueduct**
Tamagawa University ········· **7**:332b
Tama Hills ······· 多摩丘陵 **7**:332b
Tamai (field dance) ·············· **2**:86a
Tamai Katsunori · 玉井勝則 ······ **3**:140b
Tamako. 多摩湖 *See* **Tama, Lake**
Tama Kyūryō. 多摩丘陵 *See* **Tama Hills**
Tamamushi Shrine 玉虫厨子 ····· **6**:*148b*
    urushi-e ················· **8**:181a
Tamana ··············· 玉名 **7**:332b
Tamana Hot Spring 玉名温泉 ···· **7**:332b
Tamano ·············· 玉野 **7**:332b
Tamari ···················· **7**:265b
Tamatsukuri Hot Spring
    ·············· 玉造温泉 **7**:332b-333a
    Lake Shinji ··············· **7**:115a
Tamatsukuri Onsen. *See* **Tamatsukuri**
    Hot Spring
Tama Zoological Park ············ **8**:379b
Tamba Mountains
    ·············· 丹波高地 **7**:333a
Tamba ware ········ 丹波焼 **2**:295b; **7**:333a
    glaze ······················ **7**:333a
    kilns ······················ **7**:333a
    museums ··················· **5**:279b
    uses ······················ **7**:333a
Tamba-yaki. *See* **Tamba ware**
Tamba Yasuyori · 丹波康頼 ··· **7**:333a-333b
Tameie ·················· 為家 **4**:54a
Tamenaga Shunsui
    ·············· 為永春水 **5**:49b;
    7:333b-334a
    fūzoku shōsetsu ············· **2**:378a
Tamerau nakare wakōdoyo
    ·············· ためらうなかれ若人よ ··· **3**:102a

Tamezuki (method of molding paper)
    ··························· **8**:234a
Tamiya Hiroshi ···· 田宮博 **7**:334a
Tamiya Torahiko 田宮虎彦 **7**:334a
Tamjing ···················· **2**:130b
Tamon'in Diary. See Tamon'in nikki
Tamon'in nikki · 多聞院日記 · **7**:334a-334b
Tamura, Prince ··· 田村皇子 ··· **8**:303b
Tamura Denkichi ·· 田村伝吉 ·· **1**:137a
Tamura Ransui ·· 田村藍水 **1**:225a; **7**:334b
Tamura Ryūichi ··· 田村隆一 ·· **1**:82b
Tamura Taijirō 田村泰次郎 **7**:334b
    fūzoku shōsetsu ············· **2**:378b
Tamura Toshiko · 田村俊子 ···· **7**:54b, 71a,
    334b
Tan ························· **4**:193b
Tana ························· **7**:266a
Tanabata Festival ·········· 七夕 **1**:160b;
    2:260b; **7**:334b-335a
    Hiratsuka ················· **7**:*335a*
    Kantō ···················· **4**:153a
    religious symbolism ········· **6**:296a
Tanabe ·················· 田辺 **7**:335a
Tanabe Hajime ···· 田辺元 ·· **7**:335a-335b
    philosophies ··············· **5**:230b
Tanabe Hajime zenshū
    ·············· 田辺元全集 **7**:335b
Tanabe no Sakimaro 田辺福麻呂 · **5**:108a
Tanabe Seiko ···· 田辺聖子 **7**:103b, 335b
Tanabe Seiyaku Co, Ltd ····· **7**:335b
Tanabe Taichi ··· 田辺太一 ·· **7**:335b
Tanagokoro no shōsetsu
    ·············· 掌の小説 **4**:176a
Tanaka biwa ················· **7**:339b
Tanaka Chikao 田中千禾夫 ·· **7**:335b
    Shingeki ················· **7**:112a, 113a
    shingeki ··················· **7**:113a
Tanaka Chōbei 田中長兵衛 ··· **3**:333b
Tanakadate Aikitsu 田中館愛橘 · **7**:336a
Tanaka Eizō ······ 田中栄三 ·· **2**:268a
Tanaka Fujimaro
    ·············· 田中不二麿 **2**:175b; **7**:336a
Tanaka Fuyuji ··· 田中冬二 ·· **7**:336a
Tanaka Giemon. 田中儀右衛門
    See **Tanaka Hisashige**
Tanaka Giichi ····· 田中義一 · **3**:200a; **7**:55a,
    66b, 77b, 88b, 336a-336b
    cabinet ··················· **2**:277b
    Jitsugyō Dōshikai ··········· **4**:64a
    Kenseikai ················· **4**:198a
    resignation ··············· **2**:207a-207b
Tanaka Giichi cabinet
    investigation ·············· **5**:316a-316b
    Mizuno Rentarō ············· **5**:226b
Tanaka Hidemitsu
    ·············· 田中英光 **7**:336b
Tanaka Hisashige
    ·············· 田中久重 ·· **7**:336b-337a
Tanaka Kakuei ·· 田中角栄 · **2**:309b, 333a;
    7:337a
    Lockheed Scandal ··········· **5**:72a
Tanaka Kan'ichi ··· 田中寛一 ·· **2**:179a
Tanaka Kichinosuke. 田中吉之助
    See **Tanaka Fuyuji**
Tanaka Kiichi. 田中喜一 *See* **Tanaka Ōdō**
Tanaka Kinuyo ·· 田中絹代 **2**:270b; **7**:337a
Tanaka Kōtarō 田中耕太郎 · **7**:275b, 337b
Tanaka Kyūgu ··· 田中丘隅 ·· **7**:337b
Tanaka Manufacturing Works **7**:336b-337a
Tanaka Memorandum
    ·············· 田中覚え書 · **7**:337b; **8**:37a
Tanaka Mitsuaki 田中光顕 ·· **7**:337b-338a
Tanaka Ōdō ···· 田中王堂 · **7**:338a-338b
Tanaka Shōsuke 田中勝助 ·· **7**:338a
Tanaka Shōzō ··· 田中正造 ·· **1**:73a;
    7:338b-339b
    ecologist ················· **7**:339a-339b
    fight for a village ·········· **7**:339a

Fukuda Hideko ············· **2**:362b
pollution ················· **7**:338b-339a
resistance to provincial misgovernment
    ··························· **7**:338b
Tanaka Sumie ··· 田中澄江 ·· **7**:339b
Tanaka-Trudeau communique ···· **1**:238a
Tanaka Yoshio ·· 田中芳男 ·· **7**:339b
Tanaka Yutaka ···· 田中豊 ·· **7**:339b
Tanashi ················ 田無 **7**:339b
Tanasue no mitsugi 手末調 ···· **7**:264b
Tandai ··············· 探題 **7**:340a
    Rokuhara ················· **6**:335a
Taneda Santōka
    ·············· 種田山頭火 **7**:340a
Tanegashima ···· 種子島 **3**:140a; **7**:340a
Tanegashima Space Center ····· **7**:240b
Tanegashima Tokitaka
    ·············· 種子島時堯 **2**:279a; **7**:340a
Tanegashima Yukiko
    ·············· 種子島有紀子 ··· **2**:76a
Tane maku hito · 種蒔く人 · **1**:70b; **7**:175a,
    340a-340b
    proletarian literature movement ··· **6**:254b
Tang dynasty
    Dajōkan ··················· **2**:69b
    kara-e painting ············· **4**:157a
    Taihō Code ··············· **7**:295b
Tange Kenzō ···· 丹下健三 · **7**:340a
    buildings ················· **7**:340b
Tanggu (Tangku) Truce ····· **7**:340b-341a
Tango ················ 丹後 **7**:341a
Tango fudoki · 丹後風土記 ···· **8**:44b
Tango Mountains 丹後山地 **4**:337b; **7**:341a
Tang style painting ············· **6**:148a
Tani Bunchō ····· 谷文晁 · **1**:211a; **7**:17b,
    341a
    Kameda Bōsai ············· **4**:125a
Tanigawadake ···· 谷川岳 **7**:341a-341b
Tanigawa Kotosuga
    ·············· 谷川士清 **7**:341a
Taniguchi Masaharu
    ·············· 谷口雅春 **7**:341b
    Seichō no Ie ··············· **7**:49b
Taniguchi Yoshirō
    ·············· 谷口吉郎 · **1**:81b; **7**:341b
    buildings ················· **7**:341b
Tani Jichū ········ 谷時中 · **7**:341b
Tani Jōji ········· 谷譲次 · **3**:116a
Tani Kanjō ······ 谷干城 · **7**:341b-342a
    Satsuma Rebellion ··········· **7**:30a
Tanikawa Shuntarō
    ·············· 谷川俊太郎 **7**:342a
Tanimoto Tomeri · 谷本富 ·· **7**:342a
    Shin Kyōiku Undō ··········· **7**:121b
Tanin no kao (The Face of
    Another) ········· 他人の顔 · **1**:3a; **8**:15a
Tanino Setsu ······ 谷野セツ **7**:342a
Tani Tateki. 谷干城 *See* **Tani Kanjō**
Tanizaki Jun'ichirō
    ·············· 谷崎潤一郎 · **1**:3a, 313b;
    2:268a, 274a; **5**:13a, 54b-55a; **7**:26b, 100b,
    102b, 103b, 253b, 342a-343b
    shimpa ··················· **7**:108a
    Shinshichō ··············· **7**:125a
Tanizaki Jun'ichirō Prize
    Endō Shūsaku ············· **2**:214a
    Ōe Kenzaburō ············· **6**:66b
Tanka ············· **6**:296b; **7**:343b
    Hyakunin isshu (Single Poems by 100
    Poets) ···················· **3**:248b-249a
    kagura uta ················· **4**:108a
    Man'yōshū ··············· **7**:343b
    predominance ············· **4**:115b
    sakimori uta style ··········· **7**:2b
    Takechi no Kurohito ········· **7**:321b
    waka ····················· **8**:201b
Tankai ··············· 湛海 **7**:343b
    statues ··················· **7**:343b

Tanka literary groups ········· 5:19a-20a
Tanka poets, modern
  Aizu Yaichi ······················· 1:38b
  Ishikawa Takuboku ······· 3:344b-345a
  Itō Sachio ······················· 1:38b
  Kinoshita Rigen ················· 4:216a
  Kitahara Hakushū ··············· 4:225a
  Kubota Utsubo ··················· 4:301b
  Maeda Yūgure ···················· 5:81b
  Masaoka Shiki ············· 5:123b-124a
  Miyazawa Kenji ··········· 5:222b-223b
  Ochiai Naobumi ··················· 6:59a
  Orikuchi Shinobu ·········· 6:118b-119a
  Saitō Mokichi ············· 6:374a-374b
  Sasaki Nobutsuna ················· 7:23a
  Shimaki Akahiko ················· 7:99b
  Toki Zemmaro ···················· 8:43b
  Tsuchiya Bummei ················· 8:112a
  Wakayama Bokusui ··············· 8:219a
  Yosano Akiko ··················· 8:340a
  Yosano Tekkan ············· 8:340a-340b
  Yoshii Isamu ············· 8:346b-347a
  Yoshino Hideo ··················· 8:348b
Tankei ········· 湛慶 · 1:200a; 7:13a,
                        343b-344a
  works ······················· 7:343b-344a
Tankū Teisen Kyōtei. 塘沽停戦協定
  See **Tanggu (Tangku) Truce**
Tanluan ···························· 4:67a
Tannishō ············ 歓異抄 · 7:344a
  Kiyozawa Manshi ················ 4:233a
Tanno Setsu ········ 丹野セツ · 7:344a
Ta no kami ···· 4:125b-126a; 7:263b, 344a
  Daikokuten ······················ 2:60b
  scarecrows ······················ 4:115a
Tanomoshi ············ 頼母子 · 5:262a
Tanomura Chikuden
  ·········· 田能村竹田 1:211a; 6:*155b*;
                              7:344b
Tanomura Chokunyū
  ·········· 田能村直入 · 7:344b
Tansen and tammai
  ········· 段銭, 段米 ········ 7:344b
  Kaei sandai ki ·················· 4:101b
Tansu ····························· 4:161a
Tan Taigi ··········· 炭太祇 · 1:225a;
                         7:344b-345a
Tantei sōshu ···· 端艇漕手 · 7:336b
Tanuki [(raccoon dog) *Nyctereutes*
  procyonoides] ······· 4:100b; 7:83a, 345a
Tanuma Okitsugu
  ·········· 田沼意次 · 7:345a-346a
  Kansei Reforms ·················· 4:152b
Tanuma period
  kabunakama ····················· 4:100a
  merchant culture ················ 2:340b
  Tanuma Okitsugu ··········· 7:345a-346a
Tan'yū. 探幽   *See* **Kanō Tan'yū**
Tanzawasan ········ 丹沢山 · 7:346a
Tao-hsüan ························· 2:131b
Taoism ··········· 6:290a-292a; 8:372b
  holy men ························· 7:67a
  new religions ···················· 5:366b
  thought and culture ·············· 8:26b
  tolerance in Japanese religion ····· 8:70b
Taoka Reiun ···· 田岡嶺雲 · 7:51b, 346a
Taoka Reiun zenshū 田岡嶺雲全集 7:346a
Taoka Sayoji. 田岡佐代次
  See **Taoka Reiun**
Taoshuo ··························· 1:68b
Tapestry ·························· 1:189b
Tappizaki ············ 竜飛崎 · 7:346a
Taradake [(Japanese angelica tree)
  Aralia elata] ················· 7:346a
Tarashikomi ····················· 7:233a
Tariff Convention of 1866 ········ 4:113b
  Unequal Treaties revision ········ 8:148b

Tariffs ··················· 7:346b-347a
  government policy ··············· 2:325a
  after World War II ········· 7:346b-347a
  before World War II ············· 7:346b
Tariki ················ 2:293b; 7:347a
  Kiyozawa Manshi ················ 4:233a
Taru ···························· 7:347a
Taruhito, Prince. 熾仁親王
  See **Arisugawa no Miya Taruhito**
Tarui Tōkichi ······ 樽井藤吉 · 7:347a
  Futsū Senkyo Kisei Dōmeikai ····· 2:376a
Taru kaisen ········ 樽廻船 · 4:112b
Tarumaesan. *See* **Tarumaezan**
Tarumaezan ······ 樽前山 · 7:98a, 347b
Tarumizu ············ 垂水 · 7:347b
Tasaka Tomotaka
  ·········· 田坂具隆 · 2:270b, 271b;
                              7:347b
Tashidaka ············ 足高 · 7:347b
Tashiro Gengoemon
  ·········· 田代源五右衛門 · 7:226b
Tashiro Sanki ······ 田代三喜 · 7:347b
Tashiro Shigeki ···· 田代茂樹 · 7:347b
Tashiro Shōi ········ 田代松意 · 2:77b
*Task in Japan, The: A Study in Modern
Missionary Imperatives* ········· 6:289a
Tass ···························· 7:192a
Tasuki ················ 2:253b; 7:348a
Tatami ········· 1:82b, 276b; 2:371a; 4:160b;
          7:67a-67b, 249b, 273a, 348a, *348b*
  reed ··························· 4:231b
  rush production ·················· 1:27b
  standard size ··················· 1:82b
  Tatami rooms ···················· 5:8a
Tatara-buki ··········· 7:348a-348b
  Tatara furnace ··················· 3:333a
Tatari ···························· 4:126a
Tatchū ··························· 1:183a
Tateana jūkyo ··········· 6:189a-189b
Tateana sekishitsu (stone chamber)
  ······························· 4:244a
Tatebayashi ·········· 館林 · 7:348b
Tatebayashi Kagei
  ·········· 立林何帠 · 7:349a
Tatekawa Yoshitsugu
  ·········· 建川美次 · 7:349a
Tatemae. *See* **Tatemae and honne**
Tatemae and honne ··· 4:39a, 195a; 6:204b;
                          7:349a
  etiquette ························ 2:233a
Tateshakai ···················· 8:191a
Tateshina Kōgen 蓼科高原 4:127b; 7:349a
Tatewaki Sadayo 帯刀貞代 · 7:349b
Tateyama (city) ······ 館山 · 7:349b
Tateyama (mountains)
  ·········· 立山 · 7:349b
  Tateyama-Kurobe Alpine Route ···· 7:349b
Tatō ····························· 6:118a
Tatōgami ························· 4:113a
Tatsuno ·············· 竜野 · 7:349b
Tatsuno Kingo ······ 辰野金吾 · 7:349b
Tatsuta ························· 7:126b
Tatsutagawa ········ 竜田川 · 7:349b
Tatsuta Shrine ······ 瀧田神社 · 7:350a
Tatsuta Taisha. *See* **Tatsuta Shrine**
Tattoos ················ 7:350a-351a
  chronicles ······················ 7:350a
  Edo explosion ·············· 7:350a-350b
  form of punishment ·············· 7:350a
  full body ······················· 7:350b
  lover's pledge ··················· 7:350a
  meaning ························ 7:350a
  Meiji suppression ··············· 7:350b
  origins ························· 7:350a
  Shimpen suiko gaden ············ 7:350a
  today ······················ 7:350b-351a
  tools ··························· 7:351a

Tsūzoku suikoden gōketsu hyakuhachinin
  ······························· 7:350b
Taue-zōshi ······· 田植草紙 · 7:351a
Taut, Bruno ········ 4:173a; 7:351a-351b
Tawara ························· 7:351b
Tawara Kuniichi ···· 俵国一 · 7:351b
Tawara Sunao ······ 田原淳 · 7:351b
Tawarayama Hot Spring
  ·········· 俵山温泉 · 7:351a-351b
Tawarayama Onsen. *See* **Tawarayama
  Hot Spring**
Tawaraya Sōtatsu. 俵屋宗達 *See* **Sōtatsu**
Tawara Yoshizumi
  ·········· 田原良純 · 7:351b
Tax accountants ················· 7:351b
Tax accounting ··············· 7:351b-352a
Tax Account Law ················· 7:351b
Tax Administration Agency ·········· 7:55b
Tax Advisory Commission ·········· 7:353a
Taxation
  demetaka ······················· 2:84a
  Edo-period ······················ 4:267a
  recommendations by American
    specialists ················· 7:172a-173a
  revisions in system ·········· 7:172a-173a
  tax rice ························ 7:179a
  tolls ··························· 7:57a
Tax Bureau ············· 5:188a; 7:353a
Taxes ··················· 7:352a-354a
  administrative practices ·········· 7:353a
  annual reductions ··············· 7:353a
  corporate income ················ 7:352b
  early modern economy ············ 2:151b
  economic incentives ·············· 2:29a
  eidaka ····················· 2:185b-186a
  employee compensation ··········· 7:353a
  estate ·························· 7:352b
  excise ·························· 7:352b
  expense accounts ················ 7:353a
  gift ···························· 7:352b
  hanzei ·························· 3:100a
  income ························· 7:352b
  income distribution ·············· 3:285b
  industrial policy ··········· 3:296b-297a
  inheritance ····················· 7:352b
  kuchiei and kuchimai ············ 4:301b
  land
    annual (honto mononari) ···· 3:226b-227a
    handen shūju system ········· 3:95a-96a
  Land Tax Reform of 1873-1881
    ························· 4:365a-366b
  local revenue system ············· 7:353a
  military ······················ 3:69b-70a
  national and local ········· 7:354a-354b
  Occupation period ··············· 2:157a
  outline of system ··········· 7:352b-353a
  premodern economy ········· 2:148b-149a
  property ························ 7:353a
  real estate ····················· 7:353a
  records ························· 5:234a
  retirement plans ················· 7:353a
  ritsuryō system ············ 6:322a, 329a
  shōen ······················ 7:155b-156a
  special features ············ 7:353a-353b
    administrative practices ········ 7:353b
    annual reductions ············· 7:353a
    employee compensation, expense
    accounts, and retirement plans
                        7:353a-353b
    special measures ·············· 7:353a
  stipends ······················· 1:297b
  tansen and tammai ·············· 7:344b
  types ······················ 7:352a-352b
  ukiyaku ("floating tax") ··········· 8:138a
  unjō ······················ 8:171b-172a
  Urayaku ························ 8:176a
Tax law ········· 2:276b; 7:355a-358b
  individual income ·········· 7:356a-356b

juridical persons' income · · · · · · 7:356b-358a
legislation and administration · · · · · 7:358a
national income taxation · · · · · 7:355a-356a
Tax office · 7:358b
Tax returns · 1:9a
Tax revenues · 6:265a
Tax Special Measures Law · · · · · 7:353a,
                                           355a-358b
Tax system
  hanzei · 1:101b
  taxes, **national and local** · · · · · 7:354a-354a
  tax law · 7:355a-358b
Tayama Katai · · · · · 田山花袋 · · · · · 1:155b;
                                           7:358b-359a
  I-novel · 3:312a
  Ken'yūsha · 4:199a
  naturalism · · · · · · · · · · · · · · · · · · · 5:351a-351b
  Shinshōsetsu · 7:125b
Tayasu Munetake
  · · · · · · · · · · · · · · 田安宗武 · · · · · · · 7:359a
  Kada no Arimaro · · · · · · · · · · · · · · · 4:100b
  Kamo no Mabuchi · · · · · · · · · · · · · · 4:129b
  Toki Zemmaro · · · · · · · · · · · · · · · · · · 8:43b
Tayū · 4:298b
Tazaki Sōun · · · · 田崎草雲 · · · · · 7:359a
Tazawa, Lake · · · · · 田沢湖 · · · · · · 7:359a
Tazawako. *See* **Tazawa, Lake**
Tazawa volcano · · · · · · · · · · · · · · · · · · 7:359a
Tazoe Tetsuji · · · · 田添鉄二 · · · 7:359a-359b
Tchaikovsky Memorial Tōkyō Ballet Co
  · 2:76a
Tçuzzu, Rodrigues · · · · · · · · · · · · · · · 3:183b
TDK Corporation · · · · · · · · · · · · · · · · 7:359b
Tea · 7:359b-360a
  brewing · 7:360a
  history · 7:360a
  types · 7:359b-360a
    bancha · · · · · · · · · · · · · · · · · · · 7:359b-360a
    gyokuro · 7:359b
    kamairicha · 7:359b
    matcha · 7:359b
    sencha · 7:359b
Tea ceremony · · · · 4:337a, 381b; 7:64b, 71b,
                                           360a-365a
  Azuchi-Momoyama · · · · · · · · · 3:180b-181a
  Bizen ware · 1:158a
  bokuseki · 1:235b
  chakaiseki ryōri · · · · · · · · · · · · · · 2:21b-22a
  charcoal ceremony · · · · · · · · · · · · · 7:362b
  China · 1:283a
  confections · 1:350a
  drinking · 7:364a
  dry sweets · 7:364b
  Echizen ware · · · · · · · · · · · · · · · · · · · 2:144a
  examining utensils · · · · · · · · · 7:364a-364b
  flower arrangement · · · · · · · · · · · · · 2:289b
  Furuta Oribe · · · · · · · · · · · · · · · · · · · 2:373b
  fūryū · 2:374b
  gardens · 3:9b
  Hagi ware · 3:76b
  Higashiyama culture · · · · · · · · · · · · 3:132b
  historical development · · · · · · · · · · 2:295a
  Iga ware · 3:261b
  Karatsu ware · · · · · · · · · · · · · · · · · · · 4:159a
  kogikushi paper · · · · · · · · · · · · · · · · 4:113a
  Kutani ware · 4:321b
  Murata Shukō, Takeno Jōō,
    and Sen no Rikyū · · · · · · · 7:360b-361a
  nature in · 5:358a
  Nin'ami Dōhachi · · · · · · · · · · · · · · · · · 6:4b
  Oda Uraku · · · · · · · · · · · · · · · · · · · 6:65a-65b
  origins in China · · · · · · · · · · · · 7:360a-360b
  presentation of thick tea · · · · · 7:363a-363b
  presentation of thin tea · · · · · 7:364b-365a
  principal sweet · · · · · · · · · · · · 7:362b-363a
  Raku ware · 6:283a
  religion · 6:292a
  rimpa · 6:317b

Satsuma ware · · · · · · · · · · · · · · · 7:30a-30b
schools · 7:361a-361b
sencha · 7:365a
Sen no Rikyū · 7:67a
service of tea and meal · · · · · · · · · · 7:361b
Shigaraki ware · · · · · · · · · · · · · · · 7:91a-91b
Takatori ware · · · · · · · · · · · · · · · · · · · 7:320a
tatami · 7:348a
tatemae and honne · · · · · · · · · · · · · 7:349a
teabowl · · · · · · · · · · · · · · · · · · · 7:363b-364a
tea garden · · · · · · · · · · · · · · · · · 7:361b-362a
teahouse · · · · · · · · · · · · · · · · · · · 7:361b-362a
tea in Japan · 7:360b
tea meal · · · · · · · · · · · · · · · · · · · 7:362a-362b
tearoom · *7:361a*
textiles · 8:18b
thick tea ceremony · · · · · · · · · · · · · 7:363a
usucha temae · · · · · · · · · · · · · · · · · · *7:364b*
vessels · 4:140a
wabi · 8:197a
Teachers · · · · · · · · · · · · · · · · · · · 7:365a-367a
  appointment · · · · · · · · · · · · · · · 7:366a-366b
  certification · 7:366a
  composition of personnel · · · · · 7:366b-367a
  dismissal · · · · · · · · · · · · · · · · · · · 7:366a-366b
  in-service training · · · · · · · · · · · · · · 7:366a
  problems affecting profession · · · · · 7:367a
  qualification · · · · · · · · · · · · · · · · · · · 7:366a
  remuneration · · · · · · · · · · · · · · 7:366a-366b
  responsibility · · · · · · · · · · · · · · · · · · 7:366b
  training · · · · · · · · · · · · · · · · · · · 7:365a-366a
  unions · 7:366b
Teacher's Association · · · · · · · · · · · · · 6:90b
Teaching methods · · · · · · · · · · · 7:367a-367b
Tea drinking · 7:360b
Teahouse of the August Moon · · · · 4:332b
Teahouses · 7:164b
Tea-leaf Picking at Uji · · · · · · · · · · 4:320b
Tearoom · *7:361a*
Teatoro · 7:367b-368a
Teburi · 3:29a-30a
Technical colleges · · · · · 7:368a; 8:192a
Technological Art School
  (Kōbu Bijutsu Gakkō) · · · · · 2:304a; 8:327b
Technological assistance · · · · · 2:315b-316a
  foreign investment · · · · · · · · · · · · · 2:316b
Technological development · · · 7:368a-371b
  "A Model of Economic Growth" · · · 7:368a
  compared with U.S. · · · · · · · · 7:370a-371b
  contemporary · · · · · · · · · · · · · · · · · 2:161b
  history · 7:368a-368b
  17th century to 1930s · · · · · · · 7:368b-369b
  World War II to 1970s · · · · · · · 7:369b-370a
Technological innovation · · · · 7:371b-372b
  environment · · · · · · · · · · · · · · · 7:371b-372b
  fruits of · 7:372a
  future · 7:372a-372b
Technology
  development of · 6:303a-305b; 7:368a-371b
  economic growth · · · · · 2:159b-160a, 161b
  economic planning · · · · · · · · · 2:167a-167b
  electronics · · · · · · · · · · · · · · · · 2:193b-195a
  electrotechnical · · · · · · · · · · · · · · · · 2:195a
  labor unions' response · · · · · · · · · · · 2:36b
  modern · · · · · · · · · · · · · · · · · · 7:372b-373b
    characteristics · · · · · · · · · · · · · · · · 7:373a
    developments · · · · · · · · · · · · · · · · · 7:372b
    history · · · · · · · · · · · · · · · · · · · 7:372b-373a
    recent trends · · · · · · · · · · · · · 7:373a-373b
    steel production · · · · · · · · · · 3:333b, 336a
    transportation · · · · · · · · · · · · 8:103a-104a
Technology transfer · · 6:305a; 7:373b-375a
  after Meiji Restoration · · · · · · · 7:374a-374b
  cultural borrowing · · · · · · · · · · · · · 7:374a
  modes · 7:373b-374a
  postwar experience · · · · · · · · · 7:374b-375a
Tedorigawa · · · · · 手取川 · · · · · · · 7:375a
Teganuma · · · · · 手賀沼 · · · · · 7:375a-375b

Teganuma marshland
  · · · · · · · · · · · · · · · · 手賀沼 · · · · · · · · · 1:5a
Tegata · 4:163a
Tegoto-mono · · · · · 手事物 · · · · · · · 4:64b
Teigin Incident · · · · 帝銀事件 · · · 7:375b
  Furuhata Tanemoto · · · · · · · · · · · · · 2:372a
  Tanaka Kōtarō · · · · · · · · · · · · · · · · · 7:337b
Teigin Jiken. *See* **Teigin Incident**
Teihon kaeru · · · · · 定本蛙 · · · · · · 4:319a
Teijin, Ltd · · · · · · · 4:139a; 7:375b-376a
  Teijiin Incident · · · · · · · · · · · · · · · · · 7:375b
Teijin Incident · · · · 帝人事件 · · · 7:375b
Teijin Jiken. *See* **Teijin Incident**
Teijiin no Uta-awase
  · · · · · · · · · · · · · · 廷人の歌合 · · · · · · 8:182a
Tei Joshō · · · · · · · · · · 鄭汝昌 · · · 2:96b-97a
Teijō zakki · · · · · · 貞丈雑記 · · · · · · 8:358b
Teika kanazukai
  · · · · · · · · · · · · · · 定家仮名遣 · · · · · · 4:133b
Teiki · · · · · · · · · · · · 帝紀 1:151a; 2:101a;
                                     4:340b; 7:376a
  historiography · · · · · · · · · · · · · · · · · 3:152a
  Kojiki based on · · · · · · · · · · · · · · · · 4:251a
Teikin ōrai · · · · · · 庭訓往来 · · · · · 7:376a
Teikoku Bijutsuin (Imperial Fine Arts
  Academy) · 6:158a
Teikoku bunko · · · · 帝国文庫 · · · · · 4:64a
Teikoku daigaku · · · · · · · · · · · · 3:281a-281b
Teikoku Gikai · · · · · · 帝国議会 · · · 3:275b-277a
Teikoku Ginkō · · · · · · · · · · · · · · · · · · 7:375b
Teikoku Jinzō Kenshi Co · · · 7:375b-376a
Teikoku Kaigun Rengō Kantai · · · · · 1:336b
Teikoku Nōkai · · · · 帝国農会 · · · · 7:376a
Teikoku Oil Co, Ltd · · 6:182a; 7:376a-376b
Teikoku Sekiyu. *See* **Teikoku Oil Co,
  Ltd**
Teikokutō · · · · · · · · · 帝国党 · · · · · 7:376b
  Kokumin Kyōkai reorganized as · · · 4:261a
Teikoku Tsūshinsha · · · · · · · · · · · · · 1:16b
Teikoku Zaigō Gunjinkai. *See* **Imperial
  Military Reservists' Association**
Tei Kōsho · · · · · · · · · · 鄭孝胥 · · · · · 8:378b
Teimon school · · · · · · 貞門派 · · · · · · 5:18a
Teinensei · 7:376b
Teisan · 7:376b
Tei Seikō · · · · · · · · · · 鄭成功 · · · 8:378a-378b
Teisei zōyaku sairan igen
  · · · · · · · · · · · · · 訂正増訳采覧異言 · · · 4:369b
Teito Kōsokudo Kōtsū Eidan. *See*
  Teito Rapid Transit Authority
Teitoku kyōka hyakushu
  · · · · · · · · · · · · · 貞徳狂歌百首 · · · · · 4:332a
Teito nichinichi shimbun
  · · · · · · · · · · · · · 帝都日日新聞 · · · · · 8:330b
Teito Rapid Transit Authority · · · 6:264a;
                                     7:376b-377a
Teiyū Ethics Society · · · · · · · · · · · · 6:107b
Teizambori · · · · · · · 貞山堀 · · · · · · 7:377a
Tejima Seiichi · · · · 手島精一 · · · · 7:377a
Tekibo shoshi (legal wife-illegitimate
  child relationships) · · · · · · · · · · · · 6:162b
Tekichū ōdan sambyakuri
  · · · · · · · · · · · · · 敵中横断三百里 · · · · 7:349a
Tekijuku. *See* **Ogata Kōan**
Tekiya · 7:250a
Tekki jidai · · · · · · · · 鉄器時代 · · · 3:332b-333a
Tekkō · 7:377a
Tekkō Rōren · 3:335a
Telecommunications systems · · · 6:266b;
                                     7:377a-379b
  computer industry · · · · · · · · · · · · · 1:347b
  future · 7:378b-379b
  history · · · · · · · · · · · · · · · · · · · 7:377b-378a
  Kokusai Denshin Denwa Co, Ltd · · 4:261b
  services · · · · · · · · · · · · · · · · · · 7:378a-378b
Telegraph · 3:319a
Telephones · · · · · · · · · · · · · · · · 7:379b-380b
  networks · · · · · · · · · · · · · · · · · · 7:380a-380b

international calls ··············· 7:380b
modern services ··············· 7:380b
other uses of circuitry ·········· 7:380b
switchboards ·············· 7:380a-380b
transmissions routes ··········· 7:380b
Television ···················· 6:268b
children's use ············ 1:278b-279a
educational broadcasting ········· 2:179a
growth ···················· 2:192a, 193b
international communications ····· 3:319a
leisure-time activity ············ 4:382a
"Mito Kōmon" ················· 2:219b
sociocultural contribution ··· 5:129a-129b
Takayanagi Kenjirō ············· 7:321a
urban life ···················· 8:179a
Yomiuri Telecasting Corporation ··· 8:337a
Television broadcasting ······· 1:172a-173a
late-night ···················· 1:173b
mass communications ··········· 5:128b
Television Tōkyō Channel 12, Ltd 7:380b
Television viewing ············· 1:173a
Temane ··················· 3:29a-30a
Temari ···················· 7:381a
Tembimbō ················· 7:381a
Tembu ···················· 7:381a
Jōruriji ···················· 4:77b
Temiya cave ··· 手宮洞窟 ···· 7:381a
Temiyage ···················· 5:217a
Temmangū ····· 天満宮 ···· 7:381a
Temmei Famine
················ 天明の飢饉 ·· 7:28b, 345b, 381b
Temmei no Kikin. *See* **Temmei Famine**
Temmon Hokke no Ran. *See* **Temmon Hokke Rebellion**
Temmon Hokke Rebellion
················ 天文法華の乱 ··· 7:381b
Temmu, Emperor 天武天皇 · 2:55a; 5:307b; 7:96a, 381b-382b; 8:285b
Hieda no Are ················· 3:130a
historiography ··············· 3:152b
Jinshin Disturbance ············· 4:60b
Kōbun, Emperor ·············· 4:239a
Naniwakyō ··················· 5:328b
Silla relations ················ 4:277b
Temple attendants (chigo) ········ 1:274a
Temple gates ············· 3:12a-12b
Temple guarantee ·············· 8:12b
"Temple guarantee system" ······· 7:186a
Temple of the Golden Pavilion, The
··························· 4:213a
Temple of the Silver Pavilion ··· 3:33a-33b
Temple refuge ·········· 3:130b; 4:115b
Temples ··············· 8:1a-2a
Akishinodera ················· 1:42a
Asukadera ············ 1:105b-106b
Buddhist sculpture ········ 1:197b-198a
Byōdōin ··············· 1:227a-227b
construction of by Emperor Shōmu 7:166a
Honzan Shugenshū
Shōgoin ·················· 7:160a
Hossō
Hōryūji ·············· 3:231b-233b
Kōfukuji ·············· 4:243b-244a
Yakushiji ·············· 8:285b-286b
Ji
Yugyōji ·················· 8:356a
Jōdo
Chion'in ·················· 1:296b
Senjuji ···················· 7:66a
Zōjōji ···················· 8:379b
Jōdo Shin
Honganji ·············· 3:221a-222b
Ishiyama Honganji ··········· 3:346a
Nishi Honganji ·········· 6:16a-17a
Senjuji ···················· 7:66a
Kegon
Gangōji ·················· 3:6b-7a

Shin Yakushiji ··········· 7:139b-140a
Tōdaiji ················ 8:33b-34b
Nichiren
Hommonji ················· 3:217b
Minobusan ················· 5:194b
Tanjōji ···················· 1:51b
Ōbaku
Mampukuji ················· 5:89a
Rinzai
Daitokuji ·············· 2:68a-68b
Engakuji ·················· 2:217a
Ginkakuji ·············· 3:33a-33b
Kenchōji ·················· 4:195a
Kenninji ·············· 4:197a-197b
Kinkakuji ·················· 4:213a
Myōshinji ················· 5:291a
Ryōanji ··················· 6:347b
Shōkokuji ················· 7:164b
Tenryūji ··················· 8:10b
Tōfukuji ·············· 8:35a-35b
Zuisenji ··················· 8:380b
Ritsu
Mibudera ·················· 5:166a
Shingon
Chishakuin ················· 1:297a
Daianji ···················· 2:55a
Daigoji ·············· 2:57a-58a
Daikakuji ·················· 2:59b
Gokokuji ··················· 3:43a
Hasedera ·············· 3:106b-107a
Hōkaiji ··················· 3:212b
Hokkeji ·············· 3:214a-214b
Ishiyamadera ··············· 3:346a
Jingoji ···················· 4:58a
Jōruriji ···················· 4:77b
Kawasaki Daishi ············· 4:183a
Kimiidera ·················· 4:208a
Kongōbuji ················· 4:269b
Kongōfukuji ················ 1:102b
Kōryūji ·············· 4:294a-294b
Kōzanji ·············· 4:300a-300b
Murōji ··············· 5:270b-271a
Ninnaji ···················· 6:7a
Okadera ··················· 6:78b
Rokuharamitsuji ············· 6:335a
Shigisanji ·············· 7:93a-93b
Shinshōji ·················· 6:125a
Taimadera ················· 7:298a
Tōji ················· 8:38a-39a
Yakuōin ··················· 7:317b
Zentsūji ··················· 8:377a
Shingon Ritsu
Saidaiji ··················· 6:366a
Shugendō
Kimbusenji ············ 4:207b-208a
Sōtō
Eiheiji ·············· 2:186a-186b
Sōjiji ···················· 7:224a
Tendai
Chūsonji ·················· 1:314a
Daisenji ··················· 2:67a
Enryakuji ·············· 2:220a-221a
Fukidera ·················· 2:360a
Jindaiji ··················· 4:58a
Kan'eiji ·············· 4:137b-138a
Miidera ··················· 5:169a
Mōtsuji ··················· 5:259a
Risshakuji ·············· 6:320b-321a
Sanzen'in ·············· 7:19b-20a
Shitennōji ················· 7:150b
Taimadera ················· 7:298a
Yamadadera ············ 8:288b-289a
Temple slaves ················ 2:132a
Temple supporters ············· 4:362a
Temple towns (monzen machi)
·················· 5:247b-248a
urban planning ··············· 8:179b
Tempō Famine 天保の飢饉 ···· 7:87b; 8:2a

Tempō Reforms
············ 天保の改革 · 1:21a; 3:189b; 7:102a; 8:2a-3a
Domainal reforms ·············· 8:2b
fudasashi ···················· 2:340b
kabunakama dissolution ·········· 4:100a
kienrei ···················· 4:203a
Mizuno Tadakuni ········· 5:226b, 227b
Ryūtei Tanehiko ·············· 6:359b
shinden kaihatsu ·············· 7:109b
Shogunate reforms ·············· 8:2a
Tamenaga Shunsei ········· 7:333b-334a
Tokugawa shogunate ········· 8:55b-56a
Torii Yōzō ··················· 8:80a
Tōyama Kinshirō ·············· 8:88a
Tempura ········ 2:23a, 306a; 8:3a-3b
Tempyō culture ··· 天平文化 ··· 8:3b
Ten. *See* **Heaven**
Tenant farmer disputes ··· 4:363a; 8:3b-4a
cooperatives ················· 1:22a
Tenant farmers (mizunomi-byakushō)
nago ················· 4:362b; 5:308b
Tenant farming ················· 1:31a
elimination ·················· 4:364b
Tenant Rent Control Ordinance
(Kosakuryō Tōsei Rei) ········· 4:363a
Tenant rights ················· 4:374a
Tenchi, Emperor. 天智天皇
See **Tenji, Emperor**
Tenchi kakitsuke 天地書附 ······· 4:272a
Tenchi nikyū yōhō
··········· 天地二球用法 ··· 5:355b
Tenchūgumi Rebellion
············ 天誅組の乱 · 5:319b; 8:4a
Tendai sect ······· 天台宗 · 1:178b; 7:13a, 80b; 8:4a-5b
Byōdōin temple ··············· 1:227b
Chinese Tiantai ················ 8:4a
education ··················· 2:172a
Eiheiji ···················· 2:186a
Enryakuji ·············· 2:220a-221a
founding of Japanese Tendai ······· 8:4b
bodhisattva precepts ············ 8:4b
Kūkai's esoteric Buddhism ······· 8:4b
Fujiwara culture ··············· 2:347b
Fujiwara no Toshinari ··········· 2:357a
Hōnen ···················· 4:67b
Jindaiji ··················· 4:58a
Kan'eiji ··················· 4:137b
Kon Tōkō ················· 4:275b
meditation ·················· 4:67a
monasticism ················· 5:237b
musical instruments ············ 1:157a
painting ··················· 6:149b
poems and songs ·············· 8:231a
priests
Annen ···················· 8:5a
Enchin ··················· 2:213b
Enkū ················ 2:218a-218b
Ennin ···················· 2:219a
Genshin ··················· 3:23b
Ryōgen ··················· 6:351b
Senkaku ··················· 7:66a
Saichō ···················· 8:4a
raigōzu ·················· 6:277a
Saichō's successors ············· 8:4b
Sannō Ichijitsu Shintō ··········· 7:15a
Tendaishū ·········· 天台宗 · 8:4a-5b
Tendō ············· 天童 ·· 8:5b
Tendō school ····· 天道流 · 5:308a-308b
Tenement quarters ············· 7:202a
Tengu ············· 天狗 · 2:293b, 303a; 8:5a, 5b
kamikakushi ················· 4:126b
Tengutō no Ran
············ 天狗党の乱 ··· 5:204b-205a
Tenioha ··········· てにをは ·· 7:281a
Tenji, Emperor ····· 天智天皇 · 7:96a; 8:5b-6a

descendants · · · · · · · · · · · · · · **5**:308a
Fujiwara family · · · · · **2**:348a, 351b
Jinshin Disturbance · · · · · · · · **4**:60a
Ōmi Code · · · · · · · · · · · · · · **6**:101a
ritsuryō system · · · · · · · · · · · **4**:277b
Tenjikuyō · · · · · · · · 天竺様 · · · · **3**:12b
Tenjōbito · · · · · · · · · · 殿上人 · · **2**:40a; **8**:6a
Tenjōgawa · · · · · · · · · · 天井川 · · · **8**:6a
Tenjō Sajiki (Upper
Balcony) · · · · · · · 天井桟敷 · · · **8**:13a
Tenjukoku mandara shūchō.
天寿国曼荼羅繡帳 See Tenjukoku shūchō.
Tenjukoku shūchō
· · · · · · · · · 天寿国繡帳 · · **2**:200a; **4**:69a
Tenkan nōryoku · · · · · · · · · · · **8**:6a-6b
Tenka Ryūmon (Dragon Gate of the
World) · · · · · · · 天下龍門 · · · **5**:330a
Tenka taihei ki · 天下太平記 · · · · **4**:166a
Tenkō · · · · · · · · · · 転向 · **8**:6b-7b, 149b
forms of coercion · · · · · · · · · **8**:6b
significance · · · · · · · · · · · · · **8**:7b
"Thought Criminal" Probation Law · **8**:29a
types of · · · · · · · · · · · · · **8**:6b-7a
Tenkō bungaku · 転向文学 · · · · **7**:176a
Tennen kinembutsu · · · · · · **5**:352a-352b
Tenninkyō · · · · · · · · 天人峡 · · · · · **8**:7b
Tennis · · · · · · · · · · · · · · · · · · **8**:7b
Tennō · · · · · · · · · · 天皇 · · **2**:203a-209a
Tennōki and Kokki
· · · · · · · · · · 天皇記, 国記 **1**:151a; **7**:264a;
8:7b
Tennō kikan setsu
· · · · · · · · · · · 天皇機関説 · · · · · **8**:7b-8b
Kakei Katsuhiko · · · · · · · **4**:115b
kokutai debate · · · · · · · · · **4**:263b
"Tennō no bōshi"
· · · · · · · · · · 天皇の帽子 · · · · **4**:270a
Tennō no ningen sengen. See Emperor,
renunciation of divinity by
Tennōzan · · · · · · · · 天王山 · · · · · · · · **8**:8b
Tenrei banshō meigi
· · · · · · · · · · 篆隷万象名義 · · · · **1**:151b
Tenri · · · · · · · · · · · · · 天理 · · · · · · · **8**:8b
Tenri Central Library · · · · · · · · · · · **8**:8b-9a
Tenri Gaikokugo Gakkō (Tenri
School of Foreign Languages) · · · **8**:9b
Tenrikyō · · · · · · · · · 天理教 · · **2**:300b;
7:48a-48b; **8**:9a-9b
doctrine · · · · · · · · · · · · · · · · **8**:9a
historical development · · · · · · **8**:9a
kokyū · · · · · · · · · · · · · · · · **4**:264b
museums · · · · · · · · · · · · · · **5**:280a
Nakayama Miki · · · · · · · · · **5**:319a
scripture · · · · · · · · · · · · · · **8**:9b
Shinkyō kyōdōtai · · · · · · · · **7**:121b
Tenri University · · · · · · · · · · · · · · **8**:9b
Tenrō · · · · · · · · · · · 天狼 · · · · · **3**:80b
Tenryō · · · · · · · · · · 天領 · · · · **8**:9b-10a
kanjō bugyō · · · · · · · · · · · **4**:144a
rural administration · · · · · · · **4**:55a
Tenryū · · · · · · · · · · · 天竜 · · · · · **8**:10a
Tenryūgawa · · · · · · · 天竜川 · · · · **8**:10b
Sakuma Dam · · · · · · · · · · · **7**:3a
Tenryūji · · · · · · · · · 天龍寺 · **4**:336a; **8**:10b
Tenryūji-bune · · 天龍寺船 · · · **8**:10b-11a
Tenryūkyō · · · · · · · · 天竜峡 · · · · **8**:11a
Tensho (archaic script) · · · · **1**:233b; **7**:170b
Tenshō Ken'ō Shisetsu
· · · · · · · · · · 天正遣欧使節 · · **5**:203a-203b
· · · · · · · · · 天照皇大神宮教 · · · · **4**:227b
Tenshō Kōtai Jingū Kyō (Dancing
Religion) · · · · · · · · · · · · · · **8**:257b
Tenshō kyōgen-bon
· · · · · · · · · · 天正狂言本 · · · · **4**:328a
Tenshō mission to Europe · · · · **3**:350b

Tenshō naga ōban 天正長大判 **5**:242a-242b
Tenshō onna gassen
· · · · · · · · · 天正女合戦 · · · · · **4**:112a
Tenson kōrin · · · 天孫降臨 · · · · **2**:101b
Ten to chi to · · · 天と地と · · · · **4**:112a
Ten to sen (Points and
Lines) · · · · · · · · 点と線 · · · **6**:221a
Tenugui · · · · · · · · · 手拭 · · · · · **8**:11a
headgear · · · · · · · · · · · · · · **3**:119a
Terada Torahiko · 寺田寅彦 · · · · **8**:11a
works · · · · · · · · · · · · · · · · **8**:11a
Terada Tōru · · · · · · 寺田透 · · · · **8**:11a
works · · · · · · · · · · · · · · · · **8**:11a
Teradaya Incident
· · · · · · · · · · 寺田屋騒動 · · **1**:84a; **8**:11b
Terakado Seiken 寺門静軒 · · · · **8**:11b
Terakoya · · · · · · · · 寺子屋 · **1**:152b; **7**:37b,
94b; **8**:11b-12a, 174b
education · · · · · · · · · · · **2**:172b, 174b
literacy rate · · · · · · · · · · · · **5**:10b
ōraimono · · · · · · · · · · · · · **6**:115b
religious education · · · · · · **6**:295a-295b
Shingaku · · · · · · · · · · · · · **7**:112a
teaching methods · · · · · · · **7**:367a-367b
Terashima Munenori
· · · · · · · · · · 寺島宗則 · · · · · · **8**:12a
Terauchi Hisaichi 寺内寿一 · · · · · **8**:12a
Terauchi Masatake
· · · · · · · · · · 寺内正毅 · · · · · **8**:12b
annexation of Korea · · · · · · **4**:282a
Kenseikai · · · · · · · · · · · · **4**:198a
Korea's annexation treaty · · · · · · **4**:287b
rice riots · · · · · · · · · · · · · **6**:310a
Terauke · · · · · · · · · 寺請 · · · · **4**:119a;
7:185a-186b; **8**:12b
Terayama Shūji · · 寺山修司 · · **8**:12b-13a
Shinoda Masahiro · · · · · · · **7**:122a
Terazaki Kōgyō · · 寺崎広業 · · · · **8**:13a
Terebi Asahi. See Asahi National
Broadcasting Co, Ltd
Terebijon · · · · · · · テレビジョン · · · · **7**:321a
Terebijon kōgaku
· · · · · · · · テレビジョン工学 · · · · **7**:321a
Terebi Tōkyō. See Television Tōkyō
Channel 12, Ltd
Teriyaki · · · · · · · · · · · · · **8**:13a, 323b
Terrace farming · · · · · · · · · · · **1**:25a
Terrier, Japanese · · · · · · · · · **4**:45a
Territorial waters · · · · · · · **4**:2b; **8**:13b
Territory and administrative divisions.
See Japan
Territory of Japan · · · · · · · **8**:13b-14b
Terrorism, political · · · · · · · · **2**:45a
government restriction · · · · · **7**:254a
Tertiary industries · · · · · **6**:239b; **8**:14b-15a
Teshigahara Hiroshi
· · · · · · · · · · 勅使河原宏 · · **2**:274a, 292b;
8:15a
Echizen ware · · · · · · · · · · · **2**:144a
Teshigahara Sōfū
· · · · · · · · · · 勅使河原蒼風 · · · · **2**:291b
Teshikaga · · · · · · · · 弟子屈 · · · · · **8**:15a
Teshima Toan · · · · 手島堵庵 · · **8**:15a-15b
disciples · · · · · · · · · · · · · **5**:320a
Ishida Baigan · · · · · · · · · · **4**:120a
Shingaku · · · · · · · · · · · · · **7**:112a
writings · · · · · · · · · · · · · · **8**:15a-15b
Teshiogawa · · · · · · · 天塩川 · · · · **8**:15b
Teshio Mountains
· · · · · · · · · · 天塩山地 · · · · · **8**:15b
Teshio Plain · · · · · · 天塩平野 · · · · **8**:15b
Tessai. 鉄斎 See Tomioka Tessai
Tessai Art Museum · · · · · · · · · · **8**:15b
Tesshū Tokusai · 鉄舟徳済 · · · · **8**:15b-16a
Tetsudō basha. See Horsecars
Tetsugakukan · · · · 哲学館 **3**:309b; **4**:177b
Tetsugen · · · · · · · · · 鉄眼 · · · · · **8**:16a
Tetsujutsu sankei 綴術算経 · · · · **8**:231b

Tettei kojin-shugi
· · · · · · · · · · 徹底個人主義 · · · · **7**:338b
Teuchi · · · · · · · · · · · · · · · · · **8**:16a
Textbook authorization system · · · **7**:37b
Textbooks · · · · · · · · · · · · · · · **7**:37b
Textbook Scandal of 1902-1903 · · · **8**:16a
Textile industry · · · · · · · · · · **8**:16a-16b
companies
Fuji Spinning Co, Ltd · · · · · · **2**:346a
Gunze, Ltd · · · · · · · · · · · · **3**:70a
Itōman & Co, Ltd · · · · · · · · **3**:355a
Japan Wool Textile Co, Ltd · · · **4**:50b
Kanebō, Ltd · · · · · · · · · · · **4**:137b
Kurabō Industries Ltd · · · · · · **4**:311a
Kuraray Co, Ltd · · · · · · · · · **4**:311b
Ōsaka Spinning Mill · · · · · · · **6**:123a
Senju Woolen Mill · · · · · · · **7**:66a
Shikibō, Ltd · · · · · · · · · · · **7**:95b
Teijin, Ltd · · · · · · · · · **7**:375b-376a
Tōhō Rayon Co, Ltd · · · · · · · **8**:37b
Toyoda Automatic Loom Works, Ltd
· · · · · · · · · · · · · · · · · **8**:90a
Unitika, Ltd · · · · · · · · · · · **8**:168b
cotton, worker exploitation · · · · · **4**:343b
cotton spinning · · · · · · · · · · **2**:31a
female labor participation · · · · · **2**:210b
industrial structure · · · · · · · · **3**:301a
Meiji period · · · · · · · · · **2**:151b-152a
occupational structure · · · · · · · **6**:56a
technological development · · · · · **7**:369a
women in · · · · · · · · · · · · · **8**:260a
working conditions · · · · · · · **2**:241b; **4**:71b
Textiles · · · · · · · · · · · · · · **8**:16b-20a
Asuka and Nara textiles · · · · · · **8**:17a
care and preservation of · · · · · · **8**:19a
Chinese influences · · · · · · · · · **7**:195b
crepe · · · · · · · · · · · · · · · **1**:274b
design · · · · · · · · · · · **2**:90a-91a; **4**:267a
Edo period · · · · · · · · · · · · · **8**:19a
export · · · · · · · · · · · · · · · **7**:203b
folk craft · · · · · · · · · · · · · **2**:295b
Heian period and Kamakura period · **8**:18a
Jōmon period · · · · · · · · · · · **8**:16b
kara-ori · · · · · · · · · · · · · · **4**:158a
kasuri · · · · · · · · · · · · · · · **4**:164a
Kurume-gasuri · · · · · · · · · · **1**:276b
Meiji period to present · · · · · · · **8**:19b
Muromachi period and
Azuchi-Momoyama period · · · · · **8**:18b
Okinawan textiles · · · · · · · · **6**:91a-91b
Persian influence · · · · · · · · · **7**:195b
Shōsōin · · · · · · · · · · · · · · **8**:17b
aya (figured twills) · · · · · · · **8**:17b
nishiki (brocades) · · · · · · · · **8**:17b
plain weave silks and ramies · · · **8**:17b
ra and sha · · · · · · · · · · · · **8**:17b
sankechi · · · · · · · · · · · · · **8**:17b
shishū · · · · · · · · · · · · · · · **8**:17b
silk · · · · · · · · · · · · · · · · **7**:194a
tsumugi · · · · · · · · · · · · · · **8**:116a
tsuzure-ori · · · · · · · · · · · · **8**:120a
wax-resist dyeing · · · · · · · **8**:237b-238a
Yamato period · · · · · · · · · · **8**:17a
Yayoi period · · · · · · · · · · · **8**:16b
Tezuka Ryokubin 手塚緑敏 · · · **3**:116a-116b
Thai-Japanese Alliance · · · · · · · · **8**:20a
Thailand and Japan · · · · · **2**:200a; **8**:20a-21a
early relations · · · · · · · · · · · **8**:20a
Free Thai Movement · · · · · · · **2**:339b
postwar period · · · · · · · · · · **8**:20b
relations during World War II · · · · **8**:20b
1970s · · · · · · · · · · · · · · · **8**:21a
Thalidomide children · · **6**:253b; **8**:21a-21b
Thanksgiving pilgrimage · · · · · **6**:79a-79b
Theater
female impersonators · · · · · · · **7**:108a
leisure-time activity · · · · · · · · **4**:381a
onnagata · · · · · · · · · · · **6**:108a-108b

periodicals ·············· 7:112a
political drama ········ 7:112b-113a
puppet ·············· 1:212a-215b
shimpa ·············· 7:107b-108a
shingeki ·············· 7:112a-113b
Shinkokugeki ·············· 7:121a
Shinseisakuza ·············· 7:124a
traditional ·············· 8:21b-23a
　bugaku ·············· 3:1b; 8:21b
　bunraku ·········· 1:212a-215b; 8:22a
　kabuki ·············· 4:90a-97b; 8:23a
　kyōgen ·········· 4:324b-329a; 8:22a
　Nō ·············· 6:23b-29b; 8:22a
urban life ·············· 8:178b
yose ·············· 8:340b
Theater critics
　Aeba Kōson ·············· 1:18a
　Tsubouchi Shōyō ·········· 8:110a-111a
Theatrical costumes ·········· 8:23a-24a
　bugaku ·············· 8:23a
　bunraku ·············· 8:23b
　kabuki ·············· 8:24a
　nō and kyōgen ·············· 8:23b
Theocracy ·············· 8:24a
Therapy ·············· 7:83a
Theravāda Buddhism · 1:177a-177b; 6:281a
Thermal pollution ·············· 2:227b
Thermal power ·········· 2:190b-191b
Third Comprehensive National
　Development Plan ·············· 6:228a
Third Domestic Industrial Exposition
　·············· 1:71b
Third United Nations Conference on the
　Law of the Sea (UNCLOS III) ····· 8:13a
Thirty-Six Poetic Geniuses
　(Sanjūrokkasen) ·········· 3:336b; 5:166a;
　　7:12b-13b
Thirty-Six Views of Mount Fuji
　(Fugaku sanjūrokkei) ······ 8:143a, *143b*
Thistles [(azami) family
　Compositae] ·············· 8:24a
This-worldliness ·············· 8:24b
Thompson, Stith ·············· 2:302b
Thought and culture ·········· 8:24b-29a
　development ·············· 8:26a
　　community-ism versus universalism
　　·············· 8:27a
　　functionalism and classicism ······ 8:28a
　　life-centeredness versus transcendence
　　·············· 8:26b
　　stages of Chinese cultural influence
　　·············· 8:26a
　traditional ·············· 8:25a
　　community-ism ·············· 8:25b
　　functionalism ·············· 8:25b
　　life centeredness ·············· 8:25b
　　Shintō changeableness ·············· 8:25a
"Thought Criminal" Probation Law · 8:7a,
　29a
"Thought police" ·············· 6:168b
Thousand Cranes ·············· 4:176b
"Thousand-stitch" cloths ·············· 7:67a
"Three Arrows Studies" ·············· 5:214a
"Three Eccentrics" ·············· 7:320b
Threefold Pureland sutras ····· 4:67a-67b
Three Hills of Yamato
　大和三山 ······ 8:310b
"Three Labor Laws" (Rōdō Sampō)
　·············· 4:357b
"Three Lords" ·············· 3:47b
Three Magistrates, The ·············· 7:6a
Three Monkeys ·············· 8:29a-29b
Three New Laws System ·········· 5:63a-63b
Three Nonnuclear Principles · 3:137a-137b
Three Offices ·············· 7:16b-17a
"Three press-dyes" ·············· 7:13b
Three Principles of Foreign Policy 8:153b
Three Regulations for Great Crimes 2:55b

Three Successor Houses, The ····· 3:47b
Three Views of Japan ·············· 5:382a
Thrushes [(tsugumi) subfamily
　Turdidae] ·············· 8:29b
Thunberg, Carl Peter ····· 5:313a; 8:29b
Thunderbolt realm ·········· 4:269b-270a
Tianjin (Tientsin) Convention ··· 4:157a,
　280b; 7:68b; 8:29b
Tianjin (Tientsin) Incident ·········· 8:152b
Tiatong Rujing ·············· 2:186a
Tidal waves ·············· 2:141a
Tie-dyeing ·············· 8:17b, 29b-30a
Tilapia ·············· 2:282b
Time of day ·············· 1:232b
Ting Ju-ch'ang. *See* **Ding Ruchang
　(Ting Ju-ch'ang)**
Tips or gratuities ·············· 7:183a
Title Incident ·············· 7:184a
Titsingh, Izaak ·········· 5:313a; 8:30a
　works ·············· 8:30a
Toad lily ·············· 3:237b
Tōa Dōbunkai 東亜同文会 ·············· 8:30a
　Konoe Atsumaro ·············· 4:272b
Tōa Domestic Airlines Co, Ltd · 8:30a-30b
Tōagōsei Chemical Industry Co, Ltd
　·············· 8:30b
Tōa Nenryō Kōgyō ·········· 6:181b; 8:30b
Tōa Remmei ····· 東亜連盟 ·············· 8:30b
Tōa Shinchitsujo
　·············· 東亜新秩序 ··· 8:30b-31a
　international relations ·············· 3:321b
Tōa Washinkai 東亜和親会 ·············· 8:31a
Toba, Emperor ··· 鳥羽天皇 ·············· 8:31a
　Sanuki no Suke no nikki ·············· 7:18b
Toba ·············· 鳥羽 ·· 7:13a; 8:31a
　Kakuban ·············· 4:118a
　Sanzen'in ·············· 7:20a
Tobacco ·············· 8:31a
Tobacco production ·············· 1:27b
Toba-Fushimi, Battle of
　鳥羽伏見の戦 ·1:165a; 8:31b
Tōbaku no mitchoku
　·············· 討幕の密勅 ·············· 8:31b
Toba Sōjō ·············· 鳥羽僧正 ·· 2:199a-199b;
　8:31b-32a
　Chōjū giga ·············· 1:299a
Tobe ·············· 砥部 ·············· 8:32a
Tobera [(tobira)
　Pittosporum tobira]
　·············· 8:32a-32b
Tobi ·············· 4:229b
Tobiganna ("jumping trimming tool")
　·············· 1:264b
Tobira ·············· 8:32a-32b
Tobishima ·············· 飛島 ·············· 8:32b
Tobishima Corporation ·············· 8:32b
Tobiume senku ·············· 飛梅千句 ·············· 1:73b
Tōbōsaku ·············· 東方朔 ·············· 5:295b
Tōbu Railway Co, Ltd ·············· 8:32b-33a
Tochigi ·············· 栃木 ·············· 8:33a
Tochigi Prefecture · 栃木県 ·············· 8:33a
Tōchigyō (de facto rights)
　·············· 当知行 ·············· 1:274a
Tochinoki ·············· 3:228b-229a
Tochio ·············· 栃尾 ·· 8:33a-33b
Toda ·············· 戸田 ·············· 8:33b
Toda Construction Co, Ltd ·············· 8:33b
Tōdaiji ·············· 東大寺 1:182a; 4:368a;
　5:332a; 6:*106b*; 7:16b, 277a; 8:33b-34b
　construction ·············· 2:327a
　daibutsuden (great Buddha hall) · 8:*33a*
　　Taira no Shigehira ·············· 7:302a
　education ·············· 2:172a
　Ganjin ·············· 3:7b
　gates ·············· 3:12b
　Kaikei ·············· 4:111a
　Kegon sect ·············· 4:186b
　Rōben ·············· 6:333a

Shintō ·············· 7:127a
Shōsōin location ·············· 2:371a
Taira-Minamoto War ·············· 7:299b
Takaoka ·············· 7:317b
tea ceremony kō ·········· 7:360a-365a
Tōdaiji fujumon kō
　·············· 東大寺諷誦文稿 ·············· 4:132b
Toda Jōsei ·············· 戸田城聖 ·············· 8:34b
Toda Mosui ·············· 戸田茂睡 ·············· 8:34b
"Toda of the Rice Bale" ·············· 5:296b
Toda Teizō ·············· 戸田貞三 ·············· 8:34b
　works ·············· 8:34b
Tōdatsu kikō (Record of
　Travels among the
　Eastern Tartars)東韃紀行 ·············· 8:242b
Tōde ·············· 4:158b
Todoroki Falls ·等々力の滝 ·············· 8:34b
Tōdō Takatora ·· 藤堂高虎 ·· 7:56b;
　8:34b-35a
Tōei ·············· 塔影 ·············· 4:179b
Tōei Co, Ltd ·········· 2:272a, 273a-273b,
　274b, 359b; 8:35a
　Mahiru no ankoku ·············· 5:83b
　Takakura Ken ·············· 7:314a
　Uchida Tomu ·············· 8:124a
Tōfu ·············· 豆腐 ·· 2:21b, 305a,
　306a; 7:239a; 8:35a
Tōfukuji ·············· 東福寺 ·· 1:183a; 7:80b;
　8:35a-35b
Tōfutsu, Lake ·············· 濤沸湖 ·············· 8:35b
Tōgaku ·············· 唐楽 ·············· 3:1a
　composition categories ·············· 3:2b
Tōgaku no Ran · 東学の乱 ·············· 8:74b
Togakushi Kōgen
　·············· 戸隠高原 ·············· 8:35b
Togakushiyama ·· 戸隠山 ·············· 8:35b
Tōgane ·············· 東金 ·············· 8:35b
Tōgarashi ·············· 3:127b
Togariishi site · 尖石遺跡 ·············· 8:35b-36a
Togashi family ·············· 富樫氏 ·············· 8:36a
Tōgatta Hot Spring
　·············· 遠刈田温泉 ·············· 8:36a
Togawa Yūjirō · 戸川雄二郎 ·············· 4:207a
Tōgō Bakuryō Gakkō ·············· 4:69b
Tōgō Bakuryō Kaigi ·········· 4:69b-70a
Tōgō Heihachirō
　·············· 東郷平八郎 ·············· 1:87b;
　8:36a-36b
Tōgō Shigenori · 東郷茂徳 ·· 7:28a; 8:36b
Tōgyū. *See* **Bullfighting**
Tōhachiken ·············· 4:193a
Tōhaku. 等伯 ·············· *See* **Hasegawa Tōhaku**
Tōhata Seiichi ·············· 東畑精一 ·············· 8:36b
Tōhō Co, Ltd ·· 2:270b; 3:102b; 8:36b
Tōhō Gakuen School of Music ···· 8:36b
Tōhōkai ·············· 東方会 ·· 5:316a-316b;
　8:37a
Tōhō Kaigi ·············· 東方会議 ·············· 8:37a
　Yamamoto Jōtarō ·············· 8:298b
Tōhoku Electric Power Co, Inc ···· 8:37a
Tōhoku region ··· 東北地方 ·············· 4:153b;
　8:37a-37b
Tōhoku University ·············· 8:37b
Tōhō Rayon Co, Ltd ·············· 8:37b
Tōhō Strike ·········· 2:271b; 8:37b
　Watanabe Tetsuzō ·············· 8:236b
Tōhō Symphony ·············· 5:287a
Tōhō Zinc Co, Ltd ·············· 8:37b-38a
Toi ·············· 刀伊 ·············· 8:38a
Toilet training ·············· 4:38a-38b
Toimaru ·············· 問丸 ·4:122b; 8:38a
Toimisaki ·············· 都井岬 ·············· 8:38a
Toiya ·············· 問屋 ·············· 8:38a
　monopoly status ·············· 1:132b
Tōji (sake) ·············· 杜氏 ·············· 8:38a
Tōji (monastery-temple)
　·············· 東寺 ·· 2:375a;
　8:38b-39a;

construction ············ 2:327a
Kūkai's headquarters ········ 4:304a
sanjo ················ 7:12a
wooden sculpture ········ 1:198b-199a
Tōjimbō ········· 東尋坊 ···· 8:39a
Tōjin Okichi ····· 唐人お吉 ···· 8:39a
Harris, Townsend ·········· 3:104b
Tōji patriarch paintings ······· 6:227a
Tōji Treasure House 東寺宝物館 8:39a-39b
Tōjō Gimon ······ 東条義門 · 4:31b; 7:281a;
8:39b
Fujitani Nariakira ········· 2:346b
Tōjō Hideki ····· 東条英機 1:164b; 4:273a;
5:316a-316b; 7:92a; 8:39b-40a
Senjinkun ············· 7:65b
Tōjō Misao ······· 東条操 ·· 1:7a; 8:40a
works ··············· 8:40a
Tokachidake ········ 十勝岳 ···· 8:40a
Tokachigawa ········ 十勝川 ···· 8:40a
Tokachi Plain ······ 十勝平野 ··· 8:40a
Tokage [(lizard) *Eumeces latiscutatus*]
··················· 8:40a
Tōkai (city) ········· 東海 ···· 8:40b
Tōkai (village) ······· 東海 ···· 8:40b
Tōkai Bank, Ltd. ············ 8:40b
Tōkaidō ·········· 東海道 ·· 3:40a-41a,
86b; 6:229b; 8:40b-41b
development ············ 8:40b
dialects ·············· 2:92a
history ··············· 8:40b
railways ············· 6:278a
Shinkansen ············ 7:116b
stages ··············· 8:41a
today ················ 8:41b
travel ················ 8:41a
travel diary ············ 4:108b
travelers ·············· 8:41b
urban life ············· 8:177b
Tōkaidō bunken ezu
·············· 東海道分間絵図 ··· 8:41b
Tōkaidōchū hizakurige (Shank's Mare)
東海道中膝栗毛
·············· 4:61a-61b, 256a; 8:104a
Tōkaidō gojūsantsugi (Fifty-three
Stations of the Tōkaidō)
·············· 東海道五十三次 ·· 3:148b
Tōkaidō megalopolis ········· 8:41b
Gokaidō ············· 3:40b-41a
Tōkaidō Yotsuya kaidan
············ 東海道四谷怪談 ···· 8:41b-42a
Tōkai Sanshi ····· 東海散士 ···· 8:42a
seiji shōsetsu ·········· 7:50a
works ··············· 8:42a
Tōkai Shizen Hodō
··············· 東海自然歩道 ··· 8:42a
Tōkai University ············ 8:42a
Tōkamachi ········ 十日町 ··· 8:42a-42b
Tōkan kikō ······ 東関紀行 · 4:108b, 128b;
8:42b, 104b
Tokara Islands 吐噶喇列島 · 7:30b; 8:42b
Tōka zuiyō ········ 桃華蘂葉 ··· 8:42b
Tōkei ············· 1:333b-334a
Tōkeiji ·········· 東慶寺 · 4:115b, 120b;
5:133a; 8:42b
Tōkei Sūri Kenkyūjo ········· 7:246a
Toki ·············· 土岐 ····· 8:42b
Tokieda Motoki ·· 時枝誠記 · 7:281a;
8:42b-43a
Toki family ······· 土岐氏 ···· 8:43a
**Tokio Marine & Fire Insurance
Co, Ltd** ··············· 8:43a
Kagami Kenkichi ·········· 4:102b
Tokitsugu Kyō ki 時継卿記 ···· 8:43a-43b
Tokiwa Mitsunaga
··············· 常盤光長 ··· 1:137a
Tokiwasusuki ············· 7:279a
Tokiwazu-bushi · 常磐津節 · 2:301a; 4:99a;
8:43b

repertoire ············· 8:43b
Tokiwazu school ············ 4:91b
Toki Zemmaro ···· 土岐善麿 ··· 8:43b
Tōki zenshū ······· 陶器全集 ··· 4:168a
Tokkō ·········· 特高 · 7:241b-242a
Tokkōtai ·············· 4:127a
Toko ··············· 7:266a
Toko jepang ············· 7:235a
Tōkō kibun ········ 東航紀聞 ··· 4:369b
Tokoname ········· 常滑 ···· 8:43b
Tokoname ware ··· 常滑焼 · 8:43b-44a
Tokonami Takejirō
··············· 床次竹二郎 · 7:55a; 8:44a
Tokonoma ·············· 2:289a
decoration ············· 4:116a
Tokorogawa ······ 常呂川 ···· 8:44a
Tokorozawa ······ 所沢 ····· 8:44a
Tokoyo ············· 8:44a-44b
Tokto. See **Takeshima**
Toku ··············· 4:141b
Tokubetsu Kōtō Keisatsu
·············· 特別高等警察 · 7:241b-242a
Tokuda Kyūichi · 徳田球一 · 7:91b; 8:44b
Tokuda Shūsei · 徳田秋声 ··· 1:155b;
7:103b; 8:44b-45b
Ken'yūsha ············· 4:199a
works ··············· 8:45a
Tokugawa ········· 徳川 ···· 7:161a
shōgun ··············· 7:160b
Tokugawa Akitake
················ 徳川昭武 · 7:86a; 8:45b
French-Japanese relations ····· 2:331b
Tokugawa Art Museum ········ 5:276a
Tokugawa bakufu. 徳川幕府
See **Tokugawa shogunate**
Tokugawa family · 徳川氏 · 8:45b-47b
Matsudaira and Tokugawa names ·· 8:46a
origins ··············· 8:45b
shimpan ·············· 7:108a
shogunal line ·········· 8:47a
Tokugawa kinship group ······ 8:46b
Tokugawa Hidetada
·············· 徳川秀忠 · 7:9a, 64b;
8:47b
codes of conduct ········ 1:206b
daughter ·············· 8:51b
Furuta Oribe ··········· 2:373b
Saris, John ············· 7:22a
Sekigahara, Battle of ······ 7:56b
Tokugawa family ········ 8:47a
Tokugawa Ieyasu ······· 8:50b-51a
Tokugawa Ieharu 徳川家治 · 3:189a; 8:47b
Tokugawa Iemitsu
·············· 徳川家光 · 3:189a; 7:13b;
8:47b-48a
castle residences ········ 2:375a
codes of conduct ········ 1:207a
Hayashi Razan ·········· 3:117b
Kan'eiji ·············· 4:138a
local administration ······ 4:55a
sankin kōtai (alternate attendance)
system ·············· 7:14a
Tokugawa Iemochi
·············· 徳川家茂 ···· 8:48a
Chōshū Expeditions ······· 1:304a
Tokugawa Ienari · 徳川家斉 ···· 1:211a;
8:48a-48b
bakuhan state ·········· 3:189b
Tokugawa Ienobu
·············· 徳川家宣 ···· 8:48b
Tokugawa Iesada 徳川家定 ··· 8:47b
Tokugawa Iesato 徳川家達 ··· 8:48b
Tokugawa Ieshige
·············· 徳川家重 · 8:48b-49a
Tokugawa Ietsugu 徳川家継 ··· 8:47a
Tokugawa Ietsuna
·············· 徳川家綱 · 2:100a-100b;
8:49a

Tokugawa Ieyasu 徳川家康 ···· 1:11a, 83b,
151b, 156b, 193a; 7:8a, 14a, 25b, 64a, 65a,
84b, 98b, 101b, 102b, 255a, 256a, 270a,
274b; 8:49a-51a, 303a
background ············· 8:49a
China ················ 1:284b
codes of conduct ········ 1:206b
early career ············ 8:49b
Edo ················· 2:168b
Edo Castle ············· 2:170a
feudalism ············· 2:266a
Fuju Fuse sect ·········· 2:359b
Fukushima Masanori ······· 2:366b
Furuta Oribe ··········· 2:373b
Fushimi Castle residence ····· 2:375a
goningumi ············ 3:45a-45b
Hayashi Razan ·········· 3:117a
Ii Naomasa ············· 3:262b
imperial institution ········ 2:204a
Kanazawa Bunko ········· 4:136a
Kanō Tan'yū ··········· 8:49a
Kōfukuji revived ········· 4:244a
Komaki Nagakute Campaign ···· 4:265b
Korean relations ······ 4:276b, 279a
mausoleum ············ 4:154a
military practices ········ 2:279a
move to Edo ············ 8:50a
Nagashino, Battle of ······· 5:306b
Nagoya Castle ········ 5:309a-309b
paintings ·············· 4:151a
portrait ·············· 8:49a
post-station system ······· 2:188b
Sanada Yukimura ········· 7:9a
Saris, John ············· 7:22a
seal of ··············· 7:45b
Sekigahara, Battle of ······ 7:56b
shimpan ·············· 7:108a
shōgun ··············· 8:50b
Spain ················ 4:369a
vermilion seal ship trade ···· 8:190a
warrior government ······· 8:230a
Tokugawa Ieyoshi 徳川家慶 ··· 8:47b
Tokugawa jikki · 徳川実紀 ···· 8:51a
Tokugawa Kazuko
·············· 徳川和子 ·· 8:51b
Tokugawa Keiki. 徳川慶喜
See **Tokugawa Yoshinobu**
Tokugawa kinrei kō
·············· 徳川禁令考 ··· 8:51b
Tokugawa mission ·········· 7:335b
Tokugawa Mitsukuni
·············· 徳川光圀 · 1:76b; 2:65a;
8:51b-52a
Dai Nihon Shi ·········· 2:347a
historiography ·········· 3:154b
inscriptions ············ 3:314a
Kōrakuen Garden ········· 4:276a
Tokugawa Musei 徳川夢声 ··· 8:52a
Furukawa Roppa ········· 2:373a
Tokugawa Nariaki
·············· 徳川斉昭 ···· 8:52a
Fujita Tōko ············ 2:347a
Kairakuen ············· 4:112a
Tokugawa period 徳川時代 · 3:185b-192b
Tokugawa political system. *See*
Bakuhan system
Tokugawa shogunate
·············· 徳川幕府 · 7:8a-8b,
91a-91b; 8:52b-56a
achievement ·········· 8:55b-56a
administrative system ······ 8:55b
Bakuhan system ·········· 4:7a
Buddhism under ········· 7:234a
Chōsen tsūshinshi ········· 1:303b
codes of conduct ····· 1:206b-207a
collapse ·············· 4:122a
copper coins ············ 2:186b
copper mining ··········· 7:267a

decree concerning foreign ships · · · 7:125b
diplomacy · 7:220a
Edo · 2:168b
Edo city commissioners · · · · · · · · · 2:171a
emigration · 2:200b
erotic art · · · · · · · · · · · · · · · · · 7:187b–188a
feudalism · · · · · · · · · · · · · · · · · · 2:266a–267a
financial position · · · · · · · · · · · · 8:54b–55a
financial records · · · · · · · · · · · · · · · 7:263b
Gosanke · 3:47b
Gosankyō · 3:47b
government system · · · · · · · · · 7:164b–165a
highways · 4:108b
Ikeda Nagaoki · · · · · · · · · · · · · 3:265b–266a
imperial loyalism · · · · · · · · · · · 2:205a–205b
incident of bell inscription · · · · · · · 7:165b
Iwase Tadanari · · · · · · · · · · · · · · · · 3:363b
Kira Yoshinaka · · · · · · · · · · · · · · · · 4:220a
labor service under · · · · · · · · · · · · · 7:265a
military position · · · · · · · · · · · · · 8:54a–54b
missions from Korea · · · · · · · · · · · · 4:279a
Mito Civil War · · · · · · · · · · · · · 5:204b–205a
National Seclusion · · · · · · · · · 5:346b–347b
Naval forces during · · · · · · · · · · · · 7:263b
officials
ōmetsuke · 6:101a
rōjū · 6:334a
Sambugyō · 7:6a
wakadoshiyori · · · · · · · · · · · · · · · 8:217a
Ōoku · 6:113b–114a
Opening of Japan · · · · · · · · · · · · · · 6:114a
post-station towns · · · · · · · · · · · · · · 7:185a
powers · 8:53a–54a
prevention of cruelty to animals · · · 7:167a
religious inquisition · · · · · · · · · · · · 7:185b
responsibilities · · · · · · · · · · · · · 8:52b–53a
rice tax transport · · · · · · · · · · · · · · 4:112b
samurai retainers · · · · · · · · · · · 3:111a–112a
sankin kōtai (alternate attendance)
system · 7:14a
Shie Incident · · · · · · · · · · · · · · · · · · 7:89b
shimpan · 7:108a
shinden kaihatsu · · · · · · · · · · · · · · · 7:109b
social discrimination under · · · · · · · 7:209a
swordsmen · 7:124a
taxation · 7:109b
trade limitation regulations · · · · · · · 7:171a
trade with Southeast Asia · · · · · · · · 7:234b
yoriai · 8:338a

Tokugawa Tsunayoshi
· · · · · · · · · · · · · · · 徳川綱吉 · · · · · · · 7:270a;
8:56a–56b
Forty-Seven Rōnin Incident · · · · · · · 2:328a
Tokugawa family · · · · · · · · · · · · · · · 8:47a

Tokugawa Yoshimune
· · · · · · · · · · · · · · · 徳川吉宗 · · · · · · · 7:49b;
8:56b–57a
Kaitokudō patronage · · · · · · · · · · · · 4:113b
Kamo no Mabuchi · · · · · · · · · · · · · · 4:129b
Kyōhō Reforms · · · · · · · · · · · · · · · · 3:189a
Tokugawa family · · · · · · · · · · · · · · · 8:47a

Tokugawa Yoshinobu
· · · · · · · · · · 徳川慶喜 1:165a; 5:317b;
7:12b, 102a–102b; 8:57a–57b
Itakura Katsukiyo · · · · · · · · · · · · · · 3:350a
Tokugawa family · · · · · · · · · · · · · · · 8:47a
Tokuju · 8:57b–58a
Japanese economy · · · · · · · · · · · · · · 2:158a
Tokumi-doiya · · · · · 十組問屋 · · · · · 8:58a
kaisen management · · · · · · · · · · · · · 4:113a
monopolistic trade rights · · · · · · · · · 4:100a
Tokumitsukyō · · · · · · · · · 徳光教 · · 6:192b
Tokunaga Sunao · · · 徳永直 · 7:66b; 8:58a
proletarian literature movement · · · · 6:255b
Shin Nihon bungaku · · · · · · · · · · · · 7:122a
works · 8:58a
Tokunō · · · · · · · · · · · · · 篤農 · · · · · · 8:58a
Tokunoshima · · · · · · 徳之島 · · · · · · 8:58a

Tokura. *See* Dosō
Tokusei · · · · · · · · · 徳政 · · · · · · · · 8:58b
Tokusei edict · · · · · · · · · · · · · · · · · · 8:111b
Tokushima · · · · · · · · 徳島 · · · · · · · · 8:58b
Tokushima Plain 徳島平野 · 8:58b–59a
Tokushima Prefecture
· · · · · · · · · · · · · · · · 徳島県 · · · · · · · 8:59a
Tokushi yoron (Views of
History) · · · · · · · · · 読史余論 2:102a; 3:155a
Tokushu kyōiku · · · · · · · · · · · · · · · · 7:241b
Tokushu Seikō Co · · · · · · · · · · · · · · · 2:56b
Tokusō · · · · · · · · · · 得宗 7:97b; 8:59a–59b
Tokutomi Iichirō. 徳富猪一郎
See **Tokutomi Sohō**
Tokutomi Roka · · · · 徳富蘆花 1:155a; 7:103b;
8:59b–60a
Tokutomi Sohō · · · 徳富蘇峰 · · · · · 8:60a–60b
books · 8:60a
Kokumin no tomo founder · · · · · · · · 4:261a
Kokumin shimbun founder · · · · · · · · 4:261a
Tokuyama · · · · · · · · · 徳山 · · · · · · · · 8:60b
Tokuyama Soda Co, Ltd · · · · · · · · 8:60b
Tōkyō · · · · · · · · · · · · · 東京 · · · · 8:60b–66a
Asakusa Kannon (Sensōji) · · · · · · · · 8:*63a*
Azuma Ryūtarō (mayor) · · · · · · · · · 1:127b
business and entertainment center · 7:116a
cultural and recreational facilities · · 8:63b
media · 8:63b
parks and sports facilities · · · · · · · 8:63b
daily life · 8:63b
entertainment areas · · · · · · · · · 2:237a–237b
fauna and flora · · · · · · · · · · · · · · · · 8:61a
finance · 8:62a
Ginza · 8:*63a*
history · 8:61b
Imperial Palace · · · · · · · · · · · · · · · 8:*61a*
Kasumigaseki · · · · · · · · · · · · · · · · · 8:*62b*
Lake Oku Tama · · · · · · · · · · · · · · · 8:*62b*
local and traditional industry · · · 8:61b–62a
metropolitan area · · · · · · · · · · · · · · · 4:7a
modern industry · · · · · · · · · · · · · · · 8:62a
natural features · · · · · · · · · · · · · · · · 8:61a
points of interest · · · · · · · · · · · · 8:63b–66a
public institutions and services · 8:63a–63b
educational services · · · · · · · · · · · 8:63b
health services · · · · · · · · · · · · · · · 8:63a
police and fire departments · · · · · · 8:63a
utilities · 8:63a
transportation · · · · · · · · · · · · · · 8:62b–63a
urban planning · · · · · · · · · · · · · · · 8:180a
wards
Adachi · 1:11a
Arakawa · 1:73b
Bunkyō · 1:212a
Chiyoda · 1:298a
Chūō · 1:313b
Edogawa · 2:171a
Itabashi · 3:349a
Katsushika · · · · · · · · · · · · · · · · · · 4:174b
Kita · 4:229a
Kōtō · 4:298a
Meguro · 5:152a
Minato · 5:183b
Nakano · 5:317a
Nerima · 5:361b
Ōta · 6:129b
Setagaya · · · · · · · · · · · · · · · · · · 7:70b–71a
Shibuya · 7:87a
Shinagawa · · · · · · · · · · · · · · · · · · 7:108b
Shinjuku · 7:116a
Suginami · 7:258a
Sumida · 7:266b
Taitō · 7:306a
Toshima · · · · · · · · · · · · · · · · · · 8:83a–83b
See also **Edo**
Tōkyō Archaeological Society · · · · · 1:77b;
5:250b

Tōkyō Astronomical Observatory
· · · · · · · · · · · · · · · · · · 1:104b; 6:305b
discoveries · · · · · · · · · · · · · · · · · · · 1:104b
movement to Mitaka · · · · · · · · · · · · 1:104b
photographs · · · · · · · · · · · · · · · · · · 1:104b
Tōkyō Bay · · · · · · · · · 東京湾 · · · · · 8:66a
Tōkyō Bijutsu Gakkō · · · · · · · · · · 8:327b
Tōkyō Biological Society · · · · · · · 8:320a
Tōkyō Botanical Society · · · · · · · 8:320a
**Tōkyō Broadcasting System,
Inc (TBS)** · · · · · · · · · · 1:173b, 311a; 8:66a
Tōkyō Chemical Society · · · · · · · 1:268a
Tōkyō Cuban Boys · · · · · · · · · · · 6:355a
Tōkyō Daigaku Shiryō Hensanjo · 3:152a
Tōkyō Daigaku Tōyō Bunka Kenkyūjo
· 3:315b
Tōkyō Denki Kagaku Kōgyō. *See* **TDK
Corporation**
Tōkyō Earthquake of 1923 · 2:*139a*; 7:80a;
8:61b, 66a–66b
dams · 2:72b
economic impact · · · · · · · · · · · 3:199b–200a
Financial Crisis of 1927 · · · · · · · · · 2:277a
Kameido Incident · · · · · · · · · · · · · · 4:125a
magnitude · · · · · · · · · · · · · · · · 2:138b–139a
political oppression following · · · · · · 4:183a
prediction · 2:141a
transportation · · · · · · · · · · · · · · · · · 8:98b
Tōkyō Education Museum · · · · · · · 8:320a
Tōkyō Electric Power Co, Inc · · · · 1:311a;
4:151b, 153a, 205b; 8:66b–67a
Tōkyō Gas Co, Ltd · · · · · · · · · · · · 8:67a
Tōkyō Geographical Society · · · · · 8:67a
Kiuchi Shinzō · · · · · · · · · · · · · · · · · 4:231b
**Tōkyō Higher Normal School (Tōkyō
Kōtō Shihan Gakkō)** · · · · · · · · · · 8:327b
Tōkyō Hōsō. *See* **Tōkyō Broadcasting
System, Inc. (TBS)**
Tōkyō Imperial Household Museum
· 7:312a
Tōkyō Imperial University · · · · · · · · 3:281a
Tōkyō Institute of Hygienic Sciences of
the Home Ministry · · · · · · · · · · · · 7:351b
Tōkyō Institute of Technology · · · · 8:67a
Taniguchi Yoshirō · · · · · · · · · · · · · · 7:341b
Tōkyō International Airport (Haneda)
· · · · · · · · · · · · · · 1:37b; 5:370a–371b
Tōkyō Joigakkō (Tōkyō Women's
Medical School) · · · · · · · · · 8:267b, 349b
Tōkyō Kawa Kai
· · · · · · · · · · · · · · · · 東京歌話会 · · · · 5:19b
Tōkyō keizai zasshi
· · · · · · · · · · · · · 東京経済雑誌 · · · · · 7:294b
Tōkyō Kokuritsu Bunkazai Kenkyūjo.
See **Tōkyō National Research Institute
of Cultural Properties**
Tōkyō Kokuritsu Hakubutsukan. *See*
Tōkyō National Museum
Tōkyō Kokuritsu Kindai Bijutsukan
· 5:344a–344b
Tōkyō Laboratory of Hygienic Sciences
· 6:305b
Tōkyō mainichi shimbun
· · · · · · · · · · 東京毎日新聞 · · · · · · 8:330b
Tōkyō Mathematical Society (Tōkyō
Sūgakusha) · · · · · · · · · · · · · · · · · · 5:130b
Tōkyō Meteorological Observatory 6:305b
**Tōkyō Metropolitan Archives and
Records Institute** · · · · · · · · · · · · · 8:67b
publications · · · · · · · · · · · · · · · · · · 8:67b
Tōkyō Metropolitan Area · · · · · · · · 8:67b
Tōkyō Metropolitan Art Museum · 5:279a
Tōkyō Metropolitan Hibiya Library 8:67b
Tōkyō Metropolitan Police Department
· · · · · · · · · · · · · · · · · · 6:198a; 8:67b–68a
**Tōkyō Metropolitan Police Ordinance
of 1953** · 8:171a

Tōkyō monogatari
··········· 東京物語 **2**:277*a*; **3**:102*b*;
6:141*b*
Tōkyō Municipal Ordinance in 1888
········· **8**:180*a*
Tōkyō Music School ·········· **5**:286*a*
Tōkyō National Museum · **5**:276*a*; **8**:68*a*
Takami Senseki ·········· **7**:315*b*
Tōkyō National Museum of Modern Art
·········· **5**:279*a*; **7**:341*b*
**Tōkyō National Research Institute of
Cultural Properties** ········· **8**:68*a*-68*b*
Tōkyō Naval Hospital ·········· **7**:311*a*
Tōkyō nichinichi shimbun
············· 東京日日新聞 ······ **4**:170*a*
Tōkyō Olympic Games ··········· **8**:68*b*
Tōkyō ordinance decision ········· **8**:68*b*
judicial review ··········· **4**:80*a*
Tōkyō Philharmonic Society ······ **5**:286*b*
Tōkyō Police Department, Riot Police
·········· **6**:320*a*
Tōkyō Rose ··· 東京ローズ ·· **8**:68*b*-69*a*
D'Aquino, Iva Ikuko Toguri ···· **4**:15*a*
Tōkyō San'yō Electric Co, Ltd ···· **8**:69*a*
Tōkyō Semmon Gakkō ·········· **7**:311*b*
Tōkyō Shibaura Electric ·········· **3**:347*a*
Tōkyō shimbun · 東京新聞 ········· **8**:69*a*
Kokumin shimbun and *Miyako shimbun*
merger formed ·········· **4**:261*a*
Tōkyō Shiryō Collection ·········· **8**:67*b*
Tōkyō station ·········· **7**:349*b*
Tōkyō Steel Mfg Co, Ltd ·········· **8**:69*a*
Tōkyō Stock Exchange ·········· **7**:294*b*
Tōkyō Symphony Orchestra · **5**:286*b*-287*a*
Tōkyō Tower ·········· **8**:69*a*
Tōkyō Trial ·········· **8**:224*a*
Tōkyō University ·········· **8**:69*a*-69*b*, 170*a*
entrance examinations ········· **2**:222*a*
Hiraga Yuzuru ·········· **3**:142*a*
Historiographical Institute ········· **3**:152*a*
modern philosophy ·········· **5**:229*a*
research and development ··· **6**:303*a*-305*b*
Tatsuno Kingo ·········· **7**:349*b*
university upheavals of 1968-1969 · **8**:171*b*
Tōkyō University of Education ······ **8**:69*b*
Tōkyō University of Fine Arts and Music
·········· **7**:43*b*; **8**:69*b*, 294*b*, 327*b*
Tōkyō University of Foreign Studies
·········· **8**:69*b*
Tōkyō University of Science and
Literature ·········· **2**:179*a*
Tōkyō War Crimes Trial. *See* **War
crimes trials**
Tōkyō Women's Christian University
·········· **8**:69*b*
Tōkyō Women's Higher Normal School ·
7:315*a*-315*b*
Tōkyō Women's Medical School · **8**:267*b*,
349*b*
*Tōkyō-Yokohama mainichi
shimbun*
··········· 東京横浜毎日新聞 ······· **8**:330*a*
Tōkyū Car Corporation ·········· **8**:69*b*
Tōkyū Construction Co, Ltd ········ **8**:70*a*
Tōkyū Corporation ·········· **4**:188*b*; **8**:70*a*
Gotō Keita ·········· **3**:53*a*
major companies ·········· **8**:70*a*
Tōkyū Land Corporation ······ **8**:70*a*-70*b*
Tōkyū Department Store Co, Ltd · **8**:70*a*
Tōkyū group
Tōkyū Car Corporation ·········· **8**:69*b*
Tōkyū Construction Co, Ltd ······ **8**:70*a*
Tōkyū Corporation ·········· **8**:70*a*
Tōkyū Department Store Co, Ltd · **8**:70*a*
Tōkyū Land Corporation ······ **8**:70*a*-70*b*
Tōkyū Land Corporation ······ **8**:70*a*-70*b*
Tolerance in Japanese religion
·········· **7**:288*b*-290*b*; **8**:70*b*

Tolls ·········· **7**:57*a*
Tomabechi case ·········· **4**:79*b*
Tomakomai ··· 苫小牧 ·········· **8**:70*b*
Tomari Incident ···· 泊事件 ······ **8**:330*a*
Tomaso de Santo Domingo ····· **2**:330*a*
Tomato Kechappu Kōtei (Emperor
Tomato Ketchup)
···· トマトケチャップ皇帝 ······ **8**:13*a*
Tomb mounds ·········· **4**:244*a*-246*a*
decorations ·········· **3**:97*b*-98*a*
Hayatozuka ·········· **3**:118*b*
ornamented ·········· **1**:77*b*
protohistoric
excavations ·········· **1**:78*b*
dating ·········· **1**:77*b*-78*a*
Tombo ·········· **2**:133*b*
Tomb period. *See* **Kofun period**
Tombs
ornamented ·········· **6**:119*a*-119*b*
tunnel ·········· **8**:329*b*
Tomeyama ······ 留山 ······ **8**:70*b*-71*a*
Tomii Masaaki · 富井政章 ·· **7**:88*a*; **8**:71*a*
Tōmi Kemi ···· 遠見検見 ·········· **4**:191*b*
Tomikuji ······ 富籤 ·········· **8**:71*a*
Tomimoto Kenkichi
············· 富本憲吉 ·········· **2**:294*a*;
8:71*a*-71*b*
Tominaga Nakamoto
············· 富永仲基 ·········· **8**:71*b*
Tomioka ······ 富岡 ········· **8**:71*b*-72*a*
Tomioka Kenzō · 富岡謙蔵 ·········· **1**:77*a*
Tomioka Silk-Reeling Mill
············· 富岡製糸所 ··· **7**:86*a*; **8**:72*a*
Ichiyōsai Kuniteru ·········· **8**:71*a*
Tomioka Tessai · 富岡鉄斎 ·········· **1**:211*a*;
8:72*a*-73*a*, 72*b*
earliest paintings ·········· **8**:72*a*
works ·········· **8**:72*a*
Tomita Keisen 富田渓仙 ·········· **8**:73*a*
Tomita Tsuneo 富田常雄 ·········· **8**:73*a*
works ·········· **8**:73*a*
Tōmitsu ······ 東密 ·········· **2**:231*b*
Tomo ········· 伴 **1**:147*b*; **8**:131*b*
Tomobe ······ 伴部 ·········· **1**:147*b*
Tomodachi ······ 友達 ·········· **1**:3*b*
Tomoe ········· 巴 ·········· **8**:73*a*
Tomoe Gozen ······ 巴御前 ······· **8**:73*a*
Tomoko Dōmei (Friend's
League) ······ 友子同盟 ······ **8**:270*a*
Tomonaga Shin'ichirō
············· 朝永振一郎 ·········· **8**:73*a*
publications ·········· **8**:73*a*
Tōmon jissaku 答問十策 ······ **4**:101*b*
Tomo no Dainagon
ekotoba ···· 伴大納言絵詞 ······ **1**:137*a*
Tomo no Kowamine. 伴健岑
See **Jōwa Conspiracy**
Tomo no miyatsuko · 伴造 · **1**:147*b*; **8**:73*b*
uji-kabane system ·········· **8**:134*a*
Tomo no o ········· 伴の男 ···· **1**:147*b*
Tomo no Yoshio. 伴善男
See **Ōtemmon Conspiracy**
Tomura daikan ·· 十村代官 ······ **4**:112*a*
Tomuragumi ···· 十村組 ······ **4**:112*a*
Ton'a ········· 頓阿 ·········· **8**:73*a*
Kokin denju ·········· **4**:254*a*
writings ·········· **8**:73*a*
Tonami ······ 砺波 ·········· **8**:73*b*
Tonami Plain · 砺波平野 ······ **8**:73*b*
Tonarigumi · **3**:202*a*; **4**:308*a*; **5**:359*b*; **8**:74*a*
National Spiritual Mobilization
Movement ·········· **5**:348*a*
women in ·········· **8**:261*a*
Tonarigusa ······ 鄰艸 ·········· **4**:168*a*
Tondabayashi · 富田林 ·········· **8**:74*a*
Tondenhei ···· 屯田兵 · **4**:113*a*; **8**:74*a*
Tondenhei settlement
············· 屯田兵村 ·········· **1**:92*b*

Tonegawa ······ 利根川 · **4**:153*b*; **8**:74*a*
Tonegawa zushi
············· 利根川図志 ······ **8**:74*a*-74*b*
Toneri, Prince · 舎人親王 ······· **8**:74*b*
Toneri ······ 舎人 · **1**:147*b*; **8**:74*b*
ritsuryō system ·········· **6**:326*a*
Toneribe ······ 舎人部 ······ **1**:147*b*
Tong'a ilbo ·········· **4**:283*b*; **6**:159*b*
Tonghak Rebellion ·········· **8**:74*b*
Tongue twisters ·········· **8**:269*b*
Ton'ishō ······ 頓医抄 ······ **4**:114*b*
Tōno ······ 遠野 ·········· **8**:75*a*
Tōnomine ······ 多武峰 ·········· **8**:75*a*
Tōno monogatari 遠野物語 · **4**:275*b*; **8**:75*a*,
315*a*
Tonomura Shigeru · 外村繁 ······ **8**:75*a*
trilogy ·········· **8**:75*a*
works ·········· **8**:75*a*
Tonoshō ······ 土庄 ·········· **8**:75*a*
Tō no Tsuneyori · 東常縁 ······ **8**:75*a*-75*b*
Kokin denju ·········· **4**:254*a*
Ton'ya. *See* Toiya
Tō on ·········· **8**:75*b*
on readings ·········· **6**:112*b*
Tooth blackening (ohaguro; kane) · **2**:38*a*
Topaz Relocation Center ······ **8**:75*b*-76*a*
Top Food (brand name) ·········· **8**:85*a*
Toppan Printing Co, Ltd ·········· **8**:76*a*
Tops ·········· **1**:149*b*; **8**:76*a*
Topy Industries, Ltd ·········· **8**:76*a*
Toraijin. *See* **Kikajin**
Tōrai Sanna ····· 唐来参和 ······ **4**:201*b*
Torampu ·········· **6**:192*a*
Toranomon Incident
············· 虎ノ門事件 ··· **8**:76*a*-76*b*,
297*b*
Tora San ······ 寅さん ······ **8**:290*a*
Tōray Industries, Inc ·········· **8**:76*b*-77*a*
Torch Festival ·········· **4**:311*b*
Toride ······ 取手 ·········· **8**:77*a*
Torii ······ 鳥居 ·········· **8**:77*a*-77*b*
Itsukushima Shrine ·········· **3**:357*a*
Torii ga keifu · 鳥居画系譜 ······ **8**:79*b*
Torii Kiyohiro · 鳥居清広 ······ **8**:77*b*
Torii Kiyomasu I
············· 鳥居清倍(初代) ··· **8**:77*b*-78*a*,
140*a*
Torii Kiyomasu II
············· 鳥居清倍(二代) ······ **8**:78*a*
Torii Kiyomitsu I
············· 鳥居清満(初代) ······ **8**:78*a*
Torii Kiyonaga · 鳥居清長 · **8**:78*a*-78*b*,
142*a*
Torii Kiyonobu I
············· 鳥居清信(初代) ···· **8**:78*b*-79*a*
Torii Kiyonobu II
············· 鳥居清信(二代) ······ **8**:79*a*
Torii Pass ······ 鳥居峠 ······ **8**:79*a*
Torii Ryūzō ······ 鳥居龍蔵 ··· **1**:36*a*, 76*a*;
8:79*a*
research expeditions ·········· **8**:79*a*
treatises ·········· **8**:79*a*
Torii school ······ 鳥居派 · **8**:79*a*-79*b*,
139*b*, 140*a*
Torii Shinjirō · 鳥井信治郎 · **7**:276*a*; **8**:79*b*
Torii Sosen ···· 鳥居素川 ··· **8**:79*b*-80*a*
Torii Yōzō ······ 鳥居耀蔵 · **1**:141*b*; **8**:80*a*
Torikaebaya monogatari
············· とりかへばや物語 ······ **8**:80*a*
Torimono ·········· **4**:108*a*; **7**:79*b*
Torimonochō ·········· **2**:271*b*
Tori no ichi ········· 酉の市 · **8**:80*a*-80*b*
kumade ·········· **8**:80*b*
Torinomi Palisade, Battle
of ······ 鳥海柵の戦 ······ **1**:4*a*
Torishima ······ 鳥島 ·········· **8**:80*b*
Tōrō (lanterns) ·········· **4**:367*b*-368*a*
Tōrō nagashi ·········· **2**:261*a*

Toro site ········ 登呂遺跡 ·4:76a; 6:189a;
   8:80b
  excavation ··············· 1:78a
  rice cultivation ··········· 6:309a
  Shizuoka Municipal Toro Site Museum
   ··························· 7:153b
  tageta ····················· 7:294b
Tortoises. *See* Turtles
Tortoiseshell ware ········ 8:80b-81a
Torts ······················· 8:81a
  government compensation ·· 3:54b-55b
Torture, ritsuryō system ····· 6:327a
Tōryō okuri ·················· 4:195a
Tosa ··············· 土佐 ···· 8:81a
Tosa Bay ········· 土佐湾 ···· 8:81a
Tosa Diary, The ············· 6:2a
Tosa dog ·················· 8:81a-81b
Tosa Hirokane ··· 土佐広周 ··· 4:128b
Tosaka Jun ····· 戸坂潤 ·5:231b; 8:81b
Tosa Kinnōtō ··土佐勤王党··· 7:321b
Tosa Memorial of January 1874 ··· 2:234b
Tosa Mitsunobu ·土佐光信 2:200a; 6:153b
Tosa Mitsuoki ···土佐光起 ··· 5:268b
Tosa mizuki [(flowering hazel)
  Corylopsis spicata] ······· 8:81b
Tosa nikki ······· 土佐日記 1:154a; 4:133b;
   5:32a-32b; 6:2a; 8:104b
  Kino Tsurayuki ········· 4:216b-217a
Tōsanjō Palace ·············· 7:110b
Tosa school ······· 土佐派 ··· 1:210b;
  2:360b; 6:150b, 153b, 227b; 7:43a, 270a;
   8:81b-82a
Tosa Shimizu ····土佐清水·· 8:82a-82b
Tōsei ·················· 桃青··· 1:144a
Tōseiha ··········· 統制派··· 8:82b
  Kōdōha's rivalry with ····· 4:243a
  Nagata Tetsuzan ········· 5:307a
Tōsei shōnin katagi
   ········· 当世商人気質 ····· 1:18a
Tōsei shosei katagi
   ········· 当世書生気質 ··· 8:110b
Tōshiba Corporation ······· 2:317a; 8:82b
  Dokō Toshio ·············· 2:127b
  Tōshin Steel Co, Ltd ······· 8:83b
Tōshiba Machine Co, Ltd ·· 8:82b
Toshigami ··········· 2:299a; 8:83a
Tōshi kaden ···· 藤氏家伝··· 8:83a
Toshima ············· 利島··· 8:83a
Toshima Ward ···· 豊島区·· 8:83a-83b
Tōshin Denki Co ············· 7:173a
Toshi no ichi (year-end fair) 歳の市
   ········· 2:262a; 8:322b-323a
Tōshin Steel Co, Ltd ········ 8:83b
Tōshin Tetsudō ·· 東清鉄道·· 1:292a-292b
Tōshiya ····················· 7:13a-13b
Toshiyori ········ 年寄·4:160a; 8:83b
  rōjū ······················· 6:334a
Tōshōdaiji ······· 唐招提寺··· 1:182a;
   8:83b-84b
  establishment ············· 5:332a
  Ganjin ····················· 3:7a
  kondō (main hall) ········· 8:83a
  Ritsu sect ················· 6:332a
  Tankai ···················· 7:343a
Tōshōgū ········· 東照宮 ·2:376a; 8:84b
  paintings ·················· 4:151a
  "shogun art" ·············· 7:351a-351b
  Yōmeimon gate ··········· 8:84b
Tōshōgū engi ·東照宮縁起 4:151a; 7:270a
Tōshōgū engi emaki
   ········· 東照宮縁起絵巻 ··· 4:149b
Toshokan zasshi
   ········· 図書館雑誌 ······ 5:1b
Tōshoku, Ltd ················ 8:85a
Tōshūsai Sharaku. 東洲斎写楽
  See **Sharaku**
Tōson Memorial Hall 藤村記念堂 7:341b
Tosu ··············· 鳥栖··· 8:85a

Tōsuiken ········· 統帥権 ···· 8:85a
Tō Teikan ········· 藤貞幹 ·· 1:75b, 79a
Totei seido ·················· 1:71a-71b
Totoki Baigai ··· 十時梅崖 ·1:211a; 8:85b
Tōtō, Ltd ····················· 8:85b
*Tōto shōkei ichiran (Fine
  Views of the Eastern
  Capital of a Glance)*
   ········· 東都勝景一覧 ···· 8:143b
Totoya Hokkei ··· 魚屋北渓 ··· 8:85b
Tōtsubaki (*Camellia reticulata*) ·1:237a
Totsukawa (village) 十津川 ··· 8:85b
Totsukawa (river) ··十津川 ··· 8:85b
Tottori (city) ········ 鳥取··· 8:85b-86a
Tottori Plain ···· 鳥取平野··· 8:86a
Tottori Prefecture ·鳥取県··· 8:86a-86b
Tottori Sand Dunes
   ········· 鳥取砂丘 ····· 8:86b, 87a
Towada (city) ····· 十和田··· 8:86b
Towada, Lake ···十和田湖··· 8:87a
**Towada-Hachimantai
  National Park**
   十和田八幡平国立公園 ···· 1:43a;
   8:86b
Towazugatari ·問はず語り··· 7:21b;
   8:87a-87b
Townhouses ················· 5:193b
Town meetings (yoriari) ····· 8:338a
Towns and villages, consolidation of
   ···························· 8:87b
Towns and Villages Annexation
  Promotion Law of 1953 ···· 4:7b
Towns and Villages Consolidation
  Promotion Law (Chōson Gappei
  Sokushin Hō) of 1953 ····· 8:87b
Townsmen ·········· 1:300b-302b
Toxicology, medical research ·· 5:152b
Tōya ······················ 5:221a
Tōya, Lake ······· 洞爺湖··· 8:87b
Toyama ··········· 富山··· 8:87b
Toyama Bay ····· 富山湾··· 8:88a
Toyama Kametarō
   ········· 外山亀太郎 ·· 1:156a; 8:88a
Tōyama Kinshirō
   ········· 遠山金四郎 ···· 8:88a
Toyama Masakazu
   ········· 外山正一 ······ 8:88a
Tōyama Mitsuru ··· 頭山満 ·1:164a; 3:24b;
   4:340a; 7:276b; 8:88a-88b
Toyama Plain ···· 富山平野··· 8:88b
Toyama Prefecture 富山県··· 8:88b-89a
Tōya maru Disaster
   ········· 洞爺丸事件 ·· 8:89a, 122a
Tōyashū kikigaki
   ········· 東野州聞書 ···· 8:75b
Tōyo ·················· 東予··· 8:89a
Toyoake ············ 豊明··· 8:89a
Tōyō Aluminium ········· 8:89a-89b
Tōyōbō, Brazil ············· 8:89b
Tōyōbō Co, Ltd ············· 8:89b
  Tōyō Rubber Industry Co, Ltd ·· 8:94a
Tōyō Bunko ······· 7:50b; 8:89b-90a
Toyoda Automatic Loom Works, Ltd
   ········· 1:33a-33b; 8:90a
  Ishida Taizō ·············· 3:340b
  Toyoda Tsūshō Kaisha, Ltd ·· 8:90b
  Toyota Motor Co, Ltd ····· 8:93b
Toyoda Sakichi ·豊田佐吉··· 8:90a
Toyoda Shirō ···豊田四郎··· 2:270b;
   7:102b; 8:90a-90b
  films ····················· 8:90b
Toyoda Tsūshō Kaisha, Ltd ·· 8:90b
Toyogawa Canal ··········· 8:90b
Toyohashi ········ 豊橋··· 8:90b
Tōyō Ink Mfg Co, Ltd ······· 8:90b-91a

*Tōyōjin no shii hōhō (Ways of
  Thinking of Eastern Peoples:
  India, China, Tibet,
  Japan)* 東洋人の思惟方法 ··5:314b-315a
Tōyō Jiyūtō ···· 東洋自由党 ···· 8:91a
  Futsū Senkyo Kisei Dōmeikai ·· 2:376a
Tōyō kanji ······· 5:325a; 8:91a-91b
  ideographs ··············· 4:143b
*Tōyō kanji hyō (Table of Chinese
  Characters for Daily Use)* ·· 8:91a
Toyokawa ·········· 豊川··· 8:91b
Tōyō keizai shimpō
   ········· 東洋経済新報 ··· 1:50b;
   8:91b-92a
Tōyō Kōgyō Co, Ltd ········ 8:92a
  passenger car production ··· 1:122a
  rotary engine ············· 6:339b
Tōyō Kōhan Co, Ltd ········ 8:92a
  Tōyō Seikan Kaisha, Ltd ··· 8:92a
Toyokuni. 豊国 *See* **Utagawa Toyokuni**
*Toyokuni Toyohiro ryōga
  jūni kō (Illustrations of
  the Twelve Months)*
   ········· 豊国豊広両畫十二考 ··· 8:184b
Tōyō Menka Kaisha, Ltd ···· 8:92a
Toyonaka ········· 豊中··· 8:92a-92b
Toyooka ··········· 豊岡··· 8:92b
Tōyō Rayon ················ 7:347b
Toyosaka ········· 豊栄··· 8:92b
Tōyō Seikan Kaisha, Ltd ···· 8:92b
  Tōyō Kōhan Co, Ltd ······· 8:92a
Tōyō Shakaitō ·東洋社会党· 1:53b; 6:210b;
   8:92b
Toyoshima Yoshio
   ········· 豊島与志雄 ···· 8:92b
  translations ··············· 8:92b
Tōyō Soda Mfg Co, Ltd ···· 8:93a
Tōyō Suisan Kaisha, Ltd ···· 8:93a
Toyota ············· 豊田··· 8:93a
Toyota Auto Body Co, Ltd ·· 8:93a
  Toyota Motor Co, Ltd ····· 8:93b
Toyotake Wakatayū
   ········· 豊竹若太夫 ···· 4:77a
**Toyotake Yamashiro no
  Shōjō** ···· 豊竹山城少掾··· 8:93b
Tōyō Takushoku Kaisha ···· 8:93b
  historical context ········· 4:282a
Toyota Motor Co, Ltd
  Aishin Seiki Co, Ltd ······· 1:38a
  Daihatsu Motor Co, Ltd ···· 2:58b
  early automotive industry ··· 1:121b
  Ishida Taizō ·············· 3:340b
  Kantō Auto Works, Ltd affiliation ·· 4:153a
  Toyoda Automatic Loom Works, Ltd
   ···························· 8:90a
  Toyoda Sakichi ··········· 3:90a
  Toyoda Tsūshō Kaisha, Ltd ·· 8:90b
  Toyota Auto Body Co, Ltd ·· 8:93a
  unions ··················· 4:53b
Toyota Motor Corporation ·· 8:93b
Tōyō Tire and Rubber Industry Co., Ltd
   ···························· 8:93b-94a
Toyotomi Hidetsugu
   ········· 豊臣秀次 ·3:180b; 7:27b;
   8:94a
  Frois, Luis ··············· 2:340a
  kampaku ················· 4:130a
Toyotomi Hideyori
   ········· 豊臣秀頼 7:9a, 64b, 93b,
   274b; 8:94a
  Tokugawa Ieyasu ········· 8:50b-51a
Toyotomi Hideyoshi
   ········· 豊臣秀吉 ··· 1:83b, 126b,
   158a, 193a; 7:8a, 14a, 27b, 29b, 56b,
   64a-64b, 74a, 83b, 84b, 101b, 104a, 255a,
   266b, 274b; 8:94a-96a
  abolition of barrier stations ·· 7:57a
  administration official ····· 1:206a

anti-Christian edicts · · · · · · · · · · · 5:306a
China · 1:284a
chōnin · 1:301a
Christianity · · · · · · · · · · · · · · · · · · · 5:323a
corvée labor · · · · · · · · · · · · · · · · · · 1:226b
Dai Dembōin destruction · · · · · · · · 4:118a
Daigoji · 2:57a–58a
depiction in art · · · · · · · · · · · · · · · 2:377b
early years · 8:94b
Fabian · 2:241a
feudalism · 2:266a
final years · 8:95b
free markets · · · · · · · · · · · · · · · · · · 6:283a
Fuju Fuse sect · · · · · · · · · · · · · · · · 2:359b
Furuta Oribe · · · · · · · · · · · · · · · · · 2:373b
Fushimi Castle residence · · · · · · · · 2:375a
general under Nobunaga · · · · · · · · 4:256b
Imai Sōkyū · · · · · · · · · · · · · · · · · · · 3:273a
invasions of Korea in 1592 and
1597 · · · · · · · · · · · 3:326b–327b; 8:95b
Ishida Mitsunari · · · · · · · · · · · · · · 3:340a
Ishiyama Honganji · · · · · · · · · · · · · 3:347a
Kaihō Yūshō · · · · · · · · · · · · · · · · · · 4:110b
Kamiya Sōtan · · · · · · · · · · · · · · · · · 4:127b
kampaku · 4:130a
Kanemi kyō ki · · · · · · · · · · · · · · · · 4:139b
kenchi · 4:137a
kokudaka established · · · · · · · · · · · 4:257b
koku standardized · · · · · · · · · · · · · 4:256b
Komaki Nagakute Campaign · · · · · 4:265b
Korean invasions · · · · · · · · · · · · · · 4:276a
Kyūshū campaign · · · · · · · · · · · · · · 8:95a
Latin America · · · · · · · · · · · · · · · · · 4:369a
Luis Frois · 2:340a
military practices · · · · · · · · · · · · · · 2:279a
Nanzenji · 5:330a
nengu · 5:360b
Ōno Harunaga · · · · · · · · · · · · · · · · 6:110a
Ōsaka Castle · · · · · · · · · · · · 6:120a–120b
Ōsakajō kabegaki · · · · · · · · · · · · · · 4:90a
portrait · *8:94b*
Sanada Yukimura · · · · · · · · · · · · · · · 7:9a
San Felipe Incident (San Feripe go Jiken)
· 7:9b
Satake family · · · · · · · · · · · · · · · · · 7:25b
Sen no Rikyū · · · · · · · · · · · · · · · · · 7:67a
Seven Spears · · · · · · · · · · · · · · · · · 2:366b
Shimai Sōshitsu · · · · · · · · · · · · · 7:99a–99b
Shimazu Yoshihiro · · · · · · · · · · · · · 7:102b
Shinchō kō ki · · · · · · · · · · · · · · · · 7:109b
shi-nō-kō-shō · · · · · · · · · · · · · · · · · 7:122b
sword hunt · · · · · · · · · · · · · · · · · · · 7:284b
taking reins of power · · · · · · · · · · · 8:95a
Toyotomi Hidetsugu · · · · · · · · · · · 8:94a
vermilion seal ship trade · · · · · · · · 8:190a
warrior government · · · · · · · · · · · · · 8:230a
Tōyō Trust & Banking Co, Ltd · · · · · 8:96a
Toyouke Daijin · 豊受大神 · · · · · · · 3:338b
Toyouke no Ōkami 豊受大神 · · · · · · 8:236b
Ryōbu Shintō · · · · · · · · · · · · · · · · · 6:351a
Tōyō University · · · · · · · · · · · · · · 3:133a
Toys, traditional · · · · · · · · · · · 8:96a–96b
inu hariko · *8:96b*
materials used · · · · · · · · · · · · · · · · 8:96b
ohajiki · 6:73a
regional variations · · · · · · · · · · · · · 8:96b
tops (koma) · · · · · · · · · · · · · · · · · · 1:149b
Tōyūki · · · · · · · · · · · · · · 東遊記 · · · · · · · 8:106a
Tozama · · · · · · · · · · · · · · 外様 · · · · · 1:131b;
2:340b; 7:102a; 8:97a
Tōzumō · · · · · · · · · · · · 唐相撲 · · · · · · 4:326b
Track and field events · · · · · · 8:97a–97b
Trade. *See* **Foreign trade**
Trade associations (dōgyō kumiai)
· 1:66b; 2:32a
Trade controls · · · · · · · · · · · · · · · · 2:314b
Trade diversion episode · · · · · 1:116b–117a
Trademark Law · · · · · · · · · 6:164b; 8:97b

Trade name · · · · · · · · · · · · · · · · · · 8:97b
Trade secrets
"know-how" · · · · · · · · · · · · · · · · · 4:233b
protection · · · · · · · · · · · · · · · · · · 4:233b
Trade Union Law · · · · · · · · · · · · · · 4:346b
Trading companies
Itōman & Co, Ltd · · · · · · · · · · · · 3:355a
Toyoda Tsūshō Kaisha, Ltd · · · · · 8:90b
Tōyō Menka Kaisha, Ltd · · · · · · · · 8:92a
See also **General trading company**
Traditional Handcraft Products · · · · 1:261a
Traditional medicine · · · · · · · · 5:150b–151b
Training personnel · · · · · · · · · · · · · 2:318a
"Transcendental" cabinets · 6:241b; 8:97b
Transistors · · · · · · · · · · · · · · · · · · · 2:193b
Translation rights · · · · · · · · · · · · 8:98a
Translations
modern · 6:246a
publishing · · · · · · · · · · · · · · · · · · 6:268a
Transliterating, romanization of
Japanese · · · · · · · · · · · · · · · · · · 6:335b
Transmission of Dharma · · · · · · · · 7:114a
Transportation · · · · · · · · 4:336a; 8:98a–104a
and society · · · · · · · · · · · · · · · · · · 8:103a
coordination and control · · · · · · · 8:103a
new technology · · · · · · · · · · · · · 8:103b
safety · 8:103a
urban · 8:103a
history · 8:98a
Edo period · · · · · · · · · · · · · · · · · 4:108b
Heian period · · · · · · · · · · · · · · · · 4:108b
Kamakura period · · · · · · · · · · · · · 4:108b
Meiji period to World War II · · · · · 8:98b
postwar · 8:98b
postwar network · · · · · · · · · · · · · 8:99a
administration · · · · · · · · · · · · · · 8:99a
air · 8:102a
marine · 8:102a
motor vehicles · · · · · · · · · · · · · · 8:102a
railroads · · · · · · · · · · · · · · · · · · 8:99a
railroad, high-speed · · · · · · · 7:116b–119a
roads · 6:332b
Road Traffic Law · · · · · · · · · · · · · · 6:332b
ships · · · · · · · · · · · · · · · · · · 7:143b–145a
urban life · · · · · · · · · · · · · · · · · · · 8:179a
Transportation administration · · · · · 8:99a
Transportation Museum · · · · · · · · 8:104a
Transportation safety · · · · · · · · · · · 8:103b
Transportation services, land utilization
· 4:363b
Trans-Siberian Railway · · · · · · · · · · 8:255b
Travel · · · · · · · · · · · · · · · · · · 8:104a–104b
Travel diaries · · · · · · 1:294a; 8:104b–106a
distinction between kikō and similar
genres and · · · · · · · · · · · · · · · · 8:105a
language · · · · · · · · · · · · · · · · · · · 8:105a
types of kikō · · · · · · · · · · · · · · · · 8:105b
Travel sections (michiyuki) · · · · · · · 8:105a
Treasure houses · · · · · · · · · · · · · · · 5:277b
Treaties · 8:106a
Anglo-Japanese Commercial Treaty
of 1894 · · · · · · · · · · · · · · · · · · · 1:57b
Ansei commercial · · · · · · · · · · · · · 1:63a
Anti-Comintern Pact · · · · · · · · 1:65a–65b
Chemulp'o · · · · · · · · · · · · · · · · · · 1:268b
China-Japan Peace and Friendship
Treaty · · · · · · · · · · · · · · 1:291b–292a
Doihara-Qin (Doihara-Ch'in) Agreement
· 2:126b
Four-Power Treaty · · · · · · · · · · · · 2:330a
Franco-Japanese Agreement of 1907
· 2:333b
Harris Treaty · · · · · · · · · · · · · · · · 3:105a
Kanagawa Treaty · · · · · · · · · · · · · 4:135a
Kanghwa, Treaty of · · 4:140b–141a; 7:197b
Korea-Japan Treaty of 1965 · · · · · · 4:287b
Nine-Power Treaty · · · · · · · · · · · · · 6:4b
Portsmouth, Treaty of · · · · · · · · · · 6:228a

Potsdam Declaration · · · · · · · · · · · 6:231b
Russo-Japanese agreements of 1907–1916
· 6:344b
San Francisco Peace Treaty · · · 7:10a–11a
Seoul, Treaty of · · · · · · · · · · · · · · 7:68b
Shimonoseki, Treaty of 7:106a–106b, 197b
Sino-Japanese Amity Treaty of 1871
· 7:197b
Soviet-Japanese Basic Convention · · 7:238a
Soviet-Japanese Joint Declaration
· · · · · · · · · · · · · · · · · · 7:238b–239a
St. Petersburg · · · · · · · · · · · · · · · · 6:371a
Tianjin (Tientsin) Convention · · · · · 8:29b
Tripartite Pact · · · · · · · · · · 8:107a–107b
Unequal Treaties · · · · · · · · · · 8:148a–149a
United States-Japan Administrative
Agreement · · · · · · · · · · · · · · · · 8:165b
United States-Japan Mutual Defense
Assistance Agreement, (MSA or Mutual
Security Agreement) of 8 March 1954
· · · · · · · · · · · · · · · · · · · 8:165b–167b
United States-Japan securities treaties
· · · · · · · · · · · · · · · · · · · 8:165b–167b
Versailles, Treaty of · · · · · · · · 8:190b–191a
Washington Naval Treaty of 1922 · · 1:88a;
8:235a–235b
Treaty Concerning Fishing in the
Northwest Atlantic Ocean · · · · · 2:282b
Treaty for the Preservation of the
Biological Resources of the
Southeast Atlantic Ocean · · · · · · 2:282b
Treaty of Beijing · · · · · · · · · · · · · · 4:268a
Treaty of Edo (Tōkyō) of
26 August 1858 · · · · · · · · · · · · · 8:150a
Treaty of Peace with Japan. *See* **San
Francisco Peace Treaty**
Treaty of Territorial Waters and
Contiguous Seas · · · · · · · · · · · · · 2:282b
Treaty of the High Seas · · · · · · · · · 2:282b
Treaty port system · · · · · · · · · · · · · 7:78a
Trees. *See* **Plants**
Trench · 4:8b–9a
Trial · 2:50b
procedures · · · · · · · · · · · · · · · · · · 2:50b
public · 2:50a
communists · · · · · · · · · · · · · 1:340b–341a
speedy · 2:50a
Tribal chieftains · · · · · · · · · · 1:21a; 7:171b
Trio-Kenwood Corporation · · · · · · · 8:106b
Tripartite Intervention · · · 1:286b; 2:332a;
8:106b–107a
international relations · · · · · · · · · · · 3:320b
Korean-Japanese relations · · · · · · · 4:281b
Mutsu Munemitsu · · · · · · · · · · · · · 5:289a
Russia and Japan · · · · · · · · · · · · · · 6:341b
Russo-Japanese War · · · · · · · · · · · 6:346a
Sino-Japanese War of 1894–1895 · · 7:198a
Treaty of Shimonoseki · · · · · · · · · · 7:106b
ultranationalism · · · · · · · · · · · · · · 8:145a
Witte, Sergei Iul'evich · · · · · · · · · · 8:255b
Tripartite Pact · · · · · 1:57b; 1:65a–65b, 88a;
3:202a; 8:107a–107b, 272a, 344a
Konoe Fumimaro · · · · · · · · · · · · · 4:273a
Matsuoka Yōsuke · · · · · · · · · · · · · 5:139b
Tōjō Hideki · · · · · · · · · · · · · · · · · · 8:39b
United Kingdom · · · · · · · · · · · · · · 8:152b
United States · · · · · · · · · · · · · · · · · 8:158b
Triple Alliance · · · · · · · · · · · · · · · · 8:270b
Triple Entente · · · · · · · · · · · · · · · · 8:270b
Trout lily · 4:165b
Truck manufacturing · · · · · · · · · · · 3:348b
True Constitutional Party · · · · · · · · 4:198a
True Pure Land school
· · · · · · · · · · · · · 浄土真宗 · · · · 4:68a–69;
5:238a
True Seiyū Party · · · · · · · · · · · · · · · 7:55a
Truman, Harry S. · · · · · 2:157a, 158a; 3:62a;
6:302b; 8:107b

atomic bomb ·············· 1:108a
World War II ············· 8:276b
Trust ······················· 8:107b-108a
Trust banks (shintaku ginkō) ····· 1:139b; 3:327b
Trust Funds Bureau ·········· 1:140a
Trust Law (Shintaku Hō) of 1922 · 8:108a
Ts'ai O. *See* **Cai E (Ts'ai O)**
Ts'ao Ju-lin. *See* **Cao Rulin (Ts'ao Ju-lin)**
Tsingtao. *See* **Qingdao (Tsingtao)**
Tsou T'ao-fen. *See* **Zou Taofen (Tsou T'ao-fen)**
Tsu 津 ····················· 8:108a
Tsuba ·············· 8:108a-109b, *108b*
Tsubaki ················ 1:236b-237a
Tsubaki Chinzan 椿椿山 ······· 8:109b
Tsubaki Hot Spring 椿温泉 ···· 8:109b
Tsubaki Sanjūrō 椿三十郎 ···· 7:108a
Tsubakurodake 燕岳 ········· 8:109b
Tsubame 燕 ·········· 7:276a; 8:109b
Tsubo ······················· 4:308a
Tsuboi Kumezō 坪井九馬三 ··· 8:109b-110a
Tsuboi Sakae 壺井栄 ········ 8:110a
Tsuboi Shigeji 壺井繁治 ····· 8:110a
Senki ···················· 7:66b
Shin Nihon bungaku ·········· 7:122a
works ···················· 8:110a
Tsuboi Shōgorō 坪井正五郎 · 1:75b; 8:110a
kōgoishi named by ·········· 4:249a
Tsubota Jōji 坪田譲治 ······ 8:110a
Tsubouchi Shōyō 坪内逍遥 · 5:315b; 7:31a, 99a; 8:110a, *110b*, 111a
Fenollosa, Ernest Francisco ···· 2:251b
Futabatei Shimei ············ 2:375b
fūzoku shōsetsu ············· 2:378b
Shōsetsu shinzui ··········· 5:50b-51a
seiji shōsetsu ·············· 7:50a
shingeki ·················· 7:112b
Shinkokugeki ·············· 7:121a
Tsubouchi Memorial Theater Museum ···················· 8:232a
Tsuboya ware 壺屋焼 2:295b; 8:111a
Tsuburaya Eiji 円谷英二··· 8:111a-111b
Tsuburaya Special Productions ··· 8:111b
Tsuchi ·············· 土 2:*269a*; 5:307b; 8:124a
Tsuchida Bakusen 土田麦僊 ······· 8:111b
Tsuchii Bansui. 土井晩翠 *See* **Doi Bansui**
Tsuchi ikki (peasant revolts) ·········· 土一揆; 2:107b-108a; 3:268b-269a; 8:111b-112a
Tsuchimikado, Emperor 土御門天皇 ············ 8:112a
poetry ···················· 2:354b
Tsuchimoto Noriaki 土本典昭 ······ 2:275b
Tsuchi to heitai (Mud and Soldiers) 土と兵隊 ·········· 2:*270b*
Tsuchiura 土浦 ············ 8:112a
Tsuchiya Bummei 土屋文明 ············ 8:112a
works ···················· 8:112a
Tsuchiya Yasuchika ·土屋安親· 8:*108b*
Tsuda College ·············· 8:112a
Tsuda Mamichi ·津田真道·· 8:112a-112b
Tsuda Sen 津田仙 ········· 8:112b
Tsuda Sōgyū 津田宗及 ·7:67a; 8:112b
Tsuda Sōkichi 津田左右吉·· 8:112b
historiography ············· 3:157a
on *Kojiki*'s compilation ······ 4:251b
works ···················· 8:112b
Tsuda Umeko 津田梅子· 8:112b-113a
Bacon, Alice Mabel ·········· 1:129b

Tsūen 通円 ········ 4:327b
Tsugamonai hanashi no oyadama 無束話親玉 ···· 8:185a
Tsugaru Peninsula 津軽半島 ·1:69b; 8:113a
Tsugaru Plain 津軽平野 ···· 8:113a
Tsugaru Strait 津軽海峡 ···· 8:113a
Tsuga Teishō 都賀庭鐘 ···· 8:113a
works ···················· 8:113a
Tsuge [(Japanese box) *Buxus microphylla* var. *japonica*] ·8:113a-113b
Tsugumi. *See* **Thrushes**
Tsuihō. *See* **Banishment**
Tsuina ···················· 7:71b
Tsuishu ···················· 4:116a
Tsu Islanders ·············· 4:35a
Tsuitate (free-standing screens) · 7:41b
Tsuitate (single-panel screen) ···· 7:42b
Tsujigahana ·············· 8:113a
Tsujigiri ···················· 8:113b
Tsuji Kunio 辻邦生 ········ 8:113b
Tsuji Masanobu ·· 辻正信··· 8:113b-114a
Tsujimura Jusaburō 辻村ジュサブロウ ··· 8:114a
Tsujimura Sumie. *See* **Tanaka Sumie**
Tsujiura ·················· 8:114a
Tsuji Zennosuke 辻善之助 ··· 8:114a
Tsuka ···················· 4:295b
Tsukamoto Kunio 塚本邦雄 ············ 8:114a
works ···················· 8:114a
Tsukasameshi no Jimoku 官召の除目 ···· 4:57b
Tsukebito ·················· 7:273a
Tsukemono ·················· 2:305a
Tsuki ···················· 4:196a
Tsukigase 月ヶ瀬 ········· 8:114a
"Tsukigata Hampeita" 月形半平太 · 7:121a
Tsukiji Little Theater (Tsukiji Shōgekijō) ········ 7:112b; 8:299b
Tsukimi (moon viewing) · 2:*261b*; 5:248a
Tsukimi zatō ····· 月見座頭 · 4:327b, *329a*
Tsukimono ·········· 8:114a-114b
Tsukinami-e (activities of 12 months) paintings ··········· 8:309b
Tsuki ni hoeru · 月に吠える · 3:76a
Tsukinowaguma (*Selenarctos thibetanus*) ·············· 1:148b
Tsuki no yukue · 月の行方· 1:73b
Tsukioka Yoshitoshi 月岡芳年 ···· 7:306a
Tsuki wa higashi ni 月は東に ········ 8:319b
Tsuki yori no shisha 月よりの使者 ·········· 4:308a
Tsukuba Academic New Town ···· 8:114b
Ibaraki Prefecture ·········· 3:253b
Tsukubasan 筑波山 ········· 8:114b
Tsukubashū · 菟玖波集 · 5:18a; 8:114b
Shinsen tsukubashū ··········· 7:124b
Tsukuba University ··· 2:179a-179b; 8:115a
Tsukuda 佃 ············· 8:115a
Tsukue Ryūnosuke 机龍之助 ······ 5:320a
Tsukumi 津久見 ········ 8:115a
Tsukumo shell mound 津雲貝塚 ······ 6:235a
Tsukuri ···················· 7:24b
Tsukuri monogatari (courtly romances or prose fiction) ··· 作物語 ·· 5:246a
Tsukushi dōki · 筑紫道記 ······· 6:299a
Tsukushi Mountains 筑紫山地 ········· 8:115a
Tsukushi Plain 筑紫平野 ···· 8:115a
Tsukuyomi no Mikoto 月読尊 ······ 5:293a
Tsuma 妻 2:25b; 7:359a

Tsumago 妻籠 ······· 8:115a
Tsuma yo bara no yō ni (Wife! Be like a Rose!) 妻よ薔薇のように ···· 5:335a
Tsumegome ·············· 4:117b
Tsumi 2:232a-232b; 3:100b-101b; 4:186a-186b; 7:139a; 8:115a-115b
Tsumi-kegare ·············· 4:186a
Tsumugi ·········· 4:105a; 8:116a
Tsuna ···················· 7:272b
Tsunashima Ryōsen 綱島梁川 ··· 8:116a
Tsunetō Kyō 恒藤恭 ······ 8:116a
writings ·················· 8:116a
Tsunoda Ryūsaku 角田柳作 ··· 8:116a
Tsunokakushi ·············· 3:119a
Tsurane ···················· 4:94a
Tsure ···················· 4:298b
Tsurezuregusa · 徒然草 ·4:136a; 5:44a; 8:341a-342b
Tsuridono ·················· 7:111a
Tsurigane ninjin (*Adenophora triphylla* var. *Japonica*) · 8:116a-116b
Tsūron kōkogaku 通論考古学 · 1:77a, 79b
Tsuru. *See* **Ceramics**
Tsuruga 敦賀 2:364a; 8:116b
Tsuruga Bay 敦賀湾 ·· 8:116b
Tsurugaoka Hachiman Shrine 鶴岡八幡宮 4:*120b*; 8:116b
Shizuka Gozen ············· 7:152b
Tsurugidake 剣岳 ········ 8:116b
Tsurugigasaki 剣ヶ崎 ····· 7:293a
Tsurugisan 剣山 ········ 8:116b
Tsuruhachi Tsurujirō 鶴八鶴次郎 7:108a; 8:289a
Tsurukame 鶴亀 ······· 8:289a
Tsurumeso 弦召 ······ 4:59b
Tsurumi Shunsuke · 6:233a; 7:149a-149b
Tsurumi Yūsuke 鶴見祐輔 · 8:116b-117a
Tsuru nyōbō 鶴女房 ···· 8:117a
Tsuruoka 鶴岡 ······ 8:117a
Tsuruta Yoshiyuki 鶴田義行··· 8:117a-117b
Tsuru wa yamiki 鶴は病みき ···· 6:80a
Tsuruya Namboku 鶴屋南北 · 1:211b; 5:50a; 8:117b
kabuki plays ············· 4:91a-92a
plays ···················· 8:117b
Tsuryō 津料 ······ 7:57a
Tsūsanshō 通産省 ··· 5:189b-191b
Tsushima (city) ······ 津島 · 8:117b
Tsushima (island) ··· 対馬 8:*117a*, 117b, 8:117b-118a
Izuhara port ·············· 8:*117a*
role in Korean-Japanese relations ·· 4:278b
Silla pirates' attacks ········· 4:277b
Sō family ················ 7:220a
Sō Yoshitatsu ············· 4:140b
Tsushima Current 対馬海流 · 3:21a; 8:118a
Tsushima, Battle of · 3:197a; 8:118a
Russo-Japanese War ········· 6:347a
Tōgō Heihachirō ··········· 8:36a
Tsushima Incident 対馬事件 ········ 8:118a
Tsushima Senryō Jiken ········ 8:118a
Tsushima Shūji. 津島修治 *See* **Dazai Osamu**
Tsushima Strait · 対馬海峡 · 8:118a-118b
Tsūshin seido. *See* **Telecommunications systems**
Tsūshō kaisha ····· 4:184a; 8:118b
Tsūshō Sangyō Shō 通商産業省· 5:189b-191b

Tsutaya Jūzaburō
·········· 蔦屋重三郎 ···· 8:186b
Tsutsui Junkei ···筒井順慶 ······· 8:118b
Tsutsuji (azaleas) ······················1:126a
Tsutsukyahan ·························4:323b
Tsutsumi Chūnagon
  monogatari 堤中納言物語 ···· 5:36b, 42b;
                              8:118b-119a
  butterflies ·························1:226a
Tsutsumi ware ······· 堤焼 ······· 8:119a
Tsutsumi Yasujirō
  ··················· 堤康次郎 ····· 8:119b
Tsutsushimi ·············· 8:119a-119b, 347b
Tsuwabuki (Ligularia tussilaginea;
  Farfugium japonicum) ········ 8:119b
Tsuwano ·············· 津和野 ···· 8:119b
Tsuyama ··············· 津山 ····· 8:119b
Tsuyama Basin ··津山盆地 ······· 8:119b
Tsuyuharai ·························7:272b
Tsuyu no atosaki
  ··········つゆのあとさき ···· 7:176a
Tsuyu no Gorobei
  ·················· 露五郎兵衛 ···· 6:282a
Tsuzumi ···················· 8:119b-120a
  gigaku ···························3:32a
Tsuzumi no onna ··鼓の女 ······· 7:339b
Tsuzura ·············· 4:105a; 8:120a
Tsuzure-ori ························· 8:120a
Tsuzurikata ························7:51a
Tuan Ch'i-jui. See Duan Qirui (Tuan
  Ch'i-jui)
Tuberculosis ·····················5:147b
Tule Lake Relocation Center ······ 8:120a
Tuna [(maguro) Thunnus spp.] ··2:285b;
                                    8:120a
Tungusic ························· 4:18b
Tung-ya Ho-ch'in Hui ············· 8:31a
Turkic ···························4:18b
Turtles [(kame) order
  Chelonia] ················ 8:120a-120b
Tutoring schools ·················2:223a
Twenty-four Eyes ·········· 6:1a; 8:110a
Twenty-One Articles of Lord Sōunji,
  The ····························7:234b
Twenty-One Demands ··1:239b, 287a-287b;
  4:367a; 8:120b-121b, 270b, 354a
  content ·························· 8:121a
  Japanese aspirations in China ····· 8:120b
  Japanese ultimatum ·············· 8:121b
  response to ····················· 8:121a
  Shandong (Shantung) Question ···· 7:77b
  Washington Conference ············ 8:235a
Twenty-Six Martyrs ······· 5:304a; 8:121b
  Toyotomi Hideyoshi ·············· 8:96a
Two Mandalas, The ·········· 6:347b-351a
Type and Motif Index of Japanese Folk
  Literature, A ··················2:302b
Typhoons ··················· 8:121b-122a
  development and course ··········· 8:122a
  observation and forecasting ······· 8:122a
  structure ······················· 8:122a
Typhoon season ···················4:8a
Typography ······················2:296a

U

Ubasoku ·········· 優婆塞 ····· 8:123a
Ube ············· 宇部 ····· 8:123a
Ube Industries, Ltd ··············· 8:123a

U-BIX ·························4:270b
Ubusunagami ····· 産土神 ···· 6:205a;
                              8:123a-123b
Uchida Ginzō ····内田銀蔵 ···· 8:123b
  historiography ·················· 3:156b
  works ························· 8:123b
Uchida Hyakken ·内田百閒 ····· 8:123b
Uchida Kōsai ····内田康哉 ····· 8:123b
Uchida Roan ····内田魯庵 ···· 5:13a;
                              8:123b-124a
Uchida Ryōhei ···内田良平 1:164a; 8:124a
Uchida Tomu ·····内田吐夢 2:270a; 8:124a
Uchigeba ·························7:252b
Uchikake (A Robe) ···打掛 ····· 8:110a
Uchikowashi ········· 打毀 ··· 1:132b;
        7:345b; 8:124a-124b, 337b
Uchimura Kanzō ·内村鑑三 ···1:84b, 155a,
  223a; 5:262b-263a; 7:90b; 8:124a-124b
  geography ·····················3:25b
  pacifism ·················· 6:144a-144b
  works ························· 8:124b
Uchimura Naoya 内村直也 ······· 8:125a
Uchinada ············· 内灘 ···· 8:125a
Uchinada Incident ·················· 8:125a
Uchinomaki Hot Spring
  ··················· 内牧温泉 ···· 1:103a
Uchinoura ············ 内之浦 ···· 8:125a
Uchiura Bay ········· 内浦湾 ···· 8:125a
Uchiwa (fans) ······· 2:247b-248a; 5:331b
Uchū Kaihatsu Jigyōdan ············ 5:347b
Uda, Emperor ······ 宇多天皇 ·1:45a; 7:257a;
                              8:125b
  Fujiwara family ·············· 2:348a-348b
  Shinkokushi ·····················7:121b
Udagawa Yōan 宇田川榕菴 ······· 8:125b
Uda Tennō gyoki
  ················· 宇多天皇御記 ···· 8:125b
Udon ·························7:265b
Udonsuki ······················7:265b
Udo Shrine ········ 鵜戸神宮 ···· 8:125b
Ueda ··············· 上田 ···· 8:125b
Ueda Akinari ····· 上田秋成 ··· 5:11b, 48b;
                              8:126a-126b
  early life ······················ 8:126a
  Fujitani Nariakira ················ 2:346b
  Hachimonjiya-bon ··········· 3:74b; 8:126a
  Harusame monogatari ············· 8:126b
  poetry and scholarship ············ 8:126b
  Ugetsu monogatari ··········· 8:126a-126b
  yomihon ·················· 8:336a-336b
Ueda Bin ········· 上田敏 ·2:296a; 5:12b;
                        7:253b; 8:126b-127a
  Kaichōon ······················4:247b
Ueda Kazutoshi ··上田万年 ·· 2:65a, 377a;
                        7:104b; 8:127a
Ueda Mannen. 上田万年
  See Ueda Kazutoshi
Ueda Teijirō ····· 上田貞次郎 ···· 8:127a
Uehara Yūsaku ··· 上原勇作 ···· 8:127a
Uejima Onitsura ··· 上島鬼貫 ··· 3:79a; 5:16a;
                              8:127a
Ueki Emori ······ 植木枝盛 ···· 8:127a-127b
  Freedom and People's Rights Movement
  ······················· 2:334b-335a
  political groups formed by ········· 8:127a
  shigi kempō ·····················7:92b
Ueki Masayoshi ·· 植木正義 ······ 4:166a
Uemura Kōgorō
  ················ 植村甲午郎 ···· 8:127b
Uemura Masahisa 植村正久 8:127b-128a
Uemura Naomi ·· 植村直己 ······ 8:128a
Uemura Ryūichi · 上村隆一 ··· 1:125b-126a
Uemura Shōen ·· 上村松園 ···· 8:128a-128b
Uemura Sōichi. 植村宗一
  See Naoki Sanjūgo
Uemura Tamaki ·· 植村環 ······ 8:128b
Ueno ·········· 上野 7:160a; 8:128b
Ueno Basin ······ 上野盆地 ···· 8:128b

Ueno Park ······· 上野公園 ·3:94b; 8:128b
  modern architecture in ······· 8:128b-129a
Ueno Riichi ····· 上野理一 ····· 8:129a
Ueno Zoological Garden ··· 1:71b; 8:129a
Ueshiba Morihei ·植芝盛平 ····· 1:34a
Uesugi family ····· 上杉氏 ····· 8:129a
  daimyō family ··················· 8:129a
  territorial warlords ··············· 8:129a
Uesugi Harunori ·上杉治憲 ···· 8:129a-129b
Uesugi Kagekatsu
  ·················· 上杉景勝 3:179b; 8:129b
  Sanada Yukimura ·················7:9a
Uesugi Kenshin ·上杉謙信 ···· 8:129b-130a
  Kawanakajima, Battle of ··········· 4:182a
Uesugi Norizane ·上杉憲実 ····· 8:130a
  Eiryō Rebellion ·················· 4:248a
Uesugi Shinkichi 上杉慎吉 ···· 8:130a-130b
  quasi-absolute power of emperor theory
  ······························4:375a
Uesugi Yōzan. 上杉鷹山
  See Uesugi Harunori
Uesugi Zenshū, Rebellion
  of ·············· 上杉禅秀の乱 ···· 8:130b
Uetsuka Shūhei ·上塚周平 ····· 8:130b
Ugaki Kazushige 宇垣一成 ···· 1:88a;
                              8:130b-131a
Uge no hitokoto. 宇下人言
  See Matsudaira Sadanobu
Ugetsu monogatari (Tales
  of Moonlight and Rain)
  ··················· 雨月物語 ·5:48b; 8:126a,
                              336b
Ugōkai ·············· 烏合会 ···· 4:100b
Uguisu (bush warbler) ······· 1:223b-224a
Uirōuri ·············· 外郎売 ···· 4:98b
Uji (city) ············· 宇治 ···· 4:166b;
                        5:324b; 8:131a
  chieftains ······················4:89a
  firefly viewing ·················· 2:280b
Uji (political groups) ··· 氏 6:176b; 8:131a
  uji-kabane system ················ 8:131b
Uji-bito ············· 氏人 ···· 4:89a
Uji dainagon monogatari
  ··················· 宇治大納言物語 ···· 8:137b
Ujigami ·············· 氏神 ···· 7:179b;
                              8:131a-131b
  Shintō ·················· 4:362b; 7:126a
Ujigawa ·············· 宇治川 4:338a; 8:131b
Uji-kabane system
  ··················· 氏姓制度 ··· 8:131b-137a
  ason ························· 1:103a
  history ·················· 8:135b-137a
  kabane ·················· 8:134a-135b
  Taika Reform ····················7:295b
  Uji structure ·············· 8:132a-134a
Uji Kadayū ···· 宇治嘉太夫 ···· 4:77a
Ujina ·············· 宇品 ···· 8:137a-137b
Uji no kami ········· 氏上 ···· 4:89a
Uji shūi monogatari
  ··················· 宇治拾遺物語 1:137a; 2:296a,
  302b; 5:43b-44a; 7:72b, 93a, 149b;
                        8:137b, 223b
  Kobutori jijii in ················ 4:239b
Uji-Yamada ···· 宇治山田 ···· 8:176a
Ukai ·························2:26a
Ukaiki.宇槐記 See Taiki
Ukanomitama no Kami
  ··················· 宇迦之御魂神 ···· 2:375a
Ukebumi ·············· 請文 ···· 8:137b
Ukemen'i ·········· 請免居 ···· 4:191a
Ukeragahana ··うけらが花 ···· 4:167b
Ukesho ·············· 請所 ···· 4:63b
Uki-e ·············· 浮絵 8:140b, 141a
Ukigumo (Floating
  Clouds) ··········· 浮雲 ·2:272b; 375b
Uki komononari ·· 浮小物成 ···· 4:267b
Ukita Hideie ···宇喜多秀家 ···· 8:137b-138a
Ukita Kazutami ··浮田和民 ···· 8:138a

Ukitōdai ········ 浮き燈台 ······· **7**:167a
Ukiyaku ········ 浮役 **5**:360b; **8**:138a
 komononari ··············· **4**:267b
Ukiyoburo ······· 浮世風呂 ·· **4**:256a; **7**:97a
Ukiyodoko ········ 浮世床 ········ **7**:97a
Ukiyo-e ········ 浮世絵 **1**:163b; **2**:296a,
  6:153b; **7**:43a, 79b, 270a; **8**:138a-144a
 bijin-e ····················· **8**:140b
 Chōkyōsai Eiri ··············· **1**:300a
 design ······················ **2**:88b
 early ···················· **8**:138a-139a
 Edo ···················· **8**:139b-140b
 full-color printing ········· **8**:141a-141b
 fūzokuga ···················· **2**:377a
 Gaifū kaisei or *Red Fuji* ···· **8**:143b
 Genroku era ················· **3**:23a
 Golden Age ··············· **8**:142a-143a
 Hiroshige ··········· **3**:148a; **8**:144b
 Hishikawa Moronobu ········· **8**:138b
 Hokusai ····················· **8**:143b
 Ishikawa Toyonobu ·········· **3**:345a
 Iwasa Matabei ··············· **3**:363a
 kabuki actor ················· **8**:143a
 Kaigetsudō Ando ············· **8**:140b
 Kaigetsudō school ····· **4**:109b; **8**:140b
 Kambun Master ·············· **4**:124b
 Katsukawa Shunshō ······ **4**:171b-172a
 Kawanabe Gyōsai ············· **4**:182a
 kibyōshi ················· **8**:141b-142a
 Kitagawa school ·············· **4**:225a
 kyōka ···················· **8**:141b-142a
 landscape ················ **8**:143a-144a
 mitate-e ················· **8**:141b-142a
 modern prints ··············· **5**:232a
 Night View of Kanazawa in Musashi
 Province ··················· **8**:144a
 Nishimura Shigenaga ········· **8**:141a
 Okumura Masanobu ··········· **6**:97a
 Ōsaka school ················ **6**:123a
 Riccar Art Museum ··········· **6**:308a
 Sharaku ····················· **8**:143a
 shunga ······················ **8**:138b
 surimono ················· **8**:141b-142a
 Suzuki Haruobu ·············· **8**:141b
 Takehisa Yumeji ·············· **7**:324a
 Thirty-Six Views of Mount Fuji (Fugaku
 sanjūrokkei) ················ **8**:143b
 Torii Kiyomasu ··············· **8**:140a
 Torii Kiyonaga ··············· **8**:142a
 Torii school ················· **8**:140a
 uki-e ······················· **8**:141a
 Utagawa Kunisada ············ **8**:139a
 Utagawa Kuniyoshi ······· **8**:145a-145b
 Utagawa school ··········· **8**:184a-184b
 Utagawa Toyokuni ········ **8**:184b-185b
 Utamaro ····················· **8**:142b
 Western-style pictures ········ **8**:249a
 woodblock printing ········ **8**:139a-139b
 yokohama-e ················· **8**:330a
Ukiyogata rokumai byōbu
 ··········· 浮世方六枚屏風 ······· **1**:119b
Ukiyo monogatari 浮世物語 ···· **4**:136b
Ukiyo-zōshi ······ 浮世草子 ·· **2**:374b;
  3:22b-23a; **4**:136b; **5**:48b; **7**:333b-334a;
  8:144a-144b
 hachimonjiya-bon ············· **3**:74b
 Saikaku ················· **6**:370a-370b
 later Edo-period ··········· **5**:48b-49b
Ukiyo-zōshi novels
 ················ 浮世草子 ······· **6**:247a
Ukon Ujinari ······ 右近氏成 ··· **4**:270a
Ŭlsa Treaty (1905) ··········· **4**:289a
Ultranationalism ············· **8**:144b
 contradictions in interpretations
 ························· **8**:145b-146a
 genesis ·················· **8**:145a-145b
 modernization ··············· **5**:229a
 nationalism ·········· **5**:342a-343b; **8**:146a

Uma ························· **3**:231a
Umakaibe ········· 馬飼部 ···· **1**:147b
Uma no Kura ··············· **7**:248b
Umarete wa mita keredo
 ···· 生れてはみたけれど ····· **6**:141b;
  8:146a-146b
Umarete wa mita keredo (I was Born
 But . . .) ···················· **2**:269a
Umbrellas, traditional ······ **6**:280b; **8**:146b
Ume ················· **6**:192b-193a
Umeboshi ················· **8**:146b
Umeda Umpin ···· 梅田雲浜 ·· **8**:146b
Umehara Ryūzaburō
 ············ 梅原龍三郎 ······· **6**:156b;
  8:146b-147a
Umehara Sueji ··· 梅原末治 · **1**:77b; **8**:147a
 publications ················· **8**:147a
Ume Kenjirō ····· 梅謙次郎 **2**:319a; **8**:147a
Umemodoki (*Ilex serrata* var. *sieboldii*)
 ···························· **8**:147a
Umetani Matsutarō 梅谷松太郎 ···· **7**:107b
Umeyo fuyaseyo
 ············ 生めよふやせよ ····· **2**:246b
Umezaki Haruo ··· 梅崎春生 ·· **8**:147a-147b
Umezawa Hamao 梅沢浜夫 ····· **8**:147b
Umezu-Ka Ōkin Kyōtei
 ········ 梅津-何応欽協定 ······· **3**:128b
Umezu Masakage nikki
 ············ 梅津政景日記 ······· **8**:147b
Umezu Yoshijirō
 ············ 梅津美治郎 **7**:278a; **8**:147b
Umibe no kōkei
 ············ 海辺の光景 ······· **8**:319b
Umi ni ikuru hitobito
 (People Who Live on the
 Sea) ············ 海に生くる人々 ··· **6**:255a
Umi no Sachi (Gifts of the Sea) · **1**:69a-69b
Ummei ············ 運命 ······· **4**:114a
Unagi ······················· **2**:184a
Unazuki ········ 宇奈月 ····· **8**:147b
Under the Persimmon Tree ······ **8**:110a
Un Dia ····················· **7**:291a
Unebiyama ··················· **8**:310b
Uneme ············ 采女 ····· **1**:147b;
  8:147b-148a
Unemployment ····· **4**:356a; **7**:216a; **8**:148a
 hidden ······················ **8**:148a
 public employment security offices ·· **4**:265a
Unemployment Compensation Law
 (1947) ····················· **4**:358a
Unemployment insurance. See **Social
 security programs**
Unemployment Insurance Law
 (Shitsugyō Hoken Hō; Koyō
 Hoken Hō) of 1947 ······ **4**:352b; **7**:209b
Unequal Treaties ····· **1**:160a; **7**:9b, 51a-51b
 Austria ················· **1**:119b-120a
 Denison, Henry Willard ··········· **2**:86b
 foreign trade development ········· **2**:320a
 Mexico ······················ **5**:165a
 Ministry of Foreign Affairs ······· **5**:188b
 naichi zakkyo ··········· **5**:309b-310a
Unequal Treaties, revision of ······ **8**:148a
 Aoki Shūzō ················ **1**:69a-69b
 initiatives and negotiations ···· **8**:148b-149a
 1868-1874 ················· **8**:148b
 1875-1879 ················· **8**:148b
 1880-1887 ··············· **8**:148b-149a
 1888-1889 ················· **8**:149a
 1890-1894 ················· **8**:149a
 Tani Kanjō ··············· **7**:341b-342a
 treaties and problems ········ **8**:148a-148b
 United Kingdom ·············· **8**:151b
UNESCO (United Nations Educational,
 Scientific, and Cultural Organization)
 activities in Japan · **2**:175b, 181a; **8**:149b
Unfair Competition Prevention Law
 (Fusei Kyōsō Bōshi Hō) ··· **3**:297b; **8**:97b

Unfair labor practices ····· **4**:351b; **6**:312b;
  8:149b
 collective bargaining ··············· **1**:334b
Ungjin ······················ **6**:146a
Uni ······················· **7**:46a-46b
Unification, political
 before 1600 ················· **2**:149a
Unification Church. *See* **Holy Spirit
 Association for the Unification of
 World Christianity**
Unification of the spoken and written
 word ························ **3**:16b
Uniforms ········· **8**:*149a*, 149b-150a
Unionism
 labor reforms of 1945-1947 ······ **4**:357b
 labor relations ················ **4**:348b
 national labor federations ···· **4**:345a-345b
 pre-World War II ··············· **4**:345a
 reorganization and splits ········· **4**:347a
 restraints ···················· **4**:346b
 rival federations ··············· **4**:346b
 structure and function ······· **4**:347b-348a
  collective bargaining ········· **4**:347b
  employment security ········· **4**:347b
  grievance procedures ········· **4**:347b
  membership ········· **4**:347b, 348b
 wartime ····················· **4**:345b
 1945-1950 ··················· **4**:346a
Unionization ·················· **4**:344b
**Union of New Religious Organizations of
 Japan** ····················· **8**:150a
Union of Soviet Socialist Republics and
 Japan. *See* **Russia and Japan**
Unions ················· **7**:216b-217a
 bureaucracy ·················· **1**:220b
 Federation of Independent Unions
 ························· **1**:313a-314a
 labor unions ··········· **4**:358b-360a
 teachers ····················· **7**:366b
Union Theological Seminary ······· **6**:288b
Unitarian Church ·············· **5**:231a
United Church of Christ in Japan · **8**:150a
United Kingdom
 Anglo-Japanese Alliance ······· **1**:56b-57b
 Japanese studies ··············· **4**:42a
United Kingdom and Japan ···· **8**:150a-153b
 Alliance period ··············· **8**:152a
 early contacts ············ **8**:150b-151a
 interwar period ·········· **8**:152a-152b
 Japan's modernization ······· **8**:151a-151b
 Meiji period ············· **8**:151b-152a
 post-World War II relations · **8**:152b-153b
United Nations and Japan ···· **8**:153b-154b
 centrality of United Nations ······ **8**:153b
 Japan's activities ·········· **8**:154a-154b
 UN agencies and UN nongovernmental
 organizations ············ **8**:153b-154a
United Nations Conference on the Law
 of the Sea (UNCLOS I) ··········· **8**:13b
United Nations Conference on the Law
 of the Sea (UNCLOS II) ··········· **8**:13b
United Nations Conference on Trade
 and Development (UNCTAD I) ···· **2**:309b
United Nations' Economic Commission
 for Asia and the Far East ······ **7**:235b
United Nations Law of the Sea
 Conference ·················· **6**:345b
United Nations University ········· **2**:177a
United Social Democratic Party ···· **8**:154b
United States
 influence on education ······ **2**:175a-176a
 Japanese Americans ········ **4**:13a-16a
  in Hawaii ··············· **4**:16a-17a
 Japanese immigrants ········ **2**:200b-201a
 Japanese language studies ········· **4**:21a
 Japanese studies in ·············· **4**:41b
United States and Japan ·········· **6**:289a;
  8:154b-160b

armed forces in Japan ········ 8:160b-161a
economic relations (1945-1973)
·········· 2:154a-165b; 8:161a-164b
  American foreign investment
  ···················· 8:162a-162b
  American protectionism ··· 8:163a-163b
  dollar primacy ············ 8:161b-162a
  early postwar order ······· 8:161a-161b
  international economic system
  ···················· 8:162b-163a
  international monetary crisis and yen
  revaluation ·········· 8:163b-164a
  yen in new era of international financial
  relations ············· 8:164a-164b
interwar period (1920-1930) ·· 8:157a-158a
opening of relations (1853-1980)
  ···················· 8:154b-155b
postwar relations (1945-1980) 8:159b-160b
power relations in Asia (1890-1920)
  ···················· 8:155b-157a
war period (1930-1945) ····· 8:158a-159b
United States education missions to
Japan ······················ 8:164b
romanization of Japanese ·········· 6:336a
school curriculum ·············· 7:36a
teachers ··················· 7:365b
United States Immigration Acts
of 1924, 1952 and 1965 ··· 1:136b; 4:13a;
8:164b-165a
United States-Japan Administrative
Agreement ············· 8:165a-165b
United States-Japan security treaties
···················· 8:166a
United States-Japan Commercial Treaty
of 1858. See Harris Treaty
United States-Japanese Joint Committee
of Trade and Economic Affairs
Ikeda-Kennedy Agreements ······· 3:265a
United States-Japan Mutual Defense
Assistance Agreement ·········· 8:165b
Ikeda-Robertson Talks ··········· 3:266a
United States-Japan Mutual Security
Treaty
Tōkyō ordinance decision (20 July 1960)
···················· 8:68b
United States-Japan security treaties
···· 7:235b; 8:160a, 165b-167b, 344b
atomic bomb ················ 1:110b
ban-the-bomb movement ········· 1:115a
defense industry ············· 2:82a-82b
Democratic Socialist Party ······ 2:85b
Dulles, John Foster ············ 2:135a
Japan Communist Party ········· 4:12a
Japan Socialist Party ·········· 4:48b
judicial review ·············· 4:80a
Kishi Nobusuke ·········· 4:223a-223b
movement against. See Peace movement
national defense ··········· 5:336b-338b
Ōsu Incident ··············· 6:128a
reappraisal ················· 4:386a
renunciation of war ············ 6:301b
San Francisco Peace Treaty ····· 7:10a-11a
Treaty of 1952 ··········· 8:165b-166b
Treaty of 1960 ··········· 8:166b-167b
United States armed forces in Japan
···················· 8:160b
United States military bases disputes
···················· 8:168a
university upheavals of 1968-1969 ·8:171b
United States-Japan Treaty of Amity and
Commerce of 1858 ·········· 8:168b
United States-Japan Treaty of Amity,
1854. See Kanagawa Treaty
United States military bases, disputes
over ····················· 8:167b-168b
United States, mission of 1860 to ·8:168b
United States National Security Council
···················· 6:54b

Unitika, Ltd ···················· 8:168b
Universal Copyright Convention
translation rights ············· 8:98a
Wakatsuki Reijirō ············· 8:218b
Universal Manhood Suffrage Law 2:188b;
6:168b, 211a
democracy ·················· 2:84b
Hara Takashi ················ 3:103a
Ōyama Ikuo ················· 6:138a
Universal Manhood Suffrage Movement
···· 3:198b; 6:210b; 8:169a-169b
apathy and success ············ 8:169b
arguments for ··············· 8:169b
beginnings (1897-1911) ········ 8:169a
democracy ·················· 2:84b
early Diet activity ············· 8:169a
eclipse and revival (1911-1919)
···················· 8:169a-169b
Inukai Tsuyoshi ·············· 3:326a
Taishō democracy ············· 7:304b
Universities and colleges ··· 8:170a-171a
academic freedom ·············· 1:6b
Aoyama Gakuin University ······· 1:71a
associations ················· 4:10b
Atomi Gakuen Women's University
···················· 1:115a
autonomy ··········· 6:220b, 8:171a-171b
Chiba University ·············· 1:271a
Chūō University ·············· 1:313b
Dōshisha University ········· 2:131b-132a
entrance examinations ········ 2:222a-224a
finance ··················· 3:134a
Gakushūin University ······· 1:5a; 3:5a
Hiroshima University ··········· 3:150a
history ·········· 3:133a-133b; 8:170a-170b
Hitotsubashi University ······ 3:208a-208b
Hokkaidō University ··········· 3:214a
Hōsei University ·········· 3:234b-235a
imperial ··················· 3:281a
International Christian University ·· 3:318a
Japan Women's University ······· 4:50b
Kansei Gakuin University ······· 4:152a
Keiō University ··············· 4:189a
Kōbe University ·············· 4:238a
Kokugakuin University ·········· 4:259b
Kyōto University ·············· 4:339a
Kyūshū University ············· 4:341b
Meiji Gakuin University ········· 5:154a
Meiji University ·········· 5:160b-161a
Nagoya University ············· 5:309b
Nanzan University ············· 5:330a
Nara Women's University ········ 5:334a
National Defense College ········ 5:338b
Nihon University ·············· 5:384b
Ochanomizu Women's University ·· 6:59a
Ōsaka University ············· 6:123a
Ōsaka University of Foreign Studies
···················· 6:123a
Ōtani University ·············· 6:129a
present status and problems ·· 8:170b-171a
Rikkyō University ············· 6:317a
Ritsumeikan University ·········· 6:321b
Ryūkyū University ············· 6:358b
Sophia University ············· 7:229a
Tamagawa University ··········· 7:332b
technical ··················· 8:192b
technical colleges ············· 7:368a
Tenri University ··············· 8:9b
Tōhō Gakuen School of Music ····· 8:36b
Tōhoku University ·············· 8:37b
Tōkai University ·············· 8:42a
Tōkyō Institute of Technology ····· 8:67a
Tōkyō University ·········· 8:69a-69b
Tōkyō University of Education ····· 8:69b
Tōkyō University of Fine Arts and Music
···················· 8:69b
Tōkyō University of Foreign Studies 8:69b

Tōkyō Women's Christian University
···················· 8:69b
Tsuda College ················ 8:112a
Tsukuba University ············· 8:115a
Waseda University ············· 8:232a
"University, The" ··········· 2:56a-57a
University Chartering Council (Daigaku
Setchi Shingikai) ············· 8:170b
University Law
university upheavals of 1968-1969 8:171b
University Order (Daigaku Rei) ··· 8:170a
University Upheavals of 1968-1969
···················· 8:171b
Riot Police ················· 6:320b
Unjō ············· 運上 ··· 5:360b;
8:171b-172a
Unjō taxes ·················· 1:132a
Unjust enrichment ············· 8:172a
Unka ····················· 6:190a
Unkei ········· 運慶 1:186b, 199a; 8:172a
Kaikei ···················· 4:111a
Kōfukuji commission ··········· 4:244a
works ··················· 8:172a
Unknown War, The ············ 7:200b
Unkoku school ···· 雲谷派 ·· 8:172a-172b
Sesshū Tōyō ················ 7:70a
Unkoku Tōgan ··············· 8:172b
Unkoku Tōeki 雲谷等益 ··· 8:172b
Unkoku Tōgan ··· 雲谷等顔 3:182a; 7:42b,
70a; 8:172b-173a
Ōbaiin ··················· 8:172b
Unkoku school ·············· 8:172a
West Lake ················· 8:172b
works ··················· 8:173a
Unlimited partnership company · 2:31b,
37b; 6:164a; 8:173a
articles of association ··········· 2:37b
Uno Chiyo ········ 宇野千代 ··· 8:173a
Kitahara Takeo ··············· 4:225b
works ··················· 8:173a
Unohana (Deutzia crenata) ····· 8:173b
Uno Kōji ········· 宇野浩二 5:13a; 8:173b
Uno Kōzō ········ 宇野弘蔵 ·· 8:173b-174a
Uno Kōzō chosakushū
········· 宇野弘蔵著作集 ··· 8:174a
Unshū ········· 雲州 ········· 3:367a
Unshū shōsoku. 雲州消息 See Meigō ōrai
Untei ··········· 芸亭 ········ 8:174a
Untei Library ················· 5:1a
Isonokami no Yakatsugu ········· 3:347b
U Nu. See Nu, U
Uny Co, Ltd ················· 8:174a
Un'yō ·············· 雲揚 ··· 4:140b
Un'yushō. 運輸省
See Ministry of Transport
Unzen-Amakusa National Park ···
····· 雲仙天草国立公園 1:50a; 8:174a-174b
Unzendake ········ 雲仙岳 ··· 8:174b
Unzen Hot Spring
········· 雲仙温泉 ·········· 8:174a
Unzen volcano ··············· 8:195b
Uosuki ···················· 7:265b
U Ottama. See Ottama, U
Uozu ············· 魚津 ··· 8:174b
Uplands
Iwatahara ·················· 3:363b
Makinohara ················· 5:86b
Mikatahara ················· 5:170b
Nihondaira ················· 5:379a
Upright Party ················ 1:314a
Urabon'e ········ 盂蘭盆会 ··· 1:160b
Uraga ·········· 浦賀 4:135a; 8:174b
Uraga bugyō ···· 浦賀奉行 ··· 8:174b
Uraga Channel ··· 浦賀水道 ··· 8:174b
Uragami family ··· 浦上氏 ··· 8:174b
Uragami Gyokudō
········· 浦上玉堂 1:211a; 8:175a
Enkajō (Misty Landscapes Album) · 8:175a

shichigenkin ·················· 7:87b
Uragami Shunkin 浦上春琴 **1:**211a; **8:**175b
Urakami kuzure ················ **6:**178a
Uraminosuke うらみのすけ ······ 4:136b
Ura Nihon 裏日本 ·············· **8:**175b
Uranouchi Bay 浦ノ内湾 ······· **8:**175b
Uraomote うらおもて ············ 4:180a
Uraomote (Inside Outside)
··························· 4:199a
Urashima Tarō ·浦島太郎 ······· 2:302b;
5:295b; **8:**175a–175b
   prototypes ···················· 2:341a
Urasoe 浦添 ·············· **8:**175b
Urawa 浦和 ············ **8:**175b–176a
Urayaku 浦役 ·············· **8:**176a
   port or fishing official ······ **8:**176a
   tax ························· **8:**176a
Urayasu 浦安 ·············· **8:**176a
Urban administration ········ **1:**301b
Urban Construction Law ······ **8:**180a
Urbanization ···· 2:108b–109a; 4:7a; 6:223b,
225a; **8:**176a–177a
   before 1600 ················· 2:148b
   crime rate ·················· 7:209a
   Edo history ················· 3:190a
   Edo period ·········· 2:149a–150a
   housing problems ············ 3:245b
   land utilization ············ 4:363b
   Meiji period ·········· 7:202a–203a
   Muromachi history ·········· 3:176a
   postwar ···················· 3:203b
   premodern ············ 2:148b–150a
   rural society ··············· 7:214a
   studies ···················· 4:231b
   urban planning ············· 8:180a
   Urban Planning Law ···· 8:180b–181a
Urbanization Control Areas ······ **8:**180b
Urbanization Promotion Areas ···· **8:**180b
Urban life ············ **8:**177a–179b
   commerce and culture ······ 8:177b–178a
   Edo (Tōkyō) ·········· 8:178a–178b
   functions and development ··· 8:177a–177b
   leisure and entertainment ···· 8:179a–179b
   modern city ·········· 8:178b–179a
Urban planning ········ **8:**179b–180b
Urban Planning Law ····· **8:**180b–181a
   Architectural Standards Law and ···· **1:**80b
   ownership rights ············ 6:136b
Urban Planning Law of 1919 ···· **8:**180a
Urban Planning Law of 1969 ···· **8:**180b
Urban Redevelopment Act ······· **8:**180b
Urban residents ············· **1:**300b
Urban riots ··········· **8:**124a–124b
Urban slums ·········· **7:**202b–203a
Urban subcenters ········· **8:**181a
   Shinjuku Ward ·············· 7:116a
Urban transportation ········ **8:**103a
Ureshino 嬉野 ·············· **8:**181a
Urikohime 瓜子姫 ··········· **8:**181a
Urushi. See **Lacquer tree**
Urushi-e 漆絵 ······· **8:**140b, 181a
Uryū, Lake 雨竜湖 ········· **8:**181a
Usa 宇佐 ·············· **8:**181a
Usagi ····················· **6:**275a
Usagi kōmori (*Plecotus auritus*) ··· **1:**146b
Usa Hachiman Shrine
········ 宇佐八幡宮 ·**3:**74a; **8:**181b
   Shintō ····················· 7:126b
Ushi ·················· **1:**251a–251b
Ushibuka 牛深 ·············· **8:**181b
Ushin 有心 ·············· **8:**181b
   mushin vs. ················· 5:282a
Ushinotoki mairi ············ **2:**128a
Ushin renga 有心連歌 ········· **6:**297a
Usterling, Anders ··········· **4:**177a
Usu ····················· **8:**181b
Usucha Temae ·············· **7:**364b
   tea ceremony ·········· 7:364b–365a

Usui Pass ·········· 碓氷峠 ······ **8:**182a
Usuita ···················· **1:**115b
Usui Yoshimi 臼井吉見 ······· **8:**182a
Usuki ··········· 臼杵 ·**8:**182a, *182b*
Usury ···················· **2:**132a
Usuyuki shō ··· うすゆき抄 ······ **3:**151b
Usuzan 有珠山 ·· **7:**98a; **8:**182a
Uta-awase (poetry
   contest) ········· 歌合 **5:**14b–15a, 39a;
8:182a–182b
   advent ····················· 5:31a
   judgment ··················· 8:182b
   preparation ················· 8:182a
   procedure ·················· 8:182a
Uta-e 歌絵 ······ **8:**182b–183a
Utagaki 歌垣 **2:**138a; **4:**108a;
8:183a
Utagaruta 歌骨牌 ······ **4:**108a
Utagawa Hiroshige
········ 歌川広重 ·**3:**148a–149b
Utagawa Kunimasa
········ 歌川国政 ·**7:**79b; **8:**183a
Utagawa Kunisada
········ 歌川国貞 ·**5:**49a; **7:**79b;
8:*139a*, 183a–183b
   daughters ·················· 8:183b
   Kunisada II ················· 8:183b
   Kunisada III ················ 8:183b
   secondary names ············ 8:183b
Utagawa Kuniyoshi
·············· 歌川国芳 ·**1:***251a*;
8:*145a–145b*, 183b–184a
Utagawa school ···· 歌川派 ·**8:**184a–184b
   Western-style pictures ······· 8:249a
Utagawa Toyoharu
·············· 歌川豊春 ····· **8:**184b
   Utagawa school ············· 8:184a
Utagawa Toyohiro
·············· 歌川豊広 ····· **8:**184b
   Hiroshige ·················· 3:148a
   Utagawa school ············· 8:184b
Utagawa Toyokuni
·············· 歌川豊国 ·**6:***296b*; **7:**79b,
96b; **8:**184b–185a
   others with Toyokuni name ·· 8:185a–185b
   Utagawa school ············· 8:184b
Utage no ato (After the
   Banquet) ······· 宴のあと ··· **6:**250a
Utakai Hajime. See **Imperial New Year's**
Poetry Reading
Utakai Hajime ·············· **3:**278b
Uta karuta 歌骨牌 ·**3:***248b*
Uta makura ··········· **8:**185b
   waka ······················ 8:203b
Utamaro ········· 歌麿 ·**7:**79a; **8:***142b*,
185b–187a
Fujin sōgaku juttai (Ten Studies of Women's
   Physiognomies) ··········· **8:***186b*
   illustrated books ············ 8:185b
Uta monogatari (Tales
   about Poems) ···· 歌物語 ·**5:**245b–246b
   Ise monogatari ············· 3:337a
Utashinai 歌志内 ··········· **8:**187a
Utilities, public ············· **6:**266b
Utility companies
   Chūbu Electric Power Co, Inc ····· **1:**311a
   Chūgoku Electric Power Co, Inc ··· **1:**312a
   Kansai Electric Power Co, Inc **4:**151a–151b
   Kyūshū Electric Power Co, Inc ···· **4:**340b
   Nippon Telegraph and Telephone Public
      Corporation ··············· **6:**13a
   Ōsaka Gas Co, Ltd ··········· **6:**121a
   Tōhoku Electric Power Co, Inc ···· **8:**37a
   Tōkyō Electric Power Co, Inc ·· **8:**66b–67a
   Tōkyō Gas Co, Ltd ··········· **8:**67a
   Water Resources Development Public
      Corporation ··············· **8:**237a

Utility-Model Patent Law ········ **6:**164b;
8:187a–187b
Uto ············· 宇土 ······ **8:**187b
Utokusen ······· 有徳銭 ····· **8:**187b
Utsubo monogatari
············ 宇津保物語 ··· **1:**73b; **5:**34a,
246a; **8:**187b–188a
   story ······················ 8:187b
Utsukushigahara ······ 美ヶ原 ····· **8:**188a
Utsunomiya ········· 宇都宮 ·· **8:**188a–188b
Utsunomiya Daimyōjin
········ 宇都宮大明神 ······ **2:**376a
   U-turn phenomenon ·········· 8:176b
Uwai Kakuken nikki
········ 上井覚兼日記 ······ **8:**188b
Uwajima ············ 宇和島 ····· **8:**188b
Uwanari 嫐 ············ **4:**98b
Uwa Sea ········ 宇和海 ····· **8:**188b
Uyoku. See **Right wing**
Uzuragoromo ········ 鶉衣 **6:**297b; **8:**331b

V

Vaccination ················· **6:**164a
Vajra ···················· **1:***196b*
   esoteric ritual implements ···· **1:**196a
Vajradhātu ········· **4:**269b–270a
Vajraśekhara-sūtra ·········· **7:**113b
Valignano, Alessandro ·········· **1:**229b;
2:306b–307a; **8:**189a
   Jesuit mission press ·········· 4:51a
   mission to Europe of 1582 ···· 5:203a
Valleys: Four Themes ········· **8:**13a
Valor of Ignorance, The ········ **8:**323a
Value-Creating Society ········ **7:**224b
Vanguard Artists League (Zen'ei
   Geijutsuka Dōmei) ············ **6:**255a
Van Reed, Eugene ············ **4:**13b
Vassalage system ············ **1:**131b
Vaughn, Miles W. ·········· **8:**189a
Vegetables
   cucumber (kyūri) ·········· 2:52a–52b
   cucurbits ·············· 2:52a–52b
   eggplants ·················· 2:184b
   green ···················· 8:189a
   production ·················· 1:27a
   radishes ··················· 6:276a
   Welsh onions ··············· 8:241a
   Western ············ **8:**189a–189b
Vegetarian cooking ·········· **2:**22a
Vegetation
   anthropogenic period ········· 5:95b–96a
   late-glacial period ·········· 5:93a–93b
   paleolithic period ··········· 5:92b–93a
   postglacial period ··········· 5:93b–95b
Vehicles, diesel
   Hino Motors, Ltd ············ **3:**140b
   Nissan Diesel Motor Co, Ltd ······· **6:**20b
Vendetta. See **Katakiuchi**
Venereal disease ········· **2:**126a; **8:**189b
   missionary ················· 1:308a
Venereal Disease Prevention Law in
   1948 ····················· **8:**189b
Verbeck, Guido Herman Fridolin ·**1:**308a;
2:311a; **8:**189b–190a
Vermilion-seal certificate ······ **7:**184a–184b
Vermilion seal ship (shuisen) ····· **7:***144b*
Vermilion seal ship trade ····· **1:**74a, 83b;
5:306a; **7:**255b, 256b; **8:**190a–190b

Hamada Yahyōe ·············· **3**:89b–90a
licensed vessels ·············· **3**:235b
National Seclusion ············ **5**:346b
Taiwan ····················· **7**:306b
Vernacular tracts ············· **7**:80b–81a
Verny, François Léonce ····· **1**:80b, 175b;
               2:331b; **8**:190b
Versailles, Treaty of ······· **3**:199a; **7**:235a;
               8:190b–191a
  China ···················· **1**:288a
  territory of Japan ··········· **8**:14a
  "White Australia" ··········· **1**:119a
Versailles Peace Conference ····· **6**:307b
Vertical society ········· **2**:245a; **8**:191a
  paternalism ················ **6**:165a
Vice-ministers ·········· **8**:191a–191b
Victor Co of Japan, Ltd ······ **8**:191b
  Takayanagi Kenjirō ·········· **7**:321a
Vidyārāja ··················· **5**:291a
Vienna Exposition of 1873 ······· **4**:182a
Viet Minh ··················· **2**:333a
Vietnam
  activities ·················· **2**:53a
  cultural sphere ·········· **2**:141b–142a
  refugees ··················· **6**:286a
Vietnam and Japan ······· **8**:191b–192a
Vietnam Duy Tan Hoi (Reformation
  Society) ··················· **6**:182a
Vietnam War ········· **6**:166a; **8**:192a
  Okinawa ··················· **6**:90b
Viewing a Waterfall ··········· **7**:163b
Views of Sumiyoshi Handscroll ··· **6**:78a
Vijf jaren in Japan (Five Years in Japan)
  ······················· **6**:220b
Village headman ·········· **7**:177a–177b
Village Japan ··············· **4**:41b
Villages
  agricultural ················ **7**:213a
  museums ·············· **5**:278a–278b
Vinaya ····················· **1**:177a
Vining, Elizabeth Gray ········ **8**:192a
Violets [(sumire) *Viola* spp.] · **8**:192a–192b
Virilocal postmarital residence ···· **4**:217b
Virus studies ················ **4**:36b
Viscaino, Sebastian ·········· **8**:192b
Vivero de Velasco, Rodrigo ····· **8**:192b
  shipwreck ················· **4**:369a
VLSI Research Center ··········· **2**:194b
Vocabulario ················ **4**:51a
*Vocabulario da Lingoa de Japam
  com a declaração em Portugues* ·· **6**:8b
Vocabulary development ········· **4**:30a
Vocational education ······ **8**:192b–193a
Vocational Training Law ····· **8**:193a–193b
  of 1958 ··········· **4**:352b; **8**:193b
  of 1969 ··················· **8**:193b
Volcanic front ··············· **8**:193b
Volcanic zones
  Chishima ·················· **1**:297a
  Chōkai ···················· **1**:299b
  Fuji ····················· **2**:347b
  Hakusan ··················· **3**:89a
  Kirishima ················· **4**:221b
  Nasu ····················· **5**:336a
  Norikura ·················· **6**:37b
Volcanoes ········· **4**:7b; **8**:193b–195b
  caldera ··················· **8**:194b
  distribution and makeup ······ **8**:193b
  eruption disasters and prevention
    ··················· **8**:195a–195b
  Eurasia plate ··············· **8**:195a
  history and present situation of
    volcanology ··········· **8**:194b–195a
  Hokkaidō
    Daisetsuzan ·············· **2**:67b
    Komagatake ·············· **4**:264b
    Meakandake ·············· **5**:144a
    Oakandake ··············· **6**:47a

    Rausudake ··············· **6**:284b
    Shōwa Shinzan ············ **7**:177a
    Tarumaezan ·············· **7**:347b
    Tokachidake ·············· **8**:40a
    Usuzan ················· **8**:182a
    Yōteizan ················ **8**:352a
  Honshū
    Adatarasan ··············· **1**:11b
    Akagisan ················ **1**:39a
    Asamayama ·············· **1**:95b
    Azumasan ··············· **1**:127b
    Bandaisan ··············· **1**:137a
    Chōkaisan ··············· **1**:299b
    Daisen ·················· **2**:67a
    Fujisan ·············· **2**:344b–345b
    Gassan ················· **3**:12a
    Hakkōdasan ·············· **3**:85b
    Hakoneyama ·············· **3**:87a
    Hakusan ················ **3**:88b
    Harunasan ··············· **3**:106a
    Hiuchigadake ············· **3**:208b
    Hotakayama ·············· **3**:237b
    Iwakisan ················ **3**:358a
    Iwatesan ················ **3**:363b
    Kampūzan ··············· **4**:130b
    Komagatake ·········· **4**:264b–265a
    Kurikomayama ············ **4**:313a
    Kurohimeyama ············ **4**:315b
    Myōjinshō ··············· **5**:290b
    Myōkōsan ··············· **5**:291a
    Naebasan ················ **5**:300a
    Nantaisan ··············· **5**:329b
    Nasudake ················ **5**:335b
    Norikuradake ············· **6**:37b
    Nyohōzan ················ **6**:45b
    Nyūtōzan ················ **6**:45b
    Ontakesan ··········· **6**:112b–113a
    Osorezan ················ **6**:127a
    Sambesan ················ **7**:6a
    Shiranesan (Nikkō Shraine) ··· **7**:147a
    Shiranesan (Kusatsu Shirane) ·· **7**:147a
    Yakedake ············ **8**:284b–285a
    Yatsugatake ·············· **8**:320a
    Zaōzan ················· **8**:368a
  Japanese people ············ **8**:194b
  Kyūshū
    Asosan ················· **1**:103a
    Kaimondake ·············· **4**:111b
    Kirishimayama ············ **4**:221b
    Takachihonomine ·········· **7**:310b
    Takasakiyama ············· **7**:318b
    Taradake ················ **7**:346a
    Unzendake ··············· **8**:174b
    large steam explosion ········ **8**:194a
    lava dome ··············· **8**:194a
    monogentic ·············· **8**:194a
    pyroclastic cone ··········· **8**:194a
    pyroclastic eruption ········· **8**:194b
    pyroclastic flow ··········· **8**:194b
    single eruption ············ **8**:194a
    structure and activity ······ **8**:193b–194b
Volkskunde ·················· **4**:324b
Volleyball ················· **8**:195a
Volta Redonda ··············· **1**:168a
Vories, William Merrel ········ **8**:195b
Voting ················· **2**:188b–190a
Votive offerings, pictorial ····· **2**:196b–198a
VOU ····················· **4**:229a
Vukelic, Branco ··············· **7**:229b

Wa ···················· 倭 **7**:259b; **8**:197a
  Five Kings ················· **2**:287b
Wabi ················ 侘び **3**:267b–268a;
             6:361a; **7**:85b; **8**:197a
  ferns ···················· **2**:252a
Wabisuke ··················· **1**:237a
Wacoal Corporation ·········· **8**:197b
Wada ················ 和田 **8**:197b
Wada Eisaku ····· 和田英作 **8**:197b
Wada Hiroo ········· 和田博雄 **2**:168a
Wada Pass ············ 和田峠 **8**:197b
Wadatsumikai · わだつみ会 ····· **4**:206a
Wada Yoshimori · 和田義盛 **8**:197b–198a
  Samurai-dokoro (Board of Retainers) **7**:8b
Wadō kaichin. 和同開珎 *See* **Wadō kaihō**
Wadō kaihō ······ 和同開珎 · **5**:242a–242b;
             8:198a
  kōchō jūnisen ·············· **4**:240a
Waegwan ·················· **8**:198a
  Japanese envoys ············ **4**:279b
Wagahai wa neko de aru
  ············· 吾輩は猫である **5**:350a
Wagaku Kōdansho
  ········· 和学講談所 **1**:229a; **3**:155b
"Wagakuni no shigeki"
  ··········· わが邦の史劇 ······ **8**:110b
Waga seishin no henreki
  ·········· 我が精神の遍歴 ····· **4**:125a
Waga seishun ni kui nashi
  ·········· わが青春に悔なし ····· **7**:108b
Waga tō wa soko ni tatsu
  ······· わが塔はそこに立つ ···· **4**:339b
Wagatsuma Sakae · 我妻栄 **8**:198a–198b
  works ···················· **8**:198b
Wage and lifetime employment
  systems ··················· **8**:199b
Wage bargaining ·············· **7**:188b
Wage determination ············ **8**:199b
Wage differentials ····· **4**:343b; **8**:198b
  factors ··················· **8**:198b
Wage level ············ **8**:198b–199a
Wagener, Gottfried · **1**:260a; **5**:276a; **7**:51b;
             8:199a
Wages
  base ···················· **8**:200a
  bonus ··············· **1**:163a–163b
  components ··············· **7**:189a
  real ····················· **8**:199b
  regulation ················· **4**:352b
Wage system ··········· **8**:199b–200b
  government guidelines ········ **3**:287b
  income distribution ·········· **3**:285b
  nenkō ···················· **4**:345b
  problems ·················· **8**:200b
  salaries ··················· **8**:199b
  seniority system ············ **2**:211a
Wagon ···················· **4**:108a
Wagtails [(sekirei) family Motacillidae]
  ······················· **8**:200b–201a
Wainai Sadayuki
  ·········· 和井内貞行 ······· **8**:201a
Waisetsu ·················· **6**:49b–50b
Wajima ··············· 輪島 **8**:201a
"Wajinden" ········· 倭人伝 **8**:240a

Waji shōran shō

················· 和字正濫鈔·· **4**:134a, 188a,
258a; **8**:201a
Japanese language studies ··········· **4**:31a
Wajū ··············· 輪中· **8**:*201a*, 201b
Ibigawa ······························ **3**:253b
Wajū type embankments ········· **8**:338b
Waka ··············· 和歌 **6**:296b, 297b;
7:52b, 94b, 105a; **8**:201b-217a
criticism ························· **5**:14b
early classical period (794-1100)
·················· **1**:292b-293a; **8**:207b-210b
Bo Juyi (Po Chii-i) and Tang poetry
···································· **8**:210a
descriptive poetry ·········· **8**:210a-210b
Kokinshū periods ··········· **4**:254b-255a;
8:208b-209a
poetics ······················· **8**:209a
poetry contests ·············· **8**:209b
Six Dynasties poetry ······· **8**:208a-208b
early literary period (ca 610-784)
anonymous poems ············ **8**:207b
first *Man'yō* period ········ **8**:205a-205b
second *Man'yō* period and
Hitomaro ················· **8**:205b-206a
third *Man'yō* period ······ **8**:206a-207a
fourth *Man'yō* period and Yakamochi
······························· **8**:207a-207b
Edo period (1600-1868) ····· **8**:215b-216a
independents ················· **8**:216a
national scholars ··········· **8**:215b-216a
general characteristics ····· **8**:201b-202a
honkadori ······················ **3**:223b
imagery and metaphor ·········· **8**:203b
imperial anthologies ············ **3**:275b
Kokin Denju ···················· **4**:254a
late classical period (1250-1350)
······················· **8**:213b-214b
abstractions ················· **8**:214b
new styles ··············· **8**:214a-214b
other stylistic features ······ **8**:214b
Man'yōshū ················· **5**:102b-110b
mid-classical period (1100-1250)
························· **8**:210b-213b
aesthetic ideals ············· **8**:212a
conservatives and innovators
······················· **8**:211a-211b
descriptive symbolism ········ **8**:211a
harmony and balance ········· **8**:211b
"old words, new treatment" **8**:211b-212a
modern period (1867-present) **8**:216a-217a
contemporary ················ **8**:217b
early twentieth century ····· **8**:216b-217a
Masaoka Shiki and shasei **5**:123a; **8**:216b
Myōjō school ·········· **5**:290b; **8**:216b
moon viewing ·················· **5**:248a
post-classical period (1350-1600)
························· **8**:214b-215b
anti-Nijō forces ············· **8**:215a
decline of court poetry ····· **8**:215a-215b
primitive song and poetry
(ca 550-686) ··· **2**:137a-138b; **8**:204b-205a
prosody ··················· **8**:202a-203a
revival (794-905) ··········· **5**:29a-32a
rhetorical devices ········· **8**:203a-203b
engo ························· **8**:203b
jokotoba ················ **4**:71b; **8**:203a
kakekotoba ········· **4**:115b; **8**:203a-203b
makura kotoba ·········· **5**:87a; **8**:203a
uta makura ·········· **4**:185b; **8**:203a
Rokkasen ····················· **6**:334b
Shin kokinshū ··· **7**:119a-120b; **8**:212a-213b
association and progression principles
····························· **8**:213a
attenuation and decline ····· **8**:213b
other poets ·················· **8**:213a

Teika's styles ······· **2**:354a; **8**:212b-213a
Shintō ························· **7**:131b
sources ···················· **8**:204a-204b
subjects ····················· **8**:203b
subjects, themes, and modes · **8**:203b-204a
themes ························ **8**:204a
travel diaries ··············· **8**:105b
uta-awase ················· **8**:182a-182b
wabi ·························· **8**:197a
writing style ················ **4**:132b
Wakaba no uta 若葉のうた ······ **4**:139a
Wakadokoro e fushin jōjō
········ 和歌所へ不審条々 ··· **3**:272a
Wakadoshiyori ··· 若年寄· **8**:217a-217b
Wakai ····················· **8**:217b
Wakai hito (Young
People) ·········· 若い人 ··· **8**:90b
Wakaki shijin no tegami
········· 若き詩人の手紙 ··· **4**:114a
Wakakusayama ···· 若草山 · **8**:*217a*, 217b
Wakamatsu colony ············· **4**:13b
Wakamatsusama ················ **8**:83a
Wakamatsu Shizuko
·············· 若松賤子 ··· **8**:217b
Wakame (seaweed) ············· **7**:47a
Wakamono-gumi ··· 若者組 · **8**:217b-218a,
353b
Wakan ················ 倭館 ··· **8**:198a
Wakanoura ········· 和歌浦 ··· **8**:218a
Wakan rōeishū 和漢朗詠集 · **2**:353b; **5**:35a;
8:208a, 218a
compilers ··················· **8**:218a
Fujiwara no Kintō ·········· **2**:352a
Wakan sansai zue
············· 和漢三才図絵 ··· **8**:218a
Wakao Ayako ···· 若尾文子 ··· **8**:218b
films ························· **8**:218b
Waka poetry techniques ········· **3**:223b
Waka poets (modern). *See* Tanka poets
Waka poets (premodern)
Abutsu Ni ················· **1**:5b-6a
Akazome Emon ············· **1**:41a
Ariwara no Narihira ········ **1**:85b
Asukai Masaari ············· **1**:106b
Asukai Masatsune ··········· **1**:106b
Eifuku Mon'in ············· **2**:186a
Fujitani Mitsue ············ **2**:346b
Fujiwara no Akisuke ········ **2**:350a
Fujiwara no Ietaka ········· **2**:351a
Fujiwara no Kanesuke ······· **2**:351b
Fujiwara no Kintō ·········· **2**:352a
Fujiwara no Kiyosuke ······· **2**:352b
Fujiwara no Michitoshi ····· **2**:353a
Fujiwara no Mototoshi ······ **2**:353b
Fujiwara no Nobuzane ······· **2**:353b-354a
Fujiwara no Sadaie ········· **2**:354a-355a
Fujiwara no Takanobu ······· **2**:355b
Fujiwara no Tameie ········· **2**:355b-356b
Fujiwara no Toshinari ······ **2**:356b-357b
Fujiwara no Toshinari no Musume **2**:357b
Fujiwara no Yoshitsune ····· **2**:358a
Go-Toba, Emperor ··········· **3**:51a-52b
Henjō ······················ **3**:126b
Hiraga Motoyoshi ·········· **3**:142b
Hosokawa Yūsai ············ **3**:237a-237b
Ichijō Kaneyoshi ·········· **3**:256a
Ike no Gyokuran ··········· **3**:266b
Imagawa Sadayo ············ **3**:272a
Ise ························· **3**:336b
Izumi Shikibu ············· **3**:367a
Jakuren ···················· **4**:1b
Jien ······················· **4**:53b-54a
Kada no Arimaro ··········· **4**:100b
Kada no Azumamaro ········· **4**:100b
Kagawa Kageki ············· **4**:102b-103a
Kakinmoto no Hitomaro ····· **4**:17a
Kamo no Chōmei ············ **4**:128b
Kamo no Mabuchi ··········· **4**:129a

Karasumaru Mitsuhiro ········· **4**:158a
Kasa no Kanamura ············· **4**:161a
Katō Chikage ················· **4**:167b
Katori Nahiko ················ **4**:169a
Kenshō ······················· **4**:198b
Kinoshita Chōshōshi ·········· **4**:214b
Kinoshita Takafumi ··········· **4**:216a
Ki no Tomonori ··············· **4**:216a
Ki no Tsurayuki ·············· **4**:216b-217a
Kitamura Kigin ··············· **4**:227a
Kumagai Naoyoshi ············· **4**:304b
Kyōgoku Tamekane ············· **4**:329a-329b
Mibu no Tadamine ············· **5**:166a-166b
Minamoto no Sanetomo ········· **5**:178b
Minamoto no Shitagau ········· **5**:179a
Minamoto no Toshiyori ········ **5**:179b-180a
Minamoto no Tsunenobu ········ **5**:180a-180b
Munetaka, Prince ············· **5**:265a
Murata Harumi ················ **5**:269b
Nijō Tameyo ·················· **5**:387a
Nijō Yoshimoto ··············· **5**:387b
Nōin ························· **6**:32b
Nomura Motoni ················ **6**:34a-34b
Nukata no Ōkimi ·············· **6**:44a
Ōkuma Kotomichi ·············· **6**:95a-95b
Ōnakatomi no Yoshinobu ······ **6**:105a-105b
Ono no Komachi ··············· **6**:110b-111a
Ono no Takamura ·············· **6**:111a-111b
Ōshikōchi no Mitsune ········· **6**:125a
Ōtagaki Rengetsu ············· **6**:128b
Ōtomo no Sakanoue no Iratsume · **6**:131a
Ōtomo no Tabito ·············· **6**:131a-131b
Ōtomo no Yakamochi ··········· **6**:131b
Ozawa Roan ··················· **6**:140b
Reizei Tamesuke ·············· **6**:289b
Shimizu Hamaomi ·············· **7**:104a
Shimokōbe Chōryū ············· **7**:105a
Shōhaku ······················ **7**:161b-162a
Shōtetsu ····················· **7**:170b
Sone no Yoshitada ············ **7**:227a-227b
Sosei ························· **7**:232a
Tachibana Akemi ·············· **7**:291b-292a
Tachibana Moribe ············· **7**:292b
Takahashi no Mushimaro ······ **7**:313a
Takebe Ayatari ··············· **7**:321a-321b
Takechi no Kurohito ·········· **7**:321a
Tayasu Munetake ·············· **7**:359a
Toda Mosui ··················· **8**:34b
Ton'a ························· **8**:73b
Tō no Tsuneyori ·············· **8**:75a-75b
Ueda Akinari ················· **8**:126b
Yamabe no Akahito ············ **8**:287a
Yamanoue no Okura ············ **8**:302b-303a
Wakasa Bay ········ 若狭湾 **2**:364a; **4**:338a;
8:*218b*
Wakatei jisshu ("Ten
Styles of Waka")
············· 和歌体十種 ··· **8**:209a
Wakatoshisama ················ **8**:83a
Wakatsuki Reijirō
·············· 若槻礼次郎 ··· **7**:78a, 88b;
8:218b-219a
cabinet ···················· **1**:11a; **2**:277a
Kenseikai ·················· **4**:198a
Wakayama ········· 和歌山 ··· **8**:219a
Wakayama Bokusui
··············· 若山牧水 · **7**:61a; **8**:219a
works ······················ **8**:219a
Wakayama Plain
·············· 和歌山平野 ··· **8**:219b
Wakayama Prefecture
·············· 和歌山県 ··· **8**:219b
Wake no Kiyomaro
·············· 和気清麻呂 ··· **8**:220a
Heiankyō ··················· **3**:121b
Jingoji ···················· **4**:58b
Waki ························· **4**:298b
Wakiōkan ··········· 脇往還 ··· **8**:220a

Wakkanai ·············· 稚内 ······ 8:220a
Wakō (city) ·········· 和光 ······ 8:220a
Wakō (pirates) ······· 倭寇 ····· 2:148a;
             8:220a-221a
  Japanese, in Koryŏ ········· 4:278a
  Korea ······················· 8:220b
  Korean raids ················ 4:276a
  phases ······················ 8:220b
  Ryūkyū trade ··············· 6:358a
  Southeast Asia ············· 8:221a
  tally trade ·········· 7:331b-332a
Wakon kansai ···· 和魂漢才 ··· 8:221a
Wakon yōsai ····· 和魂洋才 ··· 2:34a;
            8:221a-221b, 290b
  technological innovation ····· 7:371b
Wako Shungorō
          輪湖俊午郎 ····· 8:221b
Wakun no shiori ··· 和訓栞 ··· 8:221b
Waley, Arthur David ··· 8:221b-222a
  Chinese translations ········ 8:221b
  Japanese translations ······· 8:221b
Wall painting ················ 6:148b
Wamyō ruiju shō
      倭名類聚鈔 ·· 4:50b, 188a;
             8:222a
  kites ························ 4:229b
Wamyōshō. See Wamyō ruiju shō
Wands (gohei) ··············· 3:40a
Wang Chao-ming ············· 8:222a
Wang Jingwei (Wang Ching-wei) · 3:201b;
     6:302a-302b; 8:222a
Wang Kemin (Wang K'o-min) ····· 8:222b
Wang Kōn ··················· 4:278a
Wāngsōngguk ················ 4:277b
Wang Tao (Wang T'ao) ···· 4:141a; 8:222b
"Wang Xizhi Writing on Fans" ···· 4:77b
Wang Yangming philosophy. See
  Yōmeigaku
Wang Yangming school. See
  Yōmeigaku
Wang Zhaoming ·············· 8:222a
Wang Zhengting (Wang Cheng-
  t'ing) ··············· 8:222b-223a
Wani ····· 王仁 ············ 8:223a
  Yamato court visitor ········ 4:277a
Wan Jingwei (Wang Ching-wei) ···· 7:92a
Wankel engine
  rotary ······················ 6:339b
Wa no Goō ···· 倭の五王 · 2:287b-288a
Warabe uta. See Children's songs
Warabi ····· 蕨 ············ 8:223a
Warabidemon ···· 蕨手文 ··· 2:252a
Waragutsu ········· 7:249b; 8:223a
Warai no Ōkoku 笑いの王国 ···· 8:52a
Waraji ············ 7:249b; 8:223a
Warambegusa ···· 童子草 ··· 4:328a
Warashibe chōja
      わらしべ長者 · 8:223a-223b
War chronicles ·············· 7:165b
  medieval ···················· 5:43b
War crimes trials ······ 8:223b-225b
  defendant's list ······· 8:224a-224b
  Kainō Michitaka ············ 4:112a
  Ladybird Incident ·········· 4:362a
  "minor" trials ········ 8:223b-224a
  Nanjing Incident ······ 5:328b-329a
  Tōkyō trial ··········· 8:224a-224b
  Webb, Sir William Flood ···· 8:238a
Ward, J ····················· 3:309b
Warigo ··············· 4:105a; 8:225b
Warizansho (Writings on
  Division) ········· 割算書 ··· 8:231b
War literature ········· 8:225b-228a
  Russo-Japanese War ········· 8:226a
  Sino-Japanese War ····· 8:225b-226a
  World War I ················ 8:226b
  World War II ··············· 8:226b

Warlords
  Uesugi family ·············· 8:129a
Warner, Langdon ············ 8:228a
Warplanes ·················· 1:123b
  command reconnaissance ···· 1:123b
  Hayabusa ··················· 1:123b
  Hayate ····················· 1:123b
  Model 97 ··················· 1:123b
  Shiden-modified ············ 1:123b
  Zero fighter ··············· 1:123b
War Relocation Authority (WRA)
  Japanese Americans ········· 4:17b
  centers ····················· 8:228b
"Warring States" ············· 1:99b
Warring States period ········ 7:64a
Warrior class
  eating habits ··············· 2:305b
  feudalism ··················· 2:266b
Warrior ethic ··········· 1:221b-223b
  kakun ······················ 1:222a
Warrior families
  Hatekeyama family ·········· 3:111a
  Hosokawa family ············ 3:236a
  Imagawa family ············· 3:271b
  Kyōgoku family ······· 4:329a-329b
  Matsumae family ············ 5:137a
  Minamoto family ······ 5:176b-178b
  Miura family ··············· 5:215a
  Mōri family ················ 5:249b
  Nabeshima family ··········· 5:299a
  Nitta family ················ 6:22a
  Ogasawara family ··········· 6:68b
  Ōshū Fujiwara family ·· 6:126b-127a
  Ōtomo family ··············· 6:130b
  Satake family ··············· 7:25b
  Shiba family ·········· 7:83b-84a
  Togashi family ·············· 8:36a
  Tokugawa family ······· 8:45b-47b
  Uragami family ············· 8:174b
  vassals
    ienoko and rōtō ··········· 3:261a
  women ······················ 8:259a
  Yamana family ·············· 8:300b
Warrior-farmer-artisan-merchant ·· 7:122a
Warrior government ··· 7:8a; 8:228b-230b
  Ashikaga Takauji ··········· 1:100a
  Hōgen and Heiji disturbances ···· 8:229a
  Kamakura shogunate ······· 8:229a-229b
  keishi ······················ 4:190a
  laws ······················· 1:206b
  Minamoto no Yoritomo ······ 5:182a
  Muromachi shogunate ·· 8:229b-230a
  Nobunaga and Hideyoshi ···· 8:230a
  overview ··················· 8:230b
  peerage ···················· 6:170b
  periodization ········· 6:174a-174b
  provinces ·················· 6:260a
  Taira-Minamoto War ········ 7:300b
  Tokugawa Ieyasu ············ 8:49a
  Tokugawa shogunate ···· 8:230a-230b
  warrior class ········· 8:228b-229a
Warrior leagues
  kinship ···················· 1:221b
  Tōryō ······················ 1:221b
Warrior library ··············· 5:1a
Warrior-monks ········· 8:230b-231a
  at Kōfukuji ················· 4:244a
  naginata ············· 5:308a-308b
  Taira no Tadamori ·········· 7:302a
  Temmon Hokke Rebellion ··· 7:381b-382b
Warriors
  Abe no Munetō ·············· 1:4a
  Ankokuji Ekei ·············· 1:62a
  Aoto Fujitsuna ·············· 1:70b
  Benkei ····················· 1:149b
  Date Masamune ········· 2:78a-79b
  Forty-Seven Rōnin Incident · 2:327a-328a
  Fujiwara no Hidesato ········ 2:350b

  Furuta Oribe ··············· 2:373b
  Hatakeyama Shigetada ······· 3:111b
  Hori Hidemasa ············· 3:227b
  Ii Naomasa ················· 3:262b
  Imagawa Sadayo ············ 3:272a
  Ishida Mitsunari ··········· 3:340a
  Itō Sukechika ·············· 3:356a
  Kajiwara Kagetoki ·········· 4:114b
  Katagiri Katsumoto ········· 4:165a
  Kimura Shigenari ··········· 4:211b
  Kojima Takanori ············ 4:252a
  Kōno Michiari ·············· 4:274b
  Kusunoki Masashige ········· 4:321a
  Matsudaira Ietada ·········· 5:131a
  Minamoto no Yoshinaka ······ 5:182b
  Minamoto no Yoshitomo ····· 5:182b
  Minamoto no Yoshitsune ·· 5:182b-183a
  Musashi Shichitō ··········· 5:275b
  Nasu no Yoichi ············· 5:336a
  Nitta Yoshisada ······· 6:22a-22b
  Ōishi Yoshio ··············· 6:75b
  Ōkubo Hikozaemon ·········· 6:93b
  Ōta Dōkan ················· 6:128b
  regulations for ············· 8:50b
  Sanada Yukimura ············ 7:9a
  Sasaki Takatsuna ············ 7:23a
  Shibata Katsuie ············· 7:84b
  Taira no Masakado ·········· 7:301a
  Taira no Munemori ········· 7:301b
  Taira no Shigehira ···· 7:301b-302a
  Taira no Tadamori ·········· 7:302a
  Taira no Tadanori ·········· 7:302a
  Taira no Tomomori ········· 7:302b
  Takezaki Suenaga ··········· 7:326b
  Yamanaka Shikanosuke ····· 8:300b-301a
  yoriki and dōshin ·········· 8:338b
  yorioya-yoriko relationship ···· 8:338b
  See also Daimyō
Warriors' vassals ······ 3:261a-261b
War songs. See Gunka
War stories ················· 3:68b
Wartime relocation centers
  Jerome Relocation Center ····· 4:50b-51a
"Warui nakama" 悪い仲間 ······ 8:319b
War Victim Relief Law of 1942 ··· 1:110b
Wasabi ····················· 3:127b
Wasan (mathematics) 和算 · 8:231a-232a
Wasan ···· 和讃 ············ 8:231a
  religious symbolism ········· 6:295b
  Shinran ···················· 7:123a
Waseda bungaku
       早稲田文学 7:309b; 8:232a
Waseda University ··········· 8:232a
  correspondence education ····· 2:181b
  Ōkuma Shigenobu ··········· 6:95b
Washi ··· 1:125a; 2:294a, 296a; 8:232a-234a,
                    234
  Azuchi-Momoyama period ··· 8:233a-233b
  Edo period (1600-1868) ······ 8:233b
  Heian period (794-1185) ····· 8:232b-233a
  invention and transmission ···· 8:232b
  Kamakura period ······· 8:233a-233b
  Meiji period (1868-1912) to present 8:233b
  molding ···················· 8:234a
  Muromachi period ······ 8:233a-233b
  Nara period (710-794) ······· 8:232b
  raingear ··················· 6:280a
  techniques ··········· 8:233b-234a
Washington Conference ······ 3:199a;
    7:77a-77b; 8:157a, 234a-235a, 343b
  Anglo-Japanese Alliance ····· 1:57a
  China ······················ 1:288a
  consequences ··············· 8:235a
  Four-Power Treaty ·········· 2:330a
  French-Japanese relations ···· 2:332b
  international relations ······· 3:321a
  Japan's response ············ 8:234b
  negotiations ·········· 8:234b-235a

Nine-Power Treaty ··············· 6:4b
origins ·················· 8:234a–234b
Shidehara Kijūrō ············· 7:88a–88b
United Kingdom and Japan ······· 8:152a
Wang Zhengting (Wang Cheng-t'ing)
··················· 8:222b
Washington Naval Treaty of 1922 · 8:235a
Washington Naval Treaty of 1922 ·······
1:88a; 8:157a, 235a–235b
Japan's position ············· 8:235a
negotiations ··············· 8:235a
origins ··················· 8:235a
power of supreme command ······· 8:85a
significance ··············· 8:235b
terms ··················· 8:235b
"Washington System" ············ 3:321a
Washiuzan 鷲羽山 ············ 8:235b
Wasps. *See* **Bees and wasps**
Waste, industrial ·············· 3:302b
Waste Land ·········· 1:82b–83a; 6:19b
Wasuregusa ni yosu
萱草に寄す ····· 7:293a
Watakushi no aruita michi
私の歩いた道 ·· 1:155b
Watakushi shōsetsu ·· 3:312a–312b; 8:235b
Watanabe Gen ····· 渡辺元 ········ 2:76a
Watanabe Jōtarō
················· 渡辺錠太郎 ······ 8:235b
February 26th Incident ········· 2:249b
Watanabe Kazan 渡辺崋山 · 1:211a; 7:27a,
28b; 8:235b–236a
portrait painting ············ 6:227b
Watanabe Kunio ·渡辺邦男 ······· 2:272b
Watanabe Masanosuke
················· 渡辺政之輔 ······ 8:236a
Watanabe Nangaku
··········· 渡辺南岳 ······ 8:236a
Watanabe Sadao 渡辺貞夫 ····· 8:236a
Watanabe Shikō ·渡辺始興 ····· 8:236a
Watanabe Tetsuzō
················· 渡辺銕蔵 ······ 8:236a
Watarai Shintō ··· 度会神道 2:300b; 7:128a,
263b; 8:236b
Watarasegawa ···· 渡良瀬川 ···· 8:236b
Watari yagura (tower) 渡櫓 ······· 1:248b
Watatsumi ········· 海神 ···· 5:294b
Wataya Bunko ··· 綿屋文庫 ········ 8:8b
Watches ··················· 6:233b
Water deities ·············· 7:263b
Waterfalls
Akame, 48 Falls of ············ 1:40b
Fukuroda Falls ··············· 2:365b
Kamba Falls ··············· 4:123a
Kegon Falls ··············· 4:186b
Nachi Falls ··············· 5:299a
Shiraito Falls ··············· 7:145b
Water lily [(suiren) *Nymphae tetragona*
var. *angusta*] ·············· 8:237a
Water pollution
diseases ············· 2:226a–226b
factors ··················· 2:227a
Water Quality Conservation Law · 2:227a
**Water Resources Development Public
Corporation** ·············· 8:237a
Waters, Thomas James ····· 1:80b; 8:237a
Waterwheels ·········· 8:237a–237b
Watsuji Tetsurō ·和辻哲郎 5:231a; 8:237b
emperor theory ········· 2:208a–208b
Shinshichō ··············· 7:125a
Wax-resist dyeing ······ 8:17b, 237b–238a
Wayaku Tarō. 和訳太郎
See **Ueda Akinari**
Wayland, Francis ··············· 3:4b
Wayo 和与 1:183a, 234b; 8:238a
Way of Reason ··············· 8:26b
"Way of Yin and Yang, The" ······ 6:103a
*Ways of Thinking of Eastern Peoples:
India, China, Tibet, Japan* ······ 5:315b

Waza ···················· 4:196a
Wazauta ···················· 3:59b
Wazoku dōjikun
和俗童子訓 ······ 4:108b
WCTU ···················· 4:324b
Wealth, national ········· 5:349a–349b
Weaponry, bronze ········· 1:174a–175a
Weapons
defense industry ········· 2:82a–82b
See also **Arms and armor**
Weasels [(itachi) *Mustela sibirica*] · 8:238a
Weaving. *See* **Textiles**
Webb, Sir William Flood ········ 8:238a
Weddings ·········· 5:4b; 8:238b–239a
courting procedures ··········· 8:238b
modern ··················· 8:239a
rituals ··················· 8:238b
traditional ············· 8:238b–239a
Weekly magazines ········ 8:239a–239b
Wei China
Himiko relations ········· 3:139b–140a
Weight ··················· 4:37b
Weights and measures ······ 8:239b–240a
koku ··················· 4:256b
monetary units ············· 8:240a
premodern units ········· 8:239b–240a
Wei lüe ··················· 7:264a
Wei zhi (Wei chih) ··· 魏志 · 1:78b; 2:365a;
7:69a, 264a; 8:240a–241a, 305a
history ··············· 4:28a–28b
Shintō ··················· 7:126a
Wa ···················· 8:197a
women in ··············· 8:256b
Welfare Acts for Working Women
(1972) ··················· 8:265b
Welsh onion (*Allium fistulosum*) ··· 8:241a
Shimonita ··············· 7:105a
Wen ···················· 4:123b
Wen-jen-hua ············· 1:210a–211a
Wenrenhua ············· 1:210a–211a
Wen xuan (*Monzen* or *Literary
Selections*) ·········· 4:109a; 8:208a
West
attitude toward ········· 2:311b–312a
cultural sphere ············· 2:142a
interest in Japan ········· 4:41a–42b
West Asian design composition
··············· 7:195b–196a
West Asian materials ··········· 7:195b
West Asian objects and shapes ··· 7:195b
Western-art museums ····· 5:279a–279b
Western Electric Co, quality control
··················· 6:273a
Westernization
language reforms ············· 4:29b
literary portrayal ············· 2:378b
Western Japan ··············· 8:241a
Western Learning · 7:16a, 94b; 8:241a–243a
arts ··················· 8:242b
astronomy ··········· 8:242a–242b
botany ··················· 8:242b
campaigns against
Bansha no Goku ··········· 1:141b
chemistry ··············· 8:242b
Dejima ··················· 2:83b
Dutch ··············· 8:241b–242a
Dutch Factory ············· 2:135b
education ··············· 2:174b
shogunate missions to the West · 7:161b
educational institutions
Seimikyoku ··············· 7:51b
Fuseya Soteki ··············· 2:374b
geography ··········· 8:242a–242b
Iwakura mission ············· 3:359a
Kawamoto Kōmin ············ 4:181b
Kōsei shimpen stimulated ····· 4:294b
language studies ········· 8:242b–243a
mathematics ··············· 8:242b

medicine ··················· 8:242a
Meiji Restoration ········· 5:155a–155b
military science ············· 8:242b
National Seclusion ········· 5:346b–347b
Ogata Kōan ··············· 6:69a
physics ··················· 8:242b
Rangaku kaitei ··············· 6:283b
Rangaku schools ············· 8:243a
studies
Bansho Shirabesho ········ 1:141b–142a
Titsingh, Izaak ············· 8:30a
**Western literature and Japanese
literature** ·········· 8:243a–247a
American influences ······ 8:244a–244b
characteristics ··············· 5:25a
English and Irish influences ·· 8:243b–244a
French influences ········ 8:244b–246a
German influences ············ 8:246b
Italian influences ········ 8:246b–247a
Norwegian influence ·········· 8:247a
Russian influences ········ 8:246a–246b
Spanish influences ············ 8:247a
**Western literature in Japanese
translation** ·········· 8:247a–248b
19th century ··············· 8:247b
20th century ············ 8:247b–248b
Western music ··········· 5:285b–287b
Western-style dance. *See* **Dance,
Western-style**
Western-style painting 6:155b; 8:327a–328b
Western-style pictures, early ······ 1:43b;
8:248b–249a
West Lake ··················· 8:172b
West Lake scene ··············· 8:173a
Weston, Walter ·········· 4:127a; 8:249a
Japanese Alps ··············· 4:12b
mountaineering ············· 5:259b
Weyerhaeuser Co of the United States
··················· 4:83b
Whales [(kujira) order Cetacea]
Whaling ·········· 2:284b; 8:249b–250b
history ··············· 8:249b–250a
operations and whalers ········· 8:250a
products ············· 8:250a–250b
regulations ··············· 8:250b
supply and demand of products ··· 8:250b
types ··················· 8:249b
Wheat and barley ············· 8:251a
Wheel of Life ··············· 8:335a
"White Australia" ········· 1:117b, 119a
Whitebait [(shirauo) *Salangichthys
microdon*] ··············· 8:251a
White Clouds and Autumn Leaves 3:109b
White-collar crime ·············· 2:45a
White-collar workers ········ 8:251a–251b
"White Fox, The," ··············· 7:105a
White Horse Society ····· 3:87a–87b; 8:328a
White Mountain ··············· 3:88b
White Paper on Crime ··········· 6:172a
White Paper on Labor (1950) ······ 8:251b
White Paper on Monopolies (1948)
··················· 8:251b
White Paper on the Economy
··················· 2:167b–168a; 8:251b
Economic Planning Agency ········ 4:190b
**White Paper on the National Standard
of Living** ·········· 2:167b; 8:251b
White Paper on Trade (1949) ······ 8:251b
White papers ··············· 8:251b
White Russians ·········· 8:252a–252b
Whites, attitudes towards ···· 2:312a–313a
White Tiger Brigade ············· 1:226b
Whitman, Charles Otis ········· 8:252b
Whitney, Courtney ········ 8:252b–253a
Wholesale price index ··········· 3:303a
Wholesalers, distribution system ·· 2:119b
"Why not, it's okay!" ············ 2:184a

Wild boar [(inoshishi) *Sus scrofa leucomystax*] ················ 8:253a
Wildcats [(yamaneko) family Felidae] ················ 8:253a
Wild ducks [(kamo) family Anatidae] ················ 8:253a-253b
Wild geese. *See* Geese
Williams, Samuel Wells ·········· 8:253b
Willis, William ················ 8:253b
Willoughby, Charles Augustus ··· 8:253b
Willows [(yanagi) *Salix* spp.] · 8:253b-254a
Wills ·························· 8:254a
Wilson, Horace ················ 7:242b
Wilson, Woodrow ··············· 7:192a
Wind and Thunder Gods ····· 7:232a-232b
Wind-bells ···················· 8:254a
Winding Water Banquet ········ 2:128a
Windows for the Crown Prince ···· 8:192a
Winter hazel ·················· 8:81b
Winter Seascape with Birds ··· 4:148b
Winter sports ················· 8:254b
Wire-relayed broadcasting ······· 8:254b
Wirgman, Charles ··········· 8:254b-255a
Wisdom (chi) ················· 4:141b
Wisteria, Japanese [(fuji) *Wisteria floribunda*] ················· 8:255a
Witch hazel [(mansaku) *Hamamelis japonica*] ···················· 8:255a
Witnesses ················· 8:255a-255b
Witte, Sergei Iul'evich ··········· 8:255b
Wo. *See* Wa
Wolf, Japanese [(ōkami) *Canis lupus hodophilax*] ················ 8:255b-256a
Woman ······················ 6:70b
Woman in the Dunes ············ 1:3a
Womb Realm ··················· 7:310a
Women
  changing position ·············· 4:40a
  criminality ················· 2:45a
  discrimination ················ 5:196a
  housewives ·············· 3:241a-242a
  labor force ·················· 4:343b
  legal equality ·········· 2:229b-230a
  lifestyles ················· 5:6b-7a, 8b
  poetry by ··················· 6:297b
  ritsuryō system ··············· 6:324b
  See also Women in Japan, history of
Women, rural ············· 8:266a-267a
Women Bedecked with Feathers ·· 7:196a
Women in Japan, history of · 8:257a-263b
  contemporary ················ 8:261b
    education ·············· 8:262b-263a
    family ················· 8:262a-262b
    legal changes ·········· 8:261b-262a
    life expectancy and birthrates ···· 8:263a
    political participation and volunteer work ·················· 8:263a-263b
  early high status ·········· 8:257b-258a
  Edo period ·············· 8:259a-260a
  impact of warfare ········· 8:258b-259a
  lifestyle and attitude changes · 8:260a-261a
  modernization ················ 8:260a
  Taika Reform through Heian period ························· 8:258b
  wartime ················· 8:261a-261b
Women in Japanese religion 8:256a-257b
  Buddhism ·············· 8:257a-257b
  Christianity ················· 8:257b
  new religions ················ 8:257b
  shamanism and Shintō ······ 8:256b-257a
Women in labor force ······· 8:264a-266a
  contemporary ················ 8:264b
    distribution ············ 8:265a-265b
    future problems and prospects ·· 8:266a
    increasing number ············ 8:264b
    other changes ·········· 8:264b-265a
    protective legislation ····· 8:265b-266a
    wages ···················· 8:265b

working time ·············· 8:265b-266a
  Meiji period through World War II ··························· 8:264a-264b
  modern ················· 2:210a-210b
  protective legislation ········ 8:269a
Women Lawyers' Association ····· 8:263b
Women's and Minors' Bureau of the Labor Ministry ················ 4:87a
  Tanino Setsu ················ 7:342a
Women's and Young Workers' Bureau of the Ministry of Labor ······· 8:263b
Women's Christian Temperance Union (Kyōfūkai) ············· 4:324b; 8:300a
Women's Democratic Club ········ 8:263b
Women's education ········ 8:267a-267b
  early history ················· 8:267a
  feudal times ················· 8:267a
  Japan Women's University ········ 4:50b
  junior colleges ··············· 4:84a
  modernizing ············ 8:267a-267b
  post-World War II ············· 8:267b
Women's liberation ············· 8:263b
Women's literary groups ········· 5:20b
Women's magazines ········ 8:268a-268b
Women's names ················ 5:326a
Women's rights
  national organization ·········· 7:111b
Women's Social Reform League, (Chifuren) ·················· 8:307a
Women's suffrage ·········· 8:268b-269a
  Fusen Kakutoku Dōmei ········ 2:373b
Women's Suffrage League ········ 2:374b
Women's Suffrage Movement ····· 8:169a
  Ichikawa Fusae ·············· 3:257a
Women workers ··············· 8:269a
  employment pattern ········ 4:354a-354b
  Meiji period ·················· 8:260a
  professional and technical occupations ··················· 4:354a-354b
Women workers, protective legislation for ······················· 8:269a
Wood and pulp ··········· 5:354a-354b
Woodblock painting ············· 7:187b
Woodblock printing ············· 8:246b
  Ippitsusai Bunchō ············· 3:329b
  modern ················ 5:232a; 6:245b
  ukiyo-e-style ················· 8:330a
Woodblock prints. *See* Ukiyo-e, modern prints
Wood craftwork ················ 2:295b
Wooden clogs. *See* Geta
Wooden tablets. *See* Mokkan
Woodenware ·············· 8:269a-269b
  kijiya ····················· 4:205a
Woodpeckers [(kitsutsuki) family Picidae] ··················· 8:269b
Word games ············· 8:269b-270a
  hayakuchi or tongue twisters ····· 8:269b
  kaibun or palindromes ········· 8:270a
  shiritori or capping ············ 8:269b
Word play ···················· 8:269b
Worker Farmer Artists League (Rōnō Geijutsuka Remmei)
  Proletarian literature movement ························· 6:255a-255b
Worker-Farmer Party ··········· 6:333b
Workers Accident Compensation Law ····················· 4:358a; 7:209b
  enforcement ················· 4:358b
Workers' compensation ···· 7:209b; 8:270a
  industrial injuries ············· 3:292a
  Occupation reforms ··········· 4:346a
Workers' Fraternal Society ······· 7:164a
Work hours ·············· 8:270a-270b
Working Women's Welfare Law ··· 8:262b
Workmen's Accident Compensation Insurance ·················· 2:241b
Work regulations ········· 4:352b; 8:270b

Work transfer, temporary ········ 7:185a
World Bank ··················· 3:253b
World Design Conference ········· 2:89a
World Economy Research Society ························ 1:84a-84b
World Federation of Trade Unions (WFTU) ·············· 4:347a, 360a
World Health Organization ······· 6:274a
World Intellectual Property Organization ················ 3:317b
World Trade Mart ·············· 4:51b
World War I ·············· 8:270a-271b
  China ····················· 1:287b
  declaration of war ············· 8:270b
  economic impact ·············· 3:199b
  international relations ·········· 3:321a
  military expansion and economic growth ················· 8:271a-271b
  military operations ············ 8:270b
  political relations with allies ·· 8:270b-271a
  Taiwan ···················· 7:308b
  Twenty-one Demands ·········· 8:270b
  ultranationalism ·············· 8:145a
  war literature ················ 8:226b
  Washington Conference ····· 8:234a-234b
World War II ·············· 8:271b-277a
  Allied offensives ·········· 8:275a-275b
  Attu, battle of ··············· 1:116a
  and Australia ············ 1:116b-117a
  bombings, study of effectiveness ··· 7:249a
  Cairo Conference ············· 1:229b
  casualties ··················· 6:224a
  China Incident ··············· 7:199b
  dissolution of Imperial Army ······ 1:88b
  economic reconstruction ········ 2:163a
  economy ··········· 2:153b-154a, 158b
  electronics industry ············ 2:192a
  European War ················ 8:272a
  Fujian, occupation of Taiwan ················ 7:308b-309a
  Greater East Asia Coprosperity Sphere ····················· 8:273b
  Guangdong, occupation of Taiwan ················ 7:308b-309a
  international relations ······· 3:321b-324a
  invasion of China ········ 1:289b-290a
  Iōjima (Iwojima), Battle of ········ 3:328b
  Japan after ·············· 2:154a-155a
  Japan attacks ············ 8:273a-273b
  Japanese-American confrontation ··················· 8:272a-273a
  Japanese expansionism ······· 8:271b-272a
  Japanese society during ···· 8:277a-278b
    full-scale participation ····· 8:277b-278a
    Konoe's "New Order" ··········· 8:277b
    ravages ··················· 8:278a
    war and society ·········· 8:278a-278b
    war preparations ········· 8:277a-277b
  Japan's surrender ········· 8:276a-277a
  last assaults ············ 8:275b-276a
  Luzon, invasion of Taiwan ················ 7:308b-309a
  Malayan Campaign ············· 5:88a
  Manchukuo role ·········· 5:97a-97b
  Marianas ··················· 8:275b
  nonrepatriated Japanese soldiers ························· 8:278b-279a
  Operation Number One ········ 6:115a
  Operation Victory ············· 6:115a
  Pacific deadlock ·········· 8:273b-275a
  Potsdam Declaration ··········· 6:231b
  relocation centers ········ 4:13a, 14a-14b
  reparations ·················· 2:155a
  Senjinkan ··················· 7:65b
  Tōkyō ····················· 8:61b
  United States ················ 8:158a
  war crimes trials ·········· 8:223a-225b
  war literature ················ 8:226b

Wrestling ················· 8:279a
Wright, Frank Lloyd ········ 8:279a
  Imperial Hotel ··········· 3:277b
  "Writing for Sale Association"
  ················· 1:129b-130a
Writings, inscriptions ····· 3:313b-314a
Written vernacular Japanese,
  development of. See Gembun itchi
Wu ··················· 3:46a; 6:41b
Wu Peifu (Wu P'ei-fu) ·········· 8:279b

X

Xavier, Francis · 1:150b; 2:306b; 7:30a, 64b;
                    8:281a
  Kakure Kirishitan ··········· 4:119a
Xerox Corporation ··········· 2:359a
Xianren ·················· 7:67a
Xi'an (Sian) Incident ···· 1:116b; 2:342a;
                  8:281a-281b
  Second United Front ········ 7:47b-48a
Xiliang ji ················· 7:195a
Xinmin Hui (Hsin-min Hui) 6:260b; 8:281b
Xu'an Huaichang ············ 2:187a
Xu You ··················· 4:146b

Y

Yabakei ············ 耶馬渓 ······ 8:283a
Yabakei Gorge ············· 1:70a
Yabegawa ········ 矢部川 ····· 1:83a
Yabe Hisakatsu ·· 矢部長克 ···· 8:283a
Yabukōji (Ardisia japonica) ······ 8:283a
Yabukōjishū ······ 藪柑子集 ···· 8:11a
Yabusame ······ 流鏑馬 2:261a; 4:160b;
              7:64a; 8:283a-283b
Yabusame ceremony parts ······ 8:283a
Yabuta Teijirō ·· 藪田貞治郎 ···· 8:283b
Yabutsubaki (Camellia japonica) · 1:236b
Yachiyo ··········· 八千代 ···· 8:283b
Yadake (Pseudosasa japonica) ··· 1:136a
Yaeyama Islands
        ··· 八重山諸島 ···· 7:3a, 66a;
                  8:283b
  Iriomotejima ············· 3:331a
  Ishigakijima ············· 3:340a
  Ryūkyū Islands ············ 6:357a
  Taketomijima ············· 7:325b
  Yonagunijima ············· 8:337a
Yafuki ············ 野府記 ···· 7:179a
Yagi Hidetsugu ·· 八木秀次 · 8:283b-284a
Yagi Jūkichi ····· 八木重吉 ···· 8:284a
Yagisawa Dam 矢木沢ダム ···· 8:237a
Yagi-Uda antenna ··········· 2:192a
Yagō ···················· 8:284a
Yaguramon (castle gate)
           ··· 櫓門 ···· 1:248b
Yagyū ············· 柳生 ···· 8:284a
Yagyū Munenori 柳生宗矩 ···· 8:284a
Yahagigawa ···· 矢作川 ··· 8:284a-284b

Yahata. 八幡 See Yawata
Yahikoyama ········· 弥彦山 ····· 8:284b
Yaita ············· 矢板 ····· 8:284b
Yaizu ············· 焼津 ····· 8:284b
Yajima Kajiko ···· 矢島楫子 ····· 8:284b
  Sasaki Toyoju ············· 7:23b
Yakai Incident ··· 八海事件 ···· 8:284b
Yakata ·················· 7:271a
Yakazu haikai ···· 矢数俳諧 ···· 3:79a
Yakedake ········· 焼岳 ···· 4:127a;
                8:284b-285a
Yakedake peak ···· 焼岳 ···· 1:5a
Yakimono ················ 2:306a
Yakishime ················ 1:259b
Yakke ··················· 4:194b
Yakko ············ 奴 1:147b; 8:285a
  Hatamoto ··············· 8:285a
  Machi ················· 8:285a
  Sekisho (barriers) ·········· 8:285a
Yaku ··················· 4:95a
Yakubyōgami ·········· 1:155a; 8:285a
Yakudoshi ············· 8:285a-285b
Yakukata ··········· 役方 ···· 1:137b
Yakumo mishō ···· 八雲御抄 ···· 8:285b
Yakuō Tokken ···· 約翁徳倹 ···· 4:2a
Yakusa no kabane 八色の姓 ···· 8:285b
Yakusha-e ······· 役者絵 4:171b; 8:183a
Yakusha rongo ··· 役者論語 · 6:108b; 8:21b
Yakushi ·················· 1:188b
Yakushidake ······ 薬師岳 5:352b; 8:285b
Yakushiji ········· 薬師寺 ···· 1:182a;
                8:285b-286b
  kondō (main hall) ··········· 8:285a
  Pagoda ················ 8:285a
  West Pagoda ············· 5:332a
Yakushima ········· 屋久島 4:105b; 8:286a
Yakushi Triad ·············· 1:199a
"Yakusoku" ········ 約束 ···· 8:303a
Yakuza ·············· 2:343a; 8:286b
  gambling ··············· 3:5b
  oyabun-kobun ·········· 6:137a-137b
Yakuza, The ··· ザ・ヤクザ ···· 7:314a
  urban life ·············· 8:177b
Yakuza eiga ················ 2:274b
Yakuza groups ·············· 7:209a
Yalta Conference ······ 8:159b, 286b-287a
  Occupation ·············· 6:51a
  Roosevelt, Franklin Delano ···· 6:339a
  Russia and Japan ·········· 6:344a
Yalu River, Naval Battle of ····· 8:287a
Yama ············· 2:201b; 3:329a
Yamabe ············ 山部 ···· 1:147b
Yamabe no Akahito
        ··· 山部赤人 7:13a; 8:206b,
                  287b
  poems in Man'yōshū ········· 5:107b
Yamabe no Akahito shū
           山部赤人集 ···· 8:287b
Yamabiraki ················ 8:287b
Yamabito ("mountain people") ··· 7:13b
Yama-boko ················ 2:255b
Yamabōshi (Cornus kousa) ······ 8:287b
Yamabuki (Kerria japonica) ·· 8:287b-288a
Yamabukisō (Hylomecon japonicum)
                  8:288a
Yamabushi ········ 山伏4:327b; 7:182a;
                  8:288a
  conch-shell trumpet (horagai) ·· 4:107b
  kagura ················· 4:107b
  shamanism ·············· 7:76b
  Shōgoin ················ 7:160a
Yamabushi kagura
           山伏神楽 ···· 4:107b
Yamachawan ······ 山茶碗 · 1:258b, 262a;
            7:256a; 8:288a-288b
Yamada ············ 山田 ···· 8:288b
Yamada Bimyō ·· 山田美妙 5:379a; 8:288b

Ken'yūsha ················ 4:198b
Yamadadera remains
           山田寺跡·· 8:288b-289a
Yamada Isuzu · 山田五十鈴 ··· 8:289a
Yamada Jōka ··· 山田常嘉 ··· 3:313a
Yamada Kengyō · 山田検校 ···· 7:226a
Yamada Kōsaku · 山田耕筰 ··· 8:289a
Yamada Moritarō
          山田盛太郎 ··· 8:289a
Yamada Nagamasa
          山田長政 8:289a-289b
Yamada Saburō · 山田三良 ····· 8:289b
Yamada Tomohiko
          山田智彦 ··· 8:289b
Yamada Waka · 山田わか ··· 8:289b
Yamada Yōji · 山田洋次 ·· 2:275b;
             8:289b-290a
Yamada Yoshihiko
          山田芳彦 ··· 4:202a
Yamada Yoshio · 山田孝雄 6:297a; 8:290a
  Kokugaku no hongi ········· 4:259a
Yamaga ············ 山鹿 ··· 8:290a
Yamagami Itarō
         山上伊太郎 ··· 2:268b
Yamaga Sokō ··· 山鹿素行 4:247a-247b;
             8:290a-290b
  Chūchō jijitsu ············· 1:311b
  Kogaku proponent ········ 4:246b-247b
  nature, concept of ·········· 5:357b
  Seikyō yōroku ············ 7:51b
Yamagata ··········· 山形 ··· 8:290b
Yamagata Aritomo
           山県有朋 1:86a, 91a,
     135b; 3:194b; 7:51a; 8:290b-292a
  Anglo-Japanese Alliance ········ 1:56b
  Aoki Shūzō ·············· 1:69a
  Conscription Ordinance of 1873 ·· 4:204b
  Freedom and People's Rights Movement
                  2:334a
  genrō ·················· 3:21b
  gumbatsu ··············· 3:66a
  Kabasan Incident ··········· 4:89a
  Kabayama Sukenori ········· 4:89b
  Kenseitō ················ 4:198b
  Kiyoura Keigo ············· 4:233a
  Kokumin shimbun influenced by · 4:261a
  Rikken Seiyūkai ··········· 6:315a
  rules of military conduct ···· 3:279b-280a
  Shandong (Shantung) Question ···· 7:77a
  Uesugi Shinkichi ··········· 8:130a
Yamagata Bantō ··· 山片蟠桃 · 8:292a-292b
Yamagata Basin ·· 山形盆地 ··· 8:292b
Yamagata Daini · 山県大弐 ·· 8:292b-293a
Yamagata Isoo · 山県五十雄 ··· 5:270b
Yamagata-Lobanov Agreement
     山県ーロバノフ協定 · 8:293a-293b
  Korea ·················· 4:281b
  Korea's independence ········ 4:287b
  Russia and Japan ·········· 6:341b
  Russo-Japanese War ········· 6:346a
Yamagata Masao 山県昌夫 ··· 8:293b
Yamagata Prefecture
          山形県 · 8:293b, 355a
Yamagishikai ····· 山岸会 · 8:293b-294a
Yamagiwa Katsusaburō
          山極勝三郎 ··· 8:294a
Yamaguchi ········· 山口 ··· 8:294a
Yamaguchi Basin 山口盆地 ··· 8:294a
Yamaguchi Hitomi · 山口瞳 ··· 8:294b
Yamaguchi Kaoru · 山口薫 ··· 8:294b
Yamaguchi no Atai
  Ōguchi ······· 山口費大口 ··· 8:294b
Yamaguchi Prefecture
          山口県 7:277a; 8:295a
Yamaguchi Reservoir ········· 7:31b
Yamaguchi Saburō 山口三郎 ··· 7:108a
Yamaguchi Seishi
          山口誓子 ·· 8:295a-295b

Yamaguchi Sodō 山口素堂 ······ 8:295b
Yamaguchi Yoshiko
······ 山口淑子 ······ 8:295b
Yamaha Motor Co, Ltd ······ 8:296a
Kawakami Gen'ichi ······ 4:180b
Yamaha Music Foundation ······ 4:180b
Yamaichi Securities Co, Ltd ······ 8:296a
Yamaji Aizan ······ 山路愛山 ·· 5:13a; 8:296a
Yamajiro ······ 山城 ··· 1:246b, 247b
Yamakawa Hitoshi ·· 山川均 ······ 7:3a;
8:296a–297b
Fukumoto Kazuo ······ 2:364a
Japan Communist Party ······ 4:11a–11b
Kaizō ······ 4:113b
Yamakawa Kikue 山川菊栄 ·· 7:57a; 8:297a
Fujin kōron publication ······ 2:344a
Yama kōmori (Nyctalus lasiopterus)
······ 1:146b
Yamakunigawa ······ 山国川 ······ 8:297a
Yamamba ······ 山姥 ······ 8:297a
Yamamichi ······ 山道 ······ 7:334b
Yamamoto Baiitsu
······ 山本梅逸 ······ 1:211a;
5:311a–311b; 8:297a–297b
Yamamoto Fujiko
······ 山本富士子 ······ 8:297b
Yamamoto Gombei. *See* **Yamamoto**
Gonnohyōe
Yamamoto Gonnohyōe
······ 山本権兵衛 ······ 8:297b
Yamamoto Hokuzan
······ 山本北山 ·· 8:297b–298a
Yamamoto Hōsui 山本芳翠 ······ 8:298a
Fontanesi, Antonio ······ 2:304a
pupils ······ 2:345b
Yamamoto Isoroku
······ 山本五十六 ·· 1:21a; 8:298a
World War II ······ 8:273a
Yamamoto Jōtarō
······ 山本条太郎 ·· 8:298a–298b
Yamamoto Kaichi 山本嘉一 ··· 2:269a
Yamamoto Kajirō
······ 山本嘉次郎 · 2:270b, 271b;
8:298b
Yamamoto Kanae · 山本鼎 ······ 5:232b
Yamamoto Kansai
······ やまもと寛斎 ····· 8:298b
Yamamoto Kenkichi
······ 山本健吉 ·· 5:13b; 8:298b
Yamamoto Kiyoshi
······ 山本貴誉司 ······ 8:298b
Yamamoto Sanehiko
······ 山本実彦 ··· 8:298b–299a
Kaizō ······ 4:113b
Yamamoto Satsuo
······ 山本薩夫 ·· 2:272a, 274a;
8:299a
Yamamoto Senji · 山本宣治 ······ 8:299a
birth control movement ······ 7:11a
Yamamoto Shūgorō
······ 山本周五郎 ······ 7:103b;
8:299a–299b
Yamamoto Tamesaburō
······ 山本為三郎 ······ 8:299b
Yamamoto Tōjirō 山本東次郎 ··· 4:325a
Yamamoto Yasue 山本安英 ······ 8:299b
Yamamoto Yūzō · 山本有三 · 7:125a; 8:300a
Yamamura Bochō
······ 山村暮鳥 ······ 8:300a
Yamamura Saisuke
······ 山村才助 ······ 8:300a
Yamamuro Gumpei
······ 山室軍平 ······ 8:300a
Salvation Army (Kyūseigun) ······ 7:5b
Yamamuro Kieko
······ 山室機恵子 ······ 8:300a
Yamana family ····· 山名氏 ·· 7:8b; 8:300b
Yamanaka (town) ··· 山中 2:345a; 8:300b

Yamanaka, Lake ··· 山中湖 ···· 8:300b
Yamanaka Sadao 山中貞雄 ·· 2:270a, 271a;
8:300b
Yamanaka Shikanosuke
······ 山中鹿之介 ·· 8:300b–301a
Yamanashi (city) ··· 山梨 ······ 8:301a
Yamanashi Prefecture
······ 山梨県 ·· 8:301a–301b
Yamana Sōzen 山名宗全 ······ 8:301b
Yamane ······ 2:131a–131b
Yamaneko ······ 8:253a
Yamanobe no Michi
······ 山辺の道 ······ 5:334a
Yama no kami ······ 1:20a; 8:302a
keshin forms ······ 1:122b–123a
Yama no oto (The Sound
of the Mountain) ·· 山の音 ······ 6:230a
Yamanote ······ 山手 ···· 4:176b;
8:178b, 302a
shitamachi ······ 7:149b–150a
Yamanouchi Hot Springs
······ 山ノ内温泉 ······ 8:355a
Yamanouchi Kazutoyo
······ 山内一豊 · 7:56b; 8:302a
Kōchi ······ 4:239b
Yamanouchi Pharmaceutical Co, Ltd
······ 8:302b
Yamanouchi Sugao
······ 山内清男 ·1:76a; 8:302b
Jōmon pottery ······ 4:75a
Yamanouchi Toyoshige
······ 山内豊信 ······ 8:302b
Yamanoue no Okura
······ 山上憶良 5:105a; 8:206b,
302b–303a
poems in *Man'yōshū* ······ 5:108a
poetry ······ 8:303a
Yamaoka Sōhachi
······ 山岡荘八 7:103b; 8:303a
Yamaoka Tesshū 山岡鉄舟 ·· 8:303a–303b
Yamasa Shōyu Co, Ltd ······ 8:303b
Yamashina Tokitsugu 山科言継
Tokitsugu Kyō ki ······ 8:43a
Yamashiro no Kuni fudoki
······ 山城国風土記 ······ 7:139a
Yamashiro no Kuni Ikki
······ 山城国一揆 ······ 8:303b
Yamashiro no Ōe, Prince
······ 山背大兄王 ······ 8:303b
Yamashiro Province
······ 山城国 ·· 8:303b–304a
Yamashiro Tomoe 山代巴 ·· 8:304a–304b
Yamashiroya Incident
······ 山城屋事件 ······ 8:304b
Yamashiroya Wasuke
······ 山城屋和助 ······ 8:304b
"Yamashita caveman" ······ 6:85a
Yamashita-Shinnihon Steamship Co,
Ltd ······ 8:304b
Yamashita Tarō 山下太郎 · 1:71b; 8:304b
Yamashita Tomoyuki
······ 山下奉文 ······ 8:305a
Yamatai ······ 邪馬台 · 2:103b, 365a;
8:305a–307a
Chen Shou and the *Wei zhi* ······ 8:305a
Itokoku ······ 3:354a
Kinai-Kyūshū standoff ····· 8:306b–307a
Kyūshū theory ······ 8:306a–306b
rulers
Himiko ······ 3:139b–140a
Wa and Queen Himiko ·· 8:305a–305b
Yamatai debate ······ 8:307a
Yamato theory reborn ······ 8:306b
Yamatai wa nakatta
(There Was No Yamatai)
······ 耶馬台はなかった ·· 8:306b
Yamataka Shigeri
······ 山高しげり ······ 8:307b

Yamatake-Honeywell Co, Ltd ··· 8:307b
Yamatane Museum of Art ······ 8:307b
Yamata no Orochi
······ 八岐大蛇 ······ 2:302b;
7:278b; 8:307b
Yamate Kiichirō
······ 山手樹一郎 ······ 8:307b
Yamato (city) ······ 8:308a
Yamato ("Japanese") 大和 ······ 8:308a
formation ······ 4:34b
gardens ······ 3:8b
Kinai ······ 4:211b
Yamato (battleship) ··· 大和 ······ 8:308a
Yamato Basin. *See* Nara Basin
Yamato Bunkakan ······ 8:308a–308b
iconographic drawings ······ 7:328a
museums ······ 5:277b
Yamato court ······ 大和朝廷 2:288a; 7:248a,
256a; 8:308b–309a
cooking style ······ 2:305b
court titles ······ 4:89a
economy ······ 2:147a
formation of Japan ······ 4:7a
Fujiwara no Kamatari ······ 2:351a
Hayato resistance ······ 3:118a
Imbe family ······ 3:274b
Inariyama tomb ······ 3:283b
Iwafune no ki ······ 3:357b
Iwai, Rebellion of ······ 3:357b
kikajin ······ 4:205a–205b
kokugun system to strengthen ·· 4:259b
Mononobe family ······ 5:247a
Ōjin Mausoleum ······ 6:76b
Ōtomo family ······ 6:130b
rise of ······ 4:246a
Taika Reform ······ 7:295b–296a
Takamuko no Kuromaro ······ 7:315b
Takenouchi no Sukune ··· 4:203b; 7:325a
Wani ······ 8:223a
women in ······ 8:258b
Yamato cycle of mythology ······ 5:292b
Yamato-damashii ··· 大和魂 ·· 8:309a–309b
Yamato-e ······ 大和絵 7:270a; 8:309b
development ······ 2:355b
Fujiwara culture ······ 2:348a
Fukko school ······ 2:360b
fūzokuga ······ 2:377a
Genji monogatari emaki ······ 3:20a
Kaihō Yūshō ······ 4:110b
Kanō school ······ 4:149b
kara-e ······ 4:157a
Kose no Kanaoka, as founder ··· 4:294b
Kose school initiated ······ 4:294b
modern painting ······ 6:156b
Nakamura Gakuryō ······ 5:314b
painting ······ 6:149b
rimpa ······ 6:317b
subjects ······ 6:158b
Tazaki Sōun ······ 7:359a
Yamatogawa ······ 大和川 ···· 5:332b;
8:309b–310a
Yamatohime, Princess
······ 倭姫命 ······ 8:310a
Ise Shrine ······ 3:338a
Yamato-hime no Mikoto
seiki ······ 倭姫命世記 ······ 7:263b
Yamato honzō ·· 大和本草 ······ 4:108b
Yamato koji fūbutsushi
······ 大和古寺風物誌 ······ 4:125a
Yamato Kōriyama
······ 大和郡山 ······ 8:310a
Yamato leaders, technology transfer
······ 7:374a
Yamato monogatari
······ 大和物語 5:246a; 8:310a
Obasuteyama ······ 6:48b
Yamato period ··· 大和時代 ······ 8:310a
periodization ······ 6:175b

Yama torikabuto (*Aconitum japonicum*)
·········· **8**:310b
Yamato Sanzan 大和三山 ······· **8**:*310b*
Yamato Takada 大和高田 ····· **8**:310b
Yamatotakeru, Prince
········ 日本武尊 ·· **8**:311a-311b
hero worship ············· **3**:128a
imperial regalia ··········· **3**:278b
kofun ··························· **5**:309a
Kumaso suppression ········· **4**:189a
Yamatotakeru no Mikoto. *See*
Yamatotakeru, Prince
Yamato theory ············· **8**:306b
Yamawaki Izumi no Kami Motoyoshi
········ 山脇和泉守元宣 ···· **3**:366a
Yamawaki Tōyō 山脇東洋 · **8**:311b-312a
Yamazaki 山崎 ········· **8**:312a
Yamazaki, Battle of
········ 山崎の戦 · **1**:41b; **7**:104a;
8:312b
Takayama Ukon ············ **7**:321a
Toyotomi Hideyoshi ·········· **8**:95a
Yamazaki Ansai 山崎闇斎 · **7**:27b, 263b;
8:119a-119b, 312a-312b
shasō ··························· **7**:81a
Yamazaki Baking Co, Ltd ·· **8**:312b
Yamazaki Masakazu
········ 山崎正和 · **8**:312b-313a
shingeki ···················· **7**:113b
Yamazaki Naomasa
········ 山崎直方 **1**:103b; **8**:313a
Yamazaki Sōkan 山崎宗鑑 ·· **8**:313a
Yambōshi (*Cornus kousa*) ·· **8**:287b
Yame 八女 ··········· **8**:313a
Yame tomb cluster
········ 八女古墳群 · **8**:313a-313b
Yamishio 闇潮 ········· **4**:180a
Yamizo Mountains
········ 八溝山地 ········ **8**:313b
Yanagawa 柳川 · **8**:*313a*, 313b
Yanagawa Seigan
········ 梁川星巌 ········ **8**:313b
Yanagawa Shunsan
········ 柳川春三 ········ **8**:313b
Yanagi ···················· **8**:253b-254a
Yanagida Izumi 柳田泉 · **8**:313b-314a
Yanagihara Byakuren
········ 柳原白蓮 ········· **8**:314a
Yanagi Muneyoshi 柳宗悦 **2**:293a; **8**:314a
folklore studies ············ **2**:296b
Japan Folk-Craft Museum ····· **4**:46a
Koishiwara ware ··········· **4**:250b
sashiko stitching ··········· **7**:24a
Yanagisawa Kien 柳沢淇園 ········ **1**:211a;
8:314a-314b
Ike no Taiga ·············· **3**:267a
Yanagisawa Yoshiyasu
········ 柳沢吉保 ········ **8**:314b
Yanagita Kunio 柳田国男 **2**:296b, 297b,
302a; **5**:13b; **7**:256b; **8**:*315a*, 315b
festivals ·················· **2**:253b-253b
folk religion ·············· **2**:298a
historiography ············· **3**:157a
Yanagiya Kosan V柳家小さん（五代）**6**:*282b*
Yanai 柳井 ············ **8**:315b
Yanaihara Tadao
········ 矢内原忠雄 **5**:263a; **8**:315b
pacifism ·················· **6**:144b
Yan'an (Yenan) Government · **8**:315b-316a
Yanmar Diesel Engine Co, Ltd · **8**:316a
Yano Fumio. 矢野文雄 *See* **Yano Ryūkei**
Ya no ne 矢の根 ··········· **4**:98a
Yano Ryūkei 矢野龍渓 ···· **8**:316a
seiji shōsetsu ············· **7**:50a
Yano Tsuneta 矢野恒太 ··· **8**:316a
Yao 八尾 ············ **8**:316a
Yao Keijirō 八尾敬次郎 ···· **3**:18a
Yao Shōten Co, Ltd ········· **3**:18a

Yaoyorozu no kami ("The Eight Hundred
Myriads") ················ **4**:126a
Yarigatake 槍ヶ岳 ······· **8**:316b
Yarō kabuki ··· 野郎歌舞伎 ····· **2**:75a
Yasaka 八坂 ········· **7**:126b
Yasaka Shrine 八坂神社 **4**:336a; **7**:278b;
8:316b
Gion Festival ··········· **3**:33b, 34a
Yasakayahama 八坂八浜 ··· **8**:316b
Yasan 野山 ·········· **8**:299a
Yasato 八郷 ········· **8**:316b
Yashajin Pass 夜叉神峠 ··· **8**:316b
Yashi ···················· **7**:250a
Yashica Co, Ltd ········· **8**:316b
Yashikigami ··············· **2**:300b
Yashima 屋島 ··· **8**:316b-317a
Takamatsu ············ **7**:314a-314b
Yashio 八塩 ········· **8**:317a
Yashiro Hirokata 屋代弘賢 **2**:258b; **8**:317a
Yashiro Seiichi 矢代静一 ·· **8**:317a
shingeki ·················· **7**:113b
Yaskawa Electric Mfg Co, Ltd · **8**:317a
Yasukawa Daigorō ········· **8**:319a
Yasoshima Matsuri
········ 八十島祭 ········ **3**:271a
Yasotakeru 八十梟師 ······· **4**:57b
Yasuda 安田 ···· **8**:317a-317b
Yasuda Zenjirō ··········· **8**:318a
**Yasuda Fire & Marine Insurance Co,
Ltd** ················ **8**:317b-318a
Yasuda monogatari
········ 安田物語 ········· **4**:76b
Yasuda plan ·············· **8**:364a
**Yasuda Trust & Banking Co,
Ltd** ····················· **8**:318a
Yasuda Yojūrō 保田与重郎 · **5**:13b; **8**:318a
Kamei Katsuichirō ········· **4**:125a
Yasuda Yukihiko 安田靫彦 · **8**:318a
Yasuda zaibatsu (financial
combine) ····· 安田財閥 ·· **8**:357b
Yasuda Zenjirō 安田善次郎 · **7**:52a; **8**:318a
Yasuda Bank ············· **2**:342a
Yasugawa 野洲川 ······· **8**:318b
Yasugi 安来 ·········· **8**:318b
Yasuhara Teishitsu
········ 安原貞室 ········ **8**:318b
Yasui Sokken 安井息軒 ··· **8**:318b
Yasui Sōtarō 安井曽太郎 ·· **8**:318b
Yasui Takuma 安井琢磨 ··· **8**:318b-319a
*Yasui Takuma
chosakushū* (Collected
Works of Yasui Takuma)
········ 安井琢磨著作集 ··· **8**:319a
Yasui Tetsu 安井てつ ···· **8**:319a
"Yasui-Umehara era" ········ **6**:157b
Yasukawa Daigorō
········ 安川第五郎 ······ **8**:319a
Yasukuni Shrine 靖国神社 ·· **2**:300a;
8:319a-319b
Yasumi Toshio 八住利雄 ·· **8**:319a
Yasunaka Hana 安中はな ···· **5**:267a
Yasuoka Shōtarō 安岡章太郎 · **8**:319a
Shinchō ················· **7**:109a
Yatabe Ryōkichi
········ 矢田部良吉 ······· **1**:156a;
8:319b-320a
Yatoi ···················· **2**:311a
Yatomi 弥富 ········· **8**:320a
Yatsude (*Fatsia japonica*) ··· **8**:320a
Yatsugatake 八ヶ岳 **2**:347b; **8**:320a
Yatsushiro 八代 ········ **8**:320a
Yatsushiro Kai 八代海 ····· **8**:320a
Yatsushiro Sea 八代海 ···· **8**:320a
Yautsuri ·················· **4**:195a
Yawarasugi ················ **7**:257b
Yawata 八幡 **8**:320a-320b
Yawatahama 八幡浜 ····· **8**:320b

**Yawata Iron and Steel Company Political
Donation Case** ········· **6**:202a
Yawata Iron and Steel Works · **3**:284a,
333a; **4**:344a; **5**:303a; **8**:320b-321a
Yayoi culture ·· 弥生文化 · **8**:321a-322a
affinity with Korea, Manchuria, and
northern China ·········· **4**:276b
archaeological study ····· **1**:77a-77b
belief systems ············ **8**:322a
clothing ·············· **8**:321b-322a
economy ················· **2**:147a
folktales ················· **2**:303b
food ················· **8**:321b-322a
housing ······· **3**:243a; **8**:321b-322a
Jimmu, Emperor ··········· **4**:57b
late ····················· **8**:322a
magatama ················ **8**:*320b*
pottery jars ·············· **8**:*320b*
technological advances ··· **8**:321a-321b
Toro site ················· **8**:80b
Yayoi period ····· 弥生時代 · **4**:34a-34b;
8:322a
archaeological sites ········ **7**:266a
burial mounds ············ **4**:244a
postwar research ······· **1**:78a-79a
religion ·················· **7**:126a
rice cultivation ··········· **7**:247b
Shintō ··················· **7**:126a
stone tools ··············· **7**:247b
Yayoi pottery ··· 弥生式土器 ·· **1**:76b-77a;
8:322a-322b, *323a*
fern frond design ·········· **2**:252a
jars ····················· **8**:*320b*
Karako site ·············· **4**:157b
Year-end fair ········ **8**:322b-323a
Year of My Life, The ······· **6**:298a
"Yellow peril" ········· **1**:238b; **8**:323a-323b
Yellow Sea, Battle of. *See* **Yalu River,
Naval Battle of**
Yellowtail [(buri) *Seriola quinqueradiata*]
························· **8**:323b
Yen ·········· 円 ····· **8**:240a,
323b-324a
exchange rate, monetary policy · **5**:241b
IMF ····················· **3**:274b
premodern ··············· **5**:243a
redenomination ········· **8**:324b
Yenan government. *See* **Yan'an (Yenan)
Government**
Yen credit ·········· **8**:324a-324b
Yen revaluation ············ **7**:223b
Yi Dong-wŏn ·············· **4**:285b
Yi dynasty ······· 李朝 ··· **4**:140b;
8:324b-325b
founding ················· **8**:326a
Kojong, King ············· **4**:252a
Yi Sŏng-gye established ····· **4**:276a
Yi Ha-ŭng. *See* **Taewŏn'gun**
Yi Hoe-sŏng ··············· **4**:374b
Yi Hwang ·············· **8**:325b
Yin and Yang, Bureau of ··· **6**:113a-113b
Yin-dynasty, calendrical symbols · **4**:55b
Yin Rugeng (Yin Ju-keng) ·· **8**:325b
Yin-yang ··· **4**:55b; **5**:151a; **6**:103a; **7**:191a
Yiran ················· **3**:357a-357b
Yi Sam-p'yong. *See* **Ri Sampei**
Yishan Yining ············· **3**:348b
Yi Sŏng-gye ············ **8**:326a
wakō campaigns ······· **4**:276a, 278b
Yi Sŭng-man ·········· **6**:307b-308a
Yi Sun-sin ············· **8**:326a
Yi Wan-Yong ··········· **8**:326a
annexation treaty ····· **4**:282a, 287b
YMCA ················· **8**:326a
Yobai ·············· **8**:326a-326b
Yobigoe ·········· 呼声 ·· **4**:328a
Yobikō ··················· **2**:41b
Yoda Yoshikata · 依田義賢 ·· **8**:326b

Yodogawa ·········· 淀川 **7**:140a; **8**:326b
Yodogawa Steel Works, Ltd ······ **8**:326b
Yodogimi ··············· 淀君 ······· **4**:1a;
    8:326b-327a
Yodo no koi shusse no
taki nobori (The Carp of
Yodo Climbs the Ladder
of Success) 淀鯉出世滝徳 ······· **8**:327a
Yodoya Tatsugorō
    ········ 淀屋辰五郎 ····· **8**:327a
Yōeki ················ 徭役 ······· **8**:327a
    corvée labor ·············· **1**:226b
Yōga ················ 用賀 · **8**:327a-328b
Yo ga kenshin no jikken
    ········ 予が見神の実験 ······ **8**:116a
Yōgaku ············· 洋学 · **8**:241a-243a
Yōgakusho (Institute of
  Western Learning)
    ·············· 洋学所 **1**:141b; **8**:243a
Yoidore tenshi · 酔いどれ天使 · **7**:108a
Yōjimbō ········· 用心棒 ······· **7**:108b
Yojō ············· 余情 **5**:42a; **8**:328b
    origin ·················· **8**:328b
    outside *waka* ············· **8**:328b
Yojōhan fusuma no shitabari trial
    四畳半襖の下張り裁判 ······ **8**:328b
Yōjōkun ··········· 養生訓 ····· **4**:108b;
    8:328a-329b
Yōju ··············· 遥授 ······· **8**:338a
Yōkai ···························· **1**:130b
Yōkaichi ·········· 八日市 ······ **8**:329a
Yōkaichiba ······· 八日市場 ····· **8**:329a
Yokaren ·········· 予科練 ······ **8**:329a
Yokkaichi ········ 四日市 · **8**:329a, 329b
    pollution of ··············· **2**:226b
Yokoana ·········· 横穴 ······· **8**:329a
  Yokoana sekishitsu (tomb
    chamber) ······· 横穴石室 · **4**:245a-245b
Yokohama ········ 横浜 **4**:135a; **8**:329a,
    329b
Yokohama Archives of History
    ·················· **8**:329b-330a
  Yokohama band ············· **6**:258a
Yokohama-e ······ 横浜絵 ······ **8**:330a
Yokohama Incident
    ········ 横浜事件 ······· **8**:330a
  Yokohama Kawase Kaisha ······· **4**:184b
Yokohama mainichi
  shimbum · 横浜毎日新聞 ···· **6**:245b;
    8:330a-330b
Yokohama Rubber Co, Ltd **2**:372b; **8**:330b
Yokohama Specie Bank ···· **1**:140b, 167b;
    8:330b
  establishment ·········· **1**:138b-139a
  Takahashi Korekiyo ·········· **7**:312b
Yokoi Kinkoku · 横井金谷 ···· **1**:211a;
    8:330b-331a
  Yokoi Myōdō · 横井妙幢 ····· **8**:330b
  Yokoi Shōichi · 横井庄一 ····· **8**:279a
Yokoi Shōnan · 横井小楠 · **8**:331a-331b
    fukoku kyōhei ············· **2**:360b
    Jitsugakutō (Practical Party) · **8**:331a
    schooling ················ **8**:331a
    Shōnandō ················ **8**:331a
  Yokoi Tokitsura · 横井時般 ···· **8**:331b
  Yokoi Tokiyoshi · 横井時敬 ··· **8**:331b
Yokoi Yayū ····· 横井也有 **6**:297b; **8**:331b
    haibun ·················· **3**:78a
Yokomitsu Riichi 横光利一 **2**:274a; **7**:103b;
    8:331b-333b
    early works ·············· **8**:332a
    fūzoku shōsetsu ··········· **2**:378b
    Monshō ················ **8**:333a
    psychological monologues ···· **8**:332b
    Ryoshū ············· **8**:333a-333b
    Shanhai ················ **8**:332b
    Shin'en ················ **8**:332b
    Shinkankaku school ······· **7**:116a-116b

Yokomizo Seishi 横溝正史 ······ **8**:333b
Yokoo Tadanori 横尾忠則 ······ **8**:333b
Yokose Torahisa 横瀬虎寿 ····· **8**:333b
Yokose Yau ···· 横瀬夜雨 · **8**:333b-334a
Yokosuka ······ 横須賀 **4**:135a; **8**:334a
  Yokosuka Naval Arsenal ······· **8**:334a
Yokosuka Shipyards
    ········ 横須賀造船所 · **2**:31a; **8**:334a
  foreign investment ·········· **2**:316b
  Oguri Tadamasa ············ **6**:72a
Yokota Kisaburō
    ········ 横田喜三郎 ····· **8**:334a
Yokote ·········· 横手 ······· **8**:334a
Yokote Basin ··· 横手盆地 ····· **8**:334b
Yokoyama Gennosuke
    ·············· 横山源之助 ····· **8**:334b
Yokoyama Taikan
    ········ 横山大観 ····· **6**:157a;
    8:334b-335a
  Qu Yuan (Kutsugen) ········ **8**:334b
  Yokozuna ··············· **7**:272a-272b
  Yokozuna dohyōiri ··········· **7**:272a
  Yokubō shizen shugi
    ········ 欲望自然主義 ····· **6**:204a
  Yokusan Seijikai
    ········ 翼賛政治会 ····· **3**:281a
Yōmei Bunko · 陽明文庫 ····· **8**:335a
  Konoe collection ············ **4**:273b
  Konoe family collection ······ **4**:272b
Yōmeigaku ······ 陽明学 · **1**:355a-357a;
    7:71a; **8**:335a-335b
  Kaitokudō curriculum ········ **4**:113b
  Kumazawa Banzan ··· **4**:307a-307b; **8**:28a
  Miwa Shissai ·············· **5**:216a
  Nakae Tōju ············ **5**:312a-312b
  Ōshio Heihachirō ······· **6**:126a-126b
  Satō Issai ················ **7**:27a
  Shingaku ················· **7**:111b
  Yōmeigaku philosophy ········ **5**:315a
  Yōmeimon gate ······ 陽明門 ··· **8**:84b
Yomeirikon ················ **8**:336a
Yomena (*Aster yomena; Kalimeris*
  yomena) ················ **8**:336a
  Yomi, land of ·············· **5**:293a
Yomihon ················ **1**:295a;
    5:48b-49a; **7**:18a; **8**:336a-336b
  Bakin ··················· **1**:130b
  composition ··············· **8**:336a
  history ·················· **8**:336a
  Jippensha Ikku ············· **4**:61a
  later Edo period ········· **5**:48b-49a
  origin ·················· **8**:336a
  purpose ················· **8**:336a
  Tamenaga Shunsei ········ **7**:333b-334a
  Yomi no kuni ····· 黄泉の国 ··· **1**:20a
  Yomise ·················· **7**:250a
Yomitan ········· 読谷 ······· **8**:336b
Yomiuri ········· 読売 ······· **4**:182b
  Yomiuri Kinrei (Prohibition
    of Broadsides) · 読売禁令 ··· **1**:252a
  Yomiuri Literary Prize
    Agawa Hiroyuki (1952) ······ **1**:21a
    Aizu Yaichi (1951) ········· **1**:38b
    Amino Kiku (1967) ········· **1**:52b
    Nakamura Mitsuo (1958) ···· **5**:315a-315b
    Shōno Junzō (1965) ········ **7**:167a
    Tanaka Chikao (1953) ······ **7**:335b
    Yashiro Seiichi (1972) ······ **8**:317a
Yomiuri shimbun 読売新聞 · **1**:18a; **4**:127b,
    184a, 199b, 207a; **7**:310b; **8**:336b-337a
  Baba Tsunego ·············· **1**:129b
  Occupation ··············· **6**:53b
Yomiuri Telecasting Corporation · **8**:337a
Yōmonkai ······· 陽門会 ····· **3**:145b
Yomotsu Hirasaka
    ········ 黄泉平坂 ····· **1**:69a
Yonago ········· 米子 ······· **8**:337a
Yonagunijima ··· 与那国島 ··· **4**:2b; **8**:337a

Yonai Mitsumasa 米内光政 ······ **8**:337a
  Arita Hachirō ·············· **1**:85a
Yonaoshi rebellions
    ·········· 世直し騒動 · **8**:337a-337b
  ikki ···················· **2**:269a
  Yoneda, Karl ·············· **4**:15b
  Yonemoto Masaaki. 米本正秋
    See **Tachihara Masaaki**
Yoneshirogawa ···· 米代川 · **8**:337b-338a
Yonezawa (city) ····· 米沢 ··· **8**:338a
Yonezawa Basin · 米沢盆地 ···· **8**:338a
  Yonezawa Hikohachi
    ········ 米沢彦八 ····· **6**:282a
  Yon'ichiroku Jiken. 四・一六事件
    See **April 16th Incident**
Yōnin ··············· 遥任 ····· **8**:338a
  Yōnin kokushi ··· 遥任国司 ··· **4**:262a
  Yonkakoku Jōyaku
    ········ 四か国条約 ····· **2**:330a
Yono ················ 与野 ····· **8**:338a
Yo no naka e ····· 世の中へ ··· **4**:148b
  Yonsei ··················· **4**:13b
  Yoresugi ················· **7**:257b
Yoriai ············· 寄合 ····· **4**:122a;
    8:338a-338b
  group meetings ············· **8**:338a
  linked-verse ·············· **8**:338b
  secret council ············· **8**:338a
  shogunal vassals ········· **8**:338a-338b
Yoribito ········ 寄人 · **8**:339b-340a
Yoriki and dōshin
    ·············· 与力, 同心 ··· **8**:338b
Yorimasa ········ 頼政 ······ **4**:327b
Yorioya and yoriko
    ········ 寄親, 寄子 ····· **8**:338b
Yōrō ············· 養老 ······ **8**:338b
Yoroboshi ········ 弱法師 ····· **4**:154b
Yōrō Code ······ 養老律令 ···· **7**:11a;
    8:338b-339a
  clothing styles ············· **1**:329b
  court rank ················ **2**:40a
  Dajōkan (Grand Council of State) · **2**:70a
  Fujiwara no Fuhito ·········· **2**:350b
  inheritance law ············ **3**:304a
  Rikkokushi ················ **6**:315b
  ritsuryō system ············ **6**:329b
  Taihō Code ··············· **7**:295b
Yōrōgawa ········ 養老川 ····· **8**:339a
  Yoroi kumiuchi · 鎧組打 ···· **4**:82a
Yoronjima ······ 与論島 ····· **8**:339a
  Yōrō Ritsuryō. 養老律令 *See* **Yōrō Code**
Yorozu chōhō ···· 万朝報 **1**:129a; **6**:144a;
    8:339a
  Ishikawa Sanshirō ··········· **3**:344a
  Kuroiwa Ruikō ············· **4**:316b
  Naitō Konan ··············· **5**:311a
  Russo-Japanese War ········· **6**:346b
Yorozuya Kinnosuke
    ········ 萬屋錦之介 ····· **8**:339a
  Yorozuyo Bunko · 万代文庫 ··· **8**:9a
Yoru no kutsu (Shoes in
  the Night) ······ 夜の靴 ···· **8**:333b
Yoru no nezame
    ········ 夜の寝覚 ····· **7**:257b;
    8:339a-339b
Yoru no tsuzumi ··· 夜の鼓 ···· **8**:339b
  Shindō Kaneto ············· **7**:111a
Yoru to kiri no sumide
    ········ 夜と霧の隅で ··· **4**:227a
Yoryūdo ········ 寄人 · **8**:339b-340a
  farmers and laborers ······ **8**:339b-340a
  scribes ·················· **8**:339b
  Yosa Buson ···· 与謝蕪村 · **1**:210b, 224b;
    6:297a
  Yōsai. 栄西 *See* **Eisai**
  Yōsan (mathematics) ········· **8**:231a
Yosano Akiko · 与謝野晶子 · **2**:344a; **7**:54b,
    253b; **8**:340a

Myōjō · · · · · · · · · · · · · · · · · · 5:290b
Yosano Tekkan
· · · · · · · · 与謝野鉄幹 · · · · · · 8:216b,
340a–340b
Ishikawa Takuboku · · · · · 3:344b
Myōjō · · · · · · · · · · · · · · · · · · 5:290b
Yose · · · · · · · · · · · · · 寄席 · · · · 8:340b
naniwa-bushi · · · · · · · · · · · 5:328a
Yoseba kumiai mura
· · · · · · · · · · 寄場組合村 · · · · · 1:211b
Yōshi. *See* **Adoption**
**Yoshida-Acheson exchange of
notes** · · · · · · · · · · · · · 8:340b–341a
Yoshida-Evarts Convention · · · · 8:12a
Yoshida Hideo · · · 吉田秀雄 · · 1:17a; 8:341a
Yoshida Hiroshi · · · · 吉田博 · · · · 8:341a
Yoshida Isoya · · 吉田五十八 · · 1:81a; 8:341a
Yoshida Issui · · · 吉田一穂 · · · · · 8:341a
Yoshida Kanetomo
· · · · · · · · · · 吉田兼倶 · · · 8:341a–341b
Yoshida Kasaburō
· · · · · · · · · 吉田嘉三郎 · · · · · 8:341a
Yoshida Kenkō · · 吉田兼好 · · · · 5:44a;
8:341a–342b, 380b
Tsurezuregusa · · · · · · · · · · · · 4:136a
writings · · · · · · · · · · · · 8:342a–343a
Yoshida Kōgyō · · · · · · · 8:342b, 346a
Yoshida Mitsuyoshi
· · · · · · · · · · 吉田光由 · · · · · · 8:342b
Yoshida Seiichi · · · · 吉田精一 · · · 8:343a
Yoshida Shigeru · · · 吉田茂 · · 2:4a, 333a;
7:26a, 92a, 235b; 8:341a, 343a, 343b–345a;
Dulles, John Foster · · · · · · · 2:135a
economic planning · · · · · · · · 2:168a
economy · · · · · · · · · · · 2:157a–157b
Jiyūtō · · · · · · · · · · · · · · · · · · 4:65b
Kanamori Tokujirō · · · · · · · · 4:135a
Kigensetsu controversy · · · · · 4:204a
Korean War · · · · · · · · · · · · · 4:284b
labor unions · · · · · · · · · · · · 4:347a
land reforms of 1946 · · · · · · · 4:365a
San Francisco Peace Treaty · · · · · 7:11a
Shimoyama Incident · · · · · · · 7:107a
Yoshida Shigeru cabinet · · · · · · · · 1:51a
Yoshida Shintō · · 吉田神道 · · 7:128a–128b;
8:345a–345b
Takamagahara · · · · · · · · · · · 7:314a
Yoshida Shōin · · 吉田松陰 · · 5:156b; 7:3b,
94b; 8:345b–346a
Yoshida Tadao · · 吉田忠雄 · · · · · 8:346a
Yoshida Tōgo · · · 吉田東伍 · · · · · 8:346a
Yoshida Tomizō · 吉田富三 · · 8:346a–346b
Yoshida Tōyō · · · 吉田東洋 · · · · · 8:346a
Yoshida Yoshishige
· · · · · · · · · · 吉田喜重 · · · · · · 2:273b
Yoshihara Oil Mill, Ltd · · · · · · 8:346b
Yoshiharu Shikimoku
· · · · · · · · 義治式目 · · 7:96a; 8:346b
Yoshiigawa · · · · · 吉井川 · · · · · · 8:346b
Yoshii Isamu · · · · 吉井勇 · · · 7:253b;
8:346b–347a
Yoshikawa Eiji · · 吉川英治 · 1:164a; 2:274a;
7:65b, 103b; 8:347a
Yoshikawa Kōjirō
· · · · · · · · · 吉川幸次郎 · · 8:347a–347b
Yoshikawa Koretari
· · · · · · · · · · 吉川惟足 · · · · · · 8:347b
Yoshikiri · · · · · · · · · · · · · · · · 6:285b
Yoshimasu Tōdō 吉益東洞 · · · · · 8:347b
**Yoshimi "hundred-cave" tunnel
tombs** · · · · · · 吉見百穴 · · 8:347b–348a
Yoshimitsu · · · · · · 義満 · · · · · · 3:173b
Yoshimoto · · · · · · · 良基 · · · · · · 6:298b
Yoshimoto Ryūmei. 吉本隆明
See **Yoshimoto Takaaki**
Yoshimoto Takaaki
· · · · · · · · · · 吉本隆明 · · 1:83a; 8:348a
Yoshimura Junzō 吉村順三 · · · · 8:348a

Yoshimura Kōzaburō
· · · · · · · · 吉村公三郎 · 2:271b, 275b;
7:102b; 8:348a
Shindō Kaneto · · · · · · · · · · · 7:111a
Yoshinogawa · · · · · 吉野川 · · · · · 8:348a
Yoshino Hideo · · · 吉野秀雄 · · · · · 8:348b
**Yoshino-Kumano National
Park** · · · 吉野熊野国立公園 · · · · 5:299b;
8:348b, 349b
Yoshinokuzu · · · · · 吉野葛 · · · · · 7:342b
Yoshino no tōzoku
(Yoshino Bandits)
· · · · · · · · 吉野の盗賊 · · · · · · 8:319b
Yoshino Sakuzō 吉野作造 1:313b; 7:251a,
281a; 8:348b–349a
Fukuda Tokuzō · · · · · · · · · · 2:362b
mimpon shugi · · · · · · · · · · · 5:175b
Reimeikai · · · · · · · · · · · · · · 6:288b
Yoshinoyama · · · · · 吉野山 · · 8:349a, 349b
Yōshinshi (adoptive parent-child
relationships) · · · · · · · · · · · 6:162b
Yoshioka Kinzaburō. 吉岡金三郎
See **Taiso Yoshitoshi**
Yoshioka Yayoi · · · 吉岡弥生 · · · · 8:349b
Hani Motoko · · · · · · · · · · · · · 3:96a
Yoshishige no Yasutane
· · · · · · · · 慶滋保胤 · · 1:181a; 5:37b;
8:349b
Chiteiki · · · · · · · · · · · · · · · 4:129a
Yoshiwara · · · · · · · 吉原 · 6:155b, 285b;
8:349b–351a
daily routine · · · · · · · · · · 8:350b–351a
end · · · · · · · · · · · · · · · · · · 8:351a
setting · · · · · · · · · · · · · · · · 8:350a
women · · · · · · · · · · · · · 8:350a–350b
*Yoshiwara keisei shin bijin
awase jihitsu kagami*
吉原傾城新美人合自筆鑑 · · · · 8:142b
Yoshiya Nobuko · 吉屋信子 · · · · 7:103b;
8:351a–351b
fūzoku shōsetsu · · · · · · · · · · · 2:378b
Yoshiyuki Eisuke 吉行エイスケ · · · 7:119b
Yoshiyuki Junnosuke
· · · · · · · · · 吉行淳之介 · · · · · 1:209a;
8:351b–352a
Yoshizawa Akira · · 吉沢章 · · · · · 6:116b
Yoshizawa Kenkichi
· · · · · · · · · 芳沢謙吉 · · · · · · 6:343a;
8:352a
Yōsho Shirabesho
· · · · · · · · · · 洋書調所 · · · · · · 1:142a
Yōteizan · · · · · · · 羊蹄山 · 7:98a; 8:352a
Yotsugi Soga · · · · 世継曽我 · · · · · 1:275a
Young, Ralph · · · · · · · · · 2:157a–157b
8:354b
Young Men's Christian Association
(YMCA) · · · · · · · · · · · · · · 8:326a
Young Officers' Movement · · · · · 2:250a
Youth · · · · · · · · 5:4a–4b; 8:352a–353a
deviance · · · · · · · · · · · · · · · 8:353a
education · · · · · · · · · · · · · · · · 5:4b
marriage · · · · · · · · · · · · · · · · · 5:4b
modern period · · · · · · · · · · · 8:352b
post-World War II · · · · · · · 8:352b–353a
psychology · · · · · · · · · · 8:353a–353b
social roles · · · · · · · · · · · · · · · 5:4a
traditional groups · · · · · · · 8:352a–352b
Youth clubs · · · · · · · · · · · · · 8:353b
Youth groups · · · · · · · · · · 8:217b–218a
Youth Labor Homes · · · · · · · · · · 4:87a
Yowa no nezame (Waking
at Midnight) · 夜半の寝覚 · · 5:35b; 7:21a
Yoyogi National Gymnasia · · · · 8:353b
YS-11 · · · · · · · · · · · · · · 8:353b–354a
Yūaikai · · · · · · · · 友愛会 · · · 1:2a, 72a;
4:345a–345b; 7:219a, 281a; 8:354a
Asō Hisashi · · · · · · · · · · · · · 1:102a
Tanno Setsu · · · · · · · · · · · · · 7:344a

Yuan shi · · · · · · · · · · · · · · · · 6:358a
Yuan Skikai (Yüan Shih-k'ai) · · · · 4:280b;
7:276b, 277b; 8:354a–354b
Kapsin Political Coup · · · · · · · 4:280b
Reorganization Loan · · · · · · · · 6:302a
Yuasa Hachirō · · 湯浅八郎 3:318b; 8:354b
Yuasa Jōzan · · · · 湯浅常山 · · · · · 8:354b
Yuasa Yoshiko · · · 湯浅芳子 · · · · · 5:220b
Yūbari · · · · · · · · · · 夕張 · · · · · 8:354b
Yūbaridake · · · · · · 夕張岳 · · · · · 8:354b
Yūbari Mountains
· · · · · · · · · · 夕張山地 · · · · · · 8:354b
Yūbe no kumo · · · · 夕べの雲 · · · · 7:167a
Yūbin hōchi shimbun
· · · · · · · · 郵便報知新聞 · 1:155a; 8:355a
Kurimoto Joun, editor · · · · · · · 4:313b
Yūbin Jōkisen Kaisha · · · · · · · · 3:362b
Yu Dafu (Yü Ta-fu) · · · · · · · · 8:355a
Yudanaka Hot Spring
· · · · · · · · 湯田中温泉 · · · · · · 8:355a
Yūdansha (rank holders) · · · · · · 4:196a
Yudate kagura · · 湯立神楽 · · · · · 4:107a
Yudonosan · · · · · 湯殿山 1:136b; 8:355a
Yuensai · · · · · · · · · 油煙斎 · · · · · 5:307a
Yufuin · · · · · · · · · · 由布院 · · · · · 8:355
Yuga · · · · · · · · · · · 瑜伽 · · 7:113b–115a
Yugake · · · · · · · · · · · · · · · · · 4:340b
Yugashima Hot Spring
· · · · · · · · 湯ヶ島温泉 · 1:49b; 2:342b;
8:355a
Yugawara · · · · · · · 湯河原 · · · · · 8:355a
Yugei · · · · · · · · · · · 靫負 · · · · · 1:147b
Yūgen · · · · · · · · · 幽玄 1:181a; 2:355a;
5:39a, 42a, 43a; 8:355b–356a
Jakuren · · · · · · · · · · · · · · · · · 4:1b
Yugishō · · · · · · · · · 湯起請 · · · · · 4:302b
Yugyōji · · · · · · · · 遊行寺 · · · · · 8:356a
Ji sect · · · · · · · · · · · · · · · · · 4:62a
Yuhazu no mitsugi · 弓弭調 · · · · · 7:264b
Yūhitsu · · · · · · · · 右筆 · · · · · · 8:356a
Yui · · · · · · · · · · · 結い · · · · · 8:356a
Yuiitsu shintō. *See* **Yoshida Shintō**
*Yuiitsu shintō myōbō
yōshū* 唯一神道名法要集 · · · · 7:128b
Yui Shōsetsu · · · 由井正雪 · · 8:356a–356b
Yui Shōsetsu Disturbance
· · · · · · · · 由井正雪の乱 · · · · · · 4:187a
Yūkaku · · · · · · · · · · · · · · · · · 3:15a
Yukar. *See* **Ainu language**
Yukar epics · · · · · · · · · · · · · · 1:37a
Yukawa Hideki · · 湯川秀樹 · · · · 8:356b
Yuki (town) · · · · · · 油木 · · · · · 8:356b
Yūki (city) · · · · · · · 結城 · · · · · 8:356b
Yūki family · · · · · 結城氏 · · 8:356b–357a
Yuki fujin ezu (Portrait of
Madame Yuki)
· · · · · · · · 雪夫人絵図 · · · · · · 6:221b
Yukiguni (Snow Country)
· · · · · · · · · 雪国 4:176a; 7:176a;
8:90b
"Yukihiko-Kokei era" · · · · · · · · 6:157b
Yukijirushi Shokuhin · · · · · · · · 7:206b
Yūkike Hatto · · · 結城家法度 · · · · 8:357a
Yūki Magosaburō
· · · · · · · · · 結城孫三郎 · · · · · · 4:77a
puppet theater · · · · · · · · · · · 6:270a
Yuki Matsuri · · · · · 雪祭 · · 7:206b–207a
Yukimi (snow viewing) · · · 4:381a; 7:207a
Yukinari Kyō ki · 行成卿記 · · · · · 3:45b
Yuki onna · · · · · · · 雪女 · · · · · · 8:357a
Yūki Shōji · · · · · 結城昌治 · · 8:357a–357b
Yūki Somei · · · · · · 結城素明 · · · · · 4:175b
Yūki Toyotarō · 結城豊太郎 · · · · 8:357b
Yukitsubaki (*C. rusticana; C. japonica
var. decumbens*) · · · · · · · · · 1:236b
Yukiwarisō (*Anemone hepatica* var.
japonica; Hepatica acuta) · · · · · 8:357b
Yuku haru · · · · · · · ゆく春 · · · · · 7:279b

Yukuhashi·········· 行橋 ····8:357b
Yume no shiro (Instead of
Dreams) ···· 夢の代 ·····8:292a
Yume no ukihashi
············ 夢の浮橋 ····7:343a
Yumigahama ··· 弓ケ浜 ····8:357b
Yūmoa gekijō (Humor
Theater) ···· ユーモア劇場 ··6:275b
Yuna ····················6:155a
Yun Ch'i-ho ············4:281b
Yunoyama Hot Spring
········ 湯の山温泉 ·····8:357b
Yunoyama sangin hyakuin
·········· 湯山三吟百韻 ·····6:298b
Yun Pong-gil ·········8:357b-358a
Yuragawa ··· 由良川 4:338a; 8:358a
Yūrei (ghosts) ·········· 3:30a
Yuri ·····················5:9b-10a
Yuri Kimimasa ··· 由利公正 ··8:358a
Yuriwaka legend
·········· 百合若大臣 ·····8:358a
Yūseishō. 郵政省 See Ministry of Posts
and Telecommunications
Yūshi Kyōritsu Tōkyō Hospital ··7:311a
Yushima Seidō. 湯島聖堂 See Shōheikō
Yūshi sensei ············3:91b
Yūsoku kojitsu ··· 有職故実 ···1:79a;
8:358a-358b
Yu Sŏng-nyong ···········8:358b
Yü Ta-fu. See Yu Dafu (Yü Ta-fu)
Yutai xinyong (Gyokudai shin'ei; New
Songs from the Jade Terrace) ···8:207a
Yuzawa (city) ······· 湯沢 ··8:358b
Yuzawa (town) ······· 湯沢 ··8:358b
Yūzen ······· 友禅 4:336a, 338a;
8:238a; 8:358a
kimono ················8:358b
Yūzen-zome. 友禅染 See Yūzen
Yūzonsha ······· 猶存社 ···8:359a
Yuzu ···················3:127b
Yūzuki ········ 夕月 ·····8:334a
Yuzuki no Kimi ·· 弓月君 ··4:205b;
8:359a-359b
Hata family ············3:111a
Yūzū nembutsu engi
(Buddhist hand
scroll) ···· 融通念仏縁起 ·····8:82a
Yūzū Nembutsu sect
········ 融通念仏宗 7:20a; 8:359b
nembutsu ··············4:67a
Ryōnin ················6:352b
Yūzū Nembutsu Shū
········ 融通念仏宗 ·····8:359b
Yuzurijō ········ 譲状 ····8:359b
Yūzuru (The Twilight
Crane) ········ 夕鶴 ····2:76b
shingeki ···············7:113a
YWCA (Young Women's Christian
Association) ········8:257b, 359b
Kawai Michi ············4:179a
YX project ····· 1:124a; 8:359b

Z

Za ············· 座 ···4:100a;
8:361a-361b
Zabuton ···············2:371a

Zagashira ·············4:95a
Zaibatsu ····· 財閥 1:147a; 7:214a,
267a-267b, 268b; 8:361b-363b
centralized buying and selling ··8:362b
control through credit ·········8:362b
"cordial oligopoly" ··········8:362b
defined ··········8:361b-362a
development ···········4:138a
dissolution ···· 1:8b; 2:35b; 4:364b, 378b;
8:363b-366a
economic recovery ········3:201a
Financial Crisis of 1927 ···2:277b
founders ······2:30a, 31b-32a
Furukawa ·············2:372b
general trading companies ···3:19a
growth ···············2:153a
holding companies ·······3:216a
income distribution ·····3:285b
industrial organization ····3:292b-293b
landlords ··············4:363b
Mitsubishi ············3:361b
Mitsui ···············5:209b
officer appointments and interlocks
···············8:362a-362b
older and newer ·······8:363b
ownership ···········8:362a
political parties ·······3:198b
public distrust ······8:362b-363a
reasons for growth ······2:31b
revival ··········8:363a-363b
subsidiaries ············4:189a
Sumitomo ············7:266b
Taiwan ···············7:308a
technological development ···7:369b
Yasuda ···············8:317a
Zaibatsu (film) ······· 財閥 ··8:319b
Zaibatsu dissolution · 2:372b; 7:267a, 268a,
269a; 8:363b-366a
antitrust statute ······8:364b-365a
capital levy tax ·······8:365a
Deconcentration Law ·····8:365a
dissolution program ····8:363b-364a
economical purge ·····8:365b-366a
Enterprise Reconstruction and
Reorganization Law ·····8:365b
Financial Institutions Reconstruction and
Reorganization Law ·····8:365b
Fuji Bank Ltd ·········2:342a
Law for the Termination of Zaibutsu
Family Control ·······8:365a-365b
Mitsubishi Trading ·····8:365a
Mitsui Trading ········8:365a
Occupation ·······6:52b-53a
sale of securities ······8:364b
Sanwa Bank, Ltd ·······7:19a
summary and assessment ··8:366a
Taisei Corporation ·····7:303a
technological development ···7:370a
Yasuda plan ·······8:364a-364b
Zaigō shōnin ···· 在郷商人 ·8:366a-366b
Zaikai ············8:366b-367b
Zaikata kabu ······ 在方株 ·4:100a
Zaike ············· 在家 ··8:367b
Buddhist laymen ·······8:367b
laity ···········4:362a-362b
lay Buddhist movement ···4:372a
peasants ··············8:367b
Zai Mimbukyō no Ie no
Uta-awase
······ 在民部卿家歌合 ·····8:182a
Zaisankei ······ 財産刑 ····7:140b
Zaiseigaku taikō (Principles of Public
Finance) ···· 財政学大綱 ··6:135b
Zaisei tōyūshi ···········8:367b
Zama ············ 座間 ··8:367b
Zambōritsu. See Libel Law of 1875
Zangedō to shite no tetsugaku
······ 懺悔道としての哲学 ···7:335b

Zangiri-mono
("cropped-hair"
plays) ···· 散切物 ··5:234b-235a
Zansetsu ······ 残雪 ·····7:359a
Zaō Gongen ··· 蔵王権現 ·4:208a; 6:24b
Zaō Hot Spring ·· 蔵王温泉 ··8:367b
Zaō Quasi-National Park
········ 蔵王国定公園 ·····8:368a
Zaōzan ······· 蔵王山 ·8:367a, 368a
Zappai and senryū ·····8:368a-368b
literary characteristics of senryū ··8:368b
senryū ················8:368b
types of zappai ·······8:368a-368b
Zaru (basket) ·········2:25a
Zashiki warashi ··· 座敷童 ··8:368b
Zasshu bunka ··· 雑種文化 ·4:169b
Zasso Ketsudansho
········ 雑訴決断所 ·····8:368b-369a
Zatō ·········· 5:45a; 8:369a
Zatō (blind men) plays ····4:327b
Zatsumu sata ··· 雑務沙汰 ·8:369a
Zazen (sitting meditation)
············ 座禅 ·····6:261b
monasticism ···········5:238a
See also Zen
Zeami ·········· 世阿弥 ··5:15b, 43a;
7:61b, 120b; 8:312b, 369a-369b
artistic ideals ··········8:369b
Kan'ami ···············4:135b
Kanze Nobumitsu ·······4:154b
Kanze school ··········4:155a
life ··················8:369a
works ············8:369a-369b
yūgen ················8:355b
Zeigo ········ 贅語 ·····5:214b-215a
Zeimu kaikei. See Tax accounting
Zeimusho. See Tax office
Zeirishi. See Tax accountants
Zekkai Chūshin ··· 絶海中津 ··8:369b
Zelkova [(keyaki) Zelkova
serrata] ···1:264b; 2:327a; 8:369b
Zempa ·········· 禅派 ·····8:369b-370a
Zen ·········· 禅 1:178b-179b,
185b; 7:80b, 84a; 8:370a-374b
architecture ········1:191b-192a
contemporary ·······8:374a-374b
cultural and artistic dimension ··8:374a
Eiheiji temple ·······2:186a-186b
existentialism ··········2:236b
food and eating habits ·····2:305b
Fujiwara no Nobuzane ·····2:354b
Gozan ···········3:57a-58a
Gozan literature ·····3:58a-59a
history ···········8:370a-372a
Chan in China ·······8:370a
Zen in Japan ·····8:370b-372a
Huike (Hui-k'o) Severing His Arm ··· 8:371a
influence on gardens ·····3:8b-9a
ink painting ············3:306a
intellectual background ···8:372a-373a
cosmotheism (avatamsaka) ·8:372a-372b
idealism and consciousness (yogācāra)
··················8:372a
Taoist contribution ·······8:372b
wisdom and emptiness (prajñā and
sūnyatā) ·············8:372a
Zen masters ·······8:372b-373a
Ishida Baigan ··········3:340a
meditation (zazen) ·······8:372b
monasticism ·······5:238a-238b
monks
Betsugen Enshi ·······1:150b
Chūgan Engetsu ·······1:311b
Dōgen ···············1:191b
Eisai ········ 1:191a; 2:187a
Enni ······· 1:191a, 192a; 2:219a
Gidō Shūshin ··········3:30b
Hakuin ···············3:88a

Ikkyū · 3:269b
Ingen · 3:303b
Issan Ichinei · · · · · · · · · · · · · · · 3:348b
Jakushitsu Genkō · · · · · · · · · · · · · 4:1b-2a
Keian Genju · · · · · · · · · · · 4:186b-187a
Kokan Shiren · · · · · · · · · · · · · · · 4:252b
Minchō · · · · · · · · · · · · · · · 5:183b-184a
Mokkei · · · · · · · · · · · · · · · · · · · 5:234a
Mokuan Reien · · · · · · · · · · 5:235a-235b
Musō Soseki · · · · · · · · · · · · · · · 5:287b
Ryōkan · · · · · · · · · · · · · · · · · · · 6:352a
Sesshū Tōyō · · · · · · · · · · · · · · · 8:371a
Takuan Sōhō · · · · · · · · · · · · · · · 7:327b
musical instruments · · · · · · · · · · · · 1:196a
Ōbaku sect · · · · · · · · · · · · · · · · 6:47a-47b
painting · · 1:210a-210b, 192a-193a; 6:158b
practice and enlightenment · · · 8:373a-374a
   enlightenment (satori) · · · · · · · · · · 7:28b;
                                    8:373b-374a
   kōan · · · · · · · · · · · · · · 4:234a; 8:373b
   lotus posture meditation (zazen) · · 8:373a
   psychotherapy · · · · · · · · · · · · · · 6:261b
Rinzai sect · · · · · · · · · · · · · · · · · 6:318b
Rokuon nichiroku · · · · · · · · · · · · · · 6:335b
Sasamegoto (Murmured Conversations)
· 7:24a
sculpture · · · · · · · · · · · · · 1:192a-193a
Sōjiji · 7:224a
Sōtō sect · · · · · · · · · · · · · · · 7:233a-234a
Tang (T'ang) dynasty
   tea ceremony · · · · · · · · · · · · · · 7:360a
   teachings · · · · · · · · · · · · · · · · · 3:46b
Waley, Arthur David · · · · · · · · · · 8:221b
Zen calligraphy · · · · · · · · · · · · 1:235b-236a
Zen'ei no bungaku
· · · · · · · · · · 前衛の文学 · · · · · · 4:172a
Zen'ei (Vanguard) · · · · 前衛 · · · · 1:72a
Zenga · · · · · · · · · · 禅画 · · · · 6:153b;
                                    8:374b-375a
   Circle Triangle, and Square · · · · · · · · 8:374b
   Hakuin · · · · · · · · · · · · · · · · · · 1:193a
   Sengai Gibon · · · · · · · · · · · · · · · 8:374b
Zengakuren · · · · · · · 全学連 · · · · 7:252a;
                                    8:375a-375b
   opposition to · · · · · · · · · · · · · · · 4:285b
   United States-Japan security treaties
· 8:167a
   peace movement · · · · · · · · · · · · · 6:167a
Zengo Shakkan · · · · · · · · · · · · · · 6:302a
Zenigata ("coin-shaped") · · · · · · · 7:41b
Zenitaka Corporation · · · · · · · · · 8:375b
Zeniya Gohei · · 銭屋五兵衛 · · · 8:375b
Zeniza. See Kinza, ginza, and zeniza.
Zenkōji · · · · · · · 善光寺 · · 8:375b-376a
   main hall (kondō) · · · · · · · · · · · · · 8:376b
   urbanization · · · · · · · · · · · · · · · 8:176a
Zenkoku Chiiki Fujin Dantai Renraku
   Kyōgi Kai · · · · · · · · · · · · · · · · 1:273b
Zenkoku Fujin Dōmei
   Tatewaki Sadayo · · · · · · · · · · · · 7:349b

Zenkoku hōgen jiten
· · · · · · · · · · 全国方言辞典 · · · · · · 4:31b
Zenkoku mukashi-banashi
   kiroku · · · · · 全国昔話記録 · · · · 2:302a
Zenkunen kassen emaki 前九年合戦絵巻
   Earlier Nine Years' War · · · · · · · · · 2:137a
Zenkunen no Eki. 前九年の役
   See Earlier Nine Years' War
Zen Nihon Bukkyō Kai · · · · · · · · · 8:376a
Zen Nihon Denki Kiki Rōdō Kumiai
   Rengōkai · · · · · · · · · · · · · · · · · · 2:87a
Zen Nihon Gakusei Jichikai Sōrengō
· · · · · · · · · · · · · · · · · · · 8:375a-375b
Zen Nihon Kendō Remmei · · · · · · · 4:196a
Zen Nihon Minshu Iryō Kikan Rengōkai
· 4:12a
Zen Nihon Rōdō Sōdōmei
· · · · · · · 全日本労働総同盟 2:130a; 7:219a
Zen no kenkyū · · 善の研究 · · 6:232b;
                                    8:376a-376b
Zen painting. See Zenga
Zen printing, premodern · · · · · · · · 6:248a
Zenrinkoku hōki
· · · · · · · · · · 善隣国宝記 · · · · 8:376b
Zenrō · 7:327a
Zenrō Kaigi · · · · · · 全労会議 · · · · 7:189a
Zen school · · · · · · · · · · · · · 8:369b-370a
Zensen · 8:376b
   Takita Minoru · · · · · · · · · · · · · · 7:327a
Zenshinza · · · · · · · · · · 前進座 · · 8:377a
Zenshō · 7:273a
Zentsūji (city) · · · · · · 善通寺 · · 8:377a-377b
Zentsūji · · · · · · · · · · 善通寺 · · 8:377b
   Shingon sect · · · · · · · · · · · · · · · 7:115a
ZERO · 4:10a
Zero Fighter · · · · · · · · · 5:313b; 8:377a, 377b
Zerosen · · · · · · · · · · 零戦 · · · · 8:377b
Zetsubō no seishin shi
· · · · · · · · · · 絶望の精神史 · · · · 4:139a
Zeze Castle · · · · · · · 膳所城 · · 6:133b
Zhang Jizhi (Chang Chi-chih) · · · · · 1:235b
Zhang Xueliang (Chang Hsüeh-liang)
· · · · · · · · · · 3:201b; 7:77b; 8:377b
Zhang Ziping (Chang Tzu-p'ing)
· · · · · · · · · · · · · · · · · · · 8:377b-378a
Zhang Zuolin Incident 2:207b; 7:336a-336b
Zhang Zuolin (Chang Tso-lin) · · · · 7:237b;
                                    8:378a
Zheng Chenggong (Cheng Ch'eng
   Kung) · · · · · · · · · · · · · · · 8:378a-378b
Zheng-family rule · · · · · · · · · · · · · 7:307a
Zheng Xiaoxu (Cheng Hsiao-hsü) 8:378b
Zhong Gui · · · · · · · · · · · · · · · · · · 7:163b
Zhonghua Minguo Linshi Zhengfu
· · · · · · · · · · · · · · · · · · · 6:260a-260b
Zhonghua Minguo Weixin Zhengfu
· · · · · · · · · · · · · · · · · · · 6:285b-286a
Zhou Enlai (Chou En-lai) · · · · 8:378b-379a
Zhou Hongqing (Chou Hung-ch'ing)
   Incident · · · · · · · · · · · · · · · · · · 8:379a

Zhou Maoshu Admiring Lotus
   Blossoms · · · · · · · · · · · · · · · · · · 4:147b
Zhou Zuoren (Chou Tso-jen) 8:379a-379b
Zhu Shunshui · · · · · · · · · · · · · · · 7:191a
Zhu Xi (Chu Hsi) Neo-Confucianism
· · · · · · · · · · · · · · · 3:117b; 7:190a-191b
Zhu Xi (Chu Hsi) school. See
   Shushigaku
Zōbiki · · · · · · · · · · · · 象引 · · · · 4:98b
Zōho gorin wakun no
   shiori · · · · 増補語林和訓栞 · · · · 8:221b
Zōho kai tsūshō kō
· · · · · · · · · · 増補華夷通商考 · · · · 4:369b
Zōho rigen shūran
· · · · · · · · · · 増補俚諺集覧 · · · · 6:312a
Zōjōji · · · · · · · · · · · · 増上寺 · · · · 8:379a
Zōka poetry · · · · · · · · · · · · · · · · · 5:105a
Zokkyoku no yurai (music)
· · · · · · · · · · 俗曲の由来 · · · · 6:134b
Zoku hizakurige · 続膝栗毛 · · · · 4:61b
Zoku ichinen yūhan (A
   Year and a Half,
   continued) · · · · · 続一年有半 · · · · 5:312a
Zoku sarumino · · · 続猿蓑 · · · · 4:102b
Zoku Tokugawa jikki
· · · · · · · · · · 続徳川実紀 · · · · 8:51a
Zoological gardens · · · · · · · · · · · 8:379b
   Ueno Zoological Garden · · · · 8:129a, 379b
Zoologists
   Imanishi Kinji · · · · · · · · · · · · · · 3:274a
   Ishikawa Chiyomatsu · · · · · · · · · 3:342a
   Mitsukuri Kakichi · · · · · · · · · · · · 5:213b
   Morse, Edward Sylvester · · · · · · · · 5:256a
   Toyama Kametarō · · · · · · · · · · · · 8:88a
   Whitman, Charles Otis · · · · · · · · · 8:252b
Zōri · · · · · · · · · · · · · · 7:249b; 8:379b
Zoruge Jiken · · ゾルゲ事件 · · · 7:229a-230a
Zōsen Gigoku. See Shipbuilding
   Scandal of 1954
Zōsen Oshoku. See Shipbuilding
   Scandal
   of 1954
Zōshi · · · · · · · · · · · · 蔵志 · · · · 8:311b
Zōshiki · · · · · · · · · · · · 雑色 · · 8:379b-380a
   ritsuryō system · · · · · · · · · · · · · · 6:324b
Zou Taofen (Tsou T'ao-fen) · · · · · · 8:380a
Z Revolution · · · · · · · · · · · · · · · · 8:293b
Zuihitsu · · · · · · · · · · · · · · · 8:380a-380b
   Makura no sōshi · · · · · · · · · · · · · 7:52a
   Shinkyō shōsetsu · · · · · · · · · · · · 3:312a
   Tsurezuregusa · · · · · · · · · · · · · · 8:341b
Zuisenji · · · · · · · · · · 瑞泉寺 · · · · 8:380b
Zuisho · · · · · · · · · · 隋書 · · 7:264a-264b
Zukin · 3:119a
Zuryō · · · · · · · · · · · · 受領 · · · · 8:380b
Zushi · · · · · · · · · · · · 逗子 · · · · 8:381a
Zushoryō · · · · · · · · · · 図書寮 · · · · 1:151b;
                                    5:1a; 8:381a-381b

Nengō———Japanese Era Names and Dates

A

An'ei	安永	1772–1781
Angen	安元	1175–1177
Anna	安和	968–970
Ansei	安政	1854–1860 (1855–1860)
Antei	安貞	1227–1229 (1228–1229)

B

Bummei	文明	1469–1487
Bumpō	文保	1317–1319
Bun'an	文安	1444–1449
Bunchū	文中	1372–1375
Bun'ei	文永	1264–1275
Bunji	文治	1185–1190
Bunka	文化	1804–1818
Bunki	文亀	1501–1504
Bunkyū	文久	1861–1864
Bunna (N)	文和	1352–1356
Bun'ō	文応	1260–1261
Bunroku	文禄	1592–1596 (1593–1596)
Bunryaku	文暦	1234–1235
Bunsei	文政	1818–1830 (1818–1831)
Bunshō	文正	1466–1467

C

Chōgen	長元	1028–1037
Chōhō	長保	999–1004
Chōji	長治	1104–1106
Chōkan	長寛	1163–1165
Chōkyō	長享	1487–1489
Chōkyū	長久	1040–1044
Chōroku	長禄	1457–1460 (1457–1461)
Chōryaku	長暦	1037–1040
Chōshō	長承	1132–1135
Chōtoku	長徳	995–999
Chōwa	長和	1012–1017 (1013–1017)

D

Daidō	大同	806–810
Daiji	大治	1126–1131

E

Eichō	永長	1096–1097 (1097–1098)
Eien	永延	987–989
Eiho	永保	1081–1084
Eiji	永治	1141–1142
Eijō	永承	1046–1053
Eikan	永観	983–985
Eikyō	永享	1429–1441
Eikyū	永久	1113–1118
Eiman	永万	1165–1166
Einin	永仁	1293–1299
Eiroku	永禄	1558–1570
Eiryaku	永暦	1160–1161
Eishō	永正	1504–1521
Eiso	永祚	989–990
Eitoku (N)	永徳	1381–1384
Eiwa (N)	永和	1375–1379
Embun (N)	延文	1356–1361
Empō	延宝	1673–1681
Enchō	延長	923–931
Engen	延元	1336–1340
Engi	延喜	901–923
Enkyō	延慶	1308–1311
Enkyō	延享	1744–1748
Enkyū	延久	1069–1074
En'ō	延応	1239–1240
Enryaku	延暦	782–806
Entoku	延徳	1489–1492

G

Gangyō	元慶	877–885
Gembun	元文	1736–1741
Genchū	元中	1384–1392
Gen'ei	元永	1118–1120
Genji	元治	1864–1865
Genki	元亀	1570–1573
Genkō	元亨	1321–1324 (1321–1325)
Genkō	元弘	1331–1334
Genkyū	元久	1204–1206
Genna	元和	1615–1624
Gennin	元仁	1224–1225 (1225)
Gen'ō	元応	1319–1321
Genroku	元禄	1688–1704
Genryaku	元暦	1184–1185
Gentoku	元徳	1329–1332

H

Hakuchi	白雉	650–654
Heiji	平治	1159–1160
Hōan	保安	1120–1124
Hōei	宝永	1704–1711
Hōen	保延	1135–1141
Hōgen	保元	1156–1159
Hōji	宝治	1247–1249
Hōki	宝亀	770–781
Hōreki	宝暦	1751–1764
Hōtoku	宝徳	1449–1452

J

Jian	治安	1021–1024
Jingo Keiun	神護景雲	767–770
Jinki	神亀	724–729
Jiryaku	治暦	1065–1069
Jishō	治承	1177–1181
Jōan	承安	1171–1175
Jōei	貞永	1232–1233
Jōgan	貞観	859–877
Jōgen	貞元	976–978 (976–979)
Jōgen	承元	1207–1211
Jōhei	承平	931–938
Jōhō	承保	1074–1077 (1074–1078)
Jōji (N)	貞治	1362–1368
Jōkyō	貞享	1684–1688
Jōkyū	承久	1219–1222
Jōō	貞応	1222–1224 (1222–1225)
Jōō	承応	1652–1655
Jōryaku	承暦	1077–1081 (1078–1081)
Jōtoku	承徳	1097–1099 (1098–1099)
Jōwa	承和	834–848
Jōwa (N)	貞和	1345–1350
Juei	寿永	1182–1185

K

Kaei	嘉永	1848–1854 (1848–1855)
Kagen	嘉元	1303–1306 (1303–1307)
Kahō	嘉保	1094–1096 (1095–1097)
Kajō	嘉承	1106–1108
Kakitsu	嘉吉	1441–1444
Kakyō (N)	嘉慶	1387–1389
Kambun	寛文	1661–1673
Kampō	寛保	1741–1744
Kampyō	寛平	889–898
Kan'ei	寛永	1624–1644 (1624–1645)
Kan'en	寛延	1748–1751
Kangen	寛元	1243–1247
Kangi	寛喜	1229–1232
Kanji	寛治	1087–1094 (1087–1095)
Kankō	寛弘	1004–1012 (1004–1013)
Kanna	寛和	985–987
Kannin	寛仁	1017–1021
Kannō (N)	観応	1350–1352
Kansei	寛政	1789–1801
Kanshō	寛正	1460–1466 (1461–1466)
Kantoku	寛徳	1044–1046
Kaō	嘉応	1169–1171
Karoku	嘉禄	1225–1227 (1225–1228)
Karyaku	嘉暦	1326–1329
Kashō	嘉祥	848–851
Katei	嘉禎	1235–1238 (1235–1239)
Keian	慶安	1648–1652
Keichō	慶長	1596–1615
Keiō	慶応	1865–1868
Keiun	慶雲	704–708
Kemmu	建武	1334–1338
Kempō	建保	1213–1219 (1214–1219)
Kenchō	建長	1249–1256
Ken'ei	建永	1206–1207
Kengen	乾元	1302–1303
Kenji	建治	1275–1278
Kenkyū	建久	1190–1199
Kennin	建仁	1201–1204
Kenryaku	建暦	1211–1213 (1211–1214)
Kentoku	建徳	1370–1372
Kōan	弘安	1278–1288
Kōan (N)	康安	1361–1362
Kōchō	弘長	1261–1264
Kōei (N)	康永	1342–1345
Kōgen	康元	1256–1257
Kōhei	康平	1058–1065
Kōhō	康保	964–968
Kōji	康治	1142–1144
Kōji	弘治	1555–1558
Kōka	弘化	1844–1848 (1845–1848)
Kōkoku	興国	1340–1346 (1340–1347)
Kōnin	弘仁	810–824
Kōō (N)	康応	1389–1390
Kōryaku (N)	康暦	1379–1381
Kōshō	康正	1455–1457
Kōwa	康和	1099–1104
Kōwa	弘和	1381–1384
Kyōhō	享保	1716–1736
Kyōroku	享禄	1528–1532
Kyōtoku	享徳	1452–1455
Kyōwa	享和	1801–1804
Kyūan	久安	1145–1151
Kyūju	久寿	1154–1156

M

Man'en	万延	1860–1861
Manji	万治	1658–1661
Manju	万寿	1024–1028
Meiji	明治	1868–1912
Meiō	明応	1492–1501
Meireki	明暦	1655–1658
Meitoku (N)	明徳	1390–1394
Meiwa	明和	1764–1772

N

Nimbyō	仁平	1151–1154
Nin'an	仁安	1166–1169
Ninji	仁治	1240–1243
Ninju	仁寿	851–854
Ninna	仁和	885–889

O

Ōan (N)	応安	1368–1375
Ōchō	応長	1311–1312
Ōei	応永	1394–1428
Ōho	応保	1161–1163
Ōnin	応仁	1467–1469
Ōtoku	応徳	1084–1087
Ōwa	応和	961–964

R

Reiki	霊亀	715–717
Ryakunin	暦仁	1238–1239 (1239)
Ryakuō (N)	暦応	1338–1342

S

Saikō	斉衡	854–857
Shitoku (N)	至徳	1384–1387
Shōan	正安	1299–1302
Shōchō	正長	1428–1429
Shōchū	正中	1324–1326 (1325–1326)
Shōgen	正元	1259–1260
Shōhei	正平	1346–1370 (1347–1370)
Shōhō	正保	1644–1648 (1645–1648)
Shōji	正治	1199–1201
Shōka	正嘉	1257–1259
Shōkyō (N)	正慶	1332–1334
Shōō	正応	1288–1293
Shōryaku	正暦	990–995
Shōtai	昌泰	898–901
Shōtoku	正徳	1711–1716
Shōwa	正和	1312–1317
Shōwa	昭和	1926–
Shuchō	朱鳥	686

T

Taiei	大永	1521–1528
Taihō	大宝	701–704
Taika	大化	645–650
Taishō	大正	1912–1926
Tembun	天文	1532–1555
Temmei	天明	1781–1789
Tempō	天保	1830–1844 (1831–1845)
Tempuku	天福	1233–1234
Tempyō	天平	729–749
Tempyō Hōji	天平宝字	757–765
Tempyō Jingo	天平神護	765–767
Tempyō Kampō	天平感宝	749
Tempyō Shōhō	天平勝宝	749–757
Ten'an	天安	857–859
Tenchō	天長	824–834
Ten'ei	天永	1110–1113
Ten'en	天延	973–976 (974–976)
Tengen	天元	978–983 (979–983)
Tengi	天喜	1053–1058
Tengyō	天慶	938–947
Tenji	天治	1124–1126
Tenju	天授	1375–1381
Tenna	天和	1681–1684
Tennin	天仁	1108–1110
Ten'ō	天応	781–782
Tenroku	天禄	970–973 (970–974)
Tenryaku	天暦	947–957
Tenshō	天承	1131–1132
Tenshō	天正	1573–1592
Tentoku	天徳	957–961
Ten'yō	天養	1144–1145
Tokuji	徳治	1306–1308 (1307–1308)

W

Wadō	和同	708–715

Y

Yōrō	養老	717–724
Yōwa	養和	1181–1182

N indicates era names used by the Northern Court during the period of division into NORTHERN AND SOUTHERN COURTS; the Southern Court era names are widely regarded as more legitimate.

NOTE: The dates given here for era names are those to be found in standard Japanese historical reference works. For some eras prior to the adoption of the Western calendar on 1 January 1873 two sets of dates are given. In these cases the first set are the standard dates, which have not been corrected precisely for discrepancies between the Japanese lunar and Western solar New Year, and the second set (in parentheses) are the correctly converted dates. Since the discrepancies between the beginnings and ends of Japanese and Western years are often slight, the standard Japanese practice is to assign the first or last year of an era to the Western year within which most of the Japanese year falls. The standard *nengō* tables are widely used, and to avoid confusion it is the standard dates that are given throughout this encyclopedia whenever era names are identified. The dates of specific events have been precisely converted to the Western calendar whenever possible.

Kodansha Encyclopedia of Japan (9)

英文日本大百科事典(9)

現金価格（セット定価）——140,000円
刊行記念特別定価———130,000円
（期限：昭和59年3月31日まで）

昭和58年11月25日　第1刷発行

監　修————————エドウィン・O・ライシャワー, 都留重人 他
発行者————————野間惟道
発行所————————株式会社　講談社
　　　　　　　　　　東京都文京区音羽2-12-21(〒112)
　　　　　　　　　　電話　東京 (03)945-1111(大代表)
　　　　　　　　　　振替　東京 8-3930

組　版————————Lehigh ROCAPPI(本文)
　　　　　　　　　　小宮山印刷工業株式会社(図版)
印刷所————————大日本印刷株式会社
製本所————————大日本印刷株式会社
表紙箔押————————株式会社　金栄堂
本文用紙————————北越製紙株式会社
表紙クロス————————ダイニック株式会社

N.D.C 033　　　29cm
ISBN4-06-144539-1(0)(事)